D0848574

THE
WORK
OF THE
DEAD

THE
WORK
OF THE
DEAD

A CULTURAL HISTORY
OF MORTAL REMAINS

THOMAS W. LAQUEUR

PRINCETON UNIVERSITY PRESS
PRINCETON AND OXFORD

Published by Princeton University Press,
41 William Street, Princeton, New Jersey 08540
In the United Kingdom: Princeton University Press,
6 Oxford Street, Woodstock, Oxfordshire OX20 1TW
press.princeton.edu

Jacket art: Detail of *Paris, vu des hauteurs du Père Lachaise*,
by Louise Joséphine Sarazin de Belmont.
Toulouse, Musée des Augustins. Photo © Bernard Delome.

Library of Congress Cataloging-in-Publication Data
Laqueur, Thomas Walter.
    The work of the dead : a cultural history of mortal remains / Thomas W. Laqueur.
        pages cm
    Includes bibliographical references and index.
    ISBN 978-0-691-15778-8 (hardback)
    1. Funeral rites and ceremonies—Cross-cultural studies. 2. Death—Social aspects—
Cross-cultural studies. I. Title.
    GT3150.L37 2015
    306.9—dc23   2015003565

British Library Cataloging-in-Publication Data is available

This book has been composed in Requiem

Printed on acid-free paper. ∞

Printed in the United States of America

1 3 5 7 9 10 8 6 4 2

CONTENTS

PREFACE

I am not sure when I began this book. I grew up only a phone call away from an autopsy—a "post" that is, post-mortem dissection—that took my father, a pathologist, away from the dinner table to the morgue and left me wondering what happened there and to what. What was a dead body really? He never took me with him, although I did spend hours watching him prepare the organs he had removed from it for microscopic examination and listening to him in his study as he dictated his finding. But in my first eighteen years, I knew the dead body only through hearsay or through its detached parts.

In the summer of 1964, I finally saw one—a cadaver to be more precise. It was at the University of Cincinnati, where I was working in a biochemistry lab after my freshman year; my housemate was a first-year medical student who had failed gross anatomy and was asked to try again. He was happy enough for my company. I watched him dissect but did not get my hands on the body. In the summer of 1980, at the beginning of fifteen months on an American Council of Learned Societies fellowship that I used to study medicine, I finally had—or rather shared with three others—my own cadaver. The dead body in these circumstances is a very material thing, with holes through which nerves and vessels and liquids pass, and connective tissues that connect, and tendons that, if pulled, still move muscles.

We—my tablemates and I—learned the names of hundreds of structures as we disassembled our body, our object of study. But it also had a face, at least until we started working on the fiendishly difficult anatomy of the head. I was not so blinded by the need to do well on tests not to think about how strange this thing really was—this body that now seemed to exist only instrumentally for us to learn from. It had been a person, a fact that did not sit well with its current condition. We were told to be respectful toward it and that what remained would be treated once again as human when we were done with it at the end of the summer. Perhaps my subject in this book—the relationship between the overwhelming materiality of the dead on the one hand and Death and Culture on the other—began to come into focus that summer.

But I think that the distant progenitor of an actual book—this book—was born a couple of years later: on 10 October 1983, to be exact. On that Monday, I began writing to some sixty or seventy archives and libraries, secular and ecclesiastical, asking what materials they held that might be relevant for a project I then called, I am embarrassed to admit, "The Meaning of Death in Post-Reformation Britain." "It would be impossible to answer your letter exhaustively," the Buckinghamshire County Archivist wrote back, "and the following are cited as examples." No kidding. Archives are repositories of the traces of the dead, of lost time.

The world in which I wrote my letter is lost. My file folder of kind responses is evidence of an age before on-line catalogues and instant e-mail access to everyone, a time of thin blue aerogrammes densely filled with type that can be felt through the paper punctured by an occasional hole, evidence of a period or a comma forcefully struck. It was a world of great courtesy in which archivists had the time to patiently and informatively respond to a young—but too old to be so clueless—researcher embarked on a manifestly hopeless mission.

In my defense, I did have two sets of questions in mind that I tried to capture in the beclouded phrase "the meaning of death": one was about the existential experience of death and dying; the other concerned their embeddedness in the broader social world. The first, and more intimately urgent, had to do with what we might now call the history of the emotions, or perhaps the history of attitudes toward death understood not as a progression of beliefs but of how people in the past stood, in their hearts, before the overwhelming fact of human existence: mortality and our exquisite consciousness of it. This was a search for a history of death that would go beyond the one told by demographers and doctors on the one hand and intellectual historians and scholars of religion on the other. I took meaning to be essentially an inner experience that might have an accessible history.

The question first troubled me as a doctoral student in reading the attack by Edward Thompson, one of the greatest British historians of the twentieth century, on what he took to be vicious, death-mongering eighteenth- and nineteenth-century evangelicals. By first confronting even little children with the frightening prospect of death and then holding out the false treacle prospect of a good death, Thompson's evangelicals supposedly terrified the young into submission to a life-denying and politically quietist religion. On one point, Thompson was right: death is everywhere in evangelical literature, and the prospect of meeting it with resignation, if not happily, was held out to the faithful of all ages. Dying well—holy dying, dying in peace and without fear, dying perhaps in the hope of another life, dying with acceptance of fate—was central to evangelical Christianity, as it was, in many different refractions, to all the world's major religions.[1]

More specifically, books like *The History of the Fairchild Family* by the most popular children's writer of the early nineteenth century, Mrs. Sherwood, aka Mary Martha Sherwood, seem to make his point. Listen to the father, Mr. Fairchild, speaking to his curious children about the dead body of "old John Roberts," the gardener. What begins as Mr. and Mrs. Fairchild's benevolent errand to comfort the man's widow turns into a lesson on "the subject of death"—embellished by quizzing on parenthetically cited scriptural passages—for their three children's edification. Incited by his daughter's curiosity about the dead body, Mr. Fairchild asks,

> "Have you any desire to see the corpse, my dears? You never saw a corpse before, I think?"
>
> "No papa," answered Lucy: "but we have great curiosity to see one."
>
> "I tell you before-hand, my dear children, that death is very terrible. A corpse is an awful sight."
>
> "I know that, papa," said Lucy; "but we should like to go."
>
> "Well my dears, you shall go; and you shall, if you please, see the corpse."
>
> . . . When they came to the door, they perceived a kind of disagreeable smell, such as they had never smelt before: this was the smell of the corpse which, having been dead now nearly two days, had begun to corrupt; and as the children went higher up the stairs, they perceived this smell more disagreeably.
>
> . . . [T]he whole appearance of the body was more ghastly and horrible than the children expected, and making out the words of Job: "But man dieth, and wasteth . . . away." (Job xiv. 10–12, 20.)
>
> . . . "My dear children, you now see what death is."

Mrs. Sherwood makes it perfectly clear throughout the story that the widow Roberts thinks that her husband had died a happy death, believing in his redeemer, and that she is comforted by this conviction: "I know that my poor husband loved his savior and trusted him for salvation." The theological foundation for the story is thoroughly orthodox: death is a terrible thing that is the result of sin; those who believe in Christ's redemptive sacrifice will find eternal life. While Sherwood is not shy about the gruesome details, her aim was clearly not terror but reassurance.[2]

But still, much is puzzling about this passage and about how historians have interpreted ones like it. To begin with, maybe confidence in a life everlasting *did* make death more bearable for children (and grown-ups) who faced it, as well as for the departed's survivors. My own dissertation work on the records of the Stockport Sunday School suggested that teenage scholars on their deathbeds, like the Widow Roberts, took comfort from the very evangelical religion purportedly terrorizing them. There is a great deal of reliable evidence that this was true for many others. We can never reckon how many died secure in the hopes of a life everlasting and how many suffered fear of damnation.

And then there is the terror of the corpse and of death more generally. Is it possible at a time when one-half of all children born would die before they reached the age of ten and when everyone, of whatever age, died at home, that the Fairchild children had never seen a corpse? Did it take Mrs. Sherwood to make children, who may otherwise have viewed this carnage as a part of life, fear death for the first time? Had she transformed death from a normal fact of daily life into an awful nightmare? This was a setup for moralizing. But who is being terrorized here? Maybe it is the historian. The idea of exposing children to death, their own or others, is horrible—if all too common still. I found reading modern medical anthropology on the subject so unbearable that I decided that I could not study it in the past. The book of a wise and humane German pediatric oncologist taught me that much of what adults think about death at a young age reflected their own fears and anxiety; children, even in a secular age, had the resources for holy dying. And so did some grown-ups. I realized that I could not write a history of this particular terror. I am not sure it even has a history or a trajectory. My guess is that the proportions of those who die with an equanimity born of feeling part of nature, like a tree falling in the forest (Tolstoy's fantasy of a coachman's death); those who die with the comforts of religion; and those who die in great fear have not changed much. But it would be very difficult to make this case with any sort of historical precision.[3]

When I tried to write about the history of those who were left to mourn—what parents felt about the deaths of their children through the ages, for example, but more generally of the history of loss—I got no further. On the one hand, it seemed a priori the case that in societies with high death rates (not to speak of those that practice infanticide) parents could not have emotionally survived if they had invested in each new life the passion that we do—the vast majority of us in the prosperous West—from birth or even before. Modern anthropology suggests that constant and relentless death dulls—or seems to dull—the grief of mothers. On the other hand, mountains of evidence shows that parents in the past mourned intensely their children of a certain age. The bodily language of melancholy, as far as we can tell, has remained remarkably stable since classical antiquity. And of course all we could ever hope to access from our sources is an outer expression of feeling at a moment. The soul remains hidden and mercurial.

It took me decades to realize (accept?) that I could not write a history of death as it appeared either in the inner emotional lives of those who were dying and or those who remained behind.[4]

"Attitudes toward death" seemed a way to get a more rational take on some of this. I discuss these on and off throughout this book and thought for a time that they might be my subject. There are many pronouncements about them: Buddhists think this, and Lutherans think that. Many serious books of history, theology, and anthropology try to show how ways of regarding death articulate with other, more general views, of life and the cosmos. But to tell the truth, I doubt whether such a thing as an attitude toward death exists, at least in a way that can be studied historically or with any emotional nuance.

When I think of a small arena that I know well—the attitudes of my parents toward death—I can report the following: my father went from cold, clinical detachment and annoyance at me for not understanding the pathophysiology of his hypernephroma to a sad and increasingly mute resignation toward his miserable impending end from various metastatic cancers. Those in the lung finally killed him through a massive hemorrhage. My mother faced death with absolute and unshakeable equanimity although she had, as far as I or anyone could tell, no views of an afterlife or indeed any views of the subject of death except that it was a relief from the diminishment of old age. Dying to her seemed like being absorbed into the Brahms *Requiem* or Beethoven *Missa Solemnis* or a Heine poem. As for me, I scarcely reacted to my father's death for six months; it took me years to absorb it. To this day, I have no attitude toward it. He does appear relatively often as a young man in my dreams. I miss him as perhaps the most important audience for my life. And I stand before my mother's death with awe, admiration, and disbelief. I imagine her spirit hovers over a lake in Virginia where she swam every summer for forty years. Given this muddle—my own inability to articulate the attitudes toward death of people I knew and know intimately—it seemed futile to explore the subject systematically in those whom I would know considerably less well in the distant past. I gave up on a history of death as a historical project of the inner life.

I gave up, slowly and reluctantly, after many years of false starts, trying to write about the existential experience of death and dying, about its inner world. But there remained the second set of questions shadowing my naive letters to archivists and librarians, questions about how death took on social meaning in the past. These questions were not about redeeming mortality so much as about how we lived with death as best we could: a history less of what individual people felt or thought than what they did publically in the face of death, dying, and killing and how these acts comported with other aspects of the social and political order. Over the years I wrote various essays on this subject, some of which, in new guises, found their way into this book. Others, on the history of executions and capital punishment more generally—the very strange cultural power of judicial killing that never had much to do with instrumental rationality—did not. I would have liked to have explored other topics that appear as walk-on parts in what follows more fully: the history of the passing bell and of the funereal feast, for example—that is, of collective hearing and eating in the shadow of death.

But death has remained for me an elusive topic: far too grand, far too entangled with almost everything that gives meaning to our lives to be written into some semblance of clarity. A book on the meanings of death anywhere at any time was beyond me. Like gravity or the air we breathe, it is always there, a part of being human that is so basic that it cannot be dissected out from the rest of life as we know it. One may as well write about the history of the meaning of life. And insofar as that can be written, poets, novelists and philosophers do it better than historians.

Readers will see, I hope, that I have not entirely abandoned death as a topic. I approach it through something more material, through what death leaves behind: through the dead body. This thing—this inanimate thing—that is always more than a thing has been the stuff of our imaginations since the beginning. We need it. It does massive work for the living. This is the subject of my book.

ACKNOWLEDGMENTS

It is customary to thank those who have helped bring a book into being, and I have no intention of not doing so. But it will not be easy. On 14 August 2013, when I was still some distance from finishing a first complete draft, I wrote to the Stockport Local Heritage Library in Cheshire asking the current librarian to thank one of her predecessors, Dave Reid, for sending me, back in 1971, photocopies of a memoir book recounting the deaths of local Sunday school scholars. I had just cited it, and that made me think of him. He had died in 2008, she replied; then please, I wrote back, tell his wife Naomi (a historian of Chartism who had been helpful to me when I was working on my thesis) that I was grateful to her late husband; she too was dead. My correspondent said that their son often came by and that she would tell him that I had written to thank his parents.

The first graduate student who helped me with research on what became, after many, many byways, this book was Ann Sullivan. In the late 1970s she and I laboriously went through folklore journals looking for evidence of post-Reformation survivals of what we might think of as pre-Reformation superstition: passing bells, prayers for the dead, funeral feasts. Today that task would take minutes (many of the publications we used are now online), but then it was a much bigger undertaking. She and I tirelessly transcribed text—or pasted photocopied snippets—on 5×8 notecards. I have not been in touch with her for forty years and discovered through the Internet that she is a grandmother and living in Ithaca. This sort of rummaging in the depths of memory will only make a mess of a great tumulus of intellectual and personal debts. I will make an effort at a more systematic archeology of gratitude by beginning with the most recent layers—the last to be added—and working downward in time.

My father-in-law, Siegfried Hesse, a brilliant, long-retired appellate lawyer and before that legal editor, read my page proofs with extraordinary attention to both typographical and substantive errors. In 2014—and here I already disturb the orderly excavation I intend—he went through my messy semifinal draft to get it ready for various stages of editing. A man in his late eighties might have been happier reading Proust. I am touched and proud that he gave so generously of his time and intelligence.

Terri O'Prey at Princeton University Press has seen this book through production with a wonderful combination of encouragement and efficiency; Quinn Fusting as assistant editor at the Press has attended to scores of details with care and courtesy. Beth Gianfagna was a dream copyeditor: learned, meticulously attentive to details, and appropriately strict. The wonderful and imaginative Alice Goff, once a graduate student and now an assistant professor at the University of Michigan, put together an illustration program and started the process of clearing permissions. Olivia Benowitz helped greatly to resolve the final and gnarly last-minute problems. Brenden Mackie was dogged and creative in tracking down recalcitrant endnotes during the final days of copyediting. Sheer Ganor helped clean up the texts of drafts to make them presentable.

I don't think I could have shaped a long, shaggy manuscript into a book without the help of my wonderful developmental editor Madeleine Adams, who sometimes knew what I was trying to say better than I did and who led me through final revisions with great delicacy and intelligence. But now the archeological model breaks down. A book is not like a tale, long abandoned; its topmost layers are still inhabited and reach far back in time. My editor at Princeton, Brigitta van Rheinberg, has had faith in this book for well over a decade and gave my semifinal draft a tough and demanding reading that greatly improved its clarity.

And then there are my friends and colleagues, some for more than forty years: Carol Clover was the first to read the whole thing; Carla Hesse, Mark Peterson, Jonathan Sheehan, and Ethan Shagan read, and heard about, more proto-chapters than they might care to remember before they took on all fifteen hundred pages of what had begun to look like a book; Deborah Valenze, Seth Koven, and Claudio Lomnitz read that version too and challenged me to make it better, clearer, and more consequential. James Vernon and Randy Starn read it all seriatim over the years. For each it was an act of kindness and intellectual generosity. To Cathy Gallagher, since 1973 my closest intellectual *copine*, I owe a special debt both for her preternatural ability to spot and fix a shoddy argument and for a lifetime of engagement in one another's work.

Other colleagues shared their expertise over the years, and I have tried to thank them in the notes to particular sections of this book, but I owe a special debt to Susanna Elm and to Tom Brady for reading part I and more importantly for their generosity over the decades in answering an amateur's questions about late antiquity and the Reformation, respectively. My old friend Beth Berry and my newer colleagues Nick Tackett and Carlos Norena have been my guides for matters Japanese, Chinese, and classical in that order. I have been teaching courses on death and dying with my medical colleague Guy Micco, MD, since the late 1980s he has been my expert advisor on questions about the dead body and disease as well as a great friend of this project. Every so often over the decades Martin Jay has given me just the right theoretically inflected text I needed to think with at just the right moment. His interventions on this and other projects have spanned four decades. Sharon Kaufman's breathtakingly original research on dying in modern America has informed the afterword and many other pages of this book. Patricia Williams at certain critical moments offered advice that sustained me. My walks with my dear friend Istvan Rev in the cemeteries of Budapest, as well as his work and my many conversations with him, have been formative in my thinking about the dead.

There are also moments long ago and more recently that have continued to inform my present: this present, this book. My editor for a time, Alison Mac-Keen, said something over lunch at the Princeton Institute for Advanced Study in 2008 that proved to be, in ways I cannot reconstruct, a Eureka moment. *The Work of the Dead* came into view. In the early 1980s Tom Metcalf took me to Park Street Cemetery in Calcutta, an important moment not only for my account of its history but for my thinking on spaces of the dead more generally. He has been a great friend and helpful reader of my work since 1973. In 1985 David Keightley invited me to a conference in Oracle, Arizona, on death ritual in China that opened up for me a distant world of the work of the dead of which I had known nothing. He has also shared unpublished work with me. In the late 1980s the anthropologist Doris Francis took me on a tour of one of her field sites, a dying and desecrated cemetery in East London called Woodgrange, in which broken Victorian angels shared a landscape with a patchwork of Bangladeshi and other Muslim graves, some flanked on all four corners by burning tapers, and with more or less intact old communal compounds of various sort. An elderly couple was looking for the grave of one of their ancestors so as to arrange an exhumation before the whole site went to ruin. Bodies in a landscape matter.

This book and much of my intellectual life has still deeper roots in the journal *Representations* that I helped found with friends in 1981 and in the intellectual community that grew around it over the decades. I can think of specific gifts from specific members: Francis Ferguson suggested I read Godwin's *Essay on Sepulchers*, which became a central text for me; long ago the much-missed Mike Rogin talked to me about the familial affect that informed nineteenth-century bourgeois tombs; a remark by Tim Clark at one of our evening meetings, where we discussed an early version of what became the chapters on cremation, made me recognize the crazy modernism of some of its more radical proponents; David

Henkin, learned in Judaica, sent me texts on the persistence of the dead around their bodies, which made it possible for me to think through the issues raised in chapter 3. There are specific parts of this book—those dealing with ghosts—that owe an intellectual debt to Steve Greenblatt, but far more important is a lifetime of conversations and friendship for which I am grateful. I am blessed with this community of friends, those I have mentioned and others—Lynn Hunt and Svetlana Alpers, Bernard Williams and Paul Alpers (the latter two now dead)— with whom I talked about many things that made this book possible.

Generations of graduate student research assistants and members of the Berkeley undergraduate research apprenticeship program have labored on behalf of *The Work of the Dead*, and I have tried to acknowledge them by name in the endnotes. I am sure I missed some but am no less grateful to them all. Many graduate students also read or heard parts of the book at seminars and colloquia; their challenges made it better.

And then there are the institutional "thank yous." I did not write the book I promised to write when I was fellow at the National Humanities Center in 2000–2001—I wrote another quite different one—but I did research for, and give a talk on, a very early version of chapters 6 through 9. Twice in the new millennia the Institute for Advanced Study at Princeton provided a wonderful place to think and write. I wrote some of what became a history of names and a long introduction—a first pass of what became the central idea for the whole book—at the *Wissenschaftskolleg zu Berlin*, where I was welcomed first as a guest of the rector and then as the spouse of a fellow. Fellowships from the National Endowment for the Humanities and the Guggenheim Foundation in the 1970s and 1990s supported two other books but more importantly enabled the sort of wool-gathering research that coalesced in this one. Finally, the Distinguished Humanist Award from the Mellon Foundation allowed me to take a year off from teaching in 2013 to finally—actually—write this book out of its many earlier starts and parts.

We are now deep into the excavation of those parts of my life out of which came *The Work of the Dead*. Joanna Roeber and Martin Rosendahl (she since 1970) have provided a home in London—a room, a haven, affection. I acknowledge John Walsh, my old Oxford tutor, in the endnotes for specific suggestions. But the debt I owe to him as a historian of religion and society is so imbricated in my life that I would not know where to begin thanking him. Jerry Siegel was never formally my teacher but has stood as a model for serious intellectual engagement since I was in my early twenties. Lawrence Stone shaped my life as a scholar and historian. I cherish his memory.

I think it was Alexander Nehamas who told me to read Diogenes the Cynic, whose challenge is the leitmotif of this book; he says it was, but I have no precise memory of the fact. I do have clear and distinct knowledge that he has been my friend since we were eighteen; I speak to him several times every week; he is my friend because, as Montaigne explains his friendship with La Boettie, he is he and I am I. As this book is the product of almost a lifetime's thinking and fretting, I owe him a great debt.

Finally, I dedicate this book to my colleague, friend, and wife, Carla Hesse. Yes of course she has read, as I have already acknowledged, more drafts of more chapters—and proto-chapters—than either of us can remember. And yes she has made many incisive comments. She sees big arguments and causal inferences where I want to see only the filigree of detail. But I dedicate this book to her because of the life she has made with me.

THE
WORK
OF THE
DEAD

Introduction

THE WORK OF THE DEAD

[Diogenes the Cynic] ordered himself to be thrown anywhere without being buried. And when his friends replied, "What! to the birds and beasts?" "By no means," saith he; "place my staff near me, that I may drive them away." "How can you do that," they answer, "for you will not perceive them?" "How am I then injured by being torn by those animals, if I have no sensation?"

CICERO, *Tusculan Disputations*

In the beginning was the corpse: lifeless matter from which a human had fled. Almost two and a half millennia ago, the outrageous Diogenes (ca. 412–323 B.C.E.) told his students that when he died he wanted his body to be tossed over the wall where it would be devoured by beasts. He was gone; it no longer mattered to him. This book is about how and why Diogenes was right (his or any body forever stripped of life cannot be injured), but also existentially wrong, wrong in a way that defies all cultural logic. It is about why the dead body matters, everywhere and across time, as well as in particular times and particular places. It matters in disparate religious and ideological circumstances; it matters even in the absence of any particular belief about a soul or about how long it might linger around its former body or about what might become of it after death; it matters across all sorts of beliefs about an afterlife or a God. It matters in the absence of such beliefs. It matters because the living need the dead far more than the dead need the living. It matters because the dead make social worlds. It matters because we cannot bear to live at the borders of our mortality (fig. I.1).

This book is about the body, about the disenchanted corpse, about "corpses without consciousness": bereft, vulnerable, abject. It is about that which "life breath left . . . behind" as Homer says of the bones of the fallen in the *Iliad*. The fate of this thing has been known for millennia to those who contemplate the dead. A fifth-century C.E. Buddhist text describes with great precision the "stages of foulness": "the bloated, the livid, the festering, the cut-up, the gnawed, the scattered, the hacked and scattered, the bleeding, the worm-infested, a skeleton." All the rest is commentary that modern forensic science has enriched.

I

I.1. Diogenes investigates a tomb. Jonas Umbach, 1645–1700. British Museum.

Depending on climate, happenstance, and technology, a body might be around as decaying organic matter for only a matter of weeks or months, a few years at best. It begins to devour itself within minutes, as the enzymes that had once turned food into nutriments start disassembling the body that no longer needs them in their old job. This is autolysis. Bacteria freed from the gut soon afterward also start to devour the flesh; in later stages microbes from the soil and the air join in. Putrefaction. *Eisenia fetida*—the worm in our compost bins—dines on the carnage in some climes; so do flies and other insects. There are many variations on this theme. Anything that keeps bacteria and chemical reactions from working as well as they might preserves bodies: dry, cold, wet, and sterile conditions. The deserts of Egypt and the high Andes, the frozen tundra of Siberia, the acid bogs of Denmark, tanning agents, and anaerobic conditions—all preserve the dead far longer than anyone had reason to expect. So do the desiccating clay caves of Palermo, famous for their ability to make corpses into mummies that could be dressed up to look ready for the opera. The soil of the cemetery in the old colonial city of Guanajuato yielded up mummies of nineteenth-century cholera victims that have become a major tourist attraction and an emblem of Mexico's engagement with the dead. But under most conditions, an adult corpse is lucky to survive a decade. Bodies encased in lead fare better than those in wood or in the ground; it helps to die on an empty stomach and with evacuated bowels; it helps if someone has removed the viscera; embalming helps. Collagen and hair do better than other soft tissues.[1]

Bones fare better than flesh. How much better again depends on where they lie. In the highly acidic soil of the great seventh-century Anglo-Saxon burial mound at Sutton Hoo in Suffolk, for example, only the stains of bones remain; in the more basic soil of Wharram Percy at the edge of the chalk wolds of north Yorkshire, surviving medieval skeletons are in good shape. Generally, the large bones of the leg fare better than the small bones of the foot. But it matters little. The skeletal remains of friends, of enemies, and of strangers are, as has been endlessly rehearsed over thousands of years, pretty much indistinguishable. Of course, some may bear the marks of the life that once clothed them: violence, disease, and time itself leave marks. Bones do tell tales. But without dress or some other distinguishing mark, it was hard to tell them apart before the advent of forensic DNA technology and other modern techniques. This is why in pictures of the Last Judgment the more prominent dead are shown wearing their crowns or miters to help distinguish them from the great mass of corpses. Out of context, even animal parts can be mistaken for those of humans, except by experts. Chaucer's pardoner, one might remember, "hadde pigges bones" in a bottle that the gullible took to be human: the relics of a saint. And after not so long a time, even the bones fall apart: dust to dust. Erosion and oxidation see to that. Death proves even the rich man, as Sir Walter Raleigh observed on the scaffold, "a naked beggar which hath interest in nothing, but in the gravel that fills his mouth." Everything is covered over "with these two narrow words, *Hic jacet.*"[2]

The corpse: the human body, at the edge of the abyss, soon reverts to the elements from which its physical being came and so reenters the great natural cycle of life and death. Modern ecologists welcome this, and the idea goes back to the origins of Western thinking on the matter. Heraclitus (d. 475 B.C.E.), the pre-Socratic philosopher, suggested that "corpses are more worth throwing out than dung." They serve best that serve as fertilizer. It is a view with a long and checkered afterlife. A materialist chemist and philosopher got fired from his post at Heidelberg in the nineteenth century for saying the same thing. And we will hear it again among advocates of modern cremation and from those who think it only adds to greenhouse gases and that we should find a way to treat bodies of humans as nature does the bodies of animals left to the forces of decomposition. But these pragmatic views have had little purchase over the ages. Diogenes the Cynic's request to his friends that he be "flung out unburied" has been more challenging. He made this request not for instrumental reasons but because he thought it made no difference what became of him: "What harm then can the mangling of wild beasts do me if I am without consciousness?" he asked. Or, as Euripides' Alkestis says to Admetus, right after he tells her that when he dies they will be together again: "Time will console you. The dead are nothing." The body has always been disenchanted.[3]

The Cynic's argument has had lots of admirers but has never been persuasive for very long. Just as the dead body has always been disenchanted, it has also always been enchanted: powerful, dangerous, preserved, revered, feared, an object of ritual, a thing to be reckoned with. For the living, for at least some time, it is always more than it is. "And yet . . ." and "except for . . ." have been the response to Diogenes' view, echoing from as far back as we can go. There is no more protean or more generative human endeavor than arguing, in words and action, against it. Of course, comes the collective voice in thousands of different timbres, the dead are not refuse like the other debris of life; they cannot be left for beasts to scavenge. We need to live with them in more or less close proximity. They define generations, demarcate the sacred and the profane and more ordinary spaces as well, are the guarantors of land and power and authority, mirror the living to themselves, and insist on our temporal limits. The dead are witnesses to mortality. They hear us and we speak to them even if we know that they, like all base matter, are deaf and dumb. Bones address us from the gibbet in the words of the late medieval poet François Villon:

> You see us cleaving together, five, six:
> As for the flesh, which we nourished too much,
> It is long since consumed and corrupted,
> And we, the bones, have become ashes and powder.[4]

We address bones. We live with the dead.

Conversely, the willfully brutal disposal of the dead—the treatment of the corpse as carrion—is an act of extreme violence, an attack on the order and meaning we look to the dead to maintain for us. To make the obvious point: to treat a dead body as if it were ordinary organic matter—to leave it lie as if it were the body of a beast—or willfully to desecrate and mutilate it is to erase it from culture and from the human community: to deny the existence of the community from which it came, to deny its humanity. One of the most damning pictures of the aftermath of Hurricane Katrina was that of the dead, unattended, littering the streets of an American city. If we are to believe medieval bestiaries, hyenas, the most despised and perverted of beasts, purportedly dig up the dead to eat them (plate 1). Eating human flesh for nourishment, for its protein alone, is a revolting sign of the collapse, or entire absence, of civilization. I am thinking here of the Donner Party, or the wreck of the *Méduse*, or Europeans' understanding of the practices of some of the peoples of the New World. The practice of cannibalism for the nutritional value of the dead collapses the boundary between nature and culture. It probably does not exist; the exceptions *in extremis* prove the rule. Montaigne had already understood this back in the sixteenth century. He recognized that most of the cannibalism known in his day was ritualistic: magic. It was not a practice of semihumans radically different from Europeans but rather, as the anthropologist Marshall Sahlins says of cannibalism generally, a practice symbolic even if it was real. And as such, it too, at the margins of care for the dead, constitutes a rejection of Diogenes' views.[5]

This book answers the question of why we consistently refuse Diogenes' example—why we generally do not toss the dead over the wall for the beasts to devour—in two time registers: anthropological (part 1) and historical (parts 2–4). The answer in the first of these both disregards time—we care for the dead because humans have always cared for our dead—and considers it on a scale that historians of the French Annales school called the *longue durée*. They were thinking of the time scale of climate, crops, and agricultural practices and of the patterns of life rooted in a material world that changed very slowly. These adamantine structures, the Annalistes thought, were the foundation for more temporally bound explanations of worldviews—what they called *mentalités*—and for *événements*, specific events that historians try to explain. I am thinking of the ways in which the material fact of the insignificance of dead bodies has been and is systematically and spectacularly forgotten, ignored, or reinterpreted through the millennia. Put differently, some irresistible power of the imagination, independent of any particular religious beliefs, blinds us to the cold reality of what a corpse really is. Or rather what it is not. We care about, care for, feel with a dead body, although we know that instantly or very soon after what we call biological death it notices nothing, cares for nothing, feels nothing. Part 1 plays down specific beliefs of specific groups of people at specific moments in history. It emphasizes continuity: of actors (the dead), of the kinds of work they do among the living, and of the foundational reasons we care about them.

I take this long or timeless view for four reasons. First, it lets me explain how and why very old stories are still being told in the everyday politics of today. It lets me compress time. Scarcely a week passed while I was writing this book without some new instance coming to public attention: On 9 June 2011, a black businessman and former city councilor in Stockton, California, was shocked to discover a sign that read, "Moved from Nigger Hill Cemetery" over the new graves of thirty-six anonymous black bodies that had been exhumed and reburied. "When I went up to that gravesite," he reports, "I feel like I could feel the presence of those people crying to get those things off of them." The dead do not cry out. "We know the dead are not able to speak," writes an eighteenth-century clergyman, "for they are all silent in darkness." They cannot see or walk or handle things with their hands, either. Yet they do speak, differently from the living. St. Paul preached to the Hebrews that "he being dead yet speaketh," and more generally, Rev. Abel Styles concludes, "it is common in the scriptures for inanimate

I.2. *Office of the Dead, the Grandes Heures de Rohan.* MS Latin 9471. Bibliotheque Nationale de France, 1425–1430.

I.3. The body of a U.S. soldier in Mogadishu, 1993. Jim Watson. *Toronto Star.*

things to be represented as speaking, as well as hearing" (fig. I.2). It is still common; there are cultures today in which the living regularly speak to the dead. We endlessly invest the dead body with meaning because, through it, the human past somehow speaks to us.[6]

Possessing actual dead bodies also still matters to us, as it did in the days of the early Church. National Public Radio recently reported that the children, by his first marriage, of Jim Thorpe, the great Native American football star and 1912 Olympic gold medal winner, were suing the town in Pennsylvania that was named after him and where his remains are buried under an impressive pink marble slab. They were joined in their suit by his tribe, the Sac and Fox Nation. The children wanted Thorpe's body back. "Dad's wish was that he be buried in Oklahoma," they said. Wrong and irrelevant, said "the community of Jim Thorpe." "We have a signed contract by his widow" (that is, by Thorpe's second wife), who gave the town the body in 1957 in return for the promise that it would be renamed after her husband, responded a town father. The plaintiffs were perfectly content to let the town keep its name and memorial as long as they got the body. But of course that was unacceptable to the town: an empty tomb would be a sadly diminished tourist attraction. "We have the rights to the possession of Jim Thorpe's body," insists Jim Thorpe, the town. Medieval churches fought each other for centuries over the bodies of saints.[7]

The same sort of historical escala-
tor seems to be working in the opposite sorts of stories—those that are
about the degradation of the corpse.
They too have a very long pedigree
and take on new resonance in new
times. When followers of General
Mohamed Aidid dragged the body of
a dead American soldier through the
streets of the Somali capital, Mogadishu, in October 1993, it evoked the
same raw emotional response that
Homer's story of Achilles' dragging
the body of Hector over the plains of
Troy did in the *Iliad* (figs. I.3, I.4). It
was the violation that we recognize
from Sophocles' *Antigone,* in which
Creon is horribly punished by the
gods for leaving the body of Polynices
unburied on the battlefield, prey to
birds and animals; it speaks the language of the Nazi occupiers of Paris,
who left the corpses of executed resistance fighters in the streets; it speaks
to the terror in the hearts of Jamaican

I.4. Achilles drags the body of Hector.
Diosphos painter, vase, ca. 490 B.C.E.
Louvre, Paris.

slaves excluded from burial for rebellion or for falling away from Christianity; it
evokes the effect that the Spanish conquistadors hoped for when they left the bodies of the Aztec dead for the vanquished living to see. We recognize it in the English
poor who rioted in protest against laws that made the bodies of criminals available
for public dissection. The radically different eschatologies of Bronze Age or Golden
Age Greece, sixteenth-century Mexico, eighteenth-century Jamaica or England,
and twentieth-century France or Somalia or the United States seem to melt away.

Variants on the theme of the degraded corpse are stories, echoing one another
over centuries, about getting the right dead body in the right place and excluding the
wrong body from where it is not wanted. God, through miracles, cast unworthy bodies out of early Christian burial places; Jim Crow laws kept blacks out of segregated
cemeteries; public opinion kept the body of Tamerlan Tsarnaev, the Boston Marathon bomber, out of scores of cemeteries before he finally found a place at a small
private burial ground in Virginia. And the state has its say about where a corpse can
go. In 2011, the body of Hitler's deputy, Rudolf Hess, buried in the Bavarian town of

Wunsiedel when he died in 1987, was exhumed and cremated; his ashes were scattered to the winds because his grave had become a shrine for thousands of neo-Nazis who gathered there on pilgrimage every year. The enchantment of this most profane of bodies was shattered only by reducing it into tiny particles of its constitutive chemistry and making it impossible to localize anywhere what remained.[8]

The second reason I begin with the long anthropological view and return to it throughout the book is because it lets me respond to Diogenes' challenge with a kind of answer not grounded in time or space but in more or less timeless truths. It lets me connect deep structures with historical contingencies. Three in particular are important for the rest of this book. First, there seems to be a universally shared feeling not only that there is something deeply wrong about not caring for the dead body in some fashion, but also that the uncared-for body, no matter the cultural norms, is unbearable. The corpse demands the attention of the living, however that attention is paid. We have a gut aversion to the bare, bereft dead body. Here is how an eighteenth-century clergyman put it: "The dead naturally tend to destroy the life of others," he said, "and that is really the reason Men naturally abhor the sight or the touch of the dead. . . . The natural Spirit of Life is afraid of a Dead Body and has an abhorrence of it," which is why we cannot just toss it away, at least not in sight. Dead bodies are, as we will see in chapter 5, less dangerous to health than the living. But this does not detract from his main point. A celebrated seventeenth-century preacher explained why it was the duty of children to bury the bodies of their parents: it is, he said, "a great deformity to have a man's corps lie above ground for no carcasse will bee more loathsome than a man's if it lie unburied." All sorts of reasons might be adduced for why it is so loathsome, but the preacher's sensibility is widely shared across time and culture. It is echoed in the timeless psychoanalytic anthropology of Julia Kristeva: "The corpse (or cadavre: *cadere*, to fall), seen without God and outside of science, is the utmost of abjection. It is death infecting life. . . . As in true theater without makeup or masks, refuse and corpses *show me* what I permanently thrust aside in order to live. There, I am at the border of my condition as a living being."[9]

I also believe that there is an even more fundamental reason why our species lives with, and cares for, its dead, materially and imaginatively: such attention is *a,* if not *the,* sign of our emergence from the order of nature into culture. It is, as the philosopher Hans-Georg Gadamer puts it, "the immutable anthropological background for all the human and social changes, past or present." The burial of the dead

> is perhaps the fundamental phenomenon of becoming human. Burial
> does not refer to a rapid hiding of the dead, a swift clearing away of the
> shocking impression made by one suddenly stuck fast in a leaden and
> lasting sleep. On the contrary, by a remarkable expenditure of human

labor and sacrifice there is sought an abiding with the dead, indeed a holding fast of the dead among the living. . . . We have to regard this in its most elementary significance. It is not a religious affair or a transposition of religion into secular customs, mores, and so on. Rather it is a matter of the fundamental constitution of human being from which derives the specific sense of human practice; we are dealing here with a conduct of life that has spiraled out of the order of nature.[10]

Gadamer's use of the phrase "elementary significance" puts me in mind of Claude Levi-Strauss's *Elementary Structures of Kinship,* one of the most influential anthropology books of the twentieth century, which argues that the incest taboo stands at the border between nature and culture: a liminal state, a threshold. I take "abiding with the dead" in the same spirit, to be a sign of "a conduct of life that has spiraled out of the order of nature." Burial is clearly not its only manifestation—language could be such a marker—nor is it the only way of abiding with bodies: cremating and entombing or scattering their ashes in holy places, for example, are others. It extends as well to the vast range of temporally more limited and less traceable forms of caring for the dead: all the ways in which we prepare them for more permanent disposition—for example, washing them (often the task of women in the Christian West), anointing them, dressing them, eviscerating and embalming them. And it includes the ritual forms of the disposition itself, the funeral in its endless variety. All of these acts and many others qualify and could be the subject of this book, but I concentrate on those that leave the most traces on the ground or in the historical records, those through which we live with the dead through time.[11]

There is no chronological border marked "culture" on the human time scale at which stands a guardhouse marked "the care of the dead," no clear frontier that, once crossed, definitively spirals the traveler "out of the order of nature." The idea of such a moment is the heuristic creation of fictive anthropology, meant to help us think about the foundations of the human symbolic order, to mark it as wondrous, to resist taking for granted the foundations of our existence. What actually happened in the distant past revolves around two related theoretical and empirical debates. The first is about dates: When did early hominids or humans start to care for their dead? The second is about meaning: Did beginning to care for the dead mark a cognitive border between prehistory and history, between one cognitive status and another higher one? I cannot and do not need to take sides in these sophisticated disputes. All I need for now is to observe that as far back as people have discussed the subject, care of the dead has been regarded as foundational—of religion, of the polity, of the clan, of the tribe, of the capacity to mourn, of an understanding of the finitude of life, of civilization itself. And, as far back as we can go, the archeological record seems to support the view that humans and their close hominid ancestors have cared for at least some of their dead. I do not know what this means in terms of human cognitive development or, more specifically, attitudes toward death. I do not think it matters. We must not, writes V. Gordon Childe, one of the pioneers of the study of prehistory, "imagine early hominids elaborating an eschatology and then acting on it." The deep emotions aroused by the drama of life and death "found expression in no abstract judgments, but in passionate acts. The acts were the ideas, not expressions of them." I think this is still true in our own age. But whether burial represents a great cognitive leap forward or not, for now, and for my purposes, I take Gadamer as being basically right.[12]

Third, the long anthropological view—deep time—allows me to offer another general argument against Diogenes that I will elaborate with much more historical specificity later. In 1907, Robert Hertz, a brilliant twenty-six-year-old Jewish student of the foundational sociological theorist Emile Durkheim and of the cultural anthropologist Marcel Mauss, wrote an enormously influential paper that showed that the dead have two lives: one in nature, the other in culture. There are the dead as bodies, the dead to which Diogenes limited himself: smelly, putrefying flesh that had lost whatever had made it alive and that, like any other organic matter, was in the process of decay and had become food for scavengers. Soon these dead would be only bones, and eventually they would be nothing. But there is also another way to construe the dead: as social beings, as creatures who need to be eased out of this world and settled safely into the next and into memory. How this is done—through funeral rites, initial disposition of the body and often a redisposition or reburial, mourning, and other kinds of postmortem attention—is deeply, paradigmatically, and indeed foundationally part of culture. By contrast to death in nature—anachronistically speaking, biological death—which happens in a relatively brief amount of time, social death takes time even in the West, where the other kind is regarded as more or less instantaneous. We speak of the hour of our death. Death in culture takes time because it takes time for the rent in the social fabric to be rewoven and for the dead to do their work in creating, recreating, representing, or disrupting the social order of which they had been a part. The ways in which the dead—understood as social beings—determine how we care for the dead body—the natural dead—is a central theme of part 1 and also informs the rest of the book. The relationship between the two conceptions of the dead—mere matter, on the one hand, and beings who have a social existence, on the other—is what allows bones, ashes, and names to do their work. "We humans," wrote Hertz, "are social beings grafted upon the physical individual," whose "destruction is tantamount to a sacrilege against the social order."[13]

The last reason that I begin with a long anthropological perspective is that it represents for me the foundation—the meta-reason—for all the specific reasons I will give for all the various changes that are the subject of most of this book. From there, it is turtles all the way down. As I said, there are thousands of explanations that can and have been given for why particular peoples at particular times care for the bodies of their dead in particular ways. Religious reasons, secular reasons, reasons predicated on metaphysics and reasons grounded in a materialist world-view, reasons generated by a variety of emotions and sensibilities, reasons that are difficult to articulate. There are reasons that are forever beyond us: we will never have a clue about why Neanderthals—at least some of them—ritually buried their dead. There are reasons that overreach the evidence. We can argue for a very long time about whether the focus on an afterlife really switched from the fate of the clan to that of the individual, from a concern for the cohesion of the group through time to an individual's relationship with the gods during the so-called Axial Age (ca. 800–200 B.C.E.), as some scholars of religion have claimed. There are intellectually well-articulated reasons. The medieval Church, for example, produced a highly elaborated theology to explain why the bodies of the special dead—saints—deserved extraordinary attention and why it was advantageous for the ordinary dead to be buried near them. There are whole libraries written to explain why the special dead do great things. The historical and anthropological literature is also filled with reasons of this sort for the things that the dead do in other times and places and for why we the living need to respond: for why we need to speak to them, feed them, pray for them, ingest them in some form, to name but a few possible obligations. I do not want to belittle or deny the importance of any of these; I myself cite them in the pages that follow, and I myself offer these sorts of reasons. Nonetheless, this book is fundamentally not a review of reasons but rather a commentary on them taken as a whole. It is about what the body of a Christian or a Buddhist saint and the body of Lenin share rather than what distinguishes them. It is about dead bodies as a class that I subsume, for want of a better label, under the term "the anthropological dead." In a sense, my account of why the dead matter is like the German philosopher Friedrich Schleiermacher's (1768–1834) view of the "essence" of religion. It is, he thought, "neither thinking nor acting, but intuition and feeling." It—like my subject—is not grounded in knowledge, science, morality, or metaphysics but rather in deep structures of intuition and feeling.[14]

But it also isn't. The book begins with and is supported by a cosmic claim: the dead make civilization on a grand and an intimate scale, everywhere and always: their historical, philosophical, and anthropological weight is enormous and almost without limit and compare. As such, death and the dead may not have a history in the usual sense but only more and more iterations, endless and infinitely varied, that we shape into an engagement with the past and the present. That said, most of this book is about history: the history of the work that the dead do in particular places, in particular times, and in particular ways. I ask two historical questions. First, how did the dead help to make what we think of as the modern world? And second, how was it possible for them to accomplish their work in the face of the putative disenchantment of our age? To put this second question differently: how have the kinds of reasons that we adduce for rejecting Diogenes changed in a variety of new circumstances?

My focus in much of what follows will be geographically limited to one small part of the world—western Europe and North America. In some stories—that of the cemetery, for example—I pay especially close attention to France and for a few pages also to Portugal, where the largest anti-cemetery riots of the nine-teenth century took place; the French Revolution, a world historical event, appears in almost every part of the book; the history of modern cremation begins in Italy; I take many of my examples for the history of names from nineteenth-century Germany; I draw examples of name-bearing monuments from the United States and focus for a time on the NAMES project and its AIDS quilt. But for two reasons I return again and again to England. The first is the same one that drew Karl Marx to the British, and more specifically the English, case. Even if Britain was not the first modern society, it was the place where much of what we take to be characteristic of the modern world developed relatively early and in distinctive ways: an articulate and self-conscious bourgeoisie and working class; religious pluralism in the shadow of the Reformation and revolution; the atten-uation of face-to-face relationships and autarkic communities; cosmopolitanism; commerce; industry. The world we have lost began to go missing there earlier than almost anywhere else.

But I do not want to put too much pressure on this; another historian might have chosen another country and, although the details would be different, her general story would be recognizably the same as mine. The more important rea-son I focus on England is the need for close-up examination of the work of the dead—in a place, in an encounter, in a confrontation—if we are to understand its importance in general. The story I tell is local—has to be and is always local—at the same time as it is universal. A specific literary tradition comments on it; it grows out of particular people speaking and writing to one another in particular ways. After my more than forty years as a historian, England is the only place I know intimately enough to be able to recount the work of the dead with the granularity its history demands.

No part of this book is intended to be entirely freestanding. Leitmotifs keep reappearing; the story is iterative. But each of parts 2–4 is meant to address one main question; cumulatively my answers will cash out the claim that the work of the dead is to make culture and set the boundaries of our mortality.

Part 2 is about place and space. It asks, "Where are the dead?"—by which I mean "where, geographically, are their bodies?" Peter Brown argues for the importance of place with respect to the localization of a saint's body, his *praesentia*, the ground where heaven and earth are joined: *Hic locus est*, "This is the place." I will be concerned with this idea in broader contexts and for all sorts of reasons that have little to do with holiness in his sense. Specifically, in part 2 I want to show how the dominant resting place of the dead—the churchyard—came into being during the Middle Ages and explain why the modern cemetery largely supplanted it in the eighteenth and nineteenth centuries.

Part 3 is about names. It asks, "Who are the dead?" After a survey of the deep time of the name and the list—a more detailed look at topics raised in part 1—it shows how and why, to an unprecedented extent, since the nineteenth century we have come to gather the names of the dead on great lists and memorials and, conversely, why being buried without a name (anonymously) has become so disturbing. It takes readers from a world of largely unmarked bodies to one in which hopelessly disembodied names—and even more, bodies bereft of names—are unbearable.

Finally, part 4 is about ashes. It asks, "What are the dead?" It shows how technologically sophisticated cremation—the rendering of the dead into indistinguishable inorganic matter—was begun as a modernist fantasy of stripping death of its history, which ultimately failed. Flesh and bones to ashes in less than two hours will not do.

The deep time of part 1 keeps reappearing, but most of this book is about a period stretching from the early Enlightenment to sometime in the twentieth century, roughly 1680–2000. I am not the first to argue that the work of the dead was, for better or (usually) worse, especially strenuous and effective in these centuries and, more important, that there was a break during the Enlightenment, which makes it a good place to begin the story of the dead in modern times. Michel Foucault, Philippe Ariès, Michel Vovelle, and Arthur Imhof, to take four exemplary and influential examples, all do it. And they all offer narratives of disappearance, disenchantment, loss, and secularization. For Imhof, the leading German historian of mortality, an early modern equanimity in the face of death disappeared during the Enlightenment. In the old regime of the churchyard, when children died soon after birth, parents could imagine them joining the heavenly host: "a kind of godly family planning." No more. The past two hundred years have witnessed a dramatic shortening of overall life expectancy from eternity to the threescore and ten, or at best fivescore, we might be allotted on earth. Imhof's title sums it up: *Lost Worlds*. For the Marxist historian

Vovelle, the response is good riddance: the decline of testamentary bequests for masses for the dead that he documents is evidence for large-scale secularization. Humanity is less in thrall to a Church that for millennia had used masses for the dead to keep the masses of the living enthralled. This is a longtime favorite trope of anticlericalism. For the deeply conservative and devoutly Catholic Ariès, the Enlightenment was disastrous: an epidemic of fear gripped Europe as the dying came to worry about premature burial, a result of doctors telling their patients that death was nothing but the extinction of even the tiniest flame of life. How would one really know? In the nineteenth century, sentimentalism and excessive personal grief replaced more communal and religious understandings of dying and a deeper, metaphysically rooted account of death itself. By the twentieth century, a great silence had descended; one could not speak about death at all. (Ariès bases this last point on the work of the influential English anthropologist Geoffrey Gorer.) Finally, for Foucault, death in the Enlightenment gave way to what he called the regime of life; the clinical gaze served to embrace bodies in a new web of power/knowledge that regulated life in its most intimate corners. All of these are narratives of disappearance.[15]

Mine is not. It is written under the sway of anthropology informed by history, a story of the ways in which the presence of the dead enchants our purportedly disenchanted world, of the reinvention of enchantment in more democratic forms. It is about a new and modern magic that we can believe in, and how layers of meaning from the deep past lie beneath the present, waiting to be reused and reimagined. In fact the dead have never been more prominent: from the tumble of churchyards to great acres of cemeteries, from a very small number of grand funerals making claims on public space to the funeral as a constitutive event for all sorts of communities, from anonymity to names. Even ashes have taken on new life.

I invite the reader to imagine herself as an archeologist around the year 3000, a thousand or so years from now, excavating a European city—or a city of North or South America, or Australia; much of the colonial world would work, and so might Singapore or Shanghai with some of the details changed—whose destruction could be dated with some precision to the year 1900: a city frozen in time like Pompeii. She would look, as her professional predecessors had, for evidence about what that city's inhabitants did with their dead, those strange artifacts that speak so powerfully of what matters to a civilization. Were she engaged with late antiquity and the early Middle Ages, she would be looking for the concentration of graves in the midst of human habitation, at a gathering-in of the dead from a variety of locations, each with a deep history. But archeologists a millennium from now will be looking at the ruins of the Western civilization that supplanted the old regime of the dead that had grown up by the eighth or ninth century.

Instead of the ruins of many small and not very imposing churchyards with a few modest tombs and a small number of grand ones inside the remaining walls of an adjacent church, archeologists would find at the outskirts of the early twentieth-century city huge expanses, hundreds and even thousands of acres in size, packed full of grand monuments difficult to distinguish from those of earlier civilizations: Egyptian, Greek, Roman, medieval Irish, European baroque, in relatively pure form but, more likely, each one in a strange bricolage of historical elements. Almost all of these would be stone, but perhaps by some extraordinary circumstance a great iron mausoleum might have survived if only in traces of ferrous oxide. Maybe even a photograph preserved in glass, like a fly in amber. It might well be puzzling to our excavator that instead of a tidy progression of styles through the ages there had been a sort of historical compression in which all of them came into being at roughly the same time. No churches would be found nearby.

In 1750, all the graves would have been oriented toward the east, toward Jerusalem, to greet the resurrection. In 1900 or 2000, they were oriented toward walkways or topographical features—views of a valley or a river—that might still be visible. Amidst these great tombs there would be many contemporaneous mass graves with hundreds of unnoticed and unmarked bodies in each. Places like this—the remains of Père Lachaise in Paris, or Highgate and Woking in London, or Underhill in Hull, or Olsdorf in Hamburg, or Rockwood in Sydney, or the large, beautiful, classical Jewish cemeteries at Weißensee in Berlin or Bracka Street in Lodz, or the hundreds more that had mysteriously appeared on the European urban landscape during the course of a century and, increasingly, in the countryside as well between 1800 and 1900—would demand serious attention. So too would national cemeteries and burial places all over the world, from Washington, D.C., to the gathering of the Communist elite cadre in Shanghai—all of these constituted new, self-consciously crafted communities of the dead.

Further excavation might reveal in each of these cities the ruins of something else having to do with the dead: buildings in the Romanesque, Tudor Gothic, neoclassical, or some other historical style beneath which were the outlines of high-tech furnaces that bear a remarkable resemblance to steelmaking ovens found in other excavated industrial sites. Great—unbelievable—luck in the exploration of Woking, near London, would turn up intact a modest building with an overly large chimney looking like an early Industrial Revolution ironworks, in which the British Cremation Society incinerated its members before the far grander facility at Golders Green was built in 1902. Perhaps these ruins would be rightly interpreted as crematoria, but that would be difficult at many sites because their designers had intended to hide what happened there. The templelike structure above the ground dedicated to the living was meant to disrupt the image of factory for the destruction of bodies that the regenerating furnaces below ground suggested. In fact, the whole matter would be puzzling: nothing like it could be found in any late-eighteenth- or early-nineteenth-century sites; mountains of evidence from the graveyards of almost two millennia before would have borne witness to the fact that western Europeans had stopped cremating their dead well before the year 1000, and much earlier in most places; there are no identifiable cremations after that as there had been in Neolithic, classical, and northern medieval sites before that time.[16]

And finally, our archeologist would find—assuming that weather and water had not eaten away at the stones—millions of names on gravestones and tens of thousands on very large, unprecedented, name-bearing monuments. If the excavation were of the western European countryside or the Gallipoli peninsula, the battle lines of the almost forgotten Great War would be traceable through individual names and lists of names. Our explorer might even come upon the ruins of the Vietnam Memorial. The AIDS quilt would have disintegrated, although perhaps some photographs might have survived. Perhaps the millions of names of the Jewish dead would have survived on some list: at Yad Vashem or at smaller national sites. There would be names everywhere. All this would be startling to our imagined archeologist. Between the mound and stele at Marathon and the first national cemetery at Gettysburg there had been nothing like this. Names would be relatively scarce in the churchyards of 1750 or 1800, but in the civilian cemeteries excavated from 1900, they would be everywhere.

Each of these developments, literary sources might suggest, was the result of some problem solved (an excess of urban bodies, hygienic considerations in the context of new medical knowledge) or of some new ideal or belief or taste (democracy, nationalism, death understood as sleep in beautiful surroundings, neoclassical aesthetics). And interpretations built on this sort of evidence would not be wrong. But I invite my reader to take a broader view, which is how I hope to connect my accounts of deep time with my more historical sections: to take the new sites from 1900 as seriously as we take ancient and early Christian archeology in our effort to understand the slow decline and eventual assimilation of one civilization by another. Something momentous has happened. The ruins I am imagining do more than reflect views about death; they are evidence for the social and cultural work of the dead in our era and other eras.

I want to make clear that I am not being delusional by claiming that the dead do work, in the sense that a physicist would understand the term: "weight lifted through a height," displacement of a mass over some distance in the direction of a force. Diogenes had a point: the dead—or in any case their bodily remains—can do nothing because they are nothing. They cannot even lift a stick to fend off beasts. Consequently, it would seem that they could not do the far more demanding work I have assigned them. With the exception of ghosts and other unquiet spirits—that is, with the exception of the not-quite-dead or the differently dead to which I will return (see chapter 2)—the dead as represented by the dead body are dead. They therefore do not work (or play) in the space and time of our world. This is the fundamental fact about them; it is the meaning of the universal great divide between life and death. Whatever the dead do or suffer, it is somewhere else or, in the case of spirits, in some other form. The living have stepped into their shoes, taken their property, married their wives or husbands, and in many other ways ushered them out.

My inquiry is thus, in a double sense, different from inquiries about what work the inhabitants of Berlin, Beijing, or even the farthest and most exotic reaches of the earth do. There are many kinds of the not-quite-dead: the zombies that are making such a comeback in our popular culture; the insistent spirit of Hamlet's father; the souls that cry out in purgatory; the corporeal, grotesque, monstrous undead Norse *draugar*, who are not spirits or *imagos* of the dead, as St. Augustine thought ghosts were, but rather physical beings that walk after they are dead and can wreak destruction; the Chinese dead who walk not alone but in droves to their appropriate burial places; the mournful "shadow" of Odysseus's mother, who slips from his arms and explains that he cannot hold her because a "spirit, rustling, flitters away . . . flown like a dream." Maybe they can work in some of the ways the living do. But these are my subjects only in the ways in which they affect how we regard the really dead, the remains of the dead. All of the dead, including the not-quite-dead, are different from us, whatever else they might be. It is precisely because of this that they are central to making culture, to creating the skein of meaning through which we live within ourselves and in public.[17]

The history of the work of the dead is a history of how they dwell in us—individually and communally. It is a history of how we imagine them to be, how they give meaning to our lives, how they structure public spaces, politics, and time. It is a history of the imagination, a history of how we invest the dead—again, I will be speaking primarily of the dead body—with meaning. It is really the greatest possible history of the imagination. In any given instant, the living may well be able to give an account of their beliefs about where, who, or what the dead are, or what death is, or how the dead might operate in this world or some other: roughly speaking, "attitudes toward death" or "religious beliefs" or "beliefs about the dead." But the power of bodies is remarkably independent of views of this sort. If this is the case, it might seem more appropriate in our disenchanted world to speak not of the work of the dead but rather of the living: we—not the somehow revenant dead—are the ones doing the real work. Point taken. Let me therefore be clearer. I am offering a social history of what real living people in the depths of time—and especially from the eighteenth century on—did with and through real dead bodies, and a cultural history of what their acts meant and mean to them.[18]

But the dead remain active agents in this history even if we are convinced they are nothing and nowhere. Their ontological standing is of minor importance. They do things the living could not do on their own. Federico García Lorca once claimed, "Everywhere else death is an end. Death comes and we draw the curtain." But not in Spain. "A dead man is *more alive [there] than* the *dead* of any other country in the world." I do not want to dispute national ranking, although with the massive post-Franco exhumations, Lorca has a point. But although league standings change over time, the dead are alive everywhere. (In late November 2014, Spanish archeologists began digging on a three hundred-square-meter plot where they believe Lorca's body is buried; an earlier attempt to find him failed in 2009, and no one knows if this one will succeed.) Living bodies do not have the same powers as dead ones. "The most dangerous person at a funeral," as the historian Richard Cobb once observed, "is the body in the coffin." An empty tomb, a grave marker with no body or no ashes beneath it, a funeral procession with only an empty coffin, a faux graveyard, fake bones are all greatly diminished: Hamlet without the Prince. A purposely empty tomb—a cenotaph—or an empty coffin have power precisely because they lack what is universally expected.[19]

The charisma of the dead—or *charismata*, as theologians might put it, the gift of God to man for the building of the church—exists in our age as in other ages not because of the persistence of old wine in new bottles (we are all still enchanted) but because we have never been disenchanted. This is because the care of the dead governs even where specific beliefs have no purchase. Let me end with two sets of stories that illustrate this point and also the ways in which the foundational anthropological claims with which I began are still at work in the unlikeliest modern situations.

The first begins in the cold early hours of Tuesday, 24 November 1954, still deepest night, when grave diggers exhumed the body of Karl Marx and most of his family from an obscure resting place and moved them two hundred yards up the hill to what was then—and still is today—one of the most prominent places in London's Highgate Cemetery. Lenchin (the German diminutive of Helene) Delmuth, the family's longtime servant and the mother of an illegitimate son generally believed to have been sired by Marx, had been buried, and was moved, with them. Eleanor Marx was reunited with her parents in their new location after a long, sad separation in death. She was cremated after she committed suicide in 1898. Her common-law husband, Edward Aveling, whose infidelity in secretly marrying someone else may have contributed to her despair, did not want her ashes, so they came into the hands of one of the founders of the Socialist League. He attached a dated and signed note to the urn that identified its contents as

Eleanor's remains and delivered it to the office of the Socialist Democratic Federation, where it remained until 1920 when it was moved to the headquarters of the British Communist Party, only to be confiscated there in a police raid the next year and kept in custody by the authorities for more than a decade. In 1933, they gave the urn back, and it was installed in the Marx Memorial Library, where it rested for a time in the room in which Lenin had worked between April 1902 and May 1903. Finally, in the late fall of 1954, the ashes were moved one last time: to the new grave that had been made in Highgate.[20]

Karl Marx's body had led a more sedentary existence. Russia had asked for it in 1922 so as to put it in a place of honor near the Kremlin, but the British Home Office refused, claiming that it could not obtain the required permission for an exhumation from Marx's next of kin. This may have been the real reason. The Home Office had no problem allowing the ashes of Leonid Krasim, the People's Commissar for Foreign Trade, who died in London in 1925, to be sent back home to be buried in the Kremlin Wall. When, more than thirty years later, the Marx Memorial Library asked to move the great man, it was more successful. Three great-grandchildren living in France consented to the exhumation, and the Home Office gave its permission this time but on the condition that the exhumation be carried out secretly and under cover of darkness. For three days after the reburial, "pilgrims" apparently stood unknowingly before an empty grave. On 27 November, the move was made public. It had been very costly. The Library paid £800 for the new site, exhumation, and reburial, and a huge amount, £5,000, for a new tomb: a granite plinth with a bronze bust of Marx on top that was designed by the well-known Communist sculptor Lawrence Bradshaw. The epitaph reads: "Workers of All Lands Unite."[21]

Hic locus est—here is the place. Enemies attacked it. A bomb explosion on 14 May 1970, caused £500 damage, one of at least five incidents of vandalism that year. "It naturally attracts the attention of persons of various political persuasions particularly of the younger element of the 'Right wing,'" said the commissioner of police in explaining that the site was vulnerable and that only a full-time guard—totally impractical under the circumstances—could really keep it safe. And adherents made it a sacred site. Around Marx's body the gravesites of comrades gathered as if his were the tomb of a saint: Yusof Dadoo, the South African Communist leader; Mansure Hekmat, the founder of the Communist Party of Iran, a Marxist revolutionary of Maoist persuasion who would not make his peace with the Islamic revolution and died in exile in London in 2002; "Claudia Vera Jones, Born Trinidad, 1915, Died London, 25 December 1964, Valiant Fighter against racism and imperialism who dedicated her life to the progress of socialism and the liberation of her own black people," also the founder of both the Notting Hill Carnival and Britain's first black newspaper; Paul Foot, "writer

I.5. The grave of Karl Marx
in Highgate Cemetery, London.

I.6. The grave of Eric Hobsbawm
in Highgate Cemetery, London.

and revolutionary"; and Ralph Miliband, the Jewish "Writer Teacher Socialist" and father of the current Labour Party leader, are all nearby. So is Ian Dorans, "1939–2007, Loving Family Man and Socialist to the End," who, with more famous comrades from the Workers Party of Scotland, robbed banks to pay for the hoped-for workers' revolution. Eric Hobsbawm, the greatest Marxist historian of his generation, lies only twenty-five feet away. He died on 1 October 2012 and was cremated, although this is not evident from his tomb: an upright, slightly arched tablet standing at the head of a low, full-size coffin with a stone top as if it actually held a body. Visitors have left small stones on the grave, a Jewish gesture that is probably meant to show that someone had stopped by but may also unconsciously echo the ancient practice of putting large stones in front of tombs so that the dead would stay in place (figs. I.5, I.6). Some would say that my friend Raphael Samuel, a brilliant, secular Jewish, atheist communist historian, who is buried a little farther away from Marx's tomb, to the north and up a gentle hill, hidden by trees, is part of this company. Comrades who were at his funeral certainly have thought so. And they are not entirely wrong; he did want to be buried near friends, many of whom were in the Party. But, Samuel and his wife chose his gravesite for other reasons, reasons of the sort that will find echoes throughout this book. Highgate is steeped in the history of London, whose history he had studied all his life; it is near where he grew up and near where relatives live today; and in Highgate they found a plot where they could be buried together, "connubial" in the grave.[22]

Marx might have found this very peculiar. And so should we. He certainly would have had a hard time explaining philosophically why his tomb had become a pilgrimage site. As a student, he had written his Ph.D. dissertation on the ancient materialist philosopher Epicurus (341–270 B.C.E.), who offers the most influential and long-lived argument in the Western tradition for death as a complete and permanent annihilation of body and soul. What remains of Marx or anyone are atoms—and nothing, but nothing, else. Epicurus would have given two reasons for this. First, there is no such thing as an immaterial soul that might be able to subsist as a version of the person after death. Once dead, there was no Karl Marx anywhere. And second, the material soul that enlivens a body—Marx's body, any body—could have no independent life. This means that to be dead is for the story to be over. The body loses its sentience when the soul departs—the defining moment of death in all Western and most other traditions until the advent of modern biological accounts—and, according to Epicurus, so does the departed soul. It was itself sentient only as a consequence of its having been "somehow confined within the rest of the frame." Soul and body need each other; neither can exist on its own. When specialized corporeal soul atoms leave the body at the moment of death, they both become matter of the sort they were before. A dead person instantly leaves the world of culture when its two kinds of atoms are sundered; she becomes exactly what she was before she was born, when she did not exist: plain matter. There was, in other words, no rational argument that could be given within the Marxist intellectual tradition that the place where Marx's remains rested was different from any other place.[23]

Then why would the comrades act as if they did not believe this? Lucretius, the classical philosopher who most faithfully developed Epicurus's ideas, removes any possible philosophical justification. Even if in the infinity of time all our atoms could somehow come together again in exactly the same form as they were before we died—we recognize this as an improbable thermodynamic event—the reconstituted being would not be us because "there would [have been] a break in consciousness." The new us, the reassembled replica, would no more be us than we are some possible earlier version(s) of ourselves made from the same atoms. Death ends time, just as birth begins it. And so Marx's atoms will never again be Marx. And it does not make a difference where they lie. There is no *praesentia*—no real presence, no power, no juncture of the profane and sacred—as at a saint's tomb, and none of the people buried around Marx would have claimed otherwise. Nothing that any of them would have believed about death, the body, or the afterlife explains why they or their friends wanted their bodies to be where they are, near the tomb of the founder of historical materialism, the paradigmatic modern philosophy of disenchantment.[24]

And yet there they are. Why? Not because of ideas or dogma but rather owing to delusions of the sort Lucretius exposed: the inability to recognize that what has befallen others will befall us. Complete oblivion. But more specifically, there are the two sets of reasons that inform this book. First, there is the recognition, even if unspoken, of the power of the dead in deep time to make communities, to do the work of culture, to announce their presence and meaning by occupying space. Marx's actual body is necessary for this to happen; name-bearing stones would not have sufficed for those who surround him. Second, there are the sorts of historically contingent reasons that make it possible for these men and women to announce their membership in this particular fellowship (cosmopolitan socialism) in this place (Highgate) with ashes produced by cremation in technologically sophisticated modern ovens. Bodies create a community of memory; visitors to these bodies confirm it; together they make a claim on space and on the attention of the living. We are here. We the dead even speak, as do Villon's skeletons on the gibbet.

The dead contributed also to the fall of communism and the building of something different for the same combination of reasons. "Many thousands of otherwise politically disenchanted people," writes the historian of the exhumation of Béla Bartók from a New York cemetery and his reburial in Budapest in 1988, watched a "publicity extravaganza" that occupied the media for four months and affected how an elite understood the relationship between the state and civil society, and between the Hungarian state and Europe more particularly. In 1989, the bones of Imre Nagy brought down the regime. They were translated, in a massive procession using props from the local opera company's *Aída* production, from a pit in the Budapest Zoo to the cemetery where the heroes of 1848 were buried. Janos Kadar, the old-fashioned, hard-line Communist who had ordered Nagy murdered after the failed 1956 revolution, feared for decades that the very mention of his dead enemy's name was dangerous. As it turned out, his body was more so than his necronym.[25]

And the dead contribute to creating continuities between the pre- and the post-Communist past, knitting together the parts of a fractured history. Lenin's body—a miracle of the embalmer's art—still seems indispensable to the political theology of Russia, as it was to that of the Soviet Union. A missing Romanian body makes the case with more chronological precision. In 2003, the mayor of Palermo, Sicily, promised his counterpart in Palermo's sister city, Timisoara, that he would do everything he could to repatriate the bones of Nicolae Bălcescu, "friend of Garibaldi" and hero of the 1848 Revolution, who had died in exile. The mayor's best efforts were not enough; after 150 years of fruitless searches for his remains, Bălcescu's body was irretrievably lost. He could not be found in 1977, when the Romanian Communist government sent a "shock" team of historians to Italy under an arrangement made at the highest governmental levels; he could not be found in 1942, when new documents were discovered that held out false hope of recovery; he could not be found in 1921 or in 1925, when two right-wing government missions looked for him in another Palermo site; he could not be found in 1863, when a delegation led by the hero's friend, the academician Nicolae Ionescu, looked for his body in a common grave and concluded that the case was hopeless. The search had begun in 1850, when the leader of a newly united Romania declared that those who "gave their lives for the good and glory of their country" deserved acknowledgment and expressed the wish that "the ashes of Nicolae Bălcescu . . . dead in the bitterness of exile, be brought back to the Romanian land." But if one body was missing in the making of post-1989 Europe, a hundred others were found and repatriated; new polities, like new religions, need the dead just as old polities and old religions do.[26]

The story only becomes more elaborated in our own day and more global in postcolonial contexts. For example, claims and counterclaims for the corpse of one of Kenya's most distinguished lawyers, Silvanus Melea Otiena, shook his homeland. He had wanted to be buried near Nairobi and his marital home, in a Western-style cemetery. His highly educated Kikuyu wife wanted to respect his wishes. But members of his Luo clan claimed the body for a more traditional burial in his native village, far from the sophisticated urban world of which he had been a part. At stake when the Kenyan Supreme Court decided the fate of Otiena's remains were the rights of women (his wife in particular); the role of tradition versus modernity and African versus European customs; the competing interests of tribe, of natal and of marital family, and of nation; and the meaning of the dead man's life and learning. Stories of his quoting Shakespeare in Nairobi bars were offered to the court as evidence for where his body should go. In the end, ethnic interests prevailed; he was buried at Nyamila six months after he died. Not since the great days of the medieval relic trade has there been such a high level of traffic in dead bodies as in the modern era nor such contention over their fate. Marx's translation in 1954 was but one episode.[27]

I end with my own strange story of caring for the dead. Sometime in the early nineteenth century, my great-great-great-great-grandfather, the rabbi David ben Elizer, acquired a surname. The story of how and why this happened I tell in a general way in chapter 7. That new name soon acquired a "u" and became mine. I have visited his grave on a wooded knoll that rises a few score meters from the flat Silesian farmland (fig. I.7). I know where it is because of the studies of German researchers on the Jews of this area and Polish scholars of Jewish history and culture who are transcribing names from Jewish gravestones as a way of recovering the world that the Shoah had permanently destroyed. This rabbi, born David ben Elizer, a man of considerable learning, secular as well as religious, spent his whole life in a tiny village now called Miejsce, then Stadel, set among potato fields seventy kilometers southeast of Wrocław, then called Breslau. It had both a Protestant and a Catholic church, between which sat the manor house of the local lord who, perhaps because his people already had pluralistic allegiances, welcomed a third religion. The survival of the rabbi's tombstone is remarkable. It sat in the

I.7. The grave of the rabbi, David ben Elizer, the author's great-great-great-great-grandfather, in Mjiesce, Poland.

I.8. The grave of Anna and Siegfried Laqueur, the author's great-grandparents, in Wrocław, Poland.

pathway of the Russian army's march to Festung Breslau, but, except for a few pockmark bullet holes, it has little to show for its experiences. It is unusual only in that its long Hebrew epitaph in the third person turns to a familiar second-person "you," and addresses the rabbi as "you who managed in wisdom for thirty-six years . . . you will harvest with joy." The writer imagined the dead man listening, although there would have been little left of him by the time the tombstone was set. David's wife, like Pip's mother at the beginning of *Great Expectations*, gets little more than "and also . . ." with a few words about her virtues. Abraham's first real estate purchase in Canaan may have been a cave for Sarah's burial, but from then on one hears much more about the tombs of the patriarchs.[28]

I came upon my great-grandparents' graves by accident when my wife and I toured the German Jewish cemetery in Wrocław (fig. I.8). There is an irony in the fact that a Jewish burial place is one of the very few public signs in Wrocław that there had ever been Germans in what is now a thoroughly Polish city. The other so-called German ones were unceremoniously obliterated at the first opportunity after 1945, as were almost all signs that in 1871 Breslau was the sixth-biggest city of the Kaiser Reich. Dead Jews are what little remains to witness to this history. My great-grandparents—Siegfried and Anna—are in good company: a Greek helmet adorns the gravestone of a fallen Jewish officer of the Great War; there are monuments to soldiers who died at Sedan in the Franco-Prussian War and to one who died in the Napoleonic *Freiheitskriege*. The parents of the Carmelite saint Edith Stein are here, as are those of Fritz Haber, the Jewish Nobel Prize–winning chemist who invented poison gas; Ferdinand Lasalle, the founder of what became the German Socialist Party, is twenty meters away, and Abraham Geiger, the founder of Reform Judaism, is

I.9. The grave of Walther Laqueur, Dr. med., the author's grandfather, in Friedhof Ohlsdorf, Hamburg.

not far distant. This is a cemetery of the sort I describe in chapter 5, a new kind of space where the Jews of the Enlightenment proclaimed their cultural modernity.

I have been to my grandfather's grave. He died in Hamburg in 1927 and is buried in the Jewish section of Hamburg's great, parklike Friedhof Ohlsdorf (fig. I.9). Where he lies is largely indistinguishable in its architecture and landscape from the adjacent Christian areas. I knew well what his black marble tombstone with his name in Jugendstil lettering —"Dr. Med. Walther Laqueur"—looked like, because a picture of it had stood on my grandmother's desk as I was growing up.

When my father died in 1984, he was cremated, the first in my lineage to be so disposed of. I am not sure why his father had chosen not to be; scientifically minded and self-consciously modern German, Swiss, and Italian Jews often chose cremation in the early twentieth century to show their modern bona fides. Nationalist and secularist though he was, he was also culturally conservative and probably did not relish the idea that his widow would have to fight with rabbinical authorities to be buried among Jews. In the 1920s, cremation was still a radical gesture, not just to Jews but also to others. My father specifically wanted to be cremated. As a pathologist, he was under no illusion about what dead bodies really were.

We mixed his ashes into the dirt of a flowerbed by the lake cottage in Virginia where his life ended (fig. I.10). Some of my mother's ashes are now there as well—those that we did not cast upon the waters where she loved to swim and where, it was said at her memorial, her spirit dwelled. His sister's, my Tante Elli's, ashes were put there two years before my father's. To be truthful, the body of a beloved dog is right next to the flowerbed. Frederick the Great wanted to be buried with his dogs, Byron wanted to lie next to Boatswain, but in general the

I.10. Flowerbed on Claytor Lake, near Pulaski, Virginia, where the ashes of Werner and Toni Laquer, the author's parents, and Elli Lauquer Silton, the author's aunt, are scattered.

communities of the human and the animal dead were until very recently quite separate. The bodies by the lake were a modern lot.

More than a decade after we mixed my father's ashes with the clay soil of Virginia, I was invited to lecture in Germany. My wife suggested that I take some of his ashes with me and mix them with those of his father, my grandfather, in Hamburg. I replied that, as she well knew, I had no ashes; they were by now leached away by the snows of winter and rains of summer. A body yields little more than a milk carton in volume of ash; nothing of him could possibly be left. After some discussion, I finally decided to take a small bag of dirt in which there might have been a homeopathically small number of inorganic molecules that had once been in my father and to mix these with the soil of his father's grave. This gesture of repatriation would have been regarded by my father as an act of rank superstition.

And so, I suppose, it was. If there were any molecules that had been part of my father's body in the bag of dirt, they were indistinguishable from the soil amendments one adds to one's garden: mostly calcium phosphate and calcium carbonate, some sodium and potassium salts, trace elements of this and that. But it did seem right that some of him—however attenuated and basely material— should be back where he had once felt both comfortable and troubled; and it did make me understand that he was dead. And it united him with the father he had lost when he was seventeen, with whom he had been exceptionally close. It seemed a gesture that mirrored my insistence on giving lectures in German in Germany, even to an audience like that at the Kennedy Institute for North American Studies in Berlin, where everyone's academic English is better than my academic German. Like the return of dirt pretending to be ashes pretending to be a body pretending to bear some relationship to a person I had loved, there is little reason has to say about all this. Such is the work of culture.

I number myself among the unenchanted; I take the work of the dead to be perhaps the greatest and most mysterious triumph of culture. There is, I am sure, nothing "real" behind it. It has always taken a leap to make something, but not too much, of corpses. (The past must not bury the future.) I believe that the power of the dead has always worked and still does by sleight of hand, but of a profound sort. This is what I meant when I wrote earlier that this book is written under the sway of anthropology informed, in the moment, by history.

If the things magicians did were in fact "real," they would lose much interest to us moderns. If we watched their shows always thinking of the tricks that were being played on us, they would become empty and cold. Unmasking may have its place, but this is not my purpose. Instead, as Dave Hickey writes of a show in Las Vegas, we watch elephants disappear without inquiring how this is done and we listen to a chorus asking that they be made to reappear in the same spirit. We understand that "the whole tradition of disappearing things and restoring them is located where it should be: in rituals of death and resurrection." We "simply take pleasure in seeing the impossible appear possible and the invisible made visible. Because if these illusions were not just illusions, we should not be what we are: mortal creatures who miss our dead friends, and thus can appreciate levitating tigers and portraits by Raphael for what they are—songs of mortality sung by the prisoners of time."[29]

We—we moderns and, I suspect, some of those who came before us, if they could have understood what we were talking about—have come to make meaning with corpses knowing that, if pushed very hard, we would have to admit that the work of the dead is, in this sense, magic. But it is magic that we can believe without an ironic shrug. We can and do comfort ourselves in new ways in a post-metaphysical age; we still keep the dead present, however tenuously, among the living; we still make and remake communities persisting through time as we have always done.

I will claim that what is modern about the work of the dead in our era is this: a protean magic that we believe despite ourselves. I think that death is not and has never been a mystery; the mystery is our capacity as a species, as collectivities and as individuals, to make so very much of absence and specifically of the poor, naked, inert dead body.

PART I

THE DEEP TIME
OF THE DEAD

Some day I will go to Aarhus
To see his peat-brown head,
The mild pods of his eye-lids,
His pointed skin cap.

In the flat country near by
Where they dug him out,
His last gruel of winter seeds
Caked in his stomach,

Naked except for
The cap, noose and girdle,
I will stand a long time.
Bridegroom to the goddess,

She tightened her torc on him
And opened her fen,
Those dark juices working
Him to a saint's kept body,

Trove of the turfcutters'
Honeycombed workings.
Now his stained face
Reposes at Aarhus.

SEAMUS HEANEY, "THE TOLLUND MAN"

The dead body lives on many time scales: the hours, days, weeks, or months it takes for the person to whom it belonged to leave this world and for her material remains to be put where they belong; the indeterminate time, from years to centuries, it takes for the body, flesh, and bones to become dust; the years, decades, and, for the lucky few, even longer in which a person might stay in memory with her body as its locus; the thousand or so years that regimes of the dead, notoriously conservative—pagan, classical, Christian, perhaps modern—persist; the millennia and longer in which basic forms of the care of the dead have existed since Neolithic times, if not earlier. The last of these—centuries or millennia—is the scale of deep time that is relevant to the three chapters in this part.

Most of this book is about a vast enterprise on a small stage: the work of the dead in western Europe since the eighteenth century. It is, as I have said, the history of specific practices with specific causes and specific consequences, measured in years, decades, or at most centuries, in one corner of the world or sometimes in one corner of a corner. Why the cemetery? Why modern cremation? Why are names so prominent in modern memorial practices? But these are versions of more general questions: Where are the dead? What are they? Who are they? My answers to the more limited questions depend on the long, iterative, and weighty history—the deep time—of the dead, on historical anthropological foundations that go down as far as we can see. Bodies matter; they are always much more than they seem. Personhood persists where it manifestly no longer resides; the dead, as represented by their bodies, are somewhere and are something. And finally, there is a tradition of thinking that goes from classical antiquity to contemporary anthropology that argues for the significance of the work of the dead to the making of civilizations and of communities of all sorts. Not only do the dead do work, but by their words and actions the living for a very long time have shown their reliance on the work of the dead.

The three chapters in this part will trace the dead through the *longue durée*. Here they live either in an immemorial moment or on a time scale where change works at a glacial pace. Perhaps only the incest taboo can rival the recognition of death and of the dead—that special liminal category of the human—as a civilizational ground zero: neither just biological nor just cultural but the mark of their boundary. Sharing in this foundational status—seemingly frozen at the beginning of cultural time—means that for all the immense variety in the treatment of the dead over thousands of years that historical, sociological, anthropological, and archeological research has revealed—again, only kinship as a field of inquiry is anywhere near as rich—death and the dead have always mattered everywhere in important, defining, and broadly similar ways. But all of this happens somewhere; it happens through the passing of years. I will return to deep time with respect to particular topics again and again, but its foundational importance is laid out in the part that follows. I hope here to connect the cosmic with the particular from antiquity to the beginning of the modern age.

There is another more specific feature of deep time beyond the sheer cultural weight it bears: its jagged stratigraphy. Bodies of the dead that were put to rest or abandoned hundreds or even thousands of years ago are thrust up into the present by the human equivalent of geological forces. These forgotten dead may have always been, or have become, nothing. In this state they long ago ceased doing any cultural work, if ever they did any. But then they are brought to the surface, to the notice of the living, by a variety of circumstances; they are discovered. Some in this category would include the bodies archeologists dig up and put in museums or laboratories; they have become the talismans of a lost civilization or objects of scientific study. These dead are something entirely different from what they had been before, changed from subject to object by the weight of the past.

Others emerge from oblivion to a new life as they, or more precisely their bodies, are reborn as cultural beings of a new sort. Tollund Man, killed in a fourth-century B.C.E. bog and found by peat cutters in 1950, is exemplary (plate 2). Almost magically, because of the high acidity and anaerobic conditions of where he had fallen, we know what he ate as his last meal; we know what he wore when he died—a cap of wool and sheepskin; we know how he died—he was strangled. We do not know why. Perhaps he was executed; more likely, scholars say, he was a human sacrifice. Most of his tribe died violent deaths; a few may have lost their way and fallen into a bog. Long lost and forgotten, he now has a story; glimpses of his personhood can be read from his tanned remains. He touches a great poet.

> Trove of the turfcutters'
> Honeycombed workings.
> Now his stained face
> Reposes at Aarhus.

More generally, bog people have come to live as an important community in the making of Danish identity and that of other northern lands.[1]

Even archaeological specimens, far less possessed of their humanity, have also returned to culture. I am thinking here not only of paleo-Americans—the bodies from Wizards Beach, Spirit Cave, and most famously Kennewick Man, discovered on 28 July 1996, that had lain forgotten for ten thousand years—but also of many other more recent remains that are poised today between the laboratories of anthropologists who study the origins of human settlement in North America and Native Americans who regard them as the remains of ancestors to be buried in religious ceremonies.[2]

Other communities of the historically forgotten and despised are returned to life by the living as they seek to redeem the past. In 1794, a slave burial ground in lower Manhattan was covered over by twenty-five feet of dirt and made ready for the urban development that soon followed. The cemetery and its bodies then passed into oblivion. After almost two centuries, in October 1991, much to the surprise of the General Services Administration, whose environmental impact survey of the site where it was building a $275 million federal office building found no human remains, the first of what eventually numbered 420 skeletons was unearthed. These turned out to belong to slaves, a small number of the tens of thousands who were buried on the island. Construction stopped. Ultimately, the African American community and its allies managed to force a radically altered design for the proposed building that created space for what became in 2006 the African Burial Ground National Monument: "a truly spiritual and sacred memorial to the African experience and legacy."[3]

Perhaps the possibility of historical undoing implicit in the redemption of slave graves and of lost time somehow recovered in our engagement with the bog people is a product of the modern age with its sense of progress and of loss. But even if these imaginative possibilities are especially strong after the late eighteenth century, the stratigraphic emergence of bodies is not. Dead bodies have gone in and out of being among the living for a very long time. The sixteenth-century antiquarian Antonio Bosio discovered some four thousand long-forgotten bodies in the vast catacombs of early Christian Rome; no one had visited them for eight hundred years. He essentially created systematic necroarcheology, a combination of erudition and excavation, to bring these dead—these bodies of martyrs, Bosio thought—to light and thus to map a new sacred geography of the Eternal City. More than a millennium after their deaths, these bodies worked mightily in the cause of the Catholic Reformation. The impulse to recover the special if not the ordinary dead goes back to the beginning of the writing of history. Herodotus tells of the successful Spartan effort to find the bones of Orestes, without which, so saith the Delphic Oracle, they would fail in the battle against the Tageans. In deep time the strata of the dead emerge.[4]

Finally, deep time allows us to see the extent to which the work of the dead is made possible by accretion, by the building of layer upon layer of meaning. Classicism is the perfect example, but there will be many other cases. Here is one particularly mixed-up and local case of the rich Cambridgeshire antiquarian John Underwood, who died in 1733. He insisted in his will that he be carried to his grave, not to the sound of hymns and the tolling of the passing bell, but to the voices of six friends singing the twentieth ode from the second book of the first-century Augustan poet Horace.

> No dirges for my fancied death;
> No weak lament, no mournful stave;

> All clamorous grief were waste of breath,
> And vain the tribute of a grave.

He ordered that a Greek New Testament be placed in his right hand, a little edition of Horace in his left, and the great eighteenth-century classical philologist Richard Bentley's 1732 edition of Milton's *Paradise Lost* under his feet. It is difficult to extract a historically specific attitude toward death from all this. It is, however, easy to see a highly wrought commitment to a deep tradition of classical scholarship that the dead man hoped to reaffirm as he was put into the ground.[5] Underwood's burial, still noticed in the late nineteenth century, suggests how the body in the coffin can appropriate the weight of many millennia. If not exactly timeless—without history—it rests in the very slow time of fixed structures and enduring cultural landscapes. The three chapters in this part are about the underlying cultural resources that give this little story and the whole grand work of the dead its power and efficacy.

Chapter 1
DO THE DEAD MATTER?

He looked down intently into a stone crypt. Some animal. Wait. There he goes.

An obese grey rat toddled along the side of the crypt, moving the pebbles. An old stager: greatgrandfather: he knows the ropes. The grey alive crushed itself in under the plinth, wriggled itself in under it. Good hidingplace for treasure.

Who lives there? Are laid the remains of Robert Emery. Robert Emmet was buried here by torchlight, wasn't he? Making his rounds.

Tail gone now.

One of those chaps would make short work of a fellow. Pick the bones clean no matter who it was. Ordinary meat for them. A corpse is meat gone bad.

JAMES JOYCE, *Ulysses*

Diogenes the Cynic, the dog philosopher, had an answer to this chapter's question: No, the dead do not matter. There is nothing behind the veil of the corpse but rotting organic matter. It is the answer that reason, speaking for nature, gives to culture, demanding that culture explain itself. If Diogenes had not existed, we would have had to invent him; we need a spokesman for what we believe but find unacceptable: the rupture wrought by death on the body. We need someone to insist that the dead do not matter so that we can respond with reasons for why they do. Some two or three centuries after Cicero's account of Diogenes' views (see the introduction's epigraph), the Cynic's first biographer tells an even more aggressively defiant story about him: "Some say that when dying he left instructions that they should throw him out unburied, that every wild beast might feed on him, or thrust him into a ditch and sprinkle a little dust over him. But according to others, his instructions were that they should throw him into the Ilissus, in order that he might be useful to his brethren." No one in the Western tradition makes the case against the pretensions of the dead body more uncompromisingly and with such enduring influence: a well-reported and seemingly commonsense rejection of all that decency and custom prescribe. Pierre Bayle, the first great Enlightenment historian of philosophy and a religious skeptic, gets at the qualities that make him such a worthy opponent: he was, Bayle writes, "one of those extraordinary men who are upon

1.1. Diogenes among refuse. *Diogenes Searching for an Honest Man.* Etching by Giovanni Domenico de' Rossi, after Giovanni Benedetto Castiglione, 1645–1650. The Metropolitan Museum of Art, New York. Purchase, Joseph Pulitzer Bequest, 1917 (17.50.17-54).

extremes in everything, without excepting reason [without excepting the dead, I will add], and who verify the maxim that there is no great wit without a mixture of folly." Diogenes became the great spokesman for the dead body as fundamentally profane, unenchanted, a part of nature, mere matter, carrion (fig. 1.1).[1]

His younger contemporary, Plato, described him as "a Socrates gone mad." He pushed the philosophical pursuit of virtue off the rails; his views on the dead, as on other matters, were crazy. Diogenes is said to have masturbated in public because he thought finding sexual satisfaction was no more embarrassing or private than satisfying one's hunger by having a meal in the agora. He lived on the street, in a barrel, and once told Alexander the Great, who admired him and wanted to do him a good deed, that the only favor he wanted was that Alexander "cease to shade [him] from the sun." He got in trouble for forgery. The philosopher Peter Sloterdijk gets him right: "a man who smells the swindle of idealistic abstractions and the schizoid staleness of thinking limited to the head": a clown—perhaps the most famous derelict in history—who tested the limits of culture and convention and tried to act on the fact that to be dead is to be nothing (plate 3).[2]

Socrates almost went that far. Just before he takes the poison, he tries to make his student Crito understand that he would not be "laying out, or carrying out, or burying Socrates," because Socrates would no longer be there. He cared little how he would be buried: bury me, he said, "in any way you like if you can catch me and I do not escape you." There would be no Socrates still around to bury. But the live Socrates did not ask his students to reject all that was customary. Diogenes the Cynic did. The differences between them were not metaphysical. Diogenes was not a materialist who believed that death left nothing of a person behind; like the others known as Cynics, and like Socrates, he believed in an immaterial and immortal soul. His views about what to do with the dead body had nothing to do with his views on an afterlife and everything to do with what he thought it meant to live this life virtuously. The virtuous man, he taught, ought to comport himself as closely as possible to nature, that is, to live as one who, like a dog, would do in public what others would do only in private: defecate, fornicate, and masturbate as the natural urges made themselves felt. All decency and civility worked against this sort of austerity and commitment to principle; Socrates followed convention. Diogenes did not, and the dead body had no excuse for not doing likewise. Like a dog, it could subsist virtuously (that is, according to nature) more easily than when it was alive. We humans could and should, as the saying goes, "be buried like dogs," that is, not be buried at all, assuming, of course, that dogs are buried like dogs. In fact, almost everywhere since as far back as we can go, dogs have often not been buried like dogs but in some intimate relation with humans. These dogs—those buried like humans—insist through their dead bodies that they are not part of the natural world but of the world of culture. But that is another, if related, story.[3]

For more than two thousand years, skeptics, speaking in the name of Diogenes, have mocked the social pretensions of doing things for the dead, and especially the folly of funerary practices and monuments. They have spoken for the rupture at death between nature and culture. One story from the first century B.C.E. is an embellishment of the one we have already heard. "If then you die, *who* will bury you?" the dog philosopher was asked. "Whoever wants my house," he replied. This was the Greek equivalent of "Who cares?" He was famously a street person who took shelter in a large wine cask. *Where* to be buried and *how*, he thought, were equally inconsequential. Diogenes inspired stories as few other philosophers of antiquity did. In fact, everything we might claim to know about him is from the mouths of others. A disciple supposedly asks him how to die. "Live according to virtue and nature, and that is in our power." Remember that just as one comes from nature at birth, so one will return to nature when dead; nature begets and destroys. And finally, he jokes about his dead body in such a way as to make fun of the truth that it is already back in nature: "I have no worry about my being at any time unconscious of feeling," because I am sure that "I shall be furnished with a staff after breathing my last, that I might drive away the animals that would defile me."[4]

1.2. *The Mausoleum at Halicarnassus*. Philipp Galle (1537–1612), from the series *The Eight Wonders of the World*. After Maarten van Heemskerck, 1572. Harvard Art Museum/Fogg Museum. Gift of Robert Bradford Wheaton and Barbara Ketcham Wheaton in Honor of Mrs. Arthur K. Solomon, M25955.

From this follows a long tradition, running from antiquity to Charles Dickens in the nineteenth century to Jessica Mitford in the twentieth, that much or all care for the dead is folly. In one of Lucian's (ca. 125–180 C.E.) *Dialogues of the Dead*, for example, we find Diogenes and King Mausolus of Caria (d. 353 B.C.E.), the eponymous inhabitant of the first "mausoleum," meeting as corpses in the nether world (fig. 1.2). The philosopher starts the conversation by asking the king whether he thinks he is better off than the rest of the dead because his wife was so fulsome in her grief—she is said to have made herself "a living and breathing tomb" by drinking his ashes mixed in a potion—and because she had built "the Mausoleum at Halicarnassus" for him. Near present-day Bodrum on the Aegean coast of Turkey, it was one of the seven wonders of the ancient world. Mausolus answers by recounting his deeds and by bragging about his tomb, made of the fairest marble with bas-relief ornaments that were "horses and men reproduced most perfectly." If all this does not prove his superiority, what does? he asks. "But, my handsome Mausolus," Diogenes replies, "the strength and the beauty you mention aren't still with you here." Your skull is no better than mine; we are both bald and fleshless; our teeth show; our eyes are gone; our noses snubbed. In fact, he continues, having a big tomb does not make Mausolus better than any of the other corpses except perhaps, as he says to the crestfallen king, because you can "claim to carry more weight than the rest of us with all that marble on top of you." "Will Mausolus and Diogenes be on an equal footing?" Mausolus asks, trying to make the best of it. No, not even that, Diogenes replies. He himself "has no idea whether he even has a tomb for his body, for he didn't care about all that," but if he does not have one, then all the better, because being remembered "as one who lived the life of a man . . . towers above your memorial, and is built on surer foundations." Three long-lived tropes emerge here: first, the futility of marking a particular body with a monument; second, mockery of the illusion that the dead persist in matter, that ashes are a person, and that eating them is a way of somehow re-embodying the dead; and finally, the trope of the equality of the dead.[5]

Some version of the conversation about the futility of taking care of particular bodies when the dead are all basically the same, and all equally irrelevant, became an enormously generative trope. Today it may be best known from the most famous seventeenth-century example: the grave scene (5.1) from Hamlet. Hamlet asks Horatio, as the two contemplate the skull of Yorick,

> HAM: Doest thou think Alexander looked o' this fashion i' the earth?
> HOR: E'en so.
> HAM: And smelt so? Pah!
> HOR: E'en so my lord.
> HAM: To what base uses may we return, Horatio! Why may not imagination trace the noble dust of Alexander, till he find it stopping a bung hole?
> HOR: 'Twere to consider too curiously to consider so.
> HAM: No faith, not a jot. But to follow him thither with modesty enough, and likelihood to lead it: as thus: Alexander died, Alexander was buried, Alexander returnest into dust; the dust is earth; of earth we make loam; and why of that loam, whereto he was converted, might they not stop a beer barrel.

The great king is of the same stuff—dust, clay—that might be mixed into loam to make a plug for a bunghole. Diogenes is not mentioned explicitly, and Shakespeare could have taken the idea that informs this discussion from elsewhere. But the Cynic is only a step away, if that. The emperor-philosopher Marcus Aurelius, who, like other Stoics, much admired the Cynics, reports that "Alexander of Macedon and his groom are equals now in death." Both are now no more than dust, he says, in a comment that is near the start of a long tradition of seeing the dead Alexander as the limit case for the nothingness of bones. Diogenes has been often and continuously linked to Alexander since antiquity.[6]

Less than a century after *Hamlet,* an anonymous storyteller makes the same connection between Diogenes and Alexander, on the one hand, and the undifferentiated materiality of the dead, on the other. This time, the king and the philosopher meet not in the sun but in a charnel house. Alexander asks Diogenes what he is doing there. "I am seeking your father's bones and those of my slave," the philosopher replies, but he is unsuccessful "because there is no difference between them." This story has no ancient source—the Greeks, unlike the Christians, had no charnel houses; Diogenes did not have a slave, although he was said to have been one for a time. It seems to have been invented as a parable for radical Protestants to use to criticize Catholics for their veneration of relics and more moderate Protestants for their superstitious persistence in burying the dead inside churches as if place mattered. By the nineteenth century, Diogenes' reply had become commonplace in dictionaries of quotations and source books for preachers. If the dead are indistinguishable from one another and from the dust from which they came, they really don't matter. He gives voice to the view that there is no reason to venerate one corpse over any other. If corpses matter at all, they all matter the same—which is to say, not very much.[7]

In the long history of repeating one version or another of Diogenes' challenge, the answer has almost always been "yes, you are right, the corpse is nothing": "all flesh is grass and all the goodliness thereof is as the flower of the field" (Isa 40:6, 1 Pet 1:24); dust to dust; let the body go. But at the same time, no one has been able to live with the consequences of this view. For thousands of years, Diogenes' sophism or its equivalent has earned assent and at the same time been rejected in a great variety of forms and in response to a wide range of needs, interests, and beliefs. In this dialogue, culture always has an answer to nature and to the philosopher who says we should live and die naturally, as dogs do.

One of the most important and influential these is St. Augustine's, from the fourth century C.E. He seems to take the Cynic's side when he asks, "Whether the location of [a] body is of any advantage to the soul of the dead?" It demands careful study, he says. "We should especially inquire, not according to common belief, but according to the sacred writings of our religion, if it has any effect on the souls of men for enduring or for increasing their misery after this life, whether their bodies have not been buried." If pagan philosophers—Diogenes or those influenced by him—could be indifferent to what happened to their dead, Christians should, all the more, not be ashamed to have their martyred dead left unburied: "Earth has not covered many of the bodies of the Christians, but nothing has kept any one of them from heaven and earth." Having a proper grave does not matter. The faithful should not believe the "fabulous poetic imaginings" of pagans about the fate of the unburied or uncared-for dead. Augustine is thinking here of a story from Virgil's *Aeneid* (6.348–394) that would have been known to every educated reader. The poet tells of the "horrendous banks" of the River Styx, where a "huge throng of the dead" wait: "mothers and grown men and ghosts of great souled heroes, their bodies stripped of life, and boys and unwed girls," a helpless "great rout." The ferryman Charon will not take them across "the hoarse, roaring flood," "until their bones are buried and they rest in peace." Augustine explains that this is all a silly fable: the fate of the soul is independent of the fate of the body.[8]

This is the great Church Father speaking in his soteriological voice. But he is not willing to go all the way with Diogenes in rejecting what he takes to be a fundamental human impulse: the care of the dead body. "The bodies of the dead, and especially of the just and faithful, are not to be despised or cast aside. The soul has used them as organs and vessels for all good work in a holy manner. . . . Bodies are not for ornament or for aid, as something that is applied externally, but pertain to the very nature of the man." Caring for them is therefore a sign of piety, of love, of affection, and of religious devotion. It is a "comfort for the living." It is a mark of civility and decency: exactly what Diogenes rejected. But more important, it is about linking the common dead to the divine through the bodies of blessed martyrs—the special dead—around whom they are buried. Place and proximity matter after all. Augustine recalls how, before he became a Christian, he witnessed the miraculous restoration of sight to a blind man as an immense crowd gathered for the translation of the long-lost bones of the martyrs Protasius and Gervasius into Milan's cathedral. It would come to matter a great deal where Christians were buried; in fact, for more than a thousand years to be buried anywhere but in proximity to the body of a saint or some other relic was to be "buried like a dog." Necro-sociability would become the heart of Augustine's Church. Some bodies did matter, and it was important to believers that they be buried near them rather than be thrown over the wall (fig. 1.3).[9]

1.3. The discovery of the relics of St. Gervase and Protase. Philippe de Champaigne, 1657–1660. Museum of Fine Arts of Lyon.

Almost everyone who wrote seriously about death was in conversation with Diogenes. Erasmus (1466–1536), the greatest of the Christian humanists, attributed to Diogenes the views of Epicurus, the materialist philosopher, on why being dead should be a matter of no concern. Sir Thomas Browne (1605–1682), the pious seventeenth-century physician and essayist, seems at first—like St. Augustine, but from a Protestant perspective—to agree with Diogenes. Having dissected many dead bodies, he knows from experience that they are nothing but rot and decay. And because he knows this so well, he does not, he says, care what happens to his own body. Like Diogenes, he is willing to bid "totall adieu of the world, not caring for a Monument, History, or Epitaph, not so much as the bare memory of my name to be found any where but in the universal Register of God." What is the point? "Grave-stones tell truth scarce forty years"; the names of the great concourse of the dead, in number far greater than the names of the living, are almost all lost. From the perspective of deep time it does not matter what one does with the dead; "who can but pity the founder of the pyramids?"[10]

But perhaps it does matter. Browne has an almost idolatrous relationship to dead bodies that Diogenes would have laughed at. He recounts sympathetically how Achilles and Patroclus, and again Domitian and his mistress (and niece) Julia, "affectionately compounded their bones, passionately endeavoring to continue their living union." Even in his day, he could have given scores more examples like these; from our perspective there are thousands. And Browne also had second thoughts about himself: "I am not so Cynical, as to approve the Testament of Diogenes." In his "calmer judgment," that is, when he listens to the still voices of the heart rather than the more shrill dictates of reason, he too wants to be buried so as to remain part of an imagined community of the living: like the patriarchs, he wants to "sleep by the urns of their Fathers and go the neatest way into corruption." Browne was buried beneath a rather fine monument under the chancel of St. Peter Mancroft, Norwich.[11]

More than a century and a half after Browne, the poet William Wordsworth has still another conversation with Diogenes. He refers to "varlet [knavish] Philosophers, as Diogenes, who desired to be devoured of fishes." Perhaps he was thinking here of Herodotus's claim that strange, uncivilized tribes throw their dead into the sea, since Diogenes wanted to be left for the beasts. But his real target is the view that the dead body does not matter. It does, he says, because, like "the shell of the flown bird," it was once united with a soul, an intimate association that makes the corpse matter and explains why we give the dead a proper grave: "a tribute to man as a human being." And conversely, if we really did believe that the body is just a shell, of no more importance to the human than the shells of the fowls of the forest or the chickens in the roost are to them, then we would not write epitaphs near bodies to keep the departed in memory. But we do, and since the beginning of literacy, always have. Historical anthropology—culture—Wordsworth suggests, proves Diogenes' naturalism wrong.[12]

But it doesn't. The metaphor of the flight of the bird representing the soul leaving the body was used as a common motif on New England Puritan gravestones to make precisely the opposite point. When the shell of a hatching egg breaks, "the bird does then fly away," says Cotton Mather. Likewise "our death is the breaking of the shell [i.e., the body] and we have an Immortal Soul in us, which is *We,* and in this we *Fly away.*"[13] The body that remains is not "we." Radical Puritans took this to be an argument for giving as little attention to the dead body as possible. But their views did not carry the day. For all of their condemnation of idolatry, thousands of Puritan bodies are buried on an east–west axis awaiting resurrection, under poignantly carved gravestones in scores of New England cemeteries.

There have thus been many reasons for answering Diogenes with "yes, but . . ." They depend not on any particular view of the soul, or its claim on the body, or even on the existence of an immortal or immaterial soul. In the ellipses ". . ." is the work of the dead, of the human imagination, and of this book. That work is possible only because we as a species have consistently resisted Diogenes. Or rather, we have created him in order to explain to ourselves why a corpse remains within culture, bears the mark of life, and cannot be thrown away as carrion. His answer to the question of this chapter—the dead do not matter—has had little purchase for all the many times it has been repeated. But if the answer isn't no, then why not?

The story from Augustine's *Confessions* has already hinted at one reason that has had wide resonance over many millennia and religious traditions. There is one class of the dead whose bodies are the locus of the sacred, of the divine on earth, even though their remains look like any other. (Sometimes their bodies are different—the incorruptible dead—but those of most of the early martyrs at issue for Augustine were badly mauled by beasts, fire, and other tortures.) This type of special dead survives into the present. But by the late eighteenth century, a new kind had emerged: special not because of the presence of the divine or because we subscribe to a theology favorable to them but because historical anthropology, independent of theology or ideology, implicitly underwrites the aura of bones and because nations and social movements and families and associations of all sorts need then. Whatever our religious beliefs, or lack of belief, we share the very deep human desire to live with our ancestors and with their bodies. We mobilize their power. And even as we align ourselves with skeptical Cynic tradition—all dead bodies are alike and useless—and deny that the holy exists anywhere in our world, especially in a dead body, we still want our special bodies, our special dead. A specific body. It would be a national scandal if the body of Rousseau or Zola in the Pantheon actually turned out to belong to someone else, or if some other body—especially a body with a name—were substituted for the Unknown Warrior's in Westminster Abbey. And by extension, the remains of the ordinary dead come to matter; people are upset if a funeral director mixes up one urn of chemically identical ashes with another; this book is full of other examples. The charisma—the divinely given grace—of the special dead is infectious and ubiquitous. Sir James Frazer, one of the nineteenth-century founders of anthropology, gets it wrong: not just among "primitive" people and Catholics, but other people as well, the belief persists that the dead "affect the lives of survivors for good or ill."[14]

One of the great pre-Nicene Church Fathers, Clement of Alexandria (150– ca. 215 C.E.), diagnosed brilliantly the nature of our enduring belief that some of the dead can do great things. He, unlike Protestants who more than a thousand years later who followed his lead, writes not against his fellow Christians—there were very few martyrs at the time he was writing and few signs of the cult of the saints that would flourish exuberantly after the fourth century—but against pagans for making so much of their special dead. These he said, are nothing but idols; they are false gods.

> These temples [of daemon worship] . . . , are called by a fair sounding name, but in reality they are tombs. But I appeal to you, even at this late hour, forget daemon-worship, feeling ashamed to honor tombs. In the temple of Athena in the Acropolis at Larissa there is the tomb of Acrisius; and in the Acropolis at Athens the tomb of Cecrops. And what of Erichthonius? . . . But really, if I were to go through all the tombs held sacred in your eyes, "The whole of time would not suffice my need." As for you, unless a touch of shame steals over you for these audacities, then you are going about utterly dead, like the dead in whom you put your trust.

Clement is on to something important in our own day as well as his: the almost irresistible, primal idolatry of the dead body and the near certainty in some circumstances that it—or in any case, some dead bodies—will become "sacred in [our] eyes." This sacrality attaches itself to a corpse as easily as, or perhaps more easily than, to living flesh and blood. Diogenes, he seemed to realize, would never be dangerous. In fact, the threat came from the opposite direction.[15]

There is an ample empirical record that Clement was right about pagans. The Iron Age, Bronze Age, and classical Greece were, in fact, rich in the tombs of heroes and of the progenitors of cities and demes where sacrifices and prayers were offered to daemons. Clement may have been exaggerating a little; from the perspective of modern historians, daemons are not quite immortal gods, even if they are more than men, and their tombs were not exactly temples. But they were votive sites; they had altars; people prayed there; the dead that they purportedly sheltered channeled some measure of the divine. He thinks that the distinction modern scholars might make between "tomb" and "temple" (between the profane and the sacred dead) is irrelevant. "It seems to me," he writes, "that tombs are objects of reverence in just the same way temples are; in fact, pyramids, mausoleums and labyrinths are as it were temples of dead men, just as temples are the tombs of gods." The gods in temples are as dead as the dead in tombs. It makes no difference to Clement whether the tomb is that of Antinous, the emperor Hadrian's favorite, whom he made into a divinity, or a cultic tomb that "Zeus [had] consecrated [for] Ganymedes." To entreat the help of the dead—any of the dead—is idolatry because, he insists, they are false gods, fictitious divinities that are "nothing in the world," as St. Paul put it (1 Cor 8:4). The Christian God, by contrast, lives.[16]

The idolatry of the dead that Clement diagnoses reaches well beyond the pagans whom he criticizes. Buddhists are not the "bourgeois rationalists" that we have believed them to be; in both popular and elite Buddhist practice, the "utterly profane and loathsome—the corporeal remains of the dead" (that is, of the special dead)—are the physical locus of holiness. Not icons or signs, the bits of bone and desiccated flesh that remain from the funeral pyre or mummification are "the distilled essence of human corporeality." The merest matter from a corpse of the special dead brings the holy to earth. Similarly, the Jews had their cult of holy tombs and it too seemed idolatrous to its critics. "How can I be silent while certain idolatrous practices are rampant among Israel?" came a complaint from tenth-century Jerusalem. People "pass the night among tombstones. They make requests of the dead. They light candles upon the graves of righteous ones." With variations, the same thing happened in Islam despite the prophet's manifest hostility to the cult of the dead.[17]

Within two centuries after Clement wrote, Christians would make temples of their tombs by the hundreds and soon by the thousands. They would have to defend themselves against pagans, and later fellow Christians, who made precisely the arguments that Clement had made. The special dead—the saints and martyrs who created the necrogeography of the ascendant new religion—were, as Peter Brown writes, "exempt from the facts of death." Early Christians could imagine the blood flowing back into here-and-now bones, rejoined with flesh, at the resurrection of the special dead. At their graves "the eternity of paradise and the first touch of the resurrection come into the present." Even a part of the body of a saint who died the horribly painful death of martyrdom becomes detached from its physical presence and is transformed into a sign of the great promise of Christianity: the corporeal resurrection of the dead, the divine, miraculous reversal in death of the laws of entropy. The bodies of saints, especially the early martyrs torn to pieces by beasts, were often less than nothing in their physicality, though some later saints purportedly smelled sweet or were otherwise distinguishable from ordinary bodies. But they were the remains of the house that had sheltered a soul that was now in a privileged place with God; they were a new kind of link between heaven and earth. They were, so to speak, the outward sign of a great and powerful friend who was able to intercede for the more spiritually needy. The relics of saints thus represent the limit case of the responses to Diogenes—because in their case the "nothing" of corporeality had become a magnificent something, a matrix linking heaven and earth.[18]

But this was no easy linkage. It raised for a thousand years the danger that Clement, and others as well, identified—idolatry. Nothing has been fraught with more controversy than the cultural transmutation of profane corporeal remains into vessels of holiness. Enormous intellectual energy went into the creation of an orthodox Christian theology in which the veneration of the special dead was central, in which proximity to these dead was advantageous to the living and ultimately to their souls. It was at the heart of the pre-Reformation Church at all levels and in a spectacular variety of ways. Immense pastoral effort went into the day-to-day problems of policing the holy. The miracles that were the main evidence for a relic's authenticity had to be confirmed. Special bones had to be distinguished from fake ones—the movement of relics and the documentation of their provenance had to be regulated. They were, after all, *just* bones or some other material that had been elevated into treasures because they were evidence for the existence, and the intercessory power, of a saintly life. Like paper money and credit, their power was derived from a promise of something—a status claim—and not from the material itself; they could do their work only in the context of belief in a larger world of meaning of which they were a part. Thus pastoral authorities could destroy the credit of particular relics and popular demand could restore it in turn. Making so much of the corporeal remains of saints acknowledges once again the answer to Diogenes' truth by pointing to the enormous amount of cultural work—work of the imagination—that needs to go into giving the dead body meaning. The possibility of a fake aura must not be allowed to discredit real aura and therefore has to be recognized in order to be repressed.[19]

A healthy skepticism was important, not about whether there could be such a thing as a relic, but about the authenticity of many particular cases. Under all but the best of circumstances, special bones look just like other bones; they usually did not speak for themselves and thus out of the context of a reliquary and the community that venerated them, confirmation could pose an insurmountable problem. Fakes were rife. Many experts, had they wanted to, could no doubt have caught out amateur tricksters like Chaucer's pardoner, but the problem was more difficult in the context of the huge and profitable market in stolen relics whose provenance, like that of stolen art today, had been purposely obscured. How was the famous Bishop Odo of Bayeaux (1036–1097) to be certain that the bones he had purchased with the understanding that they belonged to St. Exuperius (a shadowy fifth-century bishop of Toulouse) were not actually those of a peasant of the same name foisted on him by a church custodian? How were the claims of different churches in different places to have the bones of the same saint to be adjudicated?[20] *Caveat emptor.* Within the world of medieval Catholicism, in which the veneration of relics was an important part of religious practice, there were grounds for doubt in any particular case, grounds for wondering whether these specific bones were really something special, or just bones. But the theological principle of the special dead—of a divine aura in corporeal remains—and the imperative to venerate their bodies were not in doubt. This theological and pastoral activity kept Diogenes' challenge alive; the two were interdependent in their dialectical dance between nothingness and sacrality.

One might think that the Reformation, with its assault on idolatry, would be a turning point in this history. And in some ways it was. It is true that the whole world of the special dead, not just the abuses committed in their name, came fundamentally into question. It was a central tenant of the Reformers that a Christian did not need the help of saints or other intermediaries for salvation: *sola scriptura, sola fides, sola gratia,* and *solus Christus.* In the realm of theology and approved practice, bones and anything else belonging to them were irrelevant to human faith and redemption. To the more radical and Calvinist Reformers and to the iconoclasts on the streets who destroyed shrines and scattered bones throughout northern Europe, the veneration of saints' relics was an especially offensive species of idolatry. "Error and deception" were banished from Geneva when the putative arm of St. Anthony was exposed as the male member of a stag and then mocked in parade through the city, a sort of carnivalesque procession that turned the meaning and value of a treasured relic upside down in a public ritual of desacralization. The profanity of corporeal veneration was everywhere exposed. The brain of St. Peter was revealed to be a mere pumice stone; the voices of saints heard coming from bodies in the Church of St. Gervais were discovered to be the sound of wind blowing through "pots and pipes." Even the genuine bones and bodies of the special dead were just bones. The dead are just the dead.

"Bones are bones, and not gods," as Martin Bucer (1491–1551), the Protestant leader in Strasbourg, put it.[21] According to the Protestant story, Rome turned its back on this truth. The Reformers echoed Clement: "I appeal to you, even at this late hour, forget daemon-worship, feeling ashamed to honor tombs." In the wake of the Reformation, Clement's sensibility would find new voice in a shifted theological register. The eighteenth-century Protestant historian Joseph Bingham, for example, cited the ancient Church Father as his authority for the pagan practice of crowning the dead with garlands, which he took as evidence that the pagans' "idol Gods were only Men." By contrast, early Christians, he reported, did not crown their dead, "expecting a crown of everlasting Flowers from God." Reformers claimed to be returning to the practices of the primitive Church and assiduously rejecting the idolatrous practices of papal Catholicism. Making daemons of the dead and worshipping them as if they had power were not, by Bingham's lights, fundamentally Christian practices, but rather had crept into the true Church since its early days and perverted it with remnants of popular paganism. "Why might no one know where Moses' Sepulcher was?" asked a radical Puritan in 1642. The answer, he explained, was "for fear of idolatrous worship": "had the people known the place they would have worshiped the mould there, and kissed his bones."[22] In Protestantism, bones (and corporeal remains more generally) came to be viewed as organic iterations of dangerous images and monuments rather than the reverse. That is, they were an incitement to idolatry.

Neither this doctrinal discussion nor the widespread acts of iconoclasm that accompanied the spread of reformed Christianity spelled an end to the Christian (or, for that matter, other Western) veneration of the dead. Catholics embraced bones as never before, and even among Protestants, the dead lived on without the old soteriology. Dead bodies did not lose their aura even if they lost their institutional and theological support. Anti-relic relics are commonplace once we start to notice them. Those of Rev. George Whitefield (1714–1770) are exceptional because of their sheer incongruity. The most famous evangelical preacher in eighteenth-century America and one of the major Methodist clergymen of the North Atlantic world—an unlikely saint if ever there was one—was buried in a glass-topped coffin under the pulpit of the Old South Presbyterian Church in Newburyport, Massachusetts, after a lively and far-flung competition for his body. In 1775, Revolutionary War soldiers prevailed on the sexton to let them enter the crypt, open the coffin, and cut off pieces of his collar and waistband, which they divided among themselves as talismans to help in the arduous battles that awaited them. Like the body of a medieval saint, Whitefield's did not suffer the fate of ordinary corpses. In 1784, a visiting Englishman went down into the crypt to test the rumor that the evangelist's body was "entire and uncorrupted"; it was true. The body was still perfect in 1790, according to another visitor. By 1801 the flesh was gone, but Whitefield's gown, cassock, and bands remained in good shape. He had little rest: his skull was removed, taken to Boston to be cast, and safely returned; his arm was stolen in the late 1820s, probably by an Englishman from Bolton, and was reunited with its kindred remains in the vault only after a "no questions asked" appeal in 1849 for the return of "the venerable relic." In the thirty years after the Civil War, some six thousand people signed the visitors' book in Old South Church after visiting the crypt. Not until 1933 was Whitefield finally covered up and left in peace. The status of the special dead persisted in both popular and elite circles well after the bona fides they had acquired in the early Church were gone. Clement had a point.[23]

The case of the English Enlightenment, deist philosopher and radical William Godwin makes Clement's point again, more powerfully and in a thoroughly modern register. Godwin believed in the truth of Diogenes; that is, he believed that the dead were insensate and did not possess an immortal soul. They were gone; they were no more. But in his *Essay on Sepulchres* (1809), which is about secular necromancy, Godwin succumbs to the idolatry of which Clement warned: that is, the dead whom he proposed to honor were "utterly dead," like those in the tomb temples of the pagans. He believed nothing of what St. Augustine and St. Thomas believed, but he writes in terms they would have recognized; he cherished the last few molecules of the beloved dead as if they were alive and urged his countrymen to honor the burial places of the illustrative dead more generally.

An exemplar of post–French revolutionary Romantic sensibility, Godwin's *Essay* is, as its subtitle makes explicit, *A Proposal for Erecting Some Memorial of the Illustrious Dead in All Ages on the Spot Where Their Remains Have Been Interred*, and it was intended to be the first step of a utopian plan to map necrogeography in such a way as to resist the inevitable erosion by time. Palpably responding to the sense of cataclysmic temporal rupture experienced by the postrevolutionary generation, he sought some means to preserve memory from the ravages of change and to build on the dead the foundation of a national community rooted in deep time. He, more than almost anyone else I discuss in this book, was caught between what he believed—the infinite improvability of mankind—and what he knew in his heart: the sheer intractable fact of death. Thomas Malthus had made fun of Godwin for his claim that the human sexual impulse could be tamed, for his optimism in believing that sexual desire, overwhelmingly compelling by nature, could be made to retreat by the forces of culture. Godwin harbored no such illusions in the face of death, but still he struggled to keep the dead among the living.

His proposal seems entirely plausible by our standards: that the places where noteworthy bodies are buried should be identified by name—like today's historical signs—and should be marked on maps, like those that already existed "in which the scenes of famous battles were distinguished with a particular mark." This exercise would result in what he called an "Atlas of those who Have Lived, for the Use of Men Hereafter to be Born," and by these means it would be possible to keep in memory those who might otherwise be forgotten. He knew, anecdotally and intuitively, what modern research has confirmed: that after the passing of the generations that had known the dead directly, or through the stories of those who had, the interest of the living in those who are gone fades; gravestones become neglected and fall into ruin, they are cut down as stubble in the field. The "perishableness of monuments" and the shortness of memory were all too clear, the Romantic variation on *Sic transit Gloria mundi*. "Where is Horace's tomb now? Or where the tomb of Macenas his patron?" he asks rhetorically. His son-in-law, Percy Bysshe Shelley, would make the same point in "Ozymandias" about the broken statue of the once-great king:

> Round the decay of that colossal wreck boundless and bare
> The lone level sands stretch far away.

Godwin offers his proposal as a way to avert oblivion through perpetual care of names and bodies for the sake of mankind. The "recollection and admiration of the dead" made possible by knowing where they are buried will, he argues, make us better people and the world a more virtuous place.[24]

The civilizational claim in behalf of memory (to which I will return in chapter 3) is less important here than the arguments he makes for why dead bodies in their crude materiality are near the heart of memory. Godwin wrote this pamphlet twelve years after his wife, the writer and feminist Mary Wollstonecraft, died while giving birth to the girl who would end up marrying the poet Shelley and writing *Frankenstein*. Godwin and Wollstonecraft's courtship and marriage had been short but intensely passionate. Her death had devastated him. Six months after she died, he published his revealing (by many contemporary accounts, too revealing) *Memoir* of her life, but it did not mark the end of his mourning. The enormity of death—"the greatest of earthly calamities, and the most universal"— still weighed on his heart twelve years later. "The dead are gone," he reflects, "beyond all the powers of calculation to reach"; "the effects flowing from the mortality of man to human affairs" is incalculable. Loss is "perhaps greater to him that survives than to him that dies," not because, as St. Augustine wrote, the dead are comfortably at the mercy of God or because of the assurance of life eternal, or because, as the Epicureans or the Stoics would have it, the dead are no more— or less—than they were before birth and thus feel neither loss nor anything else. The dead do not suffer. The living suffer because they cannot be sure the dead are anywhere and because those they loved are no longer with them. The dead no longer matter—at the same time as they most desperately do.

Godwin, like Augustine in this respect, tries to bridge the unimaginably great divide between the world of the living and the world of the dead through attention to certain special dead: not saints, not those in whose bones the holy resides, but "those who Have Lived, for the Use of Men." The question is why someone who was as close to an atheist as we will find in the late eighteenth century thought that the special dead were able to do what he was asking of them. Godwin's answer takes us eerily back to the Church Fathers. He offers a psychological and anthropological theory that goes back via St. Thomas to the beginnings of the Church. For those who survive, he says, anything associated with a friend—their possessions, the furniture they used—has "the virtue which the Indian is said to attribute to the spoils of him he kills." This in itself is a remarkable emotional alliance with superstition for a man who prided himself on his civilized rationalism. Everything, he continues, "which has been practically associated with my friend, acquires a value from that consideration; his ring, his watch, his books, his habitations." (The "he" in this case is a "she"; the friend in question is "the wife of my bosom.") But a far more powerful connection to the person of the friend than what she had owned or had held near to her body was her body itself. Godwin knows he ought to accept the views of the idealist philosopher Bishop Berkeley that "the body of my friend, the vehicle through which [her] knowledge and virtue was conveyed to me, was nothing." And yet he admits he is unable to let it go at that: "I can never separate my idea of [her] peculiarities and [her] actions, from my idea of [her] person." "I cannot," he concludes, "love my friend, without loving [her] person," and if the cold, unfeeling, inert relics of a friend are the nearest thing to that person one has to love and cherish on this side of the great divide, so be it: "[Her] dead body is far closer to that person even than [her] book or watch."[25]

Godwin is painfully aware that there exists no more radical rupture than that between the living and the dead body; if its rosy hue could somehow be purchased it "would be my companion still," which it—she—painfully is not. The corpse is the great, paradigmatic reminder provided for us by the "system of the universe" that we are of a degraded nature and of humble origins, that we are mortal. We cast bodies into the ground to mold back into earth as a token of this truth. And yet, strangely, the corpse still remains the person it was, lacking only what seems so little yet so immeasurably great—the breath of life, the "rosy hue." He wants to insist that the corpse and the person are not irrevocably sundered, that there is another reality, one grounded in the emotions, that can challenge the self-evident, acknowledged reality that the dead are really gone; they are no more in this world. His unwillingness to let them go raises the next obvious, and universal, question: if the dead are not gone, then where are they? "Where is my friend?" he asks. "Close deductions of reasoning" might allow him, he says, to recover "the thinking principle which animated [her]." "Suggestions of faith" might allow him to follow the dead "through the vast regions of space and see the spirit return to God that gave it." But neither of these options is satisfying. Recollections of the wise things a person said or wrote—the remains of "the thinking principle"— are cold comfort, and the deist Godwin was famously not given to faith. He is, he insists, a "creature of sense," a creature of things that are palpable, present, touchable. The dead matter. This fact, in turn, suggests both a dispiriting conclusion—a moldering body is very far from a passionate friend and wife—and the beginning of hope. All that we have left is the epitaph *hic jacet*, "here lies, dead," over the place where "the body is deposited." *Hic locus est* in the old sense will not work. The holy is nowhere. There is only the name and the dead body beneath it. Or, to be more precise, the sign with the name points indexically to a specific body and somehow, in or through it, to a person who is no more.

As a last resort, Godwin appropriates the remarkable power of the imagination and creates a microcosm of the kinds of stories this book tells. One would have to have an impenetrable heart, he says, not to feel "a certain sacredness of the grave," a sensibility as old as writing on the subject of death, and as generative. Based on this intuition—this feeling—Godwin proposes a kind of necromancy: "the habit of seeing with the intellectual eyes things not visible to the eye of sense," "rescuing the illustrious dead from the jaws of the grave," making "them pass in review," querying "their spirits and recording their answers," and having "live intercourse with the illustrious Dead of all ages." The proposal to erect a small monument, with a name affixed, to the final resting places of the worthy dead—or even the legendary resting places of near-mythical figures like King Arthur or Homer and fictional ones like Clarissa—is thus, explicitly, an act of calling them back or willing them into being through an inner voice and the act of building memorials.

But he wants to do more than just call individuals back to life. Naming the places "hallowed by the reception of all that was mortal of these glorious beings" and erecting a "shrine to the memory" is de facto creating a community of the holy dead without believing in holiness. It is a way of communing with each and every one of them without subscribing to any traditional religious views of how and whether this might be possible. Godwin offers what he knows is a formula for necromancy and for the veneration of relics in which he does not believe and that the national church vigorously disavows. We "indulge all the reality we can now have of a sort of conference" with the dead "by repairing to the scene which, as far as they are at all on earth, *they still inhabit*" (italics in the original). The dust that covers a great man's tomb—and by extension any tomb worth paying attention to—"is simply and literally *the great man himself*" (again, italics in the original). We can attain, he says, "the craft and mystery, by which we may spiritually, each in his several spheres compel the earth and ocean to give up their dead alive." These are extraordinary claims for a virulently anti-Catholic old radical.

In the final year of his life, he would write a book—an exposé of the "credulity of the human mind"—that attacked all kinds of superstition. Necromancy was foremost among them. "No sooner are we acquainted with the laws of nature," he wrote in 1835, but we "start calling up the deceased from the silence of the grave and compelling them to disclose the secrets of the world unknown." The dead are, or ought to be, beyond "our power to disturb" because there is something sacred about their repose. And yet: Godwin is interested not in the "secrets of the grave" but in a conversation about things of this world. But he does want to rescue, query, and pass the dead in review. He wants the presence of his beloved Mary Wollstonecraft and believes that proximity to her dead body is, sadly, as close as he can get.[26]

Already in 1809, he was aware that he was sailing close to what generations of English would have branded Catholic superstition, that what he was writing might seem out of character for a man such as himself, who in "his genuine and direct sphere, is the disciple of reason." Perhaps he protests too much by assuring readers that there is "no danger in the present state temper of the European mind of falling into idolatry." But still, "no one could not be affected by the visit to a grave"—true, as far as it goes, both for his times and for ours today. If we watch visitors to the chaste grave of Elvis Presley in Graceland's Meditation Garden, or to the less chaste graves of Victor Noir in Père Lachaise, whose bronze protruding penis has been rubbed shiny by generations of women hoping for a cure to infertility, or of Jim Morrison nearby, clouded in the mists of marijuana smoke, we may wonder if "idolatry" in the present state of the modern mind is really past. At least in these cases it is benign.

Godwin, the Protestant deist, had reason to be defensive. Whether he knew it or not, Aquinas defended "the worship of relics of the saints" in terms that are essentially the same as those Godwin used to explain his attachment to the body of his beloved Wollstonecraft, and, by extension, to others whom one wants to keep near. Quoting St. Augustine as his authority, St. Thomas argued: "If a father's coat or ring, or anything else of that kind is so much cherished by his children, as the love for one's parents is greater, in no way are the bodies themselves to be despised, which are more intimately and closely united to us than any garment; for they belong to a man's very nature." Someone who loves a person who has departed will have affection for her clothes and—this seems evident to Aquinas—for her body or parts of her body. If this is the case for the ordinary bodies of the ordinary dead, it is all the more true for the special bodies of the special dead—the bodies of saints—"which were the temples, and organs of the holy ghost dwelling living and operating in them." The skeptic might respond with the syllogism that (a) it is absurd to venerate that which is insensible; (b) the bodies of saints [and of everyone else] are insensible; and therefore (c) it is absurd to venerate them. But the answer is clear. One worships not an insensible body for its own sake but for the sake of the soul to which it was once united. That is, the dead body carries with it a quality of having been something material that had an intimate relationship with the soul, just as a beloved father's ring or clothes had with his person. We are back to the aura of the dead.[27]

The philosophical and religious justifications as well as the purposes for which they sought to honor the bodies of the dead could not have been more different for Godwin, on the one hand, and for the greatest theologians of the Church, on the other. Godwin thinks that the "recollection and admiration of the dead" that come from knowing where they are buried will make us better people and the world a more virtuous place. Augustine and Aquinas believe it connects this world with God and the saints in heaven to the benefit of the living and the dead. Godwin denies an afterlife for the dead body; Aquinas believes that the self-same person, body and soul, will be resurrected on the Day of Judgment.

But for all the differences in the two accounts, taken together they show that one can go a long way toward making the dead body consequential without having particular eschatological or metaphysical commitments. It was an Enlightenment radical materialist who believed that the dead "are infected with the perishable quality of their histories," that they were "imbued with some qualifying substance, or active principle." It was the deist Godwin who believed that, unremembered, they are "barren soil," and that they "perished and left not a trace behind." But, properly buried and remembered, those clods of earth ("the dust is earth; of earth we make loam") are "admirably fertile," not of grain or flowers but of "sentiments and virtues." Godwin's proposed landscapes are thus enchanted not by a connection with a heavenly order or by bodies that had once harbored immortal souls but by history and, paradigmatically, by the history to which the dead body testifies. In other words, he tells the story of how the "nothing" of the dead body can become something on account of its having been "something" when it was alive. The corporeal remains of the body and the other objects that the departed has left behind continue to signify, whether one denies the possibility of enchantment, as Godwin does in his more sober moments, or embraces enchantment, as Augustine does.

And the body, by the fact of its physical location, infuses its meaning into the land where it rests and decomposes. The value of the body of one's beloved and of the things that belonged to her are "not merely fictitious," Godwin insists: they are constitutive of a person existing in our individual and, more broadly, our historical consciousness through the ages. The dead, he says, "have an empire" over the mind. They have always mattered, as thousands of years of answers to Diogenes suggest; they matter still in the modern era, when they seem to have little of the old sacrality left. Put differently, the status of the special dead, by whose proximity the ordinary dead profited, has been democratized. In the past two or three centuries, the sacrality that informs the dead has been excavated from the deep structures of the past and from the historical anthropology that informs our constant dialectical conversation with Diogenes.

The dead matter because we cannot bear to give them up, because the ordinary dead partake of the holiness of the special dead and its equivalent in the modern world, and perhaps simply because they have always mattered, for reasons that I will elaborate in the next two chapters.

Chapter 2

THE DEAD BODY
AND THE PERSISTENCE
OF BEING

Beneath the water people drowned,
Yet with another heaven crowned,
In spacious regions seemed to go
As freely moving to and fro:
In bright and open space
I saw their very face;
Eyes, hands, and feet they had like mine;
Another sun did with them shine.

THOMAS TRAHERNE, "SHADOWS IN THE WATER"

It is wonderful that five thousand years have now elapsed since the creation
of the world, and still it is undecided whether or not there has ever been
an instance of a spirit of any person appearing after death. All argument is
against it; but all belief is for it.

JAMES BOSWELL, *The Life of Samuel Johnson*

One of the three pillars on which the work of the dead is built, as the last chapter showed, is the enduring human resistance to Diogenes' argument that the
materiality of the dead body warrants its being treated like carrion: it matters
even if it is just matter, we insist, and hence we care for it. Although religious or
other generally metaphysical views may underwrite this resistance to letting it
simply be what it is, they are not necessary. An abiding, seemingly universal
commitment to live with the dead, identified by historical and philosophically
inflected anthropology, provides reason enough. We are speaking, I suggested,
of an originary moment of culture. This, I know is something of a tautology: we
live with the dead because we, as a species, live with the dead. We can do one

better. We live with and care for the dead because of a seemingly universal and long-standing commitment to the existence of a person after death. Her poor bereft body—bones, dust, ash, atoms eaten by the fish of the sea or the birds of the air—is a token of her continued being somewhere, somehow. I do not mean necessarily belief in an afterlife; this is certainly not a necessary condition for the care of the dead and probably not a sufficient one either. Something psychologically and emotionally more fundamental accounts for the persistence of the sense that the token we have before us—the corpse, carrion in Diogenes' view—bears some continuing relationship to a person.

There are many ways, each with arabesque refinements, to explain this. One is an adamant refusal to countenance a world in which the dead are really as dead as "the rocks of an earth that is dead," on "a homeless planet . . . wheeled through the silence of space," as the poet Alfred Tennyson (1809–1892) puts it. The dead fossil skull—the remains of a body—he wrote in *In Memoriam A.H.H.*, has to be connected to another class of the dead: those that are not really dead for eternity but either live or will live again. Faith in Christ's promise of resurrection and life everlasting supports this view, but the poet seems to be saying that not trusting in this promise is impossible, given the alternative. Another way is to remind ourselves, as my epigraph from the seventeenth-century poet Thomas Traherne suggests, that the dead—the drowned that he imaged as a child—are so like us, "eyes, hands, feet they had like mine." As they are, so shall we be also. As we are, so were they once too. But because it is so difficult to imagine ourselves not being, it is hard to imagine that the dead have really severed all connection with their remains.[1]

Exactly why this is so, I cannot say. Narcissism, perhaps? And it may be our defense against the horrible truth that, as the novelist Vladimir Nabokov says, "our existence is but a brief crack of light between two eternities of darkness." He writes about the asymmetry of this small window: we are less anxious about the time before we existed, when we were nothing, than about what follows the brief moment—our lives—when we were something. But contemplating the prenatal state can become a way of contemplating death. A young chronophobiac of his acquaintance "experienced something like a panic" when "looking at home movies of his house and his mother waving from one of its windows in the weeks before his birth. . . . Nobody mourned his absence." A baby carriage stood in front of the porch "with the smug, encroaching air of a coffin." This was, it seems, a proleptic panic that foreshadowed the other edge of the abyss. This chronophobiac—his is a common human condition—must have found it unbearable to imagine a world without him once he had lived in it.[2]

Maybe Freud's observation that "it is indeed impossible to imagine our own death" accounts for the widespread commitment to the persistence of being.

"Whenever we attempt to do so we can perceive that we are in fact still present as spectators," he claims. "Hence the psycho-analytic school could venture on the assertion that at bottom no one believes in his own death, or, to put the same thing in another way, that in the unconscious every one of us is convinced of his own immortality." Variations on this theme are Ludwig Wittgenstein's (1889–1951) aphorism that "death is not an event in life" and the French philosopher Maurice Blanchot's (1907–2003) mute claim that "what is extraordinary begins at the moment I stop. But I am no longer able to speak of it." Maybe politeness? Cultured people, as Freud says, would never express the thought, "Dear Mama, Unfortunately you are dead."[3]

Or maybe it is some strange amalgam of delusion and innate sympathy. That would be the ancient philosopher Lucretius's diagnosis. People seem to be incapable, he says, of dissociating themselves "sufficiently from the outcast corpse; they identify themselves with it and, as they stand by, [they] impregnate [taint, contaminate] it with their own feelings." Indignant at "being created mortal," we resist the fact that "in real death there will be no second self alive to lament their own end and stand by and grieve at the sight of them lying there being torn to pieces or burned." Someone who worries about rotting in the ground or being jerked around by savage beasts or about whatever else might happen to her corpse is simply railing against mortality. It is, Lucretius argued, no more or less disastrous "to be mauled by the devouring jaws of wild beasts" than to be laid on a funeral pyre or "embalmed in stifling honey," or to "grow stiff with cold reclining on a smooth surface on an icy slab of stone," or to "to be pulverized by the crushing weight of earth upon us." And worse: for those who are no longer "it makes not one speck of difference whether or not they have ever been born once their mortal life has been snatched away by deathless death." Our relationship to a dead body as a person is therefore nothing but an act of projection: attributing our own thoughts and emotions onto nature, a case of acting as if there were someone there when we know there is not.[4]

Adam Smith (1723–1790), who was deeply rooted in the Epicurean tradition, understood this when he argued that manifestly useless sympathy for the dead proved the power of sympathy generally to make us moral beings and instilled in us "one of the most important principles in human nature, the dread of death." It is an "illusion of the imagination" that makes us feel that the dead suffer from being deprived of sun, from "being prey to corruption and the reptiles of the earth," from the loss of friendship, from being obliterated "in little time, from the affections, and almost from the memory, of their dearest friends and relations." The dead do not suffer. "Fancy" causes us translate our dread of the changes that we know will befall us into sympathy with what has befallen them, to join our living souls to their "inanimated" bodies. We know they feel nothing and that we can have "no influence on their happiness." And yet, for "our own misery" we keep alive "the melancholy remembrance of their misfortune." We feel that we owe them something because we project onto their lifeless bodies our own misery at the thought of something that, when it happens, will not, we know, cause us any misery.[5]

And if we can imagine ourselves as dead, we imagine it with those we love, not in some other place—or not only in some other place—but in the grave. In the midst of the great panorama of making and maintaining civilization, there is as well a far more intimate realm of the dead making and maintaining imagined communities—friendships, marriages, family associations of all sorts. The dying king in *Fridthjof's Saga* wants to be buried near the home of a dead friend so that he can easily call greetings from grave to grave. The nineteenth-century novelist Louisa May Alcott died in 1888 but a few days after her famous father, the transcendentalist philosopher and education reformer, Amos Bronson Alcott. She asked in her will that she be buried at the foot of her parents' grave so as (she says speaking of herself in the third person) "to take care of them as she had done all her life." There is a long history in the West of friends and lovers wanting to be buried together so as to maintain postmortem lives and relationships: priests and scholars in the late medieval period who would share in the grave the brotherhood and intimacy they had shared in life; eighteenth-century friends buried near one another to unite their families; John Henry Cardinal Newman, who insisted in his will that he be buried with his friend Fr. Ambrose St. John so they could create the Second Coming of Jesus together; Heathcliff and Catherine in their parallel coffins at the end of *Wuthering Heights*. The rich and powerful, with their customary claims on the choice parts of the church and their influence over the clergy, had always been able to stay together, wives with their husbands, parents with children. More modest people did what they could. With the creation of freehold property in cemeteries, those who could afford it could begin to buy togetherness as never before. And then there is the posthumous love of poetry.[6]

Of course, we can explain our commitment to the dead's persistence of being by pointing to specific religious beliefs, to the learned eschatology or soteriology of the Christian tradition, for example. The medieval Church taught as a matter of dogma that what Adam Smith assumed to be true was false: the living *can* help the dead. They are in purgatory and suffer there from far more than corruption and the fear of being forgotten; they are in pain that could be eased by, among other things, being buried in proximity to the bodies of the special dead whose intercession in their behalf might be solicited by the living. In this account, the dead persist as sentient beings in some other place to which the living have access, albeit only through mediation.

The Reformation of the sixteenth century attacked the whole apparatus, theological and institutional, that sustained this story: the cult of saints, prayers for the dead, the efficacy of burial near relics, the existence of purgatory, and more. It offered an alternative route to salvation, but it did not offer a very satisfactory answer to the question of where the dead are if they are not in purgatory or (for a very few) already in heaven or hell. Protestant theologians offered several possibilities. "What do the dead do, uncle?" asked a boy in John Webster's play *The White Devil* (1612). "Do they eat, / Hear music, go a-hunting, and be merry, / As we that live?" It sufficed in the theater of Protestant England to reply, no, "they sleep." This was, roughly, also the view of the so-called psychopannychists—from the Greek *psyche* (soul) + *pannuchizein* (to last all night)—"soul sleepers" like the Reformers Martin Luther and William Tyndale, the first great translator of the Bible into English. The dead in their view were sleeping, more or less soundly, somewhere. Or, as Calvin would have it, the dead were already in the bosom of Abraham, more or less awake, while their bodies moldered in the ground.[7]

Even if the dead were sleeping soundly and even if, in the absence of purgatory, they did not need the help, they remained imaginatively within the embrace of the living who would tenderly make their beds. The metaphysical poet and Anglican clergyman George Herbert (1593–1633) writes about the ages since "our savior's death did put some blood" into the face of death so that we can now, "gay and glad," behold Doomsday,

> When souls shall wear their new array,
> And thy bones with beauty shall be clad.
> Therefore we can die as sleep, and trust
> Half that we have
> Unto an honest grave;
> Making our pillows either down, or dust.

The Lutheran J. S. Bach wrote his most tender lullabies to texts about the sleep of the dead: one thinks, among many examples, of the long 12/8 measures of Joseph of Arimathea's lullaby (he was the man who gave Christ his tomb) in the *St. Matthew Passion*, its melodic line hanging, like a cradle, from its tonic fulcrum: "*Mache dich mein herze rein / Ich Jesum, selbst begraben*" (Make my heart pure / I want myself to bury Jesus)—that is, to sing him to sleep. And there was no need for theological consistency. In Bach's *St John Passion*, the last chorale asks that God "send his little angels" to bear the soul to "Abraham's bosom," and to let the body "rest in its snug bedchamber without any sorrow or pain until Judgment Day." Luther himself had one of his softest moments contemplating the coffin bed of his beloved daughter Magdalena, whose death left him inconsolable. Faith in her blessedness could not overcome "the power of the flesh, the world"; the grief of "natural affection" overcame all else. He imagined her both in the grave and as a star, ever present, in the sky. This is the man who claimed to have cared nothing about where his body came to rest. We are speaking here not of theology but of the all-too-human need to remember the dead as somewhere: in the grave and in a star, for example. It is the capacity to tell these sorts of stories about the dead body and in relation to the dead that seems to stand at the beginning of our coming into consciousness as a species.[8]

Some Protestants offered a more radical answer to whether the dead persist anywhere: no, they are gone and are nothing, exactly as they were before they were born. These were the so-called mortalists, technically speaking the "thneto-psychists"—from the Greek *thneto* (mortal) + *psyche* (soul). They were the Christian heirs of Epicurus and Lucretius, with whose bad reputation for atheism they were tainted, and of the heterodox Latin Church Father Tertullian. Calvin blasted these radicals with biblical citation after biblical citation; they were the "Sadducees" who believed that the soul was made of matter and that it died when the body died: no immortality of the soul, no Christianity. He had a point. With the annihilation, even the temporary annihilation, of the material souls of the dead, the cosmos was emptied; in principle there could still be angels and devils, but an attack on one kind of immortal and immaterial spirit could be taken as an attack on all. The connections between time here on earth and God's time was severed; the dead, the mortalists seemed to claim, really were dead. Forever. Max Weber observed that Europe had tasted serious disenchantment in the sixteenth and seventeenth centuries, although he was thinking of the Calvinists when he made this argument. Those who thought the dead were really dead might have been a better example.[9]

But even these radicals represented less of a rupture with an old Christian conversation—and with the far more general belief in the dead's persistence of being—than it might first appear. Famous seventeenth-century mortalists—Hobbes, Milton, Locke, and Newton—as well as the humbler ones who were closely linked to the most democratic forces of the English Revolution and its progeny—the Muggletonian prophets John Reeve (1608–1658), his follower Ludovico Muggleton (1609–1698), and the Leveller radical Richard Overton, for example, who were the spiritual ancestors of the poet William Blake—all imagined that the dead did not exist anywhere, in any form. In that sense the plenum was empty. But, unlike their ancient predecessors, they believed that nonbeing could, and would, end in individual rebirth and resurrection. In other words, the dead had a history through time even if for great swaths of it they did not exist; they were nothing and nowhere, as Diogenes had imagined, but personal identity, in a wild leap of metaphysical faith and the imagination, subsisted across a divine chasm of nonbeing, and then became something again on the Day of

Judgment. Discontinuity did not threaten continuity; a person could exist again out of nothing.

What exactly happened was debated. Political egalitarians like Reeve and Muggleton believed that at the end of time both the damned and the saved would be corporeally resurrected. Hobbes thought that the righteous would be given eternal life in new bodies, while the damned would be eliminated for good, that is, remain nothing; there would be no hell. Milton in the first book of *Paradise Lost* imagined a fairly traditional dark fate for the newly resurrected body and soul of those whose earthly conduct had been found wanting:

> A Dungeon Horrible, on all sides round
> As one great Furnace flam'd.[10]

But whatever the specific view of heaven or hell, even the most radical Protestants imagined the dead persisting through time and bounded by God's plan. The dead were never really gone. More profoundly, at the end of the day, the radical Reformist challenge to purgatory—like its challenge to idolatry—did not lead to behaving as if the dead did not matter. The bodies of mortalists were buried just like those of other Christians. John Milton asked to be, and was, buried beside his father in the chancel under the clerk's desk in St. Giles, Cripplegate, in London (i.e., where a relic would have been a century and a half earlier).[11] And the revolutionary Muggleton tells a sweetly commonplace account of the prophet John Reeve's end. After his release from Newgate Prison, he was visiting some believers near Maidstone when the crisis came; the eldest of these, Mrs. Frances, "closed his eyes for he had said unto her, 'Frances, close my Eyes. Lest my enemies say I died a staring prophet.'" This she did, Muggleton reports, and he "gave up the Ghost and said not one word more." Mrs. Frances cut off a lock of his hair as a memorial.[12] Radical theological commitments, oddly, entailed few innovations in the rituals and practices of the deathbed or burial. People still acted as if the dead mattered.

If anything, radical English Protestants vastly expanded the sense of a shared community between the dead and the living: humans and animals alike had material souls and could be resurrected and live together eternally after very long periods of complete annihilation.[13] If the skepticism of Diogenes haunted and framed the ancient and then Christian debates about the dead, it did not overturn them. The most heterodox Christian mortalists did not break with the Christian eschatology of eternal communion, a shared world of the living and the dead, which they expanded to include beasts. And secular Enlightenment figures like Adam Smith, who had no eschatological views, explained how and why the dead persist even if we know they do not. The dead body—truly and completely dead—remained caught in a complex of meanings and social practices that have long sustained its being.

So far I have used the term "the dead" in the sense of the dead body, here on earth, and "the dead" as a class in the sense of beings who may be somewhere other than on this earth. I have suggested that humans in deep time have cared for the dead in my first sense—bodies—because they have remained part of the cultural world and have not entirely returned to nature and because of humans' deep commitment to their persistence in my second sense. The two reasons exist symbiotically. But there is a vast third category of the dead, difficult to character-ize, that I mentioned briefly in the introduction. They subsist among the living as strange doppelgangers: dead but not quite dead. There are gradations of these dead and subtle differences in their relationship to bodies, but all of them share the characteristic that they have either not yet left or have returned to this world. They are the not-quite-dead, the returning dead, and the undead—zombies—who are currently getting so much attention. I will concentrate on the middle category, the revenant, but will briefly survey the rest.

First, there are the dead who have not really left at all and who stay for some time and for different reasons near, if no longer in, their bodies. However specific to archaic Greece the conversation of Patroclus with Achilles, recounted in the *Iliad*, might be, it also structures a relationship between the living and the dead that is more universal. The dead we imagine do not want to be forgotten and are reluctant to go, and we—the living—are reluctant to let them go or forget them lest thereby we truly lose them. Patroclus could not have put this more succinctly or poignantly: "Sleeping, Achilles? You've forgotten me, my friend," his spirit, so lifelike, says to the greatest of warriors who, in his grief, has been unable to bury his friend. "Bury me, quickly—let me pass the Gates of Hades." Unburied, he roams among the "the shades of the burnt-out, breathless dead," who will not yet let him join them (fig. 2.1). The work of the hero Patroclus is no longer battle but making sure that he can definitively enter the nether world: "never, never again shall I return from Hades once you have given me the soothing rites of fire." It was an extraordinary "due," a magnificent cremation that would release his spirit from his bones and flesh. "Boundless timber" for the pyre was culled from the forests; brave Trojan captives were slain and thrown on the flames; nine dogs, their throats cut, were cast in as well; wine was poured on the fire, and all manner of other obsequies duly performed by Achilles; and finally, Achilles and his com-rades took Patroclus's bones and ashes from the center of the fire, wrapped them in the fat of a sacrificed bull, and placed them in a golden urn that was put in a burrow. Magnificent games followed. The visit of the ghost had not been in vain. He would not be forgotten.[14]

2.1. *Achilles Grasps at the Shade of Patroklos*, Johann Heinrich Füssli, 1803. Kunsthaus Zürich.

We have in general, and especially since the seventeenth century, worried relatively little about precisely how long the dead body and the person it was coexist. We have come to take death to be a precipitous severance of person and body. But the cultural weight of the question is part of our mental baggage and historical practice. Certain traditions of modern Judaism, based on Kabbalah, do worry about this and insist on very rapid burial, even at the risk of burying someone who is still alive, because of the dangers of spirits hanging around their bodies. The rabbis of the Talmud debated the matter, looking for a precise answer.[15] In the Christian tradition, Jesus waited a full four days to raise Lazarus from the dead because by then, according to popular belief, his spirit would certainly have departed and the body begun to putrefy (plate 4). He was definitively dead. Early Islam worried about similar matters and followed roughly the same timetable. And even if there is not much explicit discussion about the dead staying around the body in the modern period, mourners still act as if someone were present at the customary funeral feast. Usually three or four days after the body's death, it had its last occasion to host a meal of relatives and friends. A Durham County yeoman in 1612 left £6 to provide a dinner to make his neighbors "welcome for my last farewell to them out of this sinful world."[16]

Funerary meals continued well into the nineteenth century, although we do not know at how many of these the dead were understood to serve as host, as the Durham yeoman provided. John Ferrier, a Manchester physician of the late eighteenth century, recounts among the superstitions of the poor the idea that a soul finding it difficult to leave the body—a lingering soul—can be hastened along by stripping the dying person of her clothes and placing her on a pallet on the floor. Those who lay out the dead poor are also, Ferrier reports, anxious to open all the doors and windows of an apartment and expose the dead body to the air. He does not say whether this is to allow the departed soul easier passage, although this is the context in which he reports the practice. He does suggest, however, that such treatment sometimes revives the seemingly dead.[17]

Generally speaking, in the West, the dead who hover by their bodies before leaving for good are a relatively small and ephemeral class of beings. We see them in fifteenth-century illustrations of the *ars moriendi*—the art of dying—in which a soul seems to float above a body as angels and devils fight for its fate, but otherwise they are little in evidence. Unlike in China, death in the West is relatively precipitous. But there is a huge class of the dead who, even if they were not lingering in this world, return to it. They reengage with the living and with the lives, properties, and pleasures, the quarrels, disputes, and wrongs that they have irrevocably, but not entirely, left. They speak for dead bodies. These revenant dead come in a bewildering number of difficult-to-classify genera and species. One large division is between the more and the less corporeal: fleshy as opposed to wraithlike, incorporeal ones. But there are many ambiguities: the ghost of Hamlet's father was a wraith, but might his armor have been material? A ghost in Apuleius's *Golden Ass* seems to be an actual corpse—a reanimated body roughly in its former shape—called back to life to announce that it was his wife who killed him. In the Chinese tradition going back before the coming of Buddhism, one of a body's two souls—the *po* or earthly soul—stays with the body for generations and seems to have been understood as actually needing and enjoying the food that the living left for it or, alternatively, becoming an angry and hungry ghost if neglected. The immaterial *hun* soul, the bearer of life's breath, flees to the heavens—mourners try calling it back in the days after it leaves—but then lives for a very long time if not forever in its family's ancestral altar. In some instances, the Chinese dead can become even more material—the walking dead, for example—who, in the care of guides, traverse great distances to be buried where they belong.[18]

Western revenants of the fleshy or more material variety are usually less social and less well traveled. Some, like the vampires of fifteenth-, sixteenth-, and seventeenth-century Europe, seldom stray far: they are corpses who eat the dead with whom they are buried and thereby stay somewhat alive. But they come in many varieties. Some are the dead that archeologists find in mass graves with bricks wedged into their mouths to keep them from their meals; others are less material but still more physical than not, like the shoemaker of Breslau who "died" in 1591 and went around pinching and hitting people; still others send off vapors that kill the living. Norse ghosts, unlike most European revenants, almost all have bodies, but they differ from each other in habit: *draugar* wander far afield; *haugbúar* stay near to their barrows and sing poetry that complains about their burial companions or offers greetings to their neighbors. *Draugar* can change the weather; they ride about, occasionally, but not always, preceded by mist and darkness. Both have whole lives in the realm of the dead. Both do battle with living heroes. Sometimes just part of a dead body—the head, for example—is reanimated. But all these fleshy ghosts are relatively rare, and their numbers decline in modern times. They play a relatively minor role in imaging the being of the dead.[19]

But in this book, the ghosts that are most relevant to understanding who or what and where the dead are have a less determinant form and bear witness to the porosity of the border between nature and culture: spirituous bodies and voices of bones and ashes that cross a seemingly unbridgeable chasm. Their ontology and their veracity have always been in dispute: What are ghosts? How can we distinguish real ones from fakes? What does it mean for ghosts to be real? How do we know that what they say is true? There is a history of how such questions are answered and of their association with other questions, but the persistence of ghosts in representing the dead or in being the dead is remarkable. As Dr. Johnson said to his biographer Boswell in one of the epigraphs with which this chapter begins, the question of ghosts has remained persistently open despite five thousand years of debate. No less a rationalist than Jeremy Bentham, the man who had himself dissected by his favorite student and asked that his eviscerated body be stuffed so that it could preside over the governing body of University College London, wrote near the end of his life that the "subject of ghosts had been among the torments of his life." The artisan radical William Lovett (1800–1877) recalled in his autobiography that as a young man he felt the fear of ghosts "more severely than the labour inflicted on me." Science, Bentham thought, would free mankind from superstitions, groundless terrors, and "word magic"; it would abolish the whole category of fictions—"as ifs"—that terrorize us. Whether his project succeeded in creating rational legal and administrative structures, as he hoped, is not our question; it failed to bring the dead under the sway of reason and reality. We have not been able to shake off ghostly "as ifs" for a very long time.[20]

Ghosts were all over the ancient pagan world. Some predicted the future. When Odysseus called forth the dead in Hades, Tiresias approached and told him to put away his sword so that "I can drink the blood and tell you all the truth." "The prophet in his power" spoke, wise in death as he had been in life, and counseled the hero about all that he would encounter on his travels home. Finally, he foretold the circumstances of Odysseus's death: it shall come to you, he says, "a gentle, painless death, far from the sea it comes / to take you down, borne down with the years in ripe old age / with all your people there in blessed peace around you." Indeed, the dead might be said to see the future of nations, just as in the eighteenth and nineteenth centuries they would be imaginatively gathered into the new nations of the modern world. Anchises takes his son Aeneas to a mound above the river of Lethe, from which they scan the throng waiting by the bank: "Spirits they are to whom second bodies are owed by fate" (fig. 2.2). In this way,

2.2. Aeneas and Anchises next to the souls in the river Lethe. Illuminated manuscript of Virgil's *Aeneid*, 1515–1520.

the founding and early history of Rome can be told as if the dead—"my children's seed"—could see the future before it is thrust upon the world above. Many classical ghosts come back because they are unhappy about where their former bodies are buried, or not buried—the story of Patroclus. They are also enforcers of a sort. Pliny tells the story of a house in Athens where the rent was cheap because, as its ghost told its new tenant, its remains were unburied in the courtyard. Once properly buried, the ghost did not come back. Presumably the rents rose. A wife comes back to tell her husband that he had forgotten to bury her with her sandals. The boundary of death and being was porous.[21]

All of these kinds of reasons for coming back—new or unfinished business with this world—motivated ghosts in other times and places but, generally speaking, the monotheistic religions tried to patrol the borders between the living and the dead. Ghosts lose their independence as God asserts his authority over the traffic of the living with the dead. There is really only one important revenant dead person in the Hebrew Bible: Samuel. Saul enlists the witch of Endor to rouse him from the grave; Samuel is very unhappy about being disturbed and tells Saul that the next day the king too will be dead and that Israel will be delivered to the Philistines. There is a certain irony in this, because Saul had banned necromancy from his realm and might have known that God would be displeased by this interruption of the peace of the dead. Eighteenth-century commentators still worried about this story. Something had gone wrong, wrote an orthodox Anglican clergyman explaining the odd story to a "lady." Saul had "expected to converse with the *real* soul of *Samuel* and not with any spectre or Phantom"; perhaps the witch had cried out because there was "something extra-ordinary in the Appearance, more than she had been used to on like occasions." It was never too easy to distinguish the truly revenant from a great variety of other ghostly appearances, which is precisely what makes Dr. Johnson's observation so telling.[22]

The Church Fathers certainly "believed in" ghosts. Augustine is sympathetic to the story of a dead father who returns to tell his son where a receipt needed to settle a lawsuit could be found. But they were anxious to separate their religion from the religion of the pagans: the ghosts of antiquity were really daemon—malevolent spirits, false demigods—and not the spirits of the dead; Christians should have no truck with them. Yes, of course, God could allow genuine ghosts to return to earth, but as a matter of fact, he did so only rarely. And when he did, communication with them was to be left to experts—to priests—because necromancy was a dangerous business. In the twelfth and thirteenth centuries, the Church did not renounce its role as gatekeeper to the world of the spirits of the dead, but it did dramatically relax its standards for traffic with them. Purgatory became a prominent place in its sacred geography, and an extensive, expensive, institutionally elaborate repertoire of ways in which the living could care for the dead emerged: praying for them, paying others to pray, buying indulgences to reduce the time they spent in purgatory, and much more. To remember the dead and to care for them became one and the same thing; tens of thousands of clergy and great riches were devoted to the enterprise. More to the point, under these circumstances the dead themselves came to have much more extensive unfinished business with the living. They needed help, and they started appearing much more often than they had before to report on how things were in this nether world, to rouse the consciences of the living, and to make specific requests. Their business with the living seemed to increase dramatically, and a whole genre of literature grew up reporting directly or indirectly on these encounters; deciding on whether a visitation was real or diabolical became in itself an art. From the perspective of the historian if not the believer, the social history of the work of the dead and the institutional history of a church neatly coincide.[23]

But ghosts did not go away during the Reformation when Protestants abolished purgatory and, with it, the complaints of the dead who were tormented there. The dead kept returning. They came back to take care of unfinished business or to speak to the living about various unsettled matters as they had been doing for millennia: to warn them, like the rich man in hell who begged Lazarus to intervene with God so that he could return as a ghost to his five brothers and tell them about the consequences of sin; to give advice; to insist on being remembered; to threaten. Ghosts among Catholics continued to come back for all these reasons in addition to asking for help in leaving purgatory. The revenant haunted their old houses and workplaces. They hovered about their graves, especially at night, reluctant to leave what remained of their bodies, which is why churchyards are scary at night. They also sometimes revenged themselves for some supposed wrong done to them when they were alive. I suspect that if we could have taken a census of ghosts around 1600, we would find that their number had not decreased in Protestant Europe and might actually have increased, although there may have been a drop in the early decades when the battle over purgatory was still hot. It would be as hard for us today as it was for contemporaries in the seventeenth century to distinguish the genuine revenant dead that had returned from the other spiritual beings with business in this world: from the devil and his minions who in great number caused the epidemic of witchcraft in the sixteenth and seventeenth centuries; from the occasional beneficent messengers of God; from apparitions caused by good or bad spirits. All of these, in the great age of European witchcraft, were around in copious profusion.

The attack on purgatory and the claim that the dead, wherever they might be, were beyond the reach of the living occasioned a lively debate about ghosts between Reformers and defenders of Rome. But it had little effect on serious thinking about the ontology of these strange beings. Like miracles, ghosts were supernatural; the existence or nonexistence of purgatory made them no less so. Surprisingly, on this point the views of the greatest medieval theologian, St. Thomas Aquinas, and of one of the most widely read Calvinist writers of the seventeenth century, Richard Baxter (1615–1691), did not differ significantly.

Purgatory was relevant only because some Protestant writers thought that it exploited Catholic priestcraft, and they made much of it in their propaganda. Well into the late eighteenth and nineteenth centuries, folklorists explained widespread popular belief in ghosts as a holdover of the old Romish superstitions. And some historians have followed in this tradition: no purgatory, no ghosts. In fact, the dead for both Protestants and Catholics were *really* somewhere, and, wherever they were, they occasionally communicated with the living in a variety of ways. Confessional differences, such as they were, mattered little on this question. The problem for the Protestant clergy was how to explain the revenant dead to ordinary people for whom their presence was a fact even if they were not temporary refugees from some intermediate place.

But these explanations were very much within the terms that the Church Fathers would have understood. Ghosts still had to be accommodated in a world in which each person's experiences represented—or in any case could well represent—a cosmic reality beyond the individual and the natural world. Whether any particular ghost was real or apparitional was a matter of empirical investigation before and after the Reformation. For Catholics and for all but the most radical Protestants—the mortalists—ghosts were neither figments of the mind nor were they explicable through natural causes. Rather, they were among the company of a spiritual plenum that included devils, angels, witches, and perhaps even spirits, fairies, and other exotic creatures. The world was more or less as enchanted as it had long been. Ghosts were a representation of the unrepresentable: the dead who were somewhere.

Learned men did argue that, contrary to my speculations, there were fewer, not more, ghosts after the Reformation than before. The theologian Ludwig Lavater (1527–1586), son-in-law of Heinrich Bullinger (1504–1575), the most important Swiss Reform figure of his day, was the leading Protestant authority on the matter, and he thought that ghosts were fast disappearing. He tells the following joke: a professor of the gospel quips to a papist that the Protestant religion must be true and the papist's wrong because "since the gospel has been preached unto us, very few spirits have been seen of any man." New and better interpretations of key texts—most problematically 1 Samuel 28 (where the prophet's ghost appears to Saul) and Luke 16:23–31 (the parable of the rich man and Lazarus)—have kept them at bay. To the contrary, replies the papist on good authority, "your religion is naught and ours is good, for the devil assaulteth those whom he fearest will shortly revolt from him." Lavater admits that St. Benedict had come upon a place of holy and quiet prayer that was full of devils while a profane place had only one guarding it. A monastery full of holy men, reported Aeneas Silvius Piccolomini—later Pope Pius II—was surrounded by devils fighting with the holy fathers, whereas at a fair, full of merchandise, busy with buying and selling, there was again only one, "idle and sad." So, says the papist, there may be some truth for the claim that there were few spirits among Protestants: the devil already had them in his pocket.

But the papist misses the point, Lavater responds. Pagans could well have made the same argument when they wondered why their oracles had ceased to speak and why there were so few visions after the triumph of Christianity. The real reason in both cases—the silence of the old gods and the disappearance of ghosts—is that truth had won out. Now that we know that the souls of dead men do not return to ask for help and that we understand the devil's subtleties in making us think they do, he—the Evil One—has given up on Protestants and confines himself to deceiving followers of Rome. Ghosts disappear as the reason for tricking people into believing in them—purgatory—disappears. Others took up this tack. Edmund Grindal, bishop of London, claimed in 1564, for example, that the doctrine of purgatory was "maintained principally by feigned apparitions, visions of spirits, and other fables." Without purgatory there was no need for trickery, and so there would soon be no ghosts either.[24]

In fact, the revenant dead continued to show up just as they always had. As before, there was the possibility of fraud, but many cases were carefully examined by reliable Protestant experts who found no sign of chicanery. Ghosts, in other words, seemed to be coming back in undiminished numbers, if not from purgatory then from somewhere, and the clergy in their pastoral capacity had to help their flocks deal with them. The divide between the worlds of the living and of the dead seemed just as permeable as ever, maybe more so. We have overwhelming evidence for this from a variety of sources. There are the well-documented, much-investigated, and literarily irresistible cases like that of Mother Leakey, who on her deathbed had warned her daughter-in-law Susan that she would "come again from after her death." And at the end of March 1636, she did. Her ghost was witnessed on this and subsequent visits by Susan herself, her maidservant, a sailor on one of her husband's ships, and the local curate among others. He had at first counseled Susan to get some rest but, once he saw the black-draped figure himself, came to believe that what he had seen was real. There had been warnings. In 1634, the Leakeys' fourteen-year-old nephew lay dying of a mysterious ailment and said that he could not rest easy because of his dead grandmother. All were good Protestants. The historian who has investigated this case most carefully puts it in the context of other Reformation ghost stories: Sir Thomas Wise in Jacobean Cornwall was assured by the local clergyman that the white specter at the foot of his bed was an "angelic apparition"; in 1613, a man in Kingston near Taunton confessed to the murder of a rich widow because "the ghost of the woman he had slain was continually before him, so that his life was burdensome to him." Clergymen in the West Country continued to lay ghosts well into the eighteenth and early nineteenth centuries, often in competition with less scrupulous conjurers. If we are willing to believe, as I think we might, that many of the accounts of ghosts from late-eighteenth- and nineteenth-century folklore sources reflect what happened in sixteenth- and seventeenth-century England, then our evidence for post-Reformation ghosts increases hugely. And the same story can be told in other Protestant lands. A Swiss Reform clergyman might initially counsel a parishioner that she only imagined the ghost of the dead bürgermeister; but he himself spoke respectfully to the ghost once it was clear to him that the mayor was really back.[25]

From a sociological and polemical perspective, Reformers and the historians who follow their lead have a point: the rise of the purgatorial regime in the twelfth century may well have led priests to give more credence to the revenant dead for the obvious reason that they had an institutional interest in souls' asking for help. It provided an incentive for fraud and of the lowering of testimonial standards. And with its demise one might expect a drop in the number of dead coming back. But this did not happen, because there were much deeper cultural pressures that kept them returning and that made the living take them seriously. There is nothing about the doctrine of purgatory itself that, from a theological as opposed to pastoral perspective, would make their return more or less likely.

Compare on this question two radically different theologians of the first rank: "Doctor Angelicus," St. Thomas Aquinas (1225–1274), on the one hand, and the Calvinist divine Richard Baxter, on the other. The greatest theologian of the medieval Church had very little to say on the question of the return of the soul because it was not a pressing issue when he was writing. The early Church reclaimed the spirit world from the pagans and, as far as possible, from popular religion and tried to keep tight control of its borders. But what he did say was straightforward: it is against the laws of nature and the general practice of God for the immaterial soul, once separated from the body by death, to return to this world. It is therefore only by the special permission of God that these laws—as in a miracle—are suspended and a soul is allowed to come back from heaven, hell, or purgatory. And finally, there are great epistemological difficulties in determining whether such a miracle has happened. One cannot be sure that a ghost is actually a ghost; it may be a good or a bad angel. The Church was to be the judge of these matters, the guardian of the gates of death. These views were elaborated and refined during the Reformation by Catholic theologians into a science of specters and apparitions, but the basic outline of this position was there in St. Thomas, who himself claimed no great originality on the subject. More important, it was very close to those of one of the greatest and most respected Puritan theologians: Richard Baxter, "the chief of English Protestant Schoolmen." The big difference had to do not with ghosts but with the places they might be returning from: purgatory was not an option in seventeenth-century England.[26]

Baxter had a lot to say in defense of ghosts because, in his view, their existence was bound up with the whole spirit world that was being threatened by materialism bordering on atheism. It was, he argued, fundamentally unknowable by the senses. Just as fish do not live in cities and the sun does not shine in the womb, so we, the embodied living, do not have the capacity to know about an ethereal world, a world that will become accessible to us only when we no longer "dwell in the flesh." That is, when our souls are bound for glory, we will directly encounter unholy spirits in the lower regions and, higher up, angels and the souls of the dead. Then we will no longer see through a glass darkly. Now, all we can know is that the various souls and spirits that confront us are a reminder of "much of God's arbitrary power, and much of his wisdom, and much of his judgment, and also his love." Anything more is "unsearchable." We cannot tell how much free will God allows to "invisible intellectual powers." But we do know that their presence among us is extraordinary. God "suspend[s] his predetermining Motion, though not his General Motion and Concourse." Ghosts among us are by definition a miraculous occurrence. In fact, the spirit world of which they are members is dependent on the arbitrary power of God and not the ordinary laws of this world that are known to us through ordinary means. No spirits can do anything "but by God's will and permission"; "good spirits are servants, and evil ones slaves, of Jesus Christ"; "blessed souls and Angels" live in higher regions than their evil counterparts, so it is "no wonder if they appear more rarely to men on earth." But even the dead drawn to the bosom of Abraham, those of the Elect who go immediately to heaven, can and do return. Heaven and hell, *with God's permission*, are as permeable as purgatory ever was.[27]

The most important point that we can take from this discussion about the status of the dead and the possibility of their return was the deep conservatism of almost all the answers proposed. Purgatory or no purgatory, Protestants and Catholics had far more in common than either did with those few people who denied the reality of ghosts within a larger cosmology of good and evil.

Richard Baxter offers a good starting point, because as a Calvinist who believed that the Elect and the damned went quickly to their respective rewards he should, we might think, be hostile to the idea of ghosts who somehow still lingered about. His continued belief in them speaks to the continued permeability of the world of the living and that of the dead. Baxter is also encyclopedic: by his own account, his work is a summation of sixty years of his reflections on a vast literature: "no small number of writers on such subjects I have read, it's near three score years from the first occasion." His small tract absorbed the best thinking of the European and North Atlantic Calvinist world, as well as relevant Catholic thought. (He much admired the New England Mathers and they him; the French Catholic jurist Jean Bodin, scourge of witches, is one of his major authorities.) Baxter begins by confessing that it is very difficult to explain the many strange workings of spirits in this world. Yes, there is a great deal of fraud being perpetrated, mainly on the part of two classes of people: persons trained up by papist priests to "honour their exorcisms"—the standard Protestant propaganda—and girls and widows whose "imaginations are conquered by lust" (i.e., hysterics). But just because beggars pretend to be blind does not mean, he says, that any of us should give up on our sight. Catholic chicanery does not explain everything.

Sorting real from fake ghosts, apparitions, and other manifestations of the spirit world presents enormous and serious epistemological problems because everything about the aerial world is "unknown to us here." We don't even know whether there might not be a third class of being—neither angels or devils, on the one hand, nor the souls of men, on the other—who, like fishes in the sea, are specially created to occupy the aerial regions (for example, fairies and goblins). Baxter clearly did not subscribe to the Wife of Bath's view that these had all disappeared after the friars brought Christianity to England. As a consequence of this ignorance, when a drunk, for example, hears a knocking at the head of his bed and a voice warns him to remedy his ways, there are several possibilities: it could be a good angel sent by God; it could be "the soul of some dear friend who procureth this Leave, to try to turn and save the sinner" (that is, a ghost, a spirit, comes back from the dead, returning from the bosom of Abraham); or, it could be the devil, who against his will was forced by Christ or an angel to save a sinner. We can trace the intellectual pedigree of this list. Baxter takes from Louis Lavater the view that a ghost could be an apparition caused, most likely, by a devil but possibly also by an angel. Lavater himself was sure that the knock was never actually the revenant dead. Baxter thought it might be. He would agree with Lavater that priests encouraged their parishioners to believe that ghosts were souls from purgatory moaning for trentals—a set of thirty masses for the dead—to relieve their pain, as Reginald Scot, the great skeptic about the existence of ghosts and witches, had argued. Shakespeare read Scot and represented his views as those of Horatio about King Hamlet's ghost. But, as Baxter said in his introduction, the fact that beggars pretend to be blind does not mean that others cannot see. The other side of fraud is reality.

Reginald Scot, Johann Weyer (the German physician from whom Scot drew widely), and a few others went much further than Baxter or any mainstream Protestant was willing to go. They thought that ghosts, witches, and the whole spirit world were delusions, that people let themselves be taken in by the "many stories and books written of walking spirits and souls of men, in contrast to the word of God," and by papists who preach to the gullible that spirits wandered to have burial for their bodies and walking souls went about their business. All papists, Scot thought, believed that there was something real behind these illusions and all Protestants did not. Witches, Scot thought, were the product of a guilty conscience: someone denied a poor woman charity and then blamed her and her supposed alliance with the devil for some unexplained ill fortune. Insofar as women confessed to being in league with the devil, it was because they were tortured or mentally ill. And the same (if not for the same reasons) is true of angels and other spirit messengers: "God in times past did send down angels and appearances to men; but now he doth not so." The age of miracles is over; the ethereal realms are empty of the souls of the dead as well as of angels, devils, and other creatures. Although Scot is coy about making a definitive claim—"some say that [devils and spirits] are only imaginations in the minds of men"—his basic position is clear, and his analysis is attractive to us moderns. His insights into the social relationship between an accused witch and her accuser has been taken up by leading historians of witchcraft; we embrace his skepticism about the spirit world, and we are comfortable with the idea that good and evil are forces inside the heart of all humans. This is the sort of disenchantment that Protestantism is supposed to bring. But it does not describe Baxter's world and the truth about the Protestant dead in the sixteenth and seventeenth centuries.[28] In principle, the great majority of Protestants as well as Catholics, laypeople as well as clergy, believed that the ghosts, devils, and angels in this world represented, however obscurely, another supernatural spirit world beyond.

Baxter's *World of Spirits* and "many other treaties" to which he refers were thus addressed to a tiny minority of Protestants who denied the existence of anything beyond nature. He and others called them "Sadducees and infidels." Who were these people? "Sadducee" is a reference to the biblical sect addressed in Mark 12:27 ("He is not the God of the dead, but the God of the living") and known to us mostly through the Jewish historian Josephus, who did not believe in the immortality of the soul, the resurrection of the dead, the existence of angels, or many of the other core tenets of both Christianity and rival Jewish sects. Like all such labels, it is difficult to attach to specific people, especially almost two millennia after the term was first used. King James I, for example, wrote his famous defense of witchcraft prosecutions against the "damnable opinions" and "the errors of the Sadducees," to wit "denying of spirits," and named specifically Reginald Scot and his main source, "Wierus" (Johann Weyer), as targets. Scot denied being a "Sadducee," but in the context of sounding an awful lot like one. By the seventeenth century, it was a broad term of opprobrium in mainstream writing, meaning a materialist, an atheist, a skeptic. It meant someone who, as the learned natural philosopher, clergyman, member of the Royal Society, and one of Baxter's main sources, Joseph Glanvill (1636–1680), says, denied not only the existence of witches and apparitions but other orthodox Christian beliefs as well. He too points specifically to "Wierus." Baxter accuses Edward, Lord Herbert of Cherbury (1583–1648), one of the founding figures of English deism, of being one. His fault: he was a proponent of natural religion, that is, he denied that we have the truths of religion by special revelation but instead can rely on reason and a general built-in sense of universal religious truths. A "Sadducee" was a weirdo, someone like the profoundly heterodox Reginald Scot, whose denial of the reality of ghosts was part of his immensely learned and cogent attack on the reality of witchcraft and much else: he, unlike almost all of his contemporaries, thought that the biblical account of the return from the dead of the prophet Samuel was "mere cousenage," nothing but gossip. He was a Unitarian who denied that the Holy Spirit was part of the godhead, he did not believe in the biblical account of the Fall, and he thought that good and bad spirits were metaphors: "where it is written that God sent an evil spirit . . . we are to understand that he sent the spirit of hatred and not a bulbegger [specter]." He doubted the reality of the devil. And he was probably also a Familist, a really wild, radical Protestant sect. In short, the root and branch denial of ghosts was a position of the loony fringe.[29]

The reality of the spirit world, including the ghostly dead, stood as a bulwark against atheism and materialism. It stood against the likes of Scot. And against the likes of Thomas Hobbes (1588–1679), who argued that "phantastical forms, apparitions, or the seemings of visible Bodies in Sight, are only images"; they are the stuff of our dreams, of our imaginations. They are, he continued, "originally and most properly called ideas and Idols," no more to be countenanced than the idols of antiquity. Here was the real abyss of disenchantment, and few people were willing to take the leap. The status of ghosts did change, but it happened very slowly. The eighteenth-century antiquary John Brand, much quoted in the nineteenth, still associated the continued "vulgar ceremonies of the nation" with popery, two centuries after it had disappeared institutionally from English shores, and with the customs of the heathens that had been sustained through the "connivance of the state." Ghosts, apparitions, and "the great weakness to be afraid of walking through [churchyards]" were not gone even by Brand's time, three centuries after the fall of purgatory. Some worried that when ghosts died, religion too would "soon" expire.[30]

And they have never really gone. "Spectre and apparition make a great noise in the world," says Daniel Defoe at the beginning of his long 1736 book that tried to settle the matter. Between our ancestors who believed in them too strenuously and "the present Age endeavoring wholly to explode and despise them, the world seems hardly ever to have come at a right understanding about them." Defoe concludes that there are no actual ghosts (i.e., no wandering spirits or souls of the dead)—otherwise there would be more of them around seeing to the proper execution of their testamentary wishes—and what we see are really apparitions. These, he thinks, mostly represent kindly angels who presumably communicate some of the things people think they hear from real ghosts.[31]

Three things happened in the eighteenth century that were new. First, ghosts became the province of scientific skepticism. Not theology, but experiment and natural philosophy would determine the status of the revenant dead. In the most notorious cases, ghosts seemed of very little consequence beyond exciting controversies in the public sphere about whether they existed. Defoe had made a short foray into the question in 1706 when he wrote about the specter of Mrs. Veal, who visited a friend, a Mrs. Bargrave, whom she had grievously neglected in life, a commonplace sort of unfinished, guilt-ridden business for which the dead, whatever they really are, often return. He was unwilling to commit himself to whether any of this really happened. For a long time people thought the whole thing was a fiction, and ever since Sir Walter Scott wrote on the subject, there seemed a good case to be made that the ghost showed up with little more in mind other than praising a book about being dead that was not selling as well as its, and Defoe's, publisher might have hoped. (Defoe's tract was often appended to the book that the ghost had recommended, Charles Drelincourt's *The Christian Defence against the Fears of Death*.)[32]

The notorious "Cock Lane ghost" captivated London in late 1761 and early 1762 by rapping yes and no answers to queries put to her by the publican who owned the rooms where she had lived. She had not died of smallpox but rather had been murdered by her husband, she seems to have said by knocking on the wainscoting. In February 1762, when a distinguished committee that included the not very skeptical Samuel Johnson took up the ghost's promise—made by further knocks—that she would knock on the coffin of her sister in St. John's vault, the story unraveled. (The publican's wife was at the heart of the fraud.) It was a story that would repeat itself in the late nineteenth century's version of ghost stories, accounts of spirits who knocked and bumped tables and clouded photographic plates. This is more horseplay than the work of the dead; William James (1842–1910), in his explorations of the spirit world, wondered why the creatures he was investigating were so boring (fig. 2.3).[33]

The second change in the eighteenth century was that the assimilation of the ghost question to science and the decline of the Reformation polemic about purgatory brought the dead back among the living in a new way. They now represented the spirit world more generally, the possibility of forces outside physics—that is to say, enchantment, the magic that Bentham had hoped would be banished.

John and Charles Wesley encouraged their followers to speak to the ghosts that appeared to them; they cited no less an authority than Newton to show that a nonphysical force, a force that could not be seen or explained mechanically—gravity—could move things in this world. Indeed it, like the Holy Spirit, could only be known by its effects. The potentially unquiet souls of suicides in England were still kept in their place in the early nineteenth century by burying the body at a crossroads with a stake through the heart.[34] And the spirits of the dead in our world would find a new place in the imagination and hence the social world of the living in the late-nineteenth-century explosion of the occult as a curious rejoinder to science that was at the same time symbiotic with it.

Third, the most important eighteenth-century change is the move of the dead inward. They still

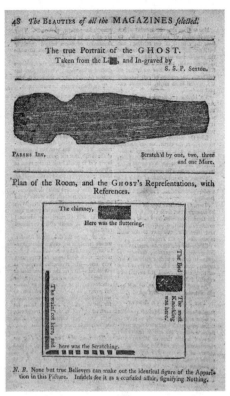

2.3. The True Portrait of the GHOST, S.S.P. Sexton. *The Beauties of All the Magazines Selected* (1762), 48.

spoke with great authority; they still made us care for their bodies. But they did it in new ways. Or to put it more precisely, the question of ghosts that in the sixteenth century was still deeply imbricated in the unsettled status of the spirit world and that haunts the opening scene of *Hamlet*—the ghost of the dead king takes his son aside and will speak only to him—had shifted. The revenant became ever more a way of representing the dead's power over our minds. "As if . . ." would come to have all the power it needed. "The souls of the Dead," writes Joseph Addison in the most important and widely read journal of the early eighteenth century, "appear frequently in cemeteries and hover about the place where their bodies are buried, *as if* hankering about the old brutal pleasures and desiring again to enter the body."[35] Almost three hundred years later but in a gentler mood, the power of "as if" is still captivating. The rural cemeteries of Bohemia, says the narrator of *The Unbearable Lightness of Being*, sparkle with tiny candles at dusk: "It looks as though the dead are dancing at a children's ball. Yes, a children's ball, because the dead are as innocent as children." No matter how brutal the times—Hitler, Stalin—these places were peaceful, "beautiful as a lullaby."[36]

In the Enlightenment, ghosts entered the mind but were no less real for all that. A Harris poll in 2003 found that 51 percent of Americans thought ghosts really exist. Mercifully, the older one gets, the less likely we are to be among this number: only 35 percent of those aged twenty-five to twenty-nine are skeptical, but 73 percent of those older than sixty-four have no belief in specters. The rationalists of the eighteenth century did not so much kill the ghosts of old as translate them into a new realm of the uncanny, into the realm of "as if," as if one were in the presence of the unnatural or the supernatural. "As if" the dead spoke. When ghosts became thoughts, as the literary critic Terry Castle argues, "the mind became subject to spectral presences. . . . [B]y relocating the world of ghosts in the closed space of the imagination, one ended up supernaturalising the mind itself."[37]

This is the world in which the German writer Arnold Zweig (1887–1968) told Sigmund Freud that a continuous stream of broken faces, death's heads, faces of men lying down, and more had started to come into the visual field of his right eye. Two-thirds of an explanation for these "optical phenomena," he writes, are of the "man in the moon" sort: moonshine, tricks of the mind. But of the last third he is not yet prepared to speak. "It could be," he writes, "that what is standing behind these always new faces of the dead is my feelings of guilt with respect to my father and my father-in-law." He wants to deal with these analytically before he reports any further. The superego speaking in the voice of dead fathers can be as compelling as real ghosts.[38]

That Zweig's images are either tricks of the eye or hauntings of the mind may seem obvious to modern readers, but their relation to history and to the psyche is worth studying. "Neither dreams for the analyst, nor hallucinations for the psychiatrist," argues a leading modern historian of the human face, Zweig's images are "but blank, physiologically explicable projections" of physiognomic types. He was, she suggests, thinking of death masks, "nearer the corpse than a picture," which became popular in the late eighteenth century and all the rage in the nineteenth. Whether this is true or not is less interesting to me than the powerful way in which Zweig's ghosts are inside and projections of what in an earlier age might be understood more straightforwardly as the product of not having put the dead properly to rest. (Zweig was a man engaged with faces who published a book of pictures of eastern European Jews in an effort to make German Jews like himself more kindly disposed toward them.) The passion for death masks was to a great extent a product of phrenology, which held that the character of a person could be read from the contours of the head. Casts of the dead could thus uncannily bring them back to life. The largest collection in the United States was assembled for this purpose; the *British Phrenological Journal* offers its readers many articles on the subject.[39] Even, or perhaps especially, in progressive scientific circles, the dead are not quite dead and remain among the living.

In fact, the dead haunt the living even when it is quite clear that they do not and cannot exist. They are dead. But not quite. The philosopher Slavoj Žižek points to the "fundamental fantasy of contemporary mass culture": the return of the dead because they were not properly buried. "Something went wrong with their obsequies," and they have come back as "the sign of a disturbance in the symbolic order." I do not think this is so historically bounded. Here I am with Freud. There is continuity between earlier anxieties and those of today. We experience, he says, the feeling of the uncanny in the highest degree in relation to death and dead bodies and to ghosts and spirits: "Yet in hardly any other sphere has our thinking and feeling changed so little since primitive times or the old been so well preserved, under a thin veneer, as in our relation to death."[40]

It is a very long way from Epicurus and Diogenes to Žižek's Lacanian psychoanalytical account of the haunting powers of the dead, but it does bring us to a place from which I can define more fully what I mean by "the dead." They are those whose bodies are treated as dead—buried, burned, tossed into the sea, left for birds to eat—but who remain powerful in the imagination of the living under very different assumptions about what or where they *really* are, whether they are anything, or whether they have efficacy in the world of the living. The dead, in short, are a powerful category of the imagination, and the corpse is their token, then and now. And, as such, they—the corpse and whatever the dead are or are not—play an important role in the affairs of this world. It appears to be impossible to live for long with the stark sophism of Diogenes, whatever one might believe. The work of the dead—dead bodies—is possible only because they remain so deeply and complexly present and because they share death with its other avatars: ancestors, ghosts, memory, history.

Chapter 3
THE CULTURAL WORK
OF THE DEAD

Liberal hopefulness
Regards death as a mere border to an improving picture.
Then there is the civilizing love of death by which
Even music and painting tell you what else to love.
Buddhists and Christians contrive to agree about death
Making death their ideal basis for different ideas.
The Communists however disapprove of death
Except when practical.
Because we have neither hereditary nor direct knowledge of death
It is the trigger to the literary man's biggest gun.
And we are happy to equate it with any conceived calm.
Otherwise, I feel blank upon this topic
And think that though important, and proper for anyone to bring up,
It is one that most people should be prepared to be blank upon.

WILLIAM EMPSON, "IGNORANCE OF DEATH"

It is impossible to see how far anthropomorphism may not extend, taking the word in its widest sense. People revenge themselves on the dead; bones are exhumed and dishonored; we empathize with inanimate things. . . . Perhaps all pronouns regarding *the other* have such an origin.

GEORG LICHTENBERG, APHORISM 80

So far I have been concerned with how humans translate their recognition of the dead body as mere matter into something that demands great care, and with how they imagine the dead themselves to persist in some other world as well as in this one. We believe that a certain aura pertains to physical remains even if we believe these remains are, in their essence, of no significance; we act as if the dead are somewhere even if we claim to believe they are nowhere; we speak as if they remain or return individually to the world of the living even when many of our rituals, practices, and professed beliefs suggest the opposite. This chapter is about the more broadly cultural consequences of material remains and the imagined afterlives of the dead. It is about the work they do collectively, about how and why the dead make civilization. Let me be clear what I mean. The dead are not, and have never been, viewed as just like the living (except perhaps by the mad); access to them was always something very different. Their work is different from ours, the living. If this were not the case, we, and they, would not be mortal. Without the gap between what they are and what we take them to be, this book—and a great deal of religion, art, politics, and poetry—would not exist. The dead body is here; the dead are somewhere. The two are connected.

One way to construe the subject of the work of the dead in this world is to survey, in contrast, the very large range of things they are said to do in some world other than this one. I am thinking here, for example, of the worker-dead in Chinese antiquity, the tens of thousands of men, women, and children who were, over the centuries, beaten into the ramparts of the tombs of the Shang emperors or great lords so as to join them in death and serve them as they had in life. Hundreds made up the largest of these brigades. Some were probably prisoners (the usual victims in human sacrifice), whose bodies were broken before they were buried—beheaded, dismembered. Others were the slaves and higher-status servants of the tomb's main resident, who were buried whole and who were clearly meant to carry on their labors in death as in life. Some emperors took with them concubines, who were freed from their labors only when royal tombs were destroyed in Chairman Mao's Cultural Revolution. Their guards were buried with helmets and realistic weapons of bronze and stone; chariots carried them to their work in the next life. Craftsmen went equipped with their knives, adzes, drills, and saws. Mesopotamian rulers also demanded this sort of otherworldly work as well. The royal dead of Ur took their retinues with them, as many as seventy at a time, sacrificed in all sorts of horrible ways. We might also tell stories of the dead of other species who serve their human masters in death as in life: the hunting dogs buried with their owners on the northern plains of America, or the dogs (perhaps just friends) found in Neolithic Scandinavian graves; the mummified cats, ibises, crocodiles, and bulls that populate Egyptian tombs by the tens of millions, some as sacrificial messengers to the gods and others—animals that were pets—as companions to dead humans; the magnificent horses that Herodotus reports were buried with the Scythian king along with one of his concubines (strangled) and his cook, groom, valet, and message bearer. But the work of these dead elsewhere is not what this chapter or this book is about.[1]

My interest is in what the dead do here, and specifically in how we imagine our own or other's people's deaths and dead bodies doing something in our world. I think this is contingently related to how we imagine what specifically happens in their world—some other world—but it is necessarily connected to our deeply grounded feeling that the dead are, somehow, still around, which makes their lifeless bodies matter to us here and now. They have not left, even if their bodies are carrion or less. Individual, relatively instantaneous biological deaths are social events that transpire over time. This connection between the individual and the social is the fundamental insight of Emile Durkheim's *Suicide*. His student Robert Hertz applied the recognition of this duality to the special case of funeral rites, which, he argued, are the occasion to begin to ease the dead gently out of this world and also to repair the social fabric rent by an individual death. I want to suggest that the philosophical, historical, and anthropological record shows us to be a species that not only lives with its dead but also is acutely aware, if not always consciously, of their continued foundational importance. And on this depends all their work.

In the beginning, even before the corpse, there was Mortality. And from this follows the fact that Death, as the poet William Empson writes, bears the burden of our very biggest ideas, of a vast, oceanic repertoire of meanings. My subject— the dead body—appropriates to itself the overwhelming fact that, much as we might want matters to be otherwise, Life (the soul, the person, or however we name it) and the Body will part company. Their intimacy will be broken, their affection will be sundered, come what may. It is a recognition that stands at a cultural ground zero. For St. Augustine, mortality "frustrated the soul's deepest wish, which was to live at peace with its beloved, the body." Like sex in the post-lapsarian world, it marked the estrangement of the soul from God, and its evil could be overcome only by the "burning love of His commandments granted by Christ to the martyrs." Death as the key to the meaning of life also has a long history in secular Western thought. Michel Montaigne's famous aphorism that "anyone who taught men how to die would teach them how to live" is an echo from antiquity. An echo of Cicero, who said that "to philosophize is to learn how to die." An echo of Socrates, who, when asked whether "the separation of the soul from the body is the preoccupation of the philosophers," answers yes, and "those who practice philosophy in the right way are in training for dying, and they fear death least of all men" (*Phaedo* 67d–e). An echo of Lucretius and Epicurus, who have a very different, materialist view of death, but who also think that it is a sign of philosophical wisdom to be able to die without fear because there is nothing to fear about returning to the nothing one had been before birth. There is a very long list of views in this tradition, and a parallel one in the teaching of most religions and secular ideologies. To make the obvious point: The dead body is a horrible reminder of death, of the fact that the human to whom it belonged has been rent from this earth.[2]

Martin Heidegger, for whom death is of central philosophical importance, offers one reason why we pay attention. It has to do with trying to understand the foundations of our existence. "In ending and in the totality thus constituted of *Da-Sein* [from the ordinary German word for existence, *dasein* (being there), but meaning in this context the human entity as a coherent Being-in-the-World] there is essentially no representation," he argues. That is, it is impossible to experience or to grasp Being when it is finished, when it is no more, even though that would be the only condition under which it could be grasped. I suggest that the dead body under these circumstances becomes a vehicle, ultimately futile, for trying to comprehend "no longer being there," by allowing us to imagine our own death—and Death—through the death of another as represented by her dead body. In other words, as Heidegger puts it, "When Da-Sein reaches its wholeness in Death, it simultaneously loses the being of the there." And, I would continue, we think we can somehow circumvent this truth by keeping the "not-being" of others in this world. Contra Diogenes, we do in fact desperately try to distinguish the "merely being objectively present" condition of the dead body from a lifeless, immaterial thing. The dead body is more; it is something *unliving* and not just a thing that is not alive. The greatest nineteenth-century collector of death masks, Laurence Hutton (1843–1904), explains in terms that Heidegger would have understood that this is precisely what makes casts of the dead face so revealing: "What life makes fugitive, death arrests. What was indefinable is defined." In other words, the relationship we maintain with the dead is a consequence of the philosophical difficulties with death itself that we translate into the phenomenology of living with the dead and their relics. The corpse becomes an icon, a way of making something present and tangible that is not present and cannot be grasped. The corpse represents something radically different from itself—the dead themselves, a soul subsisting somewhere. It works a magic we seem to need to believe in; so do things that have touched the dead.[3]

The German essayist and conservative political philosopher Ernst Junger, most famous for his youthful reflections on the Great War, gets at this beautifully in one of his later meditations on the corpse. It was something that occupied him all his life. The word *Leichnam* (corpse) is from the Old High German *lîh* (body) and *hamo* (cloth). It is etymologically more freighted than its English equivalent. *Leichnam* is explicitly the "cloth of the body" and has all of the power that good Catholics attach to relics. The deist Godwin, as we saw, wrote that something in the body of she who was gone—the dead Mary Wollstonecraft—was also there in her clothes and things. Junger makes the connection explicit. "Corpse," he writes, is "a magical word by which we characterize the dead . . . the magical life image concealed in the shrine of the body." It is connected to the Latin *imago*, which can mean a ghost or spirit, and it is this that links it to a story Pliny tells about the beginning of painting: an artist made a representation of an absent loved one. A corpse remains imbued with the person who is gone. In German, the body of Christ is his *Leichnam*. *Leiche* (cadaver) is different: "a shell [that] attracts alien powers, like an abandoned vessel." It needs to be gotten rid of lest it be taken over by the powers it attracts, but it is not itself magical on its own. A cadaver does not incite idolatry.[4]

Burying a corpse, as opposed to a cadaver—perhaps this is the distinction that all those who resist Diogenes' skepticism would want to make—is thus a representation of an imagined drama yet to unfold. The drama unfolds not only on the level of the individual corpse and the bereft mourner, but also on the level of civilizations and their histories. The rest of this book will explore the arc of this drama in the Western world, and especially in England, over the past millennium. It will trace how multiple social and cultural processes incrementally reworked the indelible relationship between the dead body and the civilization of the living. This is not, as others have suggested, a story of progressive disenchantment, but rather a history of the creation of new ways of construing the fundamentally unbreakable bond between the materiality of the corpse and the consciousness—individual and collective—of those who live with the dead.

This history moves from spaces of the dead in part 2, to names of the dead in part 3, to ashes in part 4: a progress that it would seem leads toward nothingness but in fact does not. We begin with chapter 4 to see how the practice of burying the corpse snugly in the heart of the community of the living—in, or connnected to a churchyard—first came into being and then how after at least a thousand years it came under attack from all sides. In the late eighteenth and nineteenth centuries, radical changes in assumptions about the relationship of this world with any possible other worlds, in the relative authority of different modes of knowledge, and in the nature of civilization itself combined to make new demands on the dead: they were mobilized in novel ways to re-make the world of the living. In response to these demands, the putatively disenchanted corpse, as chapter 5 shows, came to be buried in a cemetery (a huge cosmopolitan community of the dead planted in a parklike space segregated from the community of the living and outside the direct control of clerical authorities) rather than a churchyard. And here they did new work of all sorts. And so did their names in other places, mostly new and some old, as if the talismanic power of the corpse in modern life—its numen, its divine presence—had to go somewhere (conservation of psychic energy is as much a natural law as conservation of other types of energy). Part 3 is about how this happened. Finally, in part 4, we arrive at what would seem to be the greatest modern threat to the power of the dead. In the late nineteenth and twentieth centuries, burial began to give way to cremation, specifically to burning the purportedly disenchanted cadaver (now culturally understood as refuse rather than icon) in high technology ovens so as to render it into its constituent elements—that is, into nothingness—as quickly, cleanly, and thoroughly as possible. And yet again, even industrially produced ashes recuperated their aura and were recruited for cultural work. Before we turn to the historical unfolding of this story in the West, we need to understand the universal meaning assigned to the work of the dead over the *longue durée* and across civilizations: before the particular, the cosmic.

How we speak of the dead body is evidence, says the early Church Father Tertullian (160–220), of the fact that we act *as if* there were a soul or a person who lives, cares, and will be united with the "dowry of the body." If this were not so, why, he asks, would even pagans curse the memory of their enemies with the words: "May the earth lie heavy" on them and may their ashes be tormented? (The opposite sentiment, *Sit tibi terra levis* [May the earth lie lightly upon thee], was a common grave inscription abbreviated as S.T.T.L.) John Calvin, the great Genevan Reformer, who hoped to make a grand rhetorical gesture with the anonymity of his own grave, made a similar case. He argued that burial in general was a ritual ordained by God, a prelude, a mirror image of the corporeal resurrection; it was an act of faith in the foundational dogma of Christianity: an eternal soul that would be resurrected with its body because of Christ's sacrifice. But it also spoke to something universal. The fact that heathens cared for their dead is evidence that they had a sort of premonition of this great truth, even if they were to be condemned for failing to recognize it. And this was all the more the case for the Jews, whose rituals—the burning of incense, the anointing of the body with precious herbs—prefigured the doctrine of the resurrection: "What was the point of this custom of burying the dead except to make men understand that a new life was being prepared for the buried bodies?" Burial suggested that if anything slept, it was the body—hence the early Christian use of the word *coemeteria* (a place for sleep): a reminder, clear even to children, that we all await a corporeal resurrection. It is for this reason that late-nineteenth-century clerics objected to cremation: it destroyed the iconic significance of burial as a representation of the state from which the dead will rise at the end of time when the conditions for comprehending *Da-Sein* would be fulfilled.[5] The immeasurable weight of death—its cultural gravitas—bears down on the dead body and connects its materiality to a cosmic drama that transcends particular beliefs about the afterlife and journeys of the soul, even if Calvin here appropriated it to support the Christian story.

Parallel to the broad range of philosophical tradition to which I have gestured, there is an equally broad historical and anthropological record of the nature and civilizational importance of the work of the dead. In the seventeenth century, the founder of modern international law, Hugo Grotius (1583–1645), compiled a library of opinions and practices from ancient authors in support of his view that the denial of burial was so fundamentally at odds with any conceivable norm—with being human—that it was a just cause of war. His list is wide-ranging, based on the best authorities, and a good sampler of Western thinking on the subject. "The most plain and obvious Reason [for the care of the dead] is, that since Man is the Most noble of all living Creatures, it is not fit that his Body should be torn in Pieces, and devoured by Beasts." Care for the dead body is a sign "of compassion and religion"; it is "common to all civilized Nations"; it is evidence of our "common humanity." He explains what he means by this through examples: "'By the Compassion of Men,' saith Quintilian, Dead Bodies are preserved from the Depredations of Birds and Beasts. Hence it is, that this good Office of Burial is said to be performed, not so much to the Man, that is the particular person buried, as to Humanity." "Seneca and Quintilian called Burial, '*A piece of publick Humanity*'"; Petronius called it "*A piece of Humanity derived down to us from our Ancestors.*" Finally, Grotius offers a reason that connects the care of the dead with a divine order and the coming of humanity into civilization. Burial, he says, "came from the Gods." But more specifically, it marks the advent of the Olympian gods: the Giants "used to devour the dead Bodies of Men, the Abolition of which brutal practice is signified by Burial."[6]

The Jewish sages tell a similar story. It was God who taught our common parents to bury the dead shortly after Death entered the world. Adam and Eve, after they became fully human and thus mortal, were sitting about, mourning and weeping for their son, who had been murdered by his brother Cain. They had never seen a dead body before and knew nothing about what to do with it. A dog that had guarded Abel's flocks protected his master's body from the beasts and the birds that would have devoured it. Then the Lord taught our first parents a lesson on what to do. A raven fell dead; another raven came, dug a hole in the ground, took hold of his companion, and placed the dead bird in the grave. "I will do as this raven did," Adam said, and buried the body of Abel. It is a strange story about how beasts know more about the foundation of culture than humans do, about dogs who know that tossing a body over the walls won't do, and birds who teach humans about inhumation. But it is God who translates their knowledge for Adam's use and thus supports the kind of claim that Hans-Georg Gadamer made and that I discussed in the introduction: "we are dealing here with life that has spiraled out of the order of nature."[7]

The first great anthropologically informed historian, Herodotus, understood that we live with a deep belief that our own death customs in particular are irreducibly right and ethically inescapable, as if culture were in fact grounded in nature, and at the same time with full knowledge that other people, with radically different views, hold theirs to be equally dear and equally natural. This is not relativism (there is little question where civilization lies), but he understands what the stakes are. The Persian king Dareios

> in the course of his reign summoned those of the Hellenes who were present in his land, and asked them for what price they would consent to eat up their fathers when they died; and they answered that for no price would they do so. After this Dareios summoned those Indians who are called Callatians, who eat their parents, and asked them in presence of the Hellenes, who understood what they said by help of an interpreter, for what payment they would consent to consume with fire the bodies of their fathers when they died; and they cried out aloud and bade him keep silence from such words. Thus then these things are established by usage, and I think that Pindar spoke rightly in his verse, when he said that "of all things law is king."

In other words, how one disposed of the dead seems simultaneously foundational, like natural law ("it is not likely that any but a madman would make a jest of such things"), and culturally specific.[8]

The paradigmatic weirdness of the death customs of other cultures—Herodotus's anthropological point—has a long and continuous history from antiquity to the present, still retaining uncanny echoes today. The Indian novelist and anthropologist Amitav Ghosh tells of being taunted by Egyptian villagers among whom he lived. It is now the representative of the East who speaks for cremation. "Tell me, is it true what they say that in your country you burn your dead?" the jokester Khamees the Rat demands. Yes, Ghosh admits, some do. "*Haram! Haram!*" the Egyptian women shout. (Shame! Shame! Or forbidden; *haram* is the opposite of *halal*, permitted.) Maybe there is a lack of kindling in my country, his interlocutor jokes. Ghosh tries to defend himself but cannot quite figure out how to say "cremate" in Arabic, so he has to use the word for "burn," which makes what his countrymen do to their dead sound like what one does to wood or straw. Or what happens to the damned. Actually, says Khamees the Rat to a rapt audience, the Indians do it so "their bodies can't be punished after the Day of Judgment." This gets a big laugh, and there follows more teasing that Ghosh's homeland must be a world turned upside down. The joke, apparently an almost daily occurrence, is over.[9]

But the conversation starts up again in a more explicitly Herodotian way with the local imam when, a month later, Ghosh is solicited to ask him for medical help on behalf of Khamees. Ignoring the point of the visit, the imam says to a shopkeeper with whom he has been talking that in India they worship cows. Ghosh is taken aback and stumbles for a response. And that's not all, the imam continues; do you know what else they do? "He let the question hang for a moment, and then very loudly he hissed, 'They burn their dead.'" The listening shopkeeper is appalled: "Oh my God he muttered, 'ya Allah.'" The imam pushed his advantage on the strange and ironic platform of comparative civilizations. How can you allow such a barbaric and primitive practice? he shouts. Only savages would burn their dead. No nation can progress that burns its dead. Ghosh mutters in defense that the West burns its dead. Liar, retorts the imam, playing to a growing crowd. The West is not so ignorant. It has science and guns and bombs, and so do we. Ours are second only to the West's. And we have better bombs, replies ever more desperate Ghosh. "And so there we were," he concludes, "delegates from two superseded civilizations vying with each other to lay claim to the violence of the West."[10] It all started with what became of the dead.

The skeptical tradition would extend this sense of strangeness to all efforts to keep the primally material body as part of culture. For millennia, what others do that is different from what "we" do has been reckoned among the most monstrous, the most unnatural, the most irredeemably strange things in this world. One manuscript of the thirteenth-century Flemish poet Jacob van Maerlant's *Der naturen bloeme*, for example, has a lovely little illumination of people burning their dead that follows, appropriately enough, a description of Brahmins. Around it are accounts of people who kill their old parents, who are born with gray hair, who give birth to quintuplets but live only eight years, people with dogs' heads and without heads, and women with dogs' teeth, not to speak of cannibals. Burning the dead is strange beyond belief (plate 5).[11]

But, from another perspective, it too could be an entry into civilization and a synecdoche for a society's deepest beliefs. The anthropologically rich and learned travel account of the great eleventh-century Persian scholar Muḥammad ibn Aḥmad Bīrūnī makes the case for cremation in India. In the most ancient times, he reports, the people there threw their dead into the fields without any covering. This was before they were what they are. Then a legislator came along who told them to expose their dead to the wind: a move toward civilization. To comply with his wishes they built open-sided sheds that would allow the wind to pass over the dead, much as the Zoroastrians do in their grave towers. Finally, Nârâyana, the supreme Lord Vishnu, ordered that the dead be given over to fire that annihilates pollution, dirt, and smell immediately; it also releases the soul from the body. The Hindus have been following his command ever since. The claims of the dead body on the living were also specified: it is to be washed, enshrouded, and consumed by a fire with as much sandalwood as possible. Some of the ashes are to go into the Ganges, the rest into any running brook. This, Bīrūnī points out, connects them to the Buddha, who ordered that bodies be thrown into flowing water. And fire links the Hindus to the Greeks: Asclepius, among others, was raised to the angels by a column of fire.[12]

One of the most famous Renaissance humanists, Leon Battista Alberti (1404–1472), makes the same sort of argument with different facts: burial, whether of ashes or a corpse, is foundational. The places where the dead are interred have always been, he says, sacred by "the old Law"—the reference must be to Cicero—and "we still possess the same belief": "sepulchers belong to religion." In general, he thinks that places of burial are more or less coextensive with civilization. "There was scarce ever a People so barbarous as to be without the Use of Sepulchres, except, perhaps those wild Ichthyophagi in the remote parts of India," who simply throw their dead into the sea, claiming that it was irrelevant by which element—air, fire, water, or earth—corpses are consumed. Johann Heinrich Zedler, the most important German encyclopedist, is more open-minded on the subject of water burial. He cites without invidious comparison, and based on a variety of ancient sources, a whole list of African, Asian, and European peoples who put the remains of the dead in water. East Indians, Zedler adds, burned bodies first. This and all Zedler's other claims are dodgy, but their truth is irrelevant in this context.[13] What matters is that for over thousands of years the care of the dead has been a widely recognized border between savagery and civilization, propriety and barbarity, us and them.

Based on deep classical learning, eighteenth-century historical anthropologists and philosophers of history all told some version of these origin stories of the divide between civilization and barbarity and, more boldly, between nature and culture. Giambattista Vico (1668–1744) thought that burial of the dead was one of the three "universal institutions of humanity" that produced and continued to sustain civil society. The other two—matrimony and religion—are bound up with the dead: marriage binds the living to generations past (the ancestors) and generations to come (the yet unborn). It is the primal *lex*—the law of genealogy—that creates the family or the clan as an institution and connects its progeny with its dead. In the earliest ages, the dead created sacred space, and hence religion, by their presence. Vico is indebted here to Cicero, who thought much the same thing nearly two thousand years before. Religion and the dead were intimately connected through the genealogy Cicero claimed. Because "graves are the object of so much religious veneration," natural law held it wrong to bury in them corpses belonging to another family. He also thought burial should not take place on public property because it ought "not to receive a sacred character through rites performed by private individuals." Georg W. F. Hegel (1770–1831) tells a foundation story related to Vico's. In his fictive philosophical anthropology, he argues that making houses for the dead is the entry of humankind into symbol-making and into memory: houses for the living are mere shelter, structures for preserving life; a tomb is the work of the symbol-making architect. The twentieth-century Spanish philosopher Miguel de Unamuno reversed Hegel's chronology: "Stone was employed in sepulchers before it was used for houses," he said. But the idea of a primal moment in the care of the dead as a way of keeping them—housing them, we might say—among us is the same.[14]

Educated people of the eighteenth century would have known the essence of these views and their history from the major encyclopedias of the day, if from nowhere else. They were commonplaces. Denis Diderot and Jean Le Rond d'Alembert explain in their *Encyclopédie* that burial or its equivalent falls under natural law but also under human law and the concept of justice itself. It is of the essence of humanity "to not allow human bodies to rot or to leave them to be preyed upon by the beasts." Ephraim Chambers (1680–1740) in his encyclopedia, the inspiration for the French *Encyclopédie*, which began as a project to translate its English predecessor, is a little cagier but points in the same direction: "The desire of burial has been strong in most ages, and the denial of it reputed the last and severest of punishments; yet the Cynics appear to have despised it; and Pliny ranks the concern for it in the number of weaknesses peculiar to man." Pliny and the Cynics aside, though, "burial," Chambers concludes, "is an office or debt of humanity. Some found this obligation on the law of nature, others on the law of nations, and others on the divine law."[15]

The nineteenth-century founders of anthropology follow in this tradition. To take one of many possible examples, the remarkable French scholar Fustel de Coulanges argued that religion was the foundation of the ancient city (that is, of civilization) and that the dead were the reason for religion. "Our ancestors," he says, quoting Cicero, "desired that the men who had quitted this life should be counted in the number of the gods." Worship of the dead was the origin not only of Western religion but of other religions as well: among the Aryans of India, for example, who continue to believe in the necessity of offerings to the ancestors. The necessity of burial, he goes on to say, arose from the need to have a dwelling place for a soul that otherwise would roam the earth and become a malevolent spirit: "man feared death less than the privation of burial." Again, my interest in these views is not the truth or falsity of the claim that ancestor worship and thus the dead—gods of a sort—were there at the birth of religion and hence of humanity. It is rather that the status of the dead has been understood as central to debates on this question from the fathers of anthropology and sociology in the nineteenth century to our day.[16]

Modern archeology and animal ethology continue to be interested in the care of the dead because they take it to be a sign of entry into symbol making and culture more generally, as something that distinguishes the human from other categories of being. These sciences cannot, of course, settle the philosophical and cognitive psychological questions that these claims raise, but they do constitute the last stage in a tradition of thought, and they confirm the antiquity of our species' care of the dead. It goes back, among modern humans, to at least the Upper Paleolithic, 40,000–10,000 B.C.E., to what used to be called the Late Stone Age. We also know now that at least some Neanderthals buried their dead. Whether this was universal among humans and their near relatives at the time is impossible to say. There is certainly regional variation in the kinds of graves and grave goods that archeologists have found. The number of known burials we have even from more recent history is far smaller than corresponds to self-sustaining human populations; how much of this is due just to the ravages of time and how much to selectivity of care—who counted as human and hence merited burial, which would tend to preserve some remains and not others—is not known. But everyone agrees that by the Neolithic period, that is, around 10,000 B.C.E., humans cared for the dead.[17]

And we also seem to know that we are the only species to do so. The case for animals' caring for the dead, with perhaps a small exception for elephants, is thin. Some animals seem sad when another of their species dies; dogs are said to mourn the death of their masters. Some, but not all species, of elephants show an interest in the remains of other dead elephants to a greater degree than to other natural objects or the remains of other large mammals. But they do not select and visit the skulls of their own relatives more than those of unrelated elephants. And more generally, as the German essayist Ernst Junger observed, "death very quickly transforms a body for them [animals] into an object"; they are useful, perhaps as food, in the way that Heraclitus imaged human bodies as good for fertilizing the fields. I have no particular stake in the truth of various conflicting arguments about death and the beasts. My interest is in what supposedly follows: if animals care for the dead, it is because they are so marvelously like us or, the other way around, we are not so special. Since antiquity, observers have made such claims: that ants and other social insects, for example, bury their dead and can teach us a lesson in how to do it: hygienically, ritualistically, in good order. What matters to me is that ancient and contemporary ethology cares about what ants and elephants and crows do with their dead because they are interested in the boundaries of culture and the origins of civilization. The evidence suggests that we and other creatures stand on different sides of the border, but it would not matter to my theme if the border were moved a little.[18]

It does not matter whether Vico and Cicero and Grotius and all the others I have cited are factually correct, although they adduce empirical evidence for their claims that comports with modern scholarship. There are no hard answers to the sort of historical, philosophically inflected, fictive anthropology that engaged them. But they write as if it were perfectly clear, and in accord with right order, that people act as if the care of the dead—burying them, remembering them properly—stands at a cultural turning point. Necrotopology and necromnemonics, in the views of a long tradition of commentary right up the present, have been interpreted as general signs of human activity—of humanness, of entry into symbolic behavior. This deep history underwrites the specific cultural work of the dead.

When Gadamer argued that we live with our dead, he meant it in two senses: we live with them as dead bodies, and we live with their afterlives, in memory, in some other place, or when in unusual circumstances they return here. In both these senses they are, individually and collectively, the temporal extension of our present: they are us—our symbolic world—as we imagine it in deep time. Memory and death have long been understood to be the closest of relations. The first-century B.C.E. Roman author Pliny the Elder tells the story of the scholar Marcus Varro (116–27 B.C.E.), who put portraits of seven hundred famous people in his books and thus bestowed on them a sort of immortality that even the gods would envy, one that could be "dispatched . . . all over the world." (The vast photographic collections of the dead in the nineteenth and twentieth centuries are heirs to his work.) In the old days, Pliny continues, wax statues of the ancestors, representing "every member of the family that had ever existed" were present at the funeral of the latest to die. By extension, we make likenesses for our libraries "of those immortal spirits who hold converse with us in these places," even if all remembrance of how that person may have looked—Homer is the paradigmatic case—is lost. Indeed, art itself was born, Pliny speculates, in the tracing of shadows—perhaps of a dead child or absent or dead lover, other ancient sources suggest—to make loss more bearable. These stories of Pliny the Elder will inform Nicolas Poussin's widely influential seventeenth-century painting *Et in Arcadia ego* (see chapter 5), in which the shepherds discover death by tracing the outlines of a shadow on a tomb in Arcadia. Mourning the death of shepherds is of course central to the long pastoral tradition that Poussin knew. But, just as important, the ancient author and the Renaissance painter bear witness to the antiquity and solidity of the idea that we make communities of the dead: seven hundred famous people, shepherds, Christians gathered in death.[19]

The poet William Wordsworth reflects on how houses of the dead speak directly to the needs of memory. He thinks that building tombs and, in later ages, placing epitaphs near bodies—here literacy becomes the vehicle for immortality—guards the border not only of civilization but also of specific historical communities: "Never any neglect burial but some savage nations, as the Bactrians, which cast their dead to the dogs," the poet writes, quoting as his authority William Camden (1551–1623), the Elizabethan historian whose magisterial survey of the topography and history of Great Britain and its funereal monuments was meant to "restore antiquity to Great Britain and Great Britain to antiquity." With very few exceptions, even savage tribes "unacquainted with letters" put mounds of earth or rude stones over their dead in order to guard the remains of the deceased from "irreverent approach or from savage violation" and to "preserve their memory."[20]

The actors in this book—in *The Work of the Dead*—understood themselves to be engaged with creating, through bodies, specific memorial communities and specific histories. They understood the power of the dead. The dead make civilizations because those who think about this elusive term believe that they do and act as if they did. We have already seen evidence of this and will encounter more in the coming chapters. But more specifically, those who, in the eighteenth, nineteenth, and twentieth centuries, changed how they buried and named the dead, or who advocated burning them in high-tech ovens, understood themselves to be engaged in dismantling a world they had inherited from the Middle Ages and the struggles of the Reformation and in building a new one. On the one hand, they were engaged in a negative project: overthrowing what they understood to be the vast necrogeography and the institutions that maintained it that the Church had imposed on Europe, for example. If the dead were the foundation of the Church, then removing them from clerical control would weaken the institutional power of religious bodies and clear the ground for something new. On the other hand, there were a variety of positive projects: the dead could be mobilized to create new memorial communities, to make a new civic order, or to advance a particular political or social claim. All this was possible—the Christian revolution, its partial undoing, and the making of something new—because of the very long engagement of the dead. The dead are powerful in the modern era because they had been powerful for other projects in other ages over the *longue durée*.

We can divide the vast expanses of the time of the dead into chronologically more limited but still very long periods. Care of the dead has from the beginning been regarded as, and probably is, a sign of humanity and of human institutions. More recently—we are speaking here of the age of Herodotus—it came to be seen as a sign of civilization as opposed to savagery, of the ethically correct in distinction to the aberrant. It has also, in its particulars, been taken to be a distinguishing characteristic of a specific civilization. In this sense, it is long-lived but not immemorial. "Burial customs," writes the historian Peter Brown, "are among the most notoriously stable aspects of most cultures. . . . The customs surrounding the care of the dead were experienced by those who practiced them to be no more than part and parcel of being human." Therefore, when something does change, it is of some consequence. Sometime between the third and the seventh centuries, the ground shifted under this "notoriously stable" aspect of the ancient world. "You have filled the whole world with tombs and sepulchers," says Julian the Apostate about the Christians among whom he had once numbered himself. And from this is born a regime of the dead—lasting roughly from 300 to 1800 C.E., across the Reformation divide—that survived in the West until the eighteenth century, when its overthrow was part of the process of making the modern world.[21]

As far back as the archeological and literary records go, the peoples of the Mediterranean and those who came under its sway buried their dead outside of cities and—with a few exceptions—away from the gods. The dead created their own sacrality, which the state protected, independent of its support for the gods themselves. In the first century B.C.E., Cicero traces the prohibition against intramural burial to the fifth-century laws of the ancestors, the Twelve Tables, which had themselves been promulgated after a study of Greek customs. The third-century C.E. jurist Paulus explains that the reason one cannot bring a corpse inside a city is lest its "sacred places" be polluted, a commonplace opinion, widely circulated in the provinces, regularly enforced, and thoroughly taken for granted. It was a norm that died slowly: the law code of Justinian (ca. 530 C.E.) still prohibited burial inside cities or churches at a time when the very old and long-robust taboos against mingling the dead and the living were slowly crumbling almost everywhere.[22]

By the eighth century, the ancient necrogeography had been overthrown in most of Europe. The adamantine customs of burial changed, but they changed slowly. As early as the third century, a text claiming to be in the voice of the apostles addresses the faithful as those who "according to the Gospel and according to the power of the holy spirit come together even in cemeteries, and read the holy scriptures . . . and offer an acceptable Eucharist." Already then, Christians are reminded, neither the burial of a person nor an unburied corpse—nor a wet dream, for that matter—could pollute their souls. For a long time, well into the fourth century and even later, Christians often still buried their dead alongside their pagan neighbors. So did Jews. Then, the bodies of the special dead began to be carried triumphantly into churches. It is true that Ambrose's new basilica in the imperial capital of Milan, to which he brought the bodies of the martyrs Gervasius and Protasius, was outside the old city walls. The old barriers had not been definitively breeched. But the translation of bodies from outside to inside an inhabited area had a huge symbolic and practical impact. The much-frequented church was in a well-populated area, and the point was clear: the daily intercourse of living and special dead was now the norm. The same could be said for the burial of St. Martin in what had been a previously inhabited part of Rome. Soon the ordinary dead joined the martyrs and other saints.[23]

Increasingly, churches also came to be built around the bodies of the special dead in suburban areas or in the countryside. The living came to worship there even if the dead did not move into their midst right away. Far from polluting the sacred, the special dead made it visible. In some way, of course, this marks the physical erasure of ancient urban civilization and of paganism more generally. Thus in Corinth, for example, the sacred bounds of the city were still respected in the fourth century, and old prohibitions were enforced. By the next century, *martyria* and cemeteries were being built on the tombs of saints, outside new, more circumscribed walls, but well within what had been older inhabited areas. At the same time, the dead also took over pagan sacred places: the aggressive colonization in Antioch that so pained Julian the Apostate and, more than a thousand years later, Edward Gibbon (see chapter 4); the sanctuary of Asklepios; and the shrine of the Sacred Spring of Lerna—a port to the underworld in Greek mythology. (The spring became a holy well, thus adding to its attraction as a place for burial *ad sanctos*.) By the middle of the sixth century, there was a cemetery in the Roman Forum and tombs and churches in the old spaces of the city. At the end of the ninth century, the Byzantine emperor Leo VI—called "the wise," a philosopher (866–912)—formally rescinded the ancient proscriptions that had for many centuries been irrelevant or worse.[24]

The movement of the dead into cities and into—and around—churches happened at different paces in the various regions of the Roman world and its periphery. Local variation was great; where the dead were buried depended on a large number of individual decisions made within different constraints. But in general the trend was clear. The dead moved in among the living and into and around new sacred sites. There is considerable evidence for intramural burial in Italy and western Roman cities in the fifth and sixth centuries, and in Gaul, Britain, and Spain by the seventh. (Except in Macedonia and Greece, this was rare in the east, although burial within extramural churches was common.) Burial in pagan cemeteries declined slowly, and regular burial within churchyards took time. In England in the Anglo-Saxon period, there were still in use pagan cemeteries organized around the grave not of a saint but of a founding body; there were even a few old-style mounds with grave goods. But where a place was well supplied with churches—in Winchester around 675 is a good example—the dead had moved inside the city walls and were aligned in the manner that would not change until the nineteenth century. Before the Norman Conquest, burial inside the church was extremely rare; during the High Middle Ages there was increased movement of bodies to the aisle and chancel.[25] However, the point here is not to map on a fine scale this massive cultural transformation but rather to suggest its broad contours.

I could point to symbolic moments of transformation. Charlemagne issued ordinances in 786 and 810/13 forbidding the use of pagan cemeteries and giving the Church—if not necessarily the parish church—exclusive claims on the dead.

Burial in churchyards had to wait for the supply to meet the demand—for the proliferation of local churches, which took centuries to accomplish. The clergy tended to be concentrated in minsters—monasteries of sorts—and serviced surrounding villages. Even in the tenth century, many people were buried on their properties or in field cemeteries that were exclusively Christian but not consecrated. (This was clearly second best. The story is told in the saga of Eric the Red of a man who haunted the countryside because a priest's pouring holy oil into a hole over his farm grave was not enough to settle his soul.) Consecration of the churchyard in England seems to be an eighth-century innovation; if everyone cannot be inside with the relic, at least the ground in which ordinary people were buried could be made sacred. Special services for the dead developed in roughly the same period. Slowly a new social necrogeography came into view. The important people in the community, as well as monks and priests, increasingly insisted on being buried as near the special dead as possible—*ad sanctos*, as it was called—and lesser folks spread out from there into the churchyards: saints, monks, nuns, important clergy, and the prominent laity inside the church and grandly laid to rest, everyone else outside in the wet. Of course there are exceptions: ascetic modesty by holy men and devout laypeople.[26]

From the perspective of this chapter's central question—how and why do the dead make civilization?—this shift in the geography and temporality of the dead in their new places awaiting the Day of Judgment had several consequences. In the first place, the change in the organization of time and space that I have just outlined created what one historian has called a "tactile revolution"—a revolution in how the dead body felt to the living. Long a source of pollution shunned by the living, it had become, in the case of the special dead, a locus of holiness and in the case of more ordinary corpses, a part of the community and of new communal space. This revolution did not represent a rejection of ancient hygienic standards. Ritual pollution is not a health hazard. Nor was it a revolution of the senses. Perhaps the bodies of some saints miraculously did not decompose and even smelled sweet; but even if a martyr's hand or the skull or entire body did not smell at all, it would in the ancient world have been associated with the putrid and polluting body. And no one was under any illusion that the ordinary dead did not smell of corruption; the adjective "stinking" was routinely if redundantly appended to "corpse," a commonplace that informs biblical accounts, commentaries, and later pictures of the raising after four days of the dead Lazarus. Bystanders are shown holding their noses as he emerges from his shroud, as they are more generally in other contexts when a dead body comes into olfactory range (plate 3). We also have considerable evidence going back more than a thousand years that the insides of churches smelled bad, that burial grounds around churches were a crowded mess almost from the start, and that everyone knew this.[27]

The dirty had become clean not because anyone thought that the dead were in fact "clean" in a hygienic sense but because they had become part of a new kind of community with a new communal purpose: to await the resurrection of the body and life everlasting. These no-longer-polluting dead had helped make, and were sustaining, this new order. Eighteenth- and nineteenth-century reformers who led the new modern smell revolution both misunderstood and appropriated the earlier revolution for their own purposes: for the work of the dead. They wrongly attributed the ancient fear of bodies to worries about hygiene rather than ritual pollution, and they could not acknowledge the potent ritual powers of their own seemingly objective medical mandate for once again separating the dead from the living (see chapter 5).

When the places of the dead changed in the course of making Christian Europe, so also did their governance. Burial had been a private matter under the general supervision of the state: those who could afford it bought and owned their burial places; cemeteries were regulated by whoever had the right to sell *loci*. Then interment became a largely communal affair: places of the dead belonged to—or in any case were controlled by—ecclesiastical authorities; there was no private ownership of graves between the end of paganism and the early eighteenth century, although rights to graves and chapels were vastly complex affairs with infinite local variations that I will discuss as needed later on. These new arrangements meant that, with few exceptions, from the early Middle Ages to the eighteenth century, access to church and churchyard, monastic cloister, and even the freestanding chapels of the great—the only places available for honorable burial—was ultimately regulated by ecclesiastical authorities. These new communities of the dead, under new management, were exclusively for members of the Christian community in good standing; there they dwelled and there they were remembered.

It goes without saying that Jews were excluded, and likewise those who were excommunicated or had taken their own lives or were in other ways out of favor with ecclesiastical authorities. A right to burial somewhere seems to have subsisted under all circumstances; dead bodies were not left in the fields or in the street. But where they were buried came under strict supervision. Gregory of Tour tells the story of Count Palladius, who in the late sixth century committed suicide after losing a quarrel with a bishop; he was buried at a distance from the Christian community on the grounds of a monastery. A monk who hid three gold coins in violation of monastic rules, so Pope Gregory I relates, was denied burial among his brethren. And supernatural forces patrolled the new spaces of the dead even more strictly. The seventh-century nuns who had repeatedly fled their convent and failed to mend their ways each time were buried, by the abbess's orders, in segregated plots when they died. But this was not enough for higher authorities; within six months, their tombs had been scorched by fire and the bodies reduced to ash; for three years a fiery ball sat over the unconsecrated graves and screams could be heard echoing through the landscape. Jewish bodies were systematically removed from Christian burial grounds. Of course, enforcement varied and there were many loopholes, but Voltaire's fears of ignominious burial and the many fights about burial rights in eighteenth- and nineteenth-century England—and hundreds of other such battles elsewhere—were all in the context of the new symbolic and legal world of the dead. Who was in and who was out had become the decision of the religious authorities.[28]

We might imagine that this regime of the dead—the one that began in late antiquity—would have ended or at least been threatened by the Protestant Reformation. Theologically, pastorally, politically, and economically, the dead were on the front lines of the break. *Totenfresser*, devourers of the dead, the enemies of Rome called the monks and priests who, at considerable cost, prayed and said masses for the souls of the dead undergoing purification (fig. 3.1). The idea, going back to the very beginning of the cult of saints, was that not only the living but also the dead could benefit from proximity to the bodies of the special dead, whose charisma translated into having a friend in the court of heaven. These special dead, along with the Virgin, were the great intercessors of the medieval Church, to whom people could appeal in their own behalf when living and, more to the point here, on behalf of their dead loved ones and, providentially, for themselves by endowing a stream of future masses for the benefit of their own souls. By the thirteenth century, more than a thousand years of theology and tradition crystallized, as we saw in chapter 2, into the imagined geography of a far more elaborated purgatory than had existed before. And the institutions great and small through which the living could help the souls there elaborated as well. Crudely put, the Reformation began when Luther became incensed by the sale of indulgences—time off for tormented souls in purgatory that a cash-strapped Church was selling in the German lands—and launched an attack on their theological foundations.

3.1. "Die Totenfresser," based on a play by Nicolas Manuel, ca. 1530. Reproduced in Eugen Hollander, *Die Karikatur und Satire in der Medizin*, 1921.

But my interest is in the fate of dead bodies and not of the dead more generally. If, as a consequence of the Reformers' arguments against the Church of Rome, the dead did not need to be buried together around the bodies of saints or other relics, then where should they be buried? And did it matter? A group of Protestant theologians in 1526 argued that a field was as good as anywhere to put a body; Martin Luther claimed a year later that he would just as soon be buried "in the Elbe or in the forest, than in the crowded Wittenberg churchyard"; Calvin insisted on being buried in an undisclosed and unsanctified spot to make sure that no one would be tempted to make of his grave a sacred place. James Pilkington, the Protestant bishop of Durham, taught that papists were wicked in "teaching the people that one place was more holy than another to be buried in." The old intimacy between necrogeography and the fate of the soul was, Reformers argued, meaningless or worse: delusional and idolatrous. Where and how a body was put to rest had no bearing on salvation; proximity to the altar was irrelevant; so were monuments, prayers, and everything else one might do for the sake of the dead person's soul. (Luther, one might note, changed his mind about the venue of his grave; his body was transported from Eisleben, where he was born and where he died, to Wittenberg, a hundred kilometers away, and was put to rest inside the church itself very close to the altar. We still do not know exactly where Calvin was buried, although in the nineteenth century, when the idea of a nameless burial place became unbearable, a gravesite was invented for him.)[29]

A field was as good as a churchyard as a place for the dead—Luther here shared Diogenes' view—because the cultic objects, especially sacred body parts (the sine qua non of a church at the heart of the whole medieval penitential system), were, according to the Reformers, irrelevant. They were nothing, and hence there was no reason to be buried near them. As Max Weber observed in his classic study of the Protestant ethic, "the genuine Puritan even rejected all signs of religious ceremony at the grave and buried his nearest and dearest without song or ritual in order that no superstition, no trust in the effects of magical and sacramental forces of salvation, should creep in." This "genuine Puritan"—that is, this most severe Calvinist strain of Protestantism, with its belief in predestination and its abhorrence of anything that might hint of an icon—did aim to overthrow a regime of dead bodies that it believed to be corrupt and by doing so to desacralize it. Other Reformed Churches more or less followed suit in this effort to reverse history, to go back to a purer time on which to build a new future. Perhaps, as is often claimed, the world became a little less enchanted as the charisma of saint's relics vanished and the whole great apparatus built to help the souls of the dead—purgatory—was demolished.[30]

But, in fact, the Reformation did not bring down the regime of the dead that the early Church had created. Communities of the Christian dead continued to represent their connections and continuities with the living, purgatory or no purgatory. The Calvinist burghers of the Netherlands were buried just as before in churches—their walls now brilliant white and empty of icons, their saints gone, their altars stripped of relics and turned into communion tables, but their dead just where they had always been (fig. 3.2). And so were the leaders of the most Puritan and separatist of English Reformers who were in exile there. John Smyth was buried in the Niewe Kerk in Amsterdam in 1612; John Robinson, preacher of the Leyden congregation, buried two children in St. Peter's before he was laid to rest under a great stone in the floor of the same church. Gone was the purgatorial

3.2. Interior of the Oude Kerk in Amsterdam. Emanuel de Witte, 1655. Musée des Beaux-Arts de Strasbourg.

regime; gone was any theological rationale to be buried in a church or near an altar. But the communal bond between living and dead souls, as well as the hierarchical divisions of this world, continued to be represented under the soil of churches and churchyards.[31]

Only on occasion were there calls for extramural burial places on theological grounds, that is, because the case was made that there was no need to be near a church. Generally, local politics mattered more than views about salvation; the clergy was still prominent at the funeral; new tombs continued to reflect the social hierarchy of the old ones in Leipzig's St. Thomas and elsewhere. In Nuremburg, an extramural burial place—the St. Johannis Friedhof—was built ten minutes' walk outside the walls in the thirteenth century because the old churchyard had become too crowded. But neither then nor in the sixteenth century was this new burial ground regarded as representing a separation of the living from the dead. Before and after Luther, bodies from both of the city's parish churches were buried there, recorded in the same *Todtenbuecher*, with clergy in attendance, with due regard to social hierarchy. Each Reformed city had its own history and politics, its own quarrels about civic ritual and practice. But there was no systematic separation of the dead from the living anywhere. And, Catholics and Protestants in areas where they lived together insisted on being buried together in the old places, whoever now controlled them and whatever theologians thought. In the midst of the French Wars of Religion and sporadic violent attacks by both sides on the enemy's dead in their graves and tombs, ordinary people in mixed communities shared cooperatively the old churchyards. In German cities, neighbors insisted on being buried with neighbors and kin when the clergy resisted the cohabitation of Protestant and Catholic dead. In Britain, almost nothing changed in this regard. The dead kept old communities together, until they no longer did, hundreds of years later.[32]

Protestantism seems also to have had little effect on memorial practices other than prayers for the dead. We do not, and probably will never have, a record of the number of tombs and monuments built to honor the dead before and after the Reformation, in Protestant or Catholic places, in England or on the continent. Too many were destroyed for ideological or economic reasons—their materials were reused—or have fallen into ruin over the ages. We have no systematic written record of their existence. The best we can say is that probably the number of tombs began to rise after the Black Death of the late fourteenth century and continued to increase in the centuries that followed across Europe, independent of what the tomb-building classes thought about prayers for the dead. At least five thousand substantial ones were built in England between 1540 and 1660—probably more than in the previous century—not because the end of purgatory made memorial practices here on earth more exigent but because of an increase in the wealth and number of members of the tomb-building classes and because of a general increase in construction. Well before the Reformation, the dying came to have a greater interest in how they were buried because classical ideals of memory and virtue, refurbished in the Renaissance, had far more to do with the look of monuments than theology did. We also know that late medieval churches had become the stage for all sorts of individual display that had nothing to do with prayers for the dead, the importance of being buried near saints, or any of the other matters fought over in the Reformation.[33]

While there came to be obvious differences in the iconography of Roman and Protestant monuments in some cases, the aesthetics of memorial building also followed its own course. Again there was continuity. The cadaver tombs of the late Middle Ages enjoyed new popularity in the seventeenth century; medieval alabaster tombs continued to be built in all their Gothic splendor with a few Renaissance modifications after the Reformation as before; secular representations of the earthly virtues and achievements of the dead were common in medieval as in post-Reformation monuments. And the bodies of the dead with attendant monuments became even more closely identified with the parish church and its most sacred spaces underneath the altar than before, because monastic burial grounds were no longer an option and because space opened up with the removal of altar screens and shrines. But all in all, the ancient tradition of building tombs for those who could afford it found new energy in the Renaissance as a way of abiding with the dead. The supposed rupture of the Protestant Reformation had relatively little effect on burial practices.[34]

This is because tombs, like the care of the dead more generally, were believed to serve deep civilizational purposes. The great Protestant jurist Sir Edward Coke, certainly no friend of Rome, held, for example, that tombs and monuments in a church were lawful as "the last act of charity that can be done for the deceased who whilst he lived was a lively temple of the Holy Ghost with a reverend regard and a Christian hope of a joyful resurrection." In other words, if one can afford it, one should honor the dead as represented in and though the body; it remained something toward which one could act charitably. "Amongst the people of God, Sepulchre was ever held in great reverence," Coke argued, and even by the "moral heathens"—we are back to the foundational arguments with which we began— monuments were held in great respect. They are well represented among the wonders of the ancient world, he pointed out, because there were good reasons besides religious ones for building them: respect for achievement and familial memory, for example. This idea has survived even into the modern regime.[35]

Finally, we can see the power of the dead by looking briefly not at their constructive but at their destructive power: the mutilated dead, the dead whose graves and tombs are erased, individually and collectively, the dead who are severed from what was supposed to be their final resting place—all of them work, too. It is the work of unmaking. We can see this at particular historical junctures. Smashing tombs—of saints and of those wealthy enough to have tombs within the Christian community of the dead—was widespread in some areas early in the Reformation as a way of attacking the idea of purgatory and the whole inter-cessory apparatus of the Roman Church. Vandalism made the point nicely that the body here on earth and the dead that it represented were beyond human touch or care. Death was an unbridgeable chasm; wherever the dead were, they were in God's hands and of little concern for the living. But such radical rupture could not and did not survive. In England, a royal proclamation of 19 September 1560 condemned iconoclasm—an officially sanctioned policy earlier, under King Edward VI—on a number of grounds: it was politically disruptive; it violated the memory of the honorable dead and destroyed the historical record—the imag-ined correlative community of the dead that was the foundation of community; and it was almost by nature excessive and tended toward heterodoxy. Attacking the dead was and is a profoundly radical step.[36]

But it was sporadically widespread over time and space. Let me be clear. Bones and bodies over the millennia have seldom been left in peace for very long: sec-ondary burial is routine in the Christian East; the sextons of medieval and early modern churchyards routinely tossed out the debris of the long dead, sometimes into an ossuary and sometimes not; excarnation—the boiling and defleshing of a body to bring it back to where it belonged from far away—was well established by the twelfth century; regional exhumations were routine for the elite as their corpses waited for tombs to be ready or for the opportunity to join relatives. This was all commonplace but not intentionally violent or destructive—sometimes the opposite.[37]

But there was also a tradition throughout Europe of violently removing and punishing the dead. Especially in the early years of Christianity, God sometimes cast out bodies from where he thought they did not belong, and humans embraced the practice (see chapter 5). Posthumous punishment and exclusion visited on corpses was very old and widespread. Victorious armies in ancient China would erect monuments using the corpses of their defeated enemies to memorialize their triumph. The Spanish Inquisition dug up the bodies of the ancestors of some of its victims and publicly burned them. The students of the Cultural Revo-lution in China destroyed the tombs and bodies of long dead emperors, as did the French revolutionaries with their kings at St. Denis. The English did it at critical moments over the centuries. In 1428, on the pope's orders, the bishop of Lincoln had the body—or in any case, the supposed body—of the heretic John Wycliffe (ca. 1320–1384), the progenitor of English Protestantism and the first translator of the Bible into English, dug up from his grave in the churchyard of Lutterworth, where he had been vicar. He had it burned, and the ashes were then thrown into the nearby River Swift. Thus the world was to be cleansed and heresy washed away.[38]

A century later, the body of the evangelical Reformer Peter Martyr's wife was similarly dug up and humiliated: "the despightful handling and madness of the Papists toward Peter Martyr's wife at Oxford, taken up from her grave, and after buried in a dunghill," as John Foxe put it in his *Acts and Monuments* (one of the most widely read books of the sixteenth century and, next to the Bible and *Pilgrim's Progress*, a core text of English popular Protestantism), was among the most emotionally freighted charges leveled against the Marian restoration. In 1556, Foxe recounts, Cardinal Reginald Pole, the papal legate sent to receive England back into the Catholic fold and also Queen Mary's chief adviser, ordered that a commission be sent to Oxford to find evidence that Katherine Denmartin, Peter Martyr's dead wife and a former German nun, had been a heretic. The commissioners failed at their task. Potential witnesses all said that they could not understand Katherine's native tongue and thus had no idea what she thought. Undeterred—her being a married former nun and the first woman to live in the college was presumably heretical enough—Pole ordered that the body of this "honest, grave and sober matron" be dug up from its grave in Christ Church Cathedral and thrown on a dunghill. When history took a new turn, her body bore witness. In 1561, with Elizabeth now on the throne, "from Marshall's dunghill she was restored and translated to her proper place again," that is, her remains were mixed with the relics of St. Frithuswith, patron saint of Oxford, and buried in the cathedral near which she had originally been buried. "They [Catholic authorities] rage against one that is dead," said a preacher on the occasion of Katherine's reinterment. Everyone on both sides of this horrible episode understood that a dead body was *just* a dead body ("For though that the body being once dead, all estimation lykewise perished and was taken away: yet was some reverence to bee vsed towarde her for sexe and womanhoode sake"), and yet it was not—is never— just a body, which is precisely why Foxe makes so much of the insult to the dead person, to her husband, and to the Protestant nation.[39]

It was not an isolated instance. Foxe tells the story of a man who robbed a Spaniard and was hanged for it in early June 1555. But this was not the end of his punishment. Because he had spoken out against masses for the dead, saints, and popery on the gallows, a citation for heresy was issued against him in late June. When, not surprisingly, he failed to appear, he was dug up and asked: why "the sayde John Tooley that is dead, ought not to be determined and declared for such a heretic and excommunicate person. . . . When the poor dead man could not speak for himself, nor did (as they said) sufficiently answer them," he was condemned and handed over to the secular powers for execution at the stake. That is, he was not reburied in a churchyard but burned and his ashes scattered, the same technique used in the twentieth-century Holocaust to achieve ultimate *Vernichtung* (extermination) and as close to annihilation of personhood as the state was able to accomplish in the sixteenth century. In Cambridge, the famous Protestant theologian and professor Martin Bucer and the Hebrew scholar Paul Fagius were also dug up and burned to ashes. They too were restored to their graves in an elaborate new funeral. In short, the dead mattered in the great struggle over religion and politics and went from being persons to nonpersons and back through their dead bodies. The willingness of Catholics "to pierce through the graves and ghosts of men that be dead" was taken to be evidence not only of their savagery but also of their screwy eschatology.[40]

But Protestants were equally willing "to pierce through the graves of the dead" when circumstances demanded it. After the siege of Colchester in 1648, the officers and men of the Puritan army broke open the Lucas tomb (Sir Charles was one of the royalist commanders) in St. Giles Church, cut the hair off of the undecomposed bodies of Elizabeth and her daughter Mary to put in their hats, and scattered the bones of the other corpses about with "profane jests." It was, in a sense, a reprise of the violent 1642 popular attacks on the Lucas family, the king, and an anti-Puritan Church. The restoration of the Protestant Charles II was marked by a flurry of exhumations and a sorting out of bodies as the dead did their part to erase the wrongs of 1642–1660. Early in 1661, Charles issued a warrant that the body, limbs, and head of James Graham, Marquesse of Montrose, the greatest of the Scottish royalist heroes, who had been beheaded and quartered on orders of the victorious Parliamentary forces, be reassembled and given a magnificent funeral at the king's expense. His head had been put on a pike at the Edinburgh tollhouse and his arms and legs displayed in various towns before the whole lot was dumped in a field where executed felons lay. His heart, stolen by his widow from the grave or maybe from beneath the gibbet, had been sent to Flanders and was returned to the family in 1660. The body complete again, the remains were buried in St. Giles Cathedral with "a greater solemnitie than any of our Kings ever had at their burial in Scotland," according to the seventeenth-century historian Robert Baillie. More than any other single act, the funeral marked the ceremonial end of a revolutionary regime and the return of a legitimate one. When it came to humiliating or elevating the dead, there was little difference between Protestants and Catholics.[41]

If some bodies were restored to honor, others were dug up so that revenge could be exacted against them. Between 26 and 29 January 1661, the bodies of twenty-one people were dug up from Westminster Abbey and dumped into a pit in the nearby churchyard of St. Margaret, the local parish church: among others, Anne Fleetwood, Cromwell's granddaughter, and Elizabeth, his mother, who had died in her ninetieth year; William Blake, the great admiral of the Commonwealth; Thomas May, the poet, dramatist, and historian who had written in the Parliamentary cause; William Twisse, the theologian who had led the opposition to Archbishop Laud; and John Pym, one of the "Five Members" whose arrest in 1642 had sparked the rebellion against the king. These were representative corpses of a failed revolution; hundreds more would have done as well. A plaque put up by the Cromwell Association commemorates the event. A worse fate awaited the bodies of three dead regicides, one that was the mirror image of Montrose's. As a dead royalist body was reconstituted, those of three dead regicides were torn apart. On 31 January 1661, the twelfth anniversary of the death of the king whose execution warrant they had signed, Oliver Cromwell, his son-in-law Henry Ireton, and Charles Bradshaw, Lord President of the Court that had condemned Charles I to death, were ripped from their desecrated tombs in Westminster Abbey, drawn face-down to Tyburn on sleds, publicly hanged in their shrouds, taken down, and beheaded. They were thrown into a pit under the gallows. Their heads were displayed in various venues. Cromwell's began a three-century-long peregrination. In 1813, Lord Liverpool objected strongly to its being displayed in a London museum. Then for a century and a half it went underground, finally ending up on 26 March 1960 somewhere in the chapel of Sidney Sussex College, Cambridge, where Cromwell had been a Fellow Commoner.[42]

We can return to a gloss on Empson's line "death . . . is the trigger to the literary man's biggest gun" on an intimate and a more capacious scale. In 1888, a modest English elementary schoolteacher wrote about her visit to a small Norwegian cemetery. She was moved by the small iron enclosures around tombstones—"grave gardens"—and by the women watering the flowers they held. She commented also on the small seats, painted white, on which visitors to a grave sat. "Surely," she mused, "if a nation shows its civilization and Christianity by the care for the dead, these people ought to be in the first rank." At the core of her sensibility, in some ways so very nineteenth-century, there is a more universal truth. The dead, like death itself, are of overwhelming consequence. We care for them, and they work for us on making and remaking the very foundations of our species' Being, individual and communal. The dead in the ground, or anywhere that they have been thoughtfully put, constitute a symbolic system that defies cultural nihilism and carries within itself a long, iterative, slowly changing history of meaning. As such, the dead are powerful. To change the symbolic system of the dead is to change the world, as the rest of this book will show in detail.[43]

PART II

PLACES OF THE DEAD

They were camping for the last time and Coyote could see [his wife] very clearly as if she were a real person who sat opposite him. He could see her face and body very clearly, but he only looked and dared not touch her. But suddenly a joyous impulsion seized him; the joy of having his wife again overwhelmed him. He jumped to his feet and rushed over to embrace her. His wife cried out, "Stop! Stop! Coyote! Do not touch me. Stop!" Her warning had no effect. Coyote rushed over to his wife and just as he touched her body she vanished. She disappeared—returned to the shadowland. When the death spirit learned of Coyote's folly he became deeply angry. "You inveterate doer of this kind of thing! I told you not to do anything foolish. You, Coyote, were about to establish the practice of returning from death. Only a short time away the human people are coming, but you have spoiled everything and established for them death as it is."

"COYOTE AND THE SHADOW PEOPLE," NEZ PERCE STORY

Tradition authorizes the expectation that our Lord will appear in the east; therefore all the faithful are buried with their feet towards the east to meet him. Hence in Wales the east wind is called "the wind of the dead men's feet."

Curious Church Customs (1895)

Places of the dead are of two kinds: those like shadowlands that are strange and far off and those like the churchyards of Wales that are near and familiar. The first of these—"over the five mountains," or in the land of Osiris, or in the sky with the sun god Ra, or in the subterranean world of Hades beyond the River Styx, or in the most distant heavens somewhere—cannot be found on a map. Each may have its own geography, sometimes a very precise one, as in Dante's *Divine Comedy*, where the circles of Hell are arranged vertically and are precisely isomorphic with the sins of their inhabitants. Most are divided by a moral axis: places for the good and different places for the wicked.

But these sorts of places, places like that from which Coyote hoped to get back his wife, are not like distant lands that can in principle be charted and explored. Even if they are imagined as deep within the earth or over a distant horizon or across a great sea, they are beyond ordinary knowing. In another version of "Coyote and the Shadow People," the crafty ancestral figure has gone to fetch not his wife but his daughter from the land of the dead. Like Greek Orpheus, whose music had charmed the god of the underworld into freeing his beloved Eurydice, Coyote had been warned not to look back. Like Orpheus he disobeyed, but, unlike him, it was by accident. He slipped, exhausted from carrying his daughter and the five wolf brothers on his back, as he attempted to cross the last mountain. Still, like Orpheus, who lost Eurydice forever, Coyote lost his beloved daughter. But his failure had other far-reaching consequences: the establishment of the great uncrossable divide of two worlds, that of the living and that of the dead. "Now you have made death a permanent condition," his daughter told him when he begged that she continue on beyond the fifth mountain where he had faltered: "People will never return from death." The border between the two kinds of places of which I speak became secure; whatever the geographical features of the other side, transits and compasses and the other instruments of the surveyor are of little help in mapping it. Or put differently, there had once been a place (the journey perhaps, the world before humans more generally) where physical beings and spirit beings—Coyote and his daughter—could coexist. Now there was no such place.

Bodies subsist in curious ways in this first sort of place of the dead. Even if they are atom for atom identical to their earthly state, as the late medieval church imagined them to be in heaven, they have a strange relationship to space: they are not situated in cardinal or ordinal directions, no east or west, north or south; if there are an up and a down, it is not clear in relation to what these are determined; even if bodies in this world are material, they are incorruptible and do not return to earth. There is no ecological cycle in this land. And finally, there is no need for an enormous social, political, and legal apparatus to manage this place. It existed before "death as it is" became the lot of humanity.

There is second kind of space of the dead—incommensurable with those like shadowland yet bound to it as the dead on earth are bound to the dead wherever they are—that is the subject of the next two chapters: the space of corruptible bodies, the space in which the cultural norms of the living dictate their fate. Humans have to answer mundane questions of where dead bodies go and how they are to get there. Diogenes wanted his body tossed over the walls into a no man's land, with no attention to the placement or posture of the corpse, and left there to be eaten by beasts. This wish has been viewed, almost universally, as insane. Humans who bury put dead bodies into the ground in a meaningful direction. Among Christians and Jews, the body is oriented east–west, so that when it arises it will look toward Jerusalem. "Hence in Wales the east wind is called 'the wind of the dead men's feet,'" as a nineteenth-century scholar of folklore discovered. The Islamic dead are buried on their right sides, with their faces toward Mecca. A metaphysically and practically elaborated system of feng shui determines both grave orientation and location in much of China. And if bodies are not buried, they still go somewhere under the sway of culture. Ashes in India go in this, and not that, river. Birds eat bodies in special places. Corpses also exist in three dimensions. They are buried face up or curled on their sides; rarely face down. Never head down into the earth; this is a rare inversion. Directionality and cartographic location order the earthly world of the dead, and thereby also of the living, at the same time as the positions of the body in space prepare it for the other—the otherworldly—place.[1]

Maintenance of these many practices of placing dead bodies, and access to appropriate sites for exercising them, are regulated by various authorities: sometimes the state takes command of bodies; sometimes families; sometimes religious bodies; sometimes clans. Some bodies are allowed into a particular regime of care and others not; some get more privileged places within that regime than others. Some get longer occupancy in a grave; some get nice tombs and others get no tombs or memorials at all. Sometimes the ground above the body is lumpy and sometimes smooth; sometimes planted and sometimes not.

Part 2 is about the history of the places of the dead in the earthly, second sense that I have been describing: it is, broadly speaking, a cultural and historical necrogeography of where the dead are in this world, of how this is determined, and of why it matters. More specifically, it is about how the churchyard came into being in the Western world and why it came to occupy so important a place; it is about struggles over inclusion and exclusion within Christian communities; it is about the emergence of new, heterogeneous spaces in the late eighteenth and nineteenth centuries, and how they came into being. Much of the material in these chapters comes from England, because the meaning of any necrogeography can only be grasped locally, as defined by the literature, the history, the politics, and the botany of a place. But this part broadens out to include places of the dead elsewhere as well. This is because Enlightenment scandals about access to burial and, more generally, new eighteenth-century ways of imagining the dead led to the creation of a more cosmopolitan necrogeography: the cemetery.

Chapter 4

THE CHURCHYARD
AND THE OLD REGIME

Beneath those rugged elms, that yew-tree's shade,
Where heaves the turf in many a mouldering heap,
Each in his narrow cell for ever laid,
The rude forefathers of the hamlet sleep.

THOMAS GRAY, "ELEGY WRITTEN IN
A COUNTRY CHURCHYARD" (1751)

Few places are as deeply rooted in their history as the churchyard. The dead came first—the pagan and the Christian dead of Britain gathered with their clans in fields and on hillsides. A chapel or an altar might have been built among them in the seventh or eighth century. Then came churches and churchyards that slowly broke the bounds of family as they gathered bodies from outside the extended circle into an explicitly and insistently Christian necrogeography that held sway in England and more generally throughout the Western world for at least eight centuries (ca. 1000, or much earlier in some places, to ca. 1800): the old regime of burial of the dead gathered together in churchyards. The dead of a place—be they martyrs of more ordinary people—first created the places of the dead: infidels were ejected when a consecrated altar was built near graves of Christians. By the twelfth century and often much earlier, churchyards as we know them had become a naturalized feature of the landscape and a new *gemeinschaft* of bodies was born: an intelligible "congregation of the dead," as the eighteenth-century clergyman James Hervey would call them.[1]

This chapter explores in detail the churchyard as the heart of an old regime of the dead, tracing its rise, its full flower, its crisis, and its decline. I use evidence mostly from England but also other places; the churchyards of Europe have much in common. It is a history of a place that held a near monopoly on burial throughout Christendom—and hence on entrance into the community of the dead—for more than a thousand years, from the Middle Ages to the early nineteenth century and beyond in some places. After tracing competing accounts of how the churchyard came into being in the centuries from the fall of the Roman Empire to the early Middle Ages, it turns to an examination of the regime's linguistic hegemony in Europe, which for centuries made it nearly impossible to imagine, let alone speak of, an alternative. This leads not only to a thick description of the place itself—compact, congested with the dead, and intimately present in the daily life and the minds of the living: a necrogeography, necrobotany, and necrotopology that all changed remarkably little over the centuries—but also to a story of a literary topos that captured the imagination. Finally, the chapter tells the vexatious, often petty, history of the churchyard in law, particularly in the years after the rise of religious pluralism and the advent of overt skepticism: What dead bodies were excluded from consecrated ground or from the churchyard entirely? What claims did the body have on the parish churchyard, and what claims did the parish have on the dead body? How did the economics of churchyard burial affect the individual dead? By the eighteenth century, the hegemony of the churchyard was threatened by a crisis from within and from without. There were scandals—small, nasty battles for the right to be buried, as well as the great Enlightenment set pieces surrounding the deaths of two of the leading nonbelievers of the eighteenth century, Voltaire and David Hume—that revealed the vulnerabilities of the old regime. The beginning of the end of the story comes when a variety of people came to imagine a new regime—the cemetery—that would gather all the dead, the cosmopolitan dead rather than just the faithful ones, into spacious, landscaped gardens at the periphery of cities, thus creating a new kind of space in law, literature, and physical being.

The general movement traced in this chapter and the next is from one sort of place—ancient, crowded, hierarchical, exclusively for the use of a small community, grounded in faith, and seething with new burials that all faced east to await the resurrection and displaced older ones in constantly reused land in the heart of the living community—to another, to the new regime of the cemetery that is the subject of chapter 5. It was spacious, open to anyone who could pay, landscaped, gardenlike, with huge and diverse communities of the dead serenely planted in specific graves, many owned in perpetuity, gathered at the periphery of the settlements of the living, and oriented toward a calm, melancholy, but sweet eternal repose. These new venues in turn offered unprecedented new opportunities for the work of the dead on behalf of a variety of interests. Although much of the detail I examine comes from England, the historic and cultural movement traced in part 2 of this book represents the grand succession of the two quintessential physical places—first the churchyard and later the cemetery—in which the dead have done their work throughout the Western world over the past millennium.

And, with the globalization of Europe through imperialism, the cemetery became a place of the dead beyond its places of origin.

In 1817, William Jones, who had been the vicar of his parish for almost four decades, gave in to his granddaughter's wish that he go with her to *"read the dead!"* The next day he lay in bed, this time mentally "reading the parish & hamlet," thinking about how "Death has, without ceremony, or much previous notice, ejected the occupiers," of various houses, gardens, and grounds: the woodman John Smith, born on Good Friday fifty-four years earlier and buried that day, Good Friday; a poor woman who had worked in a paper mill and about whom Jones had written in his diary in 1777 that she was a "prodigy of grace" who "had more of the pith and marrow of sound divinity in her than 19/20th of the gownsmen in the University."[2] Even those no longer held in the memory of anyone living were part of an idealized community in deep time.

The parish churchyard remained powerful in language, geography, law, custom, and the common imagination even as it slowly lost its monopoly on the dead themselves. Hugely popular eighteenth-century poems like Thomas Gray's "Elegy Written in a Country Churchyard" (1751), and the melancholy meditations of the other so-called graveyard poets, endlessly anthologized and reworked over the generations, kept the old regime culturally exigent even as its claim to represent newly exigent communities of the living—Dissenters, Quakers, and others outside the Established Church that controlled these spaces, as well as *philosophes* and their followers—began to weaken during the Enlightenment in both England and elsewhere. For much longer than one might expect, the churchyard remained a place where "dead men have come and walked about."[3]

THE DEVELOPMENT OF THE CHURCHYARD

The question is why the churchyard so long remained the place where the dead labored for the community they had left. To give an answer, we have to take a step back and ask with more local precision why they were there—as a collectivity, in consecrated ground, in a church or a churchyard—in the first place. An educated eighteenth-century Englishman such as Richard Burn, chancellor of the diocese of Durham, and author, among other works, of the major eighteenth-century text on ecclesiastical law, would answer with a Protestant-inflected story that traced the custom back more than a thousand years to Pope Gregory the Great (540–604), who purportedly first allowed burial within churches for "mercenary reasons": monks and priests could earn fees by praying for the dead in their care. Cuthbert, archbishop of Canterbury, brought the practice to England in about 750, "from which time date the origins of churchyards in this island." Lanfranc, archbishop of Canterbury, seems to have been the first, he continues, to provide vaults under chancels and even under altars when he rebuilt his cathedral in 1075. There were some earlier precedents that Burn's readers would probably have known about. The Venerable Bede writes about the cult of saints in these isles: the body of Chad, the apostle to the west Saxons (died ca. 672), had been buried next to but not inside a church in a small wooden enclosure from which pilgrims took dust that they mixed with water to make potions that were said to cure both humans and cattle; the body of the learned Tobias, bishop of Rochester (d. 725), rested in a portico of a church that had been built for his remains. With this began the attraction of *ad sanctos* burial: Christians wanted their remains to rest inside or, failing that, surrounding the church because, as Gregory the Great supposedly argued, "their neighbors, as often as they come to those sacred places, remembering those whose sepulchers they behold, do put forth prayers to them unto God." And so, according to Burn, "the superstition of praying for the dead," seems to be the true origin of churchyards."[4]

Burn's narrative was not—nor was it meant to be—a scholarly account. There were outside of cities relatively few churches and no consecrated churchyards before the later ninth or early tenth centuries, and no one seemed to miss them. The inside of churches were for monks and priests: with the exception of royalty, very few laypeople were buried there until the eleventh century. And, the subsequent increase in the number of their bodies had relatively little to do with the status of prayers for the souls of the dead and a great deal to do with the increasing power and wealth of the landed classes. But in broad outline, Burn got it right; more important, his was the standard story repeated by critics, beginning in the Reformation, as evidence that intramural burial as well as the churchyard itself had outlived any conceivable raison d'être, if indeed they had ever had one.[5] Still, the old regime persisted, indeed thrived, after the Reformation robbed it of its theological foundations. There were a few alternatives by the late seventeenth century, mainly the "churchyards" of Protestant sects—Baptist, Quaker, and Congregationalist—that defined far more narrowly than did the national Anglican Church what constituted membership in the relevant Christian community. Baptism was all that mattered there. With these exceptions, neither the churchyard's dark origins in suspect Romish beliefs and practices nor pragmatic criticism of intramural and churchyard burial did much to change what English people did with their dead for a very long time. To the contrary, as this chapter shows.

Burial anywhere within the building and especially near the altar, the most sacred part of the church and churchyard, had been, until the seventeenth century, restricted largely to the local landed families or the clergy. (The great landed families came to put their dead there in significant numbers only after the possibility of monastic burial ended in 1536.) John Tomlinson, Northumberland curate, records in his diary for 28 October 1717, that there were "no graves in churches till of late." The seventeenth-century writer John Evelyn (1620–1706) noted approvingly in his diary for 1682 that his father-in-law had explicitly asked in his will for burial outside, "adjoining to the burying places of his ancestors he being much offended by the novel custom of burying everyone within the body of the church." In this wish he aligned himself with "the pious Bishop of Norwich, who would also be so interred," and against those who seemed to be willing to grant to ordinary mortals a "favour heretofore granted to martyrs and great persons." When in 1684 Edward Rainbow, the bishop of Durham, was buried in Dalston churchyard, it was to make the same point and fight a trend: the fabric of his cathedral "was for the living and not for the dead." Rainbow's self-consciously modest burial was unusual for a bishop, who would, following ancient practice, have been routinely buried in his church, and was much remarked on at the time. "How admirable was his humility . . . which his earnest desire to be interr'd among the meanest of those that own the same common Saviour and Redeemer, will testifie to all posterity." Monuments he regarded not as signs of honor but as "trophies erected by death" in memory of the fatal sin that got us expelled from Eden.[6]

Few who had the resources to do otherwise followed the bishop's example or shared his sensibility. Church vaults were necessary for holding up buildings of any size, and large vaults were needed for a large church. But they did not have to be dug out, and they did not have to be filled with bodies. They were filled by the dozens of corpses in country churches and by the thousands in cities, usually clad in lead and encased in multiple coffins. The aisles were packed with less securely wrapped corpses. Keeping them out seemed impossible. The architect Nicholas Hawksmoor (1661–1736) hoped that the vaults in the six new churches he designed in London would be "made into a School for ye Charity Children." Instead, the "novel practice of burying everyone [that is, everyone who was anyone] within the body of the church" meant that these structural elements were taken over for burial to meet the demand of wealthy eighteenth-century burghers to imitate medieval grandees.

The huge public vaults of churches like Hawksmoor's Christ Church, Spital-fields, or St. Alfege's in Greenwich are even bigger than they needed to be structurally because their floors were raised above street level to make these already very massive buildings look more massive still. They were packed with the prosperous. Archeologists removed more than a thousand bodies from Christ Church's crypt between 1984 and 2003; the crypt of St. Alfege's was already getting full after thirty years but was never excavated. After 1857 it was filled with fuller's earth, which absorbed the numerous dead. Tourists can now lunch in the crypt of St. Martin-in-the-Fields, rebuilt in 1726 and lined with grave markers from the crypt of an earlier church; in the early nineteenth century, elegantly dressed parties of visitors could view thousands of stacked coffins. Archeologists removed almost a thousand. The crypt that Sir Christopher Wren, an opponent of intramural burial, built after the fire of 1666 to hold up his new St. Andrew Holborn, on the site of the old one, held almost two thousand bodies when it was excavated in 2001.[7]

And the trend continued well into the late eighteenth century. The "large handsome brick building" that was Saint James's Church in Manchester, consecrated in 1787, was designed with vaults, dedicated to burial, separated by aisles "from which the coffins (which are prudently lined with lead) are exposed to the eyes of the visitors of this awful mansion." The author of the guidebook from which this comes also offers evidence for how the parochial system could be extended to meet the needs of vast new populations of the dead without resorting to a cemetery: next to the parish church, he reports, is a new burial ground in which a large pit—a "cavern of death"—is dug and then left open until full with the bodies "of poor persons who have *no family place of burial.*" Old churches (for example, St. Augustine the Less in Bristol) adapted to new demands for intramural burials by remodeling; new ones purposely built spaces so that ever more people could be buried *ad sanctos.*[8]

The old regime of the dead was not only very old but also very resilient. It continually reinvented itself. Almost universally until the nineteenth century, everyone rested in or around the parish church or, in London especially, on land that was perhaps not contiguous but belonged to it. It would take a great deal, as a leading ecclesiastical architect of the nineteenth century put it, to separate "the burial places of English Churchmen [and even those not committed churchmen] from the sacred precincts in which they and their forefathers had worshipped for many generations."[9] The question, again, is why?

Conservatism is the obvious but also the circular answer. It is in the nature of an old regime to seem adamantine and unending until it begins to end. This is when it becomes an "old regime." A better reason would be a cultural refinement of this truism: the work that the living demanded of the dead did not change dramatically when the religious foundations of the churchyard and of burial within the church disappeared. It did not change when it occasionally came under attack as a superstitious holdover or a gloomy, unhealthy nuisance. It did not change with the commercial and urban revolution of the eighteenth century. The dead of the churchyard, supported by history and a living tradition, did what was expected of them until there was new work to do. This chapter explains their longevity. It is about the persistence of the old regime.

LANGUAGE

There was almost no way to articulate an alternative: linguistically, the term "churchyard" has very deep roots and leaves little space for other options. The word emerged from Old English in the eleventh century not long after it became the norm for churches to have the dead buried in and around them. It meant then, and for a long time afterward, an enclosure—a yard—that, in context, was consecrated, usually walled in or somehow demarcated, on which was situated a church. In much the same way as the absence of the dead defined a Roman city's boundaries—there were no dead within its walls—the presence of the dead came to distinguish a church from other buildings used for worship. To be a church was to have a churchyard: "If a question should arise," one of the most popular eighteenth-century legal commentators explains, "whether 'tis a church or a chapel belonging to the Mother Church and any proof can be made that . . . the dead [are] buried, then 'tis by law accounted a distinct church." This doctrine had centuries of legal precedent to support it.[10]

Conversely, all places of the dead were called "churchyards" whether or not they actually were the yard of a church or consecrated or even Christian. There was no other word in common use for such places. John Stow (1524–1604), the historian of London, reports on two new cemeteries for the surplus victims of the Black Death. One was in West Spitalfields, purchased in 1349 by Sir Walter Manny, an important servant of the king, "for the burial of poore people, travailors and others that are diseased to remain for ever." It was "no man's land," Stow says, and came to be called the "Pardon churchyard" or the "new Church Haw," from "hawe," the Old English word for enclosure, a word that in Old Norse and related dialects referred to single or clan burial around a barrow. The other was in East Smithfield, the gift of Sir John Corey, another major servant of Edward III, given on the condition "that it might be called the Churchyard of the Holy Trinity." There was no church there. Unprotected by an actual parochial church, neither cemetery survived into modern times: Stow describes them as "now covered with houses and . . . inhabited by persons who are unconscious how many skeletons lie under their feet." But these churchyards may have lingered in folk memory. In 1984, a caretaker at the Royal Mint, which occupies the Holy Trinity site, told staff that ghosts had been heard and seen, and during a recent excavation, employees of the Barclay's bank nearby wanted assurances that all the bodies had been removed, because they had heard mysterious noises and footsteps.[11]

New burial grounds such as these, built over the centuries, might seem in retrospect to be harbingers of a new regime. But still they were called, and in essence were, "churchyards." And so too was the "new churchyard," outside the city walls and nowhere near a church, that was built by the city in response to a chronic shortage of parochial burial spaces. It was in Moorefields, near what is now Liverpool Street Station. We know a great deal about it because its bodies were in the way of redevelopment but could not be removed until the site had been studied by archeologists. There was nothing "churchyardlike" about the "new churchyard." It was not shrouded in the history of a place. It was, as its name suggests, new and purpose made. The very earth of which it was made up was of dubious origin. In the summer of 1569, city authorities paid scavengers 2d. a cartload for "all earth and rubbish" dug from wells and ditches; they were to include no "street soil or dirt" from the surface. The city got what it asked for—archeologists found in the cemetery Roman pottery and tile of the sort that sixteenth-century workers might unearth in their digging—but also much of what it had not: cat, dog, and rat skeletons as well as excrement and other rubbish that contractors must have found in the London middens. All of this—clean fill and garbage—reclaimed the marsh that had been there and was duly consecrated. It was distant from a church but still a consecrated churchyard; it bore almost no resemblance to the cemeteries of the new regime.[12]

Bunhill Fields, the most famous and illustriously populated Dissenting burial ground in England (Daniel Defoe, William Blake, John Bunyan, and John Foxe, the martyrologist, among many other luminaries, are there), was not the yard of a church, and it was not consecrated. It was meant to be a community of outsiders, a *salon des refusés* of the dead, for Quakers, Baptists, Independents, and other Nonconformists who had lived and died outside the national Church. All this said, a stone that once stood near its entrance announced that "this Churchyard was enclosed with a brick wall at the sole Charge of the City of London, in the mayoralty of Sir John Lawrence, Anno Dni 1665." Even distant places of the heathen dead were "churchyards." Thus, the early eighteenth-century lexicographer Nathan Bailey defines the term *Keber*, a derogatory word for a Persian sect, by explaining the Zoroastrian custom of propping up the carcasses of the dead "against a wall in the *Church-yard*" and watching to see which eye birds pick out first as a divinatory exercise.[13]

There seemed no way around it: the word "cemetery," when it first appeared in English in 1485, was a synonym for "churchyard." William Caxton, the first English printer, tells of how the dead of Charles the Great's army were buried in "two cymytoyres or chiurche-yerdes" in Arles and Bordeaux that were "sacred and blessed with seven bishops" and made "sacred and hallowed by a number of saints." These were prototypical churchyards of the old regime, not cemeteries like those of the future new regime. And when, nearly a century earlier in 1387, "cemetery" appeared as a synonym for catacomb, it only just bypassed "churchyard" by taking on its pagan-inflected archaic equivalent, "chirchehawe," and situating it, via a double anachronism, in the story of early Christianity before there were churches: "Calixus [pope, r. 217–222] made a chirchehawe at Rome, in a place þat hatte [that was called] Via Appia, for to burie the bodies of Holy Martires; now þat place hatte [is called] cimitorium Calixty."[14]

When in 1656 a lexicographer first actually defined "cemetery," he takes us back to where we started: "a churchyard." "Churchyard" itself was too easy a word to merit definition; dictionaries in the early days concentrated on hard words. "Cemetery," by contrast, was a hard word with a long, convoluted history. It comes from the Greek *koímhthrion* and its Latin cognate *coemeterium*, and originally meant a sleeping place, a dormitory. It was not used in classical antiquity as a place for the dead because, although they might be regarded as sleeping, this was only one of many possibilities and by no means the dominant one. It was the early Christians who embraced death as a temporary and, one hoped, short sleep before the end of the world, the Second Coming, and the corporeal resurrection of the dead. *Coemeterium* in the late second century thus became a special kind of dormitory, a place for the sleep of the dead. Tertullian is credited as the first to use the word in this sense when he writes about a corpse miraculously making room for a second one in a *coemeterium*. At first and for some centuries it meant a single tomb where a martyr slept. There came to be churches called *coemeteria* built around the special dead. John Chrysostom (347–407) tells his flock in his Good Friday sermon that the Christians of Antioch worshipped that day in a *coemeterium*—and not in another *martyrium*—because "we should know that the dead, while they lie here, are not dead, but are asleep and rest." From the sixth century on, the *coemeterium* became ever more of a churchyard, as the theology and practices of Christian care for the dead became ever more established. It might be only part of the churchyard—the part for the dead, while the *atrium* was reserved for other functions—but the word was not common in medieval Latin, and its nuances were absorbed by the fact that the *coemeterium* had become the churchyard or, until the Reformation, the consecrated ground of a monastery: "bodies there deposited [are] not properly dead, but only laid to sleep till the resurrection should wake them."[15]

If late antique churches were cemeteries, places built around the bodies of the special dead where the nascent church gathered to pray and to bury, by the late tenth or eleventh century cemeteries were churches. That is, the cemetery became the churchyard, an extension of the church—like it, consecrated, and, like it, inclusive of Christians and exclusive of all others. If the church was a place of collective worship, the cemetery was a place of sepulture. The word *cimiterium* was rarely used in the Middle Ages because it was not really a place unto itself, freestanding as it had been in classical antiquity and would be again in modernity, but rather was joined to the church as "a kind of matrix of Christian society."[16]

The moment in the eighteenth century when the word "cemetery" is actually thinkable, even speakable, as something other than "churchyard" represents a rejection of this history and its assignment to a place that was explicitly *not* a churchyard, not a place of rest for Christians in good standing from a particular parish, but a cosmopolitan space for a cosmopolitan people, a sort of fantasy of ancient Rome's burial places. A "great number of *strangers*" came to Bath in Roman days, wrote the antiquary John Ward in 1754. "Some of those who came from distant places," he continues, "may be supposed from time to time to have died there." Therefore, he concludes, "a public cœometery for the burial of them was highly requisite." Ward was referring not to a space that existed in his day but to one from the distant past. The next year, 1755, Dr. Johnson offered the first definition of "cemetery" that does not depend on its synonym: "a place where the dead are deposited." "Churchyard" is still defined as "the ground adjoining a church; a cemetery." The two terms for Johnson are not yet two different sorts of places: "churchyard" is a species of the genus "cemetery," and so technically it would remain. But by the early nineteenth century, the two words for places to put the dead would come to have very different resonances and very different imagined histories. "Elegy Written in a Country Cemetery" sounds strange not only because we associate cemeteries with cities but because elegiac is precisely what visitors are not supposed to feel there. They are places for different sensibilities. The many articles in nineteenth-century folklore journals on "churchyard superstitions" have no equivalent for cemeteries.[17]

PLACE

The old regime of the churchyard was grounded in much more than the conservatism of language, although the lexical stickiness of the word itself does suggest how intimately a sacred geography was conjoined with places of the dead. And ancient geography remained long after its theological raison d'être had vanished.

The Church and Churchyard in the Landscape

A churchyard was adjacent to a church; both held the bones of the dead. The three—the building, the ground, the dead—were conjoined by a common history that made them part of what by the eighteenth century was a given; if ever there were an organic landscape, it was the churchyard.[18] How the dead got to the church in the early Middle Ages is a whole story unto itself. Pre-Christian Anglo-Saxons were buried in fields, often on hillsides, usually with no other structures nearby, which is why they are difficult to find today. They were buried singly, in small groups, and in cemeteries: "places of power." The in-gathering of all these dead is the story of the Christianization of Britain, of the "appropriation, and even the 'conversion' of the ancestors." What the Saxons began, as they remade the sacred landscape that the Romans and those who came before them had left, ended with the parish church and its churchyard. From then on, even when churchyards expanded, they tended to be on land adjacent to the church;

freestanding parochial burial grounds were not common, even in London, except *in extremis.*[19]

Many churches and thus churchyards were on or near older, pre-Christian sacred places—holy wells, Roman temples or relic sites, standing stones, circular burial barrows, cemeteries where the church joined the already-present dead, or in places of secular significance. Urban churches might be on what had been the Roman forum, or at crossroads, or in street islands that had been or continued to be markets, often near guildhalls. Histories upon histories: the eleventh-century York Minster was built over a cemetery of bodies in boats and chests, burned and not burned. Some rural churches were located adjacent to manors where, before the Norman Conquest, they had served as proprietary chapels and thus were intimately connected with the landed classes. This history remained important in the seventeenth and eighteenth centuries because, while the local gentry could not own burial places in a church or churchyard, they could have rights in a vault that had become part of a church because it was construed as manorial *messuage* (a dwelling and its outbuildings) with a common law property right of occupancy as if it were a wine cellar or a barn. They could also have customary claims of other sorts. After the Reformation, the increasing number of lay patrons were responsible for chancel maintenance and had a claim to use the space beneath for burial, although technically only with the incumbent's permission. Chantry chapels descended with the estate to which they had been attached and continued to be maintained by secular owners, even if these owners were Roman Catholic. Place trumped faith. In such recusant strongholds as Arundel in Sussex or Mapledurham in Oxfordshire, Mary chapels were attached to Anglican parish churches and held the bodies of their owners. In Beoley, Worcestershire, a Catholic gentleman named Ralph Sheldon (d. 1613) actually built a new chapel at the north end of the parish church and was buried in it. As anyone who has visited an English country church knows, the presence of its patron family is not to be missed—*primus inter pares* among the dead, dominant in the hierarchy of commemoration. It is largely through their dead in the parish church, as Nicholas Penny suggests, that the "English ruling classes asserted the status and continuity of the families," a status and continuity deeply rooted in a place.[20]

Churches and their churchyards—not all of them, of course, but enough to matter—were part of the consciousness of ordinary people as well. Like trees or hedges that made landscapes intelligible, these places were part of a natural and cultural world that either was very old or felt that way. It was a world—unlike that of the suburban cemetery—in which an old woman could threaten that if she were not carried to her grave via the "Church Road" she would come back to haunt her fellow villagers. Steeples stood for towns, villages, and London parishes.

Churches and their dead, in short, were probably the oldest feature of a very old landscape.[21]

Necrogeography

In these ancient places the dead lived an ordered existence. Their graves and the churches in and around which they were gathered were aligned with some precision on an axis drawn from east to west. This orientation seems the consequence of a natural metaphor, a correlative in the earth of our common fate: "It is by the simplest poetic adaption of the Sun's daily life, typifying Man's life in dawning beauty, in mid-day glory, in evening death," argued Edward Tylor (1832–1917), the nineteenth-century pioneer of cultural anthropology.[22] The significance of the direction of the rising sun predated Christianity: man was born, the rabbis held, with his face to the east; it was the direction of the right hand—the hand of virtue—as opposed to the left hand. So, the bodies of the old regime dead lay along a compass of immemorial significance, one that pointed in the direction of the dawn and of good. That said, grave declination along this axis is not universal; neither Roman nor Greek graves were so ordered, and in the absence of churches to orient bodies, order was not so clear.

But very early in the history of Christianity, east took on a new exigency, and those who built churches and buried the dead began to take it seriously. The earliest medieval Anglo-Saxon churches were oriented true east, that is, ninety degrees counterclockwise from the geographic north, with a precision that can only have been attained by careful astronomical study. Declination was thus not a local matter dependent on locally exigent observation—the position of the rising of the sun, for example, on the feast day of the church's patron saint or on one of the solstices—but a universal fact based on the heavens. Over the centuries, a church's exact declination might shift a few degrees as one structure replaced another, as the Saxon one, for example, was followed by successive reconstructions on new foundations. But within a few degrees, the chancel and its altar were invariably in the east—the direction of Jerusalem and of the second coming of Christ—and the entrance and tower were in the west. It was in the east that the resurrection of the dead would be heralded.[23]

Medieval scrupulousness about declination persisted into the eighteenth century. Christopher Wren (1632–1723), the man who designed the new St. Paul's and was most responsible for rebuilding London after the Great Fire of 1666, proposed that architects ought perhaps to take into account convenience and topography in how they oriented, on site, the fifty new churches being built from Queen Anne's Bounty (1712). They ought not perhaps "too nicely to observe East or West." He was roundly rebuffed. Following Wren's advice, John Vanbrugh

(1664–1726), the playwright and architect of Blenheim Palace, proposed a design for a new church oriented north–south, the direction that he thought best suited the site; it was rejected by Queen Anne's Commissioners, who explicitly reaffirmed tradition in the explanation of their decision.[24]

The dead themselves in the churchyard visibly followed the orientation of the church. One can, in the excavations of archeologists, almost see this begin to happen in the seventh century: a cluster of irregular graves gives way over time to properly aligned ones; a small timber building follows. Later, the occasional gravestone, slab, or tomb might have given away how the bodies lay, but more evident would have been the heaving of the ground itself. Grassy mounds and fresh dirt rippled parallel to the fabric of the building like waves lapping a wall. Everything did not always line up so nicely in real life. The High Church antiquary Thomas Hearne insisted that his grave be aligned east–west with a surveyor's precision, so it actually looked akimbo when compared to the less carefully positioned graves. But in general, there was order throughout: the dead in the bumpy floor inside also lay along the axis of the church; one walked over them lengthwise—head to foot, west to east—as one proceeded down an aisle or across them as one entered a pew. And so too the privileged few under the chancel, where they reposed in their anthropomorphically shaped lead coffins on benches, ready to burst out on the Day of Judgment and face east. Recumbent figures on the monuments above had their pillows on that end of their palettes, mirroring the bodies below. Even the dead poor in London's large sixteenth-century "new churchyard," nowhere near a church and stacked seven to a pit, were laid in the ground so as to face Jerusalem when the Resurrection came.[25]

Shakespeare's audiences understood what this meant:

> nay, Cadwal, we must lay his head to the East;
> My father has a reason for it. (*Cymbeline*, act 4, sc. 2)

Or more to the point, they understood what burial in other than an east–west direction said about the dead. When the two clowns, spade and pickaxes in hand, enter in *Hamlet* (act 5, sc. 1) and begin discussing what is to be done with Ophelia's corpse, the audience knew the question: "Is she to be buried in Christian burial when she willfully seeks her own salvation?" (i.e., has committed suicide), asks the first. "I tell thee she is," replies the second; "therefore make her grave straight. The crowner [coroner] has sate upon her, and finds a Christian burial." "But is this law?" asks one; "ay, merry, is't; crowner's quest law," replies his companion. Rank made all the difference: "If this had not been a gentlewoman, she should have been buried out o' Christian burial," they conclude. But she was not. "Make her grave straight," Dr. Johnson explains, means "Make her grave from East to West, in a direct line with the Church; not from North to South" (fig. 4.1).[26]

So familiar was the alignment of the dead that everyone would appreciate a parody: less-well-educated Lilliputians in *Gulliver's Travels* believed that the dead should be buried standing on their heads so that when the resurrection came and the flat earth was turned upside down, they would arise standing up. The only way of burying a body that was too weird for parody or protest was to be buried face down: "Diogenes was singular," Sir Thomas Browne reports in *Urn Burial*, "who preferred a prone position in the grave."[27] In other words, as the bearers of a common history, as witnesses to a community over generations, the dead of seventeenth- and eighteenth-century England were, like their forebears, buried in

4.1. Southeast view of a church, described as St. John's of Southwark, showing the churchyard. J.W. Edy after a painting by John Buckler, F.S.A., 1799. British Library.

the direction of the rising and the setting of the sun: they would face east—Jerusalem—on the Day of Judgment.

Those who lay in any other direction did so either because they were excluded or because they excluded themselves from the community of the normative dead. There were, on the one hand, the unwanted, the irrelevant, or the despised dead, the dead one did not need to care about. The dead in disarray. We are speaking here of those in the mass graves from the twelfth century forward in the hospital cemetery of St. Mary Spital, in Bishopsgate, London; of the graves of thousands of unclaimed dead paupers lying helter-skelter in the eighteenth-century burial ground of the Bristol infirmary; and of sixteen burials from the seventeenth and early eighteenth centuries in the ground of the bailey of Launceston Castle— some bodies seem to bear evidence of hanging—with some buried along a north–south axis, sometimes with the head in one direction, sometimes the other, and a few lying, as they should, with their heads to the west. Of eight skeletons from the late seventeenth century outside the churchyard of nearby St. Petrox near Dartmouth Castle, Falmouth, three lie with their heads in the south and five to the southeast instead of to the west. They belonged probably to foreigners. Although archeologists have not specifically noted it, the excluded dead—suicides, excommunicates, the unbaptized (including sometimes young children), the diseased, women of ill repute, and others—who lay outside the precincts of the churchyard or in its obscure northern corner were probably not buried with an overly fine sense of direction either.[28]

The point is that an orderly, that is, properly aligned burial mattered in the old regime. Even in the crisis of the first great plague epidemic of 1348–1349, when the dead in their thousands were placed in the mass graves of emergency burial grounds, they were put there with care. They were not dumped. They were not scrunched up. Small coins and other signs of caring were often placed on them. They would face east when the resurrection came. Their bodies are carefully aligned. By contrast, the mass grave of soldiers after the Battle of Towton (1461) in the War of the Roses is a jumble, bodies stripped and mutilated. So were many early modern military graves. To be disordered is to be dirt.[29]

Sometimes it is difficult to tell whether bodies are misaligned out of neglect or rebellion, whether the dead would have wished the compass heading in which they lay or just ended up that way. When archeologists excavated nearly 250 bodies (out of what may have been as many as 500) in a burial ground outside the walls of an old convent in Abingdon, Oxfordshire, they thought at first that they had come upon a Roman cemetery because all of the dead lay in a north–south direction and because they found some ancient detritus in among them. Their initial dating soon proved wrong. One of the bodies had a musket ball between the ribs, another a coffin plate from sometime after 1650, a third a Scottish silver shilling from the reign of James or Charles. It was a civil war cemetery. Nine of the bodies in a mass grave might have been prisoners from a nearby jail, captured royalist soldiers perhaps, since one had the bullet in his chest. These might have been intentionally misplaced to posthumously humiliate an enemy. But the other bodies seemed those of ordinary people who were buried between 1643, after the triumph of Puritan forces over the king in Abingdon, and the Restoration, when such a massive and aggressively heterodox burial site would have been a scandal. No written record remains, and we do not know how these dead came to lie as they did. Perhaps this a case of local clerical or civic authorities taking seriously the new Calvinist mandate that the dead be taken "to the place appointed for publique burial" and not to a churchyard, and that there the dead could turn their faces against the old superstitious order of things. We don't know. The Puritans in New England did abandon consecrated ground—although not so rigorously west–east orientation—but we know little about how extensively the dictates of the new parliamentary ordinances were carried out at home.[30]

The reasons for bodies out of line are usually not so difficult to find. Folklorists have collected examples of individuals who for one reason or another wanted their bodies to be buried facing north to make a point. In the chancel of the parish church of All Saints in Fornham, near Bury in Suffolk, a tomb rests perpendicular to its axis. Engraved on it is an explanation: "as a mark of penitence and contrition." Penitence and humility, not the wish to offend, motivated William Glanvill of Wooton, near Dorking, to ask in his will that he be buried north–south. Something so small, so theologically insignificant.[31]

The playwright and pamphleteer Thomas Nashe (1567–1601) in one of the most famous tracts of the pamphlet war between Puritans and more moderate churchmen, mocks the cultural pretentions and self-important weirdness of his leading opponent, the pseudonymous Martin Marprelate. It was, like his theology and views on church governance, a world turned upside down: his mourners wore hoods and gowns of yellow; he ordered that a hornpipe—a merry dance—be played at his funeral. "*Rebuke* and a *shame*, in my opinion, were the fittest fiddles for him." He would have no minister to bury him and "would not be laid East and West (for he ever went against the haire [grain]) but North and South." "*Ab Aquilone omne mallum*" (every evil comes from the north), Nashe adds, just so his readers get the point. Martin refused a tomb altogether so as not to lead his followers into idolatry, but there would be an epitaph away from the body. Some post or tree somewhere would read "M.M.M": "Memoriae Martini magni," according to his son "Martin Jr."; "Monstrum Mundi Martininus," in Nashe's view.[32]

Necrogeography was of the essence of the old regime churchyard, and the Puritans who left Old for New England rejected it *tout corps*. Some of their burial grounds were adjacent to a church; many were not; all were ostentatiously not consecrated. They were civic spaces. As in Roman cemeteries, grave placement was a contingent matter dictated by local topography or by nothing at all. Some bodies and gravestones in New England might be more or less along the normative axis, others not. Placement did not matter; eschatology was irrelevant. Occasionally, some Nonconformists back in England—the Independents or Congregationalists from whom the New England colonists came, and the Baptists in particular—also rejected the normative alignments of bodies. But this was unusual; the hold of the old regime remained strong. In London's Bunhill Fields, by far the largest and most important of the Nonconformist burial places, they are all lined up east–west.[33]

A systematic rejection of the east–west axis of the dead was a genuinely radical gesture of self-exclusion and critique of an established order. Only the Quakers publicly and ostentatiously went so far. They were in their early days the wildest of the sects, refusing to doff their hats to those in authority as an outward sign of their radical egalitarianism and refusing to take public oaths of allegiance to the Protectorate, the king, or anything else. They rejected theology, predestination, any kind of authority—clerical or secular; they allowed women to preach and prophesize. These were people who courted martyrdom by rushing naked and smeared with ashes through the respectable churches of Boston. As they lived, so they went to their graves. Why should they bury their dead to meet the resurrected Christ in the east? Christ was in no particular direction but within every man. So vehement were the Quakers in rejecting the ceremonies of the Church and proper burial in particular that one of the sect's earliest chroniclers thought that in their fastidiousness they risked a strange kinship with their enemies. Given that the dead "have no sense or feeling, neither is it any matter where they rot," why does it matter how they are buried? asks Geradus Croese (1642–1710). Why do his coreligionists in England feel that Church rites defiled them by burying them east–west in a churchyard? This "concernedness and anxiety of theirs is indeed very strange," he writes; it is as if they "so abhorred the Superstition of others, as to favour another superstition" in its stead. If anyone should have taken Diogenes to heart, it should have been the Quakers.[34]

But they did not. They actively rejected the necrogeography of the old regime dead, and in response the Church, rather than letting the heretics go, insisted on keeping them within the civic order of the churchyard. "It's a wonder," writes Croese, "how much hatred also the odd and different way of managing and carrying their Funerals and what reproaches and Trouble it brought upon [them]." The "dead Carkasses of their friends were dug up again" and reburied; their funerals were persecuted. "Outrageous barbarity," writes William Sewel (1654–1720), one of the best of the early Quaker historians, in the case of Mary, the wife of Francis Lardner, who was "dug upon again, whereby the coffin was broken, which they tied together, and carrying it away, exposed the corps in the market place." This from a man who read the semiotics of dead bodies with some care: the traitor Cromwell was "rowled with infamy from the grave," dug up on the king's command from his grave in Westminster Abbey and dragged on a sled to Tyburn, where the corpse was executed and its head put on a pike. It was, Sewel observed a "remarkable instance of the judgment and equal justice of God."[35]

Little remains today of this turmoil. In the most carefully excavated of the seventeenth- and eighteenth-century Quaker burial grounds (Kingston upon Thames, used between 1664 and 1814), only 10 percent of skeletons were oriented east–west, 55 percent north–south, and the rest either south–north or west–east. The "traditional" 10 percent may well have been put in the ground by a gravedigger who did not belong to the Society of Friends. By the nineteenth century, when the Quakers relented and allowed members to have small tombstones, these were set neatly in rows running at ninety degrees from the traditional orientation. But they had become more like others: they allowed coffin decoration, with some buried in the usual direction, witness to the power of tradition.[36]

Even in the late nineteenth century, long after the old regime was gone in law and largely gone in practice, memories of past battles over the declination of graves could still stir passions. In 1882, the Dissenting Deputies, a body that since the middle of the eighteenth century had fought for the civil rights of non-Anglicans, brought a lawsuit against the vicar of a country parish, George Miller of St. John the Baptist, Harlow, because he had, "contrary to custom," "caused the grave [of a Dissenter] to be dug from North to South." He locked the regular churchyard gate and insisted that mourners enter through a special opening in the wall rather than through the usual gate, whose geography comported with the accustomed southeast- or southwest-oriented approach to almost all English churches. Miller's gesture cannot have been a surprise; he was active in the battle to retain tithes as an immemorial and divinely sanctioned right of the clergy, among other lost causes. The tithe was gone, and bodies were being buried by the tens of thousands in cemeteries large and small in whatever direction seemed locally appropriate. But memories of the old regime remained powerful enough to make a reactionary vicar's effort to bury a Dissenter in a north–south direction a small but still resonant *causus belli*. People who knew full well that what direction a body lay made no difference thought Miller's gesture, so self-consciously anachronistic, worth a lawsuit. Like so much about the dead, it mattered especially when it did not.[37]

The distribution of graves within the churchyard was an even more visible and fraught feature of the necrogeography of the old regime, because at the center of the graves there stood a church. In ancient Roman or Anglo-Saxon burial places and in a nineteenth-century cemetery, there would have been no such reference point for the eye. Graves would have followed natural or manmade local topography (roads and hills); they might have been around some feature of sacred geography (a sacred grove, a holy well), but it would not have made so manifest the cardinal directions. These older sites were generally also not enclosed. There was no clear back or front, no distant corner.

When the church, so carefully aligned to the east, joined the dead, this changed. Burial *ad sanctum*—close to that which is holy—for the privileged few became possible; more and more people demanded a roof over their bones, all aligned with the nave. But more evident to the eye was the evidence of the vast majority of the dead outside, spread in a morally freighted pattern that is so deeply settled in the landscape that it seems almost natural. Our eyes have become accustomed to seeing a church and its churchyard from a southern perspective, with graves in front and mostly to the west. It is difficult to imagine seeing the churchyard in any other way. Paintings and drawing reinforce this sense of inevitability. The artist's view is from the southwest or southeast; grave mounds and markers are in the foreground, a path to the western door winding through them toward the steeple. We rarely see the north side. There are few bodies there. "The most casual observer," writes a well-informed nineteenth-century clergyman, "must have been often struck with the fact that old churchyards frequently have few mounds or memorial stones on the north side while the south side may be inconveniently crowded." We have scores of eighteenth- and nineteenth-century images of the Chelsea churchyard, but none from the north, even though by then there were many graves in this unfavored corner.[38]

There might seem to be nothing culturally or historically interesting about this fact: other things being equal, buildings in the northern hemisphere tend to face in the direction of the sun in the southern sky. They are set at the back of their sites so that open space is on the sunny side, and in this open sunny space are most of the graves. Art follows nature or, more precisely, the common sense of the builder's craft. That said, there were many opportunities for alternative necrogeographies and also alternative ways of seeing a churchyard. And even if it is "natural" to enter a church from the south and to bury the dead where they are visible as one enters, they have been there so long that they have created, even if they were not created by, a meaningful necrogeography. For a thousand years, even before the parish church became the norm, people wanted to be buried on the south side of cemeteries and wanted the dangerous dead to be buried elsewhere. A resplendent light, a light from heaven, miraculously lit the place on the south side of the monastery of Berecingum, where the bodies of certain nuns were "to expect the day of the resurrection." South, the Venerable Bede tells us, is the direction of Christ's love.[39] And the south became the side of the virtuous, of those fully a part of the community of the dead.

In the late nineteenth century, the distribution of graves was still morally scrutable within the world of the parish, writes A. E. Housman in his hugely popular *Shropshire Lad*:

> To south the headstones cluster,
> The sunny mounds lie thick;
> The dead are more in muster
> At Hughley than the quick.

By contrast,

> North, for a soon-told number,
> Chill graves the sexton delves,
> And steeple-shadowed slumber
> The slayers of themselves.

The poet, however, is not judgmental: "I shall ne'er be lonely / Asleep with these or those." The north was the reprobate's quarter of the graveyard, "the place for a pauper, a poacher, or other sinners of undignified sins"; it is where Bathsheba would expect to find Fanny's grave in Thomas Hardy's *Far from the Madding Crowd*, although she would not expect to find there the "grand tomb" that she does.[40]

By Housman's and Hardy's time, and for centuries before, the justification for these beliefs, if not their power to effect where bodies went, had receded in the mists of superstition. The north was in practice the place for the unsettled dead— suicides who escaped burial in a field or at a crossroads, the unbaptized, excommunicants—whose bodies retained a civil right to a place in the parish churchyard but were far too dangerous to be kept near. The northern corners were thought by many, clergy and laity alike, to be unconsecrated ground, although anyone who knew anything about the relevant ritual would have known that this was not the case. In fact, the bishop and attending priest would have consecrated each corner of the churchyard and perambulated the periphery several times. There is no question that the church and the entire churchyard had been designated as a sacred space, but since the consecration of most churchyards had happened at least five hundred years earlier, these niceties were lost on most people.[41]

By the eighteenth century, the question of why the north side was in such disfavor and the southwest so popular demanded an anthropological explanation from those who posed it. Inevitably, it ended up being circular. Rev. Sir John Cullum, sixth baronet and a well-known antiquary, became rector of the tiny west Suffolk parish of Hawstead in 1762. He was intrigued to discover that there was still among his flock a "great partiality to burying on the south and east sides of the church-yard," despite the fact that these spaces were so crowded that "a corpse is rarely interred without disturbing the bones of its ancestors." He managed to persuade a "few persons to bury their friends" on the almost entirely vacant north side, but with no long-term effect: "the example was not followed." Parishioners continued to bury their dead in the south.[42]

The fact that his parishioners wanted to be buried on the south side, Cullum says, was certain; why was less obvious. The preference, he thinks, might have arisen from the practice of praying for the dead: the approaches to most English churches are from the south, that is, the sunny side in the northern hemisphere; the living as they entered would be reminded to pray for the dead whose mounds they passed. Everyone wanted to be remembered in the prayers of the living and therefore insisted on a southern burial, where they would be seen. This speculation is supported by the fact that in those rare cases where the church is approached from the north, more than the usual number of graves are on that side. But if this is the explanation, why, Cullum asks himself, does the preference persist two centuries after prayers for the dead were forbidden? The answer is that sentiment has replaced eschatology, or rather, a primal longing continues to find expression under new religious circumstances. The desire to be remembered remains constant. Ancient and anachronistic practices, on the one hand, and modern mourning customs, on the other—the exchange of mourning rings is his example—have the same origin deep in human psychology. They are different ways of expressing the same thing: "the fondest wishes of the heart of man, that of surviving, as long as we can, in the memory of others." Prayers or no prayers, people continue to want their dead in sight—hence on the southern side—because they continue to want to imagine themselves still in the gaze of the living when they die: graves, he suggests, "excite some tender recollection in those who view them."

But this explanation—the secularization of a pre-Reformation practice—did not altogether satisfy him either. Even in churches with a north-facing entry and with a greater proportion of graves on that side, there still was a disproportionate number in the south. Cullum turns next to what seems like a desperately clever theory: the sanctity of the east is well known because that is where our Savior—the "SUN of Righteousness"—will appear. This might be translated in the popular mind into a preference for being buried with easy access to the sun that provides warmth and light. Parishioners conflated the figurative and the literal: "so that those who are buried within the rays of the latter [the material SUN] may have a better claim to the protection of the former [the SON of Righteousness]." The explanation was a homonym. But by the eighteenth century, and long before, there was in fact no explanation for this particular feature of necrogeography other than the sanction of history and tradition. The north side was simply suspect—secluded, peripheral, the place for strangers, suicides, and the unbaptized—because that is how it had always been as long as anyone could remember. At stake were the political and cultural consequences of custom since time immemorial.[43]

John Brand (1744–1806), the learned antiquary whom Cullum cited, was less charitable. For him the old concentration of graves in the south, like their east–west alignment, was a popish holdover, a vestige of benighted, pre-Reformation England, where the superstitions of a millennium reigned, when "those who were reputed good Christians lay towards the south and east; others who had suffered capital punishment, laid violence to themselves, or the like were buried towards the north." "Every advocate of manly and rational Worship" must know that there is nothing special about the east. He was inveighing against both the aversion to burials in the north and to the insistence on an east–west declination of bodies. He wonders that "this custom was retained by Protestants," and decides, somewhat implausibly, that it must have something to do with the idea of the real presence in the Eucharist that some Anglicans maintained. If one actually ate one's God at the altar, then east did mean something. Whatever the reason—and the point is that there is really no reason—an old regime does not fall so easily to criticism like Brand's: the north continued to be suspect long after any possible eschatological justifications had ceased to be relevant.

Well into the nineteenth century, the north carried the stigma of history in the churchyards of England. William Brock, distinguished Baptist clergyman and abolitionist, records in his diary for 1866 that when his father died in 1808, he was buried "out among the gypsies," so strong was the prejudice then against Dissenters. A story circulated among folklorists about a girl (Mary C. of Sutton), dying of consumption, who demanded that she be buried in some quiet northern spot in the churchyard. Her parents objected and relented only when she threatened to come back to haunt them if they did not comply with a request that would put their daughter in a corner with strangers, suicides, and the unbaptized. This report fits into a genre of folklore that regarded the churchyard as a romantic vestige of premodern England, an England of customary rights and superstition, of an age in which unquiet spirits still rose from their graves, a world in which bodies lay in a specific relationship to the ordinal directions, and in which some bodies might not be worthy of—might even pollute—the earth of the churchyard: the old regime of the dead.[44]

As discussed in the next chapter, a new regime, self-consciously modern, supplanted it. In towns, the prolific historian of old church lore George Smith Tyack tells, "the increased value of land or the business-like arrangement of cemetery boards has not suffered the interference of such sentiments" as a predilection for burial on the south side of a church. John Claudius Loudon, the most important British landscape architect of the nineteenth century and a leading advocate of the new cemetery, suggested why such sentiments had hastened the demise of the old. Crowding in churchyards was exacerbated, he thought, by the uneven distribution of graves that followed from hoary prejudice. The root cause of that evil was where we began: the heart of the traditional necrogeography, the pesky orientation of the church in the direction of west to east. If the church could have been placed southwest to northeast or northwest to southeast, the problem would never have arisen in the first place. Loudon's point was that the demands of proper hygiene based on the latest theories of public health and efficient land use should take precedence over history and eschatology in dictating where and how the dead should be buried.[45]

Necrobotany

The ancient necrogeography of the churchyard is echoed in its necrobotany, in the presence of the long-lived European yew tree—*Taxus baccata*, the tree of the dead, the tree of poisonous seeds—that bears witness to the antiquity of the churchyard and shades its "rugged elms," and the mounds and furrows of its graves: The yew of legend is old and lays claim to immemorial presence. We are speaking here of two or three dozen exemplary giants, some with a circumference of ten meters, that have stood for between 1,300 and 3,000 years but also of many more modest and historically documented trees that have lived, and been memorialized, for centuries. At least 250 yews today are as old or older than the churchyards in which they stand. Some were there when the first Saxon and indeed the first British Christian wattle churches were built; a seventh-century charter from Peronne in Picardy speaks of preserving the yew on the site of a new church.[46]

Just how ancient any given tree might be is, and was, a matter of controversy. Estimates depended on having two or more measurements of girth over a long period of time and then applying a formula that projected rate of growth back in time. These formulas were in turn derived from other serial measurements—so many feet in so many years—supplemented by girth measurements of trees whose age was known from written evidence. In fact, precise dating is probably impossible, and everyone acknowledged it. There are too many variables that determine a tree's rate of growth to derive a reliable ratio for changes in girth per decade. But no one questions that yews live for thousands of years: "most trees look older than they are," says the dendrologist Alan Mitchell, "except for yews which are even older than they look." They have been an intimate part of the churchyard for time out of mind. They are trees of the deep past; their history vouches for the antiquity of the ecclesiastical landscape.[47]

The nineteenth-century antiquarian Daniel Rock speculates that the yew tree in the Aldworth, Berkshire, churchyard may well have been planted by the Saxons. John Evelyn, the seventeenth-century diarist and writer on forestry, measured that tree; Augustin Pyramus de Candolle (1778–1841), the famous Swiss botanist, measured it again a century later and used the difference to calculate age/circumference ratios; Rock himself measured it in 1841 and noted that it had grown a yard in girth since it was noted in *Beauties of England* (1760). Scores of other ancient churchyard yews have their own well-documented histories. These are the celebrities of the species that give voice to the antiquity of the churchyard and its dead. Thousands of ordinary yews share in the aura of the species (fig. 4.2).[48]

4.2. *Yews in a Country Churchyard.* John Burgess (1798–1863). British Museum.

It is "beneath the yew-tree's shade" that "heaves the turf in many a moulder-ing heap," as Gray's "Elegy Written in a Country Churchyard" puts it. *Taxus baccata* almost invariably casts its shadow where the dead are, on the south and west sides of the church. Like the bodies it watches over, it is rarely found on the north side, and then only in exceptional circumstances. Some believe, suggested Robert Turner, the strange, learned, and prodigious seventeenth-century translator of many mystical and medico-chemical texts, that this is because yews' branches would "draw and imbibe" the "gross and oleaginous Vapours exhaled out of the graves by the setting Sun." They also might prevent the appearance of ghosts or apparitions. Unabsorbed gases produced the *ignes fatui*, the "foolish fire" like that which travelers saw over bogs and marshes, and these, in the context of churchyards, could be mistaken for dead bodies walking. Superstitious monks, he continues, believed that the yew could drive away devils. Its roots, he thought, were poisonous because they will "run and suck nourishment" from the dead, whose flesh is "the rankest poison that could be."[49]

But Turner's fanciful claims about the yew's ecological adaptation are a bit post hoc. The more basic question is why the yew was so intimately associated with the dead in the first place. And, like all questions that seek mythic begin-nings, it is unanswerable. Or rather it has too many answers. The yew tree was sacred to Hecate, the Greek goddess associated with witchcraft, death, and nec-romancy. It was said to purify the dead as they entered Hades; the first-century C.E. poet Statius, much quoted by nineteenth-century folklorists, says that the oracular hero Amphiaraus, struck by Zeus's thunderbolt, was snatched so quickly from life that "not yet had the Fury [who lived in a yew grove] met and purified him with branch of yew, nor had Proserpine marked him on the dusky door-post as admitted to the company of the dead." Druids associated the tree with death rituals. In fact, it was the long pagan history of trees that caused the lead-ers of the Catholic Counter-Reformation to ban their planting altogether and motivated some—an early seventeenth-century bishop of Rennes was a famous case—to try, unsuccessfully in the face of popular opposition, to ban the yew in particular. Post-Reformation English clergy made no such efforts. Sixteenth- and seventeenth-century poets tell us that the yew leaf covered graves and anointed bodies. The fool Feste in *Twelfth Night* (act 2, sc. 4) sings of his "shroud of white, stuck all with yew." All this was commonplace in antiquarian histories. And so was the yew's association with the story of Christ's Passion—with Ash Wednes-day and Palm Sunday.[50] Few trees were so rooted in the deep time of the dead.

In the early eighteenth century, a rival unburdened by a long history appeared in Europe: the weeping willow. It got to England from China via Syria because a merchant from Aleppo named Thomas Vernon gave one to Peter Collinson, the most important middleman in global exchange of plants. He in turn gave the specimen to Alexander Pope for his gardens at Twickenham sometime in the

POPE'S VILLA.

Engraved by JOHN PYE, the Figures by CHᵃ HEATH, from a Picture by J.M.W. TURNER ESQᵗ R.A. and P.P. in the Gallery of SIR JOHN FLEMING LEICESTER, BARᵗ

4.3. *Pope's Villa.* Pye and Heath, after J.M.W. Turner, 1811. Tate, London.

early 1720s. There are variants to this story: Vernon was Pope's landlord and so may have given it to him directly; it may have appeared in England a little earlier. But the weeping willow was undeniably new and foreign in the eighteenth century, and early ones like Pope's enjoyed the attention paid to the new tree in town. *Salix babylonica* Linnaeus named it, mistakenly thinking it to be the tree of lamentation in Psalm 137: "By the rivers of Babylon, there we sat down, yea, we wept, when we remembered Zion./We hanged our harps upon the willows in the midst thereof." He can be forgiven his mistake. The taxonomy of willows is, as the leading expert tells us, "perplexing." True *Salix babylonica* is fragile in cold climates and may now be extinct, so our modern weeping willow is one of its cultivars, *Salix × sepulcralis*, produced by crossing it with the European white willow, *Salix alba.*[51]

The willow weeps and mourns perhaps because of its drooping leaves or because it was mistakenly called the tree of the ancient Hebrews' lamentations. But however it got its name and whatever its precise genealogy, it is the horticultural opposite of *Taxus baccata*: shallow-rooted, short-lived, and without historical baggage until Alexander Pope made it famous. His villa was torn down in 1808, not a century after the weeping willow arrived, because the new owner was tired of tourists. The painter J.M.W. Turner painted its ruins and saw the famous tree, now a dying trunk, and wrote of it (fig. 4.3):

> Pope's willow bending to the earth forgot
> Save one weak scion by my fostering care
> Nursed into life which fell on bracken spare
> On the lone Bank to mark the spot with pride.[52]

Tens of thousands of scions were sent forth from Twickenham before the sad end of Pope's tree.

Images of *Salix babylonica* or perhaps *Salix* × *sepulcralis,* the funereal willow, decorated the new commercial funeral announcements and mourning memorabilia of the eighteenth and nineteenth centuries; it shaded Rousseau's grave at Ermenonville (fig. 4.4). Gloom, thought John Claudius Loudon, the most learned horticulturalist of the nineteenth century, was the natural expression of the yew tree, melancholy that of the weeping willow. Its drooping branches made

4.4. Mourning ring showing an urn on a pedestal, shaded by a weeping willow executed in hair, 1782. British Museum.

it a natural sign of sorrow. Within a century, the foreigner without a history became the iconic tree of the parklike cemeteries of the nineteenth century. It was the tree not of the immemorial dead but of mourning, a tree not for the ages but for the three generations for which the dead can hope to be remembered.[53]

Necrotopology and Memory

The churchyard was, with few exceptions, a lumpy, untidy place. Gravediggers have always instinctively known this; they dug in ground that had been turned over for centuries. From very near the beginning they intercut, hacked through, turned over, tossed out earlier tenants to make room for new ones, and every few hundred years or so apparently leveled the ground and started again. In centuries-long cycles, the fact that there were dead bodies in the ground was made evident on its surface. The dead are really there. The lumps we can still see today in a few churchyards escaped one last round of recycling when the bodies stopped coming or when a local landscaper decided to leave them be.[54]

The majority of the parish (that is, the poor) were thus visible as a collectivity; their bodies changed the shape of the land; they were constitutive of the "mould'ring heaps" that are the churchyard's surface. They were insistent on being seen even if they could not also claim the regard that the speaker in Gray's elegy paid to them. To a large extent this is also what it was like for the middling sorts. The churchyard was not primarily a space for individual commemoration or for mourning at a family grave; indeed, there was, as we will see, technically no such thing, even if custom allowed it. Passersby would have seen a few temporary wooden markers; there were wreaths or in some cases plaques inside the church, but outside there was little that was intended to be permanent. Some of the elite of a parish had marked individual graves outside, and in sparsely populated parishes there was some hope that a family of bodies might remain for decades or even centuries together in a vault or at least in proximity to one another. There were few tombstones—five, ten, maybe twenty—in a space that we know holds thousands of bodies, and they were not set in concrete. They are invariably depicted as tilting precariously, as if to proclaim their impermanence. And since no one could claim a specific part of the churchyard, they were in fact transient. Even the occasional box tomb is usually shown in a state of disrepair. Inside there was more hope for rest but even there nothing was assured. When Samuel Pepys in 1664 arranged for his brother's interment in the middle aisle of St. Bride's, London, the sexton promised—after accepting a 6d. tip—that he would "jostle them [other bodies] but [would] make room for him." The remodeling of the parish church of Gulval near Penzance in 1897 revealed what any eighteenth-century sexton, most families, and twentieth-century archeologists would have known: that "the whole of the interior of the church had been used over and over again for interments," and thus no one had a secure place, even inside. A few great families kept their places for centuries. Outside, there was no pretense.[55]

The churchyard was and looked to be a place for remembering a bounded community of the dead who belonged there rather than a place for individual commemoration and mourning. In the many eighteenth- and early nineteenth-century images we have of them, they are represented less as small parks than as works in progress, constantly in a state of use and reuse. We see mounds of fresh dirt piled up; the grass is unmowed where it is not disturbed by digging. This is an active, working landscape. The visual image we are given is of a ground heaving with its harvest of the many generations, punctuated by a fragile sign here and there of someone in particular. It is a place—this home of the old regime of the dead—for dead bodies. If there was an epithet over a grave, it was likely to read, "here lies the body"—*hic jacet*—as if to add "amidst the other dead." In contrast, memory, and the phrase "in memory of . . . ," would become the topos of the cemeteries of the new regime, in which the poor were hidden and the prosperous were decorously covered. There were of course exceptions. Some of the great wool churches of the Cotswolds had magnificent outdoor tombs already in the early seventeenth century and maintained a tradition of memorial competition that by the nineteenth century left them looking like well-tended gardens.[56] (See the next chapter.)

When an important nineteenth-century painter takes on the subject of mortality and immortality, the scene is set in a churchyard, not a cemetery. There were no bodies evident in the latter. Henry Alexander Bowler's *The Doubt: "Can These Dry Bones Live?"* was painted in 1855 as a meditation on Tennyson's *In Memoriam* (fig. 4.5). A young woman is standing amidst the genteel disrepair of what appears to be a substantial country churchyard (but actually is the churchyard of the London suburb of Stoke Newington). The box tomb on her right has lost its siding, exposing the brick vault beneath; this is the sort of shelter that sparked late-eighteenth-century litigation, an effort that went against the nature of the place, that somehow tried to bring order to an individual grave by claiming for it a permanence that some opposed. The stone behind her has sunk almost out of sight; further back, an old-fashioned and short-lived grave board with elaborately carved posts running laterally along the body beneath is visible among a picturesque array of variously angled slabs. She rests her arms on the gravestone of John Faithful and looks onto the disturbed earth of the grave—there is no hint why it is in this condition, but it is almost a trope of churchyard representation. More specifically, she contemplates the skull that is lying there and the femur and bits of ribs that are poking out of the ground. This would have been unthinkable in the new regime of the cemetery. The red brick buttresses and a few windows of the church building itself stand out as if to make the point of a historical continuity of the Christian community of the living and the dead, represented by the field of markers in various stages of decay—its past, by the church that serves the living, and by the visit itself. John Faithful died in 1791, and the woman's costume makes clear that the scene we are witnessing occurred sixty years later, in the 1850s.

The stark fact of death is counterpoised with the promise of everlasting life: "I am the resurrection and the life," it says on Faithful's stone, which we, but not the young woman, see; "Resurgam" (I shall rise again) is written on the slab nestled in the ground at the foot of a large, very much alive and growing chestnut tree. Although topologically specific, the painting's landscape, like that in Nicolas Poussin's *Et in Arcadia ego* or the imagined landscape where Ezekiel confronted "dry bones," is prototypical: the universal country churchyard.

4.5. *The Doubt: "Can These Dry Bones Live?"* Henry Alexander Bowler, 1855. Tate, London.

To the visual record of the absence of individual memorials we can add the local knowledge of other, earlier historians. A 1690 record of St. Mary's, Nottingham, one of the oldest of the town's parish churches, shows that there were only six memorials in the churchyard. By the early twentieth century, there were in the churchyard no markers from before 1700 and few from the eighteenth century. The history of a church in Petersham, Surrey, makes a similar point. A churchyard that in 1800 was only 100 feet wide and 150 long could accommodate thousands of corpses because before the seventeenth century coffins were seldom used, and even afterward old bones were shoved out of place as new ones came in. There were no monuments there from before the 1680s. A nineteenth-century historian of Sheffield manages to turn even his three-acre churchyard—then the largest in England—into a version of the one that inspired Gray. He remembers the undulations of the earth marking a community of bodies: "how vivid in remembrance appears the picturesque irregularities of the ground and the gravestones through the halo of seventy years." Gravestones are almost irrelevant. He is not sure when the first appeared; there is little evidence of them before 1700. There were very few tombs ever, and the earliest extant one, then less than a hundred years old, was from 1776. And despite that by 1869 there were almost three thousand markers, even this number fell immeasurably short, he reminds us, of "representing the number, much less the name, sex, age and condition" of all those with whom we share a common humanity and who have "gone to dust in yonder little plot during more than seven hundred years."[57]

An early nineteenth-century clergyman, surveying his churchyard, counts the hillocks as he balances two interpretations of the graveyard: as a magazine for the "safe custody" of the dead waiting for judgment, in which some are more comfortable than others—the rich and important, the pretentious, and those blind to the fact that "the paths of glory lead but to the grave"; and as a Golgotha, where bones are scattered. He thinks of his community of the dead—176 of them in thirteen years—and wishes that he had served better as their pastor before it was too late.[58]

The Life and Afterlife of the Churchyard in Literature

In 1806, England's greatest landscape painter, John Constable, began a series of drawings and oil sketches of the church and churchyard of East Bergholt in the Stour Valley of Sussex, the village in which he had been born. In one of these, a man and two women gather around a tomb and look intently at an inscription that we cannot quite read. Those who saw the final painting would have known the allusion. An engraving published as the frontispiece to a collection of epitaphs the same year makes it explicit: the girl with her back to us blocks most of the text, but we can make out "Here rest / A Youth." Anyone in the early nineteenth century would have been able to fill in the missing words:

> Here rests his head upon the lap of Earth,
> A Youth, to fortune and to fame unknown

from Gray's "Elegy Written in a Country Churchyard" (1751). They would not have needed the words; any picture of a churchyard evoked Gray. The "Elegy" was an immediate success when it was published and remained resonant for at least two centuries. "Poem of Poems," Edmund Gosse, the late-nineteenth-century man of letters called it in his *English Man of Letters* book about Gray. Line for line, it has given more words to the English language, according to the attributions in the *Oxford English Dictionary*, than any other source; it was probably recited by more schoolchildren in the nineteenth century than any other; it was continually trans-lated—thirty-three times into Italian alone by 1850. It was endlessly reprinted and anthologized in English (plates 6, 7).[59]

The "Elegy" stands in a long history of elegiac poetry and is also one of a genre of poems, hugely popular in the eighteenth and nineteenth centuries, that taught English people how to feel and speak about churchyards. Among the first are Edward Young's immensely popular "The Complaint or Night Thoughts on Life, Death and Immortality"(1742-1745) and Robert Blair's "The Grave" (1741). Both revel in the pleasures of melancholy, the terrors of the tomb, and, especially in Young's case, a certain melodramatic hysteria occasioned by death and mourn-ing. (William Blake's twelve illustrations to an 1805 edition of "The Grave" were his most popular work in the nineteenth century.)

These poems, and many more in the same genres, were critical in defining the emotional attraction of the old regime of the dead for the generations that fol-lowed: when nineteenth-century reformers spoke of the gloom of the churchyard, they meant the gloom that the so-called graveyard poets evoked and encouraged. And when they blasted the churchyard as a place of "preternatural fear and super-stition," they correctly understood that these intensely local places were where (as Blair writes in "The Grave," lines 24–26) the not-quite-gone dead lingered:

> Where well healed ghosts, and visionary shades
> Beneath the wan, cold moon (as fame reports)
> Embody'd thick, perform their mystic rounds.

"The Souls of the Dead appear frequently in Coemiteries," writes Addison (by which he meant churchyards). They "hover about the Places where their Bodies are buried, as still hankering about the old brutal Pleasures, and desiring again to enter the Body." Ghosts stay near home: houses, pubs, the crossroads at which they were wrongly buried, and, most obviously, the parish churchyard.[60]

But Thomas Gray's "Elegy" stands apart. It is not our task to understand why it seemed so fresh and resonant to generation upon generation of readers but only to recognize that it did and that its literary vigor had historical consequences. Abraham Lincoln told a journalist that everything anyone would want to know about him could be found in one line of Gray's poem: "The short and simple annals of the poor." Part of the ideological novelty of the poem is its insistence that the humble dead have as much of a claim as do the great to live on in the imagination of posterity and in the ground of the churchyard. The poem recognizes that not everyone shares this view. Its voice is a recognizable view: that of eighteenth-century sympathy, of a certain bourgeois optimism that recognizes social distinction but embraces the possibility that virtue will or could have its just reward:

> Some village-Hampden that with dauntless breast
> The little tyrant of his fields withstood;
> Some mute inglorious Milton here may rest,
> Some Cromwell guiltless of his country's blood.

The youth in the engraving made from a Constable painting might have made his fortune and been known if death had not cut him short. We are here on the threshold of the Napoleonic "Field Marshal's baton in every knapsack," imagined in a churchyard elegy. It is also a poem of seductive mysteries and shadowy interlocutors: Who is the mourner? Who is the nameless peasant? What lives might these dead have lived in a world other than that into which they had been born? (figs. 4.6, 4.7).

4.6. Frontispiece to "Elegy Written in a Country Churchyard." In Richard Bentley, *Designs by Mr. R. Bentley for Six Poems by Mr. T. Gray* (London: R. Dodsley, 1753).

4.7. Frontispiece to *A Select Collection of Epitaphs and Monumental Inscriptions.* J. Raw, 1806.

More important to our understanding are the ways in which the "Elegy" represents the churchyard as a visible, socially and juridically defined, narrowly bounded, hierarchic parish community of the dead through time. It, more than any other work of literature, law, or religion, both shaped and articulated the sensibilities of a very wide swath of English men and women as the old regime gave way to the new in terms of where in fact the dead came to rest. It was the world "we have lost" and yet never lost entirely. The poor in this vision were as important to the churchyard as it was to them. They were the collectivity, constitutive of it and of the community it claimed to represent. Gray and those who read him understood this. We know, of course, that it is not quite correct when the poet says,

> Each in his narrow cell for ever laid.
> The rude Forefathers of the hamlet sleep.

They were all jumbled together, the rude ancestors, but they were seen to be there in the contours of the ground and felt to be there through verse.

George Crabbe, in a widely popular and much-praised poem, is closer to what modern archeology confirms about how the rude ancestors were actually "forever laid": they were not.

> Him now they follow to his grave, and stand
> Silent and sad, and gazing hand in hand;
> While bending low, their eager eyes explore
> The mingled relics of the parish poor.[61]

It turns out to be nearly impossible to do a stratigraphic analysis of churchyard excavation precisely because, over the centuries, the "narrow cells" of the rude ancestors—and even those less rude—were frequently cut into and overturned. What the poet saw is what we imagine from contemporary topographical art:

> Beneath those rugged elms, that yew tree's shade,
> Where heaves the turf in many a mould'ring heap.

Constable, as well as artists before and after him, knew their Gray. The "Elegy" is thinkable only within the space of the old regime dead; it follows from the religious, legal, and cultural history I have been telling, a history that could be and was read on the ground and, in the succeeding centuries, in poetry.

Change was also read into the world that Gray bestowed on readers. For example, the criticism of distinctions within the community of the dead—the increase in burials within the church building and of monuments, for example—became a way of articulating what some imagined as a sadly dying moral order. The eponymous heroine of the best-selling *Goody Two-Shoes* (1765) ordered that she be buried in the churchyard without an inscription on her stone, like the unknowns that Gray imagines. In this wish, she stands in contrast to the proud Lady Ducklington who "squandered away, [money that] would have been better laid out in little books for children, or in milk, drink, and clothes for the poor" than in a tomb and obsequies. She did not rest well, or in any case not solemnly. The day of her burial was a farce. Her interment was delayed because of its excessive pomp; at four in the morning the church bells started to ring; some thought it was her "ghost dancing among the bell ropes." Goody cleared up the mystery: she went into the vault and trod on Lady Ducklington's coffin; she saw no ghost; she was locked inside the church and raised a ruckus to get attention. Among her many virtues, Goody was not superstitious. That said, these were the circumstances under which a ghost might appear to the more gullible: Lady Ducklington's was a body out of place. "And oh! How needless when the woe's sincere," writes the poet Crabbe about another proud landlord:

> Slow to the Vault they come with heavy tread,
> Bending beneath the *Lady*, and her lead . . .
> Ungenerous this, that to the Worm denies,
> With niggard-caution, his appointed Prize.[62]

The trope of contrasting burials—the virtuous humble burial with a modest or "a moldering mound" and the overweening pompous burial inside the church or under an ostentatious monument outside—became more ideologically charged in the eighteenth century in ways it had not been before. No longer just a sign of the failure to appreciate the democracy of the grave—the common fate of bodies as food for worms—or the transience of fame, it became a way of representing the breakdown of an imagined parish community whose existence through time was vouchsafed by the dead at its center. The centrality and longevity of Gray's "Elegy" in the English literary canon bears witness to the ongoing power of the old regime. It never really ended.

Charles Darwin wanted to be buried in his village churchyard, and the dean of Westminster Abbey would have been just as happy if he had had his wish. But he did not. The world of science needed him in the Abbey. Thomas Hardy too wanted to lie in his village churchyard: Stinsford in his native Dorsetshire. But he too "belonged to the nation" and, after much controversy, he had two funerals: his heart was buried in Stinsford and his cremated ashes in Poet's Corner. Intimate local places of the dead did not die in the imagination even as great new cosmopolitan ones rose to prominence.

The Passage of the Dead to the Churchyard

Just as ghosts did not disappear with the Reformation, neither did the liminal dead, those still making their way out of this world and into another one, those on their way to the churchyard. They were cared for in the Protestant world—minus masses for the dead, plus the newly popular commemorative funeral sermon—much as they had been before. The ritual vocabulary changed little; the final destination of the funeral remained the same.

Members of guilds—the barbers and the bakers and the carpenters—continued to escort their brothers and their brothers' wives in procession to the grave as they had done in the Middle Ages. They buried in the same churches as before. They continued to leave small sums in their wills for a common supper and for the ringing of the passing bell. Most of the companies kept a funeral cloth or pall, and if anything, these became more ornate. In 1563, the worshipful company of coopers spent £70 on a pall in honor of the Virgin, their patron, which was embroidered with gold and silver thread and laden with pearls. Puritans or no Puritans, the pall was used until 1672, when it was sold for £8, which was put toward a new one.[63]

Giving alms also was expected at the funerals of those who could afford it in late medieval Europe. Charity was a cardinal virtue, and the deceased who had made arrangements for the gift might hope that her largesse would encourage its beneficiaries to pray for her soul. The Reformation may have changed the theological justification for such practices; it did not change the practices themselves. They flourished. We do not know, for example, exactly when Christ's Hospital, Edward VI's new Protestant educational foundation for the poor, started supplying children to funerals in return for alms. The school took in its first scholars in 1552; in 1608, the music master was given a raise in return for guaranteeing that there would always be eight of them available to sing a corpse from its home to the churchyard. By 1622, the provision of child mourners had become a major money-making operation: over the next 132 years, the children of Christ's Hospital followed more than 1,550 bodies to their churchyard graves, marching together in long columns—sixty, eighty, on one occasion as many as two hundred of them—in return for charity. By this means the school earned a great deal of money, more than £75,000. Far from declining, the practice of giving alms to the poor to accompany a body to the grave became better organized. And on a smaller and more routine basis, seventeenth-century wills customarily provided for food, drink, and small monetary gifts to the poor at funerals. Their presence, as before, signaled the generosity of the deceased as well as her wish to be associated in death with those to whom Christ had promised so much. Sensibility trumped theology. Christ's Hospital's income from providing mourners did decline after the success of the Cromwellian, that is, the Puritan, revolution: poor children attended more than 1,000 funerals between 1622 and 1649, but only 550 in the next 105 years. But the biggest contingent—two hundred children—ever to mourn for alms followed the body of one of the Hospital's governors,

Thomas Stretchley, on Tuesday, 13 September 1681. There were many more grand funerals in the late seventeenth century.[64]

The sounds of the so-called passing (or soul or death) bell, which before the Reformation had invited prayers for the souls of the dead, continued to ring over the churchyard as Thomas Gray knew it in the eighteenth century. And beyond. the practice was attacked by more reform-minded Protestants as irrelevant, superstitious, and inconsistent with scripture. Some bells did fall victim to radicals; some bishops in their visitations inquired about superstitious clangs. But the bells were not silenced, not even in Calvin's Geneva, and certainly not in the villages and towns of England. The passing bell—strictly speaking, bells rung as someone lay dying—probably declined, although they were not gone: "Perchance he for whom this bell tolls may be so ill as that he knows not it tolls for him," as John Donne says. But their sounds left echoes. The speaker in "Cross Roads," by the agrarian laborer-poet John Clare (1793–1864), learned that her friend Jenny had drowned herself when she was with child when she heard the ringing of the passing bell. In at least four parishes of late-nineteenth-century Hertfordshire there was, writes a local historian, "a near approach to the good old custom": death knells tolled as soon as notice was given to the sexton. More generally they were postponed to the next day, perhaps because of Protestant objections to praying for the dead, although he could find no evidence for this hypothesis. His informants said they had no idea why the bells did not ring sooner, except perhaps that no one wanted it to appear that anyone was glad to get rid of the deceased. Bells continued to ring in most rural and many urban parishes, announcing by so-called tellers the sex and age of the deceased: three for a man, two for a woman, one for a child, or multiples of these. Nineteenth-century folklorists report that there were between seventy and eighty ways of doing this in rural Lincolnshire. And there is a great deal of folkloric evidence from Victorian England that we can probably project backward that suggests a continuous tradition of such sounds in the popular imagination. The third bell at the Church of St. Helen's in Brant Brougham comports with Protestant theology; its inscription reads,

> Beg ye of God your soul to save
> Before we call you to the grave

Bells followed the dead as before.[65]

When they were finally silenced, it had little to do with a rigorous segregation of the dead or prohibitions against praying for their souls and a great deal with the socioeconomic forces that ruptured communities of the living. And where they survived, their subsistence in a new world could take on new and ironic meanings. Lawrence Hilliard, research assistant to the Victorian sage John Ruskin, sent him the following tidbit of information: "A tolling machine has been erected at Ealing cemetery at the cost of £80, and it seems to give universal satisfaction. It was calculated that this method of doing things would (at 300 funerals a year) be in the long run cheaper than paying a man 3d. an hour to ring the bell. Thus we mourn for the departed."[66] By then the old regime of the churchyard was rapidly becoming more memory than reality.

LAW

There was a large body of law, some statutory, most customary, born of controversies about who had what rights to be buried where, for how much money, and with what ceremonies. It falls into different categories and was adjudicated by a bewildering mix of courts, secular and ecclesiastical. But taken as a whole, it registers how deeply the old regime is imbedded in history, in local practices as well as in notions of church and state. Slowly, the dead are transformed from parishioners into citizens and members of civil society. The new law of the cemetery largely superseded the old law of the churchyard by the end of nineteenth century, but the old regime persisted for a very long time, in large measure because its legal framework represented the cultural claims of its dead.

Exclusion from the Churchyard

In English law, every body had a place and every place had its bodies. It was the parish churchyard. An ancient and statutory communal right of the dead to be buried, grounded in the utter abjection of the unattended corpse and in demands that the living made of the dead, was unquestioned. The denial of this right (that is, refusal to properly bury a dead body) constituted a posthumous exclusion from the cultural and political order, an obliteration of personhood after death, and could be sustained only under special and often contested circumstances. Thus the bodies of outlaws—criminals and traitors—were statutorily forfeit to the king, who could order that they be hung from gibbets or burnt or, increasingly after the 1720s, sent from the gallows to the anatomy theater, where surgeons cut them up before a large public audience. These bodies, so profoundly out of place, were, and were meant to be, terrifying to would-be criminals—being anatomized was repugnant to and hugely feared by ordinary subjects and by the lone passerby who, like the speaker in Wordsworth's *Prelude* could just make out the palimpsest of a body that had once been left hanging in the wind.

> . . . Mouldered was the gibbet-mast;
> The bones were gone, the iron and the woods;
> Only a long green ridge of turf remained
> Whose shape was like a grave.[67]

Excluded too from their rightful place, in this case by the sixty-eighth canon of the Anglican Church, was another category of criminals: those who had died by their own hands, the *felo de se*—the "felon [murderer] of himself." These were not left to hang in the air or to be dissected by the surgeons; they were not left unburied. But they also were not incorporated into the community of the Christian dead. We do not know what proportion of those found by coroner's juries to have committed suicide were, in fact, excluded from the churchyard entirely in the sixteenth and seventeenth centuries, when the verdict of *felo de se* was still commonplace. This is the question that the gravediggers debate in the last act of *Hamlet*; some suicides must have found their way in. Clearly, Ophelia had drowned herself and should not be buried in the churchyard, but rank made all the difference: "If this had not been a gentlewoman, she should have been buried out o' Christian burial," they conclude. And the priests attending the ceremony agree:

> Her obsequies have been as far enlarged
> As we have warrantise: her death was doubtful;
> And, but that great command o'ersways the order,
> She should in ground unsanctified have lodged
> Till the last trumpet: for charitable prayers,
> Shards, flints and pebbles should be thrown on her. (act 5, sc. 1)

A corpse could do worse than to be dumped without ceremony in a far-off, supposedly unconsecrated corner of the churchyard. In the early nineteenth century, upon occasion, the dead considered dangerous were still buried at crossroads. To the nineteenth-century laborer-poet John Clare, these were bodies paradigmatically out of place; their ghosts therefore still walk the earth:

> That grave ye've heard of, where the four roads meet,
> Where walks the spirit in a winding-sheet,
> Oft seen at night, by strangers passing late,
> And tarrying neighbours that at market wait,
> Stalking along as white as driven snow,
> And long as one's shadow when the sun is low;
> The girl that's buried there I knew her well,
> And her whole history, if ye'll hark, can tell.

One cannot quite tell whether Flora Thompson (1876–1947) is offering a ghost story or ethnographic reportage when she remembers that in her Oxfordshire village, "no one cared to go after dark to the cross roads where Dickie Bracknell, the suicide, was buried with a stake through his entrails, or to approach the barn out in the fields where he had hung himself some time at the beginning of the century." It makes no difference.[68]

Burying suicides at crossroads was certainly not a canonically sanctioned practice and had no foundation in law. It was rather an expression of popular outrage that the authorities were long loath to quell, a vestige of so-called superstitions that the Church had fought only selectively since the advent of Christianity. In any case, many clergy probably shared in the popular antipathy to suicides and were only too happy to exclude their bodies from the churchyard and from the promise of resurrection offered by the burial service of the Book of Common Prayer. As the speaker in that master of melancholy Robert Blair's hugely popular poem "The Grave" (1743) puts it:

> Forbid it, heaven! Let not, upon disgust,
> The shameless hand be foully crimsoned o'er
> With blood of his own hand. Dreadful attempt!![69]

During the eighteenth century, these "felons of the self" could, with spectacular exceptions, begin to hope for better, because coroner's juries increasingly rendered a verdict of insanity, which in principle gained the corpse entry to the churchyard and to a service, if not necessarily clerical sympathy and a good spot. Some clergy simply refused to honor a jury's decision that a body found hanging was not that of a murderer of the self. The Honorable and Reverend A. P. Percival, a future leader of the Tractarians (the High Church Anglicans who eventually went over to Rome), argued in a pamphlet skirmish that the inquest over a body that he had been asked to bury was simply wrong: the evidence for insanity was not strong, and the jury had been poorly instructed. And more generally, he concluded, neither he nor his fellow clergy could be compelled to bury a suicide, whatever a lay jury said: "clergy have shrunk from the duty in this respect." The Lord Chancellor ruled in 1856 that a clergyman had no right to second-guess a jury. None of this was to much avail, and a small number of clergymen debated what to do into the early years of the twentieth century. By the 1880s, however, the Burial Law Amendment Act and other legislation had wrested control of the churchyard from the clergy so that suicides could be buried with the same respect as others.[70]

Amid more fraught struggles over excluding corpses from burial in the churchyard, there were also occasionally some strange attempts at exclusion: a loose memorandum in a nineteenth-century Berkshire Quarter Sessions bundle tells of the body of John Mathews of Fowler being arrested for debt on 23 August 1689, on its way to the grave. He lay there for four days until the justices ordered his temporary burial to "prevent offensiveness" in a strange parish. By order of the session, the corpse was "taken up and buried in the [proper] churchyard on October 10." For the next century, there were periodic reports of holding the dead ransom for their debts (that is, keeping them from the churchyard grave to which they were entitled), but the courts never accepted this procedure, and in 1804 Lord Ellenborough ruled definitively that such a practice was "revolting to humanity" and "contrary to every precept of law and public feeling."[71]

The Claims of the Dead Body on the Parish Churchyard

The vast majority of English people had not only an immemorial right to be buried somewhere but also a more specific and geographically bounded right: "by the custom of England, to be buried in the Church-yard of the Parish where he dies," as Sir Simon Degge put it in his standard legal guide to the law of the parish. Whether this right was also based on statute law, that is, on late Anglo-Saxon legislation at the dawn of the creation of what came to be the system of parish churches, is less relevant than that it was very old and deeply embedded in ecclesiastical geography and common practice.

More controversial was whether, as Sir Simon Degge claimed, by the "Custom of England" every parishioner also had the right to "be buried in any common part of the Church or Chancel, paying the accustomed fee to the parson for breaking the Soil," by which he meant a fee, which might go to either the churchwardens or to the parson who had a freehold in the building, for actually tearing into the fabric of the church floor. The problem was that ecclesiastical and customary law diverged. The incumbent, and only the incumbent, some argued, could grant parishioners the *privilege* of being buried within the body of the church, not because of his religious authority but because his office held the freehold. Burial in the church or chancel had anciently signified spiritual merit that could be judged only by the incumbent, qua incumbent, or his superior.[72] But these are fine points: every corpse had by right its place in the parish churchyard or an extension of that churchyard, barring extraordinary circumstances.

This was an absolute right. But precisely which particular parish churchyard that might be and under what conditions was open to interpretation. Litigation refined and reaffirmed the basic claim: *Ubi decimus persolvebat vivus, sepeliatur mortuus,* reads the canon: "Where he pays the tithe while alive, let him be buried there." This was determined to mean that to belong to a parish for the purposes of having a right to be buried meant having paid a tax there; simply dying in that place was not enough to lay claim to a permanent place on its soil for some judges. So, for example, one authority held that a wealthy person dying accidentally in the parish adjoining the one where he usually lived could not claim the right to burial there irrespective of its being the actual parish of his demise.[73] But an equally distinguished judge disagreed and thought that a parishioner dying outside his parish had a right to be buried there as well as in the parish in which he had paid tithes.[74] Then there was the question of the very considerable number of the poor who paid no tithes and of impoverished outsiders: who in a parish was responsible for the dead poor who might not have had a settlement there was an issue just like the allied question of who was responsible for the living poor who were deemed out of place. Tens of thousands of migrants to London died, abjectly out of place, in the hovels, privies, and streets of the great city, as they do today in Nairobi and Calcutta. But courts generally maintained the overarching principle that everyone had a common law right to burial in the parish where she died, which was usually but not always where she had lived.

Lord Chief Justice Denman (1779–1854) held, for example, that St. George's Hospital in London, not the parish overseers, was responsible for burying paupers not normally resident in the parish who died in its care. But he made clear that this was a dispute about who paid, not about the right itself: "Every person dying in this country . . . has a right to a Christian burial; and that implies the right to be carried from the place where his body lies to the parish cemetery."[75] There is no mention of tithes, although the use of the word "cemetery" rather than "churchyard" reflects the fact that some densely populated London parishes were increasingly using sacred ground not contiguous with the church as a place to put "their" dead poor.

A foundational localism governed the old regime. Churchwardens could not, for example, invite "strange" corpses from neighboring parishes with too little space and too many pauper bodies into their churchyards. The much-cited case of "The Churchwardens of Harrow on the Hill" clarified that point. Here the defendants were admonished that they had no absolute right to grant such permission. Their motivation was clear: they and not the incumbent received the fees.[76]

At the edges there was always debate. Some authorities held absolutely, for example, that "a stranger or foreigner"—everyone from the next parish or from around the world—"had no absolute right to burial there," but then added, "except as arises out of necessity." This meant in effect that bodies of unknown origin found on roads, or in extraparochial places, or washed up on beaches were by custom the responsibility of the nearest parish. The churchwardens were not always anxious to meet these obligations, because their funds bore the burden. In at least one scandalous case—the burial without coffins in unconsecrated ground of sailors whose bodies washed ashore in 1808 from the wreck of HMS *Anson* in Mounts Bay, Cornwall—their reluctance led to legislative remedy: the Burial of Drowned Persons Act that year (48 Geo ca. 75) that mandated the decent treatment of "foreign" bodies. But "necessity" did not define the rule; almost all bodies had prescribed places where they belonged.[77]

Conversely, all parishes had a prima facie claim on particular bodies or, more specifically, on the fees generated by these bodies. This goes back at least to the reign of the eighth-century Saxon king Edgar, who imposed a "soul-scot" to be paid "to the minster to which [the soul] belongs." The notion that a body somehow belonged to an incumbent and owed him something was well established by the late Middle Ages. Excavations of a medieval churchyard found many skeletons that had been buried with a pebble on the chest, a sign, it seems, of the corpse's acceptance of the soul-scot. By the eighteenth and nineteenth centuries, ecclesiastical lawyers were debating the subtleties of a principle with a thousand years of tradition behind it. "Albeit the clergy may not demand anything for burial, yet the laity may be compelled to observe pious and laudable customs," and that went for the customary demands of others with a pecuniary interest in the church or churchyard as well. Even the poorest of the poor thus paid—or rather the overseers of the poor paid for them—a fee not only to the parish priest for a burial service but also to the sexton for actually digging the grave and to the clerk, if there was one; there was also a fee for "breaking the ground" that was paid either to the churchwardens, to be used for the maintenance of the churchyard for which they were responsible in the name of the community, or in some cases to the incumbent. That was one side of the story that bound a corpse to the parish. But in this ancient land there was also an opposing tradition that argued against collecting any money at all for burial.[78]

By canon law, anyone could be buried where he pleased and, in principle, for free; parishioners could not be forced to be buried in the churchyard to which they held common law rights (that is, the one outside their parish church) or in the church in which they might claim intramural interment. And they could not be forced to pay anything to their home parish or any other for a grave. "By the Custom of England," Simon Degge had written in his ubiquitous guidebook on such matters, "every person . . . may be buried . . . *without paying any thing for breaking the soil.*" Burial was a right, not a privilege to be bought. Ground for interment was among the holy things (*res sacrae*), as the twelfth-century theologian Stephen Langton had argued. It was simony, the ecclesiastical crime of selling a sacrament or holy office or any spiritual good, to receive money for a burial place or for reading the service. "Payment of fees is not a condition precedent to the right of interment, because burial ought not to be sold," nineteenth-century lawyers held, in conformity with this view. Places and rituals for the dead, in other words, were normatively outside the marketplace, to prevent a suspect mixing of commerce with sacrality. If the parish had any real claim at all, it was not pecuniary. Practice diverged from norms.[79]

In real life, the first principle—that a body belonged to a parish—prevailed and quarrels revolved around the question, "Who precisely belonged to the parish and in what circumstances?" In a 1618 case (15 Jac 1), for example, Edward Topsel, vicar of St. Botolph's, Aldersgate, unsuccessfully sued Sir John Ferrers for his and the churchwarden's fees for the burial of Sir John's wife, as if she had been buried in his church's chancel in the manner in which she was actually buried in another parish. The deceased had indeed expired in Topsel's parish but was not resident there. She was buried where she lived by another clergyman. Topsel sued not for the minimal churchyard fees but for the same fees as the other clergyman got. The judges in this case held that just dying somewhere did not count. If someone staying in an inn or passing through a parish happened to die there, the local vicar had no rights to the body; the supposed London tradition to which Topsel appealed was "beyond reason." But the learned Doctor Gibson (d. 1644), in a well-known digest of cases published by his grandson, holds that this only proves the rule: it *is* unreasonable, he agrees, to force someone to be buried in a parish just because he happened to be passing through it when death caught up with him, that is, to demand of a man's heirs that they pay a fee to the incumbent for the privilege of *not* burying someone in his church or churchyard just because someone happened to expire in his parish. But that said, he affirms the cultural foundations of the doctrine at the heart of the old regime of the dead: "it is agreeable to rule of canon law that everyone, after the manner of the patriarchs, shall be buried in the sepulchres of their fathers." Clerical claims on bodies do not perhaps have quite the Old Testament pedigree Gibson is here suggesting, but they are deeply embedded in the old regime. Subsequent experts agreed that the case did not in any way undermine the principle that a body owed a fee to the clergyman of the parish where it had died.[80]

The specific right litigated in *Topsel v. Ferrers* (to collect fees for bodies buried elsewhere) probably dates back to the arrangement whereby monasteries paid some portion—one-third, one-fourth—of the oblations they received for the burial of the dead in their precincts to the parochial clergy from whose parishes these dead came. What began as a kickback to avoid quarrels had become by the seventeenth century a customary if contentious claim of the parochial minister. *Topsel* did not settle the matter. In 1741, Charles Zouch, the vicar of Sandal, near Wakefield, obtained a writ of distress against two Quakers for burying a member of their meeting in an apple orchard. That was fine, but not paying the vicar's fees and the breaking the ground fee was cause for a lawsuit. Zouch won before a magistrate, and the Quakers appealed. The vicar argued in Quarter Sessions that law and custom gave him fees no matter where the body was buried if it was "his" body. The lawyer for the Quakers cited the judgment of other courts in *Topsel* and other cases that held that custom dictated that a clergyman could not take money out of a layperson's hands for a service that was not performed. In Quarter Sessions the appellants prevailed, but they did not recover their considerable costs, suggesting that the court did not find Zouch's claim especially egregious.

The Dissenting Deputies, who guarded the civil rights of non-Anglican Christians, protested a half-dozen similar cases during the eighteenth century: On 13 October 1769, they got a case in which a clergyman demanded a mortuary of 10s. for the burial of one of his parishioners who was interred in a Dissenting burial ground with no Anglican service at all. On 26 May 1787, they learned that a Dissenting minister in Essex had been threatened with prosecution for not paying the incumbent of the parish a fee for a body that he buried in the meetinghouse burial ground. In 1851, when London churchyards were finally closed, the State promised as part of its negotiation with the Church to buy out—although it never did—the rights of incumbents to the dead of their parish. Every dead body was in debt to the clergyman of her parish. And even if it cost a body nothing to escape, she had to pay extra elsewhere.[81] Although living bodies could no longer be bound to the land after the Tenures Abolition Act of 1660, dead ones still more or less belonged to a place well into the nineteenth century.

The Economics of Churchyard Burial

The charge that priests trafficked in places for the dead and other services for them, which had been a mainstay of anticlericalism in the later Middle Ages and a major complaint of the Reformation, was still made in the last century of the old regime. Although all church fees were wrong, argued Francis Sadler in a much-reprinted 1738 tract, "selling" one part of the churchyard for three times the price of another "to keep Rich and Poor asunder as if there were a difference in their dust" was especially ridiculous.[82]

There was a market in burial places in the old regime much as there would be in the new, but it was severely restricted: the church and churchyard were for the use of the parish community in perpetuity; burial was a civil right, whereas burial in any particular place was granted at the discretion of the clergy as the guardians of consecrated ground in the interests of the community; no specific place of burial could be transformed into private property. Priests and churchwardens, each with their own interests, could within these rules charge differential fees to allocate scarce resources: a place in better ground and the right to erect memorials. Furthermore, there was also no question that important families in individual parishes could put enormous pressure on an incumbent to grant interment inside the church; indeed, in some cases they had customary rights to burial in a vault inside the church if not in the churchyard. Conversely, those without resources went where it was convenient. Thus the much-quoted epitaph, with its gentle, resigned irony, on a country churchyard:

Here I lie by the chancel door;
They put me here because I was poor.
The further in, the more you pay,
But here I lie as snug as they.[83]

This, without the epitaph, constituted the default burial; almost everything cost extra. In the first place, those from outside the parish generally paid twice what those who "belonged" paid—"stranger's fees," a sort of tariff barrier to foreign bodies. People were willing to pay extra for burial in parishes other than their own largely to be near relatives. They were apparently also willing to pay for location—the chancel was a better address than the center aisle, which was, in turn, preferred to the side aisles. They were willing to pay for more permanent occupancy: lead coffins were admitted to the churchyard of St. Andrew Holborn, for a fee ten times as large as for burial in ordinary wooden ones.[84] When a new parochial burial ground was added to the old, the former might become differentially more attractive and hence a source of increased revenue for the churchwardens.[85] Burial in the vaults of new eighteenth-century churches was much dearer than burial in the churchyard. Even the time of day mattered: St. John the Evangelist, Westminster, charged an extra 5s. for burials after 10 P.M. and, beginning in 1748, after 8 P.M.[86]

By the late eighteenth century, a few London and other urban parishes had developed a fee schedule that rivaled that of the modern cemetery in its many gradations. St. James Chapel and Burial Ground, for example, had a price list three pages long that gave the cost of tombs, vaults, and common graves for adults, children, and stillborn infants in each of four separate areas, along with an account of the division of fees between the rector, clerk-in-orders, sexton, and churchwardens. The parish had borrowed £6,000 to pay for new grounds and a chapel in 1789 and so was in much the same situation as a cemetery company needing to finance its capital expenses. (The loan was paid off by 1811.)[87] All London churches by 1838 offered at the very least a distinction between "best" and "common ground," while most used three or even four levels, each with different specified fees for "strangers," "parishioners," and, in the case of St. Pancras, "lodgers."[88] Despite this market, burial remained "parochial" and governed by custom and a whole mess of historically rooted claims and counterclaims. No churchyard would be mistaken for a modern cemetery or for a Roman one that served as its model.

In the first place, with the exception of lay rectors (someone who was not a clergyman but who had acquired, probably in Henrician times, the right to the so-called great tithes and who was obligated to keep the chancel in good repair) and certain other landholders with easements (someone who owned a house, for example, whose cellar had been incorporated into the fabric of the church back in the mists of time), no one had a right to a particular burial place. There was also neither an individual freehold property nor even a set-term lease in whatever grave one might have; the place of the poorest of the poor was in this regard no less secure than that of the rich, although custom from time immemorial, enforceable through litigation, protected the latter much more carefully than the former. Fees were decidedly not statutory but rather were rooted in the history of each parish. Clergy making a claim for payment in disputed cases had to first prove in a common law court that a certain customary fee existed and that the fees were appropriate under the facts of the case at hand. Having proven custom and propriety, they had then to try to collect what was due through the ecclesiastical courts. Fees were regulated by the ordinary—the incumbent's ecclesiastical superior—and, although they clearly did reflect supply and demand of burial places or areas within the church or churchyard, they had to do it circumstantially. Parishioners making claims to burial had a similar burden. The market in places for the dead was thus very much regulated by the overarching principle that the parish churchyard and the fabric of the church belonged to a narrowly bound community of the living that was refracted in an equally bounded community of the dead.

In 1820, as the old order was on the verge of collapse, the Consistory Court of London—an ecclesiastic court that heard, among other matters, probate cases—was called on to decide a case that turned on precisely the relationship between the rights of the private dead, on the one hand, and the community of the dead, on the other, while making manifest how muddled the land law of the dead really was. It arose because the churchwardens of St. Andrew Holborn refused to allow the iron-coffined body of one Mary Gilbert into the churchyard (that is, not in the church itself, where the vicar might have had a say, but into the common ground that the churchwardens administered purportedly in the community's interest). Mary's husband, John Gilbert, first tried to get a writ of mandamus from the Court of King's Bench to compel the wardens and parochial priest to bury his wife in her iron coffin, which suggests that his lawyers hoped his demand might be construed as a matter of customary right. (A writ of mandamus is a common law remedy, issued in the name of the Crown, in which a higher court commands a lower official to meet his basic obligations.)

Gilbert's lawyer argued that Mary was a parishioner and thus "generally has a right to a place in the churchyard" and that the material of which the coffin in which she was to be buried had been constructed was, or in any case should be, irrelevant. The coffin was made, he said, of thin plates of wrought iron, one-twelfth of an inch thick, and was thus smaller than the usual wooden coffin. Iron rusts and is no less liable to decay than wood; and in any case, since the churchwardens admitted lead coffins, they had no right to refuse iron ones. But most important, he claimed that there existed a private right to the supposedly common ground.

Although admittedly no living parishioner had a prospective right to any particular place in the churchyard, Mary's dead body had such a right: "once death and interment had taken place then there is a severance of the common property—the general right has become a particular right." This follows, the plaintiff argued, from the right to inviolable sepulture, "one of the dearest and most ancient rights of mankind": *requiescat in pace*. In fact, he continued, it is precisely to preserve this right that parishioners had the duty to repair the churchyard. In short, the earth surrounding a corpse belonged to it "till the time comes when appropriation cannot be maintained," which will be at so remote a time that its extinction really cannot be contemplated. A grave is forever, he argued, with a certain common-sense logic based on the idea that the dead subsist in timelessness. As John Dunton, a late-seventeenth-century writer and magazine publisher, put it, harkening back to Horace and forward to Alexander and beyond, a man subsists in his grave in an unchanging present tense until the Resurrection. One might say, "This was his brother—That was his building—This was his Garden . . . but if we go to the Church-yard, where his body lies, 'tis said this IS HIS GRAVE."[89]

Messrs. Boyer and Buzzard, the churchwardens who rejected Mary Gilbert in her iron coffin, based their defense on the rejection of the principle that a body could hold a grave in perpetuity (that it could have an absolute claim on a particular—not just any—grave) and on disputing one fact: that iron decomposes at roughly the same rate as wood. This was relevant, they argued, because a long-lasting coffin was essentially an assertion of a private right that they were duty-bound to oppose in order to protect the communal rights of which they were the guardians. That is, they objected to the principle that "the appropriation of ground for each party of interment is for ever." All that was required, they rejoined, was that "the body be kept unmolested till it decay." And they maintained on public policy grounds that if a sizable number of parishioners started to bury in metal coffins, given "their imperishable nature," there would very soon be no space available at all in the already tiny and crowded churchyards. The court took the occasion to offer a detailed historical gloss on the right to specific modes of burial. It began by pointing out that uncoffined funerals were once not uncommon in England; old tables of church fees made clear that such burials in a shroud alone were charged less than coffined ones.[90] South American Christians continued to bury only in shrouds, the court said. The law, it held, certainly "says a parishioner has a right to burial in his own parish churchyard," but this does not convey the further right to bury a box or chest containing that body.

That said, the court admitted that all sorts of laudable feelings might make one want to put a loved one in a box. However much we may feign unconcern about what happens to the body after death, few of us have the firmness not to care at all. It is painful to contemplate the "total and complete extinction of the remains of those who were justly dear" to us; and certainly it is understandable that we would want to prevent spoliations of the dead—presumably the trepidations of grave robbers. An iron coffin is thus not an unreasonable thing to want and it is admissible to churchyards. But—and here is the critical point—it is not admissible on the same terms as wooden coffins. Equal treatment, the court held, would give credence to the more general, and spurious, argument advanced by the petitioner's counsel: that "ground once given to the interment of a body is appropriated for ever to that body," that the grave is not only *domus ultima* but also *domus aeterna*, whatever the tenant's condition. If this were true, then the permanence of the iron coffin, on the one hand, and the corruptibility of a body exposed to the wet earth, on the other, would indeed be irrelevant distinctions; both should pay similar fees.

But the learned judge went out of his way in this much-cited and admired opinion to deny the very notion of "one body, one space" and the possibility of owning a piece of the churchyard. (Both would be central features of the modern cemetery.) There can be, he says, no inextinguishable title belonging to a perishable thing: no "perpetuity of possession." "Man" and "forever" are incompatible terms. "The time must come when his posthumous remains must mingle with and compose a part of the soil in which they were deposited." The idea that it was the living who held a freehold in a grave plot in a churchyard, as they would be able to in a cemetery, was not even contemplated. The doctrine of a *domus aeterna*, at least with respect to a body in a churchyard, is thus "a mere flourish of rhetoric."[91]

Of course, bodies may decompose at different rates, depending on soil, climate, exposure, embalming, and so forth, but that is not relevant to the legal doctrine: the parish churchyard and, by extension, the soil in the church itself cannot belong to any individual. It is not "the exclusive property of one generation now departed." It is, the judge repeats, not *res unius aestatis*—something for a season—but rather "the common property of the living, and of generations yet unborn, and subject only to temporary appropriation." Over time various people have been given the distinction of exclusive title, but this is not something to be encouraged. Even brick graves—increasingly fashionable in the eighteenth century—were "an aggression upon the *common* freehold interest" and their use "carries the pretensions of the dead" to such an extent that they impinge on the rights of the living. Lead coffins were no better, but their costliness and the customarily high fees for their interment made them less of a problem.

The churchwardens were therefore vindicated: the individual rights claim of John Gilbert infringed on the rights of the community. But such trespass was not new; monuments inside and outside the church took away from a communal good but were allowed for a price. The remaining question for the court was therefore how much should Gilbert's particular and novel infringement—a long-lasting iron coffin—cost. Setting a price—and here we enter into a world of explicit economic calculation that one does not find earlier—depended, the judge held, on the facts, specifically on the differential decomposition rates of various materials. A discussion of the decomposition rates of bodies was not new. It was common enough in the sixteenth century to be put by Shakespeare into the mouth of clowns: "I' faith, if he be not rotten before he die—as we have many pocky corpses now-a-days, that will scarce hold the laying in—he will last you some eight year or nine year: a tanner will last you nine year," explains one grave digger to Hamlet during their talk about the skull of the jester Yorick. The sort of learned discussion that the judge entered into in order to set a price on a parishioner's infringement of the common rights of other parishioners is suggestive of the challenges of an explicit market in graves to the informal market of the old regime. "The declared opinions of eminent professors of chemistry" were of no help, he wrote. "These disagree, as is not infrequent." There were too many variables to allow the court to determine a universally true ratio. In dry climates like Egypt, wood and metal seem to endure forever, whereas in England—the judge notes that Charles I's coffin was much decayed despite being encased in lead—the situation was quite different. There was the quality of water to consider: wood can survive for a very long time submerged, as for example the Conway stakes in the Thames, which were supposedly set by Caesar, or the piers under Trajan's bridge in the Danube. But he also cited other archeological evidence—more relevant for this case—from ancient British burial sites in which metal artifacts are unearthed while "no particle of wood remains." And so, he concludes, charging ten times as much for metal as for wood was reasonable.[92]

Messrs. Boyer and Buzzard did not contest John Gilbert's efforts to bury his wife in an iron coffin because of an abstract interest in the communal rights of the parish dead. They wanted the extra income that came from being allowed to take into account the material of a coffin in setting their fees. They had done this before. But this whole arcane proceeding does make clear how very local the churchyard was and how much it was governed by tradition and custom. The common law court in this case responded that while it might be able to compel a clergyman to bury a parishioner—this was the ancient civil right—it could not compel burial in any specific manner.

Ten years later, in 1830, King's Bench similarly refused to issue a writ of mandamus to compel the rector of Stoke Damerel, near Plymouth in Davenport, to bury the son of a parishioner who had, in 1805, after paying all due license fees, built a family vault at considerable expense in the churchyard. At first the dispute over opening the vault was over the payment of a fee, but when the petitioner finally agree to pay what the rector asked—the body of his son had gone unburied for months—the rector still refused. The court said it could do nothing: "The clergyman is bound by law to bury the corpses of parishioners in the churchyard. . . . Mr. Blackmore had no legal right to insist on burying the corpse in any particular part of the churchyard." King's Bench would also not issue a writ of mandamus to compel a clergyman to bury someone near someone else.[93]

Little more than a decade later, Mr. Gilbert could have bought his wife a freehold in Highgate or Kensal Green cemeteries and put her in any kind of coffin he wanted without leave from anyone. Litigation is evidence of the pressures on the old regime, but also of the old regime's persistence and power. So too the intense demand for one's rightful place and for a proper burial in the face of exclusion and ignominy. "To be buried like a dog"—that is, to be buried as Diogenes the Dog Philosopher wanted to be buried in a gesture of rebellion against all that was decent, customary, and human—was the abyss.

THE RIGHT TO BURIAL
AND THE CRISIS OF THE OLD REGIME

The site of the revolutionary new regime of the dead was the cemetery; its promise of liberty, landscaping, and cosmopolitanism helped bring down the old. But the old regime also conspired in its own demise through its unbending resistance to change. The High Church architect Augustus Welby Pugin was right about his countrymen's "natural repugnance to separating the burial places of English Churchmen from the sacred precincts in which they and their forefathers had worshipped for many generations." "Churchmen" meant not just those formally adhered to the Church of England but also those who, whatever their views, regarded the churchyard as theirs. By excluding others—real or imagined enemies— conservatives of the old regime more or less forced the state to dismantle the thousand-year-old legal infrastructure that had sustained the churchyard. They were in a sense the agents of history, as they made the paradoxes of the old regime in a pluralist society unsustainable. But even as the churchyard declined, its cultural purchase did not, as it became emblematic of the world that had been lost.

Englishmen had for a very long time felt the rejection of their dead acutely, both at home and abroad. Parishioners in early-seventeenth-century Oxfordshire broke into the chancel of the Holton parish church to bury in the most sacred part of the building the body of a woman, Elizabeth Horseman, who was regarded by the vicar and higher authorities as excommunicated (to wit, a Catholic), but who was considered a member of the community by her fellow parishioners. The supporters of his Catholic majesty the exiled Old Pretender James

III made much of his ability to gain from the papacy permission to bury the bodies of Protestant members of his court in a specially designated cemetery in Rome. If he could create a space for these dead, they argued, he could be trusted to rule over a religiously pluralistic Great Britain. (It was the High Church party in England, born of the refusal of some clergy to recognize the ouster of the Pretender's father, James II, that fought most strenuously in the eighteenth and nineteenth centuries to keep their churchyards pure.) Edward Young's hugely influential "Night Thoughts on Life, Death and Immortality" (1742) "distilled his tears into song" after his stepdaughter died in Lyon and her body, as the "dust of a Protestant," was refused burial in Catholic soil. Actually, it was refused burial only by day, but the rejection still offended Young greatly.[94]

But these, and many of the battles recounted in this section, were small-scale compared with the Enlightenment scandals of old regime France. There was nothing in England comparable to the highly charged and scandalous negotiations over the burial of religiously suspect *philosophes*. There was no La Mettrie, no Voltaire, no Diderot. Hume was the closest there was within the English cultural orbit. The Anglican Church was too weak, the standards for admission to the churchyard too low, and respectable alternatives too plentiful for there to be major scandals about the bodies of important public figures threatened with the lime pit. But the right of ordinary parishioners to a place in the churchyard and the right to have the Burial Service for the Dead read at the gravesite were bitterly contentious in the eighteenth and nineteenth centuries in the way that only small wrongs in small places often become. Claims on the parish churchyard, the only churchyard, the churchyard of the Established Church, remained urgent in an age of religious pluralism when the idea of the singleness of civil and ecclesiastical authority was but a distant dream. The old regime had deep roots in law, custom, and the hearts even of its enemies.

As we have seen, common and ecclesiastical law gave every corpse a place: the churchyard of the parish in which the person had lived or where she died. The sixty-eighth canon of the Anglican Church put a high burden on the incumbent to prove that a body should not be allowed in the churchyard. The presumption of right was with the dead body. And there was a skein of local customs that gave bodies still more claims—to be buried near one's kin, to have a particular spot inside the church. But control over how its rights were exercised rested entirely in the hands of the incumbent. He could, as the gatekeeper of this communal space that was at the same time a consecrated space, question whether a body met the standards of the canon. He also held a monopoly on the Office for the Dead, that is, on the burial service as prescribed in the Book of Common Prayer. And, since no other services could be read over a grave in the churchyard, he could (or at least could claim to) deny the dead and the living words of hope and comfort.

As the freeholder, he could also—or could claim to—control the movement of the body within the sacred precincts. The Office gave him the option of taking a body inside the church before burial in the churchyard; it prescribed, but did not insist, on his meeting it at the churchyard gate; it seemed to allow him to deny it entirely entry through the proper gate. We have already seen that, *mutatis mutandi*, he could also allocate burial space and relegate unfavored corpses to the obscure north corner in what was taken to be an unconsecrated shameful place. So, while common law and ecclesiastical law seemed to guarantee a grave in the churchyard to everyone, the ecclesiastical law of the State Church, and some common law courts as well, made the clergy the exclusive arbiter of how these rights would be exercised. Without the incumbent's cooperation, the most that a rejected body could hope for was to be put in the ground—usually on the north, wrongly believed to be unconsecrated, side—without ritual or prayer.

The new cemeteries of the nineteenth century offered a resolution to this tension by offering an alternative that rejected history. The dead now had their choice: consecrated ground deeply imbricated in an ancient place under the Church's religious jurisdiction or a place open to anyone, which made no pretense of representing a local community of the dead, and which offered, in most cases, consecrated as well as unconsecrated ground, was administered by a private company or municipal agency, and had no more reason for being where it was than those that dictated the location of an insurance office or railway station. Burial places belonging to Dissenting or Methodist chapels offered another option: churchyards by another name but restricted to a narrow constituency. But in thousands of towns and villages, cemeteries were geographically and, more important, culturally distant; in some of the most bitter nineteenth-century controversies, one of more than a thousand denominational burial grounds was close at hand. Despite this, for many, and especially for the poor and humble—"the rude ancestors"—the churchyard remained the place where their dead belonged.

The history of the freeing of the churchyard from the State Church through legal reforms belongs in the next chapter. It is about the civil rights of corpses, regardless of their beliefs. Rev. Walter Camberlain, vicar of St. John's Bolton and a bitter enemy of such rights, goes to the heart of the matter: Dissenters claimed that "our churchyards" "belong to the nation," that in disputes about burial "the rights of the nation are in dispute," that a grave was "a national right," to be enjoyed by "communities of whatever kind." As the conservative Anglican clergy became ever more hostile to these "civil rights" and to the world that they represented, proponents of a more open churchyard became more stridently anticlerical. The Society for the Liberation of Religion from State Patronage and Control fought against what it called the "post-mortem Test Act," to which some bodies were subject in the same way as a series of Test Acts going back to 1673—and finally repealed in 1828—had limited the civil rights of those who refused communion in the Anglican Church. Their aim was to open the churchyard to bodies of whatever persuasion, to clergymen of all denominations, and to prayers of any sort or to the option of no prayers at all. They ultimately succeeded, the triumphant end to a story about the rise of civil liberties and secular society through the creation of a new class of the dead.[95]

There is nothing wrong with this view, but it is something like a Freudian screen memory, a cover for a deeper and more disruptive history. Battles for a place in the churchyard were for a very long time not about civil rights or secularism. The right to have a body met at the gate, to have it enter the church before it is put in the ground, to have the Office of the Dead guide its movements, to hear the talismanic words of the sixteenth-century Book of Common Prayer as it is covered by dirt—are evidence for the persistence of the old regime and not only of its end. In this sense Chamberlain was wrong. He, like so many of his brethren, did not recognize how much religion there was in his parishioners. They did not attend Sunday services; they had no interest in being catechized. But they did have deep feelings for the sanctity of the church and churchyard; they believed that to be properly buried was to be buried in the canonically prescribed way. Most disputed cases began not with the demand for alternative prayers or for no prayers, or for alternative clergy or for unconsecrated ground, but for the incumbent to do his duty: to bury the dead of his parish as law and custom required. Disputants sought a real or figurative writ of mandamus to compel an Anglican clergyman to do his duty. The continued insistence on this right through the eighteenth and nineteenth centuries bears witness to the ideal of a local democracy of the dead that was the foundation for the moral vision of Gray's "Elegy" and was resonant among ordinary people well into an age when it might have seemed completely illusory.

Each microdispute, whether it swirled around local antipathies, pride, hurt feelings, and pent-up resentments or focused on purportedly serious theological reasons a corpse did not qualify for burial according to the sixty-eighth canon, was about this: who was (or was not) one of "our" dead and thus, more generally, who was among the "we" of the parish or of the world beyond. These disputes fell into two broad categories. The first was born of antagonisms between an incumbent and his parishioners in which the fate of the dead came to represent the rights and wrongs of a relationship that demanded a great deal of negotiation and compromise. These were like marital disputes: the details differ but there are a limited number of issues to be fought over; seemingly inconsequential disagreements explode into profound chasms. The second were framed from the start as principled disputes about what did and what did not constitute entry into the community of the parish: was so-called lay baptism valid as a rite of passage into the *res Christiani?* On one side of this question were those who believed that to be an Independent or a Presbyterian or a Baptist or Methodist of some sort was not to forfeit membership in either the parish or the larger community of Christians. On the other were clergymen who thought that these people were not Christian in the sense of the sixty-eighth canon and, in addition, that they were actively subversive of local and national order. They were not only outsiders but dangerous outsiders. Keeping their dead out of the churchyard was thus, in their view, a principled defense of the parish, the national Church, and the nation. For two centuries the dead body was endlessly provocative.

To paraphrase *Anna Karenina*, "every unhappy parish is unhappy in its own way." For example, 18 May 1764: Thomas Bliss, the incumbent of Haworth, near Bradford (this would, fifty years later, be the parish of Patrick Brontë, father of three remarkable daughters), writes an anguished four-page letter to his ordinary, the archbishop of York, defending himself against what he fears is a suit against him in ecclesiastical court. The father of a child, "long ago and now excommunicated" and reputed to be a thief, came to him at two o'clock one day and demanded that he bury his daughter before four. (There was by then no effective excommunication for laity and so Bliss must have meant only that he had not come to Easter communion.) The child had died of smallpox, and although Bliss agreed to read the service at the grave, he refused, as he thought was his right, to allow the body into the church. "But my child shall go in," insisted the father. We don't know what happened next, but when Bliss came to the churchyard the next day, he found the corpse in its grave and an angry father threatening legal action. He had the grave opened at the behest of the grandfather—a man who, according to Bliss, was irreligious, never came to church, and later interrupted another burial service—and read a service over it. The rest of the letter is a protestation of his innocence and an affirmation of his standing in the parish. The archbishop assures him he did nothing wrong. But more interesting here is the passion that the right to a proper burial raised among the ordinary and supposedly irreligious poor.[96]

Or, 21 February 1767: This time the archbishop was not so understanding. The dispute was with a parishioner of considerable social standing and exposed the compromises and ambiguities that maintained the old regime of the churchyard and that his Grace probably had no interest in disturbing. On that Saturday, the vicar of the small parish of Broughton in the West Riding of Yorkshire (now North Yorkshire) sat down to write his ordinary a pained and not altogether coherent letter. The immediate reason was that Rev. Gay was being sued in King's Bench—that is, in a secular court—for his failure to allow the burial of, as he puts it, an "opulent Papist's" dead child in the Church and needed help in mounting a defense. There was some urgency in the matter because the child remained unburied. We do not know the whole chronology, but it extended over months and had a long back story.

The "opulent Papist" in question was Stephen Walter Tempest, scion of an old gentry family that went back to the days of Edward I and that had famously remained Catholic after the Elizabethan settlement. He was thus deeply of the place and at the same time not. Three years before the current controversy, a child "at nurse" (that is, old enough to have been baptized) died; Tempest himself went to the sexton and demanded that he make a grave in the church; the sexton did as he was told although he ought to have asked the incumbent's permission; the child was conveyed there by Tempest's own priest and presumably buried with Catholic prayers.

A year later another child died, this one "dead born," and was carried to the family grave even though, Gay writes, "no Protestant parishioner has ever been permitted to place such a Birth in a common burying place even in the yard." It would normally have gone to the northern fringes of the churchyard with the other dangerous dead—the suicides, the vagrants, the otherwise unsettled. Gay's claim—or rather the custom he reports—had no doctrinal foundations; the north side was still consecrated ground, but it was safely away from the more benign dead. On the other hand, Tempest did have a claim to put the baby where he wanted. He had a property right in his family burial place, although of a peculiar and ambiguous sort (see the previous section in this chapter, "The Economics of Churchyard Burial"); it could not be alienated and could not be defended at law but was a right all the same. Burial in a specific part of the church or churchyard was wholly at the discretion of the incumbent who held the freehold.

Finally—and this brings us to the point of the lawsuit—another child of Tempest and his wife, Frances Olive née Meynell, died. Gay refused it entry, demanded a proper certificate of baptism, and said that he would give way only if "the Rights, rules, and usages" of the Church in matters of interment were observed (that is, he would get his fees whether he attended the burial or not because the infant Tempest was one of the parish's and hence "his" dead). Finally, Gay adds, the family's priest had been busy "perverting" this and neighboring parishes. If someone like Tempest has "unlimited right and power to convey what and who he pleases" into the church, he warns darkly, neither he nor his parishioners can be safe. This is a dog's breakfast of self-justification: the claim for fees whether a service was rendered or not, the claim to adjudicate who was or was not baptized and hence eligible for church burial, the thorny question of private versus communal rights (Temple claimed to own the family vault), and hanging over it all the problem of religious pluralism: what to do with Christians not in communion with the Anglican Church. To Gay, control over the community of the dead was central to the orderly functioning of the community of the living.

The archbishop's secretary clearly has interest neither in Gay's whining nor in sorting all this out. "As far as your letter is intelligible . . . ," begins the archbishop's reply. Of course, Tempest has a right to a burying place in the church. In fact, he points out, an early-seventeenth-century statute (I Jac. Cap v), which compels Catholics to conform to Anglican practices, mandates that Tempest be buried there or in the churchyard on penalty of £20 levied on his estate. Section xv of this statute is a bit more ambiguous in how it might be read in this case. It demands of recusants that they be buried in a church or churchyard "according to the ecclesiastical laws of the land," in which case Tempest would not have been allowed his own priest or, probably, a claim on a particular place. Furthermore, the archbishop's clerk continues, Gay had been given proper notice of the hour when the corpse was coming to the church and thus had no excuse for not showing up and performing his duties. It is not clear what these would have been. And as for fees for burials, "the customs of the parish must be the rule." This too was not so clear. But the archbishop did not want to get involved in a fight with an important local family and had no interest in the squabbles of one of his overzealous and controversy-prone clergy. But we can have some sympathy for Gay because he was at the front line of the battle over precisely what community of the living—what history—the dead in the churchyard represented.[97]

These sorts of conflicts have a long afterlife. They are generally short on theological content and long on differences between communal rights, on the one hand, and clerical rights, on the other. There must have been lots of these in a world in which people and their parish priest were often stuck with each other for life. Like the disputes of an unhappily married couple in an age before divorce, each little contretemps would be remembered the next time. Nothing was too petty or too nasty. Sometimes it was not just the clergyman who was at fault. On 24 June 1808, the Dissenting Deputies received a letter complaining that Rev. Mr. Owen, curate of Melbourne Park, had refused to bury the body of a poor woman on any day other than Sunday within the week she died, although her mother had explicitly requested it be on Saturday instead. Upon inquiry by the bishop of Bath and Wells, to whom the deputies took the case, it turned out that the curate had been quietly doing his duty for twenty-three years and that his refusal in this case was the result of an earlier takeover by Dissenters of the choir gallery for a funeral on a weekday when there were few people around. They wanted to sing their own hymns. The case was dropped.[98]

Often quarrels did not end so peacefully. There were no higher principles at stake; they bear witness to how seriously ordinary people took their claim on the churchyard and its rituals when it was denied. A real or perceived wrong to a corpse was an act of war. The case of Cowley, near Oxford, is a *locus classicus*. In the week before 5 November 1871, Benjamin Bullock, a seventy-five-year-old laborer, died. Notice was given to the parish clerk that his friends and widow hoped to bury him in the churchyard on Sunday and requested that the incumbent read the Service for the Dead. In a loaned cart and accompanied by his aged widow and six bearers, the body duly arrived as the congregation were leaving. Then the trouble began. Rev. James Coley refused the body entry into the church and began reading, not the full but only the second part of the burial service at the graveside while the body was elsewhere. Efforts to reach a compromise failed. Coley claimed that it was his policy to read only an abbreviated service for Sunday burials; Bullock's friends, backed by a crowd of angry parishioners, argued that this was contrary to custom and especially injurious to the poor, who tended to bury their dead on the Sabbath. The bearers left the corpse in the church and retired. By now the crowd outside had reached four or five hundred; it began to throw dirt clods at Coley; a constable intervened before anyone was hurt. The next day, with different bearers in attendance, he agreed to read the full service. But this was not the end. On Wednesday, a large crowd gathered at the local pub to burn him in effigy. A figure, dressed in gown and cap, was suspended from a pole with a rope around its neck and burned on the village green. The next Sunday, eight men in black appeared at services, along with a large crowd from Cowley and surrounding villages. They were, it was said, in mourning for the effigy. The leader of all this was a local character named Frederick "Moses" Merrick.[99]

Four years later, Merrick died. Twice Rev. Coley was asked to bury his body. Twice he refused it so much as entry to the churchyard. Clearly, Merrick was no saint, and Coley had reason to hate him because of the effigy incident in 1871 and because of what appears to have been many years of antagonism between the incumbent and the common folks of his parish. Merrick was famous locally as a slow underhand bowler, as a man who liked to quote scripture (hence his nickname Moses), and as someone who liked the pub. But saint or not, he had, beyond question, been baptized in the Anglican Church. When a committee of parishioners came to insist on the burial, Coley locked himself in the house. A large crowd gathered; a policeman escorted him to safety. By the ninth day of the standoff, with Moses' body still above ground, parishioners appealed to the bishop and the sanitary authorities, a new twist to an old story. The bishop ordered Coley to do his duty, and he more or less did it by asking Rev. Mr. Green, vicar of Littlemore, to take the service.

The hapless Rev. Green now found himself trying to perform only the minimal service in the churchyard, as Coley had commissioned him to do, while he was confronted by a thousand people crying for more. The body was at the gate; the church was locked; the crowd shouted, "We'll have him in the church," and "Take him to the church." Green tried to ignore them and to read the truncated service; the cortège made its way insistently up the path toward the church and pressed the hapless Green into the church. He tried to move sideways toward the grave but was blocked; he was trapped. As things began to turn really ugly, he agreed to read the full service inside the church if he could but get in: Coley had not given him the keys. At this point, there were calls for a pickaxe; someone brought a sledgehammer. Just as men were getting ready to smash down the door, voices were heard from inside; a dozen men with crowbars had broken in through the belfry door on the northern side and were in the process of removing the locks from the main, west one. Merrick's corpse, now dead almost two weeks, triumphantly entered the church, the service was read, the body was buried, and a vote of thanks taken to Rev. Mr. Green. Police guarded Coley's house that night. It had taken a riot to get the dead old Moses into his rightful place in what the community believed to be the proper manner: in accord with the Anglican Office of the Dead.[100]

A whole other set of acrimonious disputes over the fate of dead bodies speaks to a more fundamental issue: a persistent demand by ordinary people to belong in death to the local Christian community of the churchyard and a growing resistance by a small but articulate number of the clergy not to allow in those who in life had been less than zealous adherents of the national Church. By the middle of the nineteenth century, close to half of England were in their eyes not fellow Christians but schismatics, excommunicants, who had no place in the churchyard. In litigation over burial, long-buried and seemingly anachronistic issues of religious controversy—the dangers of rebaptism, the contested liturgy of the Book of Common Prayer, the thunderbolt of excommunication, the civil functions of priests—were all suddenly unearthed, reanimated revenants of the English Reformation. For a brief moment, conflicting Victorian interpretations of the Tudor–Stuart era assumed seemingly apocalyptic significance; litigation became an act of historiography, sending lawyers skittering to the archives to fight for the soul of English Christianity. Only a few steps lie between great questions of political theology and acrimonious local quarrels about the fate of a corpse. Here is one way in which the distance shrank.

On 9 October 1794, an obscure discussion group of evangelical Anglican clergy in Elland, a market town in the West Riding of Yorkshire, determined that "Baptism by Lay persons and Dissenting Ministers is illegal." Why, one might ask, did they care and, more puzzling, why did they come to what is historically a radically restrictive view of what constituted legitimate baptism? There had been a heated debate in the sixteenth and seventeenth centuries about whether Christians should be baptized as infants or, as some Reformation sects held, should wait until they were adults. But that question had long been unambiguously resolved in the Anglican Church, *vide* article 27 of the Thirty-Nine Articles: the answer endorses infant baptism, because nothing is required to be incorporated in the body of Christ beyond the sacrament itself. There had been debates about immersion versus sprinkling, about one or several immersions, about whether the clergyman had to make the sign of the cross. All were settled by the early seventeenth century and were largely what the Church called "matter indifferent."[101]

There was one sense in which 1604, the year the Canons of the Church of England were promulgated, might still be relevant to our clerical debating society, but they would not have known it. The printed account of the conference only suggests that King James insisted on baptism by lawful clergymen. Later printed evidence suggests he softened his views. But a manuscript account of the 1604 Hampton Court conference, discovered in the early twentieth century, shows just how strongly James felt on the subject. He was not, however, specifically interested in excluding non-Anglican clergy—there were none—but rather in excluding women. According to this record, James said, "He had lief his child were baptized by an ape as by a woman." When told that if he banned baptisms by women "all antiquity would be overthrown," James responded, as a good Protestant, "that as well might they by color of antiquity bring in prayer for the dead." When the bishop of Peterborough then offered an ancient example of a baptism *in extremis* being performed with sand instead of water, the king answered in his inimitable style, "A turd for the argument, he might as well have pissed on them, for that had been more liker to water than sand." There followed two hours of debate, and "at the last it was concluded that none should baptize but ministers, and that if the fathers did require it in time of danger of death, the ministers should come home and baptize their children." So, in some ways a strict interpretation of the language of 1604 Canons supports the men of Elland and others who refused to bury those who they thought were not properly baptized. But little else does.[102]

In fact, the sacrament was not particularly fraught either before or after 1604—until the burial controversies of the eighteenth century, when conservatives who favored the old regime felt threatened and used it to support their cause. In the context of defending the validity of baptism by women and by all sorts of other "irregular" persons, no less an authority than the great Richard Hooker (1554–1600), one of the founding fathers of Anglicanism, had set down the principle that "the fruit of Baptisme dependeth onely upon the covenant which God hath Made." Nor was there ever, he also argued, a need for rebaptism. Augustine, in his battle against the Donatists, had made the same point. And practice accorded with this theological principle. People who were baptized during the interregnum, 1649–1660, when there was no Anglican Church, were considered baptized once the king was back and the Church reestablished. As a nineteenth-century court pointed out, references in support of a very broad view of the validity of baptism by almost anyone "would be endless." No one, with the exception of a tiny number of Unitarians (Socinians, as they were called), argued about the formula: "I baptize you in the name of the Father, and the Son, and the Holy Ghost." And after 1662, when religious bodies outside the Anglican Church came to be officially recognized, the 1604 phrase "none but ministers," born of a time when there was only one kind, became meaningless.[103]

So why did the men of the Elland Clerical Society, who were neither lawyers nor theologians, worry about the legality of particular baptisms? Their debate on 3 October 1800 suggests an answer that returns us to the rights of the dead. That Friday, the Society took up the same question they had discussed five years earlier, but this time in a much more precise form and one that begins to make clear what was really at stake: "Whether a child baptized by an un-ordained Methodist and brought to church should be baptized again?" "*Yes*," was the answer, the word underlined in the minutes of their meeting. It was a pastoral question then, but again one wonders why it mattered. Re-baptism was almost unheard of in the English church. But then comes a related matter: "Whether one, in the same circumstances, shou'd be admitted to Christian burial?" "Majority answer. NO." Capital letters are in the text, as if the secretary wanted to emphasize that, even if not everyone was in agreement, they really meant NO. Here in miniature a great battle was joined; there were thousands and tens of thousands of children as well as grown-ups who could be kept from a proper burial if this "no" was sustained.

These men were not High Church conservatives; they were men of roughly the same theological persuasion as John Wesley. They could not have believed that, from a theological perspective, someone who had not been baptized by a priest was really unbaptized. But they did understand that a new sort of religious community was coming into being and with it a new sort of dead body, both of the community and not. These were the dead they could not suffer to have in their churchyards, the dead who spoke for an emerging world that seemed to the clergymen of Yorkshire dangerously out of kilter. It was men like these and their even more strident successors who did more to destroy the old regime than the advocates of civil rights—by excluding many of its dead.[104]

Disputing baptism was their only real weapon of exclusion. Excommunication was no longer viable in the eighteenth century because the category was either too broad (it included all Dissenters and Catholics) or too narrow (it was not applicable to the laity). Suicide was of limited use because many disputed burial cases involved young children, and because the number of suicides in the population as a whole was small, three or four to eight per hundred thousand, depending on age and sex, and increasingly because coroner's juries were ever more reluctant to return a verdict of *felo de se* as they sat in judgment over the bodies of people who had killed themselves. In practice, denying that a body was that of a baptized

Christian was the only plausible ground to exclude it from the community of Christians. It did not belong.

The men of Elland were not being disingenuous when they debated what counted as a valid baptism, but the stakes for them were not some abstract questions about the rites of entry into the body of Christ but what to do about the dead who, in their view, were not "theirs." Baptism mobilized corpses in the culture wars of the age, mostly with Dissent but also with those who would forgive suicide under some misguided modern ideas about madness or despair. At about the time when Parliament in 1808 passed a law that required that the bodies of sailors washed ashore should be assumed to be baptized and given a proper burial in the nearest parish churchyard, the validity of the actual, documented baptism of well-known neighbors became a way for some clergymen to keep them out.[105]

"Baptized by an *un-ordained Methodist*" thus points to the broader context of the Elland discussion. John Wesley (1703–1791), his brother Charles, and many others of the early Methodist leadership were, unambiguously, ordained Anglican priests. However irritating they might have been to their colleagues, they were clergy in the apostolic succession who could legitimately perform baptism, celebrate the Eucharist, and in every way function ritually as would any other clergymen. (The run-ins they had with the authorities had to do with unlicensed preaching and other putative administrative violations.) He and the first generation of the Connection's leadership were also careful to not compete directly in their ministry with the Established Church. They tried not to meet during hours of Anglican service; they did not set up an alternative institutional structure to that of the Church in which they were ordained. All this changed on 27 July 1795. On that day, the Wesleyan Connection took a decisive step, one that it had been moving toward after the founder's death and that Wesley himself had prepared when he ordained two missionaries in 1784 to send to America: they declared that the Connection could ordain clergymen and that they could openly administer the Lord's supper and the sacrament of baptism in their meetinghouses.

From the very beginning, Wesley had been seen as a threat, less because of his theology than because of his travels. He was constantly on the road, the very opposite of the parish priest. The world, he said, was his parish, not the bounded autarchic community clustered around a church and a churchyard. This mobility, a kind of indigenous cosmopolitanism, as Max Weber recognized, is what made Wesleyanism a solvent of the old regime. Wesley's enemies understood this well before Weber articulated it theoretically, which is why he and his preachers were driven from parish after parish by pro-Church mobs led by their clergy. He had meant by "the world is my parish" only that the actions of the Holy Spirit did not recognize parish borders and that therefore those who preached the Word ought not to either. He had not directly challenged the authority of the parish clergy.

But now his followers did. For the evangelical clergymen debating in a small town in the West Riding of Yorkshire, the Methodist dead now seemed no longer their dead—the dead of the parish; they had become strangers. They were, from their perspective, the unbaptized dead and hence the dead not in communion with the Church. The enemy dead: a man whose child the rector of Belton refused to bury in 1808 was not a Dissenter with, perhaps, some rights, but "a deluded, infatuated and ignorant disciple of the lowest description of Methodist." "A Sectarian is a mutineer," as a clerical enemy of the Methodists put it later in the century.[106]

And so, the long-settled question of what counted as baptism—the ritual of entry into the Christian community—became exigent because of the question of departure: what to do with the dead. On the one side were those who insisted on inclusion in the old regime; on the other side, those who believed that certain of the dead had forfeited their rights by publicly rejecting the Anglican Church. Disputes over burial had engaged the Protestant Dissenting Deputies, guardians of Old Dissent's civil liberties (that is, the rights of Baptists, Independents, and Presbyterians) for more than fifty years before the Elland debate. Unlike the early Methodists, whose status was ambiguous, these successors of those who had refused to go along with the restoration of the Anglican Church and its episcopacy were recognized religious bodies that were licensed and officially tolerated by the State. They had legally guaranteed rights, and the deputies existed to be sure they got them: rights having to do with marriage and testamentary matters, in a few instances rights to political participation, and finally the right to burial in the parish churchyard. The deputies spent twice as much time defending the claims of corpses as combating all the other disabilities from which Dissenters suffered combined. "Instances of the refusal by the clergy [to bury]," as an early history tells us, "were brought to the committee at almost every meeting."[107]

Most are from rural areas. In London, many Dissenters chose to be buried in Bunhill Fields near the great men of their tradition, near John Bunyan and George Fox and Daniel Defoe, as if these fierce critics of relics had themselves become the special dead. And in many cities and country towns, meetinghouses of the various denominations often had their own small burial grounds. But the great majority of Dissenters, as a matter of right and custom, expected that they and their children would be buried in or around the church of their parish. The living may have been out of communion with the national Church; the dead demanded their place in its churchyards. This some clergy refused on the only plausible ground available: that they were unbaptized and hence not Christian, and therefore excluded by the terms of the governing rubric—the sixty-eighth canon of the Anglican Church.

27 January 1747: Dr. Benjamin Avery, founding member and chair of the Dissenting Deputies from 1735 to 1764, reports that he had received a letter from

Mrs. Cooke of Newington in Lincolnshire about the case of the wife of Jonathan Everingham, who had died in childbirth but had been refused burial until she produced a baptismal certificate.

28 September, 1747: Dr. Avery read a letter from Mr. Cotton of the Isle of Wight relating to Dr. Fahoor's refusal to bury a child without a certificate of his being baptized.

30 November 1748: Dr. Avery read a letter from Mr. Harmon of Watesfield, Suffolk, complaining of the refusal by an incumbent to bury some Dissenters' children on the pretense of their not being baptized

After decades of advocacy, Dr. Avery retired, but refusals of burial, prayers, and the ringing of the passing bell continued to be his successor's single biggest item of business. We do not know whether there were more cases or simply more cases reported.[108]

In general, the Dissenting Deputies were reluctant to go to law to compel even the most contumacious clergyman to do his duty. Prosecuting a case in ecclesiastical court was expensive and, so it seemed to them, unnecessarily provocative. When they got a complaint they wrote first to the clergyman asking him to do his duty, and, if they got no satisfaction from him, they sent a delegation to wait on the recalcitrant priest's bishop and explain what had happened. Almost invariably they would be courteously received and would leave with the assurance that the offending clergyman would be told that he had no right to refuse burial and that he was not to do it again. By this time, the corpse was in the ground. We do not know if a service was ever read in most disputed cases.

But an egregious refusal to bury in 1798 prompted the Protestant Dissenting Deputies to mount a full ecclesiastical court challenge. On 27 April, they received a report that the curate of Coventry had refused to bury the child of "a poor man" and also "to ring the bell announcing the death as customary." His explanation was brutal: "Your child is no Christian," he told the boy's father; he would "not bury him nor shall anyone else." The parents eventually dug the grave for their son near his ancestors with their own hands and put the body into the grave without any sort of service. There seemed little hope in changing the curate's mind by appealing to his bishop: "I will bury no Dissenter. I will only bury Roman Catholics and Churchmen," he announced to those who had taken the side of the bereaved parents.[109]

In the face of this intransigence, the deputies sought a legal opinion that would publicly and definitively make clear what the law actually said about the right to burial in a churchyard and the reasons it might be denied. They asked one of the most distinguished jurists of the day, Sir William Scott (1745–1846), lord of the Admiralty Court (and formerly king's advocate general, the Crown's senior law adviser), for his views. He delivered an opinion that confirmed all that the deputies had been saying for most of the century. Scott began by inquiring into the facts, that is, into whether the Dissenters in question actually practiced baptism. The answer was yes. They believed infant baptism to be essential, they agreed with all the doctrinal points of the Anglican Thirty-Nine Articles relevant to the subject, and they used the same form as the Church of England, leaving out certain optional ceremonies. He then inquired into the history of baptism in the English Church and concluded that the material collected by, among others, Bishop William Fleetwood (1656–1723) supported the validity of the act no matter who said the words and sprinkled the water. In short, Scott concluded, the dead child had been baptized "in the sense and intention of the founders of our Litany and Rubric" and the vicar had acted "illegally and improperly in refusing to bury" the child. Scott suggested that this was probably not a case warranting public prosecution and advised that the deputies seek the "just censure of his ordinary."[110] This they did—repeatedly—but to no avail. In August 1808, they decided to take the further step of litigating a test case.

The facts were perfect. A Dissenting clergyman, Rev. John Green of Uppingham in Rutlandshire, wrote to complain that Rev. John Wight Wickes, rector of the parish of Wardley, had refused to read the Burial Service over the body of Hannah Swigler, the infant daughter of John and Mary Swigler, who were Dissenters in his parish. Both sides agreed that a "duly qualified" and state-licensed minister of their denomination—Calvinist Independents—had baptized Hannah as an infant. He had done so in the name of the Father, Son, and Holy Ghost. There was some dispute over whether Wickes had also demanded a fee of 3s.6d. for the service he had refused to read, but none that he had asked for 5s.6d. for breaking the ground, without payment of which he would completely bar the corpse from the churchyard, service or no service. He was not some obscure, impecunious country clergyman in need of every shilling but chaplain to the duke of Cumberland (one of the sons of George III) and author of a collection of sermons. The original complaint did not mention it, but it emerged in other documents that Wickes himself made public that he rejected the father's request for the ringing of the passing bell to announce the death of this child of poor laborers; his clerk had tried to persuade him to relent, but he was adamant in his refusal.

The chairman of the deputies first sent Wickes a copy of Scott's legal opinion but got no reply. He then wrote in the name of his committee to Wickes's ordinary, the bishop of Ely, and enclosed the original complaint, supporting materials, and again Scott's opinion. After reading the packet, the bishop forwarded it to Wickes, along with a note saying that he did indeed seem to be obliged to bury anyone who was baptized and that he especially regretted Wickes's taking a fee, whatever the reasons might have been for his refusal. Wickes was unrepentant.

He wrote, and simultaneously published, a letter to his bishop in which he denied nothing except that he had received 3s.6d. and that he had tried to keep little Hannah from getting a school prize because she was a Dissenter's child. In fact, he proudly proclaimed himself guilty as charged: he had refused to bury Hannah and for good reason: she was not "regularly baptized," because only an ordained priest can "*regularly* baptize." That was his defense based on his reading of Church law. But his political motivation in refusing to bury her corpse, though not germane to a discussion of the only reasons for not burying a parishioner allowed by the canon, makes clear why he was so insistent. Her people were enemies of the Church, whose demand for the Burial Service and a place in the churchyard was nothing less than subversion. John Green's letter about his "supposed offense" is "strong, piteous, and pathetic," "evincing not less the *cant of the fanatic*, than the *artful cunning of the man*." It "deserves this and only this: MY SOVEREIGN CONTEMPT." "Johnny" Swigler, Wickes continues, isn't even a Dissenter but the lowliest of the Methodists, who keeps a private conventicle in his house with its own "mystical lubrications upon the new birth." "He is a friend and sometime rival of another infamous keeper of conventicles in his parish," claimed Wickes, whose flock was notorious for its sexual irregularities: men who had transgressed and females "that had sinned and females that wished to sin." The girl may have had water sprinkled on her and had the words of the Rubric spoken—indeed, he admits that the baptism had been duly registered in a Dissenting meetinghouse as law required—but that does not mean that she was "regularly" baptized. He would not bury the infant Hannah Swigler and would refuse again to bury a Dissenter if a similar situation arose. "We," that is, the Church of England, had to defend itself against the "iterated garbage" and "torrent of encroachments" by Dissenters and keep the churchyard pure. Clearly, keeping out the corpse of a subversive was a symbolically powerful way of trying to do just that. The bishop of Ely could do no more and advised the deputies that their only recourse was to bring a lawsuit. The parish clerk meanwhile had buried Hannah.[111]

The deputies took the bishop's advice and brought an action in the highest ecclesiastical court of the province of Canterbury, the Court of Arches, in the names of John Green, the minister who had told them about the case, and William Kemp, the local Methodist minister, who became the named plaintiff. Arguments were heard on 9 November of the Michaelmas term 1809 before Sir John Nicholl, a politically well-connected lawyer who had succeeded his friend Sir William Scott as king's advocate general in 1798 and became dean of the Court of Arches and a judge on the Prerogative Court of Canterbury—the highest ecclesiastical court of the land—with a seat on the Privy Council in early 1809. Wickes could not have hoped for a more sympathetic ear. Nicholl was a staunch Tory and well-known defender of the Established Church; he had argued that Dissenting chapels were not to be excused from paying local rates; he would, seven years later, chair a select committee in 1816 that defended tithes; he was staunchly anti-Catholic.[112]

Conservatives were therefore shocked when so seemingly loyal a Church of England man ruled in favor of the Dissenters' right to burial and in conformity with Scott's earlier opinion. There was no way around it: "It is with some degree of surprise that the court has heard the suggestion of there being no law to compel the clergy to bury Dissenters. This seems to be," he continues, "most strangely perverting, or rather inverting, all legal considerations." Like Scott, he rehearsed the history of lay baptism in learned detail with lots of quotations in Latin from medieval church councils and a careful reading of post-Reformation Anglican precedents in English. How could one read the 1604 canons to mean that only those baptized by an Anglican priest could be buried in an English churchyard, he asks, for example, when only three years later Parliament passed a law requiring that "popish recusants," who would be excluded if one read the canon as Wickes did, be buried in a churchyard by the incumbent? And like Scott, he concludes, "after tracing the law [of baptism] through the several stages of its history," that it is "impossible to entertain a reasonable doubt that the Church did at all times hold Baptism . . . though administered by a layman or any other person" to be valid. "Unbaptized" means what it means in ordinary language; the infant Swigler was baptized; Wickes had a duty to put her in his churchyard. And moreover, he ought to want to bury her to signify that in death and the last offices, "there is no separation between the Church and her Protestant Dissenting brethren." The Dissenting Deputies were vindicated and graciously decided not to seek costs or suspension and were satisfied with an admonition.[113]

The High Church clergy were furious at Nicholl's betrayal of their cause. George Hutton, D.D. (1764–1817), vicar of Sutterton and fellow of Magdalene College, Oxford, grumped that he could not understand "how any doubt could ever have arisen, or how any controversy could ever have been engaged in on the subject": "lawful baptism" means baptism by a lawful minster, and a lawful minister is a minister of the Church of England. "Anyone baptized by unlawful ministers is not baptized." End of story. Nicholl's learning was shallow and his intentions suspect. We may as well accept "any similar declaration by a trader on the Royal Exchange," Hutton argued. Nicholl was "piously laboring to subvert and destroy her [the Church] by all possible means," added another critic. But the matter of lay baptism was really only a screen. Even if one admitted that any fishwife or barrow woman could administer the sacrament, a critic pointed out, "that would not affect the legality of Wickes'" refusal. Just because a minister *could* bury a Dissenter does not mean that he *should*. Indeed he should not. The rites of the Church and the place in its churchyards was meant for its own members; in the metropolis, Dissenters had their own burial ground; they could and should find places elsewhere and not impose on the conscience of clergymen. In the view of Wickes's defenders, he was not only within his rights as prescribed by ecclesiastical law but morally in the right as well: the corpses of subversives only undermined the Church and had to be excluded.[114]

Despite this conservative reaction, the deputies hoped that their legal strategy would work. It did not. There was an 1829 case in which the body of a young man, a Baptist, was buried "without a word or a sentence from anyone," because the incumbent of Eatington in Warwickshire not only refused to bury the body but also threatened dire legal consequences if a Dissenting minister said anything at the grave or even outside the churchyard gate. If anything, the High Church clergy became more recalcitrant, perhaps because of fear of popular insurrection in this era of the great Chartist organization, perhaps because they saw the right to burial as one prong in a larger attack on Church privileges—rates, tithes, education.

On 16 February 1840, Jane Rumbold, child of Independents in Bassingbourne, Cambridgeshire, died. Rev. William Herbert Chapman refused to bury her, even though her mother and ten of her siblings lay in the churchyard and despite acknowledging that she had been baptized in the prescribed manner. The rub was that it was not by an Anglican priest. Chapman ordered that the clangs of the funeral bell be stopped. Mr. Rumbold could bury her himself if he wished, but there would be no service. The hopeful bereaved father brought the body to the gate; Chapman again refused any service; the father took the body home; it remained in his house encased in double coffins for two years. In 1841, Chapman refused to bury a second child, Esther Fisher, whose body rested in the chimney nook in her aunt's house while the deputies took the case through the legal hoops. Finally, in 1845, when they were on the verge of getting a writ of mandamus, Chapman agreed to bury the child, only to renege at the last moment and send another clergyman.[115]

But the most spectacular legal case of the Chartist era did not involve the deputies and old Dissent, but arose instead from clerical antipathy toward the Methodists and their dead. Elizabeth Ann Cliff, the daughter of Thomas Cliff, a blacksmith, and his wife, Sarah, in the tiny Lincolnshire parish of Gedney, died on 14 December 1839. She had, according to her mother, never been well and had been baptized soon after birth by a twenty-six-year-old unordained Methodist minister, schoolteacher, and preacher named Elisha Bayley. All agree that he had used the proper words. The next day, Elizabeth's father waited on Rev. Thomas Sweet Escott, informed him of his daughter's death (i.e., gave proper notice), and asked that she be buried. Escott refused. The blacksmith asked the help of a more senior Methodist minister, Mr. Overton, who the next day appealed to Escott to change his mind; he reminded him of some cases—he could not quite remember in what newspapers he had read about them—in which a clergyman had been suspended for refusing to bury a Dissenter. He testified that he "adverted to the unkindness and even inhumanity of such a course at a time when the parents' feelings were so lacerated." Escott is said to have replied that he knew nothing about their feelings; that he had read of the cases; and that he would not relent. A case was brought against Escott in the name of Frederick George Mastin, a Methodist class leader in Gedney, and made its way to the Court of Arches.

There Escott lost on more or less the same grounds that Wickes had lost. The court this time took the story back to Tertullian and Cyprian; it argued more strenuously against some deviant 1712 views of nonjurors.[116] But basically, it rehearsed *Kemp v. Wickes*. It had been asked to deal with one set of legal technicalities that, if interpreted as Escott wanted, would without question exclude Methodist corpses: the followers of Wesley, Escott's lawyers argued, were not Dissenters covered by the Acts of Toleration or indeed by any legal protections, but rather Anglican schismatics who as such had to be excluded from Church burial. The rejection of this view by the Court of Arches was one of the grounds for Escott's appeal to the Privy Council, where the queen, through her most brilliant and distinguished lawyers, discussed whether all the testimony against Escott should have been inadmissible because it had been given by purported excommunicants, and whether lay baptism, as a matter of English law, not theology, was sufficient to procure for a corpse the right to burial under canon sixty-eight. Lord Brougham, on behalf of a distinguished panel, announced in the name of the queen that the testimony was admissible and that Elizabeth's baptism had been valid. Meanwhile, she was carried in her double coffin to the churchyard gate, where a Methodist read a burial service—no one challenged the incumbent's monopoly in the churchyard itself—and then her body was carried through the gate and silently buried.

With this extraordinary case, the history of burial disputes took a turn. The Protestant Dissenting Deputies and their allies abandoned the hope that pressure from bishops or courts could persuade the conservative clergy to properly bury the dead of their community as defined by canon sixty-eight. They began instead to press for legislation that would break the Anglican monopoly on its own churchyards by guaranteeing access to it to non-Anglican clergy on an equal footing with Anglican priests, and to any body. After almost forty years of effort, they got what they wanted: the Burial Laws Amendment Act of 1880.

But in the meantime, the war of attrition continued, nasty small battle by nasty small battle. These were not the result of self-conscious provocations by Dissenters, as some Anglicans claimed, but of the expectation of humble people—the bourgeoisie were happy in cemeteries—that their dead would be properly buried in their churchyard. It is a dispiriting story. In 1846, the vicar of Warminster refused to bury a pauper woman because, although baptized in the Anglican Church, she had attended Unitarian services in her old age. When her body arrived at the churchyard gates, there was no clergyman to meet it; a few passersby said "ashes to ashes"; she had been, as one of the Guardians of the Poor put it, "buried like a dog." And this was not an isolated instance, he testified. In 1853, there was a long and much publicized correspondence between the lord bishop of Manchester, the local Poor Law authority, and James Leigh, the vicar of Leigh, over the priest's manifestly illegal refusal to read the scriptural portion of the service: "There is no justification to offer indignity to a senseless corpse and inflict a pang on deprived perhaps, and sorrowing mourners, for the supposed errors of others." In 1863, a poor old man and "respected member of the Church though a pauper" in Staffordshire remained unburied for two weeks as crowds and the vicar did battle over his body and the churchyard. In 1864, the incumbent of Lower Heyford, Northamptonshire, told a father he could bury his child only in what villagers called "hell corner," the northern section of the churchyard. Everyone understood what this meant. In the debate about a burial bill that failed in 1861, Sir S. M. Peto noted that a clergyman in Norfolk had taken fifty cartloads of dirt from the north side of his church to manure his glebe lands to indicate to all that he, for one, did not regard this as sacred soil. It was reported that when another clergyman compelled a poor man to bury his child in unconsecrated ground (i.e., the north), he said that it was "little better than a garden, a public not a private one." He threatened to make trouble with the Guardians of the Poor if the man protested.[117]

The end came with the notorious Akenham burial scandal. I will piece the narrative together from the first of hundreds of newspaper reports about what became a national preoccupation in the late summer of 1878:

> A few days since, a workingman in the employ of Mr. E. E. Golding of Akenham Hill, lost a child [Joseph Ramsey] who was two years old. Both parents [Edward and Sarah Ramsey] being Baptists, the child was never baptized.
>
> Mr. [George] Drury [the vicar] on learning that the child had not been baptized, positively and peremptorily refused to have it buried in consecrated ground, but gave permission for it to be buried in unconsecrated ground reserved for still born infants, on the condition that no religious service was performed with the graveyard. He sternly refused to bury it himself and refused and insisted that no one should officiate in the church in his stead. Very naturally the sorrowing parents did not wish to have their beloved child buried like a dog.

No bier could be procured, and the coffin was placed on the ground immediately in front of the churchyard gate. The friends gathered round it, and Mr. Tozer [a Baptist minister, who "had always been kindly disposed toward churchmen" and would have welcomed the child in his chapel burial place four miles away] commenced reading appropriate parts of scripture. The incumbent in his saintly garb . . . sailed majestically up to the path, came out of the gate, and stood about an arm's length from Mr. Tozer, facing the mourners. The situation at this point was painfully exciting.

For ten minutes they argued heatedly about whether the child was a Christian. The child's mother stopped the father from attacking the priest. Drury locked the gate and stormed off. The mourners found their way to the graveside by another route.

There, in solemn silence, the poor innocent child's remains, over which this hard and unseemly battle of words had been fought, were deposited. The party then returned to the gate, and the usual burial service was read, and the ceremony concluded.

There are many reasons this case became the last of a long lineage and led to a defining moment in the national law of burial: Drury was a Romanist who had been in trouble with his bishop; Frederick Wilson, the editor of the *East Anglia Daily Times*, was a great champion of the Dissenting interest and of "liberation," and eager for a scandal. Drury obliged by suing him for libel in King's Bench. He won the suit; he was, the jury found, legally within his rights to refuse burial because this child had unquestionably not been baptized and Wilson had impugned his honor by libelously denying that there were grounds for his refusal of burial. Drury won little else. A great deal of meanness saw the light of day and the meager 40s. he was awarded made clear what the jurors really thought about his views. Why this incident created the perfect storm is less important than that it did.[118]

The passage of the long-fought-over Burial Amendment Act of 1880 was now politically assured. Under its provisions, "churchyard" was subsumed under the more general rubric "graveyard," which included joint stock company cemeteries and cemeteries managed by publicly funded Burial Boards that had been authorized by acts of Parliament between 1852 and 1857. It lost its legal particularity. Burial in a churchyard became a civil right open to everyone; anyone could read any service they wished at the grave, or there might be no service at all. After more than a thousand years, the legal foundations for the churchyard's delicate balance as civic and ecclesiastical place collapsed. The dead became full citizens a few years before the 1884 Reform Act gave the vote to the rural laboring classes.

The great struggle between religious pluralism and a national Church that had begun in the Reformation was over.

The Anglican clergy tended to see the prospect of a civil churchyard as apocalyptic: it would result not only in disestablishment but also in "a general reign of sacrilege and confusion." Sixteen thousand of them signed a petition against passage of the 1880 act; one wrote bitterly to his superiors that by their voting for the legislation in the House of Lords they had "outraged, destroyed and deleted . . . order truth and religion."[119]

But this was not the intention of the Ramseys, who wanted only to bury their child. They did "have feelings towards [the parish churchyard] of sanctity or religious reverence," contrary to what those who wanted to exclude their child believed. More radical advocates of "liberation" took their plight in an anticlerical and antisacral direction. And to some extent they succeeded. For the Ramseys, the old regime kept much of its old aura, and so for many others. Churchyards remained largely peaceful; alternative places of burial created possibilities for alternative narratives and alternative communities of the dead. A juridical threshold had been crossed in 1880, but any reader of Thomas Hardy knows that the old places of the dead still had a firm grasp on the imagination of English men and women.

ENLIGHTENMENT SCANDALS

The ruin of the Pagan religion is described by the sophists as a dreadful and amazing prodigy which covered the earth with darkness and restored the ancient dominion of chaos and night. They relate, in solemn and pathetic strains, that the temples were converted to sepulchers and that holy places, that had been adorned by the statues of the gods, were basely polluted by the relics of Christian martyrs.

EDWARD GIBBON (1737–1794)

On its own account historiography takes for granted the fact that it has become impossible to believe in this presence of the dead that has organized (or organizes) the experience of entire civilizations; and the fact too that it is nonetheless impossible "to get over it," to accept the loss of a living solidarity with what is gone, or to confirm an irreducible limit. . . . Historiography is a labor of death and a labor against death.

MICHEL DE CERTEAU (1925–1986)

Infamous scandals did some of the same work as the microdisputes that finally brought down the old regime of the parish in 1880.[120] Edward Gibbon, in one of the most famous parts of his *Decline and Fall of the Roman Empire*, tells the story of the Christian revolution as a dreadful tale of the dead. With the persecutions of the late third century, the new religion had plenty of martyrs. Their bodies became central to the making of the new regime of the dead as Gibbon tells it. We know that it took many more centuries to take shape, but in the imagination of Gibbon and of other Enlightenment figures the details of when and how the Church came to have control over the dead does not matter. By the eighteenth century, the cult of saints had existed for a very long time. Gibbon had emblematic dates in mind for its beginning: the conversion of Constantine in 325 was one. Christians who were once persecuted and worshipped surreptitiously were now free to make temples of their tombs. St. Peter's Basilica, started that year over the bones—Gibbon calls them "trophies"—of "spiritual heroes" (that is, Saints Peter and Paul), is his paradigmatic case. "The emperors, the consuls, and the generals of the army," he notes with disgust, "devoutly visit[ed] the sepulchers of a tentmaker and a fisherman." The year 351 C.E. would be for Gibbon an alternative beginning of the Christian revolution of the dead. In that year, the Emperor Julian, he tells us, found the "holy ground" of the temple of Apollo in the ancient grove of Daphne near Antioch "profaned by the introduction of Christian and funeral rites." To wit, a dead body was brought into the precincts of the oracle. Julian's brother Gallus, the zealously Christian emperor in the east, had ordered that the corpse of Babylas, patriarch of Antioch, who had been martyred in the Decian persecutions of 253, be moved from the city to the temple. Sacred lands were usurped to support a clergy that cared for the Christian dead who wished to be buried at "the feet of their bishop." As a consequence, the oracle of Apollo, whom Julian wished to consult, ceased to speak. To give her voice again, Julian tried to reverse the tide of bodies: the church of Babylas was demolished, the saint's body sent back whence it came, and the "scene of infection purified by decently removing the bodies of the dead" more generally. But the oracle did not break her silence. A threatening crowd, intent on insulting the emperor, accompanied the corpse back to the city. Julian, we know, ultimately lost, and the rise of the cult of saints began in earnest.[121]

Gibbon and the protagonists of this section were, fourteen hundred years later, engaged in undoing the consequences of Julian's defeat. They—men of the Enlightenment—were not much concerned with redistributing the work of the dead so that it served an alternative view of how God worked and of the nature of the Christian community. This had been the Reformation project. Their aim was to take the dead into other uncharted realms: less Reformation than revolution. It was for them a revolution with no settled ideology. Anticlericalism was certainly one of their motives—the aim was to deny the church and its priests the power over the dead that they had enjoyed and purportedly abused for so long—but by no means the whole story. It was not even aggressively secular; Voltaire would have been perfectly happy in sacred ground. And it did not aim to wipe away the idea of a Christian community of the dead. But—and this is the novel element—Enlightenment controversies over burial would not be determined primarily by debates about the immanence of the divine in particular spaces or anxieties about idolatry or about maintaining the integrity of any particular Christian but, rather, about creating new spaces where new forms of enchantment could flourish.

This is not the usual story. The Enlightenment moment in the history of the dead, as I suggested in the introduction, is generally interpreted as oppositional, as negative, as subtracting from the power and importance of the dead. There is considerable evidence for this view. Gibbon was manifestly and aggressively anti-clerical, as was the secular politics of dead bodies more generally. The enemy was the Church—in some cases, all churches. The movement of which he was part was in a sense also on the side of the here-and-now world. It assumed the decline of faith and this very fact had consequences for how contemporaries understood being dead. As the distinguished German historical demographer Arthur Imhof puts it, life expectancy crashed. The few years that might have been gained through public health measures—the cemetery was one of the most publicized of these—and better food were nothing compared with the infinitude of time that was lost when faith in resurrection and life everlasting flagged. He names 1785 as a key date, the year the great Cemetery of the Innocents in Paris was closed and the bones of millions displaced. First, graves were banished from the city; then the dying were moved to hospitals; "finally, our thoughts about death and dying were then repressed from our conscious thoughts."[122] The history of death in modernity is, in this telling, a history of loss, however many years of life may have been gained.

It is also a history of the disenchantment of the dead body as it became just one more locus for the scientific study of life. The philosopher Michel Foucault interprets the clinical gaze, whether into the live or the dead body, as a founding moment for a new regime of power. Medicine, grounded in its intimate knowledge of the body and the environment, would take over the care of souls from priests and guide the state in building an "untroubled, dispassionate society restored to its original state of health." Death becomes a symptom of failure and the dead body a site for understanding what went wrong. The "birth of the clinic," the rise of pathological anatomy (the early nineteenth century was the advent of the golden age of the autopsy), and the registration of birth and death by civil authorities (medically and scientifically trained registrars in the service of the state) rather than the religiously inflected recording of baptism and burial are all signs of the new regime and its efforts to appropriate the dead for the regime of life. The dead body thus became ground zero of what Foucault called biopower, a "technology" of power that governed subjects through the regulation of live bodies, individually and, more important, collectively. From a distance, one can imagine the abyss of this technology in the Nazi death camps, where humans were stripped of God, culture, and the protections of the state and became "mere life," and then "mere death": bodies to be disposed of in a technologically more advanced version of what Diogenes had advocated.[123]

Philippe Ariès, a devout Catholic, a man of the traditional Right, and a royalist in his heart who supported Vichy, tells a differently inflected version of this story close to that of Michel Foucault, with whom he had nothing in common politically, philosophically, or spiritually except a deep suspicion of the Enlightenment and the so-called regime of life.[124] In moving from the domain of priests to that of physicians in the eighteenth century, death lost its role in a cosmic drama; in fact, the whole notion of death and the dead body having any metaphysical or transcendental importance collapsed, and they became little more than the opposite of life and the live body. Life is nothing but "the sum of all functions by which death is resisted," in Xavier Bichat's famous gnomic phrase quoted by both Foucault and Ariès. Death in this context becomes little more than a diagnostic category defined by the absence of certain signs and the presence of others; it created still further anxieties about the death of the other—and one's own death— by making premature burial, the consequence of misdiagnosing apparent as real death, a constant possibility. Doctors frightened themselves and their patients to death as they helped give birth to the regime of life. The empty godlessness of modern death and the hubris of the regime of life are the results of all this.[125]

And then there are versions of these Enlightenment stories with the opposite moral inflections—with plus rather than minus signs in front of them—but with the same denouement. A study of wills, for example, by one of the influential French Marxist historians, Michel Vovelle, shows that testamentary provision for intercessory prayers declined: death became more secular and a good thing too. The young Marx writes about Epicurus and a material soul; everywhere the monopoly of religious authorities over the dead body declined; death and the care of the dead seemed to be becoming secular—freed of superstition. Humanity had finally entered its maturity on matters of death as well as life.[126]

My interest does not lie either in the particular narratives of these scholars or in their moral diagnosis, but rather in the fact that they offer ways of characterizing the counterrevolution—the reversal of history—that Gibbon advocated. They all speak for a new age of the dead in which Diogenes' challenge will find novel, secular answers. More important, all of them link the history of death and of the dead body to broader transformations, to the making of the modern world. "No doubt," writes the literary critic Lionel Gossman, "the political and industrial revolutions, the dissolution of old traditions and communities, and the erosion of long-established religious beliefs had a good deal to do with the new preoccupation with death." Indeed, but even more the other way around. New preoccupations with death made the new order.[127]

Finally, these stories are important because they are importantly wrong, not in their substantive historical claims but in their collective interpretive thrust: they all speak only about the evacuation of enchantment. It may have "become impossible," as Certeau says, "to believe in [the] presence of the dead that has organized (or organizes) the experience of entire civilizations." But it was also impossible not to. Science did not, in fact, end up in exclusive command over death and the dead body. The dead did not become secular. History, memory, and politics, with the deep time of the dead as their resource, created a new enchantment of the dead. And the old did not disappear either. The living shared the deep historical intuition that, whatever they might actually believe about bodies, the soul, or the afterlife—the range of views that could be spoken widened considerably in the late eighteenth century—Diogenes' views remained incompatible with culture. Somewhere between 1700 and the early nineteenth century, the work of the dead in modernity was put on a new foundation through a vertiginous number of new and newly reconfigured rituals and practices.[128]

The previous section described the end of the old regime of the dead in terms of the micropolitics of a religiously, politically, and culturally pluralist society. The work of the Reformation of the dead that began in 1535 was finished in England in 1880. A cosmopolitan community of the dead had succeeded a local one. Scandals involving intellectual celebrities—hugely public and publicized spectacles— did the same sort of work on a larger scale. Together, the deaths and afterlives of the bodies of two famous Enlightenment figures suggest the consequences of the rupture represented by Gibbon and the condition of which Certeau speaks: the end of an old regime of the dead and birth of a new one in which history came to challenge, if not replace, metaphysics in creating "a living solidarity with what is gone." Collectively, they represent the new possibilities for doing this, liberating to some and terrifying to others, in the era in which we still live. I am speaking of the deaths of Voltaire in 1778 and David Hume in 1776.

Both come out of the very long tradition of judging the meaning of a life by its end—by the comportment and the last words of the dying, and by the burial of the dead. The paradigmatically dignified deaths of Jesus and of Socrates, the more contested death of Seneca, and the good deaths of saints (a fixture of the hagiographic tradition), on the one hand, and the tormented death agonies and ravings of various sinners, reprobates, and dishonorable people, on the other, represent the irresistible urge to see in death great truths. Last words mark not only an awesomely final social and cultural boundary but an interpretive one as well; we will never be able to ask for clarification: What did you mean by that?

Those of Jesus ("I thirst" and "It is finished") are clear: the scripture had been fulfilled. Those of Socrates, once he had chastised his disciples for their anxiety at his death ("I have been told that a man should die in peace. Be quiet then, and have patience") are gnomic. "Crito, we owe a rooster to Asclepius. Please, don't forget to pay the debt . . ." has engendered debate for more than two millennia. The disposition of Christ's body matters a great deal to his followers. Socrates comes just short of Diogenes: he hopes that Crito will not "be grieved when he sees my body being burned or buried. I would not have him sorrow at my hard lot, or say at the burial, Thus we lay out Socrates, or Thus we follow him to the grave or bury him; for false words are not only evil in themselves, but they infect the soul with evil. Be of good cheer then, my dear Crito, and say that you are burying my body only, and do with that whatever is usual, and what you think best." All of this is in the cultural DNA of the West and of the educated men of the Enlightenment.[129]

But there was also a more recent precedent for warring, politically fraught, and widely circulated deathbed stories of the Enlightenment, and that goes back to the Reformation and the great drama of Martin Luther's death in the early morning hours of 18 February 1546. It was the propaganda war about dying in modern history, a prelude to those of the eighteenth and nineteenth centuries. With his final illness, death, and burial, the legitimacy of the whole revolution he led seemed to hang in the balance, and everyone knew it. Luther's wife and his family doctor as well as several other doctors and the town apothecary, two of Eisleben's magistrates and its scribe, two theologians, and three or four of the nobility crowded into his death chamber and watched closely as his life ebbed away. We know the drugs he was given and the ointments with which he was rubbed; we know when he railed and when he and all those present gave up on his life. We know his last spoken word: *ja*, in answer to the question of whether he was dying in the name of Christ. But before that he is said to have repeated three times the words he had learned as a young man from St. Anselm's guide for the dying—the words of Jesus on the cross: "Herr, in deine Hände befehle ich meinen Geist." (Into thine hands I commend my spirit.) Some accounts say that he whispered, "I go there in peace and joy," a paraphrase of the words of one of his best-known hymns.[130]

The drama of his death became international news. Already, in 1522, he had been likened to Elijah, the prophet who raised the dead and ascended into heaven in a chariot of fire; a great deal was expected. After 1546, this identification with the Hebrew prophet became commonplace. The first poem about Luther's death was written almost immediately after he died and became the first of many; his last written words were carefully preserved. His peaceful countenance in death, belying Catholic propaganda that he had died in agony, was quickly documented and reproduced. A local artist, whose name we do not know, rushed to the body

4.8. *Portrait Sketch of the Dead Martin Luther.*
Lukas Furtenagel, 1546. Staatliche Museen
zu Berlin.

and made a sketch of the old man still lying in his bed and looking like a contented child asleep in his cot; within a day, Lucas Furtenagel arrived from Halle, twenty-five kilometers away, and sketched the portrait that Lucas Cranach the Younger must have received shortly after the event and that became the basis for his *Portrait of Martin Luther on His Deathbed,* signed and dated Wittenberg, 1546. (The two are very similar; the painting adds ruffled bedclothes and hands softly resting on the dead man's chest [figs. 4.8, 4.9].) Cranach, who had done more than anyone to publicize Luther's face from the earliest days of the Reformation, thus did the great man one last service: creating a much-reproduced image showing that one could die well in the new faith. A death mask, later drawn and published, made the same point. Luther's body was then moved to Wittenberg, some 140 kilometers away; his world was a small one. A beautiful black satin pall that would be preserved for more than two hundred years covered his coffin as he was laid to rest in a great public funeral near the altar of the church where almost thirty years earlier he had supposedly posted his Ninety-Five Theses.[131]

Much about the form of the battle over Luther's end prefigured battles over deathbeds to come. But the stakes were different from those that would be generated by the deaths of Voltaire and Hume. At issue in the sixteenth century was whether Luther's was the true religion, not whether religion mattered at all to the dying and the dead, or whether one should be buried in sacred ground, or whether a civilization could be built without religion as its foundation. The subject had been changed.

We have early hints in the late seventeenth century of a new and more radical public conversation. The much-discussed death of Spinoza is perhaps the first of those whose history was said to stretch back to Epicurus, Democritus, Lucian, and, implausibly, Socrates, and was embraced by his contemporaries Hobbes, Bayle, and Anthony Collins—a freethinker, at best, and one of the first to use that term. A peaceful end and honorable burial for any of these men would be seen by the commonplace interpretive conventions of the day to be a vindication of their views; a bad one proof of the contrary. The battle lines were clear. A much reprinted and translated life of Spinoza went to greats lengths to deny various charges that the great philosopher collapsed on his deathbed: No, he did not send for ministers; no, he did not invoke the name of God in his sickness. His landlady and others in the house "believe the contrary, because ever since he began to be in a languishing condition, he always expressed, in all his suffering, a truly *Stoical* constancy." On the other side of the ledger, the repentance and consequentially good death of a famous rake like the late-seventeenth-century James Wilmot, the earl of Rochester, were also widely publicized. Bishop Burnet's account of how the now-contrite writer of bawdy verses had made his peace with God went through seven editions

4.9. *Martin Luther on His Death-Bed.* Lucas Cranach, 1546. Niedersächsisches Landesmuseum Hannover.

between 1680 and 1699, another five by 1750, and thirteen in the contentious second half of the century. From there, it entered the popular evangelical literature of the nineteenth century as the point of contrast to the bad deaths of infidels. Print brought stories of these sorts to anyone who could read.[132]

Voltaire

Voltaire's deathbed story exploded the genre for two reasons. The first had to do with his fame and notoriety. He was, as Edward Gibbon said of him, "the most extra-ordinary man of the age." His return on the eve of his death to Paris from his estate at Ferney, near the Swiss border, had been a great public triumph witnessed by thousands in the streets. *Écrasez l'infâme*, "crush the infamous"—superstitions, prejudice, tyranny—had by 1760 become the closing to his many letters (15,300 survive, to more than 1,000 recipients). More than anyone else in Europe, this man represented the Enlightenment.[133] His death and the question of what would become of his body was therefore of national and international interest, the final battle of a long, portentous war: how would the great enemy of religious superstition die?

The second reason depends on the first but was more immediately political and time sensitive: what would become of his body? The question arises because, on the one hand, the Church that he had so often fought controlled burial in old regime France, and, on the other, every body, by custom and tradition, had the right to rest in the ground of its parish. Burial was a fundamental civil right. Church, state, and ordinary people needed the dead. Of course, some people were cast out with little controversy—suicides, for example. But other cases were wildly and publicly fraught. An unburied dead body or a humiliated dead body was emotional and political tinder. Voltaire's deathbed and the fate of his body became not only the most public test of whether one could die at peace without the consolation of religion but also the occasion for a complex struggle to determine whether France's most famous writer would be dumped in a lime pit. At the bedside, the negotiations were about what exactly Voltaire would have to do for the Church, whose most famous enemy he had been, to grant him a proper burial (fig. 4.10).

4.10. *The Death of Voltaire.* Samuel Percy (1750–1820). Wax relief. Victoria and Albert Museum, London.

There was a protocol for what it took: confession, absolution, extreme unction, and the viaticum or last communion. But the circumstances under which these—and hence burial—could be denied were many and were open to interpretation at all levels, ranging from local quarrels between a priest and a parishioner to disputes of national and international importance in which the priest at the bedside was taking orders from the very highest authorities in Rome and at Versailles. The year 1731 saw one such case, a battle in the war that the Church had been engaged in for almost a century against the so-called Jansenists, members of a supposedly heretical sect—crypto-Calvinists or strict Augustinians, depending on your point of view. The most public weapon at its disposal was to deny burial to these supposed heretics. This was done by forcing someone suspected of Jansenist sympathy to present a certificate of adherence to a 1713 papal bull called *Unigenitus* (from its first word in Latin, "only begotten" son of God) before she would be given the last rites by a parish priest. No *billet de confession*, no burial. (The Jansenists, for their part, regarded the bull as a work of the Beast of the Apocalypse.) Matters came to crisis—Voltaire was thirty-seven at the time—when royal authorities in support of the Church sent the police to erect a fence around the tomb of a popular Jansenist martyr.

François de Paris—a wealthy young man who had given all his money to the poor, probably died from ascetic mortification, and certainly had not signed the relevant documents—was thus "illegally" buried in the cemetery of Saint-Médard. Very soon after the interment, miracles began to happen at his grave. Worse, people started to go into dramatic public convulsions there (fig. 4.11). (These had been occurring on and off in some circles since the 1680s.) The police fence was supposed to keep supporters of the dead heretic and especially *les convulsionnaires* away. It did not. The king then issued edicts threatening imprisonment for those who showed off their religion at the tomb; the Parlement of Paris responded with a declaration against king and Church. Famously, someone painted graffiti on the offending wall saying, "By order of the King, God has been forbidden to perform miracles here." (The French doggerel rhymes: *De par le Roi, defense a Dieu, De faire des miracles dans ce lieu.*) All this time, the archbishop of Paris continued to issue orders that kept ordinary dying Jansenists from making deathbed communion and thus being properly buried. And the Crown found itself debunking the power of the special dead on whose legitimacy in general its own legitimacy depended. That is, the last thing that the regime wanted was to undermine the power of the Church by denying that the special dead—the saints—could intervene with God to cure the sick and the lame. But it did want to control which dead bodies transmitted or were inhabited by divine power and in exercising this control opened itself up to the mockery of its devout but heterodox subjects.[134]

4.11. *Les convultionnaires au cimetière Saint-Médard*, n.d. with feet coming out from under the platform on the grave. Bibliothèque nationale de France.

In 1749, the archbishop of Paris renewed the struggle, forbidding his clergy from offering last rites to anyone who had not presented a *billet de confession*. In the next few years almost all the diocese followed suit, and many legal battles followed in the high courts of the land with the king, the episcopate, and the litigants all party to the cases. A growing pamphlet press reported widely on these fights. Clerical authorities would deny someone burial as an *honnête homme*, a respectable person; relatives would sue; and depending on circumstances, the case would become more or less scandalous. The same year as the reintroduction of the *billets de confession*, the dying Charles Coffin, principal of the Collège de Beauvaisand and a known Jansenist, was, for example, refused the sacraments by his parish priest. His nephew complained to a magistrate, who referred him to the archbishop, who in turn, as a zealous anti-Jansenist, supported his priest in his refusal. Coffin died without absolution, communion, or extreme unction and only with difficulty found a place to be buried in consecrated soil. The nephew then brought a formal complaint before the Parlement of Paris, but just as the proceedings were getting going, the king let it be known that these matters were to be decided by him alone. An *arrêt* from the council of state was issued in 1759, and the court backed off. In other cases it did not. The Parlement of Paris supported the rights of a man—or more accurately his body—who had been refused a place in consecrated ground because he had not attended Easter communion. It ordered that his body be exhumed and properly buried; the offending priest was fined and charged for expenses. An aristocratic family sued and won a similar case; a magistrate ordered that an actor whose body had been preserved in brine while his case was litigated receive a church burial despite a policy of denying it to those of his profession.[135]

Actors were in fact a whole other excluded category, and the Church's refusal in 1731 to give a Christian burial to the popular actress Adrienne Lecouvreur, who had died under mysterious circumstances, greatly exercised Voltaire. He was outraged by both the hypocrisy and the cruelty of the curé of Saint-Suplice and his superiors, who had enjoyed her art when she was alive but treated her body as unfit for its sacred ground when she was dead. He made much of the fact that, by contrast, in England actors were honored in Westminster Abbey alongside the likes of Newton. "Seine's banks should now no more be deemed profane," he wrote,

> Lecouvreur's sacred ashes there remain:
> At this sad tomb, shrine sacred to thy shade,
> Our vows are still as at a temple paid.[136]

The dying Voltaire presented real political problems to his friends and enemies as well as a challenge to the Christian dramaturgy of dying well.

In a few comparable cases, hard-line atheists and anticlericals simply did not enter into negotiations and wanted to make a point of brazenly ignoring the Church. (Some, like Rousseau, had no choice; as a Protestant, he could not be buried in French sacred ground even if he had wanted to be, which he most certainly did not.) But this was a very radical action, and many people—local characters as well as many well-known Enlightenment figures and members of the progressive aristocracy with edgy relationships to the Church into which they had been born—died in a gray zone. They had to be willing to compromise enough to satisfy their priests so that they could be buried in the only places that would not signify disgrace or full-throated apostasy but not so much as to be egregiously untrue to themselves.[137]

Because one party to the negotiations was dying, the Church had a serious advantage. But it also had an interest in avoiding scandal or, in the case of Voltaire, major riots. Priests drove as hard a bargain as they could. La Fontaine, the famous writer of fables, had to express regret about his writing, but even that did not get him an honorable burial. The deathbed of the great jurist and political philosopher, the baron de Montesquieu, was an edgier affair. As *président à mortier* of the Parlement of Bordeaux, one of the major legal offices of the old regime, it was unthinkable both to him and to the Church that he not receive the burial of an *honnête homme*, a citizen of standing. It was in no one's interest for his body to become an occasion for scandal. But there was a problem. His most famous work, *The Spirit of the Laws*—an account of the anthropological rather than transcendental origin of law and of different polities—as well as the *Persian Letters*, which tended to assimilate Islam and Christianity, and indeed all religions, into one another as more or less useful—were on the Church's Index of Forbidden Books. There had to be a compromise.

On 29 January 1755, Montesquieu contracted a fever and was aggressively bled. He became delirious. In moments of lucidity he felt that his end was near, asked for a confessor, and requested that it be someone he knew—the tutor of his son—whom he knew to be sympathetic. Instead, the Jesuits sent a hardedged Irish priest named Bernard Routh, who had been told by the papal nuncio in Paris that Pope Benedict XIV was personally interested in the satisfactory outcome of this case.[138] Routh pushed the dying man hard. He insisted, first of all, that Montesquieu give permission for the normally confidential confession to be made public. Thus it was recorded and widely reported that: he had never been in a state of unbelief; he subscribed to all the mysteries of the Church; he had written his scandalous works because he "had desired to rise above prejudice and accepted maxims and to win the approval of those who shape public opinion and who approve most restlessly freedom and independence from constraint"; he had only wished for fame and had not intended to injure the Church. Satisfied, Routh called in the parish priest, who made further demands. Montesquieu, in addition to his confession, was to give some sign of the adoration of our Lord—he did this by raising his eyes heavenward—and acknowledge the "grandeur of God and the smallness of man" before he would be given the sacraments. The dying man complied.

All of this was made known to the pope, who sent the report to papal nuncios all over Europe. But the clerical triumph was not complete, and people in the dying man's circles knew this. One of his friends heard loud noises from the room in which Routh was interrogating Montesquieu and came in. She asked what the matter was, and Montesquieu told her that Routh had demanded the key to the cabinet containing his papers and that he had refused. When she berated Routh for harassing her friend, he said he was only following orders. Routh also demanded the manuscript of a revised *Persian Letters*, which Montesquieu managed to give to other friends to do with as they wished. And so the dying man navigated his last days. On 11 February 1755, he was buried in the chapel of St. Genevieve in the Church of Saint-Suplice. Of the great Enlightenment figures, only Diderot was in attendance. His bones were lost when the Revolutionary crowd destroyed most of the church's tombs.

Voltaire did not have this much negotiating space, and the Church could not hope for as much. He could not, and would not, renounce a lifetime of anticlericalism to secure burial, if for no other reason than that all of educated Europe was watching intently. It would have been too shameful to surrender at the very end. Frederick, king of Prussia, his friend and patron, kept in close touch with d'Alembert about events at the townhouse of the Marquis de Villette, where Voltaire had taken refuge to die: "he will disgrace us all," the king worried. (Frederick had quite the opposite problem from Voltaire's; he *wanted* to be buried like a dog and lie at Sans Souci next to his hounds. Instead, a mass was said for him in St. Hedwig's Cathedral—in addition to Lutheran services, of course; he was buried in the garrison church in Potsdam and only after several more moves ended up with his dogs on 17 August 1991.) Voltaire was not in a position to make the sorts of concessions that Montesquieu had made. He was, however, willing to go some way to avoid the consequences of publicly dying outside the Church and having his body treated as Diogenes would have recommended.[139] The threat was real, and we know that Voltaire worried about it. Voltaire spoke in his dying days about the infamous cases mentioned above and did not want to suffer the same fate. The dying *philosophe* wanted to be just compliant enough that, should there be any trouble, the courts would rule in his favor. This wish explains the difficulty in determining exactly what actually transpired at the Hotel de Villette in the negotiations between Voltaire's friends, various church authorities, and, in the background, public authorities desperate to avoid the consequences of a scandal in which the darling of Paris would be refused proper burial in the city where just weeks before he had made a triumphant entrée and was the hero of the crowd in the streets and in the theater.

The abbé Théophile Duvernet, a future Jacobin and an early biographer, wrote that Voltaire compromised only enough to be reassured that his body would not be thrown into a kennel like a dead dog but not enough to alarm his friends. It was disagreeable for him to have to report, he continues, that the great infidel responded to the parish curate's urging him to acknowledge the divinity of Jesus Christ, "Do not mention that name to me," but that *was* what he said. (The curate was apparently not in on the original negotiations about how far Voltaire was willing to go.) Nevertheless, "Voltaire died peacefully, with the resignation and calmness of a philosopher who is returning to his maker." The impact of the last scene must be clear: "all free thinkers will now be very much delighted" by Voltaire's response; it "was certainly calculated to make Christians shudder."[140] The translation of the memoir by the priest Louis Mayeul Chaudon claims that the primary goal of Voltaire's friends in their deathbed war was to "outwit the priests and have M. Voltaire enjoy all the ceremonials they thought his due, rather perhaps as a citizen than as a Christian." They succeeded, but just barely.[141]

Voltaire, according to the Marquis de Condorcet, confessed to the Abbé Gauthier and said that he died in the Church in which he had been born, but only, as Condorcet interprets it, to ensure that "certain scenes of intolerance should not succeed his last moments." It was a cagey statement, but it was sufficient to outflank Churchmen like the archbishop of Paris, who wanted to deny Voltaire a place in consecrated ground unless he made a full-throated recantation of very public anticlerical views. Readers needed to understand, Condorcet continues, that Gauthier was the very same priest who had "restored to the church" the Abbé de L'Attaignant, "known by offenses of another kind," a louche character known for writing comic songs and a poem about having good tobacco. Wits commented that this was altogether appropriate, since Gauthier was also chaplain to the hospital of incurables. Whether he was in his encounter with Voltaire as frivolous as Condorcet implies is less important than the fact that a minimal reconciliation was all he could hope for, and all Voltaire would offer.[142]

From here, Condorcet's story goes in the direction of farce. The curate of Saint-Suplice, Jean-Joseph de Tarsac, in whose Parisian parish Voltaire was dying, seems either not to have been in on the game or, more likely, willing to let the compromise that Gauthier negotiated suffice. "A mixture of hypocrisy and imbecility, with the persuasion of a maniac and the flexibility of a Jesuit," made him try to get Voltaire specifically to acknowledge the doctrine "to which he was more attached than any other dogma," to wit, the divinity of Jesus Christ. And when the dying man refused and forcefully asked Tarsac to leave him alone, the curé threatened to refuse him burial. This sets Condorcet off on the central point of his account: that the question of the right to burial was thoroughly political. The curé could not hope to carry out his threat alone. He and his allies had to proceed either by getting a sentence of excommunication from the Church—unlikely given that he had sort of confessed—or a secular judgment against the dying man. Voltaire's family would have prevailed before the high court of Parlement if he had chosen the latter route, because it could not "without disgrace to itself, depart from the principles on which it had acted in favor of the Jansenists," in the earlier battles over whether the "heretics" could be buried in sacred ground. In any case, younger magistrates could scarcely wait to attack the fanaticism of the Church by honoring the memory of a great man who was its enemy. He then goes on to tell the story of how the body was secreted to the monastery where Voltaire's nephew was abbé and buried before anyone—the priest or the archbishop—could prevent it.[143]

There was relatively little response to these accounts from conservatives in France or abroad. In 1786, the learned Rev. William Agutter preached at the University Church in Oxford on the deaths of the righteous as compared with those of the wicked. Dr. Johnson and David Hume were his main cases, but Voltaire's death, he said, framed the problem he was considering with particular clarity: it was difficult "to discriminate the exact features of truth." In the first place, infidelity, horrible as it was, could now be advocated in polite company; people had an interest in presenting it in favorable ways. One needs to know that "the need of the infidel is sometimes concealed with industrious secrecy and sometimes misrepresented by officious friendship." The deathbeds of the wicked, he continued, were no more transparent than the postures of politicians. And even if it were true that they by all appearance died well, one could still not take this at face value as evidence for a good end without God, because a calm countenance may in fact signal a troubled soul. The fact that Hume and Voltaire seemed to die well only shows how wicked they were. Both were like a hardened criminal whose "habitual course of guilt" had brought him to the point where he could undergo his execution calmly. Someone who could stand on "the brink of a precipice without feeling emotions of terror" manifests a blind rashness that is not courage and not worthy of applause. This oft-repeated argument undercut the theater of morality that was supposedly the foundation of capital punishment—terror—and made the hermeneutics of much-watched deathbeds impossible. There had always been problems in interpreting the final hours of a life; now they became more politically freighted. Agutter's sermon would probably have lain unpublished had it not been for the ideological battles of the French Revolution. Printed in 1800, it earned a favorable notice in the respected *Anti-Jacobin Review*.[144]

It was the Revolution that transformed an eighteenth-century debate, still well within the boundaries of anticlerical politics, about the rights to burial into a world historical conspiracy. Two things happened. First, the 1792 Civil Constitution of the Clergy set the Revolution on a collision course with the Church and set the stage for what would be two centuries of conflict. Second, and more specifically, the French revolutionaries began to use the dead bodies of mere mortals for the building of a nation. In 1790, they finished and transformed a church begun by Louis XVI in gratitude to his patron saint, Genevieve, for her help in his recovery from a seemingly fatal illness and turned it into a secular temple of worthies. The "Pantheon" was to be a place enchanted by history, by its namesake, the Roman temple dedicated to all the gods. (Westminster Abbey might have primacy as the burial place of a nation, but it maintained the balance between transcendental and historical enchantment longer; more on this later.)

Mirabeau, in 1791, was the first new "god" of the nation to be admitted to the Pantheon, but it was the "apotheosis" of Voltaire—his "deification"—that set the stage for a new counterrevolutionary politics of the body that took as its foundational moment the death scenes at Ferney. On 11 July 1791, the remains of the greatest old regime *philosophe*, the forebearer of the Revolution, were made sacred by the nation. Having narrowly escaped the lime pits thirteen years earlier, his body was now, in very different times, exhumed from the churchyard of the abbey of Selliers in the village of Romilly sur Seine, where it had been secreted by his nephew and his friends once it was clear that nothing could be done to persuade the ecclesiastical authorities allow his burial in Paris. Once back in the capital, it was placed in a sarcophagus redolent of ancient Rome, loaded onto a magnificent chariot, and paraded through the streets to a new tomb in the building that had been originally conceived as a royal gift to a saint (fig. 4.12). Voltaire's heart had gone separately in 1778 to his friend and prodigy Charles Michel, Marquis de Villette, "the most famous sodomite in eighteenth-century France," who had burned his title of nobility during the Revolution and served as a deputy in the Convention. It ended up in the Bibliothèque Nationale.[145]

4.12. *Translation de Voltaire au Panthéon français.* C. N. Malapeau, 1795.
Bibliothèque nationale de France.

Enemies of the Enlightenment saw in this "apotheosis" a vindication of their
worst fears: the *philosophes* had indeed caused the collapse of religion and the old
regime; now they showed their true colors by making their leader into an alternative god. But old guard got its revenge: in 1814, ultramonarchist thieves stole
Voltaire's body. It has disappeared. We can see in this history one of the first cases
in which Diogenes' argument is met by the magic of history and historical stage-
craft without benefit of transcendental claims. The modern age of reburial had
begun; a new aura had begun to attach itself to bones.[146]

Other enemies of the old regime followed. Jean-Jacques Rousseau in 1794
was ripped from his rural resting place on the Isle of Poplars, set in the park of
his friend and patron the Marquis de Girardin, far from priests and churches,
where half France made a yearly pilgrimage, and moved some thirty-five kilometers to Paris. He was joined there by Jean-Paul Marat, the martyr who was
murdered in his bath by Charlotte Corday on 13 July 1793, whose body had been
exhumed from the garden of the deconsecrated church of the Cordeliers in Paris.
(His heart had been separately enshrined; it too entered the Pantheon in 1794.)
Rousseau got his place because everyone in the Revolution claimed to be his follower and could embrace his memory: disinterment and divinity in the interests
of unity after the anti-Jacobin events of 9 Thermidor (24 July) 1794. The dead

Rousseau could not have been happy either to be moved from his rural Elysium to the center of Paris or to have to be reburied with Jean-Paul Marat. Marat made it to the Pantheon because his body allowed the remaining revolutionaries to reject his enemy, the newly deposed Robespierre, and still hold on to the radical tradition. There were numerous ins and outs as the nation redefined itself in fits and starts after that: Mirabeau was unceremoniously expelled out a side door when Marat came in on 21 September 1794; Marat was out by February 1795 and sent back to St. Etienne.[147] But Voltaire stayed, and his death and burial became the starting point for the major conservative interpretation of the Revolution: that it was the work of Freemasons, "illuminati," and other irreligious forces who had been conspiring for much of the century to bring down the Church and the State that supported it.

Freemasons, of whom Voltaire was one, were thought dangerous for all sorts of reasons—because of their democratic aspirations, their claims to spiritual wisdom, their independence from religious and secular authorities—and because they believed that "emancipation from the fear of death [was] . . . the greatest of all deliverances" and that it could be effected through reason. In other words, they took as their own the old Epicurean/Lucretian claim that there was nothing after death and hence nothing to worry about. This was a fundamental threat to good order. It was, argued the brilliant and distinguished Scottish physicist John Robison (1739–1805), central to the great illuminati (that is, freethinker/Masonic) conspiracy because good government and moral order depended on the belief that there would be a Last Judgment. "Our anxiety about futurity has made us imagine endless torments in a future world"; princes and their allies in the Church take advantage of these anxieties to manage "our hopes and fears, and direct them to suit their own purposes." If one could demonstrably die quietly as a Mason, that is, freed of the fear of death, the world as we know it could be shaken to the core. Never mind that this gives credence to the radical Enlightenment's argument that the Church created a terror of death in order to rule by it. D'Holbach became an atheist, he claimed, when he watched his first wife die in agony about the future of her soul. Robison's argument is in a broader sense an engagement with the origin and place of the fear of death. An anonymous English "friend to truth" argued in 1732 that because the fear of death and of being dead does not exist in nature and could not be the result of experience— one only dies once—it had to be the product of "ambitious men" who were not content with a state of equality and who used it to prey upon the ignorance of the people to bring them into subjection.

Rousseau acknowledged the primal happiness of having life and the sadness of losing it but thought we could be reconciled to this by our immortality and that our relation to death—regarding it as evil and fearing it—was the product of civilization with its "mad refinements" and "barbarous institutions." There was no fear of death in "*l'ordre de la nature.*" Montesquieu thought that a subject's primal fear of death was the primary source of despotic government's power and, more generally, that its management was central to all government. Robison did not invent a political theology of death and being dead. We can begin to see why, as another British conservative wrote, apparently without irony: "Twelve apostles, they say, were necessary to propagate [Christianity], but one Voltaire was sufficient to overthrow it."[148]

Nonetheless, it was not a Scottish physicist but rather a Jesuit émigré priest, the abbé Augustine Barruel, with whom Robison shared a publisher, who made Voltaire's death a world historical event. It became in the abbé's imagination both a synecdoche for the whole long-running, gigantic revolutionary plot that had brought Europe to ruin and its culminating moment. It is only slightly an exaggeration to say that for Barruel the events at Ferney caused the French Revolution. His chapter on the subject is called "The Anti-Christian Conspiracy." *Mémoires pour servir à histoire du Jacobinisme* (1798) was hugely influential, translated into English, Italian, German, Russian, Swedish, and Spanish before the end of the century. It quickly became the foundational text for the view that the French Revolution was the work of a cabal of Enlightenment infidels who, after 1789, morphed into Jacobins, *Philosophes*, illuminati, Freemasons, and their dupes undermined Christianity and, in so doing, the old regime itself. Voltaire was their captain. Country by country, Barruel shows his connection to the forces of darkness. In England, for example, he was pleased to support Socinians (Unitarians; he probably had Joseph Priestley in mind), "who scoffed and hated Christ, as Julian the Apostate hated and despised him." Everywhere in the higher classes of France "impiety made great strides," "everyone would be a Philosophe." And all this could be traced back to Voltaire: "the secret committees of education in Paris, the country conventicles, and the correspondence with village school masters, owed their origin to him."

The *philosophe* died in misery, crying out for God's mercy. But a secret band of hypocrites and scoundrels conspired to conceal what really happened from the public because had it become known, their whole project would have been exposed as false. God had spoken, but they could not allow His judgment to get out. Voltaire's last hours, Barruel tried to show, were in fact "the most terrible that is ever recorded to have stricken an impious man." The cover-up plot was systematic. Diderot, the editor of the *Encyclopédie*; d'Alembert, "the philosopher of mechanism"; and "twenty other conspirators" witnessed the ignominy of their master crying in his agony for Jesus but swore to keep it secret. They also suppressed the fact that he had told the abbé Gauthier that he wished to die in the Church. Condorcet kept away from the deathbed all those who might have "availed themselves of any homage done [by the dying man] to religion." And he did what he could to keep Voltaire on the path of perdition as he "ferociously combated these last signs of repentance from the dying Sophister."

This, Barruel continues, was furthermore not the only time the conspirators had been up to such tricks. Diderot, "that hero of atheism," had on his deathbed in 1783 also called for a priest and that too had "given alarm to Sophisters who would have thought themselves dishonored by the dereliction of so important a chief." He too was not allowed to have a private conversation and was said by his friends to have died calmly, but again the public was misled. In fact, the Diderot story was not as convoluted or opaque as Voltaire's nor as publicly consequent. The same curé of Saint-Suplice, Jean-Joseph de Tersac, who had tried to keep Voltaire from a proper burial, haunted Diderot. They seemed, Diderot's daughter Angélique reports, to have had many amiable conversations about theology and to have agreed about many practical ethical matters. Her mother, she continues, would have liked nothing better than to have her husband become a believer, but "she would rather have died than to have him commit the least action she would regard as sacrilege . . . she wanted to protect him from persecution, and would not leave him alone with the cure for a single instant; we took turns to guard him." When he died, Tersac's many visits and the generous charitable donations of his son-in-law were enough to avoid scandal and to assure him a grand funeral, paid for by the same son-in-law, with fifty priests at one *livre* each in attendance as one of the century's best-known atheists was laid to rest in the chapel of the Virgin in the Church of Saint-Roche.[149]

What actually happened at Voltaire's deathbed is not the issue here, nor is that question very pressing for us today. Probably, Voltaire's friends did shield him from priests, and when Gauthier came one last time, they probably did tell him that the old man was too sick to receive him. There is no reason to believe the whole deathbed agony and repentance story. What matters is the centrality of his death and burial to the making of the modern world. What might have been a private negotiation aimed at assuring the dying Voltaire that he would not be thrown into a pit became the crux of one of the most important and influential political narratives of the nineteenth and early twentieth centuries. Barruel made the *philosophe*'s last days and hours the crux of the irreligious conspiracy that unleashed the Revolution. Many others took up his cause.

Hannah More, the most popular of conservative evangelical writers for a broad audience, for example, wrote in one of the tracts of her *Practical Piety* that "the boastful accounts we sometimes hear of the firm and heroic deathbeds of popular but irreligious characters," were among the most important ways of "making worldly men" insensible to "eternal things." Whatever the "sage of Ferney"—Voltaire—might have been in the eyes of the "Encyclopedists," or the king of Prussia, or "revolutionists in the egg of his own hatching," his nurse attested to "the horror which was sedulously to be consigned to oblivion." But the real story of his agony was kept secret. And the same, she says, goes for J.-J. Rousseau. Despite the "precautions taken by his associates to bury him in congenial darkness," the fact was that this "audacious blasphemer"—infamous because, among many other reasons, his heroine Julie died without comfort of priests—also "believed and trembled at the end." The English Religious Tract Society published an account of Voltaire's death in the context of one of its best-selling—in any case, one of its most widely distributed—numbers: the "Tracts on Infidelity" that focused on Paine's death but surveyed the field more broadly. It also offered to the pious working classes many other more generic titles on the horrible deaths of freethinkers; educated readers and the happily godless poor had other accounts of the bad versus the good death at their disposal.[150]

An 1802 poem by the editor of the provincial *Hull Advertiser* contrasted the happy death of a Christian man of letters, Joseph Addison, with the miserable death of the infidel Voltaire à la Barruel. The dying Voltaire, readers are told, in the agony of his last hours dismissed his atheist colleagues, who eagerly "fly th' horrible sight." "As racked the culprit on the tort'ring wheel," he might even have been half-inclined to pray. It was too late; nothing could bring him "back from the dreadful irremediable brink." By contrast, Addison, whom the "votaries of virtue" mourn, "awaits with tranquil mind his dying hour." And so on. This poem too had an afterlife, reprinted in ordinary and presentation copies of the author's works in 1828 and again in 1879.[151] How Voltaire died and was buried mattered to conservatives for more than a century.

It mattered as well to the other side. It is hard for us to appreciate the extent to which Voltaire and his death held the popular imagination. Fifty years after it happened, Thomas Carlyle, the nineteenth-century sage and critic, surveyed the debate skeptically, ironically, but without being able to let it go. He pronounces himself ambivalent about whether Voltaire deserved, like Charlemagne, to be always called "the great." Perhaps he was not the greatest man since Noah. But with the exception of Luther, no one seems to have made a stronger impression on the European mind; he was an extraordinarily important cultural figure. And this fact in the political context of the time made his death and subsequent burial irresistible to all sides: "maledictions, expostulations and dreadful death scenes painted like Spanish *sanbenitos* [Inquisition sackcloths] by weak well-meaning persons of the hostile class," and eulogies by "open or secret friends."

Carlyle's essay is a mark of a new contentious age for the work of the dead. He quotes at length a major source for the peaceful-end version of Voltaire's death; he curses all sides; he says that it does not make any difference where one is buried; he says it is wrong to deny a great man a proper place however he died. Then

Carlyle claims that the hermeneutic problems interpreting how one dies are insurmountable while at the same time trying to sort out the facts as if they really mattered. He condemns as spurious the many idle tales on dying horrors and remorse and says that even if they were true, they would be irrelevant. Like the Puritan William Perkin, Carlyle rejects the correspondence between a peaceful death and a virtuous life. Anyone who has watched "in every age of the world" the perfectly composed dying moments of men like the legendary eighteenth-century French highwayman Cartouche or the infamous early-nineteenth-century English murderer John Thurtell and yet "continue[s] to regard the manner of a man's death as a test of religious orthodoxy, may boast himself impregnable to merely terrestrial logic." But terrestrial logic is not the point. A new kind of political enchantment is.[152]

David Hume

The death, in 1776, of the philosopher David Hume in Edinburgh is the last of my representative anecdotes about the new work of the dead. It is the most self-consciously historicist. It, like the others, is thoroughly imbricated in the politics of its day. But more than they, it illustrates the ways in which death and the dead body were, philosophically rather than theologically, in contention.[153]

James Boswell, Dr. Johnson's intimate friend who was well connected in Hume's circles, worried a great deal about Hume's seeming equanimity in the face of death but also about the generally unsettled question of what a reasonable man should think on the subject of death. He spoke in 1782 with Henry Home, Lord Kames, a major figure in the Scottish enlightenment, about a medallion that the dying lord had commissioned for his monument. Kames did not like death's heads and bones and had asked for a veiled skeleton. Boswell told him that he thought it looked like an old woman's skeleton and, besides, one ought not to tamper with these sorts of emblems: "Death is a figure well known." "Death as a skeleton, Time with Wings, scythe and sandglass, Justice with scales"—one did not alter established emblematic forms as one pleased. The dead, in short, were somehow fixed in the imagination. Lord Kames was not so sure. "Somebody," he said, had "first invented an emblem. Why should another man not invent a new one?" "But it is a universal sign," Boswell protested. Once it had become established, "no one would understand a new one." And there the conversation ended. "My Lord was so weak he could neither rise nor sit down comfortably." A little more than three weeks later, the great proponent of a naturalist aesthetic was dead. In this encounter Boswell takes the conservative position: he thinks there is something fixed—adamantly old—about how we imagine death: dead bodies and bones. Time cuts down humanity with its scythe as the laborer cuts wheat. Kames, by contrast, argues for the artificiality of such associations. Even if one cannot escape death, one can literally make up how one imagines it. Nothing about it is "unrepresentable"; death does not undo humanity but provides the opportunity for free play. Death and the dead body are up for grabs.[154]

Similar conversations were taking place on the Continent. Gotthold Ephraim Lessing, for example, the philosopher and dramatist, articulated a German version of how neoclassicism offered a way out of a very long Christian tradition of representing death as decay. His immediate object was to attack the hapless Professor Klotz, who held that death in antiquity was represented primarily as a skeleton, and to make the case that it was more usually understood as its twin: sleep. Of course, Lessing writes, "the art of antiquity offers images of the skeleton." But what does that mean? Does the skeleton have to represent the evil of death, its "personified abstraction," its "godliness"? Of course not. "Why can't a skeleton just represent a skeleton? Why does it have to be something else?"[155] More to the point, Lessing argues, the Greeks were able to imagine the process of dying as far less horrible than the moderns imagine it. There is here an acute sense that one can refashion, through argument and struggle and philology and history, how one understands death in the eighteenth century by reinterpreting classical antiquity with a more complex, nuanced understanding of death. We need not decide whether this is true, only recognize that educated men of the Enlightenment thought they could unmake almost two millennia of conceiving of the horror of being dead.

Boswell had long been worried about what to think of dying and being dead, and became acutely so as a consequence of David Hume's death. In 1776, Boswell visited him just before he died and was sufficiently unsettled by the philosopher's calm to confide to both his diary and his friends that it had left him with "right and wrong and every distinction confounded in my view." Thirteen years before his conversation with Lord Kames and seven years before Hume died, he had badgered Samuel Johnson on the subject, specifically on Hume's claim that one could get over the fear of death. Hume was, as Boswell reported to his friend, "no more uneasy to think that he should *not be* after this life, than that he *had not been* before he had existed." Hume's formulation is certainly not original. In fact, it is pretty clearly a conscious paraphrase of what the ancient materialist philosophers Lucretius and Epicurus had argued: no one is made anxious about contemplating the eternity when one did not exist before one's birth; it is therefore irrational to fear the eternity of nonexistence that is death. Whether Boswell was attracted by the wisdom and the aesthetics of a pre-Christian age and subsequently terrified by his own potential apostasy, or was repelled by Hume's calm and wanted confirmation of his sensibility, he plagued poor Johnson on the subject.[156]

The line of interrogation that Boswell pursues says little about revealed religion—that is, the rightness or wrongness of Hume's position—but concentrates instead on an empirical examination of whether it could be true. Religion does come up in a guilty aside in which Boswell confesses that he knew that despite Johnson's professed belief that death is "'kind Nature's signal for retreat' from this state of being to a 'happier seat,'" the great man could not shake his existential terror of dying and of being dead. Their discussion, as Bowell reports it, is about facts, a way of talking about this serious subject that turns it from a religious or philosophical to an empirical question. If Hume really believed what he says, "his perceptions are disturbed," Johnson insists. Would you believe him, he asks Boswell, if he claimed that he could hold his finger in a candle flame and not be burned? Boswell does not relent. Their common friend, the actor and acerbic wit Samuel Foote, claims that when he was deathly ill he was not afraid to die. Not true, Johnson replies: "Hold a pistol to Foote's breast, or to Hume's breast, and threaten to pull the trigger and you will see how they behave." But can we not fortify ourselves against death, insisted Boswell, who began to feel a little uneasy at this point because Johnson was so clearly discomforted. Johnson's mind was, as Boswell explains, like a Roman amphitheater in which the lions were death and Johnson a gladiator. He drives them back into their dens, but without killing them: "they are assailing him still." "Let it alone," Johnson insisted; "it matters not how a man dies but how he lives. The act of dying is of no importance." Dying is short and of no importance. With "an earnest look," he added, "a man knows it must be so, and submits. It will do him no good to whine."

Boswell tried to press on but Johnson was so provoked and agitated that he stopped the conversation. "Give us no more of this," he said, "in a way that alarmed and distressed me" then. Boswell continues that Johnson "shewed an impatience that I should leave," and he let it be known that he did not want to see Boswell anytime soon. For his part, Boswell thought he had been too severely dealt with by Johnson, even though he knew that he had this time, as so often before, pushed matters too far. He sent a letter of apology saying that he may have been wrong, "but not intentionally."

Perhaps. But Boswell knew his friend. Johnson was a man who throughout his life was terrified of dying and of being dead; he feared the state of not-being as a metaphysical reality; he feared damnation; he feared Death. Boswell took up the subject once again with the same combination of horror and attraction, the same eagerness to watch his famous friend in a state of high emotion, after Hume died. He was shocked, he reports to Johnson, that Hume "persisted in his infidelity when he was dying." Johnson claims not to be surprised. Hume had never seriously studied the New Testament, had never inquired about the truth of religion, and therefore one would expect him to die in ignorance, short of

God's miraculously sending an angel to set him right. Yes, Boswell responds, but still he had "reason to believe that the state of annihilation gave Hume no pain." This, Johnson responds firmly and out of a lifetime of irrepressible anxiety on the subject, is humanly impossible. He must have been simulating calm out of vanity. (There is some truth to this, and even Hume admits he was writing his own obituary.) In any case, he was faking composure, because no one could face going into an unknown state without being uneasy at "leaving all he knew." In any case, because Hume did not believe in an afterlife, he had no reason to speak the truth.

The horror of death seemed to have been gripping Johnson more than usual that night, reports Boswell, and still he persisted in pestering his friend. He suggests that because he himself had sometimes, for a few moments, not feared death, it seems at least possible that Hume could remain in such a state of calm for a "considerable state of time." Johnson confesses that he finds all this unimaginable: he had never had a moment when death had not been terrible to him, and any man who claimed the contrary must be doing so because the desire for the praise that calm might garner never leaves one. Again Boswell argues his point, but after a few more ripostes gives up: "even the powerful mind of Johnson seemed foiled by futurity." As for himself, he confesses rather unconvincingly, he would rather live with "the gloom of uncertainty in solemn religious speculation, being mingled with hope," than in the "emptiness of infidelity."[157]

One remarkable aspect of these conversations is how little they had to say about the Christian drama of resurrection, judgment, and life everlasting. Perhaps it was an unspeakable fear of damnation on Johnson's part that kept him off the subject; perhaps Boswell gave him no openings. They talked about matters of fact, about the physiology and psychology of dying, about how to interpret behavior and whether it could ever be taken at face value. Some of this is not unprecedented, but the fact that it could occupy a whole conversation on this subject is. It is the sort of debate one might stage between Sir William Osler, one of the founders of the Johns Hopkins Medical School, who in the early twentieth century did the first systematic survey of how people actually die—all but a handful of his five hundred cases expired without pain, he claimed—and Sherwin Nuland, professor of medicine at Yale, who in a recent best-selling book on the subject argued, also from empirical evidence, that, to the contrary, most people die miserably. Hume, in Boswell's and Johnson's conversations, seems to represent the possibility of an anti-metaphysical death, a death outside religion, a death that was historically staged in classical antiquity, a death that had no more—but also no less—meaning than any other event of nature or human affairs. It was, as we might say today, "Humean." It was a world-class effort to bring order and calm to nature by mind alone.[158]

But this is only part of the story. There was no question at the time, and—unlike the case of Voltaire—only a few questions subsequently, that Hume died peacefully.[159] At issue was the political meaning and decorum of his deathbed. People wrote about his deathbed as if they were reviewing a play in which Hume staged a radical ending. When it came his time to die, he behaved as his friends expected. He had already, a year and a half earlier, given a coolly clinical account of his last illness in a short autobiographical addendum to the last edition of his *History of England*. "In spring, 1775, I was struck," he wrote, "with a disorder in my bowels, which at first gave me no alarm, but had since, as I apprehend it, become mortal and incurable. I now reckon upon a speedy dissolution." He wrote that he was not in much pain, that he had never worked better, and that he continued to enjoy the company of friends. According to Adam Smith, he spent his last days reading the second-century C.E. Lucian's *Dialogues of the Dead*, an enormously self-conscious choice of a classical pagan writer famous for his revival of beautiful, golden age Greek and more specifically for writing in a genre—the letter from the dead—that would find many imitators in the eighteenth century. Great men of one era talked with their dead counterparts of another—Socrates, Alexander, Montaigne. Smith knew that his friend was being provocative. There had been one such dialogue in 1754 in which a repentant—dead—Viscount Bolingbroke tells Hume that he and Hume were wrong in their critiques of religion.[160]

Hume, with the complicity of Adam Smith, thus fashioned an explicitly pagan deathbed in a certain classical tradition that was intended for public consumption. No one would mistake his end for that of Socrates. We now know, however, that Hume was in fact not reading the relatively dignified *Dialogues of the Dead* but a still more outrageous Lucian dialogue, *Kataplous*, from which he took his much-reported deathbed banter.[161] (Perhaps Smith reported the other Lucian title because he wanted his subject to be reading something provocative but still suitable.) Hume engaged, Smith tells us, in a running joke in which he imagined himself arguing with Charon, the ferryman of Hades, about putting off for some time the ride across the River Styx to the land of the dead. It was meant to be an outrageous performance, and it was: "I have been correcting my works for a new edition. Allow me a little more time, that I may see how the public received my alterations," Or this last gambit: "If I live a few years longer, I may have the satisfaction of seeing the downfall of some of the prevailing systems of superstition." And here Charon lost his temper: "You loitering rogue, that will not happen these many hundred years. Do you fancy I will grant you a lease for so long a term? Get into this boat this instant." Hume died as he had lived, his friend Adam Smith reported, "approaching as nearly to the idea of a perfectly wise and virtuous man, as perhaps the nature of human frailty will permit." Joseph Black, professor of medicine at Glasgow and Hume's physician, confirms that his patient breathed his last "in such a happy composure of mind that nothing could exceed it." In other words, Smith wittily tells the story, with "strokes of good humor, with the most happy allusions to [Hume's] peculiar tenets," of an infidel who not only forswore revealed religion but spent his last days joking with the mythical boatman on the River Styx. Scandal multiplied by scandal.[162]

And then the battle in the press began. Smith wrote, perhaps disingenuously, that his "very harmless sheet of paper" in which he reported on the deathbed of his friend earned him "10 times more abuse" than the *Wealth of Nations*, in which he attacked Britain's monopoly-plagued commercial system: "Can anything be more frivolous, more childish, more indecently wanton and presumptuous in a dying man . . . than H[ume]'s dialogue with *Charon*?" wrote one correspondent to the *Weekly Magazine*. His well-known hostility to Christianity, wrote another, "is likely to receive more support from that jocularity, and unconcerned composure with which, we are told, he wound up the thread of life, than from all his metaphysical subtleties." The *Gentleman's Magazine* was less hostile in its generally appreciative review of Hume's deathbed but allowed that "we can not think anyone 'perfectly wise' who is not *wise to salvation*."[163]

"No proper evidence has ever been produced by Dr. Smith," grumped the Presbyterian Joseph Towers, that Hume's deathbed revealed him to be "a perfectly wise and virtuous man." To the contrary. Compare him to a London tradesman or a country clergyman who died under Christian principles; the "striking inferiority of this celebrated skeptic" is clear.[164] George Horne, bishop of Norwich and master of Magdalen College, Oxford, is more pointed in his criticisms of Smith for bringing favorable attention to Hume's wickedness. The first edition of his attack is bound in the Bodleian Library with another on a related question—his 1784 "Letter on Infidelity," promised already in the 1777 work—in which Horne argues that the philosophy of Epicurus from which Hume took his account of being dead is "ever ruinous to society," that it contributed to Greece's decline, and that it is doing the same thing in contemporary England and France. William Wilberforce in 1797 would proclaim the prescience of that prediction. He attacks Smith for praising the actions of a man who could anticipate—as he did in his joke with Charon—"as at no great distance, the more complete triumph of his skeptical principles." Hume's performance, he says, is a prelude to the later revolutionary end of religion. One need only look to France, where the effects of infidelity have produced their full effect. Although Wilberforce does not say so explicitly, it is the affective quality of Hume's last act that rankled, its humor and the admiration that it produced. "Infidelity," he says, "is in general a disease of the heart more than of the understanding."

Horne, of course, did not see the revolution in France in the deathbed of Hume. But he understood the emotional issues as Wilberforce did. Anyone who can, as

Smith did, reflect on a friend who amuses himself on his deathbed playing whist, reading Lucian, and being "droll with Charon," would smile on the destruction of Babylon and the Lisbon earthquake. Dying like "our brother philosophers, the calves in the field and the asses of the desert," that is, foolishly and insensibly, is not admirable. Smith is unwise to make widely known the purportedly praiseworthy death of a man who would destroy religion. Horne commends that the public use as a model instead the decorous death of the "learned judicious and admirable [Richard] Hooker," one of the greatest Anglican theologians, whose death in 1600 was well known and long admired.[165]

Back comes a reply in this very active pamphlet war. "Never before," claims the writer, actor, and humanitarian Samuel Jackson Pratt, "were the pillars of orthodoxy so desperately shaken" as by the unexpectedly and widely publicized peaceful death of Hume. His enemies had wished and expected a very different behavior and now, of course, they were disappointed. (He may have had Johnson specifically in mind.) It is in this context that one needs to understand Horne's "abominable prudery of sentiment." And, in any case, Pratt contends, Horne offers no evidence for the superiority in the manner of Hooker's death; he concludes, more generally, that Hume's "system, upon the rectitude of his life[,] can not be wrong."[166]

But this was not the end. The fate of Hume's body is another modern beginning, a new kind of work for the dead. He left £100 to have a tomb built over his grave in the Old Calton Burial Ground, a secular cemetery carved out of an old pasture high above Edinburgh, where he had bought a plot. (See chapter 5 for more on this place.) Designed by Robert Adam, Scotland's best-known neoclassical architect, it is a Roman-style cylinder modeled on the famous tomb of Theodoric, the Ostrogoth king, at Ravenna. An urn guards its door (fig. 4.13). For the past 150 years, it has stood near the one-hundred-foot-tall Political Martyrs Monument, built in 1844 by the "Friends of the People" to commemorate five political prisoners deported to Australia in 1794. Thousands followed Hume's funeral in the streets; the activity of the grave diggers "attracted the gaping curiosity of the multitude." "From the busy curiosity of the mob," writes Pratt, "one would have presumed them to entertain notions that the ashes of Mr. Hume had been the cause or object of miraculous exertion." Perhaps, he speculates archly, they "expected the hearse to have been consumed in livid flames or encrusted in flames of glory." "Ah," one of the crowd was overheard to say, "he was an atheist." "No," replied another, "he was an honest man."[167]

Hume's ploy was a clever one, and Charon's response the only one the boatman could have given if he was to have any hope of ferrying the philosopher over the Styx. Hume meant religious superstitions of all sorts; the Christian belief in an afterlife is only an example. And superstition of that sort is of course still with us.

4.13. Tomb of David Hume, Old Calton Cemetery, Edinburgh.

But Charon may have had something else in mind. We still "stand over or above" (*superstāre*) death and the dead body with feelings of awe or reverence or the sense that they mean a great deal. Ours is a disenchanted enchantment, a knowing idolatry. We moderns know—or at least in public we act as if we knew—that there is nothing to know specifically about the ontology of death (or life) or of the dead body. A dead body is a dead body. But we still, as before, need to live with our dead: "Historiography is a labor of death and a labor against death."

In the eighteenth century, a very old enchantment of the dead and a very old disenchantment—the quarrel with Diogenes—takes a turn away from metaphysics, away from a cosmic order and is reconfigured in the historical, anthropological, psychological, and political language of the modern era. They—the dead, individually and collectively in our imaginations—perform a magic we can believe in. A magic for our times. But it is not cynical or even ironic. I am not thinking here of a wink. My claim is not so much that we "try to distil the eternal from the transitory," as Foucault claimed Kant was doing, but rather that all those small, contingent, transitory deaths and the dead (little Ds) subsist through the power of eternal Death and the Dead: big Ds.

Around 1800, a thousand-year-old regime of the dead began to crumble. Edmund Gibbon would date it back to the middle of the fourth century, to when the body of St. Babylas was brought into the grove of Apollo in Antioch and the oracle of the old god refused to speak again. The dead of the Church in deep time—of a Christian community however fractured—became dispersed. New kinds of places—cemeteries—open to a far broader range of people and purposes came slowly into existence. Imagined already almost a century earlier as avatars of the ancient pagan Elysium, they were made real with the opening of the Cimetière du Père-Lachaise in Paris in 1804. This story is the subject of the next chapter.

Chapter 5
THE CEMETERY
AND THE NEW REGIME

In these refuges of the dead are gathered together all ranks and ages: the Russian is by the side of the Spaniard; the Protestant, the Jew, not far from the Catholic; people of radically different opinions find themselves finally meeting in the dust.

F.-M. MARCHANT, *Le nouveau conducteur
de l'étranger à Paris* (1824)

Like Diogenes, although for different reasons, Karl Marx thought that the dead should be thrown over the walls. If not, they haunt us. The bourgeois revolutionaries in France had "conjure[d] up the spirits of the past to their service" in order to disguise a new phase of world history, and the working class, he wrote, should not follow their example. Humanity needed an exorcism to bring an end to history. Leave the dead alone, he insisted; the proletarian revolution "cannot begin with itself before it has stripped away all superstition about the past." Let the ghosts go, he warned, and do not invite them back: "The revolution of the nineteenth century must let the dead bury their dead in order to arrive at its own content."[1]

Marx borrowed the maxim from Jesus, who delivered it twice: once to a disciple ("Follow me, and let the dead bury their dead," Mt 8:22), and once to an unspecified interlocutor who asked that he be allowed to put off joining Jesus in order to first bury his father ("Let the dead bury their dead: but go thou and preach the kingdom of God," Lk 9:60). Both times it had the same revolutionary implication: to follow Jesus is to forsake not only one's old life—"No man, having put his hand to the plough, and looking back, is fit for the kingdom of God" (Lk 9:62), Jesus said to a man who wanted to first say goodbye to friends—but also the dead, the bearers of the past.[2]

But the dead were *not* left to bury the dead, either by the followers of Christ or by the revolutionaries of the eighteenth, nineteenth, and twentieth centuries.

Marx was not thrown over the wall. The early-nineteenth-century cemetery and its successors offered a novel and luxuriantly protean space—almost a tabula rasa that could be furnished with a great variety of plants, trees, walks, monuments, and bodies—where the dead could haunt the living anew, to do the work of civilization. This space, the cemetery, was a historicist jumble made of borrowed bits of different pasts: Egyptian, Roman, Greek, medieval Christian, Ottoman, Moghul, and more. It belonged nowhere in particular, and the bodies that rested there had no claim on it beyond those of convenience, inclination, and either the ability to pay or (if poor) the calculations of others who paid. It followed the dictates of instrumental reason: it was meant to be clean; it was the public policy alternative to churchyard intramural burial; it comported with the latest engineering, horticultural, and aesthetic fashions. Custom, the ruling principle of the churchyard, had nothing to do with the cemetery. It was a place of sentiment loosely connected, at best, with Christian piety and intimately bound up with the emotional economics of family. In it, a newly configured idolatry of the dead served the interests less of the old God of religion than of the new gods of memory and history: secular gods. The cemetery was a cosmopolitan place, even if every corpse was not a citizen of the world: it could be anywhere; it welcomed strangers; there were no barriers beyond those of the sort that would regulate entry to a store or a railway station or an exclusive salon. National cemeteries testified to an imagined community—a nation— and its shared history as represented by its honored special dead. Religious denominations, political alliances, and fraternal organization could all create their own stratigraphies of their dead. Freehold property and very long leases allowed bourgeois families to create shrines like those that, under very different circumstances, previously had been the privilege of a landed aristocracy. The new spaces whose story this chapter tells were open to money and talent and differing points of view. They were, in short, the space for a *Gesellschaft* (a society) rather than, as the churchyard had been, a *Gemeinschaft* (a community) of the dead.

Put negatively, the cemetery was not a churchyard; it was not controlled by a church; it was not autarchic; it was not old; it did not make the dead evident in mounding soil and wavy church floors but instead hid them decorously in specially designed landscapes amid a flurry of monuments that proclaimed their memory, or in any case the memory of those who could afford it. It did not make the claims that the churchyard did: that it represented the Christian community of the living and the dead. And it rejected the deep historical roots of the churchyard in favor of other and far more secular histories. In sum, it was everything that the places of the dead in the old regime were not or claimed not to be.

More affirmatively, it was a genuinely new and spectacularly versatile stage for the work of the dead in the making of memory and community and the recollection of a history for all sorts of people for many different purposes. The ashes of Abelard and Eloise; of the Doors' Jim Morrison; of Victor Noir, who died in a nineteenth-century duel and who is buried under a life-size bronze sculpture whose genital area is rubbed shiny by tens of thousands of women who think it brings fertility or love; and of the murdered of Dachau, Auschwitz, Neuengamme, and Ravensbrück are all within a few hundred meters of one another. (There is now a fence around Noir's tomb.) This could not have happened before there were spaces like the cemetery of Père Lachaise. The epitaph "Here, in an urn, bits of earth mixed with ashes brought back from Auschwitz perpetuate the memory of martyrs" shares a field with that for Marie-Anne Bondini-Barelli, the leading soprano of the Italian opera in Paris: "O death! You have imposed silence on the sweetest sounds ever heard." Distant bodies are brought together. Beginning in the mid-nineteenth century, hundreds of famous and not so famous Hungarian, Czech, Serbian, and Greek bodies were buried—or more often reburied—in magnificent spaces where they became the bodies of the nation. The ashes of artists, musicians, writers, and political figures of all sorts were at the service of the living in their search for new cultural and social configurations. On 13 September 1833, Rapahel's tomb was opened to determine whether the skull in the Academy of St. Luke in Rome was really his. It was not. His skull was with the rest of him and was said to match the self-portrait in *The School of Athens*; his larynx was unusually large, leading some to fear that this god of painting had an inordinately loud voice. Ingres somehow got a rib, which he worshipped. Great efforts were made to identify the body and burial place of Johann Sebastian Bach, who had been lost in St. Thomas's churchyard in Leipzig but became culturally exigent in the early nineteenth century when the *St. Matthew Passion* became the epitome of German Protestant music. There are hundreds of examples. Indeed, the nineteenth century opened up an era of exhumation that rivaled all but the most fevered periods of the cult of saints. Jewish cemeteries, too, shared in the novelty as they came to look more like the great bourgeois cemeteries of their neighbors than they did the traditional burial places we have in mind after visiting Prague or seeing the paintings of Ruisdael.[3]

To take the long view: the dead in the cemetery lent their authority to a new order, just as their ancestors in churchyards had done with the advent of Christianity and as they continued to do for millennia in the cities and villages of Europe until they moved elsewhere. In the late eighteenth century, the corpse ("the magical life image concealed in the shrine of the body," which Diogenes would have us toss over the wall because it was meaningless) came to work its idolatrous magic in the service not of a transcendent God (or, more precisely, in the service of the body of Christ on earth—His church) but of other gods: family, civil society, nation, class, history.[4] Durkheim might have said that it underwrote the sacred foundations of the modern world. If the church and the churchyard were a matrix of Christians, living and dead, the cemetery was the space in which their bodies supported the interest of the major cultural and political innovations of the nineteenth and twentieth centuries.

Otto von Bismarck understood this. In 1849, he visited the cemetery in Berlin where the dead of the March Revolution of 1848 are buried. Afterward, he wrote to his wife with a heart full of bitterness; he could not forgive these dead, he told her. But more to our point, he could not "forgive the idolatry practiced at the graves of these criminals whose every tombstone boasts of 'Freedom and Rights,' a mockery of God and man." He reminds himself and his young wife that we are all full of sin and that God will judge us all, but still, he writes, he cannot stop his heart from swelling with poison when he thinks about—again the crucial term—the "idolatrousness" with which Berliners come to these graves. And they kept coming, forbidden in some years, tolerated in others, with and without disturbances. To this day, the cemetery in the Friedrichshain Park, unthinkable in the old regime, remains a site of memorial reflection for the German Left, although after 1900, when Wilhelm Liebknecht, one of the founders of the SPD was buried there, Friedrichsfelde became known as the "socialist cemetery." In Paris, the private Cimetière de Picpus, where the bodies of 1,306 victims of the last phase of the Reign of Terror are buried, has something of the same quality for the Catholic Right. Old aristocratic families still bury their dead here; Carmelite nuns pray for the dead in its chapel; the names fill its walls. It borders on the Rothschild Hospital.[5]

This chapter explains why the cemetery came to challenge and largely triumph over the churchyard and how it emerged from a wide range of imaginative possibilities. It begins by examining the purported hygienic rationale for the new regime, asserted with an urgency and certitude that belied the lack of evidence for the mortal danger corpses posed to the living—an irrational certainty that still affects even well-educated and scientifically trained twenty-first-century doctors and others who should know better. The timing and insistence of the challenge that the cemetery posed to the old regime of the churchyard had little or nothing to do with scientific discoveries about health and disease and much to do with a revolution in cultural values and eschatology mapped in the realm of the imagination. We trace the genealogies that twine together to give birth to new imaginary venues of the dead and to their physical manifestation in the great nineteenth-century cemeteries not only of Paris and London but in much of the world besides. This chapter tries to get at their essence—their necrogeography (so different from the churchyard's), their sociology, and their legal standing. It offers examples of the new work of the dead made possible by these new places: how they labored in the making of the modern world.[6]

By this I mean not just that the dead in cemeteries are symptomatic of the modern world, of its flux and lack of fixity. Yes, "all that is solid melts into air" and the cemetery is an arena for this mercurial quality. Nor that the dead in cemeteries are constitutive in the sense that they define and sacralize—in a secular way—a variety of social and political configurations, although they do that, too. They are constitutive of modernity because they set its limits. In the old regime, the dead in the churchyard were central to the whole great story of resurrection and redemption: death is not an interloper but the main foe to be defeated at the end of time. Death in the modern world is not so easily fitted into a narrative. It defies change; it defies the possibility of a sense of time that opens up infinitely into a better future. Once Thomas Malthus is done with William Godwin, the philosopher's speculation that immortality can be achieved through the working of mind over matter is in shambles. The bodies in the new spaces of the dead are fixed. Individuals may believe in this or that form of life after death, but the cemetery speaks of finitude. This is how it is. Forever.[7]

THE DANGER OF THE DEAD AND THE RISE OF THE CEMETERY

> The foundation of the whole subject [hygiene and cemetery reform] is that animal matter in a state of decomposition is injurious to health. If this is true burying grounds in town must be injurious. . . . Now it appears to me that the Evidence of that fundamental truth in your report is neither so strong, so precise nor so varied as it might be as is necessary to produce a powerful impression on the public mind. [I recommend] that the whole of this part be *greatly* strengthened if there were time for it.
>
> LETTER, THOMAS SOUTHWOOD-SMITH
> TO EDWIN CHADWICK, 1843

Edwin Chadwick, the most important sanitary reformer of his day and the author of the best-selling parliamentary report on the dangers of the dead to the health of towns, could not have been happy with this letter.[8] He had sent a draft copy of the report to his close colleague Thomas Southwood-Smith for comment. The report mattered to him: its recommendations were far-reaching; it was the only one of his many influential reports that was solely his work; he regarded it as a model for what was to come. And he knew that no one was better equipped

5.1. *Consecrated Ground.* Phiz (Hablot K. Browne), from Dickens, *Bleak House*, 1853.

to evaluate it than his friend and ally: a leading doctor who was active in public health reform and no friend of the vested interests of the old regime in Church or State. The response came back: it would be better if his evidence could be "*greatly* strengthened." It wasn't.[9]

This section asks whether Southwood-Smith was right to be cautious: are the dead really deadly? On the one hand, he knew that in principle they were dirty and dangerous: being a confirmed miasmatist, one who thought that disease was spread by bad air, he believed that stinking, decomposing matter was mortally dangerous; and dead bodies were without doubt stinking animal matter in a state of decomposition; therefore it was injurious to health to bury them in towns close to concentrated populations of the living: QED (fig. 5.1). On the other hand, he also knew that as an empirical matter the case was much less convincing. The evidence might be "sufficient to form the fact in any normal mind"—that is, any mind that is already of this opinion—but it would not sway those not already on board.

More generally, this section explores whether the deadliness of the dead ultimately matters in explaining the decline of the old regime of the churchyard and the rise of the cemetery. Historians have generally accounted for this succession in two ways. The first regards it as a consequence of a new attitude toward death itself, one that turns away from older ones: from a fascination with the horrid physical realities of corpses, from the great religious drama of an earlier age, and from the ideal of a natural death—quiet, unanguished, and unmarked, like a tree's, or in an expected and ordinary part of life. In its place comes something more terrifying, personal, and threatening. This new attitude, romantic and sentimental, is focused on what Philippe Ariès calls "the death of the other," which encourages what he took to be excessive grief and ostentatious displays of personal mourning and memory: it was individualistic, familial, and maudlin. Death had escaped its metaphysical moorings for a more quotidian, worldly, and psychologically inflected existence. The communal place of the Christian dead gave way to the bourgeois space of the cemetery and to the revolution in sentiment that accompanied it. In the new cemeteries, the living came to imagine their dead selves and their loved ones in "a cool sweet grave" quietly slumbering. For those who held these views it became ever more important to bridge the chasm of death not just with the hope for a reunion in the next life but with a venue for a continuing relationship in this one.[10]

The dead needed the same amenities as the living might want for themselves: graves with all the privacy, comfort, and honor of bourgeois life; a comfortable bed in quiet surroundings far from noise and hubbub, where they could be cared for and rest undisturbed. In the garden cemetery, as a founder of the Glasgow Necropolis put it, "death was tranquility, and the only images that were associated with it were those of peaceful repose and tender sorrow." To be precise, the causal argument here is that because death came to be understood differently than it had been before, the living demanded, and got, new spaces for their dead where these new attitudes could find full expression.[11]

As far as it goes, this story has a great deal to commend it. But it does not explain the rise of the cemetery. First, there is the question of timing. Sleep is a very old metaphor for death; "peaceful repose and tender sorrow" are not novel hopes. We know that people have for centuries imagined the dead sleeping in churchyards and other venues. And the idea of continuing the relationships of life could be played out in churches and churchyards, if not quite as freely as in cemeteries. There is also the bigger question of how changes in attitude are translated into a millennial change in the places of the dead. These new attitudes themselves are grounded in broader changes; they come to us imbricated in layers of cultural, political, and social history that we need to lay bare in order to understand how changes in a state of mind—a kind of baroque pleasure in imaging the dead as rotting corpses transforming into a horror of such an image—are translated into action. We also need to be careful in deciding which attitudes are relevant. Anticlericalism probably played as big a role in the rise of the cemetery as romantic attitudes toward death. In other words, an explanation based on changes in attitudes toward death hides the processes through which these come to have an effect and other possible causes as well. And, finally this explanation mixes up cause and effect; if death and the dead are understood in new ways in the modern age (i.e., if there are "new attitudes"), then these are as much a consequence of the cemetery as the other way around. New venues allow the dead to do new work and the living to understand them differently.

A second explanation for the advent of the cemetery and the demise of the churchyard is simpler and more commonsensical. It is also the one that the historical actors themselves gave: dead bodies are deadly. By the late eighteenth century, progressive policymakers not only recognized this universal truth but also the fact that the dead were getting deadlier all the time; there were manifestly too many of them in too little space; they smelled bad; and they were thus causing illness and death among the living. These reformers gained the upper hand politically, and the clean, tidy, and well-managed extramural cemetery was the result. Historians, following the lead of their sources who gathered and publicized vast amounts of evidence on the nuisance of the unclean dead, have tended to embrace this view and for good reason. Rotting flesh does smell bad—this is evident to anyone—and even if the slogan "all smell is disease," as Edwin Chadwick said and as most reformers of the eighteenth and nineteenth centuries believed, is not true, we still seem to believe that the dead need to be hygienically disposed of in the interests of public health. Chadwick and company must have been right even if for the wrong reason.[12]

Let us start with this evidence. There were unquestionably ever more bodies, ever more cheek-by-jowl with one another and with the living. They kept accumulating at an ever greater rate as the population increased. Cities pressed everyone—the living and the dead—closer together. The Paris story is prototypical and, in broad outline, commonplace for urban Europe and the New World. On 30 May 1780, a wall collapsed between the most recently dug *fosse*—the burial pit—of the ancient Cimetière des Innocents and a neighboring house (fig. 5.2). (This vastly overused successor to a medieval church was where the shopping center and transportation hub Les Halles now stands.) Decomposing bodies spilled into the house's cellar. And this was not the first time that the dead had caused problems. In previous years, local residents had complained of trembling, vomiting, and fainting; wine reportedly had gone bad and candles went out. With rotting flesh tumbling

5.2. Cimetière des Innocents. Charles-Louis Bernier, 1786. Bibliothèque nationale de France.

into basements and a history of strange illnesses rife in the neighborhood, the dead came under new suspicion. Something had to be done: an investigation by an expert, Antoine-Alexis Cadet de Vaux—savant, chemist, member of the Royal Academy of Sciences—determined that first suspicions were correct. The dead, or more precisely "cadaverous gases," were a problem. They had to go.[13]

Hundreds of books, pamphlets, and inquiries over the next century came to the same conclusion. In England (the case I will develop in detail), the most extensive collection of evidence for the dangers of the dead is a series of books beginning with *Gatherings from Graveyards* in 1839 by the Victorian surgeon George Alfred Walker. Everyone from his day to our own has used his data to prove just how bad things were. Because of the prevailing medical theory of the day that bad smells caused disease, he was especially attentive to the nauseating odors of burial places. The dead stank, he showed again and again: New Bunhill—"intolerably offensive"; the vault of St. Savior, Southwark—"extremely damp and . . . the most offensive smell"; St. Clements Dane Burial ground on Great Portugal Street—"reeking with fluid which diffuses a most offensive smell." But more fundamentally, there were simply too many dead bodies in too little space. They were disgusting, and nothing made the point better than the "revolting and dangerous state of Enon Chapel and the receptacle beneath it" (fig. 5.3). After visiting it at least three times and interviewing former grave diggers, he reported that it contained an unimaginably dense mass of bodies: ten thousand, perhaps twelve

5.3. Enon Chapel Cemetery and Dancing Saloon. In National Philanthropic Association, *Sanatory Progress: Being the Fifth Report of the National Philanthropic Association* (London: J. Hatchard and Son, 1850), p. 71.

thousand of them in the fifty-nine-by-twenty-nine-foot space under this Dissenting place of worship on Clement Lane; twenty new corpses were added each week, he reported. (That would come to roughly twenty-five thousand burials per acre, more than seven times the density of bodies in the churchyards of St. John's, Clerkenwell, its nearest competitor.) There were only a few inches of dirt above the top layer, and it failed to cover the horrors of the scene; "particularly long black flies . . . a product of putrefaction" crawled out of the bodies. The only way this system could be maintained, Walker pointed out, was to make room for new bodies by getting rid of those that were already there; these, he was told, were flushed down a storm sewer to the Thames. Each time he visited this "Golgotha" he was newly appalled by the "total disregard of decency," by the "numbers of coffins [that] were piled in confusion," and by the "large quantities of bones [that] were mixed with earth."[14]

Enon Chapel may have been the most crowded, but there were many others almost as grotesque. Drury Lane Burying Ground, belonging to St. Martin-in-the-Fields, had been temporarily closed because the ground was "saturated with the dead," but had recently reopened when Walker visited; the churchyard in Whitechapel was so densely packed as "to present one entire mass of human bones and putrefaction"; the soil next to the church in Stepney was "imbued with the products of putrefaction, [and was] also extremely moist." The goings-on at Spa Fields, a private burial ground, seemed beyond belief. Neighbors reported foul-smelling smoke; upon investigation in December 1843, Walker reported that in a "bone house" he saw coffins in various states of decay being burned; there were human ribs and socket bones on the grill. Witnesses reported what seemed to be wheelbarrows full of human bowels being extracted from the putrid soil; others saw grave diggers deep in flesh. It was a place, Walker concluded, "that amongst the infamous of this class was the most infamous," a place "from the contemplation of which a strong man would have passed with the most intense loathing, disgust, and alarm."[15]

Walker amplified his findings in later books, in newspaper articles and broadsheets, and in testimony for the *Royal Commission Report on the Health of Towns*. There were also hundreds of locally organized investigations in London and other cities into the dangers of the dead. And most famously, the 1842 *Supplementary Report on the Results of a Special Inquiry into the Practice of Interment in Towns*, compiled under the direction of the leading sanitary reformer of the day, Edwin Chadwick, became one of the best-selling "Blue Books" (parliamentary papers) of the century. Everyone in the political classes now read about how dangerous the dead were. Although Walker's evidence still figured prominently, there was much new material in this massive document. Even allowing for the self-referential quality of these publications, there was a great deal of evidence for severe crowding in churchyards, and it was all aimed at showing how dense masses of the dead harmed the living.[16]

But we should put all this mess in context if we are to understand why the dead, in particular, seemed so dangerous in the places where they had been for so long. Here is a back-of-the-envelope calculation. Let us assume for the sake of argument the historically contingent claim that dead bodies count as dirt ("matter out of place") that needs to be cleared out. About fifty thousand people died in London in 1840 and contributed about four million pounds (allowing one hundred pounds for each body), that is, two thousand tons, of organic filth ("animal matter in a state of decomposition") that was buried, however untidily, mostly in churchyards. The living—about two million of them—meanwhile, excreted almost one hundred times as much feces: between 320 million and 640 million pounds (160,000 to 320,000 tons) of it (based on seven to fourteen ounces per person per day). Between 160 million and 225 million gallons of urine (1.75 to 2.5 pints per person) would have added to the city's odor, if not to its compost. If one could magically travel in time, it would be useful go back to the seventeenth-century churchyard of St. Clement Dane and sniff out whether it added much to the smell of Pissing Alley, which it bordered. Some of this waste from live humans would have gone into great, open cesspits that were emptied more or less often by night soil men; a great deal was thrown into gutters. In addition to all the human waste, there were mountains of animal excrement. Henry Mayhew, one of the great collectors of statistics on dirt in the nineteenth century, claimed that twenty-four thousand horses dropped 236 million pounds—118,043 tons five hundred weight, to be exact and to use the units he used—of manure every year, about a quarter of it in the streets, the rest in their stables. Cattle on the way to Smithfield Market added another fifty-two thousand tons. (Mayhew did not calculate the excrement from 1.4 million pigs walking to Smithfield Market.) In sum: dead humans contributed roughly 2,000 tons of rotting flesh to London in 1840; living humans, horses, and cows produced between 330,000 and a little less than 500,000 tons of excrement the same year: around two hundred times as much. We could add to the ledger of "animal matter in a state of decomposition" not contributed by the human dead the weight of the dead dogs, cats, and rats and of the excretions of live ones. On any balance sheet, the contribution of bodies to urban filth is disproportionately small compared with the attention that it received.[17]

It is impossible to quantify how much of which kind of dirt contributed to bad smells, but dead bodies had lots of competition. By some estimates, early modern people produced five pounds of solid organic food waste for every pound of feces. Mayhew studied the sources of other sickening smells that we might not at first think of: great mounds of empty oyster shells, gutters of rotting fish parts, spoiled meat. We can imagine others. But the bottom line of our exercise is that although two thousand tons of dead human flesh is not inconsequential, it is a very small proportion, easily less than 1 percent, of the foul-smelling organic dirt produced in London in 1840. The extraordinary nineteenth-century focus on the particularly disgusting quality of crowded churchyards and the public health hazards they posed will need some explanation beyond churchyards' objective contribution to the mess of cities.

Part of an answer may be changes in how people regarded smells. Smell is notoriously in the nose of the inhaler; some smells are more bearable than others, even pleasant to some and not so pleasant to others. And these borders shifted in the late eighteenth and early nineteenth centuries. It was the age of what the greatest historians of smell called "olfactory vigilance," an age when, for the bourgeoisie, certain street smells and the bodily smells of the poor became troublesome and quite possibly dangerous. People in the West have always found the smell of exposed dead bodies disgusting (plate 3), but for centuries the smell of crowded burial grounds and churches whose floors bulged with the shapes of the corpses below was tolerable. The historical question in this case is why the ancient smell of hidden corrupting flesh became pollution, why a commonplace odor became a threat not just to health but also to the social and moral order. The dead became dirty and therefore dangerous. Archdeacon William Hale, the most vocal clerical opponent of extramural burial and the demise of the churchyard, made a last-ditch effort in 1854 to make clear to his contemporaries that a major cultural shift with grave consequences but no objective correlative was about to happen. He and his family lived next to the churchyard of St. Giles, Cripplegate, which Walker and Chadwick had identified as one of the most crowded and offensive in London. It was, he admits, essentially made of the compost of seven hundred years of burial, but so what? It smelled, at the surface and in samples taken from six feet down, like compost, like ammonia. "The earth," he says, "had the qualities which are attendant upon every heap of the farmer's treasure upon every highly cultivated field." How can the physiologist say about evaporating ammonia: "avoid this place because it is dangerous to health"?[18]

The buried dead as a giant compost heap was once a commonplace idea. Dr. Johnson in his *Dictionary* gives as a use of "churchyard" a quote from Sir Francis Bacon: "in *Church-yards,* where they bury much; Where the Earth will consume the *corps* in fare shorter time, than other Earth will." Johnson took this quotation from a section of Bacon's *Natural History* that is about inducing and accelerating putrefaction. Here Bacon explains that placing something that is already putrefied next to something that isn't speeds the process along, as, for example, when "a rotten apple lieth close to another one," or when already putrefied dung is added to fresher dung, or when dead bodies are packed in churchyards. What Walker took as disgusting, Hale and generations before him took as the nature of things. There were also technologies available to deal with smell if it became bothersome; a study in 1854, for example, confirmed with scientific precision what had been known since at least the ninth century: that charcoal—as little as one inch of it—"destroyed the putrid exhalations of even a large animal." The attack on churchyards has to be seen therefore as in some measure part of a new and important episode in the history of smell, of what was and was not tolerable, of how odor was to be mitigated if at all, of what sort of dirt mattered.[19]

But opponents of closing urban churchyards did not generally resort to the history of anthropology or to an attack on the miasma theory of disease generally. They argued on their enemy's turf: Walker's and Chadwick's evidence, they claimed, had been falsified or distorted in the interests of their public policy objectives. The wife and children of the late Rev. Mr. Howe, who had ministered to Enon Chapel—Walker's worst case—protested, for example, that "a foul and cruel calumny on the memory of a beloved husband and revered father" had been perpetrated. Not a word was true: there were, according to the register itself, not 10,000–12,000 bodies but 3,403; the sewer through which bodies were allegedly floated to the Thames was a small barrel-sewer through which it was impossible to pass a body, and in any case it had been bricked over, not to prevent Howe's nefarious practices but as part of an enlargement project; the parliamentary select committee that visited the chapel in 1843 smelled nothing but then attributed their failure to confirm Walker's evidence to it being a day "favorable for carrying off effluvia." All the "thrilling horrors" that Walker had put before the committee came from a few small, irregular graveyards and was wholly unrepresentative, politically biased, and far too flimsy to be the basis of a historic policy change.[20]

These opponents of the sanitary reformers were both right and wrong. Churches and churchyards *were* crowded in the nineteenth century, if not as grotesquely as Walker and others claimed. And the problem was especially acute in London, which had not only a rapidly growing population of poor people but also a notoriously high death rate. Between 1800 and 1835, fourteen burial grounds under private management had been founded, not counting the first of the new cemeteries at Kensal Green, in order to meet rising demand. But the problem itself was far from new. Churches and churchyards had always been crowded; it is in their nature to be crowded. They were crowded in the fifth century. A Gallo-Roman aristocrat writes in horror at the disturbance of his grandfather's tomb—he had been the first of his line to convert—in a pagan cemetery that had become a Christian one: "it had for a long time been so filled up with both ashes from the pyres and bodies that there was no more room for digging." They were crowded in the fourteenth century, when two of the king's servants gave land for new burial places outside the walls of the City of London. They were crowded in the sixteenth century, when Hugh Latimer, bishop of Winchester, complained in 1555 that "man taketh his death in Paul's Church Yard" and that he himself was much the worse from its "ill-favored unwholesome savour." The so-called New Churchyard that London opened in 1559 was itself soon crowded. The Lord Mayor complained to the Privy Council twenty years later that the ground was so full that no corpses could be put in without turning out others. Churchyards were crowded in the seventeenth century. The vestry of St. Botolph, Bishopsgate, noted in 1621 that its churchyard was "buried so full" that there was scarcely room for a child; it was still open in 1840. John Evelyn, when he visited Norwich in 1671, observed that churches "seemed to be built in pits" because the "congestion of bodies" had so raised the ground around them.[21] The same holds for Dissenting burial grounds that Walker made so much of. When George Fox, the founder of the Quakers, was buried in the Friends' plot at the western edge of Bunhill Fields in 1691, a contemporary witness remarked that it was large but "quite full" with 1,100 bodies, dead from the plague or martyrdom. More than one hundred thousand dead bodies followed Fox's before the great Dissenting burial ground closed in the nineteenth century.[22]

Churchyards were crowded in the eighteenth century. Churchwardens and vestrymen of Saint Stephen in Bristol petitioned the House of Commons in 1773 for permission to expand their churchyard because "the surface thereof is raised by at least five feet higher than the natural surface of the Earth." Fifteen years earlier, the churchwardens of St. Andrew Holborn had petitioned to be allowed to buy more land for burial on the testimony of the sexton, who deposed that "it has been difficult to dig a Grave without digging up Parts of dead Bodies before decayed." Little had changed in this story for well over a thousand years, and the sextons whom Chadwick interviewed almost a century later still voiced the same complaint. Crowded churchyards were not a novelty in the 1830s and 1840s.[23]

And the insides of churches, where the elite were buried, were not much emptier. There were more than a hundred burials commemorated—many others would not have had memorials—in the floor of the south quire aisle alone of Bristol Cathedral. Room in the aisle of the church in the medieval town of Cranbrook in Kent had run out by the late seventeenth century, and bodies were being buried in the north and east of the chancel, traditionally reserved for the clergy, to meet demand for inside space; a falling in of the roof in 1725 stopped the makeshift practice until 1807 but not did not solve the problem: limited floor space, ever more dead. What Voltaire said of the Gothic churches of Paris could be said of all but the smallest English churches: "You step on ugly, disjointed, uneven stones that have been lifted up a thousand times to throw coffins under them."[24]

None of this is surprising. Nineteenth-century observers, like twentieth-century archeologists, understood that the problem of crowding was a long time in the making. A public health inspector in the northern city of Huddersfield reported that the parish churchyard there had first been used in 1584—it had replaced an older one when the church was rebuilt in its current Tudor Gothic—and that 38,298 bodies had been buried since; that would be, he calculated with the precision to which nineteenth-century reports are given, nine bodies per square yard distributed in what he estimated to be twenty-one layers. Crowding was also accelerating—4,334 corpses in the previous nineteen years—but that still leaves thirty-four thousand bodies from before rapid urbanization. Holy Trinity in the county town of Dorchester had been in use for 650 years, and by the middle of the nineteenth century some of the dead were piled so high as to be "above Mrs. Dee's window," wrote another inspector. By comparison, the major Paris burial ground, the Cimetière des Innocents, the very worst case to critics of the old regime of the dead, absorbed some two million Parisians in an area of 60 by 120 meters during the seven centuries before its closure in 1780: that is, the impossible density of roughly three hundred bodies per square meter. What was left of all those bones by the end found its way to the Catacombs, where tourists today can see them artfully arranged into various death symbols: the dead representing their fate (fig. 5.4).

Nothing in England was this dramatic, but everyone who studied the matter understood that the level of crowding in nineteenth-century urban churchyards was not the work of a few decades of population growth. The compacting, composting, jostling, and intermingling of corpses and coffins in various states

5.4. La "Mort Saint-Innocent." The statue was at the center of the Cemetery of the Innocents since ca. 1530. When the cemetery was closed, it was transported to Saint Gervais, then to Notre Dame, and eventually was made part of Alexandre Lenoir's Musée des Monuments français. It is currently in the collection of the Louvre.

of repair was and always had been endemic, a permanent condition, an inevitable consequence of the doctrine of *ubi decimus persolvebat vivus, sepeliatur mortuus* (the right to be buried where one had paid tithes, i.e., where one had lived), which gave each succeeding generation of parishioners a claim on the same relatively small space. Matters were made worse by the ever more common use in the sixteenth and seventeenth centuries of coffins in place of winding clothes and by the use of sturdy boxes, lead cases, and bricked vaults by an elite.[25]

All of this, Edwin Chadwick pointed out, either makes crowding inevitable or creates the need for endless new burial space. A corpse is not in "mortmain inalienably," the grave is not a *domus aeterna,* an eternal home; bodies have no right to rest undisturbed, he argues. Indeed, the dead are not rights-bearing subjects. All that the living should be able to claim for themselves is a place to decay into dust as quickly and decently as possible; every contrivance to prevent this is an assault against the rights of future generations and makes an already bad situation worse. Crowding in churchyards was made more acute by population growth and urbanization and new cultural practices, but there was nothing dramatic going on that would make eighteenth- and nineteenth-century reformers take aim at the intramural churchyard as one of the great evils of the age. And there was also no reason, in principle, that old expedients could not have met or at least ameliorated the new challenges.[26]

In the first place, a parish could simply add dirt on top of an earlier accumulation of the dead; this was not common, but the "Stranger's Ground" in Brady Street, Bethnel Green, did it. More usual was to level the churchyard every few centuries, throw away the bones, and start again. Even the smallest churchyards in scantily populated places did that; urban ones did it more often. Less dramatically, bones and pieces of coffin were jostled about to squeeze in just one more body. More comfortable to modern sensibilities, new churches and churchyards were built and old churchyards expanded. As the population of the parish of St. Peter's in the northern industrial city of Leeds grew from six thousand inhabitants in 1700 to almost forty-nine thousand in 1820, the churchwardens found room for the increased population of the dead by periodically enlarging its churchyard. (Ninety-seven percent of all bodies in the 1730s were buried there; 93 percent between 1810 and 1820.) In the rapidly growing industrial city of Kingston-on-Hull, Holy Trinity in 1783 added 14,520 square yards, more than three acres, to its medieval churchyard; the ground inside the churchyard was by then three feet above the level of surrounding ground; St. Mary's in Kingston more than quadrupled the size of its ancient churchyard from 750 square yards by adding 2,772 square yards.[27]

Anglicans also built hundreds of new churches, and most of these had churchyards. In the eighteenth century they were paid for largely through private philanthropy and through selling to the middle and upper classes access to pews and vault space. In the rapidly growing industrial city of Manchester, for example, a new church of St. James was consecrated in 1787 with a yard for the poor, and copious well-appointed vaults—regular avenues of lead-lined coffins, many of which lay behind iron grates through which they are exposed "to the eyes of visitors to this awful mansion"—that offered accommodation for several thousand bourgeois worthies: "many thousands of bodies have been interred in this singular depôt (it might almost be said *magazine*) of mortality," claimed an early history. St. Michael's, consecrated in 1789, had a "tolerably large" burial ground next to an earlier expansion of the mother church's so-called new burial ground for paupers. And so it went throughout much of urban as well as rural England. Parliament supplemented private funds with a £1 million grant in 1818 and another £500,000 in 1824 for new churches. Some had huge churchyards—ten thousand square yards for St. Martin's in Liverpool, for example.[28]

Crowding the dead was not new; it was systemic and long-standing; a variety of expedients were tried to alleviate the problem and to some extent succeeded. By the 1830s, it became clear that it was not enough. The reformers were right on one point: the old regime was failing to keep up with the demand for burial. But what does this have to do with public health and the dangers of the dead? Very little or a great deal, depending on how we construe the question. Very little in that the barriers to creating more churchyard space were largely political, and dead bodies in general do not cause disease. Rotting bodies, however smelly, did not create a public health crisis. We know that today and, as the epigraph at the beginning of this section suggests, nineteenth-century experts knew it as well. It has a great deal to do with public health and the dangers of the dead in that the debate about where to bury the dead turned overwhelmingly into a debate about disease. And, to come full circle, this shift is also explicable only in political terms.

Churchyards failed to meet demand because of the inherent conservatism of the old system: parishioners were loyal to the old churchyard and to old church vaults; vestries were reluctant to spend money; the vastly complicated old regime system of fees made cooperation among, and reform within, parishes difficult. But more important, they failed because the world into which the churchyard was born was irrevocably changed in the industrial age, which was becoming ever more inhospitable to the old expedients. Of course, new churchyards did not have to be contiguous to or near churches; consecrated land belonging to a parish could in principle be anywhere. But greater distances from the church itself destroyed the sense of the geographic and cultural autarchy of the parish that had made the churchyard culturally resonant. This was a real problem. Land near urban churches was scarce and competition for it between the dead and the living was becoming sharper. Of course there had always been some competition:

consecrated plague burial grounds were used for all sorts of industrial purposes after the dissolution of the monasteries; bits of churchyards were always in play.

But matters worsened in the modern age. St. Christopher le Stocks was demolished to make way for the extension of the Bank of England in 1780. "All that is solid melts into air," as Marx put it; the modern city was by nature oblivious to claims for eternal rest. Or, more simply, in the words of an obscure nineteenth-century observer, "railroads seem to have affection for burial grounds." Thomas Hardy's first job as a young architect was to supervise the nightly removal of hundreds of more or less rotting coffins from the old St. Pancras churchyard—William Godwin and Mary Wollstonecraft had been buried there, but their bodies had been removed earlier—to make way for a Midland Railroad tunnel. The British naval officer and novelist Frederick Marryat reported that in the "puritanical state of Rhode Island," "the sleepers of the railway [are] laid over the sleepers in death," where they "grind down the bones of the ancestors for the sake of gain, where consecrated earth is desecrated by the iron wheels, loaded with Mammon-seeking mortals." The clergy also quit caring, at least when it came to the poor. Friedrich Engels reported that in 1842 a railway line was cut through the consecrated ground of Manchester's pauper burial ground. "If it had been a respectable cemetery, how the bourgeoisie and the clergy would have shrieked over the desecration!!" he comments archly. "But it was a pauper burial-ground, and the resting-place of the outcast and superfluous, so no one concerned himself about the matter."[29]

None of this, however, gets at the immediate problem. The main reason that the old regime of the dead could not sustain itself was the same one that explains why accommodation for the living in Anglican places of worship lagged behind population growth in so much of urban England: politically organized Nonconformists sitting on parish vestries opposed using public money to support an established Church in which they did not worship and churchyards in which their dead were often made to feel unwelcome. Westminster could and did with difficulty allocate funds for new churches and churchyards; actually building them was harder, since it meant sorting out the property rights of the Mother Church, which were sometimes so complicated as to defy the best of lawyers. But when it came to the state's supporting consecrated burial places to replace crowded intramural ones that were to be closed, Nonconformists balked. The Congregationalist newspaper the *Patriot*, in particular, mounted a long and broadly disseminated critique of the evidence for churchyard crowding largely because it opposed the parliamentary remedy on offer: the 1842 bill proposed by William MacKinnon, the reforming conservative MP for Lymington, would have replaced crowded churchyards that had been closed with extramural burial places under the control of the Anglican clergy; the same structure of fees and the same laws for admission and for holding services as governed churchyards would have applied to the new spaces. MacKinnon's related efforts to clean up the Smithfield slaughterhouses and to remove rubbish from the streets were more successful, but they, unlike burial reform, did not entail defense of a thousand-year-old regime against its nineteenth-century opponents.[30]

More limited solutions were also politically problematic. Efforts to expand churchyards paid for, as they had almost always been, by local rates ran up against the fact that many vestries, especially in the north of England, were controlled by Congregationalists, Baptists, and Methodists who refused to vote for new levies. And when, in some parishes, levies did manage to pass, Dissenters refused to pay. New churchyard space was thus hostage to the much larger and hugely fraught debate about a sacred space controlled by an established Church and the demand for the civil rights of the dead in a pluralist society, one that was at the heart of so many other quarrels about burial in the eighteenth and nineteenth centuries.

By the 1850s, when the battle for the old regime had become hopeless, some clergymen were still trying to salvage what they could of the old order. But the ground had shifted. The governing body of the new East London cemetery replied to an address of the archdeacon of London as if the care of the dead were without a history: there was no reason, it said, to have a clergyman among those in charge of burial. There were also no grounds for subdividing the cemetery so that each of London's 106 parishes would have a space of its own: the cemetery "was designed to be a burial place for the whole city." Gone was the autarchy of the parish, even if some details of commuted fees of incumbents still needed to be worked out. The Commissioners of the Sewers had spoken.[31]

The dead had moved into a new universe with new people in charge. Sir John Simon, medical officer of health for the Commission, reported in the same year as the archdeacon's petition on the progress that had been made: "cattle markets have largely been removed from the city and the new Smithfield will soon be attractive enough to the trade to allow the council to extramuralise slaughter," he said with satisfaction; Sir Benjamin Hall's Metropolis Management Act would soon cure the "extreme sanitary evils of tidal drainage." And, sandwiched in with this good news, he reported that the nearly completed new city cemetery has "terminated forever the nuisances and scandals of intramural burial and will give you the means of greatly diminishing those evils that belong to the retention of the dead within the chambers of the living."[32] Healthy places for the dead had joined sewers, slaughterhouses, and river drainage as venues for the triumph of hygiene and progress in the most progressive of centuries. In France, we would add brothels to this list.

A determined party of reform had convinced the political nation that the dead were dangerous to the living and had to be dealt with accordingly. Like ghosts, those who may have been wronged when they were alive were especially threatening: "By secret avenues . . . [miasma from the poor] reaches the most opulent, and severely revenges their neglect, or insensibility to the wretchedness surrounding them." This claim had already been used in the late eighteenth century by advocates of more churchyards in crowded cities like Manchester: "If the effluvia of living bodies are of so deleterious a nature, how much more virulent must the effluvia be of bodies deceased," reasons the local newspaper.

By the 1830s, this warning had become a thunderous commonplace that demanded a more drastic solution. Dead bodies were an existential threat. George Alfred Walker, the most frequently quoted of the enemies of the urban dead, warned darkly of the "injurious and destructive agencies" of "putrefying animal substances" (specifically, dead bodies in graveyards), armed with "invisible and irresistible powers," to which "may be attributed the violence, if not the origin of some of the most destructive diseases which have depopulated the human race." "All smell is disease," Edwin Chadwick told a parliamentary inquiry, and nothing smelled worse than a putrefying corpse. One could be more precise: specific diseases were blamed on the dead. Typhus fever owed its origin to "the escape of putrid vapors," and "overcrowded burying grounds would supply such effluvia most abundantly," testified the eminent physician W. F. Chambers to MacKinnon's Select Committee when it was investigating the problem of city interments in 1842. Cholera likewise: the superintending inspector under the Nuisances Removal and Disease Prevention Act cited Sir James Clark, Queen Victoria's physician, to support his claim that it was caused by gases from unenclosed privies, the "same kind of gases as from graves."[33]

Talk like this was everywhere in official documents and in the press. It seems to have carried the day: the public health danger of churchyards explains why they closed in favor of cemeteries. Yes and no. Yes, in that it is the reason that the successful reformers and their allies would have given. No, in that this answer begs the question of why this claim was convincing enough not only to force the closure of urban churchyards but also to bring the dead forever more under the watchful eyes of public health authorities. The answer that contemporaries as well historians and many doctors today give is that truth triumphed: that the dead, especially in great numbers, were in fact a hazard to the living. For eighteenth- and nineteenth-century commentators, this was clear from the fact that they produced a horrible odor. To put it technically, they gave off "effluvia," from the Latin *ex fluere* "to flow out," tiny, insensible particles, noxious exhalations. These in turn caused disease because, more generally, what the Greeks had called "miasma"—"pollution, bad airs" in a literal and material sense—caused disease. Pollution, meaning ritual uncleanness, had been broadened to mean an uncleanness that caused specific diseases. The policy implication of this view was that the rotting, effluvia-producing flesh of the dead urgently needed to be cleaned up, sealed, and somehow prevented from giving off its morbid exhalations. Deep burial in single graves seemed the answer.[34]

Putting this claim in a broader context shows how puzzling it actually is. The living would seem, even to nineteenth-century observers, at least as dangerous as the dead. "By the mere action of the lungs of the inhabitants of Liverpool," argued the city's public health officer, who was thoroughly committed to miasmatic theory, "a stratum of air sufficient to cover the entire surface of the town to a depth of three feet, is daily rendered unfit for the purposes of respiration." He has it right; the chances of getting consumption or some other respiratory disease from breathing the exhalations of the living was infinitely greater than from breathing in the effluvia of the dead. But crowded churchyards had come to be a stand-in for the morally repulsive, horrible, almost phantasmagoric crowding and poverty of London and other nineteenth-century cities. Disgust for the dead body became a sign of how dangerous it must be.[35]

The rise of germ theory in the late nineteenth century definitively killed the view that effluvia caused disease. It did not, however, change anyone's mind about the health dangers of the corpse. Twenty-first-century doctors who ought to know better still act as if corpses are a threat to health and, especially in the numbers that accumulate after a natural disaster or battle, need to be disposed of as quickly as possible in the interest of public health, whatever the social and cultural consequences. There is no medical foundation for this policy. The World Health Organization, Médecins Sans Frontières, and others have been trying to convince doctors that the dead are not dangerous and that "the result of this mistaken belief is the overlooked and unintended social effect of the precipitous and unceremonious disposal of corpses." They could as well be speaking to Sir Edwin Chadwick's irritation at the Irish for waking their dead. In a section titled "Myths"—defined as superstitions against which science has to take a stand—a WHO report concludes: "Dead or decayed human bodies do not generally create a serious threat." "The facts indicate that there has not been any epidemic generated from large numbers of dead bodies." It is the other way around: "a dead body is the result of an epidemic and not the cause of the epidemic." This does not mean that corpses are always innocuous: fleas on unburied bodies can spread typhus and plague; fecal material from a cholera victim can get into the water supply; the exhalations from a body that had tuberculosis can still be infectious, and doctors are encouraged to cover the faces of corpses and keep autopsy rooms well ventilated; special precautions must be taken in caring for the bodies of those who had blood-borne diseases.[36]

But in every such case a living body is more dangerous than a dead ones: fleas abandon a corpse; bacteria (especially the tubercle bacillus, to take the case in point) and viruses die quickly once their host is dead. Putrefying, stinking bodies are even more innocent than fresh ones, which are innocent enough: bacteria do not thrive in the alkaline conditions of decomposition. Rotting flesh may be disgusting, but it is not a good vector of disease. Water from cemeteries rarely pollutes a water table and, when it does, today the contamination is likely to be from embalming fluids. In the twenty-first century, the facts do not explain the insistence that the dead cause disease. WHO turns to anthropology for an explanation: "although empirical evidence suggests otherwise, strong aversion to the dead may represent a natural instinct to protect ourselves against disease."[37]

The same explanation applies in the eighteenth and nineteenth centuries: no new empirical evidence by the standards of that day explains the insistence that the dead cause disease and need to be removed from among the living. In 1771, for example, the distinguished professor of medicine and bibliophile Henri Haguenot, "one of the first among the moderns who strenuously exerted himself against the custom of burying in churches," wrote an influential report that Walker still cited almost seventy years later in 1839. In it Haguenot says that because he has had little success combating the universally accepted custom of burying the dead amongst the living in and around churches, he wished to report his observations in the hope of changing public opinion. He was called to the Church of Notre Dame; he noticed a prurient odor as he approached the crypt. It became more intense as the *cave* (the vault) was opened. He put a burning taper into the depths; it was immediately extinguished, "as if it were plunged in water." Next he lowered dogs, cats, and birds into the cave; they too died, within two minutes for the most robust of the beasts (cats) and within seconds for the most delicate (the bird). He lowered bottles into the cave and collected a gas that was still noxious but not as strongly as it had been in situ. Haguenot concluded that the "mephitis"—noxious vapors or exhalations—in the *cave commune* were dangerous not only because the air had lost its elasticity or because of the lack of air but specifically because of "the corrosive exhalations of cadavers."[38] Here supposedly was hard evidence for what Walker, Chadwick, and company wanted to do.

Not really. Haguenot's is an old and ambiguous story. Doctors before and after the famous Renaissance surgeon Andre Paré had warned about the dangers of vaults in general without any reference to the corrosive exhalations of cadavers. Haguenot's contemporary, Bernadino Ramazzini, the founding father of organic pathology and no great friend of unpleasant smells—inhaling foul air, he says, "is to contaminate the animal spirits"—might have given him pause as well. The problem of workers in the *fosse commune* (the common grave) had a lot in common with that of workers in other enclosed spaces, Ramazzini wrote: slaves in antiquity, for example, who were consigned to work in caverns of all sorts—mines, sewers, burial pits. The stale air in mines was dangerous and needed to be ventilated; Ramazzini's chapter on corpse bearers is sandwiched between one about dirty trades—tanners, oil pressers, cat gut string makers—and another on midwives, who breathe in the effluvia of various uterine fluxes. Smell in enclosed spaces, not particularly the smell of dead human flesh, was the problem. It was Haguenot and his successors who focused on corpses.[39]

The grounds for doing so were, as contemporaries noted, shaky at best. In 1792, James Curry, a distinguished physician whose research focused on distinguishing deathlike states—suspended animation—from real death offered an alternative explanation to Haguenot's of why the cats, birds, and dogs died, or appeared to have died, when thrust into a tomb. Noxious vapors arise, he pointed out, in any number of places that do not have the free circulation of air (the wells of ships, mines, sewers, pump-wells, and, yes, deep vaults) and from all manner of sources—fermenting apple or pear cider and malt-liquors and from burning brick kilns. There might be something, he admitted, in the product of fermentation and burning other than "fixed air" (carbon dioxide) that had ill consequences. Pathogenic cadaverous exhalations were not one of his alternative explanations. Curry's example is drawn from the lectures of his famous teacher William Cullen, who, when treating of the subject of apoplexy, talked about the case of a brewer who used to determine how far fermentation had gone by holding his head over his vats to test the "pungency of fixed air." Sometimes he would stay too long and fall backward from giddiness; testing the beer repeatedly in this way, Cullen thought, may have caused his subsequent seizures. By 1815, Curry, by then senior physician at St. Guy's in London, had worked out more of the chemistry of how bad air kills. Or rather, he applied the fruits of new research by others. Every gas except "vital air" ("oxygene gas," or what we call oxygen) is destructive to life when breathed alone; "nitrogene gas" and "hydrogen gas" would not sustain the vital principle but neither will they snuff it out instantly. "Carbonic acid" (carbon dioxide) in its pure state, on the other hand, kills instantly. (Not quite, but a 30 percent concentration will almost instantly cause convulsions and coma; death follows in five minutes.) An appendix refers readers to experiments by the great eighteenth-century Edinburgh chemist Joseph Black, who tried to figure out the pathophysiology of death from CO_2 inhalation by asphyxiating birds. Alternative explanations like these for why animals thrust into a long-closed burial vault die do not, of course, belie claims like Haguenot's or make them less attractive to people looking to close churchyards. There could still be mephistes at work, and Walker was happy to quote extensively from eighty-year-old studies without a nod to newer work. We know that counterevidence does not topple theories that are bolstered by far more than facts.[40]

Similarly, a great deal of epidemiological evidence against the ill effects of dead bodies had no impact on the views of reformers. Matthieu Orfila, one of the founders of forensic medicine and a professor at the Sorbonne, pointed out in 1835 that the evidence that dead bodies were dangerous was either apocryphal or exaggerated or irrelevant: purported injuries were, in any case, not due to "putrid exhalations." How else, he asks rhetorically, could he and his assistants, not to speak of the grave diggers, who have done many exhumations and autopsies, taken no special precautions and not taken ill? They all may have been lucky. Modern evidence suggests that the bacteria that cause tuberculosis may be more easily spread at autopsy than by live patients, perhaps because doctors cut into lung tissues without proper protection, thus exposing themselves to aerosol transmission. Some people think that Rene Laënnec, the inventor of the stethoscope, and Xavier Bichat, one of the founders of histology, who both died of tuberculosis, may have acquired it from cadavers. Bichat is said to have done six hundred necropsies the year he died. But still, contemporary experts thought that even intimate contact with dead bodies was not dangerous. Alexandre Parent-Duchâtelet, one of the most important French medical writers on public health in the first third of the nineteenth century, thought that the conclusions that the English were trying to draw from their data were insupportable. There were detailed technical studies on the matter easily available in the early nineteenth century. And there are always plenty of anecdotes. When the *Lancet* discussed the question in the 1840s, various correspondents pointed out that the eighteenth-century evidence adduced for the danger of bodies, even when supplemented by such massive compilations as Dr. Walker's *Gatherings*, was weak. One physician, for example, pointed out that they had all done many dissections without getting ill. There was also little consistency among the enemies of the intramural dead. Edwin Chadwick was offended by the Irish keeping their dead at home for an inordinate amount of time in order to hold a wake and thought their custom to be a hazard to health and morality. He was, on the other hand, a big supporter of the Anatomy Acts that allowed the unclaimed bodies of the poor to lie on dissecting tables for as long as they were needed. These observations are especially telling because Chadwick, unlike Walker, thought that the dead were more dangerous within the first few days after death than later.[41]

Many others, however, claimed they were not dangerous at all. In 1851, forty doctors in Leeds testified on behalf of the plaintiffs in a lawsuit to keep the church vaults open that a body buried three feet deep posed no danger. Anecdote confounded anecdote: Sir Charles Graham, the generally progressive Home Secretary in Peel's reform administration, responded to the public health argument for government action by saying that London was healthier than Paris, where bodies were so quickly removed; that the rector of Bishopsgate and his family lived immediately contiguous to the churchyard and had never been healthier; that the same could be said for the rectors of St. James and St. Giles; and so on.

Lots of grave diggers and clergy testified that they lived perfectly healthy lives surrounded by corpses. But there was no shortage of responses from those who wanted to close churchyards. Evidence counted for little. John Snow's elegant demonstration that the water in the Broad Street pump, not bad smells, was responsible for cholera in its neighborhood notoriously did not sway Chadwick and company. Hostile witnesses could be impugned. The evidence for the danger of bodies seemed too vast—or too often repeated—to be ignored.[42]

But it was not enough to convince one of the most important architects of the "sanitary idea" in England, someone who ought to have been on Chadwick's side if anyone was: Thomas Southwood-Smith, with whose views I began this section. He was a trained doctor, a leading figure in public health reform, among the most important witnesses before the 1840 Health of Towns Royal Commission, and a founder, in 1844, of the Health of Towns Association. He was also a thoroughgoing miasmatist and had about as unsentimental a view of the dead as one could hope to find. His pamphlet *On the Use of the Dead to the Living* (1824) did the intellectual heavy lifting for the 1834 Anatomy Acts, which gave the bodies of the unclaimed poor to medical schools. He publicly dissected his mentor Jeremy Bentham's body and prepared the auto-icon—the skeletal figure dressed in the great man's clothes—that still presides over meetings at University College: a corporeal relic strangely sacred to the idea that dead bones do not matter. We are back to the beginning: "the first statue was the mummified corpse itself." And the statue is the paradigmatic idol. Diogenes could not have wished for a better joke. In short, no one was more inclined to be sympathetic to Chadwick than Southwood-Smith.[43]

He was not. He read the draft report on the dangers of interments in towns and sent his friend a devastating response, the sort we all fear from our best-informed readers: "The foundation of the whole subject [hygiene and cemetery reform] is that animal matter in a state of decomposition is injurious to health. . . . Now it appears to me that the Evidence of that fundamental truth in your report is *neither so strong, so succinct nor so varied as it might be.* [I recommend] *greatly* strengthening the evidence." Southwood-Smith underlined the words in italics here. Chadwick paid no attention and published what became a best-selling report. By 1850 he had won, despite the evidence being *"neither so strong, so succinct nor so varied as it might be."* Urban churchyards were closed; burial boards were created; the administration of dead bodies passed to secular authorities.

Perhaps this is not surprising. As the World Health Organization report remarked, empirical evidence seems to have very little to do with how we care for the dead today, and there is no reason to suppose that people in the eighteenth and nineteenth centuries were any more moved by it. A very long and extensive research tradition has had no effect. The public health argument worked and still works. The dead in their corporeality have moved from the domain of culture to the domain of nature, from religion to science, from the control of priests to the control of doctors and public health officials.[44]

But what exactly were the circumstances that made this possible? One answer takes us back to anthropology. In 1724, Thomas Lewis, an Anglican clergyman, launched an attack on church burial. He recited a miscellany of ancient and Renaissance medical lore that animals die in vaults, that all corruption is dangerous, and that the danger is greatest "from DEAD BODIES when the corruption is at the highest and is fatal." A woman sitting on the grave of someone who died of postpartum vaginal and uterine discharges ("flux of loches") can get it herself; just seeing a corpse hanging after an execution can cause her to miscarry. How many women, he speculates, have suffered the same fate just from being in church? But his argument runs deeper. Like the French feminist Julia Kristeva, he thinks the corpse is abject, "death infecting life" as she puts it, and therefore is threatening to our sense of our living selves. But for Lewis this is not a psychoanalytical claim but a fact of culture grounded in an understanding of nature, a sort of rational anthropology. "Men naturally abhor the sight or the touch of the dead"; "the natural Spirit of Life is afraid of a Dead Body and has an abhorrence of it," he observes. Our experiences—pregnant women have miscarried because of exposure to dead bodies while they worshipped—and our instincts tell us that they are dangerous, which is reason enough for excluding them from churches. Evolutionary biologists make this kind of case today: disgust is the gene's way of signaling danger.[45]

But an anthropology of the dead putatively grounded in instincts will not explain why in the eighteenth and nineteenth centuries corpses became such a great threat and why disgust toward them became especially exigent. John Stuart Mill offers a macrohistorical explanation whose outlines he gets from the Roman historian Tacitus. "A moral effeminacy, an ineptitude for every kind of struggle," has crept over the refined classes, he argues; we live in an unheroic age. "One of the effects of civilization (not to say one of the ingredients in it) is, that the spectacle, and even the very idea, of pain, is kept more and more out of the sight of those classes who enjoy in their fullness the benefits of civilization." Slaughterhouses are removed from where those who eat meat can see them; executions are out of view. We delegate unpleasantness to the butcher, the judge, the policeman, the surgeon, the executioner. "The great part of refinement," Mill says, consists of "avoiding the presence of not only actual pain, but of whatever suggests offensive or disagreeable ideas." As John Simon reported to the Board of Health in 1855, Smithfield market was being moved; excrement was being removed from the streets; the dead were being excluded. All of this too is part of the process, identified by the philosopher Michel Foucault, in which the politics of life supersedes the politics of death, in which the well-being of society is guaranteed by an administrative state and a bureaucracy that exercises power through bodies. Edwin Chadwick and George Alfred Walker are exemplary instruments of biopower.[46]

Both Mill's metahistorical reflections and Simon's bureaucratic report suggest that the new metanarrative of public health succeeded because it was part of large-scale historical change. But it succeeded also because it is imbricated in the many-stranded story of how a whole new regime of the dead became thinkable. The historian Philippe Ariès is right when he suggests (in a different context) that, starting in the late seventeenth century, doctors frightened themselves to death. And so is the great defender of churchyards, London's Archdeacon Hale, when he equates "the modern Hygienist advocating the entire separation of the mansions of the dead from the houses of the living for the sake of public health" with the modern Epicurean who holds the same view because "nothing is so painful to him as the thought or sight of death." This is Mill in other language. With death stripped of superstition and revealed in all its natural boldness, doctors and the enlightened public retreated from its now exclusively materialist realities. Death, in other words, lost its lineage—its metaphysical centrality; the discourse and agitation of public health is more a symptom than a cause of the displacement of the dead into new spaces. But this leaves the question of how the old regime, so seemingly grounded, so adamantine, gave way to a new one.[47]

Félix Vicq d'Azyr, one of the leading eighteenth-century French proponents of cemeteries and a widely translated authority, offers one characterization of the process. A new group of people managed to capture smell for its worldview. In the old superstitious days, he says, we carried "our beliefs so far as to persuade ourselves that the emanations from the bodies of the saints were capable of warming the hearts of the faithful and encouraging in them impressions favorable to zeal or piety." It was against this "superstition" that the Enlightenment fought. Once it triumphed, the relation of the living to the dead would change. Carefully hidden, the body would appear only in its representation through new memorial practices that hide it and yet need it to be there. Vicq suggests cenotaphs, mausoleums, tombs, and epitaphs in new, expressly built, clean parks.[48]

Two things have happened. Because the public health argument worked, the dead in one sphere of their existence came to serve the living in new ways. In their capacity as rotting flesh they created a new and paradigmatic medical—not ritual—uncleanness. From this it seemed to follow, as the *Church of England Quarterly Review* noted at a time when it still looked as if the state would ally with the High Church clergy rather than with secular public health authorities, that

George Walker was right: "It is the positive duty of the Government to enter on the business of purification." (The occasion was a review of *Gatherings from Graveyards*.) The real villains, in the editor's view, were Dissenting clergymen who buried the dead by the tens of thousands, pretending to have the authority of priests.[49]

Concern for the health of the living—for making the dead clean—helped open spaces where a new idolatry of the dead was coming to supplant old superstitions: bodies serving a religion of memory and history would rival those gathered in communities of a transcendent God. The answer to why the public health argument worked turns out to be a series of micronarratives about how it created an alternative to the millennia-old arrangements for the care of the dead. It had the wind of a massive cultural shift in its sails.

GENEALOGIES OF THE NEW REGIME

There is no single problem or process that accounts for both the demise of the old regime and the specific nature and success of the new one. The old regime did not fall in one swoop; it persisted both institutionally and in the imagination for a very long time; the churchyard on the ground and of the mind lives still. But by the middle of the nineteenth century, a new necrogeography and a new kind of landscape had come into being, both in Europe and in its empires. This happened through the conjuncture of connected but distinct histories, which together changed how the living spoke to the dead, how the dead spoke to the living, and how the dead, singly and assembled, registered the past, the present, and the future. In this section, I trace these intertwined histories, beginning with the eighteenth-century conceit of the blessed dead inhabiting Elysian Fields or pastoral Arcadia, before examining the first of the great cemeteries—Père Lachaise in Paris—and how the new regime of the cemetery was reflected and inflected in the far-flung colonies of the British Empire and how the cemetery absorbed "exotic" Ottoman, Chinese, and Indian influences.

Imagination: Elysium, Arcadia, and the Dead of the Eighteenth Century

The telos of Elysium and Arcadia in their eighteenth-century representations was not the cemetery. But the mythological islands or fields of the blessed dead and the home of shepherds who loved, played music, and mourned at the tombs of their friends did allow Europeans to imagine their dead in places radically unlike the parish churchyard. This had little to do with attitudes toward death and almost nothing with crowding and public health, but a great deal to do with gardens and nature and painting and classicism.

We begin with the fact that between the eighth or ninth century, when the norms of Christian burial were established in Europe, and the Protestant Reformation, when these norms were challenged, the dead could scarcely be imagined outside the matrix of church, churchyard, or monastic garden. Two things happened around 1500 to make it possible to once again imagine them elsewhere. First, Renaissance classicism brought with it, in addition to much else, a new appreciation of ancient Greek and Roman temples for the dead. The great tomb became an architectural feature unto itself. Frank Lloyd Wright once remarked about what a beautiful building he could design if he did not have to cut windows in it for the living. When the tomb became a structure in its own right, it could be imagined in landscapes and settings other than a church or churchyard: in Elysium, the place of the blessed dead, or in Arcadia, known through pastoral poetry, where tombs were scattered around forests and meadows. Not in Arcadia, of course, but in forests and meadows is where, in fact, the dead were buried before the Church gathered them up around churches and monasteries.

Second, the Protestant Reformation undermined the theological argument for the advantages of the dead being buried *ad sanctos,* in or near a church. There was, reformers argued, nothing that the living could do for the dead; prayers for the dead were irrelevant, and hence one did not need to be reminded of their presence as one went to worship. Having a saint's body or some other relic nearby was equally irrelevant. In places where Protestantism triumphed, the main reason for burial *ad sanctos* thus disappeared. In reality, the dead remained in the churchyard even there, and more and more, not fewer, of them moved into the church. When Luther said in a hasty moment that he would as soon be buried in the fields as in a church, this was not a positive wish but a rhetorical gesture. An adventurous or very grand few who might earlier have been buried under the altar did begin to build tombs attached to or adjacent to the church as if to declare just a whiff of independence from the rest of the congregation, living and dead. The same thing happened in Catholic countries. More or less self-contained burial chapels in parts of Italy came to resemble classical mausoleums even if they were not called that and even if they were still intimately a part of the churches to which they were attached. For two hundred years after the Renaissance and the Reformation, no tomb broke free.[50]

In the early eighteenth century in England, one did. Around 1720, the architect Sir John Vanbrugh and his patron, Charles Howard, Third Earl of Carlisle, conceived and began to build the first freestanding mausoleum since antiquity (fig. 5.5). It was an astonishingly bold and protean effort to appropriate a long-lost past in order to reject a more recent one and in the process create something new. The mausoleum was to be a mixture of elements from at least

5.5. Mausoleum at Castle Howard, 1780. British Library.

two Roman models. One was the drumlike—eleven meters high, twenty-nine meters in diameter—first-century B.C.E. tower on the Appian Way, six kilometers south of Rome, under which lay Cecilia Matella, daughter and mother of Roman consuls and wife of one of Julius Caesar's lieutenants. To her tomb was joined a reworking of the colonnade from the third-century "tomb of Gallineus" (emperor, r. 253–268 C.E.) a few kilometers farther along the same road even more deeply in the Roman countryside. Vanbrugh died in 1726 when the tomb was still only a concept; his close colleague Sir Nicholas Hawksmoor brought it to fruition, adding elements from other classical sources and supervising the actual construction.

The mausoleum, grand as it was, would become a model for thousands of more modest—and some not so modest—freestanding tombs in every nineteenth-century cemetery and for other buildings that had no connection to the dead: a water tower in Warsaw's great baroque Bath Park, for example. (David Hume's tomb in Edinburgh acquired a classical drum in 1778, two years after he died.) But it is important for our story less because of its architectural features than because of its culturally radical setting. It stood in the vast gardens that were being built around the earl's new country house in the tiny North Riding parish of Henderskelfe. Whole villages and the parish church were razed to create a utopian setting free of peasants and their hovels, or in any case free of real peasants as opposed to imaginary Arcadian shepherds. Wisps of smoke from unseen chimneys effectively made the poor visible only through modest signs of their meager lives. Because the Roman tomb translated to rural Yorkshire was not ready for occupancy when Carlisle, racked by gout, died in Bath in 1738, he was temporarily buried in the local parish church at Bulmer (the alternative burial place in the chapel at Henderskelfe had been torn down to clear space for the gardens), and he—or more accurately his body—had a second chance to offer insult to the Christian community of the dead. In 1745, the earl's body was exhumed from the parish church, where it by all rights belonged, and was moved, as he had wished, to its permanent tomb in his unconsecrated park. A plaque in the church today tells passersby that he had moved to pagan quarters.[51]

To some extent this grand gesture was negative: Carlisle and his architects' anticlericalism bordered on active hostility to established religion and to the necrogeography in which it was grounded. The earl's burial, Vanbrugh wrote, would comport with what "has been practic'd by the most polite peoples before Priestcraft got Carcasses into their keeping." By "polite people" he meant the aristocracy of ancient Rome. In 1722, he had come close to convincing Sarah Churchill, the duchess of Marlborough, to bury John Churchill, the first duke, victor of the battles of Blenheim and Malplaquet, in a field like a Roman general instead of in Westminster Abbey or a chapel like an English lord. Carlisle was also deeply influenced by Hobbes and by the outrageous deist John Toland, who, among many impious things, spoke out about how the excessive veneration of dead men had always led to heathenish excess, by which he meant that the "new Idolatry of the Christians . . . improv'd by degrees to such a pitch by the Artifices of priests . . . always tend[ed] to the Increase of their own Glory, Power, and Profit." This sounds very much like the Protestant reformers' attack two centuries earlier on the whole purgatorial regime. But now, sans purgatory, it was a rejection of the old regime of the dead in post-Reformation England and Europe more generally.[52]

The first freestanding mausoleum since antiquity also paid homage to a radically alternative necrogeography. It was a tomb in a garden. Not Eden. Not the garden where Jesus was buried between His crucifixion and resurrection. Carlisle was in Elysium. Castle Howard was the first fully realized effort by the English aristocracy to imagine and reinvent on their estates the place where the blessed dead lived like gods in "that golden age that now, alas, is lost." The earl's daughter, in a long poem in praise of her father's new seat, wrote:

Vergil presum'd to paint th' Elysian Fields
To him my lays, but not my Subject yields.

The mythological abode of the happy, and especially the heroic, dead had come to mean a rural place of ideal happiness that invited serious reflection; it was a place of elegy, of instruction, and of memory. It was book 6 of *The Aeneid* made real; a place of memory, soft and tender feelings; a place to speak with the dead as of old; a place where the work of humans evokes, through the art of landscape design, a pure primal nature. Although Carlisle's Elysium made no explicit reference to the mythological place—no River Styx, nor explicitly named Elysian Fields—it had the distinction for almost four decades of being the only abode of the ancient dead that actually had a dead body in it.[53]

At more or less the same time that Carlisle built his great house and mausoleum at Castle Howard, Sir Richard Temple, made Viscount Cobham in 1718, began to work with Vanburgh, the earl's architect, on what became the most influential English garden of the eighteenth century: Stowe in Buckinghamshire. From there, various versions of *le jardin anglais*—asymmetric, artfully natural, deeply influenced by Virgil's and Horace's ideas of the blessedness of rural life—began their conquest of Europe from the Channel to the Urals. Vanbrugh and those who followed him had in their mind's eye the soft, classical landscapes of seventeenth-century painting, especially those of Salvator Rosa (1615–1673), Nicolas Poussin (1594–1665), and Claude Lorrain (1600–1682). Proponents of the more formal French garden would criticize Stowe's "perspective ruins" of tombs and urns as too dependent on the landscapes of Rosa. Admirers of the English style could argue that gardens should as literally as possible mirror the painterly vision. But debates about how true to these masters any given English-style garden should be does not alter the fact that Stowe and its successors set the visual terms for how ancient imagined places of the dead—Elysium and Arcadia—looked.[54]

Stowe echoed through the century. René de Girardin, the most important French proponent of the English style, thought that Julie's Elysium (from Jean-Jacques Rousseau's *Nouvelle Héloïse*), which he was re-creating on his estate at Ermenonville, was based on Stowe. The filiation is shaky. Rousseau allows St. Prieux, one of the novel's main characters, to compare the English with the novelistic Elysium, but there is also evidence that he regarded his heroine's home-made garden as far more natural than Lord Cobham's infinitely grander one. But, from the perspective of imagining new spaces for the work of the dead, the precise relationship between the fictional and the real garden makes no difference. The great philosopher of nature spent his last year in a cottage in Girardin's garden and was buried in what contemporaries regarded as Elysium (see the fuller discussion later in this section). Baron von Holbach wrote to Diderot about an English garden with urns and monuments that its owner called the mythical Greek land of the happy dead—Elysium—and that he thought of as a Roman cemetery.[55]

In the almost forty years between the first made-to-order Elysium at Stowe and the one where Rousseau was buried, the dead slowly made their way in, at first metaphorically and then in the bone. "Passing by the Church we went on to what is call'd the Elysian fields," writes the learned antiquarian Jeremiah Milles, an early visitor to Lord's Cobham's gardens in 1735. There were no actual dead there, but there was a tomb, indeed the archetypal great tomb: "a building by Kent call'd the Mausoleum." In 1733, William Kent, one of the founders of the English style, had scooped out a small valley alongside a stream which he dammed to create two lakes to represent the River Styx: forty acres, sixteen hectares of Elysium in all. (Horace Walpole famously said of Kent that "Mahomet imagined an Elysium, but Kent created many." Kent also designed Alexander Pope's famous villa garden of "memory and meditation" at Twickenham.) The "mausoleum" that Milles refers to is and was known as the Temple of British Worthies and stands opposite the Temple of Ancient Worthies—Homer, the greatest poet; Socrates, the greatest philosopher; Lycurgus, the greatest lawgiver; and Epaminondas, the greatest general—and not far from the Pantheon, a small-scale version of the Roman temple of all the gods, where Hercules is enshrined. In the mausoleum is a verse from the *Aeneid:*

> hic manus ob patriam pugnando uulnera passi,
> quique pii uates et Phoebo digna locuti,
> inuentas aut qui uitam excoluere per artis
> quique sui memores aliquos fecere merendo
> And here are troops of men
> Who had suffered wounds, fighting to save their country
> And the faithful poets whose songs were fit for Phoebus,
> Those who enriched our lives with the newfound arts they forged
> And those we remember well for the good they did mankind

These lines are from book 6, where the hero visits the kingdom of the dead and has reached "the land of joy, the fresh green fields, the Fortunate groves where the blessed make their homes." Virgil appears, like an attentive tour guide, to tell visitors to Stowe what sorts of people are assembled in the Elysian Fields (figs. 5.6, 5.7).[56]

The British Worthies comprise eight men of contemplation on one side (Milton, Shakespeare, and Bacon, for example) and eight men of action on the other (King Alfred, John Hampden, and William III among them). And to make clear

5.6. Temple of British Worthies at Stowe. Thomas Rowlandson (1756–1827).
Pen and watercolor on board. The Huntington Library, Art Collections,
and Botanical Gardens.

5.7. The Grotto and the Temple of Contemplation, Stowe. Jean B. C. Chatelain, 1752.
Yale Center for British Art, Paul Mellon Collection.

the implied historical continuities of an imagined community, there is a bust of a (then) living contemporary, each with its own Latin inscription, next to the busts of the dead: Alexander Pope on the side of the poets; the Whig politician John Barnard, honored for his opposition to the "iniquitous practice of stock jobbing," on the activist side. (Both in fact would end up being buried in a church, Pope with his parents in Twickenham and Barnard under the chancel in Mortlake.) Around the back of the mausoleum is the only inscription over an actual body, that of Signor Fido, Cobham's favorite Italian greyhound. ("He was no atheist though he believed none of the 39 articles," it says in part.) Unthinkable in consecrated ground, dogs found their way into memorial gardens in the eighteenth century because their masters imagined them as part of the community of the dead. (It was not always easy; Frederick the Great wanted to be buried with his dogs at Sans Souci but it was not until 1991 and several exhumations later that he finally made it there.)[57]

Like a churchyard, Kent's mausoleum in the Elysian Fields is meant to constitute "a congregation of the dead" that mirrors an imagined community of the living; unlike a churchyard, its dead are virtual and disparate; they are not Christians of a place in deep time whose bodies are gathered together on earth and whose souls congregate in heaven but instead a select number of great leaders and poets from different eras joined in a neoclassical paradise imagined through the poetry of Virgil and the landscaping of William Kent (figs. 5.8, 5.9). They form a national cemetery without the actual dead that would give them the power they took on in the nineteenth century. Contemporaries noticed this strange disposition of the virtual dead in relation to the dead bodies in the churchyard nearby. Unlike Carlisle, Cobham did not destroy the local church but left it in place: "closely surrounded with a wood, as to not be seen" from the adjoining classical landscapes. "A new part of the garden is called the Elysian fields," writes an anonymous visitor in 1738, "and the way to the church is designed to be through some part of them." "Unless the influence of the preacher is great indeed," he continues, "more will pay their devotions among the Antient [sic] heathens than the Modern [Chris]tians." Perhaps the oddest gesture to the churchyard went unremarked. The mausoleum's inscription is not exactly what Virgil wrote. A line is left out:

> quique sacerdotes casti, dum uita manebat,
> And those who had been pure priests while still alive

Even if visitors did not seem to notice this elision, they did notice that the tombs at Stowe were empty. Speaking of the pyramid not far from the Elysian Fields, a visitor noted that "neither the Body of the Architect, nor any person is deposited in it, and a crime it would be, since there is so fine a view from it, that the Dead should possess a Place which they are Uncapable of enjoying the particular delights of."

5.8. Arrival of Rousseau in Elysium. Macret after Jean-Michel Moreau, 1782. Bibliothèque nationale de France.

5.9. Reception of Voltaire in Elysium by Henri IV. Macret after a drawing by L. Fauvet, 1790–1796. Bibliothèque nationale de France.

By the nineteenth century, it was not a crime; pyramids and mausoleums would again, as they had in antiquity, house bodies. But first the Elysian Fields—as well as other imagined places of the pagan dead—would have to capture the contemporary imagination as alternatives to the churchyard and the congregation of the dead gathered there. They would have to be widely regarded as they were by Daniel Defoe when he visited Stowe, as "the most charming place that ever Eyes beheld." "So steals the ambrosial pleasure of the mind, We think tis heaven—and leave the world behind," wrote an eighteenth-century minor poet when he saw Stowe's Elysium.[58] This took time. The form of cemeteries of the early nineteenth century emerged from variations on Stowe's Elysium well before more than a handful of actual dead bodies were actually in such places.

At Stourhead in Wiltshire, for example, a walk around the artificial lake evokes again and at great length Aeneas's descent into the underworld: "when the road diverges," Jupiter tells him, "take the road to Elysium, the haven of the pure . . . rinse thyself with fresh pure water, for this land is Holy." Other lines of book 6 of the *Aeneid* were inscribed on monuments around the lake, as they would be in the nineteenth-century cemetery. (See, for example, the monument at the Ricoletta in Buenos Aires.) At Stourhead, Hercules was housed in a copy of the Pantheon, the perfect Roman building, modeled in this case on the temple in Claude Lorrain's painting *Aeneas at Delos,* one of the pictures of mythological subjects that deeply influenced the picturesque garden. In accordance with the advice in the Renaissance polymath Alberti's *Ten Books of Architecture,* translated into English in 1727, the garden had its share of "columns, pyramids, obelisks and other memorials to remind us of great men."[59]

It was only in 1776 that real dead bodies would find a place in a modern Elysium and, as in late antiquity, other dead would gather around them. Unlike in the cemetery churches of early Christianity, the dead in question now were only virtual, although it would be hard to tell by looking only at their monuments. In 1776, excavations began on a burial tumulus in the gardens of the Danish royal park at Jaegerspris, forty kilometers from Copenhagen; it would become the nidus—the ur-tomb—of an unprecedented memorial garden. There had never been anything like it, wrote C.C.L. Hirschfeld, the preeminent Enlightenment landscape theorist, who studied it carefully: "The temples and monuments recalling worthy Britons which are erected here and there, even the famous Elysian Fields at Stowe, are not the same as Jaegerspris," he gushed. Eighteenth-century archeologists could not have known that the tumulus was really from the Bronze Age. But all the better for our story, and for theirs. They thought it was the burial place of mythical Viking kings who could plausibly be recruited as the founders of the royal Danish monarchy. The primal idolatry of the dead had lost none of its power. And because twenty years earlier bones and tools had been discovered, thereby confirming that the royal park had belonged to Danish kings for time out of mind, it would be hard to image a more perfect ancestral shrine of sorts than Jaegerspris. A world could be built around the ancient dead.

At its center was the tumulus restored to what it was imagined to have been like and improved, like the catacombs had been once they became pilgrimage sites, for the purpose of tourism—new entrance, stairs, lighting in the burial chamber. Around it was "a national grouping of statues," as Hirschfeld called them, a national cemetery without any of the real national dead. The only real bodies remained those in the tumulus, but that was enough; the putative ancestral tomb from the mists of time joined memorials to the worthy dead of historical time. Prince Frederick chose for the project Johannes Wiedewelt, one of the leading neoclassical sculptors of the day, who was fresh from an extensive study tour of English gardens and especially of Stowe. It had impressed him deeply. The Jaegerspris project was like the Temple of British Worthies writ large: in scale, in political ambitions, and in alliance with the real dead, for which Hirschfeld especially complimented him. Wiedewelt, like William Kent, knew his classical monuments. Indeed he probably knew them better than Kent. As a student in the 1750s he had shared lodgings with the great German classicist Johann Winckelmann in Rome.[60]

The fifty-four monuments he made for this commission between 1778 and 1784 were nestled in a grove of oaks and beeches around the rebuilt and improved tumulus; a new mound with a replica of a dolmen (the type of Stone Age tomb with a rectangular flat rock held up by smaller round supports that could be seen everywhere in Denmark) was added later (fig. 5.10). The effect was of a Roman or a nineteenth-century cemetery: obelisks, stele, pedestals with surmounts, pyramids, columns, and combinations of these forms more or less randomly arrayed. Missing only are bodies of the dead. (A few years after his Jaegerspris commission, Wiedewelt designed fifteen monuments over the actual graves of prominent Danes in Copenhagen's new overflow burial grounds, the so-called Assistens Kirkegård, which fifty years later evolved into one of Europe's great cemeteries.) Each monument in the royal gardens has one or more names engraved on it, chosen by the chief minister from a recent history book about *Great and Good Deeds of Danes, Norwegians and Holsteiners*. Tycho Brahe, the Danish nobleman and astronomer who employed the young Johannes Kepler, is there (fig. 5.11). He gets a plinth with a celestial globe on top and the date on which he founded his famous observatory. (Brahe's body is buried in Prague but was briefly exhumed in the late twentieth century and again in 2010 to find out the cause of his death.) Hannibal Schested, an important seventeenth-century statesman who died and was buried in Paris, gets a pyramid; so does Niels Lembak, the improving Norwegian landlord and vicar, who is commemorated by a stele surmounted by

5.10. Burial mound at Jaegerspris, Soren Lange, 1799. National Gallery of Denmark, Copenhagen.

rocks, tools, and small coins that represent his efforts to improve peasant cultivation and to reward good work. Memorials were meant as synecdoches of the missing dead. Admiral Iver Huitfeld, whose ships blew up, for example, is represented by a sculpture of a mutilated prow on his would-be tombstone. Near this simulacrum of a national cemetery is the Normandsdahl—the Norwegian valley—where there are seventy statues by Johan Gottfried Grund, allegorical life-size figures of ordinary workers that were so lifelike, said Hirschfeld, who raved about the place, that one feels as if one could actually talk to them. They look like the naturalistic figures of people doing ordinary things that

5.11. Johannes Wiedewelt's Monuments of Tycho Brahe, the great astronomer, and Absalon, the famous noble bishop, in Christian Cajus Lorenz Hirschfeld, *Theorie der Gartenkunst*, 1779. Bancroft.

characterize nineteenth-century cemetery art. Elysium thus proved to be a serviceable place to commemorate the modern dead even if only a handful were actually there yet.[61]

The same can be said for Arcadia. This hardscrabble mountainous region of the northern Peloponnese was transformed by the poetry of Theocritus, the third-century B.C.E. Greek founder of the pastoral tradition, into the home of happy shepherds and shepherdesses who loved, played pipes, lived in rustic simplicity, and, more relevant for our purposes, mourned their dead. Theocritus's first *Idyll* is an elegy to the shepherd Daphnis, the mythic first pastoral poet, who was killed by a vengeful naiad. Throughout the *Idylls* tombs are landmarks, places to meet: "Scarce had we gone thro' half the neighboring Plain / By Brasil's tomb we met a musing Swain."[62] Virgil imitates these moments in his hugely influential *Eclogues*. Places of the dead structure landscapes and the other way around in an enormously influential literary tradition. Indeed, death informs the genre. The great German art historian Erwin Panofsky thought that Virgil, in writing about the dissonance between the shepherds' beautiful surroundings and their consciousness of loss, had "discovered" the evening. We are on the track that leads to Gray's "Elegy Written in a Country Churchyard."[63]

Almost two thousand years later in a garden in Oxfordshire there would be a new Arcadia, and in it there would be death as well as the dead. The earliest of these earthly Arcadias is at Rousham, the work again of William Kent, famous already for his Elysiums. It has a statue of Venus and also one of Mercury, the guide to the world of the blessed dead at Stowe and in Greek mythology. One would expect these gods. But Rousham also has Pan, Ceres, and Proserpina, and they do not belong in Elysium. Educated visitors would have figured out from Virgil and Theocritus why they were there: the rustic Pan was the god of Arcadia; he taught Daphnis to play the shepherd's flute. We know that Kent's mythological guidebook claimed that Ceres and Proserpina too were worshipped in Arcadia. The question now is how the dead came to be thought of in this new Arcadia, and the answer is that visitors to Rousham would have immediately associated it with Nicolas Poussin's *The Arcadian Shepherds*. This painting, one of the most important in the history of the picturesque garden, is central to understanding how the cemetery came to be imagined almost a century before one was actually built.

There are two versions of this picture. The earlier (1627) version (plate 8) at Chatsworth, seat of the dukes of Devonshire in rural north Derbyshire, shows shepherds out enjoying themselves who have discovered an overgrown tomb set in an unruly grove of old trees; the sky is cloudy and brooding; the shepherd nearest the viewer in the center is tracing the inscription with his fingers; he is intent on deciphering it. Another shepherd and a young woman with one bared breast look on intently; a fourth, his head crowned with laurels, sits pensively on the ground with his back toward us; we, but not yet they, know from the parts of the inscription that are visible how the full epitaph reads: "Et in Arcadia ego." We, but not yet they, also know what it means: there is a skull sitting in the shadows on top of the tomb; we notice it; they seem not to. A mouse crawls through the eye sockets, a sign to knowledgeable viewers but not to the shepherds of the transience of life. We, but not they, know that the "ego" of the inscription—the "I"—can refer only to death itself; the Latin phrase, if read according to its grammar, can only mean "Even in Arcadia, there I am." It is irrelevant whether anyone is or is not in the tomb. Death is speaking; this is a memento mori, however novel some of its elements were. The words had appeared for the first time in a 1618 painting by the Venetian painter Guercino that shows two shepherds looking at a far more prominent skull and mouse plus a blowfly—notoriously short-lived—resting on a small square marker instead of a large tomb. (Classically informed viewers would have recognized this as a cippus, on which, in antiquity, an informative short message was written.) "Et in Arcadia ego" is easily readable. Guercino's influence on the Chatworth version of *The Arcadian Shepherds* is clear. But the tombs and their imagined dead in an eighteenth-century garden were not there as memento mori.

A second version of Poussin's subject and of the phrase "Et in Arcadia ego" worked far better (plate 9). Painted in 1637 or 1638, it was bought by Louis XIV and today is in the Louvre. In this painting, the tomb stands in open fields; the sky is brighter; the Italian Campania, not a gloomy forest, is the background. A kneeling shepherd is tracing the inscription with his finger and at the same time seems to be tracing his own shadow. Educated viewers would have understood the reference to a story told by Pliny about the invention of drawing through the tracing of a shadow as a way to bring the lost dead to life. The woman in the foreground looks like a piece of Renaissance sculpture. There is no mouse and no skull and nothing else to make viewers think that it is a memento mori picture. Here is how Panofsky explains what happened:

> Thus Poussin himself, while making no verbal change in the inscription, invites, almost compels, the beholder to mis-translate it by relating the ego to a dead person instead of to the tomb, by connecting the et with ego instead of with Arcadia, and by supplying the missing verb in the form of a vixi or fui instead of a sum. The development of his pictorial vision had outgrown the significance of the literary formula, and we may say that those who under the impact of the Louvre picture, decided to render the phrase Et in Arcadia ego as "I, too, lived in Arcady," rather than as "Even in Arcady, there am I," did violence to Latin grammar but justice to the new meaning of Poussin's composition.[64]

More to the point, from the perspective of those who built eighteenth-century gardens and, for a much larger class of people who read about them or saw engravings of Poussin's painting, it came to be a great authority for how tombs looked in Arcadia, and by a leap of the imagination, how they looked in a pre-Christian, preclassical, mythical Europe, where the dead were buried in fields, forests, and meadows. This revolution—or rather the return to some imagined version of burial in a more bucolic age—happened not because of art historical comparison of two versions of *The Arcadian Shepherds* or an analysis of Latin grammar but because of the stories that came to be told about the Louvre's painting and in a new burst of hugely popular eighteenth-century neopastoral poetry more generally. Painting, literature, landscape, and eventually real tombs in the garden resonated with one another and changed the sensibilities of a broad audience about where the dead belonged.

Start with gardens. Sometime after 1748, to take one example, Thomas Anson, the owner of Shugborough Hall in Staffordshire, commissioned the Flemish sculptor Peter Scheemakers to produce a relief of the Louvre version of Poussin's shepherds for his gardens. It was an odd replica; the epitaph is not "Et in Arcadia ego" but a string of letters whose meaning remains to be deciphered. But there is no question of how Anson's imitation was understood (fig. 5.12). In 1759, William Shenstone, the poet and owner of one of England's most famous gardens, wrote to his friend Rev. Richard Graves asking if he had seen a drawing or print of Poussin's painting. The painting's idea was so pleasing to him, he says, that he will not rest until he has put the inscription on an urn in his park. Mr. Anson, he reports, already has a version—the one by Scheemakers. And should Graves want to understand what all this means and why Shenstone is so eager to have a drawing of the Shugborough relief, he refers him to volume 1 of the Abbé du Bois—that is, to the French lawyer, diplomat, and literary figure Jean-Baptiste Dubos's *Réflexions critiques sur la poésie et sur la peinture*. This work, published in 1719, often reprinted, and translated into English in 1748, did more than any other text to make the Louvre's *The Arcadian Shepherds* be about a dead body—indeed a specific dead person—speaking to her loved ones in Arcadia.[65]

Never mind that the two youths and two young virgins decked with garlands that Dubos describes are not in Poussin's painting; there is no statue lying on the tomb. (The descriptions of other writers, well known at the time, bear an equally tangential relationship to what is actually depicted.) But never mind. Dubos tells readers that the monument is that of "a young maid snatched away in the flower of her youth" and that she is speaking through "the sepulchral inscription [that] contains those few Latin words 'Et in Arcadia ego' [And I was an inhabitant of Arcadia.]" Dubos was not the first to tell this story—Poussin's second biographer had

said as much—but his is the one that is
most quoted and the one that became
the incitement to imagine the dead
body in Arcadia. René de Girardin,
who owned and designed the gardens
in which Rousseau's Greek tomb
would be placed in 1778, had earlier
visited Shenstone's Arcadian fantasy
at Leasomes, born of Dubos's account
of Poussin. In the 1780s, Hirschfeld
repeats the story of the maiden in
the Arcadian tomb and advises landowners to imitate Poussin's shepherds by burying loved ones in fields
and forests; it will, he thinks, support
"moral sensibilities." About the same
time, Princess Helena Przezdziecka
Radziwill built a shepherd's hut and
inscribed Poussin's epitaph on a tomb
modeled after Rousseau's in her Ark-
adia, near Lowicz, in Poland.[66]

5.12. Bas-relief of Chatsworth Hall
version of Poussin's *The Arcadian Shepherds*,
Shugorough Hall, Staffordshire, England.

The painting's inscription was a commonplace by the early nineteenth century. "And I too in Arcadia Dwelt" is the refrain of Felicia Hemans's poem on the
pastoral. It is about the scene made famous by Poussin: shepherds finding a tomb
in nature:

> What hath staid the wand'rers now?
> Lo! A grey and rustic tomb
> Bower'd amidst the rich wood gloom;
> Whence these words their stricken spirits melt.
> —"I too, Shepherds! In Arcadia Dwelt"

The poet offers the suggestion that the voice may be that of

> . . . some gentle kindred maid
> In that grave with dirges laid.

But she hesitates; no one "had yet been torn" from "the bright band of viewers." It
is death speaking, but in the voice of a person who dwelt in Arcadia.[67]

Nineteenth-century readers, even if they had known nothing about Poussin,
would have recognized this scene from the writings of Salomon Gessner (1730–
1788), a German Swiss author of neopastorals and painter and engraver of tombs

in Arcadia. Now largely forgotten, and probably for good reason ("It is somewhat difficult for us now to understand the reason of Gessner's universal popularity, unless it was the taste of the period for the conventional pastoral," comments the 1911 edition of the *Encyclopeadia Britannica*), he was almost universally admired in his day both by famous literary figures and by ordinary readers. There is a different reception history in every country; he was translated into modern Greek, for example, probably because the Theocratian *Idylls* that he imitated were said to have been written in authentic rustic Greek and to be accurate descriptions of actual practices, a link between the deep past and nationalist present. But his popularity was astonishing everywhere: readers in Sweden, France, England, Spain, Portugal, Denmark, Bohemia, and Wales, among other countries, could read him in translation. (Felicity Hemans was among his translators into English.)[68]

Gessner did not invent the image of women mourning at a tomb in Arcadia: educated readers could think of the lament for Daphnis in Virgil's Eclogue 5; English readers would recognize the lines from Milton: "Where were ye nymphs, when the remorseless deep / Closed o'er the head of your loved Lycidas." But it was Gessner in his neopastoral *Idylls* and other poetry as well as in his illustrations—cheerful, softly melancholic, quietly comforting, and, most important, sentimental—who taught Europeans what a tomb in nature looked like and how one might feel in its presence. "Oh you, my beloved," a young man calls out from his grave surrounded by flowers in a meadow; "when you visit me and tears come to your eyes, a gentle breath will touch your cheeks and a gentle shudder will run through your soul." "One day, her [the shepherdess Glicera's] eyes overflowing with tears, she visited her mother's solitary tomb . . . and suspended crowns of flowers . . . she had planted there."[69] Gessner's poetry was illustrated by the pictures of tombs and mourning that he produced, and that were imitated by others enraptured by his benign, sentimental *naturgefüh*: Theocritus's theme and Poussin's design for Everyman. In his own tomb life would mimic art; it became a cult site, as did memorials designed to reproduce its effects. Hirschfeld, who was generally opposed to putting empty tombs in gardens, argued that an exception should be made for Gessner because such a memorial would make visitors better people. The "hermitage" in the great gardens of Arlesheim near Basel was converted in 1788 to the "Gessnergrotto" in honor of the poet; the English gardens of the Hungarian princely Betthyani family had its simulacrum of Gessner's tomb. There are eighteenth-century engravings of the Gessner monument in Zurich that look like pictures of a nineteenth-century cemetery; there are paintings—a 1789 landscape by the Viennese painter Lorenz Schönberger (1768–1847), for example, somewhere between Poussin and Ruisdahl—of his garlanded tomb. And there are breathless descriptions of pilgrimages to his tomb or memorial. A long epistolary memoir records a lover's account to his beloved of a journey to the Gessner faux tomb in the Swiss Alps with its inscription: "Saloman Gessner wanted to donate a monument to nature and she allowed his name to be eternally there" (fig. 5.13). Gessner's English admirer Marguerite, Countess of Blessington (1789–1849), went to see the tomb of "the poet who so well understood and painted the attributes of nature, that deity that he worshipped." She comes to his tomb "with as much true devotion, as most pilgrims visit the shrine of some departed saint." It is Arcadia, "the ideal regions of pastoral life," into which, the countess says, Gessner's *Idylls* had transported her: "a verdant spot, embosomed in trees . . . and bounded on each side by the clear and rapid rivers, Limmat and Sil . . . [amidst] the glowing foliage of the woods . . . [beside] the limpid sparkling waters."[70] As writer, engraver, and publisher as well as icon, Gessner managed to express the normative sensibility of the cemetery decades before one existed; the power of the dead had found a new voice; the visual trope of mourning in a new space had become familiar avant la lettre; commemoration was commonplace in art before it became so in reality.

By the last quarter of the eighteenth century a historically intelligible and imaginatively rich alternative to the churchyard had acquired a respectable and long pedigree in literature, art, and landscape: Elysium, Arcadia, and less easy to categorize places as well. Like the Earl of Carlisle, Lord Hardwick, for example, tore down a whole village and an ancient church to build a splendid park. (Oliver Goldsmith's poem *The Deserted Village* is based on this clearance.) Unlike the earl,

5.13. *Landscape with Ancient Tomb and Two Wayfarers.* Salomon Gessner, 1768. Metropolitan Museum of Art, Edward Pearce Casey Fund, 2009 (2009.254).

however, Lord Hardwick did not build a freestanding mausoleum but something even stranger to hold his bones: a new church in the style of a domed Palladian temple with an Ionic portico: a church "intended as a landscape ornament." No attention was paid in the design to the convenience of worshippers, if there were any. Adjacent to this Elysian temple masquerading as a church was a garden that one entered through a Doric gate on which was inscribed a sentence from Rousseau: "Si l'Auteur de la nature est grand dans les grandes choses, il est très-grand dans les petites." (If the Author of Nature is great in great things, he is very great in small ones.) Jonathan Tyer, owner of London's famous pleasure gardens at Vauxhall, did not exactly build an Elysium but rather a sort of deathly correlative to his amusement grounds at Denbies near Dorking, a place where two skulls, male and female, greeted young strollers in the voice of death, and a pyramid by the famed French sculptor Roubiliac that showed Tyer's friend, the great horticulturalist Lord Petre, throwing aside his grave clothes.[71]

The memorial garden in various forms was rooted not only in history, but in widely articulated theories that explained why gardens mattered. John Claudius Loudon, father of the English cemetery in the nineteenth century, explains in his massive encyclopedia of gardening that everyone would agree that Addison and Pope put "the new art of gardening on the firm basis of philosophical principals." The garden as Elysium, or as Arcadia, could be traced back to Francis Bacon, John Milton, John Evelyn, and others of their contemporaries; Virgil, Horace, and Theophratus are its ancient progenitors. But Loudon was pointing to more than genealogy. By "philosophical principles" he means that Addison and Pope had articulated a theory of how the garden worked on the imagination—a Lockean physiology of memory that would inform how nineteenth-century people understood the cemetery, and a new, philosophically sophisticated view of how artificial nature worked on the human soul.

In his chapter on "The Power of Landscape over the Senses, and, through Their Interposition, over the Soul," in *Observations on English Gardening*, Thomas Whately (1726–1772) explains how it worked. (This book went through six editions, was translated into French, and heavily influenced Thomas Jefferson in the building of his Palladian mansion at Monticello. I take it as an exemplary popular version of a European-wide genre.) The actions of fluids upon solids, Whately reminds readers, moves the universe, and all progress is the result of the relationship of these objects to one another. Pleasure or repugnance felt through the senses strikes the nerves of the soul and moves it in one direction or another. In properly made gardens it is pleasure that moves the soul through smell and sight and sound and through recollections of the poetic descriptions of nature: "inscriptions on the bark of ancient oaks, urns in the wood; in the consecrated grove, a rustic temple . . . the chorus of the shepherds, assembled round the living spring, while every maid of the village becomes a wood nymph." "Peaceful and solitary, so that nothing divides our attention or interrupts that calm and delightful sentiment which penetrates the heart." It is a short step from here to the claim of the new Glasgow necropolis in the 1830s that it would re-create the blessed state of antiquity, when "death was tranquility, and the only images that were associated with it were those of peaceful repose and tender sorrow."[72]

Hirschfeld developed a general theory of how this worked. If anyone provided the *eidos* for Père Lachaise, Mt. Auburn, and their successors it was Hirschfeld. Quatremère de Quincy, who among other things oversaw the conversion of the church of St. Genevieve into the Pantheon, based his article on cemeteries in the *Encyclopédie méthodique* on Hirschfeld, who was the first to articulate what the modern cemetery was in its essence: an ideal space for the dead that is a subcategory of the "melancholic garden." It should be in a peaceful and lonely place; it should be open to "purifying winds"; it should have a wall but not be "fastidiously confined." Its sacred melancholy could be enhanced by "darkly encroaching pine forests or by the dull murmur of falling water." These new tasteful public burial places might have on their grounds buildings with walls covered in murals of painful mourning. In any case, they would be "an educational school for all classes of citizens." In other sections, Hirschfeld offers other possibilities: the softly melancholic garden modeled on a monk's hermitage—a frequent feature of the picturesque garden, with a grave that he has dug himself; the tomblike structures that remind viewers of Poussin; and, most important, the tomb of Jean-Jacques Rousseau on an island amidst poplar trees at Ermenonville, the "most famous new park in France" (fig. 5.14).[73]

Not only for Hirschfeld, but also for thousands of others, Rousseau's burial in a picturesque garden was a decisive moment. Except at Castle Howard, there had been almost no bodies in these Elysiums and Arcadias, only the promise of memory. (Jaegerspris does not count; the faux cemetery was built around long-dead tombs.) Burial outside sacred ground was a gesture of cultural defiance that very few people made. Even Voltaire hesitated. And the occasional exception proves the rule. Sir John Reynolds, high sheriff of Suffolk in 1735, built a mausoleum on his estate near Felsham because, so John Wesley tells us in his journal, he was "resolved that none of his family should be put in the ground [of the churchyard]." "Having eat and drank, and forgotten God for eighty-four years," he joined his wife and only child there in 1759.[74]

Rousseau's tomb in Girardin's Elysian gardens certainly fits into the anticlerical protest tradition. As a Protestant, Rousseau would not have been welcome in the clerically controlled burial places of France, no matter how revered he was. Ermenonville was a politically freighted refuge. "Narcissa's Burial" in Edward Young's poem *Night Thoughts*, translated into all European languages, had made a wide swath

5.14. "To sensitive souls: view of the tomb of J. J. Rousseau on the isle of poplars at Ermenonville." Engraved by Godefroy after a drawing by Gaudat, 1781. Bibliothèque nationale de France.

of readers sensitive to the emotional pain caused by the refusal of the Catholic clergy to bury properly the body of a Protestant girl—Young's daughter—who had died in France. Enlightened landowners in France had occasionally offered a place to the spurned bodies and memory of Protestants: the grave of the Lutheran tutor to Girardin's children predated Rousseau's, "humanity" thus putting "what is called religion to the blush"; Admiral Coligny, murdered by Catholics in the St. Bartholomew's Day massacre, had a monument if not a grave in the Elysium of Maupertuis. And they continued to do so after Rousseau's burial: in 1784, Antoine Court de Gébelin (1725–1784), a French Protestant clergyman, Mason, and inventor of a tradition of tarot reading, was buried in the gardens of Claude Camille François, Comte d'Albon (1753–1789), at Franconville-la-Garenne.[75] But Rousseau's tomb was far more than a protest. It was a sensation: a cult site in a new religion of memory.

In the first place, Ermenonville was already famous as a garden—a manmade Elysium, a tamed Arcadia—before Rousseau moved there in the last year of his life. J. M. Morel, the late-eighteenth-century French theorist of the picturesque garden, devotes a whole chapter to it in his 1776 book as an exemplary combination of civilized and wild. It was famous also as a real-life version of the most famous fictional garden of the century; Girardin intended it to be a scaled-up version of Héloïse's Elysium; the cottage where Rousseau spent his last year was supposed to be hers. Rousseau's body made the famous garden into a real Elysium, a place of the blessed dead. In 1781, as Hirschfeld writes, it acquired the "mysterious shrine, in no way sad or dismal, that inspires gentle melancholy." "Now he sleeps here the long night, his face toward the rising sun." Hills surround the island on which he lies in the midst of nature that "he described as truly as he experienced it." A six-foot tomb stands over the "holy Reliquiem." The dead prophet of sentiment and sensibility, the great advocate of nature against civilization, seemed to sanctify his surroundings and give them new meaning.[76]

In 1786, the sober, Protestant, English botanist J. E. Smith visited the Ermenonville theme park and was enraptured. He compared Rousseau's wish to be buried in a garden favorably to Voltaire's hypocritical insistence, after a lifetime of anticlericalism, on being buried in a churchyard through the "indulgence of grudging and insolent priests." Smith, like the deist William Godwin in his "Essay on Sepulchres," was almost embarrassed by his own idolatry. But that did not stop him. It is impossible, he writes, "to contemplate this monument without various reflections and emotions. Many people may wonder that I should bring away a little portion of moss from its top; but I know some gentle minds in England to whom such a relick would not be unacceptable and I thought with secret satisfaction that the *manes* [the ghost] of Rousseau, if conscious, would not have been offended."

Rousseau's tomb in the garden became a sensation. Thousands visited out of curiosity or conviction and wept as Rousseau, Gessner, and others had taught them to do.

They could buy cheap prints of the great man stepping out of Charon's boat and being greeted in Elysium by Plato and Montaigne, among others; they could buy guidebooks and engravings as at any tourist or pilgrimage site; they could buy a watch with the tomb painted in its back. A young man committed suicide on the grave after swimming to the island. The year 1789 brought it to Paris and other cities: even though Rousseau was by then in the Pantheon, a replica of the Isle of Poplars with its tomb was built in the Tuileries Garden to celebrate the Fête de Revolution; the citizens of Lyon carried a replica through the streets at the Festival of the Supreme Being in 1794.[77]

With Rousseau's burial, four decades after Castle Howard and the building of the gardens at Stowe and Rousham, Elysium and Arcadia fully entered the European imagination. Goethe's body may have entered the ducal tomb in Weimar in 1832, but he, like Rousseau, was also among Charon's passengers to the fields of the blessed dead. A historically, philosophically, and culturally rich alternative to the churchyard had come into being. The old idols of the dead began serving new gods: history, memory, and sentiment. They had their first major cult site at the tomb of Rousseau, "L'Homme de la Nature de la Verité," in the garden. There would be many others. When the editors of the *Builder* in 1847 commented that the new Coventry cemetery "had much more of the air of a gentleman's park than a city for the dead," it had its genealogy right. Ermenonville redux: the shrine of Princess Di, buried on an island, the Round Oval, in a lake in the great park at Althorpe.[78]

Cimetière du Père-Lachaise

In the early nineteenth century the world got its first large-scale simulacrum of Elysium filled with the dead themselves. The year 1804 is ground zero for modern necrogeography. Napoleon, Hegel's incarnation of the Spirit of History on horseback, was crowned emperor. His prefect of the Department of the Seine supervised the building of the Cimetière du Père-Lachaise, a genuinely new kind of space for the dead in the heart of Europe. The Cemetery of the East, as it was officially known, became the mother house of the new religion of memory and history, its Cluny Abbey and its Disneyland. Like the French Revolution itself, it would soon have imitators everywhere. Had the Napoleonic bureaucracy in 1802 smiled on the prefect's request for the specific piece of real estate he wanted, we could have traced a wonderfully straight line from Sir John Vanbrugh, the architect of the mausoleum at Castle Howard in the early eighteenth century, to Nicolas-Thérèse-Benoit Frochot, who built Père Lachaise in the early nineteenth. We would also have had the paradigmatic cemetery two years earlier, and it would not have been on the former property of Father François de la Chaise, Louis XIV's confessor. But history is never perfect.

In 1711, the opportunity afforded by Queen Anne's proposal to build fifty new churches in London seemed to offer Vanburgh a "glorious occasion," not seen since the birth of Christianity, to build a public garden for tombs to replace the urban churchyards that he despised. The "rich as well as the poor will by [*sic*] in," he assured his correspondent, and would find a place there, although by no means equally visible. If the proposed cemeteries were "regularly and handsomely walled in," and if they were planted with trees "in such a form as to make a Solemn Distinction between one part and another," then he was sure that "the Rich sort of people will think their friends and relations well and decently intern'd there." They would be "honorably enslumbered by lofty and noble mausoleums erected over them in Freestone," instead of having to make do with "little Tawny monuments of marble stuck up against walls and pillars," which would have been their lot in a church or churchyard. The cemetery would have been born a hundred years earlier. It was not.[79]

But nearly a hundred years later the prefect almost got acres of "lofty and noble mausoleums," a commemorative garden of some twenty hectares, which, with real dead bodies, he could have turned into a cemetery. The state owned such a property because its original owner, Philippe Egalité, the duc d'Orléans and cousin of Louis XVI, had run afoul of the Revolution and was guillotined in 1793. Frochot made a pitch for his Parc Monceau with its extensive Bois des Tombeaux. The pitch failed. With that idea off the table, the government offered him forty-four hectares to the north and east of Paris that had once belonged to the confessor of Louis XIV, Père Lachaise, which it bought in 1804 expressly for use as a cemetery. Frochot had to build from scratch what he might have had ready-made.

He commissioned for the job an architect with strong historicist credentials who was experienced in matters of commemoration. Alexandre-Théodore Brongniart had in 1780 designed the Élysée with its famous pyramid in the gardens at Maupertuis; he had been a consultant for the Pantheon, the new burial shrine to the nation's illustrious dead. (Three years later he would build the neoclassical Paris Bourse, as representative of the new world of the living as Père Lachaise would be of the dead.) For what was to become the first "true cemetery" since antiquity, Brongniart chose as a model not a mythological but a real place of the dead in antiquity: Karameikos (Ceramicus) in Athens, near the Academy of Plato. It was where the heroes of battle and the great families of Athens were buried, where the citizenry went to perform funeral games and to mourn, where Praxiteles and other renowned great sculptors of Attic Greece had their work. It was "the most interesting public work connected with that 'city of the mind,'" as an American advocate of the cemetery put it in the 1830s. Père Lachaise was intended to be the modern version of this great ancient civic space.[80]

It did not immediately succeed in becoming that: distant from Paris, unconsecrated, nonsectarian, it was so new—utopian even—that there were few customers in the first few years despite the regime's best efforts to make it appealing. Napoleon gave it the remains of a long-dead queen of France, Louise de Lorraine, wife of Henry III, that had been made homeless by the Revolution, to bolster its prestige, but the gesture had little effect. Her body had rested for centuries in the Convent of the Capuchins on what is now Place Vendôme; that was destroyed in 1790 and her remains rescued and stored. In 1817, Louis XVIII had her body exhumed from Père Lachaise and ceremoniously moved to the former royal tombs at St. Denis (where it is today), but by then it was not missed. That same year, Père Lachaise got four new arrivals that made its fortune.

In a burst of entrepreneurial modernism, Etienne-Hippolyte Godde, architect of the city of Paris, managed to get his hands on what he took to be the bones of two of the old regime's most famous bad boys: the writers Molière and La Fontaine. Militants of the Parisian "section Molière and La Fontaine" had exhumed them from their respective burial places in 1792 with the plan to rebury them with the honors that had been denied them in their day. Like so much of the French cultural patrimony, the bodies were rescued by Alexander Lenoir, who, since 1791, had been the director of the Commission on Monuments, charged with placing dispossessed art in new civic venues. He put them in the Elysium: the garden of tombs, and a cemetery in all but name, of his Musée des Monuments Français. In April 1816, with the restoration of Charles X, the museum of Revolutionary booty was ordered closed and the bodies as well as the art in its Elysian Fields were redistributed. Some of the dead went to the Pantheon. Molière's and La Fontaine's remains went to Père Lachaise on 6 March 1817. The fact that the bones were almost certainly imposters made no difference; they worked as new relics for a new day, idols of the cemetery in a postrevolutionary world. (The Restoration did not rescind the funeral ordinances of the Napoleonic regime.)[81]

Three months later, on 12 June 1817, two new arrivals assured the future of the new Elysian Fields: the bones of the medieval lovers Abelard and Héloïse. These were almost certainly genuine; their provenance is well documented. For six centuries the pair had rested peacefully, except for occasional checkups and local transfers, in the Paraclete monastery that Abelard and founded and where Héloïse served as abbess. (He died in 1141; she in 1163.) Revolutionaries destroyed their tombs, along with the monastery, in 1792; then comes almost a decade when the bones led a peripatetic existence with several close escapes; if there was a mix-up, it would have been in these years. By 1800 they were safe again. The indefatigable Lenoir rescued them, along with pieces of their tomb, and installed both tomb and bodies in his museum. With its closing in 1816 began the latest and last part of the lovers' posthumous story. An enormous funeral brought first the bodies and, six months later, their mausoleum from the old museum Elysian Fields to the new ones at Père Lachaise. And so the medieval pair from a distant world could be reimagined as bourgeois lovers in a new memorial park for the dead on the eastern outskirts of Paris where hundreds of middle-class families would build their eternal homes[82] (figs. 5.15, 5.16; plates 10, 11).

5.15. Tomb of Abelard and Héloïse in the Musée des monumants français. Jean-Lubin Vauzell, 1815. Bibliothèque nationale de France.

Tombeau d'Héloïse et d'Abeillard,

5.16. Tomb of Abelard and Héloïse in Père Lachaise. Christophe Civeton, 1829. Bibliothèque nationale de France.

It very quickly became a place to visit. On his European tour in 1816, the young American historian-to-be William H. Prescott had it on his itinerary: "Cemetery of Pere de la Chaise, tombs of Labadoyere—a black crucifix on green turf. Neys. Madame Collins, Maréchal Mortier, a pillar gilt, child's tomb with his mother in a cottage &c, excellent views," he writes in his diary of the social and aesthetic bricolage of this new place of the dead. By 1825, a standard guidebook to Paris told visitors that this new "picturesque and glowing landscape" was now being chosen "by the most distinguished personages as the place of their interment." It, like the other new Paris cemeteries only more so, "may be considered a public promenade." Statistics confirm its success: Baedeker's guide in 1865 recommends three hours for a tour because there are sixteen thousand monuments to see, from the most magnificent mausoleum to the unpretending cross. "Père Lachaise," the trademark of the modern world's first "true cemetery," became a generic term to describe a greater or smaller expanse of monuments set amongst trees, shrubs, grass, and flowers, with walkways and vistas, which hid most of the dead under its even surface and memorialized others in classical splendor.[83]

The cemetery in Copenhagen was a "miniature Père Lachaise," and the emperor of Brazil wanted one in Rio "on the extensive scale of Père Lachaise." The Merchant Adventurer's Company of Glasgow successfully built one in Scotland. "Who, for example, that has visited the romantic cemetery of Père la Chaise, would not wish that there were, in this, his native land, some more attractive spot dedicated to the reception of the dead?" the prospectus asks rhetorically. It will be in sharp contrast to the "mighty cinerial depot that surrounds the Glasgow Cathedral" and its "vast fields of rude stones and ruder hillocks," the prospectus continues. By 1857, a local writer announced proudly that the "Necropolis" was to Glasgow "what the cemetery of Père la Chaise is to Paris."

For the first time there was an international standard for what a place of the dead should be. The Boston Horticultural Society, when it started planning Mt. Auburn in 1830, announced that it wanted "a public cemetery similar in design to that of Père Lachaise in the environs of Paris." One of its leading members, and an early advocate of a new cemetery, visited Paris in 1833 with a delegation of famous Bostonians and reported that the original "truly equals our expectations." Ruskin thought that "in everything but situation and abstract beauty of sculpture," the churchyard of Peterborough Cathedral (the most beautiful in England, he thought) exceeds Père Lachaise. The stock prospectus for Kensal Green Cemetery, the first space of its kind in England, promised shareholders that it would build a Père Lachaise on the land that it had bought in a poor and run-down section of west London, and visitors to San Francisco in 1855 were told that something like this had already happened there. Sixteen acres from a "sad and desolate" scrubland in the Yerba Buena district had been transformed into a place where people built all sorts of monuments in "the best Parisian style" in imitation of "the sepulchers of Père la Chaise." The Napoleonic prefect's memorial park had become a world standard, so much so that to fail to be like it was a scandal.[84]

When in 1832 a writer for the *China Courier* visited the tiny Protestant cemetery at Macao, he complained that it was forlorn and cheerless, by which he meant that it induced "inverse reflections which occur in visiting Père la Chaise and other cemeteries." The director of the Hull General Cemetery complained that it was a national disgrace that England did not have one: anyone who has seen Père Lachaise in Paris will, he said, be "grieved that England, which has raised so high the standard of civilization and high moral feeling should in this particular lag behind." "Let anyone enter into the cemetery of Père Lachaise . . . , and compare his feelings with those created in his breast by Great Portland Street graveyard," argued an MP through invidious comparison in favor of burial reform in 1845.

It was also a place some loved to hate. A proposal to build a new cemetery in Norwich sniffed that the French managed to introduce "their national frivolity even into their burial grounds." Père Lachaise, the author thought, was a "cimetière ornée," "hardly befitting the silent city of the dead." But whatever was said about it, Paris's Cemetery of the East had become the international standard to be reckoned with for a new modern space of the dead. It was supposed to meet certain expectations: a place where "taste and affection strive to remove from the last resting place of those we love the evidences of the sad uses to which they are dedicated," a memorial park where families could mourn at an individual grave and where bodies singly and together could create new social, political, and cultural association for the living.[85]

One further answer to how the cemetery came into being is now clear: neoclassicism and the eighteenth-century picturesque commemorative garden—Elysium and Arcadia on earth—were appropriated under auspicious political conditions by a new cemetery that became the world standard. There were other routes as well to imagining alternatives to the churchyard, both as a congregation of the dead and as a kind of space.[86]

Distant Lands and the Imperial Imagination

Park Street Cemetery in Calcutta, founded in 1767, did not, like Père Lachaise, become a brand; it would be hard to say that it influenced anything. It made no claim to Elysium or Arcadia. It had no horticultural pretensions. Robert Kyd, the founder of the botanical garden in Calcutta was buried there in 1793, but only because his wish to be buried under an avocado tree in the garden without any religious ceremony was unbearable to his countrymen. Park Street does, however, provide a case study in how a new community of the dead came into being when the historical, aesthetic, and religious constraints of the churchyard were absent. The merchants of the East India Company made it in a world very far and very different from home in order to allow their dead to speak in new ways. In the evolution of the European cemetery, it shows how a new cultural ecology changed where and how the dead do their work even if it had few direct progeny itself.

English people knew of contemporary alternatives to Christian necrogeography in the world beyond Europe. Beijing, reported the seventeenth-century government official and much-reprinted travel writer Sir Thomas Herbert, included many stately buildings and mausoleums: "24,000 are numbered of the Mandarins Sepulchers; the meanest of which is not without beauty." Eighteenth-century picturesque gardens would sometimes include a Chinese monument. When Sir John Vanbrugh thought of an alternative landscape to the churchyard, the simile he first used was not Arcadia or Elysium but a place that was in its way far stranger: "the manner of internment [that] has been practiced by the English at Surrat [sic]." He is talking about the extraordinary seventeenth-century tombs of the great East India Company merchants in the Gujarati city on the banks of the River Tapti, which was the major trading port on the west coast of the subcontinent. He had signed up as a young man to be a factor for the East India Company and sailed for Surat in 1683, where he saw the tombs. But he might have heard about them anyway from the accounts of a visit to Surat by the late seventeenth-century French merchant and traveler Jean-Baptiste Tavernier that was included in a well-known 1705 compilation of some four hundred "voyages and travels." Travenier reports on a cacophony of burial places outside the city's walls: Catholics and Protestants (the Dutch and the English) adorn "their graves with Pyramids of brick whitened over with lime," a form much in evidence in Europe until the 1780s, which became popular because of its Masonic associations. "Religious gentiles"—the "pious gentiles" he had referred to earlier, that is, Muslims—had their square, domed tombs; the "banians" (local brokers and agents, mostly high-caste Hindus) cremated their dead by the riverside and let the ashes wash away. Surat allowed Europeans to encounter communities of the dead that were in every respect different from theirs, but which they joined in a style unimaginable in a seventeenth- or eighteenth-century churchyard.

They did not even have to make use of classical models. "Indian architects have proven by the tomb of baron Rheede von Drakenstein that a building may look majestic without being either of the Corinthian or Tuscan orders," wrote the eighteenth-century Dutch chaplain of a trading ship. (Drakenstein was an important naturalist and Dutch East India Company administrator who died in December 1691 off the coast of Bombay.) The high Moghul imperial style worked as well as the Greek or the Roman for British merchants. "Men [the East India merchants] who lived in such grandeur may naturally be supposed to have emulated each other in erecting ostentatious tombs to commemorate their dead," sniffed a member of the Bombay civil service in his report on two-hundred-year-old burial places. "Among the most pompous mausoleums in the English cemetery," he continues in the same vein, is that of the merchant Christopher Oxenden, who died in 1659 and is buried beneath a domed temple with four pinnacles and a long Latin epitaph.[87]

The vast Muslim cemeteries of the Middle East also captured the European imagination long before there was any thought of imitating them. A pilgrim coming from the desert to Cairo in 1335 was impressed by the vast expanses of magnificent tombs—marble, alabaster, porphyry, and other noble stones—of a scale and magnificence not to be found anywhere in all of Christendom. Another traveler, Emmanuel Piloti, saw on the outskirts of Cairo around 1400 what he called a "city of the dead"—a phrase that would come to be used to describe the new cemeteries of Europe five centuries later—that was not only walled but full of tombs and ritual dwellings, occupying a space as big as Venice.[88] By the time of Mary Wortley Montagu's letters from Constantinople in the early eighteenth century, Ottoman graveyards seem directly to prefigure Père Lachaise and its successors: more vast perhaps—larger than a whole city on the scale of London, she says—but recognizable with their individual tombstones, inscriptions, railed and landscaped plots, and, most important, isolation from the world of the living. Istanbul was ringed by a belt of burial grounds, each a distinct community of the dead representing the cultural autonomy granted to communities of the living under the *millet* system: Muslims, Jews, and Bulgarian and Greek Orthodox along a stretch of three hundred meters on a slope down to the Golden Horn; Romanian Catholics separate from Romanian Orthodox on another hillside. (Europeans generally did not comment on ways in which Muslim burial practices were like theirs; perhaps 1 percent of the dead were buried in or around mosques in the city.)[89]

It is this—"the still seclusion of a Turkish cemetery," sanctified in its remoteness "by the grove of Cypress in which it is embosomed"—that Wordsworth would find so attractive and in such contrast to the "busy, noisy, unclean, and almost graceless church-yard of a large town." Ottoman cemeteries allowed for monuments and epitaphs, for the work of memory, in great profusion; and its garden-like setting drew a veil over the unpleasant fact of decay and putrefaction. Edification—"the metaphysical instruction of death," Wordsworth calls it—by the late eighteenth century was no longer to be found in the ghastly *memento mori* of the European parish graveyard with its all too evident compost of carcasses but in the "soothing influences of [and proximity to] nature," the beauty of "the flower that passeth away." Muslim graveyards, and Turkish ones in particular, supplied these truths and inspirations and would continue to do so up to and after the founding of new British cemeteries. They were vast: "Scutari is recorded in the pages of every traveler for its cemetery, which is reputed to be the biggest in the world." They were beautiful: one small cemetery is intermingled with a "mass of smiling verdure and blossom-loaded boughs," amidst which the dark cypress, symbols of death, appear in "melancholy contrast" to the "smiling and cheerful tints"; there is no cemetery in Constantinople of equal beauty to Scutari, writes "Miss Pardoe," and she thinks that probably none in the world can match either its extent or it "pictorial effect." They were mercifully free of the gloomy associations of European burial places. And since each body has its piece of ground—hence the vast expanse—each body, as Wordsworth would have it, could have its own epitaph in close proximity. The passerby is exhorted to repeat a passage from the Koran; the details of the deceased are announced; and the survivors can address their dead: "May the Eternal deign to envelop his soul in a cloud of mercy and goodness."[90]

There were plenty of models for what a place of the dead might look like and what alternative communities they might serve. But the important point is not that these models directly influenced the burial places that Europeans built, either abroad or in the metropole. When the men of the East India Company had the opportunity to collect a community of the dead from ground zero, they started not with the churchyard but with a bricolage of classical and Eastern elements. In some measure, this was of necessity, but only to an extent. Calcutta is a good example. When Job Charnock, the founder of the British trading outpost that developed into the second city of the empire, died in 1693, there was no church and no churchyard within thousands of miles. He was buried by the River Hooghly in a Moghul-style mausoleum on the site of the grave of his Hindu—or, some say, Muslim—wife. Alexander Hamilton, one of the earliest historians of the British in the East Indies, tells the famous story of how Charnock rescued a young widow from suttee; he goes on rather disapprovingly to say that instead of his converting her, she converted him. To wit, Charnock kept the anniversary of her death by "sacrificing a cock on her tomb [the one in which he would be buried] after the Pagan manner." It is impossible determine whether this is true, but Hamilton, writing in 1726, is anxious for his readers to believe him. Pagans and Christians who were alive at the time assured him, he says, that the reports of Charnock at the tomb are "really true matter of fact." If any of it were credible, it would have made the couple's burial in a churchyard unthinkable. Others of the British dead gathered for the next half century around the Moghul-inspired tomb of the city's founder.[91]

In 1709, the East India Company directors did finally build a church, St. Anne's, some distance from the land side of Fort William. But its churchyard was a narrow collar of land tightly circumscribed by high walls despite there being thousands of acres—indeed a whole continent—of open ground adjacent. The local congregation of the dead continued to gather elsewhere: in the unconsecrated ground around Charnock's tomb. In 1756, St. Anne's and much of the city were destroyed by the troops of the Newab of Bengal, but building a new church was not a high priority for the company: "Your directions for postponing the building a Church until every other building be completed shall be duly attended to," wrote the Council to the Court in 1766. Instead, it proposed in the same memorandum that the Company buy land for a new burial place a little distance from the city. The location was justified on hygienic grounds: the present burial ground "we have reason to believe contributed greatly to its being unhealthy," the Council said. Maybe it believed this. But when it got around to building a new church, St. John's, in 1787, it was on the site of the old burial ground, with Charnock's mausoleum, looking now like a strange baroque ruin in a Piranesi engraving, at its center. Once again, the dead got there first. St. John's has a magnificent altarpiece by Zoffany, but its churchyard is tiny. The congregation of the dead started to gather in 1767 on land that had been part of the deer park of Sir Elijah Impey, a judge of the Calcutta High Court.[92]

What soon became known as the "Great Cemetery" or "Park Street Cemetery" was, from an ecclesiastical perspective, not ready. Nine months after the first body was buried it remained unconsecrated; the company chaplain asked for an extra thirty rupees to pay for bearers to get him to what he took to be a distant site, and no one seemed in a hurry to make the necessary arrangements. He got his supplement, although we do not know when he consecrated the ground. The important point is that it seemed to make no difference. The Great Cemetery soon filled with tombs: the huge whitewashed pyramid of the famed orientalist Sir William Jones and the even more massive broad-based one of Miss Elizabeth Jane Sanderson, wife of a company collector; the chest tomb of Warren Hasting's antagonist Sir John Clavering. "Obelisks, pagodas, etc. are erected at great expense," wrote Sophia Goldborne, the narrator of an anonymously published novel of late eighteenth-century Calcutta life by the shadowy feminist novelist Phebe Gibbes; "the whole spot is surrounded by as well-turned a walk as those you traverse in Kensington gardens, ornamented with a double row of aromatic trees." "Not old Windsor Churchyard with all its cypress and yews is in the least degree comparable," she adds. Death was on her mind: "the eastern world *is,* as you pronounce it, the grave of thousands," the novel begins. As in an English park, but not a churchyard, all manner of alien structures could be built over people who would never have made it past a watchful clergy. General Charles "Hindoo" Stuart was buried with Christian rites but in a tomb facsimile of a Hindu temple decorated with stone sculptures of idols from his extensive collection. (An early twentieth-century historian notes that Stuart's tomb is reminiscent of an even stranger one made for a Dutch colonial officer in Agra, which is in the form of a large sandstone replica of the Taj Mahal.) The monument to Colonel James Achilles Kirkpatrick (1805) is lost, but as a man who converted to Islam and married a Muslim woman of high rank with whom he had a daughter, he too did his part to make the Great Cemetery a strange and novel place where "all the used up machinery of the Empire is put away," as Kipling put it.[93]

Each new cemetery in the far corners of the world has its own story, some strange, some more ordinary, and together they create the tangled web from which a new place for the dead emerged in the absence of an ancient site. The burial ground just to the west of the British one for Catholics in Calcutta, for example, was bought by an Italian exile named Edward Tiretta, of dubious reputation and a close friend of Casanova's, who ended up in India after first escaping to France. He bought the land to bury securely his eighteen-year-old wife, who died in 1796 and was originally buried elsewhere. Upset by the usual churning of bodies with each new interment, he had her exhumed and moved to a new quiet and more permanent grave in 1798. There, she was soon joined by an assortment of people from all over—Brittany, Corsica, Elba, Venice. In some cases, a cemetery of the colonial dead in the midst of a city of the colonized is an overt imperial gesture. The British put their new burial ground in the midst of the native quarter of Patna, a city on the Ganges in which the East India Company had a factory. "If the dead could feel disconnected with the place of their interment," wrote Emma Roberts (1794–1840), a prolific travel writer and popular historian of her day, they would rise as specters to rid themselves of their pagan and Muslim neighbors. In Macao, on the other hand, a new European cemetery grew out of weakness. The East India Company finally purchased land for burial only in 1821, and then after long negotiations with Portuguese and Chinese authorities. It was meant for its employees, but other dead disinterred from hillside graves scattered throughout the region soon made up this peculiar new community. Not only Europeans but also Arabs, Indians, and Chinese shared the extensive eighteenth-century cemetery of the Dutch East India Company at Tanah-Abang in Jakarta.[94]

There are similar stories in Europe. In Oporto, it took British traders almost 150 years to get a burial ground; a 1654 treaty gave Protestants the right to a cemetery of their own, but the Portuguese Church—Jesuits and the Inquisition, it was said—managed to prevent its being implemented until the late eighteenth century, when a "cemetery of the British nation" was finally established. Before then, the dead were buried clandestinely along a riverbank or in the sands at low tide. Afterward, the dead of a nation, not a parish, had its place.[95] It took a century of negotiations with the papacy to finally establish the famous polyglot "English" (i.e., not Catholic) cemeteries in Rome and Florence.

British cemeteries abroad are in some measure the children of necessity: there were no historically rooted churchyard communities of the dead. But by and large, no one tried to re-create them either. Given an ecclesiastical blank slate, the disparate, polyglot, and sometimes eccentric community of the British

5.17. Watercolor of the west end of St. John's Church in Calcutta. Amelia Rebecca Prinsep, ca. 1830. British Library.

dead abroad looked elsewhere for models. The Great Cemetery in Calcutta resembled a provincial Roman burial ground far more than any Christian burial ground; a people who thought of themselves in India as servants of a new world empire did not, with but few exceptions, reject Christianity but neither did they feel bound by more than a thousand years of Christian tradition. They appropriated instead a variety of traditions, Western and local, to create a novel space of the dead unconstrained by local churchyard histories stretching back for millennia. I turn now to a discussion of the characteristic values, intentions, and meanings that found their expression in the new regime of the cemetery (fig. 5.17).

THE AGE OF THE CEMETERY

It is believed that this cemetery [New Haven's] is altogether a singularity in the world. I have accompanied many Americans and foreigners into it, not one of whom had ever seen or heard of anything of a similar nature.

TIMOTHY DWIGHT, *Travels in New England and New York*

(1821, ABOUT THE 1790S)

A garden cemetery is the sworn foe to preternatural fear and superstition. The ancients, from their minds being never polluted with the idea of a charnel house, nor their feelings roused by revolting symbols of mortality, contemplated death without terror, and visited its gloomy shrine without fear. With them death was tranquility, and the only images that were associated with it were those of peaceful repose and tender sorrow.

JOHN STRANG, *Necropolis Glasguensis* (1831)

There were many new churchyards built through the ages, some extensions of old ones, some around new churches. But whether new or old, the churchyard was meant to be ancient, to belong in its place. Cemeteries were meant to be radically novel: spaces that broke with the historical past to restore an idyllic classical one or to create a marvelous, even utopian, future.[96] No visitor whom Timothy Dwight (1752–1817), minister and president of Yale University, showed around the just-built New Haven cemetery had ever seen anything "of a similar nature": "a singularity in the world." Public burial grounds, "planted and laid out as gardens around the metropolis," said the author of a famous London guidebook, "are a novelty of our times." And their founders had high hopes for them: the prospectus of Glasgow Necropolis claimed that it would erase in a stroke "preternatural fear and superstition" and return the dead to the unpolluted calm of antiquity. Its tastefully landscaped acres and variety of monumental sculpture would underwrite a world governed by tender sentiments rather than by the terror and gloom of the churchyard and the crypt. We do not know if John Strang, the local editor and writer who was the force behind the whole venture, had read the moral philosophy of the local academic moral philosopher Adam Smith, but he had absorbed its essence. Cemeteries were also envisaged as novel because they offered a venue for other novelties: new styles, new materials, new plants. Highgate had the first macadam surface in England on its famous neo-Egyptian promenade and a steam-powered lift to get bodies from one side of the Swains Lane to the other. Neo-everything found a place in England's public Elysiums.[97]

Novelty

For Timothy Dwight, the new cemetery in New Haven was less a rejection of history than a place where history could finally catch up with itself. The original mid-seventeenth-century settlers had, he explains, followed "the custom of their native country" and buried their dead in what was in appearance, if not in law, a churchyard. (The cemeteries of Puritan New England were, and remained after the disestablishment in 1833 of Congregationalism, civil spaces.) His historical chronology is a little off. As had been the case in the European Middle Ages, the bodies in New Haven were there first—at least two of them in the town square— before the first meetinghouse was built. But his general point is well taken. As long as the "Romish apprehension" about the "peculiar advantages supposed at the resurrection to attend those who are interred" in churchyards prevailed, there was nothing strange about having the dead around a house of worship. But after the Reformation, and especially for Calvinists, there was no reason for having them there. The impropriety of burying around a church in the middle of town was certainly clear by the late eighteenth century: "groundless and ridiculous." If, on the one hand, the churchyard was a crowded meaningless anachronism, the cemetery, on the other, promised to be "a source of useful instruction and desirable impressions." It was a place of the dead of a new kind of community: orderly, private, family plots, laid out in neat parallelograms like the columns of a gigantic temple, represented its prosperous members; common graves without monuments were for the poor; and a special section was provided for slaves, Dwight boasted. He was more or less right when it opened in 1796.[98]

The novelty of the cemetery registered across the ocean in the melancholy longing for death and burial in a lost world of medieval monasticism represented in the deathscapes of the German romantic painter Caspar David Friedrich (1774–1840), for example. Images of graves scattered around ruins in organic confusion and monks processing peacefully through snow that covers the irregular body-engorged ground stand in sharp contrast to the cold and ordinary pictures he did of modern cemeteries. Especially in his *Cloister Cemetery in the Snow* (1818) and *Abbey in the Oak Forest* (1808–1809), viewers enter into the imagination of an artist who mourned the world that the dead had lost when they moved to the tidy, classically inspired, municipal urban cemeteries that were just beginning to be built in Germany. Novelty for Friedrich is spiritual estrangement.[99]

Incomprehension was a more common response. Harriet Martineau, the English journalist and writer on political economy, no enemy of modernity, went to Mt. Auburn in 1834, three years after it was founded and too early for it to have become a cliché. She could not quite figure it out. It was as if postmodernist bricolage were born in the modern cemetery. What was one to make of the neo-Egyptian entrance gate, with its winged globe and serpent, which had the first part of Ecclesiastes 12:7 inscribed on its pediment: "then shall the dust return to earth." It did not reflect an Egyptian view of death, and it did not sit well with the idea that the dead were peacefully sleeping. She was equally puzzled that the Trier-born, Boston-buried phrenologist Johann Spurzheim was lying under a tomb that was a facsimile of Scipio's (that would be L. Cornelius Scipio Barbatus, consul 298). It is not easy, she said, "to conceive how anything appropriate to Scipio would suit Spurzheim." The answer turns out to be purely circumstantial and shallow but also wonderfully liberating. The marble arrived just when Spurzheim died, and the committee appointed to honor him saved time by purchasing it instead of ordering something that might be more fitting.[100]

Martineau is also skeptical that all the decorous tombs and parklike vistas would, as was claimed, comfort those who mourn. Mt. Auburn seemed to her simultaneously beautiful—"the most beautiful cemetery in the world"—and spiritually mendacious. Mourners could not be sure of the promise of life beyond death: they send "their thoughts abroad meekly, anxiously, imploringly, through the universe, and div[e] into the deepest abysses of their own spirit to find a resting solace." This is projection; there is no evidence that she asked anyone how he or she felt. But in her view, the cemetery offered neither Christians nor anyone else an answer to the persistent question of what happens to the dead, in part because it seemed to erase death and the dead from view.

Père Lachaise, she thought, was comfortless because it was so relentlessly funereal: a landscape where "every expression of mourning is to be found; few or none of hope. . . ." "There is no light from the future shining over the place." Balzac famously disagreed. He thought that it produced just the right effect: "I seldom go out, but when I feel myself flagging I go and cheer myself up in Père Lachaise." But if Père Lachaise was too gloomy for her taste, Mt. Auburn was the opposite: "a mazy paradise where every forest tree of the western continent grows; and every bird to which the climate is congenial builds its nest." It was deceptive; doubt was muted by denying its existence. This was no solution. If Père Lachaise was shallow because it offered no future, "in Mount Auburn, on the contrary, there is nothing else." Any notion that there is a past of any sort "is little more than a matter of inference." There can be no sorrow because the landscape itself is in denial: "all the woes of bereavement are veiled"; "all tears [are] hidden or wiped away; and thanksgiving and joy abound instead." The dead simply vanish, burying the problem of where they might be: "a visitor from another planet, ignorant of mortality, would take this place to be the sanctum of creation." Offered a bricolage of mourning at Père Lachaise and a prelapsarian Eden at Mt. Auburn, the modern survivor stands "alone and most desolate." It is fine for "the living to delight in while watching the dead sleep," but those who want to be nearer to them will be disappointed. Martineau's sensibility is very far from Gray's "Elegy" and far closer to that of Caspar David Friedrich, with whom Martineau, a thoroughly modern positivist and Unitarian, would have shared little except the feeling that the cemetery was a strange and discomforting product of modernity[101] (fig. 5.18).

5.18. *The Cemetery*. Caspar David Friedrich, 1825. Galerie Neue Meister.

Like daffodils, the cemetery quickly became naturalized, but for its first few decades it remained on the front line of cultural wars. On one side stand those like the grumpy conservative critic William Mudford, who writes about his visit to Kensal Green, the first English garden cemetery to be founded by a joint stock company in 1833. He was, he said, reluctant to accompany the friend who invited him because this field trip was intended to be more than a sightseeing jaunt. The friend had an ulterior motive: that I "might be converted, and give up certain notions I entertained touching the rather cockneyish sentimentalities which we now hear about pretty, ornamental, nay even beautiful places for the dead." He would have none of it: "Death and prettiness! Beauty and the grave! What ill-assorted images. . . . What a violation of all those tender recollections of the departed, whose wellsprings are gloom, and silence, and solitude." Kensal Green, Mudford was convinced, had none of the elegiac sadness that English people associated with the burial places of the old regime. It was hopelessly urban; one took an omnibus there; "why bother?" But Mudford presents himself as open-minded and adventurous; he agreed to go because he had never been to a cemetery before. Specifically, he had never visited Père Lachaise in Paris, but he had, of course, read about it: "fripperies and frivolities." He knew that the proprietors of Kensal Green were trying to provide London with its own version of Père Lachaise. But, since he admired his friend, he was willing to give him a chance: "there must be something in these fashionable collection of graves and grave-stones which gave them a decided preference over the CHURCHYARD." It was, the guidebooks might say, *vaut le détour*: a must-see attraction.[102]

Not surprisingly, he did not like what he saw. Fancy Gray writing his "Elegy" in a cemetery, he observes, as if that were all that needed to be said: "Fancy even a ghost taking its nocturnal airings among the trim walks and gay *parterres* of Kensal Green." (He was well attuned to the ecology of ghosts: the revenant dead are creatures of particular places; they belong where they belonged, and in the cemetery no one really belonged. Ghosts are local and not cosmopolitan creatures.) Mudford admits that the cemetery was beautiful, but not in the sense that it should be. As he passed through the gates, he was ready for amusement, rather as he was when entered the Zoological Garden. And this was precisely what was wrong with the place. Everything about Kensal Green seems to take one's mind off the fact that one is "standing amidst heaps of mouldering human dust." Like Martineau, he found the absence of any evidence of the dead in a place that is full of them disconcerting and incongruous. This was not yet commonplace.

Mudford concedes that the flowers and landscaping were attractive but, because they were the product of professional landscaping ordered by the cemetery company, they had none of the emotional resonances they would have had if those who loved the buried there had planted them. A guidebook sings of the "harmonious minglings of nature and art," and of "the great truths so silently yet eloquently asserted in a *garden of the dead*." But to Mudford, Kensal Green is coercive. He does not like feeling that he is being compelled to find pleasure in its gardens; he does not like the thousands of names written in a "fantastic variety of forms"; he hates the monumental absurdities. By 1881, there were 335 tombs famous enough to make their way into the newest edition of the cemetery guide. Every name, Mudford writes, is a stranger both to the visitor and to every other; this is a public ground, and the wide public makes use of it. Nothing connects these dead: "A mob, collected together to witness a fire or an execution, are not more disconnected from each other, than are the mob of corpses that lie rotting side by side in this huge joint stock warehouse of coffins." We can hear echoes of Carlyle crying out against the cash nexus as the only bond between man and man. We can also sense the possibilities, so repellant to Mudford, of making of these dead a new, and to him uncongenial, imagined community. Most of all, he hates the absence of the historical associations that he finds in parish churchyards: "The CEMETERY—the CHURCHYARD! Pronounce the two words—write them— look at them. How cold, how unmeaning the one; how rich in recollections the other." In short, everything is wrong with Kensal Green, starting from the basic premise that a sea of graves is to be enjoyed in the way one would enjoy a park.[103]

George Collison, a leading light of Abney Park, one of London's "magnificent seven," made the same sort of criticism of its rival, Highgate Cemetery. Highgate's hilltop site and surroundings had long been a place for promenading and holidaymaking, and it had done nothing to break that association. "So little is the former feeling subdued," he sniffs, that he has seen "parties of pleasure partaking of their slight refreshments, in rural language called *pic-nics*, within the consecrated area." The dead of a Christian community do not belong in Elysium or Arcadia—or Vauxhall Pleasure Gardens, for that matter.[104]

A year after Mudford published his article, Laman Blanchard, one of editors of the popular *Ainsworth Magazine* and sometime secretary of the Zoological Society, wrote about his visit to Kensal Green and reported a very different reaction. Most of his views were conventional; he complained of the noise, desecration, and nasty smells of the city churchyard in contrast to the sweet smells and the quiet isolation of the new "Asylums for the Dead"—a telling metaphor in a world in which all sorts of people were being segregated in a variety of asylums. Smelling good, or at least smelling better, was an important sign of progress in the nineteenth century. These "asylums" were not only hygienically but also psychologically good for the living, he thought. Sorrows were soothed and anguish and terror were softened by the well-kept garden that is the modern cemetery. Standing in a cemetery might even make it possible to contemplate one's own death calmly.[105]

Responses to novelty, more specifically the dead in urban modernity, are what really divides Mudford and Blanchard. Blanchard's article begins, as if the pages of a machine-printed, nineteenth-century magazine were an illuminated manuscript, with a large ornamented majuscule "C" in the form of a neoclassical cemetery gate through which a funeral procession is about to pass. The first word is "change." "Change, so busy in this eventful century with Life, is busier yet with Death," Blanchard writes. And a good thing too: "there is no late step in the progress of opinion or the habits of society so broad as the distinction between the city Churchyard and the suburban cemetery." The dead are in the vanguard of the march of progress: it is not possible "for change to take a healthier or wiser direction." In city churchyards "the pure and exquisite sentiment that should embalm the memory of the dead is stifled"; "in sweet smelling parks it is preserved." Pleasant smells are a sign of civilization (fig. 5.19). The article ends with a full-page illustration that makes Kensal Green look like the great Scutari Cemetery in Constantinople that had so captivated Mary Ashley Montague and William Wordsworth, or like the "mysterious valley where the dust of the Egyptian kings repose" to which it aspired. Our cemeteries, Blanchard admits, are not as magnificent yet as these; but they are, by way of an excuse, still in their infancy. Already they are responding to William Godwin's plea that we put names and monuments over the tombs of those we want to remember because to the human heart the bones of the dead are sacred. The dead in the modern cemetery are thus available, by name, to the living; they are objects of calm thoughts and elevated feelings as they were once in ancient cemeteries and still are in the Ottoman East.[106]

Such radical differences of opinion as between these two journalists should not be surprising. The dead were going to places that traced their lineage back to eighteenth-century gardens and, through them, to classical antiquity. The intervening millennia seem to have disappeared. The martyr cults of early Christianity were no part of this story, nor were tales of yew trees and churchyard elegies. If there was anything sacred in the new cemeteries it was "Nature" and "Art" and "Memory" and "History." God might have been important to individuals; the great majority of cemeteries in England did have some portion of their ground that was consecrated—the market demanded it—and the portion that was not was often proudly claimed as the province of Dissent; there were crosses amidst a sea of neoclassical and neo-Egyptian tombs, angels among the

5.19. Title illustration by W. Alfred Delamotte to Laman Blanchard, "A Visit to the General Cemetery at Kensal Green." *Ainsworth's Magazine* (August, 1842), 178.

sphinxes. The dead did not lose any of their idolatrous charms, but they exercised them more promiscuously than before; the old God was considerably less evident. The founder of the Glasgow Necropolis argued that only by abandoning the cinereal heap that was the cathedral burial ground and moving the dead into beautiful places could they inspire sublime thoughts among the living as they had once done: Cicero wrote of the gods and of nature in the shadow of tombs; Montaigne wrote his finest chapters, Gray his "Elegy," Raleigh his *History of the World*, Johnson his *Rasselas* in the shadow of the dead. Byron's dreams of darkness were born of tombs in Bologna. The cemetery makes possible a magic we can believe in.[107]

At the same time, it is rational and progressive. Contemporaries put cemeteries at the front ranks of the march of progress: "with new hospitals, museums, Athenaeums, etc. . . . [Reading's] lack of cemeteries is a scandal," complained a local booster. An alderman in the Lancashire town of Rochdale was praised as a great reformer because he obtained for his city a burial ground "occupying a charming site, and laid out . . . on a plan introducing many beauties of landscape gardening, without any outrage on the reverent character which naturally attaches to a cemetery." Gone were the "gloomy notions of the churchyard." "An undoubted improvement," wrote the town historian: "a mecca of memory." Alderman Taylor, by trade a chemist, was also renowned for a widely used system of sewage utilization that he invented. "Healthy repositories of the dead" and a solution to the refuse problem for crowded cities were his legacy.

London's cemeteries "are among the features which mark the progress of the present day," a guidebook informed visitors, adding that they were really a return to classical perfection. The owners of Norwood, another one of the magnificent seven, made much of the fact that it was next to the Crystal Palace, the great midcentury temple of technology and progress: "the beauties of Nature and the appliances of art are happily blended." Change had taken a healthy and wise direction in the new "gardens of graves," the haunts of memory where there is "no impenetrable barrier between us and those we mourn." Elysium had joined the century of hope and progress.[108]

Necrogeography and Necrobotany

There would be no cemetery without the dead; a memorial is not a tomb; a cenotaph counts only in very special cases when the living can somehow imagine its empty chamber to be filled. Cemeteries need bodies, discretely hidden bodies: there are no mounds and no jumbles of bones; there is no smell; monuments refer to death or the dead body only with metaphorical circumspection and historical allusiveness. Few epitaphs direct the attention of visitors to the body: model tombstones in the shops of masons never say, "Here lies the body . . ." or "Here lies . . ." or "*Hic jacet . . .*," but instead "In memory of. . . ." In the burial places themselves, the change from marking a corpse and calling for the person to be remembered was gradual over the eighteenth and early nineteenth centuries and proceeded at a different pace from place to place. In several New England Puritan burial grounds, "memory" began to appear in the 1740s and had become dominant by the 1760s; references to the body decreased dramatically over the same period. In Père Lachaise, "memory" was always preeminent and became even more so over the course of its first thirty years. It begins to appear on tombstones in a large French Protestant burial place in Wandsworth for descendants of Huguenot refugees in the 1750s and becomes predominant in the 1770s; in one late-eighteenth-century churchyard, only one of twenty-six nineteenth-century tombstones tell us that anyone lies below the ground. Sometimes in cemeteries memory and the body are conjoined—"here lies, in the sacred memory, the body of . . . ," which speaks to the essence of the place. The cemetery was born of memorial gardens, not of repositories of the community of the Christian dead awaiting resurrection together; its physical, historical, and cultural geographies made it possible for new aggregations of the dead to do new kinds of work.[109]

This was in part done through erasure: a clean slate. Readers of Goethe's *Elective Affinities* will remember that one of Charlotte's landscaping innovations in the churchyard was to level the graves, as is done in the modern cemetery, and to keep the ground smooth for resowing. Why she insisted on this is not clear: perhaps a commitment to the democracy of the dead, perhaps because the clover cover would be beautiful and the churchyard more seemly. After some protests by a local solicitor that the right of the rich to their tombs and the poor to their humble wooden crosses had been violated, he agreed that a smooth common earth covering all would be best. Of course in the cemetery those who could afford it had it all—a monument and a garden—but the visual effect of Charlotte's impulse was clear.[110] The disruptions of the surface of the cemetery were as quickly as possible repaired in the interests of the decorum that the messy churchyard lacked. Thomas Hardy makes sad fun of our capacity to forget what was really going on. Mothers quarrel over where their children had been buried, as if the flowers they brought actually could be laid on a grave. In fact, "remarks the man of the cemetery,"

> . . . the main drain had to cross,
> And we moved the lot some nights ago,
> And packed them away in the general foss
> With hundreds more. But their folks don't know,
> And as well cry over a new-laid drain
> As anything else, to ease your pain![111]

The surface gave no signs of what lay below and little of what had been before (figs. 5.20, 5.21, 5.22).

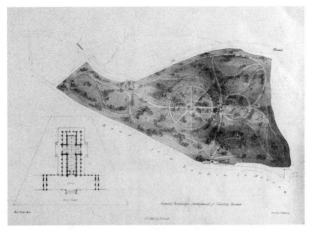

5.20. Map of Kensal Green Cemetery. From Henry Edward Kendall, *Sketches of the Approved Designs of a Chapel and Gateway Entrances Intended to Be Erected at Kensall Green for the General Cemetery Company*. London: J. Williams, 1832. The Yale Center for British Art, Paul Mellon Collection.

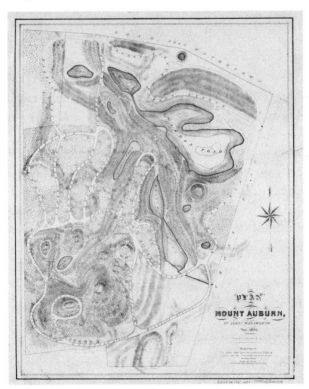

5.21. Plan of Mount Auburn Cemetery, Boston. Alexander Wadsworth, 1831. Boston Public Library.

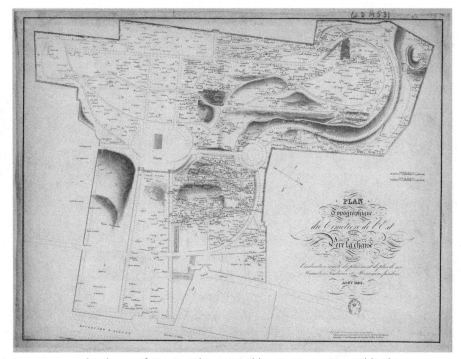

5.22. Topographical map of Père La Chiase. Giraldon-Bovinet, 1824. Bibliothèque nationale de France.

The cemetery was largely free to make its own history and memorial communities. The great majority of churches and hence churchyards were where they were for reasons that stretched back to time immemorial. They occupied pre-Roman or Roman or Anglo-Saxon burial places, sites of holy wells or places of martyrdom. They succeeded a medieval manorial chapel; they were a guildhall, a village green, a city center, a crossroads. They were of a place thick with their pasts, a complex stratigraphy of bodies over centuries or even millennia, a stage upon which much had transpired for generations of the living. Cemeteries were not. A few absorbed and made use of a truncated past: Abney Park in London had been associated with Dissent, but only for two hundred years; the Ricoletta in Buenos Aires was on land confiscated from the Jesuits and very quickly lost its right to consecration by ostentatiously burying Freemasons. But these were exceptions, as were some national cemeteries—Vysehrad in Prague, for example, which sits on an old monastic site. Mostly cemeteries appropriated a past or pasts as their managers saw fit, a *tabula rasa* eager to take on new cultural meanings.

They were discretely separated from the living. Cemeteries segregated the dead; they had no place in urban space. More successfully than the home ever was for women, they succeeded in really being a "separate sphere." Not for the dead the "tumult of a populous city . . . their business with this world is ended. . . . The price of corn, the state of the money market, or the rising or falling of the funds are matters which ought to be discussed far away from those we followed." Not in front of the servants. No wonder that William Hazlitt understands the fear of death as being the fear of no longer mattering in the world of affairs and of never having mattered at all: "People walk along the streets the day of our deaths just as they did before, and the crowd is not diminished. While we were living, the world seemed in manner to exist only for us. . . . But our hearts cease to beat, and it goes on as usual, and thinks no more of us than it did in our lifetime."[112] There is in these sentiments an almost Darwinian disenchantment of the world avant la lettre, a realization that the world cares little for the individual. But there is also an implicit hope: that away from the dirt and distractions of the city a beautiful new world for the dead can be built free of old constraints.

Cemeteries were where they needed to be, their location determined by the demands of instrumental reason, not history, not sentiment, not something holy. These came latter. In Paris they were at the cardinal compass points: Père Lachaise was officially the "cemetery of the east," Passy that of the west, Montparnasse "the cemetery of the south," and Montmartre that of the north. London's "magnificent seven" ringed the old city. In this sense they were like any other utility, near those they served. They were, with few exceptions, on land that had little other use and that could be transformed into something new. The Merchant Adventurers, a venerable guild in Glasgow, had profited over the years from their property, which became the Necropolis: some of it had been leased for farming, some used as a quarry. But by the late 1820s, returns had dropped, and a cemetery promised a new revenue stream from new customers for a new product: "it afforded a much wanted accommodation to the higher classes, and would at the same time convert an unproductive property into a general and lucrative source of profit." The prospectus argued that the land was especially suitable for its new use because it was already covered with beautiful fir trees and because the varied terrain and soil types gave the dead many choices: those who wanted to be buried like the patriarchs could have a "resting place in the hollow of a rock or sleep in the security of a sandstone sepulcher." (That was a big selling point at the Liverpool quarry-turned-cemetery as well.) Those who wanted to mix quickly with the earth could be buried in clay. The land was not good for farming but perfect for tombs; a screen for memory and the writing of history through the dead.[113]

There was a magic about cemeteries: from often unpromising land, monuments, trees, and plants they created the successors to eighteenth-century memorial parks. Sheffield and Nottingham were built on quarries and sandstone pits. Southampton put its municipal cemetery on commons that the corporation owned; Bradford's owners easily bought twenty-six acres with good views out of a hundred-acre estate that happened to be up for auction, and the interdenominational cemetery company in Leeds managed to put together two parcels of not very desirable agricultural land after prolonged scrutiny and debate. In his manual on laying out cemeteries, John Claudius Loudon pointed out that there were "thousands of acres of the poorest gravelly soil" along the tracks of the Southampton railway that could be had for 3s. or 4s. per acre and that it would be sufficient to all of London for a very long time. Brentwood in Woking was in fact built on two thousand acres of very cheap land near the London and Southwestern Railway line, which transported bodies from a special waiting room at Waterloo along the main tracks and then via a branch spur to the chapels. Good rail access determined the location of Rockwood Cemetery in Sydney. Of course, the architects and landscape architects and horticulturalists who created the new memorial parks appropriated a great deal from the past when they went to work on the raw land they were given, but they were in culturally virgin territory. Historical geography was not a constraint.[114]

Neither was the old cultural necrogeography. Graves in the churchyard were oriented east–west with the church that dominated them and directed the eye and the footstep. The most impressive monuments were generally inside and aligned with the axis of the nave; the whole assembly faced Jerusalem. There was no fixed direction in the cemetery funeral chapel and hence nothing to give the landscape an alignment. In Kensal Green, the Anglican one was on an east–west axis and the Dissenting one was not; its axis was aligned north–south, for aesthetic and not religious reasons. At Highgate Cemetery, the Circle of Lebanon, one of the cemetery's grandest features and most expensive burial sites, was aligned with St. Michael's Church just outside the borders, but the entrance gate and multidenominational chapel were not. The chaste Greek temple in Leeds faces northwest. In any case, the contingent orientation of the chapel had little impact on how an assembly of tombs was seen. Unlike a country house in its park, the chapel was often not at the visual center of a cemetery's design; and the spaces involved were too great—tens, hundreds, and thousands of acres—for all but a few areas to have an intimate relationship to it. There were micro-intimate spaces in cemeteries, but these were the work of landscape design, the subdivision of plots, and the placement of important monuments, not of an ersatz church or a millennia-old tradition (figs. 5.23, 5.24).

Tombs, great numbers of them, represented the dead of the cemetery, and they were situated to take advantage of its best features, natural and manmade. They are the buildings of the city of the dead and, like any complex of buildings, they work on the human imagination through a combination of individual qualities and their relationship to one another and to their environment. The direction of Jerusalem was irrelevant and so, for the most part, was any reference to the old

5.23. Sheffield General Cemetery, soon after it opened in 1836. Thomas Christopher Hofland, 1840. Museums Sheffield.

[Highgate Cemetery, 1841.]

5.24. Highgate Cemetery and the Circle of Lebanon. From Charles Knight, *London* (London: 1875), 652.

religion. Or, put differently, these tombs served the dead in the interest of the new deities of memory and history. Tombs faced roads as they might have outside a Roman city; they hugged a peripheral wall in magnificent array, or they looked over moorland and river valleys. The reason the dead bore witness to the power of Dissent in Bradford was that the tombs of Dissenting worthies lined a central avenue on a commanding height. There was no missing the point. And there was no mistaking the grandeur of the heterogeneous community of the dead in Highgate's Circle of Lebanon, a ring of spectacular sunken tombs that, while oriented toward a nearby church, was built around an existing old and very large cedar tree that was its visual focus. The choice plots in Philadelphia's Laurel Hill have magnificent views of the Schuylkill River.[115]

And bodies—visually the monuments under which they lay—defined its character and that of its neighborhoods: famous, high-born, rich, or variously distinguished people were cheek by jowl with one another. The poor were there too, but invisible. This was a new necrogeography in the service of a new social order. Parvenus could buy in; enough money and good or egregious taste could put a tomb on a tourist's agenda. Andrew Ducrow, the star of the longest-running equestrian drama in London and the son of the "Flemish Hercules," a circus muscle man, built an over-the-top Egyptian confection on the central avenue of Kensal Green just a few squares from the Duke of Sussex, the first royal to be buried among commoners; both were right across the circle from the Marquis of Sligo. Strange, intriguing, unexpected juxtapositions of many different styles of monuments, in no historical relationship to one another, in memory of all sorts of people, is the essence of the modern cemetery. It is the duc d'Orléan's Bois des Tombeaux on a vast scale, with the dead as its guarantor.[116]

Cemeteries, in other words, are parks, the progeny of eighteenth-century gardens—Elysium or Arcadia—adapted to accommodating diverse thousands and tens of thousands of the dead in various degrees of commemorative splendor or oblivion. They are contrived spaces—self-fashioned spaces, we would say if speaking of people. Sacred history was relevant only as the inspiration for some of a number of possible design elements: catacombs or tombs dug into a rock face in imitations of the biblical patriarchs. But history provided a palette of associations. Stephen Geary, one of earliest architects of the Egyptian revival, was among the early backers of Highgate, where he introduced a style long associated with dead pharaohs to nineteenth-century spaces of the dead. Mummy mania must have contributed to its adoption. Greek temples were the main style of the eighteenth-century picturesque garden and easily found a place among the dead of the first industrial society. Neo-Gothic—Cemetery Gothic, as it came to be called—was endemic in the nineteenth century. The battles over chapel architecture became battles about which history to appropriate for the new spaces, and they remind us again of the self-conscious artifice of cemeteries. The supporters of the still-existing Grade I neoclassical chapel in Kensal Green won a fight with proponents of the neo-Gothic. Egyptian revival "gardenesque," Romanesque, and what the leading historian of the buildings of England called "robust idiosyncratic" were among the historicist options.[117]

The same sort of decisions applied to landscapes. There may have been a few more constraints than in other kinds of parks; some people argued that consecrated earth should not be moved about as carelessly as its ordinary variant. But this sort of delicacy was rare. Earth was moved as needed for drains and grading. The old necrobotany was there only to be quoted: an avenue of young yews among many other varieties of trees and flowers as a gesture toward a lost world. John Claudius Loudon, who wrote the standard treatise on cemeteries and designed three himself, invented the term "landscape architecture" and was among the century's greatest horticulturalists. His "gardenesque" idea was hugely influential: the plantings in cemeteries were meant to make evident the artfulness of the design over its natural features. He was a horticulturalist at heart who tried to adapt his craft to the particular demands of a place. Loudon, for example, was not a great fan of the new tree of memory—the weeping willow—because it needed lots of water and he thought that cemeteries ought to be on dry, well-drained soil. But he knew what customers demanded. Men of a practical sort generally designed and oversaw cemeteries. Among them was Robert Marnock, who had been the head gardener at a great house park and designed the Sheffield Botanical Gardens before he took on the Sheffield Cemetery and the Royal Botanic Society Gardens in Regent's Park. Joseph Paxton, head gardener at the Duke of Devonshire's Chatsworth, did the design work for a proposed Birkenhead cemetery in the 1840s; after the project fell through, the work went to his pupil, Edward Kemp, a major writer on gardens who also designed Liverpool's Ansfield Cemetery. Some cemeteries in England and the United States—Abney Park, Boston's Mt. Auburn, Cincinnati's Spring Grove—were really arboretums in which the gardens enveloped the dead and their tombs to such an extent that it was not clear who served whom.[118]

If there was a specific historical necrogeographical feature of the nineteenth-century cemetery it was the marker of religious difference. Rev. Leapidge Smith, like others, might have wished that "all mingle, ashes [to ashes,] dust to dust," in the new Sheffield Cemetery and that "no lines [would divide] the Saints of God / Although they various paths have trod." It was not to be: a wall divided churchmen from Dissenters in Sheffield. There were other more or less ostentatious ways of doing the same thing elsewhere: a path in the East London Cemetery; a sunken fence, like an eighteenth-century park's haha, at Kensal Green; and, at the extreme, a six-foot-high, or perhaps better described as deep, underground wall, built at the insistence of the Catholic archbishop of Belfast, to separate his from the Protestant section of the new civil cemetery.[119]

The old necrogeographies were not gone; there were, and are still, thousands of churchyards in England and everywhere in Europe; most are more beautiful and better kept than ever in their history; the poetry and painting they inspired are still resonant. But with the advent of the modern cemetery a new kind of space had come into being that appropriated pieces of the past to make a future: as a museum of sculpture and architecture; as an arboretum; as a tourist attraction; as a pilgrimage site; as national, regional, communal, or familial place of memory; as the venue for the work of the dead that has made our modern world; as a place to make money.

Cemeteries and Capitalism

Critics from before and during the Reformation condemned the church for making money from the dead, and opponents of churchyard and intramural burial in the eighteenth and nineteenth centuries did the same. Lucre sustained the old regime, they said, and with some justice: resistance to reform came in part from the fear of losing fees. "The city has too long been poisoned by men who live by the dead," complained the mass circulation *Illustrated London News*. But no one ever claimed that the church existed primarily to make money. Before the early 1850s, all but one of the cemeteries in Great Britain were privately owned—either by old corporate bodies like the Merchant Adventurer in Glasgow or, far more commonly, by joint stock companies formed to make profits for their shareholders. The first of these was founded in 1825 by a group of London worthies who formed the General Burial Grounds Association. Two aspects of the prospectus they published are notable. First, the new burial place was explicitly not some version of a churchyard: the new company "united and associated together men of different religious sentiments." Second, their intention was to import a cultural innovation of the Napoleonic regime. The prospectus offered the public six thousand shares at £50 each and said that it planned to use the capital—£300,000—to build a "British Père Lachaise," "highly honorable to our capital and country," which would provide burial to anyone "in accordance with his own feelings, the wishes of families, and the general sentiment of mankind." Nothing came of the venture for five years.[120]

In 1830, a new General Cemetery Company tried again. Once more, the idea was to build something "after the manner of the celebrated cemetery of Père La Chaise." Nothing radical: George Frederick Carden, the barrister who was behind the earlier effort as well, rejected the idea of a giant, multistory pyramid that had been proposed by the architect Thomas Wilson at an 1824 Royal Academy show.

It would have been economical—five million bodies on five acres—but was too advanced to have much market appeal. He insisted on the Père Lachaise plan. The directors this time settled on a more modest initial stock offering: 1,800 shares at £25 each in order to raise £45,000 of capital. They also researched the market for their product carefully. There were, they discovered, 233,370 burials within the old Bills of Mortality—the seventeenth-century catchment area in which mortality statistics were first systematically collected—in the previous twelve years. They estimated that there were another 100,000 from hospitals, poorhouses, denominational grounds, and other extraparochial sites that were not included in the Bills of Mortality figure, so 333,370 would provide a large customer base. Moreover, they argued, parishes on their own could never satisfy this high demand. The expense and difficulty of obtaining ground was increasing all the time, and there was a certain delicacy about removing the bodies of people previously buried as had been done in the past.[121]

The economic prospects of the venture looked good. Liverpool had opened a cemetery in 1825 at the summit of Low Hill, which was returning 8 percent at a time when government consuls—bonds—were paying 3 percent. In its first fifteen years, it averaged 12.5 percent per year. This was encouraging. (The same young architect and city surveyor who had designed the Low Hill cemetery, John Foster Jr., had designed another cemetery in Liverpool, St. James, in an old quarry. It offered tombs in the style of the patriarchs hewn from rocks—this was the beginning of the great age of interest in the Holy Land—in addition to other kinds of plots and was said to be very beautiful. Its profits were not as great because it held only consecrated land and thus had to pay fees to parish clergymen to release "their" bodies.) Business would come from two constituencies, prospective investors were told. The middle and the upper classes would buy a freehold in a beautiful garden at a cost that was only a small multiple of the fee for burial in a parish churchyard other than their own. On their property they were free "to erect what description of monuments they pleased." And overseers of the poor in various London parishes that were strapped for burial space would enter into contracts with the company to bury their paupers. Even after paying the incumbent of every parish a fee for "his bodies"—the price for getting the bishop of London to consecrate part of the cemetery—the prospectus assured readers that there "was no doubt of an adequate return for the capital invested" in the cemetery. There was no mention of the dangers to public health of the dead in this public offering.[122]

One of the provisional trustees, the banker Sir John Peet Paul, bought fifty-four acres of land in the far west of London for £174 per acre; the company bought this land from him in 1831. Parliament passed an incorporation bill in 1832; capital demands were lowered to £45,000, and shares sold for £25 as planned earlier.

On 24 January 1833, the bishop of London consecrated the Anglican section; the first body was buried a week later. Less than ten years later, England's first garden cemetery was a big success: the stock, after an initial embargo on transfers, was selling at a 76 percent premium (i.e., £44 per share); there was a nice cash balance of £4,044; the costliness and good taste of the monuments that the middle and upper classes of society had built showed that the cemetery had become a "favorite place of sepulture." Plans were revealed to spend £10,000 on catacombs for prosperous patrons who might be attracted to this historicist venue. The directors, however, were anxious to grow the other end of the market, that is, to get more pauper funerals from the metropolis. They were working on showing people how economical Kensal Green was for overseers of the poor (25s. for a common grave), on developing a low parochial rate that would depend in part on negotiating lower transportation costs (a 50 percent discount, for example, for bringing several bodies at once), and on reducing fees owed to incumbents for removing bodies from their parishes.[123]

Less than thirty years later, the company sponsored a guidebook that told the world about its commercial success in this very special market. A city "tenanted with dust" had come into being. Well-ventilated catacombs had replaced the vaults of dark parish churches; vast sums had been spent on keeping them up. Visitors could enjoy delightful views of the Surrey Hills in the background and the rich foliage of Kensington Gardens closer by. The number of trees had been kept to a minimum so that none would interfere with the beauty of the monuments. But there is also a strange sadness in an otherwise bright infomercial. We are all acquainted, it begins, "with the noisy stream of humanity which struggles through the great thoroughfare and intersecting channel of the Metropolis." But there is another silent, sad, and mournful stream from which most of us would rather avert our eyes; the one is cloaked in gaiety, the other "in the awful paraphernalia of the dead." One of these streams has "wound its way for more than thirty years to Kensal Green." For a company that sells space for monuments and memorials, the message seems hopeless. Men and women whose "names were once familiar in our mouths as household words," have passed along the stream of the dead, "scarcely noted and almost forgotten."[124]

All but a handful of cemeteries before the 1850s worked more or less the same way; all of them both responded to and created consumer demand. "Within the last twenty years the example of Père la Chaise has become very strong," an 1854 guidebook to London pointed out, "and such establishments have been formed in the neighborhood of London": the "magnificent seven," as the capital's great new cemeteries came to be called. The same could be said of provincial cities. Local worthies got together—in Birmingham, for example, the chairman of a large button works, a malster, a banker, and a solicitor, among others—formed a company and raised capital by selling shares in what was something like those in today's real estate investment trust. (If an unmarried woman shareholder married, the deed of settlement for Brighton, for example, specifies, her husband does not automatically become a shareholder, which would be the case for her stock in other kinds of companies.) The business model was more or less the same as Kensal Green's. Companies hoped to make a profit by selling "two classes of graves," as the prospectus for Shrewsbury put it, and pricing them accordingly: "public" ones "where may be placed upon each other bodies of persons not connected by ties of family and kindred," and private ones "exclusively for the use of purchasers." The *Bradford Observer* praised the liberal spirits of the town's new cemetery in offering "freehold graves at prices quite as low as can be purchased elsewhere," and, separate from those, in sections to be chosen by the management, single interments "at the same figure as the fees now charged in the Parish Church Yard." The market was responding to two kinds of demand: that of overseers of the poor, who wanted to bury paupers as cheaply as possible and to alleviate crowding, and that of the middle and upper classes, who wanted sites of memory that they could develop, a little part of Elysium or Arcadia.[125]

Those who could afford to do so bought a plot in the cemetery, a freehold: front row 8 feet by 7.5 feet (i.e., 60 square feet); the rest the same width but only 7 feet 7 inches long—though of course it was possible to buy adjoining lots to increase one's property. The cemetery developers could thus calculate in advance the number of plots available—1,113 in one section of Manchester's Ardwick Cemetery, 420 in another—and the profits they could hope to realize from their sale. Places of burial became like speculative building projects; and occasionally, as in other real estate developments, government regulations could spoil the most carefully devised predictions. In the 1850s, a limit on the number of bodies that could be put in one grave cut into profits; a revision upward resolved the problem. Sometimes plots had to be taken off the market to effect drainage or some other improvement; sometimes they had to be repriced to reflect new developments. Leeds decided to set aside low ground on the southeast corner for children—2s.6d. under age twelve, 5s. over. There was no pretense of the cemetery being an organic space; like a modern city, it was zoned.[126]

Directors of the new cemeteries reserved the right to lower prices and shift the allocation of plots from the use of the middle and upper classes to the sole use of the poor as they saw fit. But they were clear that all were welcome. The privilege of purchasing graves, vaults, and single plots "shall be open to all persons willing to pay the price to be fixed upon," as the Trustees of the Westgate Hill General Cemetery in Newcastle on Tyne put it. Purchasers of private graves had an absolute interest in their property, forever in the case of freehold and for the duration of the lease for other tenures. The only restriction was that the land could be used solely for burial and commemoration. (Occasionally, a trust deeds specifies "for human burial.") A few cemeteries had only consecrated ground, and these were governed by the same exclusions that applied in churchyards, but all the rest offered customers "the liberty to introduce such ministers as they prefer and to use their own form of Burial service" in the unconsecrated sections, usually about one-third of the total. It was very much to the financial advantage of companies to offer both consecrated and unconsecrated ground, because public authorities were largely committed to burying the dead for which they were responsible in soil that had been sanctified by the Established Church and because a considerable majority of the population generally demanded it.[127]

Like any developer, the directors of cemeteries sold more than individual plots of land to those who wanted to put on memorials to their loved ones. Plots were valuable because of their specific location and because of the amenities of the eighteenth-century picturesque garden that cemeteries made available to a class that would not have had access to them before. The annual meeting of the Harpurhey Cemetery in Manchester urged shareholders to spread the word that "the gracefully undulated surface interspersed with flower-beds and serpentine walks [presents] a situation unrivaled in appropriateness for the favourable display of architectural taste in the erection of Mausoleums and monuments." People of relatively small means could now afford to own a little part of an Elysian field. The possibility of combining "the classic beauty of erections" in the service of memorials to living friendships required "only to be seen to be admired." A visitor's guide to Hull promises that the keeper of its cemetery "pursues his floricultural labors con amore and with such taste and industry as to make this otherwise valley of gloom a very garden of delights." It is sure that the relatives of the dead will be gratified. These sorts of appeals worked. The directors at Harpurhey noted in 1839–1840 that increasing profits to shareholders were testimony to the awakening of the public's consciousness of the need for a suburban cemetery. The directors of Ardwick reported in 1843 that more family plots were sold than ever before, justifying the expectations of the proprietors.[128]

At the other end of the market, directors maintained the right to set aside land for the "sole use of the poor, as they may think is reasonable and proper." It was their fiduciary duty to juggle the needs of two constituencies in managing their property and to lobby the government for policies that made the sale of land for the use of paupers profitable. Cemetery companies without consecrated ground—Abney Park was in the lead—opposed the 1843 version of MacKinnon's bill to close intramural burial places in favor of extramural consecrated ground because poor law authorities would have sent bodies there: the Church monopoly reasserting itself. And the directors of private cemetery companies were opposed to a provision in the 1847 Health of Towns Act that prohibited opening a grave for four years because, they said, it was prejudicial to the interment of paupers and the poorer class of society as well as to other segments of society. Cemeteries would have to charge more for private land if they could not reuse the land occupied by the poor and if they wanted to keep up their revenues. The directors at Ardwick reported reduced revenues in 1854 because they were complying with a new one body per grave rule. By 1861 profits were up again because they—and other cemeteries as well—had reached an agreement with the secretary of state to allow four bodies instead of one. "Considerable income" was generated after 1866 by granting (i.e., selling) the poor in these small communal graves the privilege of putting names on joint memorials.[129]

Capitalism thus moved into the market for memory that had been stimulated by the gardens, paintings, and literature of the eighteenth century, pioneered by state and municipal governments on the Continent—Père Lachaise was the great model—and brought to Great Britain in the 1820s and 1830s by joint stock companies. There was a demand for memory in places of the dead, and cemetery companies both met and stimulated it. Public health and crowding of urban churchyards was little discussed in prospectuses, shareholder meetings, or press reports; these matters hovered in the background. The fact that urban churchyards, given the political constraints on significant expansion, could not meet demand allowed cemeteries to offer burial at prices equal to or below that charged by any parish and to use the revenues generated by this side of the business to subsidize landscaping and the sale of private plots. To return to the question of how the cemetery came to rival the churchyard, the general answer is Marx's: the power of the bourgeoisie to tear down fixed relationships, "venerable prejudices," and social relationships. The cemetery was revolutionary, and it was deeply imbricated in the new urban world where money threatened all other ties.

The end of Balzac's *Père Goriot,* published in 1835, sets out its contours. Rastignac, the young protagonist of this and succeeding novels of *The Human Comedy,* accompanies the body of Goriot to the grave; the service is short: the choir-boy and beadle "did all one could expect them to do for seventy francs in an age when the Church is not rich enough to pray for nothing." Neither of the old man's daughters are there. After putting "a few shovelfuls of dirt on the coffin," the grave diggers stop and ask for their 5-franc fee; Rastignac has to borrow it from Christophe, the handyman, who is the only other unpaid mourner with him. "This incident, so trivial in itself, overwhelmed Rastignac and a wave of desperate sadness swept over him. Night was falling and a damp half light fretted the nerves; he looked at the grave, and in that place the last tear of his youth was shed, It was a tear that had its source in the sacred emotions of an innocent heart." He stood on the heights of Père Lachaise and looked over Paris. "He eyed that humming hive, with a look that foretold its despoilation. . . . It's war between us now."[130]

Pluralism in life demanded pluralistic communities of the dead. The consolidation of Christianity in late antiquity and the early Middle Ages gave birth to the
churchyard and to the idea that there should be a visible community of the dead
intimately bound to that of the living. Sometimes practical considerations and
extraordinary circumstances made contiguity of the church and its dead impossible: epidemic disease, lack of room in the churchyard, an increase in the numbers
of the dislocated poor who belonged nowhere and were buried where they died
on land owned by hospitals, prisons, asylums, or poorhouses in alien if consecrated ground. But the nation's dead were generally buried, parish by parish, for as
long as the story of a single community in church and state and in the eyes of God
could be maintained.

Skepticism undermined the old regime, but in its most aggressive and articulate form it was distinctly a minority taste. John Baskerville, one of the greatest
print designers of modern times and a well-known radical, wrote in his will that
he wanted to be buried standing upright in his Birmingham backyard under a
conically shaped monument—he had been experimenting with windmills—and
an epitaph that read:

> Stranger—
> Beneath this consecrated [*sic*] Ground
> A Friend to the Liberties of mankind Directed his Body to be In-
> hum'd
> May the Example Contribute to Emancipate thy mind
> From the Idle Fears of Superstition
> And the Wicked Arts of Priesthood.

It was a brave, eccentric gesture. The house and garden were gutted in the famous
antirevolutionary King and Country Riots of 1791; the body remained in the
ground until the land was needed to build a wharf for a new canal; then it made
its way to a plumber's shop and a rare showing before being secretly interred in
1829 in the vault of St. Philip's Church, near where his wife was buried. In 1893
it was moved again to a common grave in a Church of England cemetery. All this
left a legacy of sorts—George Holyoake dedicated Baskerville Hall in 1877 as the
headquarters of the local branch of his Secular Society—but not on the fate of
the dead.[131]

Radical gestures like Baskerville's were, at the most, a sign of the tensions that
eroded the old regime. The collapse of a single religious community was a far
bigger part of the story of how the cemetery and new communities of the dead
came into being. To some degree this is about the rise of negative liberty: the right

to a grave in a neutral civic space irrespective of one's beliefs or lack of beliefs, and the right to a choice in rituals of burial. In other words, the cemetery represents freedom of religion for the dead. There is also, however, a positive liberty of the dead in a pluralistic world: the capacity to create new communities in the dust. These made themselves visible as never before in public spaces.

Religious pluralism is, of course, not new in Europe. There have been Jews in Europe since the beginning—more sporadically in England, but continuously after they were allowed back in 1656—and their dead, in separate and distinct burial places by the thousands, were there as well. The New England Puritan lawyer and judge Samuel Sewall visited the Sephardic burial place at Miles End during his 1688 stay in London: "Some bodies were laid East and West, but now all are ordered to be laid North and South. Many tombs. Engravings are Hebrew, Latin, Spanish, English, sometimes on the same stone," he noted. (In fact, many must have been in Portuguese, since many of the London community immigrated from Portugal.) Jews bought land for burial in 1657, a year after they were allowed to settle; the first grave was from 1659. There was a garden and a small keeper's house; perhaps it also functioned as an *ohel*. The Puritan Sewall said that he hoped that he and the Jew would meet in heaven; yes, answered the Jew, he wished for that as well and that they might have a beer together there, which they were then doing on earth. A community that had disappeared or been underground since 1290 and had been allowed to settle openly in England only in the midst of a revolution was thirty years later well established in dust and stone. Christians had no interest in pluralism; they hoped to convert the Jews. But the living as well as the dead said otherwise. Miles End stayed in use until 1742 and can still be seen. There are dozens of other Jewish burial places from the eighteenth century.[132]

Visually this seventeenth-century Jewish burial place, the oldest in England, bore almost no resemblance to the great Jewish cemeteries of the nineteenth century on the continent. And because of the conservative nature of English Jews, neither did even the grandest of their later ones in England. Of London's "magnificent seven," only Brompton has a Jewish section, and it was modest. (Southampton's cemetery, by no means as grand as these but still impressive, has an Anglican and a Dissenting chapel and a Jewish burial house.) The largest Jewish cemetery in England, Golders Green, opened in London in 1898 and is traditional and restrained compared with those in Frankfurt, or Lodz or Warsaw or Budapest or Berlin or the Jewish section of any of Paris's great cemeteries. That said, the small Reform branch of English Jewry did participate in the new cultural work of the dead in the nineteenth century in splendid new venues. Jews too could imagine being in an Elysium of sorts, a place where a collection of memorials or grand classical porticos testify to the worth of a particular community of the dead amongst the living. The cluster of chest tombs and sarcophagi with their English inscriptions in the West London Reform Cemetery sheltered the remains of Sir Isaac Lyon Goldsmid (d. 1859), the first unconverted Jewish baronet and founding benefactor of the secular University College, London; of David Marcatto, the chief architect of the London and Brighton Railroad, who built for it a series of Italianate stations; and of Moses Montefiore before his "estate chapel," a Late Georgian–style synagogue in Ramsgate, was finished. (The Sephardic tombs in this Reform community are the old-fashioned table kind.) The Greek Revival entrance gate of the old Liverpool Jewish burial ground could be out of Stowe or any Christian cemetery. There the great Jewish families were buried in the style that the Earl of Carlisle revived: the Rothschild mausoleum in West Ham that the Baron Ferdinand built for his wife looks superficially like the one at Castle Howard; Montefiore's mausoleum built for his childless wife is modeled on the Tomb of Rachel, which he had restored in the Holy Land. Some twenty of Bradford's most prominent Jews are buried in the unconsecrated part of the Victorian Valhalla of Undercliffe in Bradford. The first inhabitant of the Glasgow Necropolis was a Jew. From being a world of the dead entirely outside the world of their Christian neighbors the Jews of England integrated their dead, more or less, into the new pluralistic regime.[133]

On the Continent, where the status of the Jew as citizen was intimately tied to debates about nation and nationality, church and state, the disposition of the Jewish dead in new cemeteries spoke directly to these great questions. All the major French cemeteries had *divisions Israelites*, which were far less demarcated from the rest of the grounds than were the consecrated and unconsecrated sections of English cemeteries. In these places of the dead "are gathered together all ranks and ages: the Russian is by the side of the Spaniard; the Protestant, the Jew, not far from the Catholic." The great battles of the Enlightenment in which Voltaire and other philosophes had been caught were over. Important Jews, like gentiles, were buried under freestanding mausoleums. In some cases they differ from their Christian neighbors in their appropriation of oriental styles—Morisco arches, mosquelike fountains—but in many not. The Königswarters' tomb in Montmartre is largely in the Egyptian style, with wrought iron gates bearing a seven-headed candelabra from the Arch Titus; the Russian French banker Baron Josef Gunzberg's tomb in Montparnasse is in the style of Violet le Duc's neo-Gothic; the actress Mademoiselle Rachel has a thoroughly classical tomb in Père Lachaise. Inscriptions are largely in French. Only a Star of David usually announces that a Jew lies beneath one of these thoroughly integrated and cosmopolitan memorials set among similar ones of other leading citizens.[134]

German Jews were generally buried in distinct communal cemeteries very much in the spirit of a people that understood its dead to be joined with the dead of the world around them. Oldsdorf, in the free Hanseatic City of Hamburg, has a separate Jewish section divided only by a road from other parts. This is an exceptionally porous landscape, but it spoke to the aims of the city fathers: to create a single, municipal cemetery and take burial out of the hands of various religious bodies. Frankfurt had a distinct and large (seventy-three thousand square meters, i.e., about fifteen acres) new Jewish cemetery on Rat-Beil Strasse, which opened in 1828 when the old one in what had been the ghetto became full. Only a wall separated it from the new, general municipal cemetery that opened at the same time next door. Friedrich Rumph, the city architect and a graduate of Paris École des Beaux Arts, designed the entry gates for both of them in the same Doric style and with similar iron gates. There is a lively contest over Jewish identity—orientalism and Hebrew versus German and classicism—on one side of the wall (and of course not the other), but sarcophagi and mausoleums in the Jewish cemetery as an assemblage hold their own compared to those next door. Architectural details give it away, but Rat-Beil Strasse is far closer to Père Lachaise than to a traditional Jewish burial place. Hanover's new Jewish cemetery, opened in 1864 when again the old one became too crowded, looks like what one would expect from the studio of the assimilated Jewish pupil, Edwin Oppler, of Violet le Duc, the leading French neo-Gothic architect of his day. Oppler had worked with his master on the restoration of Notre Dame.[135]

After National Socialism, the great nineteenth- and early twentieth-century German Jewish cemeteries with their opulent monuments to civic worthies are poignant reminders of history gone wrong. One can say the same thing about those of Budapest or Vienna or much of central and eastern Europe. Had things gone otherwise, people in the early twenty-first century might be saying of the assembled dead of Wießensee in Berlin or the Lohestraße cemetery in Breslau or of many of the other Jewish cemeteries in Germany what (substituting "Jews" for "Dissent") a national mass circulation magazine in 1886 said of the names in Bradford's Undercliffe Cemetery: they not only evoke "the memory of past epochs of local history," but also "preach an eloquent though silent lesson of the power of Dissent in this neighborhood."[136]

The commitment of Jews in their cemeteries to a national as well as communal project is unmistakable. Colonnades of Doric columns on a mausoleum in Breslau look like the front wall of a Greek temple; nearby are tombs with Ionic and Corinthian capitals proud in their detail; funerary urns of a people who eschew cremation dot the landscape, as do large and small neo-Romanesque and Gothic and Moorish confections. There is a small version of the Pantheon with an opening in the roof for light; an archaic Greek sits atop a plinth. My great-grandparents' tomb slabs are more modest than these and many others but this does not detract from the fact that the whole place is, and was meant to be, a Pantheon of local Jewry, full of pride in their place as citizens: Ferdinand Lassalle, founder of the German Social Democratic Party, is here, as are later SPD politicians; so are Ferdinand Julius Cohn, the first Jewish regular full professor in Prussia and a pioneering microbiologist; Hermann Cohn, one of the nineteenth century's most famous ophthalmologists; Clara Sachs, the painter; and members of Silesia's great banking, manufacturing, commercial, and philanthropic elites. The cemetery survived with relatively little damage from the savage battle for Festung Breslau. After the war, Poles expelled Germans and bulldozed their cemeteries. They changed the name of the city to Wroclaw. The Jewish dead of Lohestraße and their monuments are the only sign that Germans had lived here for hundreds of years.[137]

The late-nineteenth-century Jewish cemetery in Berlin is incomparably grander than this one, with every architectural style model from neo-Assyrian and Egyptian to neoclassical, neo-Romanesque, and Gothic. A cluster of identical tombstones of the local Jewish dead in the Great War bear witness to the community's commitment to the nation. Some of the most important bankers, industrialists, merchants, politicians, and academics in Germany lie here in splendor. In the large cities of Europe, Jewish cemeteries in the tradition of Elysium and Père Lachaise came to replace the small, crowded, inward-looking burial places of small, inward-looking communities. Like the new Kozma Street cemetery that bordered the larger municipal one in Budapest, these made evident to the world a confident, rich, and cultured community that stood with, if also apart from, the gentile civic world.[138]

Dissenters in England were, of course, not the equivalent of Jews on the Continent or at home for that matter. They may have for a time suffered under some of the same civil disabilities—being barred from a seat in Parliament or a fellowship at a college at Oxford or Cambridge—but their dead, as baptized Christians, had a right in principle to a place in the churchyard of their parish. When this right was attacked on the only grounds possible—that they were not properly baptized—they fought back in three ways. First, they argued locally and in the highest courts of the land for the validity of their baptisms. Second, they insisted that the churchyard was essentially a civil space to which they had a civil right that could not be denied them by ecclesiastical authorities for what they took to be specious religious reasons. The Burial Act of 1880 was the culmination of this struggle and guaranteed access to everyone with any or no religious service. And finally, they created new burial grounds that rejected consecration and that announced themselves as explicitly civil spaces with no religious tests for entry; they also refused to pay the Anglican parish clergy a fee for taking "their" bodies and burying them outside the parish.

Clifton Street in Belfast, founded in 1797, and the Rosary Cemetery in Norwich, founded in 1819 by a Unitarian minister who had been engaged in a burial dispute with an Anglican clergyman, are early examples of these new kinds of public burial places. A few years later, the "Chorlton Row Cemetery for the Use of Persons of All Denominations" argued in its prospectus that its being open to everyone was not only right but profitable; if a cemetery did not have to pay a minimum of 10s. per body to the priest from whose parish it came, it could pocket some of the savings and pass the rest on to consumers. In fact this was not quite the case. Cemeteries without consecrated ground did have a cost advantage, but they also had a narrower customer base because Poor Law authorities were loath to get into fights with the Anglican establishment by burying all paupers in unconsecrated ground. On balance, almost all the joint stock cemeteries and all those opened by tax-funded Burial Boards after 1854 provided both unconsecrated ground open to anyone to be buried with any or no religious service (although not necessarily without paying fees), as well as consecrated ground according to the Anglican Service for the Dead. Companies from the start, and the state after 1854, generally agreed to continue to pay fees to a clergyman for a body removed from his parish or to buy out this remunerative clerical right. One immediate answer to the question of how religious pluralism produced the cemetery is through the creation of alternative spaces for the dead that sidestepped restrictions on the civil right to churchyard burial and struck a blow at a hated clerical right at the same time.[139]

But the Dissenting dead were more than pawns in a battle for equal access and against payments to the priests of an alien religion. They did a great deal to create and make manifest separate and distinct identities. This is clearest with respect to Quakers, who set up separate burial grounds beginning in the seventeenth century because they wanted to distinguish themselves not only from the National Church but also from other Dissenting Christians. They often had burial grounds before they had meetinghouses. It was not easy to maintain the strict humility and simplicity demanded by the Quakers of their dead; local meetings remained ever vigilant and did not always succeed with their admonishments; the archeological record bears witness to the failure. Still, when Thomas Clarkson, the abolitionist, wrote a history of the Society of Friends in 1806, he was impressed with their austerity in the grave. Quakers have no vaults or bricked tombs; no stones or monumental inscriptions are erected over the ashes of dead men lest "by making too much of these, a superstitious awe should be produced and a superstitious veneration should attach to them." Even what Moses said of Seth and Enos and Canaan—"they lived and they died"—is too much, because these words confer merit upon the dead. "False as an epitaph," Clarkson claims, has become a proverbial expression with these people who have more or less overcome the superstitious need to "sleep with their fathers." They usually bury not in family groups but as deaths occur. In the burial grounds around meetinghouses, in the ground at the far Cripplegate extremity of London's Bunhill Field—the first freehold public burial place in England—and in their own tracts in the general cemeteries of the nineteenth century, the Quaker dead make manifest a radical spiritual and social vision.[140]

Dissenters sometimes had their own burial grounds next to their meeting-houses as well, in effect very modest churchyards for a subcommunity of the Christian dead. William Wordsworth visited one next to an unprepossessing Baptist chapel in the Vale of Hawkshead: an "obscure burial place," he says, "of a character peculiarly melancholy." The ground is "humbly fenced in like any of the surrounding fields," no trees, no adornment; a single low headstone stands out from "this little company of graves." Bunhill Fields in London is a different case. It was, as the poet Robert Southey said in commenting on the funeral of the famous and learned Presbyterian minister Samuel Chandler in 1766, "the Campo Santo of Dissent," the "first of repositories of the dead in Christ, which will at the resurrection of the just, give up so many bodies of the saints to be made like to the glorious body of the Redeemer." (His allusion is probably and ironically to the famous Campo Santa Monumentale next to the cathedral in Pisa.) More prosai-cally, bodies came from all over; Bunhill Fields, unlike a churchyard, did not serve a notionally autarchic community. There may have been a Saxon burial ground there a thousand years before there were Dissenters, and there is evidence of early-seventeenth-century burials there. But its modern history begins in 1665, when the land was enclosed and prepared as an overflow plague cemetery. It may well never have been consecrated—William Maitland in his 1739 survey of Lon-don says it was; others say not—but it certainly was never used for its intended purpose. But no matter. It came into the hands of a series of private leaseholders who sold burial places, mostly to Dissenters, who did not care. London's Com-mon Council took over the lease in 1778 and continued to manage it as before until 1855; in 1866 the Corporation of London bought it from its owners, the Church Commissioners, and turned it into the tomb-filled memorial park that it is now.[141]

At a time when many outside the Church were battling to be buried in the churchyard and when many others were without controversy choosing to be bur-ied in parish churchyards, the "Dissenter's Burial Ground" in London became a voluntaristic Pantheon of sorts for its great and good, a Westminster Abbey for a nation within a nation. The infamous publisher Edmund Curll thought that the epitaphs of seventy-two famous men and thirty-one women buried there by 1717 were of sufficient interest for him to make a profit from printing them. Over the years, others followed his lead. Here lie the saints, a very bad poet writes in a 1735 pamphlet: "In Bunhill Burial Ground crumbling to dust / There lies two generations of the just"; "A large Assembly in this Ground does lie, / When rais'd with streaming glory that shall fly." Individual verses celebrate them by name. The "great dreamer," John Bunyan, is there, and so are the grandchildren of Oliver Cromwell and the bones of Charles Fleetwood, one of his major generals. Daniel Defoe, William Blake, the hymn writer Isaac Watts (he also has a memorial in Westminster Abbey); the eighteenth-century Presbyterian minister and inventor of probabilistic inference, Rev. Thomas Bayes; and his friend Richard Price, the radical Unitarian preacher, mathematician, and mentor of Mary Wollstonecraft, are there as well. This is an illustrative company. Susanna Wesley, the mother of Methodism, also lies there. (Of her sons, John is buried behind his chapel nearby and Charles in St. Pancras Churchyard; her husband, Samuel, is buried in the churchyard of St. Andrew's in Epworth, where he was the priest.) The Baptist historian and hymnologist John Rippon (1751–1836) spent decades recording forty thousand names of those buried between 1713 and 1790, collecting as much biographical information as he could for each name, and copying all of the extant epitaphs. He began a multivolume history of Bunhill Fields that was never finished but that provided material and inspiration for generations of its future historians. Because of these labors his successors could imagine Milton, who lived nearby, meditating on the names of fellow Nonconformists and ordinary Dissenters meditating on the "great and good who have come before us" and who rest together "until the trumpet shall sound and the dead shall arise." There is no equivalent of Gray's "Elegy" for Bunhill Fields because it was so much more than a churchyard. Guidebooks told visitors whom to visit there; generations of Dissenters built and maintained monuments to the dead in danger of oblivion; it was a commemorative work in progress.[142]

Not a churchyard, Bunhill Fields is not a cemetery either. It remains, like the churchyard, a place where bodies await a communal resurrection: "Here lies the body," epitaphs begin, not "In memory of . . . ," as do most of those on the monuments of Père Lachaise and its successors. It is perhaps more like the catacombs, where tens of thousands of the ordinary dead were buried near the bodies of saints, than a nineteenth-century cemetery. But Bunhill Fields is part of the story of how the cemetery in Britain came into being. It broke the autarchy of the parish for both its special and its ordinary dead; it is not local. It is also defiantly both the product and the engine of a religiously pluralistic world; the dead of Bunhill Fields are a collective that proclaims, in the center of the capital city, that England can no longer claim to be an ecclesiastical polity, indeed that some of its most distinguished citizens chose to be buried outside the national Church.[143]

Abney Park, one of London's "magnificent seven," is the Bunhill Fields of the new regime. Other cemeteries proclaimed their openness to all comers but almost all of them provided separate consecrated ground as well. A few did not. But only Abney Park was designed to transform Bunhill Fields into a horticultural Elysium and to expand its writ. It became, writes a prolific nineteenth-century clergyman, a new and altogether different "*santo croce* or *campo santo* of revered and hallowed dust." Unlike almost all nineteenth-century cemeteries, which were built on land devoid of historical associations, Abney Park was not: the land it occupied was deeply rooted in the Dissenting tradition. The manor of Stoke Newington from which the park was carved in what is now north-central London had been owned by Puritans since the early seventeenth century. Dr. Thomas Manton, one of the most famous of the "ejected" clergy—those who refused to accept the 1662 prayer book, lost their livings, and became the first generation of Dissent—was, for a time, rector of its parish church. Through the daughter of a distinguished Puritan family—Mary, née Gunston—the manor came into the hands of Sir Thomas Abney, also a scion of the Dissenting elite. When he died in 1736, she became that rare being, the lady of the manor in her own right, and a great supporter of revivalist religion as well as of antislavery and other progressive causes. More important, the couple and then she alone were the great patrons of Isaac Watts, "father of English hymnody" and the most prominent Dissenting clergyman of the century, whose *Divine Songs* were universally known. He had been a student at a Dissenting academy in Stoke Newington in the 1690s, came for a week's visit to Abney Park in 1714, and did not leave until he died in 1748. Mary paid for his first grave monument in Bunhill Fields. His statue has stood at the center of the cemetery since 1845; he is its *genius loci*. Early-nineteenth-century lore had it that the small mound on which Watts wrote his hymns was the burial place of the bones of Oliver Cromwell that had somehow been spirited out of Westminster Abbey. (In fact, Cromwell was disinterred, hanged, drawn, and quartered; the provenance of bones claiming to be his is dubious.) Watt's room in Abney House had been a holy site for Dissenters well before the cemetery surrounded it and after: in her *Pilgrimages to English Shrines*, the prolific Mrs. S. Carter Hall (Anna Maria Fielding) reports she felt that the walls of his chamber upon which "hung the parting breath of the benevolent man might well be an object of the deepest interest to all who follow, however humbly, the faith of Jesus." No place in England was better suited historically to the land of the blessed dead of Dissent, their Elysium.[144]

George Collison, the solicitor who was the driving force behind Abney Park, made the filiation clear. First of all, it was, like the gentleman's park it had once been, a picturesque garden. But it was more than that. Collison incorporated it as a joint stock company whose income went to a trust that maintained a spectacularly varied garden: the dead paid for their many trees and flowers. A quarter of his book, 104 pages, consists of a descriptive catalog of the arboretum, the largest in the country: more than 2,500 species in all, 1,029 varieties of roses, and hundreds of different kinds of American plants around the chapel. There was a yew tree walk in the midst of the many exotic specimens to evoke old times in

England. Planting was under the direction of George Loddiges, one of the most distinguished nurserymen and horticulturalists of the century, who had founded the Hackney botanical gardens and edited a twenty-volume botanical encyclopedia. More immediately, Abney Park was the offspring of the first generation of garden cemeteries and their foreign inspirations. Père Lachaise, with its "picturesque undulations" and its freedom from "all begotten or sectarian pretensions" (that is, from "the illiberal dogmas and inventions of priestcraft"); Mt. Auburn, "perhaps the most attractive of all modern cemeteries"; and the unforgettable cemeteries of the Turkish dead are its immediate ancestors. Pera, overlooking Constantinople, where Turk, Greek, Armenian, and French "stroll together in [a] camps du mort," suggests the cosmopolitan spirit Collison hoped for (plate 12).[145]

More than any other cemetery in Europe, Abney Park presented itself as a space for the dead of liberal civil society that could be at the same time a Pantheon of interconnected strata of the great and the good. Collison structured its trust deed so that it needed only administrative, not parliamentary, approval and thus avoided any danger of protests from the Anglican party. It had no consecrated ground because this would have "destroyed and defeated [its] very scope and object," as he said repeatedly and as the national press reported widely. It paid no fees to the clergymen from whose parishes its bodies had come (this significantly lowered burial costs), it allowed anyone or no one to officiate, and it offered staff Anglican and Dissenting clergymen to officiate on a fee-for-service basis for those who wanted them: "the Labourer is worthy of his hire." Abney Park declared itself, like Père Lachaise, open "without test or interruption" to any and all of the dead: Jew and Christian, baptized and unbaptized, native, foreigner, and sojourner. And except for Jews, they were all represented.[146]

Abney Park was a favored burial place for worthies of the British antislavery movement, for antislavery missionaries, and for "natives" associated with the struggle. Joanna Vassa, the daughter of Olaudah Equiano, the most famous eighteenth-century freed slave, is there; so is Thomas Caulker, the son of the king of what is now Sierra Leone, who signed an antislavery agreement with the British. The Irish Catholic Chartist radical Bronterre O'Brien, various Labour worthies, and feminists of note share space. There are also many Anglicans. In its early months, their burials actually exceeded those of Dissenters seventeen to eight, and over the years prominent Churchmen were interred in Abney Park with the Service for the Dead read by their well-known brethren—the dean of Westminster, the vicar of Kensington, and others—as if to prove that a modern civic religious space had come into being. Their bodies were mixed in with bodies of other persuasions; no walls or walks divided anyone.[147]

Architecture proclaimed the pluralism of Abney Park's dead and the banner of historicism under which they were buried. William Hosking, who had earlier built railway bridges and went on to become the first professor of architecture at King's College, designed the magnificent neo-Gothic nondenominational chapel, perhaps the first such building in the West. It aligned not east–west, like a church, but on the axis of a path that led to where Isaac Watts and his patron Mary Abney had lived; a necrogeography of human memory replaced one oriented toward the Second Coming and the end of times. Denominational tastes were also carefully calibrated; Gothic arches that recalled medieval churches were balanced with classical ones more in keeping with Dissenting tastes. They also built a decidedly non-Christian Egyptian Revival entrance structure with hieroglyphs that supposedly said: "Abode of the Mortal Part of Man." The Dissenting cemetery in Sheffield had made this internationalist move already in 1836.[148]

It drove Augustus Welby Pugin, the High Church apostle of the Gothic revival, crazy. In his "An Apology for Revival of Christian Architecture," he drew a caricature of Abney Park's so-called Temple Lodges as an example of what not to build. The "grossest absurdities" were rife, he complained in his discussion of the gate itself and of the cemetery more generally: a superabundance of inverted torches, cinerary urns—but, of course, no ashes—and other pagan symbols adorned tombs; the entrance gate might be Egyptian—a kind of orientalist fantasy that in Pugin's view created an affiliation between catacombs for sale in Christian burial places—bad enough—with discoveries along the Nile. To make matters worse, there were Grecian capitals along with a frieze that gave the cemetery's name; on it, Osiris bore a gas lamp and various "hawk headed divinities" looked on. Hieroglyphics on a cast iron gate meant nothing: "they would puzzle the most learned to decipher." He had a point. In general, the dead in the cemetery were being made to give credence to all that was vulgar about the first industrial society, about the Low Church party, and most particularly about Dissent. Abney Park was the very antithesis of the medieval churchyard that Pugin, a convert to Catholicism, and his colleagues of the Ecclesiastical Society hoped to restore.[149]

The English cemetery came into being as part of the struggle for a religiously neutral space. In that sense it was a solution to the burial controversies that signified both the continued attraction of the old regime and its undoing, an urban prelude to the 1880 act that made churchyards as free as Abney Park. But it also allowed the dead of newly powerful and self-confident communities to make themselves manifest in new and magnificent settings. The god of history and memory was worshipped here alongside the old God. Little did children walking in Bunhill Fields with their mothers know that "there was an 'Old Mortality' dwelling among its tombs." The reference is to Rev. John Rippon, who spent decades recording tens of thousands of names there, and the literary allusion is to Sir Walter Scott's wildly popular novel about a man who in the eighteenth century went about making the names on the tombs of seventeenth-century Presbyterian religious martyrs legible again. Bunhill Fields and Rippon's books in the College of Heralds record men and women whose pedigree is "of the highest, and whose honor is of the brightest that earth can show." What had been reserved to the gentry in their country church vaults is now manifest to the world in the dead of religious minorities.[150]

Finally, the new cemeteries were the ground for an anthropological and historicist account of religion more generally. The home of the dead is sacred, writes the New England Unitarian minister and literary critic William Bourn Oliver Peabody in his review of the proposal to build Mt. Auburn Cemetery. Its ground is the primordial boundary between the living and the dead that neither can cross; its claims on the imagination are like those of a wreck at the bottom of the sea. But more than that, we continue to represent the dead as if they were alive—his authority here is Adam Smith, who was one of the great influences on his thought—and we feel bound to remember them because of our own dread of being buried with no trace. Cities are no place for such memories because they are almost like predators set on devouring the defenseless dead. And then he rehearses the deep history of his story. Reverence for the dead is primordial: Abraham paid four hundred pieces of silver for a field and all its trees in which to bury Sarah; Jacob and Joseph on their deathbeds both wished to be buried with their fathers. The Jews, Peabody speculates, learned this reverence for the dead from the Egyptians. And there was the Athenian Karameikos, where the king of terrors "imparted something of his majesty to all the victims of his power." We no longer believe that burial in churches wards off evil spirits, but we remain connected to deep-rooted feelings that we share with all humanity. Boston needs a public cemetery not because of public health dangers (these are overdrawn, Peabody says) or as a blow against the Church of Rome (that fight is long settled) but because we need to return to the dead their ancient sacrality. Thirty years later, another New England writer reviewed a history of Mt. Auburn and again reviewed ancient history, secular and biblical, as well as more recent anthropology. Diogenes was wrong: "let the heathen Cynic hang. . . . [N]othing is plainer, from all history, than that men have, with rare exceptions, regarded an honorable and peaceful burial as one of the greatest privileges for themselves, and the most sacred of duties to others." The story is not so straightforward as this implies, but it is clear that the modern cemetery was both a cause and a reflection of the triumph of the sacred secular.[151]

Reform, Revolution, and the Cemetery

In Britain, the revolutionary origins of the cemetery are obscured by the fact that its revolution, 1642–1660, gave birth not to a new polity but to permanent religious divisions in its largest kingdom. In 1662, some two thousand clergymen who refused to conform to the Restoration religious settlement, specifically to the 1662 *Book of Common Prayer* and Act of Uniformity, were ejected from their livings, from the Church, as well as from the political life of the nation.[152] (Quakers, Jews, and Catholics were separately excluded.) These "Nonconformists" and their followers became outsiders even if they remained, and fought to remain, to a very large extent a part of the parish community. The heirs of the Great Ejection were enemies of the old regime and in the forefront of social, administrative, and political reform in general, and reform of the many privileges of the Established Church in particular. They struggled for the civil rights of the living and of the dead at the same time as they claimed for their dead an honored place in national memory. Through the eighteenth and nineteenth centuries, the politics of Dissent led to the cemetery, the great-grandchild of the first modern revolution.

But the links to the more recent revolution, the one in France, were also clear and inescapable to contemporaries even in the relative calm of England. In the pages of counterrevolutionary journals like the *Anti-Jacobin Review* and the *Churchman*, conservative defenders of the churchyard made their case for excluding from burial those not baptized by Anglican clergymen and thereby forcing some Dissenters to find alternatives. W. H. Hale, archdeacon of London, in his last-ditch efforts to prevent the construction of the City of London Cemetery, argued that what was being proposed was not some minor administrative change—the commission of the sewers did all the planning and design and was poised to administer it—but an epochal rejection of a millennia-old history that had survived the convulsions of the Reformation: the regime that Gibbon dated from when the body of St. Babylas was brought into the grove of Apollo in Antioch was under mortal siege. The "practice of interring the dead in Churchyards, which is coeval with the erection of Churches until the unhappy period of the French Revolution, [and which] universally prevailed throughout the whole Western or Latin Church" was "being rapidly subverted," he told his clerical colleagues, and would soon end unless liberal forces were stopped. No churchyard, no church.[153]

He had a point. Père Lachaise was a revolutionary project, even if not as successful as some might have hoped. In 1801, the Institute National de France, successor to the royal academies of the old regime, proposed a question for an essay contest: "What ought to be the ceremonies used for funerals and what regulations should be adopted for places of sepulcher?" Simply selecting this topic was, in itself, revolutionary. The dead had become a civic, not primarily a religious, responsibility. In a new world the despotism of the Church would be overthrown and mankind's natural feeling for the sacredness of the dead would be directed toward a better purpose. It was needed; without it there would be no love of country or of family. But how was it to be reformed? Some thought that the state should be in charge of all funerals; regulated cemeteries were on every-one's list; public health and the need for administrative oversight were priorities. Some made specific proposals for landscaping that comported with the history I have recounted: there should be picturesque alleys of trees to focus meditation; there should be an "imposing structure consecrated to the father of men" but no mausoleums; nature should preside. A professor learned in the classics supported burning the bodies of those who died in combat, as the Athenians had done, in a public ceremony on the Avenue des Champs-Élysées.[154]

How much came of all these big ideas is debatable. The historian Joseph Clarke is probably correct that the Revolution did not democratize the commemoration of the dead whether or not it also demeaned it. The Church continued to be the source of solace for most French people; new ceremonies manifestly borrowed from old ones.[155] But spaces of the dead, so central to the great controversies of the Enlightenment, moved definitively outside the control of priests and into other administrative hands: bureaucrats and doctors. Twenty-five years later, the machinations that made Voltaire's death an international sensation would never have happened. The shift was huge and worked its way through various commu-nities in different countries, including England.

Nowhere was it more violently contested than in nineteenth-century Portu-gal; nowhere was the link between a new social and political regime and a new regime of the dead clearer. What in England passed as a series of squalls was in Portugal a great storm that showed that in a largely rural society, liberal Enlight-enment efforts to create a new regime of the dead were of existential importance to its opponents. In 1846, a peasant uprising, the Maria da Fonta Revolt, swept the northern part of the country. Its eponymous leader is commemorated in town squares throughout the country, and the revolt itself is a set piece of nineteenth-century Portuguese history taught to schoolchildren. Like all mass movements it had no simple cause, but it was sparked by the question of what was to become of the dead. The Liberal regime of the 1830s promoted enclosures and more generally the transformation of land from a neofeudal into a marketable com-modity; the state confiscated the lands of religious orders—about one-third of all property—and sold it; it demanded tax payments in money from peasants. The revolt might be seen as peasant resistance to the bourgeois transformation of their world. But none of these measures had prompted large-scale protest when they were first introduced. But new regulations for the dead at the same time had met with opposition. There had been some riots in response to an 1835 law that forbade churchyard burial and compelled each parish to build an extramu-ral cemetery. Angry peasants, led by women, tore down the new walls, forced priests to bury in the old places, and exhumed bodies that had been in their view misplaced. But it was specifically the 1845 health code that sparked a revolt. It went a step further than earlier liberal measures: the priest had to have in hand a certificate of inspection of a dead body before he could bury it; that certificate could be obtained only from a government-approved doctor, and that doctor demanded a fee that he shared with the state. The law was vigorously enforced; priests suddenly needed a license from state-appointed doctors for what they had been doing for a thousand years. Women led the violent and widespread revolts against this new medical regime of the dead. At issue was less a defense of the Church against liberal anticlericalism—there had been little reaction to large-scale land confiscations in the previous decade—than protest against interference by the state in the relationship among ghost, kin, and progeny. The foundations of memory and its keepers seemed threatened. The law thus took the dead body out of the collective social life of the community, and most especially women in the community, and brought it under the purview of outside professionals.[156]

Nowhere was the reaction to this shift as strong as in northern Portugal, where resistance to moving the dead from the authority of priests to that of doctors occasioned the biggest disturbances of the century. But this extreme case points to the centrality of the state in the creation of cemeteries and the new regime of the dead that it either mandated or enabled in less dramatic circumstances. For the English case, Rev. William Hale, archdeacon of London, whom we have already encountered because of his rebuttal to the arguments of public health, got it right once again. In 1834 and 1836 he wrote two pamphlets against the passage of a bill requiring the registration of births (and eventually of births, deaths, and marriages) that articulated clearly the radical nature of these measures. The shift to the date of birth that the government of the day first proposed as the category of civil registration—the entry into the social and legal order—meant the abandonment of baptism as the act that had been recorded in parish registers since the Reformation for the same civil purpose, in addition to its religious significance. This represented a major break: the state abandoned a spiritual event and proposed instead to use a biological event as the defining moment of official recognition. It would, he wrote, "un-Christianize the lower orders" and destroy the "strongest tie which binds the parochial clergyman to his flock," and—here is where he is on to the play of power that the philosopher Michel Foucault emphasizes—it could only be enforced by carrying "the officer of police into every man's house, where the stranger never thinks to enter, to the still privacy of the lying in room," and, he added in 1836, into "the solitude of the dead man's chamber." Hale was wrong about de-Christianization: the vast majority of English people baptized their children until well into the twentieth century, and most people still wanted to be buried either in the churchyard or in consecrated soil.[157]

Hale may also have been wrong that there was, as he thought, a "secret history" to the government's bill that was characteristic of the times generally and more specifically of the "party politics" of his day. But he was right about what was happening. "A man must be blind," he writes, "if he does not perceive that a great scheme is on foot, for separating religion from the state . . . and for providing, if possible, that the acquirement of all civil privileges shall be totally independent of any relation to religion." This was the project of 1789. The 1836 bill was a part of this program, and its deeper roots were clear enough. Civil registration "owes its origins in Europe to no other state of society but that of military despotism." In short, it is French. For Hale, the opposite of biopower was not, as Michel Foucault thought, sovereign power over death and the body but rather the power of civil society. But his point is the same as the philosopher's: bringing both life and death under the sway of biology, and biology at the service of the administrative state, represents a sharp break from the old regime of the dead and cleared the ground for new cultic work for the dead.[158]

Class, Family, and the Cemetery

It was the sociology of the cemetery that most impressed nineteenth-century observers. Or, more specifically, it was the way in which a memorial landscape bore witness to social configurations of the dead. The New Haven Cemetery was such a "singularity in the world" because it was designed to make easy the fulfillment of a wish that "seem[ed] to be natural" but had previously been difficult: that families be buried together. Except for plots set aside for the poor, Yale College, certain congregations, and slaves, each of the 64- by 35-foot parallelograms into which the ten-acre field was divided was in turn subdivided into roughly 22- by 18-foot burial sites that were sold in perpetuity to families; the name of the family was written on the black painted railings that divided the plots. Most of the plots had obelisks that were laid out in a line that went through all the parallelograms. There was little question what the dead were doing here.[159]

A less regular version of this scheme was followed everywhere. Family mausoleums line the walks of all the great cemeteries, houses for the dead who had once lived together and followed one another over the generations. What had been the privilege of great landed families was now within reach of the bourgeoisie. They were places of family mourning, they were cared for by families, and they were the real property of families. In this sense, the cities of the dead were havens in a heartless world for the dead over generations. Time was not, in fact, kind to most families. This was not new. But now there was no long-lived institution like the church to give graves a sense of solidity, only the fragile support of companies whose responsibility for the private property of defunct families was minimal.

The churchyard was in principle a well-defined and autarchic community: the dead of a parish who had been baptized within the Church of England or some other Christian denomination to the satisfaction of the priest. In other countries religious entry requirements differed, but the point was the same: those buried together in consecrated ground were the people of Christ of a place. "Of this parish . . ." was a common tombstone inscription that disappeared with the rise of the cemetery. This is what mattered. Again and again, nineteenth-century observers remarked on its openness: "the Russian is by the side of the Spaniard; the Protestant, the Jew, not far from the Catholic." It could be said of cemeteries in San Francisco, Glasgow, or Paris. All sorts of strangers are intimate neighbors in the dust. Madame Musurus, wife of the Turkish ambassador to the Court of St. James, could not have expected ending up in a park in an industrial area of west London. She fell ill and died at a ball in 1867 given to honor the visit of the sultan, and was buried—temporarily, it was said—by the chaplain of Kensal Green in Catacomb B beneath the Anglican chapel. Fourteen years later she was still there. Major John William Pew of the Madras Army, Lady Bonham, wife of the commander in chief of Hong Kong, Major General Casement of the Bengal Army, various East India merchants—more than twenty imperial worthies with no parish to call their own—are noted in a guidebook to the cemetery.

Cemeteries recorded Marx's "uninterrupted disturbance of all social relations." William Darby, also known as Pablo Fanque, the black owner of one of the most famous circuses of the century and one of its stars, has an impressive memorial in Leeds (now on the grounds of the university) because his wife, Sunsa Darby, died there when a circus tent fell on her. (Fanque is famous today because John Lennon borrowed the lyrics for a song on the *Sergeant Pepper* album from one of his posters.) These circus folks are the unlikely neighbors of the great congregational city fathers in prime mortuary real estate. There had always been mobility between parishes; neither people nor bodies stayed put. But the church-yard was a constrained place of a fixed order, a model in miniature for the cosmic order of the world at large. The cemetery was not: cosmopolitan to its core, it encompassed the world of the dead, largely unknown to one another but manifest to the living as a marvelous reminder of a new age of "everlasting uncertainty and agitation" that seemed tamable in its parklike surroundings.

"People of radically different opinions find themselves finally meeting in the dust," comments our Père Lachaise guidebook. This is because they molder in a civic space where a pluralistic—sometimes even cosmopolitan—community of the dead is manifest. A wide range of the dead who mattered to someone, if not to one another, could now claim a place in the landscape of memory. Witness Marx among the Churchmen and circus performers of Highgate, not to speak of his old ideological enemy Herbert Spencer just across the path. The poet Amy Clampitt thinks about how Spencer might feel after more than a half century to be intruded on:

his monumental neighbor a likeness
of Karl Marx, egregious in granite—
over incorrigible Nature, his memory red
With nosegays ribboned in Chinese.[160]

As some gained notice, others—hundreds of thousands of them—were lost as never before. This is not a statistical claim. The nineteenth century saw an expansion of the franchise of memory: a higher proportion of people by the end of the century had monuments than a hundred years earlier; there were more, not fewer, names among bodies even if many of these were four to a tombstone over a common grave of unrelated people. The working class had a better chance of getting their names on a tombstone in 1900 than in 1800, even if they shared a space with others.[161] If the poor and their names were present, it was as a contingent fact. Unlike the churchyard, which needed the "rude forefathers of the village" to be what it was, the cemetery did not. The Cambridge Cemetery Company was explicit: it existed "chiefly for the middle class." The parliamentary hearing on the 1842 bill requiring extramural burial in large cities proposed special areas for the poor; one MP asked witnesses repeatedly about the possibility of putting quicklime in the coffins of the poor to get rid of their bodies quickly. John Claudius Loudon, who opposed such measures, reassured his readers that this would be impossible; bones cannot be so easily dissolved. He also lamented the fact that the committee, along with much of bourgeois Europe, seemed to think of the dead poor as little more than animals that can be put in trenches or fifteen to a grave in pits. It may be natural, as the bishop of London put it, for the rich to hate the poor and to want to get rid of them as quickly as possible, but "cultivated nature" and "sympathy" dictated that we do a little better. Even Loudon floats the idea of temporary cemeteries for the poor on rented land that after twenty-one years would revert to agriculture. Urban churchyards had never dealt kindly with paupers; they were not terribly respectful of any bodies. They were perhaps also not, as Loudon claimed, "a local history and biography" to the uncultivated poor. But before the dead became dirt and before the religion of memory rivaled the religion of a transcendent God and His Church on earth, they were meant to be part of a commingled dust, however imperfectly it might have been arranged.[162]

This was not so in the cemetery. The monuments and landscapes of memory were for other classes, even if some working-class heroes sometimes found repose there. Freehold gravesites were completely out of reach. But the poor were financially indispensable to the modern places of the dead and their memory because they subsidized the rich. Per square meter they yielded much more in aggregate fees than more prosperous clients did when they bought individual plots. There is still a certain poignancy in reading their names in a register of a single-shaft grave. No. 3788 in Rusholme, Manchester, was opened on 13 November 1825 for the burial of Dennis Hannam, "found dead on the highway"; thirteen bodies later, on 25 November we come to Maria Bright, forty-five, who died of "decline"; and the infant Elizabeth Gibbons, who died from the same cause; and Anne Findley, twenty-six, who died in childbed. By 27 November, coffins must have been near the top of the grave, because all but one of the next fifteen occupants were children. Chris Connelly, dead of measles at fourteen months, on 7 December became the top coffin. Less than four weeks after it was opened, grave 3788 was closed. In the Bradford Order Books we do not even get names. First in grave 619 is no. 25439, eight years; then comes 25440, fifty-five years; thirteen bodies later, 25453, four months; near the end we get to 25522, nine hours; and finally 25525, stillborn. This pit yielded £23 7s.6d. for a space that must have been not much larger than a substantial middle-class plot that sold for one-third that amount.[163] In Père Lachaise, a *fosse commune*—a common grave—held the poor for five years, after which they were disinterred and tossed.

The poor responded by making a proper funeral a matter of utmost importance. Even if the body was lost, it needed to be laid in the grave with dignity. This is the subject of the next section. But the point for now is that the erasure of the poor is a consequence not so much of class antagonism directly as of a shift in the work of the dead that the cemetery made possible. The small stage of the churchyard could not accommodate the cosmopolitan dead, the dead of a nation, the working-class dead, the dead of the city and of the middle class, the dead of many religions. Whereas the churchyard gathered its local, hierarchically ordered dead to await a common resurrection, the cemetery was home to civil society, a new kind of space in which new social, political, and cultural ideals could claim their place in history and memory. It was also an arena for class.

PUTTING THE DEAD IN THEIR PLACE: PAUPER FUNERALS AND PROPER FUNERALS, BURIALS AND REBURIALS

Oh, Where are the mourners? Alas! He has none;
He has left not a gap in the world now he is gone,
Not a tear in the eye of child, woman, or man—
To the grave with his carcasse as fast as you can.
"Rattle his Bones over the stones;
He's only a pauper whom nobody owns!"

THOMAS NOEL, "THE PAUPER'S DRIVE," 1839

This ditty could only have been written in the nineteenth century.[164] Before then, in principle at least, the parish owned its poor and gave them graves in its churchyard. And, again in principle, a decent funeral even for paupers was taken for granted. Guilds and early friendly societies in the seventeenth and eighteenth centuries helped to ensure that members would be appropriately buried, but in general there was little anxiety about the matter. All this changed in part as a result of the deratiocination that the fall of the old regime brought with it to the world of the dead. On the one hand, there were new horizons: new places allowed for new funeral rituals and monuments of all sorts; they were open to bodies that before had been shunned in the churchyard. The rapid increase of funereal undertaking raised the stakes for what the dead—and the living—might want and expect. On the other hand, the old safety nets disappeared: the erasure of the pauper dead from cemeteries made the body's last claim on public notice and public space as it moved toward the grave more emotionally exigent, more poignant, more important to the poor and disposed. The possibilities of social death had increased. Finally, the bodies of the poor were ever more vulnerable to the pressures of a modern society: anatomists and artists sought and obtained them in greater numbers; the authorities in charge of the poor were ever more conscious of costs and more concerned with the political economy of poverty than with maintaining old proprieties. In this context, the funeral (proper and pauper) and the antifuneral (dissection and exhumation) became more central to the work of the dead in the modern age. This section explains why this was the case: why and how the pauper funeral became so melancholy; why the proper funeral became so culturally central; and why the dead were on the move to an extent and for a variety of reasons rarely if ever equaled in the West.[165]

The ignominious funerals of the poor became a public and a private scandal in the nineteenth century.[166] Tory radicals like William Cobbett and High Church Anglicans like Augustus Welby Pugin regarded the treatment of the pauper dead as symptomatic of the heartlessness of the industrial order (fig. 5.25). For the poor it was a more intimate danger. "Nothing" tended "to keep up in the imaginations of the poorer sort of people a generous horror of the workhouse more than the manner in which pauper funerals are conducted," wrote the essayist Charles Lamb in 1811. Almost a century later, a working-class mother in London told a social investigator that she would rather have her dead child picked up by a dust-cart than have it carted through the neighborhood by the "Black Mariar" of the parish. It was an abiding fear. To be "put away on the parish" was for the survivor's family to bear a "lifelong stigma," wrote Robert Roberts in his account of the "classic slum" of his boyhood in the 1910s and 1920s. The pauper funeral was a resonant symbol of profound degradation even to those in no danger of suffering it. The acute sensibilities of the poor to the fate of their bodies loomed large in discussions of medical teaching, burial, and cemetery reform even if only to be disregarded. Of all the horrors that the future Earl of Shaftsbury must have

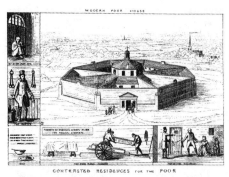

5.25. "Contrasted Residences for the Poor." In August Pugin, *Contrasts or a Parallel between the Noble Edifices of the 14th and 15th and Similar Buildings of the Present Day* (London: St. Mary's Grange, 1836).

seen as a boy in London in the first decades of the nineteenth century it was, he reports, the sight of drunken bearers unsteadily conveying a pauper to his grave that pierced his heart and converted him to a life of reform.[167]

The enormous efforts, collective and individual, to escape this fate bear witness to the terror with which it was regarded. "The poor would deprive themselves of the necessities of life for the sake of paying respect to the bodies of their departed friends," explained a witness at one of the many parliamentary inquiries investigating burial practices. It was a matter of great civic pride that four children murdered by their father, a Manchester workman, were treated well after death. Vast crowds lined the routes to Harpurhey Cemetery, where the victims were buried in a tomb whose inscription told of the fate that they had escaped: "These poor innocents were found dead on 16 May 1862 and to avoid a pauper's grave, Mr. B. Lee received in a few hours from upwards of 300 persons of all classes and sects voluntary contributions sufficient to provide a respectable funeral and purchase this monument. One touch of nature makes the whole world kin." These sorts of stories became a trope for the rest of the century. "Illustrating the feelings of this class on the question of death," Charles Booth, one of the most important social researchers and observers of working-class life in late Victorian England, tells yet another story. A factory girl was dying. "Her friends in the [burial] club when told that there was no hope of her recovery clubbed together before her death to buy a wreath for her coffin. There were exceeding anxious that she should live long enough to see it."[168]

The desire for a decent funeral, however defined, and for a place in ground where one belonged was not new in the eighteenth and nineteenth centuries. But a widespread sense that what came to be regarded as the bare necessities of civilization might well be denied, that an abyss of ignominy faced the dying poor and vulnerable, was unprecedented. And a massive infrastructure grew up to make sure that it did not happen. By 1874, two and a quarter million people, mostly men, belonged to friendly societies that provided both death and sickness benefits; millions more, their spouses, were insured for a funeral only. Six hundred and fifty thousand men and women belonged to local burial societies registered with the government, and hundreds of thousands more must have belonged to the many thousand small burial clubs that remained unregistered. In addition, more than a million belonged to so-called collection societies, commercial ventures that were founded to insure primarily women and children not covered in other ways. These societies took their names from the collectors who went door to door, mostly on Saturdays after wages were paid, to receive the weekly premium of a few pence per head. Much to the consternation of middle-class observers who thought there were better uses for hard-earned surplus income, if the Victorian working class saved for anything, it saved for death. (The worry that working-class mothers killed or neglected their children to collect funeral insurance was the fantastical version of these fears.) As one West Country woman said, justifying her membership in a burial society, "What did a poor woman work for, but in hopes she should be put out of the world in a tidy way." "Most illogical, inconsequential and light hearted, this, but travellers in the valley of the shadow of death are apt to be light hearted," as Dickens's narrator said of Betty Higden in *Our Mutual Friend*.[169]

Why would a poor woman deny herself the small pleasures of this life in order to ensure a tidy exit for her corpse? What exactly made going to the grave in "grim one hearse in a jolly round trot," as the poet writes, so sad and so terrifying that great sacrifices would be made to avoid it? The answer is probably not that the West Country woman Betty Higden feared that her death would not leave a gap in the world. The poor probably would not have imagined otherwise. And those who could afford grand funerals and proper memorials probably knew in their hearts that the same fate would befall them. The life of the city, as the essayist and critic William Hazlitt noted, does not stop even when one of its great and good dies; those who once seemed so essential are soon not missed as the world rushes on without them. The truth is that the pauper funeral takes us, and the Betty Higdens of the world, back to Diogenes. No one sheds a tear because the pauper really did not matter in the world; he makes a noise only now that his carcass—the used-up and lifeless flesh that might as well be thrown to the beasts, "his cloddy," the lump of earth—is bouncing to the grave as fast as the horse can draw it. We should not care what becomes of the dead—cloddy bodies—that are not, and cannot be, of any more use to us. But we do. Dread of a pauper funeral is in this sense like everything having to do with the care of the dead and the work they do: born of the imagination and of projection. Those who watch the wretched hearse, the poet says, "should be joyful to think, when by death you're laid low / You've a chance to the grave like a gemman [gentleman] to go." The sense of the pauper funeral as the abyss of death comes from imagining oneself dead and imagining the feelings of others as they imagine us. It is about the work of the dead at a particular time. The question now becomes more focused: what in the eighteenth and nineteenth centuries made the pauper funeral a major part of this work?

One answer is that it is a special case of sympathy for the dead that we have already encountered, a trickle-down of what philosophers were saying about the rise of sympathy in modern society more generally. Adam Smith recognized in all of us that the ground zero of sympathy is the sympathy for the body in the grave that is, in turn, sympathy for our own prospective dead bodies. It is a feeling that gives rise to the fear of mortality that besets us all and to the only antidote to it that this world offers. With the imagined prospect of our own abjection comes the hope of something better, of a continued social existence, of one last gesture of regard. We can imagine basking in its glow even if we know that it is impossible. Saving while alive to avoid a pauper funeral makes this possible for ourselves and is a kindness to kin and neighbors; it creates the conditions for the continuity of communities and of generations through the dead. That is, it creates the conditions of spectatorship and caring that we imagine for ourselves. The pauper funeral, like the new humanitarianism of the eighteenth century, is the fruit of the sentimental revolution.

But this answer pushes the question one step back: what are the specific changes in the cultural history of the corpse that make a sentimental attachment to a dead body so urgent and so demanding? They are of three sorts. First, the pauper funeral was the doppelgänger of the proper funeral. What one generation might have regarded as decent became in the next shabby and in the one after that dishonorable. No funeral, however miserable, in the nineteenth century was without a coffin; in the sixteenth and seventeenth centuries—later in some places—burial in a shroud alone was commonplace. Much more also came to be demanded of funerals than ever before: the body on its way to the grave took on new work of claiming space, power, and respect for new constituencies. As the proper funeral became more elaborate and more freighted with meaning, its opposite, the pauper funeral, became more dreadful. A theater of presence—the corpse on its way to the grave—created a theater of absence: no one was there to watch a procession that was almost too minimal to be noticeable even if anyone cared.

Second, the pauper funeral became the stage for the great nineteenth-century conversation about the new commercial and industrial order, about what would become of society—an early-nineteenth-century term—in the age of the cash nexus. The pauper funeral was a synecdoche for the meaning of poverty and pauperism. "There are so many things that cash will not pay," as Thomas Carlyle wrote in 1839, on the eve of the greatest working-class movement of the nineteenth century, Chartism. The chorus of "The Pauper's Drive"—"Rattle his Bones over the stones / He's only a pauper whom nobody owns!"—speaks in this language. The pauper while living may have owned her own labor. But after her death, no one wanted to buy it. She was unsalable. She was, in terms of the market, worthless. Since the late eighteenth century, "pauper" had come to mean not only what it had always meant—someone with no property, dependent on charity—but specifically someone who was the object of poor relief. It became an administrative category. The Poor Law reform of 1834 gave new resonance to this meaning: under its terms the state would offer the poor—this was the "principle of least eligibility"—less in relief than whatever someone in the least remunerative employment on the open market might earn. As we already saw with burials, many thought that the condition of society could be calibrated by how it cared for the poor. Theodore Lyman, scion of a distinguished Boston family, visited Europe after he graduated from Harvard in 1810. He devotes a whole chapter to burial in his published account of Italy: the poor who died in the hospital, he writes with obvious distaste, are thrown naked and without coffins into pits where they lie "rotting, ulcerated, marked with white-blueish spots and streaks of black" until the pit is full. The authorities never failed to pay for a mass, although the body was "thrown upon the pit as if it were carrion." Such, he sniffs, a proper Protestant and man of New England, "is a Christian burial."[170]

But in England, even without specific legal and administrative reforms, the poor over the course of the eighteenth century, especially in London and other rapidly growing cities and in places of "surplus population," were slipping into documented worthlessness. They consumed, over time, more than they produced: about 850,000 families, according to Gregory King (1648–1712), one of the pioneers of social statistics, decreased the wealth of England. (Some half a million supposedly increased it.) Respectable and unrespectable alike—the widow who had once kept a good house and the whore, the vagabond and the fallen artisan—were or could be reduced to worthlessness. In life the pauper was a drain on the commonwealth; in death she was pure waste, a relic that might only be redeemed if it could somehow find a use in anatomy theaters or, more fantastically, in marling the field. Anonymous mass graves in urban churchyards and in specialized new grounds belonging to poorhouses starting in the early eighteenth century and the mass graves in the nineteenth-century cemeteries largely worked to erase the poor from the community of the dead. The pauper funeral was a chief instrument of this vanishing act.

It was a *reductio* of a new kind of poverty, the ground zero of social atomism, as Karl Polanyi described it in his masterpiece *The Great Transformation*, about the defense of the social body. Alive, the pauper was alone; dead, the pauper's body was utterly bereft, without any visible link to the living. Biological and social deaths were simultaneous; the pauper was already gone. Nothing, as the poem says, seemed as desolate and isolated as the one-horse hearse with its pauper load. To be "Only a pauper whom nobody owns" was to be in the full darkest of the new social order: ownerless, unwanted, culturally unsustainable.

Third, there were new political, medical, and cultural exigencies. The modern world is a great new age of exhumation, reconstruction, and dismemberment. Bodies are dug up and reburied to right, or to revenge, some wrong of the past, to create memorial communities, to shape or reshape history, to assimilate their component parts into new scientific narratives, to advance medical knowledge and training, to entertain the curious. What was once largely a concern for the fate of saint's bodies, because they bridged our world with the world beyond, came to embrace lesser mortals. In this context, the pauper funeral became the *mise en abîme* of the dead who had no place where they belonged or anyone who wanted them; the dissected cadavers of friendless bodies are its nadir.

The pauper funeral comes into focus as its antithesis, the funeral of public standing and regard. These are part of broader changes, of course—the elaboration of royal rituals and its trickle-down effect; the rise of voluntaristic organizations of all sorts that, among other things, cared for their dead; the advent of the well-ordered parade and march that gained prominence at the expense of less disciplined forms of collective action. Not only the press but commemorative pottery, engravings, medals, and the like gave the funeral a cultural power it had not hitherto had. In sum, civil society needed the dead and gave them new platforms for action. Nation, class, and religion needed them too. But there is also a more internal history of the funeral generally that exposes the pauper funeral as a humiliating residue left when decency is stripped away.

Funereal sumptuary law, in principle at least, governed the old regime. There were rules for what the dead were entitled to, just as there were for the living. The College of Heralds, an institution of the Tudor chivalric revival that prescribed and organized the burial rituals for those with a claim to heraldic identification, from the king, aristocracy, and gentry to citizens and burgesses who were "free within the city," held a monopoly on public funerals sanctioned by a royal charter and based on the idea that one's niche in the upper reaches of a hierarchic order was more or less given. The funeral made it manifest. The heralds kept score. For the elite—for those with a claim to have their actions, words, and rituals express "the order of symbols, of values and beliefs, which govern society," as the sociologist Edward Shils puts it—the heraldic funeral was meant to represent rank with great clarity and precision. A king, for example, was allowed fifteen mourners, an earl or a viscount nine, a knight five, a gentleman two. A knight's funeral had all the regalia of a baron's with the exception of "bannerols"—extra-wide banners on which were represented the relationship of the dead to his ancestors. (The Duke of Norfolk required more than a dozen to display his pedigree.) A "citizen" could expect everything a knight received with the exception of a sword. The college and its officials ensured that the funerals it arranged were at once mirrors of hierarchy and specific mnemonic devices to remind viewers and participants of the deceased's place in the world order. In principle at least, social standing was assured, and the funeral was not a locus of anxiety: God's judgment of the soul was beyond human influence, and one's earthly reputation was too deeply grounded in the world order to be susceptible to human judgment.[171]

The funeral of the Elizabethan soldier, poet, and courtier Sir Philip Sidney, who died in storybook fashion as a knight on the field of Flanders, is exemplary of the old regime public funeral. By nineteenth-century standards, it was small, at most seven hundred people. The funeral of London's fire chief in 1861 was five times as big; Winston Churchill's funeral, to which Sidney's has been compared, was of another order of magnitude. But Sidney's was as large as it could be or needed to be, for to be larger would have been to go beyond the bounds of the community that it defined and of which it was a model. Thirty-two poor men for the "thirty-two years of his age" led the procession. Poor men, women, or children were customary attendants in elite funerals until the late seventeenth century, performing a dual role as living reminders of the deceased's benevolence and as bearers of the blessedness that was still thought to inhere in poverty. Representatives of Sidney's regiment followed the poor; then came his servants; then his heraldic devices; then, in order of precedence, sixty gentleman and yeoman servants of distinguished participants; then the esquires "among his kindred and friends" (sixty in number), followed by ten knights, the two categories distinguished by their collars; then his horse of the field and his horse for state and chivalric occasions; then more banners, followed by heralds carrying spurs, sword, and gauntlet. Following these came the corpse, borne by the dead man's friends; then came mourners of the appropriate number; then barons and earls; and then, after various others, the more ordinary, though richly dressed, folk of the grocers' company to which Sidney belonged. All was done in exquisite order to the dictates of the King of Arms, who marched as well. It was intensely inward-looking: Sidney's friends, in order, among the great; their servants in order; flags, banners, bannerols, telling anyone who could decode them of the deceased's relationship to those alive and those dead. It was hugely impressive. The diarist John Aubrey was deeply impressed and remembered seeing as a boy the magnificent visual record of this extraordinary pageant engraved on a roll that when unfurled covered the whole wall of a house.[172]

Though manifestly expensive, Sidney's funeral was not a reflection of his wealth. Nor was it a moment of judging his standing in civil society, as the nineteenth-century funeral was to become. The many "publics" of the nineteenth century that funerals helped to constitute did not yet exist. Rather the great heraldic funeral was a magnificent display of a given order. The funerals of the great were essentially rituals of inclusion for a small band of men and a show of status that expressed the deceased's place in a well-defined, if sometimes contested, community of superiors, equals, and dependents. They were said to be "suitable to the quality" (that is, the rank) of the deceased. Those that the heralds orchestrated, for a considerable fee, were in general the most elaborate and expensive; they took weeks or months to organize; they involved hundreds, even thousands, of yards of black cloth for mourning clothes, church drapes, and the like; they involved hundreds of mourners and marchers; they included great feasts. The record expenditure was for the Earl of Northumberland in 1489— more than £1,000—but funerals of the great aristocracy often cost in that range. (This sum would have the buying power of something like £400,000 in 2000, by one estimate; it was two hundred times the yearly wages of an agricultural worker.)[173]

"Decent suitablenesse to his [the deceased's] quality" was a vaguer version of sumptuary standards. Unlike the funerals of the eighteenth, and even more the nineteenth, century, the variation within social groups was huge. A knight or esquire in Kent might spend on average ten times as much as a yeoman and twenty times as much as a husbandman, but status was only loosely correlated with cost. Although the median cost of 116 gentlemen's funerals in seventeenth-century Lincolnshire was £4 2s.4d., the average of the lowest three was 9s.4d. and of the highest three £33 17s.4d. Out of seventy-one estates in the range £100–£150 (based on probate figures), the median deduction for the funerals was £2, the average of the lowest three 7s.3d., and of the highest three £9 19s.3d. Food was a far more important part of the sixteenth- and seventeenth-century funeral than a procession that made a claim on public space. How much food was loosely dictated by the "suitablenesse" criterion? Magnates fed thousands of their extended families, that is, all those in some way dependent on them: 1,900 ate at the Duke of Norfolk's funeral in 1524; twenty-eight extra cooks were hired for the Duke of Rutland's in 1612. But even very poor people, those supported by the parish, fed the humble few who saw them into the grave with bread, beer, and special cakes. Among the relatively prosperous, there were also gifts—mourning rings, hatbands, handkerchiefs—and perhaps a funeral sermon, especially in the last decades of the seventeenth century. All told, although there were status-appropriate expenditures, there was no standard respectable funeral, costing a specified amount, with specified accoutrements, to which the ordinary person or even the very great aspired. The funeral was less a parade than a specialized ritual and feast to which the greater or lesser part of the relevant community was invited to witness the beginning of the end of the social life of the dead.[174]

In the eighteenth century this began to change, in part because the material resources for creating elaborate funerals as resonant forms of consumption and social mobility became available. The late-seventeenth-century diarist Abraham de la Pryme complained that when Queen Mary died, the price of black cloth jumped from 10s. to 20s. a yard; in the nineteenth century one could get more than ten yards of French cashmere for the price of one yard at the inflated price de la Pryme reported. The Industrial Revolution had made black cloth of all sorts abundant. The first private carriage in Manchester was not acquired until 1758; by 1850, there were 1,009. Parades of the sort we see in eighteenth- and nineteenth-century funeral prints would have been impossible earlier. Relative plenty made the massive modern funeral possible.[175]

But plenty was at the service of something else. As commentators in the eighteenth century noted, money was the great solvent of the old order, and bodies, by making claims on public space, labored to create something new in the space that money cleared. As Daniel Defoe put it in an early work:

> But England, modern to the last degree
> Borrows or makes her own nobility
> Wealth however got in England makes
> Lords of mechanics, of rakes.
> Antiquity and birth are needless here;
> 'Tis impudence and money makes a peer.

"Gold and silver," said Dr. Johnson a half century later with some annoyance, "destroy feudal subordination." Of course, mobility through acquired wealth had always been possible, but never before so dramatically and so visibly. The Elizabethan world order represented by funerals like Sidney's was shattered in an age whose central concerns were not primarily rank and glory but rather, as one of the greatest historians of the eighteenth century, Sir Lewis Namier, put it, "property, contract, trade and profits."[176]

A sign of the times was that the College of Arms lost its monopoly over heraldic funerals the same year the Bank of England was founded. William III refused to renew the commissions that gave the heralds sole authority to adjudicate the use of heraldic devices and to pressure those who used them without authorization in special courts. In fact, the monopoly was never complete and was hard to enforce. Many people who were entitled to a heraldic funeral saved money by not hiring the College and made do with what they could procure locally. Nevertheless, the heralds helped organize some of the great state funerals of the nineteenth century. But something had changed. "Commerce," as a late-eighteenth-century historian of the College noted, "rewarded her votaries with a profusion of wealth." While England still had privileged orders, he continued, "they are attainable by all who merit them."[177]

Shortly after the Bank was founded and the College lost its monopoly, a new kind of tradesman was born; the term "undertaker," meaning a contractor who specialized in arranging funerals, entered English in 1698. Beginning in the late seventeenth century, anyone with enough money could buy a funeral like Sidney's. Profiting from the decline of the heralds, this novel class of men rented out cloaks, hangings, escutcheons, coach coverings, and even coaches to whoever could afford them. They arranged for the printing of invitations and the ordering of mourning rings and scarves; they organized the great processions of the urban funeral. It was a massive mobilization of resources for a great show in death. From one stock, an undertaker could furnish a hundred funerals; what had been restricted to a few could now be bought relatively cheaply. "Since the method of these undertakers have got a footing, persons of ordinary rank may, for the value of fifty pounds, make as great a figure as the nobility or gentry did formerly with the expense of more than five hundred pounds . . . the gaiety and splendour both of the nobility and gentry is hereby very much eclipsed so that not many of them do in this exceed the show of the common people." Undertakers were purveyors of falseness, men who traded in lies and deception. As a London guide to various trades noted in 1747, "the undertakers' business is to watch death and to furnish out the funeral . . . with as much pomp and feigned sorrow as the heirs or successors of the deceased chose to purchase." The poet Robert Blair wrote more pointedly about what they were hiding. Denial of death is not a twenty-first-century problem alone.

> Ye undertakers, tell us,
> Midst all the gorgeous figures you exhibit
> Why is the principle concealed, for which
> You make this mighty stir?—'Tis wisely done.
> What would offend the eye in a good picture,
> The painter casts discreetly into the shades.

That "principle" can be read as the body, "which in the nostril smells horrible" and is paraded in finery, or as Death itself, from which the living had best avert their gaze and notice. But it is also money, for which undertakers "let out their persons by the hour."[178]

The falseness of the seventeenth century became a large measure of the truth by the nineteenth. Money made the man, or at least went a long way toward doing so; and death became the occasion for a final accounting, a stocktaking of worldly success. Of course, there were other metrics: virtue, martyrdom, political standing, fraternal ties. But it took money to publicize them. The funeral became more and more a standardized commodity whose cost could be matched with exquisite precision to the class and degree of "respectability" of the deceased. When one bought a funeral, one bought a more or less splendid parade, each additional bauble, each horse, each feather or set of nails adding to the base price. Bit by bit, finery accumulated, and by looking at the account books of an undertaker who specialized in pauper funerals, we can begin to see the bounds of decency in death. J. H. Wick was under contract to the City of London Poor Law Union. It allowed the poor to add what little they could to the basics without reducing its subsidy. The unadorned pauper funeral—a plain pine coffin, four bearers, and rental of a pall made of rough woven cloth—cost the Union £1 15s. By the standards of the "grim one-horse hearse in a jolly round trot," this was generous. A name was the first luxury: an inscribed coffin plate cost 2s.6d.—desirable despite, or perhaps because, the body itself was headed for the anonymity of a common grave. For 6s.5d., the poor could buy a row of nails all round, black and shiny; at that price, such decoration was in less demand. Wick's account book makes clear that it was the making of a little finer procession that was most wanted. Aside from the plate, an extra man—presumably a mute—to attend and look sorrowful, who cost 3s.6d., and the "best pall" to cover the coffin at 2s.6d. were the most popular add-ons.[179]

The nineteenth-century commercial funeral was built in this fashion, and there was almost no limit to accessories that could be had from the stores of funereal consumer goods produced by the new industrial economy. Coffin furniture became a staple of the Birmingham metal trades beginning in 1769, and great quantities of decorative metal fell from its presses. From one catalog an undertaker could order wholesale angels and flowers, white for infants at 1s.9d. each; for children, white at 5s.6d., and black at 8s.6d. Pairs of small angel handles cost 15s. (white) or 18s. (black) by the dozen. Cotton, wool, and silk mills produced staggering amounts and varieties of cloth to be made into drapes, mourning clothes, hats, scarves, or gloves. By 1870, more than fifteen hundred people in the town of Whitby (where the fictional Count Dracula disembarked in England) worked making jet mourning jewelry. And of course one could choose from coffins of oak, elm, or pine, decorated with various qualities of nails, lined with various qualities of cloth, and furnished with the mattress of one's choice. Very expensive funerals added a lead inner coffin. Even feathers for the mutes hired from the undertaker, for the horses, and for various coaches were available in astounding variety.[180]

The funeral of a respectable workingman was constructed from a modest collection of such items. From the advertisement of a London burial society we learn in almost obsessive detail what kind of a funeral a 2d. per week subscription would buy:

> a strong Elm Coffin, covered with fine Black, and finished with Two Rows all around close drove with Black Japanned Nails, and adorned with rich ornamental Drops, a handsome Plate of Inscription, Angel above the Plate and Flower beneath, and four Pair of handsome Handles with wrought Gripes. . . . For Use, a handsome Velvet Pall, Three Gentlemen's Cloaks, Three Crepe Hat bands, Three Hoods and Scarfs, and Six Pairs of Gloves: Two Porters equipped to attend the Funeral, a Man to attend the same with Band and Gloves.[181]

A reasonably posh bourgeois funeral required more items from the shopping list; like a Victorian parlor, it was burdened with materiality. One bill, for example, lists a shell for the body, covered with crepe, £2; a lead coffin, £7; an outside coffin covered in silk with furniture, £7 7s.; a brass plate, £2 12s. Omitting several items but still on the first page of the accounting: a set of velvet and feathers for the coach, £3 7s.6d.; another set for the hearse and horse (each animal had a feather on its head), £7 19s.; and yet another set for the chariot and horse, £1 17s. This excludes wages for bearers, feathermen, undertakers' assistants, and the like, scarves, gloves, and many other items. The meaning of the funeral as a consumer good that defined the place of the deceased in society could thus be made clear to all. (The effect of all this on mourning is of course another matter. I am speaking here only of the corpse cutting a figure in the world.) Cassel's *Household Guide* in its 1870 edition listed various classes of funerals from £3 5s. for the poorest to £53 for the respectable middle class. In 1843, however, a parliamentary report announced that, at least in high-priced London, the lowest tradesman, in station "not much beyond that of a mechanic," needed a £10 2s. funeral, while the average prosperous tradesman required one for £50; "a professional person's" cost at least £100.[182]

The police chief of Stockport, near Manchester, testified at another parliamentary investigation in 1854 that the funeral expenses of a child (though the same could be said of adults) depended on "the differences in the parent's notions of respectability . . . in a very low class of life £2, others £4, £8 and some even £10." The point is not the exact amount—his estimates are probably high—but that a precise relationship could be established between social standing and the cost of a funeral, and that cost was manifest in the parade that was presented to the public.[183]

As the standards of respectability went up, the opportunity for the poor to meet them declined. The old regime norm of a place in the churchyard was under threat; the new cemeteries lived off of but hid the poor as much as possible in unmarked mass graves. There was also a significant expansion of burial places dedicated exclusively to paupers. Archeologists have unearthed more than one thousand bodies from the late eighteenth and early nineteenth centuries on the grounds of the Bristol infirmary. None were in coffins: these were the completely disposable poor. More than six hundred bodies, dating from the 1750s to the mid-nineteenth century, were excavated from the burial ground of the Newcastle infirmary. Of those intact enough to be studied, many showed signs of post-mortem surgery—autopsy or dissection. Archeologists have also found "medical waste" from the Nottingham General Hospital, probably from a teaching collection discarded after the Anatomy Act. Most of the new eighteenth-century hospitals must have had burial grounds for those unfortunate enough to die there, even if they have not been dug up. (No one of substance died in hospitals, which generally tried as best they could to keep out those who were mortally ill.) The workhouses and asylums of eighteenth-century London and other cities also had dedicated burial places. As the living poor were segregated, so too were the dead.[184]

In this context, the pauper funeral became the final stamp of failure. It is almost as if it had been consciously or unconsciously wrought as a new marker of status in eighteenth- and nineteenth-century England. The poor, instead of being those who would always be amongst us and who indeed occupied a spiritually privileged category, became those who could not or would not sell their labor and who consequently had to be supported, more to assure political stability than by reason of benevolence, at some minimal level above starvation. With the 1834 Poor Law Amendment Act, the so-called New Poor Law, this notion was finally given its full legal articulation; its evolution since the seventeenth century had been slow and irregular. Similarly, the pauper funeral as a distinguishable category of burial and a sign of the new poverty appeared in different places at different times. In Oxfordshire's house of corrections as late as 1775, an anonymous deaf-mute woman who died while in custody was buried with a full complement of bearers, not just a cart to the churchyard, and with a small party of beer, bread, and cheese for those who laid her out and those who carried her to the grave, as well as with the accustomed peal of bells at the church. As late as 1830 in rural parishes, beer, cheese, and bread for bearers, candles for a wake, and the use of a pall, all costing 18s. to 22s., were still common at a time when these same parishes, on the roundsman system, forced unemployed men to break stones from dawn to dusk for a shilling per day. A respectable funeral was among the last of the old communal rights to go.[185]

The right to decent burial disappeared first in cities and in parishes burdened by large numbers of the extraparochial poor, those without a settlement that entitled them to the rights of the parish. It fell victim to the process by which the poor went from being objects of charity to being objects of administration, a process evident in petitions to Parliament for new burial grounds to serve newly authorized workhouses and in the increasingly skimpy funerals offered the poor by urban, and in particular London, parishes. A sprig of rosemary costing only 3d., for example, disappeared from accounts about 1730. An old woman, who was paid 3d. to follow pauper funerals to St. John's Wood and thereby add a bit of dignity, disappeared in the early nineteenth century. Most poignantly, pauper funerals as a category of degradation emerge in contracts between authorities responsible for the poor and those who were to provide the actual services. Manchester, which in 1715 still bought coffins of an ordinary sort as needed for the dead poor, in 1811 contracted for specially built pauper ones: ribbed only on the lid, made of the cheapest pine, specified to be only one inch thick on the sides, one-half inch on the lid and ends for small coffins, and only somewhat thicker all around for the bigger ones. Another page of the contract gives a set of estimates with higher prices marked out and a new rock bottom price for each size, without any ribs, noted by the clerk as "lowest price."[186]

The contract between Nicholas Soan and the churchwardens of St. Botolph, Bishopsgate, London, in 1780 is almost a parody of this trend. In fact, contemporaries thought it went too far. He agreed to a whole list of provisions with regard to the maintenance of the poor in the workhouse that was to be under his management. Then somewhere in the middle of the contract there is a clause in which he committed himself to "provide the sick poor with physic, Surgery, and midwifery (doctor excepted), all hospital expenses (lunatics excepted), to pay all expenses of Burials, to pay the emptying of the Necessary [i.e., the privy, the cesspit] when occasion requires." Thus, he promised to provide certain care while his poor charges were still alive; he would bury them, and, as part of the same thought, he would cart off the workhouse excrement.[187]

The New Poor Law of 1834 intensified and codified the attitudes and practices that made such contracts possible. The pauper funeral was but the final ignominy; even in death the poor were marked as social outcasts. As late as 1795 in the industrial town of St. Helens, the overseers contributed 7s. to drink and other niceties at the funerals of the poor. By 1840, the Assistant Poor Law Commissioners had convinced the new Poor Law Unions, the administrative units that consolidated parish poor law administration and were governed by centrally promulgated rules, to put everything they needed up for bid: food, fuel, cogs, coffins. No extras at a pauper burial under this regime. In London, that part of the burial service carried out inside the church was omitted for the pauper dead if their relatives couldn't come up with the required fee. Unions were authorized by new legislation to purchase special burial grounds solely for paupers who died in the workhouses of the new regime. It was routine in big cities for several pauper funerals to be combined, thus giving the poor no choice as to when their relatives or friends were to be buried and creating through the display of identical unmarked parish coffins a striking image of anonymity and individual worthlessness. Sunday was the most common day. Whether it was Edwin Chadwick or his rival Lewis who forbade Unions to pay for the ringing of bells at pauper funerals is irrelevant; the point is that the degree of shabbiness had become a question for administrative adjudication.[188] In the same spirit in which the commissioners disallowed public funds for workhouse Christmas dinner on the grounds that some of the working poor might not have it so good, they created the degrading spectacle of the pauper burial. Just as the proper funeral came to be defined quite precisely by its cost, so also the pauper one. Gone was the variation of the eighteenth-century churchwardens' accounts; neatly lined "Relieving Officers' Application and Report Books" give the standard entries, depending on the size of coffin or grave and fees; nothing more.[189]

By 1850, the pauper funeral had become perhaps the dominant representation of that vulnerability, of the possibility of falling irrevocably from the grace of society, of exclusion from the values of one's culture. It was an image that worked on the poor; they would, as one observer put it, "sell their beds out from under them sooner than have parish funerals." Anxiety about pauper burial did not, of course, stand alone in drawing—pushing might be the better verb—the poor into industrial civilization, but ignominious burial was one of the most powerful ways in which the relationship between money and standing was made manifest, a metaphor for the meaning of consumption, a vehicle for the creation of desire that made the new economic order possible. To avoid a pauper funeral the poor saved through burial clubs, friendly societies, or the large "collecting" societies; they borrowed and repaid pawn-shop loans; they tried to live frugally. The rules of the various burial clubs and societies in many cases denied benefits to families of those who died as a result of profligate lives (e.g., from alcoholism or venereal disease), and they demanded sobriety and civility at meetings. Thus, to provide oneself with a dignified burial was, consciously or not, to abandon the plebian ways of the old order and to participate in the respectability of the new.[190]

Before the late eighteenth century, the bodies of the humble dead had only rarely claimed the streets of Europe's cities. In the modern era they did so in considerable numbers and to great effect. The other side of the pauper funeral is not only the proper funeral but the extraordinary funeral. Whether their funerals were the technically public—paid for or organized by the state—or private is less important than that their bodies did public work. The funerals in 1793, planned by the painter Jacques-Louis David, of the child soldier-martyrs of the French Revolution, Joseph Bara and Agricol Viala, who died fighting the enemies of the nation, begin a new era. There was the unprecedented and remarkable burial procession on 22 March 1848, of 189 dead workers who had fallen on the barricades in Berlin on the night of 18–19 March. The authorities had wanted a common funeral with the soldiers who also died; the middle-class liberals and their working-class supporters insisted that only separate funerals would make clear that a revolution had happened. Rich and poor paid for the sad festivities; theaters held fundraisers—Lessing's *Nathan der Weise* was on offer at one. Jewish, Protestant, and Catholic officials met the bodies as they entered the cemetery. And, most important, the autocratic Prussian King Frederick IV doffed his helmet in "forced homage" as the coffins and carts rolled by: "———, father of six, shot down at the barricades . . ." A name, an identification, a revolutionary act made publicly manifest through the bodies of the dead. (The king also promised a constitution, a promise that the failure of the Frankfort Parliament allowed him to renege on.) Adolph Menzil's unfinished picture offers only the promise of an extraordinary mass funeral moving through the public spaces of a capital city that Sunday (fig. 5.26). In other words, the dead were very much still on the barricades.[191]

There were many more such moments, on a much smaller scale, in the making of the English working class. In some cases, it is the forensic dissection table and the coroner's inquest that bear witness to political repression. John Rhodes

5.26. *Victims of the March Revolution in Berlin Lying in State.* Adolph Menzel, 1848. Hamburger Kunsthalle.

took a sabre wound in the head and was "dreadfully crushed in body" when the yeomanry cleared the great reform meeting that he was attending at "Peterloo" Fields in Manchester on 16 August 1819. The magistrates who had ordered the attack ordered that the coroner perform an autopsy to find the cause of Rhodes's death, one of eleven. Rhodes, it was found, "died of natural causes." The inquest on Edmund Dawson was slightly less absurd: "Willful murder not allowed." But investigations of death did not always go so smoothly for the authorities. The jury in the inquest on the body of John Lees, the son of Robert, a small factory owner, produced a minor *cause célèbre*. Sitting in Oldham and dominated by radicals, it produced the most complete account of the yeomanry's attack that we have. Lees's father had refused to accept that his son's death on 7 September was the result of anything other than the saber wound and trampling he had sustained from the cavalry when it unlawfully cleared what he regarded as a peaceful demonstration from St. Peter's Field. The surgeon whom the son consulted on the day after the attack insisted on an inquest; two well-known radical solicitors represented his bereaved father. At stake in the examination over John's corpse was the interpretation of 16 August: an illegal attack on unarmed citizens or a justified suppression of a potentially violent revolutionary gathering.[192]

The local coroner did what he could to suppress the hearing: sending assistants who would not carry on without him; refusing to hear witnesses; failing to view the body. The solicitors who represented the interests of Lees and of the radicals more generally insisted on as many witnesses as they could muster. They brought them to Oldham by the coachload. Most had not actually seen what happened to John but testified to what they took to be the unprovoked violence of the mounted yeomanry. Their aim was to create a record of illegality. Some had intimate knowledge of John's fate. "I have seen many dead people," said the wife of a shoemaker who had laid out the body, "but I never saw such a corpse as this in all my life." There was a dark purple bruise on his right shoulder; there was scarcely a place on his back free of bruises as if he had been "tied to a halbard and flogged." She insisted that she had seen the body before it was cold, she understood that death brought with it discoloration, but what she had observed was not natural. Thomas Ferrand, the coroner, had not thought it necessary to view the body himself. Under pressure, he ordered that it be exhumed. He was awakened at 3:00 A.M. to be told that a crowd had gathered at the churchyard, thinking that his men were stealing the body that he had planned to view at six o'clock. There were, he said, thousands of people in the Oldham churchyard to prevent him from filling up the grave again before the arrival of Lees's solicitor. The crowd, like that at the inquest, was, he said, out of control. In the end, Ferrand managed to avoid rendering a verdict by citing a technicality in the Court of King's Bench: the law required that the coroner and the jury see the body at the same time. This had not happened. There was considerable protest that the government of the day had managed to suppress a finding, but verdict or not, 618 pages about how the body of young John Lees came to be dead are the most complete record we have of England's most notorious case of political repression.[193]

The public fate of others of the dead of Peterloo was more poignant, comic, sentimental, and strange. When the horse belonging to Orator Hunt, editor of the major radical paper of the day and a speaker at the great reform meeting in Manchester we know as "Peterloo," died en route home after his master was released from prison on bail, he was given a funeral attended by thousands of ordinary people and buried under a weeping willow with a headstone that read, "Alas Poor Bob." Seven years later, his bones were exhumed, like so many, to serve other purposes: in his case, to make snuff boxes, one of which was presented to his former owner.[194]

Some working-class funerals were self-consciously epic in scale. "Nothing is more calculated to give more exalted feelings" to kin and comrades "than to witness a respectable and numerous attendance at the last rites of a brother," wrote the newspaper of the Grand National Consolidated Trades' Union in 1834, just months before the government cracked down on it. The story was of the burial service of a Barnsley linen operative: "what man, that has a rational feeling for himself, his family, and his country, would not be a unionist, . . . all to be surrounded with laurels in life, and when dead to be clad with them." The funeral parade was spectacularly large and iconographically rich: a band and mutes dressed in black, the officers of various lodges with black sashes and white rosettes, then bearers of white rods and crepe, then several choirs four abreast, then the body borne by three officers clothed in white on each side, then other officials, then the secretary of the deceased's lodge carrying the Bible on a black velvet cushion, then his whole lodge, then other lodges all wearing rosettes. Fifteen hundred marchers in all, it was reported, with five thousand spectators. (*Pioneer*, the weekly reporting all this, had a circulation of twenty thousand, with many times that number of readers and those who heard it read out loud. Thus the funeral was far more public than was reflected in the numbers who actually watched or participated in it.) "How elated did every spectator appear, and with what amazement did they gaze upon the whole movement." The dead in procession made the movement manifest to itself: a hundred women in black robes with white hoods and five hundred trade unionists carrying springs of ivy followed the coffin of a worker in Hinckley; women in white hoods and members of eleven trade societies made up the procession of a Derby carpenter; all the building trades were in the funeral of a Birmingham woodsawyer. Funerals, like initiation rituals, created new collectivities, new communities of the dead and the living.[195]

This was true of the Chartists later in the century and of Methodists and other denominations earlier. Political martyrs claimed the streets as never before. The elaborate funeral of Samuel Holberry, a young militant Sheffield Chartist and unemployed distillery worker of the humblest of origins—he was one of nine children of an agricultural laborer—who died at age twenty-seven from tuberculosis and harsh prison treatment, drew a crowd in the tens of thousands. His corpse mobilized all the material accessories of a grand bourgeois funeral—the mutes, the mourning coaches, the beautifully decorated hearse—but also the political banners ("Is Chartism Dead?" CLAYTON and HOLBERRY, The Martyrs of the People") and, most important, the crowds: conservatively twenty thousand, said the Whig Sheffield Iris; nearer fifty thousand, said the Chartist Northern Star; somewhere in between, said another witness. But whatever the number, the multitude was gloriously manifest: the Star describes several views but thought that "it was on Sheffield Moor that the mighty multitude showed to the best advantage." (This notion, borrowed from the theater, of "showing off well" was central to making nineteenth-century funerals public in a new way.) No previous assemblage in Sheffield of any sort, the paper said, had been on the scale of this funeral. And an active press made events like this even more public, even larger in the public imagination. The Northern Star had a circulation of around fifty thousand and as many as four hundred thousand readers. This was not a singular event. At the height of revolutionary agitation in June 1848, London Chartists stopped their round of meetings and plotting for the massive funeral of an East London silk weaver who had died, the coroner's jury insisted, of injuries inflicted by the police at the last of the decade's great demonstrations in Bethnal Green on 4 June 1848.[196]

And memories of the movement were kept alive by the dead in the decades afterward. On 19 June 1853, Benjamin Rushton, age sixty-eight, died—"poor, as many reformers had done"—in a village two miles from Halifax. "It was decided by the Chartists of Halifax that his funeral expenses should be borne by them," perhaps because he was in many ways a prototypical figure in the movement. Like a disproportionate number of the working-class leadership, he was a handloom weaver; he was a New Connection Methodist preacher, a Sunday School teacher, and a man who was all his life engaged in progressive causes, opposition to the New Poor Law, for example, before he embraced the People's Charter. His funeral was grander than the greatest aristocratic funerals of the seventeenth century, a requiem for a movement and a celebration of the community it had mobilized. The old Halifax Chartist Benjamin Wilson reports on Rushton's funeral in the memoir he wrote many years afterward in 1887. On Sunday, 26 June, Ernest Jones, a radical barrister, and R. C. Gammage, a shoemaker and the movement's first historian, led a procession of six of the oldest Chartists as pallbearers and twelve of the younger ones as "conductors," wand bearers, followed by one hundred forty Oddfellows (members of England's biggest working-class fraternal organization), to Rushton's house to pick up his double-lined coffin. The cortège then began the two-mile walk to Halifax's new Lister Hill Cemetery, with its neoclassical chapel and fine bourgeois monuments. As it went, it gathered numbers. Five special trains brought people from Bradford. The local paper put the number marching at between six thousand and ten thousand. Wilson says that he will decline to give numbers but says that he saw more people that day than ever before or since and all other public funerals he had seen paled by comparison. Jones spoke at the graveside about the burial of a patriot and the "resurrection of a glorious cause." "There rests a working man, there rests a producer," he intoned. The funeral ceremony closed and a reform meeting began.[197]

When Jones himself, firebrand of the movement and a friend of Marx, jailed for his role in 1848, died in 1869, the *Manchester Guardian* reported that "many thousands of persons, for the most part of the working class," crowded the streets, and probably a thousand marched six abreast to the sounds of a brass band playing the "Dead March" (from Handel's *Saul*) as his body made its way to the grave. Six very old Chartists who were identified by their radical lineage—"veterans of Peterloo," men who had witnessed the great radical massacre of 1819—led the procession. The coffin bearers were other old Chartists "associated," as the *Times* put it, "with Mr. Jones in the agitation of 1848." Then behind the coffin were his pallbearers: Mr. Jacob Bright, MP; Sir Elkanah Armitage, Lord Mayor of Manchester; Mr. C. H. Bazeley, the factory owner and liberal worthy; Mr. T. B. Potter, MP; among others. Thus the body of a man who had been jailed as a dangerous revolutionary nineteen years earlier was buried to the cheers of tens of thousands of his fellow citizens. His procession was an uncannily precise model of the political history of Manchester and of the fate of radicalism: the tumultuous uncertainty of the post-Napoleonic years when troops were garrisoned near the city to prevent serious unrest was glimpsed safely through aged Peterloo survivors; Chartism was manifest in the corpse of one of its leaders; and the representatives of Gladstonian liberalism, triumphant, brought up the rear.[198]

Feargus O'Connor's funeral in 1855 was the last and one of the largest Chartist demonstrations of the age. O'Connor had many passionate opponents and detractors, but, for better or worse, he was the most prominent and fiery of the movement's leaders: editor of the *Northern Star* (the major Chartist newspaper, with a circulation in the tens of thousands) and chair of the great April 1848 demonstration at Kennington Common that was both the apogee and the end of Chartism as a mass movement. He died on 30 August, penniless and insane, and was buried by subscription. G.W.M. Teynolds, a radical publisher and one of the most famous writers of his day, thought that, with the exception of the funerals of

Admiral Nelson, Queen Caroline, and the Duke of Wellington, "no ceremonial of this description . . . has attracted during the present century such vast crowds to witness it." People started gathering in the working-class districts of the east, in the City and Finsbury; they marched to Bloomsbury and then on to his sister's house in Notting Hill; from there they went—between thirty thousand and forty thousand of them, according to the *Times*, which had every reason to play down the numbers; fifty thousand, others said—to Kensal Green. When the cemetery management closed the gates "against this vast mass of people," the crowd tore them down. Then O'Connor joined conservative politicians, generals, and circus managers. "He lived and died for us," read one of the banners.[199]

The dead of new religious communities also became more public as they went to their graves. We do not know how many small funerals made claims on the space of the parish in the name of one group or other. John Wesley saw near Bath a group of children attending a coffin that was being carried into St. George's Church; when he came closer he saw that they were "our own children," and they were attending the corpse of one of their schoolfellows, who had died of smallpox. God thereby touched their hearts, he thought. Far more public was the funeral of Sammy Hick (1758–1829), a man who worked as a blacksmith well into his old age while on the side preaching conversion and witnessing its signs before large audiences of "gentle and simple" people. Some hundreds, we are told, went to Micklefield, a small village east of Leeds, and then formed a procession to carry the body to Aberford, a village two miles west. It swelled as it neared the churchyard to "no less than a thousand." The funeral was magnificent and, like many, it was reexperienced by the larger virtual community who read about it at the time and for decades to come.[200]

There was a similar history at the other end of the social scale as funerals expanded in scale, access, and publicity. In the fifteenth, sixteenth, and seventeenth centuries a "public funeral" had meant one organized by the College of Arms. Public funerals, in the sense that the state paid for them and oversaw their protocols, were essentially nonexistent for private citizens before the nineteenth century: three before 1800. Almost eighty years separated Isaac Newton's in 1727 and Admiral Nelson's in 1806. There were at least six more, besides Nelson's, by 1900. (Royalty, whose bodies and persons were public, are another story.) The French state, which, at its revolutionary birth, invented the modern state funeral with the Pantheonization of Voltaire and Rousseau, was much more profligate in using its dead great men in the nineteenth and twentieth centuries than was Britain: thirty-six state funerals under the Second Empire, eighty-one in the Third Republic. There were no dead women thought worthy, not even Madame Curie, except for the wife of the chemist Marcelin Berthelot, who died about the same time he did and was buried with him.[201]

Great public funerals of the new age represented a level of pageantry and engagement of ordinary citizens unknown before; they were, so to speak, the official, state-sanctioned version of the community-making processions of the corpse that defined various forms of popular class politics and religion. Enormous crowds followed the body of the hero of Trafalgar, Admiral Nelson, in 1806 as his body traveled from Greenwich, along the river, and into the City. Once there, it rode in a funeral car shaped like a ship. Queen Caroline, the people's hero during her infamous trial for adultery in 1819, aroused great passion and great crowds also when she was dead. Lord Liverpool, the prime minister, feared that the mob might seize her cortège or use the procession for radical purposes; he ordered that it skirt the City of London as it made its way from Hammersmith to the sea on its way back to where she was born in Brunswick. A crowd stood in the way; shots were fired and people killed as the body was forced onto the Marylebone Road; another barricade forced it south down Tottenham Court Road toward the city. There had been considerable reluctance on the part of the lord chamberlin's office about having a funeral at all, but because she remained technically queen of England, protocol had to be followed.[202]

Few nineteenth-century public funerals were so politically fraught as the queen's. The Duke of Wellington's in 1852 had its problems: managing an overwhelming demand for tickets to the service in the cathedral and for the right to have a carriage in the parade, organizing the lying in state so that hundreds of thousands of people could file by the casket. But they were solved; as an example of a dead body bringing people into a common space, physically and emotionally, it was wildly and unprecedentedly successful. By conservative estimates, a million people, 5 percent of the kingdom's population, were physically there; tens of millions more read about it. It was to the dead body what Britain's 1851 Great Exhibition was to the Industrial Revolution: the grand occasion to show off a civilization. Its very scale bore witness to the productive capacities of industrial England: mechanical steam presses working around the clock could not keep up with the demand for the *London Illustrated News*'s account of the funeral. Two million copies were ultimately sold, but only after temporary shortages resulted in scalpers' prices up to five times the normal cost. The twenty-seven-foot-long by sevente-foot-wide monstrosity of a funeral cart, modeled on that of Alexander the Great, was a triumph of the metal trades, which managed to melt down and mold twelve tons of old Waterloo cannons into some semblance of decorative form. (Never mind that it could not navigate the funeral route.) Because the railroads provided cheap transportation for the masses, almost a half million people could file by the coffin as Wellington lay in state. "Why, more visitors to London have come by the railroads to see the mighty Duke's coffin than all London and Britain furnished as spectators to any royal funeral, or all royal funerals put together, since any living man was born," proclaimed the *London Illustrated*. And more. The funeral was a sign of social cohesion; even thieves mingled with the public as ordinary subjects and purportedly did not ply their trade. It was a celebration of London, "the empress of cities," and of England, in which "this event is to be solemnized as becomes the mightiest nation in the world." It was a commentary on spiritual and "higher" things, the day on which the dominant utilitarian spirit of the age was to be forgotten; it was the final event of the French Revolution, its two great sons, Wellington and Napoleon, now dead—the one, as the papers all pointed out, having early on fought and destroyed the other. There was no end to the allegorical interpretations that could be attached to the funeral of the Great Duke.[203]

Perhaps only Victor Hugo's and Adolphe Thiers's funerals and the Pantheonization of Zola rivaled Wellington's in bringing a crowd into the streets in the nineteenth century: numbers that amounted to half the population of Paris. Many, many more saw the funeral train of the dead President Lincoln as it made its way from Washington to Springfield. These were the dead in service to the nation. But there were thousands of nineteenth-century funerals in Europe and the New World that, while technically private (that is, arranged and paid for by friends and family without state subsidy), were really public, in the sense that they engaged the public and openly affirmed not only the values of a civilization generally but of specific communities. The worth of an individual, the regard in which he—and rarely she—was held was publicly made manifest. Thus, the deaths of Dissenting clergymen were marked by displays of denominational solidarity as well as of respect for someone in particular. "Multitudes" followed the body of the Methodist Rev. William Dawson for a mile and a half as it left Leeds; eighty-six carriages "containing friends of various ranks" continued on to the village where he was buried. Provincial culture celebrated itself in the funeral of its worthies. Forty thousand saw John Dalton, the great chemist and lion of the Manchester Literary and Philosophical Society, lie in state. The account of the various parts of the almost mile-long procession takes thirty columns of small type: group by group, carriage by carriage all associated with the hero by virtue not of his place in a God-given hierarchy, but by his great energy and intelligence.[204]

The funeral of the great manufacturer, Titus Salt, made different sorts of claims. In part it appropriated the charisma of aristocracy to the new industrial order, aping in a curious way the great heraldic funerals of two and three centuries earlier. As one report noted with stunning clarity, "a stranger might have thought a prince had fallen, and the people had come to witness the funeral pageant on its way to the tomb of his royal ancestors." His barons-in-chief, the foremen of his various departments, were bearers; loyal retainers, some four hundred who had been in his employ twenty years or more, were privileged to be allowed on the chapel grounds. The crowds and the procession, as might be expected, would make even Queen Elizabeth's funeral seem puny: forty thousand, many arriving by special trains, crowded the model factory village of Saltaire for the last stages of its eponymous founder's funeral alone. But of course it was again not the size that differentiated Salt's from early modern funerals. It told a very different story. Salt was a leader of Congregationalism; his life had been a testimony to the power and moral fiber of Independency. He entered Bradford a poor youth in the early decades of industrialization, and at his death, as one of many memoirs points out, "men of middle age, who as they gazed on the spectacle [of his funeral] and remembered the successful career now ended, must have received an incentive in prosecuting their own life work." The dead valorized the worldview of the living.[205]

DISRUPTED BODIES

Bones and bodies over the millennia have never been left in peace for very long: secondary burial is routine in the Christian East; the sextons of medieval and early modern churchyards routinely tossed out the debris of the long dead, sometimes into an ossuary and in England usually not; excarnation—the boiling and defleshing of a body to bring it back to where it belonged from far away was well established by the twelfth century; regional exhumations were routine for the elite as their corpses waited for tombs to be ready or for the opportunity to join relatives. The bones of saints were often on the move. The dead fell victim to all sorts of more immediate dangers: iconoclasm, the demands of the living for space, time. But there is also a modern politics of disrupting bodies that is engaged with a variety of fraught juridical, cultural, and scientific questions. These gave potency to the funeral—pauper and proper—as a moment of reckoning.[206]

The juridically and broadly politically motivated disruption of the dead body is not new and over the years took many forms. There was a long European-wide story of violently removing and punishing those who had retrospectively become personae non gratae (that is, first *personae* again after some gap of time, and then *non gratae*). God, especially in the early years of Christianity, on occasion cast out unworthy bodies from where he thought they did not belong. Mortals followed the practice. The effort to purge the world of some evil by cleansing it of the unwanted dead may be nearly universal: the students in the Chinese Cultural Revolution who scattered the remains of a former party chairperson probably knew nothing about either the French Revolutionaries who in 1793 attacked the royal tombs at St. Denis, collected a few souvenir bones, and threw the rest in a pit or, closer to home, the Manchu destruction of Ming tombs in retaliation for the Ming despoilation of a tomb from an earlier dynasty. "Let all the coffins of these divinized monsters be broken open!" wrote the journalist and politician Pierre Henri Lebrun, "Let their memories be condemned!" The sansculottes who broke into the Sorbonne and cut off the head of Cardinal Richelieu's corpse in 1793 were mimicking the guillotine and following in the footsteps of fifteenth-century iconoclasts. (The head, along with a bit of linen, first went to the leader of the local section, a hosier named Cheval, and after 1805 went the rounds until Napoleon III united it with the body.) This particular political theater of dismemberment and reassembly, directed as it was against powerful individuals, basically ended in the eighteenth and early nineteenth centuries. The mass disruption of burial places to purge whole cultures did not. And when it did happen, it came to be regarded as an unseemly atavism. When Queen Victoria learned that the bones of the Mahdi had been exhumed to prevent them from being enshrined by his rebellious followers, she wrote to Lord Kitchener that she did not approve: the destruction of the body of a man savored "too much of the Middle Ages"; the graves of our people had been respected, and we should show similar respect to those of our enemies. He explained to her satisfaction that they had been decently reburied in secret.[207]

The denial of a proper funeral in the first place—posthumous mutilation or neglect—also has a long history as an act of judicial terror. In chapter 18 of his *On the Rights of War and Peace*, Grotius writes that the antiquity, universality, and moral centrality of the right to burial make its denial a just cause of war. In the next chapter he suggests that there are some exceptions: "some" people, he says, would deny certain criminals the right to burial, but only the very worst. For a long time in England and the rest of Europe, surgeons could get bodies of criminals from the scaffold—they belonged to the state—and they might end up on public display or, at the edge of possibility, as food for dogs: the fate of Hogarth's idle apprentice. This was the sort of *reductio* that so disturbed Diogenes' students; dogs in execution pictures, including those of the crucifixion of Christ, bear testimony to the carnality of the dead. But in 1751 in an "Act for Preventing the Horrid Crime of Murder" (25 Geo 2 c 37), the state took up Grotius's suggestion. It made public dissection, if not being fed to dogs, part of the punishment for what it regarded as particularly heinous crimes by allowing judges to add the penalty of public dissection to that of being hanged until dead. The intent was clear: it was to add "some further terror and peculiar mark of infamy" so as "to better prevent the horrible crime of murder." The new law gave judges the discretion of sentencing to either anatomization or hanging in chains, but "in no case whatsoever shall" they allow "the body of the murderer be suffered to be buried unless after [having been] dissected and anatomized." It was an open question whether they could order both dissection and hanging in chains, and the answer seemed to be yes. It was also unclear whether judges could order hanging in chains without dissection; the language of the act suggests not, but we know—as did the speaker in book 12 of Wordsworth's *The Prelude*—of bodies whose fate was precisely hanging intact on a lonely gibbet. One point is clear: the law was outrageous, and the learned jurists knew it. The popular classes responded to it with riot and with the fear that Parliament had meant to instill. "When I reflect that my poor remains, the tokens of mortality, must not sleep in peace," wrote a convicted mail robber to his wife from his jail cell in York, "but [rather] be buffeted by the storms of Heaven or parched by the summers sun while the Traveller shrinks from them with disgust and terror. . . . [It] freezes my blood." "Why," he continues, "will the Laws continue with the wretched after life is at an end." Indeed. Few could bear it, and the wronged dead demanded vindication.[208]

Digging up and reburying them was one way of doing this. On Friday, 8 September 1820, two Scottish radicals, Andrew Hardie and John Baird, were executed as traitors in front of a crowd of thousands at Stirling Castle for their part in an aborted armed resurrection. An eighteen-year-old medical student clumsily cut off their heads, as was appropriate for their crime. The "mangled bodies of Hardie and Baird were not allowed to be delivered to their grieving relatives" because the authorities feared a great public funeral and procession. Instead, they were spirited by night to the local churchyard and their graves guarded by soldiers for the next six weeks to prevent the bodies from being retrieved. "Thus ends one of the Government Tragedies of 1820!" But not quite. Fifteen years later, the muckraking Glasgow journalist Peter Mackenzie proved that government spies had entrapped the men: the innocent had been "confounded with the guilty"; history had come full circle; reform had triumphed. "Blessings on the French Revolution." And twelve years after that, in 1847, the Home Office gave permission to exhume the bodies of the two martyrs and allowed them to be taken to Sighthill Cemetery in Glasgow to be reburied under a new memorial.[209]

Two American examples from the same period make the point: heroes and counterheroes dug up and put where they belonged. General John André had been hanged in 1780 for conspiring with Benedict Arnold and buried ignominiously under the gallows. (His request to be shot as a soldier rather than hanged as a spy was denied by General Washington.) Forty years later, things were different. André was exhumed and taken back to England, where his remains rest in Westminster Abbey. Sixty years after the Battle of Lexington, 19 April 1775, which began the American Revolution, the dead made another contribution to the writing of history. The bones of seven soldiers from the town itself were exhumed and reburied under a monument that had been built in 1799 and already bore their names. Ten of the last eleven survivors of the battle watched—"a small and venerable remnant of those who took the field in the dawn of that Revolution"—as living witnesses to a glorious past that would soon be remembered only through bones. The speaker at this event was the young classicist Edward Everett, who would go on to have a distinguished career and almost thirty years later would give the main address over a far larger number of the dead at the founding of the world's first national cemetery in Gettysburg.[210]

Each story of exhumation is different, and rewriting history is only one among many reasons to disrupt the dead. The body as corpus delicti—the body of the crime—has been the object of dozens of forensic exhumations since the middle of the twentieth century and continues to function in this way. Tens of thousands of bodies have been dug up to get them in the right place. The point for now is to use a range of examples of nineteenth-century disrupted bodies to show how they create new domains for the work of the dead. The deathbed politics of Tom Paine, author of the immensely popular *Common Sense* and the *Rights of Man* and hero of two eighteenth-century revolutions (the American and the French), was a major force behind the peregrinations of his body. The facts in his case were clear: he did not die crying for Jesus, and he made no overtures to any religious authority except to ask the Quakers for a burial place. There were no claims about a conspiracy. That left the core question—whether he died in agony or peacefully—and another one as well: of what significance was his body and, more specifically, its many afterlives.

That Paine died an infidel is undisputed; whether he suffered spiritual anguish in his last days as a consequence was disputed for more than a century. Body ulcers, discolored blisters on his feet, coughs, and vomiting fully account for his physical pain, his supporters argued. Radical publishers in the first half of the nineteenth century dined out on Paine biographies and on vindications of his death: James Watson, a leading Chartist, freethinker, and radical publisher, advertised his wares in a pamphlet about Paine's body as often as he could. G. J. Holyoake, the leading secularist of his day, attacked the idea of a deathbed renunciation as slander's "weakest invention" before once again presenting pages of evidence for Paine's steadfastness. The testimony of a Quaker servant who said she heard him cry out for Jesus when she brought him food was impugned because she supposedly was paid to lie. Robert Ingersoll, the German-born leader of Anglo-American free thought, was still writing poignant accounts of Tom Paine's end in the late nineteenth century and still defending his—and Voltaire's—resistance to the Christian belief that, without God, dying was unbearable. In 1877, he issued a challenge: he would offer $1,000 gold to any clergyman who could prove that Paine died in agony. When the Presbyterian *New York Observer* asked for the money, he issued a scathing attack on the "Sunday school papers, the thousands of idiotic tracts, and other countless stupidities called sermons" that claimed that Voltaire and Paine were terrified in their last hours, and proposed a tribunal to adjudicate the matter with the loser paying the costs.[211]

Although the debate over his deathbed was remarkably stable, for a century Paine's body shared the fate of many nineteenth- and twentieth-century politically and culturally important bodies in its travels, gaining or shedding meaning as circumstances changed. It, like so many, was a body on the move. Once the American Revolution had succeeded, Paine's unrepentant secular radicalism made him less welcome in the new United States than before. When he died in 1809, even the Quakers abandoned him. His body was denied entrance to the burial ground where his father was buried on the grounds that he was the author of the deistical, if not atheistic, *Age of Reason*. Paine had deep Quaker roots and had every reason to expect that the Friends would give his body a place. Rejected, it was buried on his farm in New Rochelle, New York, attended by two black men who had walked more than twenty miles to be there, a Catholic woman, and a Quaker supporter. It was a pointedly syncretic funeral.

Surrounded by walls and trees, the grave went unnoticed. A decade later, Paine's bones became relics in the hands of men who did not believe in relics and who used them, each for his own purpose, as they worked to give them a proper and honored burial. The eccentric British radical journalist William Cobbett dug up Paine in 1819 and shipped his body back to his native England so as to rebury him under a grand memorial. How this ambition grew is another little stream in the history of the corpse. Cobbett had escaped from England in 1817 to avoid the prison term he had been sentenced to for seditious writing and lived in exile near where Paine was buried in New York. There he was a neighbor of Elias Hicks, the leader of a Quaker schism that emphasized the autonomy of the inner light and played down the importance and divinity of Jesus. Elias was a cousin of Willet, the man who had unsuccessfully defended Paine's right to Quaker burial. The poet Walt Whitman, who grew up near the Paine farm, thought that Hicks might well have converted Cobbett to Paine's views because Cobbett had often been hostile to Paine. The exhumation was seen in radical circles as something of a retraction, a way for the age's most influential radicals—one dead, the other alive—to make amends. Nothing came of the memorial. The bones made a brief appearance on the Liverpool docks and then went into a box in Cobbett's living quarters; he wrote his name on the skull to register ownership. This seems to have been a well-established way of registering ownership of corporeal relics.[212] Identified or not, the history of Paine's skeleton now becomes clouded.

When Cobbett died in bankruptcy in 1835, the auctioneer of his estate refused to include it in the sale, whose proceeds were to go toward settling his debts. Their status as property was dubious, as more generally was the dead body's in common law. Unlike the bones and bodies of animals, human bodies could not really be owned because the *only* thing that could be done with them was to put them in the ground, that is, they were legal refuse, although even as such their fate was further regulated to meet common law standards of decency. On the other hand, bones could become something other than a body—relics of a sort—in which case other rules applied. Indeed, much of the history of body peregrination is about this duality. With nothing legally resolved, the bones ended up in the possession of the man who took over Cobbett's farm or perhaps in the hands of a laborer who worked there. It is possible that Cobbett's publisher and accomplice in the exhumation, William Benbow, as near to a revolutionary as Britain had at the time, held them for a while. We know that the leading "ultraradical" James Watson (1799–1874), secularist, printer, and founder of the London Working Man's Association, who had made money from selling Paine's works, bought them at auction in 1853. (Some parts of the skeleton may have ended up in the possession of an Anglican priest. A finger, it was said, was left in the United States.) When Watson died, they made their way, as did so many other skulls, through phrenology circles; the brain, separated from the bones, was sold at auction in 1897. A simple oblesisk, erected 1839, sat over Paine's empty tomb near New Rochelle until it was replaced by a new, more elaborate one in 1881.[213]

As the most careful historian of his body concludes, Paine is thus everywhere and nowhere. But, the point of this strange tale from the perspective of the work of the dead is that it mixes up so many stories, each with a deep historical heritage: there is the long-lived controversy over his deathbed, very much born of modern culture wars around the theme of revolution and irreligion. There is the story of the peripatetic bones that has hundreds of antecedents stretching back through the Christian centuries, but this time without claims of old school sacrality. No one claimed that Paine's body parts channeled the divine or that it would help anyone to be buried near him. The story, like so many in the late eighteenth and nineteenth centuries, is a strange brew of the new and the old—radical publishing, phrenology, hoary claims to hold a body for the payment of debt, new demands to give Paine, through his body and his monument, their political due. Moncure Conway, a prominent abolitionist, freethinker, and Paine's first biographer, played a prominent role in this effort. Paine shared with Diogenes a cultivated disrespect for established institutions and would perhaps not have minded what became of his body, an equal of all other bodies in the "perfect republic of the grave." The moment that Death "obtains a conquest he loses a subject," Paine wrote. He is right, of course; the dead are not subjects; they are nothing. But they are at the same time something: witnesses to lost causes, lost genius, lost pasts of which they might be made to speak.[214]

Versions of this story can be multiplied a thousandfold since the eighteenth century, in many registers. Consider the bones (and in some cases, organs) of native people that had been bureaucratically changed from human remains to objects of scientific study. Every ethnographic museum in the world is full of them, and most in the United States are working overtime to return them to various claimants for ritual burial: that is, to comply with the Native American Graves Protection and Repatriation Act of 1990 by changing them back into culturally human remains again and returning them to their descendants. Sometimes this story is painfully strange: Ishi, the last Yahi Indian, died as an inhabitant of the Lowie (now Hearst) Museum at Berkeley. His body was cremated and buried in a private mortuary in Colma, the city of the dead near San Francisco; his brain went to the Smithsonian. They remained separated from 1916, the year he died, to 2000, when, after considerable controversy about what Indian tribe he belonged to, because it no longer existed, the two together—ashes and pickled brain—were returned to those deemed his closest relatives and secretly buried.[215]

Bones and bodies can also become trophies of conquest. Five months after the suppression of the Sepoy mutiny and the death of two thousand Indians in the Sikanderbagh in Lucknow, the photographer Felice Beato showed up to document the imperial victory. There was little to see except for a ruined building. To make the point, he arranged to have hundreds of skeletal corpses of Indians exhumed and scattered around a large courtyard, where they bore witness to their fate and to the success of the British soldiers (fig. 5.27).[216] There are phrenological bones and historical bones and many, many political bones and bodies constantly on the move. Mirabeau out and Marat in to the Pantheon; Diderot may finally be in, three hundred years after he died, if indeed they are his bones; still few women have made it. Napoleon's bones came back from St. Helena in 1840 to the Invalide in a gigantic funeral. (He had hoped to be buried in St. Denis as had been the kings of France.) In central and eastern Europe, 1848 is commemorated through incorporating the dead into a national story that is still being told. New stories of restitution and reversal are legion. But for now I want to finish with two cases of bones that speak for great nineteenth-century topics: genius and history—one case English, one not.

First, genius, or how Joseph Haydn's skull became an idol. The great composer died in Vienna in 1809 in the middle of the Napoleonic wars. He was given a perfectly respectable funeral; nothing like Beethoven's, an unprecedentedly massive event for the paradigmatic modern musical genius, but respectable enough (fig. 5.28). Mozart's *Requiem* was played at a memorial service; those who were meant to attend did so. But his body did not go to where it seems to have belonged: his longtime employer, the Prince Esterhazy, had planned to move it to his estate in Eisenstadt, where Haydn had spent most of his working life. Various things intervened, and Haydn's body was not moved. More than a decade after the funeral, Adolphus Frederick, Duke of Cambridge, who was visiting Vienna, reminded the prince of his plans for Haydn's body after the two heard a performance of the *Creation* in the composer's honor. Esterhazy ordered that it be

5.27. Interior of the courtyard of the Secundra Bagh [a villa on the outskirts of Lucknow] after the slaughter of 2,000 rebels by the 93rd Highlanders and 4th Punjab Regiment, Lucknow 1857. Ann S. K. Brown Military Collection, Brown University Library.

exhumed and was shocked to discover when he got it home and opened the coffin that the great composer's head was missing. A wig had taken its place. Suspicion immediately fell on Haydn's friend and a former accountant of the prince's, Joseph Karl Rosenbaum, and on Johann Nepomuk Peter, the governor of the local prison. Both were followers of Franz Joseph Gall and his even more famous pupil, Johann Spurzheim, the cofounders of phrenology (as it came to be called), the science of reading character from external features of the skull. The theories of these two men, put to many different uses, accounted for the collection of more skulls in the nineteenth century—not to speak of death masks—than all the relic collectors of Christendom. In Haydn's case, Rosenbaum and Peter had bribed the grave digger to sever the composer's head, which they kept in a black wooden box with glass sides and a golden lyre on top. It would have been a reliquary in another age. (Seventeen years later, people tried to bribe Beethoven's grave diggers but failed, perhaps because friends who got wind of the plot stood guard. History has had to make do with his death mask and a thorough autopsy report by the most famous pathologist of the day.)[217]

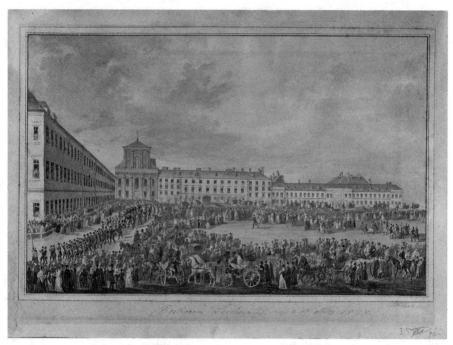

5.28. A ceremonial procession of Beethoven's body in front of the former cloister of the Schwarzspanierhaus in Vienna. Franz Xaver Stöber, 1827. Beethoven-Haus Bonn.

Esterhazy was furious. He alerted the police, who searched Peter's house; Peter told them that he had given the skull to Rosenbaum. The police proceeded to Rosenbaum's house but failed to turn up anything there because his former lover and now wife, an imperial court soprano who had been the first to sing the role of the Queen of the Night in Mozart's *Magic Flute*, had taken Haydn's head to bed with her. Foiled, the prince changed tactics. He offered to pay for the return of the composer's head. The pair gave him a skull, or maybe two. If there were two, the first one was of a youth and was rejected. That of an old man passed for Haydn's and was buried with the body. Only when Rosenbaum died and bequeathed the skull to Peter on the condition that he, in turn, leave it in his will to the Society of the Friends of Music, did the prince learn that the skull he had taken to be Haydn's was a fake. And when Peter died, the skull in its reliquary did indeed go where its thieves had wanted. But the Esterhazy family did not give up; in 1932, the then prince got the Society to agree to hand over the real skull so that the intact Haydn could finally be buried in a new mausoleum at Eisenstadt. Now the city fathers refused to let it go; presumably, local pride required keeping it in Vienna. In 1954, his body was made whole.

Disrupted bones in the service of history are stranger still. In 1842, the Victorian sage and historian Thomas Carlyle had writer's block. He was stuck in his biography of the greatest of his heroes: Oliver Cromwell. A visitor diagnosed the problem: Carlyle had entered the grave of history "wherein with his hero who he was seeking to disinter, [he] himself was descending—a giant mastered by the spirit of his time." He could find no way to translate a living Cromwell onto the page; he had lost faith in communing with his hero's specter. "A dead man does lie buried under [a] waste continent of cinders," and the struggle was to make him speak. At stake is not the sort of forensic investigation that motivated many nineteenth-century exhumations: an interest of confirming some fact or other. Carlyle is scathing about the mutilation of "the Patriot [John] Hampden" in 1828 when his biographer, Lord Nugent, had him dug up to confirm details of his death. Nor was he hoping for the sort of direct confrontation with sacrality that Abbott Samson experienced when he pulled back some of the outer linen wrappings from the body of "the glorious martyr, holy Edmund," and touched his face and body still veiled in linen. That was at least a genuine contact: "Shining luminous effulgent as the lights of St. Edmund do though the dark night." "Let the modern world look earnestly on that midnight hour . . . shining yet on us, ruddy bright, through the depths of seven hundred years," and "consider mournful what our Hero-worship once was," writes Carlyle.[218] But he was not really after holiness. Carlyle needed to make the dead speak in the age of history; to imagine that which was irrevocably gone based on its traces in archives, on the land, and on bodies.

In the early autumn of 1842, the dead found their voice; in any case, Carlyle heard it in his mind's ear. His friend Edward Fitzgerald lived on the battlefield of Naseby. "You will do me and the Genius of History a real favour," wrote Carlyle, "if you will persist in these examinations and excavations to the utmost length possible." (We do not know whether Carlyle knew of or gave any credence to the legend that Cromwell had not been buried in Westminster Abbey—and thus had not been exhumed and drawn and quartered—because he went instead to Naseby. According to this legend, he was buried there by moonlight, and the field was then plowed to conceal his final resting place.) Fitzgerald did as his friend asked. He dug deep into the field of battle; he found skeletons, aligned east–west, head to toe, and reported on what he found. This "opening of the burial heap blazes strangely in my thought," responded Carlyle. It "brings the matter home to one with strange veracity." The battle could not be a fantasy or a theory; it was irreducibly "dire fact." He asked to be sent the relics, and Fitzgerald complied by forwarding two molars and part of an arm bone. "To think," Carlyle wrote to his brother John, that "this grinder chewed its breakfast on the 14th of June 1645, and had no more eating to do in this world"; it is now in his drawer and exists to "be a horror." There is, he added, "something sternly impressive in such a horrible pair of relics." Carlyle imagines the jaws "clenched together in deadly rage," the arm bearing its weapon. The dead had been unsilenced.[219]

Carlyle was under no illusion about the fundamental materiality of the relics that Fitzgerald had dug up and sent. If the farmer from whose field they came can thriftily make a few usable turnips from five thousand wasted men, why not? he wrote. Heraclitus, of course, had beaten him to the punch. And so had Lord Byron, who had written to his publisher John Murray that one could tell where the bodies at Waterloo lay from the health of the grain growing above them. But for Carlyle, the magic of relics triumphed over cool flippancy. His writing block lifted; the book began to move apace because the teeth and bones made the "past vitally present into the present," until they were no longer needed. Carlyle periodically reminded his friend to put up a monument on the spot where the bones were taken. It never happened. Fitzgerald responded to the last of his friend's reminders in 1871 by admitting that it would never happen. He no longer owned the site of the Naseby battle; he could arrange to have a stone cut but he did not have the courage to go back and there was no one else who could take his place. Those who were with him when the bones were dug up are dead and no one remembers them anymore; the plow "has long ago obliterated the traces of sepulture." This is high historicist melancholy.[220]

Jane Carlyle, the great sage's wife, had had enough of Fitzgerald's gift; it had done its work. Thomas had one of the teeth and a forearm bone set on filigree silver mounts in a small velvet-lined, glass-topped box. Next to the fragment of arm there is a note in his handwriting that reads: "Arm bone from Naseby Battlefield, sent to me in September 1842 by E. Fitzgerald, now presented to John Child of Bungay, 18 Feb. 1848." Next to the tooth in its holder is a similar message, even more precise: "Jaw-tooth, dug up from burial mound (near Cloisterville) in Naseby Battlefield on 23 September 1842, by E. Fitzgerald and sent to me soon thereafter." The provenance of the relics was without a gap. Somehow the box made its way from the radical publisher Child into the hands of the mid-twentieth-century advertising executive Norman Strouse, chair of J. Walter Thompson, who gave it to the library of the University of California, Santa Cruz. Archives, Carlyle once said, house the "dull pedantry of history that gives us only the ashes of it." Maybe not. His reliquary shares space with the archives of the Grateful Dead.[221]

All of this only whispers about the great age of exhumation in which we live. Millions of bodies in the Great War moved in the interests of memory; scores of famous and thousands of less famous dead moved in eastern Europe after 1789. Federico García Lorca's comment, "In *Spain*, the *dead* are *more alive than* the *dead* of any other country in the world," which I have already quoted, was made seventy years ago and is probably not exactly true. The competition is fierce. But after 2007 and the Law of Historical Memory (*Ley de la Memoria Histórica*), tens of thousands in Spain are newly alive. The Association for the Recuperation of Historical Memory (Asociación para la Recuperación de la Memoria Histórica, ARMH) as well as private individuals are searching for and exhuming the bodies of Spaniards murdered by the fascists after the civil war. Some 30,000–40,000 of more than 110,000 are still lost. And then there are the bodies of an unknown number of republicans that were surreptitiously taken from mass graves and reburied among the tens of thousands in Franco's grotesque shrine because there were not enough nationalist ones to serve its purposes. There they are bearing witness to a cause they hated.

Modern exhumation is a huge story, a story of corporeal unrest in a world of mass political upheaval in which the dead are called on to rewrite history and commemorate a newly exigent past. How much of the early modern, eighteenth-, and nineteenth-century history of corporeal disruption—political, historicist, phrenological, recreational—touched the popular classes is hard to say. We know that the long tradition of posthumous punishment was felt deeply, that people cared where they were buried, that anatomical dissection was intimately linked to the scaffold, and that what to a poor person was her body, dead as well as alive, was to others a means to an end. Being tossed over the walls—having no funeral or an ignominious one—whether to make a political or juridical point or for some other reason, was a horror.

The knife was imagined as a particular existential threat to the corpses of the poor. Judicial anatomies were anathema: their point was a social death that was as humiliating as possible. It struck terror as it was intended to do. But in the late eighteenth century and after, the chances of poor people ending up in anatomy theaters or art studios was just as powerful and far more likely an outcome. In 1782, Charles Byrne, an Irish giant, 7 feet 8 inches tall, appeared in London thanks to a local entrepreneur who had convinced his impoverished parents to allow him to be exhibited first around his home village, then more widely in Ireland, and finally in the capital. John Hunter, the most famous surgeon of the age and the first professor of anatomy at the Royal Academy, was determined to have Byrne's skeleton when he died and stalked his prey relentlessly. In the spring of 1783, he was ready to move in. Byrne's life had begun to ebb; he had a brain tumor and probably also tuberculosis; he was an alcoholic. Hunter decided to try to get the giant to sell him the right to anatomize his body when he died (i.e., to grant him a future interest in his body for payment now). The idea of getting living people to sell rights in their dead bodies persisted well into the nineteenth century, but, in addition to being generally thought disgusting, it also ran into a major legal problem: the right was not enforceable. The person who made the contract was gone, and his heirs did not have the right to do anything with the body but bury it properly. In Hunter's estimation, Byrne was worth far more in death than in life. But Byrne did not see it that way. Despite the fact that he was virtually penniless—his nest egg had been stolen, and his popularity had dropped to the point that he was getting 1s. per show, if that—he rejected Hunter's offer. In fact, he made elaborate plans to avoid the dissecting table. On his deathbed he extracted a promise from his friends that they would dump his body into the sea, a fate less awful than the anatomy lab. And that is what they did, or at least what they thought they did. They took his coffin to Margate, chartered a boat, sailed out a ways, and dumped the giant coffin overboard.[222]

Unbeknown to them, Byrne's corpse was not inside. John Hunter's early nineteenth-century biographer takes up the story, which had been in every newspaper and journal of its day. The surgeon's "eagerness to obtain rare and valuable specimens for his museum often led him to pay more than its worth for an object he desired to make his own," a weakness that became legendary. His passion for collecting seems to have often gotten the best of economic rationality. He had just overpaid outrageously for a whale skin and was not about to let a giant's skeleton get away. He paid a shady character and regular retainer, adept at body snatching and general skullduggery, to keep watch over the mortally ill Byrne. The giant died on June 1. Hunter found out where the men who were guarding the body for the undertaker went for their drinks and offered one of them a £50 bribe to turn a blind eye to his having the body kidnapped; the undertaker's man said he needed to talk it over with his friends; they realized how eager Hunter was for his prey and the men worked him up to the staggering sum of £500 to turn a blind eye to body snatching. Hunter's carriage whisked Byrne's corpse away, and a coffin filled with rocks was thrown into the North Sea. Meanwhile, Hunter was so nervous about being discovered that he did not follow his usual procedures but quickly cut the body into pieces from which he boiled the flesh away. "Hence has arisen the brown colour of the bones, which in all other respects form a magnificent skeleton," concludes his biographer.[223]

The fate of this one special body that belonged to a man who died penniless and abject—worthless while alive—represents the abyss that threatened all those who were in danger of dying poor or friendless. Byrne had once not been destitute; he was robbed of his considerable savings. His story, like so many others, makes clear that almost anyone could end up on the anatomist's table or preparation kettles. Already in the early eighteenth century, before the demand for bodies approached nineteenth-century levels, dissection was the king of workhouse cruelties. Several inmates "who died in the same manner [as Mary Whistle]" were anatomized, reported an exposé of the worse abuses. She had been left to die in a basement and then subjected to autopsy. The bones of one inmate were supposedly broken "because she could not be put in to the coffin by reason of her crookedness." A nurse who blew the whistle when she discovered that "a child was to have been made an anatomy of, after their common custom," was punished by the contractor who ran the workhouse.[224] Scandals of this level were rare, but the pauper whom nobody owned had a culturally resonant, if relatively small, chance of belonging first to thieves and then to surgeons.

This was the case in some measure because there was a great deal of legal muddling about who owned a pauper's, or indeed anyone's, body. To those who had friends and kin to bury them properly, it did not matter. They could trust the kindness of others. But the friendless body was a sort of *homo sacer*, an outlaw who could be killed with impunity. A corpse subsisted outside both civil and criminal law. In some respects, wrote a nineteenth-century American judge, it is "the strangest thing on earth." "Still and cold, and all that is visible to the mortal eye of the man we know," it is a jurisprudential misfit. But still, "the law—that rule of action that touches all human things—must also touch this thing of death." The opening scene of Dickens's *Our Mutual Friend*, a novel about dust and gold, makes clear how difficult this is. Gaffer and Rogue Riderhood, two watermen who make a living retrieving and despoiling corpses that they find drowned in the Thames, are discussing the problem: "Has a dead man any use for money? Is it possible for a dead man to have money? What world does a dead man belong to? 'Tother. What world does money belong to? This world. How can money be a corpse's. Can a corpse own it, want it, spend it?" In the same novel, Silas Wegg tries to buy back his leg bone, which Mr. Venus, the taxidermist, had purchased as part of an odd lot from St. Thomas's hospital. It should be cheap, says Wegg, because it was crooked—that was the reason for its amputation in the first place—and because Venus bought it as part of an assorted batch of bones. But no, argues Venus, it may have had no use or value while attached to Wegg, but now it could be worth something as a curiosity; and in any case, its market value was up simply because Wegg wanted it, so as not to be, as he says, "dispersed."[225]

Lawyers, unlike Dickens's characters, were quite sure for a very long time that dead bodies could own nothing and that no one could own them. There was no one to hold possession and there was nothing to own. Edward Coke, the seventeenth-century chief justice of the King's Bench and the most famous jurist of his age, explains in the context of the law of buildings that in every sepulcher there are two things: the monument and the body buried under it. Monuments have a purpose—as proof of decent and pedigree, as a record of the time of decease, as a chance in an epitaph to exhort passersby to do good, as an occasion to remind the sons and daughters of Adam that death awaits them all. Monuments also have an owner, and an action is given at the common law for defacing them. On the other hand, "the burial of cadaver, (that is *caro data vermibus* [flesh given to worms]) is, *nullius in bonis*," which means "among the property of no man" or "no body's property," or more literally "nothing in goods," in the sense that the dead body cannot be property because it is nothing and because it is good for nothing. It lacks that which makes something ownable by someone and that would hence be of interest to the common law. It "belongs to Ecclesiastical cognizance." (Or, as Locke might put it, its original owner no longer exists in this world. A dead person cannot own anything.)[226]

When William Blackstone, the greatest English legal scholar of the eighteenth century, looked into the matter, he came to the same conclusion. An heir has property in the monuments and escutcheons of his ancestors but none in "their bodies and ashes." A parson may bring an act of trespass against those who dig in his church or churchyard; it is larceny to steal a shroud, even if those who buried the body and own its grave clothes are unaware of the theft. Prosecution can go forward without them. "But stealing the corpse itself, which has no owner (though a matter of great indecency) is no felony." And it has no owner for the purposes of criminal law because it is no good, more like a dog in that regard than a cow that gives milk. Blackstone is aware that this is not a universal view; in the law of the Franks (Salic law), he points out, anyone who digs a corpse out of the ground is an outlaw and is banished until he has satisfied the kin. But not among us, he says.[227]

In the 1800 edition of the *Commentaries on the Laws of England*, there was, however, a new footnote. "It has been determined," it reads, "that stealing dead bodies, though for the improvement of the science of anatomy" (i.e., even for a good cause and not for "indecent exhibition") was an indictable offense. It refers readers to 1 T. R. 733. The defendant had been convicted of entering a burial ground and taking a dead body for the purpose of dissecting it. On appeal, his lawyer moved that the conviction be vacated on the grounds that what the man had done was not a crime for the reasons Coke and others gave and because there never had been a conviction for this purported crime. Disturbing the ground, yes; stealing a shroud, yes; but stealing a body, impossible. The sexton and grave digger of St. Andrew Holborn, in London were convicted and sentenced to transportation in 1747 for stealing a lead coffin worth 13s., but not for digging up the body and having it secretly reburied. That the dead are no worse off for the crime was not accepted as mitigation; "Give me leave to assure you," said the prosecutor, "'tis an offense and robbery against the living." There were only two possible precedents for the 1788 conviction, the accused thief's lawyer argued, and neither was on point. One was based on a Jacobean statute that made it a crime to steal a body for purposes of witchcraft; in the only reported case of this sort, the defendant was charged with sorcery, not theft. His client was not a witch. The other gets us closer to the fears of the poor. The master of the Shoreditch workhouse, a surgeon, and a third person were indicted not for theft but for conspiracy to prevent the burial of a person who had died in the workhouse.[228]

The judges took all this under advisement and decided not to issue a writ of error. Common decency dictated, they said, that something be done to prevent an act that was manifestly against the common good, something "at the bare idea of which nature revolted." In other words, they skirted the question of property entirely. But inasmuch as the defendant may have committed the crime merely from ignorance because no one had ever been punished for doing what he did, they let him off with a fine of five marks, a little over £3. Later editions of Blackstone added further footnotes on the subject of what one could do with the dead. In 1822, the case of *Rex v. Cuddock* held definitively that it was an indictable misdemeanor to sell the body of an executed criminal for dissection when dissection was not part of his sentence. This was a bit of a change of course. The Company of Barber Surgeons, by a Henrician statute (i.e., well before 1752, when dissection became a part of some sentences), had the rights to a certain number of executed bodies every year. And in the early eighteenth century, they fought to keep unauthorized people from carrying away what they took to be "their" bodies from the gallows at Tyburn—roughly where the Marble Arch is now—and selling them for dissection. They paid their beadles to fetch the bodies to which they thought they were entitled; and they chastised members who somehow procured bodies for a "private" anatomy at the same time as the guild's public one. King's Bench moved to regulate all this anew. So, even if Coke had the law right, he was wrong about the usefulness of bodies. Between the middle of the seventeenth century and the last decades of the eighteenth, corpses became something more than *caro data vermibus*, even if it was not quite clear what they were. But a market in dead bodies emerged that was supplied almost entirely by the most defenseless: a few criminals and many of the poor whose shallow, unguarded, common graves were far easier marks than deep and often guarded bourgeois graves.[229]

Demand for cadavers grew on two fronts, and the dead body entered into the creepy world of the market from which it had always been and to some extent still is excluded. First, museums. The Hunterian collection, with its skeleton of the Irish giant and some 10,500 other specimens, was only the most famous and extensive of thirty-nine new anatomical museums founded in England between 1739 and 1800. All those body parts—diseased, grotesque, or simply curious— came from someone: the pauper and the outcast dead.

So did the beautiful and eerie bodies that artists studied as part of their training and that the public admired in galleries as paintings and sculptures. Hunter prepared at least three écorché figures—casts from the flayed dead meant to display the musculature—before he posed his most famous model. We still don't know who he was. Maybe one of a pair of smugglers condemned to death and dissection for killing an excise agent, who were hanged on 27 May 1776. Possibly James Langar, a former soldier, who was convicted of two Hyde Park robberies and hanged for his crimes on 12 April 1776. Whoever he was, he became a classical statue whose stone surface had somehow been removed to reveal, for the edification of art students, what lay beneath. First, before rigor mortis set in, his dead body was posed. It was then stripped of skin, fat, and interstitial material to the desired depth. Hunter probably dried it overnight. Next, Augustino Carlini, one of the founders of the Royal Academy and a well-known sculptor, cast the now day-old cadaver first in plaster and then in bronze. And so an obscure criminal became "The Dying Gladiator," a "very beautiful representation of one of those wretches," as a critic noted. The figure was a copy of a famous Roman copy of a lost Greek statue prominent enough that it had been noted with approval by Pliny. Carlini may have seen it in one of the Capitoline museums in Rome but probably worked from a cast in the Academy's collection. Smugglerius—"a name jocosely given to this cast which was moulded on the body of a smuggler"—thus has a pedigree that connects it with one of the most reproduced and admired sculptures in the Western canon, a work less affecting because of "the visible perfection of a Grecian chizzel than . . . the inhumanity of the Romans," as the author of a contemporary guidebook noted. We do not know what happened to the original corpse or to Carlini's bronze. The flayed dying gladiator, aka Smugglerius, survives today in a beautiful drawing by a student, William Linnel, who submitted it in 1840 as part of his application for art school and in two copies made in 1854 by an obscure sculptor named William Pink. (Linnel got in and eventually became an academician and had a successful career as a genre and landscape painter; Pink's copies are in the Royal Academy and the Edinburgh School of Art and have been much exhibited of late.) Everyone in the world of art knew this story. We do not know how much the poor whose bodies at the time might end up in the service of medical or art education knew.[230]

The making of the écorché of James Legg, on the other hand, was very public and ostentatiously grotesque. Seventy-eight years old and a Chelsea pensioner, he was sentenced to death, although not to dissection, for the murder of a fellow pensioner and was hanged along with another man at Tyburn on 2 November 1801. He ended up flayed and then crucified near the place of execution in order to satisfy the curiosity of some eminent artists and to bear witness to their commitment to nature over tradition. Benjamin West, among the best-known painters of his day and president of the Royal Academy, and two colleagues, Richard Cosway, a specialist in miniature portraits, and Thomas Banks, a sculptor famous for his bas-relief of Shakespeare accompanied by "painting" and "poetry," were having a discussion about whether the many pictures of Christ hanging from the cross were anatomically accurate. They thought not and that most had been done from écorchés either lying on their sides or nailed up only after rigor mortis or, more likely, from copying other paintings. To finally settle the matter, they secured the services of the well-known surgeon and popular freelance anatomy teacher, Joseph Constantine Carpue, who knew a thing or two about snatching bodies. Carpue got hold of Legg's freshly dead corpse, moved it to a nearby temporary building, and nailed it to a cross that he had provided for the experiment. Still warm, it sagged into the position of someone who had died from crucifixion; much was made of the hands. (The experiment was flawed because the Romans probably secured the hands with ropes and then broke the legs of the victim so that he suffocated, but that is another story. Everyone thought that Christ was hanging from nails.) Carpue let the body cool, and Banks, one of the trio who arranged the crucifixion, made the first of two casts. "When the mob had dispersed," Legg was taken to Carpue's anatomy theater, where he was flayed; Banks made the second and best-known of his casts, the most accurate anatomical rendering we have of how the muscles of a crucified body hanging by nails through its hands might look. Both casts were used by Banks in his teaching of art students; the first is now lost; the second escaped a Zeppelin bombing in 1917 and is now in the life drawing room of the Royal Academy and a star at many contemporary exhibitions.[231]

Spectacular as these displays were, the revolution in medical education was more important for the rise in demand for bodies than anatomical museums or the need of art students or their teachers for models. A new organ- and tissue-based pathology came to dominate medical schools and teaching hospitals beginning in the late eighteenth century, even if old Galenic ideas still influenced everyday clinical practice. It was the beginning of the great age of the autopsy; Baron Carl von Rokitansky, the lion of the Vienna School, was said to have performed twenty-five thousand, including Beethoven's. Dissection, disassembling the body to look at what is beneath the skin, became newly important not just as a medical rite of passage, but as practice for ever more daring and skilled surgery. But anatomical dissection became a requirement not only for surgeons but for all licensed medical men. Only Edinburgh and London in the British Isles had medical teaching establishments on anything like the scale of the Continental capitals, but here too the new appetite for bodies was voracious. The provinces too, on a smaller scale, needed cadavers.[232]

There are no precise figures for this rise of demand and supply of bodies to dissect in the eighteenth century. The chief of the anatomical department of the medical faculty in Paris, the mother church of advanced medical research and training, sent a carriage around to different hospitals to collect about two thousand per year, not counting those used in the Hôpital de la Pitié; by the 1820s, the rise in the number of autopsies performed in various hospitals reduced the number collected for anatomical teaching to 1,000–1,220 (i.e., they kept the bodies for themselves). How anatomy teachers coped we do not know. In London, grave robbers who gave testimony estimated that they had sold 305 adult bodies and 44 children in 1809–1810, earning for themselves 1,328 guineas, without figuring in what they got for teeth. (Dentures created a whole other market.) This estimate is almost certainly low. There were more than a thousand new medical and surgical students in London every year in the early nineteenth century; seven hundred in Edinburgh. Most major cities also had schools. The Apothecaries Act of 1815, which required attendance at anatomical dissection for admission to the licensing examination, added to the demand. Not every student got a body of his own—one estimate is that because of shortages only 150 to 200 students had a chance to dissect in Edinburgh in the 1820s. On the other hand, young men preparing to be surgeons supposedly needed at least four or five full dissections to gain even the most basic competency. Precisely how many bodies these thousands of medical students of different sorts actually used is unknowable. The general answer, for the early nineteenth century, is many, and later on, many many more: sixty thousand whole bodies, by the best estimate, in London alone between 1834 and 1929, mostly those of the poorest of the poor—prostitutes on the lowest rungs of their trade, the destitute and homeless who died on the streets, paupers of all sorts who ended their miseries in a workhouse—and another sixty-five thousand in the provinces. Without them, argued advocates for making the dead poor more easily available for dissection, doctors and surgeons would have to practice on the living, where they would do real and not just symbolic harm.[233]

Under these circumstances, "persons employed in procuring subjects for dissection" could not exhume bodies fast enough. Inflation proved the point. In the 1790s, "the price of a subject" was said to be between 1 and 3 guineas. (When this was written, in the early nineteenth century, a guinea was 21 shillings.) By the late 1820s, it was up to an average of 8 to 10 guineas, with especially fine specimens or a particularly tight local market pushing the price up to 16. No one liked this situation. One of the most articulate proponents of anatomical teaching and advocates for finding a regular legal supply of cadavers agreed that digging up the dead was "a repulsive employment," "disgraceful to a hoard of savages," and "revolting to the highest degree." But it was a necessary evil under the circumstances. James Doherty, a leading trade unionist of the 1820s and 1830s, agreed: an "odious and disgusting traffic in human flesh," he called the trade in cadavers. "Not content with the people's toil while living, the rich insist upon having their bodies cut up and mangled when dead," he wrote in defense of the rioters accused of ignorance and brutality for demolishing the Manchester infirmary, brick by brick. "We have seen the bodies of the poor stolen from the grave, and carried away to be sold, like port, to the highest bidder." During the 1832 cholera epidemic, someone noticed that "somebody had taken the liberty of chopping off the head of a child, and of substituting, in its stead a brick." The likely suspects for making the switch, discovered when the coffin was opened, were of course the doctors. Doherty thought it worth his time to spend much of 1831 exposing the rector of Stockport, an industrial town near Manchester, for having allegedly been in league with resurrection men to take bodies of the poor from his churchyard and convey them to his brother-in-law, a surgeon. Others told their own versions of this story. The radical journalist William Cobbett, after a long account of the iniquities of the New Poor Law, ended it with a condemnation of the "Dead Body Bill"—the 1832 Anatomy Act—which, he asserted, would authorize the keepers of the workhouse "who may be a negro-driver from Jamaica, or even a negro, to dispose of the body to the cutters-up." (Wage slavery was a common metaphor, as was the idea that black slaves had it better than white workers.) If science needed bodies, let it have the bodies of the rich who benefited from it, Cobbett concluded. Mammon had triumphed over feeling; it haunted the poor beyond the grave.[234]

It haunted some into the grave. Exhumation for sale was illegal, carried out clandestinely by men at the fringes of society. If caught, grave robbers faced serious consequences. There had been fourteen convictions in 1823; one man was sentenced to two years in jail and stayed longer because he could not pay the £20 fine. Another man died after being sentenced to Cold Bath Fields for stealing the dead. Punishment did little to deter grave robbing, but it did raise the price of bodies, and that tempted some to go a step further: murdering people in order to sell their bodies to the doctors. The first of these scandalous crime sprees gave English a new verb: "to burke" (to suffocate; figuratively, to suppress quietly, i.e., to murder without leaving a trace that an anatomist would immediately notice). The eponymous William Burke, an Irish navvy who rose to being a weaver and cobbler in Edinburgh, and his accomplices killed upward of seventeen people between November 1827 and October 1828 for sale on the Edinburgh market. All of them ended as cadavers seemingly untouched by any violence beyond poverty. Burke's customer was one of the city's best-known teachers of anatomy, Robert Knox. The first corpse Burke and his accomplices sold was that of an aged tenant who died from natural causes in his mistress's boardinghouse ("a pensioner who led a good for nothing life [and whose] debauched habits sufficiently account for his death," as a contemporary source puts it). The others were clearly the product of bespoke murder: a poor tenant who owed rent; an old woman and her blind grandson, she dead of an overdose of opiates, he of a discretely broken back; a homeless woman and her daughter who had sought shelter in Burke's stable were cleanly burked; likewise two prostitutes, a woman who had been released by the police to Burke's custody, and a retarded eighteen-year-old with a limp called Daft Jamie. Burke was hanged before a great crowd in Edinburg on 28 January

1829. His body was publicly dissected by Alexander Munro, Darwin's anatomy teacher and the son and grandson of more famous and gifted Monros. His skeleton and death mask are in the Edinburgh University Anatomical Museum, along with a label written by Munro in Burke's blood. On average, the gang got £8 per body for these, the friendless poor, who "left not a gap in the world."[235]

London saw copycat murders. On Saturday, 5 November 1831, John Bishop and Thomas Williams, two well-known resurrection men, who eventually confessed to having successfully exhumed and sold five hundred to one thousand bodies in the regular course of business, appeared at the dissecting room door of King's College, carrying a large wicker basket. They asked the porter whether "he wanted anything." "Anything in particular?" he replied. "A male subject," they answered; to be precise, a fourteen-year-old boy for which—for whom, perhaps—they wanted £12. The porter said that he was sure that his bosses would not pay so high a price, but he checked. They came down to £10 and agreed to settle for £9. They left the body while the anatomy demonstrator went off, supposedly to change a £50 note. He instead examined the body, discovered that it was too fresh to ever have been buried and found upon closer examination signs that the boy had died a violent death. He alerted the police, who investigated and found that the fourteen-year-old victim was not an Italian boy named Ferrari, as originally thought, but a boy from Lincolnshire whom the men had found homeless and seeking shelter. They took him to their house, asked him to wait in the privy, then gave him a spiked drink and murdered him in his sleep. First there had been Fanny Pigburn, whom they found sitting in a doorway with her four-year-old child; when asked why she was there, she said she had no home since her landlord had evicted her; they offered her food and shelter and then killed her for sale. Cunningham, around eight years old, they found "under the pig-hoards in the pig market at Smithfield." They offered him warm beer with sugar laced with rum and laudanum and then suffocated and sold him. These, like the Scottish victims, were the poorest of the poor, the most vulnerable, the least likely to be missed of a great city's poor. "Subjects" at the anatomy theater door, they were the grotesque limits of the friendless pauper on the shabby one-horse cart. The London Burkers were themselves "anatomized"; thousands watched.[236]

Only a tiny part of the demand for bodies was supplied through murder, but these two spectacularly awful cases exposed what had long been known in some circles: that doctors were complicit in the fate of pauper bodies generally and that they relied on a criminal underworld to supply them with the cadavers that the medicine and surgery of the day demanded. The profession recognized that at the heart of the problem was the stubborn challenge Diogenes had posed long ago. The horror of dissection did not spring, at least not in Great Britain, from an ideological objection to anatomy per se (the subtle and unfair suggestion being that maybe in Catholic Europe it did). Rather, as the anatomist R. D. Grainger said as he stood over the body of Jeremy Bentham, the "repugnance to dissection sprang from a feeling strongly implanted in the human breast—a feeling of reverence towards the dead." It was not to be condemned. From respect for the body sprang "some of the purest principles of our nature." But, as Bentham had argued, "an undue indulgence to this feeling procures incalculable mischief." Fear of being anatomized, indeed about the fate of one's fleshly remains, may in earlier ages have given rise to healthy emotions. It was not an incomprehensible reaction. But in the modern world, it was superstitious and therefore could be modified by reason.[237]

Southwood Smith, in the same anatomy theater, made the case in his speech over the body of his dear friend as it lay before him on the dissection table. Yes, there is a dread of being in the presence of the dead; "but behold," he says, pointing to Bentham's cadaver, "that revered and beloved countenance . . . a body purer and innocent." Yes, he says, we cannot separate our ideas of "the peculiarities and actions of our friend," of the "delicious emotions" felt in his company from his body and now from his corpse. (Southwood Smith for a page quotes from Godwin without attribution.) But all that said, dissection was indispensable for the progress of human knowledge. What was about to transpire was the greatest happiness principle in action. "Health is the first of human enjoyment," he says, while disease causes physical pain as well as psychological distress that is "oftentimes far greater than the physical." Bentham's insistence that his body be dissected was a gesture toward making acceptable a practice that would minimize pain and maximize health. It was unfair to the "humbler classes of the community," Grainger had pointed out, to ask only them to sacrifice their feelings. Rich and poor shared alike in the benefits of medicine. This is why Bentham wanted to make an example of his body: "the last act of this illustrious man was a special and solemn act of conformity to his principle." "Brave Bentham! All week I have thought of that dissecting table with a feeling of solemnity," wrote Thomas Carlyle to his friend J. S. Mill.[238]

Bentham was not the first to make a public display of the fact that he had transcended deeply ingrained conventions of reverence for the dead by asking to be dissected, although he was the most famous and principled. Messenger Monsey, a famous eighteenth-century freethinker and physician, had been insistent that he be dissected in public. "Many have ridiculed and censured that part of his will which directed that his body to be sent to the anatomist after his death," wrote one of his biographers. He only wanted to show that he was willing to have performed on himself something that he had recommended to all his patients in the hope that young men of genius and learning might follow his example. He wrote to William Cruickshank, perhaps England's most famous surgeon, a year before he died asking him to dissect his body because he was worried that his own surgeon might not arrive in time from Norwich. He did. Monsey was anatomized before an audience of students at Guys Hospital in December 1788.[239]

But the Benthams and Monseys of the world could not meet the need for thousands of cadavers every year. Far too few people who had the means to do otherwise were brave enough to take Diogenes at his word. "Unclaimed" pauper bodies—bodies with nowhere else to go—were thus the only possible source of "material" on the scale that was required. The 1832 Anatomy Act would regulate precisely which bodies would be made available, to whom, at what cost, and under what conditions. An 1824 pamphlet by the Vienna-trained Glasgow ophthalmologist William Mackenzie offered the first clear proposals for how this might be done. Thomas Southwood Smith, soon to be one of Jeremy Bentham's closest allies, his executor, and the man who oversaw his dissection, reviewed it at great length. It is this review, "The Use of the Dead for the Living," reprinted and supplemented in various editions, that translated Mackenzie's ideas into legislative form (fig. 5.29).[240]

5.29. Head of Jeremy Bentham. Special Collections, University College, London.

Many pages are devoted to defending the importance of anatomy to an audience that still regarded it as a dodgy business. In a few decades, its arguments would be commonplace: if doctors were going to be able to cure people they needed to understand what makes them sick, and this can be discovered only in the body. And furthermore, if they were going to intervene through surgery it was better to practice on the dead than on the live poor. Anatomy was the royal road to modern medicine. The question, once this was established, became how doctors were going to procure bodies honorably. A reliance on criminals—or, more precisely, on those who were being criminalized for providing a socially necessary but distasteful service—was no answer. Handling the dead is always suspect: exhuming them for one's private use was distasteful and unseemly; exhuming them for sale was outrageous. The only answer was for the state to intervene to ensure a culturally legitimate supply of bodies. Three things needed to happen. First, dissection had to be destigmatized by decoupling it from punishment; dissection was a medical, not a juridical, act. Second, the supply of bodies had to be regulated, one source suppressed and a new one opened up. Exhumation was to be made illegal and a category of legally acceptable, dissection-appropriate bodies identified. Mackenzie's suggestion was capacious: the body of anyone who died in any hospital, workhouse, poorhouse, house of correction, or foundling hospital in designated large cities, or, if supply was short, in any town or country parish should be available for dissection as long they were "unclaimed by immediate relatives" or who had "decline[d] to defray the expenses of burial." These were the bodies that no one owned or even wanted to own for the purpose of a proper burial: the pauper in purest form. Instead of marling the fields as Heraclitus had suggested, they could be of use on dissection tables.

Mackenzie's proposals were taken up wholesale by other advocates. Thomas Rose, surgeon of the St. James Parochial Infirmary, argued for this administratively straightforward solution before an 1828 parliamentary committee on the subject. It solved the supply problem in one stroke. In 1827, 3,744 people died in the workhouses alone of London's 127 parishes, he pointed out; 3,103 of these were buried at public expense and thus would be in principle eligible for dissection; 1,108 bodies were attended to the grave by no one. Sending those in this last category to the anatomy theater would thus offend no one. But all of them owed their bodies to society. Rose thought that relatives of the dead had forfeited any rights they might have had to "interfere," as he put it, with the disposal of their kin's bodies because they had failed to provide for them while they were alive. Their corpses were, in short, payment for society's providing a roof under which to die.[241]

Southwood Smith was sympathetic but not entirely supportive of Mackenzie's and Rose's views. There was, he admitted, merit to their case: it was indisputable that "those who are supported by the public die in its debt," and it would be no injustice if they were "converted to public use." But he objected to the plan for asking for more than was needed, for "making the bodies of the poor public property." It served only to alienate would-be supporters. Doctors needed for dissection only "that portion of the poor who die unclaimed and without friends and whose appropriation to this public service could, therefore, afford pain to no one." "The fittest persons in society for dissection," remarked a witness to the parliamentary committee, were those who had no friends to care about them, "those who died friendless."[242]

Finally, in addition to removing dissection from the menu of punishments and designating a class of subjects who could be dissected, Mackenzie's proposal, Southwood Smith's review, and the 1832 act had to set the rules for procurement and disposal of bodies. Those in lawful possession of the dead—mostly but not entirely Poor Law unions, asylums, and hospitals—could give them up to anatomy for a specified fee as long as no relative objected and the anatomist agreed to bury the remains once science was done with them. It is not hard to imagine how this system could be gamed by medical schools anxious for bodies and Poor Law authorities and others in possession of the dead eager for fees. It is also not hard to understand the fear and hatred that this system generated among those who might end up among its numbers. The British working-class Left was reluctant to sign up for cremation—it was popular with Continental socialist parties—because it reminded its members of the smoke in workhouse chimneys that was believed to come from pauper remains being burned after dissection. The Anatomy Act of 1832 was the corporeal correlative of the despised 1834 Poor Law Amendment Act, like it a product of Benthamite radicalism, like it an insertion of the bodies of the poor into a triumphant political economy and a program of rational administrative reform.

But more specifically, the 1832 act gave a new twist to the old stories. Not only the bodies of criminals, enemies, and those with the courage of their radical convictions but now also the friendless, unclaimed, unwanted, culturally worthless bodies were for the first time legally designated as subjects specifically destined not for burial but for cutting up by strangers. That what remained after that was to be buried in consecrated ground by a clergyman was a very thin veil of decency. Or the other way around: to be available for dissection was of the mark of the pauper whom no one owned. The pauper funeral announced this condition to the world.

There is more to it than that. Some of the bodies given to surgeons might indeed have been friendless with no one to speak for them, the detritus of workhouses, asylums, hospitals, and the streets. But others might have had friends who "decline[d] to defray the expenses of burial" because they could not afford it or who could not bear the humiliation of walking behind a corpse buried "on the parish." It was better to leave the dead to dissection. Part of the answer of how the pauper funeral came into being is the emergence of a new and brutal designation of pauper—one whose body is *homo sacer,* not mere life but mere death—and nothing more. The body defined the funeral. But the status of the funeral changed as well; the chasm between dignity and degradation widened.

The glass that the dead held before the eyes of nineteenth-century men reflected something new. Diogenes was now wrong for different, or rather additional, reasons than before. On the dead was now projected an anxiety about earthly standing, and on it could be etched in perpetuity the definitive record of the place of the dead in a social order in which that place had, during life, been tenuous. The celebratory rituals of the worthy refracted the threadbare ones of those who had fallen away. This was a world, one can already see in eighteenth-century London, that was enormously conscious of the fragile nature of respectability, and even of civilization. All sorts of imaginative literature as well as works of social investigation play on this theme. One thinks of heroines "ruined," it was said, by a single false step; one thinks of the image of bankruptcy and of debtors' prison; and one thinks of charities ministering to those who had fallen from grace. As a clergyman soliciting support for the Manchester Night Asylum put it: "there is but a thin gauze veil between virtue and crime, which once broken through . . . can never be wholly repaired."[243]

Far from being a time for reflection on the transience of earthly glory, death had oddly become the occasion to exult in it. The funeral, as a rite of passage, spoke not of the world hereafter but of the history of the deceased and of his and sometimes her status in civil society. It was the final pronouncement on earthly existence: only a pauper whom nobody owns or wants except perhaps medical students. In the funeral of others one could contemplate the meaning of one's own life. "What draws the reader to a novel is the hope of warming his shivering life with a death he reads about," Walter Benjamin observed.[244] What repelled the poor in the pauper funeral was precisely that they could find no warmth in its contemplation; they were left shivering.

1. Hyena eats the dead. In *Medieval Bestiary*. England, thirteenth century. Royal 12 C XIX f. 11v, British Library.

2. The Tollund Man, fourth century B.C.E. Silkeborg Museum.

3. A corpse-like rendering of Diogenes. Jules Bastian-Lepage, *Diogène*, 1873. Musée Marmottan.

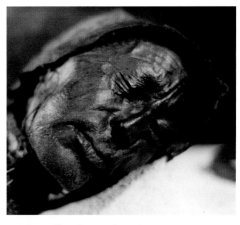

4. Maestá Altarpiece. Panel from the back predella section showing an onlooker holding his nose at the raising of Lazarus, 1308–1311. Kimbell Art Museum, Fort Worth, Texas.

5. "People who burn their dead." In Jacob van Maerlant, *Der naturen bloeme*, 1350, KA 16 folio 40v. The Hague, Royal Library. National Library of the Netherlands.

6. *The Church Porch, East Bergholt.* John Constable, 1810. Tate, London.

7. *Scene in a Churchyard on a Hill.* John Constable, 1833. British Museum.
Illustration to Thomas Gray's "Elegy," stanza V, which follows the line,
"The rude forefathers of the hamlet sleep."

8. *The Arcadian Shepherds (Et in Arcadia Ego)*. Nicholas Poussin, ca. 1627, Chatsworth House. Derbyshire, UK.

9. *The Arcadian Shepherds (Et in Arcadia Ego)*. Nicholas Poussin, ca. 1650. Louvre, Paris.

10. View of Père-Lachaise. To the left, the monument of General Foy, Christophe Civeton, 1829. Bibliothèque nationale de France.

11. View of the garden of the Musée des Monuments Français. Alexandre Lenoir. Louvre, Paris.

12. View of Constantinople from the cemetery at Pera. Unknown artist, ca. 1860. Victoria and Albert Museum, London.

13. Aids Memorial Quilt at the Washington Monument, National Institute of Health.

14. Gang der Erinnerung, Holocaust Memorial at the
Jewish Center in Munich. andreasgregor.com.

15. *The Field of Waterloo.* Joseph Turner, ca. 1818. Tate, London.

16. *The Field of Waterloo.* (Watercolor.) Joseph Turner, ca. 1817. Fitzwilliam Museum, University of Cambridge, UK.

17. Memorial of poppies at the Tower of London on the 100th anniversary of Armistice Day, Tom Piper, London 2014. https://commons.wikimedia.org/wiki/File:Tower_of_London_Poppy.jpg.

18. *The Funeral of Shelley.* Louis Edouard Fournier, 1889. Walker Art Gallery, National Museums, Liverpool.

19. Interior of the Manchester Crematorium.

PART III

NAMES OF THE DEAD

Particles of matter are measured
The heavenly bodies weighted
and only in human affairs
a criminal neglect runs rampant
a deficit of precise data
a specter is haunting
the map of history
the specter of indeterminacy
how many Greeks perished at Troy
—we don't know
how to give the exact losses
on both sides
in the battle of Gaugamela
Agincourt
Leipzig
Kutno
and also the number of victims
of the white terror
the red
the brown—ah the innocent colors—
—we don't know
we really don't know.

ZBIGNIEW HERBERT, "MR. COGITO ON
THE NEED FOR PRECISION"

The unmoored name, even more poignantly than the dead body, is a perfect representation of what Freud in his essay on mourning calls the "verdict of reality." Bereft of the person to whom it belonged, it is—or rather it has become—meaningless as a consequence of the fact of death. "Mary Wollstonecraft" inscribed on a tombstone over her grave refers to nothing: a shadowy record, like the name on a coffin "dropped into the darkness," that may as well be read only by worms for all that it does to recall its previous owner. It is what linguists would call a "space deixis," an indexical sign that depends on its place: here is Mary Wollstonecraft, to whose dust it directs our gaze. But she is not here; she is no more and nowhere. Her name, as her husband William Godwin admits, is at best a formula with which to conjure up the dead.[1]

The very long commitment that we as a species have to the names of the dead is therefore an even more remarkable feat of imagination than that which we mobilize to care for their bodies. When we ritualistically breathe life into the flesh or the bones or the dust of the dead, we do so in the belief that these remains belonged to one (and only one) person, the person in question, the dead herself. She is the one we want safely out of the way, the one we want to honor, the one we want back. A body's "remains" are presumed to be unique even if very soon they differ little from what remains of all other bodies. Diogenes' friends were reluctant to throw his body to the beasts not only on general principles—because the corpse was a token of the human, a category that for many reasons made insistent claims on the living—but because it was "his" that needed to make its way safely to the underworld; "him" to whom honor was due; "he" had a specific claim to dignity—however much the dog philosopher tried to play that down—and it was to "him" that a monument was eventually raised. Our friends feel the same sorts of things. But names, unlike bodies, are not uniquely anyone's. Three hundred and twelve "William Jenkinses" fought in the British army during the Great War: nineteen were privates in the South Wales Borderers, and two of them died; thirteen were sappers in the Royal Engineers, and two of them died as well. How, asked a frustrated official in the Imperial War Graves Commission, was one to know whose name was honored on a memorial without adding a regimental number, which presented other problems?[2]

The same is true in civilian life. To return to our example, the Christian—that is, baptismal—name "Mary" belongs to "Mary Wollstonecraft" only through a strenuous exercise of the imagination. It was shared by millions. "Wollstonecraft," by which her husband, William Godwin, and we distinguish this particular "Mary" from all others, was her surname—sur-nom—her extra or added name. By etymological sleight of hand and custom it might also be her father's name—"sire or sir name." If this Mary had had a more common surname there would have been thousands more of her. We are still far from a name that is truly a body's—this Mary's—and even further from the material specificity of her, or any, body.

The disembodied names of the dead are thus the strangest of that strange category of noun, the proper name, because they are shadows of shadows: more insubstantial than ghosts. Even more poignantly than the dead body, they are a reinscription of loss, one of its poor avatars, a substitute, a placeholder, a trace of a trace. Whether writ on stone, parchment, paper, bronze, or cloth, whether sung or recited, singly or collectively, the names, like the bodies, of the dead have served the living. There are countless naming practices, but in each case names, and the names of the dead in particular, are deeply embedded in the cultures that employ them. More specifically, beginning in the late nineteenth century, accelerating after the American Civil War, and ever more so in the century of the Holocaust, the Great War, the Soviet terror and so much more mass death, Mr. Cogito's demand for precision—the demand to know, to count the names of the dead—has become ever more exigent. We live in an age of necronominalism; we record and gather the names of the dead in ways, and in places, and in numbers as never before. We demand to know who the dead are. We find unnamed bodies and bodiless names—those of the disappeared—unbearable.

There are two questions here. The first asks about the universal connection of the names of the dead with their memory and with the dead themselves. This is the same sort of question I asked about bodies, and I want to answer it in a similar way by pointing to a similar historical anthropological conjuncture of names and the dead in deep time. The second question is the more strictly historical: it asks why Mr. Cogito's demand to know has become more exigent in the modern era than ever before. How do we account for the advent and the life of the age of necronominalism? Part of an answer is that names themselves have become far more exigent than before through the actions of the state, of civil society, and of individuals. They are part of public history and of the history of private life and of the emotions as well. The rest of the answer comes from individual circumstances: how the new bureaucratic, civic, and emotional power of names became the nidus of memory or oblivion.

Chapter 6
THE NAMES OF THE DEAD
IN DEEP TIME

It [the name] is an instrument of exchange: it allows the substitution of a nominal unit for a collection of characteristics by establishing an equivalent relationship between sign and sum: it is a bookkeeping method in which, the price being equal, condensed merchandise is preferable to voluminous merchandise. . . . [It] is *filled* with a person (civic, national, social), it is to insist that appellative currency be in gold.

ROLAND BARTHES, *S/Z*

This chapter, like the three chapters in *part 1*, makes a broad historical if not universal claim. It is not about the bodies but about the names of the dead, which, like bodies, evoke, commemorate, beckon, stand, and speak for the dead, singly and collectively. A survey of the names of the dead in deep time exposes the philosophical, anthropological, historical, and emotional infrastructure of the changes in how the question "Who are the dead?" is answered in the modern era.

We must not take names for granted, or perhaps we should; they are both profoundly commonplace and profoundly strange. They come in many different varieties; their meaning and power have a variety of explanations. But to some extent they are always, as Roland Barthes claims, "filled with a person." Their existence, like the care of the dead, has been taken to be a kind of primal touchstone of humanity, a practice that defines the border between nature and culture. Homer knew this. Alcinous says as much to the wily Odysseus: "Surely no man in the world is nameless, all told. Born high, born low, as soon as he sees the light, his parents always name him, once he's born." He is not quite right. The giving of a name does not coincide with the baby's emergence from the womb but with its acceptance into the family and the human community: into a certain minimal status of personhood. Naming marks the entry not into biological but into human life. Herodotus, the first historical anthropologist, made that point. He thought that on the coast of Ethiopia there lived a people so primitive that they cast their dead into the sea: Ichthyophagi. And by analogy he thought that there were people, in what is now Libya, so deeply strange that they purportedly had no names: "ten days' journey from the Garamantes [Garama]," live the Atarantes, who, he claims, are "the only men known to us who have no names, for the whole people are called Atarantes, but no man has a name of his own." Pliny makes the case explicit. This "Atlas tribe has fallen below the level of human civilization, if we can believe what is said; for they do not address each other by any names." Having no names is evidence for primal strangeness. They hate the sun and share their women, and they "do not dream like the rest of mankind." That is, the people without names have no inner lives.[1]

Ancient anthropology still had purchase in the seventeenth century. In 1623, the English antiquarian William Camden, who produced the first great genealogically informed topographical atlas of England, thought it important to ground his project in deep history. "Every person had in the beginning only one proper name, as among Jews, Adam, Joseph, Solomon . . . among the Greeks Diomedes, Ulysses," he writes. The same is true for all other nations, he continues (having given many more examples), except "the sages of Mount Atlas in Barbary which were reported to be both nameless and dreamless." Camden goes on to explain that different cultures gave their children names at different times: eight days after birth—the feast of the circumcision among the Hebrews (he does not mention girls); the eighth day for females and the ninth day for males—the *dies lustricus* (cleansing day for males) among the Romans; the day of birth for the Anglo-Saxons. If, as he suggests, naming constituted an entry into the social order, it was done for the same sort of reasons that humans have so long cared for the dead: the maintenance of a human community in deep time. From "the most ancient times among all nations," names were imposed "upon the future good hopes conceived by parents of their children." Almost three centuries after Camden wrote, an expert on the common and statute law of naming, informed by nineteenth-century anthropological research, introduced his treatise by saying that naming goes back to the "remotest period of human law as opposed to natural law"; it began, he says, at the point when human nature advanced from savagery to civilization, when individuality came into existence. Herodotus's fictive anthropology of names, like his strikingly similar story about the dead, has a very long pedigree.[2]

The insights of Homer and Herodotus and of the sages of other traditions on the power of names, and consequently on the power of the names of the dead, have their roots in the nature of proper naming itself. This turns out to be terribly difficult to specify. An early-twentieth-century English barrister begins his treatise on the law of names by lamenting the "very abnormal difficulties [that arise from] the initial obstacle that it is almost impossible to properly define a name." And philosophers are of little help. A proper name, say followers of J. S.

Mill, take its meaning solely from what it refers to; it has no connotations but only a denotation: it points to a person without saying anything about her. This view matters to our discussion of the work of the dead for two reasons. First, the claim that a name has meaning only because it is intimately linked to *a* person links it to the sense of specificity and exclusiveness we associate with a body as well. And second, it raises the question of how the dead matter in a new and more abstract register. If we believe Mill, then the names of the dead mean nothing, because what they referred to is gone; one name adds as much semantic content to a statement as any other name of something that does not exist—Atlantis or El Dorado.[3]

Others, the so-called descriptivists, avoid some of the logical problems of Mill's view and also help, for our purposes, to connect names to the dead. They claim that names are a form of definite description: "*the* F" instead of "*an* F." From the perspective of the names of the dead, we might translate the meaning of the name "Eric Pinks" as follows: "the man, a private soldier, who was shot by a sniper near Ypres on August 14, 1917, whose body was never recovered, and whose name is recorded on Menin Gate." (The more usual example is "Aristotle" = "the teacher of Alexander the Great.") In this sense a name becomes a mnemonic that recalls or tells a story of the departed dead to whom the name applied.

Finally, there are those—the philosopher Saul Kripke is the most famous— who think of naming as a sort of baptism, an originary event. A name follows a person from this primal moment; names pertain in all possible worlds, and they keep their meaning through a chain of use even if someone gets a description of a person wrong. Aristotle would be Aristotle even if he had not taught Alexander the Great. Kripke argues for a "causal" theory of how names refer: all uses of a name take their meaning from a historical moment. They are the most rigid of rigid designators: they refer to that person in all places and times, presumably forever into death. Another way of putting this, although not one of great interest to philosophers, is that becoming a person is getting a name: like the first cry or the first bite of food, the moment of naming has in many cases been the divide between counting as a human being and not. For almost two thousand years, to take just one example, unbaptized children could not be buried in what was taken to be the consecrated part of churchyards; hence having a baptismal name meant having a body that required care.[4]

Fortunately we do not have to sort out the logic of names, because the history and anthropology of naming lore, as we humans tell it, is messy. Sometimes, as J. S. Mill thought, names do not mean anything. And sometimes they do. Names were once descriptive and then became just a way of denoting a particular person. English surnames, for example, said something about the person who first had that name or about a succession of different people with that name: sometime in the twelfth century the aristocracy came to take their names from the lands with which they were associated and more ordinary folk from what they did—Smith = a blacksmith, Farrier = a specialist blacksmith who takes care of horses' hooves, Currier = someone who works with leather once it is tanned. English surnames became fixed and thus less descriptive at the beginning of the fourteenth century. Names of descriptive derogation are ancient. These so-called bynames have in some cases and places became surnames: Alice Smalwhor, one of the "anilepiwymen"—the landless, unmarried, submerged—who eked out a bare living as best she could around 1290 in Holkham, Norfolk. The record is full of such bynames. And finally, names are treated as the sort of rigid designators given at a historical moment and forever bound to a person. So-called Christian names—baptismal names—were once regarded in common law as essentially Adamic names. In the seventeenth century, the most famous of the common-law-lawyers, Chief Justice Coke, said that when it counted (in land purchases, for example), "a man may have divers names at divers times, but not divers Christian names." The baptismal name is inseparably connected with religion and thus cannot be changed. The first human names are of this sort: God created and named Adam and Eve. And that is who they—and indeed all the creatures that Adam named—were before the entry of sin into the world made language a glass through which to see the world darkly.[5]

The deep history of naming is thus a mirror of a great drama. "Adam" is both the name God gave to his first human creation—the primal naming moment—and it has been interpreted by the rabbis to be a generic form of "man" or "mankind" or "humanity," and thus a description of him. Jacob, after wrestling with the angel, becomes who he is by being named: "But now thus saith the LORD that created thee, O Jacob, and he that formed thee, O Israel, Fear not: for I have redeemed thee, I have called thee by thy name; thou art mine" (Isa 43:1). These words still have resonance in the twenty-first century. In the German military cemetery of the Great War at Langemark in Belgium, the epitaph in bronze over a mass grave borrows from this verse. The man who wrestled with the angel goes from being Jacob, "heel puller" (a reference to trying to beat Essau out of the womb), to Israel, "god redeemer" or "he who perseveres with God." Abram becomes Abraham, father of nations.[6]

"All people have names of one kind or another," claims the Irish novelist Flann O'Brien, as well as hundreds of anthropologists, historians, linguists, and others who have studied the matter. "Some are arbitrary labels related to the appearance of the person," O'Brien goes on to say, "some represent purely genealogical associations but most of them afford some clue as to the parents of the person named." They "confer a certain advantage in the execution of legal documents," he concludes, but they also do much more. To be specific, proper names, the names by which individuals distinguish self from other—autonyms, indeed, the names that create them as individuals—are universal; but aside from this basic, anthropological fact, all else varies among cultures and over time: 40 percent of naming systems have only one name; 30 percent have patronymic surnames. There are clan names and sacred names and secret names; many cultures have semantically meaningful names—Robert really is a smith—and many do not. The great majority of naming systems distinguish men and women. In most, names are stable; the ease with which we in the West today change our names is both recent and rare.[7]

There are also relational names, names that define the bearer's status vis-à-vis someone else (i.e., someone else's name): a teknonym, for example, in which an adult is known as the father or mother of a child; necronyms, the names of the dead, which are a sort of negative category, since these cannot be spoken; names taken at marriage—a teknonym of a sort—that until very recently submersed, for public purposes, the baptismal name of a woman in the name of her husband: the wife of Hans Schmid becomes Hans Schmidin, even if at home or among friends she is still known by her autonym, her first name. There are endless naming practices, but the point for now is that, in a great variety of ways, names universally are deeply embedded in the cultures that employ them.[8]

And so are the "just so" stories of the anthropology of naming, memory, and in particular caring for the dead. Humans have clan names, according to a compilation of Chinese ritual and ceremonial texts written before the Han period (206 B.C.E.–220 C.E.), in order to distinguish themselves from beasts, to order the generations, and to induce men to "love each other during life and to mourn each other in the case of death." They are also forbidden to marry persons of the same clan names—which once again links the beginning of the incest taboo and that of the care of the dead as a liminal moment between nature and culture. In one of the foundational works of Anglo-Saxon scholarship, the late-sixteenth-century poet, antiquary, spy, and Protestant polemicist Richard Verstegan offers a similar deep-time historical anthropology. Before Babel, there was no problem with the semantic meaning of proper names: an almighty God would not have allowed humans to give one another names in an "unintelligible and frivolous kynde of speech." They were easy monosyllables. After the confusion of languages, proper names were made up of syllables whose purpose was to express, "as it were, some precept, remembrance or encouragement for the enticing of some kynde of virtue or nobleness which they [parents] wished their children should effect," or to create the remembrance of some "praiseworthy memory."[9]

There are many versions of the ancient story from other traditions, and it has its resonances in many other Western origin stories as well. The eighteenth-century anthropological and philosophical tradition that regarded the tomb and the grave as signs of our coming into humanity interpreted the name on the tomb as an advance of the civilizational process. If burial, as Hegel thought, was meant to stop, for a time at least, the reversion of a body to nature, names on the burial site were a further shield against oblivion.

Wordsworth, for example, coming out of this tradition, thought that as soon as people learned to write they began to put names and epitaphs on their tombs, not so much because of particular beliefs—although all the civilizations produce accounts of what happens to the dead—but because they gave expression to a primordial feeling: the desire to remain part of this world. Funerary inscriptions, he thought, "proceed from the presage or forefeeling of immortality" and are, "if not a co-existent and twin birth with reason, then . . . among the earliest of her offspring." Wordsworth's authority for this anthropological claim was the early-seventeenth-century antiquarian and poet John Weever, whose *Antient Funeral Monuments of Great Britain* was edited in 1767 by the learned clergyman and historian William Tooke. It begins with a lengthy "Discourse" on the subject of monuments in general and epitaphs in particular that reviews evidence from classical texts. Naming the dead—more generally, building a monument that bears an epitaph—grows out of the feeling that there is "some part of our nature that is imperishable." This is the space of this, named, person. Every man, Weever writes, "desires a perpetuity after his death." Without this idea "man could never have awakened in him the desire to live in the remembrance of his fellows." And without it, human life in the shadow of death would be unbearable and unrecognizable: "the social affections could not have unfolded themselves un-countenanced by the faith that Man is an immortal being." Our love for one another differs from the love animals might feel for one another in that an animal perishes in the field without "anticipating the sorrow with which his associates will bemoan his death," whereas we "wish to be remembered by our friends." Naming the dead, like care for their bodies, is seen as a way to keep them among the living. And maybe it is a way around Diogenes. "The grave stele," writes the classicist Jean-Pierre Vernant, "is a permanent witness to the identity of a being who, together with his body, finds his definitive end in absence." It will "remind generations of men of his name." Vernant is speaking of heroes, but later generations would appropriate the practice, the only mortal hope to live forever, unchanged and beautiful, like the gods on earth.[10]

Naming the dead is deeply imbricated not just in Western histories of the human commemorative capacity and of the desire to live forever but also in the techniques of memory itself. Cicero and Quintilian (ca. 35–100 C.E.), the most influential of the ancient rhetoricians, are the source for the story of how the late-sixth-century B.C.E. lyric poet Simonides invented, or in any case first demonstrated, the art of memory when he was able to identify—to attach names to—otherwise unidentifiable dead bodies by remembering where they had been when they were alive. This happened as follows. Once upon a time, the poet exceeded his brief in an ode that was supposed to celebrate the victory in a chariot race of his patron, King Scopas of Thessaly. He gave excess praise to Castor and Pollux. The king refused to pay the full price because the divine twins had shared too much of the glory that was his alone. After that and for no apparent reason, two mysterious strangers called Simonides out of the room. Just as he crossed the threshold, the strangers—presumably Castor and Pollux—vanished, and the roof of the room he had just left fell in. All the guests, except of course Simonides, were killed, indeed crushed beyond recognition, not "merely the faces, but even the limbs of the dead." Proper burial would have been impossible under these circumstances. But Simonides "remembered the order in which the guests had been sitting, [and] succeeded in restoring to each man his own dead," showing that "it is an assistance to the memory if localities are sharply impressed upon the mind."[11]

Finally, there is a phylogenetic version of the deep history of the names of the dead: the claim that name itself carries kinship over the generations. The God of the Hebrews, for example, promised a pious eunuch that even without progeny his name would not be lost: "even unto them will I give in mine house and within my walls a place and a name [*yad vashem*] better than of sons and of daughters: I shall give them an everlasting name, that shall not be cut off." Yad Vashem, the "place of names" of the murdered of the Holocaust and the national shrine of Israel, is a reference to this promise. The premise of this story is that to die in name as well as body—to become nameless, to lose that by which the dead were known among the living—is a profound and deep kind of death: mortality in flesh and in memory. God offers the eunuch an alternative. Absalom, the beloved and rebellious son of King David, tried it for himself: "in his lifetime [he] had taken and reared up for himself a pillar, which is in the king's dale: for he said, I have no son to keep my name in remembrance: and he called the pillar after his own name: and it is called unto this day, Absalom's place" (2 Sam 18:18). But God also threatened extinction: "he shall deliver their kings into thine hand, and thou shalt destroy their name from under heaven," the Lord promises the Children of Israel after their liberation from Egypt (Deut 7:24). Conversely, generations of their names correspond to generations of the dead who "sleepe by the urnes of their Fathers."[12]

Psychoanalysis also speaks to this fundamental and seemingly universal human relationship with the necronym. Freud thought it strange that among savages, speaking the names of the dead is forbidden with "extraordinary severity." But, he continues, the taboo might be understood "if we bear in mind that the savage looks upon his [the dead person's] name as an essential part and an important possession of his personality, and that he ascribes the full significance of things to words." For my purposes, the point is not the conflation of things and words that Freud points to, but the elision of the distinction between name and person. This, as he knew, was not limited to savages and required no particular view about where the dead are and what they are doing. Children succumb to it, Freud says, and so do neurotics, who are "just like savages in regard to names." He reports on a patient who was afraid of writing down her name because she feared that it would fall into someone's hands and that she would consequently lose "a piece of her personality." This was true at the end of the twentieth century among the Communist elite. Exemplary, and brilliantly told by Istvan Rev, is the case of János Kádár, who murdered and usurped the place of Imre Nagy in the Hungarian Revolution of 1956 and believed—rightly it turned out—that speaking his rival's name would mean his own downfall. Kádár is a special case. It is true of the Roma in France today, who fear not only to speak the name of the dead but to camp where she had camped or eat foods that she had enjoyed eating. There are many such examples and many explanations. At the bottom, the fear of the necronym, as Freud understands it, is grounded in the fear of the dead—or more specifically in the ambivalent emotions that the dead arouse. The names of the dead are placeholders. Why people fear the dead, or at least some of the dead, is a larger question and not immediately at issue here. It may be, Freud speculates, because of the "natural horror that a corpse inspires," or because of "the double feelings—tenderness and hostility against the deceased," or because of the bad conscience that is aroused by actual wrongs done to the dead or by the guilt of feeling both guilty of the death and in some horrible and secret way pleased. This list is far from exhaustive. But two things are clear. First, the names of the dead are proxies for persons, not just among "savages" but also among the people whom Freud encountered in twentieth-century Vienna and whom we might encounter today. And second, whether taboo or embraced, this identity of the name and the dead remains totemic. "As long as you call my name, I live," says a voice from an early nineteenth-century slave burial record.[13]

The existence and cultural import of names—those of the living and those of the dead—extends to the deepest reaches of time. It seems to exist before history. And this is almost true of the form in which we remember the names of the dead, although their number has increased logarithmically in the past two centuries. I am speaking of lists. We encounter lists at the birth of oral epic poetry; they are promiscuously present in the earliest records of literate societies. Umberto Eco may be exaggerating when he says that "the list is the origin of culture," but he is probably right that "we like lists because we do not want to die"; death is disordering, and lists, like funerary rituals, bring order to a world rent by mortality. But there are other reasons to like a list. The crucial insight of his "Infinity of the

List" show at the Louvre in 2009 is that there is a poetics of catalogs, that lists constitute a literary form with many variants and purposes but a recognizable form nonetheless.[14]

In all lists—of people, whether alive or dead, of things, of tasks, of debts, of taxes, of food, of aspirations and resolutions, of pictures, of books—there is an insistent logic of inclusion or exclusion. Lists have a purpose: this family in the ancestral tables of China, where names are a safe haven for the *hun* or cloud soul that has left a body; these donors to a monastery or a church; these members of a guild or their friends who will be named in prayers; this assemblage of dead soldiers; these great men; the dead of this school or village; these martyrs. More mundanely, lists denote this inventory, these things to do, these articles to read. Some lists have a "use by" date; they have a short-term instrumental purpose which, once fulfilled, makes them no longer relevant. The names of the dead in any form, and more specifically their names on lists, are not of this sort; they are there to be remembered, forever; others—not on the list—are forgotten, either purposely excluded or, more commonly, having never counted in the first place. Lists of the names of the dead that matter, like churchyards, cemeteries, even rivers into which ashes are thrown, constitute communities of the dead that live from generation to generation.

NAMES OF THE DEAD IN TIMES OF WAR

Modern practices of gathering the names of the dead, with their bodies and without them, have a number of genealogies. Let me trace one of these: that of the national cemetery at Gettysburg in Pennsylvania. Its root lies in the soil of the Soros on the plains of Marathon on the northeast coast of Attica, forty kilometers from Athens, where in 490 B.C.E. 192 Athenians died in the defeat of the Persians. When the geographer Pausanius (110–180 C.E.) visited the site of the epochal battle, he reported that the ten pillars on which the names of the Greek dead had been inscribed were still standing. The epitaph on one of these was more than likely written by Simonides, the founding father of memory. It must have been an extraordinary place to visit. Pausanius could imagine the topography of a battle that in antiquity, and in some circles to the present day, was regarded as a turning point of Greek, and hence Western, civilization.[15]

Almost two thousand years later, in 1815, we pick up the genealogy again. In that year the classicist, politician, and future president of Harvard University, Edward Everett—he was in his early twenties and had just been elected to a professorship—followed in the footsteps of Pausanius. Nearly a half century later, by then the country's most famous classicist, this man whom his student Ralph Waldo Emerson regarded as "almost comparable to Pericles" explicitly clothed the new democracy in the memorial mantle of the old when he translated his youthful experience into his speech for the dedication of the world's first national cemetery at Gettysburg. Like "those who rolled back the tide of the Persian invasion and rescued the land of popular liberty, of letters, and of arts, from the ruthless foe," he said, the men who lay in the graves among which the audience gathered had also "rolled back the tide of an invasion, not less unprovoked, not less ruthless, than that which came to plant the dark banner of Asiatic despotism and slavery on the free soil of Greece." The new Marathon at Gettysburg in the green farm-land of western Pennsylvania was, he said "holy ground." He had once "gazed with respectful emotion on the mound that still protects the dust" of the Greeks who died at Marathon, he told his audience. The name-bearing stelae had long since disappeared "beneath the hand of time and barbaric violence," but the spirit in which the stelae were built had not vanished; it still lived at Gettysburg. Erected around 490 B.C.E. to mark the bodies of the war dead more or less where they had fallen, the stelae of Marathon became the model for U.S. military practice during the Civil War. Like the dead of Marathon, those at Gettysburg lie where they fell.[16]

There is another branch of this genealogy, not as direct but just as important, that Lincoln and his listeners understood well and that articulated with Everett's speech about Marathon. If we were to be sticklers for historical accuracy, the president in his Gettysburg Address was being anachronistic by a generation or two. His speech was in the form of the Periclean funeral address that we know (as did Lincoln) through the report of the historian Thucydides. By the time Pericles delivered his famous oration around 431 C.E., the bodies of the war dead—their ashes and bones in any case—were no longer being left on the battlefield as they were at Marathon (even then it was not common practice) but were being brought back to Athens. Their names would be recorded on casualty lists chiseled with exquisite lettering on monuments in the Demosion Sema of the Keramakis, the beautiful burial place outside the city that became a model for the nineteenth-century cemetery. Lincoln spoke on the site of the Battle of Gettysburg itself; his model Pericles spoke over the ashes of men that had been brought home from distant battles. But the chasm of two millennia was bridged, and our genealogical line remains clear: both men spoke in the presence of the names of the dead in order to rhetorically reconstitute the community of the living through an evocation of the dead.[17]

We can narrow our focus to one particular lineage: lists of names of the dead of war. The form is ancient, and it offers the sort of precision that Mr. Cogito wants. But such lists are by turns common or rare over the millennia. Archeologists have discovered and epigraphers have identified between thirty and forty casualty lists on Athenian monuments and sixteen in other places, going back to a black lava stone with nine names, magically preserved from the eighth century

B.C.E., which was discovered on the island of Thera. A meticulous study of public burials (the so-called Patrios Nomos) from the fifth and fourth centuries B.C.E. has provided a cumulative record of the names of almost fourteen hundred dead soldiers, many with their tribes and a few with their ranks given. All of this, of course, is in addition to the names on individual tomb memorials (*mnema*) described in the *Iliad*, which "remain without moving, changeless . . . over the tomb of a man or woman who has died," fixed in stone in contrast to the mutability of flesh. Given the custom in ancient Athens of reading inscriptions aloud, every voice gave life again to the names on the stone (figs. 6.1, 6.2).[18]

These lists are so precise and so carefully constructed because their makers needed to know the names of the dead. This was not always the case in antiquity. Sometimes, only some names mattered. The *Iliad*, the archetype of Western memorial poems, records 234 names. This is explicitly a select number. Thersites, the one ordinary soldier who is named among the thousands who must have died on the plains of Troy, is present as a cautionary joke, a reason the list is short. "Insubordinate, baiting the kings—anything to provoke some laughter from the troops," he makes a cameo appearance in book 2 to speak for the commonality and announce that he and his like have had enough and would like to go home. Odysseus tells him to shut up or be stripped of the clothes that cover his private parts and be whipped back to the ship: "So stop your babbling, mouthing the names of kings." Exit Thersites. The Romans, in so many ways heirs to the Greeks, did not collectively commemorate their war dead by name at all.

And in the feudal armies of Europe no one demanded to know

6.1. Greek inscription: List of citizens killed on the field of honor (the dead of the Athenian tribe of Erechteides). Athenian Casualty Lists, ca. 460–459 B.C.E. Louvre, Paris.

PATTON EUGENE G · · · SIGNALMAN 3C · · · USNR
PAUL LEWIS FRANKLIN · · SEAMAN IC · · · USNR
PAULEY ERNEST CALVIN · APPRENTICE SEAMAN · · USNR
PAULLIN DELMER L · · · SHIP'S COOK 3C · · · USN
RAYNE WEST A · · · SEAMAN IC · · · USN
PEACOCK HAROLD C · · LIEUTENANT · · · USN
PEACOCK JAMES T · · · SEAMAN 2C · · · USN
PEARCE STANLEY B · · GUNNER'S MATE 3C · · · USN
PEARSON GEORGE A · · MACHINIST'S MATE 3C · USNR · PE
PEASE HARRY NORMAN · · APPRENTICE SEAMAN · · USN
PECHAR ARTHUR J · · · SEAMAN IC · · · USN
PECKHAM JAMES R · · · COXSWAIN · · USNR · · C
PEDERSON WENDLE A · · APPRENTICE SEAMAN · · USN
PEEBLES DORIES R · · APPRENTICE SEAMAN · · USN
PEELER CLARENCE N · · FIREMAN 3C · · USNR · · NORT
PELLETIER PAUL ROMEO · SEAMAN 2C · · USN · · MA
PELTIER WALLACE J · · SEAMAN IC · · · USNR
PELUCH MARTIN FRANK · · MACHINIST'S MATE 2C · · US
PENCEK RICHARD V · · AVN RADIOMAN 2C · · USNR
PENDLETON ANDREW J JR · RADIOMAN IC · · USNR
PENDLETON ROBERT G · · SEAMAN IC · · · USNR
PENNINGTON JESSE M JR · LIEUTENANT (JG) · · USNR
PEOPLES ROBERT G · · · FIREMAN IC · · USNR
PERATT GARRETT H JR · · SHIP'S COOK 3C · · USN
PERCIVAL PETER S · · · USNR
PERISTERE VICTOR L · · PHARMACIST'S MATE 3C · · US
PERKINS GEORGE A · · · QUARTERMASTER 3C · · USN
PERKINS ROBERT L · · SEAMAN IC · · USN · · NO
PERRAULT JOSEPH L C · · SEAMAN 2C · · USNR
PERRY DEWEY PORTLAND · APPRENTICE SEAMAN · · US
PERRY DONALD D · · · ENSIGN · · USNR
PERRY HOWARD B · · MACHINIST'S MATE IC · · USN
PERRY JOHN · MACHINIST'S MATE 2C · · USNR · · M
PERRY LEROY E · · BOATSWAIN'S MATE IC · USNR
PERRY NORMAN A · · GUNNER'S MATE 2C · · US

6.2. List of casualties at the Second World War Memorial in Battery Park, New York.

with any precision either the number or the names of the multitudes of those dead in battle. They did not matter. We know the names, in fiction and in archives, of those who did matter for the story at hand, and no more. Twelve peers are named in the *Song of Roland;* we know the names of the hero's sword (Durendal) and his horse (Veillantif); we know the names of seventy of his slain aristocratic Saracen enemies; but of the twenty thousand soldiers he is said to have had with him we know nothing. The same is true of Japanese feudal armies. Of thirty thousand horsemen—the number is fantasmic— who purportedly marched from the capital to Muro in Harima on the twelfth day of the ninth month in the battle of Uji Bridge, the medieval *Tale of Heike* lists twenty-six, with a few more named later; of a force of "twenty-eight thousand riders [that] crossed Kohatayama and bore down on Uji Bridge," the war tale names thirteen.[19]

If we imagine Mr. Cogito's need to know names and numbers as the product of cultural gene, we might say that it is found at the very beginning of recorded history and that the way it is expressed—its phenotype—has changed little. Greek lists are very much like twentieth-century ones in spirit if not in length. But this imagined gene is relatively inactive in certain times and places; the names of particular dead, like particular bodies, matter because of the ways in which the living want to know and care for them. An example from the most famous instance of naming—and not naming—the dead of war in Western literature illustrates the point. Shakespeare puts in the mouth of Henry V before the late medieval battle of Agincourt a speech that might lead us to expect that, after the battle, the audience would hear a complete list of the names of dead:

> . . . then shall our names,
> Familiar in his mouth as household words
> Harry the king, Bedford and Exeter,
> Warwick and Talbot, Salisbury and Gloucester
> Be in their flowing cups freshly remembered.
> This story shall the good man teach his son:

And Crispin Crispian shall ne'er go by,
From this day to the ending of the world,
But we in it shall be remembered;
We few, we happy few, we band of brothers;
For he today that sheds his blood with me
Shall be my brother; be he ne'er so vile,
This day shall gentle his condition.

But we know that those "vile" will not get a name either in the play or in any public forum. That is, they will be gentled and made a brother on the day of Saints Crispin and Crispian, martyred twin patrons of leatherworkers and shoemakers. The reason is not that no one knew their names but that for memorial purposes no one had an interest in them.

After the battle, Henry reads the names of the dead. "Where is the number of our English dead?" he asks his herald, who hands him a list. It says:

Edward the Duke of York, the Earl of Suffolk,
Sir Richard Ketley, Davy Gam, esquire:
None else of name; and of all other men
But five and twenty.

This is far too low a number for the nameless dead, and Shakespeare knew it. His source, Holinshed's *Chronicles,* says twenty-five is believable only "if you will credite such as write miracles." "Writers of greater credite," he says "affirme that were slaine about five or sixe C. persons." But of course Shakespeare did not have to credit miracles. He had plenty of excuses in case he needed any. How many names an audience would listen to, for example. And he was being true to both the historical setting of the play and his own time. It was difficult to determine the precise number of deaths on a battlefield, or anywhere for that matter, before the advent of twentieth-century record-keeping and identification techniques. But the great disparity in this case and in others for centuries to come was the result of neither artistic discretion (although that explains *Henry V* in particular) nor technological failures but rather of having no reason to obtain accurate totals of the dead—in the Hundred Years' War or in any other war during those centuries—or to publicly proclaim their names. The wildly different figures given mattered mostly for propaganda purposes, and the names of particular causalities mattered only for administrative ones.[20]

Contemporaneous English accounts of the battle of Agincourt list between fourteen dead on the English side—the four that Shakespeare names plus ten archers—and one hundred. Generally reliable contemporaneous French sources offer estimates of the English dead that range from four hundred to sixteen hundred. The discrepancies between these and other estimates were the result of each chronicler's decision about which of the dead needed to be counted—"esquire," a category of the gentry just below knight, is about as far down the social ladder as any English commentator was willing to go (or French source, with respect to the French dead). "None else of name," in the context of the criteria for counting the dead, has a technical meaning in late medieval feudal armies. Davy Gam, or David Gamme as he appears in his Indenture of Jewels, is the lowest-ranking man who made a direct contract with the king to provide troops for his army. He engaged to serve with one lancer and three archers, and in return the king contracted to pay a certain amount, guaranteed by the value of jewels, to cover the costs for which the king was responsible. By contrast, Edward, Duke of York, the king's first cousin, indented to bring with him one baronet, four knights, and three hundred archers; in return, he had one of the royal crowns in pledge. From the point of view of the king and his administrators, these were the names that mattered after the battle. The French cared just as little about who, below the armorial-bearing classes, became a casualty of war: one list claims that 10,000 men died and names 228, a little over 2 percent; another gives the names of 75 out of an estimated 4,075 dead, a little under 2 percent; a source called "Religeaux" (after the monk of nearby St. Denis to whom it is attributed) names 11 out of 4,011, a quarter of 1 percent of the dead.

Under other administrative conditions, however, the king and those who entered into an agreement with him were more interested in who died. Muster or retinue rolls recorded who actually showed up at various times, from the departure of troops from England to their entering the battle itself. When accounts were finally submitted to the exchequer at the end of the campaign, the king and those to whom he owed money had to arrive at an accounting of who was in Normandy and for how long, based on these records. The Crown, for example, might not have to pay for men who had died in the port of Honfleur before the battle started. And historians can use these documents to construct for their own purposes a remarkably complete list of the names of soldiers below the rank of esquire. We now know the names of 5,116 archers present at Agincourt. Some names of the dead that we have learned from contemporary reports are absent from some lists because they fell outside the scope of the paperwork needed to put men on the field of battle. The bishop of Norwich, for example, died on the expedition, but since he held no indenture with the king, he is not noticed in the rolls. The names of men who went to France but were not part of a military entourage—carpenters, blacksmiths, doctors, priests—are also absent.[21]

It would have been irrelevant to Shakespeare's or anyone else's poetic, political, or memorial purposes to find the names of the many hundreds more English soldiers and to determine their fates. Sir Robert Bapthorpe, comptroller of the king's household, prepared a list down through the ranks that trailed off as it descended the social scale well below esquire: "Thomas Fysh with other Labourers of the Hall," "William Temple, master carpenter with other carpenters," "Robert Mitchell and other fletchers" (makers of arrows). The four archers in the service of the fallen Sir Richard Ketley were William de Holland, John Greenleaf, Robert de Bradshaw, and Gilbert Howson. We do not know their fates. And we know that the social cutoff for being named became more stringent. When Robert Glover, Somerset Herald from 1571 to 1588, copied Bapthorpe's list more than a century later, he left off everyone below Men-Arms (i.e., esquire), giving only the numbers present. In a sense, the ordinary dead did not have names of the sort that Barthes imagines in this chapter's epigraph. The names of ordinary soldiers, as in the *Iliad*, are there mostly as comic relief. They are generic, not real names: Pistol, a nickname; Michael Williams, a stock Welshman.[22]

By contrast, "name" in this play and others as well—*Coriolanus, Richard II, Much Ado about Nothing*—takes its meaning from blood, rank, and place in a feudal order, and from membership in a "band of brothers" that presumes a fictive kinship subsumed in the name of the king. A messenger replies to Leonato's question, "How many gentlemen have you lost in this action?" with the news, "but few of any sort and none of name." Percy says to Northumberland in *Richard II* (2.3.56–59):

> There stands the castle, by yon tuft of trees,
> Manned with three hundred men, I have heard
> And in it are the Lords of York, Berkeley, and Seymour
> None else of name and noble estimate.

Name designates (that is, refers uniquely to) a person of consequence. "Thou desireth to kill my name in me," John of Gaunt says: "Oh how that name befits my compositions." Ultimately, it designates the king's body as encompassing his eternal body and his kingdom. As Richard II asks, is not the king's name twenty thousand names?

"Arm, Arm my name." York, Berkeley, Suffolk, Seymour, Northumberland, and Talbot are names that collectively constitute a body politic. Political theology determines their claim to a place on the list. Dead or alive, these are names that have public consequences, and the name of the king above all: "Oh that I were as great as my grief or lesser than my name," bemoans Shakespeare's Richard II. "Must he lose," he says, speaking of himself in the third person, "the name of King? A God's name, let it go." As he becomes not-king, he becomes a man of no name. The name "King," so sacred, so seemingly solid, is so terrifyingly fragile that "the breath of worldly man can dispose of it."[23]

The names of the dead in Shakespeare, in the various chronicles and accounts on which he drew or could have drawn, on Greek stelae, on Chinese ancestral tablets, or in epics of various sorts were all collected and written down to recover and preserve those who mattered for the making of a particular memorial community. The names of the dead that figured in narratives or genealogies were worth writing for a variety of public or private reasons. They were filled with the lives of those who needed a denouement. Specifically, "none else of name" in *Henry V* makes a political and cultural claim; it is ostentatiously not a statement of fact. "Of all other but four and twenty" bears no more relationship to reality than any of the other numbers given by various chroniclers from whom Shakespeare might have drawn. Sufficient unto the day are the collection of names that count.

NAMES OF THE DEAD IN TIMES OF PEACE

Names of the civilian dead are mobilized for different purposes than those of the dead of war but share a common genealogy. Again, the forms for the deployment of these names—their genetic code, and most of the ways in which it is expressed—are very old. Their appearances resemble those of the war dead. But the frequency and purposes for which these dead are named—or not named—have changed dramatically over time. I survey the history of these changes in deep time not to make a specific causal connection between two historically distant instances of naming the dead—the medieval *liber memorialis* and the AIDS Memorial Quilt, for example—but to demonstrate their phylogenetic connections and to suggest that their cultural ecologies are structurally similar.

The number of names of the dead proportionate to population has fluctuated over the past several thousand years. The names of the dead are ubiquitous in classical antiquity: thousands of the dead of war; hundreds of thousands of others. They proclaim lives and deaths and relationships to those who pass by and to an imagined community of the living more generally. Their numbers declined sharply at the end of the classical era, although probably not directly as a result of Christian beliefs about death and memory. There are tens of thousands of paleo-Christian tombstones and markers that connect the living—those who write the name—to the special dead and the bodies nearby. But as the care of the dead became less and less the responsibility of families and more and more that of the Church, names became rarer and rarer. By the sixth century, even the tombs of important people went unidentified. Decline in literacy played some part in this; a community of the dead became more important than their individual identities and numbers; the public to whom names might be proclaimed shrank. These were the Dark Ages of the necronym.[24]

But Christianity found new ways and new reasons to write the dead in memory, not over their bodies but in texts that were the parchment version of collective burial places on which certain of the dead could be singled out to be remembered. Lists hundreds of names long began to appear on hinged tablets—diptychs—in the early Middle Ages, first in the Eastern and then in the

Western Church. They were read out during mass—those of the living and the dead—begging mercy for their souls. By the eighth century, a specialized form, a new kind of list of the dead, took their place: the monastic *liber memorialis*. As these memorial books were written in codices rather than on tablets, the scale of naming increased dramatically. A book compiled by the Benedictine Abbey at Reichenau on Lake Constance in the ninth century held the names of forty thousand men and women who were remembered in the prayers of the monks. Fifty-eight scribes, many of them nuns, compiled a helter-skelter list of 11,500 names in the *liber memorialis* of the Benedictine convent and abbey of Remiremont in the Vosges over a period of three centuries: name after single name, "NOMINA DEFUNCTORUM. Hiltibrahit, Vogo, Rihgovuo, Gerhart, Meginuuarc ... Judit ... Goca ... Emma," and on and on. An enormous geographically dispersed library thus made a whole host of the dead present (fig. 6.3).[25]

These codices of names had a specific function that is different from most of the lists of the names of the dead in the past few centuries: they named the names of those to be remembered during the celebration of the mass. But they also, like the modern list, made the dead present to one another and to a wide community of the living. The men and women whose names appeared in the *liber memorialis* were not related by blood and were not, in fact, buried together in a common place. But, by virtue of being together in a book kept by a monastery, they became fictive kin in fictive sacred ground. If the dead in the parish churchyard or on the grounds of a monastery constituted the Christian community of

6.3. *Liber Memorialis* of Remiremont. Facsimile edition in the *Monumenta Germaniae Historica* (Weidemann, 1970).

a place, a piece of ground that bore layers of bodies, in deep time, then, by analogy, the *liber memorialis* wrote a distant and dispersed group of the dead together over many centuries. It included monks and nuns in the house on whose altar the "Book of Life" was placed as well as those from other houses with which they had fraternal relations, but written into the book too were lay men and women who, as patrons and donors to these houses, became allied with one another. Many were alive at the time they were inscribed, but over the decades and centuries the lists became an overwhelming record of the names of the dead. The lists are untidy; they are not written in chronological order and are not meant to tell a story. Each page is as lumpy as a churchyard full of bodies. Names are squeezed in near other names through which an alliance was being made, just as a body might be squeezed into an ancestral tomb or into a monastic burial ground near the body of one of the special dead. The names of those still living when they were first inscribed join the dead so that they all came together as if their bodies rested in the same ground where succeeding generations could visit them. Parchment became a common space. It was laid on an altar during masses; the names were present as a priest offered prayers for the salvation of this particular carefully knit together community of the dead—this book of life—that was the earthly representation, one hoped, of the record kept by God of those that live in Him.[26]

Still more names of the dead were listed in the new necrologies that began to appear in the middle of the ninth century, shortly after the first *liber memorialis.* By definition, necrologies included only the names of the dead, mostly the dead of a particular monastic community, and were organized chronologically by date of death of the person who once filled that name. Unlike the *liber memorialis,* these necrologies were not laid on the altar during mass but were meant to remind celebrants to offer prayers for the souls of this particular cohort of the dead on the anniversary of their deaths at a specific point in the liturgy: a reminder to speak the names to God. In addition to these long necrologies another new form developed: more or less individual circulating necrologies, so-called mortuary rolls (fig. 6.4). To produce these, monasteries and convents would write the names of particularly distinguished members who had died on a scroll, which was then carried around by a special messenger to other houses, which added an epitaph or comment of some sort and a promise to pray for the deceased on the anniversary of his or her death (i.e., added his or her name to its necrology, its calendric reminder list of names for which to pray on the death date of the person to whom the name once belonged). Eventually, the names of less distinguished members were appended as strips, the equivalent of medieval "sticky notes," to these rolls. The longest among these rolls were more than ten meters and joined one name to all sorts of commemorative poetry from all over Europe; some take sixty, seventy, eighty pages of print to make them available to modern readers. A few might make the rounds to two or three hundred monasteries and convents, a kind of traveling parchment tombstone that joined name, commentary, and the fictive presence of the dead whose bodies were in but one place. Maps that modern scholars have prepared look at first like the dense European railway maps of the nineteenth century but, on closer viewing, lack their metropolitan focus. The names of these dead followed paths—more intricate and less geometrically organized—that connected communities of memory paths.[27]

The soteriology of the medieval Church and of a particular universe of religious institutions dedicated to preserving the memory of the dead in the interests of souls became ever more generative of necronyms in the High Middle Ages. Monasteries kept lists of the names of the dead who had left bequests to ensure that the monks would pray for their souls for some number of years or forever. Endowments of land called chantries, dedicated to paying for one or more priest or priests to pray for a list of benefactors and their kin, kept their lists too. Because they required licenses under thirteenth-century statutes of mortmain that were meant to keep inheritances out of Church hands as much as possible, we know the numbers of these in England by the fifteenth century with some precision: 2,734. Some were freestanding; many were attached to parish churches and competed openly with monasteries in the market for memory and the work of helping the souls of the dead. An even larger number of names in England appeared on so-called bede rolls, which were lists of people from a parish or a guild who were to be prayed for. These names of the dead too, like the dead in the churchyard, constituted a legible collectivity, a palimpsest of a community—a parish, a guild, a confraternity—over centuries. As with all lists and maps and landscapes, the bede rolls were meaningful because

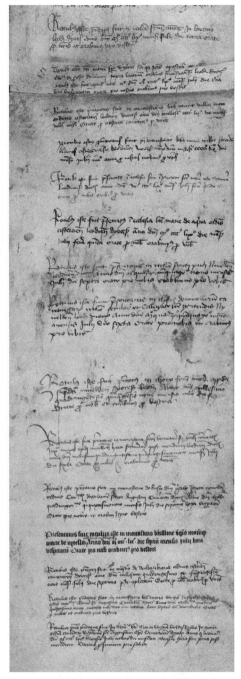

6.4. Mortuary Roll of Elizabeth Sconincx, 17th abbess of Foret, now Vorst, 1458–1459. Rylands Medieval Collection, Manchester University, Latin MS 114.

of whom they excluded as much as whom they included. The names written on the bede rolls of a parish were distinguished by being remembered, not as just one of a great anonymous population of the dead like those who lay unnamed under the mounds of the churchyard, but as someone in particular, as a person of note: someone who had provided the parish with a cloth or a chalice or who had repaired the fabric at some time in the building's long history. The price for entry onto such a roll could be low, affordable by modest people. Guilds, as corporate bodies, also kept lists of these names, but getting one's name on one of these was more expensive. They included current members, but these names were soon dwarfed in number by the names of the dead, stretching back for centuries, that the living had obligated themselves to remember in perpetuity. These lists could be very long. The Bede Roll of the Fraternity of St. Nicholas, the brotherhood of parish clerks in London, for example, accumulated seven thousand names between 1449 and 1521: nine hundred are the names of clerks; the rest comprise the names of their wives, of a sprinkling of honorary members, and of more than six hundred Londoners of the middling sort who hoped for a better sort of funeral mass and subsequent prayers for their souls than could be provided by the average parish.[28]

Over several millennia and in very different places and situations, names and aggregations of the names of the dead have abided with the living. They bring the dead into the present and keep them there for a time. The reasons for doing this for so long vary enormously: a Christian necrology shares little of what we might call theological function with a medieval Jewish memorial book that records the names and deeds of the most learned of the community; the six hundred named dead from Crusader violence in medieval Mainz share very little of the civic military culture of fifth-century B.C.E. Attic Greece and are also far from the memory books of post-Holocaust towns and villages that bind together a worldwide network of survivors. The reasons for making monastic necrologies and *liber memorialis* share little with the reasons for making the AIDS Quilt (plate 13).

But all of these cases are phylogenetically linked. They share the meaning of names; they share the enormous anthropological weight of the names of the dead that are filled with the person they once denoted. They also share, although in very different ways and to different degrees, the ways in which the names of the dead, like the names of the living, like the name of Mme de Guermantes for Swann, live in each of us: "At an age when Names, offering us the image of the unknowable that we have invested in them and simultaneously designing a real place for us, force us accordingly to identify the one with the other to a point where we go off to a city to seek out a soul that it cannot contain but which we no longer have the power to expel from its name[,] . . . [s]ometimes, hidden deep in her name, the fairy is transformed by the needs of our imaginative activity through which she lives; this is how the atmosphere surrounding Madame de Guermantes . . . began to lose its colors."[29]

They also share the capacity of names, like bodies, to create community between the living and the dead over time. The Corpus Publicum that is manifest in modern collections of the names of the dead is in one sense completely foreign to the Corpus Christi of the necrology or memory book: one is exclusively of this world, the other bridges the earthly and the divine. But in another sense it is not. By a magic that we can believe in, we secular moderns make worlds of the names of the dead. It is a magic that works at the individual level. We write the names of the dead and particulars of their age and sex on a coffin: "records how shadowy," as the early-nineteenth-century essayist Thomas De Quincey put it, "dropped into darkness as messages addressed to worms." And it is a magic that works collectively as we gather names as if to make the death once again present to us.[30]

The next two chapters address two questions about the modern appropriation of the dead. First, by what means—technical, political, and emotional—have we come to record names on the unprecedented scale that is now available to us? What makes it possible, and what drives our desire to write and speak the names of the dead? And second, what are the consequences of change—quantitative and qualitative—in the history of the names of the dead? At the intersection of the state, civil society, and the inner lives of millions, the age of necronominalism comes into existence.

Chapter 7

THE RISE OF THE NAMES OF THE DEAD IN MODERN HISTORY

the exact number of dead
in an airplane catastrophe is easy to determine

it's important to the heirs
the insurance companies
plunged into mourning

we take the list of the crew
and passengers
after each name
draw a cross

a little harder in the event of
a rail accident

you must reassemble the bodies torn apart
so that not one head
remains ownerless

at the time of natural
disaster
counting
becomes
complicated

we count the survivors
and an unknown remainder

neither known to be alive
nor definitively deceased
are given the bizarre name
of the lost

they still have a chance
to return to us
from fire
water
the center of the earth

ZBIGNIEW HERBERT, "MR. COGITO ON
THE NEED FOR PRECISION"

Some of the dead—those who die in an airplane crash, for example—are easier to count and then to draw crosses beside their names than others. But not all of those who plunge from the air are counted: not the deported migrant workers who died in flames at Los Gatos Canyon, near Coalinga, in 1948, remembered in Woody Guthrie's last great protest song, "Deportee (Plane Wreck at Los Gatos)." They seem beneath notice:

> Goodbye to my Juan, goodbye, Rosalita,
> Adios mis amigos, Jesus y Maria;
> You won't have your names when you ride the big airplane,
> All they will call you will be "deportees."

The names of the pilot and security guards were printed in the *New York Times* and other papers; the twenty-eight Mexican workers who died with them were unnamed—"just deportees"—and buried anonymously.

> The sky plane caught fire over Los Gatos Canyon,
> A fireball of lightning, and shook all our hills,
> Who are all these friends, all scattered like dry leaves?
> The radio says, "They are just deportees."

These dead, beneath notice, were buried in a mass grave—"Mexican Nationals 1–18"—in a nearby Catholic cemetery. Sixty years later, through the efforts of the poet and novelist Tim Hernandez and an aged cemetery worker, their names were recovered. And the site became a memorial around which the dead hovered: "Abuelo, Tio, estoy aqui" (Grandfather, Uncle, I am here). The nameless had a resting place: "Mi'jo, I can go in peace now that I know where my brother was buried." And yes, the counting does become harder at the time of natural disaster but not always for technical reasons. We know that 439 miners died in a purported "natural disaster" in the Senghenydd coal pit explosion of 1913, their bodies in some cases mutilated beyond recognition. Only in 1981 was a memorial bearing their names erected near this small Welsh town: after each name a cross at last.[1]

It has always been the case that names have stood in for, or pointed to, the bodies of the dead. They are their spectral mates. But the names of the dead have also multiplied dramatically for two sets of reasons. First, administrative changes: insurance companies do need to know; so do lawyers; so does the state, which tracks natural disasters, among so much else, for its own reasons. And second, this burgeoning of records results from moral and emotional exigencies that have their own historical trajectories: Mr. Cogito's "need for precision" arises from the heart.

Let me work from an imaginative ending to this story of comprehensive naming back to its beginning. The narrator in a short story by the Serbian writer Danilo Kiš discovers an "Encyclopedia of the Dead" in a Swedish library. A strange sect, he reports, had undertaken the "difficult and praiseworthy task" of recording "everything that can be recorded concerning those who have completed their earthly journey"; the narrator is struck as he begins to examine this gargantuan corpus—there are thousands of "M" volumes alone—by the absence of famous names; it turns out that no names that have appeared in any other encyclopedia or that are in any way well known appear. "Mazuranic," who wrote the grammar book his father used in school, is not in it, and neither is Dagoslav Maksimovic, a "lathe operator and socialist deputy his grandfather had known." On the other hand, the date of birth of his peasant grandmother, the cause of her fatal illness and death, the names of those who laid her out and who made the casket, and where they got the wood, and many other details are there: everything that "could be recorded concerning those who have completed their earthly journey." Somehow the Great War is there too: "trains clanking past a market town, a brass band playing, water gurgling in the neck of a canteen, glass shattering, kerchiefs fluttering . . ." Perhaps this is a hint of the millions of names soon to be added to lists of the dead.[2]

The sect that kept the encyclopedia stressed "an egalitarian vision of the world of the dead" that aimed at "redressing human injustices and granting all God's creatures an equal place in eternity." The fictional "Encyclopedia of the Dead" had a relatively limited chronological reach; it began only after 1789 and depended for its information on the labors of teams of "erudites" who pored over obituaries—a form of necrology that blossomed beginning in the late eighteenth century—and imagined bits of posthumous biographical information, name by name, for everyone who had died over almost two centuries. None among the dead were lost.[3]

This ledger, this "Book of Life," this impossible Borgesian mnemonic fantasy, in which, as in the mind God, there is no forgetting, would drive a reader to insanity. But it serves to introduce the political, technological, and emotional foundations of the new expansive modern regime of naming the dead. It represents an egalitarian view not just of the world of the dead but also of the world of the living: every person has recorded, and deserves to have recorded, a life and a death. Records exist—obituaries, for example—that begin to make this possible. And there are people who have a commitment to the task of naming and describing the ordinary dead without exclusion, as did the sect Kiš describes, those who may already have been noticed elsewhere. The imagined "Encyclopedia of the Dead" depends on the changes that made possible the vast project of naming the dead in the past two centuries.

Kiš claimed in a posthumously published postscript to have discovered that there is in real life a religion with a commitment similar to that of the sect he imagined: it is the Mormons. The Church of Jesus Christ of Latter-day Saints owns the greatest storehouse in the world of the names of the dead and has the greatest institutional expertise in elaborating their genealogical connections. Of the 26 billion people that LDS estimates were born between 1500 and 2010, about 8 billion are documented. It has already indexed and published online 3.3 billion names and believes that in the 900 million photographs of records that it has also published, many more unindexed names appear. Vast as the number born since 1500 is, the number born before then is even larger. Demographers calculate that between 82 billion and 108 billion people have been born and died since the beginning of humankind; if we subtract 26 billion from these estimates we get 56 billion to 82 billion people born before 1500. Very few names of this multitude survive in extant historical records.

These dead have almost entirely disappeared, some because records in which they might have appeared have been destroyed, many more because their names were never written down anywhere. These vanished into the air. The remaining 26 billion names—those born after 1500—fare much better. Almost a quarter of these are documented in some record or another, the portion rising at the beginning of the nineteenth century. These named names, the known survivors among the dead, are stored in six gigantic vaults, protected against even the most devastating hydrogen bomb attack, below seven hundred feet of granite in the Wasatch mountain range; access to them is through three tunnels guarded by fourteen-ton doors. A laboratory sits a few hundred feet higher up, under three hundred feet of rock.[4]

This archive reflects the two parts of my story. The chronological contours of the collection are the result of administrative changes after 1500 and even more far-reaching ones after the late eighteenth century. But the reason for collecting names in the first place is rooted in civil society—a religious organization—and in the hearts of its nineteenth-century founders. Perhaps it was God who told Joseph Smith that the dead were imprisoned and that it was the duty of the members of his new church to release them from darkness through baptism. The idea was old—some early Christian churches baptized the dead. And it had roots in prophecy: the Messiah would "bring out the prisoners from the prison, and them that sit in darkness out of the prison house"; "he hath sent me to bind up the brokenhearted, to proclaim liberty to the captives, and the opening of the prison to them that are bound" (Isa 42:6 and 6:1). Jesus preached to the spirits of the dead. In its execution it was very nineteenth century. Brigham Young impressed upon the followers of Smith—the people who became the Church of Jesus Christ of Latter-day Saints—that "the doctrine of baptism for the dead is a great doctrine, one of the most glorious doctrines that was revealed to the human family," that it entailed redeeming "the nations of the world," and that it was done "for the inhabitants of the earth" without exception.[5] This required identifying with genealogical precision specific unredeemed dead souls and retroactively baptizing them in a special temple ritual.

The vast storehouse of names in Utah was assembled to make this possible, to mobilize the dead into a new communion. Not everyone is happy with these activities. There was a great controversy when in 1995 it was discovered that the LDS had retroactively baptized many Jewish victims of the Holocaust, including Simon Wiesenthal's mother, who had been murdered in Belzec. Leaving baptism aside, these names belonged on the lists of others of the living. The Church apologized, but controversies keep flaring up. According to a former member—a whistle-blower—Anne Frank was retroactively baptized in February 2012 by a temple in San Salvador, thus violating a 2010 agreement to stop the practice; Daniel Pearl, the journalist murdered by Islamic radicals in 2002, was baptized in the summer of 2011 by a temple in Twin Rapids, Idaho.[6]

The archive as it stands is possible because of the dramatic rise in the state's interest in names, in births and deaths, and in record keeping more generally. The parish register (with respect to the names of the dead) and the rise of the census (for names more generally) represent a huge shift in the class of names thought worth recording. The year 1500 is not a magic moment in world history, of course, but we can take it as a sign of the age of necronominalism to come. In 1538, Henry VIII ordered that each priest maintain and keep safe a register of all baptisms, births, and burials in his parish. In 1539, Francis I, probably influenced by English practice, issued the so-called ordinance of Villers-Cotterêts, which required priests to record baptisms and burials. (Marriages were added in 1579.) The ordinance also codified and froze medieval naming practices so that an increasingly circumscribed set of surnames was now passed on through the generations. French revolutionary laws of naming also had the effect of both limiting the number of permissible names and making them very difficult to change. It was the church authorities, Lutheran and Catholic, who also started to insist on parish registration during the course of the sixteenth century. Various states mandated parish records of births and deaths in the course of the seventeenth century: Sweden started to do so in 1686, and those areas controlled by Denmark came under such orders in 1646.

There were earlier precedents for a public interest names—for example, records of births, deaths, and marriages in medieval ecclesiastical jurisdictions, some far better than in others. And there are censuses. The Roman census, for example, especially in the republican period, was not primarily an exercise in determining how many people lived in any given jurisdiction and even less in recording their names but a civic and moral exercise of enumerating one category of people: citizens. It was a representation in writing of the names that mattered for a specific purpose or purposes, especially the declaration of taxable property and the assertion of membership in the class that enjoyed the legal protections of a Roman. Only citizens were required to appear before the office of the Censor to be named and to be counted: no minors, no women (unless they were not under anyone else's potestas), no slaves, generally no subject people. The remarkable Florentine Catasto of 1427 is far more thorough. It enumerates more than 260,000 people, many by name, because there were social and legal incentives for a head of family, especially a prominent one, to hand in as many names as possible. But the states came late to keeping lists of the names of those who were born and had died. Systematic censuses began only in the late eighteenth century with the rise of state interest in population. These did not record deaths, and at first recorded only heads of household by name—women were excluded, except if they fell into this category—but they did provide fodder for contemporaries and for modern demographers to find out who—at least which men—had died in intervals between each canvass. The surge in names from after 1500 and even more so after 1800 in the caves of Utah are to a large extent the product of the administrative state and its classification of those under its power; having a name entailed having a place within a juridical and political order. And inversely, not having a name meant the opposite. Slaves in the American South had no legally recognized names and are enumerated under the name of their owner by age, sex, and color—black or mulatto. There was a space reserved for noting whether any of the nameless slaves were deaf, dumb, blind, insane, or idiotic.[7]

Getting a fixed surname and subsequently also a necronym represented for some, starting in the eighteenth century, a state-mediated entry into civil society. The cases of slaves in the United States and of Russian serfs after emancipation are the most obvious: they had no legally recognized names of any sort before emancipation. "We were cussed for so many bitches and sons of bitches and bloody bitches . . . we never heard our names scarcely at all," a former Arkansas slave told an interviewer. Insofar as slaves had a surname, it was that of the master. When given a chance after emancipation, most slaves kept their first names, although many renamed themselves. Some, for the sake of historical or family connections, kept the surname of their former master; many did not and took new ones. But the big point is that to get a name was to become a person. "It is through our names that we place ourselves in the world," wrote Ralph Ellison, "our names being the gift of others must be made our own," meaning that the whole sordid history of slave names has to be imaginatively both incorporated and reimagined in the time after emancipation.[8]

In Britain, the modern pattern of a Christian and a surname had been in place since the thirteenth century. In law, everyone, including Jews and foreigners of other sorts and with the exception of only the crown and peers of the realm, had two names that differed profoundly from one another: the Christian name, given at baptism and confirmed later by a bishop, was Adamic—*the* name in all times and places—and could be changed only with the greatest difficulty. The surname was easily changed as long as there was no hint of fraud. In practice, however, some people's names counted more than others. "Even today," the barrister and heraldry expert Arthur Fox-Davies claimed in the early twentieth century, "there are hundreds of the lower classes who are only known by a Christian first name and nickname." He might have said: "their putative betters use only their first names." Women could, and almost universally did, take the surname of their husbands, but they were not required to do so. There is thus a long history of having fixed names but a shorter one of having them count.[9]

In much of continental Europe, the story for many people is closer to that of slaves in the United States. Various states demanded that, for civil purposes, those who did not have two names must get them: fixed and unchangeable ones. For Jews, the only people in Europe (with the exception of small groups in peripheral areas and large numbers of serfs in eastern Europe) who had no surnames, this was a major part of what has been called "emancipation." I take the Jewish case as exemplary of a longer and more diffuse history of one of the paths—state action—through which names came to matter in civil life and in death. In 1787, Emperor Joseph II issued a decree that all Jews in Hapsburg lands have a "constant" surname; the Napoleonic decree of 20 July 1808 did the same thing in France and areas under French control and insisted that Jews not adapt biblical patronymics. In Prussia, to take the best-known because the most tragic case, Jews were required, and had the right, to have two fixed names under the emancipatory degree of 11 March 1812. Acquiring civilly recognized names, like emancipation generally, raised with new intensity the question of what it meant to be a Jew as a member of a national community rather than a tolerated minority in a society of ranks and orders. Onomastics—the study of naming practices—became an instrument of government in the nineteenth century; just over a century later, National Socialist laws of naming would become an important part of the exclusion of Jews from civil and political life. But this was not inherent in the 1812 Prussian law; there were opportunities for those who got new names.[10]

The surnames that Jews took were sometimes traditional ones and sometimes names that marked them as Jews. Some were horrible, the malicious work of local clerks; some, the Jewish joke goes, were the sad result of not being able to pay a big enough bribe for a good name. Some were simply Jewish, the choice in a liberal era of those who wanted to keep old names: Levi, for example, or transliterations of classic Jewish first names: Bendix for Baruch, Markus for Mordechai. As names became fixed in a polity in which name change was difficult and expensive, anti-Semites in the late nineteenth century had no trouble naming the archetypal Jew: Cohn and Levi were traditional examples in German. There were famously ambiguous names—Rosenberg—and ones in which a small difference in spelling made all the difference: the old, aristocratic, Rhineland Katzenelnbogens and the rabbinic Rhineland Katzenellenbogens. Many new names followed general vernacular naming patterns: profession, place, patronymics—Davidsohn, Liebersohn. Women and children got real names for the first time, derived from those of their husbands or fathers. Thus, Gella Davidim, wife of David Bauer—a perfectly German surname—became Regina Bauerin; Brendl Gerstlin, daughter of Gerstle Jacob, became Regina Schwarzin when her father took the name Gottlieb Schwartz, a more ambiguous surname. Names were gendered: Jakob Gerstl, Gottlieb's son, became Jakob Schwartz. My own name, acquired in Prussian Silesia in the first decades of the nineteenth century, does not fit into any of these categories, but the souvenir book for the five hundredth anniversary celebration of the Johaneum Gymnasium in Hamburg attempts an explanation: opposite my father's name it says "Netzstricker (franz.)," meaning "from the French for fishnet maker."[11]

Jewish first names have a more conflicted story because they seemed to signal more acutely than surname the dangers of assimilation. On 6 July 1836, King Friedrich Wilhelm III of Prussia promulgated a decree that forbade Jews to "bear Christian baptismal names," which he hoped would finally put Jews back in a nominal ghetto. The decree led to considerable bureaucratic confusion because Jews and Christians, as numerous officials kept pointing out, shared many names. What to do about "Julius" for example? And all those German pagan "Christian" names? My great-grandfather, born in 1844 in Prussian lands, was Siegfried, and his father was named Joachim, I assume not after the husband of St. Anne; my grandfather, born in 1872, was Walther, and my father, born in 1910, was Werner.

And what about Christian women named Abigail and men named Abel, perfectly good saints with Jewish names? A battle for repeal of the Jewish naming law began.[12]

Leopold Zunz, a member of Heinrich Heine's circle and one of the founders of what we might call Jewish studies, made the case that the king's whole premise was nonsense: there was no such thing as a "Jewish name." One suspects that Zunz's massively researched *Namen der Juden* did little to assuage Friedrich Wilhelm's anti-Semitic scruples. Written as much for his fellow Jews as it was for the Prussian state, it showed that Jews had always taken the names of the people they lived among; the onomastic assimilation that the king feared was a historical reality. Antigonus of Soco was a great first-generation teacher of Mischna; Alexander, Amyta, and Andromicus begin the alphabetical list of names of Jews under Herod the Great; in the works of the great first-century Jewish historian Josephus, Zunz points out, there are a few old biblical names, there are a few newer ones, and there are lots of Persian and Syriac names in addition to the customary Roman and Greek ones. It was, he thought, only natural to take on the names of host nations and, in general, these nations through the ages expected no less. So, yes, of course: taking German names meant becoming German, assuming the status that the original Enlightenment emancipatory degrees had promised. He does not make the point, but a shift in civil status might (although it need not) result in a name change precisely because names were not as coded as they would become later on. Of the 3,330 Jews who converted to Christianity in Vienna between 1748 and 1868, only 45 percent changed their first names and less than 5 percent their surnames. Priests seemed content to regard a Jewish name as a Christian name at the baptismal font. The names of the Jewish dead—those of the Great War massed together at Weissensee in Berlin, for example, or in the vernacular cemeteries of the nineteenth century—represent an important, if unbearably sad, claim to be German (fig. 7.1). It could be made because of the Enlightenment history of getting a name in the first place.[13]

7.1. Graves of Jewish soldiers who died in World War I, Jewish Cemetery at Weissensee, Berlin.

There are similar changes in the relationships among civil status, names, and the state elsewhere. In Japan, for example, until the Meiji restoration, surnames (that is, family or clan names) were generally restricted—with the exceptions of a few famous writers or artists—to aristocratic and military families.

Everyone else was known by only one name. In 1868, everyone was allowed to take a family name, and in 1875, family names became compulsory. That is, everyone was allowed the sort of name that "onomastically linked . . . the individual's self to the self of the entire group, including his political office and territorial holding." All the things attached to the name—the rights, the ancestors—could now be claimed in the form of Everyman's name.[14]

One answer to the question, "What changed in the history of the names of the dead?" is the rise of vast new archives of names and facts about these names, created largely but not entirely at the behest of the state. It is a history intimately tied to the history of civil status. This is a necessary but not a sufficient answer. Why, we still need to ask next, does anyone outside of an administrative context come to care? We know the specific reason why the nineteenth-century Mormons cared. The question now is why people more generally came to care. And the answer to that question lies at the intersection between the intimate and the bureaucratic, the intersection of an administrative and a psychic infrastructure.

José Saramago's novel *All the Names* lives in this space. The protagonist, Senhor José, is nearly fifty but still only a junior clerk in the registry of births, marriages, and deaths in an unnamed city. He lives adjacent to its vast, limitless archive, in which the records of the long dead are closest to the desks of the clerks and the more recently deceased are in such deep recesses that those who need to examine them leave a thread, like Ariadne, so that they can find their way back to their desks. One genealogical researcher who did not take this precaution was found after a week in which he had survived by eating old death papers. Through a small, unused door in his flat, Senhor José has secret access to this great storehouse of names.

He customarily brightens his dull life by gathering from it information about famous people, but one day he steals by mistake the record card of an "unknown woman" and becomes driven to know more and more about her: about her life and about the circumstances of her death. He will use whatever tricks are necessary to rescue her from the obscurity of the labyrinthine cavern of forgotten names. The novel is about this obsession and the scrapes it gets him into as his search becomes ever more consuming and his superiors begin to suspect something. There is, he realizes, something absurd about the recovery of the dead through the written traces of their names: "It is a macabre exaggeration to call this the archive of the dead," he thinks to himself. The papers he has in his hands "are just paper, not bones, they're paper, not putrefying flesh." "That was the miracle worked by your Central Registry, transforming life and death into mere paper," he concludes.[15]

Senhor José's search takes him finally to a graveyard where, in a delirious dream, he sees Death, who with her scythe sweeps the ground "to make sure that the dead resign themselves to remaining dead." He encounters a surreal shepherd who walks with his sheep around the cemetery changing the names on tombstones so that all the dead get their fair share of mourning. And Senhor José discovers the grave of the young woman he has been searching for; he has in the course of his adventures learned a great deal about her, including the fact that she committed suicide. Meanwhile, the all-powerful godlike figure of the director of the archive has decided that the dead and the living will no longer be radically separated in the registry office that he rules. All the names will bridge the chasm of the two worlds that the cemetery keeps apart; the living, the recently dead, and the long dead come onto a continuum with those just born. There is a "double absurdity" in separating the dead from the living as had been the case: from an archival perspective it is stupid, because "the easier way of finding the dead would be to look for them among the living." But, the narrator continues, "it is equally absurd from a mnemonic point of view," because "if the dead are not kept in the midst of the living sooner or later they will be forgotten and then . . . it's the Devil's own job to find them when we need them, which, again, sooner or later we always do."[16]

Another way of asking the historical question becomes: What is it that makes Senhor José emotionally and psychologically plausible; what makes his quest, surreal as it is, comprehensible to readers? Broadly speaking, we already have a partial answer: the recognition of a right, a universal right to be written in death, to be mourned as a name that is filled by a person; the right to have a denouement. Or put differently, since the dead have no rights, the right of the living to the stories of the dead, which comes down to keeping them until "we need them." But this right is neither universal nor timeless. How then did it come to be, or more precisely, how did it come to be claimed by ever more people?

Let me put this concretely: How does one name of a working-class soldier, among the names 34,785 others who died in the Arras sector of the Battle of the Somme between early 1916 and August 1918 and who have no known grave, come to matter? The soldier was W. J. Martin, an infantry private and onetime groom. He wrote his fiancée, Emily Chitticks, a farm servant, seventy-five letters between August 1916, when he enlisted, and 27 March 1917, a couple of days before he was killed; she wrote twenty-three to "her Will," including five that he had not read; they were returned to her unopened and marked "KILLED." In 1921, she collected Will's letters into a bundle to which she added a chronology of their relationship, a penciled verse about how she won't see him on earth again, and a couplet in ink that read, "Sleep darling sleep, on foreign shore / I loved and love you dearly, but Jesus loves you more." There is also a note saying that she wanted the packet buried with her, just as her heart was already buried in Flanders' Field. Her life, she said, had ended with his. Emily Chitticks never married and died alone in a council estate. She left no known heirs. A neighbor found her papers after returning from her funeral and gave them to the Imperial War Museum.[17]

It is a remarkable letter exchange, for two reasons: it allows both of the correspondents to reveal their inner selves, to think themselves into each other's lives, and more specifically to imagine death and burial with a quite characteristic nineteenth-century sensibility. And, it exposes the infrastructure for these feats of the imagination: literacy, habits of letter writing, and a postal service, of course, but also a whole complex of genres—deathbed accounts in novels and other places, obituaries, ego-documentation of all sorts, poetry—that collectively sustained a new relationship of the living to the dead. Lives so connected, so imbricated in new narrative forms and new sensibilities, demand a different sort of closure than in earlier times. Writ small, the age of the necronym is built on an interstitial matrix of the emotions. "I have dreamt that you were back home with me dear," writes Emily, "and the most strange thing about them, you are always in civilian clothes when I dream of you, & I have never seen you in those dear, so it seems very strange. I hope that will come true. I only wish you were in civilians now." "You must forgive me dear," he writes to her, "if I was reserved on Tuesday night. I wanted to say a lot dear, but I knew that you couldn't stand it. I didn't want to make it worse for you dear. If I do not mistake dear I think you gave vent to your feelings before I was out of hearing." They share all manner of small news, the sort that produces texture—the reality effect—in domestic novels. "Two dear little puppies at Suffolk House," Emily reports in one of the five letters that were returned with "KILLED" on the envelope, "two little sheep dogs they are and they are so pretty and playful one cannot help loving them." He tells her about death at the front: "I have seen some graves today dear of Officers and men who were killed in action. They had wooden crosses and wood railings around the grave. They were really done off very nicely. Well dear Emily I hope you have received all my letters. . . ."

When she learns of his death, she is desperate to fit it into the sort of story that the two of them had been creating; she demands a denouement. Emily Chitticks wanted to know the exact circumstances of Will Martin's end. His comrades offered some details: "How can I thank you for the information you sent me." Emily writes back to a friend of his, "regarding my sweetheart Will Martin. It is a terrible blow to me, no one knows but myself what it means to me."

Emily's inquiries to the War Graves Commission regarding the location of Will's grave at first elicited what might have been a comforting reply. She was told in a letter dated 22 October 1917 that Pte. W. J. Martin was buried "at a point just S.W. of Ecoust St. Mein [a tiny commune in the Pas de Calais] which is S.E. of Arras." Subsequent inquiries asking for more precise details about his burial place brought forth more disturbing news. The site was in the midst of a battlefield and was destroyed in the back and forth of artillery duels and trench excavation.

No trace could later on be found of Will Martin; whether his body was unearthed without bearing any marks that would identify it or whether it disappeared into the general carnage cannot be known. After several inquiries, the WGC assured Emily Chitticks, however, that she could "rest assured that the dead who have no known resting place will be honoured equally with the others, and that each case will be dealt with upon full consideration of its merits as regarding the site and place of the memorial." Pte. Will Martin's name, along with more than thirty thousand others in similar circumstances, is on the memorial to the missing at Faubourg d'Amiens for soldiers lost in the Arras sector of the Battle of the Somme.

This exchange is dependent, of course, on the needs of the state: record keeping in the army. The state, however, had very little interest in satisfying the demands of Emily Chitticks until it was pushed. This letter exchange is predicated on an emotional and administrative infrastructure that came into being and is responding to "Emily Chitticks's Need for Precision," to paraphrase the title of the poem that stands at the head of this chapter. Most obviously, the postal service in war and peace offers the emotional skeleton for what happened between Will and Emily. This too has a history, albeit a short one. By one estimate, 180,000 letters passed through the hands of American Civil War soldiers every single day. This means that, on average, any one of them might well have received word from a loved one once a week. The making of what Drew Faust has called the "republic of suffering" is built to a great extent on this communicative infrastructure. By the early twentieth century, it had grown even further. During the Great War, the Home Depot staff that handled outgoing mail to the British army grew from a few dozen to more than 2,500 clerks; 5,500 clerks distributed it in the daily mail calls of the overseas troops; by September 1914, each corps on the western front had its own post office; by one well-informed estimate, two billion letters and papers moved through postal channels. By the first quarter of 1918, there were twelve million outbound letters. We do not know how many of these were the Field Service postcards issued free to soldiers after September 1914; an old history of the British Post Office says that all other responses to war by the Royal Mails pale by comparison to the hundreds of new items brought on line during the Great War. (The next war, it suggests, will "no doubt wipe out the Post Office altogether, along with the rest of such civilization as we have succeeded in attainting to.") And the communications avalanche does not count packages: just under five million in the month before Christmas 1916; a million a week in the following spring. The much-discussed chasm between the horrors of the trenches and the relative safety of home was real enough, but the army could get a letter from London to the front in a day.[18]

It is inconceivable that with so intense a communications nexus the humble Will Martins of this world could simply be allowed to disappear, as they largely had before the American Civil War. Or put differently, intimate connections were made and sustained by post that, in turn, had public consequences. Letters made possible the thousands upon thousands of inquiries and responses that constituted the enterprise of identifying, accounting, numbering, and caring. In civilian life, too, the sheer volume of letters per capita increased dramatically, and news of deaths was a common subject of ordinary familial correspondence.

The correspondence of Will and Emily is predicated also on the expectation that she would be interested in how her Will had died—in the denouement of his life—and would want to have precise details of where he was. In a general way, of course, this is what we might expect. The tradition of wanting to know the exact circumstances of death—last words, looks, gestures, signs of any sort—has a long history in the West. But now letter exchanges made it possible to know on a much broader stage through an infrastructure of literacy and communication. Both Emily and Will could write; both were born after the advent of universal compulsory primary education in 1880. Both read, or in any case they had absorbed, the psychological and literary tricks of the novel and other nineteenth-century literature. And the state helped them to keep in touch.

The new institutional and emotional infrastructure in which their correspondence could take place began to emerge in the eighteenth century in many different registers. At its most general and material level it grows out of the expectation that the deaths of humble people would, or ought to, be written: on stone, on paper, in stories of many different kinds. They demand attention; even the poor, also women, come to have names in death. The anxiety about the pauper funeral is evidence of this nascent sensibility. And so is the rise of the idea that Everyman might have an epitaph that had traditionally been reserved for the great and glorious.

In 1791, a minor poet named John Bowden published in Chester a three-part collection of epitaphs—*The Epigrammatic Microscope*, he called it on the last page—that was intended "for the use of those Artists who write and engrave epitaphs for the middle and lower ranks of society." It filled a niche. There already existed large and beautiful books of model epitaphs, but these are more suited to libraries than for purchase and use by artisans. He would not presume to give "satisfaction to the Gentry and Nobility," who had at their disposal far more learned poets than he to write inscriptions for their monumental tombs. His audience, he repeats, is the "middle and lower ranks of people," who have generally not been members of the epitaph-owning classes. Bowden, without recognizing it in his work, also fits into a shift in the attributes for which the ordinary dead might be remembered. Dr. Johnson had suggested that "the best subject for epitaphs was private virtue," virtues that the bulk of humanity might have a hope of attaining. Freeing his country from oppression or ignorance was not among these; overcoming poverty without succumbing to evil was more likely. Bowden thought that he was making a significant cultural contribution if he could show how to better remember the ordinary dead.[19]

There was, of course, always a danger that monuments would be false and pompous. People had been complaining about this problem since King Mausolus, and they did not stop in the eighteenth century. Vicisimus Knox, a much-read Anglican minister, schoolmaster, and moralist whom Bowden quotes, gives the old canard an eighteenth-century English inflection: "there is an elegance and classical simplicity in the turf-clad heap of mould which covers a poor man's grave, though it have nothing to defend it from the insults of the proud but a bramble." Again we hear the echo in that most culturally resonant of modern English poems, Thomas Gray's "Elegy Written in a Country Churchyard." But ordinary people are as much deserving of the mark of friendship that an epitaph represents as the great and mighty. The first fifty-three epitaphs Bowden proposes are short—only two lines; then come longer ones for specific categories of people—"a poor man strictly honest"; "a poor but laborious and honest man." About forty years later, in 1832, George Mogridge, a popular children's and religious book writer, published a new collection of five hundred epitaphs in the democratic mode that Bowden had begun (fig. 7.2). He would, he promised, make "little reference to rank and those distinctions in society, which in this life are so precarious, and which death destroys utterly." A classical genre that had been reborn in the Renaissance now seemed in reach of Everyman; quite ordinary people could imagine having their deaths and their names being written in stone. Critics took the point: the *Monthly Review* likened Bowden's "wholesale" couplets and stanzas to the work of the slop-tailor who makes coats and breeches "of all sizes and patterns, ready for chance customers." Epitaphs were no longer bespoke.[20]

The correspondence of Emily Chitticks and Will Martin and her insistence that she know the details of his life, death, and burial are part of a vast new narrative world in which the names of all sorts of the dead are written not only on tombstones but in many other ways as well. From the perspective of the sixteenth and seventeenth centuries, the mounting denseness of accounts of the lives and deaths of ordinary people in the late eighteenth and nineteenth centuries is astounding. We take it for granted: of course Emily Chitticks would want to know the exact circumstances of her Will's death. There had come to be recognizable forms, gestures, and moral norms that organized the couple's emotional world; an intimate domestic place had been made for Private W. J. Martin's distant death in the mud of the Somme. And Emily had a right to a narrative of her beloved's death and burial. That right grew from many small literary streams, across a range of genres that were engaged with how we die.

Recording narrative details of dying and of the care of the dead is not new; as a genre it has a long history in the West from Socrates and Seneca to Jesus and the saints to less distinguished deaths. But there were new forces at work after the eighteenth century that explain the demand for a precise accounting and collecting of the names of the dead of ordinary people. The literary marketplace in fiction and in reportage was one. Joseph Kaines's *Last Words of Eminent Persons* is a good example with which to begin because he self-consciously claims that he is offering his readers something new: a collec-

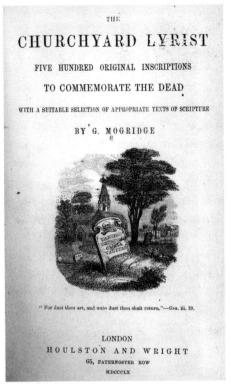

THE

CHURCHYARD LYRIST

FIVE HUNDRED ORIGINAL INSCRIPTIONS

TO COMMEMORATE THE DEAD

WITH A SUITABLE SELECTION OF APPROPRIATE TEXTS OF SCRIPTURE

BY G. MOGRIDGE

"For dust thou art, and unto dust thou shalt return."—*Gen.* iii. 19.

LONDON
HOULSTON AND WRIGHT
65, PATERNOSTER ROW
MDCCCLX

7.2. George Mogridge, *The Churchyard Lyrist* (London: Houlston and Son, 1832).

tion of vernacular deathbed scenes. Kaines was a well-known positivist lecturer, the treasurer of the London Anthropological Society, and a compiler of various other anthologies. He was well aware of the historical depth of his market and of his own innovative contribution. He was not a hagiographer, he insisted; he had no particular denominational interests to further; his aim was to bring the death-bed story squarely into the world of commercial publishing.[21]

Kaines begins with conventional wisdom; it is almost irresistible when speaking about or caring for the dead to know the details of their deaths: "the last words of dying persons are always interesting." We demand stories not just of lives but also of deaths of our fellow creatures because we are drawn to the liminal condition of those on the brink of death: "they are nearest to the gods"; they are about to "be initiated into grand mysteries by the highest intelligences." Walter Benjamin, a century later, would speak of the authority that "even the poorest wretch in dying possesses for the living around him." Dying, Kaines thought, also mirrors living in edifying ways. Those who were calm and self-possessed in their prime die "with ease and resignation"; and more generally, "we meet death with more or less fortitude, as we have met troubles and difficulties in active life."

(He knows this is not really true and takes it back later.) Kaines offers many old-fashioned accounts of pious deaths across an ecumenical range of people: Loyola "raising his eyes towards heaven and feebly pronouncing the one word, 'Jesus'"; Luther falling asleep after he distinctly replied "yes" to the question of whether he died peacefully in the faith that he had taught. There is nothing from Jewish sources, because Kaines probably did not know about the tradition of "last words" from great rabbis on their deathbeds that came to be recorded in the early second century.[22]

But religion as understood in his day is not central to Kaines's work. He writes that the dying are near to "the gods" not "God," and he allies himself both with older pagan forms and with modern, secular ones that treat of lives and deaths: newspaper accounts; controversialist tracts; the vast print culture generated by the institutions of civil society—religious and not; biographies and autobiographies; private letters; and, perhaps most important, the novel. Memory and the way it is sealed in the moment of death is what matters; the afterlife is an afterthought; nothing seems to be left of the dead but their last words. These allow us, as it did for the "grand old Romans," to "imagine meanings for those that are meaningless." "Last words" are what the dead leave the living to "awaken emotions in the heart," to thrill us, to melt us, to allow us to "commune with the spirits of those we loved." Last words are the last sign of intelligence, inspiration, and affection that we have of the once-living. They, or something like them, have come to be expected. "Don't let it come to this," the Mexican revolutionary Pancho Villa supposedly said to the journalists awaiting some word around his deathbed; "tell them I said something."[23]

Kaines recognized that his book was not the first compilation of deathbed stories. It was an old genre. But he is at pains to distinguish his work from what he thinks is its main rival, *The Book of Death*, and to declare his own disinterested modernity. That book, he thinks, is too much about "notable Christians" and draws too heavily on "the most obvious sources." He, by contrast, has "no theory to prove—no sect to serve"; his purpose is psychological, not religious. There had already been enough written in the deathbed wars genre—infidels versus Christians, and Catholic versus Protestant in the old days—and he had nothing to add. Others did: "The Rev. Erskine Neale has not thought it beneath his dignity to compose an extensive series of these holy frauds, under the title of 'Closing Scenes,'" writes C. W. Foote, fifty years later, in his *Infidel Death-Beds*, which shows that one can die quite nicely without the comforts of the Christian religion.[24]

None of this is Kaines's problem. His principle of ordering deathbeds is alphabetical. The atheist Tom Paine—his death was by this time already the subject of a small library—comes just before the archdeacon and influential theologian William Paley, without any effort to compare the two. Paine on his deathbed confounded his interlocutor by insisting, in answer to the question, "Do you wish to believe that Jesus Christ is the Son of God?" that he had "no wish to believe on that subject"—this despite his having repeatedly called out, "Jesus help me!" Paley worked until a few days before his death getting some sermons ready for publication; his mind to the end was unshaken in its "habitual confidence and self-possession." His last words were to ask his surgeon to move him to a more comfortable position despite the medical dangers in such an operation.

In other words, how one died had become a topic of broad vernacular interest that transcended whatever religious or philosophical portents it might once have had. Kaines insists that it is not an "irrefragable test of a man's religious convictions and opinions," and that it is very difficult to read how a man has lived from how he died. Many people, good and bad, distinguished and not so distinguished, died without saying much of anything, or in any case without anyone bothering to record what they might have said or not said: the "wise man dieth even as a fool" (Eccles 2:16). Pathophysiology also mattered. Kaines cites a long account in his preface by Sir Henry Halford, the most distinguished physician of early-nineteenth-century London, on the ways in which the nature of the fatal disease affects the deathbed. Some people, Halford explains, meet their end by asphyxia: black venous blood in every part of our bodies instead of red arterial blood. Memory falters, the senses numb, faculties dim, the body breaks down, and finally tranquil sleep interrupted by delusional dreams. A peasant "babbles of" green fields; Napoleon expires "amidst visions of battles" with "tête d'armée" on his lips. In short, "the man is not intact."[25]

Kaines helps to transform an old genre; it became more democratic in other forms as well. Emily and Will's correspondence is shaped on a great surge of deathbed accounts and life stories of more humble men and women in a variety situations. More and more deaths in the eighteenth and succeeding centuries— fictional and real—were publicly noticed. There is no ground zero in the literary tradition for this shift, nothing as startling as Courbet's *A Burial at Ornans*, the enormous painting of the artist's obscure peasant great-uncle's funeral that gives it the attention usually reserved for works depicting great historical events and famous people. But the cumulative shift in how death was written and in the social standing of those whose deaths were noticed is just as dramatic and more widely diffused.[26]

We might begin with the rise of the obituary. The word itself, meaning a newspaper announcement of a death and, more generally, an appreciation of someone who had recently died, entered English in 1738. Earlier uses referred to necrologies or registers of obits, prayers for the dead or lists of the date of someone's death on which prayers for her soul were to be said. It was a vernacular genre: domestic virtues were more important than public ones, which meant also that an increasing number of women's deaths received public notice. There were several thousand of these in the leading journals of the eighteenth century, almost all of the wealthy urban middling sorts or of the gentry. But they were the first fruits of a genre that would reach much further down the social scale in the burgeoning press of the next century. Everyman and Everywoman and even Everychild could have a place, if not a full life story, on a death roll that had been the preserve of the great and pious. By the late nineteenth and early twentieth centuries, a death notice and, increasingly, an in memoriam notice on the date of someone's death—a vernacular obit in a solidly Protestant world—would become commonplace and affordable by the working classes.[27]

A large part of the increase in narrations of life and death in the eighteenth century comes not from obituaries in *Gentleman's Magazine* or its rivals but from religious publications of various sorts. Published funeral sermons, small in absolute number but a generic guide for other kinds of writing, began to increase in the late seventeenth century. Some are anodyne, but others bear the "testimonies" of members of new and persecuted religions—the Quakers most prominently—whose good lives and deaths bore witness to the truth of their faith. The death of Judith Fell, daughter of a well-known Quaker family, is recounted day by day over the last eight days of her mortal illness in 1682; the last days of Amariah Drewet are merged with stories of persecution in Cirencester so that her death becomes the occasion for reflecting on the status of Quakers more generally and not just on her life. The numbers of funeral sermons and publications that recounted the last days and hours of the faithful grew in the eighteenth century and increased logarithmically in the next, as the deaths of more and more ordinary people came to be written. Never before had writing the dead been so democratic.[28]

Some of the new stories were entirely generic, representative of the deaths of pious humble people rather than of any particular person, but even so, they helped establish expectations of what details readers might want to know. These circulated widely. The Religious Tract Society, for example, claims to have published 227,175 copies of *The Happy Death Bed*, in its Narrative Series. Most stories were of particular people in particular places. The teachers of the Stockport Sunday School, almost all of them from the working class, regularly visited sick students and fellow teachers and wrote accounts of the last days of those who died. Some of them were printed. As the management that published these accounts remarked, the writers were not well educated, and they did not necessarily use exactly the expressions that the children might have used or that would have been used had the memoirs been written by an educated clergyman. Yet, they "state simple fact" and "will be perfectly intelligible to all": for example, "25 October 1796, Joseph Lodge came to the affliction that would end his life; he was a good singer and instrumentalist; he hoped the whole Sunday school band would visit him, which it did; he was depressed but not afraid of death; November 1 his fever increased; Friday, 11 November, he died to join the 'grand central chorus above.'" There were probably tens of thousands of such accounts in local memoir books as well as in the pages of religious and other periodicals.[29]

Women's deaths came to be written in proportionately large numbers in the magazines of various new denominations and in secular venues. They are perhaps more prominent in the journal of the Primitive Methodists, who welcomed women cottage preachers long after they had been eased out of more respectable denominations, but their number increased everywhere. They are notable for their quotidian detail: Elizabeth Bell of Highbaldstow near Brigg in Lincolnshire was a housekeeper for a gentleman when she was a young woman; a poor laboring man befriended her, and she started to come to religion; then she faltered; he died; she married and had six children and was left a widow at twenty-five. And so on. Stories, often in novelistic detail, of those whose names would before never have been "uttered beyond the narrow circle in which they toil and suffer" multiplied. Mary Barton raised her stature by going into service, where she learned to read and write; she was seduced by an upper-class lover who left her when she became pregnant: "he had rifled my treasure, the only thing for which he cared for." Shades of Hardy's Tess. He was already married. She moved to the nearby town and had her child; there she met another man and lived with him as his wife until he too abandoned her when she became pregnant. She gave up her children to the workhouse and "plunged deeper and deeper into all the vices accompanying such a life." Then she developed tuberculosis, began spitting blood and returned to her mother Anne's house, where John Warton spoke with her. She came to God before she died. We know from accounts of the death of the wool dresser Abraham Lockwood (1792–1871) about his last walks to the tree where he had over his life conversed with God and of how "Abe went on quietly severing himself from one tie after another, which bound him to this world and getting ready for his departure to another and a better one." This is the stuff of intimacy that fills the correspondence of Will and Emily.[30]

There are also many secular versions of this sort of story, new volleys in the deathbed wars that recounted the lives and last days of the heroes of socialism and free thought that touched upon the lives of people who were socially far less prominent than Paine and Voltaire. John Jacob Holyoake, for example, spoke movingly of the infidel Emma Martin at her funeral in Highgate, where he, in the names of "friends of the *Reasoner*," the secularist journal that he founded, had purchased a grave for her: "square 31 at the head of grave no. 4267." She died on 12 October 1851, age thirty-nine, after a year of suffering from "phthisis" (tuberculosis). She had grown up in religious circles in Bristol and had married a man from that milieu whose "company it was a humiliation to endure"; she left him despite having three young daughters that she would have to support by herself. She subsequently met another man, Mr. Joshua Hopkins, the "husband" at her bedside with whom she lived without the benefit of a "priest-made" marriage: "no affection was ever purer, no union ever more honourable." She was reading volume 2 of Strauss's *Life of Jesus* as she lay dying and complained, between labored breaths, that he was trying to explain rationally what was not worth explaining. Holyoake concludes: as Emma Martin went into the unknown, truth remained her guiding principle. And in a footnote to the printed version of this speech, he added that the various published accounts of her deathbed recantation are nonsense. Her name, written in stone and on paper, appeared many times over because Holyoake's address was printed in the radical newspaper *The Leader* as well as in other venues.[31]

Most accounts of the names and deaths of ordinary people are less contentious and, like the bodies of the dead, they work to constitute communities and expectations of remembering. They write lives that would have gone publicly unnoticed in earlier ages. Benefit organizations like the mostly working- and lower-middle-class Odd Fellows regularly printed death notices beginning in the 1820s: date of the death, the cause, whom and how many he left behind, the lodge where the deceased belonged and any special services he rendered there, and often the number of brothers who accompanied the coffin to the grave. Sometimes, they might mention if the brother had been "on the box"—the coffer where the weekly contributions were kept well into the nineteenth century because members distrusted savings banks—when he died, or had never been on the box, or if, had he died one day earlier, his widow would not have received the benefit. There were longer and more professionally written obituaries for lodge or provincial grand masters. These might stand for the tens of thousands of obituaries in the publications of the many voluntaristic organizations of civil society.[32]

Printed working-class autobiographies also write the dead to an unprecedented extent. "England expects every driveller to do his memorabilia," as the *Quarterly Review* lamented. We know about the death of the mother of the Cornish miner turned poet, John Harris; we know that one of his earliest recollections is of the white coffin in which his eldest sister was conveyed to the grave. We know that two of the siblings of James Dawson Burn, the Scottish "beggar boy," died while his family was on the road with their father looking for work: "one pretty little girl lie[s] in the quiet sequestered churchyard of Staindrop, in the county of Durham." And of course, deathbeds are a mainstay of nineteenth-century "lives and letters," and along with mountains of letters allow a detailed look into how the middle classes of the age died. We know about the death of scores of relatively humble women because John Wesley thought them important enough to include in his magazine along with those of many more men.[33]

It should be clear by now how much the sensibility of the correspondence between Emily and Will and of her desire to know about his death, burial, and name owes to the sorts of accounts I have been citing and, perhaps most important, to the novel. Deathbed scenes and, to a lesser extent, funerals are so pervasive in the adult novel and in a new literature for boys and girls that it is easy to forget how generically new they were. There are no natural deaths in the plays of Shakespeare, but the exquisitely detailed death scene of the heroine in Samuel Richardson's *Clarissa* goes on for a hundred pages, and Ruskin counted nine deaths in *Bleak House* alone. One turns out not to be a death, and one, Mr. Tulkinghorn's, is by assassination, so there are seven natural, unheroic deaths in all. And novels have plenty of the other kind: some of those in the novels of Scott are "magnificently heroic," thought Ruskin.[34]

Deathbed scenes of Everyman are ubiquitous in adult and children's fiction. Young Charles Trueman's end in the first volume of Mary Martha Sherwood's unrelentingly evangelical but hugely popular *The History of the Fairchild Family* prefigures what might be the most famous death scene in nineteenth-century literature: that of Little Nell in chapter 71 of *The Old Curiosity Shop*, which Charles Dickens famously performed on tour to rapt audiences. This is the scene about which Oscar Wilde said, "One must have a heart of stone to read the death of little Nell without laughing." He was probably in the minority. And Little Nell is in a vast and good company: little Paul in chapter 16 of *Dombey and Son*, with its premonitions of another and better world; Eugene's death, complete with its attentive nurse in *Our Mutual Friend*; many maternal deaths; the violent deaths of Tess on the scaffold in *Tess of the D'Urbervilles* and Tom and Maggie in the flood at the end of *The Mill on the Floss*; Heathcliff in *Wuthering Heights*; Uncle Tom in Harriet Beecher Stowe's *Uncle Tom's Cabin*; Beth in *Little Women*, which we can follow also in the letters and diaries of Louisa May Alcott and her father; Emma Bovary. Any reader could add many more. It is easy to image that Engels had read Flaubert's *Madame Bovary* or *A Sentimental Education* when he spoke at the gravesite about his friend Marx's last days: "A number of complications have set in, the most serious being an abscess of the lungs. . . . Despite this, however, the general course of his illness was proceeding favourably. . . . [O]ne of the foremost young doctors in London . . . gave us the most brilliant hope for his recovery. But anyone who has but once examined the lung tissue under the microscope, realizes how great is the danger of a blood vessel being broken if the lung is purulent. . . . [W]hen we came in, he lay there asleep, but never to wake again. His pulse and breathing had stopped."[35] This is literary realism in real life and suggests the ways in which the novel informed how we moderns write the dead.

Fiction set new standards. It is as if the deathbed were a guarantee of the fictive facticity of the novel, the key to the reality effect. "Only in death," writes one critic, "can Dickens find an image of complete release from the human economy." Or perhaps in death—specifically in dying scenes—is hidden the secret of the novel itself: "the ultimate power of fiction to entertain him [the reader]," thought Ruskin, "is by varying to his fancy the modes, and defining for his dullness the horrors, of Death." Perhaps we rely on knowing about death—the name, the details—to make it real.

> Because we have neither hereditary nor direct knowledge of death
> It is the trigger of the literary man's biggest gun
> And we are happy to equate it to any conceived calm,

as the poet William Empson put it.[36]

Finally, in the penumbra of Will and Emily's correspondence and her efforts to find his grave was the poetry of death, the almost endless poetry of death that every late-nineteenth-century English schoolchild—and very probably Will and Emily—could recite: at least some lines from Gray's "Elegy Written in a Country Churchyard," and, more likely than not, all of Felicity Dorothea Hemans's 1826 poem "Casabianca." A ballad, easy to memorize—and to parody—it celebrates the bravery and death of a French cabin boy, son of a ship's commander, who stayed at his post and died when its gunpowder magazine blew up during the Battle of the Nile in 1798. The poem begins:

> The boy stood on the burning deck
> Whence all but he had fled;
> The flame that lit the battle's wreck
> Shone round him o'er the dead.

And it ends with the image of "that young, faithful heart," of a boy deeply entwined with the hearts of those who read about his death:

> With mast and helm and penion fair,
> That well had borne their part,—
> But the noblest thing that perished there
> Was that young, faithful heart.

Whether children reciting Gray or Hemans understood the irony of the silent "rude ancestors" or exactly why the thirteen-year-old son of a naval officer remained at his post, awaiting word from his father, as the deck on which he stood went up in flames and the ship exploded is less relevant than that the denouement of ordinary lives seemed to matter: a commander's son can become Everyboy; the "rude ancestors" were Everyone.[37]

The deep time of the dead began to shift with legal and administrative changes that constitute part of the modern history of names. But the imaginative possibility of Kiš's "Encyclopedia" was the result also of new social realities and new affective relations, new expectations, and new audiences for what is written of the dead. John Ruskin, in his discussion of the death scene of *Père Goriot*, grasps these realities, their geographical and anthropological specificity: "A village grocer," he writes, "cannot make a large fortune, cannot marry his daughters to titled squires, and cannot die without having his children brought to him, if in the neighbourhood, by fear of village gossip, if for no better cause."[38] Ruskin is thinking about the role of the city in Balzac's novel, but the same sort of argument could be made about the ways in which social changes demanded more of the dead and their names.

The narrator's summary of the rest of Dorothea's life at the end of Eliot's *Middlemarch* suggests another of the conditions that made Will and Emily's correspondence and his name on the memorial in Arras both possible and necessary. The age of the necronym is the age of stories about ordinary lives: "But we insignificant people with our daily words and acts are preparing the lives of many Dorothea's, some of which may present a far sadder sacrifice than that of the Dorothea whose story we know." Her nature "spent itself in channels which had no great name on the earth. But the effect of her being on those around her was incalculably diffusive: for the growing good of the world is partly dependent on unhistoric acts; and that things are not so ill with you and me as they might have been, is half owing to the number who lived faithfully a hidden life, and rest in unvisited tombs." This glance at Dorothea's grave reminds us of where we began, with names on tombstones.

In *Great Expectations*, Pip imagines his parents in the epigraphy of their tombstone in an age before photography, when the mind's eye unaided had to conjure the dead.

> As I never saw my father or my mother, and never saw any likeness of either of them (for their days were long before the days of photographs), my first fancies regarding what they were like, were unreasonably derived from their tombstones. The shape of the letters on my father's, gave me an odd idea that he was a square, stout, dark man, with curly black hair. From the character and turn of the inscription, "Also Georgiana Wife of the Above," I drew a childish conclusion that my mother was freckled and sickly. . . . At such a time I found out for certain, that this bleak place overgrown with nettles was the churchyard; and that Philip Pirrip, late of this parish, and also Georgiana, wife of the above, were dead and buried; and that Alexander, Bartholomew, Abraham, Tobias, and Roger, infant children of the aforesaid, were also dead and buried.

By the middle of the nineteenth century, writing and reading the ordinary dead had become culturally possible, even necessary. It is almost as if, as we will see in the next chapter, the staggering memorial at Thiepval with its seventy-three thousand names of soldiers with no known resting place killed in the Battle of the Somme and the Vietnam Veterans Memorial had to be.

The final resting place of Will's name is a tiny part of the great expansion of names of the dead that, I have argued, are grounded in administrative history and the material and cultural history of many different sorts of narratives: more and more of the names of the dead matter because more and more lives matter in the huge variety of stories that people, at all levels of society, told themselves about many subjects. The claim to have a life whose end matters, a life that cannot just vanish, lies at the core of Emily and Will's letter exchange, which, in turn, is the emotional foundation of the great naming monuments of the First World War and what followed them. Naming the dead is thus not a reflection or sign of democracy; it is constitutive of it.

Finally, the age of the necronym is one aspect of the great shift of the dead from a transcendental sphere to an imminent one, from a religion based in a cosmic reality to one grounded in memory. This brings us back to the beginning. The demand for names of the dead—that is, the demand that more and more lives be noticed—thus grows in part out of the fact that, as the philosopher Michel de Certeau recognized, it "has become impossible to believe in this presence of the dead that has organized (or organizes) the experience of entire civilizations," while at the same time it has proven impossible "to get over it," to "accept the loss of a living solidarity with what is gone, or to confirm an irreducible limit."[39]

Chapter 8
THE AGE
OF NECRONOMINALISM

Now Mr. Cogito
reaches
the highest swaying
rung of indeterminacy

how hard to establish the names
of all those who were lost
battling inhuman power

the official data
diminish their number
once again mercilessly
decimating the fallen

and their bodies vanish
in abyss like basements
great police compounds

eyewitnesses
blinded by gas . . .

But in these matters
Accuracy is necessary
One can't get it wrong
Even in a single case
In spite of everything
We are our brothers' keepers

ZBIGNIEW HERBERT, "MR. COGITO ON
THE NEED FOR PRECISION"

"We are our brothers' keepers." The poet Zbigniew Herbert speaks this time about the moral imperative to know the exact numbers and names of the dead of the great disasters of the past century: "the names of all those who were lost battling inhuman power"—the dead of the Shoah, Stalin's Great Terror, the Argentinian dirty war, of so many wars and evils. We could know the numbers of the dead that official sources seek to diminish without knowing names: this dead body and this dead body and this dead body. Sometimes we search for precision when we have neither names nor bodies. The moral and political imperatives of which the poet writes have encouraged demographers to do their best to fill gaps where they might have expected people: I am thinking here of their estimates of the numbers of the Southern dead in the American Civil War, of the Vietnamese dead, of civilians in the two U.S.-led wars in Iraq. But this will not do, although it is better than complete erasure: acting as if these dead had never existed. In our age, names are filled with human life; each one demands a denouement. In the past two centuries Mr. Cogito's need for precision has come to be grounded, as the previous two chapters suggest, in the social, cultural, and political history of names and in the history of the new intimate psychological infrastructure in which names came to matter more than ever before.

This chapter is about how, in specific cases, these two histories have produced a proliferation of the names of the dead or, more precisely, a moral imperative to hold on to them in public settings: to read them from books and lists; to inscribe them in stone or steel; to trace them on paper; to treat them as if they were actual remains. Ours is the age of necronominalism: the precise counting and marking of the dead, one by one, in the way that children "add apple to apple / subtract grain from grain." It is an age in which a French Holocaust survivor, trying to construct a convoy-by-convoy list of deported children, struggled to imagine phonetic misspellings of the name of a five-year-old boy in order to determine on which train and on which day he—his name recorded in orthographically correct form—was sent to Auschwitz. I survey this vast undertaking by going from the most concrete to the most abstract instances, from names over bodies to the names of the vanished dead, a whole new category that gestures toward bodies dropped into the sea or in some other fashion made to vanish. Between these two poles are two further categories. Nearer to the beginning are the names of absent/present dead, unidentified—gone—yet imagined as being nearby, present. And nearer to abstraction are monumental names, those that identify precisely the dead as a claim on public space and notice without a commitment to the location of their bodies. I make no claim for the status of these taxonomic categories beyond the hope that they allow us to explore the vast new world of necronominalism.

These are the names of the dead with which we are most familiar, names that, as Wordsworth said of epitaphs more generally, bear a "close connection with the bodily remains of the deceased," names that serve as "a tribute to a Man as a human Being." They announce that this human who once lived and is now dead lies here; that her name was ———, that she was born, that she died, that she is to be remembered. The numbers of epitaphs probably increased after the Reformation; whether because of it or not is another question. Ben Jonson in the early seventeenth century was the first great writer of epitaphs in English, although the form is classical. But we can be more precise: a higher proportion of the dead in churchyards were named in the nineteenth and twentieth centuries than at any time since churchyards began. A hundred years earlier it would have been unlikely that young Pip at the beginning of *Great Expectations* could have recalled his father, mother, and siblings from the dead through the form of an inscription on their tombstone. One generally knew, roughly speaking (and Wordsworth appreciated this), who was buried where in country churchyards—but not because of signs pointing to bodies. The dead were mostly remembered as part of the Christian community of the parish as a collectivity over time.[1]

By the time Dickens wrote, names of the dead on tombstones were common enough that the shape of the letters on a tombstone could become the stuff of the imagination through which Pip could recognize his parents as if in a photograph from the grave. Epigraphy—the physical features of the name in stone, the qualities of the graphemes themselves—seemed to mimic their physical qualities. Their bodies lay beneath the sod, but their features are in the lettering of their names: square, dark, stout, "Philip Pirrip, late of this parish, and also Georgiana wife of the above." Today a far greater proportion of men and women are, in this ancient form, "written in death" over their bodies than at any other time in history.[2]

The new places for the dead in the nineteenth century—Père Lachaise, Mt. Auburn, Kensal Green, and their hundreds of imitators—opened up a vast frontier for names over bodies: the "most continuous presence of exhibited written testimony imaginable," as Armando Petrucci, the most insightful and brilliant historian of the long history of epigraphy, puts it. "To go into a nineteenth-century European cemetery" (and, one might add, European-style cemeteries in much of the rest of the world), he continues, "means entering upon a great universe of writing." And at the heart of this vast archive—the poems, epitaphs, and genealogies (husband of . . ., wife of . . .)—are the names of the dead that direct the visitor's gaze to the precise ground that holds a body or several bodies.

Independent of the state, nationalism, and all public demands on the dead, a vast new civil society of their names came to identify their remains.[3]

That said, writing of the dead is never entirely either a private or a public function, especially in writing of war dead, which took on new meanings in the nineteenth century—new since Greek antiquity, in any case—both for the state and for families and civil society. Names on the tombstones of soldiers were the avant-garde of the age of necronominalism, not in absolute numbers but in the proportion that were marked. Hundreds of thousands of them, many in churchyards or in the new nineteenth-century memorial parks, others with their comrades in dedicated spaces, others still in specially designated local spaces, appeared over bodies during and after the American Civil War: an orgy of new names. Atlanta's magnificent Oakland Cemetery holds 6,900 Confederate bodies, of which almost 4,000 are named, among its 70,000 graves. Of the 3,580 Union soldiers who died and are buried on the Gettysburg battlefield, 1,883 are in named graves and 116 are partially identified by initial, unit, or state; the rest are marked "unknown," in sharp contrast to the others and as a reminder of the time when this fact went without saying, when "unknown" was the default. (More than a thousand others were taken from the Gettysburg battlefield by relatives and buried under tombstones elsewhere.) Of about 10,000 northern soldiers who fell in the protracted battle for Atlanta, 7,045 are written in death on the grounds of the Marietta National Cemetery, and nearby, of 3,000 Confederate dead from various campaigns, more than 1,900 are named on their tombstones.

The federal government became involved in 1901 with the naming of the dead of its former enemy, and more actively after 1906 with the creation of the Commission for the Marking of Confederate Graves. At the same time, white veterans of the northern and southern armies met amicably—black Union soldiers were excluded. Together, the dead and the living seemed to give their blessing to national reconciliation under Jim Crow. Of some 4,000 Confederate soldiers who died at a prisoner-of-war camp near Point Lookout Cemetery in Maryland, 3,382 names are written on brass tablets that were affixed to a monument there in 1911; 4,250 names were added in 1911 to the four sides of a new base for a monument in Oak Woods Cemetery, Chicago, dedicated in 1895 to those who died in a prisoner-of-war camp near there.[4]

Identifying bodies also became an important part of a southern civilian commemorative culture in which women played a critical part. Memorial Day in the United States is one manifestation, and so are thousands of tombstones. Between 1904 and 1915, the Confederate Ladies Memorial Association of Lynchburg, Virginia, for example, placed stone markers bearing the initials, state of origin, and unit over the graves of about three thousand soldiers who had died in a military hospital nearby. This information can be matched to the meticulous records, grave by grave, kept by George Duiguid, who organized the burials. The women's work continues.[5]

Writing the names of war dead over their bodies became still more common in the Great War of 1914–1918; the numbers of the dead increased dramatically, and the proportion of those whose bodies were identified increased as well. There are 557,520 names on tombstones of soldiers of the British Empire who had some-how—through the thick of battle and in most cases the perils of reburial—man-aged to keep their identity. Most were along the western front—and are joined there by comparable numbers of German and French and smaller numbers of other belligerents. Tens of thousands are in Gallipoli, where they are joined by the Turkish dead. (On the eastern front, millions of Russian and Serbian soldiers lie unidentified and unmourned.) All told, the Great War led to a logarithmic increase in the number of names over bodies for reasons explored in chapter 9.

NAMES AND THE ABSENT BUT PRESENT BODY

Names over bodies are rhetorically simply: deictic signs—signs that depend on where they are; here lies; that lump there belongs to so-and-so. Memorial lists demand more of the reader. They are, as we have seen, of great antiquity, but the florid commemorative culture of the nineteenth and twentieth centuries pro-duced many, many new ones in a variety of venues and forms. And the Great War of 1914–1918 witnessed a novel kind: memorial lists of the absent but present dead, the dead who had vanished but could not be let go, the dead who were hovering around somewhere. These are the dead whose names, like those on ep-itaphs, bear a "close connection with the bodily remains of the deceased" but whose bodies are unidentifiable or have disappeared: buried anonymously or so fragmented as to be essentially gone but belonging to men who, based on last sightings or platoon records, were presumed to have died nearby. Together the names on this sort of list forever float close to, but never quite on, bodies them-selves. They are inscribed securely on a memorial wall as the unmoving shadows of men, as stand-ins for the dead whose bodies are nowhere yet everywhere close by. This kind of memorial list of names from the early twentieth century is the aesthetic progenitor of the twenty-first-century wall of names at New York's 9/11 Memorial that stands over the unidentified remains of some or all of those com-memorated.[6]

To take the case of Great Britain as an example once again: between 1914 and 1918, 180,861 unidentifiable dead bodies were put each in a separate grave marked "known but to God," or variants of anonymity—"An Australian Soldier of the Great War" (*Ein deutscher Soldat* and *Ici repose un soldat inconnu* are the German and French variants). In addition, 336,912 bodies had disappeared as recognizable human forms. (There was some debate about what do with disarticulated body parts.) These were the dead blown into the air or pounded into the mud of abandoned trenches and mine craters during the back-and-forth movement of the front lines over the ground where they had fallen and been buried; others were lost at sea or shot out of the sky. They were, in a sense, the predecessors of the still more absent dead of the Holocaust, lost in smoke, sometimes from a furnace whose location is unknown, and whose disappearance was not a contingent fact but an essential feature of their murder. But unlike the naming monuments of the Holocaust that gather together "bodies buried in air"—bodies that are nowhere—those of the Great War hold names, almost 518,000 of them, that are as close as possible to where a soldier was last known to be alive; in the case of sailors, this was one of three major ports of embarkation. A staggering amount of research, name by name, went into making this possible. The sites of monuments now stretch, following the contours of battle, from the North Sea south and the east toward Verdun: Thiepval in the Somme, 72,194 names; Menin Gate in the Ypres Salient, 54,382; Loos-en-Gohlle, 20,610, and Richebourg-l'Avoué, 13,389, from the Battle of Loos and from earlier fighting in the same area; and so on, battle by battle, country by country.[7]

The label "unknown" that marks almost two hundred thousand graves of the British dead in the Great War has a short history in relation to names. It is little seen before late in the nineteenth century because it described the default condition of war and also of peace. Most soldiers were buried in unmarked graves, and purportedly permanent markers over the vernacular dead were relatively rare. "Unknown" became a common designation in the American Civil War cemeteries when, for the first time, this fact about a casualty was no longer taken for granted. A similar trend subsequently developed in civilian life. The death mask of the "inconnue de la Seine," the "unknown woman of the Seine," figured widely in European art and literature after 1900; being identified as *inconnue*—rather than just another of the hundreds of bodies dredged from the river who, even after days of being on display at the Paris morgue, remained unidentified—became a new and emotionally evocative category of the dead. We have already seen the power and horror of the unnamed, unowned, unclaimed pauper whose name is meaningless, and the length to which the poor went to avoid the ignominy of such deep obscurity. "Unknown" became a marked category for lists of the dead and, by extension, the essence of an entirely new cult predicated on deep namelessness in the Great War. On the one hand, hopelessly nameless bodies came to stand for all such bodies, for loss of name, for loss of life and personhood: the universal body. "The unknown soldier" would become in different variations a shrine in scores of countries and contexts. And the collective plural form—a distinct category—developed from it. Chaim Kaplan, writing in his diary of the

Warsaw ghetto, imagines a "time when the Jewish people will erect a memorial here, where the common grave holds all these brothers forever. Here lie our 'unknown soldiers' whom all of us should honor and respect." (The quotations marks are in his text.) Sisters are part of neither this band of brothers nor the public recognition of namelessness generally. In what was perhaps the first public demonstration of the French women's liberation movement, a group of feminists on 26 August 1970 put flowers on the tomb of the Unknown Soldier at the Arc de Triomphe in memory of "one more unknown than the unknown soldier, his wife."[8]

The namelessness of the dead, once so common, has become a moral rebuke that lists—and the encompassing category of "unknown" as a kind of apology for not knowing—are meant to mitigate. Woody Guthrie's song about the unnamed Mexican migrant dead has had a long resonant history. The New York artist Melinda Hunt in an emotionally related gesture has spent years of research in order to publish the names of as many of the 850,000 paupers who lie in the 101 acres on Hart Island where the city buries its anonymous dead. The Department of Corrections, which is in charge of this enormous paupers' field—the irony is too delicious to belabor—has just opened a database where families and descendants can search for their loved ones; the Interfaith Friends of Potter's Field holds memorial services there.[9]

The lost and unidentified dead are imagined somehow to be present in the lists of their names as they are imagined to be present in their bodies, as if each inscription were itself a tomb and the monument in a giant churchyard or cemetery. Siegfried Sassoon, one of the most famous of the poets of the Great War and one of the bitterest critics of any effort to redeem the suffering he had witnessed, loathed the memorial at Ypres—the Menin Gate—when he visited a couple of days before its dedication on 25 July 1927. He recognized the walls of names for what they were: a cemetery that should not do what all cemeteries invariably do, make the dead fit for the living.

> Here was the world's worst wound. And here with pride
> "Their name liveth for ever," the Gateway claims.
> Was ever an immolation so belied
> As these intolerably nameless names?
> Well might the Dead who struggled in the slime
> Rise and deride this sepulchre of crime.

The literalness of the names of the dead being the dead themselves had been a trope of antiwar poetry for more than ten years before the Menin Gate monument was dedicated. Helen Hamilton, a far more obscure poet of the war, shares

Sassoon's revulsion at the list of the dead as a sort of blood feast for foolish old men who exploit the dead for sustenance and the distant pleasures of patriotism:

> You strange old ghouls,
> Who gloat with dulled old eyes,
> Over those lists,
> Those dreadful lists
> To see what names
> Of friend of relation
> However distant
> May be appended
> To your private Roll of Honour.
> Unknowingly you draw, it seems,
> From their young bodies,
> Dead young bodies,
> Fresh life.[10]

On the other hand, *The Ghosts of Menin Gate*, painted by the Australian war artist Will Longstaff after he attended the monument's dedication, depends on the same sleight of hand, the same evocation of the dead by name, to make more reverential and benign claims. He depicts a vision he purportedly had during a midnight walk in which he saw the helmeted dead rise from their graves in front of where their names were inscribed; in the foreground are the red poppies that were said to grow so profusely over the war's carnage. The painting was, and is, displayed in a darkened room at the Australian War Memorial as if it were actually a tomb and viewers were in the presence of the dead. Longstaff's specific references were spiritualist: he painted the dead rising from an empty tomb—the Cenotaph—in the 1928 painting, and later he pictured the phantom dead on a hillside beneath the Canadian monument, with its 11,169 names, on Vimy Ridge (*Ghosts of Vimy Ridge*, 1931) (figs. 8.1, 8.2).

But the sense that the dead are present in their names goes far beyond any particular view of where or who the dead are more generally or whether their spirits can and do return. R. J. Campbell, leader of the so-called New Theology and a major figure in London's religious circles for almost a half century, encouraged his readers in 1915 to be a little less Protestant, to believe that the dead need us as they did when they were alive. "Our dead," he preached, "are not only not dead, but more alive than we." The visitors' books at war memorials today are still full of messages from the descendants of the dead claiming to have found, in a name, a lost ancestor, addressing the dead as if at a grave, announcing to the world what they are doing: "We came to pay our respects to great grand dad Herbert Davies missing in the Somme. Rest in Peace"; "we have found you at last"; and the like, by the thousands.[11]

8.1. *Immortal Shrine*. Will Longstaff, 1928.

8.2. *Menin Gate at Midnight (Ghosts of Menin Gate)*. Will Longstaff, 1927.

MONUMENTAL NAMES

Since antiquity, monuments—"human creation[s], erected for the specific purpose of keeping single human deeds or events (or a combination thereof) alive in the minds of future generations"—have borne names and often a great deal of biographical material. This person's—her or, much more likely, his—achievements are to be remembered on this site, they proclaim. Whether because they were purposely built or, more commonly today, because of something beyond their builder's intention or because of some combination of intent and accident, their numbers increased dramatically in the great age of commemoration that began in the nineteenth century. Monuments are a great venue for names. Together, the ubiquitous monument and its names represent many, many different memorial purposes; but, in general, like the bodies of the dead, they make a claim on public space and attention. Of course, the names on the western front I have been describing—the ghosts of absent present bodies—are at the same time monumental names in the sense that I am discussing here. But there was also a vast increase in the names that have no precise relationship with necrogeography.[12]

War probably accounts for a large proportion of nineteenth- and twentieth-century monumental names, although there is no survey to prove it. But in addition to those on battlefields, there are millions of names on tens of thousands of monuments to the dead of war far from where their bodies lie. Most of the 600,000 dead of the American Civil War are listed on local monuments somewhere; 102,000 names fill the walls and rolls of the Australian War Memorial that forms one end of the great axis of official Canberra, the country's capital; almost 30,000 names of the New Zealand war dead are inscribed in a book kept in the Hall of Memories in its capital, Wellington. Almost every village in Europe has a war memorial, most with long lists of names of the dead of the Great War, to which shorter lists from subsequent wars are appended. Sometimes only by inference, sometimes in poignantly explicit ways, these names replace absent bodies. An intense localism is counterpoised to the enormity of mass death on a global scale. In Oldham, for example, a roll of honor was buried in the "sacred chamber" beneath the town's memorial. The memorial committee in Blaydon, an industrial village five miles west of Newcastle-on-Tyne, suggested that since so few people could actually visit the graves of their dead loved ones, "it will be of some consolation to them to come to the beautiful monument and lay their tributes of affection at its base": names—201 of them—fill up the four sides of a pedestal on which stands a bronze soldier in greatcoat with his head bowed as if standing watch over the bodies of his comrades. Of these 201, only 104 are buried anywhere in identified graves that could be visited on a pilgrimage to the battlefields; the remaining 97 are "missing." The 259 names of the dead of Saddleworth are arranged on a monument high on a hill in Lancashire with churchyardlike attention to necrogeography: there "the names of the fallen [are] as nearly as possible on that side which looks over toward the men's old homes." We know from archives how much labor went into preparing these tens of thousands of lists. There are 158 names on the war memorial in Atherstone, Warwickshire. One by one, the last few years of their lives were researched and recorded. Private Joseph William Austin enlisted on 1 November 1914; he was wounded in the head; he had typhus and pneumonia and died from gas poisoning near Bethune in France on 24 June 1917. Private Frank Manning served first in France and then in the Balkans, was reported missing 25 April 1917, and was "probably killed in action at Jumeaux Ravine Dorian Sector." His name is among more than 2,000 on a memorial at Dorian in Greece; 2,800 others died in action in the army of Salonika, 1,400 more from wounds, and 4,200 from disease.[13]

Every Oxbridge college has its list of the dead of the Great War—here the controversy was whether to list members who had died for Germany—and so do many schools. Questions about whom to include on such lists have a history and a future: Harvard's magnificent Memorial Hall has the names of 136 men who died fighting for the Union, written on twenty-eight white panels; those who died for the Confederacy are not named. Yale did not build its memorial until well into the age of regional reconciliation (1909), and it included the southern dead. At Princeton, a proposal to list both the Union and Confederate dead, but on distinct lists, was vetoed by the president in 1921; together they were engraved in alphabetical order. The Johaneum Gymnasium in Hamburg, where my father graduated in 1929, lists together the names of those of its students who died fighting for Germany and as victims of the Holocaust.[14]

Thousands of insurance offices, railway stations, and other places of work also name the dead of the Great War on monuments of widely varying scale and artistic significance. Among the most heartbreaking is the Great Western Railway War Memorial in Paddington Station, London, which has a greater-than-life-size statue, by the gifted sculptor Charles Sargeant Jagger (1885–1934), of a soldier, clad in a thick greatcoat, reading a letter from home, a synecdoche of the bond that would not, as in past times, let the names of the dead be lost. An inscription tells viewers that inside the plinth behind it, written on a vellum scroll, are the names of 2,542 employees of the company who died in the 1914–1918 war. And then there are the monuments to the civilian dead of that war. The names of eighteen children, fifteen no older than age five, who died in a Poplar, East London, school from a German zeppelin attack are recorded on a monument in their East London neighborhood.

But names on other sorts of monuments besides those to the war dead also proliferate. A few examples will have to represent a multitude. Beginning in 1866, the famous "blue plaques" began going up on buildings around London. The person named had to have been dead at least twenty years, done something useful for humanity, and lived or worked on the site where plaques were affixed: a major impetus of the project was to "mark in a permanent manner" the houses of notable people and by increasing "the public estimation of such places," to preserve them from "modern destroyers and improvers." The names of these dead were more successful than their bodies were in keeping burial places out of the hands of land speculators, and they were an important part of the broader historical preservation movement. There are by now almost a thousand of these guardian-like memorial names; scores of other cities now have such blue plaque schemes. Similarly, political causes insist that the names of their dead be remembered. The

Martyrs' Memorial in Sighthill Cemetery, Glasgow, bears the names of the two radicals executed for treason in 1820 (whose bodies were moved there in 1847), of a third man executed and buried in Sterling, plus the names of nineteen others who were transported for their role in the 1820 Rising. Variants on a name were inscribed with scrupulous care to ensure that precisely the right man was remembered: "Thomas Pike or Pink," "William Clackson or Clarkson." There are five names on the political martyrs monument in Calton Hill, Edinburgh, dedicated to radical causes.[15]

Many acts of naming the dead, like putting their bodies in the ground, are explicitly political: these and not other names—or bodies—can legitimately claim space, and attention, and a part in a publicly important narrative. Two examples could be multiplied a thousand times everywhere. First, the Marker of Change monument in Vancouver: it consists of a circle of coffin-shaped granite benches, each with the name of one of the fourteen young women who were murdered by an avowed misogynist gunman in Montreal in the so-called École Polytechnique massacre of 1989. Together these fourteen empty stone coffins with their fourteen names are dedicated to "the memory of all women who have been murdered by men." (The monument in Ottawa in the form of roughhewn name-bearing tombstones is more modest in its claims but has also been attacked for "blaming men.") Second, an 1891 monument in a prominent place in New Orleans that commemorates an 1874 insurrection against the mixed-race Reconstruction regime that governed the city: it bears the names of members of the White League who had died fighting for the restoration of the racial old regime. In the post–civil rights movement world, many would rather forget. After decades of racially fraught struggle over who and what and where to remember, the names of eleven policemen who died in the line of duty defending the government were added in 1993 to the names of the dead who had fought to overthrow it. Names of the dead, like exhumed bodies, can remake history for the present.[16]

The Vietnam Veterans Memorial and the AIDS Memorial Quilt are but two of the most famous examples of monumental assemblages of names, but they deserve special attention because of their scale and the exemplary status they have attained. They take in whole worlds; they seem able to evoke the dead almost as Saul summoned the ghost of Samuel, one by one, even when the dead themselves—that is, their bodies or anything substantive that was theirs—are nowhere near. They mobilize the magic of names. When Maya Lin began thinking about what became the design for the Vietnam Veterans Memorial in an undergraduate class on funereal architecture, she had previously encountered Edwin Lutyens's memorial at Thiepval with its more than seventy thousand names (fig. 8.3). She also knew the lists of the names of Yale undergraduate Civil War dead, 113 who died for the Union and 54 for the Confederacy, in Woolsey Hall where they are surrounded by walls covered with the names of the dead of twentieth-century wars; she witnessed the engraving of new names. Names were thrust upon her. While she was working on an imagined World War III memorial for a class project, a colleague passed to her a call for proposals, along with the design program for a memorial to those who had died in the Vietnam War: all fifty-seven thousand names of the dead and of the missing, it insisted, had to be part of it. This in itself is evidence for the exigency in the twentieth century of the question, "Who are the dead?" But Lin's response is evidence too. Names, she wrote, reflecting back on her experiences, "bring back everything someone could remember about a person . . . far more realistic and specific and much more comprehensive than a still photograph." The one is frozen at a point in time: subject rendered object, "death in person . . . wounding to the observer in its detail," as Roland Barthes puts it. Photographs of the dead, especially when young, almost scream mortality, a life not lived. Names, by contrast, point to a life. The question "Where are the dead?" finds an answer in the response to another question: "Who are the dead?" They are where their names are, an even more remarkable fact than the almost universal human capacity to make the dead body, at least for a time, represent a dead person.[17]

The Vietnam Veterans Memorial directly—and the AIDS Quilt by reflection—owe an obvious debt to the great innovation of First World War commemoration: the monumental listing of the names of the missing dead. Vincent

8.3. Thiepval Memorial to the Missing, names.

Scully's lecture on Lutyens's monument in the Somme, if not a direct influence on Lin, enabled her, she says, to write the essay that explicated her design for the competition. There are enormous formal and narrative differences between old and new: a soaring brick structure that alludes stylistically to the nearby bombed church at Albert whose steeple remained erect through all the fighting, and an abstract, polished, black, reflective two-winged surface cut into the ground far from the jungles of Vietnam. Thiepval faces east toward the terrifyingly close German front line. It is set in a small cemetery amidst hundreds of thousands of graves stretching north and south along the western front for hundreds of kilometers. "There is no cover," Scully writes. "We imagine the machine guns sweeping the gentle slopes." Thiepval is of that and no other space. Its ground is haunted. The Vietnam Memorial, by contrast, is on the Washington Mall, where the dead are little evident. Other things hallow its site. Its orientation has no particular meaning. Something about it even survives translocation; there are various large- and small-scale traveling models, as well as fixed replicas; there is also a virtual wall. And the mood of the two is radically different. Lutyens's tower is "the open mouth of death, the ultimate 'portrait' of landscape art that rises to consume us all. . . . [W]e are enveloped by the creature's great gorge." In Scully's account, Thiepval is a monster. Maya Lin's reprise of it is not. It is almost elegiac.[18]

But as she understood what her teacher was saying, entering into the maw of Thiepval through its arches was also "a journey to an awareness of immeasurable loss, with the names of the missing carved on every surface of this immense archway." Names are at the heart of the matter. The question was the form they would take. At Thiepval, they—the vanished and unidentified dead—are on sixteen panels that resemble altar screens and are organized alphabetically by regiment. Collectively, they resist a chronological narrative: they proclaim the fact that, after substantial research, a staggering number of bodies—72,203 to be exact— are somewhere close but without their names, some, we do not know which ones, are in graves marked "unknown"; the majority are lost: "Here lies recorded . . . ," "Their names liveth evermore." Lutyens had no story, perhaps only a statement: "there they stand, the men, [the dead] unbroken."[19]

Maya Lin, against considerable opposition, insisted on a narrative. The names of the dead on the Vietnam Veterans Memorial—57,939 of them on the day it was dedicated—are in chronological order of death, beginning at one end of a wing and tapering off at the end of the other; the beginning and end of American involvement gesture to one another. The central portion, the highest and most photographed part, represents in space the modal years, 1964–1969, when the great bulk of deaths occurred. Like all lists, the principle that orders this one represents choices and has consequences. Veterans had wanted an alphabetical ordering of names because, they felt, it would making finding a comrade easier; the very large number of "Smiths" made it clear that this was not necessarily the case. Groups representing those missing in action wanted a separate section with the names of servicemen and -women who were lost but not proven dead. This, Lin argued, would break the narrative "and interrupt the real time experience of the piece." She prevailed: a diamond before a name (on the west wall) or after (on the east wall) would denote a man or women confirmed dead; a cross would identify MIAs or prisoners unaccounted for at the end of the war. If the status of a name changed, a diamond was to be superimposed on a cross. Practically, but not politically, the stakes were small. Almost all of the dead of Vietnam are accounted for—only about 1,200 out of 57,000 names, 2 percent of those on the memorial, represented MIAs or unaccounted-for POWs. Even the remains of the "Unknown Soldier" of the Vietnam War were identified, using mitochondrial DNA techniques, in 1998—Michael Joseph Blassie—and returned to his kin for burial. The chronological ordering of the names of the dead, the rise and fall in their density over time, was retained; form becomes content in response to Lin's answer to "Who are the dead?"[20]

Despite all the differences, Thiepval and the Vietnam Veterans Memorial share the power of the names of the dead, both in aggregate and one by one. The overwhelming presence of bodies at one and their absence at the other seems to have little effect on the fictive presence of the dead. They are visited and offerings are left for them as if they (that is, their bodies) were present or nearby. Both monuments are votive shrines; Lin's more so because its names are far more accessible. The actor Jimmy Stewart claimed that he visited Maya Lin's great black, reflecting marble every time he was in Washington. "There are 57,000 names there." His voice became soft as he spoke of his son Ronald, a marine lieutenant killed at Danang. "But I can pick out my son's name almost with my eyes closed." "Walker, I miss you dear friend. Hope things are peaceful for you," writes a friend on a scrap of paper; a single piece of cellophane attached the note and a picture identified as "Walker Smith Fullback" to the wall. Tens of thousands of visitors photograph their reflections in the name-bearing surface, as if this brings them and the dead together somehow, a shiny face punctuated by the duller gray of letters cut in stone: names a ghostly presence over the image of those who gaze upon it. Visitors make rubbings of names on paper and trace them with fingers on the stone. The Park Service worries that the surface might be worn away and eventually need to be replaced because of this intimate contact with visitors. The letters, as they did for Dickens's Pip, bring the dead into some sort of presence (fig. 8.4).[21]

8.4. A visitor pointing to a name at the Vietnam Memorial, Washington D.C.

More than a hundred thousand objects—this is only the number collected by the National Park Service—have been left at the Vietnam monument as if it were a gigantic votive shrine or a collection of thousands of such shrines: funeral notices and dog tags and gifts for the dead of all sorts—cans of fruit cocktail (a reference to C rations), crutches, cans of beer (Budweiser, the "King of Beers," is especially popular), church keys, cigarettes, a motorcycle. Some gifts come with messages; some messages are left on their own: "Sorry Greg, I named my kid after you and here's the beer we would have drunk." "Why you did not take my life on that trail at Chu Lai I will never know," writes a man to the name of someone whose photograph he has carried for twenty-two years. Precisely what the tens of thousands who leave these offerings think or believe is less important than the fact that they act as if they were in the presence of the dead body or, more precisely, in the presence of the dead.[22]

The AIDS Quilt began as names of the dead; it soon came under the care of the small NAMES project, and today is administered by its successor, the Atlanta-based NAMES Project Foundation. In the fall of 1985, marchers wrote the names of friends and lovers who had died of AIDS on placards and carried them in a candlelight parade. They were stuck with tape on the San Francisco Federal Building at a time in the history of the disease when it was little understood, often seen as a stigma, and invisible to those in power. In the late spring of 1987, Cleve Jones, a San Francisco activist, spray-painted the name of his best friend, Marvin Feldman, who had died of AIDS, on a quiltlike memorial panel. By 11 October, just after sunrise, with 1,920 panels stretched out before him on the Washington Mall in front of the Capitol Building, Jones began to read the names of the dead. (There was not a one-to-one correspondence of names and quilts; some people's names were on several quilts; some quilts had multiple names.)

The grid of walkways, the maps, and the directions all suggested a cemetery; for some it provided, as Peter Hawkins of Yale Divinity School put it, "a surrogate burial site for those whose ashes are scattered in the wind . . . or may indeed have been excluded from the family plot." As mourners might do at a tombstone or in front of a name on a memorial, they left objects and messages, stitched or painted onto the fabric that defined the three- by six-foot plot: baseball caps and teddy bears and favorite items of clothing became one with the materials of the name. Those who planned and those who came that day imagined the dead themselves to be present among the names, just as they could be imagined to be among the bodies beneath tombstones. Or, put differently, it is not just in the commemorative practices of the early medieval church that naming the dead brings them into presence.[23]

"Jerry will always be in the quilt," writes a loved one he left behind in one of at least fourteen thousand personal letters (as of 1992) addressed to the dead through the NAMES Project. The ensemble became a graveyard: "There is no Arlington Cemetery, no monument to this disease. I think people need something tangible, physical to touch, to look at," said Jones in anticipation of the first public display of the quilt. "Each of us has made a panel . . . all men can now see what has happened . . . it is our Vietnam War Memorial," Lisa Heft, the project coordinator, told a New York gay newspaper. "Blades of grass visible between panels and walkways suggested . . . verdant grave sites," said one visitor, "and then, as though I were visiting a graveyard that sported many mounds of freshly laid dirt each name came alive. . . . [I]t hurt too much to see the epitaphs that made up this quilt cemetery."[24]

There was a section for "unknowns," the death from AIDS that could not be, or was not, publicly acknowledged: "This is my brother but I cannot out his name." All this of course is in the context of the political work of the names of the dead of a shunned minority who had died from a disease that could not be spoken of: a "great physical symbol of survivor's resistance to the denial of AIDS." "If there were a meadow, and there were one thousand corpses lying out here," Jones said to a friend, "people could see it, they would have to respond at some level." The Quilt was the Vietnam Memorial of the activist gay community. By May 1991, there were fourteen thousand quilt panels, many with several names on them; today there are eight thousand blocks with eight panels in each, with perhaps as many as a hundred thousand names.[25]

The longest single monumental list of the names of dead is on Chris Burden's 1991 sculpture, *The Other Vietnam Memorial*, first shown at the Museum of Modern Art in New York and now owned by the Chicago Museum of Contemporary Art. He set out, he says, to make a book: six 7-foot by 12-foot copper sheets etched in a tiny six-point, unadorned typeface "sort of like Moses' tablets, that would be an official record of all these three million names." It would, he hoped, be "a presentation of fact." As in the making of any list, this is not an easy thing to do. All lists are to some extent fictions that depend on how they are defined, that is, on their principles of inclusion and exclusion. They are, by their nature, artifices. The years 1959 to 1975, the chronological span of Maya Lin's memorial, is not writ in heaven as the interval of American involvement in a war in Vietnam; some advisers died before then; those who died of injuries or suicide after 1975 should, or perhaps should not, be included. In Burden's case, a list might plausibly, but does not, encompass the dead—civilian and military, difficult as they are to disentangle—from as early as 1945, the beginning of the French colonial war, right up through the end of the American war in 1975.[26]

But there are two particular fictions at the heart of *The Other Vietnam Memorial*. However precariously, the narrative circle in Lin's Vietnam Veterans Memorial is closed: a putatively precise correspondence holds between a complete list of the accounted-for dead—bodies identified, bodies not identified, bodies missing and presumed dead—and each name engraved in stone. One name, one body. This is not the case in Burden's installation. In the first place, no one knows how many Vietnamese died. The estimate available to Burden at the time, based on the work of the reporter Stanley Karnow, was 3 million. A figure close to this number was confirmed by the Vietnamese Ministry of Labor, War Invalids, and Social Affairs in 1995: 1.1 million military and 2 million civilian deaths for a total of 3.1 million dead between 1955 and 1975, the dates usually given for the so-called Vietnam War. Recent careful and sophisticated demographic research has shown that this and Karnow's estimate are impossibly large: the number of Vietnamese war-related deaths is probably somewhere between 791,000 and 1,141,000, that is, about one-third of the number on Burden's memorial. (Later in this chapter, I will deal with the problem of the arithmetical sublime, with death on such a scale that one hundred thousand is a rounding error.)[27]

If the number of Vietnamese dead is difficult to specify, their names are even harder to come by. There is nothing close to a list from which Burden could have worked. Some of the names he inscribed correspond to specific deaths; most do not. He created—perhaps invented is a better word—the list of names on his "Moses' tablets" by first extracting four thousand Vietnamese names from telephone books and then combining and recombining them according to the syntactic rules of Vietnamese name formation until he had generated 3 million. (There is a sort of "screwball empiricism," here, as there is in much of Burden's work; this is an artist who used fifty thousand matchsticks placed on top of fifty thousand nickels to represent the fifty thousand Soviet tanks that supposedly were the reason for the U.S. decision to build a neutron bomb.) The names are in no discernable order and are separated from one another by dots: Vien Moc Lan·Phan Ngoc Ho·Vien Trong Phuong. The probability is very high that every dead body will correspond to one of these names but, in the absence of a sophisticated analysis of Burden's algorithm and name frequencies in Vietnamese, no way of knowing how many bodies any given name represents.[28]

All lists are overtly rhetorical, instrumental, and political exercises. *The Other Vietnam Memorial* is unabashedly so. Its artifice makes its case: these are the forgotten dead, the dead outside of a Western narrative, whose names should be remembered like those on one of the most visited sites in Washington. These dead are in the book of life, even if we have done everything to erase them and to separate them from the bodies to which they once belonged. But it also suggests how tenuous is the hold of the names of the dead on the dead themselves. A great deal of work goes into creating "a magic we can believe in."

NAMES OF THE VANISHED DEAD

Billions and billions of the dead—at least 90 percent and probably nearer to 95 percent of all those who ever died—have disappeared without leaving a name behind. Only in the early twentieth century were the names of some of these, the inadvertently vanished dead (specifically, soldiers lost in the muck of the battlefront), gathered together to represent an absent present dead. These are the contingently disappeared dead. Only later, in the middle decades of the century, did the absent dead more generally become a proper new species unto themselves: the dead who were made to disappear, the secretly "Disappeared." The term was first used in 1947 as an adjective to describe the secret dead—the "disappeared" Polish officers of Katyn Forest; in 1977, it became a collective noun, a derivative of the Spanish *desaparecido*, when Amnesty International used it to refer to a class of people who, as a consequence of state action, had vanished without a trace. The category has become so useful that the Spanish word has since migrated to English.[29]

There were many ways that people could be made to disappear: dropped at sea or in rivers, shot and cast into mass graves, left to rot. Thus the body disappeared. But even if it was not literally disappeared, it was erased. Although the exact number is not known, most of the corpses of the nine thousand "disappeared" were, it seems, buried in clandestine or recognized cemeteries in Argentina during the "dirty war." They lie there anonymously: "N.N." ("*nomen nescio*" in the Latin of the law, "*ningún nombre*," "no name"). Finding and then giving these bodies back their names is an act of making them reappear both as an individual commemorative act of mourning and a collective act that establishes a disappearance as a fact—an act that had a cause—and tries posthumously to undo that fact. The Mothers of the Plaza de Mayo and the forensic teams that took up their work of identification of each victim did so that they could, one by one, mourn their dead properly but also to establish proof that a singular horror had happened. "A lot of people didn't believe what happened. People said it was a lie, that the disappeared were in Europe," a young volunteer on a forensic team told a reporter. "When we find a skeleton with a bullet through the cranium, it's a way of showing that these people aren't travelling in Europe." Someone was taken from somewhere and killed in this and that way and, now, all of this is revealed and the body can go back to where it belongs under a name on a stone prepared by those who loved that person. Naming here is an act of redeeming the private past, returning "to the requesting families the remains of their murdered, formerly 'disappeared' loved ones," as well as an act of public memory, a step in the "reconstruction of the usually denied recent history" and an act of faith in the moral imagination. There is here a move from the intimate and personal (mothers demanding to know what happened to their children, articulated as a demand for a name and a body) to the political (a demand by the victims of wrongs committed by agents of the state for an accounting, for recognition, and for the insertion of this crime into history in such a way as to make it less likely to happen again). With different twists, this is a story that can be told in Guatemala, South Africa, Cambodia, Bosnia, Rwanda, Spain, and all too many other places. In each case, recovering the names and narratives of the murdered is a major juridical and commemorative act.[30]

There were, of course, the disappeared *avant la lettre*, before the category came into use: the dead of the Shoah and of the Great Russian Terror, to take two horrific examples. I will focus on the first of these because the naming of the Holocaust dead is probably the single biggest effort in world history to answer the question "Who are the dead?" and because their murders have become of overwhelming cultural significance for the West. I intend no invidious comparisons with the 1,300,000 names in the memorial database of those murdered by Stalin, or with the names of hundreds of thousands of Armenians that have been recovered. The Holocaust is also the world's limit case of erasure: 437,000 Hungarian Jews, deported to Auschwitz in the late spring and early summer of 1944, were murdered in a six-week period and their bodies incinerated—they disappeared. The overheated crematorium ovens were barely up to the task.

He shouts scrape your strings darker you'll rise then as smoke to the sky you'll have a grave then in the clouds there you won't lie too cramped.[31]

Of course not all of the nearly six million murdered by the Nazis and their helpers were rendered into ashes; some millions—we will never know with precision—were disappeared in less technologically advanced ways. But the Holocaust—"a grave in the sky"—is the limit of the vanished dead. Those turned into ash and the others did not just happen to be unidentified; they did not just disappear from society; their bodies were not falsely registered. The utter disappearance of these dead was intentional, and naming them has become a hopeless and heroic act of recovery, of reincorporation of these dead into a narrative and into life: a restitution of identity; a funeral of sorts even if the disappeared body is never found or has been rendered unfindable. There is an intimate, vernacular form of this sort of naming—the restitution of names to a place from which they disappeared—as well a grander, more public and collective ingathering of names, and much in between.

The German *Stolpersteine* (stumbling stones) began as a project of the conceptual artist Gunter Demnig to put the dead back in place, back into the topography of everyday life. He had long had an interest in reinscribing traces of lost pasts on landscapes and public spaces. In 1990, Demnig wrote in white paint the words "May 1940—1,000 Roma and Sinti" on the pavements of Cologne to document the facts that they had been there and that they were gone. From this developed the idea of permanent brass markers—nameplates, microhistories—embedded in pavement as close as possible to where someone murdered in the Holocaust had lived. They are not tombstones, both for the obvious reason that there is no body but also because *Stolpersteine* do not claim to be a substitute for an absent body or grave. They announce where someone lived, not died. That said, passersby are often reluctant to step on them; the dead seem present. Each name is given in large, unadorned capital letters—clean, modernist, sans serif—with an identifying text in smaller type: "Hier Wohnte Arthur Abrahamsohn JB. 1889, Deportiert 1943, Ermördet in Auschwitz," and next to it, "Hier Wohnte Margarete Abrahamsohn, Geb Jacobsohn, JB. 1901, Deportiert 1943, Ermördet in Auschwitz." (Here lived Arthur Abrahamsohn, born, 1889, deported 1943, murdered in Auschwitz; Here lived Margarete Abrahamsohn, formerly Jacobsohn, born 1901 . . . .) Like the names on the lists of the disappeared or unidentified dead soldiers of the Great War, each name on a *Stolperstein* elides the extensive research in public and private archives—in this case, carried out by volunteers—that made it possible to record these names in this one particular place, to rediscover key dates in the narrative of a life and a death that belonged there. There are now more that forty thousand such plaques in Germany and elsewhere in Europe.[32]

Christian Boltanski's Berlin installation, *The Missing House* (1990), makes the same sort of liaison between the names and the places of the disappeared dead, but for those of the Holocaust in a strange and ironic way. Some of the outlines of the floors and rooms of a bombed-out apartment building on the Grosse Hamburger Strasse in Berlin are still visible on the walls of the two buildings still standing on either side of the gap: traces of rooms and flats, ghost spaces. Boltanski, then a visiting professor at a local art academy, led a small team of students to find out who had lived there: name, occupation, date of birth, and when they had lived in the building. This information he placed on plaques that corresponded to each person's flat. The project began as part of a celebration of German unification, a memorial to the dead of the former East Berlin. But there had, in fact, been layers of death. Twenty former inhabitants, it turned out (not surprisingly because this had been well known as a religiously and socially diverse area), had been Jews, deported in 1942 and murdered by the Nazis. Those who were actually hit by the bomb in 1944 were "Aryans." So the names and dates of the disappeared dead became palimpsests of waves of destruction: ghosts who had met their ends in different ways in ghost spaces.[33]

Elsewhere too the names of the disappeared dead reoccupy the spaces of the living. On 16 and 17 June every year, they are in the windows of hundreds of buildings in the Marais and elsewhere in Paris, telling passersby that "Here lived . . . ," who on those days in 1942 were rounded up by the French police and taken to the detention camp at Drancy, from which they were taken by train to Auschwitz. These were the days of the notorious *rafle du Vél' d'Hiv* (the roundup of the Winter Velodrome), the biggest single French police action against Jews, when 13,152 men, women, and children were seized and kept for a time at the velodrome near Drancy before being sent east. Seventy-six thousand names are now on the Shoah Memorial; the official documents—some reconstructed, some saved from destruction—that allowed the authorities to identify Jews are kept there as well. The *Stolpersteine* and the Boltanski installation and the window signs in Paris are entirely the work of civil society. There are many more memorials in this genre. And there are also projects to satisfy Mr. Cogito's demand for precise numbers but without names: Gleis 17 Memorial at the Grunewald S Bahn station in Berlin, where the German national railway company lists, transport train by transport train, the numbers of Jews in each shipment east from this track, for example (figs. 8.5, 8.6).[34]

8.5. Memorial at platform 17, Grünewald Station, Stiftung Denkmal, Berlin.

8.6. Holocaust Memorial by Rachel Whiteread, Jewish Museum, Vienna.

8.7. Identification passport issued to visitors by U.S. Holocaust Memorial Museum.

In addition to these efforts of civil society, major projects have been launched by governments to recover the names of the vanished dead, of which Yad Vashem, the "Place of Names," in Jerusalem is by far the biggest. It has gathered and made accessible some four million names of those murdered in the Shoah; there are smaller lists of names on official Holocaust memorials and in museums by the hundreds; and there are state-supported monuments that depend on names to represent the fact of erasure: Rachel Whiteread's structure, *Nameless Library*, with its row upon row of inside-out and hence unreadable metal cast books built at public expense on Vienna's Judenplatz in Vienna—officially designated the Mahnmal für die 65,000 ermordeten österreichischen Juden und Jüdinnen der Shoah (Memorial for the 65,000 Murdered Austrian Jews of the Shoah). Visitors are handed a card with the name of a victim of the Shoah as they enter the United States Holocaust Memorial Museum in Washington (fig. 8.7).[35]

Serge Klarsfeld's record of the 11,400 murdered Jewish children, exhumed from official archives, out of the total of 75,724 Jews deported from France during the Holocaust offers an exemplary case of the private recuperation of names. It is, as he puts it, "a new reference work in the domain of memory and feeling," "a full memorial book to the Jewish children deported from France," a book born of "an obsession to be sure that these children are not forgotten," by a man whose father sacrificed himself to the SS so that his family, huddled behind a false wall, would escape discovery. I take it as exemplary of an important class of recuperative efforts to redeem—make bearable if not undo—past wrongs through the recovery of the names and the stories of the disappeared dead, through the juxtaposition of the cosmic and the particular. It is a massive response to Mr. Cogito. On the one hand stand vast numbers, often hard to come by:

> the official data
> diminish their number
> once again mercilessly
> decimating the fallen

as the poet writes. In this case, "the official data" probably did not intentionally decimate the number. The official *fichier juifs* that contained police information on the Jews living in the Department of the Seine had indeed been destroyed after the war, but the large number of files on foreign Jews that Klarsfeld discovered in 1991 in the Veterans Administration Archives had not been kept hidden to hide Vichy complicity.[36]

But there is a general problem. Murder on the scale of the Shoah, or the Stalinist Terror, or the Armenian genocide, or even one or two powers of ten smaller than those, is difficult to organize in one place; archives of death at this level are usually dispersed; it takes many hands. This means that there is often no choice but to add one murder to one murder extracted from diverse repositories to arrive at a total.

> one can't get it wrong
> even in a single case
> in spite of everything
> we are our brothers' keepers

Implicit in these verses is another difficulty that names and their aggregation must address. In a happier age, Immanuel Kant identified it: the problem of the mathematical sublime. The arithmetician has no more difficulty in principle comprehending one murder than six hundred thousand—the number murdered in the Armenian atrocities of 1916–1917 or by the Nazi Einsatzgruppen on the eastern front in 1941 before the death camps were fully geared up—or five million to six million, the best estimates we have of the number of Jews murdered in the Shoah. At a purely cognitive level, any number can be understood by adding it, unit by unit, to the unit that comes before. The quantity "three" is no more difficult to understand than "three million." But, Kant says, actually being able to take in great magnitudes—to feel their sublime terror—is ultimately an aesthetic act, one that depends on gaining the right distance on the subject. His example comes from the memoirs of Anne Jean Marie René Savary, one of Napoleon's generals in Egypt, who worried about how to feel and convey to others the emotional effect of the pyramids. Too close, he could see only stone by stone and could not take in the full sweep; our imagination, Kant explains, forgets the lower tiers as our eyes move toward the apex. Too far away, "the parts that are apprehended (the stones piled on top of one another) are represented only obscurely, and their representation has no effect on the aesthetic judgment of the subject."[37]

Names, singly and together—communities of the dead that the investigator brings into being—offer a hope of bridging the spaces between the particular and the cosmic, between each single case and the vast, morally ungraspable size of their aggregation. Klarsfeld was of course not the first to embrace this strategy. An article in the *Montreal Gazette* of 25 January 1930 also appropriates the necronym. The great lists of names and fields of graves, it says, are "without parallel in history," erected so that "future generations seeing these things must realize how great was this conflict, how tremendous the effort, and how dear the cost." The names at Yad Vashem are read out loud each year; so too those on the Vietnam Memorial. If I were to read the names of the children murdered during the Holocaust in France at a rate of thirty-two per minute—barely two seconds for each name—it would take me five hours and fifty-six minutes to pronounce them all. In short, the mathematical sublime can be imagined as space, as a wall filled with letters, or as time filled with the sound of voices intoning names (plate 14).

French Children of the Holocaust is a more intimate and emotionally profound exploration of two other projects that speak to Mr. Cogito: Klarsfeld's *Le mémorial de la déportation des juifs de France* and his *Le calendrier de la prosecution des juifs de France*. The first of these lists the names, birth dates, nationality, and convoy number of all 75,721 Jews deported from France, beginning on 27 March 1942 (convoy 1, Drancy, the main transit camp on the northeast outskirts of Paris, to Auschwitz: 1,112 men, mostly French nationals, none chosen for immediate gassing, 22 survivors in 1945); through 9 February 1943 (convoy 46, the first of several that day: 1,000 deportees, of whom 816 were gassed on arrival and 22 survived (15 men, 7 women) through the last poorly organized departures—17 August 1944 (convoy 79, carrying 51 "special Jews," whom Eichmann's man on the spot, SS Hauptsturmführer Alois Brunner, managed to transport by trading some pigs for three cars that belonged to an aircraft battery); and 22 August 1944 (convey 82, from Clarmont-Ferrand, about which little is known except that it arrived at Auschwitz on 8 September, that it contained 3 adolescent girls, and that 39 men were selected for work). (Convoy numbers, like names, are printed in boldface as if to enlist typography in the process of making them adamantine realities.) The *Calendar's* 1,300 pages provide the scaffolding: a week-by-week, month-by-month, sometimes day-by-day chronicle of the legislation, the meetings and negotiations, the roundups and arrests, interments, loadings, unloadings, and shipments east, the precise how, where, and when of 73,157 murders (75,721 deportations less 2,564 survivors) arranged on French soil with active French assistance (fig. 8.8).[38]

The 1,881 pages of *French Children of the Holocaust* shifts attention from the bare facts of murder—name, arrest, convoy—to the person, to the fact that she was a child with a life largely unlived, to the fate that inhabited the name. It gathers material of all sorts—letters, lists, ancillary details of apprehension, transport, and arrival at camps that, taken together, allow Klarsfeld to produce the microhistories of many dead children, just as Emily wanted to create a death narrative for her Will. Most important, photographs—thousands of them—bear testimony to the fact that the dead were once alive, just as we are. More than any other art form, the photograph informed the names in the age of the necronym since the late nineteenth century.[39]

Madame de Guermantes's photograph, Swann confesses in *Remembrance of Things Past*, "had seemed to me an almost forbidden spectacle." The prolonged encounter in the present with that frozen moment of the past—which evoked the sense that she had paused nearby him and which had given him for the first time the leisure to look at her rounded cheek, at her neck, at her tapering eyebrow—was both a voluptuous pleasure and dangerous necromancy. The photographic image became the medium for thrust-

8.8. List of names of French Jews taken to concentration camps during the Holocaust. From Serge Klarsfeld, *French Children of the Holocaust* (New York: NYU Press, 1996).

ing the past into the present, for revivifying in the imagination a lost world in all its pain and pleasure. But however much we might treasure these images as relics, as testimony to the existence of a person in particular past surroundings, in a particular light, wearing particular clothes, in one fleeting, forever-past moment in their lives, we now apprehend them in the present with our present knowledge of their fate. Memory erases time. And even if the viewer does not know the subjects of a photograph and thus cannot literally remember them, they are not really past. Photographs are archetypally memorial.

Old photographs almost demand that we see them as memorials; by their nature they bear witness to their subject's irrefutable existence in the past, to the death of an instant—a second or two in the nineteenth century, a hundredth of a second or less by the 1930s—which was frozen through the chemistry of light on some sort of emulsion and preserved on glass, metal, or paper. Then suddenly this thing of the past is brought into the present like the image of a star whose light, we know, has traveled for years to reach us. (Photography, of course, flourished beginning in the late nineteenth century precisely as a memorial practice. In part it was a way of remembering the dead through studio pictures of bodies laid out for burial or of dead children, dressed as if they were alive and nestled in a mother's arms. But it was also about capturing for memory moments in life, for chemically freezing them for posterity.) Kodak prospered by inventing the snapshot camera, which made it all possible, and many of the pictures in this book are the product of this revolution. Living as we have for so long with a superabundance of photographic images, the terrible magic of the art is perhaps not so apparent. But it is nevertheless magic. Nadar, the great mid-nineteenth-century French pioneer of photography, looking back from 1900, thought that it was far more disturbing, far more astonishing than the other momentous discoveries of his century—the steam engine, the electric light, the telephone. In its sheer "peculiarity" the photograph surpassed these and other wonders. It "endowed man," he thought, "with the divine power of creation: the power to give physical form to the insubstantial image that vanishes as soon as it is perceived." It captures "the ripple on the surface of the water," the moments that in their succession make up a life. Maurice-Mandrel Mildiner will always look out at us, on his bar mitzvah day, wrapped in his tallis. He was deported to his death nine months later on convoy 24.[40]

Perhaps all photographs—but certainly the ones in this book—subsist in the present perfect conditional. History on whatever scale is written in the past tense or the historical present. Liki Bornsztajn was born 27 August 1927, in Nancy, had taken refuge in the Vienne department in central France, lived in a Jewish social services home for children in Vauquelin, and was arrested there and deported on convoy 77, which carried her and 326 other children to Auschwitz on 31 July 1944; 726 out of the 1,300 men, women, and children on this particular convoy were gassed on arrival at Auschwitz. All this is in the past indicative. 16–17 July 1942: "The Vel d'Hiv roundup begins as planned before dawn, at 4 A.M. . . ." Historical present. But Liki's picture exists in another tense: She "would soon have been 17," the caption tells us. Her half-brother Wolf, born on 21 October 1933, also in Nancy, is shown as a two-year-old, very much the child of another age: his baby shoes could be hand-me-downs; his tunic is that of the twenties. He would be three, four, five, and so on in the present conditional until 31 July 1944, when he would have been eleven on his next birthday. The Wolf we see is of course not the Wolf who was deported, and indeed the world he came into was not that which would destroy him. The baby girl Myriam Piper we see in 1928 or 1929, stark naked, her face peering just a bit to her right in this, the only surviving picture of her, taken five years before Hitler came to power. She is not the fifteen-year-old who was deported with her mother on 19 August 1942; France still welcomed immigrants. This mixing up of time, this invitation to project what we know will happen, is irresistible if suspect, indeed indefensible.[41]

In fact it is a vertiginous *mise en abyme* of memory. Hundreds of the pictures are actually pictures of pictures on tombstones. Some are not unlike those that abound in Mediterranean cemeteries, although the sort of family groupings one finds here—a father in fine business suit fills the frame of the studio portrait with his children, both deported, in the lower right third, for example—are relatively rare. Some are pictures of broken images—Albert Szipdbaum's face is almost completely gone next to the intact luminous face of his younger sister Monique, both deported in convoy 6, 3 February 1944—as if to announce some eternal truth about the transience of all things, including memory.[42]

There are close-up pictures in which the vitreous overlay of tomb pictures produces a ghostly haze through which the faces seem to shine. Cracks in the surface give these extreme close-ups the quality of old master paintings coming through the layers of paint and old varnish. Scores of pictures are embedded in what look like photography albums covering what we know to be an empty grave in a cemetery. Suzanne Kappe, born in Paris in 1931 and deported with her older sister and mother on convoy 24, 23 August 1942, looks out at us from the oval cutout with slightly embossed borders that determined the placements of pictures. Her mother and sister fill the other slots. The album is in white marble, and it sits on a black polished slab on which we can just see, at the very bottom of the image, four stones, two black and two white, which are put on Jewish graves by visitors. The legend in black reads, "Mortes en déportation." On each page, the images threaten to sweep the reader into the abyss. For example: Henri Flamenbaum, not quite age five, dressed in a double-breasted suit, arm on pedestal, hand in the jacket pocket—the nineteenth-century statesman pose—looking out at us and the camera with the apprehensive smile of a little boy who wants to please in unfamiliar circumstances. (We know his age because a legend in ink cursive script across the top of the picture identifies it as taken on "24-1-42," and the caption gives his birth date.) This rectangular photograph of a photograph is positioned on the page to cut at a right angle into a stone representation of an Edwardian photo album, one in which some paper lace work—a rose in this case—pops out as the book is opened. Here the head from the lower portrait appears again—a picture upon picture upon picture—in a framed oval below others that contain images of the faces of his two almost grown-up sisters and their mother. On the right of the book there is a note in French that reads, "To my dear wife and children, whose death broke my heart, which ever bleeds and weeps and which will never forget their woe. Died during the deportation to Auschwitz." (They were on convoy 20, Drancy to Auschwitz, 17 August 1942: 878 of 1,000 deportees were gassed on arrival. No women survived.) Behind this album we can just glimpse another that lies open on the same black slab; the word "Deportes" is just visible; the name P——OFF" is obscured by the rose.[43]

It is the pain that some small detail of each photograph elicits—what Barthes called its "punctum," its barb, its capacity to pierce—that makes this book a "memorial." Images of the dead wound the hearts of the living. The abyss—the superabundance of particularities is endless, each disturbing in its fashion: the boys and girls holding furry lambs and teddy bears, sometimes completely absorbed in them, like seven-year-old Jeanine Gotainer, who holds a stiff creature almost her own size and plays with the ribbon around its neck, and other times bearing them less personally, as signs of childhood and objects that bridge the unnatural milieu of the studio with the world of the nursery; the twins Claude and Guy Goteiner absorbed as naked infants in the furry rug whose individual soft hairs are visible against the shadows of their bodies; the fingers of Stella Radomysler's hand as it peeks out from between her father's thumb and index finger as they walk down the street, two years before they were deported to Auschwitz, he secure in a three-piece suit, she in a white dress trimmed with fur and wearing a hat with pom-poms; the shaving brush wielded on the smiling, lathered face of his father by a laughing three-year-old Jean-Pierre Guckenheimer; two five-pointed stars cut in the wooden doors of a garage—meaningless decoration—that contrast so poignantly with the six-pointed "Juif" badge worn by a resolute-looking man sitting for this picture with his wife and three daughters (André May, age fourteen, survived from this group). There are stereotypically happy pictures of the age, scores of girls in Shirley Temple poses; stereotypically serious poses—boys and girls with violins or holding books, the titles of which are just visible—*Contes de.* . . . There are pictures that pierce in other ways; a little girl with bare chest, a heart locket around her neck; a bracelet barely visible on her wrist; she is looking straight at the camera—at us—arms folded below her exposed nipples; long blond hair. On the facing page she stands, fully dressed in a smock this time, next to her naked doll on the table. The first of these pictures was used for a poster advertising an exhibition on the Loiret concentration camp. Innocence protests too much, as if the innocence of every man, woman, and child in this book were not as great.[44]

Finally, the photographs with their names are signs of murder; they are *corpus delicti*. At Beate Klarsfeld's urging, and with her help, Fortunee Massouda, who survived Auschwitz, sat with an enlargement of the only picture that she had of her three children—Jacques, thirteen; Richard, six; Jean-Claude, five—in front of the office of the German prosecutor bearing a sign that read, "I am on a hunger strike as long as the investigation of Klaus Barbie, who murdered my children, remains closed." The story of political action to force state action has to be told elsewhere. Here we have only the picture of the three boys, all with dark, deepset eyes and delicate lips. The oldest boy, whose last, adoring Mother's Day letter to Fortunee is reprinted, rests his hand on his little brother's shoulder. Jacques wears the Bermuda shorts of a teenager held up with a belt; he wears laced shoes. Six-year-old Richard's shorts are held high by cloth suspenders; he wears androgynous buckle shoes. The youngest brother is in a knit shirt and toddler pants. They stand in front of a ludicrously picturesque studio background. Victims of murder. The remains.[45]

If the photographs and names are signs of the dead, the list and the chronology explain how they came to be that way. Consider the raid on the orphanage in Izieu, a tiny village between Lyons and Chambéry. We know that at the end of 1943 and early 1944 the Oeuvre de Secours aux Enfants (OSE, Organization to Save the Children) had managed to disperse children to safer havens throughout rural southern France. Izieu was uniquely vulnerable in part because of its isolation. We also know that by the anti-Jewish raids of 10–11 January 1944 in Bordeaux, Vichy authorities had given up any pretense of protecting even French Jews; foreign ones had long since been written off. It had already happened elsewhere, Pierre Laval is quoted to have said in sanctioning the raids over the initial objection of his regional prefect. The stage was thus set. We have, on page 87, a copy of the telex in which Klaus Barbie announces to his bosses in Paris what he had achieved. (Every shipment was accompanied by a telex announcing to the next stage that so-and-so many Jews were en route from A to B.) It is worth quoting in full to show just how easy it is to represent this corner of the Holocaust. I translate from the German, retaining as much as possible its telegraphic style.

> 6.4.44 2010 Subject: Jewish children's home in Izieu. In today's morning hours the "Jewish Children's Home" "Children's colony" [first in German, then in French] was emptied out. [The verb is *ausheben*, perhaps better translated as "robbed," as one would eggs from a nest.] A total of 41 children aged 3 to 13 years were taken into custody. Further success in securing the entire Jewish staff consisting of 10 head, of which 5 are women. Cash and other valuables could not be secured.

Klarsfeld juxtaposes this to another microhistory of the same event. Many of the children had already been arrested with their parents and had subsequently been freed to the custody of the OSE. We know from other sources that they were having a breakfast of hot chocolate and bread when the SS came and threw them into trucks "like parcels." Klarsfeld reprints letters of some of the children to their parents as captions to their pictures. Henri Goldberg, age fourteen, to his mother: "I'm going to study hard to make you happy . . . and the headmistress and our teachers happy, and myself too, so that after the war you'll find us intelligent and not consider us [him and his brother Joseph] dunces." Aspiring artists, the picture shows him, his brother, three unidentified kids, and an adult—perhaps the farmer for whom he worked occasionally—looking at a sketch pad.[46]

The list in this case, as in all cases of naming the dead, bears a metonymic relationship to those who are being commemorated. It is disconcerting that the form of commemoration here is determined so much by a part of murder itself. Klarsfeld's categories are perforce Nazi categories, since his sources are the lists of various sorts that the murderers used to identify, classify, locate, arrest, deport, and ultimately kill Jews. Like a strange version of Christian Stations of the Cross—the Via Dolorosa—Klarsfeld's memorial practice follows the paper trail of criminals. Paper was murderous. In the first place there are lists of the names of those who are to be arrested; there were adjustments to these lists. Klarsfeld reproduces two neatly typed registration cards from the Drancy camp. Rene Levy, born in France on 27 May 1934, arrested as part of the "Allg. Massnahmen gegen Juden" (General Measures against Jews), was released despite both his paternal grandparents being Jewish: "Mutter Arierin." His card is marked in pencil, "Libere." Ten-month-old Arlette Chabbat's card, on the other hand, is marked, "Evakuiert, 20 Mai 1944." She too had two Jewish grandparents. But her card reads: "Uneheliches Kind Mutter Jüdin" (illegitimate child, mother Jewish). She got onto the list for convoy 74 and, along with ninety-nine other children, went to her death. There were sixteen sublists for convoy 36. It is a testimony to the extraordinary energy, time, and intelligence of Klarsfeld and his coworkers that they were able to reconstruct for us to contemplate so much of the horrible bureaucratic skein of lists upon lists of names: four names from Besançon; fifty-three from Claivaux, without date of birth or nationality; one hundred thirty five names sent from the camp of Leland to Durance, many children without parents. There are fifty-one last-minute additions on a sublist to convoy 26, mostly people wanting to leave with members of their families, but also one child listed as "a boy of 3" and "a little girl wearing placard #36." No effort was spared to make these lists monuments to the actual victims. Bernard Dziubas, pictured in a dark wool jumpsuit and wearing knee socks, a great mess of dark locks surrounding his face, was known to have been deported at age five, but Klarsfeld was not able to find his convoy number. By imagining a phonetic version of his name as a five-year-old might pronounce it—Jubes, Bernard—he was able to determine that Bernard Dziubas left for Auschwitz on convoy 49, March 2, 1943.[47]

Although one cannot, mercifully, actually still see the microgeographies of this terror—the transit camps, the rail sidings, and the bus depots—Klarsfeld does offer the means to imagine with precision, stairway by stairway, convoy by convoy, car by car, the spaces in and through which the Jews of France were destroyed. In stairway 9 at the transit camp at Drancy were sixty-four people, all adolescents and young children, whose names we know are on the list of those slated for convoy 27, which left for Auschwitz on 2 September 1942; car 7 of convoy 24 held one man and thirty-three children; car 8, forty children and seven adults, including Ita Epelbaum, age thirty-one, and her seven children, ages eleven, nine, seven, two six-year-old twins, Henri, five, and Arlette, three. We have photographs of them in better circumstances. Many of the kids in this convoy had already been through various other camps en route to this, their final French stop before their 26 August 1942 departure for Auschwitz (937 out of 1,002 were gassed on arrival).[48]

Klarsfeld tells us precisely and in mundane detail what happened in each small step of the French Holocaust. On 9 February, police acquired lists of children in the Rothschild Foundation; at 6:30 in the morning on 10 February, five inspectors broke into a dormitory, awakened twelve children, and took them away; at one in the morning on 11 February, they came to take away four girls aged fifteen and sixteen. But the coolness of this account takes on a different resonance when we turn the page and see a picture of nineteen children with pillowcase sacks slung over their shoulders—at the far left a little boy clowns, looking straight into the camera—leaving an orphanage in secret on their way to refuge with non-Jewish families.[49]

I dwell on this one history of the names of the Holocaust not because it is unusual (although it is beautifully researched and artfully presented) and not because it is particularly influential, although it is (Klarsfeld's work led to the prosecution of leading Vichy figures and a reexamination of the French role in the murder of its Jews), and not because it has found echoes elsewhere, although it has (a 100-meter-long, 13-meter-high memorial in Roglit in Israel bears the names of all the 73,157 murdered Jews of France, 962 more than Thiepval in the Somme, which had, until 1981, been the greatest assemblage of names in stone in the world), but because it is exemplary. Nothing has generated names on the scale of the Shoah, not even the Great War. The age of necronominalism had come to its terrible maturity.

This suggests the question, What explains the rise of a democracy of naming and its triumph in the twentieth-century age of necronominalism? One explanation would invoke democracy more generally: the democracy of naming had its origins in the age of the democratic revolutions of the late eighteenth and early nineteenth centuries. But this is little more than a redescription—a tautology—unless we understand democracy as a subjective state, a sensibility, a way of living among others and of publicly narrating a life, a condition of being human, a relationship with God and with religious authorities. From all this might flow certain rights and obligations. But certain of these conditions can and have influenced the history of the naming of the dead with nothing even remotely connected with democracy as a set of political arrangements. The claims of the names of the dead are parallel to the claims of the names of the living: a claim to a life equal to other lives, a claim to a life story with a meaningful denouement, a claim to a part in the making of history and the social order at different levels. And more. In this sense, naming the dead is less a result of than a constituent of democracy as a set of subjective conditions. More generally, like changes in the places of the dead, the age of necronominalism arises from new demands by the living on the dead. Mr. Cogito needs to know because of a new moral orientation toward the dead.

A fuller explanation of the age of necronominalism works on three levels. First, the names of the dead draw on deep anthropological and historical roots for their power; the weight of a deep past is felt still today. Second, there are important changes, beginning in the sixteenth and seventeenth centuries and accelerating dramatically in the late eighteenth and nineteenth centuries, in the function of names—of the living and of the dead—at all levels. Finally, as my discussion of the names of the dead of the Shoah has shown, and as a case study of the Great War in the next chapter will develop more fully, the age of the necronominalism in full flower is born of a conjuncture of the interests of the state, of civil society, and of the individual psyche, each of which for its own sometimes overlapping, sometimes disparate and incompatible, reasons needs the names of the dead.

Chapter 9
THE NAMES
OF THE GREAT WAR

My own dear Mother. . . . We were marooned on a frozen desert. . . . There is not a sign of life on the horizon and a thousand signs of death. Not a blade of grass, not an insect . . . but extra for me is the universal pervasion of ugliness. Hideous landscapes . . . everything unnatural, broken, blasted; the distortion of the dead, whose un-buriable bodies sit outside dug-outs all day, all night, the most execrable sights on earth. In poetry we call them the most glorious. But to sit with them all day, all night . . . and a week later to come back and find them sitting there, in a motionless group, THAT is what saps the soldierly spirit.

WILFRED OWEN, *Letters . . .,* SUNDAY, 4 FEBRUARY 1917

ignorance about those who are lost
undermines the reality of the world
casts us in the hell of appearance
the diabolical net of the dialectic
which says there is no difference
between substance and specter
we must therefore know
draw up exact accounts
summon them by name
ready them for the road
in a clay bowl
millet poppyseed
an ivory comb
arrowhead
a ring of fidelity
amulets

ZBIGNIEW HERBERT, "MR. COGITO
ON THE NEED FOR PRECISION"

The English poet Wilfred Owen writes in this letter to his mother not only about the battlefield of Flanders—the cold that left him numb and some of his companions dead; the thirst he suffered because Sterno cans were not hot enough to melt enough snow to drink; the near madness from the bursting of high explosives; "the universal pervasion of ugliness"—but also about the most execrable sight on earth: the unburiable dead. He indulges in the grotesque irony that would inform so powerfully the memory of the Great War: "in poetry we call them the most glorious." But he gives voice also to the immemorial abjection of the dead and to the expectation that in a normal world they will, they can, they should be buried properly instead of remaining in their distorted forms among the living. He writes too in the knowledge that these dead have an audience: his mother and other mothers. The dead of the Great War died and were unburiable by the hundreds of thousands on the battlefront, but they subsisted also within the narrative embrace of a wider world. The attention to the names of the Great War makes this clear.[1]

The Polish poet Zbigniew Herbert, whose verses have informed the previous two chapters, speaks here again precisely on the theme of this chapter: not knowing who is lost "undermines the reality of the world." And knowing who is lost, name by name if possible, remakes it. So does creating an apotheosis of namelessness. No grave at Westminster Abbey was more visited than that of the Unknown Warrior, both by its Dean, who dwelled with it, and by uncountable others to this day. Amulets are left on the grave. He is readied "for the road." There had never before in history been so massive an effort to "draw up exact accounts/to summon them by name" as there was during and after the Great War, never a time when an "unknown soldier" stood singularly for a great multitude of names bereft of their bodies and bodies bereft of their names, never a time when the reality of the world seemed more shattered. It began an era.

This chapter puts the names of the dead in the Great War in the context specifically of the modern history of naming the dead of war but also in the broader context of the previous three chapters. It shows, in fine grain, the advent of a new era of the work of the dead at the level of the state, of civil society, and of the individual—of the Emily Chitticks of the world. It might have been about the American Civil War: its dead and its living were the pioneers of the full-blown age of necronominalism. But that history has already been written, and sometimes sheer quantitative scale—the tenfold or greater increase in the dead of the First World War—speaks for something new.

These years produced the greatest assemblage of names in world history and probably also the greatest number of memorials. There are tens of thousands of local monuments in Great Britain alone on which are inscribed lists of the names of men—and in some cases women too—who died between 1914 and 1918.

Nearly every French, German, Italian, and Austrian village, town, and city has one as well. Thousands of schools, businesses, places of worship, and clubs have their lists of the names of the dead. There is a monument to the squire's son in many a village church. This most bureaucratic and global of wars produced the most intense local writing of the names of the dead ever seen.[2]

The same can be said at a national level. By 1930, 587,117 soldiers of the British Empire had been buried, or reburied, in identified (named) graves. Another 180,861 unidentified bodies—each marked on a 1 cm–to–40,000 km map to within ten meters of where it was found—were put in separate, unidentified graves, for a total of 767,978. (There are very few British, as opposed to German, mass graves.) The names of these men and of an additional 336,912 whose bodies had disappeared, the newly exigent category of the "missing"—a total of almost 518,000—were inscribed on imposing major monuments that stretch for hundreds of miles along the western front. The density of names on stone is new in world history; just producing the list for the stonemasons to engrave took hundreds of thousands of hours. Nothing like it had "been dreamt of before," wrote Sir Reginald Blomfield, one of the three senior architects in charge.[3]

And the difficulties of building them were commensurate with their novelty; writing the dead in stone by the thousands and tens of thousands now seems so sadly commonplace that it is easy to forget what a prodigious epigraphic challenge this seemed a century ago. "I had to find space for a vast number of names, at first estimated at 40,000," Blomfield writes. That number went up to 58,000, but despite trying to cram 1,200 panels up all of the major columns, along stairs, and on the walls of terraces that abut the ramparts of tunnel arches that led from Ypres to the battlefield beyond and to the town of Menin, it could be made to hold only 54,896. "So interminably many," the German novelist Stefan Zweig wrote, "that as on the columns of the Alhambra, the writing becomes decorative." But it never quite did; the names remained clear and distinct. Blomfield asked for, and got, from a notoriously parsimonious patron, an extra £500 (something like five years of wages for a fully employed craftsman in the building trades) to build a mockup of one panel just to see whether the calculations about letter size, spacing, leading (spacing between lines), and so on would give the required density and legibility. Miscalculations of one-eighth inch, he pointed out, would result in more than two thousand too many or too few names. He proclaims himself apologetic for continuing negotiations but points out that this is a "matter so important . . . every precaution should be taken to see that we get it right." He excuses his persistence "over the question of the name panels for the Menin Gate," because "in many ways they will be for the interested public the most important feature of the Memorial." He was right (figs. 9.1, 9.2).[4]

9.1. Interior of Menin Gate, Ypres, Belgium.

9.2. Exterior of Menin Gate, Ypres, Belgium.

The names that remained from the Ypres Salient, defined arbitrarily to relieve Ypres of the number of names it could not bear as those who died after the night of 15–16 August 1917, are inscribed on the seemingly endless walls of Tyne Cot, just to the south. The date marks the night of the Battle of Langemarck near Passchendaele, a village close to Ypres. Producing the lists themselves, deciding whose name went where, was another novel and enormously difficult task to which I will return. But the point here is that the big problem was to give each list meaning—these men lost their names or their names lost their bodies near here—while dividing it up so it could be inscribed. "Was there," the bureaucrat in charge asks his boss, "any reasonable interpretation of the term that would give us as low a figure as 50,000 'missing' [for Menin Gate] and if so what interpretation?" The date 15–16 August 1917 was chosen because it left Blomfield's memorial with a number that it could accommodate. And so the 34,888 names that were sent east surround 11,908 individual gravestones at Tyne Cot. The disembodied names of another 11,447 men—the dead of battles from Armentiers and Aubers Ridge in 1914 to Hazebrouck and Scherpenberg in 1918—are on the colonnades of the Ploegstreert Memorial a dozen or so kilometers to the south. I cannot list every memorial. Thirty kilometers further south is the Duds Corner Memorial, where visitors enter a courtyard formed by panels with 20,589 names from the battles around Loos. Then ten kilometers on, more than eleven thousand names of Canadians with no known graves stretch out on the stone walls to either side of Walter Allard's two monumental figures on Vimy Ridge. Thirty kilometers to the south-southwest is Cambrai, with 7,048 names. In the heart of the Somme bat-

tlefield near a destroyed village stands Lutyens's towering monument at Thiepval (fig. 9.3), where sixteen weight-bearing columns hold up the massive structure, each one faced on three or four sides with panels holding a total of 73,367 names of men with no known resting place who died and were lost in this sector (see chapter 8).

There are other British repositories of names, not to speak of hundreds of cemeteries, each with from a score to more than ten thousand grave markers, some with names, others with the notation that here lies a soldier whose name is known

9.3. Thiepval Memorial to the Missing.

but to God. Even the pyramids pale by comparison with the sheer scale of British, let alone German, French, Belgian, and Portuguese commemorative imposition of the landscape: millions of bodiless names hovering near where those they belonged to died; millions of names over bodies. The first monument to ordinary dead soldiers was built in Lucerne in 1821 and is dedicated to the memory of the Swiss Guard killed during the French Revolution in the attack on the Tuileries Palace, 10 August 1792, that captured Louis XVI and his family: there are on it the names of 760 men who were killed and of 350 who survived. The first democratic monument was to soldiers who died defending a king against the Demos. There are 509 names of citizens who died in the battles of the Revolution of 1830 on the Colonne de Juillet built between 1835 and 1840. The quantitative change over the next century defines a qualitative revolution in the naming of the dead.[5]

This gigantic effort to name dead soldiers at or near where their bodies lie is radically new in British military practice and a dramatic expansion of domestic practices. Mass graves had disappeared from the nineteenth-century cemeteries of Britain by the 1860s, but the poor were still routinely buried four to a grave, and a majority of the dead were still laid to rest anonymously. By contrast, we know the name, rank, and regiment of the first British soldier killed in the Great War: Private John Parr of the Middlesex Regiment, who was wounded by a German patrol two days before the Battle of Mons in Walloon, Belgium, just north of the French border. He died on 23 August 1914 and is buried at St. Symphorien cemetery, where the Germans had begun to bury their earliest casualties. At 9:30 in the morning on 11 November 1918, in the last hours before the armistice that would end the carnage, Private George Edwin Ellison of the 5th Irish Lancers, was mortally wounded near where the war's first battle was fought. He lies a few yards from Private Parr. (Some claim that the strange honor of being the last soldier of the British Empire to die before the Armistice was a Canadian, Private George Lawrence Price, shot by a sniper at 10:58 A.M. I am less interested in adjudicating these claims than in the fact that we know enough to even discuss the matter.)[6]

Now the question is how and why this massive writing of the dead—local as well as on the fields of battle—happened as it did. To answer this question we need to go back in a more focused way to the story I began earlier of how the names of the dead became exigent in public and private life.

Both Private John Parr of the Middlesex Regiment and George Edwin Ellison, of the 5th Irish Lancers, as well as George Lawrence Price of the 28th North East Battalion, Second Canadian Brigade, lie less than twelve miles from the site of the Battle of Malplaquet where, in 1709 during the War of Spanish Succession, the Duke of Marlborough lost twenty thousand men in his much-celebrated and famously bloody victory over the French. Soldiers in the Great War marched by on the way to and from Mons and stopped by the solitary obelisk on the fields that silently witnessed one of the deadliest battles in Western military history. We do not know—to be precise, there is not commemorated on the battlefield—the name of a single one of those who died on that 11 September more than three centuries ago. Anonymity was the norm. It is impossible to give precise numbers, but of the many hundreds or even thousands of men in the Revolutionary army who died from wounds or disease with Washington at Valley Forge, not one is named where he died. Less surprisingly (Wellington famously referred to the British soldier as the scum of the earth), we can search up and down Spain at the sites of great battles and sieges of the Iron Duke's famous peninsular campaigns between 1808 and 1814—Vimierea (eight hundred Allied dead), Corunna (a thousand British losses), Albuera (seven thousand dead, including half the entire British force), Badajoz and Burgos (five thousand and seven thousand dead, respectively)—without finding the name of even one common soldier or a memorial to them collectively. One of the most recited poems of the nineteenth century—a standard of the school canon in Britain and the United States—mourns the anonymous burial of Sir John Moore, the British commander at Corunna, with a sensibility that a century later would embrace Everyman:

> No useless coffin enclosed his breast,
> Not in sheet or in shroud we wound him;
> But he lay like a warrior taking his rest
> With his martial cloak around him.
> Slowly and sadly we laid him down,
> From the field of his fame fresh and gory;
> We carved not a line, and we raised not a stone,
> But we left him alone with his glory.[7]

Waterloo, the last great battle of the French Revolutionary wars, is missing most of the names of the dead, but its history hints at the emotional and aesthetic infrastructure that would support necronominalism in the next century. On 18 July 1815, Wellington's army lost fifteen thousand men, their bodies in some cases fallen with the geometrical precision of the battle formations of the day: "the 27th [Inniskilling] were lying literally in a square." There is a monument on the battlefield to Victor Hugo commemorating his stay at the Hotel des Colonnes when he was writing the Waterloo chapters of *Les Misérables*; there is none to any of the dead Inniskillings. In the nearby village church, there are the names of twelve private soldiers of the Twelfth Light Dragoons. There are a few names of officers here and there. Otherwise nothing. "Shoveled into a hole . . .

and so forgotten," as the novelist William Makepeace Thackeray wrote after a visit to the battlefield in 1844. "English glory," he continues, "is too genteel to meddle with these humble fellows. She does not condescend to ask the names of the poor devils whom she kills in her service."

"Earth," Robert Southey writes,

> had received into her silent womb
> Her slaughtered creatures; horse and man they lay,
> And friend and foe, within the general tomb.
> Equal had been their lot; one fatal day
> For all, . . . one labour, . . . and one place of rest
> They found within their common parent's breast.

Only "the breeze upon its breath" bore "a taint of death." The "shoe, and belt, and broken bandoleer / And hat which bore the mark of mortal wound" were all that marked the thousands who did not return from Waterloo.[8]

But there is something new in Southey's sensibility: the battlefield had become a ruin, a site of pilgrimage to be cherished, a reminder of the ravages of time and the fragility of memory. It was the first such secular place since Marathon.

> The passing seasons had not yet effaced
> The stamp of numerous hoofs impressed by force
> Of cavalry, whose path might still be traced.
> Yet Nature every where resumed her course;
> Slow pansies to the sun their purple gave,
> And the soft poppy blossomed on the grave.

The farmer, frustrated in his labors by battle, now turns the "guilty ground" with his plough; green corn will grow; weeds fertilized by the dead will thrive. It had also become a pilgrimage site, a place of relics, the first battlefield *lieu de mémoire* of modern times: a self-conscious place of memory born of a moment when there was, or was perceived to be, "the increasingly rapid slippage of the present into a historical past that is gone for good, a general perception that anything and everything may disappear." Byron visited; so did the Wordsworths—twice—and the architect and collector John Soane and thousands of others. They carried away skulls—Sir Walter Scott had one—and fingers and teeth and bullets and cannon balls; an entrepreneur put Napoleon's coach on display in London. When the painter William Turner visited Waterloo, he had with him a copy of "A walk over the field of battle . . ." from a well-known guidebook to Belgium. A century later such battlefield tourism would flourish even if its more gruesome collecting tastes were suppressed.[9]

Most immediately important for the history of naming the dead is that Waterloo was the first modern battle where the missing and unnamed soldier became an object of emotional and aesthetic engagement. The poet in Southey's *Pilgrimage* speaks of a father who had come to the battlefield to find his son in a common grave:

> That soldier's name
> Was not remembered there, yet may the verse
> Present this reverent tribute to his herse.

And Turner's *The Field of Waterloo* (plate 15) may be the first painting we have of women looking for their men—a prefiguring of the Emilys of the Great War in search of their Wills. Most striking to contemporaries was what the painting was not: it was not in the heroic tradition of battlefield pictures; it was not patriotic. A great heap of dead men and animals, friends and enemies, lie in bloody heaps. Three women, perhaps the wives or sweethearts who had accompanied their men to the battlefield and had been waiting at its edges until the fighting was over, are trying to make sense of it. We do not know who they are; some of the men shown are ordinary soldiers, some officers. One of the women who are standing looks aristocratic; the one who is kneeling less so, and she is directing her gaze toward the French dead. By torchlight and light from the afterglow of the burning manor house at Hougoumont, where some of the most intensive fighting of the day had occurred, they search for their men. The painting was made with scrupulous attention to topographical details: "4,000 killed here," "1,000 killed here," Turner writes on his sketches. Each hollow, road, and copse of trees is carefully identified.

The *Field at Waterloo* was not a popular painting; it was shown with verses from Byron's *Childe Harold's Pilgrimage* at the Royal Academy in 1817 and not shown again in the painter's lifetime. It had little effect on what was done with the dead of war. These remained overwhelmingly unnamed, buried in anonymously in mass graves. But Turner's searching figures are striking. In a watercolor study (plate 16) they are absent; it shows only bodies, a fiery sky, and scarred earth. In the oil painting, by contrast, they represent the subjective world of emotions—needing to know where the dead are, to know that a loved one really is dead—in a scene of great historical, great public, significance: a kind of modern Marathon; a landscape already pregnant with memory.[10]

The Napoleonic Wars had a memorial afterlife at a more modest level, thanks to the nascent historical preservation movement that was invented in the nineteenth century. An "increased interest felt in these historic spots," says the author of an 1878 pamphlet on the Guards' Cemeteries in St. Etienne, Bayonne, has given him hope that sales will generate enough funds to build a memorial tower at Biarritz to the memory of the officers and men who fell in the south-west of France in 1813–1814. In addition to pictures of the extant graves—all of officers—the author appends an alphabetically arranged list of the names of the officers of the British army who died in these campaigns: Major Ackland Dudley to Captain Charles White. "And men . . ." is a gesture to new late nineteenth-century sensibilities.[11]

But these took time to find expression in stone. Forty-five thousand men died from battles and disease between 1853 and 1856 in the Crimean War, and they were mostly, as in earlier wars, not worth knowing by name. Their suffering, however, had come to public attention through the efforts, most famously, of Florence Nightingale but also those of war correspondents and photographers. Neither they nor their graves were as entirely forgettable as they would have been before. We know there were at least 139 cemeteries. Prince Albert thought it worth acquiring a photograph of individually named graves of the dead of war, the first of its kind: the war photographer James Robertson's salt print of an unidentified burial ground. The National War Museum owns one of his prints: officers' tombstones in the 77th Regiment's cemetery, modest but tidy. There are at least three more of this genre, two by Roger Fenton of the graves on Cathcart's Hill and another of an unnamed site.

While most cemeteries did not contain individual memorials, some did: 51 out of 324 in one of the burial grounds of the Second Brigade, Light Division; 22 out of 1,334 in the cemeteries of the Third Division. One of these cemeteries was said to resemble a "humble imitation of Kensal Green, and contain some handsome monuments, in design and execution far from inferior to many in England." As in Kensal Green Cemetery back home, the poor were largely packed into common and often unmarked graves. But some were not. Private soldiers were occasionally written in death: "Sacred to the memory of Pte Martin Dowd 63rd Regt Died 30th Sepr 1855"; "Sacred to the memory of Private James Lewis Lt. Co. 57th Regiment who was killed in the Trenches on the 24th day of May 1855 Aged 22 years"; "Beneath this humble tablet lie the remains of James Brodie Band 72nd Highlanders who died June 19th 1855 Aged 19 years. This small tribute of respect erected by his comrade Corpl Jams Stewart 72nd Highlanders."[12]

The state had nothing to do with any of this and did not take responsibility for maintaining the cemeteries of the Crimea in the decades to come. They began to vanish into the landscape, but now the public noticed: "Over the graves of our dead heroes, and their no less heroic hospital nurses and attendants, browsed three donkeys belonging to some wandering Yuruks," a letter writer tells the *London Times* about the cemeteries around Smyrna. "The grass, nourished into life by the autumn rains, was greening upon the nameless and undistinguished graves of our countrymen." Wooden crosses were down, stone monuments off their foundations, inscriptions barely legible. Grazing cattle did not help. Still, contemporaries thought this state of disrepair worth investigation. It was no longer the default condition. Civil society noticed namelessness and the ravages of time even if the state did not.[13]

Perhaps in light of this neglect we should not expect much for the dead of Queen Victoria's little imperial wars. But parody sometimes announces the dawn. At the Battle of Maiwand (27 July 1880) in the Second Afghan War, 962 officers and men died. A burial party returned in September, reinterred the hastily covered dead, and erected a single marker: to Major Blackwood of the Royal Horse Artillery. A pet dog survived the rout and managed to catch up with the bedraggled retreating British forces. He shipped back to England and, once home, was invited to visit Queen Victoria at Osborne House, her residence on the Isle of Wight. She gave him a medal. When this brave dog died, he was stuffed and installed in the regimental museum. We know his name: "Bobbie" of the Royal Berkshires. A few years before, during the Franco-Prussian War the German army became the first in Europe to introduce the "hundenmark" in Germany, a reference to the dog tags that the dogs of Berlin were required to have at about the same time. Pets, if not humans, had to be identified, and the British army noticed. (In fact, even this strange story speaks of a new age. The officer who returned to rebury the dead did identify some of them, although we do not know how or why their names are nowhere noted.)[14]

In 1899, Thomas Hardy published one of the last of the much-recited death poems of the nineteenth century, a common boy's version of Charles Wolfe's "Burial of Sir John Moore after Corunna." (The others are Gray's "Elegy" from the century before and Felicia Hemans's "Casabianca"—"The boy stood on the burning deck.") Hardy's is about an anonymous burial of an unknown young man, as if to claim for him what Wolfe had claimed for a lieutenant general:

> They throw in Drummer Hodge, to rest
> Uncoffined—just as found:
> His landmark is a kopje-crest
> That breaks the veldt around:
> And foreign constellations west
> Each night above his mound.

It ends with a poignant reversal of Rupert Brooke's sonnet "The Soldier," written on the eve of the Great War, in which England is incorporated in the dead body:

There shall be
In that rich earth a richer dust concealed;
A dust whom England bore, shaped, made aware,
Gave, once, her flowers to love, her ways to roam,
A body of England's, breathing English air,
Washed by the rivers, blest by suns of home.

Young Hodge—the name is a stand-in for a country lad—"never knew the meaning of the broad Karoo." "The bush the dusty loam" becomes a body of the place where he lies:

Yet portion of that unknown plain
Will Hodge for ever be.[15]

After the South African Boer War (1899–1902), the war in which young Drummer Hodge died, the state was willing to provide small iron crosses to mark the graves of those among the almost six thousand dead who were not privately commemorated: memory of last resort. Nothing more. Most of the twenty-two thousand dead from battle or disease sank quickly into oblivion. But this did not happen without protest; the days of the complacent erasure of the names of the ordinary dead had passed. The secretary of state for war opposed the consolidation of the more than 170 burial places, and thus the creation of substantial commemorative sites; he suggested that a cairn might be set up with the names of the dead in any given place, but he was against individual tombstones marking graves and against the consolidation of graves more generally: soldiers were to be buried where they fell. The largest congregation of the dead consisted of 421 bodies; only six sites held more than 100; most were tiny, with no more than 10 graves. It was civil society, in particular women's groups, that did the work of memory. The Loyal Woman's Guild assumed responsibility both for the maintenance of scattered burial places and for communication with kin searching for loved ones. Ordinary people cared. Mary Curry, the guild's secretary, wrote to an official in 1903 that the graves are "impossible to preserve." Those at Magersfonteirn, she reports, had been "disturbed by jackals and other animals burrowing" and were "causing great grief to those concerned." Nothing was done officially, but the women raised the money to register and care for graves, to photograph them and send the pictures to relatives so that they could imagine where their sons were buried, and to maintain lists of the names of the dead. Their bodies remain scattered and haphazardly remembered. Then there was case-by-case work: where, asked the family of Private F. Houghton (No. 2394) of the Royal Scots Fusiliers, was his body? The Canadian patriotic women's organization, the Federation of

Daughters of the British Empire, sought its help to preserve the distant graves of dead countrymen.[16]

And so things stood on the eve of the Great War except for one other great precedent that was neither causally nor administratively linked to what happened after 1914 but born of a common sensibility. When, after the Boer War, the South African Guild of Loyal Women proposed National Cemeteries based explicitly on the model of the American Civil War, nothing happened. But the guild was on to something important. Mourning and memory embraced civil society, both in the North and South, after 1861 and led to both state and civil society efforts to keep track of the dead: to name them, to mark their bodies, to keep them as a part of families, to make of them members of local communities, of the Lost Cause and of the Nation. The exchange that we witnessed between Emily Chitticks and her Will Martin and between her and the authorities to discover what happened to his body is an echo of earlier exchanges like it in America. I give but one example to suggest that a new emotional and communicative world was already in place and that the dead and the living were together building a Republic of Suffering.[17]

On 24 May 1864, the family of Private Abram Clendening of the 5th Ohio Sharpshooters received a sad letter from one of his comrades: "I cant right mutch at this time," it began, but "I want to tell you that your son is with us no more for ever he only live one hour after he was shot." On 15 July of the next year, one of Abram's brothers received another, much more detailed and literate letter, this one from the sexton of the military hospital cemetery in Bridgeport, Alabama, in response to a query about Private Clendening's body. There was, the sexton admits, a discrepancy between the date of death and the date on a wooden board that he thought identified the grave: it said 13 May 1864, but Abram was supposed to have died on 12 May. But there were no unknown graves near it prior to 5 April 1865; so the nameless grave marked 13 May is certainly a soldier's grave and not that of a citizen: "You are certain," he assures his correspondent, that "this being the only unknown grave between the dates above written and corresponding to your brother's death fixed in my mind the final resting place of your brother." And again, after giving more forensic detail, a summary: "The Sexton's records harmonizing with each other leaves but little or no doubt of it as I have said the no. of the grave is 236 marked 'died May 13, 1864 Unknown.'" A final P.S.: "My assistant has just told me that 'soldier' is also written on the head board." This letter seems to have been lost, because on 20 January 1867, the brother writes once again to the superintendent of the military cemetery. He refers to two earlier letters that seem not to have survived—of 14 January and 8 June 1865—and to the letter that we have, which, the brother recalls, mentioned grave number either 230 or 236 and offered evidence the grave in question was indeed his brother's. The oak tree on a hill that had originally marked the grave had been cut down. Could the commander confirm these details so that "he may know to a certainty almost whether it is his or not. I will send on directions about marking it." He asks also whether the government is taking as great pains in gathering in the dead, enclosing their burial places, and fixing head boards as it is where he lives in Mill Creek, Berkeley County, West Virginia. Stories like this could be multiplied in the tens of thousands. They are part of the changes we have seen that collectively make writing the dead a cultural if not a political imperative. The much more extensive involvement of the state in these matters is a response not just to the great forces of history—nationalism, bureaucracy, democracy—but also to a world in which more and more lives demand a denouement and their bodies a known resting place.[18]

None of the states that went to war in late July and early August 1914 imagined that the conflict would be as long or as deadly as it turned out to be and had no plans to name, record, or bury the dead beyond the half-measures of the nineteenth century. The Battle of Mons shattered delusions. In the British case, it became clear almost immediately that the public would no longer tolerate the chaos that had ruled in South Africa and that, in the absence of any state organization interested in or equipped to keep track of the dead—or for that matter the missing and the wounded—a voluntary organization, the Red Cross in this case, would have to assume the task. It very early on began preparing lists of the dead; the poet T. S. Eliot writes in a letter to his brother on 8 September 1914 how he had been awakened by cries of "Extra, extra!" and seen in the newspaper the headline "GREAT GERMAN DISASTER!" and a list of the dead and wounded. Common soldiers ceased to be "buried where they fell—in the fields, in the roadsides, sometimes singly, sometimes together," writes a member of a British Red Cross unit in his war diary; he and his colleagues began "to search for graves, identify soldiers, mark them with a cross, register their position." He reported that "no unit of the army existed to do such registration work." The Red Cross also tried to bring order to the emotional detritus of war: "Letters addressed to soldiers picked up on the Marne battlefields were brought to the office, which undertook to return them to the writers." (The return of letters and personal items is a common trope in the writing of those who cared for the dead. A chaplain reports, to take a random example of the desperately sad task of going through the papers taken from the bodies of the dead, that he found "a child's first letter to 'Daddy,' printed crooked, ill-spelt . . . a paper of peppermints . . . the pictured face of an old woman.")[19]

The Red Cross continued throughout the war to help relatives get news of their missing relatives; 150 volunteers, a small staff, and 15 typists worked to find men who were for the time being neither dead nor alive. But other agencies took over its other roles. In October 1916, a new Central Prisoners of War Committee within the War Ministry began keeping track of prisoners, although the Red Cross worked closely with it. More important, registering a man's death became the job of a new bureaucracy: the "War Office Casualty Branch." The determination of this irreducible fact—death—was the first step in the process of notifying kin. Generally, but not in all cases, the families of officers got a telegram, and the families of those in the ranks a letter. The great cascade of state and civil processes that had by the early twentieth century descended on the dead followed: issuance of a death certificate, payment of pensions and death benefits, probate and return of property found on the body. This beau modern Charon of a bureaucracy ferried men from the world of the living to the dead. It was a staggering task.

The Casualty Branch grew from a handful of staff to more than seven hundred clerks who managed ten million index cards that occupied 42,000 square feet of office space. Four or five people did nothing but prepare the lists of the dead that were published every day in newspapers throughout the country. State bureaucracy on a previously unimagined scale enabled not only instrumental rationality but eventually also the writing of the names of the dead on monuments, local memorials, and hundreds of thousands of tombstones. Intimacy was dependent on its opposite, and vice versa.[20] But the Casualty Branch only handled the formalities. In March 1915, the bodies of the dead (and eventually the collection of their names) became the province of another new bureaucracy, the Graves Registration Commission, which in February 1916 morphed into the Directorate of Graves Registration and Enquiries. This agency was loosely integrated into the military bureaucracy through the office of its chief administrative officer, the adjutant general. Like the Casualty Office, its number of staff grew: from 10 to 109 to 608 to 777 by February 1918. Of these, 497 were women on the home front who kept the voluminous files generated by the men at the battle lines. By March 1916, the Directorate had chosen two hundred cemetery sites and had plans for an additional three hundred to three thousand, depending "on the extent of future fighting." For the first time in British military history, scattered bodies were to be gathered together, reinterred, and if at all possible individually marked, photographed, and mapped. The Imperial War Graves Commission (IWGC), later the Commonwealth War Graves Commission, received a royal charter in 1917 and between the armistice in 1918 and the early 1930s employed thousands of people to create permanent cemeteries and memorial sites of the Great War (fig. 9.4, plate 17).[21]

9.4. Burial service near the trenches at the Somme, September 1916. Imperial War Museum.

It was soon very clear at the highest level that the care of graves and the writing of the dead of war was rooted not in the interests of the military and only partially in the politics of the nation but rather in the intimate lives of citizens. Field Marshal Douglas Haig, commander of the British armies on the western front from late 1915 to the end of the war, understood that the dead of war could no longer simply disappear as they had in the Napoleonic wars and that *raison d'état* was not the reason, at least not the whole reason. "I fully recognized," he wrote, "that the work of the [Graves Registration Commission] is of purely sentimental value, and that it does not directly contribute to the successful termination of the war." But it has "extraordinary moral value" both to the troops and to the "relatives and friends of the dead." The nation, he concludes, "will demand an account from the Government" as to what it had done to "mark and classify the burial place of the dead." Edmund Whitman, a former army quartermaster who became responsible for setting up the National Cemetery System in the United States fifty years earlier, when it was a wholly new enterprise, had understood this: "Such a consecration of a nation's power and resources to a *sentiment* the world has never witnessed." He was speaking of the discovery, ingathering, reburial, and commemoration of soldiers' bodies after the Civil War. The Great

War would magnify that enterprise more than tenfold, and it would be driven by sentiment—by the intimate connection of the living and dead—as well as by an imperative to gather together those who died for the nation.[22]

The diary of one army chaplain, Ernest Crosse, contradicts Haig's claim about the irrelevance of burying the dead to the actual war effort. It was a matter of "real military significance," he wrote, worth the risk of having burial parties killed, because "nothing is more depressing to the living than to see unburied men around them." He recorded the burials at which he presided on the War Graves Registration map and then wrote to the families of men from the ranks. He remarked that officers who were killed had friends who usually supplied details to next of kin, but the families of enlisted men, who also had lives and deaths worth noting—they are perfectly well known to their comrades—received officially "nothing more than the cold official fact notified to them by the War Office." In fact, we know from the archives that men of the ranks wrote in great numbers to the families of their dead comrades, but Crosse's point remains: the dead of this war lived in a new emotional economy.[23]

And this emotional economy demanded something new from the state. As Haig's predecessor, Field Marshal Sir John French, recognized in the context of negotiations with France on a treaty to protect cemeteries, the "care, registration, etc. of graves now assumes a national character" and should therefore become the responsibility of the state. To meet this responsibility, the Directorate and later the War Graves Commission insisted on state control over the bodies of the dead and on determining both the location and the commemorative treatment of their final resting places. Sir Lionel Earle, permanent secretary of the Ministry of Works and member of the new National Committee for the Care of Soldier's Cemeteries (founded 28 December 1915), "laid great stress," the committee's minutes say, "on the necessity for taking strong action to prevent the public from putting up unsuitable effigies in cemeteries and thought that the monuments on all graves should be uniform." (That Earle had a voice on this matter is the result of an anachronism. He served on the IWGC because in the nineteenth century the Office of Works was responsible for the few scores of graves of dead soldiers abroad for which the state did assume responsibility.)

The assumption of state responsibility had less to do with the kind of community of the dead that those in charge wanted to create (although they had strong views on this subject) than with public demand for equality of treatment and with the fact that only the state had the resources to meet the new need for knowing about the names and places of the dead. As we will see later, there was in fact a lot of grousing by some very important people—Churchill, Asquith, and thousands of the British upper classes who signed petitions—against the insistence of the War Graves Commission that the dead belonged collectively together near where they fell and more pointedly that they belonged to the state. There were rumors, both during and after the war, that some bodies were smuggled home rolled up in rugs and transported by small fishing boats or by other means. More about this controversy in a moment. The point for now is that there was no going back; the sort of selective naming and commemoration of earlier wars was politically impossible. In a sense, a new national community of the dead made itself not in the service of, but often despite, some of the most powerful of the land.[24] How did this happen?

There was in the beginning a touching and, in retrospect, naive sense that the dead of war could be buried as they might have hoped for in civilian life. The Red Cross congratulated itself very soon after it began recording graves of the war dead by reporting that "the remains of soldiers have been saved from the common grave and interred in private plots." In fact, more usual were reports on the collapse of civilian decency in death: "the blackness of their exposed features told me that they had long lain thus: in the bustle of preparing for a push the small services due to the dead were often overlooked. I felt sad; there was no peace here even for the dead."[25]

Naming and burying under the conditions of this war was a heartbreaking enterprise. The bureaucratic procedures put in place by the army and the Graves Registration Commission—general orders, forms, chaplains' reports, the orders of the day—all hid reality. They hid the dangers and the backbreaking labor. Reginald Bryson's commander was killed watching the bombardment on the Ypres–Menin Road, but only after surviving the "many occasions [on which] he would go into the front line trenches in order to put a cross on a grave or to see a chaplain." A military chaplain went with fifty men to collect the dead: "163 Devons covered up in a copse"; "crew dead beat—task of filling trench was awfully slow." A photographer attached to the Red Cross was constantly pressed to hurry, to utilize every minute of daylight he could, to record as many graves as possible. He was exhausted. Tens of relatives requested photographs of the graves of their dead loved ones from the Red Cross and the IWGC; when the grave could be found and the battle had moved a few kilometers off, pictures were taken and sent home. Pictures of unburied dead bodies were strictly, indeed obsessively, forbidden. Lord Curzon perhaps understood the primal terror of the uncared-for dead; at the very least, they were dangerous to the morale of the home front.[26]

Hidden too in the bureaucratic forms and procedures was what the writer Edmund Blunden recognized as "the insoluble problem of burying the dead in modern conditions." These included the phantasmagoric moments that Wilfred Owen wrote to his mother about and the more systemic nature of this war. Blunden recounts the fate of an area east of Festubert, a tiny commune in the Pas-de-Calais. In May 1915, British forces launched an attack on the Germans there over swampy ground. There was little movement; as soldiers built or rebuilt trenches, they could hardly dig without discovering the remains of their countrymen or enemies. "Hamlet and Horatio might have meditated there many a dark hour." Then came the next summer and the Battle of the Somme, so fierce and so mired in miles of mud that thousands of bodies were irrecoverable. Relief battalions in the "fire-splashed night" stumbled over corpse after corpse.[27]

It was all very well, if not very cheery for his men, that Captain M. Alexander of the 141st Infantry Brigade, 47th Division, ordered that graves be dug before each battle—six at Bedford House cemetery and six at Chester Farm cemetery (both just south of Ypres)—and that the graves used be replenished by digging fresh ones. "All dead bodies are to be buried as soon as possible." Reality was different: "Moved into trench where Lt. Kidder, Prvt Coombs and White were blown to bits. We gathered their remains in sad bags and buried them 25-7-17." The next day, R. A. Walker reports, he went up to the front again to look for the missing: "no trace of them but we saw lots of dead bodies." It was hopeless. "Often when we moved in the trenches you trod and slipped on rotting flesh."[28]

F. M. Packham, a sergeant, found himself assigned to a burial company along with two corporals and fourteen men; he reported to a chaplain who seems to have himself taken direction from an officer of the IWGC. Every day his company got a detailed map and went as far up the system of duckboards as they could, looking for bodies. They passed men knee-deep in water and mud, men in trenches and shell holes, and stopped at the end of the tracks. They searched for the driest land they could find. Usually no luck. The ground was everywhere too waterlogged to dig individual graves, so they put men into a shell hole, feet to the center. Some looked as if asleep; "others had limbs missing and were horribly mutilated." Sergeant Packham's men took from each body its personal papers and put them in a black bag identified by the man's dog tag. (By 1916, soldiers were supposed to carry two tags, and one was to be left on the body when it was buried. There is little evidence that this happened, which accounts for why so few bodies, stripped of all that belonged intimately to them, could be identified when initial identifying grave markers were destroyed in the course of battle.) "The horses and mules must not be forgotten. It was terrible to see them," deep in the mud trying to drag artillery, Packham concludes, before he starts telling about his company's being reassigned from burial to raiding.[29]

In the midst of all this there is sometimes an almost unbearable intimacy about the archival files that speak today about the urgency of writing the names of the dead in this war: an enormous web of official but also unofficial correspondence from the comrades of the dead to families back home and from families to one another when they had heard something from the front. Gunner E. Handley wrote to the mother of his dead mate Dick Skitt, with whom he had been pals "since we were at Southport together" that her son was hit by shell splinters, taken to a dressing station, and died there. Or at least so he learned from the lads. He was buried in a cemetery not far away from where he—Handley—was when he wrote. Two weeks later, he thanks Dick's mother for sending him a package and acknowledges that she was right about "Fritz not letting the dead alone as he sends his shells all over the place," but that "the place where Dick was buried was alright the day I came away as I went to look." He is happy to report that he—Handley—is in the pink of health.[30]

The parents of Private E. K. Foreman had been in regular contact with him by mail until, on 13 November 1915, a letter was returned unopened: in blue pencil was written "casualty." Foreman had been killed in his trench by the shock waves of a shell blast on 10 November; his body was intact. The father writes to one of his son's mates that since Edgar's letters had all been "bright and breezy" so as to cheer up his parents, they wanted in their grief to know the details of his death and burial. "The fact that we shall never see him again or hear his dear voice gives us deep and bitter anguish," they wrote. They craved news from Edgar's friends. His staff sergeant responded that after the shell hit two bays away, he went to search for survivors. He had hoped that Edgar might still be alive under the rubble but was saddened when he found him dead. He and three comrades were buried behind the trench. "I have tried to indicate as well as I can on a rough sketch the position of the grave," he concluded. Another comrade writes that it will be impossible for Mr. Foreman to visit the grave at the present time, but it was marked with a wooden cross with Edgar's name engraved on it. He hoped that the company officer who took charge of Edgar's diary could find it. (In fact, the map was to no avail; Edgar's grave was hopelessly lost. We do not know whether the body survived, unidentifiable, or if it merged unrecognizably with the muck. We do know from the IWGC files that Private E.K. Foreman's name appears among twenty thousand others similarly lost to their bodies on the Loos Memorial to the missing. It is on panel 132.)[31]

The poet's "Mr. Cogito" wants to know because beginning in the late nineteenth century ordinary people wanted to know. The massive records of the Great War bear witness to both the technology and the emotional infrastructure that made knowing possible and necessary. We know a great deal about Sapper [combat engineer] S. L. Poole because his family knew a lot. He enlisted on 14 August 1914 and went to France on 7 October; he moved to the front of what became known as the First Battle of Ypres on 21 November and was killed between the lines on 18 December, a few days more than four months after he joined. We know from the last entry in his diary on the day he died that he "wrote letters to Fanny, Mr. Portland, Sarah, Harold, and Lizzie wishing them all Happy Christmas." We know what was in the last package his family sent to him. It was returned in the brown paper wrapper on which was written in pencil: "Killed P.P. no. 38, Undelivered Package returned to sender Free, 28-12-1914"; in it, according the list on the wrapper, were socks, a cake, chocolate, and sweets. We know from his captain that he was "buried with two other RE's [Royal Engineers] between the German trenches and ours at about 400 yards S.E. of where the RIVDES-LAYES crosses the SAILLY-FROMELLES road." A map sketch was enclosed. We know that at the time this little archive was accumulated by the Poole family they, of course, did not know that his grave would be lost. His name is one of the 11,320 on the Ploegsteert Memorial in Flanders. There are hundreds and thousands of letters and maps like those to the Foremans and the Pooles and Emily Chitticks in the archives of this war, a fraction of the web of correspondence that connected the dead to their loved ones.[32]

Once the war was over, the battlefield needed to be cleaned up and its dead properly situated with one another and among the living. As modern critics, echoing contemporaries, have rightly pointed out, this constituted an aesthetic obfuscation of reality. But there was no alternative. As the history of sites of horror makes clear, they cannot remain as they were to become shrines to themselves. It was also impossible not to memorialize the dead of war. The cleanup of the battlefield and the exhumation of vast numbers of bodies were less dangerous work than caring for the dead in wartime but in its first stages only slightly less gruesome, an enterprise bedeviled by the sorts of snafus common to large-scale military operations, by disease, and by unexploded ordnance. In the fall of 1919, for example, Captain W. E. Southgate was sitting with his men in the Cambrai subsector, in the Pas-de-Calais in the far north of France. He had been ordered to exhume and rebury two hundred bodies. He was worried that his team's performance would be unfavorably compared to that of other groups; he had no canvas; he had only thirty picks, not enough shovels, and no crosses. Even if he had the equipment that he needed, he couldn't get it to the burial site because promised transportation had failed to appear. In fact, the problem of insufficient army support for gathering together the bodies from some 180,000 scattered graves generated considerable worries in the highest circles. "I need scarcely point out," wrote Sir Robert Borden, the Canadian prime minister, to Lloyd George, "that if there were any carelessness or avoidable failure in this work it would be most unfortunate." Clearly here was an issue the public in Britain and in the empire generally cared about deeply. "Nothing," Borden wrote in one report to the British prime minister, "could be more calculated to produce a public outcry." "Any reasonable suspicion that there has been negligence or inattention with respect to the graves of our soldiers in France would arouse a feeling of stern resentment in Canada and I believe in every one of the dominions." The Army Council apologized for any avoidable delays.[33]

The task was monumental. Photographs not seen at the time show how horrible and abjectly untidy this war of stasis had been. Thousands of laborers, British and foreign, did the hard labor. Almost 1,500 Chinese laborers died on the job, many no doubt from the 1918–1920 influenza epidemic; their bodies rest with those of dead soldiers but with Chinese inscriptions on their tombstones (fig. 9.5). "The vastness of the work of exhumation and concentration of scattered graves" slowed progress, pleaded the War Graves Commission in 1920, by which time it had already overseen the reburial of 128,577 men, of whom 6,273 had been identified for the first time and 66,796 were still, and thus probably would forever remain, unknown. A year later, when systematic efforts to find bodies ceased, the remains of 204,650 dead had been reburied; by 1938, 38,000 more bodies, 80 percent unknown, had been found by farmers, metal searchers, and others. There is a curious letter from Lord Littleton to the secretary of state for war, marked private and confidential, in which he complains that at Ypres they were still finding fifty corpses a week and that he doubted whether "quite such elaborate gardening operations should be involved in their interment" as Sir Fabian Ware and the IWGC were insisting on.[34]

All of this labor was in the service not only of bringing order to the chaos of death but specifically of creating permanent communities of the dead—cemeteries—some large with thousands of graves, some small with a few score bodies. They are, still today, a great palimpsest of mortality that traces the contours of war. There is a sense in which some sort of consolidation of bodies was a political and cultural as well as practical necessity. The Great War—especially, but not only, on the western front—left not the highly localized squares of the dead as at Waterloo or Malplaquet or a few tens of thousands of bodies in a few hundred locations in the South African veld but millions of bodies in tens of thousands of places amidst the heavily cultivated beet and wheat fields of Belgium and France. It would have been inconceivable to let the bodies of dead Anzac troops and those of their British comrades lie here and there at Gallipoli.

But the nature of the places of the dead and the ways in which their names would be gathered were very much in dispute. Whether the IWGC, a quasi-official body, would or should have dominion over all the dead and their public memory was an open question. In general, by the late nineteenth century, the state—or rather the state as the representative of the nation—had a greater need for its dead than in earlier times, largely because of demands made on it by civil society. The number of public funerals rose, and the interests of the nation and civil society could well trump the private interests of families. There were two very public cases of this in the decades before the war. The first involved the body of Charles Darwin, who died on 19 April 1882. His eldest son, William Erasmus Darwin, did not want his father's body to belong to the nation or be appropriated to the glory of some learned society. The great man had hoped to be quietly laid to rest. But the pressure to turn over the body was soon irresistible. Francis Galton, Charles's cousin, wrote to William the next day that he hoped that the family would assent to a burial in Westminster Abbey: "The feeling of the scientific community is deeply touched," he argued. On 23 April, William got a letter from his father's intimate younger friend, Sir John Lubbock, saying that "though individually I should of course have preferred that he should have rested in our quiet little churchyard at Down, where someday I should have joined him," he hoped that the dean of Westminster would give permission for Charles's burial there. "From a national point of view it is only right that he should be buried in the Abbey," Lubbock wrote two days later. The next day, there he was bur-

9.5. Gravestone of a member of the Chinese Labour Corps at the Chinese Cemetery at Noyelles-sur-Mer (Somme).

ied. The story was over in a week. On 29 April, Charlotte Passé, who identifies herself only as "an insignificant and unknown woman," wrote to William that she was happy that, contrary to first reports, he had not refused to let his father's remains be taken away from the family house and that "the great immortal is laid in the only spot that is worthy to him." But her most important argument is one that would be made in other circumstances after 1918: "England had a right to claim this grave."[35]

Forty-six years later, Thomas Hardy's family was even more reluctant to give over the poet's body to the nation than Darwin's had been; and this time the dean of Westminster was not keen on having it either. After he had agreed to accept the body, there was so much controversy that he wrote to Hardy's wife's vicar to inquire whether the poet had been a Christian. But again the demands of the nation as represented by key representatives of civil society prevailed, as if somehow, by burying Hardy in the Abbey, the religious and spiritual muddle of the age could be made to recede, if only for a day. The man who in 1867 had written to his wife, "I could only ask thereof that my worm should be thy worm, love" (that is, that they should be buried together in their churchyard), was in fact buried to prayers that affirmed the life eternal before a great congregation. There was something at once ridiculous and suggestive of the power of the dead in the whole affair. There was no food for worms anywhere; Hardy had been cremated, and the tiny casket with his ashes sat ludicrously on a large bier set up to bear a body in Westminster Abbey. But in the end, the nation got only his body. Two days after he died, a pair of local surgeons removed his heart and put it in a borrowed biscuit tin to await transfer to a small coffin. (There is apparently nothing to the rumor that the cat of one of the surgeons for a time made a claim on the tin and its contents.) That coffin with his heart in it is buried, as he had wished for his body, by the side of Emma in the churchyard of the Dorset parish of Stinsford.[36]

So it was with the great: the state and the public generally won. But the hundreds of thousands of dead soldiers lying in foreign lands raised a more demanding, far-reaching, and politically sensitive question: To whom did the bodies of the dead of war belong? In early 1919, the *Spectator* announced that it had received a copy of an appeal from Lady Florence Cecil, daughter-in-law of the former Conservative prime minister Lord Salisbury and wife of the bishop of Exeter, in which she argued against both the policy that all the dead would remain overseas and more specifically against the IWGC regulation that prohibited crosses and any kind of private commemoration. A flurry of letters and articles in support of her views followed. In the months to come the *Times* would also publish a petition to the IWGC that asked it to give back the bodies it had gathered if families demanded them and also to allow gravestones of a family's choosing on the graves of those that remained abroad. She told readers that she "would be glad to hear from bereaved wives and mothers who feel strongly against the proposed uniform and almost secular memorials erected on the graves of our soldiers." Many responded. So did important statesmen. Arthur Balfour, the former prime minister and foreign secretary between 1916 and 1919, was on her side; so was Herbert Asquith, prime minister when the war began; so was Winston Churchill, the secretary of state for war. In 1919, he wrote to colleagues that for several reasons, emotional and aesthetic, the Commission ought not to stick to its position that "no individual memorials are to be allowed": "in this matter, more perhaps than any other, people have the right to have their feelings studied," he argued, and furthermore, "large areas filled with uniform stones like those that mark kilometers by the roadside" would look horrible.[37]

All this came to naught. The arguments of the IWGC's supporters won. Sir Fredric Kenyon, director of the British Museum and the Commission's main artistic adviser, argued successfully that allowing some bodies to come home and individual monuments over those that remained behind would leave a land-scape "of inequality, haphazard and disordered." Some monuments might be fine but others would not. Edwin Lutyens, one of the IWGC principle architects, opposed leaving bodies where they fell and allowing individual graves because a concentration of graves would allow more "beautiful treatment." Crosses instead of slabs were rejected both for aesthetic reasons and because the IWGC and its advisers were determined to keep religious symbolism out entirely except for small signs of faith not readable at a distance. Fabian Ware, the director, refused to have a religious adviser; the debate about religious symbols had to be stopped before it got going. If crosses were allowed, then why not crucifixes for Roman Catholics? "Keep the poisonous sculptures out of the plan," advised a group of artists and architects.[38]

The quarrel was, of course, about far more than landscaping and aesthetics. At stake in the discussion was the nature of the community of the dead that was being created with the bodies and the names of the dead. Beatrix Maud Palmer, the Countess of Selborne, conservative suffragist, sister-in-law of Lady Florence Cecil, and wife of the second Baron, a conservative politician and son of a Lord Chancellor, published a piece in the *National Review* whose very title got to the heart of the matter: "National Socialism of War Cemeteries." The arrangements negotiated by the IWGC through which Great Britain gained the right to bury its dead abroad were the problem. The rights of the next of kin had been "abro-gated by a secret treaty with a foreign power"; the House of Commons, "capti-vated by the Socialist ideal" of the state, had refused to intervene. The result, she argued, was mediocrity and the end of individual freedom: "the common condi-tions of state action are very obvious. Absolute uniformity." "The final tyrannical decree," as she called it, "that no one is to have the right to move his relation's body from the national cemeteries," had not yet been approved by Parliament at the time she was writing but de facto it had been in place since the war began. The very idea, she continues as her rhetoric heats up, represents "pure Socialism of the most advanced school." Indeed, "the conscription of bodies is worthy of Lenin" in its "contempt of liberty . . . exaltation of the State . . . and the aspiration for similarity and equality."[39]

The Countess had a point. The treaties that the IWGC had negotiated and its claim on the dead were unprecedented and new: the nation of the dead was inherent not in the bodies of the aristocratic classes alone but in the bodies of all those who died. A delegation of five Labour MPs joined by Ernest Bevan, head of the Transport Workers Union, went to France because they "wished to satisfy ourselves, on behalf of thousands of those we represent in Parliament who have not been able to visit the graves of those dear to them, that these graves are being fittingly cared for by the Imperial War Graves Commission." They returned home satisfied that "our brothers of every class" were lovingly cared for, that "equality of treatment" meant that they saw "every rank of soldier from General to Private, lying side by side, under the same simple headstones, silent witnesses to future generations of the world's greatest tragedy." The argument that prevailed in the House—that "what is done for one should be done for all," made by William Burdett-Coutts, the American-born MP for Westminster and husband of the great philanthropist the Baroness Burdett-Coutts—stands in stark opposition to the aristocratic principle that had dominated the remembrance of the dead of war since Agincourt and that was eroding in the late nineteenth century.[40]

All bodies—aside from the Unknown Warrior and some few putatively smuggled back—remained abroad and all were remembered equally with a standard-size tombstone and a standard inscription. Relatives were allowed for a fee to add 64 characters. Few took up the offer. Against considerable pressure, the IWGC also held firm to the principle that there would be a body for each grave and a grave for each body; or put differently, there would be no empty graves, no tombstones without bodies beneath them. Memorials and graves were to be kept distinct. There was, over the years, much discussion of this matter, but one case makes the point: a grave demands a body, and only graves will have tombstones. In March 1924, a time when the building of cemeteries and the consolidation of bodies was in high gear, Sir Fabian Ware, the Commission's vice-chair and chief executive officer, received a memorandum from Sir Lionel Halsey, equerry to the Prince of Wales, who was the Commission's titular head. Five typed pages long, it represented the views of two distinguished military men with a personal stake in the matter: one was William G. Middleton, a lieutenant colonel in the Scots Greys; the other, William Boyd, a member of the King's Body Guard for Scotland. Each had lost a son, and they were asking for HRH's help in having them commemorated together. As Middleton and Boyd represented their case, their sons had died in the intense shelling and machine gun fire of the German resistance to an attack that they had led on 25 April 1915 at St. Julien near Ypres. It took two nights before the dead and wounded of the engagement could be recovered. Bodies that were then retrieved were buried a few hundred yards from where the attack had finished, but it was uncertain whether Lt. Boyd's and Capt. Middleton's were among them. They were reported first "wounded and missing," then "missing, believed killed," and finally "killed." On 13 October 1917, a comrade had written to Mr. Boyd that he and some men had put up crosses where "our fellows were buried" and had put up one for the two missing men with no identifiable graves. The bodies of the two young officers were, it seemed, among the hundreds of thousands that disappeared.

In 1922–1923, the IWGC removed all the bodies of the officers and men of the 2nd Battalion of the historic Seaforth Highlanders, the boys' regiment, to a nearby small cemetery, transferred the original wooden crosses, and eventually substituted for them granite headstones. But since no bodies could be identified as those of Capt. Middleton and Lt. Boyd, no stones with their names on them were put up. The two fathers recognized, and thought it appropriate, that the names of their sons would be among those on the Menin Gate but they wanted in addition to have a tombstone put up in the small—one-sixth of an acre—cemetery near where their sons' bodies undoubtedly lay. It was to read, "To the Memory of Capt. W.A.A. Middleton and Lieut. W.N.L. Boyd, both of the 2nd Battn. Seaford Highlanders. Killed in Action 25th April 1915 but whose bodies were not recovered."[41]

Ware wrote back to the Prince of Wales's equerry saying that he would be happy to see the boys' fathers but that he could not possibly accede to the request, that is, to make "a distinction between the commemoration of these officers as opposed to those of others who have no known graves." More telling is his handwritten note on the typed letter. The "fundamental point" is that there are at least two hundred thousand missing bodies in France and the IWGC had consistently rejected the suggestion—from no less than the prime minister of Australia, among others—that a tombstone should be raised for each of these "though they had no graves." If this policy were adopted, there would have been hundreds of thousands of what Rudyard Kipling, one of the artistic advisers to the Commission and the father of a lieutenant whose body was missing, had called "dud graves." Tombstones by definition marked tombs that contained bodies. If we were to give in to the request that he had been forwarded, Ware wrote, then the rejection of empty graves more generally would become indefensible. Considerable effort had gone into the grave/memorial distinction. "We have always opposed anything that might lead relatives to imagine that a body was buried when it is not," read the "memo to file." Exhumations in the future might find nothing beneath a memorial masquerading as a tombstone, causing "relatives considerable anxiety as to whether or not graves are genuine." The graves by the tens, and hundreds, and thousands across the vast front, Ware insisted, each had to represent real dead bodies. The names that had lost their bodies would be represented as a collectivity not by tombstones but by long poignant lists on which they were joined with the names whose bodies were buried somewhere namelessly.[42]

The IWGC had made an extraordinary commitment to creating an accurate surface representation of the dead that lay below. It is nowhere clearer than in one particular investigation of a failure to live up to its impossible ideal: mistakes—in the naming of the dead and in having a body in each grave—must have been routine during the exhumation, relocation, and identification of hundreds of thousands of decomposed bodies spread across thousands of miles of battlefront.

Officials, when they were compiling lists of the missing to be engraved on memorials near where they were last known to be alive, estimated that the error rate might have been as high as 3 percent. But only one specific screw-up has come to light, and its investigation was kept secret, not because the IWGC did not care about accuracy—it cared desperately—but because from the intimate perspective of kin, the whole enterprise of naming and burying depended on a shared belief that a body was where it was claimed to be and a name near where the person to whom it belonged was last seen. Unmasking the magical belief that this could really be so in a half million instances was unthinkable. But even if no outsider could audit the IWGC's accuracy, its internal culture demanded the greatest possible care. In October 1920, "as a result of the reported duplication of the grave of a certain soldier, the grave reported to be in the cemetery known as Hooge Crater Cemetery, on the Ypres Menin Road was opened and alleged to contain the remains of a soldier other than that described on the temporary wooden cross marking the grave." It is remarkable that record keeping in the field was good enough to catch the error and that it was not just let to pass. As part of an investigation, 134 other graves were opened and further discrepancies found.[43]

The investigating committee laid the blame on the 68th Labour Company, which, in the months after the war, had given greater priority to simply cleaning the battlefield than to "minute accuracy in establishing the identity of those bodies that were found." By July 1919, procedures had been put in place that would "ensure not only the elimination of error but also the exhaustive examination of the remains for every clue to identity." Better and more detailed record keeping was enforced; more weight was to be given to the detailed examination of bodies than to replacing crosses, which might have been moved, with gravestones. An analysis of the work company's efforts showed that it had been possible to identify three out of eighty unknowns and to disprove the identity of five out of fifty-five unknowns. It was not clear to the committee that a 3.75 percent rate of new identifications made it worthwhile doing further exhumations and tests in this cemetery of five thousand dead, especially since the bodies were in trenches, so disturbing one would disturb others and potentially make even more of a muddle. It admitted that there had been carelessness in five instances of exhumations; the investigating committee concluded with a general recommendation that the errors already discovered be corrected and that elaborate new procedures be enforced. A grave-by-grave analysis of the particular graves in question follows in the report.[44]

In many ways, collecting the names severed from bodies and writing them in stone was a more complex task, conceptually and bureaucratically, than burying the bodies themselves. A list has to be made to mean something; all lists have to have a principle of inclusion and exclusion, and the possibilities after the

Great War were many. The creation of the great monuments with their lists of names was the most culturally innovative and administratively taxing part of the IWGC's work. Burial and the consolidation of bodies had been going on since early 1915. Naming apart from burial was not mooted until late 1918. The first suggestions seem to have come in a memo from Sir Fredric Kenyon, the IWGC artistic adviser, a month after the war ended; he thought that the "propriety of some memorial in which their [the missing's] names would be recorded is obvious." It would be good, he thought, if the names on any list corresponded to where the men to whom they once belonged "are believed to have fallen." This became known as the "geographic principle." A letter from a marine engineer in Satlburn-by-the-Sea in the IWGC files makes a similar suggestion: that the names of those whose bodies "be where they fell—at the bottom of long disused craters and elsewhere over wide battlefield . . . sunk deep in Flanders mud . . . blown to fragments by shell fire"—be recorded somewhere. Even if their bodies are lost, their names and, with effort, also the dates when they disappeared could be recovered. This gathering of names was to be an act of recuperation.[45]

But the principle that was to guide the construction of the proposed lists, specifically their relationship to the dead, was another matter, taxonomically and practically. By far the easiest and cheapest way of proceeding would have been, as many in the councils of the War Office, Ministry of Works, and the IWGC recommended, to group the names of the missing by regiment and put them in special chapels. Officials would go through regimental records and subtract from the total number the names of those with a known burial place and those still alive; the residuum—the missing and unknowns—would go on the list. It would have borne no relationship to where a man was killed or buried before his grave was lost; the names would be completely disembodied; they would be reinscribed as a subsection of an army unit's records from which they—rather than the live soldiers—had been struck. That said, this principle of listing would have been bureaucratically relatively simple. The IWGC did not adopt it. It took to heart the views of those in its ranks who complained that the regimental principle was "cruelly practical": "a considerable savings in cost . . . and a considerable savings in time," as the Director of Records put it, missed the point that in "dealing with the missing, one touches upon the saddest phase of the war." Their kin, "all these poor souls," know nothing but "the place where their dead dear one was last seen." Regimental identification means "practically nothing, while the place means everything."[46]

The question of what a list should mean was still being debated in early 1921, but no one denied that the "geographical system" was "more generally attractive and more interesting," even if it was far more costly to implement. It carried the day. The principle for inclusion in the lists of the lost dead that the Commission would use to inscribe their names in stone was that they would stand for bodies that had been torn from their names near where the list was located. The ancient principle of place won. But actually putting the names in place was an enormous enterprise. First, the size and location of the monuments themselves had to be determined. At the time the decision was taken, no one knew how many missing there would eventually be; two hundred thousand to a quarter million was the best estimate, less than half the actual number. And then the names had to be allocated to monuments in particular battle zones. These two matters are related. As the number of missing grew, so did the need for new space for their names. Potentially more than one hundred thousand could plausibly have gone on the Menin Gate at the center of the three battles of Ypres: an impossible number. Equally impossible was the suggestion by the director of works to Ware in 1926 that one hundred thousand could go in Amiens. Where should they go, if such aggregations were not practical, so as to maintain some geographical and emotional relationship to where a man had died? "In dealing with the missing, one touches upon the saddest phase of war," wrote Col. Lord Arthur Browne to the Commission; "place means everything" "A desperately difficult question," wrote Fredric Kenyon, hoping to find a solution by cramming ever more names on every walkway and rampart. Speaking just of the Menin Gate, an official of the IWGC on the ground wrote to his boss that he was not sure when he could complete his list "because there has been no precedent for this kind of work." And even when he had a list, it was never definitive: "whatever number is given there will always be some who fall just outside it." So it was on the frontiers of naming the dead.[47]

The sorts of decisions facing the IWGC depended on other technical and conceptual decisions: font size and name spacing, estimate of average name length, for example, but also whether or not a missing soldier's regimental number would be used to identify him—"Arthur Jones" followed by his number so as to distinguish the dead man that this iteration of the name identified from all others of the same name. Numbers posed a technical problem as well as an emotional one. They take space, which would push names to other memorials; and the amount of space they might take was unpredictable because there was no consistent regimental numbering system and because no one knew how many names on a list might require a number to distinguish this "Arthur Jones" who had lost his name from that one. But the use of numbers would also ostentatiously imbricate the name in a bureaucratic web that many found repellant. The Commission cited "Tommy's proverbial dislike of regimental numbers," to support the decision that only in the rare cases in which two men of the same name in the same regiment were both missing in the same sector of the battlefield would numbers be used to specify *this* Arthur Jones. We are back to the problem of how names create meaning with which I began chapter 6. Well into engraving the names of Canadians on the Menin Gate, the man in charge discovered that names at the end of the alphabet are on average longer than ones at the beginning, and he ended up with more names on his list than he had room to accommodate. He began searching for a way to assign some Canadians, as needed, farther south to Vimy Ridge.[48]

The public was watching as scores of bureaucrats read tens of thousands of official war diaries and filled hundreds of thousands of index cards and sent endless memos back and forth to compile great ledgers of names that bore some relationship to what had taken place and to comport as well with other commemorative interests. The Canadian Memorial at Vimy Ridge, for example, held mostly the names of men lost in the Somme, but it made some sense to send the names of those killed farther north to Vimy if there ended up being more names than there was space for on the monuments around Ypres and nearby battlefields. The bereaved cared. Mrs. Isabel Baynes wanted to know where the name of the son she had lost on 14 October 1918 would be; she wanted to be at the unveiling of the new Menin Gate. Ware told her that work on it had not begun. But the detailed, life-by-life exploration to compile the names before the Menin Gate or any other memorial could be built was staggering: 451772 Pt. A. W. Abrams should not be on the missing list for Ypres because he was found buried near Zillebrucke with some others under a memorial at New Irish Farms, the Director of Records responds to a man in the field; "Query to the Directors of Records— Sapper R.J.G. Campbell 502006 was drowned in the Dunkirk-Furnes Canal. An accident; no grave has been found; should he be included in the Vimy Memorial or do these isolated circumstances warrant his inclusion on Menin Gate?" What is to be done about "CONNELL, Hugh Tripney," who enlisted as "James McDonald"? asks the assistant keeper of records in Ottawa of the IWGC. He is to be included under "C" at Vimy Ridge, is the answer. The question of what to do about the names of Rhodesian porters is a whole other issue. Chinese laborers who died in the cleanup were given tombstones but buried separately from soldiers; the IWGC insisted on getting the tombstones done quickly because only Chinese stonemasons could engrave calligraphy, and they needed 1,500 of them before the Chinese were sent home. Tens of thousands of pages of corrected and recorrected lists were sent back and forth between keepers of records in imperial capitals and the IWGC in London and between the central office and men in the field. To this must be added the process of building the memorials, engraving names, and making corrections as new findings came while the names on a list were actually going up. This was and remains the greatest exercise in writing the names of the dead in history. A similar story, on an individually smaller but cumulatively even larger scale, could be told about each of the many thousands of lists in nearly every city, town, and village of England (figs. 9.6, 9.7).[49]

9.6. Engraving a headstone for a Canadian casualty of the First World War, Doullens Communal Cemetery. Imperial War Museum.

9.7. Carving names at the Vimy Memorial.

There is another story, however, that has as its main, indeed only, character the almost spectral doppelgänger of the list: the Unknown Warrior buried in Westminster Abbey. The names and markers that gird the battlefields of France and Belgium and fill village memorials cry out in their specificity, in their one-to-one correspondence with a body at, or near, or imagined to be near, the place of death of the person who once bore that name. The epitaph at the intersection of nave and aisle at Westminster Abbey does the opposite. It proclaims its universality

BENEATH THIS STONE RESTS THE BODY
OF A BRITISH WARRIOR
UNKNOWN BY NAME OR RANK

It points not just to another one of the hundreds of thousands of bodies marked "Known but to God" but to the great mass of "unknowns" that have been recognized in increasing numbers since the American Civil War: in other words, to *an* unknown warrior. *The* Unknown Warrior is a cipher that can mean anything, the bones that represent any and all bones equally well or badly. It is the universal body severed from its name. He was, as a nurse said in her memoirs about a soldier who died without anyone knowing who he was, among those "poor fellows" who had "given even their names."[50]

It is the unlikeliest of shrines: without precedent, its origins obscure. In the British case, some say the idea belonged to Dean Ryle of Westminster Abbey who wrote the epitaph; others credit the Reverend D. Railton, vicar of St. John the Baptist and son of the first commander of the Salvation Army, who says that the idea came to him in his billet near Armentieres in 1916 and that he wrote to Lord Haig with the proposal. He claimed that the only part of his proposal that was not accepted was its suggestion for a name: "the unknown comrade" instead of "the unknown warrior." The idea, of course, emerged at roughly the same time everywhere, so that these local beginnings are rivulets feeding a larger current. Profound and absolute anonymity was the essence of the figure: forever unnamed and unnamable; "unidentified and unidentifiable." The body would be buried at the intersection of the aisle and the nave of Westminster Abbey, in a spot unused by any other body in the eight-hundred-year life of the building—or at least since the reign of Henry III—an eternally nameless body that came to represent the poignancy of absolute loss of a name, both specific in the body in question and for all similarly situated bodies (figs. 9.8, 9.9).[51]

9.8. The selection of bodies for the Unknown Warrior in France, n.d.
Imperial War Museum.

9.9. The coffin of the Unknown Warrior at
Westminster Abbey. Imperial War Museum.

No one foresaw the overwhelming resonance of this act. The archbishop of Canterbury was, he said, "at first inclined against" a funeral service for "an unknown man." The king was doubtful. Brig. Gen. B. J. Wyatt, who had been ordered to deliver an appropriate body, reported that twenty-three of the twenty-four people at a luncheon party where he spoke about the project felt that it would "never appeal to the British." This was not the Protestant thing to do. They were wrong. Wyatt's men extracted four parcels of bones from the muck of 1914—they chose the oldest graves they could find—and put each in a plain coffin that was then loaded onto a horse cart, taken to a Quonset hut and placed on a table. At midnight Gen. Wyatt, blindfolded, chose the bones destined for sacrality. The others were returned without any due notice to their graves: ordinary bodies of the "missing," "Known but to God." (The French buried their also-rans in specially marked individual graves near Verdun.) Someone proposed that the bones be cremated to make anonymity certain; the dean of Westminster was amenable, but the War Cabinet did not like the idea, and nothing came of it. In the morning, the handpicked bones were taken by cart to Calais, transported across on a Royal Navy destroyer to Dover, and from there guarded as the most precious of relics until the ceremonies on the next day. Along with the body came bags of soil, whose transformation from ordinary to sacred is mundanely documented. Receipts dated 10 November 1920, written on Office of Works, Supply Division, forms, acknowledge that Lt. Swift had received the sixteen barrels from Lt. H. P. Allum. He, in turn, accompanied the consigned "16 barrels, numbered 1–16," onto the Dover ferry. As Rupert Brooke would have it, the English body rested still—at least would eventually rest—in French soil in Westminster Abbey.[52]

More than a million and a quarter people filed slowly past the open grave in the days after 11 November. The unnamed body, the universal unnamed body, representing all bodies that had lost their names, struck powerful chords of sentiment. The burial ceremony was almost unbearably freighted with emotions: amidst the great and good of the empire were one hundred mothers who had lost not only their husbands but also all of their sons. "Enough to say that the great symbolical act of allowing an unidentified body to represent all the mighty inarticulate sacrifice of the nation is justified, because all people heartily understand it and approve of it." What makes "every heart, in however simple or poor a body it beats," intimately engaged in "the great symbolic act" is that "every bereaved man or woman can say, 'That body may belong to me.'" This, of course, is possible only through a mighty suspension of disbelief; it could not be an unknown soldier from Gallipoli or Greece; it could not be a sailor. But the fact that anyone could say this speaks again to the power of a magic we can believe in. Even those on the political Left who might be unhappy about making a shrine out of a nameless decomposed body acknowledged that it struck the popular imagination. A writer in the *Bradford Pioneer*, the independent Labour newspaper in which Siegfried Sassoon had published his famous declaration "Finished with the War," lamented that whoever thought of the public burial of the unknown soldier had "plumbed the depths of our incorrigible sentimentalism with his master scheme." Hundreds of thousands of "living soldiers are on the industrial scrap heap," a half million are struggling with inadequate pensions, and yet "one dead [body] can stir a whole population to an orgy of sentimentalism such as these islands have never before witnessed." But there was no master scheme.[53]

The Cenotaph—the empty tomb on Whitehall honoring the dead who were buried elsewhere—was dedicated on the same day as the burial of the Unknown Warrior, 11 November 1920, and was an even more unlikely candidate to move the hearts of those who had lived through the Great War. The prime minister, Lloyd George, seemed to have the idea for some sort of catafalque, past which troops could march and salute the dead in the 19 July 1919 Victory Parade that celebrated the signing of the Versailles Treaty and the formal end of the war in the West. No one in the War Cabinet loved the idea. Curzon, leader of the House of Lords, thought it would be "foreign to the Spirit of our people . . . too Latin" or (as the minutes express it as a general view) so "foreign [i.e., French] to the temper and custom of the nation that it might not be easy for the public to assume a properly reverential attitude." The king was said to be against the idea. Sir Alfred Mond, the minister of works, came right out and said it was simply too Catholic.[54]

With so little expected of it, no one gave much thought to its design or to what exactly it was to be. It was Sir Edwin Lutyens who designed the austere temporary monument—he actually dashed off his first sketch of it while having dinner with his mistress, Lady Sackville—and suggested that it be called a cenotaph. Very little was made of the unveiling. To everyone's surprise, the general public showered the empty tomb with wreaths; the press was full of reports of how moved all who saw it were. "Never before has there been such a proclamation, gladly made, that we are all equal, all members of one body, or rather one soul." "All of us were members of one orchestra . . . [there was] one forgetfulness of self in that quiet ritual, one desire that prophecy be fulfilled . . . that we may, indeed, all become members of one body politic and of one immortal soul." Hundreds of thousands came from nearby and more than a million from the rest of the country came to see it.[55]

Still officialdom thought of the cenotaph as but a temporary structure. Sir Lionel Earle (1866–1948), permanent secretary of His Majesty's Office of Works, lamented that "it is rapidly becoming a war shrine" and that the longer the public was allowed to lay floral tributes at its base, the more politically difficult it would be to dismantle it. He worried about traffic and crowds on the busy Whitehall thoroughfare. On 21 July 1920, the commissioner of works decided to give the plaster of paris monument a one-week reprieve because of the "very general desire from the public to that effect": "Many people will be coming from the country to see it as an outward symbol of the nation's gratitude to its sons who have made the great sacrifice."[56] A week later, the decision was taken to make the Cenotaph permanent; the new granite version was officially unveiled on the day the Unknown Warrior was buried.

By 1920, two central features of a new regime of naming the dead were in place, and a third was on the way to realization: the sacral unnamed body and the empty tomb that stood for all bodies. Plans were well under way to list the names of the missing on memorials and to place a tombstone over those bodies that could be identified. In the fifteen or twenty years after the beginning of the Great War, the number of the names of the dead recorded in public would increase logarithmically, and a new kind of shrine to namelessness—not just in Great Britain but by now almost everywhere else—had come into being as if willed by the forces of history. How to explain this in the broader contexts we have considered earlier?

Politics is one possible, and in some ways, the obvious answer: the dead and their names had work to do in the interests of the state. Elias Canetti says somewhere that without the dead of the First World War, Hitler would not have existed. Hitler had planned to repay his debt with a great monument of their names had the next war—the Second Great War—turned out differently. As it was, Field Marshal, now President, Paul Hindenburg, dressed as colonel in chief of a Prussian regiment, told a great crowd in 1926 at the dedication of a memorial to the unknown soldier at Tannenberg, where in August 1914 Germany had destroyed the Russian 2nd Army, that it was "with clean hearts" that German soldiers had marched to war in 1914 and that the country "is ready at any moment to prove this fact before an impartial tribunal." Jews and socialist parliamentarians had been excluded from the ceremony. Soon after coming to power, Hitler spoke at the shrine about how Germany was shamed by its loss in a war it never wanted. The appropriation of the unknown dead and of the bodies of the dead more generally for overt political purposes could not be more obvious.[57]

But we need not go to the most egregious case. Sir Fabian Ware, director of the IWGC, managed to oversee the creation of an empire of the dead: great legions of tombstones and names that could be grasped as one. He fought relentlessly, as we have seen, against those who wanted the dead for any other purpose, public or private. Perhaps nowhere else is Britain, as the world imperial power it was then, more evident than along the battle lines of the Great War. The Unknown Warrior in Britain and elsewhere—there are now hundreds—became a new kind of being in the political theology of nationalism. In the old regime, Richard II had it right: "Is not the king's name 20,000 names?" The new *corpus mysticum* of the Unknown Warrior assumes all names by having none.[58]

In addition, there are immediate practical political considerations, recognized on all sides, for what naming the dead might do for the state and the established order. Allowing the general public an opportunity for seats in the Abbey at the burial ceremonial for the Unknown Warrior would, an adviser of Lloyd George hoped, "be a bold and dramatic stroke, because you might find the Duchess next to the Charwoman; it might even have its effect, however small and imperceptible, upon the industrial situation." In a war fought purportedly for freedom and democracy, it was symbolically important that the Princess Beatrice, visiting the grave of her only son, Prince Maurice of Battenberg, met, and was known to have met, "an aged fellow" from New Zealand who was on a pilgrimage to the identically marked and cared-for grave of his only son. The *News of the World* published the account of their commiseration in a cemetery near Ypres. Dead bodies elided the divisions among the living. Efforts of protestors to disturb the moment of silence were apparently met angrily. By remarking on the painful irony of this fact, newspapers on the Left acknowledged that the new symbolic regime had struck a deep chord. The communist *Workers Dreadnought* complained that "millions of bereaved people [were] impressed by the thought that their dead son, their brother, their father, husband or friend they will see no more, has been honored" while unemployment remains high and the government does nothing. The Glasgow socialist newspaper *Forward* joked that perhaps it was fine for a landlady to collect a 30 percent rent increase during the moment of silence: "Of course, the rustle of Treasury Notes wouldn't really disturb anybody."[59]

But all of this is to say little more than that the names of the dead on local and national memorials and the birth of a new kind of shrine were together a force to be reckoned with. The state wandered, as if sleepwalking, into the new regime; great swaths of the elite opposed it; specific plans emerged from a chaos of possibilities. The emotional power of what emerged surprised almost everyone. Of course naming the dead of war and burying them together had political consequences, but this explains little about its causes. The terms might better be reversed: the nation, and local communities as well, discovered themselves in the memorial response to the Great War.

We would be closer to an explanation if we understood the history of forgetting. There was during and after the war a hopeless, poignant, desperate anxiety about what Samuel Beckett would later, referring to Proust, call the "poisonous ingenuity of time." Of course, knowledge of the transience of earthly things is neither new nor modern. But in the ruin and in the monument and in the hearts of ordinary people it came to have new resonance. One thinks here of the end of *The Mill on the Floss*, a novel that insists that "the future will never join on the past again"; that the "book is quite closed," while also insisting on the power of history and the necessity for its constant recollection:

> Nature repairs her ravages—repairs them with sunshine, and with human labour. The desolation wrought by that flood [one might read: war], had left little visible trace on the face of the earth, five years after. The fifth autumn is rich in golden corn-stacks, rising in thick clusters among the distant hedgerows.

But time has been irreparably rent:

> Nature repairs her ravages—but not all. The uptorn trees are not rooted again; the parted hills are left scarred: if there is a new growth, the trees are not the same as the old, and the hills underneath their green vesture bear the marks of the past rending. To the eyes that have dwelt on the past, there is no thorough repair.

Nor did there seem any repair for the gaps between, on the one hand, the mute, dead, quick to decay, and stolidly material dead body, about which war journals, diaries, and letters speak incessantly, and, on the other hand, the imperative to give it some more permanent meaning, to make something cultural of it, to make it part of national and personal memory. In a sense, this awareness of a chasm might be regarded as a symptom of a more acute modern anxiety of erasure. But it is also more specifically an anxiety about the corporeal integrity and individuality of the dead in an age when the omnipotent God of John Donne's sermons could no longer be relied on to appropriately collect every atom at the day of judgment to make the dead fully live again in their bodies. More generally, it is about maintaining the dead as part of the world of the living.[60]

Modern arts of memory are preoccupied with chronicling this poisonous ingenuity of time. The filmmaker Alain Resnais's camera follows the weed-, grass-, and wildflower-filled track to the gate of Auschwitz; it is the central image of *Night and Fog*. The building that housed Josef Mengele's putative hospital looks more like a slightly dilapidated late-eighteenth-century mill in the russet colors of fall than a house of torture. *Night and Fog* has given way to the work of time. Claude Lanzmann's *Shoah* uses the same device. It demands again and again that we take in the lovely countryside around the grass-covered ruins of what had been death camps. All that transpired there—the pain, the victims and the perpetrators, the dead, all the ugliness—is gone.

These responses to the possibility of forgetting the Holocaust had powerful precursors in the Great War and in the century that came before it. Even before the slaughter ended, the poison of erasure—or perhaps it was the balm—was at work. A young lieutenant in June 1916, a month before he was to die in the Somme, wrote home about the "multitude of lives [that] have been simply wasted"; but in the same letter he imagined what would happen when the war ended: the trenches "which in February were grim and featureless tunnels of gloom . . . are already over arched and embowered with green." Children will play there "as in a garden" before summer comes again. Very quickly, the bodies and the scars vanish, almost as if they were never there, as if there were nothing to ascribe meaning to. The earth that during the war seemed "diseased, pocked, rancid, stinking of death in the morning sun" appears to a writer of battlefield guidebooks only a few years later as being "nursed back to health" by nature: "many of the scars have softened; soon they will be gone altogether, and the old familiar landmarks will be gone forever." A postcard to his wife from a soldier visiting Ypres after the war captures the same feeling: "The war is gone forever—only a memory now. What we last saw as a vast desert of shell holes, bare tree stumps, mud, filth, smashed guns and tanks and dead men is all waving cornfields, pretty gardens . . . quarreling children and flighty girls. The only things left to remind one that memories once were realities are the cemeteries and the poppies." "Your death means nothing to these fields," wrote one soldier in the context of musing that all this death meant nothing in any case, no more than if "you had died in your bed, full of years and respectability." "We travel humbly and happily over battlefields already become historic," writes the poet Edmund Blunden about his journey home: "lengths of trenches twisting in and out . . . where amateur soldiers, so many of them accepted death in lieu of war-time wages."[61]

Earlier, the American Civil War battlefields generally had been allowed to revert to pasture with nary a notice. It marked a change, which the Great War took further. Ruins became a reminder of suffering and a caution to remember. Winston Churchill was only the most prominent person to propose—the first such suggestion in history, I think—that an entire city, Ypres, be kept in ruins to bear testimony to the fact that the British Empire had bled there. A great deal of serious discussion went into making this a reality; negotiations were undertaken to buy the land or to get Belgium to donate it. They ultimately failed. Australian units fought unsuccessfully after the war to keep Caberet Rouge, the site of one of their greatest efforts in the Battle of the Somme, out of cultivation and as close to its ruined state as possible. And, of course, the actual lists and cemeteries mark, if in a sanitized and aesthetic way, the contours of death. Trenches are still visible on almost every site. In this way, the Great War began what we might think of as self-memorialization: the thing standing for itself, the ruin as the witness to something beyond itself. *Híc locus.* Charles de Gaulle ordered that Oradur-sur-Glane, burned by the Germans along with 642 of its citizens, be kept in ruins as a "martyred village," the spatial equivalent of a saint's body; the ruins of concentration camps and railway sidings and other sites of the Holocaust, similarly, are heirs to memorial creations of the Great War and of the nineteenth century.[62]

We could search for an explanation for the explosion of names and nameless-ness in the Great War microscopically. We might ask: Why would someone like Catherine Stevens, sister of the poet Wallace Stevens, feel that when she saw still another lone cross on the field of battle that she "just had to go to it and see if I could read the name"? Her journal, along with her body, was returned home when she was killed. Or we could provide an answer that harkened back to the more general story of the names of the dead and memory: namelessness of the dead had become unbearable. "Very hard to believe," writes Vera Brittain early in the war, "that far away men were being slain ruthlessly, and their poor disfigured bod-ies heaped together and crowded in ghastly indiscrimination into quickly pro-vided common graves as if they were *nameless* vermin." In short, as if Diogenes had triumphed and we humans would no longer care for our dead. "Nothing in life or death, amidst all the varied scenes of pain and sorrow in wartime," wrote a future member of Parliament who worked at grave registration for the Red Cross from the very beginnings of the project in October 1914, "impresses the mind with so dark a picture of utter loneliness and desertion as does the sight of a soldier's grave standing alone . . . with nothing to mark it but the remains of a tiny flag or a forage cap or a dilapidated cross." Under these circumstances, a continuation of the previous two millennia's practices of military burial was impossible.[63]

There is, finally, a body-by-body explanation. In 1914, no one knew that the men who died in the Great War lived in a new world, one in which an enormous bureaucracy would be held accountable for the denouement of individual lives. Perhaps, after the American Civil War, everyone should have known. But they didn't. The unprecedentedly massive enterprise of naming of the dead in the Great War might be seen as a result of hundreds of thousands of small histories: the story of Emily and Will writ over and over again.

In 1917, Private Eric Pinks's mother was told in a penciled note, on thin Church Army Recreation Hut stationary, written by a corporal in his company, that her son had been killed by sniper fire but that he "has got a good grave" whose pre-cise location the corporal could not reveal. Ten years later, Mrs. Pinks wrote to the War Graves Commission asking for its location; it was, she thought, near Langemarck in the Ypres Salient. By return mail she was told that her son's grave could not be located: "in many areas military operations caused the destruction of crosses and grave registration marks, and completely changed the surface of the ground," the letter said. "His *name*," the reply continued, had however "been com-memorated on the memorial which has been erected at Menin Gate, Ypres." The IWGC sent along two photographs of the list, where his name appeared between those of W. Pilling and J. H. Pinney and opposite a great long list of Smiths.[64]

This is the end of the story. Its earlier chapters—Eric Pinks's correspondence with his working-class family—fills hundreds of pages: a postcard to his sister,

"To dear little Eva, with much love and kisses, Eric." A letter from his Uncle Bill, 17 May 1917, "You are passing through a rough time now my dear boy but keep smiling for I think the good times are coming." "What a little begger old Spot is," writes Eric to his mother in response to her report that the family dog won't allow itself to be dried after its bath; on 5 August he writes home that he is "glad that Spot is getting on alright," that he "is so glad to hear old chap that you have got over having those teeth drawn alright and that dear old Gran and Harold are better and that all the rest of you dear ones are well and so hope that all the rest of you dear ones will keep well." He asks for one or two razor blades. There is a 6 August standardized postcard on which Eric acknowledged receiving his family's letter of 2 August and crossed out all the alternative messages to the phrase "I am quite well." And then there can be only the name.

Sometimes we have only fragments of this history in an archive: a sheet of brown wrapping paper on which is written the contents of the package it once encircled (foot powder, peppermint, socks, cake) and in capital letters "RETURNED— RECIPIENT KILLED," along with official notices of death and burial site. John Bennett had given his little daughter a watch, which she promptly overwound; it was repaired, but he told her that he had better keep it until she was old enough to take care of it; it did not come back with his effects because, we learn from a comrade, his left arm had been severed by the shrapnel from which he died. Three days

9.10. Grave of a German soldier.

before his death, his diary reads, "Bright sunny day. O.P. [our position] had warm time. 200 shells dropped near." His name is on the Arras memorial.[65]

The strange connection of intimacy and slaughter was brought home to me by a watercolor of a grave of a German soldier that was sent to me by his grandson the distinguished Renaissance scholar Klaus Reichert (fig. 9.10). It shows a cradlelike bower of twigs over a lone grave, as if the soldier whose body lay beneath were in his cradle back home. The grave disappeared, as did the body. I do not know if the dead man's name appears anywhere. Probably on a village memorial.[66]

PART IV

BURNING THE DEAD

The organized movement for cremation which has become pretty lively lately, started certain thoughts in me which might be of interest to others. . . . I am certain that this question is quite different from cases where a human being died through accidental fires, or in the Middle Ages by the burning of heretics and witches. . . . These cases are . . . hardly comparable to modern cremation, where in special crematoria by means of excessive heat, cutting off atmospheric air, etc., total destruction is methodologically aimed at and probably achieved, so that nothing remains of the human being after death but a small heap of ashes.

DANIEL PAUL SCHREBER, *Memoirs of My Nervous Illness* (1901)

If one thinks about the formal demands of early crematorium design one comes to understand it as an aesthetic struggle against the chimney.

FRITZ SCHUMACHER, *Die Feuerbestattung* (1939)

Mad as he was, the Austrian jurist Daniel Paul Schreber, whose mental illness so engaged Sigmund Freud and later psychoanalysts, had a point. Modern cremation as the world came to learn about it in the early 1870s was different from anything that had gone before. It relied on sophisticated new technology borrowed from the steel industry; it claimed to represent "the final triumph of reason"; it promised the complete destruction of the dead. In not much more than an hour, specially adapted furnaces could reduce a body to its elements. Most of it went up into the air. The rest was reduced to common nitrogen, potassium, calcium, phosphorus, and chlorine with traces of other elements, "nothing but a heap of ashes." The funeral pyres of antiquity and of contemporary India took ten times as long to do a much less thorough job.

Finally, in coke and gas ovens materialism was triumphant; a long history of care for the dead was cast aside; Diogenes' rejection of the demands of culture seemed to have won out. It was outrageous. And Schreber, for all his paranoia, knew it; so did the faithful of all Western religions, Protestants and Catholics and Jews. So did the great majority of people.

Cremation had not always been so fraught. It had never before had much to do with technology and hence with science and progress. There had been almost no changes in how the dead were burned from the earliest times until the 1870s. Wood was the usual fuel, and because it generated relatively low temperatures, especially in open-air pyres, it left recognizable bits of bone that could be accommodated as local customs required. Something of the dead body remained.

It had also over the ages generated little conflict as one of the ways of treating the dead body. Burning and burying had a long and generally peaceful coexistence. Greeks in the age of the Homer usually, but not always, cremated their dead, as did the Greeks of the classical age. (Antigone asked only that the body of Polynices, her brother, be decently covered with earth.) The ancient Romans buried; those of the late Republic generally cremated; and by the second century of the empire, burial was back for more or less everyone. Neither specific religious ideas, nor the influence of Eastern mystery religions (the Pythagoreans, for example, opposed cremation, but to little effect), nor the slow growth of Christianity, nor a shortage of wood explains the final shift from cremation to burial. It was, as the distinguished classicist Arthur Darby Nock concluded more than a half century ago, nothing more than another turn of fashion, a change in the "habits of the rich" that trickled down. No one has come up with a better explanation.[1]

By the time that Christians were threatening enough to be worth persecuting, almost all societies in the Mediterranean world were burying their dead. Cremation was not an issue. Burning someone to death or destroying her remains by fire as judicial acts were something else: acts of state terror, vengeance taken on the body of an offender, forms of radical exclusion. But these posed no danger to the soul. Eusebius, the early fourth-century Church historian, speaks of the martyrs in Gaul whose bodies "were abused in every possible manner" for days and then "burnt and reduced to ashes" and thrown into the River Rhone so not a vestige remained. "They did all this as if they were able to overcome God, and destroy their resurrection," he concludes. But of course they could not. The faithful will rise again. (Proponents would confront the Church with this and other passages in the late-nineteenth-century battles over cremation.) The souls of the witches and heretics whose bodies, by the thousands, were consumed by flames in the late Middle Ages and early modern period were already damned from the perspective of the authorities. The bodies of those convicted of treason were burned and their ashes scattered so as to enact publicly the complete eradication of the enemy of good order. In all of this, fire was but one way of enforcing exile from the community of the dead that represented the living in deep time. The Church did retrospectively look for a history of opposition. After secular, materialist proponents of cremation began to make their case in the late nineteenth century, authorities responded by finding precedents to their opposition in decrees from the thirteenth century issued by Pope Boniface VIII. These had little to do with cremation and a great deal to do with dividing up special bodies in order to increase their relic value.[2]

There were moments of cultural conflict concerning cremation but not until well after everyone in western and southern Europe had for no discernable reason abandoned it in favor of burial. Charlemagne forbade cremation, along with all sorts of other pagan practices, as part of his campaign to force the conversion of the Saxons in the late eighth century.[3] Christianization also hastened the decline of cremation among the Vikings, but the two methods had long and happily coexisted for centuries in any case apart from religious change. By 1000, and much earlier in parts of western and southern Europe, Christians buried their dead, and they did so in churches and churchyards. With the irrelevant exception of some early thirteenth-century prohibitions against boiling the bodies of the special dead in order to distribute their parts as relics, which nineteenth-century clerical defenders of the old regime of burial brought up to give some historical weight to their position, cremation was a nonissue.

It was this thousand-year history—this old regime of the dead, this regime of gathering the bodies around a church as the representation of the Christian community in deep time—that briefly allowed cremation to become an issue in the French Revolution. Here, some Jacobins thought, was a past to be overthrown; here was a history (albeit one that the revolutionaries seriously misunderstood) to be revisited; here was a way of returning to an earlier and nobler past. Cremation could be an expression of anticlerical neoclassicism.

But this is not what bothers Freud's famous paranoid patient. He is worried about the way in which cremation seems intended to dash all hope of an afterlife. Writing as a modern, educated layman, he has no interest in spiritual substance; he believes that the soul, the seat of what makes us human, rests "*on a material substrate, the nerves*" (his italics). And, even if he claims no special expertise on the physiology of nerves, he is sure that the high temperature of the modern crematorium definitively "precludes their re-awakening in the life beyond." If pushed, he might admit that the decay of the grave could have similar consequences. But he, like many others, understood the symbolic import of mobilizing advanced industrial technologies for burning the dead. The transition from body to ashes was slow; one could imagine that something of a person might survive even if reason dictated otherwise. But a blast furnace left little room for such reveries. The advent of modern cremation on the world stage was a breathtaking, almost lunatic, exercise in disenchantment, modest in scale at first but huge in ambition. Diogenes seems at last to have won: the dead body really was matter that could be transformed into nothing more than a "small heap of ashes" that bore no relationship to what it had once been. It belonged to science, whose object was the natural world, and it was to be managed in the ecological and hygienic interests of society.

Why did this happen, or rather, why, beginning in the 1870s, did some people want it to be the case? There were no new discoveries that would support the view that burning the dead was better for public health than burying them, and beautiful, clean new cemeteries had recently triumphed over overcrowded old churchyards. Cremation, at least under any conceivably acceptable conditions, was not cheaper than burying bodies. There was no new attitude—not toward death or the dead, in any case—that favored cremation, no sudden turn to Hinduism or Buddhism, which believed in cremation on religious grounds. There was no great necessity: cremation grew at different rates in different Western countries but did not become a common way of disposing of the dead until the middle of the twentieth century. The best that a suburban governmental committee in England at the end of the nineteenth century could argue in giving permission to build a crematorium was that it was not a nuisance. Certainly, the 870 cremations that had occurred over a period of eleven years did not suggest a high demand; the authorities at the Dogs' Home burned thirty thousand to forty thousand bodies each year with no problem.[4]

Cremation by the 1870s had become a way of mobilizing the dead in a whole range of overlapping enterprises and projects: modernism and the march of progress, the regime of life, radical and not-so-radical new classicism, anticlericalism and laicization, spiritualism, heterodox and liberal religions, socialism and materialism. The story begins with what the mad Paul Schreber feared and continues with how the ashes and the techniques for creating them were reinscribed in history and culture. Even the most alienated possible form of the dead—a form indistinguishable from a few kilos of light, powdery calcium phosphate and various other elements that the bones might have picked up in life—could and did work for the living in various ways. And so did the technology and the venues that created them.

Chapter 10

DISENCHANTMENT
AND CREMATION

The body of Lady Dilke, who died five weeks ago in London, was burned on the 10th inst. at Dresden. The ceremony was performed in the furnace recently invented for burial purposes by Herr Siemens, and the relatives of the deceased lady permitting strangers to be present, a large number of scientific men attended the experiment. When the company had complied with Herr Siemens' request to offer up a mental prayer, the coffin was placed in the chamber of the furnace; six minutes later the coffin burst; five minutes more and the flesh began to melt away, ten minutes more and the skeleton was laid bare; another ten minutes and the bones began to crumble. Seventy-five minutes after the introduction of the coffin into the furnace all that remained of Lady Dilke and the coffin were six pounds of dust, placed in an urn. The brother-in-law of the deceased was present.

Times (LONDON), 14 OCTOBER 1874

The first move to strip the corpse of its history was publicly announced on 1 May 1873. The exact place was exhibit #54 of the Italian section of Group 26—"*Erziehungs, Unterichts und Bildungswesen*" (Educational, Instructional and Cultural Materials)—in the Northern Cross Gallery of Exhibit Hall 6B of the Vienna World Exposition of that year. It belonged to Ludovico Brunetti, professor of anatomical pathology at the University of Padua. Its title was unrevealing, if not positively deceptive: *Gegenstande der Anatomie* (Anatomical Apparatuses). *Kultur und Erziehung* (Civilization and Education) was the fair's overall motto and the context for the tens of thousands of contributions listed in its bulky, green, 3-inch-thick catalog. Two hundred twenty Italians shared with Brunetti this small corner of the 70,000 square meters of packed exhibition space—six times the size of the Paris 1867 World Exposition—which opened on a day when Europe stood at the very pinnacle of its nineteenth-century economic prosperity. (Just over a week later, on 9 May, the Vienna stock market crashed, ushering in the so-called Long

495

Depression, which would last until the end of the decade. Cholera struck in July, and so it was not until September that big crowds started coming to the fair.)[1]

Brunetti's so-called anatomical objects must have seemed strangely out of place both to his countrymen and countrywomen in Group 26 and to visitors more generally. In size it paled to insignificance compared with the full-scale model of a Kyoto temple and a large-scale model of the new Mont–Cenis Tunnel. Egyptian artisans engaged in their crafts, and a huge array of industrial machines, technologies, and products probably attracted more touristic interest. And, it did not fit in with its neighbors. On one side, at #55, was the plan, history, statement of purpose, and statutes of an industrial school. Just up the aisle, at #59, was a display of books from a Venetian Christian publishing house for teaching French in Protestant schools; at #93, further along, the Milan Commission for the Statistics of Bee Keeping had a stand. Brunetti's "apparatuses," really glass cubes filled with bones and flesh in various stages of carbonization, as well as the first models for cremation technology, were of a different order.

He wrote a pamphlet that may have been available at his booth; it was published in French instead of Italian, probably so as to reach a large international audience, on 1 May, the opening day of the exposition. He begins with the promise that he will present the conclusions that might be drawn from his work in a separate communication to the International Medical Congress that was to be held in conjunction with the world's fair and would meet on the fairgrounds at the end of the summer. There had never been such a series of experiments publicly reported before; they represent the beginning of a new era in the history of the dead body.[2]

"Falsely impressed by the extreme smallness of Roman funerary urns," and "led astray" by those who thought it would be easy to reduce to a pile of ashes the remains of a human being, Brunetti says that he decided to set "himself the task of burning a whole body." (There had, especially in Italy, been a number of published calls for cremation in the previous decades, but none addressed the technical questions that engaged Brunetti.) He would have to go well beyond the "well-known calcination of bones." "Calcinated bone" (bone ash) was indeed well known in industrial circles. It was produced by burning off organic matter as carbonic acid and leaving the mineral shell, which consisted mostly of phosphate of lime: chemists had calculated precisely 86.4 percent for human bones, 90.7 percent for cattle. Ground up, it was used for polishing material and in the manufacturing of other phosphates. By contrast, burning bones in closed vessels and then grinding the much-reduced remains made the commercially more important "bone-black" (animal charcoal). This technique would be nearer to the process that Brunetti embraced as a result of his experiments.[3]

Brunetti's first effort, dated 10 March 1869, was low tech and would have been more or less familiar to visitors. In this preindustrial cremation, a strongly built thirty-five-year-old woman who had died of pneumonia was placed over 90 kg of walnut fuel on an iron platform in an open brick furnace with an ordinary chimney. Four hours later the soft tissue had been fully carbonated and the 55.55-kilogram corpse transformed into 2.512 kilos of calcined bone; its volume was reduced from an estimated 37.4 liters (assuming that it had the density of water) to a cube 16.2 cm on a side, that is, just over 4 liters. (One can only assume that the unnecessarily precise measurements were there to vouch for the exhibit's scientific bona fides.) Visitors could see the remains of what shortly before had been a human body in "vitrine 1," which looked boxier but otherwise not terribly different from the glass coffins in which visitors from Catholic countries would have been accustomed to viewing the bodies of saints. Brunetti reported that he was not happy with the results of this experiment; he was still very far from his goal of cremating a substantial number of bodies rapidly and completely. He needed a new approach.

For experiment 2 he built a three-tiered rack of perforated iron (0.23 m and 0.21 m between levels two and three) that would, he hoped, resolve the problem of the overly thick basket that, he speculated, may have militated against the success of his first experiment. This time, instead of trying to incinerate a corpse whole, he would try cutting it into pieces. On 20 January 1870, Brunetti reports, he put the limbs of a forty-five-year-old man who had died of tuberculosis on level 1 of his new device; the head, trunk, and pelvis he put on level 2; the viscera went on level 3. He used 60 kilos of wood as fuel in the same furnace he had used before. After two hours, when all the soft parts had been carbonized, he removed what remained on levels 2 and 3 put it on level 1 for two more hours. Once again, the results were disappointing. "Anyone competent would say that this was long and slow." (In fact, the results were slightly better than in experiment 1: a cadaver weighing 43.1 kilos was reduced to 1.294 kilos, a weight loss of 97 percent versus just over 95.5 percent before.) Experiment 3 consisted of putting the remains from experiment 2 in an iron-reinforced marmite that Brunetti put in the vault of a coke-fired glassmaking furnace. The extra heat made the bones curl up but did not carbonize them. (Brunetti was, however, on the right track here. The design technology of pottery and glass kilns would soon become directly applicable to crematorium furnaces. The French industrial engineer Emile Bourry worked productively in both areas.)[4]

Frustrated but "not willing to give up [his] ideal of incinerating a whole cadaver," Brunetti tried again, this time using "an enclosed vessel" in a hotter oven. In two further experiments on 25 February and 10 March 1870, he put parts of bodies into an enormous "gasometer retort," one of the coke-fired furnaces that produced the so-called town or coal gas that illuminated the cities and factories of the nineteenth century. These gasometer retorts, Brunetti reports, were several hundred degrees hotter than the glass furnace and much more effective for his purposes. After six hours, the bone was "beautifully carbonized." He checked to be sure that the sparks he had seen in the process of carbonization were, in fact, bits of incandescent bone by reproducing the results on a small scale using a blowtorch. Once the resulting sparks had cooled, he examined them under a microscope and determined that they were indeed bone: white in the case of the spongy parts and gray for the hard parts.

"Absolute incineration," Brunetti concluded, "is impossible with fire alone." He struck out on a new path: "it remained for me to find a method of cremation with which I could obtain incineration of the bone in a manner complete and economical." Clearly, his account is written in some measure for its literary effect, but this should not detract from its denouement: modern cremation, as he conceived of it, was a problem for science and technology. However much it might hearken back to the practice of the ancient Greeks or Romans or Germanic tribes, whatever its affinities it might have with contemporary Hindu and Buddhist practices—all this would be much discussed in the decades to follow—it was the first time the dead body had received this kind of attention. Not fire but superheated hot gases would efficiently consume bodies.

A model of Brunetti's successful apparatus and a glass cube—vitrine 9—testify to the results of his final, ultimately successful experiment. The critical new element—and the most important technical feature of modern cremation—was what Brunetti called his *appareils à réverbation,* a reverberating or regenerating furnace, in which the heat of the burning fuel is bounced from a curved ceiling and walls back toward the furnace's contents. The heat "reverberates" within a chamber or chambers, recirculated through flues, and as it does, it gets hotter and hotter, indeed hot enough to melt steel and bodies. Neither fuel nor flames touch the furnace's contents; burning is indirect, as in an alchemist's retort or a nineteenth-century metallurgical furnace. Brunetti's own portable reverberation device was on display for visitors to the Vienna fair, and he explains it in detail. But the technical fine points need not concern us here except to say that there would be a great deal of debate over the succeeding decades about which precise furnace technology, adapted from metallurgy, was best for cremation (fig. 10.1). All produced a great deal of heat and required special precautions when employed on human bodies. Because the cadaver, once it reaches the stage of "spontaneous combustion," will "twist and make strange movements" and because there is a danger that "some member will fall into the embers," Brunetti proposes, for example, an iron strap to prevent these alarming contingencies from happening.

At the end he allows himself to acknowledge that all of these experiments are about burning a special sort of rubbish: a human body. The "spontaneous combustion of a cadaver," he allows, "is a solemn moment, grandiose, something sacred." It "always produces in me"—there must have been unreported experiments—"sadness and ecstasy." As long as the incandescent corpse retains its form, his "amazement" is sustained, and then when it disappears and there is no more than carbon, a kind of "moral

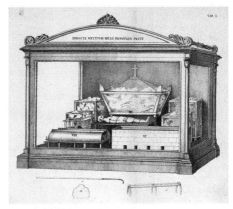

10.1. *Cremation Des Cadavres.*
Ludovico Brunetti. Padua, 1873.
British Library.

prostration seizes one." Lest his readers become too absorbed in this unexpected reverie—Brunetti's Masonic side here seems temporarily to have triumphed over his materialist and coolly scientific persona—he points out that if the pyre is well set up, there is no reason to watch and that two hours suffice to completely carbonize the cadaver. One can avoid all the emotion. Between 70 and 80 kilos of wood are needed. He set out to do what he said he had wanted: the complete carbonization of a cadaver. A fifty-year-old man, very weak, dead of pneumonia, emphysema, and chronic bronchitis (COPD, we would say), weighing 45 kilos was reduced to 1.770 kilos of ash that fit in a 17.6 cm high cube for all to see. In some sense this may have seemed disappointing; all that technology had burned off very little more of the body's weight. But it left nothing recognizably human, so the fine ash would now fit easily into an Etruscan urn; its product was clean; and it showed the way to more efficient apparatus.

In September 1873, on the occasion of a much-publicized Third International Medical Congress that met in the Jury Pavilion in connection with the Universal Exhibition, Sir Henry Thompson, England's leading urological surgeon, stopped by Brunetti's booth. The Archduke Rainer opened the medical meeting by telling the assembled scientists that while the world's fair represented "results that had already been gained," they were like an intellectual atmosphere surrounding past triumphs. It was their job to use it to prepare for future times. This is what Thompson did.[5]

Brunetti's achievements opened Thompson's eyes to the virtues of high-tech methods for disposing of bodies. In 1874, a few months after he returned home from Vienna, he founded the British Cremation Society, the first such advocacy group in the world.[6] And he undertook a new round of industrial experiments on the dead. The Italian's results, Thompson thought, were impressive; converting an adult human to 1.7 kilos of delicate white ash in three and a half hours with 150 pounds of wood was a good start. But the process was still in the research and development stage of what might become a routine process.

Thompson moved cremation nearer its full technological promise. Soon after he got back to London he got hold of what he describes as an emaciated 47-pound body, perhaps a child (it could only have belonged to a pauper, but he does not tell readers how he came by it), and burned it to 1.75 pounds of ash in the furnace of Maudslay, Sons and Field, one of Britain's leading engineering works. The firm was famous for, among other things, having built the engines and propeller screw for the *Great Western*, the first steamship built specifically to cross the Atlantic Ocean. It took only twenty-five minutes to fully carbonize the body, Thompson reported: a clear improvement over Brunetti's results. Another more challenging corpse, that of a robust 140-pound pauper, was converted, without producing an odor, to only 4 pounds of ash in less than an hour. (A 33:1 reduction in weight, compared with 25:1, Brunetti's best.) "Nothing can be purer tested by sight or smell than they are," he enthused, with all the brio of a scientist whose experiment has gone perfectly: a "portion of refuse" (i.e., a dead human body) had been successfully turned it into a "refined sublate."

In an interview that Thompson some years later gave to Edmund Yates, muckraking journalist and writer of sensational novels, he offered to show his interlocutor a "curiosity" that he kept in his study: two glass cubes no more than 5 inches on a side—one containing the remains of a twelve-stone (168-pound) human body, the other of an eighteen-stone (234-pound) pig. These, he proudly announced, were entirely mineral in content and small in volume. "There is nothing offensive about either specimen," he pointed out. The a pig was probably the one he cremated in Birmingham at the invitation of his friend William Siemens, the German-born electrical engineer and metallurgist whose regenerative furnace revolutionized steel making beginning in the late 1860s; the other, he says, was cremated at "Maudslay's." But the original weights do not correspond to those of either of the bodies in the initial experiments that he had described earlier. Perhaps these ashes were the result of further trials; perhaps he mixed up the details.[7]

With Brunetti and even more publicly with Thompson, the ground shifted under the dead. Being dead was unbearable if one paused to give the matter any thought, the early advocates of cremation argued, and the sooner the evidence of decay and corruption—the disgusting inevitable consequences of being dead—could be purged from the imagination the better all around. And especially better from the only relevant perspective, the perspective of life and hygiene, of "the art of preserving health."[8] All the rest is commentary.

Cremation was another instance of the march of progress through the mobilization of scientific knowledge. Reports of the first public, as opposed to private, experimental, high-tech cremation were in this genre and made news all over the globe. The young wife of the English politician Sir Charles Wentworth Dilke was estranged from the Church of England and had requested that she be cremated should she die in childbirth. On 20 September 1874, she did. It was impossible to fulfill her wishes in England, so the body of Katherine Mary Eliza Dilke, née Sheil, age twenty-four, was embalmed and taken to Dresden by her brother-in-law. (Lady Dilke's husband, driven temporarily mad by her death, had repaired to Paris, shaved his head, and was saved from ruin by Leon Gambetta, who recognized him in the street. He did not witness his wife's body's posthumous adventures.) Once there, and after elaborate legal maneuvering to prove that a public experiment on cremation was in the interests of science, her body was burned in a modified industrial furnace before a crowd of local worthies, all male as far as one can tell from reports.[9]

The world soon knew about it. The *Hobart Times* in Australia says that it got its account from the *Cologne Gazette*, which, in turn, based its story on the correspondent of the *Swäbische Merkur*; the *New York Times* quoted the *Times* (London). (The fact that Charles Dilke had spent some time in Australia may account for why a Tasmanian paper would report on a cremation on the other side of the world.) All reports tell a roughly similar story. Friedrich Siemens—brother of the English Siemens who had helped Thompson and coinventor of the regenerative furnace—had used their invention in a glass factory that he opened in 1867. He modified it for the cremation of Lady Dilke so as to allow guests to look inside as it consumed her body. The temperature must have been around 1100–1200°C, almost twice as hot as the air in an ordinary fireplace or funeral pyre.[10] (The minute-by-minute details of what the guests saw is described in the epigraph to this chapter.) There were over the next decade scores of further experiments, less publicly heralded but well known in scientific circles with human and various kinds of animal bodies that were incinerated using different sorts of fuel—coal and gas made from coal were the main ones because wood was too expensive—utilizing furnaces of varied designs.[11]

But, of course their innovation had and was meant to have far broader political and cultural consequences. It was a huge and fraught claim that the dead ought to belong exclusively, and for as short a time as practicable, to those who could most efficiently and hygienically dispose of organic refuse (chemists, sanitary engineers, metallurgists, doctors, and technicians of various sorts) and to no one else. Of course, they acknowledged that they would have to make concessions to "sentiment"—Siemens had suggested a silent prayer as Lady Dilke's body entered the retort of his reverberating furnace, just as Brunetti had had his moment of contemplation—but this was of secondary importance to the fact that the actual dead body had quickly and cheaply been reduced to ashes. The early proponents of cremation made only the most instrumental concessions to what anthropologists were discovering about diverse cultures of death: that the transition from being alive to being dead might be gradual, that the living might remain vested in the body even if it was buried; that bodies were and had long been central to the geography of civilization; that for millennia no one had ever quite taken the advice of Diogenes.

An austere technological modernism seems finally to have disenchanted the dead body: instead of being left to be eaten by beasts in the field as Diogenes proposed—much too messy, unpleasant, and unhygienic—it was to be quickly decomposed into its constituent elements through the 1100°C heat of a blast furnace. Then perhaps the ashes that remained could be used as fertilizer, or scattered, or done with as one pleased. Cremation, as a Zurich doctor said in 1874, represented "the final triumph of reason and common sense." Anyone who knew anything about the science of decomposition knew that the grave did slowly, inefficiently, and dangerously what the blast furnace could do a thousand times—indeed, tens of thousands of times—more quickly: turn a body to dust. So get on with it. At death, Thompson insisted, the stages that created life are retraced, "with another end, still formative, in view." No longer synthesis but deterioration, decay. "The problem which Nature sets herself to work in disposing of dead animal matter is always one and the same."[12]

In this world the dead body would finally lose its special status. As a thing unto itself, it was inconsequential, best left to feed the beasts or to marl fields. Speedy, clean, technologically sophisticated cremation represented the maximum modernist program of nineteenth-century science in the face of death, indeed in the face of all human history. It was revolutionary. But it did not spring from nothing. Enlightenment doctors had already begun the appropriation of death in the interests of the regime of life, stripping away death's metaphysical, mythic, and purportedly superstitious accretions and making possible its assimilation into biology. Death could now become a largely negative category, a word for the abyss toward which all that lived was hurtling more or less quickly. The novelist José Saramago in *Death with Interruptions* takes us back to a time when there was not one great figure Death with her scythe but many lesser deaths—demigods—each with her own helper who brought a different sort of mortality to the world's various kinds of creatures. Of course this is still the case to a very great extent. None of us want to see ourselves as bit players in the great cosmic drama of extinction that Darwin laid before the world so powerfully in the nineteenth century. Not in the Enlightenment, not since, and not ever have we reconciled ourselves to Death as "just" the end of life, as it purportedly is for animals and all other living things.

But the pedigree of Death as something more came to be seriously challenged around 1750. Its metaphysical and its physical aspects began decisively to go their separate ways: the death of humans and the death of animals, once so distinct, came together in a new and powerful language of science. For experimental cremationists of the late nineteenth century, horse, pig, dog, and human carcasses could be used more or less interchangeably. A carcass was a carcass was a carcass.

We can date this shift from many deaths to Death with some precision. It had not happened by the middle of the seventeenth century. Thomas Browne, for example, writing in 1642 as the well-trained physician that he was about matters medical and religious, still makes a clear distinction between the death of humans and animals: "I believe that the whole frame of the beast doth perish and is left in the same State after Death as it was materialled into Life." But it is not so simple for humans. Browne is fully aware of the "Anatomies, Skeletons, or Cadeverous relicks" evident in "raking into the bowels of the deceased." That is, the human frame decays just like an animal's. And in his later short book on urn burials, bones in jars, he mobilized archeology to reflect on the fragility of the human frame. But his naturalism is thoroughly Christian. The souls of humans "know no corruption" and "subsist beyond the body" by "the privilege of their proper Natures, and without a Miracle." (The resurrection of the body is a different matter.) The status of the soul is a fact of nonmaterial nature; its separation from the human body is what constitutes death; even if, on Browne's account, a body is merely animal matter, human death is not just, or even primarily, a bodily affair. The human body is not just the elements that it was before life; it had a soul with which it will be reunited.[13]

Eighty years later this was still the common wisdom. Chambers's *Cyclopedia*, the first of the great eighteenth-century compendia of knowledge, defines "death" laconically: "*Mors*, is generally considered as the Separation of the Soul from the Body; in which Sense it stands opposed to Life, which consists in the Union thereof. See Life." (The first edition of the *Encyclopeadia Britannica* in 1771 would repeat this definition verbatim.) "Life," not very helpfully, is defined as "the Duration of Animal Being, or the Space of Time that passes between their Birth and Death," that is, the period between the body getting a soul and losing it, although Chambers's *Cyclopedia* distinguishes this sense of life from what it calls "a strictly physical sense," namely, "the Circulation of the Blood," and a rather vaguer sense of "the Principle of Heat and Motion that animates Bodies, and makes 'em Perceive, Act, and Grow." There is an uneasy asymmetry here: human death is not quite comprehended by the nature of animal death because the human (the rational) soul is not the same as the animal (the locomotive or sensitive) soul that makes the blood circulate and maintains the other motions of the body—and yet it is. Life is the period of animal existence between birth and its end in death.

This mirrors again the truth that the dead body is no more horrible than that of any dead animal bereft of its warmth and motion and yet is more so.[14]

Heinrich Zedler's far more massive German encyclopedia makes the case even more explicitly than Browne and Chambers do, although it presents the view in the context of an anthropological survey, suggesting that its warrant is cultural and not metaphysical. The death of a beast, Zedler says, is by definition the end to its corporeal frame and the processes that kept it animated: "In the case of animals death means the complete dissolution of the machinery out of which the body is put together or the pure cessation of the circulation of blood and the materials of life." Human death, however, is something altogether different: "In the case of humans, according to the most generally held view, death is the departure of the soul from the body as result of an absence of warmth and motion that have stopped for contingent reasons [disease, accident]." In other words, while death in humans is a consequence of natural causes and presumably has the same natural consequences that it has in animals—decomposition of the body into its elements—it is also essentially different, something more, in "the most generally held" (Christian) view. And the same argument goes for life. Animals and humans share warmth, mobility, and strength—a common physiology—and a multiplicity of wonderfully organized parts. But "the life of humans that in its corporeality has all this in common with animals" is constituted also by "an inseparable community of body and soul," and in that sense life continues as long as they "remain in this state of mutual union." Life and death are thus mutually implicated via the hugely complicated but still self-evident relation of flesh to spirit.[15]

With Diderot and d'Alembert's *Encyclopédie*, the great monument of the Enlightenment, this would no longer be the case. What Death *is* remains contested today, perhaps because it is not anything. But the distinction made by Faust before his death and damnation at the end of Marlowe's play would have little public resonance soon after the 1750s. No one, even believers, today would say, with Faust, that they wished they were animals so that their souls would not be damned:

> O no end is limited to damned soules,
> Why wert thou not a creature wanting soule?
> Or, why is this immortall that thou hast?[16]

Death, at least for a moment in the rarified context of what was meant to be a practically oriented summary of all knowledge, was represented as a wholly natural phenomena that stood outside of culture and sacred history. In the context of Louis de Jaucourt's *Encyclopédie* entry for "Death, Natural History of Man," it is defined as "the destruction of the vital organs in such a way that they cannot be revived," a gradual process, one that begins at birth and continues to the end, a gradual extinction of life that goes on slowly and without a sharp break. In fact, thought Jaucourt, there was a greater difference between youth and old age than there was between decrepitude and death. He means this point to be reassuring. Dying is not, as the old image of a skeleton with a scythe suggests, a violent process but rather a gradual fading away; most people, he claims on the basis of doctors' reports, settle painlessly and imperceptibly into death. We thus fear it only because of "habit, education, and prejudice," because we do not know any better. This is an extraordinary claim that challenges millennia-old antidotes to the fear of death. Well-publicized empirical observations, Jaucourt claims, will offer the consolations that had before been provided, inadequately, by philosophy and religion.[17]

The article under the heading "Death, Medicine," by the chemist and royal physician Paul-Jacques Malouin, strips death of its pedigree even more explicitly. It begins with a rejection of the old distinction between human and animal death—between death in culture and death in nature—by declaring that it is groundless and pointless to discuss. There is only one Death. "The separation of the soul away from the body, a mystery that is perhaps more incomprehensible than its union, is a dogma of theology affirmed by religion and consequently is beyond discussion. Neither consonant with the light of reason nor supported by any medical observations we will not make any mention of it in this article." Consequently, an answer to the question, "When is a body dead?" depends on determining how and, more urgently, precisely when life is irretrievably over. And life, like death, is no longer, as it had been for Chambers and Zedler, a question of body and soul but only of the body. Life is the opposite of death: "the continual movement of solids and fluids through the whole living body." The "smallest bit of life is that which the body cannot do without, without which death ensues"; without that spark of life there is death.[18]

These views had three hugely important consequences for the work of the dead and for the work of the modern cremated body in particular. First, death, and by extension the dead body, became ever more absorbed in what would, by the early nineteenth century, be called "biology," the science of life. It became an essentially empty category not only for mechanists like Jaucourt but also for vitalists, men like Xavier Bichat—one of the most important physiologists of the late eighteenth century and the founder of histology—as well as for agnostics and for those with no public views on what constituted life. "Life," Bichat wrote in a famous gnomic tautology, is "the totality of those functions that resist death."[19] But it did not matter for the purposes of defining death that one have deep views about its opposite. "If we are aware of what indicates life," wrote a pragmatically inclined doctor in a forensic medicine textbook, "which everyone may be supposed to know, *though perhaps no one can say that he truly and clearly understands what constitutes it*, we at once arrive at the discrimination of death. It is the cessation of the phenomena with which we are so especially familiar—the phenomena of life."[20]

A corollary of this story is that the dead body became part of the science of life. One aspect of this is the golden age of pathology, in which doctors appropriated the bodies of tens of thousands of the poor to study the disease processes that had led to their demise. Another is the matter of the disposal of the dead. They were not as dead as the lay public might think. The life of the dead underwrote the late-eighteenth- and nineteenth-century opposition to churchyards, where putrefying flesh sent its deadly effluvia into the air. They were refuse, like the remains of the stockyards and the privy. And it was a major premise of the new cremationists. The dead body was teeming with life, wrote Sir Henry Thompson shortly after seeing Brunetti's exhibit. But the life was not its own. "Rest! Not for an instant." Never was there such activity. Thousands of changes have begun. "Forces innumerable have attacked the dead." "The rapidity of the vulture" is nothing compared to the rapidity with which the forces of synthesis that constituted life are reversed. Nature "has another end in view": decomposition. She "acts herself to work in disposing dead animal matter" by resolving it into carbon dioxide, water, ammonia, and various minerals. In other words, cremation does rapidly what nature, in her slow, old-fashioned, messy, artisanal way takes much longer to do.

As death drifted into biology, the metaphysically clear notion of a dead body as one from which a soul—or something—had departed gave way to the metaphysically empty, but empirically thorny, question of *how* one could tell that life was *really* gone. (The deeply engaging question of what exactly life was and how it emerged was sidestepped in the way that doctors today are able to identify cancer without having the foggiest idea what the disease actually is, if it indeed is *a* thing.) Attention shifted to finding signs, short of putrefaction, that life had in fact been irretrievably, and not just temporarily, lost. If it was gone for good, then a body was dead; if only temporarily hiding, then it was not. Death became a diagnostic category, and the question of what it meant to be dead became, like the problem of how to fully and hygienically burn a body, a matter of technical skill.

How could one tell that life was *really* gone? The "continual movement of solids and fluids" whose cessation entailed death could be very, very slight and therefore difficult to recognize. If, by definition, the "smallest bit of life is that which the body cannot do without, without which death ensues," one has a real diagnostic problem on one's hands. What if there were still enough life present to keep death from happening but too little to readily detect and too easy to miss by all but the most careful, experienced, and skilled observers? "In this delicate state," as the *Encyclopédie* admitted, "it is difficult to distinguish the living from the dead."[21] Determining whether life was gone became an exercise much like cancer screening today and fraught with the same problems. It required real diagnostic skill to detect reliably and was subject to false positives.

The *Encyclopédie* did not exactly invent the diagnostic problem of death. Physicians in antiquity had occasionally commented on the uncertainty of its signs. Telling the difference between a trance and genuine death was enough in the consciousness of ordinary people to play a central role in the plot of *Romeo and Juliet* and, more happily, in Boccaccio's *Decameron*, where a man disinters his prematurely buried lover, who subsequently bears him a son. King Lear's hope to see the breath of life in a fogged mirror held to Cordelia's nostrils had a long pedigree. But the problem became vastly more acute in 1740.

In that year there appeared an eight-page Latin thesis, *An mortis incertae signa* (*The Uncertainty of the Signs of Death*), that would conquer the Western world. It was by a relatively obscure doctor, Leander Peaget, and would probably not have made much of an impact if he had not been a student of the famous Jacques-Bénigne Winslow, member of the Academy of Sciences, noted anatomist, and one of the lions of the Paris medical faculty. (Winslow's textbook appeared in thirty-two different versions and five languages in the eighteenth century.) His imprimatur made all the difference. In 1742, thanks to Jacques-Jean Bruhier d'Ablaincourt, a well-known doctor, client of Winslow's, and soi-disant literary figure, Peaget's little tract morphed into French, with mountains of new anecdotal evidence and a scary new subtitle: *And the Evil of Premature Burial and Embalming*. Bruhier gave the problem of diagnosing death a sharp and culturally exigent form that would engage the international reading public until the twentieth century. His book grew exponentially. Eight pages of Latin gave rise to 364 of French right off; 34 pages more in 1746; 609 by the two-volume 1749 edition; the two English editions of the 1740s were only in the range of 200 pages, but the first German version, in 1754, came in at 800. An enormous literature grew up in the eighteenth and nineteenth centuries—there are four densely packed pages of bibliography in the major medical encyclopedia of the 1880s, not counting the many textbook discussions and mountains of fiction—that echoed again and again how difficult it was to tell if someone was really dead and that offered many, many suggestions for how the problem might be resolved.[22] Gothic fiction lived off the fear of mistakes, or premature burial; "humane societies" grew up to teach laypeople how to resuscitate the apparently dead; ordinary people took action to be sure that it did not happen to them. In fact, cremation was held out as one such remedy, more refined if not surer than a slit wrist or punctured carotid; there was no danger of waking up in a cold dark grave if one was reduced to ashes in a fiery oven. The nature of death as a physiological problem scarcely existed in 1740, but it had become an anxiety throughout the Western world less than two decades later.

The advent of widespread fear on the subject cannot be attributed in any specific instance to a broad vernacular trend of descralization or dechristianization or disenchantment: that is, to the story that corpses that had once bled or perspired or failed to decompose for miraculous reasons were replaced by those that did all this because they were not really dead at all but only the victims of misdiagnosis. Winslow, who started it all, was a Danish Protestant who was converted to Catholicism by Bossuet and whose piety and orthodoxy were beyond question. The aggressive secularism of the *Encyclopédie* is the exception rather than the rule in the writing about apparent death that soon made its way into popular culture.

The epidemic of fear that apparent death would be mistaken for the real thing, for example, fueled Gothic fiction: Poe's "The Fall of the House of Usher" and "The Premature Burial" (fig. 10.2) are but the most famous of a genre about the nightmare of being trapped in a tomb. (Roger Corman's 1962 film, *Premature Burial*, starring Ray Milland, brings the genre nearly into the present.) False death also plays a part in later-nineteenth-century novels. Wilkie Collins's *Jezebel's Daughter* has a long-drawn-out scene in which a dead woman in a Frankfurt *leichenhaus*—the place where, by law, corpses were kept for three days before burial to be sure they were really dead—comes back to life, for example. It gave rise to "humane societies" that taught laypeople to be careful about acting on apparent death as if it were the real thing and also how to resuscitate those who might still have a spark of life in them. A mainstay of modern first aid, "artificial respiration," was developed to make those who seemed dead breathe again. And all sorts of devices were invented to allow would-be corpses in the grave to alert those above that a mistake had been made. The state developed an interest in being sure that everyone who was buried really was dead, and more recently in promulgating rules for when a body could be considered dead for some purposes and alive for others. Doctors became the main experts on the question as "really dead" became a matter of biology. Death shifted registers in a way analogous to how the dead body would become rubbish to be efficiently burned in high-tech furnaces.

10.2. Illustration by Harry Clarke for Poe's "The Premature Burial."

And the anxiety does not end just because doctors develop better diagnostic strategies and feelings of superiority to their benighted predecessors 150 years after they set the problem on track. At the limit, even today physicians find themselves in a muddle between an old, deep sense of death and the *Encyclopédie*'s version. The capacity for consciousness or neural integration has replaced the presence or absence of the soul as an ontological sign because of the pragmatic need to have a body be dead for a particular purpose (the harvesting of organs) and at the same time alive for another (that it not be buried or hustled off to a morgue before its parts are salvaged). When no such need exists, people seem content to keep a dead body alive for a very long time—or to "pull the plug"—for all sorts of emotional, administrative, and assorted other reasons. If death can be "chronic," it can be almost anything. The important point is that two culturally exigent accounts of what it is to be dead, one deep and grounded in what it is to be human, the other avowedly shallow, pragmatic, and diagnostic, came into sharp focus in the age of the Enlightenment. At its birth, modern cremation was intended, like modern death, to be as culturally spare as possible.[23]

And finally, the demotion of death to its physiological basics by the *Encyclopédie* and its advocates helped to create a new space for political action around the dead. They became imbricated in the late-eighteenth-century culture wars that produced modernity, just as advocates of cremation in the nineteenth century were combatants in new but related wars one hundred years later. On occasion, the participants explicitly spelled out the stakes: "enlightened" Jews in Germany led by Jewish doctors, for example, welcomed, as a step toward modernity and away from tradition, the regulation, promulgated first by the Duke of Mecklenberg-Schwerin in 1772, that Jews, like others, had to wait three days before burying the dead to avoid making the horrible mistake of premature burial. The self-consciously modern among them would later embrace cremation. A furious and long-running battle over burial followed, in which Moses Mendelssohn, founder of Enlightenment Judaism, negotiated a compromise: Jews could bury within the traditional twenty-four hours if they obtained a physician's assent. At the same time—and here is where the trouble started—he argued that waiting three days was not a serious violation of Jewish law and that custom would need to accommodate itself to reason. Even doctors who opposed the new rules did so on empirical rather than religious grounds: that the Jewish custom of remaining with the newly dead until the time of burial ensured sufficient scrutiny to avoid the acknowledged problem of premature burial.[24]

As a matter of fact, it is not difficult, and does not take very long, to know for sure that a body is dead: one waits for a matter of days, and then putrefaction definitively confirms death, or rather, the cessation of "the smallest bit of life." The great philosopher Bishop Berkeley was among the first famous people to publicize this insight.

Afraid of a misdiagnosis, he insisted in his will that his body "be kept five days above ground, or longer, even till it grow offensive by the cadaverous smell." It was to "lye unwashed, undisturbed and covered by the same bedclothes, in the same bed, the head being raised by pillows." When, after six days, he was finally buried in Christ Church Cathedral, the matter was beyond dispute.[25] His body was exactly how the early cremationists regarded all of the dead: stinking, disordered, and filthy. Matter out of place. Dirt. And so, it might seem that the late-nineteenth-century advocacy of cremation was just a continuation of the Enlightenment project to collectively clean up the dead, to relocate them in the interest of public health.

And in one sense it was. The modern cemetery was the first great triumph of this campaign and cremation the next stage: the definitive surrender of the dead to the regime of life. But cremation as it emerged in the 1870s was far more radical than anything that had been proposed in the previous century. In the first place, there were no day-to-day exigencies that gave it its initial impetus: the many new, and some of the old, cemeteries of Great Britain were far from full; there was room in the burial places of the rest of Europe as well and more than enough in the United States. The abuses of the 1820s–1840s, always exaggerated, were everywhere almost eradicated. The soggy urban churchyards that supposedly once breathed poisonous miasmas into dense urban populations had been or were being turned into parks, insurance offices, or railway yards. The most notorious old regime burial place—the Cemetery of the Innocents—had been emptied into old quarries under Paris almost a century earlier. (The entrance today is by the Saint-Jacques Metro stop.) In short, the dirty dead were not, and were not seen as, a threat to health by anyone in the years before cremation offered itself as a way to rid the world of a problem it did not know it had.

While earlier reformers had claimed that they opposed churchyards of the old regime because they regarded them as breeding places for disease, they did not attack burial itself. The industrial annihilation of bodies was not on their horizons. They also did not want to expose the magic that made the collective burial of the dead a culturally resonant act. Père Lachaise and many imitators were intended to be an alternative communal space for the dead with its own aesthetics, its own necrogeography, and its own affective associations. Ashes would eventually be treated like bodies—that is, burial would reassert itself. But the question of what was to become of the remains of the coke oven was scarcely mentioned for decades after Brunetti, Thompson, and their colleagues first put cremation on the international agenda. They used some of the old arguments, but in the interest of something far more radical than the progenitors of nineteenth-century cemeteries could have imagined. Thompson reported that even the few supporters of his initial proposals—most of the more than eight hundred letters he received condemned them as pagan and un-Christian—considered them to be so novel that they did not come "within the range of practical policy."[26] Bodies safely tucked away in spacious and salubrious gardens still mattered to the great majority of people. For the early stalwarts of cremation, bodies were to be gotten rid of as soon as possible; they constituted a problem that needed to be solved by engineers of different sorts and by political economists. The effort to strip them of any claims to cultural regard was relentless and driven.

There is very little about heart and sentiment, about mourning and aesthetics, as there had been among the hygienists who had earlier advocated cemeteries. Cremation was for a time all about cleanliness. Sanitation, argued one early advocate to members of the Sunday Lecture Society meeting in St. George's Hall, Langham Place, on 14 March 1886, was the true—the chief—raison d'être of modern cremation. Experiments would prove or disprove "the system" superior to burial. George Wotherspoon knew that his audience would not take this quietly at face value; the series in which he spoke had been addressed by the distinguished psychologist Henry Maudsley on the lessons of materialism and by the pioneer statistician and freethinker Karl Pearson on matter and the soul; subscribers to the series had heard about the history of eighteenth-century English free thought and about the triumph of science over superstition. They had not paid to hear only about the technicalities of drains and sewers.

And Wotherspoon quickly assured them that he would also talk about the moral and the economic aspects of cremation; he would address too its ancient historical roots in what he thought was a combination of fire and ancestor worship. Even with respect to sanitation he, like many who spoke on the subject, could turn poetic: the idea that "fresh earth is the best disinfectant is itself a delusion"; ask Nature "what is the great purifier," he suggests, "and her very echoes will answer Fire." There was always more at stake than pure *techne*. But that said, mundane arguments about the connection between inhumation and disease loomed large in the 1870s and offered a thin disguise—perhaps it would be more precise to say, an alternative register—for what was, in fact, a radical turn to thinking about the dead as mere, abject matter.[27] Fifteen years into the agitation, Thompson still needed to "explain the sanitary laws which must inevitably render cremation, or some method of disposing of the dead other than burial, inevitable."[28]

Buried bodies, he wrote, caused untold amounts of misery and disease. Thousands of lives, he said, are "cut short by the poison of decay," offering some fifteen pages of evidence ranging from the hoary eighteenth-century stories deployed by the enemies of the churchyard back in the day to the latest experiments of Louis Pasteur on the dangers to livestock from grazing in pastures where animals who had died of anthrax were buried. Twenty-two pages more, based on the previous fifteen years' research, give added weight to these views in the expanded 1889 edition: 73,747 out of 537, 276 people who died in Britain in 1886, for example, succumbed to so-called zymotic disease, diseases caused by "ferment," which included smallpox, measles, scarlet fever, diphtheria, whooping cough, typhus, enteric fever, simple fever, dysentery, and cholera. All of these newly dead could be blamed on the decaying dead who preceded them.

Thompson was clearly not keeping abreast of the medical literature on infectious diseases. Robert Koch's discovery of the anthrax bacillus in 1878, the tubercle bacillus in 1882, and the cholera vibrio in 1884, as well as the discovery of the causes of some of the other infectious diseases he lists—for example, in 1883 and 1884 *Corynebacterium diphtheriae* was shown to cause diphtheria—made nonsense of "ferments." But rhetorically such lapses did not matter. Even if one cannot prove that cemetery air produces endemic epidemic illnesses, writes an early French advocate of cremation, one cannot deny that it "diminishes the general vitality" and favors propagation of epidemics like typhus. Of course one could, and people did, deny it. But the idea of the dead as profoundly polluting was so powerful as to make counterevidence irrelevant. The founding text of modern cremation insisted that science had proven that "putrefaction affecting organic matter disseminates the germs of fatal disease," and that, through the very act of interment itself, we "literally sow broadcast throughout the land innumerable seeds of pestilence," that lie dormant until, at some future time, they "fructify in premature death and ruined health for thousands." Cremation stops the process before it can begin, as no other method of disposing of the dead short of feeding them to fish does. Even well-regulated cemeteries allow for mistakes that society simply cannot afford. (Plague is not on Thompson's list, but his reference to supposed epidemics of that disease in Eyam and Minchhampton, where churchyards from the sixteenth century were disturbed in the nineteenth, makes the same point: dead bodies are like time bombs.)[29]

Anecdote could be piled on anecdote. One speaker in Hull explained in a series of "health lectures for the people" how Louis Pasteur had shown that earthworms living a few feet below the ground where cows with splenic fever had been buried spread germs through their guts. He had already given his listeners a full account of how even new cemeteries were becoming crowded, a common theme, and that regulation was for naught. ("Your new burial code is a paper constitution . . . futile," as one of the founders of the Cremation Society put it.) A chemist speaking before the Reading Literary Society reminded his listeners that Prof. Bianchi—perhaps he meant Giuseppe Bianchi, a politically and socially engaged astronomer—had shown that the 1828 plague in Modena was a direct result of excavating a three-hundred-year-old churchyard.[30] And so on.

Colleagues filled in the many intermediate details. Once one thought of dead bodies as reagents in a laboratory retort—fifty-two thousand of them in London alone producing 2,572,580 cubic feet of gas, which, if it wasn't absorbed by soil, went into the water supply—the terms of the discussion were clear. The sooner society rids itself of this odiferous garbage the better. In short, decay in the grave is but slow burning, as a sympathetic clergyman said. Or alternatively, fire—and, for that matter, being devoured by wild beasts or being lost at sea—is just a faster way for bodies to be rendered "into their compound atoms," disbursed, and "recontributed to the vast material world, to an ever living and changing Cosmos, from which they were originally borrowed." What had once been the horrible fate of placeless dissolution would become a culturally resonant gloss on what happens when a dead body is ingested or cremated. But the new reality was that dead bodies were being claimed by sanitary engineers.[31]

William Eassie, who became secretary of the newly formed Cremation Society upon its founding in 1874, made his name first in the Crimea, where he supervised the building of the Erenkoy Hospital. Back home he was well known as the author of what became the standard handbook for building healthy houses, a work dealing in a detailed technical way with proper drainage, ventilation, and "kindred subjects." But he thought of himself as engaged in a far grander, world historical project: "at length, the sanitary day is dawning." Mankind will at last be "restrained from committing suicide by setting at defiance all the laws of Health." The preservation of public health, he argued, was crucial if we—we British—are "to hold our own in the rapid race for pre-eminence amongst the nations of the earth." "Science is to triumph"; "facts not fancies must be our guides." Finally rotten back drains, the infiltration of sewage into wells, and disused drains would get their due; "permanent sanitary temples" like the one built in Leeds in 1871 would, he hoped, soon serve as shining examples.[32]

In fact, only the preface of his book offers such high-flown thoughts. The rest is devoted to the details of getting rid of waste—mostly of bodily origins—and its smells: water closets should not be placed in cramped quarters; they, and sinks too, must have proper traps, which he described in detail; the state of urinals is the best index to the sanitary condition of an establishment; earth closets are fine as long as "all possible smell" is avoided. Avoid ammoniacal dust—suggestive of the smell of composting bodies—when choosing chemicals for wetting streets, he counsels.

From here it is a small step to cremation and its history. From the earliest times forward, people had burned bodies, Eassie argues, on sanitary grounds to "protect the living from corruption." Now we know in detail why. Foreign doctors have done basic research about carbonic acid levels in graveyards; we know that, only recently, graves have poisoned wells in Finchley. His colleague from the Crimea, Edmund Parkes, to whom he looks for authority, had set up the terms of the problem clearly. Basically, the dead, like excrement, are a waste product. A section of Parkes's much-reprinted *Manual of Practical Hygiene* on "ordinary London sewage" explains that feces produce 1–1.5 cubic inches of gas/hour/gallon: asphyxiating gases—carbonic acid, sulfurated hydrogen, sulfide of ammonia, and a residue category of "putrid organic vapors." Fungi and "germ infusoria" abound. Dead bodies do the same. The section on air in churchyards follows the one on sewage. Parkes rehearses the figures, first calculated by the distinguished chemist Sir (later Lord) Lyon Playfair in the 1850s, that 2.5 million cubic feet of carbonic acid are produced by fifty-two thousand dead bodies in London; again fungi and infusoria abound.[33]

Parkes, who founded a much-publicized Temple to Health in Leeds in the early 1870s, had no systematic ideas before 1874 about what to do with all this human sewage, but he knew that something had to be done. He warns about the accumulation of bodies that one finds in the great cemeteries of Anatolia; he explains that bodies are eventually oxidized into simpler components—gases and volatile salts that go back into the soil. The question is how to best accommodate a mass of dead organic material so that it decomposes harmlessly into its elements. Deep burial has advantages in terms of keeping pollution away from the living, even if it is a slow way to recycle; charcoal helps with smell but is expensive; burning costs more than burial at sea, which is cheap and allows the body "to go at once to support other forms of life." It is unlikely, however, that any government would send fifty thousand corpses down the Thames to Southend and the Channel beyond. But Eassie could still make much use of all this.

By 1883, Parkes had discovered the cremationists, who had already discovered him. (He had also discovered Haden's earth coffin, which he thought had possibilities because it hastened decomposition and was sanitary if it was buried deeply enough.) The new editions of his book add a long and approving section on what the Germans and French had learned about disposing of bodies in their 1870–1871 war. Simply digging up superficially buried bodies and burning them by covering them with pitch and straw—one ton for every fifteen to twenty bodies—met with mixed results; only the surface of the dead soldiers were burned by this technique, leaving a charred mess. But there was a cleverer plan that worked in Metz in 1870. French authorities dug a pit 17 feet deep; a row of bodies was placed side by side; a second was placed across them; and so on with gunpowder placed between the rows. Filled to within six feet of the surface, 8,400 of the dead were swiftly incinerated.

There was, even at the time, something embarrassing about this; it was clear to early advocates of cremation that even if the dead were rubbish, they needed to be burned reasonably and efficiently. A young French doctor, Jules-Octave Laurent, in his 1882 thesis bemoans the Russians, who burned mounds of cadavers that the French army left there after the failed Napoleonic campaign, and the Germans, who after the 1814 battles burned four thousand cadavers in such a primitive way as to give cremation a terrible popular image. Even Parkes must have understood that what he was describing was less than appealing. There was a nicer way to achieve the same result: Mr. Eassie, Laurent tells his readers, has recently proposed an "ambulatory cremation furnace," which would "unquestionably be of advantage from a hygienic point of view."[34]

But the central point remained; the dead were, before all else, refuse and had to be treated as such. They constituted an acute problem for the military sanitary engineer in times of war and a chronic everyday problem for his counterpart in civil society. There were, one lecturer warned, some 4 million stone (56 million pounds) of putrefying flesh produced in Great Britain every year; Hull alone produced 28,791 stone (403,074 pounds) every year, assuming that the average body weighed 8 stone. Burying this mass merely preserved "scaly germ covered bodies instead of destroying them." Refuse is refuse. "No sound arguments can be urged" against the cremation of dead animals and garbage, argued an American proponent of cremation with reference to his British colleagues. Eassie had shown how important it was to burn dead horses in the Crimea; an article in the *British Medical Journal* had reported on how animal bodies cut up into chunks could be burned in the furnaces of gas works. In short, "science has shown that cremation merely produces quickly what putrefaction takes a long time to accomplish."[35]

The technical differences between various competing ways to burn bodies are of little interest today except for the fact that they were compulsively interesting to the early advocates of cremation. Books and pamphlets are full of competing designs by Muller and Fichet and Cadet and Lagénardière and Terruzi-Bertti and Gorini and Polli and Clericetti and Brunetti—who improved on his own original experimental apparatus—and Poma, and of course Friedrich Siemens, who designed the furnace that consumed Lady Dilke. Technology had become the new way to render the dead clean and suitable for subsistence among the living; the line between hygiene and ritual pollution taboo became blurred. Karl Freiherr von Engerth, scion of one of Europe's great railway engineers and second president of the Austrian Cremation Society, wrote as if it were a commonplace that the practices of the ancients would repulse us moderns and that cremation today is "only possible" if the ashes of the deceased remain "unmixed" with fuel. And this, in turn, is possible only if there is no direct contact between the body and the flame. (Gas-fired furnaces avoided this problem entirely.) Furthermore, the ashes of the body needed to be kept apart from those of the coffin in which the body was brought to the crematorium and in which it awaited its fate before being moved into the furnace. Thompson recommended wrapping it in cloth like an old fashioned shroud in which it could be gently lifted onto the slab on which it would be incinerated.[36]

He himself remained faithful to his friend Siemens's regenerating furnace. Like others of similar design, it reheated the products of combustion from one chamber in a second one and then channeled the hot gases back to the original chamber for further combustion. The process had all sorts of advantages for fuel economy. And it had revolutionized steel production: by the 1890s, the Siemens process had outstripped Bessemer's in tonnage manufactured. It likewise made possible the incineration of bodies without fouling the air or mixing human ash with coke ash.

The potential of particulates going up the chimney was a problem for those who thought of the dead as waste. Thompson, as vice president of the British Sanitary Institute, took up airborne stray matter more generally in his last reform crusade. His object was the elimination of "the abominations which are loading the air with unknown mischief": the lighter particles and scraps of garbage that escaped from the wicker baskets used by London's dust men to transfer each house's "dust" to a collecting cart. The closed collectable bin—the garbage can—that we still use today was his lasting contribution to metropolitan cleanliness.[37]

Burning bodies could potentially be even more polluting than collecting rubbish the old-fashioned way, and that issue too had to be addressed. The *Sanitary Record* in 1879 noted the "horrible effect" of the possibility of "imperfectly decomposed cadaverous molecules escaping" but pointed out that it could be prevented by a grate of coke in the chimney. (This would not be the preferred solution.) Several councilors of the Imperial Board of Health in Vienna, for example, had suggested that cremation was not as clean as advocates claimed: one brought to the attention of his colleagues reports from India that the air was poisoned for miles round after a suttee. The Indian comparison was immediately relevant because William Eassie, the sanitary engineer who was also secretary of the Cremation Society, had described how a poor person could be burned in Poona "with all necessary respect" and at "low cost." An old paper by an English doctor working in India which claimed that simply building a fifty-five-foot chimney for each burning ghat would do the trick was apparently not widely read.[38] The matter was referred to committee.

Thompson and his colleagues were on the case. A 227-pound animal body, Thompson reports—this the pig whose carbonated remains he so proudly showed the journalist in the interview twenty years later that I mentioned near the beginning of this chapter—was burned in one of Siemens's furnaces to less than 5 pounds of ash in fifty-five minutes with not a particle of smoke or stray flesh: only "heated hydrocarbons in gaseous form" and hot air escaped. Walter Smith, speaking to the Salford Gas Department Mutual Improvement Society—there may have been professional self-interest here—described a mortuary plant that was perhaps less sophisticated than Siemens's furnace but one whose seventeen banks of six retorts each could burn a day's worth of dead bodies from metropolitan Manchester in just five hours. The idea was to make double use of the retorts: distilling coal to produce town gas—mostly methane and carbon monoxide—and using the heat to distill bodies. Surplus gases would go up the chimney with no more prejudice to the environment than one factory chimney.[39]

Other more farfetched schemes were mooted. Even if the Siemens furnace was the top of the line, new and harebrained technologies seemed on the

FIG. 26. — Crématoire de Woking.

10.3. Britain's first crematorium in
Woking. From Prosper de Pietra Santa,
"La crémation en France et Italie,"
Journal d'hygiene 8 (18820): 73.

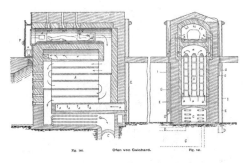

Fig. 140.   Ofen von Guichard.   Fig. 141.

10.4. The oven design of Guichard.
From Dr. Th. Weyl, "Neuere Apparate zur
Leichenverbrennung," *Gesundheits-Ingenieur* 15.12
(30 June 1892), 387.

horizon: the body might be shrouded in sheets of asbestos and large cooper
plates could be placed at head and feet. It would be like a "filament in an incandescent lamp" that, when a current was passed through it, "would be instantly
carbonized."[40] The image does not quite work, of course, because filaments are
meant to glow and not burn up and the amount of electricity required would
be staggering. No one ever tried so madcap a scheme. The British Cremation
Society settled on a furnace for its new facility at Woking designed by an Italian
anatomist named Paolo Gorini. Culture and history had been left far behind
(figs. 10.3–10.6).

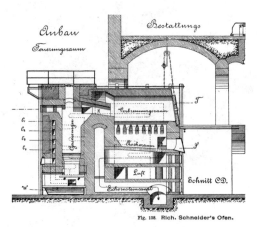

Fig. 138. Rich. Schneider's Ofen.

10.5. The oven design of Richard Schneider. From Dr. Th. Weyl, "Neuere Apparate zur Leichenverbrennung," 386.

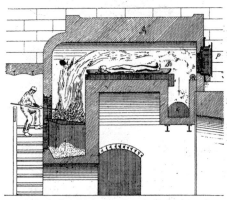

Fig. 136. Paris (Père-Lachaise).

10.6. The oven at Père Lachaise, designed by Gorini. From Dr. Th. Weyl, "Neuere Apparate zur Leichenverbrennung," 382.

With this step, then, the dead also became more explicitly than ever before a part of the political economy—in fact, the management of resources more generally—and were subject to its laws.[41] The defunct human, like manure and other organic remains, is part of nature's capital, Thompson argued, and "capital is intended to bear good interest." Burying bodies is like burying money or anything else valuable, preventing them from being fruitful, whereas cremating them makes them available for reinvestment. Consider, he suggests, that there are 80,430 deaths in greater London each year. These could yield 206,282 pounds of ash—six to eight times more valuable than an equal weight of dried but still extant bones—plus another 5,584,000 pounds of gaseous food for plants that would otherwise not be available for fifty to one hundred years. Multiply these numbers by nine and one gets an astounding figure for what the whole country's dead would yield.

Thompson goes on to make the same point in terms of national income accounting. Britain imported £409,590 worth of bones in 1866, £600,029 in 1869, and £753,185 in 1877 because the nation was "hoarding" its own bones six feet underground. (These figures would translate into hundreds of millions of pounds today.) Add to this the cost of freight for imported bones and the cost of funerals and burials, £10 on average, times eighty thousand dead in London alone, and the economic madness of current burial practices becomes clear. Or, as a colleague recalculated the matter, at £42 per ton of ash, the bodies of London alone were worth ninety-two times that, which, if added to the 683 tons from the country as a whole, would produce £30,660 worth of fertilizer. This does not seem to articulate with Thompson's figures for the savings in bone imports, but never mind.[42]

The numbers matter less than the breathtaking materialism of these claims and counterclaims. Louis-Sébastien Mercier, the French Revolutionary playwright, father of science fiction, and passionate follower of Jean-Jacques Rousseau, opposed cremation when it first became a political possibility after 1794 by arguing that corpses do not belong to us but to the earth from which their elements came. Fire, he says, robs the soil of what it "has a right to expect for the reproduction of vegetable life and the building up of chalky soils," because most of the cremated body goes up in smoke. And cremation wastes whole forests for fuel.[43]

Fifty years later, the physiologist Jakob Moleschott, a Dutch-born lecturer in physiology at Heidelberg, would argue on the same terms but come to a different conclusion. Moleschott was the subject of the first academic freedom case on record when he lost his position at Heidelberg because of, among other things, his insistence on speaking about the dead primarily and exclusively as sources of mineral salts that were needed for the tissues of the living. He was, his accusers argued, mixing politics and science; he was being *unsittlich* (immoral, unethical). (His radical materialist view of life—and death—was welcome first in Zurich and then in professorships at Turin and Rome, where he traveled in the same circles as Brunetti and the other Italian cremationists.) Phosphorus salts in particular, Moleschott argued, were the foundation of the brain: "without phosphorous no thoughts." By burying the dead instead of cremating them, the human race deprived itself of this crucial element; bodies were being left to greedy worms, which presumably had little need of them.[44]

In other words, beginning with the French Revolution, corpses could be spoken of as vitally important recyclable material. By the time Thompson wrote, the boundaries of decency had shifted even more dramatically. In 1845–1846, the revelation that paupers' bones—and, it was hinted, bones from the local churchyard—were outstripping the number of animal bones being converted into fertilizer meal at the Andover Workhouse caused a scandal for eliding the boundaries between the worthless poor and valuable skeletal remains. Now the pre-Socratic philosopher Heraclitus's idea that the dead were best suited to marling fields was being presented as a real public policy option.[45]

There were still limits to how far proponents might want to take the ecological argument. William Eassie admitted that the case for cremation had suffered from an early proposal that the dead might be used to produce illuminating gas.[46] And all the early writers on cremation were a little embarrassed by the mass incineration of dead soldiers. But even if it was not clear how, technologically or within the limits of what society would tolerate, bodies could be effectively recycled, it was clear that this was the goal. One might hope that in the future "some higher use may possibly be made of our bodies by enabling them to increase the food and wealth of others" once they were of no more use to us. (The same writer looked forward to the day when "dust to dust, ashes to ashes" will no longer be words without meaning.)[47]

But until bodies could be made into fertilizer, the question of what to do with cremated remains hovered between discussions of rational land-use policy and utopian necrogeography. One needed to economize on space, for example. A coffin commanded a surface area of at least 18 square feet; 40 or more cubic feet by volume. A cremated body, on the other hand, fit into a cube 6 inches on a side, Eassie pointed out; Thompson's experimental subjects had fit into a 5-inch one. With such a radical reduction in volume, one million corpses—a year's worth of mortality in England—would take up no more than one acre if placed in appropriate-size urns; a square mile of earth could contain the dead of six hundred years. (By contrast, a single cemetery in Woking, where Britain's first crematorium was built in 1878, takes up almost a square mile; more than a century and a half after its founding in 1854, it holds only 0.0004 percent of the bodies it could if all of them had been cremated.)

Or suppose, another argument goes, that we were to convert the ashes, especially of poor people, into cubic-foot-size cubes. Then we could build a pyramid of these—the "one indestructible form of architecture"—with a base of 9,801 square feet. Going fifty feet high, with four sides, we would get a 166,650-cubic-foot structure that contained precisely that number of bodies. Multiply by four and we get 666,600 corpses in four pyramids that could easily fit onto a one-acre plot that would be equivalent to twenty acres of cemetery. (Actually it would be a squeeze, leaving just over 4,000 square feet to spare.) Or alternatively, bury the urns in 20-foot-deep graves, and fifteen acres would have room for 13,680,000 remains, with room for another 50,000 more prosperous bodies in exposed urns set in niches around a wall and 5,000 more in vaults: total, 134,118,000 bodies per acre.[48] Consider the alternative. The costs in land alone for finding a place for bodies could be enormous: Manchester had just spent £100,000 for a new cemetery; lands out of cultivation and recreational use would cost the metropolis £270,000; half a million dead required seven thousand new acres of cemeteries per year; and so forth. That said, one of the most effective opponents of cremation argued his case by raising the ecological stakes in favor of inhumation. If one used wicker baskets, as the prominent physician Francis Seymour Haden argued, then bodies and their temporary coffins would quickly compost into rich soil; the churchyard at Holborn had been raised 15 to 18 feet; what rich alluvial soil awaited the lowlands of Kent and Essex if bodies could be composted there. The slow, natural decay of the three thousand people who died weekly in London would enrich the soil far more than their ashes.[49] More utopian late-nineteenth-century calculations harkened back to the most spectacular funerary fantasies of the eighteenth century—the neo-Egyptian cenotaph of the architect and academician Étienne-Louis Boullée, a pyramid set in a bleak desert that would comfort humankind with the prospect of entombment in what he took to be an embodiment of nature, or the mausoleum dedicated to the "illustrious men of the republic" of Jean-Jacques Lequeu, that won a prize in an architecture completion in the year VII, for example—although there is no evidence that these were in the minds of the new cremationists.[50]

The most radical of the cremationists seemed to accept the most radical claim suggested by Diogenes' argument: there was really no such thing as a dead human body. Death constituted a radical rupture, and what remained when life had departed was really nothing more than matter shorn of its past. But there is a difference. Diogenes had made his argument against cultural norms more generally and in favor of a life lived in accordance with nature. The bourgeois modernists—the engineers, doctors, scientists, and political radicals of the eighteenth and nineteenth centuries—fought for their vision of the dead as a synecdoche of a rational society.

The dead in regenerating furnaces, their ashes fertilizing plants or neatly stored in the ground or in pyramids, were soldiers in the march of progress: "more than every novelty" it would bring about an age of reason. The doctor who wrote these words also thought that all the world's religions would be welded into one by the recognition of fire as the ultimate purifier. Cremation in its technological, economic, and ecological registers thus embraced a hopelessly utopian high modernism. But it was, of course, already and always entangled with many different histories that could not be shrugged off and that determined its meaning. Ashes would come to stand for bodies, new kinds of necrogeographies would come into being, and old ones might become newly possible again. The work of the dead would broaden beyond the confines of cremation's efforts to erase its own history.

Chapter 11
ASHES AND HISTORY

The ways in which the human corpse is treated today by so-called civilized people shows how far from civilized they really are. . . . Large cities should take the lead in instituting cremation because they are the places of greatest intelligence and least prejudice. The inhabitants of the countryside and the mountains will follow.

JOHANN-JAKOB WEGMANN-ERCOLANI,
Ueber Leichenverbrennung als rationellste Bestattungsart (1874)

For men like Wegmann-Ercolani, speaking to a large, enthusiastic crowd of Zurich's most forward-looking citizens—2,200 of them who debated the subject with a degree of thoughtfulness and thoroughness rarely seen, according to the local newspaper—cremation stood for the advancement of humanity: more than technical advances like vaccination, chemical matches, and steam power, more than the destruction of medieval fortifications and the incorporation of churches into a program of historic preservation, burning the dead in ovens adapted from the steel industry was on the right side of history. It was its cutting edge.

Even friends of cremation recognized that might be claiming too much. The Italian doctor Prosper de Pietra Santa accused his Milanese colleagues of mixing advocacy of cremation with political opinions and religious beliefs. They suffered, he thought, from an inflated sense of their own importance: it was "nothing more than a useful technical novelty," and "orthodox fanatics [who] mischievously mix it up with questions of morality and religion" are both wrong and unrealistic. But his own work, deeply imbued with the laicism and positivism of Third Republic social policy, shows how hard it is to draw boundaries. Technology is never just technology. Something has to bridge the chasm of the crazy ahistorical practicality of Brunetti's pamphlet reporting on his experiments with the flesh-consuming furnace (see chapter 10), on one side, and the dead body that is still part of culture, on the other: matter and personhood.[1]

This chasm has always existed. To those who haul the bodies or dig the graves or hoist the dead onto funeral pyres, or, in the past few centuries, to those funeral professionals who whisk the dead away for embalming or burial, the materiality of the body has been what matters. But modern cremation has made the gap much more evident. This was brought home to me some years ago when I gave a memorial lecture at the University of Manchester in honor of Professor Donald Cardwell, a pioneer in the history of technology or, more precisely, when I delivered my talk on the subject of this chapter at the Manchester Crematorium. It is a large, beautiful Romanesque building with a cloister set among tombstones in what looks like, but isn't, a churchyard. It could be. Light streams into the chapel—lecture hall, for my purposes—from three large bays of clerestory windows and one rosette over what would be, but isn't, the altar. Pews fill the aisles, and plaques with the names of the dead on the wall identify each columbarium niche where the corresponding ashes are kept. My pulpit-lectern was to the right of the altarlike fixture on which a cross or some other religious symbol could be affixed. All this is the cultural side of cremation. The front of the altar is a door onto a track that takes the dead to the other side of the wall. I asked for a tour before my talk.

On the other side of the wall, things are different. It was late afternoon, and workers wearing rubber boots had been hosing down a concrete floor. Tracks shuttled coffins into furnaces that looked as though they might have been used for small-scale steel production or efficient waste disposal. The scene was not brutal or disrespectful to the dead so much as matter-of-fact: on this side of the wall were the industrial guts of the building. Once the work is done here, the product—that is, the ashes—return to the other side again, and the cycle of culture and material engineering will have come full circle.

DIFFERENT ENCHANTMENTS

Fire and ash took their place on the front line of the culture wars more than a century before the 1873 Vienna World Exposition, beginning with Enlightenment interpretations—or rather misinterpretations—of antiquity: if the Christians had suppressed cremation, then embracing it again in the Enlightenment and nineteenth century was a way of honoring the classical world that had been lost and more or less aggressively rejecting the new one that had supplanted it. Frederick the Great, always ready to show his philosophical hand, supposedly asked that he be "burned in the Roman fashion." Of course that did not happen; he even failed to be buried as he had wished—with his dogs. But one of his aunts fared better. In 1752, she was cremated "for aesthetic reasons." It may have been the first cremation in the West in modern history.[2]

Cremation in its neoclassical inflection was on the side of progress in the sense of a return to a long-gone and better time. But it was not necessarily on the side of revolution, secularism, materialism, and the new cult of reason. Jacob Grimm, the philologist and collector of folktales, in his learned address to the Berlin Academy in 1849, could make the case that the advent of cremation in preclassical antiquity had represented a step forward in the spiritual or mental cultivation of a people: the use of fire distinguished humans from animals. He could argue that it coincided with the advent of religion: spiritlike fire rises to heaven, whereas flesh is earthbound; burnt sacrifices were a way of connecting humans and the gods. Broadly speaking, there were thus "aesthetic merits of a fiery grave." But cremation is practical as well, Grimm continued: ashes are easier to transport. And it is rational: fire does quickly what earth does slowly. Finally, he said simply, to burn the dead was to honor antiquity. In other words, cremation is on the side of classicism and civilizational progress. But Grimm does not go on to draw the conclusion, as others would, that burial—dank, morbid, the quintessence of baroque darkness—is therefore retrograde. Nor does he think that a return to ancient practices would be easy: burial was too deeply embedded in the whole Christian symbolic system of the sleeping dead and their eventual rising into a life everlasting for that. Perhaps Grimm's most important contribution was to show his contemporaries the civilizational stakes of how people dealt with the dead and thus to put the French Revolutionary reinvention of cremation in the context of deep time.[3]

In 1794, a new history began in earnest, and with it burning the dead took on new meaning. After a thousand years in which all the dead—excluding heretics—were buried, Jacobin revolutionaries in France reintroduced public cremation to Europe: an explicitly public alternative to Christian burial. More precisely, they produced the first full-scale, Roman republican–style cremation in almost two thousand years and the first cremation of any sort in France for a thousand. (Sometime in the late tenth century near the Breton village of Ile de Groix, the body of a Viking chieftain was burned in his ship, itself a strange backward-looking gesture in a strange land. By that time the Vikings were mostly burying their dead.)[4]

The eighteenth-century body in question once belonged to Charles Nicolas Beauvais de Préau, a doctor, a member of the National Assembly from the Department of the Seine, and, at the time of his death, the representative of the Convention to the politically divided city of Toulon. After a royalist takeover, he was put in prison; there he fell mortally ill. When the city was retaken by the armies of the Convention in late December 1793—the siege of Toulon was one of Napoleon's first great moments—de Préau was too sick to travel the more than eight hundred kilometers back to Paris and was moved instead to Montpellier. There he died on 28 March 1794.

On the next day, 29 March, the revolutionary municipal government reinvented cremation: the body of this "martyr of liberty would be cremated in a civil ceremony," it announced, "and his ashes gathered in an urn which would be conveyed to the Convention [in Paris]." In what is almost an act of historical enactment, de Préau's body was laid on an old-fashioned wood-fueled pyre, like what would have been used in the *Iliad* or the Rome of Cato. (There would be no better way until the age of Siemens and Bessemer.) The flames took all day and well into the night to consume the body. The next morning the ashes were collected and taken first to the local Temple of Reason—the site since 1793 of the explicitly anti-Christian Cult of Reason and its festivals—and from there sent on to the capital, where they were received by de Préau's colleagues, who ordered them ensconced in the National Archives. (How, and indeed if, they were separated from wood ash is not discussed in the sources. At stake here is neither pollution nor the utilization of cutting-edge technology but homage to pagan antiquity.)

The link between cremation, on the one hand, and support for an alternative to Christianity (that is, the Cult of Reason), on the other, became even more explicit when by the law of 21 Brumaire in the year V—11 November 1795—cremation was made legal. It is hard to say that it was ever illegal, because not since Charlemagne had anyone prohibited it. It was a nonissue in Europe for more than a thousand years. But no longer. Its political bite was clear: "Whereas, the greater part of the people in antiquity burnt their dead," begins the decree, and "[whereas] this practice was abolished, or in any case fell into disuse, only because of religious influences [read Christianity]," it would now become available again as part of an effort to create a new national cult of the dead and to discredit the old one. (The tyranny of the Church over the dead had become a national scandal eighteen years earlier when it tried to prevent Voltaire from being properly buried. See chapter 4.)

Never mind that the law of 21 Brumaire got its history wrong: Christianity had not caused the decline of Roman cremation. But the fact that men of the Enlightenment and Revolution believed that it had was enough to make reinstating it both an anticlerical protest and a neoclassical alternative to long-established practice. It also set the stage for the battles of the next century. The same year—1796—the Convention solicited ideas for the reform of funeral rites intended to make them less dependent on the Church. Père Lachaise, the innovative new kind of space for the dead that would sweep the world, was a product of this cultural ferment; many harebrained schemes that were suggested came to nothing. Cremation stood in between. Having been made legal—or rather, having entered the cognizance of civil law—for the first time in European history in 1796 as part of the cultural reform program of the Directorate, it could be made illegal when political winds shifted with the Concordat between Pius VII and Napoleon in

1801. That same year, Pierre Giraud, who in 1795 had been appointed as the first "architect on monuments and conserved buildings" in France, suggested in a last gasp of funereal utopianism that French men and women might turn ashes into glass that could then be made into commemorative medals. The Third Republic made cremation legal again in 1889: the laicization of the dead.[5]

At issue in all this was not a particular view of the consequences of cremation versus burial; cleanliness, which would loom so large in later debates and in contemporary arguments for closing churchyards, played almost no role. Materialist philosophy played no part; there was no interest in technology. Cremation was meant to strike a blow at a millennium-old community of the dead buried in sacred ground and to offer a historically based alternative. The reasons that the Church opposed it are clear. But even Louis-Sébastien Mercier, who opposed cremation on ecological grounds, disliked it for a number of aesthetic and sociological reasons: the pyres were hateful; the flames were cadaverous; and the private sepulchers made possible by having one's dead grandfather and uncle in urns that could be put in the cupboard were "an affront to the calm and repose of society."[6] For seventy years, little would be heard of this kind of talk, and when it reappeared, it was to make the opposite case. Ferdinando Coletti, a distinguished Italian medical academic and liberal reformer—the cremation society of Padua was named after him—reflected on the French experience. Having the urns of one's relatives at home would exercise "a very healthy influence on the morality of the individual"; they would become a "sanctuary of the family, which is the eternal base of social order ... [because] it is uncontestable that the genealogy of the people would be a great element of moral regeneration."[7] This makes a would-be collection of ashes seem like an Italian version of a Chinese ancestral altar. And so it might as well be. The differences between the French science fiction writer and the reformist Padua pathologist about ashes and ancestors could not be resolved empirically. There were far too few cremations to decide the question back then anyway, and no one has tried since. The debate is about how the remains of the dead, ashes in this case, call the living to imagine a moral order.

Relatively little was said about this question in the first few decades of modern cremation—from the 1870s to the late 1890s—because the necrogeography of ashes mattered less than the process of making them in the first place. Recreating the republican funeral pyres of antiquity would have been enough of an alternative representational strategy because of its more recent association with revolutionary anticlericalism and neoclassicism. Employing high-tech methods married that pedigree to progress, materialism, and reason. The political sons—and to a lesser extent daughters—of the revolutionary tradition would embrace and embellish it all.

Nowhere was cremation more politically and religiously charged than in Italy. The Italian pioneers of cremation were doctors, scientists, progressives, Positivists; they were republicans and supporters of the Risorgimento; they were anti-clerical. Most important—or rather, representing all these ills, from the perspective of the Church—they were Freemasons. For religious conservatives, Masonry connected the French Revolution and all its sins with the rebirth of cremation in the second half of the nineteenth century. The pope had condemned it first in 1738 and did so again many times after that. More pointedly, the Abbé Barruel's much-reprinted, widely translated, and immensely influential history of Jacobinism argued that the Revolution itself could be summed up as a Masonic conspiracy: "what evil is there not to be feared" from them, "deists, atheists, sceptics," begetters of "Liberty and Equality," plotters all?[8]

The Masonic lodges of Italy, especially those of Milan and Turin, provided the institutional infrastructure for advocacy of cremation as well as for the invention of new rituals and for construction of purpose-built crematoria. Jacob Salvatore Morelli, one of the main early publicists for cremation, was a freethinker, feminist, campaigner for more liberal divorce laws, and a Mason. The noted Milanese physician Gaetano Pini, secretary of the Italian Cremation Society, was both a leader of Italian Freemasonry and the main force behind the building of the first crematorium in Italy. The minister of the interior who gave permission for the first legal cremation in Italy—22 January 1876—was a Freemason, and so was Alberto Keller, the German Lutheran businessman whose body provided the occasion. He had died two years earlier and been embalmed in the hope that when technology reached an advanced enough stage he could be cremated. Before a great concourse of worthies and in a thoroughly up-to-date crematorium modeled on a Roman temple, Keller finally got his wish. His ashes were placed in a tomb that he had built in the Protestant part of Milan's municipal cemetery. There, according to the *New York Times*, it was visited by "great numbers of Milanese who are desirous of looking upon the ashes of one who had been the originator of an epoch in the civilized world" (fig. 11.1).[9]

Giuseppe Garibaldi, a representative of populist democratic nationalism in the wars that led to a united Italy—and a Masonic grand master—wanted to be cremated too. For him it would be one last blow against the clerical establishment whose hold on the dead, he thought, was the foundation of its power. (The papacy was of course bitterly opposed to the Risorgimento.) He wanted to go in the style of republican Rome and had no interest in proving the hygienic virtues of the regenerative furnace or in the politics of funeral reform. The great man had left his widow precise instructions for the size of the old-fashioned pyre (no modern coke or gas oven for him), for the kind of wood to be used, and for the disposal of his ashes. They were to be put in an urn and placed near the graves of

11.1. The cremation of Alberto Keller.

his daughters. Like a Roman gentleman, he wanted to rest with his family. The whole ceremony was to take place privately and before his death was announced.

No one was interested in following Garibaldi's wishes. Burning him on a Roman pyre would clearly be a snub to the Church. When he died in 1882, cremation was legal only under special circumstances. The so-called Crispi Laws of 1888—named after Francesco Crispi, the Garibaldian, decidedly leftist, strongly anticlerical premier—made cremation generally legal and mandated access for ashes to state-supervised cemeteries. (He was threatened with expulsion from the Italian Masonic order late in his career because some thought that he was getting soft on Catholicism.) But as for the rest of Garibaldi's wishes, they represented to almost everyone the hero's posthumous refusal of one last public service to the secular state. No one was for it, not even the cremation societies, which abandoned the young widow in carrying out her husband's wishes. In the end, Garibaldi went to his grave with great civic pomp; his dead body had waited patiently for six weeks while his followers quarreled.[10]

When the Church officially condemned cremation on 19 May 1886 with the decree *Quoad cadaverum cremations* and on 15 December 1886 with a second decree, *Quoad cremationem aliena voluntate peractam*, it supported its case not on theological but rather on sociological and political grounds. It forbade membership in cremation societies and demanding cremation for oneself or for others, not as acts contrary to dogma but as acts hostile to the Church. Missionaries, for example, were never to condone the practice, but they could baptize high-caste Hindus on their deathbeds even if they knew that they would have themselves cremated. "Assent of the will to the deed" was never acceptable, the archbishop of Freiburg declared in 1892, but material cooperation—helping in the act—was lawful as long as the cremation was not "a distinctive mark of a Masonic sect" and was not actively "in contempt of the Catholic religion." A modern conservative Catholic journal understands cremation as hubris. The deceased "orders that his body become not dust, but ashes. It is he himself who imposes this destruction, not God. . . . [He] escapes God's authority and the duty to submit to him." Death, it reminds readers, was inflicted on mankind to punish sin. Cremation was a show of human power in the face of death, a gesture at mastering the dead even if mortality itself could not be mastered. Cremation self-consciously represented, much more than the cemetery had, the disruption of a cult of memory that Christianity had helped create and sustain. The author of the 1908 *Catholic Encyclopedia* sums up the case: cremation was making a "public profession of irreligion and materialism." And so it was with variations elsewhere on the Continent.[11]

In Germany, the impetus came not from Freemason lodges but from municipal and military doctors (advocates of hygiene), from working-class movements, and from others who wanted to align themselves with progress, with the forward march of history defined in a number of ways. The fact that some of the nineteenth century's most hard-line radical materialists—Moleschott and Vogt, among others—embraced cremation helped make it attractive to many on the Left. In 1920, when one might think more consequential matters were at hand, a small debate took place between German communists and social democrats about whether members of cremation societies should be obliged to remove their children from religious instruction in public schools. Yes, argued the communists, because at stake was cultural revolution; half steps were not enough.

And indeed they weren't when the Bolsheviks came to power in Russia. They very quickly took up the cause of cremation because it was both practical and scientific ("Side by side with the car, tractor, and electrification—make way for cremation," read one poster), because it was a rejection of religion, and perhaps most important, because it seemed to offer an alternative to the dangerous space of the cemetery where citizens might create alternative communities outside of the socialist sphere. In 1927, the new revolutionary Russian cremation society would identify itself unabashedly as "militantly Godless." The first crematorium in Moscow was built in 1927 on the site of the great Donskoi Monastery, technology on the site of the old religion. (A pit within its walls would hold the ashes of cremated victims of Stalin's purges.)[12]

Socialists in Germany also aligned modern cremation with their freedom-loving ancestors who had burned their dead in the primeval forests. Progress was rooted in nostalgia. Those with "an ardent zeal for progress . . . might not be sorry to find from the records of history . . . that with the Teutonic race also cremation was once the ruling custom," writes Karl Blind, the German revolutionary and member of Marx's circle since 1848 days. A half century earlier, the philosopher Johann Gottlieb Fichte (1762–1814) had imagined a future history: a strange utopian vision of Germany in the twenty-second century in which burning the dead had become a unifying ritual. Populist, free of an aristocracy, and national-ist, the Christian churches in this Germany had all agreed among themselves to cremate their dead: the ashes of a soldier who had fallen in battle would be put in an urn and sent back to the place of sepulcher in his hometown where it would be placed—along with his name—on the highest shelf; a rung below would come the urns of those who had counseled the state wisely; then those of good house-holders, men and women, and their good children, all identified by name. On the lowest level would come the nameless, presumably those not brave, nor wise, nor good. Through this intensely local and intimate columbarium, Fichte was able to imagine a new community of the dead, defined not by the churchyard or by old hierarchies but by service to home, heart, and nation.[13]

Whichever appreciative interpretation of cremation one took in Germany or elsewhere on the Continent, the alternative was always clear: religious cus-tom. And opposition came from the expected places: the Evangelical churches opposed the burning of the dead because of its association with socialism and radical materialism, its general disregard for religion, and its seeming lack of interest in communities of the dead rendered into ashes. In the Catholic south it was unthinkable. Priests were forbidden to give last rites to those who had asked that their bodies be cremated; ashes were excluded from burial in Church ceme-teries. It was beyond the pale. There could be no doubt what the mass member-ship of working-class socialists—not just in Germany but in the Netherlands and in Austria—signified. (Of course, this claim too is contingent on contact. In 1934, the same year that cremation was put on an equal footing with burial in Germany, a new conservative and pro-Church government in Austria confiscated the assets of the Labour Cremation Society.)[14]

For almost all Jewish authorities, cremation meant the same thing: apostasy. There were a few exceptions to the almost total rabbinic condemnation. When the chief rabbi of Rome, Hayim (Vittorio) Castiglioni, died in 1911, he was cre-mated and his ashes buried in the Jewish cemetery in Trieste. A Reform rabbi in the United States argued in 1891 that cremation was practiced by the ancient people of Israel and it had fallen into abeyance only for practical or contin-gent reasons: wood was expensive, burning bodies had become associated with execution at the stake and thus had horrible associations. Modern cremation, on the other hand, was aesthetically attractive and avoided "the slow loathsome dissolution of the body in a pit" with all the attendant poisons in the air and water and all the dangers to health that these created. Even most of his Reform colleagues demurred. And in Europe the only real question was not whether it was lawful to cremate—the answer was no—but whether the ashes could be buried in a Jewish cemetery. This in turn raised a number of religio-legal issues: Were ashes a dead body? If so, were they ritually impure and hence did they need to be dealt with properly? Did they require burial as did other bodies, no matter how sinful the deceased had been in asking to be cremated?

The resolution of the cremation question varied from place to place. The British burial society condemned cremation but permitted ritual care of the dead and burial in Jewish cemeteries; some rabbis in Germany allowed burial and prayers but would not themselves attend the body to the grave. In Wurzburg, the state in 1906 forced the Orthodox rabbi to allow a separate building for ashes. In other places there were integrated and exclusive Jewish cemeteries and more or less permissive rabbis. In general, cremation emerged as a symbolically defining issue for modern Jewish communities in the late nineteenth and early twentieth centuries, and even more so after the Holocaust, a new litmus test for how far one could deviate from historical practices and remain Jewish. An astonishing percentage opted for modernity over tradition: in Frankfurt, Dresden, Hamburg, Nuremberg, and Stuttgart, in Turin and Bologna, a higher proportion of Jews were cremated than were Protestants. Significant numbers chose cremation in Budapest and Vienna as well. Perhaps the Holocaust changed the calculus. (Although 10 percent of Israeli Jews today claim they want to be cremated, fewer than one hundred in fact availed themselves of Israel's only crematorium, which opened in 2005 and was burned down by arsonists two years later.)[15]

In the British case, neither anticlericalism—battles over Church rates and access to churchyards were essentially over—nor a strong revolutionary tradition, nor an explicit commitment to materialism (the implicit connections are evident) had much to do with the advent of cremation. The organized working class was indifferent if not affirmatively hostile to cremation. What a local newspaper in 1874 called an "exciting demonstration" by women, identified as being from the humbler parts of town, against a motion before the West Hartlepool Improvement Commissioners set the tone. Instead of burning the dead—a "revolting idea"—the commissioners should spend their time providing "suitable burial-ground for their decent interment. The Labour Party, unlike Continental socialist parties, never took up the cause of cremation. Perhaps hostility to the Anatomy Acts went too deep; smoke in a poorhouse chimney signaled a pauper body not decently buried. No writer in Britain was quite as outspoken as the widely read American freethinker Augustus Cobb, who saw in the history of burial the heavy hand of benighted clerisy: "by adroit management [the grave] became a connecting link between things seen and unseen, and was the most potent factor that the Church possessed for retaining its hold over its prostrate votaries." Edward Gibbon had it right, Cobb thought, when in *The Decline and Fall of the Roman Empire* he scoffed at the late imperial emperors, generals, and consuls who out of "superstitious reverence" "devoutly visited the sepulchers of a tent maker and a fisherman."[16]

Cremation was the cause of the cultural avant-garde, the professional upper middle class allied with a sprinkling of aristocrats (the dukes of Bedford and Westminster, for example), hygiene specialists, Freemasons, eccentrics of various sorts—it was a Welsh Druid who got cremation legalized—religious progressives, spiritualists, and Romantic socialists like Robert Blatchford, the Fabian follower of William Morris, who loved Sir Thomas Browne's *Urn Burial* because it evoked a layered English deep time: archeological remains of an ancestral and communal past. (Blatchford was also an atheist and later a spiritualist, so it is difficult to pinpoint the intellectual and affective roots of his support of cremation.) Set beside the bracing discourse of cleanliness, ecological efficiency, expertise, and progress—cremation as a force in world history—there was in the British cremation movement a sense that it was also a way to allow everyone to imagine and care for their dead as they wished. The 1882 Burial Reform Act had dealt the final blow to the churchyard as the place of a single Christian community—the definitive end of the old regime. Cremation offered all sorts of new opportunities.[17]

Most obviously, it furthered the appropriation of the dead for the regime of the living by doctors and their allies. Of the fourteen original members of the council of the British Cremation Society, three were prominent medical men: Sir Henry Thompson; Sir T. Spencer Wells, Britain's leading gynecologist; and Ernest Hart, a successful surgeon before he became the editor of the *British Medical Journal* and the *Sanitary Record*, among others. Another two more were sanitary engineers: William Eassie and Sir Douglas Strutt Galton, inventor of the ventilating grate and, like Eassie, a prolific author on matters of hygiene, who wrote books on healthy houses and hospital design and tracts on smoke-abatement policy and the virtues of the Royal College of Sanitary Engineers. John Glaister, who held the chair in forensic medicine and public health at the Glasgow Infirmary, was a stalwart of the Scottish Burial Reform and Cremation Society. Sir Henry Duncan Littlejohn, who held the comparable chair of forensic medicine in Edinburgh, was the major figure in the Scottish sanitary reform movement and also a founding member of the Scottish society in 1888. If there was such a thing as an expert on death, it was Littlejohn.

Sir Henry Thompson, however, was the undisputed leader of the movement both in Britain and internationally. His embrace of Brunetti's experiments did more than anything else to bring technology to the dead. He was the face of the movement; no one seemed better qualified to advocate for a new standard of cleanliness among the dead. Wildly gifted in art and literature and a bon vivant with a wide circle of friends, Thompson was also tremendously distinguished as a doctor. Physician to Queen Victoria, the founder of modern urology—his *Diseases of the Prostate* was often reprinted and translated—and one of Europe's most eminent surgeons, he was at the top of his profession. He was rich: a bladder stone operation on King Leopold of Belgium, for which he pocketed £3,000, set the bar; he treated Napoleon III for a £2,000 fee. And he was famous in the best medical circles. It was to Thompson that the great German surgeon Theodore Bilroth sent his epochal papers on gastric surgery for possible publication in English. Cremation was only the last of his big passions. He wrote about healthy ways to eat, served as vice president of the British Sanitary Institute (which among other things campaigned for more effective rubbish collection on London's streets), and, as a member of the Sunday Society, advocated opening museums to the working classes on the day of rest. Thompson was on the side of progress; he moved easily within the intellectual and artistic avant-garde of the late nineteenth century.

Sir Herbert Spencer's copy of the *History of Cremation*, given to him by Thompson, sits now in the Princeton University Library. That strangely un-Victorian, internationally influential sage who thought that all social, political, and ethical relations could be derived from scientific principles and discoveries ranging from cell theory to the chemistry of compounds must have taken the book to heart. He arranged to have himself cremated in 1903, one of only 477 in the United Kingdom that year. When a petition from various natural and social scientists failed to win him a place in Westminster Abbey, his ashes were placed in a sarcophagus and buried in the eastern section of Highgate not far from where Karl Marx, the apostle of another science, would be reburied fifty years later (see the introduction).

Thompson enjoyed something of a literary reputation whose fiction played on the power of medicine. His best-selling novel *Charley Kingston's Aunt* is about a gung-ho medical student who lives near the hospital so as not to lose any time from his studies in getting to and from work. He bribes the porter to get him, ahead of his classmates, the very first body that becomes available. As he unwraps the head of his new cadaver, alone amidst the nineteen dissecting tables, he begins to imagine that it resembles someone he knew, although he cannot quite identify who it might be. He decides to take a walk. Suddenly it comes to him in Regent's Park: his "subject," the friendless body that was about to enlighten him on the anatomy of the neck, is almost surely his long-lost aunt who had gone to America and who must have returned under terrible circumstances. He needs to go back to be sure. Claiming to have left his wallet with important documents that had to be sent first thing in the morning, he obtains the key to the lab from the porter and goes off, in high spirits, for a closer look. A small tattoo—A.M.P., with an American eagle below it—confirms his identification. Our hero calmly asks for a meeting with his professor, tells him that his cadaver was someone he knew as a child, and asks for permission to have it properly buried. He arranges with the hospital and Poor Law authorities—who give him the clues he needs to start discovering his aunt's story—to have the body returned to the world of the respectable dead and have it sent via Eastern Counties rail to his village, where it is buried, as a long-lost relative, in the local churchyard. This was published in 1885—before cremation was possible.

That doctors knew how to get at the truth, to cut through the sentiments of the laity is the premise of the cremation movement in its hygienic voice. Our medical student hero consults with the great "Dr. Wynchester": "how easily and yet how completely will the mist of folly and error which has obscured the essential points of the case be scattered to the winds after a few questions from the doctor." "A few decided words" and "pitiless logic" soon dispel "absurd speculations." To "the thoroughly practiced examiner of morbid signs and symptoms," the nature of a disease is instantly recognizable and demonstrable before five minutes is out. No need for much talk.[18]

Doctors knew about the dead. Beginning with the great frontispieces of Renaissance anatomy texts, they had displayed to the world their mastery over bodies. Dissection was on the side of modernity against superstition: when the young Peter the Great was on tour of the sites of Western culture, he visited the Leiden anatomical theater of Dr. Boerhaave. When one of his courtiers showed a certain unease, he supposedly ordered him "to bite into the muscles of a cadaver with [his] teeth." This would not have endeared him to the cremationists, but it did make the point: the dead are just dead meat. Nothing more.[19]

At the periphery of medicine were people of a populist Enlightenment, people like Leopold Hartley Grindon (1818–1904), who taught botany at the Manchester Royal School of Medicine and wrote extensively about natural history. He thought that nature offered an essential guide to culture across a broad front and embraced cremation as congruent with the lessons he had learned from it. "Truth Seeker," the name under which he published a pamphlet on the subject, had views about putrefaction in the grave. On the one hand, he set himself against traditions that he thought distorted reality: the cemetery with its memorials were an agent of what Marx would have called false consciousness. People ought to know what it was really like underground: jaws without lips, horrible things crawling in the sockets that "once were beautiful eyes." In fact, it was clear to Grindon that wreaths and chapels only masked "slow conversion into slimy pestilence," while fire could reduce the body quickly to "a handful of pearly ash." In other words, fire made the filthy clean. The only excuse for not recognizing these truths was sentiment, and sentiment was merely "historically grounded prejudice." In other words, to make cremation a reality, one had to change how people imagined the dead, and this required the rejection of what had by then been many centuries of thinking about them as slumbering peacefully and an even longer tradition of thinking that bodies matter for memory.[20]

Heterodox religious views also gave to cremation what Victorians and Edwardians would have called its moral—as distinct from its pragmatic, hygienic—attractions. If the soul—as sharply distinct from and independent of the flesh—was the real foundation of immortality, then intact, or even naturally decomposing, bodies lost much of their relevance. Corporeal resurrection, like a real and palpable Hell, was increasingly irrelevant to educated Victorians. And if, in addition, the spirits of the dead actually spoke with the living, memory and memorial space were doubly useless. One did not need to remember the departed who were not really gone and who continued to be in regular correspondence. Spirits had no need for cemeteries or churchyards.

Madame Blavatsky, the theosophist, supported cremation. So did Sir Oliver Lodge, professor of physics in the University of Liverpool, pioneer of radio, and from early in his life a passionate believer in psychical phenomena, especially the ability to communicate with the dead through a medium: he spoke at the dedication of the Birmingham crematorium in 1903. J. Page Hopps, another spiritualist and a liberal nondenominational preacher whose "churches" attracted tens of thousands, came to cremation not through theosophy or American-style spiritualism but via the teaching of the eighteenth-century mystic, scientist, and theologian Emmanuel Swedenborg, who conversed with both heavenly and extraterrestrial spirits. Hopps was also a peace activist and opponent of vivisection and, like so many others of the first generation favoring cremation, was linked to not just one but several radical causes. He explicitly rejected theology in favor of something much more all-embracing: God was himself a spirit and not a body, so corporeal resurrection was irrelevant; doctrine mattered not a bit in any case. His was a root and branch rejection of burial. When he preached on the "etherialization of the body" at the cremation of Alice Dunn, a leading contralto at the Free Christian Church in Croyden, he welcomed the time when there would be no memorial, no places associated with the dead, and where the only "fitting shrine" would be "the loving spirit." Cremation offered not so much hygiene in any literal sense but rather a cleansing of the dead body from a sort of primitive foulness. "What is more beautiful than that the poor dead body, purified, should be dismissed into the sunshine?" To the body itself, fire was like a "bath of fragrance of summer roses," which stood in sharp distinction to the "defilement" of burial.[21]

There were others. Charles Voysey was rejected from a curacy in 1861 for preaching against the doctrine of eternal punishment. He was appointed vicar of a dockland parish in 1863 but was deprived of his living in 1871 for wholesale heresy: he rejected all creeds, the divinity of Christ, and the whole sacramental system. Three years later he had begun a new theistic church of his own and was one of the signers of the Cremation Society's founding document. The answer to the overriding question of death, captured with such immediacy in H. A. Bowler's painting *The Doubt: Can These Dry Bones Live?* of a young widow contemplating a grave on which lies a broken skeleton (see fig. 4.5), was for him relatively simple. The body in all its materiality did not matter; one could abandon belief in corporeal resurrection with psychological impunity. It was "an absurdity" to believe in corporeal resurrection, argued Voysey. None of the apostles saw Jesus die or be resurrected. But everyone, through direct experience as well as through "experiment and demonstration," "knows that the dead are still alive." Orthodox Christianity may be a thing of the past, but a God in whom one still had to have faith is a principle of order. How did he know that he was "not a house of flesh"? Because "I am what I am . . . because the author of my being is what He is." Voysey writes eloquently about how modern learning supports the hope for a future life: even Ernst Haeckel, the great materialist biologist, seems to posit "cell souls." But now it is evolution that makes it rational to believe that man has "acquired sufficient subtlety and unity of being to enable him, the thinking, and self-conscious man, to hold together, to persist, to march out and on, when cells disintegrate." He embraced cremation because it got rid of the messy and irrelevant remains more efficiently than other methods.[22]

As corporeal resurrection became less theologically and emotionally exigent, the representational power of putting a dead body in ground from which it would rise again incorruptible diminished; cremation—in a sense the rapid release of a spirit from its fleshly prison—became more plausible. The Hon. and Rev. W. H. Lyttelton, a country clergyman of gentry origins with a bit of German liberal theological training but generally no radical views, for example, makes the whole issue seem terribly commonsensical. Few people, he claims, have any specific views about the resurrection of the body one way or the other. He personally believes that we will not have the same bodies—maybe not even a particle of our present ones—although we probably will have the faculties that we have now. But these are more idle speculations than serious theological propositions. If it is God's will to raise our bodies, he will manage even if we have been cremated. There is not a hint of the obsessive materialism that haunted medieval and early modern discussions of how we would continue to be ourselves in eternity. "No educated person now believes that immortality is chained to the dead body," said Lord Playfair, the distinguished chemist and scientific statesmen, in an epigram below a picture of a lovely marble urn in one of the Cremation Society's booklets.[23]

All that Lyttelton asked for in Christian disposal of the dead is reverence for the past, not a regard for the next life. We should take comfort that through cremation our bodies will be rapidly reduced to "their component atoms" and "re-contributed to that vast material world, or ever living and changing cosmos, from which they were originally borrowed." The language of an orthodox clergyman comes very close to the language of spiritualism, Eastern religion, and sanitary reform. In any case, if experts might differ with respect to physiology and sanitation, Christian theology should stay neutral on the question of what to do with the dead. (Hints of the cultural world that Lyttelton inhabits come from an advertisement in his book's front matter for Herbert Spencer's *Morals of Trade* and lots of references to Eassie and Thompson.) He himself died a peaceful, wholly Victorian death, in the bosom of his family: an old and, in his later years, lonely widower, living in a vicarage of the parish where he had spent his life, Hagley in Worcestershire. He is buried in its churchyard.[24]

Other churchmen—the reforming bishop of Manchester, for example—also supported cremation, often as part of a more general sentiment against the excesses of the Victorian funeral and memorial culture. Cremation was on the side of reason and progress. There was also a low-key Church Funeral Reform Association that had a voice in these discussions. It seemed more sympathetic to the surgeon and renowned artist/critic Sir Francis Seymour Haden's papier-mâché, earth-to-earth coffin than to cremation. Haden himself was a fierce opponent of cremation. Still, he and the funeral reformers, on the one hand, and the cremationists, on the other, spoke much the same language.

Rev. Brooke Lambert, an Anglican clergyman of evangelical theology and broad church sympathies with perfectly ordinary theological views, was one of the founders of the Cremation Society. Like almost everyone else who was connected with it in its early days, he was a reformer; his efforts concentrated on the slums of Whitechapel and later Greenwich, and he was also past grand chaplain of English Freemasonry. The advocacy of cremation was part of a larger project of what we would call social justice. Others, however, made Voysey seem almost ordinary. The strangest of the religious figures among early cremationists was H. R. Haweis. He, like so many others, was a spiritualist at the same time as he was an Anglican priest. Less than five feet tall, he was also a charismatic preacher, a gifted violinist, a major proponent of Wagner, and one of the first to write appreciatively about *Parsifal* in English. His book *Ashes to Ashes* has it all: a clergyman goes to visit a friend on the Yorkshire coast; on his first day there, a storm sweeps over the churchyard and wrenches open the graves of the dead who are exposed to the ignominy of human sight. Again and again this theme returns: the dead are not safe in the modern age. French-style revolutions—women in the forefront—dig up and violate their bodies; railways blast through churchyards (it was only a few years since St. Pancras had given itself up to the tracks and yards of the Great Northern); insurance buildings are built on graves with nary a thought. Eternal rest is a delusion.

In Yorkshire he meets a French doctor named Legrande who enjoyed nothing more than dissection, a practice that like no other clearly reveals the truth about humanity. Legrande lectures the narrator about the evils of burial in spreading diseases; the local clergyman's daughter falls in love with him; Legrande succumbs to an epidemic caused by dead bodies and has a miserable funeral that is emblematic of how irrational modern death practices have become; after some time the local clergyman's daughter marries the narrator. Had cremation already replaced burial, she could have been with her first love, the doctor.[25]

A nineteenth-century reprise of Homer would have made it possible for at least some educated English people of the sober sort, not frightened by medical Gothic tales, to believe that burning the dead, per se, was not outside the bounds of the thinkable: the funeral rites of the poet Percy Bysshe Shelley, who drowned just a few weeks short of his thirtieth birthday in 1822. As a model for public policy it would not do, but it did transport an archaic precedent into modern times. Edward John Trelawny, Shelley's wild and wooly friend, arranged it all. A friend also of the poet Byron, whom he accompanied to Greece, Trelawny was notorious first because of a spectacularly public divorce trial from his unfaithful young wife in the 1810s and then because of his profound eccentricities in retirement: no meat, no overcoats, no underwear. He himself died in 1881, four years before cremation became legal in England; to comply with his wishes for the disposal of his body, his friends arranged to transport his corpse to Gotha, the city where the German Social Democratic Party held its first convention in 1875 and where in 1878 the first crematorium was opened. He was reduced to ashes in its new regenerative furnace and these were taken by his young mistress—his "niece"—to Florence and buried next to Shelley's. Cremation has proved a great boon to the mobility of the dead in the past two centuries.

Shelley's cremation itself was radical only in its nostalgic neoclassicism. There was nothing technological about it. And it was not just a historical reenactment. There were practical considerations: the decomposing body had to be somehow brought back to civilization. But this does not explain the drama as it unfolded. Trelawny stage-managed a scene fit for his "Hellenic bard." The necessities were transported to the cremation site by boat: a furnace of iron bars and sheet metal, plenty of wood, and, as he said, "such things as were used by Shelley's much loved Hellenes on their funeral pyres." Englishmen—Byron and Leigh Hunt were there too—played at being Greeks of the Homeric age. It was a sultry summer day,

16 August 1822, on that Mediterranean beach near Viareggio, one hundred kilometers west-northwest of Florence on the coast of Tuscany, where the poet's body had washed up. It was a "ghastly indigo color" from the lye that had been spread over it when it was first found and from having been buried in the sands for a month before its exhumation. Unlike the body of Shelley's drowned companion, cremated the day before, the poet's more or less stayed in one piece. Oil and salt were poured over it, making "the yellow flames glisten and quiver"; the "brains literally seethed, bubbled and boiled as in the cauldron" before the front of the skull fell off. When the body burst open, Trelawny, to whom we owe this account, burnt his hands badly as he retrieved what was supposedly Shelley's intact heart—it may have been his liver—from the inferno. Afterward, the ashes were buried in the English Cemetery of Rome, a decorous, domesticated place of the dead that has no extravagant pagan associations. Louis-Edward Fournier's painting *The Cremation of Shelley* (plate 18) shows an altogether more modest, mournful ritual: a fire burning dully by the wintery shores of the Gulf of Spezzi, the body visible only in general outline. By 1889, the outrageousness of the scene Trelawny staged had been transformed into a melancholy neoclassical tableau vivant with kneeling women and all sorts of other non-Homeric touches.[26]

The transformation of cremation from an ancient practice to a legally sanctioned if culturally radical way of dealing with dead bodies was the work of a man who did not belong to, and would not have been welcomed in, the comfortably professional, bourgeois company of the Cremation Society and its sister organizations in Europe and the United States. It was his craziness that made him such a perfect representative of the new radical freedom to employ the dead in any fashion one wanted. His prosecution for the cremation of his five-month-old son in 1884 failed and produced instead a landmark judgment that ended the hegemony of burial, which had begun in Anglo-Saxon times. William Price (1800–1893) is listed in the *Dictionary of Welsh Biography* under the category "eccentric." The reality behind some of his more heroic exploits is disputed: maybe he was not at the head of five thousand men from the valleys of Monmouthshire in the great Chartist march on Newport in November 1839, and maybe he did not meet Heinrich Heine during his exile on the Continent. But much is clear: he was a Chartist spokesman in southern Wales; like so many of the others associated with creating modern cremation, he was a medical man, a surgeon, who qualified in London in the 1830s. He was more unconventional in more realms than most: an opponent of smoking who refused to treat those who indulged; a vegetarian who wore a whole fox's pelt on his head; an opponent of marriage and advocate of free love who seems to have fathered his last child when he was over ninety; an archdruid who led worship around a stone circle that still stands in the city park of Pontypridd. This is a man of whom the writer Rys Davis said that he "tried to stand outside his period . . . to escape the herd . . . to return to that mysterious druidic life whose savour remained in his ancient Welsh blood." And through him cremation became legal.[27]

On 18 January 1884, he took his dead infant son, Jesu Grist, to a field near the Glagmorganshire town of Llantrisant, chanted some druidical prayers over the body, put it in a cask of paraffin oil, and set it aflame in accordance with what he took to be ancient Celtic custom. Respectable local society was outraged by what it saw. It was not enough that Price had named his son—the last of more than a dozen illegitimate children—after our Lord and Savior; now he was trying to dispose of his body in an ostentatiously anti-Christian, pagan, and extremely public way: a huge, smoky bonfire. The authorities were called. Constables removed the partially burnt body from the cask and took it into custody for an inquest. They arrested the eighty-three-year-old archdruid and threw him in jail. But the coroner's jury ruled that Jesu Grist had died of natural causes. Price was absolved of any blame in the death and got the body back even though he refused to promise to bury it properly.

On his next try, 21 March, he put his infant son's body on top of a pyre fueled with one-half ton of coal. And this time, the cremation succeeded. Once again, Price was arrested and once again he was vindicated. The distinguished judge Lord Stephens—Virginia Woolf's uncle—ruled that "a person who burns instead of burying a body does not commit a criminal act, unless he does it in such a manner as to amount to a public nuisance in law" and held that what the accused had done with his Jesu Grist did not meet this standard of offense. "It would be strange," wrote the *Daily Telegraph*, on 8 March 1884, "and at the same time highly advantageous to the cause of sanitary reform if the fantastic tricks recently played by an eccentric Welsh octogenarian with the body of a dead baby became indirectly the means of inducing the public to bring a little more common sense and a little less prejudice to bear on the important subject of cremation."

Cremation, if not quite legal yet, was after Price's second effort and Stephens's ruling not illegal either. The next year, the Cremation Society built its first crematorium and publicly burned its first body. Price managed to collect damages for false imprisonment against one of the police constables who had arrested him for his first failed attempt in January. And he was free to irritate his neighbors. An attempt to gather subscriptions for a public crematorium failed; he did produce and sell some three thousand medals commemorating the cremation, and he would periodically cremate one of his dead cows.

Then, on 23 January 1893, Price himself died; he had at length married and had another son whom he also named Jesu Grist. After lying in state, his body was taken to East Caerlen Field near Pontypridd, placed in a makeshift furnace on top of two tons of coal, and cremated before a crowd of some twenty thousand that included three well-dressed young children in the front row and a minister of the Church of England, who read the burial service in Welsh, substituting "consigned to the fire" for "consigned to the earth." His friend Robert Anderson, said to be the hangman of Carmarthenshire, lit the flames. Souvenir hunters rummaged among the remains.[28]

A great deal separates the austere modernism of the Italian pathologist Ludovico Brunetti and the self-proclaimed Welsh archdruid William Price. The dead had come to the service of the living in a number of ways: the disenchantment of death and its reenchantment, the erasure of the dead from history and their reinsertion, as enemies of old religious beliefs and as friends of new ones. Cremation opened up all sorts of new work for the dead, but it did so slowly and in many ways conservatively.

ASHES IN THEIR PLACE

Cremation, as it was spoken of and to a large extent practiced, in the first two decades following the experiments of Brunetti and subsequent researchers was not humanly sustainable. "The ancient pyre was poetic; the history of modern crematorium is cynical," wrote the famous Italian hygienist and anthropologist Paolo Mantegazza, who had undergone a change of heart after his initial support of cremation. All the "distinguished chemists, ingenious architects and ardent humanitarians," speak only "of hygiene and no one of sentiment." Opponents of cremation were pushed into making excuses and asking forgiveness if they "appealed to the heart and to religion," when in fact the problem was completely one of sentiment and not hygiene.[29]

"It is the utilitarianism of Henry Thompson that rankles," said a letter writer to the *Richmond and Twickenham Times*. "Couldn't human hair be converted to something of public utility?"; "intestines to fiddle strings?" asked another newspaper. "Love of parents for their children gone, utilitarians will soon brace our minds to an oblivion of all our past imbecilities," bemoaned the *Gloucester Mercury*. Only in the limit case were the dead just dirt, and those who embraced cremation knew it. The dead are dirt only when they had before death subsisted as bare life, biological but not cultural being. Cremation became civilized.[30]

The fiercely anticlerical and scientifically minded members of the Milan Cremation Society decided that they had to draw women to the cause—it was everywhere overwhelmingly a male project—on the grounds that their presence would "soften" the issue and spread the idea that cremation was not such a disgusting and repugnant spectacle. They built a "temple" in which to hold services before a cremation and then afterward the ashes were buried as if they were an intact dead body. The Italian League of Cremation Societies issued a statement that the technology of incineration needed to be kept discretely out of sight and that the league would commit itself to increasing ceremony and solemnity at its facilities.

It proposed that on the next All Saints' Day all "crematorium Temples" would be open to the public and that perhaps members could put flowers on the urns of the deceased there or in cemeteries to which they would make a "pious pilgrimage."[31]

When on 26 March 1885, Jeanette Pickersgill, author of a volume of Orientalist poetry (among other works) and wife of the successful portrait painter Henry William Pickering, became the first person to be legally cremated in Britain's first crematorium, there was little ceremonious about the occasion. The apparatus had been built in 1879 and tested by cremating a dead horse. The building that housed it made no effort to hide its function; two men watched the hour-and-fifteen-minute procedure. Fifteen years later, it attached a lovely Arts and Crafts chapel with grave markers to its side but there was still no mistaking that this was basically a furnace.

But after this, architecture of crematoria in Great Britain became relentlessly, almost comically, conservative, as if to make the conveyor belts, motors, and hidden furnaces seem just like other bits of clerical apparatus hidden away in a vestry room. Golders Green's had the towers, arches, and windows of a northern Italian Renaissance brick church and cloister; the City of London's and those of Leeds, Bradford, Nottingham, and Ipswich were Arts and Crafts versions of late medieval styles; Manchester's is Romanesque with lots of terra-cotta work (plate 19). Hull has a red brick copy—and Pontypridd a stone one—of the early Tudor perpendicular architecture that one sees in so many country churches; Blackpool's crematorium is in the late Tudor style; Stockport's is neo-Byzantine. Services could thus take place in familiar, historically informed settings while the body was being burned offstage. There was invariably an organ; it took about as long to complete the on- as the off-stage business. Britain's horticultural king and leading garden magazine publisher was an early stalwart of cremation and a leader of the Cremation Society. Crematoria came to take on the look of a cemetery.

Diogenes' impulse to make the dead mere matter had run its course; indeed, it never got very far. By 1939, Fritz Schumacher, Hamburg's former director of city planning and an expert on the architecture of cremation, recognized that the biggest problem of housing a furnace for burning bodies was hiding the machinery: the pulleys, hydraulic lifts, tracks, vents, and retorts that got the job done. Whatever form the building took—he thought that architecture had no higher calling than to offer its art as a balm to those who mourn—it ought decidedly not to follow function. To repeat an epigraph from the beginning of this part: "If one thinks about the formal demands of early crematorium design one comes to understand it as an aesthetic struggle against the chimney."[32]

Unlike the churches they mimicked, crematoria did double work. Like churches, they provided, in the liminal moments between death and disposal, a space in which survivors could say their last farewells to the body; could take comfort from music, art, ritual, and beautiful architecture; and, in the case specifically

Abb. 39. Hamburg. 1892

11.2. Crematorium in Hamburg, 1892.
From Fritz Schumacher,
Die Feuerbestattung (Leipzig, 1939), 51.

Abb. 21. Öfen im Hamburger Krematorium. System Volckmann-Ludwig

11.3. The furnaces in the basement
of a crematorium in Hamburg. From
Schumacher, *Die Feuerbestattung*, 29.

of crematoria, could contemplate the beautiful cleansing power of fire, so near yet out of sight, that rapidly freed the soul from its prison. Unlike churches, their guts were of a different order entirely from the sanctuary. Above ground, Hamburg's crematorium is a Renaissance confection; below ground there is some very heavy machinery. Above ground, the Dortmund columbarium is a neoclassical rotunda; below ground are the pipes and retorts and regenerating chambers that made smokeless modern cremation possible (figs. 11.2–11.5).

11.4. Crematorium and columbarium in Dortmund. From Schumacher, *Die Feuerbestattung*, 59.

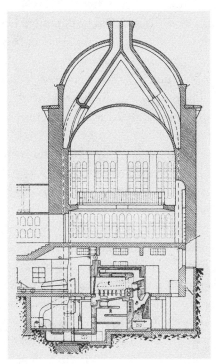

11.5. Cutaway of Dortmund crematorium and columbarium. From Schumacher, *Die Feuerbestattung*, 59.

Modern technology and rational city planning could be adapted to an older aesthetics: crematoria were clean as well as compatible with religious sensibilities and the comforts of ritual more generally. Two visual genres and the two categories they represent—an architectural engraving or photograph of a civic or quasi-sacred building in modern or historical styles, and a blueprint or schematic drawing of machinery that with some modifications could be in a steel mill or a concentration camp—happily coexist. Engineering and religion, furnace technology and worship, can together serve the living and the dead.

Ashes came to be treated as if they were bodies. Of the 112 people in the United Kingdom who, according to their biographies in the new *Dictionary of National Biography*, died before 1945 and were cremated, the ashes of only 6 (5 percent) were not somehow interred: D. H. Lawrence's were either mixed into the fabric of a so-called chapel on the New Mexico ranch where he had lived or scattered over the Mediterranean Sea after he was cremated in the French Riviera town of Vence; Sir Richard Geddes, part-time chairman of Imperial Airlines, had his scattered by a company plane over the English Channel off the Isle of Wight. As for the rest, their ashes were usually put in urns—some still used the more familiar coffin—which, in turn, were meant to have historicist associations and to be buried in traditional places (ashes could be deposited in churchyards that had been for a long time closed to bodies) or in new columbaria. Henry Thompson published designs of his own based on classical models. Etruscan models were available in the British Museum, and these appeared as illustrations in literature advocating cremation. The possibilities, in short, were seemingly limitless. (After 1945, the ashes of 33 out of 152 cremated worthies in the *Dictionary of National Biography*—22 percent—were scattered.)

The ancient link between name, body, place, and memory that seemed on the verge of being broken never quite dissolved. In 1945, the president of the British Cremation Society was still hoping that someday we might simply scatter the ashes of the dead in a garden with, "it may be, a tree or a shrub to act as 'recordium' and an inconspicuous tablet to carry his name." The columbarium, with its columns and colonnades, fixed niches, and after the 1930s, library shelves for ash-filled books of life, and certainly the cemetery, would soon be things of the past. That never quite happened. In 1936, the last body was buried in Westminster Abbey; all the distinguished dead buried there since have arrived as ashes. Burial *ad sanctum* became possible once again in the twentieth century for the first time since the dead were banned from churches in the late eighteenth and nineteenth centuries. By the 1950s, even the Catholic Church relented and allowed cremated remains to be buried with religious services as long as the ashes remained together and were not scattered, as long as they remained tied to the body that would be resurrected (figs. 11.6–11.10).

THE CREMATION BUILDINGS AT ST JOHN'S, KNAPHILL, WOKING

11.6. The cremation buildings at Woking. From Prosper de Pietra Santa, "La crémation en France et Italie," *Journal d'hygiene* 8 (18820): 73. Private collection.

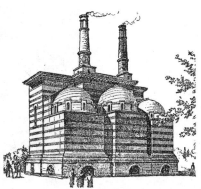

Abb. 120. Paris (Erster Zustand)

11.7. Paris crematorium. From Schumacher, *Die Feuerbestattung*, 79.

Abb. 123. Reims

11.8. Crematorium in Reims. From Schumacher, *Die Feuerbestattung*, 79.

Abb. 124. Marseille

11.9. Crematorium in Marseilles. From Schumacher, *Die Feuerbestattung*, 79.

11.10. Religious service in a chapel
with crematorium. Bilderarchiv
Preussichar Kulturbissitz.

At the same time, all sorts of new things have become possible as well. Relatives can abandon their dead; some small percentage of ashes are never collected from American funeral homes, though only rarely are funeral directors told that the deceased was a jerk and they could just throw him out.[33]

What the dead will do in the future I cannot say. I can contribute to this enterprise a brief, anthropological account of what happened to the remains of an old man, a hunting buddy of one of my childhood friends in rural Appalachia and a lifelong Christian. He died at eighty and had a traditional open-casket funeral at the Jordan Methodist Church in Pulaski, Virginia. His body was there for all to see. Then he was cremated. His ashes were widely disbursed among friends and relatives. Some went to his fellow deer hunters, one of them my friend. They took their share and headed for the cabin Ed had owned along Little Walker Creek and apportioned it as follows: some was loaded into cartridges and shot into the air using the musket loaders that Ed had made; some was scattered on the deer lick to be ingested by the game which in future seasons they would kill and eat; and some was scattered around the rock where it had been their custom to pee together. These rituals—leaving out what his wife and sons did with their shares—takes syncretism to new levels and makes one despair of a coherent hermeneutics of practice. They also show that the work of the dead has a future.[34]

AFTERWORD: FROM
A HISTORY OF THE DEAD
TO A HISTORY OF DYING

In our age, when men seem ever more prone to confuse wisdom with knowledge, and knowledge with information, and to try to solve problems of life in terms of engineering, there is coming into existence a new kind of provincialism which perhaps deserves a new name. It is a provincialism, not of space, but of time; one for which history is merely the chronicle of human devices which have served their turn and been scrapped, one for which the world is the property solely of the living, a property in which the dead hold no shares.

T. S. ELIOT, On Poetry and Poets (1957)

Eliot is writing about the loss of a tradition, specifically the European classics. Without Virgil's Latin poetry, a new provincialism, he thinks, has beset the West; history is at a discount; the dead have lost their claim on the living. We no longer care about them and what they held dear.

Over the years I have been working on this book, I have been told by many people that they are indifferent to what happens to their own bodies, if not to those of others. For them at least, Diogenes seems to have triumphed, and the story I have been telling has come to an end. If the work of the dead was once to embrace the generations of our species in an explicitly sacral order and, after the eighteenth century, to incorporate them into a variety of communities defined more by history than by divinity, then that work has now ceased—at least in the minds of those who claim not to care. Even a magic we can believe in has been exposed to such an extent that and the dead body really is just a dead body. Perhaps, "the world is the property solely of the living."

There is, in addition to the voices of people I have spoken with, some anecdotal evidence to support this view. Cremation in the United States today, for example, can be arranged online, without ever speaking to, much less seeing, a human being: the bill is paid by credit card on a secure site; the body is picked up by anonymous employees of a service provider; it is burnt to ashes; these are sent by registered mail to whoever ordered the service. The problems of life are solved by engineering, as Eliot lamented. A small percentage of people leave the ashes of a relative with the undertaker, as they would leave with the veterinarian the remains of a pet that had been put down.[1] Of course, none of this is evidence of what the dead wanted, but it is a sign that mortal remains do not matter much in some circles. I cannot say whether this sort of unceremonious treatment of the body is more common today than in previous decades or centuries, or whether it is increasing. I doubt it, because I think that, in general, mortal remains continue to matter.

The purportedly disenchanted body is enchanted again and again. I ended the last chapter with a strange story that transpired in an out-of-the-way place—a hunting cabin on the banks of Wolf Creek in rural southwest Virginia—to make this point in microcosmic detail. The dead still hold a share in our world or, to be more precise, the living are endlessly inventive in finding new work for the dead. Even in the most provincial of settings, a deep anthropological past as well as the helter-skelter of more recent history still inform what we do.

I might say also that I have heard many more stories of care than of neglect of mortal remains as I spoke with people about this book: a woman I met at a dinner told me that the tattoos on her knuckles were made from ink that had been formulated with her grandmother's ashes; a colleague whom I met after a lecture told me that she and her mother had taken the ashes of her father, a professional photographer, and put them in 35-mm film canisters that they would be leaving in the venues around the world where he had taken pictures; a friend's family was in a considerable quandary when they learned, upon belated receipt of an urn, that the ashes they had buried in a family grave had not been those of their parent but of someone else. People still care; the dead still do work for the living in private and also in public.

THE FUTURE

In a sense, this book has no afterword because there is no afterward to its claims. I began working on it many years ago, expecting to find ruptures, stages—overlapping perhaps, but discreet and distinguishable—that follow one another rather like those explored in Philippe Ariès's monumental *Hour of Our Death*: "tamed death," "one's own death," "thy death," and "forbidden death." At least I expected a "from . . . to . . ." story: from the sacred to the profane body. Instead I found continuity. Of course there was change: the dead came to work in the interests of historically, as opposed to divinely, defined communities in the Enlightenment. Put differently, in many contexts history and memory replaced metaphysics. The history of the dead body—in deep and more recent time—still resonates and will, I suspect, continue to hold power over the living for a very long time. I suspect that, like the story of this book, the future holds iterative enchantment.

But if this afterword were to look forward, if I were to switch to the role of the prophet from that of the historian, if I were to imagine writing a book similar to this one some centuries from now, I am pretty sure I would be writing a history marked by rupture: a rupture not in the history of care of the dead body but in the experience of dying. We are entering a new age—not of being dead but of becoming dead. It is impossible from the vantage of 2015 to say how historians of the future will construe our present: "Historians tell it like it was," read a bumper sticker I once owned. But more important, there is little precedent for how we die today, both from the perspective of the body—from the perspective of its descent into death—and from how we talk about it in various registers. By "we" I mean, of course, we in the prosperous first world; tens of millions die each year in old-fashioned ways from old-fashioned diseases more or less as people have always died. But for us, dying has spiraled out of the orbit of nature and has also left its history behind; engineering is at the bedside, as are lawyers and social workers and many others. In a sense this afterword is a foreword to an imagined book of the future, more like conventional history books, perhaps, because it will be organized around a radical change.

Perhaps the strangest sign of rupture is the discovery and widespread acceptance of a so-called right to die. We can only imagine what this claim would have sounded like to our ancestors if they had taken it for what it seems to demand: the right to be cursed by mortality? the right to follow the course of nature, as if one needed to demand that the tides ebb and that winter comes as it does? Understood in this perhaps too literal way, it has no negative correlative: no "freedom from" is possible. Unlike the right to free speech or assembly or privacy that authorities can deny, there is no way on earth to deny the right to die.

As a new positive claim, it was born in the late nineteenth century, when suicide lost its legal, if not its moral, stigma and physicians came to have a monopoly on the procurement of opiates. It was a demand for so-called physician-assisted suicide—euthanasia—and was an extension of the old argument for suicide with a new twist. Those who were now increasingly charged with overseeing dying, it was said, should be allowed, indeed mandated, to provide aesthetically more pleasing and physically less painful ways for people to take their own lives at some time before life came to a natural end: morphine rather than the razor or rat poison or a pistol. Care in the last hours. The right to die was a claim for a medically mediated good death.

There were only sporadic and low-key assertions of this purported positive right over the subsequent seventy or eighty years, and these mostly involved a demand that doctors and relatives and friends be spared from criminal charges for an act of mercy: freedom from legal liability. The right to die meant the right to euthanasia, a good death. Occasionally, our contemporary sense of the right to die as a negative rights claim—as a claim for freedom from something—was articulated before the late 1970s as a call for freedom from medical intervention and interference. In 1956, the views of Francis T. Hodges, an otherwise obscure Sausalito physician, made national news when he questioned the efforts of doctors to extend "a 'hopeless' patient's life by extra-ordinary feats of medicine." "There has been too little said," he argued, "for a legitimate, a God-given, right of the dying man. That is his right to die." This was not a call for euthanasia, which Hodges rejected, but rather for freedom from the efforts of others to temporarily prevent dying.[2] It was from such small beginnings that a new right found a vast new constituency in the 1970s.

First, the American Medical Association promulgated a Patient's Bill of Rights in 1972 that included the right to refuse treatment—that is, to die. Then in 1976, California passed a Natural Death Act: a joke in any other age, the first time in history that a legislature felt compelled to proclaim the right to demand the sort of death—a natural one—that humans had had from the beginning of time. But the legislation had a point: with the rise in the 1960s of intensive care units—places in a hospital where death could be put off just a little bit longer through technology—dying naturally had become increasingly difficult. The act gave legal weight to advance directives and so-called living wills—documents that told doctors what a patient wanted when she was no longer able to tell them directly—and absolved physicians from liability for failing to treat a patient as a consequence of doing what a patient asked. The fact that these documents have proven obdurately ineffective is another story.

The same year that California legislated the right to a natural death, the New Jersey Supreme Court decided the first of a series of internationally reported court cases about dying: it allowed the parents of Karen Ann Quinlan, who had gone into an irreversible persistent coma after a drug overdose, to ask her doctors to disconnect her respirator on the grounds that, as her surrogates, they had the authority to say what she would have wanted. In other words, the court held that a patient's autonomous right to decide when to die, or more specifically the right to corporeal integrity exercised by refusing treatment, was transferable. To everyone's surprise, Karen Ann Quinlan—shriveled and unconscious—lived without a respirator for eight more years. The possibility of not feeding her intravenously and thereby allowing her to die was not raised.

It was in another case, seven years later. Elizabeth Bouvia, a quadriplegic suffering also from cerebral palsy and degenerative arthritis, sued a California hospital for the right to receive comfort care as she starved herself to death. She lost the case and as a consequence was force fed. She put up what little resistance she could by biting the feeding tube. In 1986, Bouvia won on appeal: she had, the appellate court ruled, an "absolute right" to refuse treatment. By then she had either changed her mind about living or discovered that her original plan was too difficult to execute; she had, she told a reporter in 1992, "begun a morphine regimen [for pain relief] whose side effects made the process of starvation unbearable." In 2008 she was still alive.[3]

Finally, in 1990, the right to die was enshrined in the U.S. Supreme Court decision in the *Cruzan* case. Twenty-five-year-old Nancy Beth Cruzan, the litigant by proxy, was in a horrible car accident in January 1983; her heart and her breathing stopped for at least twelve minutes, causing irreparable brain damage. She went into a persistent vegetative state in which she could still breathe on her own but could do little else; she was fed through a surgically implanted tube. Her deeply religious parents thought she was gone and wanted treatment to stop. After a great deal of litigation, the Supreme Court held that the State of Missouri had been right in placing a very high evidentiary burden on the parents to prove that this is what their daughter would have wanted. But autonomy won in the end: a competent adult, the Court held, had a liberty interest in the right to refuse treatment. Six months later, a state court ruled that the testimony of three friends was enough to prove that Nancy Beth would indeed have made this choice. She died less than two weeks after feeding stopped. The freedom to die, so long unquestioned and unquestionable, had become the law.

There are three reasons why all this litigation and legislation was necessary— why it is so hard to die today. The first is the vast legal, professional, and bureaucratic structures in which the process of dying is imbricated. Dying is far more restrained than ever before.

A second and more fundamental reason undergirds the first: the rise of technologies and treatments that allow life to be prolonged and death to be kept at bay longer than what would have been, in another age, the moments of its final triumph. For the first time in human history, there is always something that can be done to gain extra hours, days, or even months of life. The importance of this is clear if we track the use in English of the terms "intensive care unit" and "chemotherapy": their use follows precisely the increasing use of the phrase "death with dignity"—reserved in ages past for descriptions of how Roman senators or famous generals died—and of the previously nonexistent term "right to die." The right to die, and to have a death with dignity, arises because we now have the means to slow dying in circumstances that are far from dignified. Thus, in an age when we are prone to try to solve not just the problems of life but also the problems of death in terms of engineering, care for the body—for mortal remains—has evolved to encompass passionately held beliefs about whether to use technology to postpone death. In the twenty-first century, we press not just the dead but also the dying into cultural service of the living. At stake in our conflicting beliefs about proper and dignified care of the bodies of the dying is unresolved ambivalence about the power of our technology and the extent of our alienation from nature.

Finally, the claim for a right to die is a result of a new and unprecedented claim for individual autonomy at the end of life. Perhaps one always died alone, but never so explicitly could one dictate the terms of one's own dying, often down to the last detail. Death had and still has the upper hand in any negotiation with us mortals, but now we—each of us as individuals—try to drive a harder bargain.

The negative rights claim against doctors, hospitals, and the state that I have sketched also has a positive correlative. In a world where it is ever more common for doctors to be willing to give up on treatment sooner than their patients accept the fact of dying, those at the end of life now demand not to die—that is, demand to live.

Even when, by medical standards, a patient is dead, there are those who insist on the contrary and demand life support to stave off death. In 2013, a thirteen-year-old girl, Jahi McMath, in Children's Hospital Oakland suffered massive blood loss from complications of a routine adenotonsillectomy intended to relieve her sleep apnea. As a result, she died. Or, to be more precise, her doctors diagnosed her state as whole brain death: she was dead, and the hospital therefore wanted to stop life support. Leaving aside the ethical question, hospitals are not paid for treating dead people. From the medical and administrative perspective, there was no life to support. McMath's parents felt differently and sued to overturn the diagnosis of death. After considerable litigation, the body was released to the Alameda County coroner, who had issued a temporary—pending an autopsy—death certificate but who, under the terms of a court-mediated compromise, gave over the purportedly dead body, still on a ventilator, to the parents, who took it to an undisclosed location in New Jersey, where state law allows a religious exception for refusing to accept brain death as death.[4]

In part, this thoroughly modern story is a consequence of the peculiar quality of brain death: it is grounded in the oldest and most deeply rooted sign of death, one that we humans have intuitively embraced since well before anyone knew anything about physiology, much less oxygen: the absence of breath, of the spirit that informs matter and makes it live. To be brain dead is not to be able to breathe or, more precisely in modern terms, to respond at the level of a reflex to carbon dioxide in the blood. But the test for the departure of breath, although close to what King Lear employed—physicians still listen carefully for breath and try to sense the movement of air—is done on a body that, until the test is made, retains the rosy hue of life. It is being mechanically maintained. A ventilator provides the energy that keeps the entropy of death artificially at bay. The machine is removed, and then the presence of life force is tested. If in two minutes there is no breath, brain death becomes "real death." All very sensible.

Both the right to die and the right not to die represent the limit cases of our unprecedented contemporary difficulty in dying more generally. More usual are the quotidian decisions made every day in the hospitals of the world about when to give up. These are difficult for many reasons. First, they take place in venues and situations not well suited for delicate negotiations between people who scarcely know one another—hospitalists, in-house specialists with no knowledge of the life of their patients, on the one side, and the dying person and families, who operate with very different interests and constraints, on the other.

Dying has also entered realms of decision making where it never appeared before. It has become part of rational—or not so rational—economic behavior, like choosing a college or a car: *Dying Better: The Consumer Experience at the End of Life* reads the title of an informative recent English guide on the subject.[5] Social workers develop scenarios of dying down to a level of detail undreamed of before: Would the dying person want someone who breaks down in tears to leave the room? Would she want to be awakened if there was a visitor?

This level of individual decision making fits all too well into the imaginative realm of war that so often defines the end of life today: dying is losing a battle, a sad but seemingly contingent surrender, as if there were a choice. At issue seems to be the bravery and daring of patient and doctor: to die or not to die—a terrible personal choice whether to stay at one's post as long as possible at whatever cost. It seems almost an act of cowardice to give up. Patients will go with us to the bitter end, Jerome Groopman, the Harvard oncologist, says approvingly, of those who are willing to try new but largely futile treatments that might prove of some scientific interest and have a tiny chance of prolonging life in any individual case. "There may be times when you'll wish for a lesser dose due to the side effects. But we've got to go full-force . . . the maximum dose to be of any use," says Dr. Kelikian, the chief of the oncology service at Johns Hopkins, in the play W;t, to his patient, Professor Bearing, who is dying of ovarian cancer: "You must be very tough. Do you think you can be very tough?" "You need not worry," she responds, as if she were a solider being sent on a hopeless mission. Even without such dramatic warfare, dying has become something new when one seems to have so many choices: another stem cell transplant? more chemotherapy? a dangerous operation that may buy weeks or months of life? or surrender? Decisions of life and death, an option confined to suicide in ages past, cannot be easy. Put differently, the seldom-asked question of suicide—choosing to die—has almost become the norm.[6]

Finally there are, at the bedside, all the microemotional decisions that have to be made by the dying person or her family, on the one side, and representatives of the vast professional, institutional, bureaucratic, and financial infrastructures that make up modern medicine, on the other. For those who die in the intensive care unit (as many as 20 percent of the 50 percent or so of people who die in the hospital) the time of death itself must be negotiated at the mutual convenience of doctors and family: usually the end of the shift for busy anesthesiologists finished with their surgery or pulmonary specialists who have taken care of more urgent cases. But even for those who don't die in the ICU, there are choices: a fifty-year-old man who is on dialysis has suffered a severe stroke that has left him in a persistent vegetative state and on life support. His advance directive says he did not want to have such treatment. But his wife points out that if he died she would lose his pension and thus her house; he would, she says, have wanted to live on life support under these circumstances. He did live, for three more years. A ninety-two-year-old woman suffering from dementia who had said, in better times, that she did not want to go into the hospital when she was dying, fell and broke her hip. Is she to have surgery or to die, bedridden, of pneumonia or some other infection that used to take the old? She had her operation, walked a bit again, and died in five weeks from complications of surgery. And so on.[7]

The work of the dead—the subject of this book—is still bound up with history and with the communal needs of the living. There are new twists to old stories: eco-burial revives the idea of the Victorian wicker coffin; controversies about replacing burial with cremation in China and Singapore are replays of the debates discussed in chapter 6. But dying has come unhinged from its past. Humans have never lived exclusively in nature; dying has always been culturally mediated. There has always been some choice. But in the past fifty years or so, the natural history of disease, which had been the subject of medicine and pathology textbooks and before that of folk and learned wisdom, has all but disappeared. New technologies are ever more effective in manipulating the end of life, in channeling nature, if only for a time. And at the same time, the burden on the autonomous, rights-bearing-to-the-very-end individual has increased beyond what our ancestors would have recognized.

None of this is itself to be regretted, of course; we all want to live longer and in good health, and modern medicine makes this possible. We all want to be in control until the very end. But we have no cultural history to guide us when health and well-being fade and dying becomes a branch of bioengineering. For the time being, our hope as individuals who have friends and family is, as Atul Gawande suggests, to take back dying into the realm of human communities of all sorts; to make it intimately social again; to listen to the dying, to find spaces outside of institutions in which to die—home or hospice; to know when to accept the inevitable.[8]

It is not clear how this humanistic strategy will comport with and become part of a new social order of dying. And if the dreams of some come to fruition—that aging is put off indefinitely and that we do not die at all or only in a very distant future—then we are in another universe entirely. A history written from the perspective of centuries hence will have to tell that story, the story of modern dying or perhaps of not dying at all.

NOTES

1. Edward Thompson in *The Making of the English Working Class* (New York: Vintage, 1966), 374, is quoting and then paraphrasing the nineteenth-century historian William Lecky.

2. The story comes from Mary Sherwood, *History of the Fairchild Family* (London: Harchard, 1818), 146–147, 151, and more generally her chapter "On Death." My own account of the death of children, first written when I was twenty-six and a graduate student at Oxford, is in the book that grew out of my dissertation: *Religion and Respectability: Sunday Schools and Working Class Culture, 1780–1850* (New Haven, Conn.: Yale University Press, 1976).

3. I learned a huge amount about who was afraid of what from conversations in Berlin with Dietrich Niethammer during the academic year 2005–2006 and from his book that has now been translated into English by Victoria W. Hill as *Speaking Honestly with Sick and Dying Children and Adolescents* (Baltimore: Johns Hopkins University Press, 2012). I read the typescript of its German version, *Das Sprachlose Kind* (Stuttgart: Schattauer, 2008). I am thinking of Tolstoy's short story "Three Deaths."

4. See Nancy Scheper-Hughes, *Death without Weeping: The Violence of Life in Brazil* (Berkeley: University of California Press, 1992). Robert Woods, *Children Remembered: Responses to Untimely Death in the Past* (Liverpool: Liverpool University Press, 1988). See also Jean Clair, ed., *Melancholie: Genie und Wahnsee in der Kunst* (Berlin: Neue National Galerie, 2006).

INTRODUCTION: THE WORK OF THE DEAD

Epigraph: Cicero, *Tusculan Disputations*, trans. J. E. King, Loeb Classical Library (Cambridge, Mass.: Harvard University Press, 1927), 1.43.

1. Andrew T. Chamberlaine and Michael Parker Pearson, *Earthly Remains: The History and Science of Preserved Bodies* (Oxford: Oxford University Press, 2001), 12–44 and ff. See the excellent summary in Kathryn Powell, *Grave Concerns: Locating and Unearthing Human Bodies* (Bowen Hills, Qld.: Australian Academic Press, 2010), 336–346. Homer, *The Iliad*, trans. Robert Fagles (New York: Penguin, 1990), bk. 16, p. 436. Bhadantácariya Buddhaghosa, *Visuddhimagga: The Path of Purification*, trans. from the Pali by Bhikkhu Ñáóamoli (Kandy, Sri Lanka: Buddhist Publication Society, 2010), 169 and 169–185 passim. This is said to be the authoritative treatment of death in general, 225ff., and the dead body in particular in the section I cite, in contemporary Theravada Buddhism (the Buddhism of Southeast Asia). I am grateful to my colleague Robert Sharf, professor of Buddhist studies at Berkeley, for his advice and guidance.

2. Simon Mays, *The Archaeology of Human Bones* (London: Routledge, 1998), 16–25. The question of bone preservation is also dealt with in the books cited above. Geoffrey Chaucer, "The General Prologue," in *Canterbury Tales*, ed. Robert Boenig and Andrew Taylor (Peterborough, Ont.: Broadview Editions, 2012), 59. Walter Raleigh, *History of the World* (Edinburgh: Archibald Constable and Co., 1820), 6:370. See Christopher Joyce and Eric Stover, *Witnesses from the Grave* (Boston: Little Brown, 1991).

3. Diels-Kranz, *Die Fragmente der Vorsokratiker* 22b96 (p. 172). Heraclitus, most famous for his views on change ("You cannot step into the same river twice"), got there first. He also had a biographical association with dung. When he developed dropsy, he covered himself with dung in the hopes that its heat would dry him out. Then he died, either because the treatment failed or because he couldn't get the dung off and dogs tore him apart. On this, see Diogenes quoted in Cicero, *Tusculan Disputations*, 1.43. This is the first instance I know in Western literature of a trope that will appear again and again in this book, dead bodies, in this case a couple, living together in ashes and dust:

    > I'll have myself placed in the same cedar box as you
    > My body next to your body
    > Never separate again
    > You alone are faithful to me.

    Euripides, *Alkestis*, in Anne Carson, trans., *Grief Lessons: Four Plays* (New York: NYRB Classics, 2006), translation lines 290ff., for Adametos's plans to be with his dead wife—as an effigy, in a dream, eventually in the grave. Alkestis's response, which I quote, is at 341. For an elegant, modern ecological perspective, see Bernd Heinrich, *Life Everlasting: The Animal Way of Death* (New York: Houghton Mifflin, 2012), ixff. I will come back to the antithesis between the natural and the (for want of a better word) culturalist perspective in part 1.

4. Vous nous voyez ci-attachés cinq, six
    Quant de la chair, que trop avons nourrie,
    Elle est pieça devoree et pourrie,
    Et nous les os, devenons cendre et pouldre.

François Villon, "Ballade des pendus" or "Frères humains" (human brothers)—we the living—whom the dead address in the poem's first line. *Complete Poems*, ed. and trans. Barbara Sargent Baur (Toronto: University of Toronto Press, 1994), 264 (with some modifications in the translation).

5.   Michel de Montaigne, "On the Cannibals," in *The Essays: A Selection*, trans. M. A. Screech (New York: Penguin, 2003), 81–92. D. Tuzin, ed., *The Ethnography of Cannibalism* (Washington, D.C.: Society for Psychological Anthropology, 1983), 88. Hyenas do not in general dig up the dead, and they eat carrion far less frequently than lions. S. E. Glickman, "The Spotted Hyena from Aristotle to the Lion King: Reputation Is Everything," *Social Research* 62, no. 3 (1995): 501–537.

6.   See reports in the *New York Times*, 21 July 2011, A1, and 9 June 2011, A14. Abel Styles, "Death God's Minister to the Living [on Heb 11:4]" (Providence, in New England: Sarah Goddard, 1768). Piers Vitebsky, *Dialogues with the Dead: The Discussion of Mortality among the Sora of Eastern India* (Cambridge: Cambridge University Press, 1993). The dead, even among the Sora, a tribal people of India, do eventually die. Literary exchanges with the dead is common in the West.

7.   I quote from the NPR story at http://www.npr.org/2011/08/03/138524619/a-fight -for-jim-thorpes-body. The AP reported in September 2013 that a U.S. district judge ruled in favor of the Thorpe family members fighting for the body to be released, finding that the town of Jim Thorpe constitutes a museum and thus falls under the jurisdiction of the 1990 Native American Graves Protection and Repatriation Act. The town appealed the ruling in the Philadelphia 3rd Circuit Court, which on 23 October 2014 overturned the lower court decision, thus allowing the body to stay where it was. Michael Rubinkam and Keith Collins, "Jim Thorpe, Pa. Fights to Keep Body of Namesake," Associated Press, 5 September 2013, http://bigstory.ap.org/article /jim-thorpe-pa-fights-keep-body-namesake; "Pennsylvania Town Can Keep Jim Thorpe's Body, Associated Press, 23 October 2014, http://www.sfgate.com/nation /article/Pennsylvania-town-can-keep-Jim-Thorpe-s-body-5843362.php.

8.   Mark Bowden, *Black Hawk Down* (New York: Atlantic Monthly Press, 1999). Vincent Brown, *The Reaper's Garden: Death and Power in the World of Atlantic Slavery* (Cambridge, Mass.: Harvard University Press, 2008), 136–137, 218–219. Brown's perspective has influenced my thinking more than these brief page references reflect. Winnifred Sullivan, *The Impossibility of Religious Freedom* (Princeton, N.J.: Princeton University Press, 2005).

9.   "A Clergyman" [Thomas Lewis, 1689–1737], *Churches Not Charnel Houses: Being an Enquiry into the Profaness, Indecency, and Pernicious Consequences of Burying the Dead in Churches and Churchyards Shewing . . . That the Original of This Practice Was founded in Pride, Improved by Superstition, and Encouraged for Lucre* (London: A Bettesworth, 1726), 54–55. William Gouge, *Of Domesticall Duties* (London: George Miller, 1634), 270a. As Sir Thomas Browne wrote—and his views could be extended to all people—"Christians have handsomely glossed the Deformity of Death by careful Consideration of the Body, and civil rites." See Thomas Browne, *Religio Medici and Hydriotaphia or Urne-Buriall*, ed. Stephen Greenblatt and Ramie Targod (New York: New York

Review of Books, 2012), 124. Glossing over death, whatever that might mean, is why people care for bodies. See Julia Kristeva, *Powers of Horror: An Essay on Abjection*, trans. Leon S. Roudiez (New York: Columbia University Press, 1982), 3–4. There is a whole literature on the psychoanalytic interpretation of widespread ways of dealing with the dead. Theodor Reik, for example, argues that the modern Jewish custom of putting stones on graves is a continuation of the practices of prehistoric peoples who feared the dead and put large stones over their burial places to keep them at bay. I am less interested in the specific explanation than in the long history of the fear of the untended dead. Theodor Reik, *Pagan Rites in Judaism* (New York: Farrar Straus, 1964), 44ff.

10. Hans-Georg Gadamer, *Reason in the Age of Science*, trans. Frederick G. Lawrence (Cambridge, Mass.: MIT Press, 1981), 75.

11. Claude Lévi-Strauss, *The Elementary Structures of Kinship*, trans. James Bell and John von Sturmer (Boston: Beacon Press, 1969).

12. V. Gordon Childe, "Directional Changes in Funerary Practices during 50,000 Years," *Man* 45 (January–February 1945): 13, and 13–19. On the absence of a break between the prehistoric and historic, I am convinced by Daniel Lord Smail's *On Deep History and the Brain* (Berkeley: University of California Press, 2008). For the purposes of this book I have no view on history and neurophysiology. I might add that the basic divisions among how the dead are cared for—cremated or buried; if buried, whether near or far from where the living dwell; whether once or with secondary burial—also stretch far back to the middle Neolithic and even earlier to the beginnings of agriculture. See, for example, Åsa M. Larsson, "Secondary Burial Practices in the Middle Neolithic: Causes and Consequences," *Current Swedish Archaeology* 11 (2003): 153–170. Larsson presents her own research and a very considerable body of literature to argue for the antiquity of cremation and of secondary burial. She also makes the general point, one that is important to this book, that there is no necessary relationship between ritual care of the dead and any particular social structure. The farmers in the earliest known Neolithic agricultural settlement, Çatalhöyük in Turkey, and certain bands of aborigines in modern Australia buried their dead under or near their houses. Nothing per se follows from this. Let me also say that I have no commitment to the idea of a genderless human. It is quite possible that the male dead were cared for more extensively and earlier than the female. A 1984 paper by Margaret W. Conkey and Janet Spector, "Archaeology and the Study of Gender," *Advances in Archeological Method and Theory* 7 (1984): 1–38, raised a whole range of new questions. The inadequacies of my engagement with them is clear from the papers in Bettina Arnold and Nancy Wicker, eds., *Gender and the Archaeology of Death* (Walnut Creek, Calif.: AltaMira Press, 2001). I am, however, less interested in establishing a genderless category "human" than I am in arguing that in whatever way we understand the term "human," caring for a dead body is a sign for membership in this group. Finally, I am not interested here in debating whether language or tool making has an equal claim to the imaginary boundary of culture. My case for the primacy of caring for the dead is elaborated in the next chapter.

13. Robert Hertz, "A Contribution to the Study of the Collective Representation of Death" (1907), in *Death and the Right Hand*, trans. Rodney Needham and Claudia Needham (Aberdeen: Cohen and West, 1960), 36–37. Maurice Bloch and Jonathan Perry, eds., *Death and the Regeneration of Life* (Cambridge: Cambridge University Press, 1982), 1–6, nicely place Hertz in the great nineteenth-century anthropological tradition next to Bachofen and Frazer. My interest in his work, in addition to its development of a general Durkheimian framework, grows out of the fact that his basic insight does not depend on what he takes to be the ultimate ends of death rituals but on the general claim I quoted.

14. Friedrich Schleiermacher, *On Religion*, ed. Richard Crouter (Cambridge: Cambridge University Press, 1996), 22. Robert Bellah and Hans Joas, eds., *The Axial Age and Its Consequences* (Cambridge, Mass.: Belknap Press, 2012). Had I been able to read the learned and provocative book by Robert Bartlett, *Why Can the Dead Do Such Great Things? Saints and Worshippers from the Martyrs to the Reformation* (Princeton, N.J.: Princeton University Press, 2013), before I was in the last stages of revision, I would have been spared much labor. The snippet is from his title; the book is largely about the theology and practice of saintly corporeal relics, whole or in pieces.

15. Arthur Imhof, *Lost Worlds: How Our European Ancestors Coped with Everyday Life and Why Life Is So Hard Today*, trans. Thomas Robisheaux (Charlottesville: University of Virginia Press, 1996), 6–87, 172. I do not believe that we moderns are in general any more accepting of death than our ancestors, but I will return to this point later. Michel Vovelle, *Piété baroque et déchristianisation en Provence au xviiie siècle* (Paris: Editions du Seuil, 1978). Geoffrey Gorer, *Death, Grief, and Mourning in Contemporary Britain* (London: Cresset Press, 1965). Philippe Ariès, *The Hour of Our Death*, trans. Helen Weaver (New York: Knopf, 1981). Michel Foucault, *The Birth of the Clinic*, trans. A. M. Sheridan Smith (New York: Vintage, 1975).

16. This formulation is from Gustav Schlyter, *Die Feuerbestattung und Ihre Kulturelle Bedeutung: Der Tempel Des Friedens* (Leipzig: Wilhelm Hemp Verlag, 1922), 4–5.

17. Robert Fagles, trans., *The Odyssey* (New York: Viking, 1996), 256. On the *draug* and its relationship to other kinds of Norse undead, see the especially informative article by Ármann Jakobsson, "Vampires and Watchmen: Categorizing the Medieval Undead," *Journal of English and Germanic Philology* 110, no. 2 (July 2011): 281–300.

18. I have no stake in the distinction between a social and cultural history generally, and with respect to the history of the dead in particular, except to insist that real dead bodies matter and that they matter because of how we, the living, give them meaning. On the ill-conceived distinction, see Carla Hesse, "The New Empiricism," *Cultural History and Social History* 1 (2004): 201–207.

19. Federico García Lorca, "Play and Theory of the *Duende*," in *In Search of the Duende*, trans. Christopher Mauer (New York: New Directions, 1998), 55. *Duende* for Lorca is some admixture of soul, of a sort of demonic possession, and of an intimacy with death, all of which informs art. On the search for his body, see "Archaeologists Hope to Uncover Playwright García Lorca's Resting Place," *Guardian*, 17 November 2014, http://www.theguardian.com/culture/2014/nov/17/spain-archaeology-federico

-garcia-lorca-mass-grave. On exhumations and the remaking of history through bodies in Spain and elsewhere, see chapter 5. Richard Cobb, *The Police and the People: French Popular Protest 1789–1820* (New York: Oxford University Press, 1970), 8.

20. On Eleanor Marx Aveling's ashes, see Yvonne Kapp, *Eleanor Marx* (London: Lawrence and Wishart, 1976), 2:703–704.

21. On the reinterment of Marx and his family, see the Burial and Cremation files of the Home Office, PRO HO 282/35; on the erection of the monument, see PRO CP/IND/DUTT/23/01. On Bradshaw, see *Morning Star*, 3 April 2007. Bradshaw was something of a specialist in busts of communist luminaries: W.E.B. DuBois and of the Scottish poet Hugh MacDiarmid, for example. It is always difficult to give monetary equivalents, but the most reliable database, MeasuringWorth (http://www .measuringworth.com), calculates that the relative value of £800 in 1954 would be between £18,000 and £70,000 in 2014; £5000 in 1954 pounds would be worth between £102,000 and £378,000 in 2014.

22. On damage to the tomb, see the Metropolitan Police file PRO MEPO 28/5. Martin Kettle, *Guardian*, 21 December 1996, as well as a number of his friends, interpret the location of Samuel's grave in a way that makes it part of the public story of the dead around Marx; I have the alternative, more intimate story in an e-mail, 12 January 2015, from his widow, Alison Light. She says that Raphael "loathed the hideous monument" put up by the Communist Party and that his grave's location so near Marx's is "ABSOLUTELY FORTUITOUS."

23. A. A. Long, "The Socratic Tradition: Diogenes, Crates, and Hellenistic Ethics," in R. Bracht Branham and Marie-Odile Goulet-Cazé, eds., *The Cynics: The Cynic Movement in Antiquity and Its Legacy* (Berkeley: University of California Press, 1996), 9–30 and 28–46 passim.

24. For Lucretius's views, see chapter 2, note 4.

25. Susan Gal, "Bartók's Funeral Representations of Europe in Hungarian Political Rhetoric," *American Ethnologist* 18, no. 3 (August 1991): 440–458. The story of Nagy's reburial figures centrally in István Rev, *Retroactive Justice: Prehistory of Post-Communism* (Stanford, Calif.: Stanford University Press, 2005). This brief allusion to Kadar and Nagy only gestures toward the importance that Rev's work and friendship has had for this book. He will be cited again.

26. Katherine Verdery's *The Political Lives of Dead Bodies: Reburial and Postsocialist Change* (New York: Columbia University Press, 1999) has clearly informed this paragraph and my work generally. All of the material upon which this summary of the search for Bălcescu's body is based is in Romanian. I thank Mircea Rainu, once a member of my undergraduate research apprentice group and now a graduate student at Harvard, for creating and translating a dossier on this case. For the search for the burial place of the Bulgarian national revolutionary hero Vasil Levski, who was hanged by the Ottoman authorities in 1873, see Maria Todorova, *Bones of Contention: The Living Archive of Vasil Levski and the Making of Bulgaria's National Hero* (Budapest: Central European University Press, 2009), 21–38. On Lenin's body, see Alexei Yurchak, "Bodies of Lenin: The Hidden Science of Communist Sovereignty," *Representations* 129 (Winter

2015). The remains of the Cossack general Anton Denikin were exhumed from St. Vladimir's Cemetery in Jackson, New Jersey, in 2005 and transferred by authority of President Putin to Russia, where they were reburied in the ancient necropolis of Donskoy Monastery in Moscow. His body had already been exhumed once before from a grave in Detroit. Various factions of the materialist, communist Left are just as likely to need the bodies of their leaders in support of their positions as are those of any religious or bourgeois political movement. For one remarkable example, see Claudio Lomnitz, *The Return of Comrade Ricardo Flores Magón* (New York: Zone Books, 2014), 493–523.

27. David William Cohen and E. S. Atieno Odhiambo, *Burying SM: The Politics of Knowledge and the Sociology of Power in Africa*, Social History of Africa (Portsmouth, N.H.: Heinemann, 1992).

28. I am grateful to my former student Daniel Usshiskin, now at the University of Wisconsin, for translating this epitaph.

29. Dave Hickey, *Air Guitar: Essays on Art and Democracy* (Los Angeles: Art Issues Press, 1997), 189–190.

PART I: THE DEEP TIME OF THE DEAD

Epigraph: Seamus Heaney, *Open Ground: Selected Poems, 1966–1996* (New York: Farrar, Straus and Giroux, 1988), 62.

1. Peter Glob, *The Bog People: Iron-Age Man Preserved*, trans. from the Danish by Rupert Bruce-Mitford (London: Faber and Faber, 1969). For a good short account, see Andrew Chamberlain, *Human Remains* (Berkeley: University of California Press, 1994), 40–44; and Andrew Chamberlain and Michael Parker Pearson, *Earthly Remains: The History and Science of Preserved Human Bodies* (Oxford: Oxford University Press, 2001), 45–82, and more generally 45–143, to include frozen and mummified bodies. For the place of bog people in modern national consciousness, see Karen Sanders, *Bodies in the Bog and the Archaeological Imagination* (Chicago: University of Chicago Press, 2009).

2. On Kennewick Man, named after the town in Washington State near which his remains were found, see the excellent summary and bibliography in Douglas W. Owsley and Richard L. Jantz, "Kennewick Man—A Kin? Too Distant," in Elazar Barkan and Ronald Bush, eds., *Clothing the Stones: Naming the Bones* (Los Angeles: Getty Research Center, 2002), 141–161. Among the dozen paleo-American skeletons, that of Kennewick is the most intact. The final disposition of the body had not been determined by the time this essay appeared. In February 2004, the Ninth Circuit Court of Appeals ruled that this body remained outside culture, that is, that it could not be linked to any extant Native American tribe and that hence it could be studied as a specimen. It belongs to the Army Corps of Engineers, which discovered it. It is held by the Burke Museum of Natural History and Culture, which makes it available for study and for ritual visits by tribal leaders. See Burke Museum, "Kennewick Man:

The Ancient One," http://www.burkemuseum.org/kennewickman. This particular body is so significant because it seems to belie the then-prevalent thesis that the early settlers on this continent came from Asia via the Bering Strait; it suggests that, to the contrary, paleo-Americans were of more varied origin.

3. On the burial site, see the African Burial Ground webpage and the extensive archeological report that is available there: http://www.nps.gov/afbg. The quotation is from the National Parks Conservation Association website: http://www.npca.org/parks /african-burial-ground-national-monument.html.

4. I take Bosio's story from my graduate student Talia di Manno's paper "Digging in Rome: *Roma sotteranea* and the Antiquarian Tradition." See Irina Oryshkevich, "Cultural History in the Catacombs: Early Christian Art and Macarius's Hagioglypta," in Katherine van Liere, Simon Ditchfield, and Howard Louthan, eds., *Sacred History: Uses of the Christian Past in the Renaissance World* (Oxford: Oxford University Press, 2012), 250–266. Deborah Boedeker, "Hero Cult and Politics in Herodotus: The Bones of Orestes," in Carol Dougherty and Leslie Kurke, eds., *Cultural Poetics in Archaic Greece: Cult, Performance, Politics* (New York: Cambridge University Press, 1993), 164–177.

5. I take this anecdote from Paul Fussell, who cites the case in his *The Rhetorical World of Augustan Humanism* (Oxford: Clarendon Press, 1965), 11, based on a notice in the 1733 *Gentleman's Magazine*. It was famous for centuries and often reprinted for the next 150 years as evidence for unusual last wishes.

CHAPTER 1: DO THE DEAD MATTER?

Epigraph: James Joyce, *Ulysses* (New York: Modern Library, 1992), 114.

1. Diogenes Laertius, the third-century C.E. biographer, in his *The Lives and Opinions of Eminent Philosophers*, trans. R. D. Hicks, Loeb Classical Library (Cambridge, Mass.: Harvard University Press, 1972), bk. 6, chap. 2, p. 81. The Ilissus is the river that borders on part of the ancient walls of Athens. For Pierre Bayle, see the translation, faithful to the 1702 enlarged original, that would have been familiar to eighteenth-century Englishmen: *The Dictionary Historical and Critical . . . the Second Edition . . .* , vol. 2 (London, 1734–1738), s.v. Diogenes, the Cynic, 665. Bayle offers a wonderfully learned and critical account of the many sayings attributed, rightly or wrongly, to this sage. French edition: Pierre Bayle, *Dictionnaire historique et critique* (Rotterdam: Leers, 1697), 1:972.

2. Plato clearly disliked him; see Diogenes Laertius, *Lives and Opinions of Eminent Philosophers*, 55; the Alexander story is at 41. My understanding of the filial relationship between Socratic and Cynic moral philosophy comes from Susan Prince's essay "Socrates, Antishenes and the Cynics," in Sara Abhel-Rappe and Rachana Kamtekar, eds., *A Companion to Socrates* (Oxford: Blackwell, 2006), 88–89 and 75–94 more generally. Prince makes the point that Diogenes' first entry into philosophy was specifically a gesture of cultural repudiation. *Currency* in Greek, she tell us, had the same root as *custom*, and *defacing* has a common root with the word for stamping. Thus, when

Diogenes was accused of "defacing the currency," the charge had the sense of violating customary norms. See Peter Sloterdijk, *Critique of Cynical Reason*, trans. Michael Eldred (Minneapolis: University of Minnesota Press, 1987), 102 and passim, on the philosophical status of what Sloterdijk calls Greek "Kynicism," a higher- (or perhaps lower-) order cheekiness.

3. *Phaedo,* 115d–116a, in John Cooper, ed., *Complete Works of Plato* (Indianapolis: Hackett, 1997), 98.

4. "The Epistles of Diogenes," trans. Benjamin Fiore, S.J, in Abraham J. Malherbe, ed., *The Cynic Epistles* (Missoula, Mont.: Scholars Press for the Society of Biblical Literature, 1977), 117. On the burial of dogs, see the exhaustive survey by Darcy F. Morey, "Burying Key Evidence: The Social Bond between Dogs and People," *Journal of Archaeological Science* 33 (2006): 158–175.

5. Lucian of Samosata, *Dialogues of the Dead*, in M. D. McLeod, trans., *Lucian*, Loeb Classical Library (Cambridge, Mass.: Harvard University Press, 1961), 7:167. The story about Mausolus's wife, Artemesia, and the potion—she can be identified in Renaissance and baroque pictures by her goblet—is from the first-century C.E. Roman collector of anecdotes Valerius Maximus, *Memorable Deeds and Sayings*, ed. Henry J. Walker (Indianapolis: Hackett, 2004), 146, in a section on "love in foreign lands." In fact, Diogenes has—or had—a tomb. The Roman travel writer Pausanias (ca. 110–180 C.E.) reports that "as one goes up to Corinth there are tombs, and by the gate is buried Diogenes of Sinope, whom the Greeks surname the Dog." Pausanias, *Description of Greece*, trans. W.H.S. Jones, Loeb Classical Library (Cambridge, Mass.: Harvard University Press, 1977), bk. 2, p. 257. For ideas of the dead in ashes, even more distant from personhood than a decaying body, see chapter 11. One striking example of this general theme is the following: the great diva Maria Callas's ashes were scattered at sea by the Greek navy and were blown by the wind back to the ship, where they were inhaled by sailors. In Federico Fellini's *E la nave va* (*And the Ship Sails On*) (1983), "We hear her voice only once," notes Michal Grover-Friedlande, "originating from a gramophone, as her ashes are blown away in the wind: her voice is 'attached' to her disappearing body." Grover Friedlander, "The Afterlife of Maria Callas' Voice," *Musical Quarterly* 88, no. 1 (Spring 2005): 37, and 35–62 more generally.

6. *Hamlet*, act 5, sc. 1; "Men are but gilded loam or painted clay," *Richard II*, act 1, sc. 1, l. 179. Marcus Aurelius Antoninus, *The Meditations of Marcus Aurelius Antoninus*, trans. John Jackson (Oxford: Clarendon Press, 1906), bk. 6, p. 116. Shakespeare almost certainly knew what Diogenes represented in the Western tradition, if only from Montaigne's *Essays* in the Florio translation. Michel de Montaigne, *Shakespeare's Montaigne: The Florio Translation of the Essays, a Selection*, ed. Stephen Greenblatt (New York: New York Review Books, 2014): Diogenes "thought us worth so little that contact with us could neither trouble him nor corrupt him: he avoided our company not from fear of associating with us but from contempt. He thought us incapable of doing good or evil." "Of Democritus and Heraclitus," in Michel de Montaigne, *The Complete Essays*, trans. M. A. Screech (London, England: Penguin, 2003), 340.

7.	The origin of this story is obscure. In a note by one of its most regular correspondents, signing himself as W. Winters, *Antiquary* 1 (1871): 142, attributes it to someone writing to a "Dutch Spectator" in 1736 against "Romish superstition" and the communion of the living with the dead. It reappears, among many other places, in the oft-reprinted *Cyclopedia of Moral and Religious Anecdotes*, ed. George Barrell (London, 1849), and the equally popular *Mirror of Literature, Amusement, and Instruction* (London, 1828), edited by, among others, the well-known antiquary John Timbs and by Reuben Percy, who claimed to be a Benedictine monk and was the editor of many collections of anecdotes. George Seaton Bowes's *Illustrative Gatherings for Preachers and Teachers* (London: Wertheim, Macintosh and Hunt, 1860), offers it as a comment on the question of honor, 233.

8.	Augustine, *De cura mortuum gerenda*, 2.3–4.6, 18.22. English translation from Augustine, "The Care to Be Taken for the Dead," in *Treatises on Marriage and Other Subjects*, ed. Roy J. Deferrari (New York: Fathers of the Church, 1955), 3.5, pp. 353, 383 (cf. *De civitate Dei*, 1.12–13, English translation from *The City of God against the Pagans*, ed. R. W. Dyson, Cambridge Texts in the History of Political Thought [Cambridge: Cambridge University Press, 1998], 20–22). (Addressed to Paulinus of Nola, who had asked about the propriety of other burials in the Basilica near the body of Saint Felix the Confessor [chap. 1].) Paula Rose, *A Commentary on Augustine's "De cura pro mortuis gerenda"* (Leiden: Brill, 2013), 154–155. I found Louise Shea's *The Cynic Enlightenment* (Baltimore: Johns Hopkins University Press, 2010) extremely useful in tracing the *longue durée* of Diogenes' influence. It might not have been Diogenes directly, but rather Cicero, Seneca, or Lucretius who reported on and elaborated his arguments. The Church Fathers had a love-hate relationship with him, and with the Cynics generally, who were, of course, in the minority among the pagans. Jerome praised Diogenes as "mightier than King Alexander in that he conquered human nature." See Saint Jerome, "Against Jovinianus," bk. 2 in *Saint Jerome: Letters and Select Works*, trans. W. H. Fremantle, *A Select Library of Nicene and Post-Nicene Fathers of the Christian Church* (Oxford: Parker and Co., 1893), 6:398. Augustine found his lack of decency less attractive. S. Matton, "Cynicism and Christianity from the Middle Ages to the Renaissance," in R. Bracht Branham and Marie-Odile Goulet-Cazé, eds., *The Cynics: The Cynic Movement in Antiquity and Its Legacy* (Berkeley: University of California Press, 1996), 241–242, 262–263, and 240–262 passim. Augustine's mockery of the Virgil story is from Dyson, *The City of God against the Pagans*, bk. 22, sec. 8, p. 1121. For the story in Virgil, see *The Aeneid*, trans. Robert Fagles (New York: Penguin Books, 2006), 6.348–394, pp. 192–193.

9.	Augustine, "The Care to Be Taken for the Dead," in Deferrari, ed., *Treatises*, 3.5, p. 356. Saint Augustine of Hippo, *Confessions*, trans. Henry Chadwick (Oxford: Oxford University Press, 1991), 9.7, p. 165.

10.	Sir Thomas Browne, *Religio Medici*, new ed., corrected and amended (London, 1737), 111–112. Thomas Browne, *Religio Medici and Urne-Buriall*, ed. Stephen Greenblatt and Ramie Targoff (New York: New York Review of Books, 2012), 46. Chap. 5 of *Hydriotaphia: Or Urne Buriall*, in ibid., 131–139, is devoted to elaborating on oblivion: the quote is from chap. 3. A. A. Long, "The Socratic Tradition: Diogenes, Crates, and Hellenistic Ethics," in Branham and Goulet-Cazé, eds. *The Cynics*, 29–30 and 28–46 passim. Death, according to Erasmus's Diogenes, is not an evil, because as long as death is not present, all is fine: "As long as a man hath perfect sense and feeling, he is alive, so then death is not yet in place, that if the same [death] be present, then sense and feeling is away. And evil is it not, that is not felt." "This manner of argumentation or reason," Erasmus's learned sixteenth-century translator adds, "certain writers ascribe to Epicurus." Nicolas Udall, *The Apophthegmes of Erasmus* (London, 1542; facsimile ed., Boston: Robert Roberts, 1878), bk. 1, paragraph 203, p. 169. I have modernized the spelling.

11. Sir Thomas Browne, *Hydriotaphia*, chap. 3, 116. "And when distance of death denied such conjunctions, unsatisfied affections conceived some satisfaction to be neighbours in the grave, to lie urn by urn, and touch but in their manes. And many were so curious to continue their living relations, that they contrived large and family urns, wherein the ashes of their nearest friends and kindred might successively be received, at least some parcels thereof, while their collateral memorials lay in minor vessels about them." Julia's and Domitian's ashes were mixed together by their common nursemaid. Browne's source for this would have been Suetonius. For Browne's remains, see his *Dictionary of National Biography* entry. He did not altogether rest peacefully. His skull was exhumed in 1840 and subjected to tests that were meant to certify the authenticity of his portrait. His great admirer Sir William Osler supervised its reinterment in 1923). His reference to the Patriarchs is probably an allusion to the story of Jacob who, as he lies dying, says to Joseph that he does not want to be buried in Egypt and hopes that his son will deal kindly and truly with him by carrying him out of Egypt to the burying place of his fathers. Joseph had him embalmed; this took forty days; he was mourned for seventy; then Joseph carried him to Canaan to where Abraham and Isaac are buried in the cave that Abraham had bought from Ephraim the Hittite (Gen 50:1–14).

12. William Wordsworth, "Essay on Epitaphs, I," in *The Prose Works of William Wordsworth*, ed. W.J.B. Owen and Jane Worthington Smyser (Oxford: Oxford University Press, 1974), 2:49–53. I am not sure what "ancient philosopher" or what text Wordsworth had in mind. Professor Paul Kalligas of Athens University suggests the comparison of the body with an oyster shell (*ostreon*) in the *Republic*, cf. 10.611c. He writes, "It is on this basis that some later Neoplatonists such as Proclus used to describe the body as a shell-like envelope (*ostreodes soma*). Combine this with the image of the soul as a bird with wings in the *Phaedrus* and you can see that the Neoplatonic imagination was not too far from Wordsworth's imagery. Plotinus is using the latter image, but not the former."

13. Quoted in Allen Luwig, *Graven Images: New England Stonecarving and Its Symbols, 1650–1815* (Middletown, Conn.: Wesleyan University Press, 2000), 214–215.

14. James George Frazer, *The Fear of the Dead in Primitive Religion* (London: Macmillan, 1933), 1:11–12.

15. Clement of Alexandria, *Exhortation to the Greeks*, trans. G. W. Butterworth, Loeb Classical Library (Cambridge, Mass.: Harvard University Press, 1982,), 99–101. The dead doing great things is a paraphrase of the title of Robert Bartlett's massively learned new book that I encountered only in the last stages of revising this manuscript. It gives the fullest history I know of the vast Christian archipelago of theology and practice centered on the special dead. Robert Bartlett, *Why Can the Dead Do Such Great Things? Saints and Worshippers from the Martyrs to the Reformation* (Princeton, N.J.: Princeton University Press, 2013).

16. On the tomb of Antinous, see Pausanias, bk. 8, chap. 9, 7–8. Clement, *Exhortation*, 111. Clement is also exaggerating the extent to which Greek and Roman temples were tombs. In truth, a very, very small number of Roman dead were declared gods and their tombs made into temples. By and large, death and the dead body in the ancient Mediterranean world were seen to be deeply polluting; we learn this from *Antigone*; we learn it from *Iphigenia*; we learn it from many other sources. Of the hundreds of thousands of Roman gravesites that have been found, perhaps twenty are located inside the sacred bounds of a city. The Olympian gods would also have no traffic with human corpses; ordinary houses had to be ritually cleansed when a death occurred in them; mourners needed ritual ablutions before they could enter temples or offer prayers. Clement, in short, picks his examples selectively and without any commitment, of course, to scholarly balance. On death and pollution, see Robert Parker, *Miasma: Pollution and Purification in Early Greek Religion* (Oxford: Clarendon Press, 1983), 32–43 and 33–73 more generally.

17. I base this on the Buddhologist Robert H. Scharf's, "On the Allure of Buddhist Relics," *Representations* 66 (Spring 1999): 75–99, and quotations, 76–77, 82. Bartlett, *Why Can the Dead Do Such Great Things?*, 627. For the story of early Islam and the dead, see Leor Halevi, *Muhammad's Graves: Death Rites and the Making of Islamic Societies* (New York: Columbia University Press, 2007), which has been influential in my thinking beyond what one endnote can suggest.

18. Peter R. L. Brown, *The Cult of the Saints: Its Rise and Function in Latin Christianity* (Chicago: University of Chicago Press, 1981), 78 and passim.

19. I owe this formulation to discussion with David Ganz, Kings College, London, who kindly sent me a communication on saints' bones as offering "credit"—spiritual liquidity—in the context of our discussions of his work at the Institute for Advanced Study, fall 2009.

20. See, on this particular case, Jay Rubenstein, *Guibert of Nogent: Portrait of a Medieval Mind* (London: Routledge, 2002), 124–130, esp. 125. The problem of stolen relics in particular is made in Patrick J. Geary, *Furta Sacra: Thefts of Relics in the Central Middle Ages*, rev. ed. (Princeton, N.J.: Princeton University Press, 1990), 5–9, 124–125 and passim.

21. Martin Bucer, *Deutsche Schriften* (Gütersloh: Gütersloher Verlagshaus Mohn, 1960–), 1:274, quoted in Carlos M. N. Eire, *War against Idols* (Cambridge: Cambridge University Press, 1986), 91 (on Geneva, 150–151). While in exile in England, Bucer would have an important role in writing the 1552 resolutely Protestant *Second Book of Common Prayer*, which makes very little of the dead body.

22. Joseph Bingham, *Origines Ecclesiastcae or the Antiquities of the Christian Church* (London: Robert Knaplock, 1726), 2:438. *The Crosses Case in Cheapside* (London: For T.V., 1642), 16–17. Moses in this regard stands in sharp contrast to Joseph, whose bones he retrieved before leaving Egypt; they were carried in an ark by the Children of Israel during their forty years in the desert and came to rest in the land of Canaan. Their presence there created a claim by his descendants to the land. The translation of his bones is reported in Gen 50:26, Exod 13:19, and Josh 24:32, and is alluded to on several other occasions in the New Testament. For a modern study of their significance, see Joseph M. Segal, *Joseph's Bones: Understanding the Struggle between God and Mankind in the Bible* (New York: Penguin, 2007). The incitement to idolatry on the part of the dead was a major theme among reformers. The longest of John Jewell's many times reprinted homilies *Against the Peril of Idolatry*, for example, cites Augustine to the effect that "such as worship the dead are not Catholic Christians" (*The Second Tome of Homilies* [London: Edward Allde, 1575], no pagination but marked as 118 in STC 513:04). On iconoclasm and the dead, see Margaret Aston, "Art and Idolatry: Reformed Funeral Monuments," in Tara Hamling and Richard L. Williams, eds., *Art Re-formed: Re-assessing the Impact of the Reformation on the Visual Arts* (Newcastle: Cambridge Scholars Publishing, 2007): "The dead were dangerous for reformers," she argues, 246ff., although the importance of keeping order made the authorities oppose the destruction of tombs. Philip Lindley, "'Disrespect for the Dead?' The Destruction of Tomb Monuments in Mid-Sixteenth-Century England," *Church Monuments* 19 (2004): 53–79, esp. 68—argues that iconoclasm threatened tombs despite the Edwardian Act, Statues IV/1, III; 3–4 Ed Vi, cap 10.

23. Horace Hovey, ed., *Origin and Annals of "the Old South" First Presbyterian Church and Parish* (Boston: Damrell and Upham, 1896), 189–191; Robert E. Cray, Jr., "Memorialization and Enshrinement: George Whitefield and Popular Religious Culture," *Journal of the Early Republic* 10, no. 3 (Autumn 1990): 339–361. I am grateful to Erik Reinhart for bringing Whitefield's sainthood to my attention.

24. William Godwin, *An Essay on Sepulchres, or, A Proposal for Erecting Some Memorial of the Illustrious Dead in All Ages on the Spot Where Their Remains Have Been Interred* (London: W. Miller, 1809). All subsequent quotations are from this edition.

25. Godwin's insistence on the male "his" is unrelenting, perhaps because he means to suggest that what he says is true in general—the masculine pronoun as universal—and is not to be interpreted as an idiosyncratic personal expression of grief. Jeremy Bentham's friend and executor, the physician Thomas Southwood-Smith, would repeat Godwin's words—without attribution—in his lecture at the great philosopher's public dissection in 1832. If anyone believed that the dead are really gone, it would have been Bentham and his pupil Southwood-Smith (see chapter 5). Godwin's views on immortality are stranger than I can suggest here. He did not believe in an afterlife, but he seemed to believe in the possibility of physical immortality, of a very prolonged if not infinite life extension—another version of the belief in perfectibility that Malthus mocked.

26. William Godwin, *Lives of the Necromancers* (New York: Harper and Brothers, 1835), iv–v, 42.

27. Thomas Aquinas, *Summa theologica*, pt. 3, question 25, "On the Adoration of Christ."

CHAPTER 2: THE DEAD BODY
AND THE PERSISTENCE OF BEING

Epigraphs: Thomas Traherne (1636–1674), *Poems, Centuries and Three Thanksgivings*, ed. Anne Ridler (London: Oxford University Press, 1966), 116. James Boswell (1740–1795), *The Life of Samuel Johnson*, ed. R. W. Chapman (Oxford: Oxford University Press, 1998), 900.

1. Alfred Lord Tennyson, "Despair," in *Poems*, ed. Christopher Ricks, 2nd ed. (Harlow: Longman, 1987), 3:90.

2. Vladimir Nabokov, *Speak Memory: An Autobiography Revisited* (New York: Knopf Everyman's Library, 1999), 9.

3. Sigmund Freud, "Thoughts for the Time on War and Death," in *The Standard Edition of the Complete Psychological Works of Sigmund Freud*, trans. James Strachey (London: Hogarth Press, 1957), 14:289. Ludwig Wittgenstein, *Tractatus Logico-Philosophicus*, 6.4311, trans. D. F. Pears and B. F. McGuinness (New York: Routledge, 2001), 87. Maurice Blanchot, *Death Sentences*, trans. Lydia Davis (New York: Station Hill, 1978), 30.

4. Lucretius, *On the Nature of Things*, trans., with introduction and notes by Martin Ferguson Smith (Indianapolis: Hackett, 2001), bk. 3, lines 844–850, 880–894, 869.

5. Adam Smith, *Theory of Moral Sentiments*, ed. A. L. Macfie and D. D. Raphael, in *The Glasgow Edition of the Works of Adam Smith* (Indianapolis: Liberty Fund, 1984), 1:12–13. Esther Schor, *Bearing the Dead: The British Culture of Mourning from the Enlightenment to Victoria* (Princeton, N.J.: Princeton University Press, 1994), offers an account of how these views fit into a long literary tradition.

6. Harriet Reisen, *Louisa May Alcott* (New York: Holt, 2009), 297. I draw these examples, except for the invention of Emily Brontë and *Fridthjof's Saga*, from Alan Bray's remarkable book, *The Friend* (Chicago: University of Chicago Press, 2003). On the general wish to stay roughly together in churchyards, see Vanessa Harding, *The Dead and the Living in Paris and London, 1500–1670* (Cambridge: Cambridge University Press, 2002), 61–62. See Ramie Targoff, *Posthumous Love: Eros and Afterlife in Renaissance England* (Chicago: University of Chicago Press, 2014). I owe a great deal more to conversations with Targoff than this brief note can acknowledge.

7. John Webster, *The White Devil* (1612; reprint, London: Methuen Drama, 2008), 72.

8. George Herbert, "Death," in Mario Di Cesare, ed. *George Herbert and the Seventeenth-Century Religious Poets* (New York: W. W. Norton, 1978), 66–67. On Magdalena Luther, see Craig Koslofsky, *The Reformation of the Dead: Death and Ritual in Early Modern Germany, 1450–1700* (London: Macmillan, 2000), 153–154.

9. There were also non-Christian mortalists, most important the Jewish heretic Baruch Spinoza, who fit roughly into this tradition as well. I rely for the theology of

mortalism on William Spellman, "Between Death and Judgment: Conflicting Images of the Afterlife in Late Seventeenth-Century English Eulogies," *Harvard Theological Review* 87, no. 1 (1994): 49–65; Norman H. Burns, *Christian Mortalism from Tyndal to Milton* (Cambridge, Mass.: Harvard University Press, 1972); Bryan W. Ball, *The Soul Sleepers: Christian Mortalism from Wycliffe to Priestly* (Cambridge: James Clarke, 2008); and Nicholas McDowell, "Dead Souls and Modern Minds? Mortalism and the Modern Imagination," *Journal of Medieval and Early Modern Studies* 40, no. 3 (Fall 2010): 559–592.

10. *Paradise Lost*, bk. 1, in *Milton's Poetical Works* (Edinburgh: James Nichol, 1853), 5. For Hobbes, Locke, and Milton, see Philip Almond, *Heaven and Hell in Enlightenment England* (Cambridge: Cambridge University Press, 1994), 47–51, 88–89, 140–142 and passim 38–162. For the Muggletonians, see William Lamont, *Last Witnesses: The Muggletonian History, 1652–1979* (Aldershot: Ashgate, 2006).

11. That he was disinterred and despoiled of his hair and teeth by those who found and opened his coffin in 1790 in the course of searching for the exact location of his grave prior to erecting a monument is a story of another age, to be told later; see Philip Neve, *A Narrative of the Disinterment of Milton's Coffin . . .* (London: T. and J. Egerton, 1790).

12. The word "ghost," as it was used in the King James translation of the Bible, would not have meant "immaterial soul," to these mortalists, as it did to more orthodox Christians. They might have explained, if pressed on the subject, that it meant something closer to its ancient Hebrew sense of "to breathe out," "to give up breath," that is, to give up life without a commitment to what exactly was being given up. Ludowick Muggleton, *The Acts of the Witnesses of the Spirit* (London, 1699), 78–80.

13. In ancient Israel, the phrase "to give up the ghost," meant "to die," that is, to breathe one's last. Job 14:10: "But man dieth, and wasteth away; yea, man giveth up the ghost, and where is he?"

14. *Iliad*, trans. Robert Fagles (New York: Penguin, 1990), 23.61–158 (pp. 561–563). Hector's body was saved from an ignominious burial not by his ghost but by the intervention of the gods, who make Achilles return the body to his father.

15. R. Hisda: "A man's soul mourns for him [after death] seven whole [days] for it is said, And his soul mourneth for him; and it is written, and he made mourning for this father seven days"; R. Abbahu says "a dead man knows all that is said in his presence until the top-stone closes the grave," which is interpreted by others until the coffin lid is closed. They base this on Ecclesiastes 12:7 "And the dust return to the earth as it was, and the spirit return unto God." In other words, as soon as the body—dust—is buried, that which animated it is with God; R. Simeon and in a different context, R. Isaac disagree. The dead man knows what is said in his presence and feels pain until his flesh rots away, for it is written that "his flesh upon him hath pain and his soul within him mourneth." Simeon makes the case more pointedly: "Worms are as painful to the dead as a needle in the flesh of the living" (*Babylonian Talmud*, Tractate Shabbath 152a–b).

16. Quoted in Ralph Houlbrooke, *Death, Religion and Family in England 1480–1750* (Oxford: Clarendon Press, 1998), 275.

17. John Ferriar, *Medical Histories and Reflections* (London, 1798), 3:198–203.

18. Apuleius, "Thelyphron's Ghost Story," in *The Golden Ass*, trans. W. Adlington, Loeb Classical Library (Cambridge, Mass.: Harvard University Press, 1915), bk. 2, pp. 81–97. On this story, see also Gertrude C. Drake, "The Ghost Story in *The Golden Ass* by Apuleius," *Papers on Language and Literature* 13, no. 1 (January 1977): 3–15. I merely want to gesture here to the Chinese story, about which the literature is enormous. I found the following to be especially useful, and I thank my colleague Nick Tackett for his help in understanding them: Ying-Shih Yü, "'O Soul, Come Back!' A Study in the Changing Conceptions of the Soul and Afterlife in Pre-Buddhist China," *Harvard Journal of Asiatic Studies* 47, no. 2 (December 1987): 363–395; Arthur P. Wolf, "Gods, Ghosts, and Ancestors," in Wolf, ed., *Religion and Ritual in Chinese Society* (Stanford, Calif.: Stanford University Press, 1974); and Myron L. Cohen, "Souls and Salvation: Conflicting Themes in Chinese Popular Religion," in James L. Watson and Evelyn Rawski, eds., *Death Ritual in Late Imperial and Modern China* (Berkeley: University of California Press, 1988), 180–202. These walking dead seem to be *jiangshi*, from the root *jiang* (stiff and dried out), but such zombielike creatures are also more than just skeletons. At a conference on the dead in modern China that I attended on Chinese death rituals in Oracle, Arizona, 2–5 January 1981, I heard Prof. Anthony Yu of the University of Chicago, a Western-trained scholar of both Chinese and European classical literature, tell the following story. An e-mail from him on 11 July 2014 confirms my retelling of it, with some minor emendations that I have made here. His (late) father, a Kuomintang general, decided to make camp near a particular village during one of the battles against the Chinese Communist troops during the late 1940s. He was approached by the village headmen and asked to move out of sight of the road that passed through it because they had been told that a large contingent of the dead (the well-known name throughout much of China territorial regions was *xing-shi*, literally moving corpses) were to walk through that night. If they were disturbed by the sight of encamped soldiers, then very bad things would happen. General Yu, a UK-trained military officer (at the Royal Military Academy of Wolwich), was skeptical; he feared a ploy meant to allow Communist troops to pass through undetected. They assured him this was not the case and that if he would move his troops out of sight, he could watch for himself from a hiding place. To this he agreed. At night he witnessed a large contingent of the dead, lanterns on their heads and led by a driver, come to rest at the local tavern. They were leaned against the wall while the driver refreshed himself. Then the band set off again. Unlike most ghost stories, this one is only one degree removed from the person who witnessed the ghosts and is framed not as a tale but as an anthropological report from a source both inside and outside the events being described. On Norse ghosts, I have relied on N. K. Chadwick, "Ghosts (A Study in the *Draugr* and the *Haugbúi*)," pts. 1 and 2, *Folklore* 57, no. 2 (June 1946): 50–65, and no. 3 (September 1946): 106–127; and on the wildly learned and informative article by Hans-Joachim Klare, "Die Toten in der Altnordischen Literatur," *Acta Philologica Scandinavica* 8, no. 1 (1923): 1–57. On reanimated severed parts, see Hilda Roderick Ellis, *The Road to Hell: A Study of the Conception*

of the Dead in Old Norse Literature (Cambridge: Cambridge University Press, 1943), 156–158. The world of Haitian and African zombies are still another part of this story.

19. On European vampires, see Koen Vermier, "Vampires as Creatures of the Imagination: Theories of Body, Soul, and Imagination in Early Modern Vampire Tracts (1659–1755)," in Yasmin Haskell, ed., *Diseases of the Imagination and Imaginary Disease in the Early Modern Period* (Turnhout, Belg: Brepols, 2011), 341–373.

20. Bentham quoted in C. K. Ogden, *Bentham's Theory of Fictions* (London: Kegan Paul, 1932), xi, xix. On the persistence of ghosts, see Gillian Bennett and Kate Mary Bennett, "The Presence of the Dead: An Empirical Study," *Mortality* 5, no. 2 (July 2000): 139–157. William Lovett, *Life and Struggles of William Lovett* (New York: Knox, 1920), I:11.

21. *Odyssey*, trans. Robert Fagles (New York: Penguin, 1996), 252–253. Virgil, *Aeneid*, trans. H. Rushton Fairclough, revised ed., Loeb Classical Library (Cambridge, Mass.: Harvard University Press, 1986), 6.713–715, which introduces Aeneas's tour of the underworld. On Greek and Roman ghost stories, see R. C. Finucane, *Appearances of the Dead: A Cultural History of Ghosts* (London: Junction Books, 1982), chap. 1; and Alan E. Bernstein, *The Formation of Hell: Death and Retribution in the Ancient and Early Christian World* (Ithaca, N.Y.: Cornell University Press, 1993), 84–106 ("Porous Death").

22. Thomas Dawson, *Dissertations on the Following Subjects' viz Samuel's Appearance at Endor . . . Written at the Request of a Lady . . .* (London, 1727), 21–22.

23. These paragraphs draw heavily on Jean-Claude Schmitt, *Ghosts in the Middle Ages: The Living and the Dead in Medieval Society*, trans. Teresa Lavender Fagin (Chicago: Chicago University Press, 1998). On these themes, see also Stephen Greenblatt, *Hamlet in Purgatory* (Princeton, N.J.: Princeton University Press, 2001), 105–137. His account of the fourteenth-century *Gast of Gy* is a wonderfully rich account of a text that deals with what the dead want with the living, with how the Church mediates the conversation, and with the psychological responses of all sides. For the history of purgatory, I, like Schmitt, rely on Jacques Le Goff's *The Birth of Purgatory*, trans. Arthur Goldhammer (Chicago: University of Chicago Press, 1981, 1984).

24. Lewes Lavater, *Of Ghostes and Spirits Walking by Night*, trans. R[obert] H[arrison] (London, 1572), facsimile reprint ed., with an introduction by J. Dover Wilson and Mary Yardley (Oxford: Oxford University Press, 1929), 183–184. Richard Baxter says of his *De spectris* that it "is a book so common and well known, (by him a Learned Godly Protestant Divine) that I will suppose the Learned Reader to have read it and will not recite what is therein." See Richard Baxter, *The Certainty of the World of Spirits and Consequently of the Immortality of Souls . . . Written as an Addition to Many Treatises for the Conviction of Sadducees and Infidels* (London: T. Parkhurst, 1691), 135. E. Grindal, *Remains*, ed. W. Nicholson (Cambridge: Printed at the University Press for the Parker Society, 1843), 24, quoted in Peter Marshall, *Beliefs and the Dead in Reformation England* (Oxford: Oxford University Press, 2002), 235; see 232–264 for an excellent account of orthodox Protestant views about ghosts. See also the survey in Owen Davies, *The Haunted: A Social History of Ghosts* (Basingstoke: Palgrave MacMillan, 2007), 101–133.

25. The case of Mother Leakey is widely reported, but I take this account from Peter Marshall, *Mother Leakey and the Bishop* (Oxford: Oxford University Press, 2007), 1–37. The rest of the book is taken up with how this case articulates with the sodomy prosecution of an Irish bishop and is not my concern. The story is also told, as are many others of ghost laying, in Bruce Gordon, "Malevolent Ghosts and Ministering Angels: Apparitions and Pastoral Care in the Swiss Reformation," in Bruce Gordon and Peter Marshall, eds., *The Place of the Dead in Late Medieval and Early Modern Europe* (Cambridge: Cambridge University Press, 2000), 87–109. Theo Brown, *The Fate of the Dead: A Study of Folk Eschatology in the West Country after the Reformation* (Ipswich: D. S. Brewer for the Folklore Society, 1977), also tells the story of Mother Leakey and gives accounts of many conjurations and ghost appearances. Alexandra Walsham, "Invisible Helpers: Angelic Intervention in Post-Reformation England," *Past & Present* 208 (August 2010): 77–130.

26. *Supplementum* to the *Summa Theologica*, quest. 69, art. 3 and *Summa Theologica*, quest. 89, art. 8. See also May Yardley, "The Catholic Position in the Ghost Controversy of the Sixteenth Century," in Wilson and Yardley, eds., *Of Ghostes and Spirits*, 221–251. The phrase is Dean Stanley's.

27. Baxter, *Certainty of the World of Spirits*, 2:viii, 3–5.

28. Reginald Scot, *Discoverie of Witchcraft* (London: Henry Denham, 1584), 462–463, 461.

29. Baxter, *Certainty of the World of Spirits*, title page. Joseph Glanvil[l], *Saducismus Triumphatus: Or Full and Plain Evidence Concerning Witches and Apparitions, in Two Parts, the First Treating of Their Possibility and the Second of the Real Existence* (London, 1681). Glanvill was a member of the Royal Society and investigated each apparition carefully. Thus, for example, he offers evidence and counterevidence that the ghost of Thomas Goddard's father-in-law, Edward Avon, had appeared to Goddard in order to show the son-in-law the grave of a man Avon had murdered and to ask Goddard to repay a debt of 20s. that he had insisted he had paid while alive, but had not. The probity of Goddard is examined and he is found reliable. The details of the story check out. He did see the apparition. But was it really the ghost of his father-in-law? It could have been a demon, because these sometime "impersonate the souls of the deceased." On the other hand, the fact that the body was, after forty years, not where the ghost said it was did not argue against the existence of the ghost. Many soils turn a body to dust in a twentieth of the almost forty years that had elapsed. Or the ghost of Edward Avon could have forgotten. Still, the "rest of the story will still naturally import that it was the very ghost of Edward Avon." But either way, what matters is "that it was a real apparition," evidence of a spirit world and of the dead communicating with the living (1700 ed., 336–342).

30. Thomas Hobbes, *Leviathan* (Cambridge: Cambridge University Press, 1996), 4.45.667–668. There is a whole genre, popular in all European countries, of conversations with the dead. For the English case, see Frederick M. Keener, *English Dialogues of the Dead: A Critical History, an Anthology, and a Check List* (New York: Columbia University Press, 1973). John Brand, *Popular Antiquities* (1849 ed.), 1:x. The first edition appeared in 1777 and is based on Henry Bourne, *Antiquities vulgares: or the Antiquities of the*

Common People (Newcastle, 1725), from which I quote 60 and 60–64 passim. Richard Polwhele (1760–1838), a Cornish clergyman and man of letters quoted in Carl Watkins, *The Undiscovered Country: Journeys among the Dead* (New York: Vintage, 2014), 127. I came upon Watkins's fine book only in the copyediting stages of my own and so have not been able to incorporate into my work his extensive research on ghosts through the ages.

31. Daniel Defoe, *An Essay on the History and Reality of Apparitions: Being an Account of What They Are and What They Are Not . . .* (London, 1727), preface, n.p. There is a well-documented modern edition that sets this text in context, ed. Kit Kincaid (New York: AMS Press, 2007).

32. C. H. Firth, "Defoe's True Relation of the Apparition of Mrs. Veal," *Review of English Studies* 7, no. 25 (January 1931): 1–6. The *Eighteenth Century Short Title Catalogue* suggests that Drelincourt's book did eventually sell well. It lists nineteen editions, one of which declares itself to be the twenty-second. There are at least thirteen freestanding editions of Defoe's short tract.

33. For this, see E. J. Clery, *The Rise of the Supernatural Fiction* (Cambridge: Cambridge University Press, 1995), esp. 13–32. The contemporary literature on this ghost is enormous—she held the popular press's undivided attention for weeks, and no less a writer than Oliver Goldsmith collected and embellished on her clippings. Later nineteenth-century writers connected her to further rappings, knocking, and the like elsewhere by other unquiet spirits. William James, *Essays in Psychical Research* (Cambridge, Mass.: Harvard University Press, 1986), 367.

34. This formulation owes a great deal to Sasha Handley's *Visions of an Unseen World: Ghost Beliefs and Ghost Stories in Eighteenth Century England* (London: Pickering and Chatto, 2007). On the ways in which Newton's views on gravity were used to account for conversion, that is, for how the Holy Spirit worked in the world, see my student David Anixter's forthcoming thesis. I make the extension of his argument explicitly to ghosts. For the burial of suicides at crossroads, see *Cheshire Notes and Queries* 4 (29 March 1884): 43. Until the late eighteenth century, murderers were still being gibbeted at Stockport Moor, causing passersby to avoid the place. At some point, neighbors cut down the pole, buried the bones, and sold the iron to a blacksmith. Suicides were buried at the intersection of Turncroft Lane and the Roman road near Vernon Park.

35. Dr. Johnson uses this quotation from *Spectator* 99 (italics mine) in his dictionary to illustrate the word "cemetery."

36. Milan Kundera, *The Unbearable Lightness of Being*, trans. Michael Henry Heim (New York: Perennial Classics, 2004), 104.

37. Terry Castle, *The Female Thermometer: Eighteenth-Century Culture and the Invention of the Uncanny* (New York: Oxford University Press, 1995), 8. Castle's work provides the context for the next two paragraphs, as does Colin Davis, *Haunted Subjects: Deconstruction, Psychoanalysis and the Return of the Dead* (London: Palgrave MacMillan, 2007), 1–19, although his whole book is about the reappearance of the dead among the living in contemporary popular culture.

38. Freud–Zweig, *Briefwechsel* (1968), S. 22ff., quoted in Claudia Schmölders, "Das ewige Antlitz ein Weimarer Totenkult," in Schmölders and Sander L. Gilman, eds., *Gesichter der Weimarer Republik* (Cologne: Dumont, 2000), 250–251 (my translation). Thomas Laqueur, "Un-mastered Remains: Dead Father in Freud and Me," in Stuart Taylor and Lila Kalinich, eds., *The Dead Father: A Psychoanalytic Inquiry* (London: Routledge, 2007).

39. Schmölders, "Das ewige Antlitz," 254. See Lawrence Hutton, *Death Masks: Portraits in Plaster* (New York: Harper and Row, 1894). Hutton's collection is in the Princeton University Library.

40. Slavoj Žižek, *Looking Awry: An Introduction to Jacques Lacan through Popular Culture* (Cambridge, Mass.: MIT Press, 1991), 22–23. Sigmund Freud, *The Uncanny*, trans. David McClintock (London: Penguin, 2003), 148.

CHAPTER 3: THE CULTURAL WORK OF THE DEAD

Epigraphs: William Empson, "Ignorance of Death," in *The Complete Poems*, ed. John Haffenden (London: Allen Lane, 2000), 78. The poet himself seems attracted to a sort of impersonal immortality. "Who first in Europe," he writes to his friend Christopher Ricks, "ever thought that the soul after death returns like a drop of water to the sea?" The answer, from his reading of Norman Cohn, seems to have been Plotinus, whom Empson vows to try to read again (*Selected Letters of William Empson*, ed. John Haffenden [Oxford: Oxford University Press, 2006], 3 August 1967, 456–457. Georg Christoph Lichtenberg, *Philosophical Writings* (Notebook K83), trans. Steven Tester (Albany, N.Y.: SUNY Press, 2012), 153.

1. Kwang-chih Chang, *Shang Civilization* (New Haven, Conn.: Yale University Press, 1980), esp. 110–124. See also David N. Keightley, for the Neolithic origins of the custom: "At the Beginning: The Status of Women in Neolithic and Shang China," *Nan nü: Men, Women and Gender in Early and Imperial China* 1, no. 1 (1999): 1–62; and his *Working for His Majesty* (Berkeley, Calif.: Institute of East Asian Studies, 2012). On the transition from actual sacrificed bodies to figurines accompanying the dead, see Wu Jung, "Art and Architecture of the Warring States Period," in Michael Loewe and Edward L. Shaughnessy, eds., *The Cambridge History of Ancient China* (Cambridge: Cambridge University Press, 1999), 732–739. Sir Leonard Woolley, *Ur of the Chaldees: A Revised and Updated Edition of Sir Leonard Woolley's "Excavation at Ur"* (Ithaca, N.Y.: Cornell University Press, 1982), 61–64 and 61–103 more generally. Christine El Mady, *Mummies, Myth and Magic* (London: Thames and Hudson, 1989), 158–169. Herodotus, *The History*, 4.71, trans. David Grene (Chicago: University of Chicago Press, 1987), 306.

2. Peter Brown, *The Body and Society: Men, Women and Sexual Renunciation in Early Christianity* (New York: Columbia University Press, 1988), 405. Michel de Montaigne, *The Complete Essays*, trans. M. A. Screech (London: Penguin, 2003), 100, in a section titled "To Philosophize Is to Learn How to Die."

3. Martin Heidegger, *Being and Time*, trans. Joan Stambaugh (Albany: State University of New York Press, 1996), II:1, 237–238, pp. 221–222. Laurence Hutton, *Portraits*

in Plaster: From the Collection of Laurence Hutton (New York: Harper, 1894), xiv. He is quoting the eighteenth-century German father of physiognomy, Johann Kaspar Lavater.

4. Ernst Junger, *The Adventurous Heart*, trans. Thomas Freise, 2nd ed. (Candor, N.Y.: Telos Publishing, 2012), 87 and 84–87 more generally. Junger is most famous as the author of *Storm of Steel*, his youthful memoir glorifying the violence of the Great War.

5. Tertullian, *Testimony of the Soul*, trans. Rudolph Arbesmann, O.S.A., et al. (Washington, D.C.: Catholic University of America Press), 137–138. Heinrich Quistorp, *Calvin's Doctrine of Last Things*, trans. Harold Knight (London: Lutterworth Press, 1955), 136–137. See the excellent account of burial in Calvin's Geneva, with many quotations from his works, in Ursula Rohner-Baumberger von Rebstein, *Begräbniswesen in Calvinistischen Genf* (Basel: Stehlin AG, 1975), 20–27.

6. Grotius, *On the Law of War and Peace*, ed. Stephen C. Neff (Cambridge: Cambridge University Press, 2012), bk. 2, chap. 19, 926–931. It was because the right to burial was so fundamental that its denial as a punishment was so horrible.

7. Angelo S. Rapport, *Myth and Legend of Ancient Israel* (New York: Ktav, 1966), 1:197–198, based on the ninth-century Midrashic text *Pirke de Rabbi Eliezer*, trans. Gerald Friedlander (London: Paul, Trench, Trubner, 1916), chap. 21, which I read online at https://archive.org/details/pirkderabbielioofrieuoft, p. 156; and on a later medieval homiletic compilation, *Yalkut Shimeoni*, Prov. 963, p. 156. Leor Halevi, in *Muhammad's Grave: Death Rites and the Making of Islamic Society* (New York: Columbia University Press, 2007), 165, 206, tells a similar story from the Quran. Hans-Georg Gadamer, *Reason in the Age of Science*, trans. Frederick G. Lawrence (Cambridge, Mass.: MIT Press, 1981), 75.

8. Herodotus, *The Histories*, 3.38, p. 228.

9. Amitav Ghosh, *The Imam and the Indian: Prose Pieces* (New Delhi: Ravi Dahal, 2002), 6–11, and 1–13 more generally.

10. Ibid.

11. I thank Beate Fricke for bringing this illuminated manuscript to my attention. Jacob van Maerlant, *Der naturen bloeme* (The Hague, KB, 76 E4). The Brahmins and the burning of the dead are drawings 18 and 19; the others I mention are 20, 23–24, 28, 33, 40, and 30 in order. For a copy of this manuscript, see Koninklijke Bibliotheek, http://www.kb.nl/en/themes/middle-ages/der-naturen-bloeme-jacob-van-maerlant.

12. *Alberuni's India*, English ed. with notes by Edward C. Sachau (London: Kegan Paul, 1910), 2:167–169, and chap. 73, "On What Is Due to the Bodies of the Dead" more generally. I am grateful to my colleague Abhishek Kaicker for this reference and for discussing it with me.

13. Leon Battista Alberti, *Ten Books of Architecture*, ed. Joseph Rykwert, based on the Venetian architect James (Giacomo) Leoni's (1686–1746) eighteenth-century translation of Alberti's 1452 masterpiece (London: Alec Tiranti, 1955), 163–164. Johann Heinrich Zedler, *Grosses vollsändiges Universallexicon aller Wissenschaften und Künste* (1732–1754), vol. 53, s.v. "Waßer-Begräbnisse."

14. Giambattista Vico, *The New Science*, trans. Thomas Goddard Bergin and Max Harold Fisch (Ithaca, N.Y.: Cornell University Press, 1984), para. 12, p. 8. On this passage, see Robert Pogue Harrison, *The Dominion of the Dead* (Chicago: University of Chicago Press, 2003), xi–xii, 81–82. Harrison's book has been far more important to my thinking than one endnote can suggest. Cicero, *The Laws*, trans. Clinton Walker Keyes (Cambridge, Mass.: Harvard University Press, 1968), 2.22.55, 2.23.58 (pp. 439 and 445). The appropriation of the special dead to create new sorts of public—"communal" is probably a better word—places is, of course, exactly what fourth- and fifth-century Christians did and what the founders of nations did in the nineteenth and twentieth centuries. There is also a huge amount of social historical evidence for the general drift of Vico's argument. Where one sees mounds of earth marking the places of the dead, there one sees not only the work of civilization *tout court* but also the particular work of a particular civilization: burial mounds are evidence of human work and, in Anglo-Saxon Britain the burial mounds of previous owners of land constituted border markers of holdings. Legitimate possession of land was to know its provenance, to know where those who had held it before were buried. Enseng Ho tells an extraordinary story of how the people of the Hadrami (a town in Yemen) marked their collective story of diaspora through the movement of burial places. "Burial" he writes "is the act of combining a place, a person, a text and a name on a gravestone. This simple act carries great creative, communicative potential" (*The Graves of Tarim* [Berkeley: University of California Press, 2006], xxiii, and 3–97 more generally). Claiming land with the dead goes back to the translation of Joseph's bones, if not earlier. On Hegel, see Tony Vidler, *The Architectural Uncanny: Essays in the Modern Unhomely* (Cambridge, Mass.: MIT Press, 1992), 122ff. Much of the book, and especially the chapter "Buried Alive," is on my themes. Hegel's views on tombs follow from his more general account of how humans come into subjectivity through the confrontation with death—"the violence of negativity." On this, see Achille Mbembe, "Necropolitics," trans. Libby Meintjes, *Public Culture* 15, no. 1 (2003): 14, and 11–40 more generally. Miguel de Unamuno, *Tragic Sense of Life*, trans. Anthony Kerrigan (Princeton, N.J.: Princeton University Press, 1972), 46. Of course the tomb, the marker of what Sally Humphries has called "static immortality," is not universal; Melanesian funerary exchanges produce "processual" immortality in its place. Individual tombs are far from everywhere. The Merina grind up the bones of their dead and create a tomb of group unity. See Sally Humphries and Helen King, eds., *Mortality and Immortality: The Anthropology and Archaeology of Death* (London: Academic Press, 1981), 5–6, and the essays in this book more generally. The point I take away is that while there are "Western" patterns, there is also a remarkable coincidence between practices in very different cultures: remembering dead heroes in Greece, India, and Melanesia, for example.

15. Denis Diderot, Jean Le Rond d'Alembert, Pierre Mouchon, *Encyclopédie, ou dictionnaire raisonné des sciences, des arts et des métiers* (Paris: Briasson, 1751–1765), s.v. "sépulture" (*droit naturel*): "Le droit de sépulture est fondé sur la loi de l'humanité, & en quelque façon même sur la justice. Il est de l'humanité de ne pas laisser des cadavres humains pour-

rir, ou livrés en proie aux bêtes." Ephraim Chambers, *A Supplement to Mr. Chambers's Cyclopædia: or, Universal Dictionary of Arts and Sciences* (London, 1753), vol. I, s.v. "burial."

16. Numas Denis Fustel de Coulanges, *The Ancient City: A Study on the Religion, Laws and Institutions of Greece and Rome* (Baltimore: Johns Hopkins University Press, 1980), 10, 13, 14, and 7–17 more generally. The foreword to this edition by Arnaldo Momigliano makes clear the extent to which Fustel de Coulanges was part of a larger conversation about the evolution of culture. He also points to the empirical failures of this book, although none of the points he raises have to do with the specific claims of the dead. Sally Humphries in her foreword argues that Coulanges's major contribution is to point out the centrality of the *gens*, and more generally the role of culture rather than nature, for determining the bounds of kinship. And here the dead, i.e., ancestors, are crucial. On these debates generally, see chap. 2, "The Study of Mortuary Rituals," in Jack Goody, *Death, Property and the Ancestors* (Stanford, Calif.: Stanford University Press, 1962), 13–30.

17. For the latest on Neanderthals, see William Rendu et al., "Evidence Supporting an Intentional Neanderthal Burial at La Chapelle-aux-Saints," *Proceedings of the National Academy of Sciences* 111, no. 1 (December 2013): 81–86. We now know of one certain burial site before the appearance of *Homo sapiens*. For an earlier round in this debate, see Robert H. Gargett, "The Evidence for Neanderthal Burial" (with fourteen replies), *Current Anthropology* 30, no. 2 (April 1989): 157–190. The author thinks all earlier evidence is suspect and that the placement of skeletons can be interpreted as the result of geomorphology. Commentators disagree. Giacomo Giacobini, "Richness and Diversity of Burial Rituals in the Upper Paleolithic," *Diogenes* 54, no. 2 (May 2007): 19, and 19–39 passim, pushed the evidence for human burial back. He uses Italian evidence of graves to date the upper Paleolithic to around 40,000 B.C.E. Paul Mellars, the leading expert in the field, thinks burials do define a moment ca. 40,000 B.C.E. but pushes "modern" humans back to ca. 70,000 B.C.E. and to Africa, based on evidence of tools (review article, "Neanderthals and the Modern Human Colonization of Europe," *Nature* 42 [25 November 2004]: 461–465). On the more general question of when the care of the dead began, see Julien Riel-Salvatore and Geoffrey A. Clark, "Grave Markers: Middle and Early Upper Paleolithic Burials and the Use of Chronotypology in Contemporary Paleolithic Research," with the appended debate, *Current Anthropology* 41, no. 4 (August–October 2001): 449–479. Gargett is one of their harshest critics. Three enormously useful and cautious articles both support the antiquity of burial and warn how hard it is to say anything with precision about the cultural meanings of these burials or cremations: Richard Nathalia, "Did Prehistoric Man Bury His Dead? Early Debates on Paleolithic Burials in National Contexts"; Jacqueline McKinley, "Cremation: Excavation, Analysis, and Interpretation of Material from Cremation-Related Contexts"; and Julien Riel-Salvatore and Claudine Gravel-Miguel, "Upper Paleolithic Mortuary Practices in Eurasia: A Critical Look at the Burial Record," all in Sarah Tarlow and Liv Nilsson Stutz, eds., *The Oxford Handbook of the Archaeology of Death and Burial* (Oxford: Oxford University Press, 2013), 27–47, 147–173, and 303–347. My interest is not to resolve

the question but to point to the centrality of burial evidence in various answers. Whether, in fact, burial rather than cremation was the aboriginal mode of disposing of the human dead was as much debated in the nineteenth century as it had been in the Roman Republic. Cicero thought that burial came first, a sort of natural return to one's mother. Nineteenth-century proponents of cremation argued for the symbolic primacy of fire. But for the history of living with the dead, the answer is irrelevant.

18. Claudius Aelianus, a second-century C.E. pagan, wrote *On the Nature of Animals*, which was widely read by Christians and tells us that the Stoic philosopher Cleanthes "was forced against his will and in spite of his vehement arguments to the contrary, to make a concession to animals and to allow that they too are not destitute of reasoning power. Cleanthes . . . observed how some were conveying a dead ant out of one track to a nest belonging to other ants not of their own kin. And they paused on the edge of the nest with the corpse while the others came up from below and met the strangers seemingly with a view to some consultation; the same Ants then went down to the nest. And this happened several times until finally they brought up a worm, as it were a ransom. And the other party accepted it and surrendered the dead body which they had brought. And the Ants in the nest were glad to receive it, as though they were recovering a son or brother." More than a thousand years later, the seventeenth-century English compiler of animal lore Thomas Mouffat tells his readers that "it is sufficient to prove the cleanliness of ants" that they "carry out their dead in the husks or bladders of trees and corn as of old time the Romans buried their dead in pots." See Aelian, *On the Nature of Animals*, trans. A. F. Scholfield, Loeb Classical Library (Cambridge, Mass.: Harvard University Press, 1958), bk. 6, chap. 50, pp. 69–70. The Renaissance naturalist Ulisse Aldrovani (1522–1605) picks up this story, as does the Swiss naturalist Conrad Gessner, through whom it got to Thomas Mouffat, *The Theater of Insects or Lesser Living Creatures* (London, 1658), bk. 2, 1076. This is the third volume of Edward Topsell's more famous series, *The History of Four-Footed Beasts* and the *History of Serpents*. The ant story was still popular among the followers of Darwin, who wanted to show that behavior that seems to have been uniquely human in fact evolved from lower animals who did the same thing. For a critical review of nineteenth-century views on ants, see Margaret Floy Washburn, *The Animal Mind* (New York: Macmillan, 1917), 8–9. For modern evidence against the ritual behavior of ants and other social insects with respect to their dead or even their use of systematic burial—eating them and tossing them out are also practiced—see Thomas Chovenc et al., "Burial Behavior by Dealates of the Termite Species *Pseudacanthotermes spineger* Induced by Chemical Signals from Termite Corpses," *Insectes Sociaux* 59 (2012): 119–125; and M. Renucci et al., "Complex Undertaking Behavior in *Temnothorax lichtensteini* Ant Colonies: From Corpse-Burying Behavior to Necrophoric Behavior," *Insectes Sociaux* (August 2010), doi: 10.1007/s00040-010-0109-y. See also I. Douglas-Hamilton, S. Bhalla, G. Wittemyer, and F. Vollrath, "Behavioural Reactions of Elephants towards a Dying and Deceased Matriarch," *Applied Animal Behaviour Science* 100 (2006): 87–102. George Wittemyer

writes in a private correspondence that there is very little literature on the subject because there is so little evidence that animals care for their dead. Karen McComb et al. are considerably more critical in "African Elephants Show High Levels of Interest in the Skulls and Ivory of Their Own Species," *Biology Letters* 2 (2006): 26–28. I am grateful to the immensely learned Steve Glickman of the Department of Psychology, UC Berkeley, for his guidance on this matter, on hyenas, and on everything I know about animals. Chambers's *Encyclopedia* (1753 ed.), s.v. "burial" can represent the long tradition that these articles question. He first quotes Pliny on the uniqueness of humans in caring for their dead and then goes on: "Yet it is said, we find something like it in some species of brutes. Naturalists assure us, that elephants, passing by the corpse of others, gather grass, and break branches of trees with their trunks, where-with they cover the dead." Pliny, *Natural History*, trans. H. Rackham (Cambridge, Mass.: Harvard University Press, 1952), 2:509. Junger, *Adventurous Heart*, 87.

19. Pliny, *Natural History*, 9:267, 271.

20. William Wordsworth, "Essay on Epitaphs, I," in W.J.B. Owen and Jane Worthington Smyser, eds.; *The Prose Works of William Wordsworth* (Oxford: Oxford University Press, 1974), 2:49–53. The eighteenth-century antiquarian Richard Gough was the first the translate Camden's *Britannia* into English (1789) and continued in the tradition of mapping tombs as a way of mapping the history of a nation and a community. See his *Sepulchral Monuments of Great Britain, Applied to Illustrate the History of Families, Manners, Habits and Arts at the Different Periods from the Norman Conquest to the Seventeenth Century* (London: J. Nichols, 1786, 1796, 1799).

21. Peter Brown, *The Cult of the Saints: Its Rise and Function in Latin Christianity* (Chicago: University of Chicago Press, 1981), 24. Julian the Apostate, *Against the Galileans*, trans. Wilmer Cave Wright, in *The Works of the Emperor Julian* (Cambridge, Mass.: Harvard University Press, 1962–1969), 3:415.

22. Cicero, *Laws*, 2.58. Paulus, *Sententiae* (*Opinions*), 1.21.2, in Valerie Hope, *Death in Ancient Rome: A Sourcebook* (London: Routledge, 2007), 129–130.

23. R. Hugh Connolly, ed., *Didascalia apostolorum* (Oxford: Clarendon Press, 1929), 252. Jill Harris, "Death and the Dead in the Roman West," in Steve Bassett, ed., *Death in Towns: Urban Responses to the Dying and the Dead, 100–1600* (Leicester: Leicester University Press, 1992), 60–61, and 56–67 more generally. Donald Bullough, "Burial, Community and Belief in the Early Medieval West," in Patrick Wormald, ed., *Ideal and Reality in Frankish and Anglo-Saxon Society: Studies Presented to J. M. Wallace-Hadrill* (Oxford: Basil Blackwell, 1983), 179, and 175–201 more generally. On Christian and pagan burials together, see the evidence from legal, ecclesiastical, and archeological sources in Mark J. Johnson, "Pagan-Christian Burial Practices of the Fourth Century: Shared Tombs," *Journal of Early Christian Studies* 5, no. 1 (1997): 37–59.

24. For this example, see Eric A. Ivison, "Burial and Urbanism at Late Antique and Early Byzantine Corinth (ca. A.D. 400–700)," in N. T. Christie and S. T. Loseby, eds., *Towns in Transition: Urban Evolution in Late Antiquity and the Early Middle Ages* (Aldershot: Scholar Press, 1996), 97–125. On the creation of open-air churches around tombs and the segregation of Christian and pagan dead, see François Decret, *Early Christi-*

anity in North Africa, trans. Edward W. Smither (Eugene, Ore.: Cascade Books, 2009), 17–19.

25. Birthe Kjølbye-Biddle, "Dispersal or Concentration: The Disposal of the Winchester Dead over 2000 Years," in Bassett, *Death in Towns*, 221ff., and 210–247 more generally. Warwick Rodwell, *The Archaeology of Religious Places* (Philadelphia: University of Pennsylvania Press, 1989), 157ff.

26. Luce Pietri, "Les sepulchres privilégiées en Gaule d'après les sources literraires," in Y. Duval and J.-Ch. Picard, eds., *L'inhumation privilégiée du IVᵉ au VIIIᵉ siècle en Occident* (Paris: De Boccard, 1986), 133–142.

27. The quote is from Polymnia Athanassiadi, *La lutte pour l'orthodoxie dans le platonisme tardif: De Numénius à Damascius* (Paris: Les Belles Lettres, 2006), 224. Frederick Paxton in his hugely informative book writes, for example, about the ways that monasteries become the loci of noble family tombs and how Gertrude (d. 659), the daughter of Pippin I, asked to be buried in a simple shroud. This show of modesty apparently helped to ease out the elaborate dressing of bodies and the issue of grave goods in Frankish tombs (*Christianizing Death: The Creation of Ritual Process in Early Medieval Europe* [Ithaca, N.Y.: Cornell University Press, 1990], 63–64).

28. I have these stories from Bonnie Effros, "Beyond Cemetery Walls: Early Christian Funerary Topography and Christian Salvation," in *Early Medieval Europe* 6, no. 1 (1997): 2–3, 14–15, 19, and 1–23 more generally for regional variations on the theme.

29. Peter Sherlock, *Monuments and Memory in Early Modern England* (Aldershot: Ashgate, 2008), 119. James Pilkington, *Works of James Pilkington* (Cambridge: Cambridge University Press, 1842), 317. The Luther quote is from Craig Koslofsky, *The Reformation of the Dead: Death and Ritual in Early Modern Germany, 1450–1700* (London: Macmillan, 2000), 46.

30. Max Weber, *The Protestant Ethic and the Spirit of Capitalism*, trans. Talcott Parsons (New York: Scribner's, 1958), 496. Jonathan Sheehan, "Temple and Tabernacle: The Place of Religion in Early Modern England," in Pamela H. Smith and Benjamin Schmidt, eds., *Making Knowledge in Early Modern Europe* (Chicago: University of Chicago Press, 2007).

31. Henry Martyn Dexter, *The Congregationalism of the Last Three Hundred as Seen in Its Literature* (New York: Harper and Brothers, 1880), 321, 391–392.

32. Koslofsky, in *The Reformation of the Dead*, argues for the shift to extramural burial as a very public representation of the Reformation's rejection of intercessory masses and the role of the clergy, saint, and so on in the drama of salvation. Clearly this was part of the story, but in fact most towns kept their churchyards or had already moved to new extramural ones because old intramural ones had become crowded before there was any talk about the end of purgatory. Politics of all sorts played a part in the allocation of the sacred in various cities. Thus in Augsburg, the city fathers after the Thirty Years' War insisted on continuing burial because sacred space had strategic worth in interconfessional conflict. See for this case, J. Duane Corpis, "Space and Urban Religious Life in Augsburg, 1648–1750," in Will Coster and Andrew Apicer, eds., *Sacred Space in Early Modern Europe* (Cambridge: Cambridge University Press,

2005), 322, and 302–325 more generally. I am grateful to Hannah Murphy for the material on Nuremberg. For the French case, see Keith Luria, "Separated by Death? Burials, Cemeteries, and Confessional Boundaries in Seventeenth-Century France," *French Historical Studies* 24, no. 2 (Spring 2001): 185–222. For the Reformation and burial in the German lands, see David M. Luebke, "Confessions of the Dead: Interpreting Burial Practice in the Late Reformation," *Archive for Reformation History* 101 (2010): 55–79.

33. The argument that classical ideals of honor and virtue spurred the growth of monuments is Keith Thomas's in *The Ends of Life: Roads to Fulfillment in Early Modern England* (Oxford: Oxford University Press, 2009), 247. The argument is made in a more local context by Lorraine C. Attreed, "Preparation for Death in Sixteenth Century Northern England," *Sixteenth Century Journal* 13, no. 3 (1982): 64 and passim. Nigel Llewellyn, *Funeral Monuments in Post-Reformation England* (Cambridge: Cambridge University Press, 2000), 10, on numbers, and 257, on the many different Protestant views about monuments and idolatry; to see how the trajectory of monument building follows that of other construction, compare fig. 5a with the data in W. G. Hoskins, "The Rebuilding of Rural England, 1570–1640," *Past and Present* 4 (1953): 44–59. Regarding wills and the role of the Black Death, see Christopher Daniel, *Death and Burial in Medieval England 1006–1550* (New York: Routledge, 1997); Samuel Cohn, *The Cult of Remembrance and the Black Death* (Baltimore: Johns Hopkins University Press, 1992); and Andrew Martindale, "Patrons and Minder: The Intrusion of the Secular into Sacred Spaces in the Late Middle Ages," in Diana Wood, ed., *The Church and the Arts* (Oxford: For the Ecclesiastical History Society by Blackwell, 1992), 143–178, and esp. 149ff.

34. Sherlock, *Monuments and Memory in Early Modern England*, 50. Arthur Gardner, *Alabaster Tombs of the Pre-Reformation Period in England* (Cambridge: Cambridge University Press, 1940), 81–83.

35. Edward Coke, *Institutes of the Laws of England*, 6th ed. (London, 1681), 3:202–203. Coke is at pains to note that whatever authority the Church has over bodies, the safety of memorials is protected by common law.

36. *A Proclamation against Breaking or Defacing of Monumentes of Antiquitie, Being Set Up in Churches or Other Publique Places for Memory, and Not for Superstition* (London: Richarde Iugge and Iohn Cawood, Printers to the Quenes Maiestie, [1560]), accessed on ESTC.

37. Estella Weiss-Krejci, "Excarnation, Evisceration, and Exhumation in Medieval and Post-Medieval Europe," in Gordon F. M. Rakita et al., *Interacting with the Dead: Perspective on Mortuary Archaeology for the New Millennium* (Gainesville: University Press of Florida, 2005), 155–172.

38. The students in the Chinese Cultural Revolution who destroyed the Ming tombs and scattered the remains of their inhabitants probably knew nothing about the French revolutionaries who in 1793 attacked the royal tombs at St. Denis, collected a few souvenir bones, and threw the rest in a pit. "Let all the coffins of these divinized monsters be broken open!" wrote the journalist and politician Pierre Henri Lebrun. "Let their memories be condemned!" The sansculottes who broke into the

Sorbonne and cut off the head of Cardinal Richelieu in 1793 were mimicking the guillotine. (The head, along with a bit of linen, first went to the leader of the local section, a hosier named Cheval, and after 1805 went the rounds until Napoleon III united it with the body.) Lebrun is quoted in E.A.R. Brown, "Burying and Unburying the Kings of France," in R. C. Trexler, ed., *Persons in Groups* (Binghamton, N.Y.: Medieval and Renaissance Texts and Studies, 1985), 282. A. Rébellon, "La tête de Richelieu en Bretagne," *Annales de Breatagne* 69, no. 3 (1962): 295–304. Alexandre Lenoir, the founder of the museum of French antiquities, was wounded by a bayonet as he was defending not Richelieu's body but his monument, the work of the great seventeenth-century sculptor François Girardon. Mark Edward Lewis, *Sanctioned Violence in Early China* (Albany: State University of New York Press, 1990), 26.

39.   The story is in John Foxe's hugely influential *Actes and Monuments of These Latter and Perillous Dayes, Touching Matters of the Church*, which quickly came to be known as Foxe's *Book of Martyrs* (London, 1563), 1639–1640. The reburial in a saint's grave was either, depending on one's views, an anti-Catholic gesture or insurance against the remains being disturbed again should winds of religion change once more. The story was repeated in future editions. I have used the 1563 variorum edition provided online by the University of Sheffield: John Foxe, *The Unabridged Acts and Monuments Online* or *TAMO* (Sheffield: HRI Online Publications, 2011), http://www.johnfoxe .org, accessed November 3, 2014, which has an excellent introduction to the sources for Foxe's accounts. For the chronology, see Sherlock, *Monuments and Memory in Early Modern Britain*, 169–170. The *Dictionary of National Biography* and the 11th ed. of the *Encyclopaedia Britannica* differ on years but not on the general story line. James Calfhill tells the story and justifies his counterexhumation and reburial in his short tract *De Katherinae nuper vxoris doctissimi viri D. Petri Martyris vermilij Florentini, regij theologiae apud Oxonienses tempore Edwardi sexti professoris, Cardinalis Poli mandato, regnante Maria, effossae exhumatione, ac eiusdem ad honestam sepulturam sub Elisabetha* (London, 1561), from which Foxe took his information. The preacher James Pilkington is quoted in Peter Marshall, *Beliefs and the Dead in Reformation England* (Oxford: Oxford University Press, 2002), 123, and more generally 122–123, on the polemics of exhumation.

40.   Foxe, 1537ff. This story has an international circulation. Foxe more or less reprinted an English version by Arthur Golding (a famous Elizabethan translator)—*A Brief Treatise concerning the Burnygne of Bucer and Phagius* (London, 1562), of a Latin work by Bucer's secretary, Conrad Hubert, *Historia vera de vita, obitu, sepultra condemnatione D. Martin Buver . . .* (Strasbourg, 1562). There was also a German translation. The Tooley story is no. 285 in Foxe.

41.   On Colchester generally, see John Walker, *Understanding Popular Violence in the English Revolution* (Cambridge: Cambridge University Press, 1999), 11–68, 336–337, and passim. The spot where General Sir Charles Lucas was executed became a local pilgrimage site marked by the failure of grass to grow there. Concerning the tombs of the family of Margaret Lady Cavendish in Colchester, see Historical Manuscripts Commission, 12 Rep. pt. 9, 1891, 27–28, quoted in Katie Whitaker, *Mad Madge: The Extraordinary Life of Margaret Cavendish* (New York: Basic Books, 2002), 105. Margaret learned from the fate

of her mother and sister that "it was but folly" to plan costly tombs "since not only time but wars will ruin them," 106. This account on Montrose is based on the *Dictionary of National Biography* entry for James Graham. The warrant is in the Parliamentary Register, Edinburgh, 4 January 1661. The body of Sir William Hay of Delgetie, Montrose's adjutant, also executed in 1650, was ordered to be exhumed and reburied. The quotation is from the *Dictionary of National Biography*, citing Robert Baillie, *Letters and Journals* (Edinburgh: Robert Ogle, 1842), 3:466. The account of the execution is from *A Relation of the Execution of James Graham Late Marquesse of Montrosse* (London: E. Griffin, 1650), no pagination. The most through modern examination of the embalming of Montrose's heart suggests that it was re-embalmed just before the funeral and that its casket of precious metals became a family heirloom. This is according to James Cameron Robbie, "The Embalming of Montrose's Heart," in *The Book of the Edinburgh Club* (Edinburgh: T. and A. Constable, 1908), 1, 31–47. There is another tradition: Montrose's heart, unlike Robert the Bruce's, did not actually make its way back. It went off to India where it was stolen by a local prince before it was brought back to Europe and lost in 1792 during the French Revolution, when the government requisitioned the silver urn in which it was kept. This shaggy heart story is well told by Sir Alexander Johnson, "The Heart of Montrose," in Mark Napier, *Montrose and the Covenanters* (London: James Duncan, 1838), 559–565, as well as 176 and 553–554. His ancestor had had the heart in Flanders.

42. There are all manner of stories alleging that Cromwell had shuffled around the bodies of dead kings, so that the head that was supposedly his might be royal. Samuel Pepys tells this unfounded story, as well as a canonical version of the execution of the dead regicides. I rely on Jonathan Fitzgibbon, *Cromwell's Head* (Kew: National Archives, 2008), for the general narrative. Fear of retribution against the dead may have affected the burial of the martyred Charles I. The doctor who was present at the opening of his coffin in 1808 claims that Edward Hyde, Earl of Clarendon, the first great historian of the English revolution and a major figure in the Restoration government of Charles II, was vague as to where the executed king's body was buried, because he was worried that, should there be another reversal of political fortunes, the same fate as befell the corpses of the regicides might befall Charles's. Henry Halford, "An Account of What Appeared on Opening the Coffin of King Charles the First . . . April 1, 1808," appendix to *Essays and Orations* (London: John Murray, 1831), 159–130. Clarendon is not exactly vague. He says that in order to stop fanciful speculation as to why Charles II did not immediately, as he is said to have planned, remove his father from his obscure burial place in Windsor Chapel and rebury him in Westminster Abbey, he would tell the full story of Charles I's original burial and of the failed attempt to locate the body in 1660. According to Clarendon, none of the still-living lords who attended the body nor their servants could reliably say where it had been placed; one effort to dig where some thought it might be was unsuccessful. Halford points out that in fact the body was exactly where it was said to be in a written account left by one of the servants present for the occasion. Edward Hyde Clarendon, *The History of the Rebellion and Civil Wars in England, Begun in the Year 1641. . . . Written by . . . Edward Earl of Clarendon, . . .* (Oxford, 1702), 1:200–201. On the crowds

at the execution of the regicides, see Tim Harris, *London Crowds in the Reign of Charles II* (Cambridge: Cambridge University press, 1987), 39. Nine living regicides were hanged, then drawn and quartered in 1660, beginning with the particularly gruesome and brave death of Thomas Harrison on 13 October 1660. He was said to have boxed the ears of the executioner, as he was being quartered and was still alive when he was disemboweled. There were great cheers when his head and heart were held up after his martyrdom was finished.

43. Whitelands Archive (no author named), "A Journey to the North Cape," *Whitelands Annual* 9 (1888): 10, cited in Christopher Bischof, "Making Good: British Elementary Teachers and the Social Landscape, 1846–1902" (Ph.D. diss., Rutgers University, 2014), 226. I am grateful to him for this reference.

PART II: PLACES OF THE DEAD

Epigraphs: Archie Phinney, *Nez Perce Texts* (New York: Columbia University Press, 1934; reprint, New York: Arno Press, 1969), 285, 282, and 278–285 more generally for both versions of the story. (I thank Prof. Beth Piatote, Native American Studies, University of California, Berkeley, for this reference and for discussing it with me. Nez Perce funeral ritual today recreates the journey to the shadowlands, where the living then have to leave the dead.) England Howlett, "Burial Customs," in William Andrews, ed., *Curious Church Customs* (London: Simpkin, Marshall, 1895), 136.

1. My interests in the experiences and politics of space have been influenced by Yi-Fu Tuan, *Space and Place: The Perspective of Experience* (Minneapolis: University of Minnesota Press, 1977), esp. 8–85. See also, on the specific Welsh belief, Stephen Wickes, *Sepulture: Its History, Methods and Sanitary Requisites* (Philadelphia: Blakiston, 1884), 138.

CHAPTER 4: THE CHURCHYARD AND THE OLD REGIME

Epigraph: Thomas Gray, edited by H. W. Starr and J. R. Hendrickson, *The Complete Poems of Thomas Gray* (Oxford: Clarendon Press, 1966), 37. Subsequent quotations from this poem are from this edition.

1. The most learned synoptic account is John Blair, *The Church in Anglo-Saxon Society* (Oxford: Oxford University Press, 2005), "The Birth and Growth of Local Churches," 368ff. and 236. See also Helen Hamerow, *Early Medieval Settlements: The Archaeology of Rural Communities in Northwest Europe, 400–900* (Oxford: Oxford University Press 2002), 122–123.

2. William Jones, *The Diary of the Rev. William Jones, 1777–1821, Curate and Vicar of Broxbourne and the Hamlet of Hoddesdon, 1781–1821*, ed. O. F. Christie (London: Brentano, 1929), 267, 155–156.

3. The line is from Robert Blair's (1699–1746) celebrated poem "The Grave." See Robert Blair, *The Grave: A Poem* (1743; reprint, Los Angeles: University of California Press, 1973), 5.

4. Richard Burn, *Ecclesiastical Law* (London: H. Woodfall and W. Strahan, 1767), 1:234–236. Venerable Bede, *Ecclesiastical History of the English People* (Oxford: Oxford University Press, 1994), 178.

5. I base this on the excellent summary in Helen Foxhall Forbes, *Heaven and Earth in Anglo-Saxon England: Theology and Society in the Age of Faith* (Farnham, U.K.: Ashgate, 2013), esp. 273–278.

6. "Diary of John Thomlinson" (curate of Rothbury, Northumberland, in the early eighteenth century), in *Six North Country Diaries*, Publications of the Surtees Society, 118 (Durham, U.K.: Surtees Society, 1910), 87–88. *The Diary of John Evelyn*, ed. Ernest Rhys (London: Everyman's Library, 1907), 2:177. Jonathan Banks, *The Life of the Right Reverend Father in God, Edw. Rainbow, D.D. Late Lord Bishop of Carlisle to Which Is Added, a Sermon Preached at His Funeral by Thomas Tully, His Lordship's Chaplain, and Chancellor of the Said Diocese of Carlisle; at Dalston, April the 1st. 1684* (London: Printed by Samuel Roycroft, for Robert Clavell, 1688), 8.

7. On Hawksmoor and the architecture of vaults, see Pierre de la Ruffinière du Prey, *Hawksmoor's London Churches: Architecture and Theology* (Chicago: University of Chicago Press, 2000), 54–55, 64–67; Margaret Cox, "Eschatology, Burial Practices and Continuity: A Retrospective from Christ Church, Spitalfields," in Margaret Cox, ed., *Grave Concerns*, CBA Research Report 113 (York: Council for British Archaeology, 1998), 112; and, for a fuller account, Cox's *Life and Death in Spitalfields, 1700–1850* (York: Council for British Archaeology, 1996). On vaults generally and Spitalfields's in particular, see Max Adams and Jez Reeve's remarkable report "Excavations at Christ Church, Spitalfields, 1984–86," *Antiquity* 61 (1987): 247–256. On St. Andrew Holborn, see *Post Medieval Archaeology* (2002): 193, and (2003): 242. I am grateful to Rev. Christopher Moody, vicar of St. Aphege's, for the information on his church (e-mail correspondence, 24 September 2014).

8. Eric Boore, "Burial Vaults and Coffin Furniture in the West Country," in Margaret Cox, ed., *Grave Concerns: Death and Burial in England, 1700 to 1850* (York: Council for British Archaeology, 1998), 67–84. Joseph Ashton, *A Picture of Manchester* (Manchester, 1816), 83–84.

9. Ben Ferry, *Recollections of A. N. Welby Pugin, and His Father, Augustus Pugin* (London: E. Stanford, 1861), 49.

10. Hans Kurath, *Middle English Dictionary* (Ann Arbor: University of Michigan Press, 1959), s.v. "chirche-yerde." Kurath lists as its source the Anglo-Saxon *Peterborough Chronicle* for the year 1137; the primary meaning, he writes, is "the sacred space surrounding a church," from which follows its secondary meaning as a burial ground. [Jacob Giles], *The Complete Parish Officer*, 11th ed. (London: Henry Lintot, 1747), 119. The other defining feature was that the sacraments were administered there.

11. John Stow, *A Survey of London* (1603; reprint, Oxford: Clarendon Press, 1971), 2, 81–82, 124. Ian Grainger, Duncan Hawkins, Lynne Cowal, and Richard Mikulski, *The Black Death Cemetery, East Smithfield, London*, MoLAS Monograph 43 (London: Museum of London, 2008), 10, 28, 32.

12. Penelope Hunting et al., *Broadgate and Liverpool Street Station* (London: Rosehaugh Stanhope Developments, ca. 1991), 33–34 and 11–37 more generally. See also Vanessa Harding, "'And One More May Be Laid There': The Location of Burials in Early Modern London," *London Journal* 14 (1989), and, more generally, her definitive *The Dead and the Living in Paris and London, 1500–1670* (Cambridge: Cambridge University Press, 2002).

13. Thomas Allen, *The History and Antiquities of London* (London: Cowie and Strange), 4:417. N. Bailey, *Dictionarium Britannicum: or A More Compleat Universal Etymological English Dictionary* (London: T. Cox, 1730). Richard Rawlinson, *The Inscriptions upon the Tombs, Grave Stones, &c. in the Dissenters Burial Place near Bunhill Fields* (London: E. Curll, 1717), 1. I have been unable to find out what exactly a *Keber* is, but Afsaneh Najmabadi, the Iranian historian and gender theorist now at Harvard, tells me it is probably a version of *gabr* or *guebre*, which in Persian today is a derogatory way of referring to Zoroastrians. Francis Joseph Steingass's nineteenth-century *A Comprehensive Persian–English Dictionary*, to which she kindly referred me, gives: "An ancient Persian, one of the Magi of the sect of Zoroaster, a priest of the worshippers of fire; a pagan, infidel." Bailey's little tidbit has a long life, oft repeated, but in the late-nineteenth-century versions of his dictionary the word "churchyard" is gone—it no longer meant, in general, a place of burial—and the corpses are simply set against a wall. Nathan Bailey, *An Universal Etymological Dictionary . . . Revised* (London: E. Bell, 1730).

14. For the dates of the first uses of the word "cemetery," see the *Oxford English Dictionary*; for the uses in context, see William Caxton, *The Lyf of the Noble and Crysten Prynce Charles the Grete*, ed. Sidney J. H. Herrtage (London: Early English Text Society, 1880), 243; and in relation to catacombs, see Joseph Rawson Lumly, *Polychronicon Ranulphi Higden . . . together with the Translation of J. Trevisa . . .* (London: Longman, 1874), 5:64–65. Higden (ca. 1280–1364) was one of the most popular of late medieval chroniclers. John of Travisa (1342–1402) was also involved with Wyclif's Bible translation. Caxton first printed his translation of Higden in 1482.

15. For the first definition of "cemetery," see Thomas Blunt, *Glossographia, or, a Dictionary, Interpreting the Hard Words of Whatsoever Language . . .* (London: Printed by Tho. Newcomb, 1656), s.v. "cemetery." Edward Phillips, *The New World of Words, or a Universal Dictionary*, 5th ed. (London: R. Bentley, 1696), likewise gives for "coemeterie" the synonym "churchyard." John Kersey's *The New World of English Words* (London, 1708) does not define "Church-yard" but gives a definition for its tricky West Country form, "church-litten" = "Church-yard." Tertullian is cited as the first to use *cimeterium* in Lewis and Short. For the etymology, see Éric Rebillard, *The Care of the Dead in Late Antiquity*, trans. Elizabeth Rawlings (Ithaca, N.Y.: Cornell University Press, 2009), 3–7 and 113 for *coemeterium* as an actual sleeping place. The whole book is essentially about how the martyr's tomb became only slowly, in the course of the fifth and sixth centuries, a place for communal Christian burial and for how the Church and not the family became responsible for the dead, that is, the story of the rise of the Christian *coemeterium*, aka churchyard. For a full and learned discussion of the etymology, see Rebillard's "KOIMHTHRION ET COEMETERIUM: Tombe, tomb sainte, nécropo-

le," in *Mélanges de l'École Française de Rome. Antiquité* 105, no. 2 (1993): 975–1001. On divisions in the churchyard based on German material, see Reiner Sörries, "Kirchhof oder Coemeterium? Anmerkungen zum littelalterlichen Friedhof, zu den Sonderfriedhöfen und der Auslagwerung vor die Stadt," in Norbert Fischer and Markwart Herzog, eds., *Nekropolis: Der Friedhof als Ort der Toten und Lebenden* (Stuttgart: W. Kohlhammer, 2005), 23–35, esp. 24–32. Joseph Bingham, *The Antiquities of the Christian Church* (1708–1722; reprint, London: H. G. Bohn, 1846), 1230.

16. This is based on the excellent treatment in Michel Lauwers, *Naissance du cimeterière: Lieux sacrés et terre des morts dans l'Occident medieval* (Paris: Aubier, 2005), 120, and 117–125 more generally. The whole book speaks to this subject.

17. For the full text of what, according to the *Oxford English Dictionary*, is the first modern use of the word "cemetery," see John Ward, "An Attempt to Explain an Antient Roman Inscription, Cut upon a Stone Lately Found at Bath . . . ," *Philosophical Transactions* 48 (1754): 337. Dr. Johnson in his *Dictionary of the English Language* (London: W. Strahan, 1755). Thomas Sheridan's *A General Dictionary of the English Language* (London, 1780), follows Johnson. Earlier uses of "cemetery" as a burial place are explicitly references to antiquity or to exotic places. When a modern cemetery like Forest Lawn in Los Angeles appropriates the church of St. Giles in Stokes Poges, where Gray purportedly wrote his elegy, it is in the spirit of bricollage—a quotation of a tradition, not an adoption.

18. To a lesser degree, this might have been said about monastic burial grounds, which in England, more than elsewhere, took in bodies of those for whom the monks prayed. But after the suppression of the monasteries by Henry VIII, burial there and by chantry chapels stopped, and churchyards held a virtual monopoly on spaces for the dead. The transition still had implications for burial fees three centuries later, about which more below.

19. Howard Williams, "Mortuary Practices in Early Anglo-Saxon England," in Helena Hamerow, David A. Hinton, and Sally Crawford, eds., *The Oxford Handbook of Anglo-Saxon Archaeology* (Oxford: Oxford University Press, 2011), 255, and 238–265 more generally. Sarah Semple, "Sacred Spaces and Places in Pre-Christian and Conversion Period Anglo-Saxon England," in Hamerow et al., *Oxford Handbook of Anglo-Saxon Archaeology*, 751, and 742–763 more generally.

20. D. M. Hadley, "Late Saxon Burial Practice," in Hamerow et al., *Oxford Handbook of Anglo-Saxon Archaeology*, 289, and 288–311 more generally. Howard Colvin, *Architecture and the Afterlife* (New Haven, Conn.: Yale University Press, 1991), 355–357, and more generally 327–363. Rodwell Warwick, *The Archaeology of Religious Places* (Philadelphia: University of Pennsylvania Press, 1989), 152–156. Richard Morris, *Churches in the Landscape* (London: J. M. Dent, 1989), 152–155, 210–213, and passim. Warwick cautions that much more work needs to be done on the locations of churches, but the general point holds. Nicholas Penny, *Church Monuments in Romantic England* (New Haven, Conn.: Yale University Press, 1977), 2.

21. Rev. J. C. Atkinson, *Forty Years in a Moorland Parish: Reminiscences and Researches in Danby in Cleveland* (London: Macmillan, 1923), 219. He had this story from others; the incident

occurred before he arrived. The context is an account of popular belief in spirits. The woman in question seemed to have had the power to foretell the timing of an individual's death. Because she had predicted her own accurately, her threat was taken seriously.

22. Edward B. Tylor, *Primitive Cultures* (London: Murray, 1871, 1920), 2:48.

23. See Walter Johnson, *Byways of British Archaeology* (Cambridge: Cambridge University Press, 1912), "The Folklore of the Cardinal Directions," 324–359. See also the study of 181 central and southern English churches by Peter G. Hoare and Caroline S. Sweet, "The Orientation of Early Medieval Churches in England," *Journal of Historical Geography* 26, no. 2 (2000): 162–173. Italy offers the only real exceptions in western Europe.

24. Du Prey, *Hawksmoor*, 63n.44 and 110.

25. See John Blair, *Church in Anglo-Saxon Society* (Oxford: Oxford University Press, 2005), 235–236. The story of Hearne is told in John Brand, *Observations on Popular Antiquities, Arranged, Revised and Greatly Expanded by Sir Henry Ellis, Principle Librarian of the British Museum* (London: Charles Knight, 1842), 2:181. Hearne was a nonjuror and a Jacobite who lost his Oxford fellowship because he refused to take an oath to George I.

26. I got the Dr. Johnson quote from John Brand's much-reprinted *Observations on Popular Antiquities* (Newcastle on Tyne, 1777), 53; it was originally published in Samuel Johnson, *Notes on Shakespeare* (Los Angeles: Augustan Reprint Society, 1957), 3:176. For the question of grave declination more generally, see P. A. Rahtz, "Grave Orientation," *Archaeological Journal* 135 (1978): 1–14; and Rahtz, "The Archaeology of the Churchyard," in P. V. Addyman and R. K. Morris, eds., *The Archaeological Study of Churches* (London: Council for British Archaeology, 1976).

27. Thomas Browne, *Religio Medici and Urne-Buriall*, ed. Stephen Greenblatt and Ramie Targoff (New York: New York Review of Books, 2012), 126.

28. See Brian Connell, Amy Gray Jones, Rebecca Redfern, and Don Walker, *A Bioarchaeological Study of Medieval Burials on the Site of St Mary Spital: Excavations at Spitalfields Market, London E1, 1991–2007* (London: Museum of London, 2012); Jan Willis, "Archaeological Review No. 27," *Transactions of the Bristol and Gloucestershire Archaeological Society* 121 (2003): 267–289; and Andrew Saunders et al., "The Structural Sequence," in Saunders, ed. *Excavations at Launceston Castle, Cornwall,* Society for Medieval Archaeology Monograph 24 (Leeds: Maney Publishing, 2006), 161–165. The bodies did not lie in ordered groups, so the pattern of declination seemed disordered. R. E. Freeman, "Post-Medieval Burials near Dartmouth Castle," *Devon Archaeological Society* 43 (1985): 131–134.

29. Grainger et al., *Black Death Cemetery*, 12–22. D. Hawkins, "The Black Death and the New London Cemeteries of 1348," *Antiquity* 64 (September 1990): 637–642. For comparison with Towton, see Roberta Gilchrist, "Dust to Dust: Revealing the Reformation Dead," in David Gamster and Roberta Gilchrist, eds., *The Archaeology of the Reformation, 1480–1580* (Leeds: Maney, 2003), 406.

30. Tim Allen, "Abingdon," in *Current Archaeology* 11, no. 1 (September/October 1990): 24–27. Roman burials were in fact not consistently aligned in any particular direc-

tion. Some are random—in Essonne, France, for example: Pascal Murail and Louis Girard, "Biology and Burial Practices from the End of the 1st Century A.D. to the Beginning of the 5th Century A.D.: The Rural Cemetery of Chantambre," in John Pierce et al., eds., *Burial, Society and Context in the Roman World* (Oxford: Oxbow Books, 2000), 105–106; or in Cirencester: Ian Morris, *Death Ritual and Social Structure in Classical Antiquity* (Cambridge: Cambridge University Press, 1992), 83–85. Others followed the contours of the land or of nearby roads, the pattern that nineteenth-century neoclassical cemeteries adopted. See, for example, Giles Clarke, "The Roman Cemetery at Lankhills," in *Winchester Studies*, pt. 2, *Pre Roman and Roman Winchester* (Oxford: Oxford University Press, 1979), 131–132 and foldout. The phrase I cite replaces the word "churchyard" in the relevant section of *A Directory for the Publique Worship of God throughout the Three Kingdoms . . . Ordered Printed 13 March 1644* (London, 1645), 35.

31. Brand, *Observations on Popular Antiquities* (1842 Ellis ed.), 181–182. Johnson, *Byways in British Archaeology*, 245.

32. "Mar-phoreus" [Thomas Nashe], *Martins Months Minde, That Is, a Certaine Report, and True Description of the Death, and Funeralls, of Olde Martin Marreprelate, the Great Makebate of England, and Father of the Factious. Contayning the cause of His Death, the Manner of His Burial . . .* (London: Thomas Orwin, 1589), n.p. The anonymously produced Marprelate tracts, so called after their pseudonymous author Martin Marprelate, were the most important radical Protestant attack on the Elizabethan settlement. The title refers to a commemoration service called "month's mind" traditionally held four weeks after a death. This pamphlet is the most famous of a whole genre of anti-Marprelate literature.

33. There are no systematic studies of New England cemetery or grave alignments. The earlier the burials in the Cambridge cemetery, the more jumbled; later ones tended to align east–west, or more precisely, southeast–northwest. The graves in the Granary Cemetery in Boston line up with a boundary road that happens to run more or less east–west. Its reference point is a granary, not a churchyard. In Concord, the graves are regular in placement, roughly northwest–southeast. My thanks for Mark Peterson for his help with this.

34. Geradius Croese, *A General History of the Quakers, Containing the Lives, Tenants, Suffering . . .* (London: John Dutton, 1696), 181.

35. Ibid., 183. William Sewel, *History, Rise, Increase and Progress of the Christian People Called Quakers* (London: J. Sowle, 1722), 528 re the Larder case in Norfolk, 283 re Cromwell. Sewel wrote his history because he thought Croese's was inaccurate; both were Dutch; both works were translated. On the points I discuss, they agree.

36. Louise Bashford and Tony Pollard, "'In the Burying Place'—The Excavation of a Quaker Burial Ground," in Cox, *Grave Concerns*, 159 and 154–166 passim. Later Quaker burial grounds show a regression toward the norm; that is, as the Quakers became less radical in the eighteenth and nineteenth centuries, their grave orientation became more usual. John Gough, in *A History of the People Called Quakers. From Their First Rise to the Present Time. Compiled from Authentic Records . . .* (Dublin, 1789), 2:188,

laments in a footnote that the Quakers abandoned the early simplicity of their burials. Archeological evidence suggests that some Quakers began burying their dead in the traditional direction. The burial ground of the Leominster Friends is aligned east–west. Dating, however, is impossible.

37. "Dissenting Deputies Minute Books," Guildhall MS 3083/1S, 1881–1890, f 80–83, 21 April and 21 November 1882. Miller wrote extensively on tithes and other clerical privileges. See, for example, his "Prospectus of a Publication Entitled 'Cataloguing of Authorities Bearing Witness to the System of Tithes as a Divine Institution of Perpetual Obligation'" (London: Rivington, 1842), vi, viii.

38. George Smith Tyack, *Lore and Legend of the English Church* (London: William Andrews, 1899), 65.

39. Venerable Bede, *The Ecclesiastical History of the English Nation, from the Coming of Julius Cæsar . . . till the Year of our Lord 731: Written in Latin by Venerable Bede, and Now Translated into English from Dr. Smith's Edition . . .* (London, 1723), Eighteenth Century Collections Online, bk. 4, chap. 7, 297–298.

40. A. E. Housman, *A Shropshire Lad*, "The Vane on Hughley Steeple." I am grateful to my former student Catherine Robson, who has been discussing these matters with me for years. See her "'Where Heaves the Turf': Thomas Hardy and the Boundaries of the Earth," *Victorian Literature and Culture* 32, no. 2 (2004): 495–503.

41. There is little scholarship on the history of consecration. See Helen Gittos, "Creating the Sacred: Anglo-Saxon Rites for Consecrating Cemeteries," in Sam Lucy and Andrew Reynolds, eds., *Burial in Early Medieval England and Wales* (London: Society for Medieval Archaeology, 2002), 195–209. More generally, see the learned account in John Wordsworth, "On the Rite of Consecration of Churches, Especially in the Church of England: A Lecture" (London: SPCK, 1899).

42. Rev. Sir John Cullum, *The History and Antiquities of Hawsted* (London, 1784), 38–39. Sometimes setting a good example helped. In 1790, the vicar of St. Mary's Overton in Hampshire was buried on the north side of his church. Once he was there, various prominent families followed, and it came into regular use. Christopher K. Currie, "Archaeological Recording in the Churchyard of St. Mary's Church, Overton, Hampshire," SU 51484998, available at http://archaeologydataservice.ac.uk.

43. Cullum, *History and Antiquities of Hawsted*, 38–39, 29. Cullum is generally not worried by so-called superstitious practices. Even if prayers for the dead are of no use, they direct the mind to serious matters and redound to spiritual welfare. Nineteenth-century folklorists cited the case of Benjamin Rhodes, the late-seventeenth-century steward of Thomas, Earl of Elgin, who wanted to be buried on the north side for the same reason.

44. Brand, *Observations on Popular Antiquities* (1777 Newcastle ed.), 53 and 51. Brand's collection of popular customs was, in expanded form, often reprinted in the nineteenth century and became the standard first work of reference on the subject. *Notes and Queries* (March 1908): 233–234. Charles M. Birrell, *Life of William Brock* (London: James Nisbet, 1878), 238.

45. Tyack, *Lore and Legend of the English Church*, 65.

46. There is a huge antiquarian and modern botanical literature on the yew. The three richest compendia from which I draw are Johnson, *Byways of British Archaeology*, 360–408, and more generally 205–324, for questions of grave and church orientation that are relevant to the yew; Hal Hartzell Jr., *The Yew Tree* (Eugene, Ore.: Hulogi, 1991); and T. N. Brushfield, M.D., "Yew Trees in Churchyards," in William Andrews, *Antiquities and Curiosities of the Church* (London: William Andrews, 1897), 256–278. See Hartzell, 117, for numbers of ancient trees. John Lowe, in *Yew-Trees of Great Britain and Ireland* (London: Macmillan, 1897), 95, lists by name twenty-seven trees that are at least thirty feet in circumference. One can add others from other sources. Lowe's list of trees at least 10 feet round is on 80–92. Thomas Pakenham, *Meetings with Remarkable Trees* (New York: Random House, 1998), has beautiful pictures of some celebrity yews. A. F. Mitchell, V. E. Hallett, and J.E.J. White, *Champion Trees in the British Isles*, Forestry Commission Field Book, no. 10 (London: HMSO, 1990), lists as the *Taxus beccata* of largest girth one of 29 feet at Belvoir Castle, and the tallest at 334 feet (13 feet around) in Ulcombe Churchyard, Kent.

47. Mitchell is quoted in Pakenham, *Meetings with Remarkable Trees*, 22.

48. On Saxon yews, see Della Hooke, *Trees in Anglo-Saxon England* (Woodbridge, U.K.: Boydell Press, 2010), 208–209 and passim, on the yew in various Anglo-Saxon contexts. For Aldworth, see Daniel Rock, *The Church of Our Fathers* (London: C. Dolman, 1859), 2:321–323. I could find no reference to the Aldworth yew in any edition of *Beauties of England* before 1776, when it appears in *A New Display of the Beauties of England*, 3rd ed. (London: R. Goadby, 1776), 1:241. For the Fortingale, see *Notes and Queries* 5th.V, 477; for the Scottshall and Evelyn, 5th S, XII, 495; for the Darley, 5th S,V, 376. Gilbert White, *The Natural History and Antiquities of Selborne, in the County of Southampton* (London, 1789), 324. The Fortingale yew was described in *Philosophical Transactions* in 1769; again in 1833 in the *Edinburgh Philosophical Journal*; again around the same time by the century's great horticulturist, John Claudius Loudon, in his *Hortus Britannicus* (by then it had two distinct stems, which funeral processions passed between); and finally in *Notes and Queries* for 1876, from which I get this genealogy. There are such stories about the Brabourn yew and the Scottshall yew in Kent; the Darley yew in Northumberland and the Tanbridge yew in Surrey. These are "the fraternal four," one lost in 1883, made famous by Wordsworth's poem. The yew in the churchyard of St. Cuthbert in Lorton, Cumbria, was there before the church but it is not one of "Wordsworth's yews," one of those that "to this day stands single in the midst / Of its own darkness as it stood of yore." John Fox the Quaker preached under its branches in the seventeenth century. The yew in Much Marcle, Herefordshire, close to the church door may have been there for one thousand years; the one at Claverley, Shropshire, probably shaded a Britano-British burial site before it became a churchyard. The yews at Loughton and Ashford Carbonell and Acton Scott and Uppington in Shropshire were there before the Norman Conquest, and so were the "twin yews" by the door of St. Edwards in Stow on the Wold. The yew in Selborne made famous by the eighteenth-century naturalist Gilbert White was "of great age . . . and probably coeval with the Church," he said in his popular *Natural History*. (A friend made for me a chair carved from the

wood of a yew that once stood over the grave of "Chronometer" Harrison in St. John's churchyard in Hampstead.)

49. On the placement of the yew, see Johnson, *Byways of British Archaeology*, 405–407. Robert Turner, *Botanologia: The British Physician, or, The Nature and Vertues of English Plants* (London: Obadiah Blagrave, 1687), 362–363. Brushfield, "The Yew . . .," 257. (The ecology of the yew was delicate. One nineteenth-century historian thought there are so few of them in urban churchyards in part because there was so little room but also because the rising of the ground from too dense a mass of putrefaction for them to grow well.)

50. See notes 45, 46, and 48 above. Johnson, *Byways of British Archaeology*, 382–385; and Lowe, *Yew-Trees*, 96–107, are particularly rich in references to this lore. See also John Claudius Loudon in *Arboretum et fruticetum britannicum: or, The Trees and Shrubs of Britain . . .* (London, 1838), 2082. The original decree is S. Carlo Borromeo, *Instructiones fabricae et supellectilis ecclesiasticae* (Milan, 1577). On Charles Cardinal Borromeo's efforts to forbid all plantings, see Richard Etlin, *The Architecture of Death* (Cambridge, Mass.: MIT Press, 1984), 90, 380. For the Rennes case, see John McManners, *Death and the Enlightenment* (Oxford: Oxford University Press, 1981), 350.

51. Biblical scholars are no help either. Linnaeus might have known that Jerome translated the Hebrew *'aravah* (singular) or *'aravim* (plural), Arabic cognate, as *salix*, the Latin for willow, but that does not get us very far.

52. Jack Lindsay, ed., *The Sunset Ship: The Poems of J.M.W. Turner* (Lowestoft, U.K.: Scoprion Press, 1966), "On the Demolition of Pope's House at Twickenham," 117. Turner also wrote several poems on the subject of burial. For a short history of the willow in England, see Pakenham, *Meetings with Remarkable Trees*, 152. On the problems of willow classification and on *Salix babylonica* in particular, see R. D. Meikle, *Willows and Poplars of Great Britain and Ireland* (London: Botanical Society of Great Britain, 1984), 54–55, and section 3a generally. The "uncertainties" of *Salix* classification are also discussed (4). As usual on matters of biblical scholarship, I thank my friend Ron Hendle.

53. See Loudon, *Arboretum et fruticetum britannicum*, 1507, for one origin story, and Pakenham, *Meetings with Remarkable Trees*, 77, for a variant. See Loudon's *The Encyclopedia of Gardening* (London, 1835), 1:1117, para. 6301 re mourning and melancholy.

54. P. A. Rahtz, "The Archaeology of the Churchyard," in Addyman and Morris, *The Archaeological Study of Churches*. Rodwell, *Archaeology of Religious Places*, 146–147. Morris reports that at Conway Gwd in Wales the soil from the churchyard still pressed against the windowsills in the late nineteenth century. Morris, *Churches in the Landscape*, 421. Readers of Goethe's *Elective Affinities* will remember that one of Charlotte's landscaping innovations in the churchyard was that graves were to be leveled, as they are in the modern cemetery, and the ground kept smooth for resowing (pt. 2, chap. 1).

55. *Gulval Church and Churchyard, Past and Present* (Penzance: Beare and Sons, 1898), 6.

56. The most famous and best tended of these is in Painswick, Gloucestershire. Roy Truman, "Chest Tombs and Tea Caddies," *Painswick Chronicle* 4 (2000): http://www.painswicketc.org.uk/plhs/history/histtombs.htm.

57. A. Stapleton, *The Nottingham Graveyard Guide—Historical Descriptive, Genealogical* (Nottingham, 1911), 6ff. Charles D. Warren, *History of St. Peter's Church, Petersham, Surrey* (1938; reprint, Petersham: Manor House Press, 1978). John Holland, "Our Old Churchyard: A Paper Read before the Sheffield Literary and Philosophical Society, Oct 5, 1869" (Sheffield: Paulson and Brailsford, 1869), 27–28.

58. Alexander Dallas, *My Churchyard: Its Tokens and Its Remembrances* (1828) (London: John Nisbet, 1848), 7–8.

59. The deep imbrication of the "Elegy" in English public culture and particular in schools is beautifully told by Catherine Robson, *Heart Beats: Everyday Life and the Memorized Poem* (Princeton, N.J.: Princeton University Press, 2012), 123–191. James D. Garrison, "Pietoso stile: Italian Translations of Gray's 'Elegy' to 1900," *MLN* 121, no. 1 (January 2006). On a more general history of the translations, see Thomas N. Turk, "Search and Rescue: An Annotated Checklist of Translations of Gray's Elegy," *Translation and Literature* 22, no. 1 (March 2013): 45–73.

60. Blair, "The Grave," 4. Joseph Addison, *The Spectator*, ed. Gregory Smith (London: J. M. Dent, 1945), no. 90, p. 279.

61. George Crabbe, "The Village" (London: J. Dodsley, 1783), bk. 1.

62. *The History of Little Goody Two-Shoes; Otherwise Called, Mrs. Margery Two-Shoes. With the Means by Which She Acquired Her Learning and Wisdom* . . . , 3rd ed. (London, 1766), 46–47, 50–51. George Crabbe, *The Parish Register*, pt. 3, "Burials," in *The Complete Poetical Works*, ed. Norma Dalrymple-Champneys (Oxford: Clarendon Press, 1988), 1:254.

63. The obligation to attend funerals is mentioned in almost all guild histories for every city. Particularly useful in this context is Sylvia Thrupp, *A Short History of the Worshipful Company of Bakers of London* (London, 1933), 94–95, 155–156. Sir William Foster, *A Short History of the Worshipful Company of Coopers in London* (Cambridge: Cambridge University Press, 1944), 3–4, 81. Edward Basil Jupp, *An Historical Account of the Worshipful Company of Carpenters . . . Compiled Chiefly from Records in Their Possession* (London, 1887), 22–23, 244.

64. Christ's Hospital "Burial Book," uncataloged MS, Guildhall Library, London. See a brief summary of the practice in E. H. Pierce, *Annals of Christ's Hospital* (London: Methuen, 1901), 136, 228–231. By the time the poor were finally no longer wanted in the funerary processions of the rich and no longer fed at their funerary feasts, it was not because of Protestant theology but because of a more general change in the moral valence of poverty. God's poor, who represented special virtues and divine favor, became the poor as a social problem, an emblem of fecklessness and an expensive burden on the ratepayer. When, in 1791, John Wesley, that supposed champion of capitalist accumulation, was—as he had directed—borne to his grave by six poor men, each of whom received a pound sterling, it was a self-consciously old-fashioned gesture. Wesley could not have been further removed from late medieval theological justification for this last act of charity—that the poor would pray for the welfare of his soul. But he was a Franciscan in his belief that the poor were especially close to Christ, to whom he committed his body. Continuities persisted over the Reformation divide. "I give six pounds," said Wesley in his will "to be divided among the six

poor men, named by the Assistant, who shall carry my body to the grave; for I particularly desire there may be no hearse, no coach, no escutcheon, no pomp, except the tears of them that loved me, and are following me to Abraham's bosom. I solemnly adjure my Executors, in the name of God, punctually to observe this." See John Walsh, "John Wesley and the Urban Poor," in *Revue Française de Civilisation Britannique* 6, no. 3 (1991): 17–30. Walsh quotes these lines of Wesley's last will and testament. It is available in full at http://www.godrules.net/library/wesley/274wesley_d12.htm.

65. John Donne, "Devotions upon Emergent Occasions" (1623), meditation 17: "Nunc lento sonitu dicunt, Morieris" (Now, this bell tolling softly for another, says to me: Thou must die). Thomas North (completed by J.C.L. Stahlschmidt), *The Church Bells of Hertfordshire* (London: Elliot Stock, 1886), 80–83, gives detailed ethnographic accounts of the subject. Florence Peacock, "Church Bells: When and Why They Were Rung," in William Andrews, ed., *Curious Church Customs* (London: Simpkin, Marshall, 1895), 48 and 33–48 more generally. For the north of England, see William Andrews, *Old Church Lore* (Hull: William Andrews, 1891), 210–217.

66. *The Works of John Ruskin*, ed. E. T. Cook and Alexander Wedderburn (London: G. Allen, 1903–), 28:285.

67. William Wordsworth, *The Two-Book Prelude* (1799), in *The Prelude, 1799, 1805, 1805* (New York: Norton, 1980), p. 8, lines 310–313.

68. John Clare, "The Cross Roads," in *The Early Poems*, ed. Eric Robinson (Oxford: Clarendon, 1989), 2:620. Flora Thompson, *Lark Rise to Candleford*, with an introduction by H. J. Massingham (Oxford: Oxford University Press, 1975), 261.

69. Robert Blair, "The Grave," 22–23.

70. Michael Macdonald, "The Secularization of Suicide in England, 1660–1800," *Past and Present* 111 (1998). The debate with Percival began with the coroner, Henry Wood, *A Few Leading Facts in Defence of Truth and Character in a Letter Addressed to the Hon. and Rev A. P. Percival* (Goldaming: Richard Stedman, 1833); to which Percival replied in *A Few Remarks on the Letter of Henry Wood, Esq.* (Guildford, 1833), in which he argues that he is being attacked solely to force him out of his parish, 20–21; and in the far more prestigiously published *A Clergyman's Defence of Himself for Refusing the Use of the Office of Burial of the Dead over One Who Has Destroyed Himself* (London: J. G. and F. Rivington, 1833), 11–13. In general, the Anglo-Catholic clergy and those who went over to Rome were willing to bury alleged suicides on the grounds that God would make the final call regarding salvation. See Olive Anderson, *Suicide in Victorian and Edwardian England* (Oxford: Clarendon Press, 1987), 276–278, on this and on the Lord Chancellor's decision. Both because this particular Lord Chancellor was a Dissenter and because the High Church clergy denied that secular law had any bearing on what they did, they paid little attention.

71. Berkshire Record Office D/P 115/111; *Jones v. Ashburton* 4 East 460, 1804.

72. Sir Simon Degge, *The Parson's Counsellor, with the Law of Tythes or Tything*, 5th ed., rev. and enlg. (London, 1695), 175–176. Robert Phillimore, *The Ecclesiastical Law of the Church of England*, 2nd ed. (by his son Sir Walter George Frank Phillimore) (London: Sweet and Maxwell, 1895), 1:651–652. R. H. Helmholz, John Hamilton Baker, et al., *The*

Oxford History of the Laws of England, vol. 1, *Canon Law and Ecclesiastical Jurisdiction from 597 to the 1640s* (Oxford: Oxford University Press, 2004), 24.

73. Francis Newman Rogers, *Practical Arrangement of Ecclesiastical Law* (London: Saunders and Benning, 1840), 126.

74. Henry William Cripps, *A Practical Treatise on the Laws Relating to the Church and the Clergy* (London: S. Sweet, 1845), 674.

75. *Reg. v. Stewart*, 12 A & E. 776.

76. Phillimore, *Ecclesiastical Law*, 1:654. In *Littlewood v. Williams* this case was opened up a bit and the churchwardens allowed to use their discretion if parishioners would suffer no ill effects.

77. Rogers, *Practical Arrangement of Ecclesiastical Law*, 126.

78. The "soul-scot" is discussed in Dawn M. Hadley and Jo Buckberry, "Caring for the Dead in Late Anglo-Saxon England," in Francesca Tinti, ed., *Pastoral Care in Late Anglo-Saxon England* (New York: Boydell Press, 2005), 122. Richard Burn, *Ecclesiastical Law* (London, 1763), 1:193.

79. Degge, *Parson's Counsellor*, 6th ed. (London, 1703), 174 (my emphasis). A. J. Stephens, *A Practical Treatise on Laws Relating to the Clergy* (London: W. Benning, 1848), 216–217.

80. *The Reports of That Reverend and Learned Judge Sir Henry Hobart* (London: R. J. Kennett, 1829), 315. Gibson is cited in Phillimore, *Ecclesiastical Law*, 2nd ed. (1895), 675. See, more generally, the history of case law related to Topsel and fees, 674–680. (Topsel is famous today as the author of the most important bestiary of the seventeenth century. I take my spelling of his name from that book's title page.)

81. Friends House, Portland MS 32/127. Dissenting Deputies Minute Books, Guildhall, 3083/2.

82. Francis Sadler, *The Exaction and Imposition of Parish Fees Discovered: Showing the Common Fees Demanded for Performing . . . Christening, Marrying, and Burying the Dead & c. to Be Contrary to Law . . . with the Opinion of Mr Strange, Solicitor General to His Majesty*, 2nd corr. ed. (London: printed for D. Farme, 1738), 43. This tract went through at least four more editions during the eighteenth century.

83. Cited in D. J. Enright, *The Oxford Book of Death* (Oxford: Oxford University Press, 1983), 322.

84. These differentials came up in the case of *Gilbert v. Buzzard*. See note 90 below. Ordinary fees for parishioners were 1.15.0 and for nonparishioners, 2.10.0. Metal coffins were an extra 10s. for parishioners, and 20s. for nonparishioners.

85. Vanessa Harding, "'And One More May Be Laid There': The Location of Burials in Early Modern London," *London Journal* 14, no. 2 (1989): 112–129.

86. J. E. Smith, *St. John the Evangelist* (Westminster: Parochial Memorials, 1892), 121.

87. "St. James Chapel and Burial Ground Minute Book, 1789–1847," Westminster City Archives, D 1715.

88. James Turner, *Burial Fees of the Principle Churches, Chapels, and New Burial Grounds in London and Its Environs* (London: n.d. but ca. 1838), Guildhall, Pam 5713. This was a publication for the trade.

89. John Dunton (1659–1733), *The Art of Living Incognito* (London, 1700), 215. Dunton was a major bookseller and publisher. This strange text is made up of autobiographical fragments followed by an account of a sort of counter- or alternative life: "how he'd Think, Speak, and Act, might he Live over his Days again."

90. *Gilbert v. Buzzard and Boyer*, Consistory Court of London, Hilary term, 1820; reported in Joseph Phillimore, *Reports of Cases Argued and Determined in the Ecclesiastical Courts at Doctors Common* (London: Joseph Butterworth and Son, 1827), 3:335–367. The case is discussed in all the relevant professional texts. See, for example, the summary in Cripps, *Practical Treatise*, 680–684. On the question of the relatively late arrival of coffins, the judge, Lord Stowell, is certainly right. William Andrews, *Old Church Lore* (Hull: William Andrews, 1891), 98–108, cites considerable evidence for a dual fee structure for burial with and without coffins during the seventeenth century, and that in some Yorkshire parishes burial without a coffin was still common in the late eighteenth century, when reforming clergymen put an end to the practice. Lincolnshire Folklore Society, *County Folklore* (London: David Nutt, 1908), 5:245, cites a 1717 terrier of lands, fees, etc., from Caistor Vicarage: "For every grave in the churchyard without coffin, four pence, if with coffin one shilling."

91. *Gilbert v. Buzzard and Boyer*, reported in Phillimore, *Reports of Cases. . .* , 356.

92. *Gilbert v. Buzzard and Boyer*, reported in Phillimore, *Reports of Cases. . .* , 362.

93. Richard Vaughan Barnewell and J. L. Adolphus, *Reports on Cases Argued and Determined in the Court of King's Bench* (London: Saunders and Benning, 1831), 1:122–23, ex parte Blackmore. *Freyer v. Johnson*, 2 Wels 28.

94. On the case of Mrs. Horseman in 1631, see David Cressy, *Travesties and Transgressions in Tudor and Stuart England: Tales of Discord and Dissension* (Oxford: Oxford University Press, 2000), 116–138. *Gentleman's Magazine* 2, no. 20 (August 1732): 930. A. Shield and Andrew Lang, *The King over the Water* (New York: Longmans, Green and Co., 1907), 390, cited in Andrew Keating, "The Empire of the Dead: British Burial Abroad and the Formation of National Identity" (Ph.D. diss., University of California, Berkeley, 2011), chap. 1, which discusses the vexed problem of the burial of Britons abroad. H. Forster, *Edward Young: The Poet of the "Night Thoughts" 1683–1765* (Alburgh, U.K.: Erskine, 1986), 149–150.

95. Walter Chamberlain, M.A., *The Case against the Burial Bill . . .* (Manchester: T. Roworth, 1875), 3, 6, 23. Chamberlain was a curious figure whose other great passion was the study of how the Jews would be converted before the End of Times. In this case, I think he represents the mainline conservative clerical position. J. Carrell, *A Plea for a Free Churchyard or the Case in Support of the Burial Laws Amendment Act* (London: Society for the Liberation of Religion from State Patronage and Control, 1870), 11. He is speaking here specifically of the children of Baptists, who were unbaptized and hence not eligible for churchyard burial because the denomination practiced only adult baptism.

96. Borthwick Institute, York, R. Bp. 8/25a.

97. Borthwick Institute, York, R. Bp. 5/280–281.

98. The "Deputies," founded in 1732, represented the descendants of those Christians who had not come back into the Anglican fold when the Church, along with its bishops within the monarchy, returned in 1660—the Baptists, the Presbyterians, and the Congregationalists. This case is from their minute books in the Guildhall Library. The standard authority on their history as a struggle for civil rights is Bernard Lord Manning, *The Protestant Dissenting Deputies*, ed. Ormerod Greenwood (Cambridge: Cambridge University Press, 1952), and I have followed his invaluable narrative in the relevant sections that follow.

99. Bodleian Library, Gough Adds. Oxon. 9, 5–7, "Cowley Burial Cases."

100. Ibid., 10–15. Both of these cases received considerable attention in the national daily and periodical press.

101. Informal MS notes taken by John Coates at the Elland Clerical Society, 9 October 1794. I am grateful to my former teacher John Walsh for transcripts of this material, as I am for so much else. He is currently writing an introduction to an edition of these manuscripts, but they are not currently publicly available. There were ongoing disputes about the role of so-called prevenient grace in baptism that grabbed national attention, but these are not relevant here. My interest in a case in which a bishop refused to accept a clergyman who held what he took to be heterodox views, *Gorham v. Bishop of Exeter*, has to do with whether a lay court was the final arbiter of an ecclesiastical matter. As in the burial disputes, Privy Council insisted that it was not passing judgment on theological doctrines but on whether the procedures whereby a clergyman was denied a living or the dead were denied burial—both civil as well as ecclesiastical matters—passed judicial muster. For a full discussion of the Gorham case, see Francis Warre, *The English Church in the Nineteenth Century, Part 1* (London: Macmillan and Co., 1910), 319–337. Except for a Ph.D. thesis on the Catholic response to this judgment—many clergy on the losing side went over to Rome—there is no modern study.

102. Robert E. Rodes, Jr., *Lay Authority and Reformation in the English Church: Edward I to the Civil War* (Notre Dame, Ind.: University of Notre Dame Press, 1982), 103, 130. The material on 1604 comes from an coauthored article with Ethan Shagin now in progress and is based entirely on his research.

103. See the *Edinburgh Review* 121 (January–April 1865): 121, commentary on *Mastin v. Escott*. Richard Hooker, *Lawes of Ecclesiastical Polity: The Fifth Book* (London: John Windet, 1597), sec. 62, p. 146 and sec. 62, pp. 139–151 passim, more generally.

104. *Edinburgh Review* 121 (January–April 1865): 121. "Cases," 3 October 1800. The Society started taking formal minutes beginning 7 August 1795.

105. Robert E. Rodes, Jr., *Law and Modernization in the Church of England: Charles II to the Welfare State* (Notre Dame, Ind.: University of Notre Dame Press, 1991), 140–142. On suicide verdicts generally, see Macdonald, note 70 above, but we do know that some clergymen ostentatiously continued to refuse burial whatever the verdict. A. P. Percival, one of the leading Tractarians, got himself into a pamphlet war in 1833 for refusing to bury someone whom he thought had committed suicide—he attended the inquest himself—even though the jury found "insanity." See Percival, *A Cler-*

gyman's Defence of Himself, 11–13. See also Henry Wood, *A Few Leading Facts in Defence of the Truth*, in which he argues that Percival was disrespectful during the inquest and refused all efforts to reach a compromise. Percival replies in "A Few Remarks on the Letter of Henry Wood, Esq.," where he claims that the issue is not a few words at the grave but an effort to drive him out of his parish. Rev. Mr. Coley, of the Oxfordshire Parish of Cowley, refused, despite the entreaties of her sister, to read the burial service over the body of a forty-two-year-old woman in despair over the death of her father. She had been a regular church attendee and had lived long enough to ask to be taken to the infirmary. An inquest found "insanity." See the file in Bodleian Gough Adds. Oxon c. 9, 2. The law about bodies washed ashore is "The Burial of Drowned Persons Act 1808" (48 Geo III c.75), also known as Grylls' Act, after Thomas Grylls, the Cornish solicitor who did the most to have it passed. In general, bodies of unknown origin found on roads, or in extraparochial places, or washed up on beaches were, by custom, the responsibility of the nearest parish. But the churchwardens were not always anxious to meet these obligations because their funds bore the burden. It was one scandalous case—the burial without coffins in unconsecrated ground of sailors whose bodies washed ashore in 1808 from the wreck of HMS *Anson* in Mounts Bay of Cornwall—that led to its passage. The corpses that the sea tossed ashore became an almost obsessive mission for an eccentric Cornish clergyman who hated the Methodists, fought with them over burial, but was gripped by the fear that unquiet, unburied, and often mutilated decayed bodies of shipwrecks threatened, as ghosts, to haunt the living. Whether they had been baptized did not seem to concern him.

106. *An Extract of the Minutes of Several Conversations Held at Manchester, 27 July &c. 1795* (London: G. Faramore, 1795), 32.

107. *Sketch of the History and Proceedings of the Dissenting Deputies Appointed to Protect the Civil Rights of Protestant Dissenters* (London: S. Burton, 1814), 16, 67. Manning, *Protestant Dissenting Deputies*, 286. Testamentary cases were under ecclesiastical jurisdiction; political rights often depended on how to interpret the category "occasional conformity."

108. MS 3083/1; MS 3083/2; in the Guildhall Library. See *Sketch of the History and Proceedings of the Dissenting Deputies*, 66.

109. MS 3083/3. For the debate about Deists, see *Orthodox Churchman's Magazine*, November 1807, with a response in the December issue and a rejoinder in January 1808.

110. *Sketch of the History and Proceedings of the Dissenting Deputies*, 67. Scott's query about the views of Dissenters on baptism and the deputies' response is in the *Minute Books*, 27 April 1798. Although Scott does not give the citation, he must be referring to Fleetwood's fifty-page *The Judgment of the Church of England in the Case of Lay-Baptism and of Dissenter's Baptism* (London: A. Baldwin, 1712).

111. John Wight Wickes, *Perlege si vis: A Letter Addressed to the Bishop of Peterborough in Answer to an Appeal Made to the "Society for Defending the Civil Rights of the Dissenters" Relative to Church Burial by the Established Clergy* (Stamford, 1808), 21, 15, and passim.

112. On John Nicholl, see the *Dictionary of National Biography* entry; see also Manning's narrative of the case in *Protestant Dissenting Deputies*, 293–299.

113. Joseph Phillimore, *Reports of Cases Argued and Determined in the Ecclesiastical Courts at Doctors Common,* vol. 3, *Containing Cases from Trinity Term 1818, to Michaelmas Term 1821 Inclusive* (London: Joseph Butterworth, 1827), 273, 278, 295, 305, and 264–306 passim.

114. George Hutton, *Remarks upon a Late Decision in the Court of Arches on the Question Whether a Person Not Baptized by a Lawful Minister of the Church of England Be Entitled to the Burial Service of That Church* (Boston, 1811) 5, 8–11. The attack on Nicholl's learning is by the anonymous author of a review of a tract attacking Nicholl in *Anti-Jacobin Review* 139–142 (1810): 375, 385, and 374–386 passim. This tract, *A Letter to Sir John Nicholl on His Late Decision in the Ecclesiastical Court . . .* by "A Clergyman" (London: J. J. Stockdale, 1810), goes on for 67 pages in this vein and is one of a number of learned, pained, and vituperative attacks by conservative clergy, most famously the 144-page "Respectful Examination" (1811) by the High Church "controversialist" Charles Daubeny (1745–1827). See the *Dictionary of National Biography.*

115. On Eatington, see *Minutes,* 29 March 1829, Guildhall MS 3083/7. On the Bassingbourne cases, see Manning, *Protestant Dissenting Deputies,* 299–301; and the *Annual Reports of the Protestant Dissenting Deputies* for 1840–1845, esp. 30 December 1839, transcribed in the *Minutes* 3083/10. Hostility to the Methodist dead extended beyond refusing burial; a controversy covered by the national press broke out in 1873 when the vicar of Owston in North Lincolnshire asked the bishop if he could remove a gravestone of a Methodist minister that read, "In Memory of ——— a happy labourer in the Wesleyan Methodist Church"; it is not a church, he insisted, and he wanted to spare his parishioners (*A Pastoral Letter to the Methodists in the Diocese of Lincoln* [Lincoln: James Williamson, 1873], esp. 8; a new edition in 1875 notes that while this may seem an insignificant matter, the questions involved are "of serious importance"). Refusal to allow the title "Rev." on the tombstones of Methodist ministers was endemic.

116. The question of lay baptism became an issue in the late seventeenth and early eighteenth centuries among mostly High Church clergyman—nine bishops and about four hundred clergy—who in 1688 refused to take an oath of allegiance to William and Mary. They were deprived of their sees and their livings, and these were given to clergy willing to take the oath. These so-called nonjurors argued that all sacraments, including baptism, performed by those uncanonically installed were invalid and, more generally, that the Church ought to be autonomous from the State. This schismatic faction became increasingly insignificant after the early eighteenth century. Commentators on nineteenth-century baptism/burial cases point to the ludicrous consequences of their views—that George III, for example, had not been properly baptized because Archbishop Secker, who baptized him, had himself been baptized by a "layman." *Full Report of the Case of Mastin v Escott* (London: Crofts, 1841), 274–275.

117. William Morgan, *A Letter to the Rev. Arthur Fane, Vicar of Warminster . . .* (Warminster: R. E. Vardy, 1847), 5–6. John Carvell Williams, *A Plea for a Free Churchyard* (London, 1870). "Speech of Sir S. M. Peto, on Asking Leave to Introduce the Nonconformists' Burial Act, February 19th, 1861; together with the Proposed Bill" (London: Robert K. Burt, [1861]).

118. All the documents in this case are collected in Ronald Fletcher, *The Akenham Burial Case* (London: Wildwood House, 1974).

119. Cited in S. C. Carpenter, *Church and People 1789–1889: Part 2* (London: SPCK, 1933, 1959), 344.

120. Epigraphs: Edward Gibbon, *Decline and Fall of the Roman Empire*, ed. J. B. Bury (New York: Modern Library, 1995), 2:898, summarizing Eunapius (born ca. 347), *Lives of the Sophists*, 3, 93. Eunapius is perhaps more bitter, derisive, and angry than solemn and pathetic. He speaks of the monks who moved into the ruins of sacred places as "men in appearance [who] led the lives of swine. . . . They collected the bones and skulls of criminals, . . . made gods of them, haunted their sepulchers and thought that they became better by defiling themselves at their graves. . . . 'Martyrs' the dead men were called[,] . . . 'ambassadors' from the gods to carry men's prayers." All this, he concludes, "greatly increased the reputation of Antoninus [the emperor Antoninus Pius, father of Marcus Aurelius] also for foresight, in that he had foretold to all that the temples would become tombs." Eunapius, *Lives of the Philosophers*, trans. Wilmer Cave Wright, Loeb Classical Library (Cambridge, Mass.: Harvard University Press, 1952), 423–425. Michel de Certeau, *The Writing of History* (New York: Columbia University Press, 1988), 5.

121. Gibbon, *Decline and Fall*, 2:898–899. On the question of sacred spaces, see the fine summary by Béatrice Caseau, "Sacred Landscapes," in G. W. Bowersock, Peter Brown, and Oleg Grabar, eds., *Interpreting Late Antiquity* (Cambridge, Mass.: Harvard University Press, 2001), 36–38 and 21–59 more generally. I have supplemented Gibbon's telling of the story with the accounts in G. W. Bowersock, *Julian the Apostate* (London: Duckworth, 1978), 99; Robert Browning, *The Emperor Julian* (London: Weidenfeld and Nicolson, 1975), 180–181; and Peter Brown, *Cult of the Saints* (Chicago: University of Chicago Press, 1981).

122. Arthur Imhof, *Lost Worlds: How Our European Ancestors Coped with Everyday Life and Why Life Is So Hard Today*, trans. Thomas Robisheaux (Charlottesville: University Press of Virginia, 1996), 172–173, 180, and 162–192 more generally.

123. Michel Foucault, *The Birth of the Clinic: An Archaeology of Medical Perception* (New York: Vintage, 1994); quote is on 36.

124. Foucault, grounded in the Left, and Nietzsche wrote an appreciative obituary of his friend Philippe Ariès in *Nouvel Observateur* 12 February 1984, 31–32.

125. Philippe Ariès's *The Hour of Our Death*, trans. Helen Weaver (New York: Knopf, 1981) is much influenced by Geoffrey Gorer's famous claim that death in our age is unspoken and unspeakable, much in the way that sex supposedly had been in the nineteenth century. I think Gorer is wrong about this and that his view is a reflection of an anthropological wistful thinking of the sort that historians too engage in, that primitive people—or people in the past in our case—somehow get death and dying right because they, unlike us, can still believe in the efficacy of ritual. Although I disagree with some of his views, I have profited greatly from Patrick Hutton, "Of Death and Destiny: The Ariès–Vovelle Debate about the History of Mourning," in Peter Homans, ed., *Symbolic Loss: The Ambiguity of Mourning and Memory at Century's End*

(Charlottesville: University Press of Virginia, 2000), 147–170. Xavier Bichat, *Physiological Researches on Life and Death*, trans. F. Gold (1827; reprint, New York: Arno Press, 1977), 10.

126. Michel Vovelle, *Piété baroque et déchristianisation en Provence au XVIIIe siècle* (Paris: Editions du Seuil, 1978).

127. Lionel Gossman, *Basel in the Age of Burckhardt: A Study in Unseasonable Ideas* (Chicago: University of Chicago Press, 2000), 149. Burckhardt was one of Ariès's bêtes noirs.

128. Certeau, *Writing of History*, 5.

129. Plato, *Phaedo*, in *Euthyphro, Apology, Crito, Phaedo*, trans. Benjamin Jowett (1892; reprint, Amherst, N.Y.: Prometheus Books, 1988), 136. Glenn Most, "'A Cock for Asclepius,'" *Classical Quarterly* 43 (1993): 96–111, seems to cite almost every conceivable interpretation of these words for 2,500 years and comes to the tendentious conclusion that they refer to Socrates' illness. Emily Wilson's *The Death of Socrates* (Cambridge, Mass.: Harvard University Press, 2007) gives a more nuanced history of what the episode has meant in the cultural history of the West.

130. Luther was the first of the great reformers to die in circumstances in which one could test his faith on his deathbed. Zwingli had died in battle in 1531, and his body was mutilated by his enemies; his colleague Heinrich Bullinger tried to show that he expected death and was a thus a latter-day exemplar of the martyrs of the early Church. In fact, despite exhaustive research on Zwingli's death, Bullinger had very little evidence on which to base his interpretation. See Bruce Gordon, "Holy and Problematic Deaths: Heinrich Bullinger on Zwingli and Luther," in Marion Kobelt Groch and Cornelia Niekus Moore, eds., *Tod und Jenseitsvorstellungen in der Schriftkultur der Frühen Neuzeit* (Wolfenbüttel: Harrassowitz, 2008), 47–62. For Luther's death, see the scholarly and exhaustive doctoral thesis of Christof Schubart, *Die Berichhte über Luther's Tod und Begräbnis* (Weimar: Hof-Buchdruckerei, 1917). Bodo Brinkmann, ed., *Cranach: Exhibition Catalogue* (London: Royal Academy of Art, 2008), 196–197.

131. Brinkmann, *Cranach: Exhibition Catalogue*, 196–197. Schubart, *Die Berichhte über Luther's Tod und Begräbnis*.

132. On the tradition of the deaths of skeptics, and esp. Spinoza, see Jonathan Israel, *The Radical Enlightenment: Philosophy and the Making of Modernity 1650–1750* (Oxford: Oxford University Press), 295–301, 340–341. On a new deist pantheon, see Alberto Radicati, count de Passeran, *Twelve Discourses, Moral, Historical and Political . . .* (London, 1737). Radicati was one of the earliest Italian enlightenment figures. This collection is translated from the French and went through at least three editions. On Spinoza, see John Colerus, *The Life of Benedict de Spinosa* (London, 1706), 87 and 81–89 more generally. (Colerus was the sympathetic German Lutheran minister in the Hague at the time of Spinoza's death.) This book too had an afterlife. It was republished in the nineteenth century and much used by the aesthete Walter Pater in his story on Spinoza, "Sebastian van Storck," in *Imaginary Portraits*, ed. Eugene Brzenk (New York: Harper and Row, 1964), 114–137. Gilbert Burnet, *Some*

Passages of the Life and Death of the Right Honorable John Earl of Rochester (London: Richard Chiswel, 1680).

133. Nicholas Cronk, ed., *The Cambridge Companion to Voltaire* (Cambridge: Cambridge University Press, 2009). Gibbon is quoted on 5. For the question of Voltaire's place, see Daniel Brewer, "The Voltaire Effect," in ibid., 205–218.

134. The narrative, pictures, and relevant documents are in Catherine-Laurence Maire, *Les convulsionnaires de Saint-Médard: Miracles, convulsions et prophéties à Paris au xviiiᵉ siècle* (Paris: Gallimard, 1985), on which I have relied. McManners, *Death and the Enlightenment*, 260. He paraphrases the contemporary witticism that the Church was oppressing communion on unbelievers who did not want it and denying it to believers who did.

135. William Henley Jervis, *The Gallacian Church* (London: John Murray, 1872), 2:310–312. McManners, *Death and the Enlightenment*, 260–261.

136. Voltaire, "On the Death of Adrienne Lecouvreur, a Celebrated Actress," in *The Works of Voltaire*, ed. Tobias Smollett and William Fleming (New York: E. R. Dumont, 1901), vol. 10, pt. 2, p. 77. See also Voltaire, *Letters on England*, trans. Leonard Tancock (Harmondsworth, U.K.: Penguin, 1980), 112:

> The English have even been reproached for going too far in the honors they award to mere merit. They have been criticized for burying in Westminster Abbey the famous actress Mrs. Oldfield with nearly the same honors that were paid to Newton. It has been suggested by some that they had affected to honor the memory of an actress to this extent in order to make us appreciate still more the barbarous injustice they reproach us with, namely of having thrown the body of Mll. Lecouvreur on to the garbage heap.
>
> But I can assure you that in the funeral of Mrs. Oldfield interred in their Saint-Denis, the English consulted nothing but their taste; they are very far from finding infamy in the art of a Sophocles or a Euripides and from excluding from the body of their citizens those who devote themselves to declaiming in front of them works that are the pride of their nation.

137. I base my discussion of these negotiations on McManners, *Death and the Enlightenment*, 258–269.

138. For La Fontaine, see McManners, *Death and the Enlightenment*, 248. For Montesquieu, see the account in Robert Shackleton, *Montesquieu: A Critical Biography* (Oxford: Oxford University Press, 1961), 392–398.

139. Voltaire had both men in mind, see McManners, *Death and the Enlightenment*, 266. Although there is a great deal about Voltaire's death scene in Frederick's correspondence with d'Alembert, I could not find a letter expressing precisely this concern. Frederick the Great on Voltaire is from McManners, *Death and the Enlightenment*, 258.

140. Abbé Duvernet (Théophile Imargeon), *The Life of Voltaire: With Notes Illustrative and Explanatory*, trans. G. P. Monke (London: T. Becket, 1787), 1:327–328. The French original, also published in London, appeared the year before. Precisely the words I quote about making freethinkers happy were picked up in many of the reviews in 1787.

141. [Louis Mayeul] Chaudon, *Historical and Critical Memoirs of the Life and Writings of M. de Voltaire . . . Translated from the French* (London: C. G. and J. Robinson, 1786). The quote is from an introductory anonymous translator's note (vi), which cautions readers against believing everything Chaudon says. He is, after all, a priest. Chaudon was also the author of a well-known antiphilosophical dictionary, compiled in opposition to Voltaire. But the book memoir is relatively even-handed and must have been regarded sympathetic enough to Voltaire to prevent its publication in France. The 1785 French edition appeared in Amsterdam.

142. *The Life of Voltaire, by the Marquis de Condorcet*, trans. unknown, 2 vols. (London: G.G.J. and J. Robinson, 1790), 1:431–438. The allusion to the Abbé de L'Attaignant is perhaps to his writing a poem in honor of Voltaire, whom he admired; perhaps to his barely aborted efforts to marry a sixteen-year-old girl; or perhaps to the raucous songs he wrote. Here is what Voltaire signed, 2 March 1778: "Je soussigné déclare qu'étant attaqué depuis quatre jours d'un vomissement de sang à l'age de quatrevingt quatre ans, et n'ayant pu me trainer à l'église Monsieur le curé de saint Sulpice ayant bien voulu ajouter à ses bonnes oeuvres de m'envoier monsieur l'abbé Gautier pretre, je me suis confessé à lui, et que si dieu dispose de moy, je meurs dans la sainte relligion catholique ou je suis né, espérant de la miséricorde divine qu'elle daignera pardonner touttes mes fautes, et que si j'avais jamais scandalisé l'église j'en demande pardon à Dieu et à elle." *Complete Works of Voltaire*, vol. 129, *Correspondence: July 1777–May 1778*, ed. Theodore Besterman (Oxford: Voltaire Foundation, 1976), 359–360.

143. There is even more to the plot. The body was originally bound for Ferney in the diocese of Amiens, but the bishop there threatened to have it excluded. And there had been earlier even wilder schemes in which the dead Voltaire would be dressed as if alive and carried to Ferney so that Tarsac could not refuse it burial in Paris and it would not look as if the corpse was taken elsewhere to avoid ecclesiastical penalty. On this, see Ian Davidson, *Voltaire in Exile 1753–1778* (New York: Grove Press, 2004), 296–392. This part does not appear in the eighteenth-century accounts I have read.

144. William Agutter, "On the Deaths of the Righteous and the Wicked, Illustrated by the Instance of Dr. Samuel Johnson and David Hume, . . . Preached before the University of Oxford at St. Mary's Church on Sunday, July 23, 1786" (London: J. Richardson, 1800), 6–7. *Anti-Jacobin Review* 8 (1801): 191.

145. Darrin M. McMahon, *Enemies of the Enlightenment: The French Counter-Enlightenment and the Making of Modernity* (Oxford: Oxford University Press, 2001). For the characterization of Michel, see *Who's Who in Gay and Lesbian History: From Antiquity to World War II*, ed. Robert Aldrich and Garry Wotherspoon (London: Routledge, 2001), 1:547–548, s.v. Charles Michel, Marquis de Villette. The best single account of Voltaire's last days and apotheosis, as well as of the fate of his various body parts and properties, is Jean Orieux, *Voltaire* (Paris: Flammarion, 1999), 766–795.

146. On conservative interpretation of Voltaire's so-called second apotheosis—the first was his return to Paris amid wild acclaim in the months before his death—see McMahon, *Enemies of the Enlightenment*, 83–86.

147. On the role of the Pantheon and French Revolutionary funerals, see Avner Ben-Amos, *Funerals, Politics and Memory in Modern France, 1789–1996* (Oxford: Oxford University Press, 2000), 17–53. Ben-Amos classifies these funerals by their political purpose; thus Voltaire's and Rousseau's were funerals of integration; Marat's first funeral was "exclusive"—he was buried in the former church of the Cordeliers because the radical Jacobins rejected the seemingly centrist associations of the Pantheon. Ben-Amos then claims that his move to the Pantheon in the early days of Thermidor was integrative, an effort to create political continuity at a time of rupture. I follow him on this point, but it is open to debate. Maybe, having decided on moving him, the Convention had to follow through even as the political situation changed. And in any case, the new funeral provided the body for what was perhaps more important: a celebration of its army escort. Joseph Clark's *Commemorating the Dead in Revolutionary France: Revolution and Remembrance, 1789–1799* (Cambridge: Cambridge University Press, 2007) makes these latter points and offers a more fine-grained account of the high politics of public funerals. On Marat, see 170–215 on what his death meant in 1793, and 218–220 for the very different days of fall 1794.

148. "A Philiosophical [*sic*] Dissertation upon Death Composed for the Consolation of the Unhappy" (London, 1732), 22–23 and passim. John Robison, *Proofs of a Conspiracy against All the Religions and Governments of Europe, Carried on in the Secret Meetings of Free Masons, Illuminati, and Reading Societies: Collected from Good Authorities . . .* (London, 1797), 37; see also 36 and 106. The term "illuminati" meant, strictly speaking, a Bavarian secret society of freethinkers founded in the 1770s. By this time it referred, I think, in the minds of Robison and others who thought that the Revolution was the work of a conspiracy, to any group of freethinkers or would-be freethinkers. Robison was a highly productive professor of natural philosophy at Edinburgh from 1774 until his death and a prolific contributor to the *Britannica* 3rd edition. He was a great friend of James Watt and of the chemist Joseph Black and devoted most of his life to the rigorous pursuit of theoretical and applied sciences. But he is most famous today as author of the virulently anti-Jacobin tract from which I quote and as one of the most important proponents of the conspiracy theory of the Revolution. For Rousseau, see his letter to M. de Franquières (1769) in Ronald Grimsley, ed., *Rousseau Writings* [documents in French] (Oxford: Clarendon Press, 1970), 389–390; and also Grimsley, *Rousseau and the Religious Quest* (Oxford: Clarendon Press, 1968), 57, 65–67. William Jones, *The Scholar Armed against the Errors of the Time or, A Collection of Tracts on the Principles and Evidences of Christianity . . .* (London: Society for the Reformation of Principles, 1800), 2:338, and its article on "Voltaire," 229–339, more generally.

149. Augustin Barruel, *Memoirs Illustrating the History of Jacobinism* (London, 1797), 1:353, 356, 358, 362, and passim 347–369. Diderot did talk to a priest two or three times a week, but his wife and son-in-law were there to keep the conversation from being too strenuous. See P. N. Furbank, *Diderot: A Critical Biography* (New York: Knopf, 1992), 428 and 426–430 more generally.

150. Hannah More, *Practical Piety* (New York: Richard Scott, 1812), 2:192–193. *Infidelity Exposed, by Some Account of the Writings and Death of T. Paine, or the Churchman Confirmed in His*

Religion (Bristol: Publications of the Church of England Tract Society, 1824); vol. 3, for example, is one of a series that includes *The Contrasts; or an Interesting and True Account of the Last Hours of a Learned Infidel* (RTS 543), which compares Voltaire's deathbed with that of Dr. [Philip] Doddridge, the nonconformist hymn writer and clergyman (RTS 543 [864 e32/13]); and *Christians and Infidels, Showing the Difference between the Lives and Deaths of Several Striking Instances*, which goes way back by contrasting Beau Nash, the famous Bath man-about-town in the early eighteenth century, and a Mrs. B of London, who suffered three days of terror, with John Hervey, the Earl of Bristol, and Bishop Bedell, presumably the pious seventeenth-century bishop of Kilmore (RTS [864 e 32212/14]).

151. [Isaac Wilson], *The Infidel and Christian Philosophers or, The Last Hours of Voltaire and Addison Contrasted: A Poem* (Kingston upon Hull: Printed for the author by W. Rawson, Ludgate, 1802). The poem was reprinted in the author's *Miscellany* (1829) and quoted at length again in his biographical entry in R. W. Corlass, *Sketches of Hull Authors* (Hull: Bolton, 1879), 140.

152. Thomas Carlyle, *Critical and Miscellaneous Essays* (Boston: Brown and Taggard, 1860), 2, 12, 53–54. The essay "Voltaire" was written in 1829, but Carlyle had already engaged with him seriously in his biography of that other great eighteenth-century figure whose death was also controversial, because he insisted that he be buried with his dogs—Frederick the Great.

153. A large section of James Fieser's *Early Responses to Hume's Life and Reputation*, 2 vols. (Bristol: Thoemmes Press, 2005) reprints documentary evidence for this discussion. Although very good, it does not even scratch the surface of his deathbed's afterlife.

154. James Boswell, *The Applause of the Jury, 1782–1785*, ed. Irma S. Lustig and Frederick Pottle (New York: McGraw-Hill, 1981), 29.

155. Gothold Ephraim Lessing, "Wie Die Altren den Tod Gebildet," in *Werke* (Munich: Carl Hanser Verlag, 1974), 6:411 (my translation).

156. Boswell told Johnson in 1769 that Hume had actually spoken these words to him; he wrote elsewhere that Hume said this to him in a 1776 interview, just before his death. Fieser, *Early Responses*, 156, thinks that Boswell inserted them into his life of Johnson as a literary device. This is possible, but so is the hypothesis that Hume's views were long known. Something like what he quotes probably did set him off on his earlier conversation with Johnson. James Boswell, *The Life of Samuel Johnson*, ed. R. W. Chapman, Oxford World's Classics (Oxford: Oxford University Press, 1980), 426.

157. Boswell, *Life of Samuel Johnson*, 838–839.

158. Osler conducted this study on 486 patients at Johns Hopkins Hospital. He never wrote up the data—I am grateful to McGill University Library for sending me photocopies of the raw forms—but he did mention in a lecture, "Death and Mortality," that 104 patients (21 percent) suffered some sort of physical or mental distress. For the rest, "death was a sleep and a forgetting." A recent analysis of the data shows that in fact 186 patients, or 38 percent, suffered distress.

159. In 1810 there appeared a short account, supposedly provided by his nurse, that he "*died in horror.*" Twenty-one years after that, the *Christian Observer*, probably the most

widely read Anglican magazine, published a more detailed piece in which the nurse admitted that he did seem cheerful in front of his friends and that he tried to stay composed even in her presence but that in unguarded moments she and other servants heard "his involuntary breathings of remorse and frightful startings." This account too had an afterlife for decades more. Fieser, *Early Responses*, 1:323–334.

160. Fieser, *Early Responses*, 1:10–24.

161. On what Hume was reading, see the elegant essay by Annette Baier, "Hume's Deathbed Reading," in her *Death and Character: Further Reflections on Hume* (Cambridge, Mass.: Harvard University Press, 2008).

162. The much-admired and attacked source for Hume's imaginary conversations with Charon and for his peaceful death is Adam Smith, "Letter to William Strahan" [Hume's—and Johnson's—London publisher and one of the most important and successful bookmen of the eighteenth century], appended to *The Life of David Hume, Esq. Written by Himself* (London: Strahan and Cadell, 1777). Fieser, *Early Responses*, 1:297–300.

163. For the comments from the *Weekly Magazine* and from *Gentleman's Magazine*, see Fieser, *Early Responses*, 1:406, 416.

164. Joseph Towers, *An Essay on the Life, Character, and Writings of Dr. Samuel Johnson* (London: Chartles Dilly, 1786), 111–112. Needless to say, Johnson comes off much better than Hume. The "country clergyman" was the important sixteenth-century theologian Bernard Gilpin. I do not know who Thomas Firman, the tradesmen to whom he compares Hume, was.

165. [George Horne, bishop of Norwich], *A Letter to Adam Smith on the Life, Death and Philosophy of His Friend David Hume . . . by One of the People Called Christian* (Oxford, 1779), 11, 29, 32. The pamphlet went through at least five editions (the first in 1777, the last in 1799 by the SPCK). Much of the "Letter on Infidelity" is spent attacking Hume's view of suicide. William Wilberforce, *A Practical View of the Prevailing Religious System of Professed Christians in the Higher and Middle Classes in This Country Contrasted with Real Christianity* (London, 1797), 387–388, 474.

166. [Samuel Jackson Pratt], *An Apology for the Life and Writings of David Hume with a Parallel between Him and the Late Lord Chesterfield . . . an Address to One of the People Called Christian . . .* (London, 1777), 1, 6, 157, 167. This book went through at least three editions. Fieser reprints thirty responses to Smith.

167. Mr. Pratt [Samuel Jackson], *A Supplement to the Life of David Hume, Esq. Containing Genuine Details of His Death and Funeral . . .* (London, 1777), 42–44.

CHAPTER 5: THE CEMETERY AND THE NEW REGIME

Epigraph: F-M. Marchant, *Le nouveau conducteur de l'étranger à Paris* (Paris: J. Moronval, 1824), 266. This description of cemeteries does not appear in the 1818 edition.

1. Karl Marx, "The 18th Brumaire of Louis Bonaparte," in *the Marx-Engels Reader*, 2nd ed. (New York: W. W. Norton), 595.

2. Jacques Derrida, *Specters of Marx*, trans. Peggy Kamuf (New York: Routledge, 1994), haunts these paragraphs.

3. Epitaphs are from Christian Charlet, *Le Père Lachaise au coeur du Paris: Des vivants et des morts* (Paris: Gallimard, 2003), 107, 102. On Raphael, see Marie Lathers, *Bodies of Art: French Literary Realism and the Artist's Model* (Lincoln: University of Nebraska Press, 2001), 65–66; and Sarah Betzer, "Artist as Lover: Rereading Ingres's *Raphael and the Fornarina*," *Oxford Art Journal* (Summer 2015): 5. I am grateful to Professor Betzer for these references.

4. See chapter 3, note 4.

5. I came upon this passage from Bismarck at the historical exhibition that interpreted the Friedhof der Märzgefallenen in Friedrichshain Park when I visited in 2013. It reads in full: "Gestern war ich mit Malle [Malwine von Arnim-Kröchlendorff, Schwester Bismarcks] in Friedrichshain, und nicht einmal den Todten konnte ich vergeben, mein Herz war voller Bitterkeit über den Götzendienst mit dem die Gräber dieser Verbrecher, wo jede Inschrift auf den Kreuzen von 'Freiheit und Recht' prahlt, ein Hohn für Gott und Menschen. Wohl sage ich mir, wir stecken alle in Sünden, und Gott allein weiß, wie er uns versuchen darf; aber mein Herz schwillt von Gift, wenn ich sehe, was sie aus meinem Vaterland gemacht haben, diese Mörder, mit deren Gräber die Berliner noch heut Götzendienst treiben." 16 September 1849. *Führt Bismark's Briefe an seine Braut und Gattin* (Stuttgart: Cotta), 143–144. The organized working class resisted the destruction of this cemetery for use as a train station; it has remained what Durkheim would have understood as a sacred site. On the site, see Heike Abraham, *Der Friedrichshain: Die Geschichte eines Berliner Parks von 1840 bis zur Gegenwart* (Berlin: Kulturbund der DDR, 1988); Heike Naumann, *Der Friedrichshain: Geschichte einer Berliner Parkanlage* (Berlin: Heimatmuseum Friedrichshain, 1994); and Kathrin Chod, Herbert Schwenk, Hainer Weißpflug, *Berliner Bezirkslexikon Friedrichshain-Kreuzberg* (Berlin: Haude & Spener, 2003). On the revolutionary cult of the dead and the connections between the dead of 1848 and 1918, see Hettling, *Totenkult statt Revolution: 1848 und seine Opfer* (Frankfurt am Main: S. Fischer, 1998); and Heinz Warnecke, *Opfer der Novemberrevolution 1918 auf dem Friedhof der 1848er Märzgefallenen Stadtbezirk Friedrichshain-Kreuzberg* (Berlin: Geschichtskommission der PDS Friedrichshain-Kreuzberg, 2003). I am grateful to Alice Goff for this research. On Picpus, see the material on the Northwestern University website: "Picpus, Walled Garden of Memory: Digital Archives," http://picpus.mmlc .northwestern.edu/mbin/WebObjects/Picpus.woa/wa/overView. For Friedrichsfeld Cemetery, see Élise Julien and Elsa Vonau, "Le cimetière de Friedrichsfelde, construction d'un espace socialiste (des années 1880 aux années 1970)," *Le Mouvement Social* 237 (April 2011): http://www.cairn.info/revue-le-mouvement-social -2011-4-page-91.htm.

6. I hope it is evident how much I have borrowed here, and throughout this book, from Émile Durkheim's *Elementary Forms of Religious Life*, trans. Joseph Ward Swain (New York: Free Press, 1965), esp. 78ff. and 465 ff. The force of the dead, like religious forces more generally, are "human forces, moral forces."

7. William Godwin's views are in the 1st ed. of *An Enquiry Concerning Political Justice* (London: G.G.J. and J. Robinson, 1793), bk. 8, chap. 7, 860–895. Malthus's devastating critique of Godwin's and Condorcet's ideas of progress is in the introduction of his *Essay on Population*.

8. Thomas Southwood-Smith, M.D. (1788–1861), to Edwin Chadwick, MS, University College London. Emphasis in original.

9. On the status of this report in Chadwick's work, see Samuel Finer, *The Life and Work of Edwin Chadwick* (London: Methuen, 1952), 231.

10. Philippe Ariès, *The Hour of Our Death*, trans. Helen Weaver (East Rutherford, N.J.: Penguin, 1983). The reference to "a cool sweet grave" is from the text cited in the next note.

11. John Strang, *Necropolis Glasguensis* (Glasgow: Atkinson, 1831), 59.

12. Chadwick quote is cited in Sandra Hempel, *The Strange Case of the Broad Street Pump* (Berkeley: University of California Press, 2007), 115 and 35–37 more generally. Finer, *Life and Work of Edwin Chadwick*, 352, 230. See Christopher Hamlin, *Public Health and Social Justice in the Age of Chadwick* (Cambridge: Cambridge University Press, 1998), 251–256, for the broader political context of policing dead bodies and the lives of the poor more generally.

13. David Barnes, *The Great Stink of Paris* (Baltimore: Johns Hopkins University Press, 2006), 239.

14. On density of burial in London, see Edwin Chadwick, *Supplementary Report of the Results of a Special Inquiry into the Practice of Interment in Towns* (London: W. Clowes, 1843), Volume 12.395 [509], p. 274. This was a supplement to the 1842 *Inquiry into the Sanitary Condition of the Labouring Population of Great Britain*, 1842 (006) [House of Lords] XXVI.1, one of the founding documents of public health reform. Both of these documents were published as parliamentary papers and as self-contained best-selling books on their own.

15. George Alfred Walker, *Gatherings from Graveyards* (London: Longman, 1839; reprint, New York: Arno Press, 1977), 162, 168, 170; Walker, *Burial Ground Incendiarism: The Last Fire at the Bone-House in Spa-Fields* (London: Longman, 1846), 25 and passim. At the beginning of this book, Walker gives an account of his life's work going back to 1835, although his interest goes back to his boyhood in Nottingham, where he was shocked by the churning of human remains in local churchyards. See Walker's *Dictionary of National Biography* entry.

16. See Chadwick, *Supplementary Report*, 274.

17. "Matter out of place" is the anthropologist Mary Douglas's definition of dirt in *Purity and Danger: An Analysis of Concepts of Pollution and Taboo* (New York: Praeger, 1966), 41. Estimates for human feces production vary greatly; some sources go as low as three ounces per day. I have used here the numbers used in Martin Carver, *Underneath British Towns: Interpreting Urban Archaeology* (London: B. T. Batsford, 1987), 97, but since I am speaking here of orders of magnitude, the precise number is not of critical importance. For the weight of dead bodies, I take each to weigh on average one hundred pounds. This is probably high, given the proportion of infants and young

children among the dead, but I am interested only in orders of magnitude here. Henry Mayhew, *London Labour and the London Poor* (1861–1862; reprint, New York: Dover, 1968), 196. Mayhew is quoting annual figures from Charles Cochrane, an official at the Tax and Stamp Office, who he thinks overestimates things a bit. Mayhew himself estimates one thousand tons a week, or fifty-two thousand tons a year. On sheep to Smithfield and the nuisance posed by abattoirs generally, see the richly documented article by Ian MacLachian, "A Bloody Offal Nuisance: The Persistence of Private Slaughterhouses in Nineteenth-Century London," *Urban History* 34, no. 2 (2007): 228 and 227–254.

18. William Hale, *Intramural Burial in England Not Injurious to the Public Health, Its Abolition Injurious to Religion and Morals: A Charge, Addressed to the Clergy of the Archdeaconry of London, May 16, 1855*, 2nd ed. (London: Gilbert and Rivington, 1855), 26–27. On the history of smell, see Alain Corbin, *The Foul and the Fragrant: Odor and the French Social Imagination* (Cambridge, Mass.: Harvard University Press, 1986).

19. Sir Francis Bacon, *Sylva Sylvarum: or, A Natural History in Ten Centuries*, in *Works of Francis Bacon*, ed. Spedding et al. (New York: Hurd and Houghton, 1864), 4:320. It is followed by a section on doing the opposite, i.e., preventing putrefaction. The use of charcoal in English graves has been thoroughly documented for medieval England: see Carver, *Underneath British Towns*, 95ff.; Robert Gilchrist and Barney Sloane, *Requiem: The Medieval Monastic Cemetery in Britain* (London: Museum of London Archaeology, 2005), 120–123; and John Stenhouse, "On the Economical Applications of Charcoal to Sanitary Purposes," *Notices and Proceedings of the Meetings of Members of the Royal Institution of Great Britain* 2 (1854–1858): 53.

20. *"Health of Towns": An Examination of the Report and Evidence of the Select Committee; of Mr Mackinnon's Bill and of the Acts for Establishing Cemeteries around the Metropolis* (London: John Snow, 1843), 47–54 and passim. This thorough and generally sensible critique is a collection of "Letters to Dissenters" that had been published in the respectable Congregationalist journal, the *Patriot*.

21. MS text accompanying the engraving, vol. 8, no. 180, British Museum, Dept. of Prints and Drawings, Pennant Collection, British Library. Brent Elliot, typescript, "Notes on the Rosary: England's First Non-denominational Cemetery" (1982), Norwich Local History Library. John Evelyn, *Diary of John Evelyn*, ed. William Bray (Washington, D.C.: Walter Dunne, 1901), 73 (17 October 1671).

22. Mrs. Basil Holmes, *The London Burial Grounds* (New York: Macmillan, 1896), 192. Sidonius Apollinaris, Epistle 3.12, ed. F. Luetjohann, *MGH, AA VIII*, 47–48, quoted in Donald Bullough, "Burial, Community, and Belief in the Early Medieval West," in P. Wormald et al., eds., *Ideal and Reality in Frankish and Anglo-Saxon Society* (Oxford: Blackwell, 1983), 187. Latimer's "Sermon, 3rd Sunday of Advent, 1552," quoted in J. H. Markland, *Remarks on English Churches* (Oxford, 1842), 109. For St. Paul in 1582 and St. Botolph, see Vanessa Harding, "'And One More May Be Laid There': The Location of Burials in Early Modern London," *London Journal* 14, no. 2 (November 1989): 112–129. The problem of space was by no means unique to urban churchyards. In the 1840s, the churchwardens of the tiny Oxfordshire parish of Combe and the rector

of Lincoln College quarreled about whether, as they claimed, everyone was entitled to a private burial place and whether outsiders might be buried in the churchyard. The rector solicited the sexton's testimony; even as things stood, the sexton said, "he scarcely knows where to put a spade" and that "he digs up human bones almost every time he digs a grave." *Correspondence between the Churchwardens of Combe and the Rector of Lincoln*, 2nd ed. (N.p., 1850). William Beck, *The London Friends' Meetings: Showing the Rise of the Society of Friends in London, Its Progress . . . with Accounts of Various Meeting-Houses and Burial-Grounds, Their History . . .* (London: F. B. Kitto, 1869), 329–330. Beck recounts controversies over whether cattle or sheep should be allowed to graze in the burial ground—not finally forbidden until 1769—and whether washerwomen and leather dryers should be able to use the space for their work, 330–333. Hugh Latimer, *Select Sermons* (Boston: Hilliard and Gray, 1832), 276.

23. *Journals of the House of Commons*, vol. 34 (1773): 659, and vol. 25 (1758): 274 and 243, for original petition.

24. William Tarbutt, *The Annals of Cranbrook Church* (Cranbrook, 1873), 26. R. Latham and W. Matthews, eds., *The Diary of Samuel Pepys* (Berkeley: University of California Press, 1971), 5:90 (18 March 1664). Warwick Rodwell, *Archaeology of the English Church* (London: B. T. Batsford, 1981), 157. *Dictionnaire philosophique* (Paris, 1764), quoted in Michel Ragon, *Spaces of Death*, trans. Alan Sheridan (Charlottesville: University Press of Virginia, 1983), 199. When Samuel Pepys in 1664 asked to have his brother buried in the middle aisle of St. Bride's in the City, the sexton, after accepting a 6d. tip, promised to find him a berth: "I will jostle them [other bodies] but I will make room for him." Voltaire, "Questions sur l'*Encyclopédie* (C–E)," in *Collection complète des oeuvres de M. de Voltaire* (Geneva: [Cramer], 1768–1777), 617. My translation. The quote comes from the entry "cadavres," which is worth reading if only to show how a man who was so disdainful of mortal remains and hostile to the traditional burial place would care so much about what happened to his body upon death.

25. *Report of the General Board of Health: A Inquiry as to the State of the Burial Grounds in the Township of Huddersfield, William Lee, Superintending Inspector under Nuisances Removal and Diseases Prevention Act* (London: W. Clowes, 1850), 9. Robert Rawlinson, *Report to the General Board of Health on an Inquiry as to the Burial-Grounds in the Borough of Dorchester, and the Outlying Part of the Parish of Fordington, in the County of Dorset* (London: Eyre and Spottiswoode, 1852).

26. Chadwick, *Supplementary Report*, 270.

27. George Milner, *Cemetery Burial or Sepulture, Ancient and Modern* (London: Masters, 1847), ix–x. Mrs. Basil Holmes, *The London Burial Grounds* (New York: Macmillan, 1896), 156. Jim Morgan, "The Burial Question in Leeds in the Eighteenth and Nineteenth Centuries," in Ralph Houlbrooke, ed., *Death, Ritual and Bereavement* (New York: Routledge, 1989), 95–104.

28. Joseph Aston, *A Picture of Manchester* (Manchester: Printed and published by the author, 1816), 83–85. When the new burial ground was opened up, the old one, more than full, at the top Hunt's Bank, was closed. On Liverpool, see *Picture of Liverpool or Stranger's Guide* (Liverpool: Thomas Taylor 1834), 125–126.

29. Walter E. Brown, *A Short History of St. Pancras' Cemeteries* (London: E. Mitchener, 1896). Some of the demolished churchyard's soil was recycled in a strange way. When the bishop of London refused to consecrate the famous Methodist preacher George Whitfield's new chapel burial ground in 1780, Whitfield managed to salvage cart-loads of dirt of consecrated ground. Frederick Engles, *The Condition of the Working Class in England* (1844; reprint, Oxford: Oxford University Press 1993), 163. On Hardy's work for Blomfield in 1866, see Claire Tomalin, *Thomas Hardy* (New York: Penguin, 2007), 80–81. Captain Frederick Marryat, *Diary in America* (New York: H. Colyer, 1839), 25–26.

30. See *"Health of Towns": An Examination of the Report . . . .* This extensive pamphlet reprints material from a Congregationalist newspaper, the *Patriot*, produced by a committee opposing the bill for the "Improvement of the Health of Towns."

31. *Report of the Committee of the Commissioners of the Sewers for the City of London Acting as the Burial Board for the Said City . . . upon the Address of the Archdeacon of London, on November, 1855* (London: M. Lownds, 1856).

32. Sir John Simon, *Report on the Sanitary Condition of the City of London for the Year 1854–55* (London: M. Lownds, 1855), 10.

33. John Ferriar, M.D., *Medical Histories and Reflections*, 4 vols. (Warrington, 1792), 1:241 and 218ff. generally. *Manchester Mercury*, 28 February 1786, back page, not numbered. Walker, *Gatherings from Graveyards*, v. Chadwick to Metropolitan Sewage Committee Proceedings, *Report from the Select Committee on Metropolitan Sewage Manure*, Parliamentary Papers 1846 (474), p. 109. Letter from W. F. Chambers, M.D., FRS, RCP, to the MacKinnon Committee, in "Effect of Interment of Bodies in Towns," *Report from the Select Committee on the Improvement of the Health of Towns*, House of Commons Papers 1842 (327), p. 196.

34. For the Greeks, I rely on Robert Parker's wonderful *Miasma: Pollution and Purification in Early Greek Religion* (Oxford: Clarendon Press, 1983). Miasma theory in many guises is endemic in nineteenth-century thinking. There is a good summary in A. S. Wohl, *Endangered Lives: Public Health in Victorian Britain* (London: Methuen, 1984).

35. *First Report of the Commissioners for Inquiring into the State of Large Towns and Populous Districts.* Parliamentary Papers, 1844, XVII.1. [572], p. 17.

36. World Health Organization, "Mortuary Service and the Handling of the Dead," in B. Wisner and J. Adams, eds., *Environmental Health in Emergencies and Disasters: A Practical Guide* (Geneva: WHO, 2002), chap. 14, 198ff. Médecins Sans Frontières, *Public Health Engineering in Precarious Situations*, 2nd. ed. (2010), 8.1, http://refbooks.msf.org/msf_docs /en/public_health_en.pdf. C. de Ville de Goyet, "Stop Propagating Disaster Myths," *Lancet* 356, no. 9231 (26 August 2000): 762. I am, of course, not suggesting that dead bodies are never dangerous. I was almost not born because my father got hepatitis by cutting himself while doing an autopsy on someone with the disease. See also note 38 below.

37. Wisner and Adams, *Environmental Health in Emergencies and Disasters*, 198–201. The dead should be promptly buried, the authors say, because their presence and their odors are deeply disturbing to the living. *Disaster Manuals and Guidelines Series*, no. 5 (Washing-

ton, D.C.: Pan American Health Organization, WHO, 2004), 71ff. and passim. See Oliver Morgan, "Infectious Disease Risks from Dead Bodies Following Disasters," *Revista Panamericana de Salud Pública / Pan American Journal of Public Health* 15, no. 5 (2004): 307–312, for the precautions that need to be taken when dealing with diseased bodies, living and dead. All of these works do a thorough review of the literature.

38. Walker, *Gatherings from Graveyards*, 92. M. [Henri] Haguenot, *Melanges curieux et interessans de divers objets rélatifs à la physique, à la medicine, à l'histoire naturelle* (Paris: Chez Joseph Robert, 1771), 6 ff. The North and Central American striped and spotted skunk belongs to the genus *M. mephitis*; in Roman mythology Mephitis was a divinity who had a grove that was thought fatal to enter; she seems also to have been a goddess who protected against dangerous emanations. As late as 1854, a Select Committee tried to get John Snow, the well-known anti-miasmatist who had correctly identified the water at the Broad Street Pump, to comment on the long tradition that Haguenot had begun. No, he told the committee, ordinary decomposing animal matter was not dangerous. They asked him about vaults; yes, gases were dangerous in extremely concentrated amounts, but had no ill effect in the long run if they didn't kill instantly. Vomiting was caused only by great concentrations, mostly "by sympathy . . . persons [being] influenced by the imagination." *Report of the Select Committee on the Public Health Bill*, 1854–1855 (244) xiii, 122.

39. Bernardino Ramazzini, *Diseases of Workers*, trans. Wilmer Cave Wright (1700; reprint, New York: Hafner, 1964), chaps. 14 and 18.

40. James Curry, *Popular Observations on Apparent Death from Drowning, Suffocation etc. with an Account of the Means to Be Employed for Recovery* (Northampton: W. Birdsall and T. Burnham and J. Johnson, 1792), 62–63; and Curry, *Observations on Apparent Death*, 2nd ed. (London: E. Cox, 1815), 72–73 and n. 22 in the appendix. CO_2 gas is today used in animal euthanasia. The mechanisms for carbon dioxide toxicity were not determined until the twentieth century by Hans Winterstein, who discovered carbon dioxide's role in triggering respiration.

41. Metthieu Orfila and Octave Lesueur, *Traité des exhumations juridiques* (Paris: Bechet Jeune, 1831), 10. Parent quoted in Jacques Alphonse Guerard, *Des inhumations and les exhumations sous la rapport de l'hygiene* (Paris: Felix Loquin, 1838), 33, who cites English evidence that putrid vapors are not dangerous. His articles appeared in *Annals d'hygiene*, vols. 5, 8, and 9. No one is quite sure why necropsy seems to be more dangerous than nursing live TB patients, but this is the current view. See Gary L. Templeton et al., "The Risk of Transmission of *Mycobacterium tuberculosis* at Autopsy," *Annals of Internal Medicine* 122, no. 12 (15 June 1995): 922–925; and John A. Sbarbaro, "Tuberculosis: Yesterday, Today and Tomorrow," *Annals of Internal Medicine* 122, no. 12 (15 June 1995): 955–956, for editorial comment. Cases of TB transmission among embalmers—that is, their having been infected by the TB bacillus, although not necessarily either having a latent or active case of the disease—are common enough to warrant a report in a leading journal: J. L. Burton, "Health and Safety at Necropsy," *Journal of Clinical Pathology* 56 (2003): 254–260. The article speculates that transmission may be via an aerosol created by aspirating blood and other fluids. See Timothy R. Sterling,

"Transmission of *mycobacterium tuberculosis* from a Cadaver to an Embalmer," *New England Journal of Medicine* 342, no. 4 (27 January 2000): 246–248. In some diseases, ebola, for example, cadavers may spread the disease both because the fluids of the body are so exposed—blood leaks from open sores, bodies are often covered in vomit—and because some traditional African funeral rituals involve contact with the body far more intimate than was common in Europe. Heinz Feldmann and Thomas W. Geisbert, "Ebola Haemorrhagic Fever," *Lancet* 377 (5 March 2011): 849–862.

42. For Leeds, see Sylvia M. Barnard, *To Prove I Am Not Forgot: Living and Dying in a Victorian City* (Manchester: Manchester University Press, 1990), 15. On Snow, see Sandra Hempl, *The Strange Case of the Broad Street Pump: John Snow and the Mystery of Cholera* (Berkeley: University of California Press, 2007), 278.

43. Biographical details from the *Dictionary of National Biography*. Southwood-Smith, like Walker and unlike Chadwick, thought that the putrefying dead were more pathogenic than the fresh. Regarding the mummy and the statue, see Robert Pogue Harrison in his discussion of Michel Serres, *The Dominion of the Dead* (Chicago: University of Chicago Press, 2003), 20–21 and chap. 2 more generally. As I said in the acknowledgments, I owe more to Harrison than my occasional references attest.

44. Louis Bertaglio, *Les cimetières au point de vue l'hygiene et de l'administration*, chaps. 6–7, gives an up-to-date survey as of 1889. Dr. du Mesnil put four rabbits and six chickens at the same level as bodies in a nearby grave; no ill effects. No ill effects after five months of direct contact with putrefying bodies; Prof. Colin killed rabbits, chickens, and dogs with anthrax and buried them at various depths. He penned animals above their graves; no effect; injected them with water from the soil; no effect. Mr. Carrot tested water from Parisian cemeteries; no taste, dissolved soap well; no evidence that it would compromise public health, etc.

45. "A Clergyman" [Thomas Lewis, 1689–1737], *Churches Not Charnel Houses: Being an Enquiry into the Profaness, Indecency, and Pernicious Consequences of Burying the Dead in Churches and Churchyards Shewing . . . That the Original of This Practice Was Founded in Pride, Improved by Superstition, and Encouraged for Lucre* (London: A Bettesworth, 1726), 54–55. Lewis's *Dictionary of National Biography* entry identifies him as a "religious controversialist." His opponents in this tract are Roman Catholics but also Low Church clergy who make money from the practice he abhors. His ideal church is that of St. Cyril, bishop of fifth-century Alexandria. I quote him not because he is at all typical in his views but because he illustrates the historical depth of the argument from abjection. Lewis's views find echoes in other traditions. According to Mishnah Ohalot 18.8, a Jew who enters to live in a house in Eretz Israel that previously belonged to a goy should examine it for buried abortives because of corpse impurity, since according to the sages, the Goyim are suspected to be buried in their houses. My thanks to David Nirenberg for sending me this reference.

46. *The Collected Works of John Stuart Mill*, vol. 18: *Essays on Politics and Society, Part 1*, ed. John Robson (Toronto: University of Toronto Press, 2006), "Civilization" (1836). Online version provided by Liberty Fund. I am of course only hinting at a vast and

controversial discussion of biopower. For a conspectus, see Timothy Campbell and Adam Sitze, eds., *Bio-politics: A Reader* (Durham, N.C.: Duke University Press, 2013).

47. Hale, *Intramural Burial*, 16. Ariès, *Hour of Our Death.*

48. Vicq d'Azyr, *An Exposition of the Dangers of Interment in Cities, Illustrated by an Account of the Funeral Rites and Customs of the Hebrews, Greeks, Romans and Primitive Christians; by Ancient and Modern Ecclesiastical Canons, Civil Statutes and Municipal Regulations; and by Chemical and Physical Principles* (New York: W. B. Gilley, 1823), 357.

49. *Church of England Quarterly Review* (London: William Painter) 7 (1840): 270.

50. Howard Colvin, *Architecture and the After-Life* (New Haven, Conn.: Yale University Press, 1991), 190–363; the remark by Wright is on 332. Along with Colvin, Richard A. Etlin's *The Architecture of Death: The Transformation of the Cemetery in Eighteenth-Century Paris* (Cambridge, Mass.: MIT Press, 1984); and James Stevens Curl's *Death and Architecture* (London: B. T. Batsford, 1993) provide the basic chronological basis for this section. Blanche M. G. Linden, *Silent City on a Hill: Picturesque Landscapes of Memory and Boston's Mount Auburn Cemetery* (Amherst: University of Massachusetts Press, 2007) offers an exemplary history of how their story was translated into an American context.

51. An authoritative account of the building of Castle Howard and its mausoleum, based on extensive archival research, is Charles Saumarez Smith, *The Building of Castle Howard* (London: Faber and Faber, 1990), esp. 159–192. The quotations from Vanbrugh are on 161; on Toland's biography, see the *Dictionary of National Biography*, and for Carlisle's relationship to him, see Smith, 167. For the parts I quote, see John Toland, *Letters to Serena* (London, 1704), 97, 123; on 127 he writes about "the worship of dead men and women." See also Colvin, *Architecture and the After-Life*, 316–322. On questions where the two differ—Colvin claims, as did contemporary sources, that the Earl of Carlisle was interred in his completed mausoleum when he died in 1738—I follow Smith, who shows clearly that this was not the case. By 1760, according to Colvin, there were at least twenty-five freestanding monuments in England and Scotland, although only a handful were outside churchyards. There were some, but very few, mausoleums in the churchyards of Europe, and none outside their bounds, before Castle Howard. Of course, having a neoclassical mausoleum was not in itself a rejection of Christianity. Christian emperors after Constantine, and others of the Christian imperial aristocracy as well, continued to build tombs in the grand pagan manner, but this bit of transitional history is not referenced in Hawksmoor's design. On this, see Frederick S. Paxton, "Communities of the Living and the Dead in Late Antiquity and the Early Medieval West," in Mark Williams, ed., *The Making of Christian Communities in Late Antiquity and the Middle Ages* (London: Wimbleton, 2005), 56–57. On the elimination of all signs of the rural population, see John Barrell, *The Dark Side of the Landscape: The Rural Poor in English Painting, 1730–1840* (Cambridge: Cambridge University Press, 1980). For a survey of mausoleums in churchyards and outside them, county by county, see Lynn F. Pearson, *Mausoleums* (Princes Risborough: Shire Books, 2002).

52. Toland, a materialist and deist who was in constant trouble with authorities of various sorts, came into high Whig circles through the Third Earl of Shaftesbury and

would later be influential on d'Holbach and Diderot. He failed to make Leibniz appreciate the troublesome Giordano Bruno, with whom he identified and who was burned at the stake for heresy in 1600. When Sarah Churchill died in 1744, the First Duke's bones were exhumed from Westminster Abbey and buried with her in the chapel on the estate. See *Dictionary of National Biography* entry. The Duchess almost went along with Vanbrugh's plan; in 1723, Hawksmoor designed a triumphal arch at the Woodstock entrance to their estate, and Lord Burlington convinced her to build a 137-foot victory column; a tomb would have completed the classical fantasy.

53. "Castle-Howard, the Seat of the Right Honourable Charles Earl of Carlisle" (London: E. Owen, 1732), 7, 5. For the Elysian Fields association more generally and the attribution of this poem to the Earl's daughter, see Etlin, *Architecture of Death*, 171–172.

54. For Rosa, see Baron de Tschoudy's article "Bosquet" in the 1776 *Encyclopédie*, cited in Dora Wiebenson, *The Picturesque Garden in France* (Princeton, N.J.: Princeton University Press), 28, and for the influence of Stowe more generally, 3–63 passim.

55. See Peter Willis, "Rousseau, Stowe, and le Jardin Anglais: Speculation on Visual Sources for *La Nouvelle Heloise*," in Theodore Bestermann, ed., *Studies on Voltaire in the Eighteenth Century* (Oxford: Voltaire Foundation, 1972), 15:1791–1798. Denis Diderot to Sophie Volland, 6 October 1765, in Diderot, *Correspondance*, vol. 5: *January 1765–February 1766*, ed. Georges Roth (Paris: Editions de Minuit), 130.

56. For Milles's remark, see G. B. Clarke, *Descriptions of Lord Cobham's Gardens at Stowe* (Aylesbury: Buckinghamshire Record Society, 1990), 61. Walpole's quip is in *Anecdotes of Painting in England: With Some Account of the Principal Artists and Incidental Notes on Other Arts* (Strawberry Hill: Thomas Kirgate, 1771), 4, 11. Virgil, *The Aeneid,* trans. Robert Fagles (London: Penguin Books, 2006), lines 764 ff., p. 204; the definition of Elysium is from p. 203, line 742. Contemporaries not good at Latin would have looked up these lines in John Dryden's already famous and often reprinted 1697 translation.

57. The epitaph to Signor Fido was well known and much imitated at the time. Indeed, pet elegies and epitaphs were something of a minor genre. See Ingrid H. Tague, "Dead Pets: Satire and Sentiment in British Elegies and Epitaphs for Animals," *Eighteenth Century Studies* 451, no. 3 (2008): 289–306.

58. Geo[rge] Bickham, *The Beauties of Stow* (London, ca. 1756), 20. Clarke, *Descriptions of Lord Cobham's Gardens at Stowe*, quotes the anonymous "Lord Cobham's Gardens" (1742), on 69, 74. Daniel Defoe [and Samuel Richardson], *A Tour thro' the Whole Island of Great Britain*, appendix to the 3rd ed. (1742), on 88. Samuel Boyse, "The Triumphs of Nature" (1742), on 106.

59. Kenneth Woodbridge, *The Stourhead Landscape* (London: National Trust, 1982); and his *Landscape and Antiquity: Aspects of English Culture at Stourhead, 1718 to 1838* (London: Clarendon Press, 1970), 3–9, 24–26. For a classic article that traces a long century's debates about how to re-create Elysium, see H. F. Clark, "Eighteenth Century Elysiums: The Role of 'Association' in the Landscape Movement," *Journal of the Warburg and Courtauld Institute* 6 (1943): 165–189.

60. C.C.L. Hirschfeld, *Theorie der Kartenkunst* (Leipzig: M. G. Weidmanns Erben und Reich, 1780), 3, 200. The most useful article on Wiedewelt is Else Marie Bukdahl,

"Wiedewelt's Memorials in Memorial Park at Jaegerspris: 'A Breakthrough into New Territory,'" in Marjatta Nielsen and Annetter Rathje, eds., *Johannes Wiedewelt: A Danish Artist in Search of the Past, Shaping the Future* (Copenhagen: Museum Tusculanum Press, 2010), 175–205. On why Hirschfeld regarded Jaegerspris as important, see Annie Christensen, "Thoughts on Nordmandsdal, Fredensborg, Denmark," *Garden History* 17, no. 2 (1989): 154–165; and Margarethe Floryan, "*Hortus moralis:* C.C.L. Hirschfeld and Other Eighteenth-Century Actors in the German Borderland," *Studies in the History of Gardens and Designed Landscapes* 29, no. 4 (2009): 246–256. On Jaegerspris's connection to archeology, see Karen Sanders, "'Upon the Bedrock of Material Things': The Journey to the Past in Danish Archaeological Imagination," in Karen Povlsen and Karen Klitgaard, eds., *Northbound* (Aarhus: Aarhus University Press, 2007), 147–166.

61. On individual memorial stones and their allegorical meanings, see Bukdahl, "Wiedewelt's Memorials"; and Hakon Lund, "Two Danish Gardens in the Age of Enlightenment," *Journal of Garden History* 17, no. 4 (1997): 233–244. I am grateful to Mette Skougaard for sending me an annotated copy of her talk "The Norwegian Garden Theatre—The Nordmandsdal in Fredensborg," which is based on her thoroughly researched Danish thesis.

62. The translation from Idyll 7 is from *The Idylliums of Theocritus: With [René] Rapin's Discourse upon Pastorals; Made English by Mr. Creech* (London, 1721), 99, an edition available to the landscape architects of the period. Rapin points out in his introduction that funeral rites are on occasion the subject of pastorals and that they are innocent, even cheery occasions: "the shepherds scatter flowers on the Tomb and sing rustic songs," 20. No one knows who Brasilas was—a local hero or a mythological character—but W. Geoffrey Arnott thinks the reference is to an actual tumulus on Cos, i.e., that we should take the topography of tombs in the poem seriously ("The Mound of Brasilas in Theocritus' Seventh 'Idyll,'" *Quaderni Urbininati di Cukltura Classica*, n.s. 3, no. 3 [1979]: 104–105).

63. My thanks to conversations with my friend Paul Alpers on this subject and to his book *What Is Pastoral?* (Chicago: University of Chicago Press, 1996). Alpers thinks that "if anything Virgil perceives a consonance between suffering and ideal landscape. Rather than expressing nostalgia, the poem anatomizes it" (68).

64. Edwin Panofsky, "Et in Arcadia Ego," in *Meaning in the Visual Arts* (New York: Doubleday, 1955), 316.

65. W. Shenstone, *The Letters of William Shenstone*, ed. M. Williams (Oxford: Blackwell, 1939), 524–525 quoted in D. Coffin, "The Elysian Fields of Rousham," *Proceedings of the American Philosophical Society* 130, no. 4 (December 1986): 413–414.

66. On the history of later misdescription and Giradin's visit, see Margaret Denton, "Death in French Arcady: Nicolas Poussin's 'The Arcadian Shepherds' and Burial Reform in France c. 1800," *Eighteenth Century Studies* 36, no. 2 (2003): 201–206 and 195–216 passim.

67. Hemans is most famous for her "Casabianca," about the death of Louis de Casabianca and his son, which was one of the most recited poems of the century. I discuss it in chapter 9.

68. See John Hibbred, *Salomon Gessner: His Creative Achievement and Influence* (Cambridge: Cambridge University Press, 1976), 140–141 and passim.

69. The first line is my translation from his *Vermischte Gedichte, Salomon Gessners* Schriften 1, (Zurich: Beim Verfasser, 1776), 139–140; the second from *New Idylles by Gessner*, trans. W. Hooper, M.D. (London, 1776), idyll 13, 41.

70. F*J*B** [Franz Joseph Bueler], *Geschichte von Salomon Gessners Denkmal im Clönthal* (Bregenz, Austria: Brentano and Heissler, 1789). Bueler (1751–1816) was a Swiss amateur composer who made his living as a government official. Marguerite, Countess of Blessington, *The Idler in Italy* (London: Henry Colburn, 1839), 1, 33.

71. Nikolaus Pevsner and Jennifer Sherwood, *The Buildings of England: Oxfordshire* (Harmondsworth: Penguin, 1974); the quote is on 724–725, see 725–730 more generally. *Description of Nuneham-Courtenay, in the County of Oxford* ([Oxford?], 1797), 11. Nicholas Penny, "The Macabre Garden at Denbies and Its Monument," *Garden History* 3, no. 3 (1975): 58–61. The Lyde mausoleums in Ayot St. Lawrence, Hertfordshire, are another stunning example of a tomb, i.e., mausoleum, that looks like a large Greek temple with ancillary wings (Pearson, *Mausoleums*, 18).

72. Thomas Whately, *Observations on Modern Gardening* (London: T. Payne, 1770). The literature on the philosophical and psychological theory of eighteenth-century gardens is huge, but a useful introduction is Agnieszka Morawinska, "'Paysages Moralisés,'" *Journal of the History of Ideas* 38, no. 3 (1977): 461–475; and on the English garden in particular, John Dixon Hunt and Peter Willis, eds., *The Genius of Place* (New York: Harper and Row, 1975). John Loudon, *An Encyclopedia of Gardening* (London: Longman, 1835), 319, entry 1151. The quotation about Glasgow comes from a well-known promotional pamphlet by the man behind the new necropolis in that city, John Strang. See *Necropolis Glasguensis* (1831), 62, which I discuss below. But I cite it here from a long review in *Gardiner's Magazine* 19 (1843): 103, of a book by its own editor, J. C. Loudon, *Principles of Landscape-Gardening Applied to Public Cemeteries*, to suggest the cultural currency of these views. Loudon was the leading horticulturist of the nineteenth century.

73. Hirschfeld, *Theorie der Kartenkunst*, 2:59–60. No one, writes the German historian of gardens Barbara Happe, has influenced the development of the cemetery more than Hirschfeld. After him, the place of burial was a category of the garden (*Der Entwicklung der deutschen Friedhöfe ven der Refomration bis 1870* [Tübingen: Vereinigung für Volkskunde, 1991], 223ff.). Morel's chapter begins with the statement that "*le pays*" in the sense of "landscape" is a "great machine demanding of an enormous imagination and talent; it is to art what the epic poem is to poetry." In Ermenonville, he says, we find "*le pays*" in both its forms, wild and civilized, "*partie champêtre and en partie sauvage*." Morel is explicitly committed to the sort of sensationalist psychology used to explain why gardens, and by extension the dead in gardens, affect the soul. J. M. Morel, *Théorie des jardins* (Paris: Chez Pissot, 1776), 236, 240, and 236–263 more generally.

74. Lynn F. Pearson, *Mausoleums* (Princes Risborough, UK: Shire Publications, 2002), s.v. "Reynolds Mausoleum." *The Journal of John Wesley*, ed. Nehemiah Curnock (London: Epworth Press, 1960), 5:435.

75. James Stevens Curl, *Journal of Garden History* 14, no. 2 (1994): 92–118. Sandra Beresford et al., *Italian Memorial Sculpture, 1820–1940* (London: Frances Lincoln, 2004), 18–19. Regarding the tomb of the tutor Herr Meyer, see James Edward Smith, *A Sketch of a Tour on the Continent, in the Years 1786 and 1787* (London, 1793), 1:100.

76. Hirschfeld, *Theorie der Kartenkunst*, 5:259–262. Hirschfeld's description in general owes much to Morel's, which he footnotes.

77. The quotation is from J. E. Smith, one of the founders of the Linnean Society, *Sketch of a Tour on the Continent*, 1:100–101. On the significance of the tomb, see Joseph Clarke, *Commemorating the Dead in Revolutionary France, 1789–1799* (Cambridge: Cambridge University Press, 2007), 13–21. Clarke rightly sees the tomb as one aspect of the effort to create a new civic culture of virtue through a revolution in burial practices. He thinks this failed because of the deep conservatism of Catholic France. Because I think the idolatry of the dead transcends religion, I will emphasize instead the success of the new necrogeography. See also the excellent survey by Gordeon McNeil, "The Cult of Rousseau and the French Revolution," *Journal of the History of Ideas* 6, no. 2 (1945): 197–212; and Hippolyte Buffenoir, "L'image de J. J. Rousseau dans les sociétés de la Révolution en province," *La Révolution Française* 71 (1918): 50–54. My thanks to Carla Hesse for this reference.

78. *Builder* cited in A. Taigel and T. Williamson, *Parks and Gardens* (London: Batsford, 1993).

79. Sir John Vanburgh, Bodleian MS. Rawlinson B. 376, fols. 351–352, "Suggestions for the Building Q. Anne's Fifty New Churches in London, and for the Establishing Cemeteries in the Outskirts of the City." My thanks to Max Jones, now of the University of Manchester, for transcribing the manuscript for me.

80. The appellation is Quatremère de Quincy's, quoted in Etlin, *Architecture of Death*, 300. On Brongniart, see *Oxford Dictionary of Architecture and Landscaping*; for the suggestion that he was influenced by the Karameikos, see Linden, *Silent City*, 74, although she gives no reference. That said, any literate person in the eighteenth century would have known from reading Jean-Jacques [Abbé] Barthélemy's best-selling and much translated novel *The Travels of Anacharsis the Younger in Greece*, if not from Thucydides and Pausanius, that the war dead of Athens and those "whom their country thought of the most distinguished honours" were buried in the Karameikos and that it was intimately tied to Greek civic life. The *Voyage du jeune Anarcharsis en Grèce*, in the voice of a descendant of the semi-mythic sixth-century B.C.E. Scythian philosopher Anarchsis—a sort of proto-Diogenes, it was said—probably did more than any other single work to create widespread philohellenism and the Greek revival in architecture and design in Europe and the Americas. My short quote is from vol. 2 (out of 7), 107–108 of the 1794 London edition. [Stephen Duncan Walker], from whose *Rural Cemetery and Public Walk* (Baltimore: Sands and Nielson, 1835), 12–13, I quote, might well have learned about Karameikos from an 1830 Baltimore edition of the *Travels*,

although it could have become known to him from scores of earlier U.S. and English editions as well.

81. See Ulrich Rehm, "Ein Schlafplatz der Geschichte: Alexander Lenoir's 'Jardin Elysée,'" in Claudia Denk and John Ziesemer, eds., *Der bürgerliche Tod: Städtische Bestattungskultur von der Aufklärung bis zum frühen 20. Jahrhundert*, ICOMOS, no. 44 (Regensburg: Hefte des Deutschen Nationalkomitees, 2007), 122–131. Molière was immensely popular during the French Revolution. On this and the fate of the bodies, see Michele Leon, "The Poet and the Prince: Revising Molière and *Tartuffe* in the French Revolution," *French Historical Studies* 28, no. 3 (2005): 447–465. There is, curiously, no good scholarly history of Père Lachaise. I piece the story together from Christian Charlet, *Le Père-Lachaise: Au coeur du Paris des vivants et des morts* (Paris: Gallimard, n.d.); Michel Dansel, *Au Père-Lachaise: Son histoire, ses secrets, ses promenandes* (Paris: Fayard, 1973); and Domenico Gabrielli, *Dictionnaire historique du Père-Lachaise, XVII–XIXᵉ siècles* (Paris: Les Editions de l'Amateur, 2002).

82. Roland Recht, "L'Élysée d'Alexandre Lenoir: Nature, art et histoire," *Revue germanique internationale* 7 (1997): http://rgi.revues.org/605. This is the best single source for visual evidence of Lenoir's Elysium.

83. The quote is from William Hickling Prescott, manuscript, "Travel Diary, 1815–1817" (Massachusetts Historical Society, Boston; call number Ms. N-2180), 19 September 1816, leaf 37; my thanks to my colleague Mark Peterson for sending it to me. Prescott's writings on the Conquest of Mexico and of Peru are among the great works of the new scientific history of the nineteenth century. *Gaglignani's New Paris Guide or Stranger Companion* (Paris, 1825), 706, 693. Baedeker, *Paris* (Coblenz: Baedeker, 1865), 122 and sec. 16, 120–130 generally.

84. John Claudius Loudon, *An Encyclopedia of Gardening*, new ed., rev. (London: Longman, 1835), entries 790, 1562. Strang, *Necropolis Glasguensis*, 28. Helen Marcia Bruner, *California's Old Burial Grounds* (San Francisco: National Association of Colonial Dames, 1945), 22 (quoting an 1855 source). Milner, *Cemetery Burial in Sepulture, Ancient and Modern*. Ruskin, "Further Contribution to Loudon's *Architectural Magazine*," in *Works of John Ruskin*, ed. E. T. Cook and Alexander Wedderburn (London: G. Allen, 1903) 1:245–246. He writes to ask Loudon why he had not recommended the weeping willow for churchyards, and Loudon replies that it is associated with wet soils and water, not what one would want in a cemetery.

85. *China Courier* (8 December 1832) quoted in Lindsay Ride and May Ride, *An East India Company Cemetery: Protestant Burials in Macao*, ed. Bernard Mellor (Hong Kong: Hong Kong University Press, 1996), 68. Hansards, 76, col. 1567, 30 July 1845. *A Few Thoughts on the Necessity and Means of Establishing Forthwith a General Public Cemetery in the Immediate Vicinity of the City of Norwich, Addressed to Edward, Lord Bishop of London* (Norwich: Charles Muskett, 1848), 8. The author likes, by contrast, German cemeteries and refers readers to Murray's *Handbook for Northern Germany*.

86. For a generally informative survey of the genealogy of the cemetery in England, see Sarah Tarlow, "Landscapes of Memory: The Nineteenth-Century Garden Cemetery," *European Journal of Archaeology* 3, no. 2 (2000): 217–239.

87. Sir Thomas Herbert, *Some Yeares Travel into Africa and Asia* (London: Jacob Blome, 1638), 337. The book was translated into French and Dutch; each edition was larger than the one before through the addition of ever more secondary material. John Harris, *Navigantium atque itinerantium biblioteca: or A Complete Collection of Voyages and Travels . . .* (London: Thomas Bennett, 1705), 2:350. A. F. Bellasis, "Old Tombs of the Cemeteries of Surat," *Journal of the Bombay Branch of the Royal Asiatic Society* (January 1861): 146–156 and 146–148 in particular.

88. P. H. Dopp, "Le Caire vu par les voyageurs occidentaux du moyen-âge," *Bulletin de la Société Royale de Geographie d'Egypte* 23 (1950): 123, and 24 (1951): 153. Another late medieval traveler says that the burial place of the sultan and of the great aristocracy forms a huge city, as big as a good part of Nuremberg: *Voyage en Egypte de Felix Fabri, 1483,* ed. and trans. from Latin by Jacques Masson, S.J., 3 vols. ([Cairo]: Institut Français d'Archéologie Orientale du Caire, 1975), 527 [103b]. I am grateful to Christopher Taylor, professor of Islamic studies, Drew University, for these references.

89. *Letters during Mr. Wortley's Embassy,* 29 May 1717, in *The Works of the Right Honourable Lady Mary Wortley Montagu* (London: Richard Phillips, 1803), 2:193–194. Joseph Pitton de Tournefort noted that the cemeteries of Constantinople were so large that "were they till'd, [they] would bear Corn enough to feed that great City for half the year"; quoted in Hans-Peter Laqueur, "Cemeteries in Orient and Occident: The Historical Development," *Cimetières et traditions funeraires dans le monde islamique* (Ankara: Turk Raiih Kurumu Basimevi, 1996), 3, and 3–7 passim. As Laqueur points out, the vast size of these Islamic cemeteries is due to the fact that, by and large, graves were not reused. Burial, in short, was extensive in contrast to the European intensive pattern. For more accounts by Europeans of Ottoman burials, see Laqueur, "Grabsteine als quellen zur osmanischen geschichte," *Journal of Ottoman Studies* 3 (1982): 21–44. For the general pattern, see his *Osmanischen Friedhöfe und Gransteine in Istanbul* (Tübingen: Ernst Wasmuth Verlag, 1993). I am also grateful to Hans-Peter Laqueur for his informative letter of 19 January 1997.

90. William Wordsworth, "Essay on Epitaphs" (1810), in W.J.B. Owen and Jane W. Smyser, eds., *The Prose Works of William Wordsworth* (Oxford: Clarendon Press, 1974), 2:54. "An American," *Sketches of Turkey in 1831 and 1832* (New York: J. and J. Harper, 1833), 384. John Auldjo, *Journal of a Visit to Constantinople* (London: Longman, Rees, Orme, 1835), 134. Miss [Julia] Pardoe, *The City of the Sultan and Domestic Manners of the Turks, in 1836* (London: Henry Colburn, 1837), 1:149 and 98–99, 138–153, and 2:53–55, 166 more generally. Pardoe was a widely published travel writer and popular historian who wrote biographies of Francis I and Marie de Medici among others; Auldjo was a diplomat, traveler, and climber—the first Briton up Mt. Blanc. Thomas Thornton, Esq., *The Present State of Turkey or a Description of the Political, Civil and Religious Constitution, Government, and Laws of the Ottoman Empire* (London: Joseph Mawman, 1809), 2:225 and 221–225 generally.

91. Pradodh Biswas, "Job Charnock," in Sukanta Chuadhuri, ed., *Calcutta: The Living City* (Calcutta: Oxford University Press, 1990), 1, 6–8. See also, regarding Charnock, Sir William Wilson Hunter, *The Thackerays in India and Some Calcutta Graves* (London:

Frowde, 1897), 50–51 and 1–64 more generally. Capt. Alexander Hamilton, *A New Account of the West Indies . . . from 1688 to 1723* (Edinburgh: Thomas Mosman, 1727), 2, 8–9.

92. There are disputes about details that may in other circumstance be worth trying to resolve. Some sources, for example, say that the church I call St. Anne's was, like the new church, named St. John's because of the influence of the Society of Freemasons who helped pay for it; those who hold this view seem to follow the account in *Histori-cal and Ecclesiastical Sketches of Bengal* (Calcutta: Oriental Press, 1831), 194. There is much difference of opinion on whether the tomb in what had been the old burial ground and became the churchyard of St. John's was actually Charnock's tomb, or a cenotaph, or just a memorial; his wife is cipher and no one is sure whether his daughter and her husband are really there either. Contemporaries thought this was his tomb, which is what matters here, and some historians believe them. I piece together my account in this and the following paragraphs from J. P. Losty, *Calcutta: City of Palaces* (London: British Library, 1990), 16–33 and 55–57 (on St. John's); Kathleen Blechynden, *Cal-cutta, Past and Present* (London: W. Thacker, 1905), 68–78; Sir Evan Cotton, *Calcutta Old and New: A Historical and Descriptive Handbook* (Calcutta: W. Newman, 1907), chap. 7; and Henry Elmsley Busteed, *Echoes from Old Calcutta*, 4th ed. (Calcutta: W. Thacker, 1908). For the building of St. John's, the clearing of its churchyard, and new burials, see Holmes and Co., *Bengal Obituary* (London, 1851); and Losty, *Calcutta: City of Palaces*, 55–57. The best source on the monuments themselves in Park Street and elsewhere in India is Sten Nilsson, *European Architecture in India*, trans. A. Zettersen and E. George (London: Faber and Faber, 1968), 130–151 and the accompanying illustrations. See also Aurelius Kahn, *The South Park Street Cemetery, Calcutta*, 2nd ed. (London: BACSA, 1986), which is useful for its descriptions of particular memorials. More generally on our topic, see "Extracts from a General Letter from Bengal to the Court, November 28, 1766, para 62–64, 66," in C. R. Wilson, *India Records Series: Old Fort William in Bengal* (London: John Murray for the Government of India, 1906), 2:181.

93. On Stuart and Kirkpatrick, see *Dictionary of National Biography* entries and Cotton, *Calcutta Old and New*, 571–572, 577, 502–508. Hindus do not traditionally bury their dead or build monuments, but the eighteenth-century aristocracy of Rajasthan had started to imitate Persian, i.e., Moghul styles, and built large mausoleums in honor of the dead even if they may have been empty. Although Kirkpatrick's grave is in Park Street, there is a magnificent cenotaph to his memory in St. John's Church. [Phebe Gibbes], *Hartly House, Calcutta* (London: J. Dodlsley, 1789), 1:2 and 2:9–10. Goldborne compares the "monumental erections" in the Bengal burial grounds to those of London's St. Pancras Churchyard, which is odd because there were few monuments there and no trees to speak of. Rudyard Kipling/Sir William Wilson Hunter, 15 January 1897, thanking him for his essays, "Some Calcutta Graves" is in Francis Henry Skrine, *Life of Sir William Wilson Hunter, President of the Royal Asiatic Society* (London: Longman, 1901), 451. In this strange, new world, Kirkpatrick's daughter converted to Christianity and became for a time a love interest of Thomas Carlyle.

94. On Tiretta, see Cotton, *Calcutta Old and New*, 566–567; and Busteed, *Echoes from Old Calcutta*, 341–342. Adolph Heuken, S.J., *Historical Sites of Jakarta* (Cipta Loka Caraka, 1982), 177 and chap. 10 generally. On Patna, see Emma Roberts, *Scenes and Characteristics of Hindoostan* (London: William Allen, 1835), 1,185–1,186, quoted in Rebecca, M. Brown, "The Cemeteries and Suburbs: Patna's Challenges to the Colonial City in South Asia," *Journal of Urban Studies* 29, no. 1 (2003): 167–168 and 151–172 more generally. On Macao, see Ride and Ride, *An East India Company Cemetery*, 58–70.

95. John Delaforce, *The History of the Chaplaincy and Church of St. James at Oporto* (London: SPCK, 1982), 17.

96. Epigraphs: Timothy Dwight, *Travels in New England and New York*, ed. Barbara Miller Solomon (1821–1833; reprint, Cambridge, Mass: Harvard University Press, 1969), 1:138. Strang, *Necropolis Glasguensis*, 62.

97. John Timbs, *Curiosities of London Exhibiting the Most Rare and Remarkable Objects of Interest in the Metropolis* (London: John Camden Hotten, 1855, 1867), 81. Timbs points out that Sir Christopher Wren had proposed something like the modern cemetery after the Great Fire. Strang, *Necropolis Glasguensis*, 59.

98. Dwight, *Travels in New England*, 1:138–139. Henry T. Blake, *Chronicles of New Haven from 1638 to 1862* (New Haven, Conn.: Tuttle, Morehouse, 1898), 247ff.

99. Carl Whittington, "Caspar David Friedrich's Medieval Burials," *Nineteenth Century Art Worldwide* 11, no. 1 (Spring 2012).

100. Harriet Martineau, *Retrospect of Western Travel* (London: Saunders and Otley, 1838), 3:281.

101. Ibid., 2:229–230. The Balzac sentence reads: "Je sors rarement, mais lorsque je divague, je vais m'égayer au Père-Lachaise." *Correspondance, oeuvres complètes* (Paris: Calman Lévy, 1876), 24:6.

102. *Bentley's Miscellany*, "Cemeteries and Churchyards—A Visit to Kensal Green," 9 (January 1841): 92. Mudford was a Tory journalist and writer of sensational fiction that, like ghosts, did not do well in cemeteries. Poe drew heavily on his "The Iron Shroud" for "The Pit and the Pendulum." See his *Dictionary of National Biography* entry.

103. Ibid., regarding Mudford. H. J. Croft, *Guide to Kensal Green Cemetery*, rev. and enlg. ed. (London: J. Howell, 1881), 10.

104. George Collison, *Cemetery Interment: Containing a Concise History of Modes of Interment . . .* (London: Longman, 1840), 171. Collison, one of the founders of Abney Park (see above), insists that his views are not motivated by competition; he knows few people will share them, and Highgate was immensely popular with its particular clientele.

105. Laman Blanchard, "A Visit to the General Cemetery at Kensal Green," *Ainsworth Magazine* 2 (July 1842): 177 and more generally 177–188. Most of the article is taken up with a tour of the tombs of prominent people. Ainsworth was an important Scottish novelist and journalist. He, like Dickens, published in *Bentley's Miscellany*, in which Mudford's article appeared.

106. Ibid.

107. See, for example, the sphinx guarding the Illingworth mausoleum at Undercliffe Cemetery in Bradford, ca. 1860. Pearson, *Mausoleums*, 6 and passim.

108. William Robertson, *Rochdale, Past and Present* (Rochdale: Schofield and Hoblyn, 1875), 57, 90–94; and its companion volume *Old and New Rochdale and Its People* (Rochdale, 1881), 247. Accounts like this could be found for almost any city. "Essay on Cemetery Interments Awarded the Prize Offered by the Reading Cemetery Company by a Well Wisher" (London: Pelham Richardson, 1843), 13; T. P. Grimsted, *Norwood Cemetery: A Descriptive Sketch* (London: George Hill, 1857), 4, 7.

109. Joseph B. Robinson, *Memorials: A Series of Original Selected Designs for Works Executed in Various Parts of the United Kingdom* (London: N.p., 1859), one of a half-dozen similar books produced by this Derby sculptor. Thomas Travis Mount, *A Burial Ground of the Huguenots at Wandsworth, Surrey* (Lymington: R. E. and C. T. King, 1887).

110. Johann Wolfgang von Goethe, *Elective Affinities*, trans. David Constantine (Oxford: Oxford University Press, 1994), 118.

111. Thomas Hardy, "In the Cemetery," in *The Collected Poems of Thomas Hardy* (New York: Macmillan, 1926), 393.

112. William Hazlitt, "On the Fear of Death," in *Selected Essays of William Hazlitt*, ed. Geoffrey Keynes (London: Nonesuch Press, 1930), 168.

113. Strang, *Necropolis Glasguensis*, 38.

114. "Remarks on Extramural Sepulture, with a Short Account of the London Necropolis" (London, [1859]). London Necropolis Company, *The London Necropolis and National Mausoleum (Woking Cemetery)* (London: R. Clay, 1884). David A. Brookwood Weston and Laurel Burge, *The Sleeping City: The Story of Rookwood Necropolis* (Sydney: Society of Australian Genealogists in conjunction with Hale & Iremonger, 1989). John Loudon, "Principles of Landscape Gardening Applied to Public Cemeteries," *Gardener's Magazine* 19 (1843): 298.

115. Unlike Latin American cemeteries, higher ground in western European ones, where there were important elevation differences, tended to be the most desirable.

116. Croft, *Guide to Kensal Green Cemetery*, 21, 26, 23.

117. No survey of existing or once existing cemetery architecture exists. About a third of the buildings in cemeteries for which Nikolaus Pevsner gives information in his surveys of the buildings of Lancashire, Cumbria and Northumberland, Gloucestershire, Worcestershire, and London were some kind of Gothic. This is at best a crude indicator. Stephen Geary is quoted in Howard Colvin, *A Biographical Dictionary of British Architects*, 4th ed. (New Haven, Conn.: Yale University Press, 2008), 413–414.

118. John C. Loudon, *On the Laying Out, Planting and Managing of Cemeteries. . .* (London: Longman, Brown, Green and Longman, 1843), 90.

119. The same sort of dividers of communities of the dead are visible elsewhere, perhaps nowhere more evidently than in Barcelona. See Carme Riera and Colita Pilar Aymerich, *Els cemetiris de Barcelona* (Barcelona: Edhasa, 1981). Of course, various civic groups—Masons, Oddfellows—as well as Jews and later Muslims bought and demarcated areas within cemeteries.

120. *Illustrated London News*, 29 September 1849, 221. The exception to private ownership was Southampton. I have relied for the basic story in the following paragraphs on the well-documented account in "Kensal Green," *Survey of the History of London* (London:

London City Council, 1973), 37:333–339. For the founding itself, see "Prospective of a General Cemetery Company for Providing Places of Interment, Secure from Violation, Inoffensive to Public Health, and Ornamental to the Metropolis" (no pagination or publisher), and on the MS Minute Books of the company, held at Kensal Green.

121. "Prospective of a General Cemetery Company," ibid.

122. The details for Liverpool are from Collison, *Cemetery Interment*, 183–184. Collison says £10 shares were selling at a premium of £100. For Kensal Green, see note 121.

123. The General Cemetery Company, Annual Report, 9 June 1842 (London: C. and E. Layton, 1842), no pagination.

124. Croft, *Guide to Kensal Green Cemetery*, 3.

125. John Weale, ed., *Pictorial Handbook of London* (London: H. G. Bohn, 1854), 287. Weale was a well-known publisher of scientific works. "Deed of Settlement of the Brighton Extra-Mural Cemetery Company" (London: Edmund Fullford, 1850). *Bradford Observer*, 8 June 1854. I quote from the manuscript version of the prospectus that was sent before publication in 1844 by J. Watts of Shrewsbury to Rev. James Rawson, in the Leeds University Brotherton Collection, MS 421/121/41. [William] Wilson, *A History of the Church of England Cemetery, Warstone Lane, Birmingham* (Birmingham, 1900).

126. Manchester Central Reference Library, MS 42/121/44. Property rights in cemetery plots followed national land law and so were different in every European jurisdiction. But the point is the same. Those who could afford it, could buy freeholds.

127. *Declaration of the Trusts of the Westgate Hill General Cemetery near Newcastle upon Tyne* (Newcastle: Finlay & Charlton, 1832), in the British Library, p. 13.

128. W. Arthur Deighton, *The Manchester General Cemetery, Harpurhey, from 1836 to 1911* (Manchester, n.d.), in the John Rylands Library, p. 10, quoting from the cemetery's "General Report" for 1839–1840.

129. For Manchester's Ardwick Cemetery, see note 126.

130. Honoré de Balzac, *Old Goriot*, trans. Marion Aynton Crawford (London: Penguin Books, 1985).

131. Ralph Straus and Robert Dent, *John Baskerville: A Memoir* (Cambridge: At the University Press for Chatto and Windus, 1907), 117, 135–138.

132. Samuel Sewall, *Diary 1674–1729* (Boston: Massachusetts Historical Society, 1878–1882), 1:301, quoted in Michael Hoberman, *New Israel/New Jerusalem: Jews and Puritans in Early America* (Amherst: University of Massachusetts Press, 2011), 58; see also 11ff. and 56–60. Sharman Kadish, *Jewish Heritage in England: An Architectural Guide* (Swindon: English Heritage, 2006), 28–29. Some eighteenth-century tombstones with crossbones and skulls, although without the New England cherub, would have been familiar to Sewall.

133. Kadish, *Jewish Heritage in England*, 34–36, 61–63, 140. She suggests that Montefiore's mausoleum bears witness to the imperial connection between Britain and the Holy Land, 62. For photos of the West London Reform Cemetery, see http://www.cemetery scribes.com/showmap.php?cemeteryID=13.

134. Fredric Bedoire, *The Jewish Contribution to Modern Architecture, 1830–1930*, trans. Roger Tanner from the Swedish *Ett Judiskt Europa* (1998) (Jersey City, N.J.: Ktav, 2004); on Frankfurt, see 141–146; on Paris, 157–162.

135. Ulrich Knufinke, *Bauwerke jüdischer Friedhöfe in Deutschland* (Petersberg: Michael Imhof Verlag, 2007).

136. *Illustrated Weekly News*, 4 December 1886.

137. Maciej Lagiewski, *Das Pantheon der Breslauer Juden* (Berlin: Nicolai, 1991). I am grateful to Herr Lagiewski for this book and for his patient guided tour of the cemetery. Michael Meng, *Shattered Spaces: Encountering Jewish Ruins in Postwar Germany and Poland* (Cambridge, Mass.: Harvard University Press, 2011), 184.

138. Andreas Nachama, *Jüdische Granstätten und Friedhöfe in Berlin* (Berlin: Hentrich, 1992), 36ff.

139. Joe Baker, *Clifton Street Cemetery: North Belfast's Historic Gem* (Belfast: Glenravel Local History Project, n.d.), 13. *Chorlton Row Cemetery for the Use of Persons of All Denominations: The Trustees with the Proprietors Declaration of the Trusts. Of a Certain Close or Field, in Rusholme-Lane, Chorlton-Row, Purchased for a Cemetery, or Place of Burial, with Monies Subscribed in Six Hundred Shares, of Ten Pounds Each* (Manchester: M. H. Richardson, 1821). The vicar of a large parish like St. Pancras in London might, for example make £500 a year in an age when an artisan was lucky to make £50. The struggle over fees bears testimony to the staying power of a medieval system in late industrial England but is not immediately relevant here.

140. See notes 34–36 above. Vivian Rowe, *The First Hertford Quakers* (Hertford: Religious Society of Friends, 1970), 20. Thomas Clarkson, *A Portraiture of Quakerism* (New York: Stansbury, 1806), 2:30.

141. William Wordsworth, *A Guide through the District of the Lakes: A Unpublished Tour*, in Owen and Smyser, *Prose Works of William Wordsworth*, 2:324–325. John Wood Warter, ed., *Southey's Commonplace Book* (London: Reeves and Turner, 1876), 3:161. William Maitland, *The History and Survey of London from Its Foundation to the Present Time* . . . (London: Osborne, Shipton & Hodges, 1756), 2:1370. For the general history, see Sir Charles Reed, *History of the Bunhill Fields Burial Ground: With Some of the Principal Inscriptions* (London: Skipper and East, 1893, by order of the Lands Committee of the City of London); and for the tangled history of its ownership and its conversion into a park, see *Bunhill Fields Burial Ground: Proceedings in Reference to Its Preservation with Inscriptions on the Tombs* (London: Hamilton, Adams, 1867). The process was pushed forward by Dissenting interests who argued forcefully that the Ecclesiastical Commission had failed "to appreciate the social and historical considerations involved" in maintaining this area. I am not clear how a long-term leaseholder could sell burial places, but contemporaries and later commentators claim that he did. Much of the business was selling common graves with single or multiple occupancy to people from all over London and beyond. The dead from fourteen different parishes were buried in Bunhill Fields in February 1807, for example. *Internal Order Books*, M1092, Guildhall Library.

142. *The Inscriptions upon the Tombs, Grave-Stones in the Dissenters Burial-Place near Bunhill-Fields* (London: E. Curll, 1717). T[homas] Gutteridge, *The Universal Elegy, or a Poem on Bunhill Burial Ground: In Which Are Hinted Many of the Dead, and Particularly Described . . .* (London, 1735), 15–16. Gutteridge wrote a number of elegies that he printed as broadsheets and sold at his shop in Shoreditch. Rippon's material for a history of Bunhill Fields is in the British Library, "Collections Relating to the Dissenters' Burial Ground at Bunhill Fields, London," by John Rippon, D.D., F.S.A., 14 vols., now numbered as 11, Add MS 28513–28523. His collection of names is in the library of the College of Arms: see *Notes and Queries*, 8th ser., 24 November 1884. Samuel Cowling, *The Dead in Christ or the Baptist of Bunhill Fields* (London: Baptist Tract Society, 1871), 5, 36. For a good example of a guidebook to famous graves, which also gives an account of their preservation, see Alfred Light, *Bunhill Fields*, 2nd ed. (London: C. J. Francombe, 1915). Light offers a useful sketch of Rippon, for which see also *Dictionary of National Biography*. New grand monuments often replaced smaller ones as the memorial needs of the community changed. The box tomb of Isaac Watts, for example, was built as a replacement for one commissioned by Lady Mary Abney. Of course, not everyone chose this distinct venue. Sir Thomas and Lady Abney, Dissenting royalty, whose estate became the site of England's greatest Dissenting cemetery, Abney Park, for example, chose to be buried with their forbearers in the vault of St. Peter, Cornhill.

143. None of the epitaphs collected by Curll speak of memory.

144. E. Paxton Hood, *Isaac Watts: His Life and Writings, His Homes and Friends* (London: Religious Tract Society, n.d.), 223. Paul Joyce, *A Guide to Abney Park Cemetery*. Hackney: Save Abney Park Cemetery Association in conjunction with the London Borough of Hackney, 1984). On Watts, see in particular Collison, *Cemetery Interment*, 297. Hall, the prolific wife of a prominent journalist who wrote under his name, is quoted in James Branwhite French, *Walks in Abney Park* (London: James Clarke, 1883), 6. Hall and French (who report a similar experience) are reporting on visiting the house where Watts lived when they were young. It was torn down in 1843, but its site remained one end of the major axis of the cemetery.

145. Collison, *Cemetery Interment*, 86, 92, 104, 283. The yew tree path is evocatively described in French, *Walks in Abney Park*, along with accounts of the people buried along it.

146. Collison, *Cemetery Interment*, 92. The first inhabitant of the Glasgow necropolis was a Jew.

147. Collison, *Cemetery Interment*, 92, 282. There is a long list of the distinguished dead in French, *Walks in Abney Park*; and in Joyce, *A Guide to Abney Park Cemetery*. The website of the Abney Park Trust, which now cares for the cemetery, has an extensive list, http://www.abney-park.org.uk/Abney_Park_Trust.

148. See Joyce, *A Guide to Abney Park Cemetery*. Bridget Cherry and Nikolaus Pevsner, *The Buildings of England: London 4: North* (London: Penguin, 1998).

149. A. Welby Pugin, *An Apology for the Revival of Christian Architecture in England* (London: John Weale, 1843), 12 and plate 5. Pugin at the time was professor of ecclesiasti-

cal antiquities at the Roman Catholic seminary, St. Marie's College, Oscott, whose building he had designed.

150. Reed, *History of the Bunhill Fields Burial Ground*, 22–23. There is a large bas-relief of "Old Mortality" guarding the entrance to Philadelphia's Laurel Hill.

151. William Bourn Peabody, "Mount Auburn Cemetery," *North American Review* 33, no. 73 (October 1831): 397–400, 403–404, and passim 397–406. On Peabody's biography, see the *American National Biography*. Rev. A. D. Gridley, "Cemeteries," *New Englander* 85 (October 1863): 599 and 597–619 passim.

152. The introduction to Brian Cummings, *The Book of Common Prayer: The Texts of 1549, 1559 and 1662* (Oxford: Oxford University Press, 2011) gives a good account of the procedural and theological causes of this rupture in the national church, which would have repercussions for more than two centuries.

153. Hale, *Intramural Burial*, 4.

154. See Pierre Dolivier, *Essai sur les funéraílles* (Versailles: An 9 [1801]), esp. 1–69; the rest of the pamphlet, 72–112, is an imagined debate between the author and a state official. Général [René Jean de] Pommereul, *Mémoire sur les funéraílles et les sépultures* (Paris, An 9 [1801]). Pommereul was a notoriously anticlerical prefect, iii–21. C. Détournelle, *Mémoire sur les funéraílles et les sépultures* (Paris, An 9 [1801]). An architect, he provides near the end detailed drawings for neoclassical cemetery memorials and for official mourning wagons.

155. Joseph Clarke, *Commemorating the Dead in Revolutionary France: Revolution and Remembrance, 1789–1799* (Cambridge: Cambridge University Press, 2007).

156. I follow here the anthropological interpretation of Joyce Riegelhaupt, "Camponeses e estado liberal: A revolta da Maria da Fonte," *Estudos Contemporâneos* 2, no. 3 (1981): 129–138, which is heavily influenced by the work of Natalie Davis. Maria de Fátima Sá e Melo Ferreira, "A luta contra os cemitérios públicos no seculo XIX," *Ler História* 30 (1996): 19–35, is the most complete account of the creation of Portuguese cemeteries. Ferreira argues that the rural protests against the health laws were part of a struggle to maintain local control against a centralizing bourgeois state. She sees them as a culmination of a long cultural struggle that in the case of making burial subject to hygienic scrutiny goes back to late-eighteenth-century, French-inspired reform measures. Manual Pinto gives primacy to class and argues that a generally passive posture toward liberal reforms in land, tax, and ecclesiastical policy over the previous fifteen years was sparked into active resistance by new burial laws. "A igreja e a insurreicão popular no minho de 1846," *Estudos Contemporâneos* 0 (1979): 83–134. Miriam Halpern Pereira, even more than Pinto, emphasizes the economic background of the revolts, specifically the change in property relationships. The dead become the agents of protest: "A revolução da Maria da Fonte e o movimento dos Patao-leo," in *Livre-câmbio e desenvolvimento economico: Portugal na segunda metade do século XIX*, 2nd rev. ed. (Lisbon: Sá da Costa, 1983), 293–301. I am grateful to Shawn Parkhurst, now associate professor of anthropology at the University of Louisville, who, as my graduate research assistant, prepared for me an extensive dossier on the Maria da Fonte revolt. I summarize his learning.

157. William Hale, *Remarks on Two Bills Now before Parliament Entitled a Bill for Registering Births, Deaths and Marriages in England, and a Bill for Marriages in England* (London: J. G. & F. Rivington, 1836), 9, 4, 7, 10; and Hale, *Some Remarks on the Probable Consequences of Establishing a General Registry of Births and Legalizing the Registration of Dissenters' Baptisms* (London: J. G. Rivington, 1834), 10–11. In 1538, Thomas Cromwell ordered that every parish keep a register of baptisms, burials, and marriages. Only in the reign of William and Mary had clergymen been asked to note the day of "birth" but that only, and specifically, to allow the state to collect a heavy tax on every birth, marriage, and burial for the purpose of fighting the war with France. Civil registration meant exactly that: anyone could now be born, married, and buried without the Church taking cognizance. Birth and death had to be civilly registered; unlike the French case, in England marriages could be contracted in church or chapel without need of a registrar.

158. Hale, *Remarks on Two Bills Now before Parliament*, 7.

159. Dwight, *Travels in New England*, 1:161.

160. Amy Clampitt, "Highgate," in *Archaic Figure* (New York: Knopf, 1987), 45.

161. K.D.M. Snell, "Gravestones, Belonging and Local Attachment in England, 1700–2000," *Past and Present* 179 (May 2003): 103n11. Julie-Marie Strange, "Only a Pauper Whom Nobody Owns: Reassessing the Pauper Grave, c. 1880–1914," *Past and Present* 178, no. 1 (2003): 148–175; and more generally her book *Death, Grief and Poverty in Britain 1870–1914*, Cambridge Social and Cultural Histories Series, no. 6 (Cambridge: Cambridge University Press, 2005).

162. Loudon, *On the Laying Out, Planting, and Managing of Cemeteries*, 47.

163. Bradford Order Books 28D77/1415. Probably the young were overrepresented in common graves. Of ninety-three general burials at Manchester Cheetham Hill, thirty-four were less than one year old, and twenty-five between the ages of one and five (more than 65 percent), when we would expect something on the order of one-fifth. Establishing this claim would entail much more research.

164. Epigraph: Thomas Noel, "The Pauper's Drive," in *Rymes and Roundelayes* (London: William Smith, 1841), 200–202. The poem was set to music in 1839 by Henry Russell, who is buried in Kensal Green under a monument shaped like an old armchair, the title of one of his most popular songs. *Rymes and Roundelayes*, like so much popular nineteenth-century poetry, is relentlessly engaged with death and dying.

165. The term "social death" comes from Orlando Patterson's discussion of slavery in *Slavery and Social Death* (Cambridge, Mass.: Harvard University Press, 1997).

166. I am, as before, concentrating on the British case, but the fear of a pauper funeral, and more generally a dishonorable funeral, was widespread among the poor and disposed in other places and contexts: among slaves, immigrants, and the vulnerable.

167. Charles Lamb, "On Burial Societies; and the Character of an Undertaker," *Reflector*, no. 3, art. 11, (1811). Robert Roberts, *The Classic Slum* (1971; reprint, Harmondsworth, Penguin, 1973), 87 and 84–88 passim; his study is based on Salford, next to Manchester. Mrs. Pember Reeves from *Round about a Pound a Week* (London: Bell, 1913); the chapter "A Horrible Problem" is reprinted in Peter Keating, ed., *Into Unknown England*

(Manchester: Fontana, 1976), 304–305. Edwin Hudder, *The Life and Work of the Seventh Earl of Shaftesbury, K. C.* (London, 1887), 25.

168. *Select Committee of the House of Commons, on the Improvement of the Health of Towns*, 1842 (327), X.Q. For an account of the funeral and the crowds, see *Manchester Guardian*, 20 May 1862, in clipping file Manchester Central Ref MSP 334–8MI. Interview with Miss Jean Prince, Charles Booth Papers, London School of Economics, 1897 B178.

169. Membership statistics derived from the *Fourth Report of the Royal Commission on Friendly and Benefit Building Societies with Appendices*, 1874 (349), XXIII (2). See, for a more general discussion of these figures, P.H.J.H. Gosten, *The Friendly Societies in England, 1815–75* (Manchester: Manchester University Press, 1961), chap. 1. Margaret Fuller, *West Country Friendly Societies* (Reading, 1964), 87, as cited in Pamela Horn, *Labouring Life* (London: Gill and Macmillan, 1976), 197. Charles Dickens, *Our Mutual Friend* (London: Chapman and Hall, 1868; reprinted as part of the *Clarendon Edition of "Our Mutual Friend"*), 327. For a broader perspective, see Marcel van der Linden, *Social Security Mutualism* (Bern: Peter Lang, 1996), 16–19, 58, 440–449. Burial expenses were one of the benefits of freed slave benefit societies from the very beginning. See Richard J. Harris, "Early Black Benevolent Societies, 1780–1830," *Massachusetts Review* 20, no. 3 (1979): 603–625. The *chevra kadisha*, specialized burial societies, buried Jews rich and poor. On their history, see Anne-Sylvie-Goldberg, *Crossing the Jabbok: Illness and Death in Askenazi Judaism in Sixteenth- through Nineteenth-Century Prague*, trans. Carol Cosman (Berkeley: University of California Press, 1997).

170. Theodore Lyman, Jr., *The Political State of Italy* (Boston: Wells and Lilly, 1820), 212–213.

171. See A. R. Wagner, *The Records and Collections of the College of Arms* (London: Burke's Peerage, 1952), 4–22. John Paul Rylands, ed., *Cheshire and Lancashire Funeral Certificates* (London: Record Society, 1882), v–xxiii. T. W. King and R. F. Raines, eds., *Lancashire Funeral Certificates* (Manchester: Chetham Society, 1869), 75:1–3. Edward Shils, *Center and Periphery: Essay in Macrosociology* (Chicago: University of Chicago Press, 1975), 3 and chap. 1 generally.

172. See the extraordinary illustrated roll by Thomas Lant, *Sequitur celebritas et pompa funeris [of Sir P. Sidney]* (1587), STC 15224, engraved by Theodore de Bry from sketches by Lant. Aubrey is quoted in Richard Hillyter, *Sir Philip Sidney, Cultural Icon* (London: Palgrave, 2010), xi. For the funeral of Superintendent James Braidwood, 30 June 1861, see the *London Illustrated News*, 6 July 1861, 17–18.

173. Lawrence Stone, *The Crisis of the Aristocracy* (Oxford: Clarendon Press, 1965), 572–581. Costs may have gone down over the seventeenth century, and there were other changes—embalming may have declined—but in general this picture holds, I think, for the old regime.

174. Thomas Wentworth, *The Office and Duty of Executors* (1656), uses the "suitability" criteria for how much an executor was permitted to spend for a funeral out of estate funds. Clearly, however, this was only the vaguest of guides. The cost estimates are from Clare S. T. Gittings, "Funerals and Their Social Context in England, 1580–1645" (B.Litt. thesis, University of Oxford, 1977), tables 2.5–2.11, based on almost five thousand inventories and executors' accounts from Lincolnshire, Oxfordshire,

Berkshire, and Kent. See Gittings, *Death, Burial and the Individual in Early Modern England* (London: Routledge, 1984). My much less comprehensive analysis of one hundred administrators' accounts from 1690 to 1711 from Kent Record Office PRC 19/5–6, and PRC 1/18, confirms these findings. It is impossible to document the claim about food expenses quantitatively, since the only systematic record of funeral expenses—the administrators' accounts—do not generally itemize funeral expenditures. Thus one must rely on random accounts that remain. That of the funeral of Alice Clayton, d. 1706, daughter of John, a modest gentleman in Little Harwood Lanes, lists expenditures of £4 5s.3d. (excluding the apothecary's bill), of which £3 0s.4d. was for food and drink and another 12s. to the poor (Manchester Central Reference Library, L1/10/130/2–5). The £3 11s. expended for the early-seventeenth-century funeral of William Onyon, more or less the median expenditure for a yeoman on Gittings's evidence, was accounted for as "for burying of the corps . . . for making of the grave, for rings on the daie of the burial and for entertaining of the neighbors on the date of the burial" (MS Wills Berks 206/95, Bodleian Library). Stone, *Crisis of the Aristocracy*, makes the case for aristocratic funerals. For a well-documented example of variations on the scale of lavish but not heraldically organized funerals and of high gentry funerals more generally, see Ralph Houlbrooke. "'Public' and 'Private' in the Funerals of Later Stuart Gentry: Some Somerset Examples," *Mortality* 1, no. 2 (1996): 163–175.

175. Abraham de la Pryme, *Diary*, ed. Charles Jackson, Surtees Society, no. 54 (Durham, U.K.: Andrews and Co., 1869), 48–49. William E. A. Axon, *Annals of Manchester* (Manchester: A. Haywood, 1886), 92, 255.

176. Daniel Defoe, *The True Born Englishman* (London, 1701), 24. James Boswell, *Life of Johnson* (Oxford: Oxford University Press, 1980), 924. Sir Lewis Namier, *England in the Age of the American Revolution*, 2nd ed. (London: Macmillan, 1961), 32.

177. Rev. Mark Noble, *A History of the College of Arms* (London, 1804), 44.

178. T. T. Merchant, *Some General Considerations Offered Relating to Our Present Trade . . .* (1698), 6–7, quoted in J. S. Burns, *The History of Parish Registers in England* (London, 1862), 109–110. Undertakers upgraded funerals by using gentlemen's carriages borrowed, with the connivance of servants, from their unsuspecting masters. This relatively cheap way of putting on a good show was made illegal by 1 Geo St. 2.c57, para. 4, *Statutes at Large*, 13:321, although judging from the great lines of carriages in eighteenth-century funerals, this ban was more honored in the breach. R. Campbell, *The London Tradesman* (London, 1747), 329–330. Robert Blair, "The Grave," in Dennis Davison, ed., *The Penguin Book of Eighteenth-Century Verse* (Harmondsworth: Penguin, 1973), 103, 104.

179. *Accounts of Parish Burials for the City of London Union*, Guildhall Library, MS 11, 446. "Respectability" as a description of the state of being respectable or maintaining a status of decency came into English in the late eighteenth century and became common in the nineteenth.

180. G. C. Allen, *The Industrial Development of Birmingham and the Black Country* (1929; reprint, London: Cass, 1966), 18. See the price list "to the trade" in Joseph Turner, *Burial Fees of the Principal Churches, Chapels and New Burial Grounds . . .* (n.d. but ca. 1838), Guildhall

Library pamphlet 5713. Diana Cooper and Norman Battershill, *Victorian Sentimental Jewelry* (Newton Abbot: David and Charles, 1972), 23–26; coffin furniture and mourning jewelry were among the industrial products shown at the Great Exhibition of 1851, where three English firms won honorable mentions. *Reports by the Juries, Exhibitions of the Works of Industry of All Nations, 1851* (London: W. Clowes and Son, 1852), 13, 493, 508.

181. From an advertisement by John Middleton in the John Johnson Collection, Bodleian Library, funeral box 3.

182. From a bill rendered by W. Briscoe, "Upholsterer, Appraiser, Cabinet Manufacturer and Undertaker," Bath, for the funeral of Miss A. Bayard, 1839, MS Victoria and Albert Museum. *A Supplementary Report on . . . the Practice of Interment in Towns,* 1843 (509), xii, pp. 50–51 and 69–71.

183. *Report from the SCHC on the Friendly Societies Bill,* 1854 (412), vii, Q 781.

184. On these excavations, see Annia Cherryson, Zoë Crossland, and Sarah Tarlow, *A Fine and Private Place: The Archaeology of Death and Burial in Post-Medieval Britain and Ireland* (Leicester: University of Leicester, 2012), 199, 206, 230. On workhouse burial in London, see Holmes, *London Burial Grounds,* 173ff.

185. Oxfordshire Quarter Sessions Accounts, T, 1775, no. 4, Oxfordshire Record Office. I base the claims in this paragraph on accounts of the overseers of the poor in some thirty parishes in Oxfordshire, Lancashire, the West Riding, Berkshire, Kent, and Middlesex. In 1816, the parish of Wooton-Bassett spent for one pound of cheese, two pecks loaf bread, six quarts of beer, and a pint of gin—not common—a total of 6s.1d., plus the cost of the coffin, laying out, and fees, i.e., 17s., on the funeral of George House. While alive, he got 1s.6d. per week (Oxfordshire Record Office, Pc iv, iii, 4 Wooton). In the tiny parish of Garsington, the usual funeral expense was just over £1 around the turn of the century. The rates for roundsmen between 1804 and 1807 were 6s.9d. for nine days (Garsington Overseers' Accounts MSS DD Garsington 6.11, Bodleian). The accounts of Kidlington (ORO K II/a/1–3) provide a particularly complete 150-year view of life and death in a rural parish, 1684–1836. There are similar accounts in every county record office.

186. Manchester Poor House Book, Manchester Central Reference Library M3/3/5, 1 June 1811, fr. 322–333. I base my assessment of London on the following records in the Guildhall Library: St. Anne, Blackfriars, Overseers Accounts MS 7746/2–7, now bound in one volume; All Hallows, London, Wall Churchwardens Accounts MS 5090/3; St. Catherine Coleman, Accounts MS 1124/2, 1672–1720; S. R. Broadridge, "The Old Poor Law in the Parish of Stone," *North Staffordshire Journal of Field Studies* 13 (1973): esp. 14; *Walthamstow Vestry Minutes, Churchwardens' and Overseers' Accounts* 1710–1740, 1741–1771, 1772–1794, Walthamstow Antiquarian Society Publications, nos. 13–14, 16 (1925–1926, 1927), ed. Stephen J. Barns; Leeds Overseers' Accounts, 1801–1805, Leeds Record Office MSLO/A/1; F. M. Cowe, ed., *Wimbleton Vestry Minutes* 1734, 1743–1788, Surrey Record Society xxv (1964); *Report of the Select Committee on Anatomy* 1828 (568), vii, p. 20 re: St. Johns Wood.

187. St. Botolph, Bishopgate, *Annual Accounts* MS 4525.

188. T. C. Barker and J. H. Harris, *A Merseyside Town in the Industrial Revolution: St. Helens 1750–1900* (Liverpool: Liverpool University Press, 1959), 132–142, 307–311. *Report on a General Scheme for Extra-mural Sepulture* (1850), Manchester Reference Library pamphlet 21196, 54–55. *SCHC Health of Towns* 1842 (327), x, Q 1882–1891 and Q 1926–1929. Regarding the ringing of bells, see *Report SCHC to Inquire into the Administration of the Poor Laws in the Andover Union* 1846 (663), v. Q 2260 and *Times* (London), 12 August 1846. Chadwick, it appears, was the more liberal: see *2nd Annual Report of the Poor Law Commissioners* 1836, app. C., 536–537.

189. Regarding the issue of Christmas dinners, one of considerable emotional charge in the debate over the New Poor Law, see W. G. Lumley, *The General Orders Lately Issued by the Poor Law Commissioners* (London, 1842), 212, citing a letter of 18 March 1840; privately funded dinners were said to be beyond the purview of the commissioners.

190. The notion already in evidence in early friendly societies that "since Men of wicked and disorderly Lives are more exposed than others to Sickness, Lameness and Infirmity . . . no one remarkable for Cursing, Swearing, Lewdness and Drunkenness . . . shall be capable of becoming a Member of this Society" (*Rules and Orders to Be Observed by a Friendly Society, Hitchen* [London, 1752], 66). Members of collection burial societies lost not only their benefits but all previous contributions if they fell into arrears with their weekly payments. In short, providing for a proper burial entailed a strong measure of discipline and self-denial. See Penelope Ismay, "Trust among Strangers: Securing British Modernity 'by Way of Friendly Society,' 1780s–1870s" (Ph.D. diss., University of California, Berkeley, 2010), for the more general context of these points. I make no original claim here.

191. On Bara and Viala, see Ben-Amos, *Funerals, Politics and Memory*, 40, 43–47. There were also counterfunerals to those of the popular classes. A massive and more "respectable" procession bore the bodies of Count Lichnowsky and other conservative members of the Frankfurt parliament who had been killed in a radical uprising on 21 September 1848 to their graves in what was a semiofficial response to the populist work of the dead. It too gained a large public through print. Hettling, *Totenkult statt Revolution*, 12–51.

192. Eighteen people died directly or indirectly as a result of the attack at St. Peter's Square. One was a babe in arms knocked out of his mother's hands; two were special constables killed by their colleagues, by friendly fire. Fifteen were protesters. The fate of other bodies came out in various trials and were widely reported. See M. L. Bush, *The Casualties of Peterloo* (Lancaster: Carnegie Publishing, 2005), 44–45, 88, 139. For a short account of the Lees inquest, see Joyce Marlow, *The Peterloo Massacre* (London: Rapp and Whiting, 1969), 160–164; and John Augustus Dowling, *The Whole Proceedings before the Coroner's Inquest at Oldham, &c. on the Body of John Lees, Who Died of Sabre Wounds at Manchester, August 16, 1819* (London, 1820), 22–23, 32–33, and the conclusion. The title is misleading: he died early on 7 September of wounds and bruises that were inflicted on the day of the great radical meeting, 16 August. Dowling was a court reporter who published the transcripts of nearly a dozen important cases.

193. The court's decision and related papers are reprinted in Dowling, *The Whole Proceedings*; see on this inquest in a broader context of coroners' inquiries more generally, Ian Burney, "Making Room at the Bar: Coroner's Inquests, Medical Knowledge and the Politics of the Constitution in Early-Nineteenth-Century England," in James Vernon, ed., *Re-Reading the Constitution* (Cambridge: Cambridge University Press, 1996), 123–154, and 129–136 in particular.

194. The account of the funeral is in the *Manchester Observer*, 11 September 1819, under the title "Alas! Poor Bob!!!" On the exhumation, see Marlow, *The Peterloo Massacre*, 158.

195. *Pioneer*, 1 February 1834, 177–178; 29 March 1834; and 12 April 1834, 298; see also 22 February, 213–214; 29 March, 278–279; 31 May, 384; and 7 June, 396–397, 400. For engravings of Union funeral badges, see 14 June 1834, 407. See Clive Behagg, "Secrecy, Ritual and Folk Violence," in Robert C. Storch, ed. *Popular Culture and Custom in Nineteenth Century England* (London: Croom Helm, 1982), 160–161 and more generally 154–179. See Joel H. Weiner, *The War of the Unstamped: The Movement to Repeal the British Newspaper Tax, 1830–1836* (Ithaca, N.Y.: Cornell University Press, 1969), 192–193, on the relationship of numbers of papers printed and number who were touched by them.

196. On the funeral, see the *Northern Star*, 12 April 1842, 5. Almost an entire page of the paper is taken up with the report. See also R. C. Gammage, *History of the Chartist Movement, 1837–1854* (London, 1894), 213–216. For circulation figures, see the authoritative work on the *Star*'s editor by James Epstein, *The Lion of Freedom: Feargus O'Connor and the Chartist Movement* (London: Taylor and Francis, 1982), 68–75. On Holberry himself, see Joyce Bellamy and John Saville, eds., *Dictionary of Labour Biography* (London: Macmillan, 1997), 4, 93–96; and Malcolm Chase, *Chartism: A New History* (Manchester: University of Manchester Press, 2007), 151–157. John Clayton, age fifty-two, had died earlier in the same prison from disease and exhaustion after being forced to walk hours on the treadmill every day despite his increasingly ill health.

197. For Rushton's place in the movement, see Dorothy Thompson, *The Chartists: Popular Politics in the Industrial Revolution* (New York: Pantheon, 1984), 225–230. For the funeral, see Benjamin Wilson, *The Struggles of an Old Chartist* (Halifax: John Nicolson, 1887), reprinted in David Vincent, *Testaments of Radicalism: Memoirs of Working Class Politics 1790–1885* (London: Europa, 1977), 219–221.

198. For Jones's funeral, see *Manchester Guardian*, 1 February 1869, 5.

199. On O'Connor's funeral, see Chase, *Chartism*, 342; and *Times* (London), 4 September 1855, 8, and 11 September 1855, 5. *Reynolds's Newspaper*, 16 September 1855, is quoted, along with other sources that I have drawn upon, in Paul Pickering, *Feargus O'Connor: A Political Life* (Monmouth: Merlin Press, 2008), 154–155 and 163n72.

200. *Journal of John Wesley*, 5:31 (23 September 1763). James Everett, *The Village Blacksmith; or, Piety and Usefulness Exemplified in a Memoir of the Life of Samuel Hick*, 15th ed. (London: T. Woolmer, 1863), 167–168. I happen to quote from this edition, announced as "forty-seventh thousand." The first edition appeared in Manchester in 1831, the fifth in 1834, the tenth in 1845. Everett's *Memoirs of the Life, Character and Ministry of William Dawson* (London: Hamilton, Adams, 1842), 495–498, describes the funeral of its hero, a

popular local preacher from Barnbow, near Leeds, as it made its way from Keighly where he died, to Leeds, and then to Barwick-in-Elmet, in whose churchyard he wished to be buried along with his ancestors. Eighty-six coaches had joined the procession by the end, followed by multitudes. On Hick, see W. J. Townsend et al., eds., *A New History of Methodism* (London: Hodder Stoughton, 1909), 412–413.

201. The definition of public funeral in the United Kingdom was slippery. Strictly speaking, it was one arranged—the Lord Chamberlain's office was in charge—and paid for by the state and arguably also approved by Parliament. By that criteria, in addition to royal and royal family funerals, only Nelson's, Wellington's, and Gladstone's qualify, but public funds paid for others as well—Darwin's, Livingston's, and Palmerston's, for example. On the rise of the public funeral in its more general sense as one that engaged and created a public, see John Wolffe, *Great Death: Grieving, Religion, and Nationhood in Victorian and Edwardian Britain* (Oxford: For the British Academy by Oxford University Press, 2000), and for the technical details, 287–293. On France, see Ben-Amos, *Funerals, Politics and Memory*, appendixes A and B.

202. *Memoirs of the Professional Life and Glorious Achievements of the Late Vice-Admiral, Lord Nelson: To Which Is Added, a Circumstantial Account of the Grand Funeral Processions, and of the Interment of This Illustrious Hero; With an Engraved Representation of the Funeral Car, on Which His Mortal Remains Were Conveyed from the Admiralty to St. Paul's Cathedral, on Thursday, Jan. 9, 1806* (Norwich: Printed and sold by Stevenson and Matchett, [ca. 1806]). *Fairburn's Edition of the Funeral of Admiral Lord Nelson* (London: J. Fairburn, 1806). Queen Caroline, wife of the much-hated George IV, was the subject of an impeachment trial instigated by a husband who had hated her from the moment they met and, after his father George III finally died, hoped to divorce her and keep her from becoming queen. The effort failed, but the trial was the focus of six months of intense popular agitation in favor of Caroline, whom the radicals construed as a fellow victim of royal and ministerial tyranny. I include the funeral here despite its being officially a royal funeral, because it was so clearly part of the street politics of the year before. See Thomas Laqueur, "The Queen Caroline Affair: Politics as Art in the Reign of George IV," *Journal of Modern History* 54 (1982): 417–466, esp. 421.

203. The public press wrote incessantly on the death of Wellington between September and December 1852. Two pages of fine type index the articles in the *Times* alone. I have drawn primarily from the *London Illustrated News*, 25 September, 2 October, 20 November, and 27 November (supplement) 1852, because its coverage was the most thorough I encountered. Leopold Ettlinger, "The Duke of Wellington's Funeral Car," *Journal of the Warburg and Courtauld Institute* 3 (1939–1940): 254–259. The best modern account of each stage in the planning of the funeral and of its broader implications is Wolffe, *Great Death*, 27–55.

204. *Manchester Guardian*, 16 August 1844, for Dalton. For Dawson, see Everett, *Memoirs of the Life, Character, and Ministry of William Dawson*, 478–482. For reports of the other funerals of men who, as one account puts it, "represent the culture, the industry, and the enterprise of the North of England," see R. V. Taylor, *Biographia Leodiensis* (Lon-

don, 1865); or Richard Welford, *Men of Mark 'twixt Tyne and Tweed*, 3 vols. (London: Walter Scott, 1895), passim, and quote on 1:489.

205. B. Allsop, *The Late Sir Titus Salt, Bart.: A Brief Resume of His Life and Works* (Bradford, 1878), 14–22; and R. Balgarnie, *Sir Titus Salt, Baronet* (London, 1877), 303–319. See, for another example, George Lander, *An Answer to the Pamphlet of Mathew Robinson . . . Relative to His Father's Funeral* (Birmingham, 1811), Guildhall Library. Lander, an undertaker, is defending himself for not having produced a funeral grand enough to warrant the £544 17s. 2d. he was paid for the job. Five hundred men and sixty women from the Boulton and Watts works marched in the parade, all dressed in deep mourning; in addition, there were twenty-three carriages and scores of assistant undertakers, friends, and other worthies.

206. Estella Weiss-Krejci, "Excarnation, Evisceration, and Exhumation in Medieval and Post-Medieval Europe," in F. M. Gordon et al., eds., *Interacting with the Dead: Perspective on Mortuary Archaeology for the New Millennium* (Gainesville: University of Florida Press, n.d.), 155–172.

207. Frederic Wakeman, Jr., "Mao's Remains," in James L. Watson and Evelyn S. Rawski, eds., *Death Ritual in Late Imperial and Modern China* (Berkeley: University of California Press, 1988); and his *Great Enterprise* (Berkeley: University of California Press, 1986), 164. Lebrun is quoted in E.A.R. Brown, "Burying and Unburying the Kings of France," in R. C. Trexler, ed., *Persons in Groups* (Binghamton, N.Y.: Medieval and Renaissance Texts and Studies, 1985), 282. A. Rébellon, "La tête de Richelieu en Bretagne," *Annales de Breatagne* 69, no. 3 (1962): 295–304. Alexandre Lenoir, the founder of the museum of French antiquities, was wounded by a bayonet as he was defending not Richelieu's body but his monument, the work of the great seventeenth-century sculptor, François Girardon. The Mahdi in this case was the Sudanese sheik who claimed to be the redeemer promised at the end of time in the Muslim tradition. He died in the rebellion against the British that ended with his death at the Battle of Omdurman. *Letters of Queen Victoria*, 3rd ser. (London: John Murray, 1932), 3:354.

208. Peter Linebaugh, "The Tyburn Riot against the Surgeons," in Douglas Hay et al., eds., *Albion's Fatal Tree* (New York: Pantheon Books, 1975). Hugo Grotius, *The Rights of War and Peace*, ed. Jean Barbeyrac and Richard Tuck (Indianapolis, Ind.: Liberty Fund, 2005), bk. 2. I am grateful to Prof. Scott Shapiro of Yale Law School for pointing out to me the significance of Grotius's juxtaposition of chapters. Grotius's larger point is that soldiers in a just war have the right to burial, because killing in war is not a crime. I found the mail robber's words quoted in a manuscript letter from J. Broughton to his wife. He says their source was "the Chester paper 5th month 1792," MS D102/10 Buckinghamshire Record Office, Aylesbury.

209. Peter Mackenzie, *An Exposure of the Spy System Pursued in Glasgow* (Glasgow: Muir, Gowans, 1833), 3:232.

210. Michael Maranze, "Major André's Exhumation," in Nancy Isenberg and Andrew Burstein, eds., *Mortal Remains: Death in Early America* (Philadelphia: University of Pennsylvania Press, 2003), 123–136. Edward Everett, *An Address Delivered at Lexington on the 19th April, 1835, Appendix* (Charlestown, [Mass]: William W. Wheildon, 1835), 6, 51–52.

For the history of the Lexington episode within a broader Puritan and revolutionary context, see Mark Peterson, "Stone Witnesses, Dumb Pictures, and Voices from
the Grave: Monuments and Memory in Revolutionary Boston," in David Gobel and
Daves Rossell, eds., *Commemoration in America: Essays on Monuments, Memorialization, and
Memory* (Charlottesville: University of Virginia Press, 2013).

211. See Thomas Laqueur, "The Dead Body and Human Rights," in Sean T. Sweeney and
Ian Hodder, eds., *The Body* (Cambridge: Cambridge University Press, 2002). [G. J.
Holyoake], *The Life of Paine by the Editor of "The National"* (London: J. Watson, 1851), 47
and 44–53 generally. The British Library gives in brackets G. J. Holyoake, one of the
nineteenth century's most important religious radicals—he began as a Unitarian, but
when prosecuted for blasphemy in 1842, he became a militant atheist—as the author
of an 1840 and 1893 edition and the engraver and newspaperman W. J. Linton as
the author, noted in brackets, of the 1851 edition from which I quote. I think it is
Holyoake in all cases, given his sustained interest in religious matters. On his death
and the servant girl question, see Moncure Conway, *The Life of Thomas Paine* (New
York: G. P. Putnam, 1908), 2:421 and 417ff. more generally. See also his *Dictionary of
National Biography* entry. Robert G. Ingersoll, *Tom Paine's Vindication: A Reply to the New
York "Observer's" Attack upon the Author-Hero of the Revolution . . .* (New York: Truth Seeker
Company, 1887), 4ff. Michael Kammen, *Digging Up the Dead: A History of Notable Amer-
ican Reburials* (Chicago: University of Chicago Press, 2010), 74–77, 146–150, puts
Paine's movements in the larger context of exhumation as both a consequence and a
cause of cultural and political change as well as a response to commercial opportunity: the exhumation of the body of the outlaw Jesse James, for example.

212. The story of Paine's body is well and briefly told in the revolutionary context by
Kammen, *Digging Up the Dead*, 43–82. On Whitman, see Conway, *Life of Thomas Paine*,
422–423. The provenance of Descartes' skull can be traced from 1666 when, sixteen
years after the philosopher's death, they were exhumed by the French ambassador to
Sweden, until the twentieth century because each new owner wrote on it his name.
See Russell Shortohave, *Descartes' Bones: A Skeletal History of the Conflict between Faith and
Reason* (New York: Random House, 2008).

213. Anon., *A Brief History of the Remains of the Late Thomas Paine from the Time of His Disinterment
in 1819 by the Late William Cobbett, M. P. down to the Year 1846* (London: J. Watson, 1847),
5–8. For the later history of the body, see Paul Collins, *The Trouble with Tom: The Strange
Afterlife and Times of Thomas Paine* (London: Bloomsbury, 2005). The story about the
Anglican priest is told in Kammen, *Digging Up the Dead*, 76 and 73–76 more generally.

214. Thomas Paine, *Collected Writings*, ed. Eric Foner (New York: New American Library,
1995), 151–152. The context is an open letter dated 21 March 1778 to General Sir
William Howe, the British commander in the colonies, in which Paine plays on the
idea that Howe is essentially already dead: he has already exited "from the moral
world" and has written "HERE LYETH" over his honor; arguing with him is "like ad-
ministering medicine to a dead man."

215. Orin Starn, *Ishi's Brain: In Search of America's Last "Wild" Indian* (New York: Norton, 2004).

216. Beato was a British photographer of Italian origin. These pictures are "among the earliest known photographs of corpses." He made something of a specialty of documenting colonial defeats. See *Grove Dictionary of Art Online*, http://www.oxfordartonline.com/subscriber/article/grove/art/T007115, s.v. "Beato." I learned of these pictures through Zahid Chaudhary, "Phatasmagoric Aesthetic: Colonial Violence and the Management of Perception," *Cultural Critique* 59 (Winter 2005): 63–119.

217. Ann Fabian's *The Skull Collectors* (Chicago: University of Chicago Press, 2010) is a superb history of the nineteenth-century U.S. side of this story. Helen MacDonald's *Human Remains: Episodes in Human Dissection* (Melbourne: Melbourne University Press, 2005), 86ff., documents the terrifying traffic in Tasmanian bones within Australia and abroad. Karl Geirginger, *Haydn: A Creative Life in Music* (Berkeley: University of California Press, 1963), 191–192. "The Skull of Joseph Haydn," *Musical Times*, 1 October 1832, 942–943. Daniel Heartz, *Haydn, Mozart, and the Viennese School, 1748–1780* (New York: W. W. Norton, 1995), 45. For the attempted theft of Beethoven's head, see William Meredith, "The History of Beethoven's Skull Fragments, Part One," *Beethoven Journal* 20, nos. 1–2 (Summer–Winter 2005): 6–7.

218. For a brilliant account of the use of the dead body—necrophilia—to imagine intimately the past, see Mario Wimmer, *Archivkörper: Eine Geschichte historischer Einbildungskraft* (Konstanz: Konstanz University Press, 2012), who shows how a major German archivist took the Rankean imperative to extremes both by stealing documents and body parts. On Carlyle's problem, see Amos Bronson Alcott, *The Letters of A. Bronson Alcott*, ed. R. L. Herrnstadt (Ames: Iowa State University Press, 1969), 78 (2 July 1842), cited in David McAllister, "'A Subject Is Not Worth Presenting': Cromwell, the Past and the Haunting of Thomas Carlyle," *Romanticism and Victorianism on the Net* 59–60 (April–October 2011). McAllister is interested in arguing that Derrida's and Paul De Man's accounts of haunting help to account for Carlyle's difficulties in making the dead speak. *Notes and Queries*, 6th ser., vii, Jan. 6, 1883, 12, gives a good account of the exhumation of Hampden. I suggest throughout this book that making the dead speak is in all circumstances both necessary and impossible. That said, the article was invaluable to me and alerted me to, among other things, the location of Carlyle's relics. See on this subject, K. J. Fielding, "Carlyle and Cromwell: The Writing of History and DRYASDUST," in Jerry James and Rita Bottoms, eds., *Lectures on Cromwell and His Era* (Santa Cruz, Calif.: University Library, 1985), 45–68. *Past and Present*, in Thomas Carlyle's *Collected Works* (London: Chapman and Hall, 1870), 152–153. Edmund supposedly met his death when he refused the Danish army's demand in 869 that he renounce Christ. Samson was abbot of the Monastery of St. Edmunds, 1181–1211; because he died when England was under interdict, he was buried in unconsecrated ground and after four years was exhumed and reburied. Carlyle was referring to the exhumation of the parliamentary leader John Hampden, carried on at the behest and under the supervision of George Nugent-Grenville, Second Baron Nugent, Hampden's biographer, to determine whether "the Patriot" had died from a shoulder wound or from a pistol exploding in his hand. It was the hand wound that turned mortal was the conclusion. The report in *Gentleman's Magazine* 98, no. 2 (1828):

123–127, is not as inflammatory as Carlyle's but gives enough eyewitness testimony to confirm that indeed the body was disarticulated and the hair "came off like a wig."

219. The letters are quoted from the Duke University edition of the *Complete Carlyle Letters*, available online (T. C. to Edward Fitzgerald, 29 September 1842; doi: 10.1215/lt-18420929-TC-EF-01). Teeth were a conventional battlefield souvenir after Waterloo. Henry Crabb Robinson, most famous for his diary accounts of the great figures of English romanticism, had a dentist implant one in his mouth. See Stuart Semmel, "Reading the Tangible Past: British Tourism, Collecting, and Memory after Waterloo," *Representations* 69 (Winter 2000): 9–37.

220. Byron had purchased a trove of Waterloo souvenirs that were held for him by his publisher, John Murray. *The Letters of John Murray to Lord Byron*, ed. Andrew Nicholson (Liverpool: Liverpool University Press, 2007), 22 January 1817, note 190. Fitzgerald to T. Carlyle, 20 December [1871], in Edward Fitzgerald, *Letters and Literary Remains* (New York: Macmillan, 1903), 3:6.

221. University of California at Santa Cruz Archives. The quotes are a transcription from the notes in the box. The archivists are worried that their relic may soon be dust, because the bone is flaking, and the conservation department does not know what to do. Cloisterville is in no gazetteer.

222. I take this account from the best of the modern biographies of John Hunter: Wendy Moore, *The Knife Men* (New York: Broadway Books, 2005), 199–202, 206–209, 211–215.

223. Drewry Ottley, *The Life of John Hunter* (Philadelphia: Haswell, Barrington, 1839), 77–78.

224. The stories are told in a ballad that is then expanded into a pamphlet, *The Workhouse Cruelty: Workhouses Turn'd Gaols and Gaolers Executioners* (London: Printed for Charity Love-poor, 1731), British Library, 816 m.9, as quoted and discussed by Tim Hitchcock in his still unpublished "'The Workhouse Cruelty': Paupers, Workhouses and Community in Early Eighteenth-Century London," and discussed by Tim Hitchcock and Robert Shoemaker in *London Lives: Poverty, Crime and the Making of a Modern City, 1690–1800* (Cambridge: Cambridge University Press, 2015), 126–133. I am grateful to him for this material in addition to the comments I have already acknowledged.

225. *Louisville & N. R. Co. v. Wilson*, 5 S. E. 24, 25 (Ga. 1905), quoted in Ray D. Madoff, *Immortality and the Law: The Rising Power of the American Dead* (New Haven, Conn.: Yale University Press, 2010), 16. Dickens, *Our Mutual Friend*, bk. 1, chap. 1 and chap. 7. My interest in this passage comes in the first instance from teaching it with Catherine Gallagher. She develops her views in *The Body Economic* (Princeton, N.J.: Princeton University Press, 2006).

226. Edward Coke, *The Third Part of the Institutes of the Laws of England* (London: M. Flesher, 1644), chap. 97 ("Of Buildings"), 203. The ownership of church monuments was clouded because the freehold of the church was in the incumbent, and the monuments and pews were affixed to it. That said, they were also inheritable. But this is not the issue here. Damaging a monument was damaging someone's property. Coke's views and those of the common law lawyers who followed him are still in play. The

Appellate Division, First Department of New York rejected the defendant's claims of *nullius in bonis*; the plaintive who was suing Mt. Sinai Hospital for mistakenly sending his brother's body for dissection in 2001 did have what was essentially a property right in the corpse. Debates about owning bodies were not always in medical contexts but might have involved, for example, rival claims by relatives to have the rights to disposal of a corpse. I have found Paul Matthews, "Whose Body? People as Property," *Current Legal Problems* 36 (1983): 193–239, an invaluable guide. The New York case is 2009 NY Slip Op 03404 [64 AD3d 26] *Melfi v. Mount Sinai Hospital*. (Bodies, even though they were nothing, did have the right to a burial place and to a funeral according to their station. This seems to have been a consequence of testamentary law that allowed executors to pay for last rites even at the expense of creditors.) There is a good short summary of Anglo-American law on this subject in Madoff, *Immortality and the Law*, 12–21 or 12–56 more generally, including broader questions of consent for autopsies and the status of the rule against perpetuities in the context of new technologies that aim at reanimation. Alan Hyde, *Bodies of Law* (Princeton, N.J.: Princeton University Press, 1997), 48–79, argues that there is a notion of a sacred body, seat of the individual, that resists being turned into property, although he is not especially concerned with those that are dead.

227. William Blackstone, *Commentaries on the Laws of England* (London, 1765–1769), 2:429 and 4:236. Prosecutions did go forward for larceny from the dead.

228. William Blackstone, *Commentaries on the Laws of England*, 13th ed., with notes by Edward Christian, professor of the laws of England at Cambridge (London: A Straham, 1800), 4:236. The footnote reference on this page is to note 4 on 2:429, which refers the reader to 1 T.R. 733. Blackstone's editor miscites: the reference is to 2 T.R. 733–734, i.e., the second volume of the reports for King's Bench, the most important of the common law courts, in its Michaelmas term of 1788. Frederick Pollock, *Revised Reports* 1, 1785–1790 (London: Sweet and Maxwell, 1891), 607–608. On the theft of a lead coffin, see *Old Bailey Proceedings on Line*, October 1747 trial of John Lamb, William Bixby (reference number t17471014–11.)

229. Pollock, *Revised Reports*. The court also claimed as precedent that the Old Bailey, the criminal trial court for the City and Middlesex, had punished similar offenses. I could not find relevant cases in the online database. The nearest case to that of the stolen lead coffin involved the acquittal of a grave digger for stealing 5s. worth of coffin nails, the property of persons unknown. The court decided that it was his right to collect the nails from coffins that fell apart when he unearthed them to bury new tenants (17 December 1766). Blackstone, *Commentaries* (1820), 4:236–237. In 1804, King's Bench finally put a stop to the very old custom of "arresting" a body on the way to burial for debt. Sidney Young, *Annals of the Barber Surgeons* (London: Blades, East, 1890), 349 (6 March 1711); 360 (November 1740); 421 (1723); the dispute about the private anatomy involved the distinguished surgeon William Chiselden, 568–569 (25 March 1714). Even if bodies could be owned under certain circumstances, they did not own themselves and could not dictate their fate. The friend of a man who asked to have himself cremated failed, in a 1882 lawsuit, to prevent

his kin from burying him in a Roman Catholic cemetery (*Williams v. Williams*, 20 Ch. Div. 659).

230. In the twentieth century, the ancient sculpture has been identified as being of a Gaul—that is, a Celt—that was probably made to celebrate a Greek victory over the Celtic Galatians in Anatolia ca. 230–220 B.C.E. William Kemp, ed., *Dr. William Hunter at the Royal Academy of Arts* (Glasgow: University of Glasgow Press, 1975), 16–19 and 41–42 on Hunter's teaching of art students more generally. *Spectacular Bodies: The Art and Science of the Human Body from Leonardo to Now*, exhibit curated by Martin Kemp and Marina Wallace at London's Hayward Gallery (Berkeley: University of California Press, 2000). *British Magazine and Review* (April 1783): 264, in its account of a Royal Academy show. Joseph Baretti, *Guide through the Royal Academy* (London: T. Cadell, n.d.), 21. The *British Magazine* took its text from p. 24 of Baretti. The body from which this piece was cast had until recently been identified as that of either one of two smugglers, Benjamin Harley or Thomas Henman, who were sentenced to be hanged on 27 May and then to be dissected. In 2008, as part of a Heritage Lottery Fund project to restore the Edinburg cast collection, the artist and anatomy teacher Joan Smith and the anthropologist Jeanne Cannizzo challenged this provenance on the basis of a young artist's letter, dated 1 May 1776, that mentions the écorché. If that date is to be credited, then the body must have come into Hunter's hands earlier and would be the body of either John Langar or Samuel Whitlow, who were hanged on 12 April but had not been sentenced to dissection. The cast with a new name was exhibited with much public notice at the opening of the university's Talbot Rice Gallery in 2010 in a show provocatively called *Smugglerius Unveiled*. Tim Hitchcock, the creator of Old Bailey Online and the leading expert on eighteenth-century crime, disputes their claims at http://www.executedtoday.com/2012/05/27/1776-benjamin-harley-thomas-henman-smugglerius/. I am grateful to him for his generosity in helping with material for this and the following paragraph.

231. I take my account from Julius Bryant, "Thomas Banks's Anatomical Crucifixion: A Tale of Death and Dissection," *Apollo: The International Magazine of the Arts* 133, no. 352 (June 1991): 409–411, which in turn is based on Carpue's account that is reproduced in his obituary notice in the *Lancet*, 7 February 1846, 1:167. The London papers speak of Legg's bravery on the scaffold, although he could not have guessed his fate, but says that the body was taken down right away and taken to the anatomy theater. It does not mention the intermediary stage. For Carpue, see the *Dictionary of National Biography* entry. He was famous enough for his exploits to make their way into Thomas Hood's poem "Mary's Ghost," each verse of which tells of what became of yet another of her parts dug up by resurrection men from her grave at St. Mary-bone. As we might expect by now, the dead speak.

> I can't tell where my head has gone
> But Dr Carpue can.
> As for my trunk, it's all packed up,
> To go by Pickford's van.

The results of the experiment pleased those who ordered it. See *Selected Poems of Thomas Hood, Winthrop Mackworth Praed and Thomas Lovell Beddoes*, ed. Susan Wolfson and Peter Manning (London: Penguin, 2000), 33. West apparently remarked that until seeing Legg, he had never really seen what a human hand looked like. In November 2012, the *Anatomical Crucifixtion* (plaster cast; wooden cross) is both the "Object of the Month" at the Royal Academy and the centerpiece for an exhibition at the Museum of London called *Doctors, Dissection, and Resurrection Men*.

232. The influence of Ruth Richardson's *Death, Dissection and the Destitute* (Chicago: University of Chicago Press, 2002) about the making of the 1832 Anatomy Act on this aspect of my work is manifest. She has been an important interlocutor since I send her a draft of what became my first article on this subject, and she sent me to a very early version of her ideas, "A Dissection of the Anatomy Acts," *Studies in Labour History* 1 (1976): esp. 8–11. I first toured Kensal Green with her.

233. The Paris estimate is in the version of Thomas Southwood-Smith, "Use of the Dead to the Living," *Westminster Review* 2 (July–October 1824): 96. On the numbers of bodies used in England, see Elizabeth T. Hurren, *Dying for Victorian Medicine: English Anatomy and Its Trade in the Dead Poor, c 1834–1929* (London: Palgrave Macmillan, 2014), 303–305.

234. Southwood-Smith, *Use of the Dead to the Living* (London: Baldwin and Cradock, 1827), 30–31.

235. *West Port Murders or an Authentic Account of the Atrocious Murders Committed by Burke and His Associates* (Edinburgh: Thomas Ireland, 1829), 135 and passim for the most complete documentation of the case. The cases I cite are from Southwood-Smith, *The Use of the Dead* (1827), 32. In fact, it was not so easy to murder without leaving a trace. Burke and his colleagues succeeded. Autopsy evidence helped convict the London killers. See below.

236. There are many accounts of the confession, trial, and execution of Bishop and Williams. I have drawn primarily on the *Morning Chronicle*, 5 and 6 December 1831; and the London *Examiner*, 4 December 1831. "John Bishop and Thomas Williams, *Notorious Body-Snatchers*, who murdered People and Sold Their Bodies to Hospitals, and Were Executed at NEWGATE," 5 December 1831, *Newgate Calendar*.

237. Grainger's speech is reported, among other places, in *Isis* 11 February to 15 December 1832, 303–304. This journal was edited by "A Lady," to wit Elizabeth Sharples Carlile, wife of the radical journalist, Richard, and herself a major figure in the Rotunda radicals.

238. Thomas Southwood-Smith, "A Lecture Delivered over the Remains of Jeremy Bentham, Esq. in the Webb-Street School of Anatomy, 16 June 1832," in James E. Crimmins, ed., *Bentham's Auto-icon and Related Writings* (Bristol: Thoemmes Press, 2002), 64, 67–69, 73, pagination as in the original. Grainger, in *Isis* (see note 237). *The Collected Letters of Thomas Carlyle* (Duke University Press online complete edition; see T.C. to John Stuart Mill, 16 June 1832; doi: 10.1215/lt-18320616-TC-JSM-01; *CL* 6:173–176). Bentham died on 6 June; Mill's "Death of Jeremy Bentham," appeared in the *Examiner*, the leading progressive paper of its day that published everyone from Keats and Shelley to Mill, Thackeray, and Dickens. On 11 June, the *Times* announced that Bentham had been anatomized two days after his death.

239. *A Sketch of the Life and Character of the Late Dr. Monsey, Physician to the Royal Hospital at Chelsea; with Anecdotes of Persons of the First . . .* (London: J. Cooper, 1789), 80. *The Life and Eccentricities of the Late Dr. Monsey, Physician to the Royal Hospital at Chelsea* (London: T. Hughes, 1804), 104–105. The story about Cruickshank is from the *Dictionary of National Biography*. Monsey was ninety-four when he died and suffered from illnesses that he thought would be interesting to students. Everyone who was anybody in the eighteenth century knew him as disgusting, ill-mannered, and brilliant.

240. *An Appeal to the Public and to the Legislature, on the Necessity of Affording Dead Bodies to the Schools of Anatomy, by Legislative Enactment* (Glasgow: Robertson and Atkinson, 1824). Thomas Southwood-Smith, "The Use of the Dead to the Living," *Westminster Review* 2 (July–October 1824): 59–96, with many later reprints. The *Westminster* was the main journal of the Benthamite radicals.

241. *Reports from Committees*, 1828, vol. 8, p. 78.

242. Southwood-Smith, *The Use of the Dead*, 37.

243. *Manchester as It Is* (Manchester, 1839), 67.

244. Walter Benjamin, *Illuminations* (New York: Fontana, 1971), 100–101.

PART III: NAMES OF THE DEAD

Epigraph: Zbigniew Herbert, *The Collected Poems, 1956–1998*, trans. Alissa Valles (New York: HarperCollins, 2007), 404–405.

1. The phrase "verdict of reality" is from Freud's *Mourning and Melancholia* (1917), in *The Standard Edition of the Complete Psychological Works of Sigmund Freud*, trans. James Strachey (London: Hogarth Press, 1957), 14:254: "Each single one of the memories and situations of expectancy which demonstrate the libido's attachment to the lost object is met by the verdict of reality that the object no longer exists." Freud argues that in mourning, "the ego, confronted as it were with the question whether it shall share this fate, is persuaded by the sum of the narcissistic satisfactions it derives from being alive to sever its attachment to the object that has been abolished," and that after some time very little energy is needed to let go. Keeping names in memory is not mourning.

2. The problem of too many "Jenkinses" is discussed in H. F. Chettle, "The Director of Record's Memo Regarding the Problem of Naming the Missing," in IWGC 219, pt. 2, box 1009, marked Ref 17/F22/301/R/2. For the debate about using numbers and the so-called regimental principle, see below.

CHAPTER 6: THE NAMES OF THE DEAD IN DEEP TIME

Epigraph: Roland Barthes, *S/Z*, translated by Richard Miller (New York: Hill and Wang, 1974), 95.

1. Homer, *Odyssey*, 8.550ff., trans. Robert Fagles (New York: Viking, 1996), 209. Herodotus, *Histories*, 4.184, trans. A. D. Godley, Loeb Classical Library (1921; reprint,

Cambridge, Mass.: Harvard University Press, 2006), 2:387. Pliny, *Natural History*, 5.45, trans. H. Rackham, Loeb Classics Edition (Cambridge, Mass.: Harvard University Press, 1969), 2:251. These texts on ancient views on the origins of names and civilization were cited by the great classical linguist Anna Morpurgo Davies in her Sather Lecture on 23 February 2000. Sadly, the six series of which this one was a part are not yet published.

2. William Camden, *Remaines Concerning Britaine* (London: Nicholas Okes, 1623), 40–31 [*sic*]. Arthur Charles Fox-Davies and P.W.P. Carlyon-Britton, *A Treatise on the Law Concerning Names and Changes of Name* (London: Elliot Stock, 1906), 2–3. Sir Edward Burnett Tyler's *Primitive Culture: Researches into the Development of Mythology*, as well as his *Researches into the Early History of Mankind and Civilization*, are full of the anthropology of naming lore that informed the introductory sections of books like that by Fox-Davies.

3. Arthur Charles Fox-Davies and P.W.P. Carlyon-Britton, *A Treatise on the Law Concerning Names and Changes of Name* (London: E. Stock, 1906), 1. I have over the years read relatively widely in the literature on the philosophy of names, but I take this brief summary from the clear and thoroughly documented entry by Sam Cumming, "Names," in *The Stanford Encyclopedia of Philosophy* (Spring 2013 ed.), http://plato.stanford.edu/archives/spr2013/entries/names.

4. Saul Kripke, *Naming and Necessity* (Cambridge, Mass.: Harvard University Press, 1980) is the most important account of the philosophy of naming in the past half century. An even more dramatic example of the unnamed and hence not-yet-human dead not mattering is the well in the Athenian agora filled with dead neonates. It would have been inconceivable to pollute the city with dead humans, but dead babies did not seem to count. I learned of this in Susan Rotroff's 2011–2012 Pritchett lecture at Berkeley, "The Agora Baby Well: Neonatal Mortality and the Disposal of the Dead in Hellenistic Athens." She speculates that the well may have been closed up because the nearby priests of Apollo did not appreciate the smell. See Rostroff and Maria Liston, "Babies in the Well," in *The Oxford Handbook of Childhood and Education in the Classical World* (Oxford: Oxford University Press, 2013).

5. Alice Smalhor is among the marginal women, mostly unnoticed by historians, who are the subjects of a wonderful paper by Judith Bennett given as the keynote address to the 2012 North American Council on British Studies conference. I am grateful to her for sharing it with me subsequently and for advice on English medieval surnames. For more on these sorts of names, see David Postles, *Naming the People of England, c 1000–1350* (Newcastle upon Tyne: Cambridge Scholars Publishing, 2006). Postles has written superb books on regional naming practices. The overarching point of his work is that the mapping of naming practices tracks cultural exchange as well as the politics of gender and rank. There is no stable naming system. Coke was citing a 1594 case. Edward Coke, *A Systematic Arrangement of Lord Coke's First Institute*, ed. J. H. Thomas (London: S. Brooke, 1818), 2:217–218. At the moment of Adamic naming, names were, to use John Stuart Mill's terms, connotative—i.e., descriptive—as well as denotative: Thomas = twin. Names with meaning play a huge part in an-

cient literature. See the brilliantly evocative chapter "Polytoropos: The Naming of the Subject," in John Peradotto, *Man in the Middle Voice: Name and Narrative in the Odyssey* (Princeton, N.J.: Princeton University Press, 1990), 94–119.

6. Midrashic name derivations, MNDs as scholars call them, via anagrams and subtle letter shifts could get almost anything out of "Adam"—e.g., "ground" or "grave." Adam, in his prelapsarian state of uncorrupted nominalism—the names he gave corresponded to the way the world really was—named the first woman "Eve," which, at least in some MNDs, meant "serpent," in addition to "source of life." The great biblical moments of naming play on precisely the intimacy of naming in an originary moment and descriptive meaning; in fact, there is a massive exegetic tradition based on the literary ingenuity of the biblical writers and on the rabbis who examined every vowel shift for meaning. The earlier name "Abram" is interpreted to mean "the father is exalted," so the change to Abraham signals the change of meaning to "father of many nations." God said to Abram, as he was named, just before He made with him his covenant, that he would be from that moment be named Abraham—"Neither shall thy name any more be called Abram, but thy name shall be called Abraham; for a father of many nations have I made thee" (Gen 17:5, 17:12; Abram first appears in Gen 11:26 in a genealogy: "Terah . . . begat Abram. The "r" is excluded from the reasoning behind this derivation of meaning; ab = after, hmwn = multitude). My thanks to Ron Hendel on this and almost all questions of Hebrew etymology in these pages. My examples come from the encyclopedically learned book by Moshe Garsiel, *Biblical Names: A Literary Study of Midrashic Derivatives and Puns,* trans. Phyllis Hackett (Rama Gan: Bar-Ilam University Press, 1991).

7. Flann O'Brien [Brian O'Nolan], *The Third Policeman* (London: Picador, 1974), 35. It was written in 1939 but remained unpublished until 1967.

8. The locus classicus for this account of names is Claude Levi-Strauss's *The Savage Mind* (London: Weidenfeld and Nicolson, 1966), 191ff., but it is also the common-sense account that twentieth-century English readers would have encountered.

9. John Steele, *The I–li or Book of Etiquette and Ceremonial,* 2 vols. (London: Probsthain, 1917), 33.203. Traditionally it was dated to ca. 1000 B.C.E. [Rowlands] Richard Verstegan, *A Restitution of Decayed Intelligence in Antiquities* (Antwerp: Robert Bruney, 1605), 242–243. On Verstegan's biography, see the *Dictionary of National Biography* entry.

10. Wordsworth, "Essay upon Epitaphs I," in *The Prose Works of William Wordsworth,* ed. W.J.B. Owen and Jane Worthington Smyser (Oxford: Clarendon Press, 1974), 2:53. John Weever, *Antient Funeral Monuments of Great Britain, Ireland and the Islands Adjacent,* ed. William Tooke (London: W. Tooke, 1767), xix, in the context of discussing Absalom, the wayward son of King David, who built his own tomb because he did not have a son who would ensure that his name would be remembered. Jean-Pierre Vernant, *Mortals and Immortals,* ed. Froma I. Zeitlin (Princeton, N.J.: Princeton University Press, 1991), 40–41.

11. Quintilian. *Institutes of Oratory,* 2.2.7–16, trans. H. E. Butler (London: Heineman, 1922), 4:215–219. Some ancient sources tell us that the Castor and Pollux part is

not true, but the connection between names, memory, and space represented by the story became canonical.

12. Thomas Browne, *Religio Medici and Urne-Buriall*, ed. Stephen Greenblatt and Ramie Targoff (New York: New York Review of Books, 2012), 46.

13. Sigmund Freud, *Totem and Taboo*, trans. A. A. Brill (New York: Collier, 1919), 92, 95–96, 102–104, and the section "The Taboo of the Dead," 86–107 more generally. Rev's account of the necronym was first published as "The Necronym," *Representations* 64 (Fall 1998): 76–108, and in longer form in *Retroactive Justice: The Pre-history of Post-communism* (Stanford, Calif.: Stanford University Press, 2005). Patrick Williams, *Gypsy World: The Silence of the Living and the Voice of the Dead* (Chicago: University of Chicago Press, 2003), 4–28. Dorothy Spruill Redford, comp., *Somerset Place Slave Burial Register, 1785–1865* (Somerset N.C.: Somerset Place, 2001). I am grateful to Jean Hebrad for these two references and in general for his comments on this section.

14. Interview with Umberto Eco conducted by Suzanne Byers and Lothar Gorris, *Der Speigel,* English language ed., 11 November 2009, in the context of an exhibition that he curated at the Louvre called "Mille e tre" (the reference is to the number of Spanish women, out of a total of 2,063 by my count on Leporello's list of Don Giovanni's conquests); accessed at http://www.spiegel.de/international/zeitgeist/spiegel-interview-with-umberto-eco-we-like-lists-because-we-don-t-want-to-die-a-659577.html; see also the interview with Marie Laure Bernadac, who commissioned the exhibition in "Vertige de la Liste," *Louvres* 2 November–13 December 2009, accessed at http://www.louvre.fr/sites/default/files/medias/medias_fichiers/fichiers/pdf/louvre-louvre-invite-umberto-eco.pdf, July 18, 2013. Eco is rehearsing the insights of Jack Good, *Domestication of the Savage Mind* (Cambridge: Cambridge University Press, 1977), 74–111. It resonates with the beginning of Foucault's *The Order of Things*, where he quotes from a Borges story purporting to be a Chinese encyclopedia.

15. Pausinius, *Description of Greece*, 1.32.3, trans. W.H.S. Jones, Loeb Classical Library (1918; reprint, Cambridge, Mass.: Harvard University Press, 2004), 175.

16. Edward Everett, *Address at the Consecration of the National Cemetery at Gettysburg, 19th November, 1863* (Boston: Little, Brown, 1864), 32. Time was relatively kind to the ruins at Marathon. Excavations on the ten-meter-high tumulus beginning in 1890–1891 yielded bones, pottery, and Persian brazen arrowheads to the scrutiny of a team of scientists. In the First World War and subsequent wars, the United States—like the Athenians soon after Marathon (and unlike the British in the Great War)—tended to bring their dead home.

17. The return of bodies probably began around 468 B.C.E. and became common practice around 465 B.C.E. My views on the Athenian funeral oration and on the role of the dead in civic life comes from Nicole Loraux, *The Invention of Athens: The Funeral Oration in the Classical City,* trans. Alan Sheridan (Cambridge, Mass.: Harvard University Press, 1986). The link between Lincoln's and Pericles' speeches is made by Gary Wills, *Lincoln at Gettysburg: The Words That Remade America* (New York: Simon and Schuster, 1992).

18. I have taken as my reference the remarkable survey in W. Kendrick Pritchett, *The Greek State at War,* pt. 4 (Berkeley: University of California Press, 1985), 125, 139, 145, 157, 167, and 250 in particular, and the whole of chapter 2, "Burial of the Greek War Dead," 94–259. I counted the number of names in appendix 1, "Prosopography of Athenian Casualties," in Christopher W. Clairmon, *Patrios Nomos: Public Burial in Athens during the Fifth and Fourth Centuries* B.C. (Oxford: BAR International Series 161[1], 1983), 2:323–363. The two volumes present an enormous amount of epigraphic, cartographic, and literary evidence; see esp. plates 65 and 67. See also Armando Petrucci, *Writing the Dead* (Stanford, Calif.: Stanford University Press, 1998), 5–9; and Jesper Svenbro, *Phrasíkleia: An Anthropology of Reading in Ancient Greece,* trans. Janet Lloyd (Ithaca, N.Y.: Cornell University Press, 1993). *Iliad,* 17.432–35, quoted in Vernant, *Mortals and Immortals,* 69.

19. *The Iliad of Homer,* trans. Robert Fagles (New York: Penguin, 1998), 2:246–326. For the battle of Uji Bridge, see *The Tale of the Heike,* trans. with introduction by Helen McCullough (Stanford, Calif.: Stanford University Press, 1994), 152, 155, 156–157, 353ff.

20. Holinshead, *Chronicles of England, Scotland, and Ireland* (1577), 4:1164. I used the electronic edition available on the Holinshead Project website of Oxford University Press.

21. Joseph Hunter, *Agincourt: A Contribution towards an Authentic List of the Commanders of the English Host . . .* (London: John Russell, 1850), 22–23, 44. The most recent and scholarly treatment of the battle is in Anne Curry, *Agincourt: A New History* (Stroud, U.K.: Tempus, 2005), and I take both the numbers and my account of the administrative occasions in which the names of the dead did and did not matter from her. See appendix C, 276–279, 236–238, and 225–245, "The Aftermath" more generally. These two sources suggest the same conclusion on this point.

22. The names of the four dead archers are in Hunter, *Agincourt,* 32. Sir Harris Nicolas, *History of the Battle of Agincourt . . . to Which Is Added the Roll of the Men at Arms in the English Army . . . ,* 2nd ed. (London: Johnson and Co., 1832,), 134–136, 401; the list of names begins on 373. Thanks to a quite extraordinary collaborative research effort, we now can know not only the names of thousands of English soldiers during the Hundred Years' War but also some details of their lives: see Adrian Bell, Anne Curry, Andy King, and David Simpkin, *The Soldier in Later Medieval England* (Oxford: Oxford University Press, 2013). Shakespeare's contemporaries could have imagined knowing the names of thousands of ordinary soldiers at Agincourt but not having them read by a herald. About 12,000 men sailed for Normandy; that is 1 in about every 150 of the population in 1400, and 1 in 300 two centuries later, when *Henry V* was written. Every village and city neighborhood must have had a man among those who sailed for France. Parish churches read the lists of the local dead on All Saints' Day.

23. This paragraph is of course grounded in Ernest Kantorowicz, *The King's Two Bodies* (Princeton, N.J.: Princeton University Press, 1957).

24. Petrucci, *Writing the Dead,* 24–25.

25. Megan McLaughlin, *Consorting with Saints: Prayer and the Dead in Early Medieval France* (Ithaca, N.Y.: Cornell University Press, 1994), 98, and 90–101 more generally.

Petrucci, *Writing the Dead*, 48. I choose this example at random from a beautifully printed edition, produced by Eduard Hlawitschka, Karl Schmid, and Gerd Tellenbach, *Liber Memorialis von Remiremont* (Dublin: Weidmann, 1970), 127.

26. These two paragraphs rely on Geoffrey Koziol, *The Politics and Memory and Identity in Carolingian Royal Diplomas: The West Frankish Kingdom (840–987)* (Turnhout, Belgium: Brepois Publishing, 2012), 269–271, 333–340. I am grateful to Koziol for alerting me to these sources.

27. Each of the four volumes of Jean Dufour, *Recueil de rouleaux des mort: VIIIe siècle–vers 1536* (Paris: Académie des Inscription et Belles-Lettres, 2005), has an appendix of maps that portray the peregrinations of select mortuary rolls. On necrologies, see McLaughlin, *Consorting with Saints,* 93–95. Medievalists distinguish carefully between these different kinds of lists. But for my purposes, the point is their proliferation as a genre.

28. Alan Kreider, *English Chantries* (Cambridge, Mass.: Harvard University Press, 1979), 8–9, where he disputes the number. It is the one most cited, and Kreider gives no evidence for its being far off. Ken Farnhill, *Guilds and the Parish Community in Late Medieval East Anglia, 1470–1550* (Rochester, N.Y.: York Medieval Press in association with the Boydell Press, 2001), 42ff. "Bead" is a modern spelling of the old English word *bede*, meaning "prayer." On bede in general, see Peter Marshall, *Beliefs and the Dead in Reformation England* (Oxford: Oxford University Press, 2002), 37–39; and esp. Eamon Duffy, *Stripping of the Altars* (New Haven, Conn.: Yale University Press, 1992), 335, where he makes the case for the democratization of memory in the late medieval church. N. W. James and V. A. James, *The Bede Roll of the Fraternity of St. Nicholas* (London: London Record Society, 2004), 1:xxvi–xxvii, and the introduction more generally, xiii–xxxviii.

29. Marcel Proust, *Guermantes Way*, trans. Mark Treharne (London: Penguin, 2002), 8.

30. Thomas De Quincey, *Autobiographical Sketches* (New York: Riverside Press, 1876), 45.

CHAPTER 7: THE RISE OF THE NAMES
OF THE DEAD IN MODERN HISTORY

Epigraph: Zbigniew Herbert, *The Collected Poems, 1956–1998*, trans. Alissa Valles (New York: HarperCollins, 2007), 404–405.

1. For the Los Gatos memorial, see *Los Angeles Times,* 9 July 2013, http://www.latimes .com/local/la-me-deportees-guthrie-20130710-dto-htmlstory.html. For the Welsh memorial, see National Library of Wales, http://www.llgc.org.uk/index.php?id=seng hennydddisaster.

2. Danilo Kiš, *The Encyclopedia of the Dead*, trans. Michael Henry Heim (New York: Farrar Strauss), 43–45, and 39–65 passim.

3. Ibid., 44.

4. I owe the information about numbers to Paul G. Nauta of the Public Outreach Division of the Family History Department, personal e-mails, 2 and 3 July 2013. Alex Shoumatoff in "The Mountain of Names," *New Yorker* 13 May 1985, 64, reports that

the Genealogical Society of the LDS claimed to have documented 1.5 billion names as of 1985. By 2013, it estimated that it had indexed 3.3 billion out of a possible 8 billion names that could be documented from among the roughly 20 billion people born between 1500 and 2010. "It is difficult," Nauta writes, "to say how many unique people are documented in these records, since many people are mentioned multiple times. A person born in the late nineteenth century might be mentioned in a half dozen censuses, government records of birth, marriage, and death, church records of christening, marriage, and burial, multiple deeds, military service and pension records, probate records, and other miscellaneous records." On the storage of names, see *In a Granite Mountain* (Salt Lake City: Genealogical Society, n.d. [ca. 1960]), no pagination. I am grateful to my former student Amy Harris, Brigham Young University, for making contact for me with the Genealogical Society and to another former student, Kyle Brinkman, who left graduate school to found Myspace, for his research assistance on the Mormons and names.

5. *Teachings of Presidents of the Church: Brigham Young* (Salt Lake City, Utah: Church of the Latter-day Saints, 1977), 308–311. For the LDS view of how its doctrines fit into their long history of the baptism of the dead, see David L. Paulsem, Kendel J. Christensen, and Martyin Pulido, "Redeeming the Dead: Tender Mercies, Turning Hearts, and the Restoration of Authority," *Journal of the Book of Mormon and Other Restoration Scripture* 20, no. 1 (2011): 28–51.

6. J. F. Smith, *The Way to Perfection: Short Discourses on Gospel Themes, Dedicated to All Who Are Interested in the Redemption of the Living and the Dead* ([Salt Lake City?]: Genealogical Society of Utah, 1931), 315–319. *Genealogical Society of Utah Guide for Leaders* (Salt Lake City, 1929), 5–9, 19–28. The foundation for this practice is in the revelations given to Joseph Smith the prophet in 1841–1842 and recorded in *Doctrines and Covenants*, especially 128 and much of 124.

7. On Florence and names, see David Herlihy and Christiane Klapish-Zuber, *Les Toscans et leurs familles* (Paris: Fondation Nationale des Sciences Politiques: École des Hautes Etudes en Sciences Sociales, 1978), as well as Herlihy's article "Tuscan Names, 1200–1500," *Renaissance Quarterly* 41 (1988): 561–582. On the Roman census—and much of this applies to the Greek case—see C. Nicolet, *The World of the Citizen in Republican Rome*, trans. P. S. Falla (London: Batford Academic, 1980), 49–88. There are Buddhist necrologies in Japan that go back to the thirteenth century and names on land registries that go back to the seventh.

8. Leon F. Litwack, *Been in the Storm So Long: The Aftermath of Slavery* (New York: Knopf, 1979), 247–252. Ralph Ellison, *Shadow and Act* (New York: Vintage, 1995), 147–148, quoted in Litwack, 247.

9. Arthur Fox-Davies and P.W.P. Carlyon-Britton, *A Treatise on the Law Concerning Names and Changes of Name* (London: E. Stock, 1906), 22. On women's names and on the history of British surnames more generally, the fullest account is Ewen C. L'Estrange, *A History of Surnames in the British Isles* (London: Kegan Paul, 1931), 389–393, 427.

10. Esther Benbassa, *The Jews of France: A History from Antiquity to the Present* (Princeton, N.J.: Princeton University Press, 1999), 89–90. On the Prussian case, see Deitz Bering, *The Stigma of Names: Antisemitism in German Daily Life, 1812–1933*, trans. Neville Plaice (Ann Arbor: University of Michigan Press, 1992), 14–43.

11. Rudolph Kleinpaul, *Die deutschen personennamen, ihre entsehung und bedeutung* (Leipzig: G. J. Göschen, 1909), 115ff. (on "the New Creation of Names: Jewish Names). On 118, he recounts the joke that a Jew who got the name "Weisheit" (Wisdom) asked another who got "Schweiszhund" (Sweatdog) why he had failed to pay the needed bribe. Good god, said the second, "I paid a fortune for a single 'w.'" (Otherwise it would have been "Scheiszhund," now spelled *scheisshund* = "shitdog.") Freud quotes Kleinpaul's work on the anthropology of the dead extensively in *Totem and Taboo*. Bering, *The Stigma of Names*, 36–37. Lenka Matušíková, "Namesäderungen in Jüdischen Familen im Jahre 1787 am Beispiel der Jüdischen Gemeide Kanitz," *Judaica Bohemiae* 34, no. 2 (1998): 107–125; the examples are on 112. *Festschrift . . . zur feir des vierhudertjährigen Bestehens der Hamburger St. Johannischule 1529–1929* (Hamburg, 1929), 23. The book is perfectly happy to identify names as Jewish; next to Theodore and Walther Levis it says, "Hebrew for the 'unjoined.'"

12. On this battle, see Bering, *The Stigma of Names*, 44–75.

13. Dr. [Leopold] Zunz, *Namen der Juden: Eine geschichtliche Untersuchung* (Leipzig: L. Fort, 1837), 9, 26–27, 34, to take more or less random examples. Anna L. Staudacher, "Kovertitennamen: Der Nameswechsel jüdischer Konvertiten in Wien von 1748 bis 1868," *Oestrreich in Geschichte und Literatur* 46, no. 2 (2002): 82–104.

14. Fox-Davies and Carlyon-Britton, *A Treatise on the Law Concerning Names and Changes of Name*. *Kondansha Encyclopedia of Japan* (Tokyo: Kodansha, 1983), 5, cols. 324–327, s.v. "Names." Herbert Plutschow, *Japan's Name Culture: The Significance of Names in a Religious, Political and Social Context* (Folkestone, U.K.: Japan Library, 1995). He suggests that even after the reforms that seemed to strip away the older meanings of names, an element of the old animistic beliefs in the magic of names remains in modern Japanese naming practices. I am grateful to Prof. Plutschow for sharing his work and ideas with me before he died.

15. José Saramago, *All the Names*, trans. from Portuguese by Margaret Jull Costa (San Diego: Harcourt, 1997), 149.

16. Ibid., 176–177.

17. All of what follows is based on the "Private Papers of W. J. Martin," Imperial War Museum (IWM) Documents, 2554.

18. Drew Gilpin Faust, *The Republic of Suffering* (New York: Vintage, 2009). As I made clear in my acknowledgments, I owe a great deal to the organizing principle of Faust's book: the idea that communion with the dead is an act of social solidarity. See also Thomas Laqueur, "Among the Graves," *London Review of Books*, 18 December 2008; Edward B. Proud, *History of the British Army Postal Service*, vol. 2, *1903–1927* (Dereham, U.K.: Proud-Bailey, n.d.), 7, 18.; C. F. Dendy Marshall, *The British Post Office from Its Beginnings to the End of 1925* (London: Humphrey Milford, 1926), 93, 228 (for quota-

tion); and Duncan Campbell-Smith, *Masters of the Post: The Authorized History of the Royal Mail* (London: Allen Lane, 2011), 223–224, and 213–257 more generally.

19. John Bowden, *The Epitaph-Writer Consisting of Upwards of Six Hundred Original Epitaphs . . . Chiefly Designed for Those Who Write or Engrave Inscriptions on Tomb-Stones . . . to Which Is Prefixed, an Essay on Epitaph-Writing* (Chester: J. Fletcher, 1791), iv. Samuel Johnson, *The Idler: By the Author of The Rambler. In Two Volumes . . . the Third Edition. With Additional Essays*, vol. 2 (London, 1767), 299.

20. Bowden, *The Epitaph-Writer*, vi, xiii, and passim. George Mogridge, *The Churchyard Lyrist* (London: Houlston, 1832), iv. George Wright, Esq., *Pleasing Melancholy or a Walk among the Tombs in a Country Church Yard, in the Stile & Manner of Hervey's Meditations* (1793), takes as its theme the central trope of Hervey on churchyards: "congregations of the dead," but unlike Hervey, he is interested in what individual tombstones said. The *Monthly Review* (the first English journal to regularly publish reviews, founded by Ralph Griffith, who also published *Fanny Hill*) 6 (1791): 458; and the explicitly radical *Analytical Review* (Mary Wollstonecraft wrote for it but, like all its reviewers, wrote anonymously) 10 (1791): 193, made fun of Bowden's *The Epitaph-Writer* as being indeed the first book to offer epitaphs for people of all descriptions but in doing so it tries to "supersede the whole public stock of wit and genius" of sextons, grave diggers, and clergy whose uncouth rhymes make visiting country churchyards so much fun.

21. Joseph Kaines, *Last Words of Eminent People Comprising, in the Majority of Instances, a Brief Account of Their Last Hours* (London: George Routledge, 1866), "advertisement."

22. Ibid., vi–x. Walter Benjamin, *Illuminations*, trans. Harry Zohn (New York: Harcourt, 1968), 94. On the Jewish tradition, see Anthony J. Saldarini, "Last Words and Deathbed Scenes in Rabbinic Literature," *Jewish Quarterly Review* 68, no. 1 (July 1977): 28–45.

23. Kaines, *Last Words*. For the last, widely quoted, words of Pancho Villa, see Laura Ward and Robert Allen, *Famous Last Words: The Ultimate Collection of Finales and Farewells* (London: Robson Books, 2004), 92.

24. He is referring to the *Book of Death* [*Sketching the Deaths of Celebrated Persons Collected from Chalmers Biographical Dictionary*], compiled by Samuel Dobree (London, 1819). Erskine Neale (1804–1883) was a socially progressive and widely read clergyman; the correct title is *The Closing Scene* (1848); see his *Dictionary of National Biography* entry. *Closing Scene* (London: Longmans, 1848) went through two editions that year, and another the year after; it inspired an illustrated version in 1887. G. W. Foote's book is subtitled *Idle Tales of Dying Horrors* and was published by the Truth Seeker Press, of which he seems to have been a principal partner. Kaines, *Last Words*, 285–287.

25. Kaines, *Last Words*, ix–x. Halford himself wrote about how people died, emphasizing the physiology of death with occasional comments on their behavior. His "The Deaths of Some Illustrious Persons of Antiquity" can be found in Sir Henry Halford, *Essays and Orations* (London: J. Murray, 1833), 145ff.; and "On the Deaths of Some Eminent Persons of Modern Times" is in the *Medical Magazine* (1835): 3, 17, 538–543. There Halford notes the disadvantages under which "unprofessional writers necessarily labor, in their attempt to develop motives of human conduct, on account of

their inability to appreciate the effects of disease on the Ind." (543). Halford was present at the opening of the tomb of Charles II and was accused of having stolen the king's fourth cervical vertebrae, which he then displayed at dinner parties. See the *Dictionary of National Biography* on this.

26. T. J. Clark, *Image of the People* (Berkeley: University of California Press, 1999), 80ff.

27. Sheila Adams, "Women, Death, and In Memoriam Notices in a Local British Newspaper [*Coventry Evening Telegraph*]," in Kathy Charmaz et al., eds., *The Unknown Country: Death in Australia, Britain and the USA* (New York: St. Martin's, 1997), 98–112. By 1915, in memorium notices had come to exceed death notices. The notice taken of women's death and loss tracks changes in their legal status.

28. "Funeral sermon" appears in the title of 188 of the 125,000 titles listed in Early English Books Online of books published between 1454 and 1700 and in 524 of the 188,000 titles of eighteenth-century publications.

29. William Jones, *The Jubilee Memorial of the Religious Tract Society* (London: The Religious Tract Society, 1850), app. 5. *Extracts from the Memoir Book of the Stockport Sunday School* (Manchester: J. Clave, 1911 [*sic*] [1811]). There had apparently been an earlier compilation published in 1798 that is now lost. As the school grew, it became impossible, the editors tell us, to gather memoirs of most students, but now the practice has been reinstated and they will once again publish "short accounts of any of our young people, whose lives and deaths where [*sic*] particularly interesting" (unpaginated preface and 13–15).

30. For Bell, see *Arminian Magazine* 25 (1802): 555ff. The phrase is from *The Symbol and Oddfellows Magazine* 1–2 (1843): 179. The story of Mary Barton is in John Warton [pseud. William Wood, vicar of Fulham], *Death Bed Scenes and Pastoral Conversations*, ed. by his sons, 2 vols. (London, 1827), 1:198ff. This book went through many and ever bulkier editions in both England and the United States. Unlike the accounts of lives and death in periodicals, we do not know for sure whether the person spoken of here is really Mary Barton and if her mother is really Anne or whether these are pseudonyms. My interest here is in the recording of the deaths of people whose passing would have gone unnoticed; it is in the increasing ubiquity of a narrative form. Older exemplars of this genre that recounted the lives and death of well-known men were reprinted and circulated widely; see, for example, Richard Burnham's new edition with a "large appendix" containing more biographies of *Pious Memorials; or The Power of Religion upon the Mind in Sickness and at Death . . . with a Preface by the Rev. Mr. Hervey* (London: George Caldwell, 1788); and F. Jewell, *Little Abe; or The Bishop of Berry Brow, Being a Life of Abraham Lockwood* (Manchester, 1880), 215–222.

31. *Christian and Infidels; Showing the Differences between Their Lives and Death in Several Striking Instances* is among a collection of RTS tracts in the British Library, 864e 321 14. It may be so well known because the RTS and others published numerous pamphlets about it. George Jacob Holyoake, *The Last Days of Mrs. Emma Martin, Advocate of Free Thought* (London: J. Watson, 1851). There is additional biographical detail in Sara A. Underwood's *Heroines of Free Thought* (New York, 1876), 231–242.

32. I am grateful to my former student Penelope Ismay for these examples. For more see her Ph.D. dissertation, "Trust among Strangers: Securing British Modernity 'by Way of Friendly Society,' 1780s–1870s," University of California–Berkeley, 2010.

33. We have no good accounts for how many autobiographies there are in England; in the Netherlands, the number of what scholars of the subjects call "ego documentation" increased from the 1,600 that are known from before 1814 to almost 5,000 up 1914, although we do not know the social background of these writers. The term "autobiography" enters English around 1800, another sign of the advent of a culture that values how those who lived them narrate their lives. The *Quarterly Review* is quoted in David Vincent, *Bread, Knowledge and Freedom: A Study of Nineteenth Century Working Class Autobiography* (London: Methuen, 1981), 30. John Burnett, David Vincent, and David Mayall, *The Autobiography of the Working Class: An Annotated Bibliography*, 3 vols. (Brighton, U.K.: Harvester Press, 1984) is the best bibliographical source we have, and it is where I found references to the works I quote. John Harris, *My Autobiography* (London, 1882), 7, 102–103. Harris's works are filled with death. He came to public attention when a clergyman heard a dirge he had written for the accidental death of miners in Cornwall. James Dawson Burn, *Autobiography of a Beggar Boy* (London, 1855), 30; see 130–134 for the deaths of his wife and brother. Vicky Tolar Burton, *Spiritual Literacy in John Wesley's Methodism: Reading, Writing, and Speaking to Believe* (Waco, Tex.: Baylor University Press, 2008), 200.

34. John Ruskin, *Fiction Fair and Foul*, in *Complete Works*, ed. E. T. Cook and Alexander Wedderburn (London: G. Allen; New York: Longmans, Green, 1903–1912), 34: 271–273. The many deaths that he enumerates in the novels of Walter Scott are often violent, reflecting the historical settings of their stories.

35. Friedrich Engels, letter to Friedrich Adolph Sorge, 15 March 1883, in Karl Marx and Frederick Engels, *Selected Correspondence 1846–1895*, trans. Dona Torr (New York: International Publishers, 1942), 414.

36. The quote about Dickens is from John Kuchic, "Death Worship among the Victorians: *The Old Curiosity Shop*," *PMLA* 95, no. 1 (January 1980): 63, which is more generally wonderful on the literary function of death in Victorian novels. Ruskin, *Fiction Fair and Foul*, in *Complete Works*, 34:271. William Empson, "Ignorance of Death," in *The Complete Poems of William Empson*, ed. John Haffenden (London: Penguin, 2000), 78. The best book on the subject of death in fiction is still Garrett Stewart, *Styles of Dying in British Fiction* (Cambridge, Mass.: Harvard University Press, 1984). Judith Kegan Gardiner, "A Wake for Mother: The Maternal Deathbed in Women's Fiction," *Feminist Studies* 4, no. 2 (1978): 146–185, surveys five twentieth-century novels. The Sussex shopkeeper Thomas Turner's *Diary*, covering the years 1754–1765, reports on the shared enjoyment of Clarrisa Harlow's funeral: "My wife read to me that moving scene of the funeral of Miss Clarissa Harlow. Oh, may the Supreme Being give me grace to lead my life in such a manner as my exit may in some measure be like that divine creature's" (*Sussex Archaeological Society Collections* 11 [1859]: 186).

37. Catherine Robson, *Heart Beats: Everyday Life and the Memorized Poem* (Princeton, N.J.: Princeton University Press, 2012), 91–92.

38. Ruskin, *Fiction Fair and Foul*, 34:269.

39. George Eliot, *Middlemarch*, ed. Gregory Maertz (Toronto: Broadview, 2004), 640. Charles Dickens, *Great Expectations*, ed. Margaret Cardwell (Oxford: Oxford University Press, 2008), 3. Michel de Certeau, *The Writing of History*, trans. Tom Conley (New York: Columbia University Press, 1988), 5.

CHAPTER 8: THE AGE OF NECRONOMINALISM

Epigraph: Zbigniew Herbert, *The Collected Poems, 1956–1998*, trans. Alissa Valles (New York: HarperCollins, 2007), 404–405. This poem is also quoted in the second paragraph of this chapter.

1. Wordsworth, "Essay upon Epitaphs I," in *The Prose Works of William Wordsworth*, ed. W.J.B. Owen and Jane Worthington Smyser (Oxford: Clarendon Press, 1974), 2:53.

2. "Written in death" is the central trope of Armando Petrucci's *Writing the Dead: Death and Writing Strategies in the Western Tradition*," trans. Michael Sullivan (Stanford, Calif.: Stanford University Press, 1998). I owe a great deal to the learning and the insights of this book; on the history of epitaphs, I rely on Joshua Scodel, *The English Poetic Epitaph: Commemoration and Conflict from Jonson to Wordsworth* (Ithaca, N.Y.: Cornell University Press, 1991), 15–49.

3. Petrucci, *Writing the Dead*, 113.

4. Committee on Interior and Insular Affairs, "Data on National Cemeteries" (Washington, D.C.: U.S. Government Printing Office, 1962). See Kelly Merrifield, "From Necessity to Honor: The Evolution of National Cemeteries in the United States" and its links to particular cemeteries, National Park Service, http://www.nps.gov /history/nr/travel/national_cemeteries/Development.html. In 1914, the federal government authorized payment for distinctive headstones to be erected over the dead of both sides in every cemetery and churchyard in America and also allowed the burial of the Confederate dead in all national cemeteries.

5. David G. Martin, "Editor's Preface" to John W. Busey, *The Last Full Measure: Burials in the Soldiers' National Cemetery at Gettysburg* (Hightstown, N.J.: Longstreet House, 1988), xxix, and xi–xxix more generally. Both the preface and the listings make clear how fantastically difficult it was to produce a semblance of order on the scene of slaughter and to arrive at a stable number of the dead, named and unnamed. Some Confederate soldiers were buried among Union troops; some men were said to be buried who were alive; some bodies were wrongly identified. The effort itself is evidence of the new imperative to name. Evelyn Lee Moore, *Behind the Old Brick Wall* (Lynchburg, Va.: Lynchburg Committee of the National Society of the Colonial Dames of America, 1968), 39 and 187–240, which reproduces a facsimile of Duiguid's list of names and plots.

6. See http://www.911memorial.org/ for a description. I hope the genealogy will become clear below.

7. Fabian Ware, *The Immortal Heritage* (Cambridge: Cambridge University Press, 1937), 47.

8. See Namscar Shaktini, *On Monique Wittig* (Urbana: University of Illinois Press, 2005), 8. *Scroll of Agony: The Warsaw Diary of Chaim A. Kaplan*, ed. and trans. Abraham I. Katsh (Bloomington: Indiana University Press, 1999), 302.

9. The fact that scores of famous artists have recorded this song over the years—Bruce Springsteen, Joan Baez, Dolly Parton, John Stewart, among others—speaks to the resonance of namelessness in our times. Diane Marcum, "Names Emerge from the Shadows of 1948 Crash," *Los Angeles Times*, 9 July 2013, http://www.latimes.com/news /local/la-me-deportees-guthrie-20130710-dt0,0,2642231.htmlstory. On Potters Field, see *New York Times*, 13 September 2013, editorial by Francis X. Cline, as well as Melinda Hunt's website, Hartisland.net, for further references.

10. Siegfried Sassoon, "On Passing the New Menin Gate," in *Collected Poems of Siegfried Sassoon* (London: Faber and Faber, 1961), 188. Helen Hamilton, "The Ghouls," in Catherine W. Reilly, ed., *Scars upon My Heart: Women's Poetry and Verse of the First World War* (London: Virago, 1981), 47. I was directed to this poem and to the whole genre of poetry that calls up the dead of the Great War by Elizabeth Marsland, *French, English and German Poetry of the First World War* (London: Routledge, 1991), 74–81 and 151–155.

11. On all three of these paintings, see the brochure produced by the Australian War Memorial for its November 2001–February 2002 exhibition of Longstaff's work, "Art and Remembrance," http://www.awm.gov.au/events/special/longstaff _brochure.pdf. R. J. Campbell, *The War and the Soul* (New York: Dodd, Mead, 1916), 10. The phrase made its way around: see, for example, the American *Theosophical Outlook* 3, no. 1 (5 January 1918): 318. On Campbell, see Keith Robbins, "The Spiritual Pilgrimage of Rev. R. J. Campbell," *Journal of Ecclesiastical History* 30, no. 2 (April 1979): 261–278. The first quotation is from James Tatum, *Mourner's Song* (Chicago: University of Chicago Press, 2006), 15; the second is at Sikhchic.com, http://www.sikhchic .com/history/letter_to_an_unknown_soldier_a_new_kind_of_war_memorial. Every cemetery has a visitors book; some comments are about war and peace; most speak to or of the dead.

12. The definition of monument and the distinctions between intentional and unintentional ones is from Alois Riegl, "The Modern Cult of Monuments: Its Character and Its Origin," trans. Kurt Forster and Diane Ghirardo, *Oppositions* 25 (Fall 1982), a central text for me in the history of monuments.

13. "Unveiling the War Memorial, 28 April 1923 [in Oldham]," IWM 26(=427.2): 36. "Blaydon War Memorial Unveiling Ceremony" IWM 26 (=428): 36. I am grateful to Steve Davidson, a local historian, for information about numbers and about what became of the dead. There are fifteen distinct war memorials in the neighborhood of Gateshead. "Saddleworth War Memorial Unveiling Ceremony, October 6, 1927," IWM 26 (=427.4), 36. "Atherstonians Who Fell in the Great War," MS, Imperial War Museum.

14. On Yale's Wolsey Hall, see http://ctmonuments.net/2011/08/woolsey-hall-new -haven and http://www.chs.org/finding_aides/ransom/077.htm. J. M. Winter, "Oxford and the First World War," in Brian Harrison, ed., *The History of Oxford* (Oxford:

Clarendon Press, 1994), 8:22–23. W. Barksdale Maynard, "Princeton in the Confederacy's Service," *Princeton Alumni Weekly* 111, no. 9 (23 March 2011).

15. Emily Cole, ed., *Lived in London: Blue Plaques and the Stories behind Them* (New Haven, Conn.: Yale University Press, 2009), 5, and Cole's introduction more generally, 1–33. Cole's book offers a borough-by-borough survey of the plaques and their fate. For blue plaque schemes elsewhere, see the English Heritage website, http://www.english-heritage.org.uk/content/imported-docs/p-t/plaques-register.pdf.

16. For the New Orleans case, see Sanford Levinson, *Written in Stone: Public Monuments in Changing Societies* (Durham, N.C.: Duke University Press, 1998). The murderer is reported to have yelled at the engineering students he was about to shoot, "You're all a bunch of feminists; I hate feminists." One of the dead was a staff member. See Laurie McNeill, "Death and the Maidens: Vancouver's Missing Women, the Montreal Massacre, and Commemoration's Blind Spots," *Canadian Review of American Studies* 38, no. 3 (2008): 378, and 375–400 more generally.

17. See Lin's account of how she came to design the Vietnam Veterans Memorial in the *New York Review of Books*, 2 November 2002, and more expansively in Maya Lin, *Boundaries* (New York: Simon and Schuster, 2000), 4:10–4:14. On the chronology of the evolution of Lin's design and description, see Vincent Scully, "The Terrible Art of Designing a War Memorial," *New York Times*, 14 July 1991, sec. 2. Roland Barthes, *Camera Lucida*, trans. Robert Howard (New York: Hill and Wang, 2010).

18. Vincent Scully, *Architecture: The Natural and the Manmade* (New York: St. Martin's Press, 1991), 359–360, and 356–360 more generally.

19. Lin, *Boundaries*, 4:11. Scully, *Architecture*, 360. "It is not to be borne," Scully concludes.

20. Lin, *Boundaries*, 4:11 Almost everything written on the Vietnam Veterans Memorial has views on the subject of its genealogy. I found most enlightening Gavin Stamp's *The Memorial to the Missing of the Somme* (London: Profile, 2003); and James Tatum's *The Mourner's Song: War and Remembrance from the "Iliad" to Vietnam* (Chicago: University of Chicago Press, 2006). There is spurious precision in any narrative collection of names; of the 58, 272 names currently on the monument, 333 have been added since the dedication. These, of course, not in chronological order.

21. Larry Rother, "James Stewart Nods at Lady Luck for His Golden Age Film Career: From a 3-Month M-G-M Contract in 1935 to 'It's a Wonderful Life,'" *New York Times*, 23 April 1990, c11. I have the picture from the Washington Project for the Arts brochure *War and Memory in the Aftermath of Vietnam*, prepared for a program 15 September to 19 December 1987. It is by Lloyd Wolf and comes from a beautiful book of his photographs called *Facing the Wall: Americans at the Vietnam Memorial* (New York: Macmillan Books, 1986).

22. Kristin Ann Hass, *Carried to the Wall: American Memory and the Vietnam Veterans Memorial* (Berkeley: University of California Press, 1998), 98–102, and more generally 87–102. Sal Lopes, *The Wall: Images and Offerings from the Vietnam Veterans Memorial* (New York: Collins, 1987). This sort of encounter happens as well when the bodies are said to be near. An aged veteran of the most horrible day of the most horrible battle of the twentieth century—the first day of the Battle of the Somme, 1 July 1916, told a

BBC 4 interviewer that he had felt bad about a comrade whose wounded body had been left in a German trench, subsequently abandoned. It was never found. The old man's spirit came to rest on this matter, he says, when he found his comrade's name among the seventy-three thousand of the missing on Lutyens's monument. Only in 1986, more than a half century later, could he say in the presence of the name that he felt that "I had not abandoned him."

23. Peter Hawkins, "Ars Memoriandi: The NAMES Project AIDS Memorial Quilt," in H. Spiro, M. Curnen, and L. Wandel, eds., *Facing Death* (New Haven, Conn.: Yale University Press, 1996), 166–179.

24. "Alwyn's" letter to "Jerry," in Joe Brown, ed., *The Names Project Book of Letters* (New York: Avon, 1992), 143. Marita Struken cites many similar encounters with the dead—"Clyde is that you?" "Hey, wait a minute. Where did you go?"—in her early article on the AIDS Quilt, whose title makes it the main point, "Conversations with the Dead: Bearing Witness in the AIDS Memorial Quilt," *Socialist Review* (October/November 1992), 65–95. Cleve Jones quoted in the *Sacramento Bee*, 31 August 1987; Lisa Heft quoted in *New York Native*, 24 August 1987; the last quote appears in Robert Atkins's article in the *Village Voice*, 27 October 1987.

25. Janet Goldstein in *And Justice for All . . . A Tribute to the March on Washington, Oct. 11, 1987* (Baltimore, Md.: William W. Wolfe Foundation, 1988), 28. *Frontline*, 26 October 1987; *Washington Blade*, 14 October 1988. Struken, "Conversations with the Dead," 73, for Jones quote. I have all of the material in this and the preceding note from the clipping files at the NAMES Project archive that I read during the time when it was in kept in San Francisco.

26. Burden is quoted in Robert Storr, *Dislocations* (New York: Museum of Modern Art, 1991), 43.

27. My thanks to my colleague Peter Zinoman, a historian of Vietnam, for suggesting the most exacting article to date on this difficult subject, one that reviews past efforts like Karnow's and arrives at the best number we have: Charles Hirschman, Samuel Preston, and Vu Manh Loi, "Vietnamese Casualties during the American War: A New Estimate," *Population and Development Review* 21, no. 4 (December 1995): 783–812. The authors first survey what is known about prewar mortality and population and then try to estimate excess mortality during the war years using evidence from more reliable postwar censuses and surveys. These sorts of demographic techniques have been employed to try to get estimates for losses of Iraqis and Afghan civilians in recent wars. On the general question, see Nicholas P. Jewell, Michael Spagat, and Britta Jewell, "Accounting for Civilian Casualties: From the Past to the Future," forthcoming, 2015 (http://www.springer.com/social+sciences/population+studies/book/978-3-319-12035-5).

28. See Christopher Knight, "A Monumental Burden," *Los Angeles Times*, 28 June 1992; the phrase "screwball empiricism" is Robert Storr's, quoted in Randy Kennedy, "The Balance of a Career," *New York Times*, 6 September 2013. On the making of Burden's piece in relation to the long history of naming, see James Tatum, *The Mourner's Song:*

War and Remembrance from the "Iliad" to Vietnam (Chicago: University of Chicago Press, 2004), 23–27.

29. On the term "disappeared," see the *Oxford English Dictionary*.

30. I quote from the statement of purpose of the Equipo Argentino de Antropologia Forense. The annual reports of the EAAF document hundreds of cases of recovery, i.e., of the reentry of a disappeared dead body into the community of the living. Regarding "N.N.," see Gabriel Gatti, *El detenido-desaparecido: Narrativas posibles para una catástrofe de la identidad* (Montevideo: Trilce, 2008), 49n.21. On the question of naming the disappeared in Argentina more generally, see Pilar Calveiro, *Poder y desaparición: Los campos de concentración en Argentina* (Buenos Aires: Colihue, 2008), esp. 164; and Zoe Crossland, "Buried Lives: Forensic Archaeology and Argentina's Disappeared," *Archaeological Dialogues* 7 (2000): 146–159.

31. Paul Celan, "Todesfuge," in John Felstiner, *Paul Celan: Poet, Survivor, Jew* (New Haven, Conn.: Yale University Press, 1983), 31–32.

32. See the anthology put together by Joachim Rönneppe, *Stolpersteine von Gunter Demnig: Ein Begleitbuch* (Gelsenkirchen: Arachne-Verlag, 2010). Demnig had thought that the brass plaques, and by extension the memory of those names, would be polished by the feet of pedestrians, but apparently people avoid stepping on them because they regard them as tombstones.

33. Abigail Solomon-Godeau, "Mourning and Melancholia: Christian Boltanski's *Missing House*," *Oxford Art Journal* 21, no. 2 (1998): 3–20. Documentation was originally placed in vitrines that were part of the installation; they are no longer there in a book. See *La maison manquante*, originally exhibited in *Die Freiheit der Endlichkeit* in Berlin, summer 1990.

34. See note 36 below.

35. The Holocaust Museum was created by an act of Congress in 1980 and sits just off the Washington Mall, the closest thing to a sacred space in the civic religion of the nation that can exist in a secular republic.

36. Serge Klarsfeld, *French Children of the Holocaust: A Memorial*, ed. Susan Cohen and Howard M. Epstein, trans. Glorianne Depondt and Howard M. Epstein (New York: New York University Press, 1996), xv. See the summary of the *fichier juif* affair in Rebecca Clifford, *Commemorating the Holocaust: The Dilemmas of Remembrance in France and Italy* (Oxford: Oxford University Press, 2013), 113–116. None of this is meant to deny the fact that France as a nation was deeply reluctant to address its role in the murder of its Jews. Only 2,564 of all those deported survived.

37. Immanuel Kant, *The Critique of the Power of Judgment*, ed. Paul Geyer (Cambridge: Cambridge University Press, 1992), bk. 2, A 25–26, 135–136.

38. *Le mémorial de la déportation des juifs de France* (1978), translated as *Memorial to the Jews Deported from France, 1942–1944: Documentation of the Deportation of the Victims of the Final Solution in France* (New York: B. Klarsfeld Foundation, 1983). There have been four supplements published since then. There is also a searchable database at http://www .ushmm.org/online/hsv/source_view.php?SourceId=31063 that seems to be based on Klarsfeld but also "differs in scope and content." *Le calendrier de la prosecution des juifs*

de France (Paris: Association les Fils et Filles des Déportés Juifs en France and Beate Klarsfeld Foundation, 1993).

39. Examples are almost limitless, but for a poignant example, see the Yale University Cambodian Genocide Program Photographic database of more than five thousand images of Khmer Rouge victims: http://www.yale.edu/cgp/photographs.html.

40. Felix Nadar, "My Life as a Photographer," trans. Thomas Repensek, *Photography* 5 (Summer 1978): 8. See Jay Ruby, *Secure the Shadow: Death and Photography in America* (Boston: MIT Press, 1995); and Anne Carol and Isabelle Renaudet, *La mort à l'oeuvre: Usages et représentations du cadavre dans l'art* (Aix-en-Provence: Presses Universitaires de Provence, 2013) for two among many examples of nineteenth-century postmortem photography.

41. See Michael André Bernstein, *Foregone Conclusions: Against Apocalyptic History* (Berkeley: University of California Press, 1994). Klarsfeld, *Memorial*, 544, 1708.

42. Klarsfeld, *Memorial*, 1277.

43. Ibid., 861, 660.

44. Barthes, *Camera Lucida*, 42–47 and passim. Klarsfeld, *Memorial*, 731, 732, 1126, 765, 1016.

45. Klarsfeld, *Memorial*, 489.

46. Ibid., 713.

47. See ibid., 80–81. Bernard Dziubas is on 624.

48. Ibid., 637.

49. I rely on Michael Marrus and Robert Paxton, *Vichy France and the Jews* (New York: Basic Books, 1981) for the general background to Klarsfeld's story, although there is by now a very large literature that builds on this pioneering and still definitive work.

CHAPTER 9: THE NAMES OF THE GREAT WAR

Epigraphs: John Bell, ed., *Selected Letters of Wilfred Owen* (Oxford: Oxford University Press, 1985), letter 482, 216–218. Zbigniew Herbert, *The Collected Poems, 1956–1998*, trans. Alissa Valles (New York: HarperCollins, 2007), 404–405.

The citations in this chapter to material generated by the Imperial War Graves Commission is not as consistent as I might wish. The Commission's archives in Maidenhead were closed to research in the 1990s when I began working on the question of names in the Great War. I therefore used other archives that held copies of some of the material I wanted to see: the Public Record Office and the Royal Archives at Windsor. (The Prince of Wales was the chair of the IWGC and its administrative predecessors.) Once I did gain access to the Maidenhead archive, I used material in various stages of cataloging. Copies of some documents that were given to me by members of the staff had only their original archival markings. I have not been able to return to Maidenhead to track down all the sources generated by the IWGC but have tried to provide a clear enough citation to allow other researchers to follow my tracks.

1. My and everyone else's attention to irony and memory is of course informed by Paul Fussell's *The Great War and Modern Memory* (New York: Oxford University Press, 1975).

2. Catherine Moriarty, now curatorial director of the University of Brighton Design Archives and professor of art and design history in the Faculty of Arts, began a major effort by the Imperial War Museum to catalog all war memorials in Great Britain in the 1990s. It continues on a still larger scale today. See http://www.ukniwm.org.uk/server/show/nav.15.

3. Sir Adrian Blomfield, *Memoirs of an Architect* (London: Macmillan, 1932), 176.

4. Ibid. 186–187. Commonwealth War Graves Commission, Maidenhead, uncataloged archive, Tyne Cote file no. 2, 23 November 1923–28 July 1924, Blomfield/Col. F. R. Durham. See also Richard Fellows, *Sir Reginald Blomfield: An Edwardian Architect* (London: Zwemmer, 1985), 112–113. Stephan Zweig in *Berliner Tageblatt*, 16 September 1928.

5. The so-called Lion monument in Lucerne, completed in 1821, was famous enough by 1847 to appear in Carlyle's *The French Revolution*, published in that year. Mark Twain in *A Tramp Abroad*, chap. 26, called it "[t]he most mournful and moving piece of rock in the world."

6. The very fact that we know so many details about Private Price's death speaks to the intense interest in the denouement of ordinary lives. On the proximity of burial, see most recently the *Sunday Independent*, April 5, 2015, http://www.independent.co.uk/news/world/europe/first-world-war-centenary-could-this-be-the-most-moving-ceremony-of-all-9645308.html. On Price's story, see Nick Lloyd, *Hundred Days: The End of the Great War* (London: Viking, 2013), 266–267.

7. The figures are from the *Encyclopaedia Britannica*, 11th ed., s.v. "Peninsular campaign." It points out how difficult it is to disaggregate the numbers killed, wounded or missing. "The Burial of Sir John Moore at Corunna," by the twenty-five-year-old Irish poet Charles Wolfe (1791–1823), who follows the narrative in Robert Southey, *History of the Peninsular Campaign*. A monument to Moore was erected on the battlefield. On the impact of the poem, see Catherine Robson, "Memorization and Memorialization: 'The Burial of Sir John Moore after Corunna,'" *Romanticism and Victorianism on the Web* 53 (February 2009).

8. The description is from the autobiography of Sir Harry Smith, a brigade major at Waterloo, quoted in Henry Rose-Lewin, *With the "Thirty Second" in the Peninsular and Other Campaigns* (Dublin: Hodges, Figges, 1914), 276. Charles Dalton's *The Waterloo Roll Call* (1890; London: Eyre and Spottiswoode, 1904), 250–255, lists only the officers present at Waterloo except for the noncommissioned officers and private soldiers in the short section on a few regiments of dragoons and, in a new section in the 1904 edition, noncommissioned officers and men who were latter given commissions. Thackeray continues: "Why was not every private man's name written upon the stones in Waterloo Church as well as every officer's? Five hundred pounds to the stonecutters would have served to carve the whole catalogue, and paid the poor compliment of recognition to men who died doing their duty. If the officers deserved a stone, the men did." Five hundred pounds would not have paid to write all the

names, and the church could not have held them, but that is another matter. See *Little Travels and Roadside Sketches* in *The Complete Works of William Makepeace Thackeray* (https://archive.org/details/completeworkswi08thacgoog) with introd. by William P. Trent and John Bell Henneman (New York: T. Y. Crowell [1904]), 473. Robert Southey, *The Poet's Pilgrimage to Waterloo* (Boston: Wells and Lilly, 1816), pt. 3, "The Field of Battle," verses 35 and 39.

9. Pierre Nora, "Between Memory and History: Les Lieux Mémoire," *Representations* 26 (Spring 1989): 7–24. Stuart Semmel, "Reading the Tangible Past: British Tourism, Collecting, and Memory after Waterloo," in "Grounds for Remembering," ed. Thomas Laqueur, special issue, *Representations* 69 (Winter 2000): 9–37; and more generally Stuart Semmel's *Napoleon and the British* (New Haven, Conn.: Yale University Press, 2004).

10. Southey, *The Poet's Pilgrimage to Waterloo*, 55. Monika Wagner first got me thinking about this painting in 2005 at Wissenschaftskolleg zu Berlin. Her earlier papers on Turner are summarized in her recent book, *William Turner* (Munich: C. H. Beck, 2011), 81–83, but it is her article "Turner's Orte der Erinnerung: Über die Undarstellbarkeit von Geschichte," in Stefan Germer and Michael Zimmermann, eds., *Bilder der Macht—Macht der Bilder* (Munich: Klinkhardt and Biermann, 1997), 231–256, that informed my views. Turner's sketches are in his MS Rhine Journey sketchbooks at the Tate, f. 16. The indispensable guide to these sketches is A. J. Finberg's chronologically arranged *Complete Inventory of the Drawings of the Turner Bequest* (London: HMSO, 1909). This paragraph is based also on Fred G. H. Bachrach, *Turner's Holland* (London: Tate Gallery, 1994), entry 7, "The Field of Waterloo," 37ff.; and Bachrach's "The Field of Waterloo and Beyond," *Turner Studies* 1, no. 2 (1981): 3–11.

11. [Philip A. Hurt], *The Guards' Cemeteries, St. Etienne, Bayonne with a Concise Narrative of the Campaign in S.W. France* (London: Bemrose and Sons, 1878), preface, n.p, and 59–61 for the list. There were several printings of this pamphlet and a French translation.

12. Capts. the Hons. John Colborne and Frederic Brine, *The Last of the Brave; or Resting Places of Our Fallen Heroes* (London, 1857), iv and statistics throughout.

13. Brig. Gen. J. M. Adye and Col. C. G. Gordon, *Report on Crimean Cemeteries* (London: HMSO, 1873), 1–4. *Times*, letter re Smyrna, 30 November, from Greville J. Chester on 31 August 1864, p. 8. Chester had written about the scandalous state of the grave in the same place five years before.

14. This story is from *Chowkidar (Journal of the British Association for Cemeteries in South Asia)* 2 (March 1980–March 1982): 1, 1–2.

15. Thomas Hardy, "Drummer Hodge," in *Collected Poems* (New York: Macmillan, 1926), 83. Rupert Brooke's "The Soldier" is in *The Poetry Anthology 1912–2002*, ed. Parisi and Young (Chicago: Ivan Dee, 2002), 19.

16. This material is from Public Record Office (PRO), WO 32/6023, "Care of Cemeteries in the Colonies" folder. There is an excellent scholarly account on which I base much of this paragraph by Elizabeth Van Heyningen and Pat Merritt, "'The Healing Touch': The Guild of Loyal Women of South Africa 1900–1912," *South African Histori-*

cal Journal 47, no. 1 (2002): 31–38 and 24–50 more generally. The English poet Cicely
Fox Smith wrote "To the South African Guild of Loyal Women" in 1900:

> When the thunder of the battle rolls no more,
> And the last bugles blow o'er the plain,
> They'll be many in old England mourning sore
> For the men who must remain;
> Yet when they think upon their glorious dead,
> They shall know that their memory shall not fade,—
> That sacred, where their dear ones fought and bled,
> Is the ground where they are laid.
> When, as the years bring round the time again,
> Beneath their names our tribute wreaths we lay,
> Who sleep full sound in some Southern plain
> From their Isle far away,
> Tho' they rest afar across the sundering foam,
> 'Neath a turf never wet with English showers,
> We grieve not, since we know that, far from home,
> Their graves are glad with flowers.

17. The reference is of course to Drew Gilpin Faust's *The Republic of Suffering* (New York: Vintage, 2009). For the centrality of the mail in the U.S. case, see David Henkin, *The Postal Age: The Emergence of Modern Communications in Nineteenth-Century America* (Chicago: University of Chicago Press, 2006).

18. I chose this case almost at random from among those in but one archive: Virginia Tech Special Collections, Blacksburg, Va., MS 91-067.

19. Reginald Harold Bryson, clerk, "My War Diary," p. 10, Imperial War Museum (IWM) MS. 72/88/1. Joint War Committee, Red Cross, Report 1914–1919, pt. 16, 319, p. 359 (London: HMSO, 1921). A. H. Mure, *With the Incomparable 29th* (London: W&R Chambers, 1919), 87. It seemed impossible to contemporaries to bury this evidence of a normal life in the distant world of civilian life. On the other hand, once stripped of all that was personal and in the absence in many cases of dual dog tags, it made the identification of bodies that had lost their names in the back and forth of the trenches nearly impossible. *The Letters of T. S. Eliot*, ed. Valerie Eliot (New York: Harcourt Brace, 1988), 1, 1898–1922, 55.

20. PRO, "History of the MS3 Case during 1914–1919 (officers)," WO 32/9317. "Organization of the Branch to Deal with Casualties of Wartime," WO 32/9315. "History of Procedures in the War 1914–1918," 1/Gen. No/2084.

21. This history is authoritatively told in Philip Longworth, *The Unending Vigil: A History of the Commonwealth War Graves Commission, 1917–1984* (London: Leo Cooper, Secker and Warburg, 1985), 1–29.

22. Quoted in ibid., 7. Whitman is quoted in Faust, *Republic of Suffering*, 123.

23. Rev. Ernest Courtenay Crosse, 8th and 9th Battalion, Devonshire Regiment, Somme 1916, typed from MS diary by his son John Anthony Crosse, IWM, 27–28.

24. PRO, WO 32/5847. Minutes of the Imperial War Graves Commission (IWGC), Windsor Castle Archives, box 244, folio 27, 6 March 1917.

25. Private E. N. Gladston, 1917, quoted in C. B. Purdon, *Everyman at War* (London: J. M. Dent, 1930), 117.

26. Imperial War Museum, 75/89/1, I.L. The quote from a military chaplain is from Ernest Crosse's diaries.

27. Blunden, introduction to *Immortal Heritage* by Fabian Ware (Cambridge: Cambridge University Press, 1937), 17.

28. For Alexander's orders, IWM, Misc. 111, item 1766; Private Papers of R. A. Walker, ms Diary, June 1915–August 1920, IWM Documents, 977. The last quote is from the diary of W. Clarke, IWM 87/18/1, p. 6.

29. IWM, item 1766, "Official Orders and Messages, 47th Division." IWGC, 88/11/1, R. A. Walker file. Diary of F. M. Packham, typescript, IWM, pp. 21–24.

30. R. Skitt file, two letters, 4 and 20 September 1917, IWM, p. 360.

31. E. K. Foreman Private Papers, 26 October 1915 to 23 November 1915, IWM Documents, 21950.

32. S. Poole, IWM Letters, 15 January 1915.

33. IWM, Misc. 2118, Papers Relating to the Eighty-Third Labour Group; House of Lords, Lloyd George Papers F/5/3/46 (30 April 1919) and F/5/3/65 (15 May 1919).

34. PRO, WO32/3136, 12 April 1928.

35. All of these letters are in the Darwin Papers, Cambridge University Library, DAR box 215.

36. See the *Manchester Guardian* report on Hardy's funeral, 17 January 1928. On the arrangements for his body, see Claire Tomalin, *Thomas Hardy: The Time-Torn Man* (New York: Penguin, 2007), 372–375.

37. *Spectator*, 4 April 1919, 7; *Times* (London), 17 February 1919 and 8 February 1919. W. Churchill/Lord Peel, 3 March 1919, in PRO WO 32/5853. For the question of equality of treatment, the return of bodies, and the rights of relatives to put up individual memorials exercised by the National Committee on the Care of Soliders' Graves and, after 1917, its successor the IWGC, see the minutes in Windsor Castle Archives, box 240.

38. Kenyon's comments in his report "War Graves" (HMSO, 1918), submitted to the IWGC 22 November 1918, p. 5, found in IWGC, box 2056 marked Add 1/1/5 and labeled "Headstone Documents 1918–1920." Memo from Luytens, 28 August 1917, and other comments in IWGC 18, box 1137, folder marked "Adornment of Cemeteries."

39. *National Review* 76 (3 July 1920): 713–715.

40. "Labour Representative Delegation Report on the Work of the Imperial War Graves Commission," typescript, n.d., JSM/IWGC/1, Labour Party Archives, National Museum of Labour History, Manchester.

41. There were some mass graves, but these are carefully camouflaged. IWGC tomb-stones in Great Britain mark those who returned home alive but subsequently died of their wounds. Windsor Castle Archives 244; and Ware's reply to Halsey, Ref 20/c24/301/V; IWGC box 1009, pt. 1, 12.3.1919; IWGC 219, box 1009, 12-3-19.

42. Ibid. (Ware's reply). In fact, there were exceptions: near Zillebeck there is a circular arrangement of named graves that represent soldiers buried nearby whose graves were destroyed. They are "missing" but seem present; their names do not appear on the Menin Gate or on any other memorial.

43. This file was given to me by an archivist at the IWGC in Maidenhead. It is marked 45/1/675 and dated March 1921. I am not sure whether it has been assigned an ar-chive number.

44. Ibid.

45. IWGC 219, pt. 1, box 1009.

46. Ibid. In discussions around 12 June, the adjutant general makes the case that regi-mental numbers would not even be useful in distinguishing men of the same name.

47. IWGC 219/211, pt. 1, box 1009, esp. the typescript "'Missing' Memorials"; IWGC Acon 56, box 2054, Director of Works/Ware, 19 June 1926.

48. IWGC 219/211 pt. 1, box 1010. IWGC 360 pt. 1, box 1029.

49. IWGC 210/11/1, box 1017, 228/8/1924.

50. S. MacNaughtan, *My War Experiences in Two Continents* (London: J. Murray, 1919), 70. There is no good history of the Unknown Warrior, but A. M. Gregory's *The Silence of Memory: Armistice Day 1919–1946* (Oxford: Oxford University Press, 1998) has a suc-cinct account of the day of burial itself and wonderful history of the sacrality of the eleventh hour of the eleventh day of the eleventh month, the moment of armistice and of the burial.

51. Windsor RA Geo V o 1637/16. For the Railton controversy, see the letters at RA Geo V 1637/ 17 and 18. The man of letters Ronald Blythe in *The Age of Illusion* (Bos-ton: Houghton Mifflin, 1964), 13–14, makes a good case for Railton's primacy. For David Railton, see the *Dictionary of National Biography*. In Italy, the body of its unknown soldier was chosen from among eleven unidentified candidates by a woman whose son was killed but never found. For more on the Italian case, see Laura Wittman, *The Tomb of the Unknown Soldier, Modern Mourning, and the Reinvention of the Mystical Body* (Toronto: University of Toronto Press, 2011). I am grateful to her for discussing her work with me prior to its publication. Regarding undisturbed soil, see the *Sphere* 83, no. 1086 (13 November 1920): 146.

52. Archbishop/Lord Stamfordham, 13 October 1920, Windsor Castle Archive, RA Geo IV. o 1637/6; the king's views are at O1627/1. Brig. Gen. L. J. Wyatt file, IWM, 69/84/A. PRO, WO 12K 20/1/3 174019.

53. *Bradford Pioneer*, 12 November 1920, 7. *Forward*, 27 November 1920: "I have seen and endured the sufferings of the troops and I can no longer be a party to prolong these sufferings for ends which I believe to be evil and unjust," Sassoon wrote. His friend Robert Graves managed to have him declared insane and thus escape a court martial.

54. War Cabinet meeting, 4 July 1919. On the Cenotaph, see Eric Homberger, "The Story of the Cenotaph," *Times Literary Supplement* (London), 12 November 1976, 1429+, accessed Times Literary Supplement Historical Archive website, 28 August 2014; and Alex King, *The Memorials of the Great War* (Oxford: Oxford University Press, 1998), 141–149.

55. *Times*, Armistice Day supplement, 12 November 1920.

56. See also Stephen Heathorn, "The Civil Servant and Public Remembrance: Sir Lionel Earle and the Shaping of London's Commemorative Landscape, 1918–1933," *Twentieth Century British History* 19, no. 3 (2008): 259–287. In his memoir, *Turn Over the Page* (London: Hutchinson, 1935), 132–133, Earle blames opposition on local authorities. He offers here more details of the burial of the Unknown Warrior—the fact, for example, that the simple wooden coffin was strapped in wrought iron fashioned by "a very capable Welsh smith, Mr. Williams, from Carnarvon," 131.

57. The full text of the speech (in German) is in *Schultess Europäischer Geschichtskalender* (Munich, 1927), 153.

58. David Crane, *Empires of the Dead: How One Man's Vision Led to the Creation of WWI's War Graves* (London: William Collins, 2013). The case is made with even more archival precision in Andrew Keating, "The Empire of the Dead: British Burial Abroad and the Formation of National Identity," Ph.D. diss., University of California, 2011.

59. Lloyd George Papers, House of Lords Record Office, F/24/3/20, Storr/Davies, 28 October 1920. *Workers Dreadnought*, 20 November 1920, 4, and 19 November, 4. See also "Communist Discord: Public Anger with Men Who Broke Silence," *Times* (London), 12 November 1920, an admittedly biased source; and *Forward*, 27 November 1920, 2. The question of reverence for the Unknown Warrior and the degree of respect that he and the moment of silence demanded was still exigent in 1981 when Michael Foot, the Labour leader, was much criticized—and defended—for wearing a "donkey jacket," a navvy's coat, an inappropriate bit of cover gear by some other name, to the remembrance ceremonies. In fact, his wife had bought the usually ill-dressed Labour leader a new overcoat and had seen to it that he wear a nice suit and tie to the remembrance ceremony. The Queen Mother told him she liked the coat. As Foot's biographer says, "the whole episode was absurd," but it sadly became a defining image in Foot's public life. My interest in it is motivated by the continuing reverence demanded at a national shrine. See Kenneth O. Morgan, *Michael Foot: A Life* (London: Harper, 2007), 390–391.

60. Samuel Beckett, *Proust* (New York: Grove Press, 1994), 4–5. George Eliot, *The Mill on the Floss*, ed. Gordon Haight (Oxford: Clarendon Press, 1980), 459–460.

61. Second Lt. Stephen Hewett to Mrs. Robertson, 2 June 1916, in Laurence Housman, *War Letters of Fallen Englishmen* (London: Victor Gollancz, 1930), 137–138. H. A. Coulter, HAC 9, IWM. Edmund Blunden, *Undertones of War* (Garden City, N.Y.: Doubleday, Doran, 1929), 274.

62. PRO WO 32/5853, "Suggestions for the Preservation of the Battlefield at Ypres as a War Memorial," and for the most optimistic assessment of this possibility, see Alfred Mond/Churchill, 7 February 1919, in this file. See also WO 32/5569 on the question

of memorials. Sarah Farmer, *Martyred Village: Commemorating the 1944 Massacre at Oradour-sur-Glane* (Berkeley: University of California Press, 1999).

63. Catherine Stevens is quoted in James Longenback, *Wallace Stevens* (New York: Oxford University Press, 1991), 51. Vera Brittain, *Testament of Youth* (1933; reprint, New York: Penguin, 2005), 97. Ian Malcom, *War Pictures behind the Lines* (London: Smith Elder, 1915), 50–51.

64. Private Papers of E. A. Pinks, IWM Documents, 3759.

65. IWM 85/43/1.

66. I am grateful to Prof. Dr. Emeritus Klaus Reichart of the University of Frankfurt for sharing this family picture and allowing me to reproduce it here.

PART IV: BURNING THE DEAD

Epigraphs: Daniel Paul Schreber, "Concerning Cremation," in *Memoirs of My Nervous Illness,* trans. and ed. Ida MacAlpine and Richard Hunter (London: Dawson, 1955), 296–297. Fritz Schumacher, *Die Feuerbestattung: Handbuch der Architektur* (Leipzig: J. M. Gebhardt, 1939), 16.

1. Arthur Darby Nock, "Cremation and Burial in the Roman Empire," *Harvard Theological Review* 25, no. 4 (1932): 321–359.

2. Eusebius, *Ecclesiastical History,* bk. 7, chap. 2, trans. C. F. Cruse (London: George Bell and Sons, 1894), 168. On the legislation of Boniface VIII, see Elisabeth Brown, "Authority, the Family and the Dead in France," *French Historical Studies* 16 (1990); and "Death and the Human Body in the Later Middle Ages: The Legislation of Boniface VIII on the Division of the Corpse," *Viator* 12 (1981): 221–270.

3. Ruth Mazo Karras, "Pagan Survivals and Syncretism in the Conversion of Saxony," *Catholic Historical Review* 72, no. 4 (1986): 553–572, esp. 557–558. Henry Mayr-Harting, "Charlemagne, the Saxons, and the Imperial Coronation of 800," *English Historical Review* 111, no. 444 (1996): 1113–1133, esp. 1116ff.

4. *Report of the Crematorium Sub-Committee, Appointed June 8, 1897, Camberwell London,* Cremation Society Archives, Durham University, Durham, UK, 17. At issue is the English Cremation Society's furnace at Woking Cemetery.

CHAPTER 10: DISENCHANTMENT AND CREMATION

Epigraph: *Times* (London), 14 October 1874, reprinted in scores of newspapers.

1. This and the following information about Brunetti's place at the Vienna exhibition is based on *Welt-Austellung 1873 in Wien, Officieller General-Catalog* (Vienna: Verlag der General Direction, Zweite vermehrte Auflage, 1873), 235ff., describing the Italian exhibitors of Group 26.

2. The description of his experiments are from Ludovico Brunetti, *Crémation des cadavres* (Padua: Typographie Prosperini, 1873). The preface is dated 1 May, Vienna, and

makes the promise of a further communication. All the quotations below are from the pamphlet.

3. James Curtis Booth, assisted by Campbell Morfit, *The Encyclopedia of Chemistry, Practical and Theoretical*, 2nd ed. (1850; Philadelphia: H. C. Baird, 1862), s.v. "bone ash" and "bone-black."

4. Charles-Emile Bourry's "Les fours crématoires" (a broadside with diagram) appeared in Paris in 1886. The design was widely adopted, especially in Sweden. An oft-reprinted 1901 translation of an 1897 French work became the standard work on ceramic technology: *A Treatise on Ceramic Industries*, trans. Wilton P. Rix (London: Scott Greenwood, 1901).

5. *New York Times*, 27 September 1873, p. 2, reporting on the 7 September opening.

6. There is a discrepancy here that I have been unable to resolve. Thompson says Brunetti's exhibit, with its apparatuses and glass cubes as I have described them based on his 1 May paper, was #4149, not as in the General Catalogue, #53 of group 26 of division 6b. I assume that medically relevant exhibits from the Exhibition generally were restaged for the Congress and that Brunetti has this in mind when he said in May that there would be further communications the following September.

7. Zavhary Cope, *The Versatile Victorian: Being a Life of Sir Henry Thompson, 1820–1904* (London: Harvey and Blythe, n.d.), 124.

8. This is the definition given by Edmund Parkes, MD, FRS, in his widely circulated and much reprinted *Manual of Practical Hygiene: Prepared Especially for the Use of Medical Service on the Army* (London: John Churchill and Sons, 1864). There were editions of this book in 1866, 1869, and 1873; these would have been the ones quoted approvingly by the early advocates of cremation. Parkes makes the case that the Report of the Royal Commission of 1857 that investigated the public health debacle of the Crimean War changed the role of the army doctor and, by implication, of doctors generally. They were no longer to be concerned just with the care of the sick but also with preserving the health of the living.

9. For Charles Wentworth see his *Dictionary of National Biography* entry.

10. For the circulation of this report in the American press more generally, see *The Letters of Mark Twain*, ed. Michael Berry Frank (Berkeley: University of California Press, 2002), 6, 276n.6.

11. For the detailed "protocols" of Siemens's experiments, see Friedrich Küchernmeister, *Die Feuerbestattung* (Stuttgart: Enke, 1875), 718–755. He says he witnessed many of the preliminary experiments. See also A. Cadet, "Hygiène, inhumation," in *Crémation: ou Incinération des corps*, 2nd ed. (Paris: Germer-Baillière, [1877]), 133–174.

12. Henry Thompson, *Modern Cremation: Its History and Practice* (London: Paul Trench, 1891), 46–47.

13. Sir Thomas Browne, *Religion medici: or The Religion of a Physician*, 11th ed., corrected (London: 1738), 106–107, 111–112. All of this is in the specific context of how he—Browne—apprehends his own death: he does not fear it; he admires those who welcome death most ostentatiously (soldiers) and thinks that, if the ancient pagans

could famously meet their end without fear, Christians should do so all the more easily. In all of this, the death of the body is of little moment.

14. Ephraim Chambers, *Cyclopaedia, or, An Universal Dictionary of Arts and Sciences* (London: Printed for J. J. Knapton, 1728), 168, s.v. "death." *Encyclopedia Britannica, or a Dictionary of Arts and Sciences Compiled upon a New Plan* (Edinburg: A. Bell and C. Macfarquhar, 1771), 2:309, s.v. "death."

15. *Grosses vollstaendiges Universal-Lexicon aller Wissenschafften und Kuenste* (1732–1750), s.v. "Tod": "bey den Theiren heisset der Tod eine ganzliche Auflösugn der Gewercke, woraus der Cörper zusammen geseset, ode rein Stillstand des Umlauffs des Gebluts und der Lebens Schiffe"; "bey den Menschen ist der Tod, nach der gemeinsten Meinung, ein Abscheden der Seele von dem Leibe, aus Mangel der Wärme, und der Bewegung, wenn sie durch zufällige Ursachen verhindert worden." See "Leben, Via, Vie," 16:1261–62.

16. Christopher Marlowe, *The Tragicall History of D. Faustus* (A text), from the Perseus Online edition, ed. Hilary Binda, http://www.perseus.tufts.edu/hopper/text?doc=Perseus :text:1999.03.0010:scene=14), sc. 14, ll. 1489–1491.

17. "Mort, histoire naturel de l'homme" (Louis de Jaucourt), *Encyclopédie ou Dictionnaire raisonné des sciences, des arts et des métiers* (Paris, 1765), 10:716. "Mort = destruction des organes vitaux, ensorte qu'ils ne puissent plus se rétablir." Jaucourt, an independently wealthy naturalist and doctor, wrote more of the *Encyclopédie* than anyone else, more than 30 percent of the volume in which this article appears, 45 percent of some, and on average an astonishing 25 percent of the whole. He was a committed mechanist.

18. Paul-Jacques Malouin had an apartment at Versailles, was physician to the queen, and member of the Academy of Sciences; he was a wealthy member of the medical establishment. "Mort, medicine," 10:718: "La séparation de l'ame d'avec le corps, mystere peut-être plus incompréhensible que son union est un dogme théologique certifié par la Religion, & par conséquent incontestable; mais nullement conforme aux lumieres de la raison, ni appuyé sur aucune observation de Médecine ainsi que nous n'en ferons aucune mention dans cet article purement medicinal." This is near the beginning of a nine-page, double-column article. 17:249: "Vie, c'est l'opposé de la mort, qui est la destruction absolue des organes vitaux, sans qu'ils puissent se rétablir; ensorte que la plus petite vie est celle dont on ne peut rien ôter, sans que la mort arrive; on voit que dans cet état délicat, il est difficile de distinguer le vivant du mort; mais prenant ici le nom de vie dans le sens commun, je la définis un mouvement continuel des solides & des fluides de tout corps animé." This very short piece is also by Jaucourt.

19. Xavier Bichat, *Physiological Researches upon Life and Death*, trans. Tobias Watkins (Philadelphia: Smith and Maxwell, 1809), 1. The first Paris edition appeared in 1800.

20. J. G. Smith, *The Principles of Forensic Medicine* (London: Underwood, 1821), 16.

21. "On voit que dans cet état délicat, il est difficile de distinguer le vivant du mort."

22. Leander Peaget with Jacobus Winslow, *Resp. Quaestio Medico-Chirugrica, Praes J. P. Winslow, An Morits Incertae Signa Minus Incerta A Chirurgcus, Quam Ab Aliis Experimentis?* ([Paris], 1740). Jacques-Jean Bruhier with Jacob Winslow, *Dissertation sur l'incertitude*

des signes de la mort, et l'Abus des enterremens, et embaumemens précipités (Paris, 1743). *Dictionnaire encyclopédique des sciences médicales: Publié sous la direction de MM. les docteurs Raige-Delorme et A. Dechambre* (Paris: P. Asselin, S' de Labé, V. Masson et fils, 1865–1889), 2nd series, vol. 9, s.v. "Mort," 708–711.

23. D. A. Shewmon, "Chronic 'Brain Death': Meta-analysis and Conceptual Consequences," *Neurology* 51, no. 6 (1998): 1538–1545. On the definition of brain death in relationship to the needs of transplant surgeons, see M. L. Tina Stevens, "Redefining Death in America, 1968," chap. 3 of *Bioethics in America: Origins and Cultural Politics* (Baltimore, Md.: Johns Hopkins University Press, 2000). In a recent exchange about the incoherence of current medical definitions of death, one doctor writes, "brain death is to death as legally blind is to 'actually blind.'" But what precisely actually dead is remains elusive in medical discussion. Letter to the editor from Robert D. Truog, *Critical Care Medicine* 40, no. 4 (2012): 1393.

24. Jeffrey Freedman, "The Limits of Tolerance: Jews, the Enlightenment, and the Fear of Premature Burial," in Charles Walton, ed., *Into Print: Limits and Legacies of the Enlightenment; Essays in Honor of Robert Darnton* (University Park: Penn State University Press, 2011), 177–197. Eberhard Wolff, *Die Architektur einer modernen jüdischen Identität: Medizin und Ärzte im deutschen Judentum der Reformära (1750–1850)*, Schriftliche Habilitationsleistung zum Habilitationsgesuch an die Philosophisch-Historische Fakultät der Universität Basel (Gottingen: Vandenhoeck & Ruprecht, 2009). Gerlind Rüve, "Scheintod: Zur kulturellen Bedeutung der Schwelle zwischen Leben und Tod um 1800" (Ph.D. diss, Bielefeld University, 2008).

25. Alexander Campbell Fraser, *Life and Letters of George Berkeley* (Oxford: Clarendon Press, 1871), 4:344–345. Berkeley died on Sunday, 14 January 1753, and was buried on Saturday the 20th.

26. Sir Henry Thompson, *Modern Cremation: Its History and Practice*, 2nd ed. (London: Kegan Paul, 1891), 4.

27. George M. A. Wotherspoon, *Cremation, Ancient and Modern: The History and Utility of Fire-Funeral* (London: Sunday Lecture Society, 1886), 12, and passim.

28. Thompson, *Modern Cremation*, vii.

29. Jules-Octave Laurent, *La crémation aux points de vue historique et hygiénique* (Lille: Camille Robbe, 1882) (doctoral thesis in medicine at Lille), 27–28. This is an odd claim in itself, because typhus was usually associated with jails, prisons, and army camps—jail fever, prison fever, camp fever. Sir Henry Thompson, *Cremation: The Treatment of the Body after Death* (London: Henry S. King, 1874), 7, 25–39. *Modern Cremation*, 107–135, takes up the theme again, 107, 111ff.

30. Emrys-Jones Abraham, *Disposal of the Dead* (London: John Haywood, 1888), 77.

31. Ibid., 21. Thompson and others got these figures for gas from the calculations of Sir Lionel Playfair, who, when he first produced them had no interest in cremation but was aligned then with burial reformers. Hon. and Rev. W. H. Lyttelton, *Scripture Revelation of the Life of Man after Death* (London: Dolby, Isbisher, 1875), xxii–xxiii.

32. William Eassie, *Healthy Homes: A Handbook to the History, Defects, and Remedies of Drainage, Ventilation, Warming, and Kindred Subjects* (London: Simpkins, Marshall and Co., 1872),

i–iv. *Sanitary Arrangements for Use of Officers of Health, Architects, Builders and Householders* (London: Smith Elder, 1874) 2, 12; see, for the mundane but important details of the project, 85–86 on the evils of cesspits or 60 for the perfect arrangement of the seat and trap of the water closet.

33. Parkes, *Manual of Practical Hygiene*, 76.

34. Laurent, *La crémation aux points de vue historique et hygiénique*, 15.

35. Edward J. Bermingham, *The Disposal of the Dead: A Plea for Cremation* (New York: Bermingham and Co., 1881), 75, 48. William Holden, *Cremation versus Burial: An Appeal to Reason vs. Prejudice* (Hull: A. Brown and Son, 1891), 20–21.

36. Karl Freiherr von Engerth, *Fortschritte der Feuerbestattung in Deutschland* (Vienna: Adolph Holzhausen, 1892), 4. Thompson, *Modern Cremation*, 22–23.

37. Thompson's letter on the subject of dust collection is in the *Times* (London), 1 January 1904, and reprinted in Cope, *The Versatile Victorian*, 125.

38. "The Crematory at Woking," *Sanitary Record*, 24 January 1879, 49–51, collected in the *Sanitary Record* (London: Smith, Elder and Co., 1879), 10:50, describes the technical details. *Academy*, 29 February 1874, Notes and News section, 5:238. Major Thomas Martin, *Specifications of a 'Cinerator' for the Use of Brahmins and Hindo Castes . . .* (Bombay: Chesson and Woodhall, n.d.).

39. Henry Thompson, *Cremation: The Treatment of the Body after Death*, 3rd ed. (London: Smith Elder, 1884), 27.

40. J. Cuthbert Welch, *Cremation: The Best Mode of Sepulture* (Reading: Turner Bros., 1889), 11.

41. Readers of *Our Mutual Friend* and of Catherine Gallagher's writings about it will not be surprised at this extension of a mid-nineteenth-century theme. See Catherine Gallagher, *The Body Economic* (Princeton N.J.: Princeton University Press, 2006).

42. He uses a low estimate because London's death rate is higher than the national average; its population is more like 10 percent of the whole population. Thompson, *Cremation: The Treatment of the Body after Death*, 3rd ed., 6–7; see also his footnote.

43. L. S. Mercier, *Corps législative*, Conseil des Cinq-Cents. *Sur les sépulchres privées* (Paris: 18 Frimaire, Year V-1796), quoted in Michel Ragon, *The Space of Death: Study of Funerary Architecture, Decoration and Urbanism*, trans. Alan Sheridan (Charlottesville: University Press of Virginia, 1983), 283–284.

44. Jakob Moleschott, *Der Kreislauf des Lebens* (Mainz, 1852), 480. More generally see Ursula Staiger, "Die Auseinandersetzung um die Feuerbestattung in Deutschland im 19 Jahrhundert" (Ph.D. diss., University of Mainz, 1981), 6–9. For biographical information, see *Complete Dictionary of Scientific Biography* (Detroit: Charles Scribner's Sons, 2008), 9:456–457, s.v. Moleschott, Jacob.

45. Ian Anstruther, *The Scandal of the Andover Workhouse* (London: Geoffrey Bles, 1973).

46. William Eassie, *Cremation: Its History and Its Bearings upon Public Health* (London: Smith, Elder and Co., 1975), 2.

47. Teresa Lewis, *Cremation* (London: Thomas Scott, n.d. but ca. 1880), 6, 10.

48. Rev. H. R. Haweis, *Ashes to Ashes* (London: Daldy Isbister and Co., 1875). See 258–260 for the full mathematical justification of these bizarre calculations.

49. These calculations come from a supporter of earth burial who argued that by putting bodies in wicker coffins they would decay quickly and thus free up room for more bodies. Emrys-Jones, *Disposal of the Dead*, 77. Haden, *Earth to Earth: A Plea for a Change of System in Our Burial of the Dead* (London: Macmillan, 1875), 19–20 and passim.

50. Richard Etlin, *The Architecture of Death: The Transformation of the Cemetery in Eighteenth-Century Paris* (Cambridge, Mass.: MIT Press, 1984), 108–110, 282, 284.

CHAPTER 11: ASHES AND HISTORY

Epigraph: Johann-Jakob Wegmann-Ercolani, *Ueber Leichenverbrennung als rationellste Bestattungsart: Eine Abhandlung den gesunden Menschenverstand gewidmet* [Cremation as rational funerary practice, dedicated to commonsense] (Zurich, 1874), 13, 53.

1. Prosper de Pietra Santa, "La crémation en France et Italie," *Journal d'Hygiene* 8 (1882): 589–590.

2. Prof. Dr. Robert Nagel, *Wege und Ziele der modernen Feuerbestattung* (Suttgart: Wilhelm Ruppermann, 1922), 4. On Frederick, see Georg Aufhauser, *Leichenverbrennung und das in Bayern geltende öffentliche staatliche und kirchliche Recht* (Munich: J. Schweizer, 1912), 2 (Ph.D. diss., Erlangen University legal faculty). For his aunt, see Max Pauly, *Die Feuerbestattung* (Leipzig: J. J. Weber, 1904), 12. Pauly was the director of the Berlin Cremation Society and editor of its journal, *Die Flamme*.

3. Jacob Grimm, "Über das Verbrennen der Leichen," read 29 November 1849, and published first in *Abhandlung der Königlichen Akademie der Wissenschaften zu Berlin* (Berlin: F. Dümmler, 1850), 6–7, 83, and passim.

4. The ship burial at Ile de Groix represents arguably the most famous Viking archeological site in France.

5. Paul Pasteur, "Les débuts de la crémation moderne en France," *Le Mouvement Social* 179 (April–June 1997): 59–80. There is no good history of cremation in France. For an old "in-house" account, see G. Saloman, *La crémation en France (1797–1889)* (Paris: Publications de la Société de Crémation, E. Dentu, 1890). Joseph Clarke, *Commemorating the Dead in Revolutionary France* (Cambridge: Cambridge University Press, 2007) deals with the matter briefly.

6. L. S. Mercier, *Corps législative*, Conseil des Cinq-Cents, *Sur les sépulchres privées* (Paris: 18 Frimaire, Year V-1796), quoted in Michel Ragon, *The Space of Death: Study of Funerary Architecture, Decoration and Urbanism*, trans. Alan Sheridan (Charlottesville: University Press of Virginia, 1983), 283–284.

7. F. Coletti, "Sulla incinerazione dei cadaveri," *Rivista Periodica dei Lavori della Regia Accademia di Scienze, Lettere ed Arti* (Padua: Angelo Sicca) 5 (1857): 11.

8. Abbé (Augustin) Barruel, *Memoirs, Illustrating the History of Jacobinism, Written in French by the Abbé Barruel, and Translated into English by the Hon. Robert Clifford, F.R.S. & A.S. Part I. The Antichristian Conspiracy*, 2nd ed., rev. and corrected (London, 1798), 1:iv, 277, 356, and 273ff. for more than two hundred pages of the theory and practice on Masonic conspiracy. See also 1:45, 120.

9. *New York Times*, 19 February 1876.

10. Lorenzo Gestri, *Le ceneri di Pisa* (Pisa: Nistri-Lischi, 2001), 18–22. Daniel Pick, "'Roma o morte': Garibaldi, Nationalism, and the Problem of Psycho-biography," *History Workshop Journal* 57 (Spring 2004).

11. *The Catholic Encyclopedia* (New York: Robert Appleton Co., 1908), vol. 4, s.v. "Cremation"; online edition, 2003, http://www.newadvent.org/cethen/04481c.htm. Fr. Olivier Parent du Chatelet, "Burial or Cremation," originally published in English in *The Angelus*, July 2003. See the website of DICI, Documentation et Information Catholiques International, the press agency of the Mother House of the Priestly Order of Pius X.

12. Quotation in *Encyclopedia of Cremation*, s.v. "Russia and the USSR," 369. On cremation in Russia, see the background material in Victoria Smolkin, "'A Sacred Space Is Never Empty': Soviet Atheism, 1954–1971" (Ph.D. diss., University of California, Berkeley, 2010). As she points out, in fact the Soviet authorities did not really take on the problem of a serious alternative to the old death culture until the Brezhnev era, by which time it was too late. I am grateful to her for discussions of the Soviet case.

13. Karl Blind, "Fire Burial among Our Germanic Forefathers," *Fraser's Magazine*, 11 n.s. (June 1875): 730 ff. Johann Gottlieb Fichte, "Die Republik der Deutschen zu Anfange des zwei u. zwanzgigsten Jahrhunderts unter ihrem fünften Reichsvogte" (1807), *Gesamtausgabe II (Nachgelassene Schriften)* 10 (1994): 412–420.

14. Wilhelm Bahnsen, *Die Stellung der Evangelichen Kirche zu Feurbestattung* (Berlin: Alexander Dunker, 1898). He was himself inclined to accept cremation but spoke here for the Lutheran conference more generally. See Simone Ameskamp, "On Fire: Cremation in Germany, 1870s–1934" (Ph.D. diss., Georgetown University, 2006), 192–193.

15. The most thorough discussion of rabbinic views on cremation is Rabbi Isaac Klein as edited by Rabbi David Golinkin, "Does Jewish Law Permit Cremation?" *Responsa* 2, no. 3 (December 2007): 1–14 (Schechter Institute of Jewish Studies); the American Reform view is on p. 12. I draw heavily on Adam S. Ferziger, "Ashes to Outcasts: Cremation, Jewish Law, and Identity in Early Twentieth-Century Germany," *AJS Review* 36, no. 1 (April 2012): 71–102. For the Wurzburg case, see Falk Weisemann, "Jewish Burials in Germany: Between Tradition, the Enlightenment and the Authorities," *Leo Baeck Institute Year Book* 37 (1992): 17–31. I am grateful to Prof. Asher Colombo, Department of Political and Social Sciences, University of Bologna, for sharing with me prior to publication his data on the religious distribution of cremation. His work more generally offers the most statistically detailed study of the spread of cremation in both western and eastern Europe that we have.

16. *South Durham Herald*, 17 September 1874, accessed in the clippings files of the Cremation Society, Durham University, CRE/H2. Augustus G. Cobb, *Earth Burial and Cremation: The History of Earth Burial and Its Attendant Evils and the Advantages Offered by Cremation* (New York: G. P. Putnam, 1892), 13, vi ("superstitious reverence" is Cobb; the rest of the quote is Gibbon cited in Cobb). This is an expansion of an article in the famous and mainstream *North American Review* (1 September 1882), 135, 266ff.

17. Robert Blatchford, *My Favorite Books* (London: Clarion Office, 1901), 45, for example, where he ranks Browne just below Spenser and on par with Shakespeare and Browning. *Hydrotaphia, or Urn Burial* enjoyed something of a revival in the nineteenth century, see his *Dictionary of National Biography* entry.

18. Pen Oliver [Sir Henry Thompson], *Charley Kingston's Aunt* (London: Macmillan, 1885), 29–50, 146–147.

19. Olga Matich, "Postskriptum o velikom anatome," *Novoe Literaturnoe Obozrenie* 11 (1995): 181. The leading nineteenth-century Russian historian, Vasily Klyuchevsky, according to Matich, wrote, "Noting that some of the members of his retinue expressed disgust for the dead body, Peter forced them to tear up the muscles of the corpse with their teeth." It is disputed whether this actually happened, but the image has a power of its own. Dmitry Merezhkovky, a twentieth-century literary historian, writes that Peter was a "great anatomist who dissected Russia's decrepit body" with the purpose of revitalizing it. There was, however, a sense of wonder in the face of certain dead. When Peter visited Dr. Ruysch, he was, it is said, so struck by the life-likeness of an embalmed child that he kissed it. For this information, I am grateful to Olga Matich, who translated parts of her article for me.

20. "A Truth Seeker" [L. H. Grindon], *Cremation Considered in Reference to the Resurrection* (London, 1874). Grindon also had strong and heterodox views about the living that do not entail his views about cremation but that do put him in the company of those who recognized in dead bodies a culturally important category of being. Abolishing tradition in one realm spilled over into another. His *Sexuality of Nature* mixed science, religion, and metaphysics in strange ways. How he came to it is not clear. Grindon, like so many of those who advocated cremation in its early days, was in the orbit of medicine. He was a skilled pharmaceutical botanist. He also had a certain family connection to the dead: his father had been the city coroner of Bristol. Grindon read lots of poetry and literature. But his biography does not explain how he came to regard inorganic matter as alive: nitric acid is a "yellow ferocious liquid." Nor does it explain why he thought that human marriage was but one form of "all unions analogous to the human, in the history of both matter and spirit" and that sex refers not just to male and female but "to the separate qualities or natures by which things universally fall into two great sections or divisions." Matter and spirit, vowels and consonants, aspirated and nonaspirated sounds are all aspects of a universal duality. So are hard-boiled and soft-boiled eggs, the *Nation* joked in a scathing review.

21. J[ohn] Page Hopps, *The Etherialisation of the Body* (London: Williams and Norgate, n.d. [1898]), 2–3. See also his *Thirty Nine Questions Concerning Thirty Nine Articles* (Ramsgate: Thomas Scott, 1871).

22. On Voysey, see his *Dictionary of National Biography* entry; and Rev. Charles Voysey, "Cremation: A Lecture" (Southampton, 1884). Cell-souls are explained in Ernst Haeckel, *Freedom in Science and Teaching* (New York: Humbolt Library, 1888), 26–31.

23. Hon. and Rev. W. H. Lyttelton, *Scripture Revelation of the Life of Man after Death* (London: Dalby, Isbisher and Co., 1875), xviii–xix, xxiii, xiv, 89. *Cremation in Great Britain* (1909), frontispiece.

24. Lyttelton's death is recounted in the memoir by his niece Lucy Cavendish in the 1893 edition of his *Scripture Revelation of the Life of Man after Death*; quotation is on xxii–xxiii. She says that her uncle was a man fascinated by science, if done with reverence for God's creation.

25. Rev. H. R. Haweis, *Ashes to Ashes* (London: Daldy Isbister and Co., 1875).

26. The painting is in the Walker Gallery, Liverpool. Edward John Trelawny, *Records of Shelley, Byron, and the Author* (Harmondsworth: Penguin, 1973), 168–173. I quote from this edition of a text first published in 1878 because it is readily available; the sections I quote, however, are unchanged from Trelawny's 1858 *Recollections of the Last Days of Shelley and Byron: Biographical Information from Edward Garnett's Introduction to Adventures of a Young Son* (London: T. Fisher, 1890), 7–25; and the *Dictionary of National Biography*. The latter's entry suggests that Trelawny's eccentricity was taken as a sign of sincerity and made even his most outrageous claims about himself and others believable. That said, he was never cited in the cremation literature.

27. Quoted in Tony Brown, "The Ex-centric Voice: The English-Language Short Story in Wales," *North American Journal of Welsh Studies* 1, no. 1 (Winter 2001): 35.

28. This account is put together from the *Dictionary of Welsh Biography*'s two entries; T. Islwyn Nicholas, *A Welsh Heretic: Dr. William Price, Llantrisant* (London: Foyle's Welsh Co., n.d. [c. 1940]); and Richard Hutton's *Blood and Mistletoe: The History of Druids in Britain* (New Haven, Conn.: Yale University Press, 2009). For pictures of this event, see http://ljh.d2g.com:81/photos.

29. Paolo Mantegazza, "La cremazione," *Nuova Antologia* 27, no. 9 (1874): 12. Cited in Fulvio Conti, Anna Maria Isastia, Fiorenza Tarozzi, eds., *La morte laica*, vol. 1: *Storia della cremazione in Italia (1880–1920)* (Turin: Scriptorium, 1998), 15.

30. Cremation Society archives clipping file, Durham University Library, CRE H3.

31. Conti et al., *La morte laica*, 57–58; citing "Lega, *Italiana delle Societa di Cremazione* (Milan: Comitato Centrale, 12 October 1886), circulated in the press and preserved in 'AcLodi, b. 343.'"

32. Fritz Schumacher, *Die Feuerbestattung* (Leipzig, J. M. Gebhardt, 1939), 16; see also 14. Schumacher, a man of the social democratic Left, lost his job for political reasons in 1933; he died in 1947.

33. My thanks to Kim Stacy, who writes for the funeral director trade press, for taking a survey of her readers on this subject.

34. I am quite sure that my friends knew nothing about Hunter Thompson's wish—spectacularly followed on 20 August 2005—to be cremated and have his ashes shot out of a cannon over his ranch.

AFTERWORD

Epigraph: T. S. Eliot, *On Poetry and Poets* (1957; reprint, New York: Farrar, Strauss, Giroux, 2009), 72.

1. Caitlin Doughty, *Smoke Gets in Your Eyes* (New York: W.W. Norton, 2014), 100–101, and more generally 99–114.

2. Reported in *Sausalito News*, 20 January 1956, California Digital Library, http://cdnc .ucr.edu/cgi-bin/cdnc?a=d&d=SN19560120.2.24, accessed 24 March 2015. *Time* reported Hodges's views on 9 January 1956.

3. Quoted in Rosann M. O'Dell, "The Bouvia Case Revisited," *Online Journal of Health Ethics* 7, no. 2 (November 2011): 2.

4. The Jahi McMath case was widely reported in both local and national print and electronic media. It is endlessly bizarre. The parents, for example, can sue for only $250,000 under California law if their daughter is dead but for an unrestricted amount if she is alive, which she is from their perspective but not from that of the California courts. A less spectacular assertion of a claim to a right not to die is the message the thirty-four-year-old MTV star Diem Brown tweeted three days before her death from ovarian cancer: "My doctors are seemingly giving up but I won't & can't rollover. Whatever option I have to LIVE I'm grabbing!" (reported in the *New York Times*, 14 November 2014.)

5. Which?, http://www.staticwhich.co.uk/documents/pdf/dying-better---the-consumer -experience-at-the-end-of-life-398283.pdf.

6. Margaret Edison, *W;t* (New York: Faber and Faber, 1999), 11–12. Jerome Groopman, professor of medicine at Harvard, is among the best-known, most articulate, often-cited supporters of the value of fighting to the bitter end. He represents that view, for example, in the *Frontline* documentary *Facing Death*, first aired on 10 November 2010, and is part of the intellectual foundation for Susan Sontag's final struggle as documented in her son David Rieff's *Swimming in a Sea of Death: A Son's Memoir* (New York: Simon and Schuster, 2008).

7. On the failure of advance directives to make bedside decision making comport with the purported wishes of the patient, see "A Controlled Trial to Improve Care for Seriously Ill Hospitalized Patients: The Study to Understand Prognoses and Preferences for Outcomes and Risks of Treatments (SUPPORT)," *JAMA* 274 (22 November 1995): 1591–1598. Perhaps things have become better. On dying in the hospital, see Sharon Kaufman's remarkable *And a Time to Die: How American Hospitals Shape the End of Life* (Chicago: University of Chicago Press, 2005), esp. the introduction, chapter 4 ("Moving Things Along"), and chapter 7 ("Life Support"). This endnote does not begin to do justice to what I owe to Kaufman for years of conversation on these topics.

8. Atul Gawande, *Being Mortal: Illness, Medicine, and What Matters in the End* (New York: Metropolitan Books, 2014), esp. those parts interspersed throughout the text about the death of the author's father.

IMAGE CREDITS

Collections, San Marino, California. 5.10: © SMK Photo. 5.13: © The Metropolitan Museum of Art. Art Resource, New York. 5.17: © British Library. 5.18: bpk, Berlin / Galerie Neue Meister / Jürgen Karpinski / Art Resource, New York. 5.26: Hamburger Kunsthalle, Hamburg, Germany / Bridgeman Images. 5.27: Felice Beato. 6.1: © RMN-Grand Palais / Hervé Lewandowski / Art Resource, New York. 5.29: © University College London, The Bentham Project, 2011. Photographer: Tony Slade. All Rights Reserved. http://www.ucl.ac.uk/Bentham-Project, http://www.ucl.ac.uk/transcribe-bentham. 6.2: Album / Art Resource, New York. 7.1: Fabian Fröhlich. 8.3: Andy Malengier, 2009. 8.4: Erich Hartman, 1987. Magnum Photos. 8.7: © United States Holocaust Memorial Museum. 9.1, 9.2: Stad Ieper-Tijl Capoen. 9.3: Chris Hartford, 2005. 9.4: John Warwick Brook. 9.5: Félix Potuit, 2007. 9.8: © IWM (Q 109517). 9.9: © IWM (Q 31492). 10.1: © British Library. 11.1: © Tarker / Bridgeman Images. 11.6: © Look and Learn / Illustrated Papers Collection / Bridgeman Images.

INDEX

Page numbers in italics refer to figures.

Anglicans: cemeteries and, 226, 228, 236, 284,
290, 295, 298–99, 303, 306, 310, 313, 341;
churchyards and, 115, 122, 128, 132, 149–50,
155, 162–73, 175, 177–80, 182, 209,
601n98, 609n159; cremation and, 538;
names of the dead and, 402
Anglo-Saxons, 3, 95, 121, 123, 129, 151, 282,
368, 371, 540, 580n14
Annalistes, 5
Anne, Queen of England, 123–24, 260
Anson, Thomas, 252
anthropology: cannibalism and, 5; care of the
dead and, 8–11, 14, 18, 27; cemeteries and,
223, 232, 236, 305; churchyards and, 123,
131, 193, 210; cremation and, 502, 504, 542,
548; deep time and, 10–11, 31–32, 43–44,
50, 54–55, 82, 86–91; informed history
and, 14; Levi-Strauss and, 9; names of the
dead and, 367–72, 386, 403, 411, 446
Antigonus of Soco, 396
Apothecaries Act, 354
Apuleius, 64
Arcadia: cemeteries and, 238–41, 250–60,
265–66, 277, 286, 291; churchyards and,
139; cultural work of the dead and, 92;
pastoral poetry and, 239; Reformation and,
239; Theocritus and, 250
Archbishop of Belfast, 288
Archbishop of Canterbury, 114, 481
Archbishop of Freiburg, 530
Archbishop of Paris, 191–92, 195
Archbishop of York, 165
Argentinian dirty war, 414
Ariès, Philippe, 13–14, 185, 237, 550, 604n125
Aryans, 90
ashes, 4, 9–10, 13–14, 18; Bălcescu and, 23;
burning and, 490–94; celebrities and,
213; cemeteries and, 213, 223, 266, 287,
299, 304, 342, 350; churchyards and, 127,
145, 180, 192, 209; deep time and, 38–39,
44, 62, 65, 84–85, 88, 104–5; different
enchantments of, 524–42; disenchantment
and, 496, 500, 502, 507, 510, 515, 520–21;
Domitian and, 569n11; Hardy and, 470;
Hess and, 8; history and, 524–48; Hume
and, 209; mailed, 550; Marx and, 19, 22;

mixing of, 25–26, 546; names of the dead
and, 375–76, 429, 433, 470; personhood
and, 567n5; repositories for, 550; in their
place, 542–48; volume of, 26
Ash Wednesday, 135
Asklepios, 95
Assistens Kirkegård, 248
atheists, 20, 50, 60, 72, 75, 193, 199–202, 209,
245, 340, 404, 528, 533, 640n211
Austin, Joseph William, 422
Australian War Memorial, 420
autolysis, 2
Aveling, Edward, 18
Avery, Benjamin, 173–74

Bach, Johann Sebastian, 59, 213
Bacon, Francis, 222, 243, 256
Bailey, Nathan, 119
Baillie, Robert, 105
Baird, John, 338
Bălcescu, Nicolae, 22–23
Balzac, 274, 293, 411
banians, 266
Bapthorpe, Robert, 380–81
baptism: cemeteries and, 298, 308; certificate of, 166, 174; Christians and, 115, 164,
166–79, 184, 298, 308, 365, 369–71, 392,
394–96, 600n95, 603n116, 606n101,
632n157; churchyards and, 115, 164, 166,
169–77, 179, 184; of the dead, 652n5;
infant, 169, 175; legitimate, 169–72,
603n116; Mormons and, 652n5; names of
the dead and, 365, 369–71, 392, 394–96;
rebaptism and, 169–70; as rite of passage,
164; Villers-Cotterêts ordinance and, 392
Baptists, 115, 119, 127, 129, 132, 165, 173, 178,
180–81, 229, 300–301, 479, 600n95,
601n98
Bara, Joseph, 327
Barbie, Klaus, 442–43
Barnard, John, 245
Barruel, Augustine, 200–201
Barthes, Roland, 367
Baskerville Hall, 294–95
Bath Park, 240

names of the dead and, 389, 393, 404, 471, 482; papists and, 69–70, 73–74, 99, 104, 165; purgatory and, 17, 58–59, 61, 67–76, 98–101, 103, 241, 575n23; Reformation and, 12, 33, 46–47, 59, 68–71, 76, 93–94, 98–103, 115, 120, 122, 132, 135, 145–47, 155, 169, 177, 182–83, 186–88, 239, 241, 273, 288, 306, 308; regime of the dead and, 99–101; relics and, 47; St. Bartholomew's Day massacre and, 259; suicide and, 125, 598n70

Catholic Right, 214

Caulker, Thomas, 303

Cecil, Florence, 470

cemeteries: age of the cemetery and, 271–312; Anglicans and, 226, 228, 236, 284, 290, 295, 298–99, 303, 306, 310, 313, 341; Arcadia and, 238–41, 250–60, 265–66, 277, 286, 291; ashes and, 213, 223, 266, 287, 299, 304, 342, 350; authority of dead and, 213–14; baptism and, 298, 308; capitalism and, 288–93; Catholic Church and, 214, 239, 259, 266–67, 270, 288, 296, 303–4, 306, 310, 328, 340, 357, 617n45, 622n77, 643n229; Chadwick and, 215, 218, 220, 222–24, 226, 230–32, 234–35, 237, 327, 612n12, 617n43; Christians and, 216, 223, 239, 241, 245, 247, 249, 252, 261, 266, 268, 271, 274, 277, 280, 294–300, 303–4, 308, 310, 317, 336, 339, 341, 590n15, 601n98, 618n51, 625n93; churchwardens and, 151–59, 224, 226, 326–27, 599n76, 601n105, 613n22; class and, 309–12; coffins and, 220, 224–28, 277, 293, 311–12, 314, 316–17, 323–36, 343, 348, 350, 355, 635n185, 643n228, 643n229; as community of memory, 22; consecrated ground and, 216, 228, 245, 268, 292, 294, 299, 301, 303, 310, 360, 615n29, 641n218; as cosmopolitan place, 212; crowding and, 133, 220, 223–28, 231, 238, 291, 293; custom and, 212; danger of the dead and, 215–38; decomposition and, 215–16, 218, 221, 232, 235, 616n38; Diogenes and, 211, 213, 235, 305, 315, 337, 341, 356, 358, 360; disrupted bodies and, 336–61; distant lands and, 265–71; elegies

and, 250, 274, 276, 278–79, 301, 619n57, 630n142; Elysium and, 210, 236–39, 241–43, 250, 255–62, 265–66, 272, 277, 279, 291, 295, 298, 301–2, 386; embalming and, 232, 278, 616n41, 633n173; Enlightenment and, 247, 296, 307; epitaphs and, 237, 251–53, 267–68, 279, 299–301, 349, 619n57; exhumation and, 192, 197–98, 213, 234, 241, 245, 248, 262, 270, 307, 313, 318, 329–30, 336–47, 354–59, 618n52, 640n211, 640n212, 641n218; family and, 309–12; funerals and, 261–62, 278, 284, 290, 300, 306–7, 312–42, 347, 360–61; genealogies of the new regime and, 238–71; ghosts and, 229, 259, 276, 308, 366, 626n102; Great War and, 240, 298, 346; heaven and, 245, 247, 295, 338, 364; Hume and, 240–41; hygiene and, 214–15, 218, 229, 237, 269, 277, 631n156; idolatry and, 238, 241, 247, 259, 622n77; immortality and, 215; imperial imagination and, 265–71; Jews and, 15, 24, 211, 213, 267, 295–98, 303, 305–6, 310, 323, 328, 627n119; linguistics and, 117–21; Magnificent Seven and, 277, 279, 283, 290, 295, 301; martyrs and, 224, 278, 282, 305, 323, 327, 331, 338, 345; mausoleums and, 15, 38, 45, 237–47, 257, 260–62, 264, 266–69, 292, 296–97, 307, 309, 344, 521n71, 618n51, 625n93, 626n107, 628n133; memorials and, 214, 224, 237, 245, 247–49, 254, 256, 264–65, 279–80, 282–84, 290–96, 300, 309–10, 315, 318, 340, 342, 620n61, 625n92, 630n142, 631n154; Middle Ages and, 13–14, 173, 294, 337; monuments and, 116, 124, 141, 143–45, 160, 203, 209, 212, 225, 243, 247–49, 252, 255, 259, 261–69, 272–73, 277–80, 283–84, 286, 289–94, 297–302, 311, 313–14, 332, 338, 341, 346, 349–50, 618n51, 625n92, 625n93, 630n142, 632n164, 639n207, 642n226; murder and, 213, 259, 314, 329, 337, 347, 352, 355–56; national, 15–16, 212, 245, 248–49, 282, 284, 339, 375–76, 416, 459, 462, 471; necrobotany and, 279, 287; necrogeography and, 238, 241, 260, 266, 279, 284, 286–88, 304, 622n77; novelty and, 272–79;

cemeteries: age of the cemetery and (*continued*)
pagans and, 223, 241, 247, 268, 270, 304,
618n51; photographs and, 342–43, 641n216;
as protean space, 212; Protestants and, 239,
241, 257, 259, 265–66, 270, 280, 288, 296,
310, 317, 328; public health and, 215–38,
289, 293, 305, 307–8, 612n14, 617n44;
Puritans and, 228, 272, 280, 295, 302,
639n210; putrefaction and, 220, 222, 230,
232, 267, 596n49, 613n19, 617n43, 617n44;
reason for, 31; reburial and, 10, 19, 22, 103,
198, 312, 336, 417, 462, 468, 502, 562n12,
564n25, 586n39; reform and, 305–9; Reformation and, 230, 241, 273, 288, 306, 308;
relics and, 235, 239, 259, 262, 317, 340–41,
343, 345–46, 641n218, 642n221; religious
pluralism and, 294–305; resurrection and,
113, 120, 123–26, 130, 139, 150, 158, 184,
206, 215, 241, 273, 280, 300–301, 312, 332,
338, 356; revolution and, 305–9; rise of,
215–38; *Royal Commission Report on the Health
of Towns* and, 220; sanitation and, 220, 223,
229, 235; secular gods and, 212, 214; segregated, 7; shrines and, 243, 248, 255, 259–61,
272, 302, 337, 347; smells and, 218–23,
227, 230, 232–33, 235, 237, 256, 277–79,
322; socialist, 214; as society, 212; soldiers
and, 319, 327–28, 338, 342, 352, 639n208;
Southwood-Smith and, 215–16, 235,
357–60, 571n25, 617n43, 645n235; special
dead and, 212, 230; Stranger's Ground and,
226; suicide and, 260; superstition and, 231,
237–38, 272, 294, 299, 357; *Supplementary
Report on the Results of a Special Inquiry into the
Practice of Interment in Towns* and, 220; tombs
and, 213–14, 223, 237–69, 273–74, 277–
80, 283–89, 295–300, 304, 310–11, 314,
335–36, 341, 618n51, 626n105; tombstones
and, 267, 279–80, 298, 416, 628n132,
654n20n, 661n32, 667n41; triumph of over
churchyard, 214–15 (*see also* churchyards);
urban development and, 32–33; Voltaire
and, 224, 226, 257, 259, 296, 307, 333,
339; Walker and, 219–20, 222–24, 230,
232–34, 237–38. *See also specific cemeteries*
Cemetery of the Innocents, 184

cenotaphs, 18, 237, 279, 420, 482–83, 521,
625n92, 625n93
Certeau, Michel de, 182, 186
Chabbat, Arlette, 444
Chad (apostle to Saxons), 115
Chadwick, Edwin, 215, 218, 220, 222–24, 226,
230–32, 234–35, 237, 327, 612n12, 617n43
Chamberlain, Walter, 163–64, 600n95
Chambers, Ephraim, 90
Chambers, W. F., 230
Chandler, Samuel, 300
Chapman, William Herbert, 178
Charlemagne, 95–96, 202
Charles I, 106, 160
Charles II, 105
Charles the Great, 119
Charles X, 262
charnel houses, 40
Charnock, Job, 268–69
Chartists, 178, 303, 331–32, 339
Chaucer, 3, 46
Child, John, 346
Childe, V. Gordon, 10
China, 64, 81, 103, 110, 135, 265, 307, 375, 556,
574n18
Chitticks, Emily, 398–403, 405, 407, 409–10,
412, 448, 459, 467
cholera, 2, 230–31, 235, 354, 496, 512, 616n38
Christ Church, 116
Christians, 7, 9, 11, 25; baptism and, 115, 164,
166–79, 184, 298, 308, 365, 369–71, 392,
394–96, 600n95, 603n116, 606n101,
632n157; catacombs and, 13, 119, 225, 248,
286, 290, 301, 304, 310, 590n14; cemeteries and, 216, 223, 239, 241, 245, 247, 249,
252, 261, 266, 268, 271, 274, 277, 280,
294–300, 303–4, 308, 310, 317, 336, 339,
341, 618n51, 625n93; churchyards and, 110,
112, 115, 118–24, 132–33, 139, 149–50, 152,
155, 158, 165–66, 169–74, 181–84, 193, 195,
200–213, 590n15, 601n98; cremation and,
491–92, 496, 503–4, 508, 510, 524–26,
530–31, 533, 536–38, 541, 548, 670n13;
crowning the dead and, 48; Cult of Reason
and, 526; cultural work of the dead and, 80,
85, 92–99, 102–3, 106; Day of Judgment

and, 54, 60–61, 87, 96, 124–25, 485; deep
time and, 31, 33, 40–48, 58, 60–61, 64,
67, 70, 73–76, 80, 85, 92–99, 102–3, 106,
568n8, 570n15, 573n12, 580n14, 582n18,
583n23, 583n24; infidels and, 74, 112, 189,
195–96, 200, 202, 205–8, 339, 404, 407,
590n13; Jacobin revolutionaries and, 525;
Jesus Christ and, 58–59, 64, 72, 186–87,
195–96, 200, 211, 241, 302, 339–40, 392,
398, 403–5, 408, 537; names of the dead
and, 365, 370, 382–83, 386, 392, 394–96,
404, 415, 434, 444, 469; paradise and, 45;
suicide and, 124
Christ's Hospital, 146–47
Chrysostom, John, 120
Church Fathers, 41, 44, 47, 50, 60, 67, 69, 85,
568n8
Churchill, John, 241
Churchill, Winston, 319, 470, 486
Church of Notre Dame, 232
Church of Rome. *See* Catholic Church
Church of St. Helen's, 147
Churchyard of the Holy Trinity, 118
churchyards: afterlife and, 141–45, 167, 202,
206, 209; Akenham burial scandal and,
180–81; Anglicans and, 115, 122, 128, 132,
149–50, 155, 162–73, 175, 177–80, 182,
209, 601n98, 609n159; Arcadia and, 139;
ashes and, 127, 145, 180, 192, 209; baptism
and, 115, 164, 166, 169–77, 179, 184;
Catholic Church and, 101, 104–5, 122, 135,
161–62, 166–67, 171, 174, 177, 185, 187,
211, 598n70, 601n101; Christians and, 110,
112, 115, 118–24, 132–33, 139, 149–50, 152,
155, 158, 165–66, 169–74, 181–84, 193, 195,
200–213; churchwardens and, 151–59, 224,
226, 326–27, 599n76, 601n105, 613n22;
claims of parish on dead body and, 153–55;
claims of the dead body on parish and, 151–
52; coffins and, 116–17, 124, 126, 128, 141,
145, 156–61, 178–79, 181, 188, 192, 599n84,
600n90, 602n105; as community, 212;
consecrated ground and, 113–14, 120, 126,
131, 152, 155, 163–64, 166, 180, 192, 195,
602n105; crisis of old regime and, 161–82;
crowding and, 133, 220, 225–28, 231, 238,

291, 293; custom and, 212; decomposition
and, 158–60; deep history of, 112; development of, 114–17; Dissenting Deputies and,
128, 155, 167, 173–74, 177, 179; economics
of burial in, 155–61; elegies and, 112, 114,
121, 135, 138, 591n17, 597n59; Elysium and,
199; embalming and, 159; Enlightenment
and, 111, 113–14, 162, 182–210; epitaphs
and, 127, 141, 143, 155–56; exclusion from,
148–51; funerals and, 127–28, 137, 145–48,
158, 167, 178, 183, 188, 209; ghosts and,
105, 118, 135, 142, 145, 149, 211, 602n105;
Gregory the Great and, 114–15; as heart of
old regime, 112–13; heaven and, 109, 123,
130, 150, 187, 194; Hume and, 113, 186, 188,
196, 203–10, 607n144, 609n156, 610n162,
610n164; hygiene and, 133, 214–15, 218,
229, 237; idolatry and, 127, 184, 210, 212,
214; immortality and, 139, 142, 162, 199;
in the landscape, 121–23; linguistics and,
117–21; martyrs and, 111, 116, 119–20,
127, 182–83, 191, 198, 209, 213, 590n15,
604n120, 605n130; memorials and, 110,
123, 129, 132–33, 137, 139, 141, 151, 155, 157;
Middle Ages and, 112–13, 120–21, 146,
153, 155; murder and, 149–50, 198, 203;
necrobotany and, 113, 133–37; necrogeography and, 110–13, 123–33, 214; necrotopology and, 113, 137–41; passage of the
dead to, 145–48; Protestants and, 114–15,
132, 146–47, 162, 166, 170, 173–74, 177,
179, 193, 211, 213, 593n32, 597n64; public
health and, 133, 184, 215–38; Puritans and,
126–27, 146, 203; putrefaction and, 220,
222, 230, 232; Reformation and, 115, 120,
122, 132, 135, 145–47, 155, 169, 177, 182–83,
186–88; relics and, 122, 144, 173, 182, 201;
right to burial and, 161–82; Roman Empire
and, 113; sanitation and, 168, 220, 223, 229,
235; shrines and, 193, 198, 212–13; smells
and, 218–23, 227, 230, 232–33, 235; soldiers
and, 126; special dead and, 120, 173, 191;
suicide and, 124–25, 130, 132–33, 149–50,
166, 171–72, 190; SUN of Righteousness
and, 132; superstition and, 115, 117, 121, 126,
128, 130, 132–33, 135, 142, 145, 147, 150, 185,

churchyards: afterlife and (*continued*)
189, 207, 209, 211, 594n43; Thirty-Nine
Articles and, 169, 175; tombs and, 15, 110,
120, 124, 126–28, 130, 138–42, 145, 156,
183, 191, 193–94, 197, 209, 590n15; tombstones and, 128, 138, 603n115; Voltaire and,
113, 162, 184, 186, 189–203, 207, 606n139,
607n141, 607n142, 607n143, 607n145,
607n146, 608n147

Cicero, 1, 35, 89–91, 94, 279, 372

Cimetière de Picpus, 214

Cimetière des Innocents, 218, 225

Cimetière du Père Lachaise, 15, 53, 210, 213;
age of the cemetery and, 274, 276, 280,
283, 288–90, 293, 296–98, 301, 303, 310,
312; cremation and, 510, 518, 526; genealogies of the new regime and, 238, 257,
260–65, 267; names of the dead and, 415

Clampitt, Amy, 310

Clare, John, 147, 149

Clark, James, 230

Clarke, Joseph, 307

Clarkson, Thomas, 299

class, 309–12

Claudius Aelianus, 582n18

Clavering, John, 269

Clement of Alexandria, 44–49, 570n15

Clendening, Abram, 459

Cliff, Elizabeth Ann, 178–79

Cliff, Thomas, 178–79

Cobb, Richard, 18

Cobbett, William, 313, 340–41, 355

Coffin, Charles, 192

coffins, 20, 556; cemeteries and, 220, 224–28,
277, 293, 311–12, 314, 316–17, 323–36, 343,
348, 350, 355, 635n185, 643n228, 643n229;
churchyards and, 116–17, 124, 126, 128, 141,
145, 156–61, 178–79, 181, 188, 192, 599n84,
600n90, 602n105; cremation and, 495,
497, 514–15, 520–21, 524, 538, 546; deep
time and, 34, 48, 56, 58–59, 76, 573n11,
585n38, 587n42; earth, 514; empty, 18;
furniture and, 634n180; glass, 48, 497; lead,
124, 156, 158–59, 227, 324, 350, 643n228,
643n229; nails of, 643n229; names of the
dead and, 365, 387, 408, 424, 453, 457, 470,

480–81, 668n56; wicker, 556, 674n49;
wood, 157, 159, 668n56

Cohn, Ferdinand Julius, 298

Coke, Edward, 102, 349–51, 370

Coletti, Ferdinando, 527

Coley, James, 168–69

collagen, 3

Collins, Anthony, 188

Collins, Wilkie, 508

Collinson, Peter, 135

Commission for the Marking of Confederate
Graves, 416

Condorcet, Marquis de, 195–96, 200

Confederate Ladies Memorial Association,
416

confession, 43, 69, 191–92, 194

Confessions (Augustine), 43

Congregationalists, 115, 127, 228–29, 601n98,
613n20, 615n30

conquistadors, 7

consecrated ground: cemeteries and, 216, 218,
222, 225, 227–28, 230–31, 234–38, 245,
268, 289, 292–94, 299, 301, 303, 305,
307–8, 310, 360, 615n29, 641n218; churchyards and, 113–14, 120, 126, 131, 152, 155,
163–64, 166, 180, 192, 195, 602n105

Constable, John, 141, 143–44

Corday, Charlotte, 198

Corey, John, 118

corpses: afterlife and, 1, 3, 11, 21, 37, 54, 56,
85, 141, 167, 186, 202, 206, 209, 404,
455, 493, 571n25, 605n132, 609n153,
609n159; Annalistes on, 5; cannibalism
and, 4–5; care of, 11; as carrion, 3–4, 7,
10, 35; decomposition of, 2–3, 6–8, 31;
degradation of, 6–8; Diogenes on, 1, 3–5,
8, 10, 12, 16, 35–37, 39–40; as dirt, 221;
disrupted bodies and, 336–61; dissection
of, 7, 234, 313, 325, 328, 337–38, 347–48,
351–60, 535, 539, 571n25, 642n226,
644n230; embalming and, 3, 9, 22, 57,
159, 232, 278, 501, 507, 524, 528, 569n11,
586n41, 616n41, 633n173, 676n19; excess
of, 16; fear of, 8; as fertilizer, 3; forgotten bodies and, 32–34; importance of
the dead and, 35–54; inability of, 16–17;

invested meaning of, 5; need to care for, 8–10; pebbles on chest and, 153; personhood and, 31; possession of, 6–7; public health and, 133, 184, 215–38, 493, 510, 513, 533, 612n14, 617n44, 670n8; putrefaction and, 2, 10, 64, 220, 222, 230, 232, 267, 397, 506, 509, 512, 515, 535, 596n49, 613n19, 617n43, 617n44; ransom for debts and, 150–51; secularism and, 164, 508, 525; smell and, 46 (*see also* smell); unidentifiable, 417–20; veneration of, 40, 46–48, 52–53, 89, 241, 299; washing of, 9; without consciousness, 1

Cosway, Richard, 352

Coteiner, Guy, 442

Coulanges, Fustel de, 90

Coyote, 108–9

Crabbe, George, 144–45

Cranach, Lucas, 188

cremation, 8–9, 13, 562n12, 675n14, 676n20; afterlife and, 493; Anglicans and, 538; anonymity and, 481; as anticlerical neoclassicism, 492; ashes and, 22, 523–48 (*see also* ashes); banians and, 266; beginnings of in Italy, 12; British Cremation Society and, 15; Brunetti and, 495–501, 506, 510, 515, 519, 523, 534, 542; Catholic Church and, 491–92, 497, 508, 527, 529–31, 546; cessation of in Europe, 16; China and, 556; Christians and, 491–92, 496, 503–4, 508, 510, 524–26, 530–31, 533, 536–38, 541, 548, 670n13; cleanliness and, 511, 516, 527, 533–34; coffins and, 495, 497, 514–15, 520–21, 524, 538, 546; competing designs for, 515–16; concept of death and, 502–12; Crispi Laws and, 529; cultural consequences of, 501–2; cultural work of the dead and, 85, 87–88, 581n17; de Préau and, 525–26; different enchantments of, 524–42; disenchantment and, 495–522, 672n31; Druids and, 533, 540–42; embalming and, 501, 507, 524, 528, 676n173; England and, 15, 360, 499, 517, 532–42, 546, 669n4; Enlightenment and, 502, 504, 509–10, 524, 526, 535; France and, 674n5; funeral pyres and, 45, 57, 62, 223, 491, 499, 501, 523, 526–29, 539, 541–42; Germany and, 530–32, 543; Greeks and, 297, 491; greenhouse gases and, 3; Hardy and, 145, 470; heaven and, 525, 536; Hobsbawm and, 20; Holocaust and, 432; hygiene and, 493, 500–502, 506, 511, 513–15, 528, 530, 533, 535–36, 542; immortality and, 536–38; India and, 238, 266, 310, 491; Ishi and, 342; Italy and, 495–96, 499, 517, 523, 527–29, 542–43; Jews and, 25, 491, 509, 531–32, 675n15; law of 21 Brumaire and, 526; legal issues and, 526, 529, 643n229; martyrs and, 492, 526; Marx and, 18–19, 22, 531, 534–3, 564n21; Masons and, 499, 528–30, 533, 538; materialists and, 491–93, 499, 511, 519, 525, 527, 530–32, 537; memorials and, 524, 535–36, 538; Middle Ages and, 490, 492; modern, 3, 12, 22, 31; monuments and, 504, 527; necrogeography and, 510, 520, 522, 527; organized movement for, 490; pagans and, 492, 510, 526, 540–41, 670n13; particulates and, 516; Père Lachaise and, 510, 518, 526; persistence of being and, 62; politics and, 501–2, 518–19, 527–29; pollution and, 516; premature burial and, 507–9; as progress, 493–94, 524–25; Protestants and, 491, 496, 508, 528, 532; public health and, 493, 510, 513, 533, 670n8; as radical, 25; relative cost of, 493; resurrection and, 492, 503, 536–37; Russia and, 530, 675n12; sanitation and, 501, 511, 513–16, 533–34, 538, 541; science and, 501; secularism and, 508, 525; Singapore and, 556; smells and, 500, 510, 513–14; soldiers and, 514, 520–21, 531, 670n13; special dead and, 492; status of body and, 502–3; suicide and, 513; superstition and, 502, 511, 533, 535; technology and, 491, 495–501, 546; Thompson and, 499–502, 506, 510–12, 515–16, 518–20, 533–34, 538, 542, 546, 677n34; tombstones and, 524; United States and, 540, 549–50; Vienna World Exposition and, 495–96, 524; Vikings and, 492, 525; Voltaire and, 526; waste and, 513, 516, 519, 524; Western culture and, 88

Creon, 7

Druids, 135, 533, 540–42

Drury, George, 180–81

Dubos, Jean-Baptiste, 252–53

Ducrow, Andrew, 286

Dudley, Ackland, 456

Duds Corner Memorial, 451

Duke of Marlborough, 452–53

Duke of Wellington, 334–35, 453, 638n201, 638n203

Dunn, Alice, 536

Dunton, John, 158

Durkheim, Emile, 10, 82, 214, 563n13, 611n5

Duvernet, Théophile, 195

Dwight, Timothy, 271–73

Earle, Lionel, 463, 482–83

Eassie, William, 513–14, 520, 533

East India Company, 266–70

École Polytechnique massacre, 424

Edgar (Saxon king), 153

Edward, Duke of York, 380

Edward, Lord Herbert of Cherbury, 75

Edward I, 166

Edward III, 118

Edward VI, 146

Egalité, Philippe, 261

Egypt, 2, 15, 81, 87, 160, 212, 272–73, 278, 286–87, 296, 298, 304–5, 373, 437, 496, 521

Eisenia fetida, 2

elegies: cemeteries and, 250, 274, 276, 278, 279, 301, 619n57, 630n142; churchyards and, 112, 114, 121, 135, 138, 591n17, 597n59; Gray and, 112, 114, 135, 138, 142, 145, 164, 250, 274, 276, 279, 402, 410, 457, 597n59; names of the dead and, 402, 457

"Elegy Written in a Country Churchyard" (Gray), 112, 114, 135, 138, 142–45, 164, 250, 274, 276, 279, 402, 410, 457, 597n59

Elementary Structures of Kinship (Levi-Strauss), 9

Eliot, T. S., 411, 460, 549–50

Elizabeth, Queen of England, 105

Elizer, David ben, 23–24

Elland Clerical Society, 171–72, 601n101

Ellison, George Edwin, 452

Eloise, 213, 262, *263*

Elysium: cemeteries and, 210, 236–39, 241–43, 250, 255–62, 265–66, 272, 277, 279, 291, 295, 298, 301–2, 386; churchyards and, 199; as place of blessed dead, 239; Reformation and, 239

embalming: cemeteries and, 232, 278, 616n41, 633n173; churchyards and, 159; corpses and, 3, 9, 22, 57, 159, 232, 278, 501, 507, 524, 528, 569n11, 586n41, 616n41, 633n173, 676n19; cremation and, 501, 507, 524, 528, 676n173; deep time and, 569n11, 586n41; disenchantment and, 501, 507; materiality of body and, 524; persistence of being and, 57

Emerson, Ralph Waldo, 375–76

Empson, William, 80, 82

Engels, Friedrich, 228, 409

England, 7, 12, 18; Act for Preventing the Horrid Crime of Murder and, 337; Anglo-Saxons and, 3, 95, 121, 123, 129, 151, 282, 368, 371, 540, 580n14; cremation and, 15, 360, 499, 517, 532–42, 546, 669n4; Cromwell and, 105–6, 128, 142, 146, 301–2, 345, 587n42; cultural work of the dead and, 92–93; Enlightenment and, 49, 573n10; Great Fire of London and, 123; Norman Conquest and, 95, 122, 595n48; Poor Laws and, 180, 292, 299, 317, 323, 325–26, 331, 355, 360, 535, 636n189; suicide and, 77; Westminster Abbey and, 44, 105–6, 128, 145, 192, 197, 241, 300–302, 338, 345, 448, 469–70, 479–81, 534, 546

Enlightenment, 13–14, 25, 550; cemeteries and, 247, 296, 307; churchyards and, 111, 113–14, 162, 182–210; cremation and, 502, 504, 509–10, 524, 526, 535; deep time and, 35–36, 49, 54, 61, 78; England and, 49, 573n10; Hume and, 113, 186, 188, 196, 203–10, 240–41, 607n144, 609n156, 610n162, 610n164; Italy and, 605n132; names of the dead and, 396; scandals and, 182–210; Voltaire and, 98, 113, 162, 184, 186, 188–202, 189–203, 207, 224, 246, 259, 296, 307, 333, 339, 407, 526

Enon Chapel, 219–20, 223

Frederick IV, 328

Frederick the Great, 25, 524

Freemasons, 199–200, 282, 528–30, 538, 608n148, 625n92

French, John, 463

Freud, Sigmund, 56–57, 78–79, 164, 365, 373–74, 491, 493, 646n1, 653n11

Friedrich, Caspar David, 273, 274

Friedrichshain Park, 214

Friedrich Wilhelm III, 395–96

funerals: cemeteries and, 261–62, 278, 284, 290, 300, 306–7, 312–42, 347, 360–61; churchyards and, 127–28, 137, 145–48, 158, 167, 178, 183, 188, 209; corpses and, 18 (*see also* corpses); deep time and, 44–45, 57, 64, 82, 92, 101, 105; endless varieties of, 9; grand, 14, 147, 201, 315, 639n205; Marx and, 20; pauper, 290, 312–18, 323, 325–27, 336, 360–61, 401, 632n166; proper, 312–23, 327, 337; pyres and, 45, 57, 62, 223, 491, 499, 501, 523, 526–29, 539, 541–42; rites of, 10, 82, 183, 526, 539, 620n62

Fysh, Thomas, 381

Gadamer, Hans-Georg, 8–10, 92

Gall, Franz Joseph, 343

Gallineus, 240

Gallipoli, 417

Galton, Douglas Strutt, 533

Gam, Davy, 380

Ganz, David, 570n19

Garibaldi, Giuseppe, 528–29

Gatherings from Graveyards (Walker), 219, 234, 238

Gaulle, Charles de, 486

Gawande, Atul, 556

Gay (clergyman), 165–67

Gébelin, Antoine Court de, 259

Geddes, Richard, 546

Geiger, Abraham, 25

General Services Administration, 33

George, Lloyd, 467

George III, 175

German Socialist Party, 25

Germany, 12, 15; death camps and, 185, 437, 485; Friedhof Ohlsdorf and, 25; Holocaust

and, 105, 366, 373, 386, 392, 414, 418, 423, 432–39, 443, 445, 485–86, 532, 661n35; Nazis and, 7, 185, 433–34, 437, 443. *See also* Great War

Gessner, Salomon, 253–55

Gettysburg cemetery, 16, 339, 375–76, 416

Ghosh, Amitav, 87–88

ghosts: Bible and, 67, 69; Catholic Church and, 67–69, 71–74; cemeteries and, 229, 259, 276, 308, 366, 626n102; church-yards and, 105, 118, 135, 142, 145, 149, 211, 602n105; deep time and, 40, 53, 61–79, 84, 573n12, 573n14, 574n18, 575n20, 575n21, 575n24, 576n25, 576n29, 577n33, 577n34; Enlightenment and, 78; giving up the ghost and, 573n13; murder and, 71, 76; names of the dead and, 420–22, 424, 427, 434, 441; pagans and, 66–67; persistence of being and, 61–79; photographs and, 76; Prot-estants and, 68–76; science and, 73–77; uncared-for dead and, 40–41; as unquiet spirits, 17

Gibbes, Phebe, 269

Gibbon, Edmund, 210, 306

Gibbon, Edward, 95, 182–86, 189, 533

Gibbons, Elizabeth, 312

Gibson, Doctor, 154

Gilbert, John, 157–61

Gilbert, Mary, 157–61

Girardin, René de, 242, 253

Giraud, Pierre, 527

Glaister, John, 533

Glanvill, Joseph, 75, 576n29

Glover, Robert, 381

Godde, Etienne-Hippolyte, 262

Godwin, William, 49–54, 83–84, 215, 228, 259, 278, 357, 365, 571n25

Goethe, 260, 280

Goldberg, Henri, 443

Goldborne, Sophia, 269

Golders Green, 15, 295, 543

Goldsmid, Isaac Lyon, 296

Goldsmith, Oliver, 255

Gollison, George, 277, 302–3

Good Friday, 114, 120

Gorer, Geoffrey, 14

Gorini, Paolo, 517

Gosse, Edmund, 142

Gotainer, Jeanine, 442

Goteiner, Claude, 442

Goteiner, Guy, 442

Graham, Charles, 234

Graham, James, 105

Grainger, R. D., 357

Grand National Consolidated Trades' Union, 330

grave diggers, 18, 128, 137, 149, 160, 209, 219–20, 234–35, 293, 343, 350, 643n229, 654n20

graves: catacombs and, 13, 119, 225, 248, 286, 290, 301, 304, 310, 590n14; common, 23, 85, 145, 156, 232, 273, 290, 294, 312, 323, 351, 455, 464, 487, 629n141, 632n163; consecrated ground and, 113–14, 120, 126, 131, 152, 155, 163–64, 166, 180, 192, 195, 216, 228, 245, 268, 292, 294, 299, 301, 303, 310, 360, 602n105, 615n29, 641n218; crowding and, 133, 220, 225–28, 231, 238, 291, 293; crypts and, 35, 48, 116–17, 232, 272; exhumation and, 5, 8, 18–19, 22, 80, 102, 105, 192, 197–98, 213, 234, 241, 245, 248, 262, 270, 307, 313, 318, 329–30, 336–47, 354–59, 424, 436, 467–68, 473–74, 540, 564n26, 569n11, 586n39, 586n41, 618n52, 640n211, 640n212, 641n218; hell and, 59, 61, 68, 71–72, 109, 180, 447, 536; Imperial War Graves Commission (IWGC) and, 365, 369, 461, 463–66, 468, 470–77, 483, 487; importance of place and, 40–41; mass, 15, 65, 125–26, 317, 325, 347, 370, 389, 431, 449, 452, 455, 563n19, 667n41; mausoleums and, 15, 38, 45, 237–47, 257, 260–62, 264, 266–69, 292, 296–97, 307, 309, 344, 521, 618n51, 621n71, 625n93, 626n107, 628n133; necrogeography and, 123–33; orientation of, 15; pilgrimages and, 20, 248, 254, 260, 288, 302, 422, 454–56, 484, 543, 586n41; public health and, 133, 184, 215–38, 289, 293, 305, 307–8, 612n14, 617n44; putrefaction and, 2, 10, 64, 220, 222, 230, 232, 267, 397, 506, 509, 512, 515, 535, 596n49, 613n19, 617n43, 617n44; reburial and, 10, 19, 22, 103,

198, 312, 336, 417, 462, 468, 502, 562n12, 564n25, 586n39; resurrection and, 15, 27, 43, 45, 56, 60, 74, 85, 97, 102, 113, 120, 123–26, 130, 139, 150, 158, 184, 206, 215, 241, 273, 280, 300–301, 312, 332, 338, 355–56, 492, 503, 536–37; tombs and, 213 (see also tombs); uncared-for dead and, 40–41; Unknown Warrior and, 44, 213, 417–20, 427, 448, 455, 472, 479–84, 667n50, 668n56, 668n59; vandalism of, 102–3

Graves, Richard, 252

Gray, Thomas, 112, 114, 135, 138, 142–45, 164, 250, 274, 276, 279, 402, 410, 457, 597n59

Great Ejection, 306

Great War, 16; Battle of Mons and, 452–53, 460; Battle of the Somme and, 398, 400, 412, 659n22; Casualty Branch and, 461; cemeteries and, 240, 298, 346; Commonwealth War Graves Commission and, 461; deep time and, 83, 579n4; exhumation and, 467–68, 473–74; Imperial War Graves Commission (IWGC) and, 365, 369, 461, 463–66, 468, 470–77, 483, 487; martyrs and, 486; memorials and, 448–51, 453, 455–61, 467, 470–79, 483–84, 486–88, 663n2, 666n37, 667n42; monuments and, 25, 448–53, 456–57, 461, 463, 468, 471, 475–77, 482–84, 663n5, 663n7; names of the dead and, 365–66, 370, 390, 396, 400, 417–19, 422–23, 433, 445–88, 649n16, 658n10; photographs and, 456, 458, 461, 464, 468, 487; Red Cross and, 460–61, 464, 487; Unknown Warrior and, 44, 213, 417–20, 427, 448, 455, 472, 479–84, 667n50, 668n56, 668n59; Versailles Treaty and, 482; War Graves Commission and, 399, 461, 463, 468, 471, 487; waste of, 486; Ypres and, 369, 418–19, 449–51, 464–66, 468, 472, 474, 476–77, 484, 486–87, 668n62

Great Western Railway War Memorial, 423

Green, John, 168–69, 175–76

Gregory of Tour, 97

Grimm, Jacob, 525

Grindal, Edmund, 70

Grindon, Leopold Hartley, 535–36

Grist, Jesu, 541

names of the dead: absent but present body
and, 417–20; age of necromonialism and,
413–46; ancient, 367–69; Anglicans and,
402; ashes and, 375–76, 429, 433, 470;
baptism and, 365, 369–71, 392, 394–96;
Bede Roll and, 386; Book of Life and,
383–84, 391, 431; Catholic Church and, 389,
393, 404, 471, 482; census and, 393, 651n4;
Christians and, 365, 370, 382–83, 386, 392,
394–96, 404, 415, 434, 444, 469; civilly recognized, 394–95; clans and, 371; coffins and,
365, 387, 408, 424, 453, 457, 470, 480–81,
668n56; cultural import of, 374–75; deep
time and, 363–87; descriptivists and, 369;
elegies and, 402, 457; Enlightenment and,
396; epigraphs and, 35, 56, 65, 227, 376, 381,
411, 415, 449, 501, 543, 650n18; epitaphs
and, 370, 372, 375, 384, 401–2, 415, 417,
429, 479, 654n20, 657n2; exhumation
and, 424, 467–68, 473–74; fiction and,
409–11; first names and, 394–96; ghosts
and, 420–22, 424, 427, 434, 441; Great War
and, 365–66, 370, 390, 396, 400, 417–19,
422–23, 433, 445–88, 649n16, 658n10;
heaven and, 373, 404, 430; Holocaust and,
366, 373, 386, 392, 414, 418, 423, 432–36,
438–39, 443, 445, 485–86, 661n35; immortality and, 372; Jews and, 386, 392, 394–96,
404, 419, 432, 434, 436–41, 443–45, 483;
Kaines and, 403–5; Kiš and, 390–91, 411;
LDS storehouse of, 392; logic of, 369–70;
Martin/Chitticks letters and, 398–403,
405, 407, 409–10, 412; martyrs and, 375,
379, 424, 486; memorials and, 365, 376–86,
389–90, 400, 411–12, 416–41, 444–45,
448–51, 453, 455–61, 467, 470–79, 483–84,
486–88, 658n11, 658n13, 659n17, 659n20,
663n2, 666n37, 667n42; Middle Ages
and, 382, 385; Midrashic name derivations
(MNDs) and, 648n6; monuments and,
365, 372, 376, 383, 401–2, 412, 414–16,
418–30, 444, 448–53, 456–57, 461, 463,
468, 471, 475–77, 482–84, 658n12, 659n20,
659n22, 663n5, 663n7; murder and, 373–74,
392, 418, 424, 432–34, 436–38, 442–45;
necrogeography and, 422; necronyms and,
22, 371, 373–74, 382, 385, 393, 399, 411–12,
437–38, 649n13; occupational, 369–70;
over bodies, 415–17; pagans and, 395, 404;
phonetics and, 414, 444; photographs and,
411, 415, 425–28, 438–44, 456, 458, 461,
464, 468, 487; Protestants and, 371, 404,
406, 420, 481; relational, 371; relics and,
430, 454, 481; rise of in modern history,
388–412; Shakespeare and, 378–82, 409,
465; shrines and, 373, 418, 421, 427–28, 467,
479, 481–84; soldiers and, 369, 375, 377–81,
396–400, 412, 416–23, 427, 431, 433,
447–88, 650n22, 657n5, 658n11, 663n8,
667n42, 667n51; special dead and, 382, 384,
425, 474; suicide and, 398, 430; surnames
and, 23, 365, 369–71, 393–96, 647n5; in
times of peace, 382–87; in times of war,
375–82, 398–403, 405, 407, 409–10, 412;
tombs and, 365, 371–72, 377, 382, 384, 398,
401–2, 411, 415–20, 424, 429, 433, 440–41,
454, 456, 458, 461, 468, 472–73, 477,
482–83, 648n10, 654n20, 654n25; tombstones and, 45, 106, 128, 138, 267, 279–80,
298, 382, 398, 402, 411, 415–17, 424, 429,
433, 440, 456, 458, 461, 468, 472–73, 477,
483, 628n132, 654n20, 661n32, 667n41;
unidentifiable bodies and, 417–20; vanished
dead and, 431–46; Voltaire and, 407; Yad
Vashem and, 373
NAMES project, 12
Napoleon, 25, 143, 260–62, 265, 288, 335, 342,
394, 405, 437, 454–55, 514, 525–26, 562
Napoleon III, 337, 534, 585n38
Narcissism, 56, 646n1
Nashe, Thomas, 127
national cemeteries, 15–16, 212, 245, 248–49,
282, 284, 339, 375–76, 416, 459, 462, 471
National War Museum, 456
Native American Graves Protection and
Repatriation Act, 342
Natural Death Act, 552
Nazis, 7–8; death camps and, 185, 437, 485;
Holocaust and, 105, 366, 373, 386, 392, 414,
418, 423, 432, 432–39, 444, 445, 485–86,
532, 661n35
Neale, Erskine, 404

Patroclus, 42

patterns of life, 5

Paul, Apostle, 5

Paul, John Peet, 289–90

Paulus, 94

pauper funerals, 290, 312–18, 323, 325–27, 336, 360–61, 401, 632n166

Pausanius, 375

Paxton, Joseph, 287

Peabody, William Bourn Oliver, 305

Peaget, Leander, 507

Pearson, Karl, 511

Penny, Nicholas, 122

Percival, A. P., 150

Père Lachaise. *See* Cimetière du Père Lachaise

persistence of being: Adam Smith and, 57–58; cremation and, 62; Day of Judgment and, 54, 60–61; Diogenes and, 60–61, 79, 550–56; embalming and, 57; epigraphs and, 35, 56, 65, 227, 376, 381, 411, 415, 449, 501, 543, 650n18; Freud and, 56–57, 78–79; ghosts and, 61–79; Hades and, 62, 66, 109, 135, 207; Kabbalah and, 63–64; mortalists and, 60–61, 69, 572n9, 573n12; purgatory and, 58–59, 61, 67–76; relics and, 61; tautology of, 55–56; Western culture and, 64–65

Peter, Johann Nepomuk, 343–44

Peter the Great, 535

Peto, S. M., 180

Petronius, 86

Petrucci, Armando, 415

Pew, John William, 310

photographs, 15–16; cemeteries and, 342–43, 641n216; ghosts and, 76; Great War and, 456, 458, 461, 464, 468, 487; modern technology and, 546; names of the dead and, 411, 415, 425–28, 438–45, 456, 458, 461, 464, 468, 487; Varro and, 92

phrenology, 78–79

Pickersgill, Jeanette, 543

Pietra Santa, Prosper de, 523

pilgrimages, 20, 248, 254, 260, 288, 302, 422, 454–56, 484, 543, 586n41

Pilkington, James, 99

Pilling, W., 487

Pini, Gaetano, 528

Pink, Eric, 369, 487, 488

Pinney, J. H., 487

Pious VII, 526–27

places of the dead: cemeteries and, 211–361 (*see also* cemeteries); churchyards and, 112–210 (*see also* churchyards); Hades, 62, 66, 109, 135, 207; shadowlands and, 108–10; strange vs. familiar, 109

Playfair, Lyon, 514

Pliny, 84, 90, 92, 251

Poe, Edgar Allen, 508

Point Lookout Cemetery, 416

Poland, 24–25, 253

Polanyi, Karl, 317–18

Pole, Reginald, 104

Polynices, 7

Poole, S. L., 466

Poor Laws, 180, 292, 299, 317, 323, 325–26, 331, 355, 360, 535, 636n189

Pope, Alexander, 135–37, 245, 256

Pope Benedict XIV, 193–94

Pope Calixus, 119

Pope Gregory I, 97

Pope Gregory the Great, 114–15

Pope Pius II, 70

Portugal, 12

Poussin, Nicolas, 139, 242, 251–54

Préau, Charles Nicolas Beauvais de, 525–26

premature burial, 14, 185, 507–9

Presbyterians, 48, 165, 173, 208, 300–301, 304–5, 339, 601n98

Presley, Elvis, 53

Price, George Lawrence, 452, 663n8

Price, Richard, 301

Price, William, 540, 542

Priestley, Joseph, 200

Prince of Wales, 472–73

Princess Di, 260

Privy Council, 176, 179, 224, 601n101

Protestants, 23; cemeteries and, 239, 241, 257, 259, 265–66, 270, 280, 288, 296, 310, 317, 328; churchyards and, 114–15, 132, 146–47, 162, 166, 170, 173–74, 177, 179, 193, 211, 213, 593n32, 597n64; cremation and, 491, 496, 508, 528, 532; deep time and, 40, 42, 44, 47–48, 53, 59–61, 68–75,

98–105, 570n21, 575n24, 585n33; ghosts and, 68–76; names of the dead and, 371, 404, 406, 420, 481; Reformation and, 12, 33, 46–47, 59, 68–71, 76, 93–94, 98–103, 115, 120, 122, 132, 135, 145–47, 155, 169, 177, 182–83, 186–88, 239, 241, 273, 288, 306, 308; regime of the dead and, 99–101

Prussia, 25, 194, 201, 298, 328, 394–96, 483

public health: bacteria and, 231–32; cadaverous gases and, 219; cemeteries and, 215–38, 612n14, 617n44; churchyards and, 133, 184, 215–38; cremation and, 493, 510, 513, 533, 670n8; hygiene and, 133 (*see also* hygiene); putrefaction and, 2, 10, 64, 220, 222, 230, 232, 267, 397, 506, 509, 512, 515, 535, 596n49, 613n19, 617n43, 617n44; sanitation and, 168, 220, 223, 229, 235, 501, 511, 513–16, 533–34, 538, 541; Walker and, 219–20, 222–24, 230, 232–34, 237–38; World Health Organization (WHO) and, 231–32, 235

Pugin, Augustus Welby, 161, 304, 313

purgatory: deep time and, 17, 58–59, 61, 67–76, 98–101, 103, 241, 575n23; persistence of being and, 58–59, 61, 67–76

Puritans: cemeteries and, 228, 272, 280, 295, 302, 639n210; churchyards and, 126–27, 146, 203; deep time and, 43, 48, 72, 99–100, 105

putrefaction: cemeteries and, 220, 222, 230, 232, 267, 596n49, 613n19, 617n43, 617n44; churchyards and, 220, 222, 230, 232; corpses and, 2, 10, 64, 220, 222, 230, 232, 267, 397, 506, 509, 512, 515, 535, 596n49, 613n19, 617n43, 617n44; effluvia and, 230–31

Pym, John, 106

pyres, 45, 57, 62, 223, 491, 499, 501, 523, 526–29, 539, 541–42

Quakers, 114–15, 119, 127–28, 154, 224, 299–300, 306, 339–40, 406, 593n36, 595n48

Queen Anne's Bounty, 123

Quinlan, Karen Ann, 552

Quintilian, 86, 372

rabbis, 23–25, 64, 123, 370, 395, 404, 531–32, 648n6, 675n15

Radziwill, Helena Przezdziecka, 253

Railton, D., 479

Rainbow, Edward, 116

Ramazzini, Bernadino, 232–33

Ramsey family, 180–82

Raphael, 213

reburial, 10, 19, 22, 103, 198, 312, 336, 417, 462, 468, 502, 562n12, 564n25, 586n39

Red Cross, 460–61, 464, 487

Reeve, John, 60

Reformation, 12, 33; Calvinists and, 47, 59–60, 69, 71–73, 85, 99–100, 126, 147, 175, 191, 273, 579n5; cemeteries and, 230, 241, 273, 288, 306, 308; churchyards and, 115, 120, 122, 132, 135, 145–47, 155, 169, 177, 182–83, 186–88; deep time and, 46–47, 59, 68–71, 76; Luther and, 59, 99, 101, 187–89, 202, 404; regime of the dead and, 99–101. *See also* Protestants

Reform Judaism, 25

Reign of Terror, 214

relics, 45; anti-relic, 48; burning and, 492, 503; cemeteries and, 235, 239, 259, 262, 317, 340–41, 343, 345–46, 641n218, 642n221; cherishing of, 51; churchyards and, 122, 144, 173, 182, 201; cultural work of the dead and, 83, 96, 99–100, 104; decomposition of, 642n221; documentation of, 46; importance of the dead and, 40–41, 46–48, 51–53; medieval trade in, 23; names and, 430, 454, 481; necro-sociability and, 41; persistence of being and, 61; saints and, 3, 23, 36, 40–41, 46–48, 51–53, 61, 83, 96, 99–100, 104, 122, 144, 173, 182, 201, 235, 239, 259, 262, 317, 340–43, 345–46, 439, 454, 481, 492, 503, 563n14, 570n20, 641n218, 642n221; veneration of dead and, 40, 46–48, 52, 89, 241, 299

religion, x; afterlife and, 1, 3, 11, 21, 37, 54, 56, 85, 141, 167, 186, 202, 206, 209, 404, 455, 493, 571n25, 605n132, 609n153, 609n159; comfort from, xi; consecrated ground and, 216, 228, 245, 268, 292, 294, 299, 301, 303, 310, 360, 615n29, 641n218; cremation and,

religion, x; afterlife and (*continued*)
536 (*see also* cremation); Day of Judgment
and, 54, 60–61, 87, 96, 124–25, 485;
French Wars of, 101; hell and, 59, 61, 68,
71–72, 109, 180, 447, 536; heretics and,
103–4, 128, 191, 196, 490–92, 525, 572n9;
holy dying and, xi; importance of the dead
and, 570n20; pluralism and, 294–305;
purgatory and, 17, 58–59, 61, 67–76,
98–101, 103, 241, 575n23; Reformation
and, 12, 33, 46–47, 59, 68–71, 76, 93–94,
98–103, 115, 120, 122, 132, 135, 145–47, 155,
169, 177, 182–83, 186–88, 239, 241, 273,
288, 306, 308; sacrilege and, 10; saints and,
3, 11, 23, 36, 40–41, 46–48, 51–53, 61, 83,
96, 99–100, 104, 122, 144, 173, 182, 201,
235, 239, 259, 262, 317, 340–43, 345–46,
439, 454, 481, 492, 503, 563n14, 570n20,
641n218, 642n221; treatment of corpses
and, 1; uncared-for dead and, 40–41. *See
also specific faiths*
Religious Tract Society, The, 406–7
repatriation, 19, 22–23, 26
Resnais, Alain, 485
resurrection, 104; cemeteries and, 215, 241,
273, 280, 300–301, 312, 332, 338, 356;
churchyards and, 113, 120, 123–26, 130,
139, 150, 158, 161, 165, 169, 171, 179, 184,
197, 206; cremation and, 492, 503, 536–37;
from death, 15, 27, 43, 45, 56, 60, 74, 85, 97,
102, 113, 120, 123–26, 130, 139, 150, 158,
184, 206, 215, 241, 273, 280, 300–301, 312,
332, 338, 355–56, 492, 503, 536–37; deep
time and, 43, 45, 56, 60, 74, 85, 97, 102;
Jesus Christ and, 64, 537; Jews and, 85;
Lazarus and, 64, 68–69, 96
resurrection men, 355–56, 644n231
Rev, Istvan, 374, 564n25, 649n13
Rhodes, John, 328–29
Richard II, 483–84
Richardson, Samuel, 409
right to die, 551–55
Rippon, John, 301, 304–5
River Styx, 40–41
Robert, Emma, 270
Roberts, Robert, 313

Robertson, James, 456
Robison, John, 199–200
Rock, Daniel, 134
Rockwood, 15, 284
Rokitansky, Carl von, 353
Rosa, Salvator, 242
Rose, Thomas, 359
Rosenbaum, Joseph Karl, 343–44
Rousseau, Jean-Jacques, 43, 137, 193, 198–99,
202, 242–43, 246, 253, 256–60, 333, 519,
608n147
Routh, Bernard, 193–94
Royal Scots Fusiliers, 458
Rumbold, Jane, 178
Rushton, Benjamin, 331
Ruskin, John, 147–48, 411
Russia, 19, 22, 24, 200, 211, 296, 310, 393, 417,
432, 483, 514, 530, 564n26

Sac people, 6
Sacred Spring of Lerna, 95
Sadducees, 60, 74–75
Sahlins, Marshall, 5
saints, 11, 13, 25; cemeteries and, 235, 239, 259,
262, 317, 340–43, 345–46; churchyards
and, 122, 144, 173, 182, 201; deep time and,
40–41, 45–48, 51–53, 61, 83, 96, 99–100,
104; names of the dead and, 439, 454, 481;
relics and, 3, 23, 36, 40–41, 46–48, 51–53,
61, 83, 96, 99–100, 104, 122, 144, 173,
182, 201, 235, 239, 259, 262, 317, 340–43,
345–46, 439, 454, 481, 492, 503, 563n14,
570n20, 641n218, 642n221
Salt, Titus, 335–36
Samuel, Raphael, 20
Samuel (Biblical prophet), 67, 69
Sanderson, Jane Elizabeth, 269
sanitation: cemeteries and, 220, 223, 229, 235;
churchyards and, 168, 220, 223, 229, 235; cremation and, 501, 511, 513–16, 533–34, 538, 541
Saramago, José, 397–98, 502
Sassoon, Siegfried, 419
Saul, 67, 69
Savary, Jean Marie René, 437
Scheemakers, Peter, 252